PHILIP'S

NAVIGATOR® Britain

Contents

www.philips-maps.co.uk

First published in 1994 by Philip's,
a division of Octopus Publishing Group Ltd
www.octopusbooks.co.uk
Carmelite House, 50 Victoria Embankment
London EC4Y 0DZ
An Hachette UK Company
www.hachette.co.uk

Fourth edition 2017
First impression 2017

ISBN 978 1 84907 434 6

Cartography by Philip's
Copyright © 2017 Philip's

Map data

While every reasonable effort has been made to ensure that the information compiled in this atlas is accurate, complete and up-to-date at the time of publication, some of this information is subject to change and the Publisher cannot guarantee its correctness or completeness.

The information in this atlas is provided without any representation or warranty, express or implied and the Publisher cannot be held liable for any loss or damage due to any use or reliance on the information in this atlas, nor for any errors, omissions or subsequent changes in such information.

The representation in this atlas of any road, drive or track is no evidence of the existence of a right of way.

Data for the caravan sites provided by The Camping and Caravanning Club.

Information for the selection of Wildlife Trust nature reserves provided by The Wildlife Trusts.

Information for National Parks, Areas of Outstanding Natural Beauty, National Trails and Country Parks in Wales supplied by the Countryside Council for Wales.

Information for National Parks, Areas of Outstanding Natural Beauty, National Trails and Country Parks in England supplied by Natural England. Data for Regional Parks, Long Distance Footpaths and Country Parks in Scotland provided by Scottish Natural Heritage.

Information for Forest Parks supplied by the Forestry Commission

Information for the RSPB reserves provided by the RSPB

Gaelic name forms used in the Western Isles provided by Comhairle nan Eilean.

Data for the National Nature Reserves in England provided by Natural England. Data for the National Nature Reserves in Wales provided by Countryside Council for Wales. Darparwyd data'n ymwneud â Gwarchodfeydd Natur Cenedlaethol Cymru gan Gyngor Cefn Gwlad Cymru.

Information on the location of National Nature Reserves in Scotland was provided by Scottish Natural Heritage.

Data for National Scenic Areas in Scotland provided by the Scottish Executive Office. Crown copyright material is reproduced with the permission of the Controller of HMSO and the Queen's Printer for Scotland. Licence number C02W0003960.

Printed in China

Road map symbols

M25	Motorway
16 17	Motorway junctions – full access, restricted access
	Toll motorway
Pease Pottage Services	Motorway service area
	Motorway under construction
S	Primary route – dual, single carriageway, services – under construction, narrow
Cardiff	Primary destination
25 26	Numbered junctions – full, restricted access
	A road – dual, single carriageway – under construction, narrow
	B road – dual, single carriageway – under construction, narrow
	Minor road – dual, single carriageway
	Drive or track
	Urban side roads
	Roundabout, multi-level junction
2	Distance in miles
	Tunnel
Toll	Toll, steep gradient – points downhill
CLEVELAND WAY	National trail – England and Wales
GREAT GLEN WAY	Long distance footpath – Scotland
YATTON ROPLEY	Railway with station, level crossing, tunnel — Preserved railway with level crossing, station, tunnel — Tramway
	National boundary — County or unitary authority boundary
	Car ferry, catamaran — Passenger ferry, catamaran
CALAIS	Ferry destination
	Hovercraft
V P	Internal ferry – car, passenger
✈ ✈	Principal airport, other airport or airfield
MENDIP HILLS	Area of outstanding natural beauty, National Forest – England and Wales, Forest park, National park, National scenic area – Scotland, Regional park
	Woodland
	Beach – sand, shingle
KENNET AND AVON CANAL	Navigable river or canal
6 6	Lock, flight of locks, canal bridge number
C CF CS LS	Caravan or camping sites – CCC* Club Site, Camping in the Forest Site – CCC Certificated Site, Listed Site *Categories defined by the Camping and Caravanning Club of Great Britain
☀ P&R ▲965	Viewpoint, park and ride, spot height – in metres — Linear antiquity
29	Adjoining page number
SY 70 / 80	Ordnance Survey National Grid reference – see inside back cover

Road map scale 1: 112 903 or 1.78 miles to 1 inch

0   1   2   3 miles
0   1   2   3   4   5 km

Road map scale – Isle of Man and parts of Scotland
1: 225 806 or 3.56 miles to 1 inch

0   1   2   3   4   5   6 miles
0 1 2 3 4 5 6 7 8 9 10 km

Tourist information

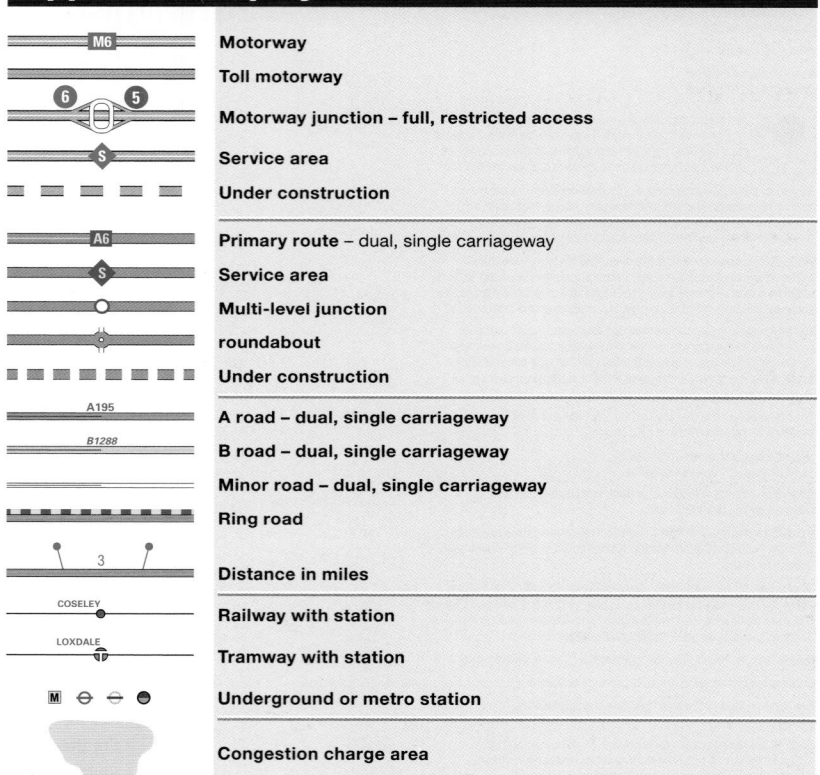

BYLAND ABBEY	Abbey or priory
WOODHENGE	Ancient monument
SEALIFE CENTRE	Aquarium or dolphinarium
CITY MUSEUM AND ART GALLERY	Art collection or museum
TATE ST IVES	Art gallery
1644	Battle site and date
ABBOTSBURY SWANNERY	Bird sanctuary or aviary
BAMBURGH CASTLE	Castle
YORK MINSTER	Cathedral
SANDHAM MEMORIAL CHAPEL	Church of interest
SEVEN SISTERS LOCHORE MEADOWS	Country park – England and Wales – Scotland
ROYAL BATH & WEST SHOWGROUND	County show ground
MONK PARK FARM	Farm park
HILLIER GARDENS AND ARBORETUM	Garden, arboretum
ST ANDREWS	Golf course – 18-hole
TYNTESFIELD	Historic house
SS GREAT BRITAIN	Historic ship
HATFIELD HOUSE	House and garden
CUMBERLAND PENCIL MUSEUM	Museum
MUSEUM OF DARTMOOR LIFE	– Local
NAT MARITIME MUSEUM	– Maritime or military

	Marina
SILVERSTONE	Motor racing circuit
	Nature reserves
HOLTON HEATH	– National nature reserve
BOYTON MARSHES	– RSPB reserve
DRAYCOTT SLEIGHTS	– Wildlife Trust reserve
	Picnic area
WEST SOMERSET RAILWAY	Preserved railway
THIRSK	Racecourse
LEAHILL TURRET	Roman antiquity
THRIGBY HALL	Safari park
FREEPORT BRAINTREE	Shopping village
PRINCIPALITY STADIUM	Sports venue
ALTON TOWERS	Theme park
	Tourist information centres – open all year – open seasonally
NATIONAL RAILWAY MUSEUM	Transport collection
LEVANT MINE	World heritage site
HELMSLEY	Youth hostel
MARWELL	Zoo
SUTTON BANK VISITOR CENTRE GLENFIDDICH DISTILLERY	Other place of interest

Approach map symbols

M6	Motorway
	Toll motorway
6 5	Motorway junction – full, restricted access
S	Service area
	Under construction
A6	Primary route – dual, single carriageway
S	Service area
	Multi-level junction
	roundabout
	Under construction
A195	A road – dual, single carriageway
B1288	B road – dual, single carriageway
	Minor road – dual, single carriageway
	Ring road
3	Distance in miles
COSELEY	Railway with station
LOXDALE	Tramway with station
M	Underground or metro station
	Congestion charge area

Mobile Layby Cafés – gourmet or gruesome?

Do you drive on by?

Stephen Mesquita,
Philip's On the Road Correspondent

▲ Roadside snack van sign in Herefordshire *Jeff Morgan / Alamy*

Have you ever done this? You're driving along on one of Britain's A-Roads. It's sometime between 6am and 2pm. You're feeling a bit peckish. You see a layby coming up. There's a notice by the road. Something about hot food. There's a van flying a Union Jack. There are a couple of truck drivers there, queueing up. You might even catch a tempting whiff of something frying.

And you drive straight past. Not really for you? You've never eaten in a layby so you'll wait for a place you know and recognise. Or buy a sandwich at the next petrol station.

Well, that's what I've always done. Up until yesterday. That's when I set out, with my trusty accomplice (and Philip's Sales Supremo) Stuart, to see if my lifelong prejudices were justified.

Butty Vans

A quick word about terminology first. We're going to drop the 'Mobile Layby Cafés' and go with 'Butty Vans'. Stuart and I were out to beat The Breakfast Buns from Butty Vans in One Morning Record.

▲ The first bacon butty of the day in a layby alongside the A43

And so it was with some trepidation that we set off from Northampton and headed for our first Butty Van. Here's confession number one: as soon as we'd photographed the bacon roll that we'd ordered, we polished it off.

This was a good start – and in stark contrast to our Motorway Service Area research, where the fare was so unappetising that we tried only a tiny portion of each item and left the rest.

And as the day started, so it went on. Of the eight buns, only one really disappointed. The other seven were tasty, hot, great value and came with friendly chat. Stuart and I polished almost all of them off – and two especially good ones were down the gullets of Philip's intrepid breakfast critics before you could say 'another bacon roll please'.

Eight in a Day

Would I recommend eight in a day? As a gastronomic experience, no. It's too much salt intake (my car was littered with empty bottles of water by the end of the day). And I did long for a freshly made flat white by the end of the day.

But a Butty Van breakfast or snack every now and again? Absolutely. Now I've done it once, I'll be very happy to do it again. In fact, I'm rather ashamed I hadn't managed to overcome my prejudices before now.

So to answer my question. Gourmet: no. Gruesome: certainly not. A tasty roadside snack, piping hot, cooked to order and served with a smile – definitely. I'll have one of those.

Butty Vans vs. Motorway Service Areas– how they compare

If you're expecting Butty Vans to serve up the fare you get at your local deli, you probably don't need to read on. The buns are not made of artisanal sourdough ciabatta. The butter isn't Danish unsalted. The bacon didn't cost £15 a kilo. The eggs probably aren't fresh from the farm that morning. Butty Vans aren't posh.

But the point is this – all the Butty Vans we ate at were owned by people who took great pride in what they did. We met one real foody proprietor who told us he'd been to a burger fair the weekend before and always offered specials ('Codfinger'; 'Blue Burger Special'). All of them were aware that, to compete against the big brands, they had to offer good food at good prices.

The ingredients were perfectly decent. The bacon was almost universally of a better quality than we tasted last year in our Full English Breakfast campaign in Motorway Service Areas. And it was all cooked to order in front of you, which gave it one spectacular advantage over the Motorway Service Areas. It was hot.

And it was a fraction of the price.

The only disappointment was the tea and coffee. But at £0.70–£0.80 a cup, you should know what you're getting and you get what you pay for – although at one Butty Van, the teabags were Yorkshire Tea.

You can compare further in our
Butty Van vs. Motorway Service Area checklist:

	Butty Vans	Motorway Service Areas
Good Value for Money	✔	✗
Proud of what they do	✔	✗
Cooked to Order	✔	rarely
Meal Hot	✔	✗
Quality of ingredients	See above	See above
Quality of hot drinks	✗	✗
Friendly Service	✔	✗
Parking	✔	✔
Easy to find	✗	✔

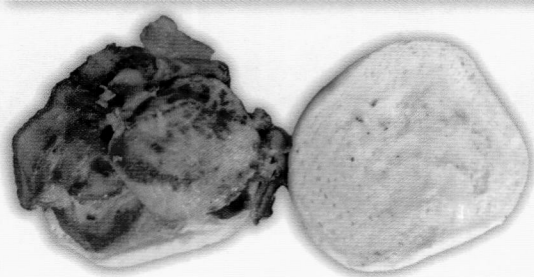

Meal in a Bun One:

Location	A43 West of Northampton
Meal:	Bacon roll plus tea
Price:	£2.50 plus £0.60

Verdict: Generous helping of tasty bacon, cooked in front of us and piping hot. The tea was wet and warm.

Meal in a Bun Two:

Location:	A43 Brackley
Meal:	Sausage and Bacon roll plus tea
Price:	£3.20 plus £0.50

Verdict: A breakfast on its own served with a smile and lots of chat. The ingredients were nothing special but all tasty.

Meal in a Bun Three:

Location:	A422 between Buckingham and Milton Keynes
Meal:	Bacon and Egg roll plus coffee
Price:	£3.00 plus £0.80

Verdict: Another very decent breakfast in a bun, with the egg cooked to order. Yorkshire Tea teabags spurned for instant coffee. Should have had the tea.

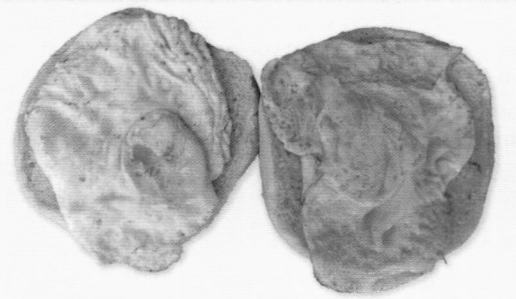

Meal in a Bun Five:

Location:	Yardley Road Industrial Estate, Olney
Meal:	Double egg roll
Price:	£2.50

Verdict: I was stupid. I had a double egg sandwich (which was tasty) but I was rightly berated by Mr Sizzler for not being more adventurous and having one of his speciality burgers or chicken dishes. The things I sacrifice to make these surveys fair.

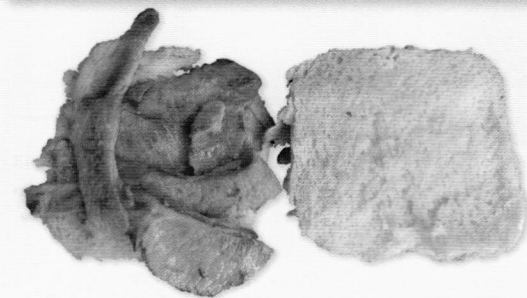

Meal in a Bun Six:

Location:	A505 West of Royston
Meal:	Bacon Roll
Price:	£2.00

Verdict: The best bread (slightly toasted) and loads of decent bacon for £2.00. I rest my case. I should have added: cooked by Italians. They know how to cook, the Italians. Even good old English Bacon butties. Buonissimo!

Meal in a Bun Seven:

Location:	A505 West of Royston
Meal:	Bacon Roll
Price:	£2.50

Verdict: A bit disappointing. Bread tough, bacon tough. Our only below par experience of the day.

DOM'S DOORSTEPS
Est 1997
Phone Orders Taken

Hotdog	£1.75
Hotdog With Cheese	£1.95
Bacon	£1.75
Egg (2 Eggs)	£1.75
Sausage	£1.75
Sausage & Onion	£1.75
Sausage & Mushroom	£1.75
Sausage With Cheese	£2.25
Sausage & Tomato	£1.95
Sausage & Bacon	£2.25
Sausage & Egg	£2.25
Sausage & Egg With Cheese	£2.25
Sausage & Egg With Bacon With Cheese	£2.45
Sausage & Egg With Mushroom	£2.45
Sausage & Egg & Bacon With Mushroom	£2.75
Egg & Bacon	£2.25
Bacon & Mushroom	£2.25
Egg & Mushroom	£2.25
Egg & Bacon With Mushroom	£2.25
Egg & Cheese	£2.75
Sausage & Egg With Bacon	£1.95
Sausage & Egg With Bacon + Cheese	£2.75
Sausage & Egg With Bacon + Mushroom	£2.95
Sausage & Egg With Bacon + Tomato	£3.25
Sausage & Egg With Bacon + Tomato	£3.25

Meal in a Bun Four:

Location:	Harding Road, Milton Keynes
Meal:	Sausage and Egg roll plus tea
Price:	£2.25 plus £0.50

Verdict: Sausage and egg: not expensive ingredients but properly cooked, nice and hot and at a nugatory price.

Meal in a Bun Eight:

Location:	A505 East of Royston
Meal:	Sausage roll
Price:	£3.00

Verdict: This café was called Smell the Bacon but the sausages were from Musks of Newmarket. They were delicious! They seemed to disappear remarkably quickly, Stuart.

How to find Butty Vans

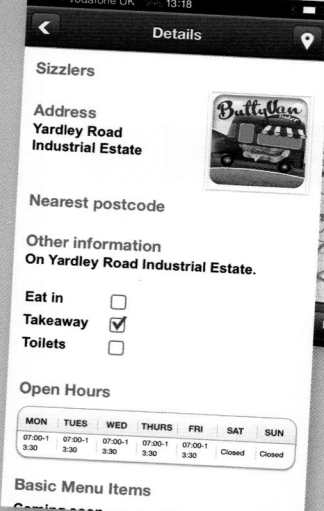

Most Butty Vans are either an 'impulse buy' (you see them as you pass by) or have their regular customers who know where they are. But say you are planning a journey and you want to know for sure there's a Butty Van at a point on your route. Then you need the free app from Butty Van Finder (go to buttyvan.com). We don't even need to describe it: these screen grabs say it all.

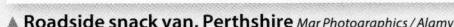

▲ Roadside snack van, Perthshire *Mar Photographics / Alamy*

▲ An unusual takeaway van menu spotted in Wales *Gari Wyn Williams / Alamy*

Butty Vans – what you need to know

- **Layby cafes are licensed by the local authority**, normally annually, to do business in a particular layby.
- **Food Hygiene is an important part of their credibility** – most of them display their certificates prominently.
- **You can't go there for dinner.** Most open early (often around 6am) and shut up around 2pm (sometimes 3pm).
- **They aren't just found in laybys on A Roads.** Some are on industrial estates and business parks.
- **The good ones are there come rain or shine** (bad weather can be good for business) most days of the year.

- **Most of them have a name:** we sampled the fare at *Dom's Doorsteps, Taste Buds Snacks, Sizzlers, Delicias* and *Smell the Bacon.*
- **It's a competitive business** – and their regulars (mostly truck drivers and white van men on A Roads) are discerning customers who expect tasty food at reasonable prices. We heard one van driver say he draws the line at paying £1 for a cup of tea.
- **We were made very welcome**, even though it was obvious we weren't their usual clientele.

Our thanks to all the proprietors who answered our questions about their businesses so openly.

Restricted motorway junctions

M1 Junction 34

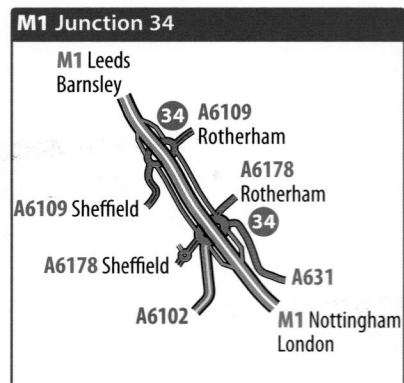

M1 Junctions 6, 6A
M25 Junctions 21, 21A

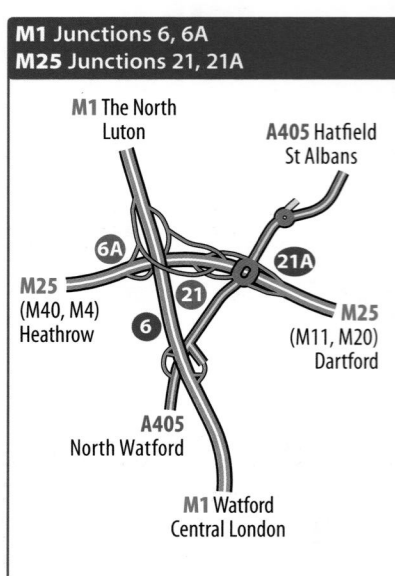

M4 Junctions 25, 25A, 26

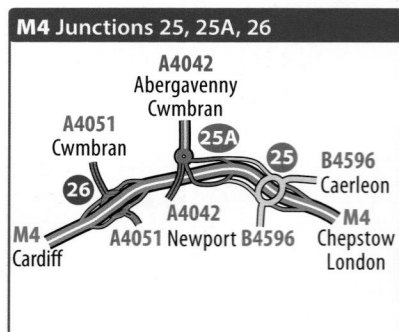

M8 Junctions 8, 9 · M73 Junctions 1, 2 · M74 Junctions 2A, 3, 3A, 4

M1	Northbound	Southbound
2	No exit	No access
4	No exit	No access
6A	No exit. Access from M25 only	No access. Exit to M25 only
7	No exit. Access from A414 only	No access. Exit to A414 only
17	No access. Exit to M45 only	No exit. Access from M45 only
19	No exit to A14	No access from A14
21A	No access	No exit
23A		Exit to A42 only
24A	No exit	No access
35A	No access	No exit
43	No access. Exit to M621 only	No exit. Access from M621 only
48	No exit to A1(M) southbound	

M3	Eastbound	Westbound
8	No exit	No access
10	No access	No exit
13	No access to M27 eastbound	
14	No exit	No access

M4	Eastbound	Westbound
1	Exit to A4 eastbound only	Access from A4 westbound only
2	Access from A4 eastbound only	Access to A4 westbound only
21	No exit	No access
23	No access	No exit
25	No exit	No access
25A	No exit	No access
29	No exit	No access
38		No access
39	No exit or access	No exit
41	No access	No exit
41A	No exit	No access
42	Access from A483 only	Exit to A483 only

M5	Northbound	Southbound
10	No exit	No access
11A	No access from A417 eastbound	No exit to A417 westbound

M6	Northbound	Southbound
3A	No access.	No exit. Access from M6 eastbound only
4A	No exit. Access from M42 southbound only	No access. Exit to M42 only
5	No access	No exit
10A	No access. Exit to M54 only	No exit. Access from M54 only
11A	No exit. Access from M6 Toll only	No access. Exit to M6 Toll only
20	No exit to M56 eastbound	No access from M56 westbound
24	No access	No exit
25	No access	No exit
30	No exit. Access from M61 northbound only	No access. Exit to M61 southbound only
31A	No access	No exit
45	No access	No exit

M6 Toll	Northbound	Southbound
T1		No exit
T2	No exit, no access	No access
T5	No exit	No access
T7	No access	No exit
T8	No access	No exit

M8	Eastbound	Westbound
6	No exit	No access
6A	No access	No exit
7	No Access	No exit
7A	No exit. Access from A725 northbound only	No access. Exit to A725 southbound only
8	No exit to M73 northbound	No access from M73 southbound
9	No access	No exit
13	No exit southbound	Access from M73 southbound only
14	No access	No exit
16	No exit	No access
17	No exit	
18		No exit
19	No exit to A814 eastbound	No access from A814 westbound
20	No exit	No access
21	No access from M74	No exit
22	No exit. Access from M77 only	No access. Exit to M77 only
23	No exit	No access
25	Exit to A739 northbound only. Access from A739 southbound only	
25A	No exit	No access
28	No exit	No access
28A	No exit	No access

M5 Junction 11A

M9	Eastbound	Westbound
1A	No exit	No access
2	No exit	No access
3	No access	No exit
6	No access	No exit
8	No exit	No access

M11	Northbound	Southbound
4	No exit	No access
5	No access	No exit
9	No access	No exit
13	No access	No exit
14	No exit to A428 westbound	No exit. Access from A14 westbound only

M20	Eastbound	Westbound
2	No access	No exit
3	No exit Access from M26 eastbound only	Exit to M26 westbound only
11A	No access	No exit

M23	Northbound	Southbound
7	No exit to A23 southbound	No access from A23 northbound
10A	No access	No exit

M25	Clockwise	Anticlockwise
5	No exit to M26 eastbound	No access from M26 westbound
19	No access	No exit
21	No exit to M1 southbound. Access from M1 southbound only	No exit to M1 southbound. Access from M1 southbound only
31	No exit	No access

M27	Eastbound	Westbound
10	No exit	No access
12	No access	No exit

M40	Eastbound	Westbound
3	No exit	No access
7	No exit	No access
8	No exit	No access
13	No exit	No access
14	No access	No exit
16	No access	No exit

M42	Northbound	Southbound
1	No exit	No access
7	No access Exit to M6 northbound only	No exit. Access from M6 northbound only
7A	No access. Exit to M6 southbound only	No exit
8	No exit. Access from M6 southbound only	Exit to M6 northbound only. Access from M6 southbound only

M45	Eastbound	Westbound
M1 J17	Access to M1 southbound only	No access from M1 southbound
With A45	No access	No exit

M48	Eastbound	Westbound
M4 J21	No exit to M4 westbound	No access from M4 eastbound
M4 J23	No access from M4 westbound	No exit to M4 eastbound

M49	Southbound	Northbound
18A	No exit to M5 northbound	No access from M5 southbound

M53	Northbound	Southbound
11	Exit to M56 eastbound only. Access from M56 westbound only	Exit to M56 eastbnd only. Access from M56 westbound only

M56	Eastbound	Westbound
2	No exit	No access
3	No access	No exit
4	No exit	No access
7		No access
8	No exit or access	No exit
9	No access from M6 northbound	No access to M6 southbound
15	No exit to M53	No access from M53 northbound

M57	Northbound	Southbound
3	No exit	No access
5	No exit	No access

M58	Eastbound	Westbound
1	No exit	No access

M60	Clockwise	Anticlockwise
2	No exit	No access
3	No exit to A34 northbound	No exit to A34 northbound
4	No access from M56	No exit to M56
5	No exit to A5103 southbound	No exit to A5103 northbound
14	No exit	No access
16	No exit	No access
20	No access	No exit
22		No access
25	No access	
26		No exit or access
27	No exit	No access

M61	Northbound	Southbound
2	No access from A580 eastbound	No exit to A580 westbound
3	No access from A580 eastbound. No access from A666 southbound	No exit to A580 westbound
M6 J30	No exit to M6 southbound	No access from M6 northbound

M62	Eastbound	Westbound
23	No access	No exit

M65	Eastbound	Westbound
9	No access	No exit
11	No exit	No access

M66	Northbound	Southbound
1	No access	No exit

M67	Eastbound	Westbound
1A	No access	No exit
2	No exit	No access

M69	Northbound	Southbound
2	No exit	No access

M73	Northbound	Southbound
2	No access from M8 eastbound	No exit to M8 westbound

M74	Northbound	Southbound
3	No access	No exit
3A	No exit	No access
7	No exit	No access
9	No exit or access	No access
10		No exit
11	No exit	No access
12	No access	No exit

M77	Northbound	Southbound
4	No exit	No access
6	No exit	No access
7	No exit	
8	No access	No access

M80	Northbound	Southbound
4A	No access	No exit
6A	No exit	No access
8	Exit to M876 northbound only. No access	Access from M876 southbound only. No exit

M90	Northbound	Southbound
1	Access from A90 northbound only	No access. Exit to A90 southbound only
2A	No access	No exit
7	No exit	No access
8	No access	No access
10	No access from A912	No exit to A912

M180	Eastbound	Westbound
1	No access	No exit

M621	Eastbound	Westbound
2A	No exit	No access
4	No exit	No access
5	No exit	No access
6	No access	No exit

M876	Northbound	Southbound
2	No access	No exit

A1(M)	Northbound	Southbound
2	No access	No access
3		No access
5	No exit	No exit, no access
14	No exit	No access
40	No access	No access
43	No exit. Access from M1 only	No access. Exit to M1 only
57	No access	No access
65	No access	No access

A3(M)	Northbound	Southbound
1	No exit	No access
4	No access	No exit

A38(M) with Victoria Rd, (Park Circus) Birmingham

Northbound	No exit
Southbound	No access

A48(M)	Northbound	Southbound
M4 Junc 29	Exit to M4 eastbound only	Access from M4 westbound only
29A	Access from A48 eastbound only	Exit to A48 westbound only

A57(M)	Eastbound	Westbound
With A5103	No access	No exit
With A34	No access	No exit

A58(M)	Southbound
With Park Lane and Westgate, Leeds	No access

A64(M)	Eastbound	Westbound
With A58 Clay Pit Lane, Leeds	No access from A58	No exit to A58

A74(M)	Northbound	Southbound
18	No access	No exit
22		No exit to A75

A194(M)	Northbound	Southbound
A1(M) J65 Gateshead Western Bypass	Access from A1(M) northbound only	Exit to A1(M) southbound only

M6 Junctions 3A, 4A
M42 Junctions 7, 7A, 8, 9
M6 Toll Junctions T1, T2

M62 Junctions 32A, 33 · **A1(M)** Junctions 40, 41

M6 Junction 20 · **M56** Junction 9

M3 Junctions 13, 14 · **M27** Junction 4

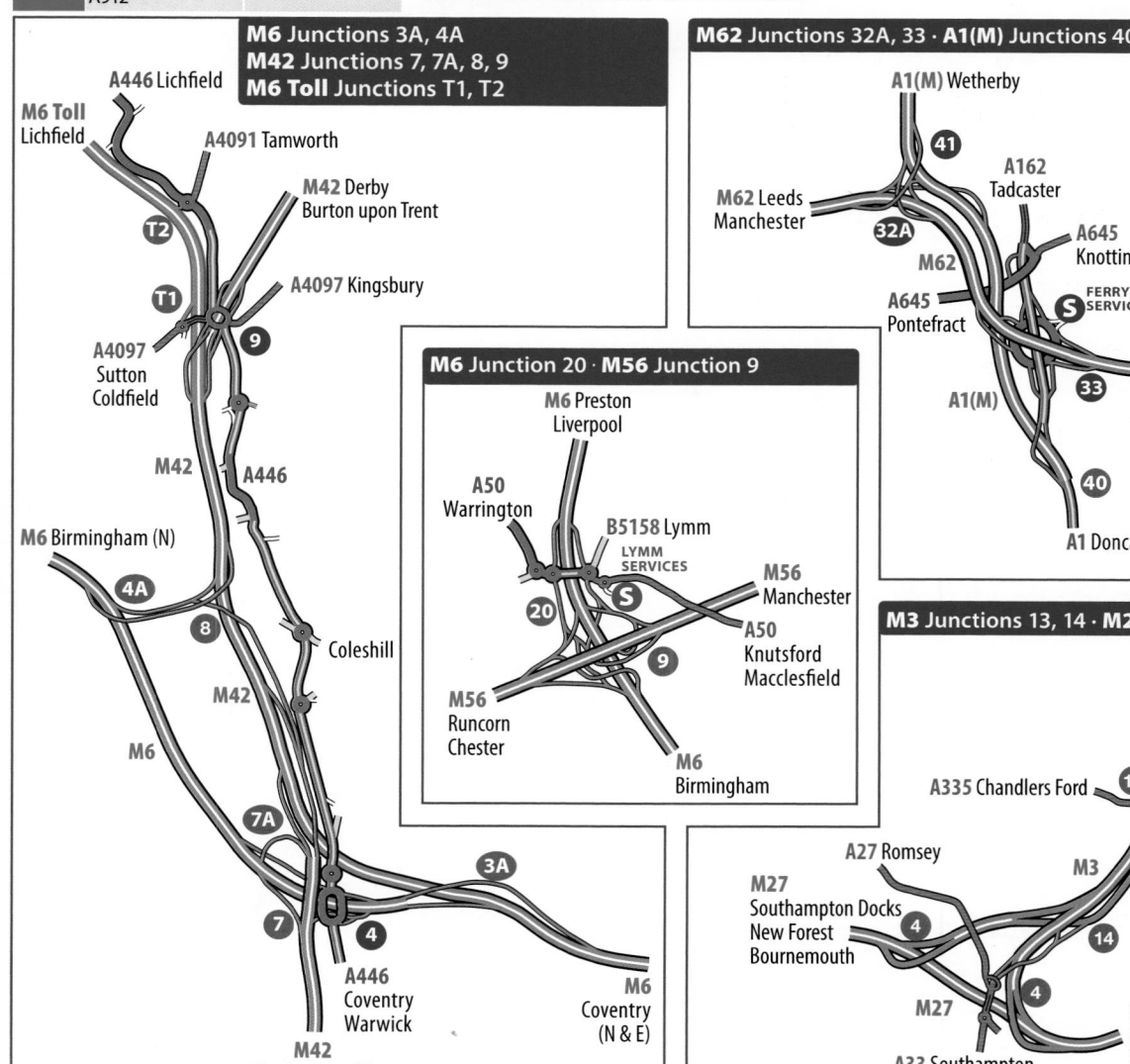

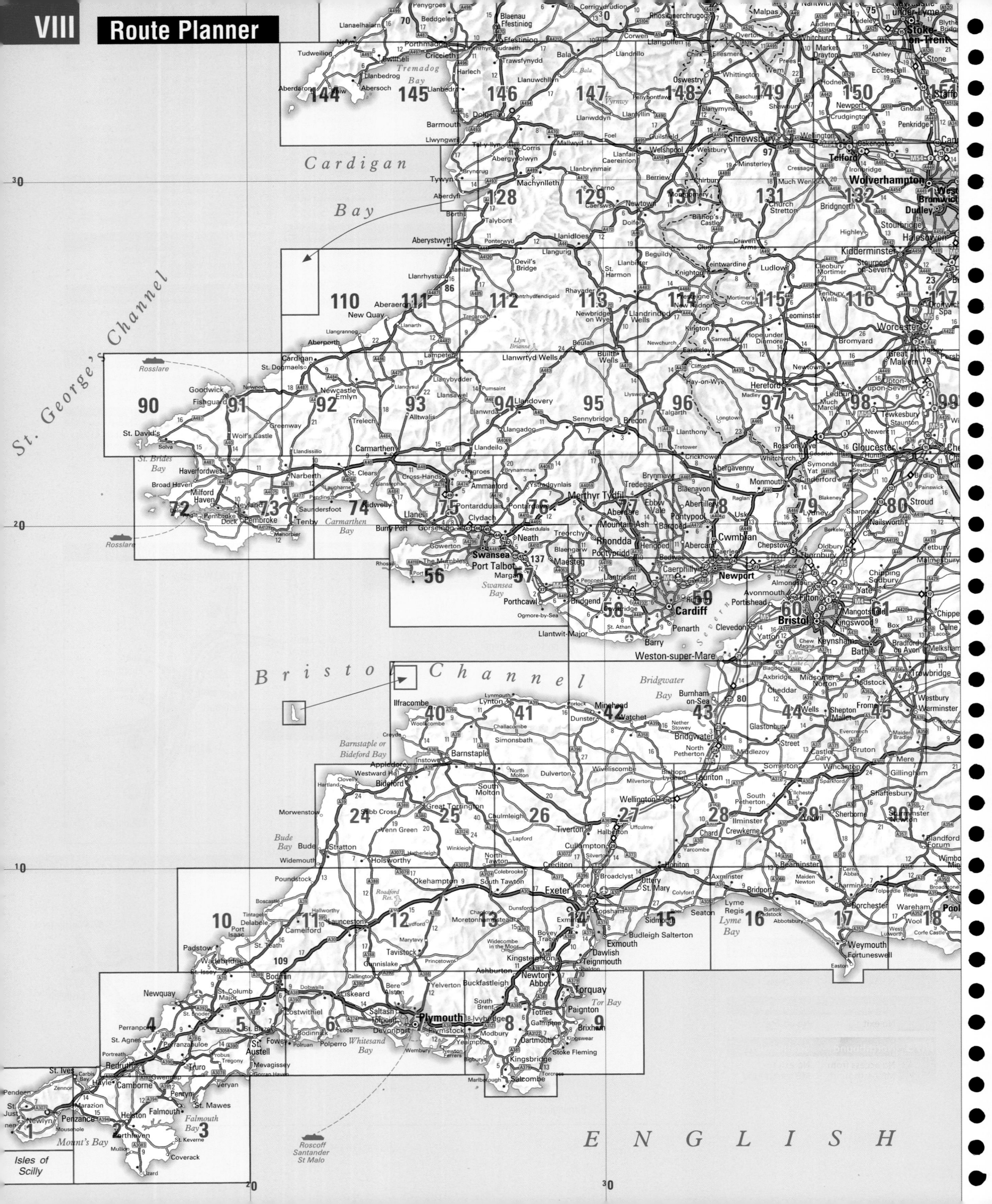

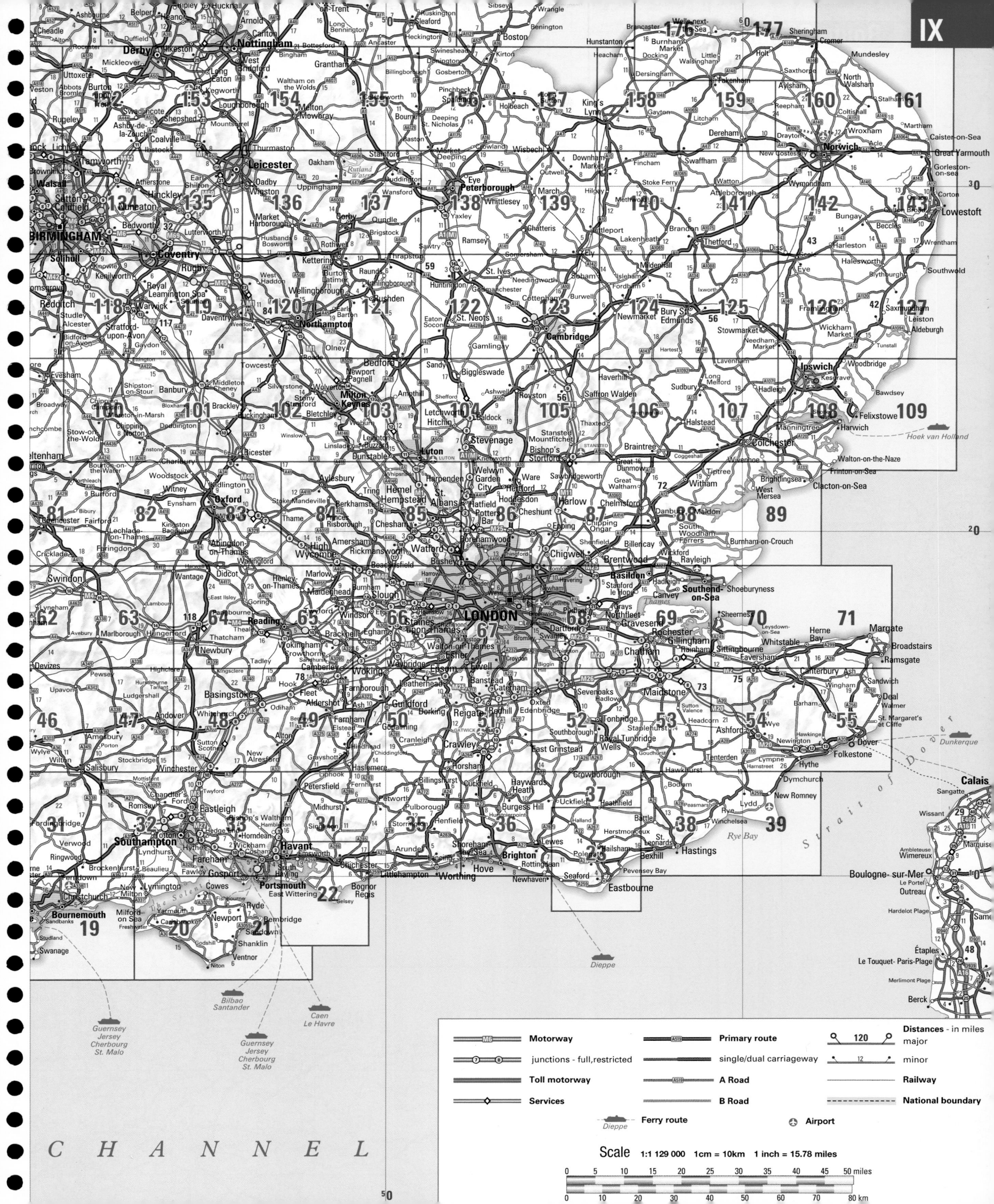

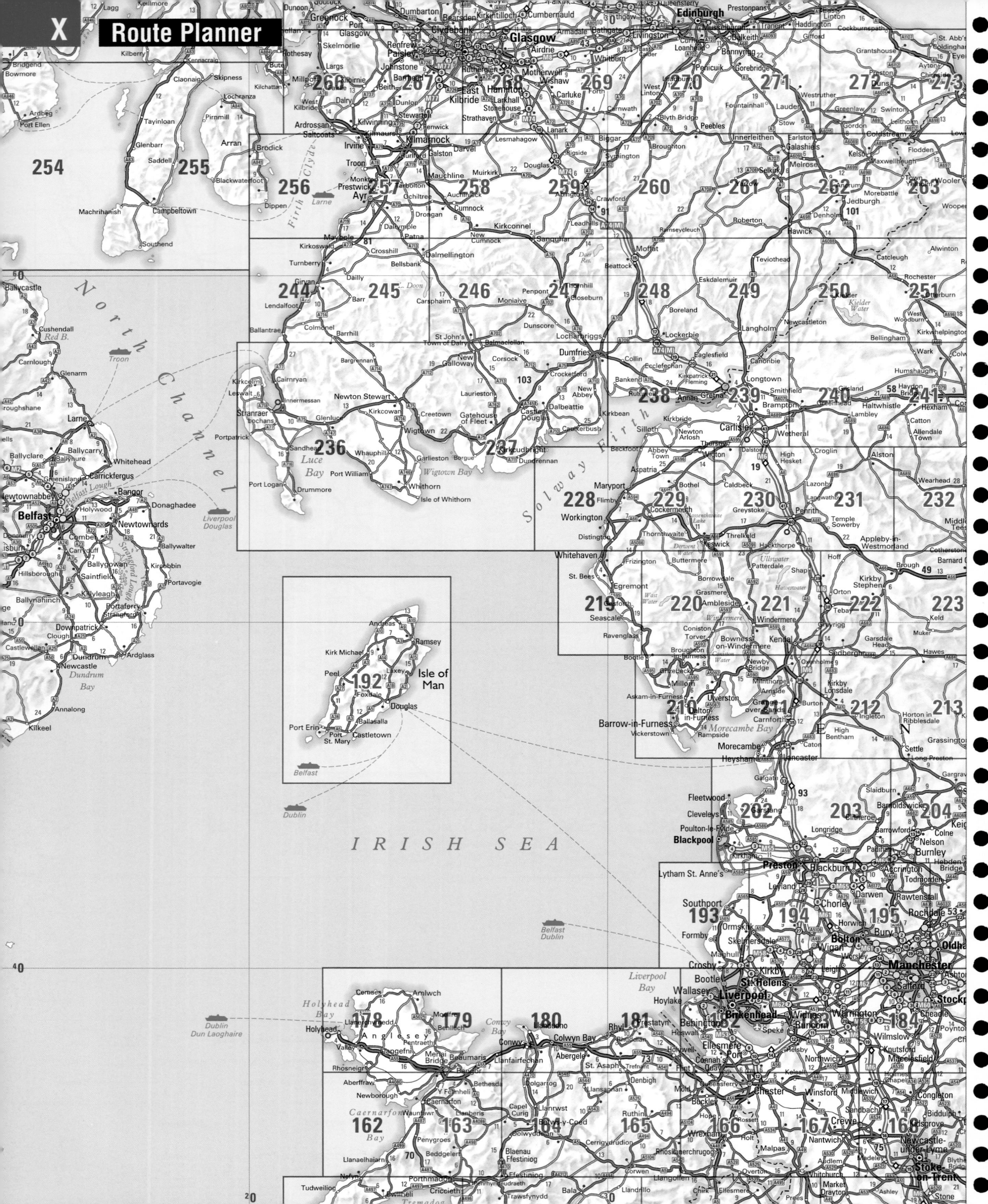

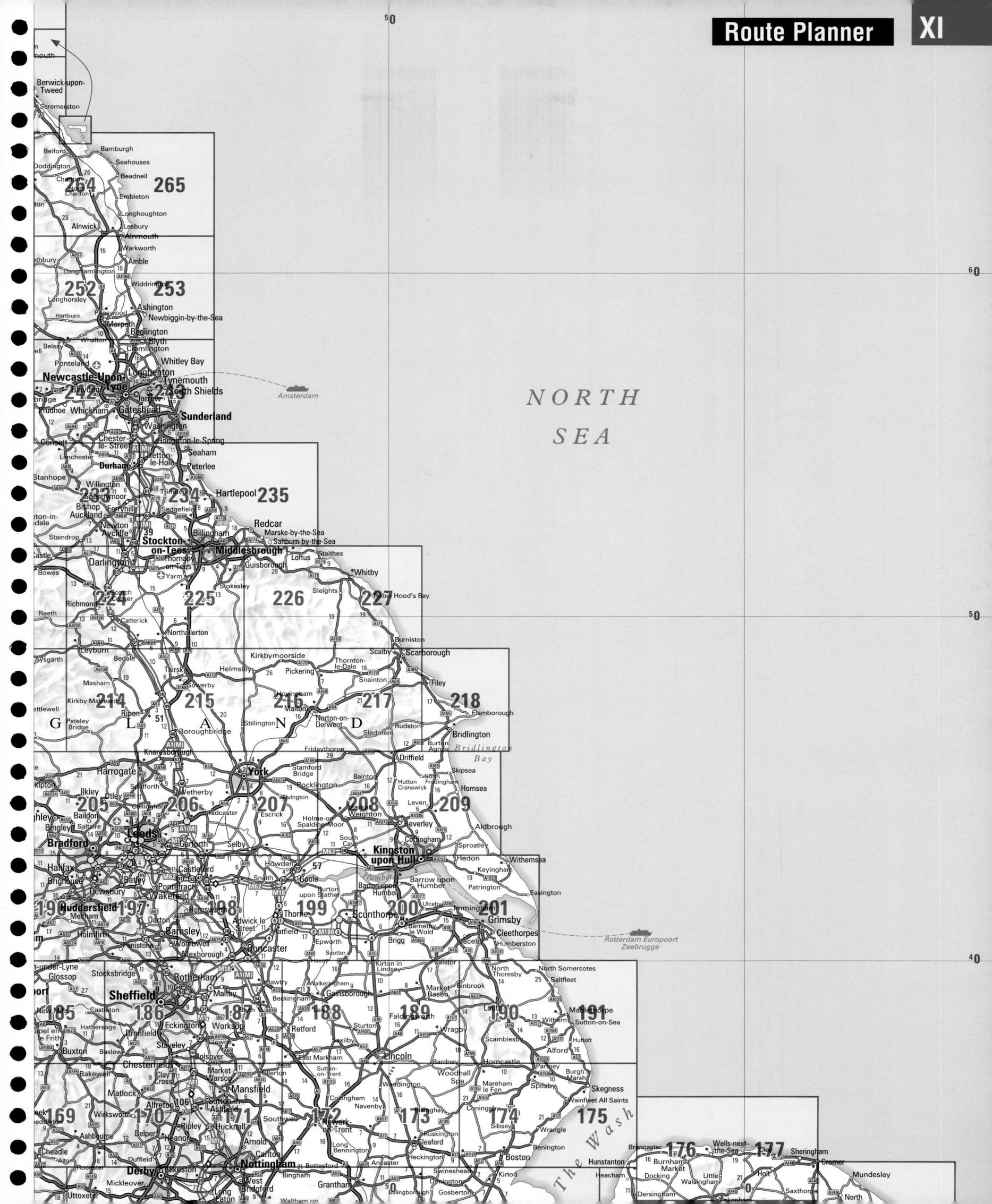

NORTH SEA

Bridlington Bay

The Wash

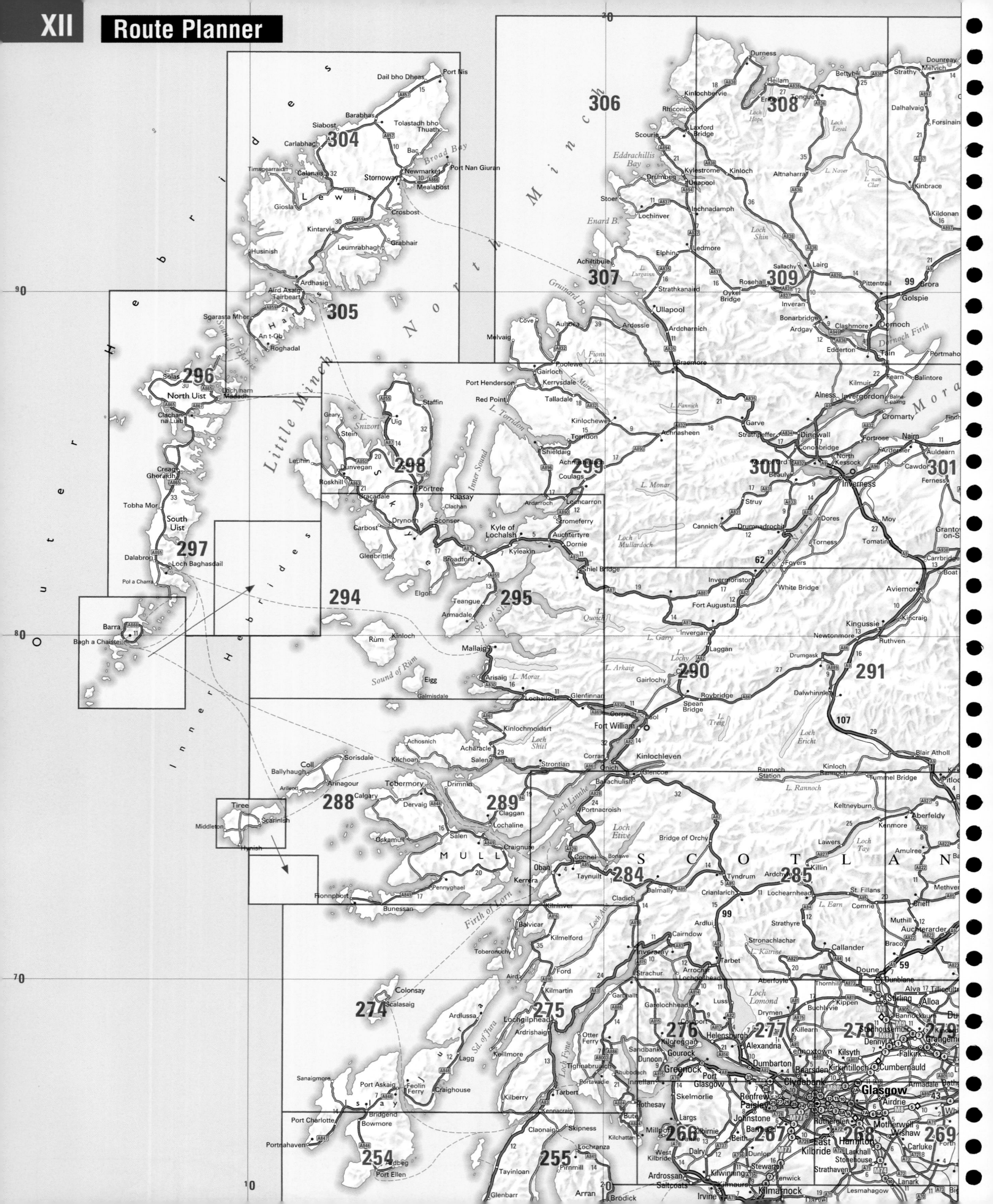

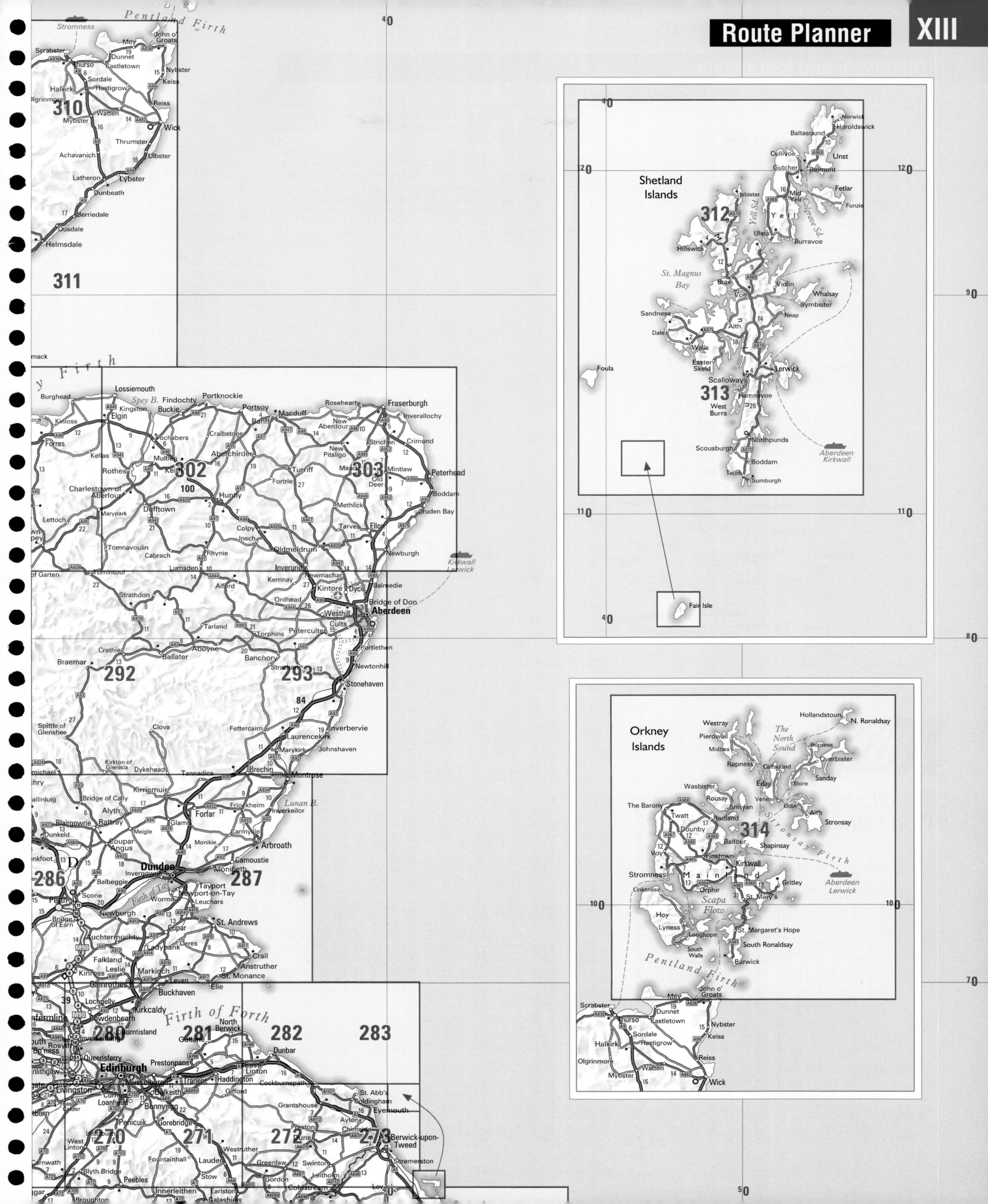

Distances and journey times

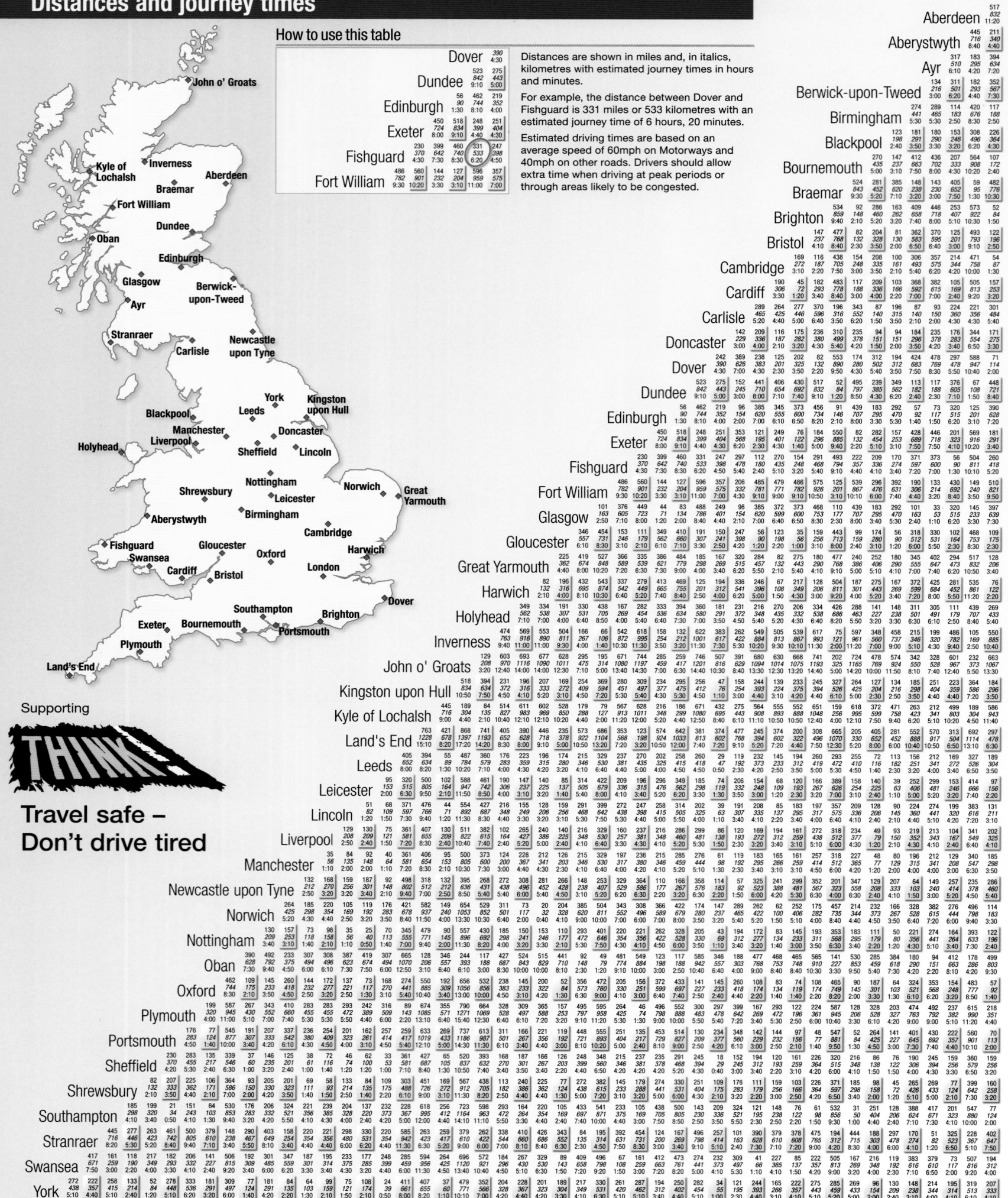

How to use this table

Distances are shown in miles and, in italics, kilometres with estimated journey times in hours and minutes.

For example, the distance between Dover and Fishguard is 331 miles or 533 kilometres with an estimated journey time of 6 hours, 20 minutes.

Estimated driving times are based on an average speed of 60mph on Motorways and 40mph on other roads. Drivers should allow extra time when driving at peak periods or through areas likely to be congested.

Supporting

THINK!

Travel safe –
Don't drive tired

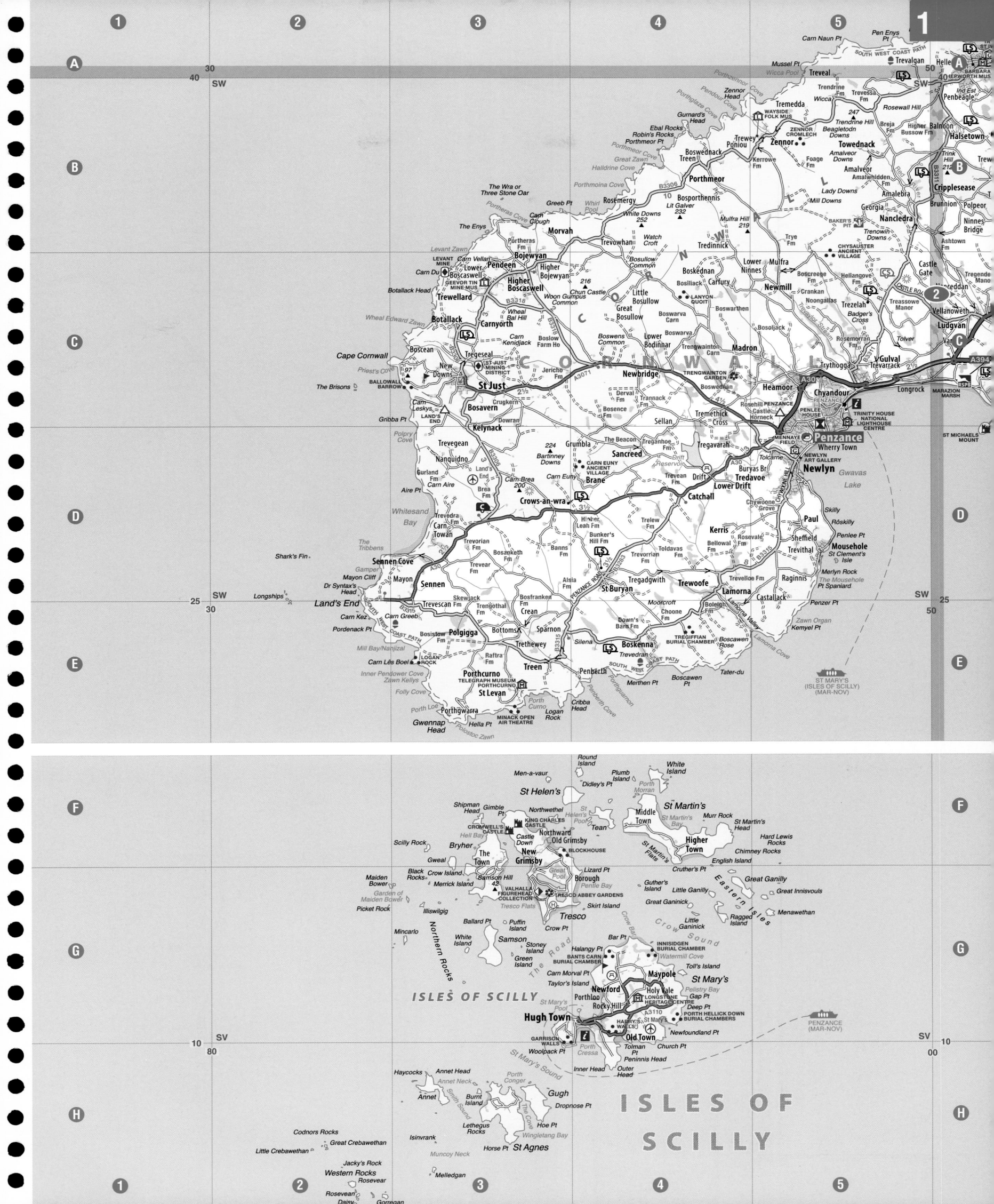

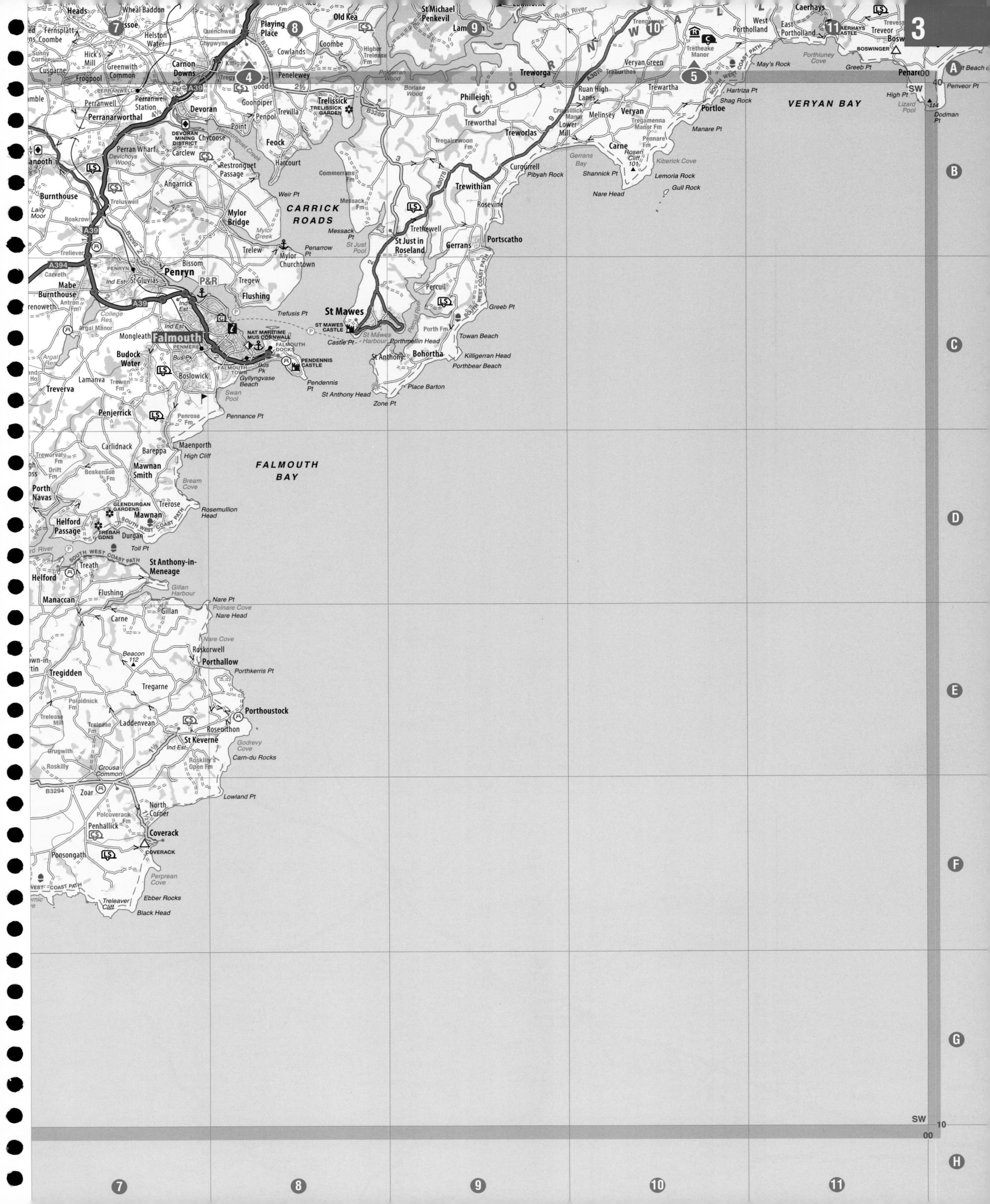

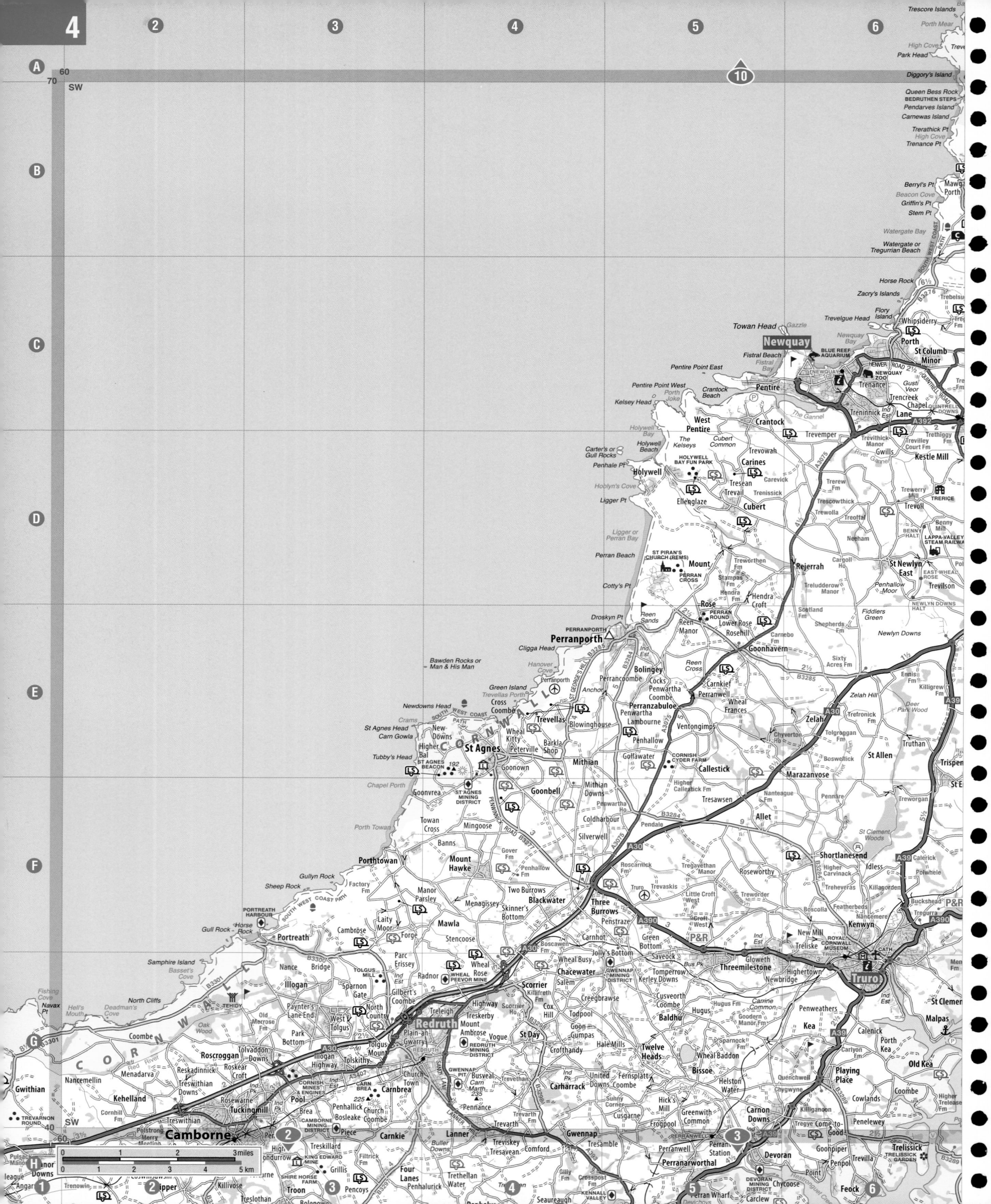

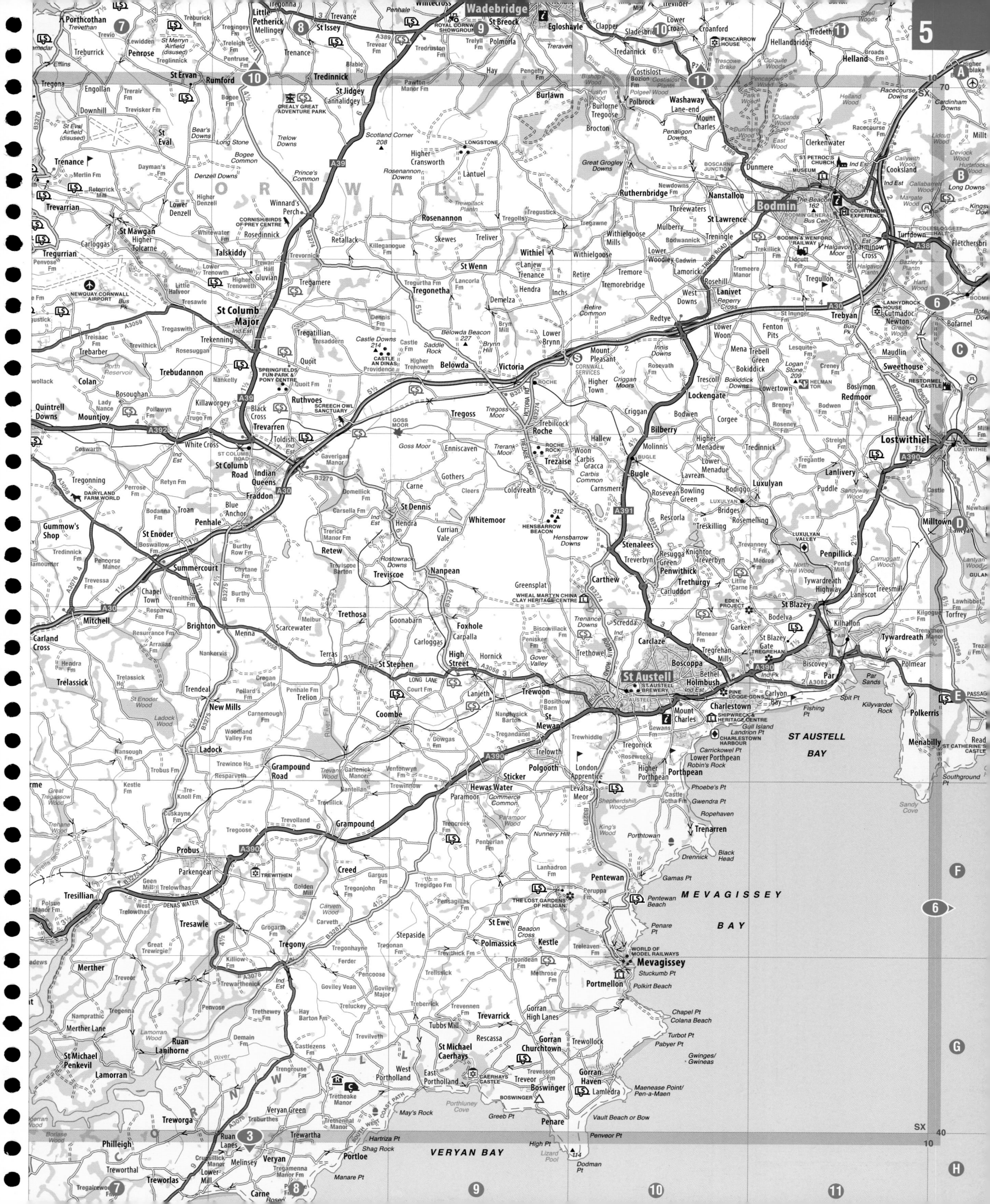

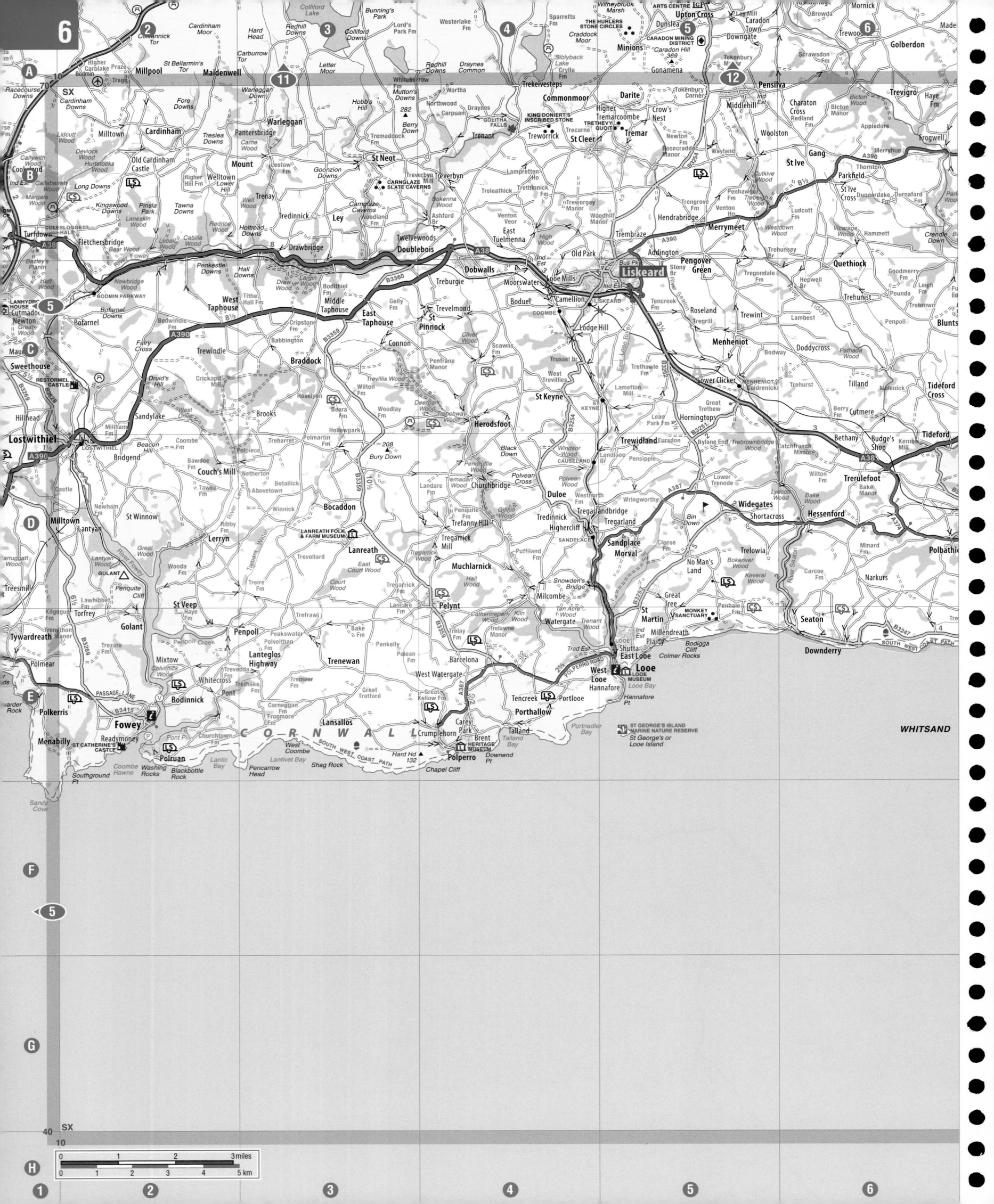

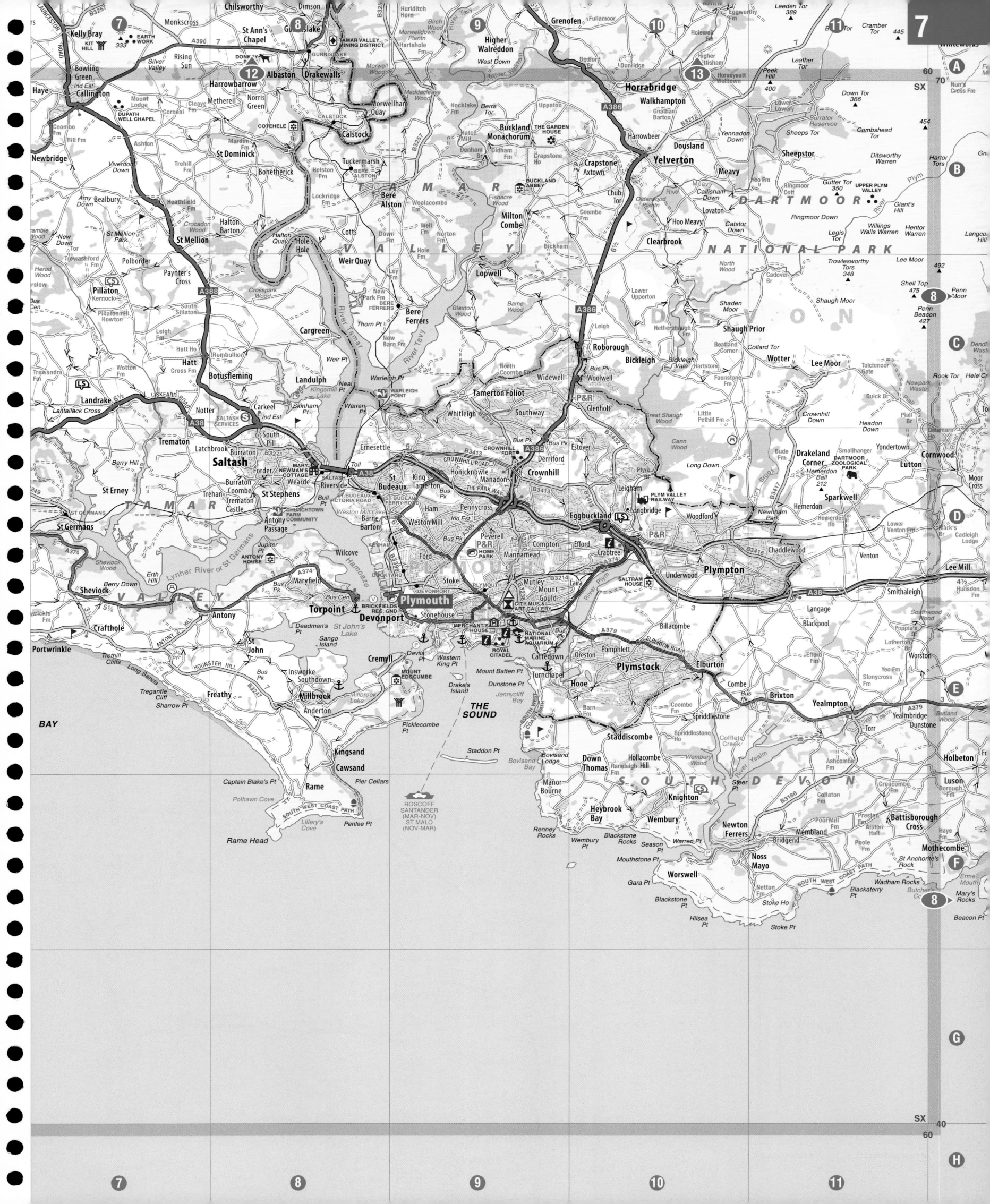

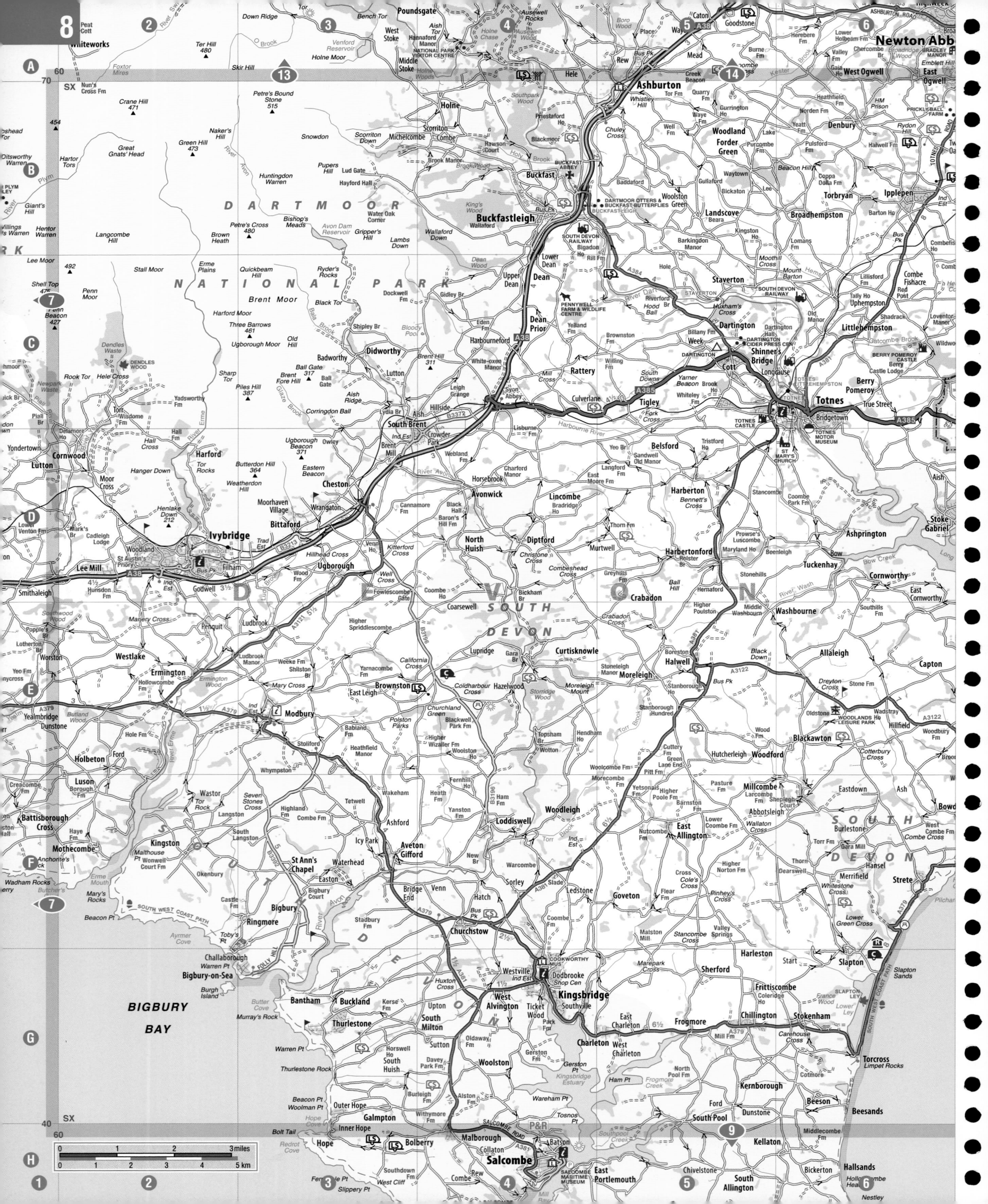

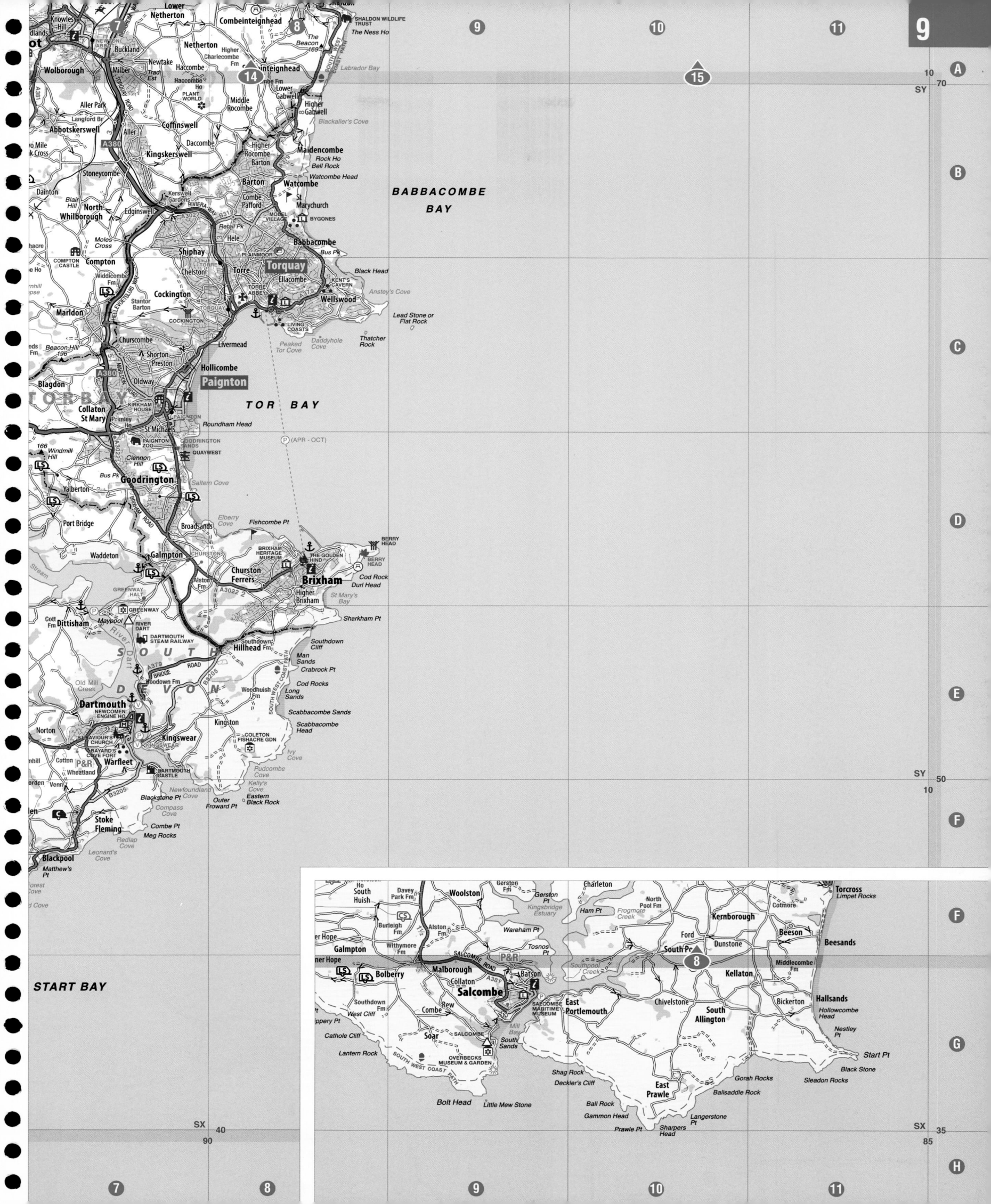

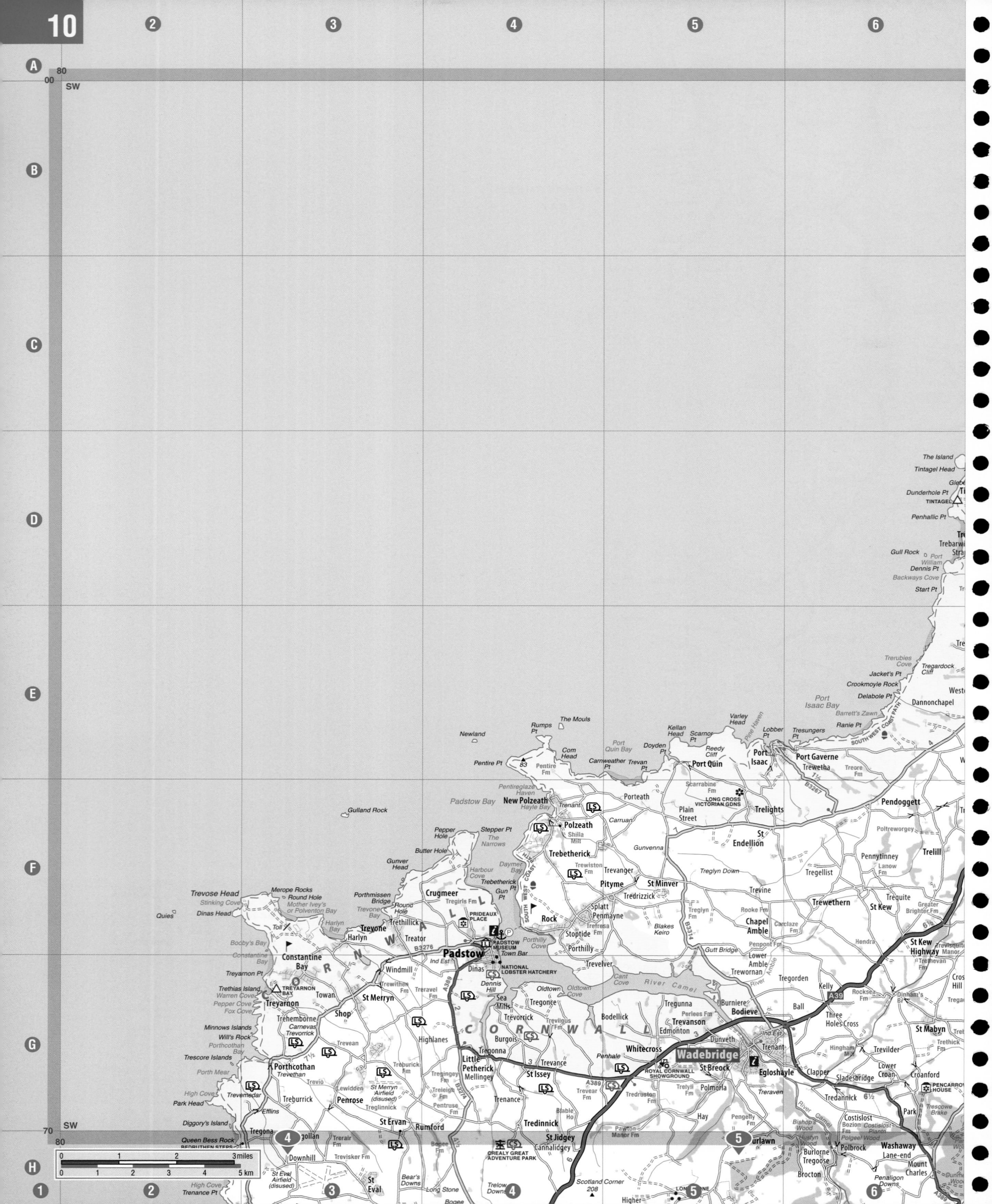

2 3 4 5 6

A
80
00
SW

B

C

D

E

F

G

H

1

The Island
Tintagel Head
Glebe
Dunderhole Pt Ti
TINTAGEL △
TINTAGEL
Penhallic Pt

Tre
Trebarwi
Stra

Gull Rock   Port
William
Dennis Pt
Backways Cove

Start Pt   Tr

*Trerubies
Cove*   Tregardock
Cliff
Jacket's Pt
Crookmoyle Rock
Delabole Pt   Dannonchapel Weste
Port
Isaac Bay *Barrett's Zawn*
Ranie Pt

Varley
Head
*Rumps
Pt* *The Mouls* Kellan Scarnor
Head   Pt *Reedy
Cliff* Lobber
Tresungers Pt
*Port
Quin Bay* Doyden
Pt Trevan
Pt Port Port Gaverne
Newland   *Com
Head*   Port Quin Isaac
Pentire Pt   83 *Pentire
Fm* Carnweather
Pt Trewetha Treore
Fm
B3267

*Pentireglaze
Haven* Scarrabine
Fm LONG CROSS
VICTORIAN GDNS Trelights Pendoggett Tr
Padstow Bay   New Polzeath Porteath Plain
Street St
Endellion
Trenant Polzeath
Hayle Bay Carruan Poltreworgery
Gulland Rock   Shilla
Mill Pennytinney Lanow Trelill
*Pepper
Hole*   *Stepper Pt*
*The
Narrows* Trebetherick Gunvenna Tregellist Trevine
Butter Hole   Daymer
Bay Trewiston
Fm Trevanger Tregyln Down Trewethern St Kew Trequite
*Gunver
Head*   Pityme St Minver Greater
Brighter Fm
Trevose Head   Merope Rocks Porthmissen *Harbour
Cove* Tredrizzick Rooke Fm
Round Hole   Bridge *Round
Hole* Trebetherick Trefresa Tregyln
Fm Chapel Carclaze
Stinking Cove   Mother Ivey's Trevone Gun
Pt Crugmeer Rock Fm Amble Fm St Kew
Dinas Head or Polventon Bay   Treyone Trethillick Splatt Blakes
Keiro B3314 Hendra Highway
Quies   Treator Penmayne Penpont Fm Trevisquite
Manor
Harlyn PRIDEAUX Stoptide Lower
Trevean Fm
Toll *Harlyn Bay* PLACE Porthilly Amble
B3276 Porthilly
Cove Gutt Bridge St Mabyn
Booby's Bay   Padstow NATIONAL Cant Trewornan Tregorden Kelly Rockhead
Fm Cros
Constantine PADSTOW MUSEUM LOBSTER Cove River Camel Hill
Bay Town Bar HATCHERY A39
Constantine Ind Est Dinas Oldtown Burniere Dinham's
Bay Windmill Dennis Cove Bodieve Br
Treyarnon Pt Hill Oldtown Tregunna Trevanson Ball Three
Trethias Island   TREYARNON Sea Perlees Fm Holes Cross St Mabyn
Warren Cove △ BAY Towan St Merryn Mills Tregonce Bodellick Edmonton Dunveth Hingham Trethick
Pepper Cove Treyarnon Shop Trevorrick CORNWALL MIK Lower
Fox Cove   Trevio Highlanes Burgois Trevance Whitecross ROYAL CORNWALL St Breock Trevilder Croan
Trehemborne Tregonna SHOWGROUND Egloshayle Croan
Minnows Islands   Carnevas Penhale Wadebridge Clapper Sladesbridge Croanford
Will's Rock Trevorrick Little Dunveth PENCARROW
Porthcothan Shop Petherick Trevance HOUSE
Bay Trevean Mellingey St Issey Tredruston Trelyll Tredannick Trescowe
Trescore Islands   Trevance A389 Trevear Polmorla Brake
Porthcothan Burgois Treglieth Hay Pengelly Bishop's Costislost Park
Porth Mear   Fm Bozion Wood Costislost
△Porthcothan   A389 Nanstallon Polgoose Wood
Trevethan Trivio Pentruse Tredannick Pawton Bozion Polgeel Washaway
High Cove   Treburrick Lewidden Blable Manor Fm Burlorne Polbrock Lane-end
Penrose Bo Bishop's Tregoose Mount
Park Head Treglinnick Hustyn Brocton Charles
St Merryn
Diggory's Island   Tregona Airfield Tredinnick Sunfl
SW   *(disused)* St Jidgey Penaligon Wo
70
80   Queen Bess Rock Scotland Corner Downs
BEDRUTHEN STEPS   Tregona 4 gollan Trerair St Ervan Rumford 5 urlawn 208

0   1   2   3 miles
0   1   2   3   4   5 km

*St Eval
Airfield (disused)* Treviskar Fm St Eval Bear's Long Stone CREALY GREAT Trelow Scotland Corner LON NE Higher·
ADVENTURE PARK Downs 208

2   *High Cove*   3   4   5   6
Trenance Pt   Downhill   St Eval   Bogee

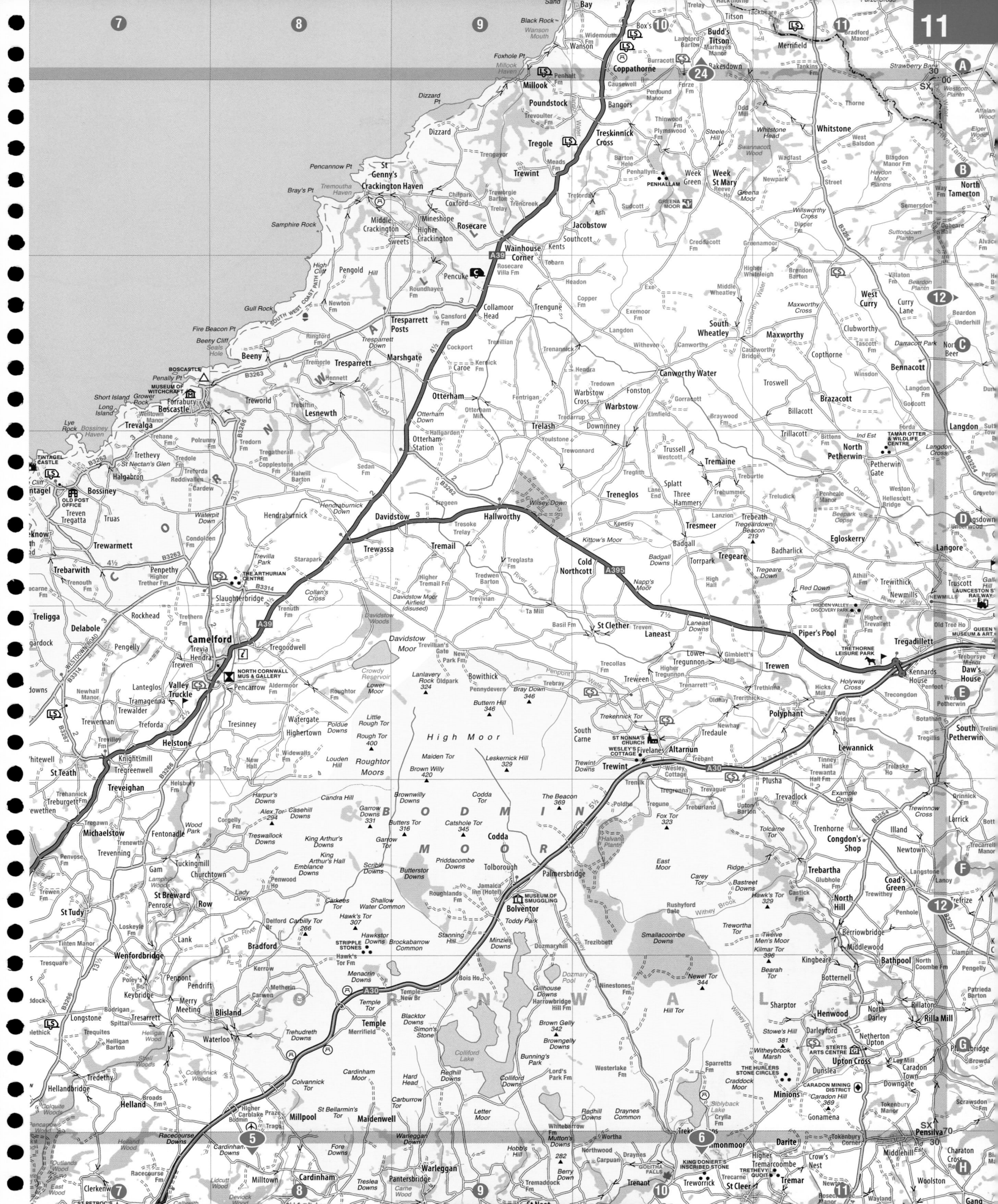

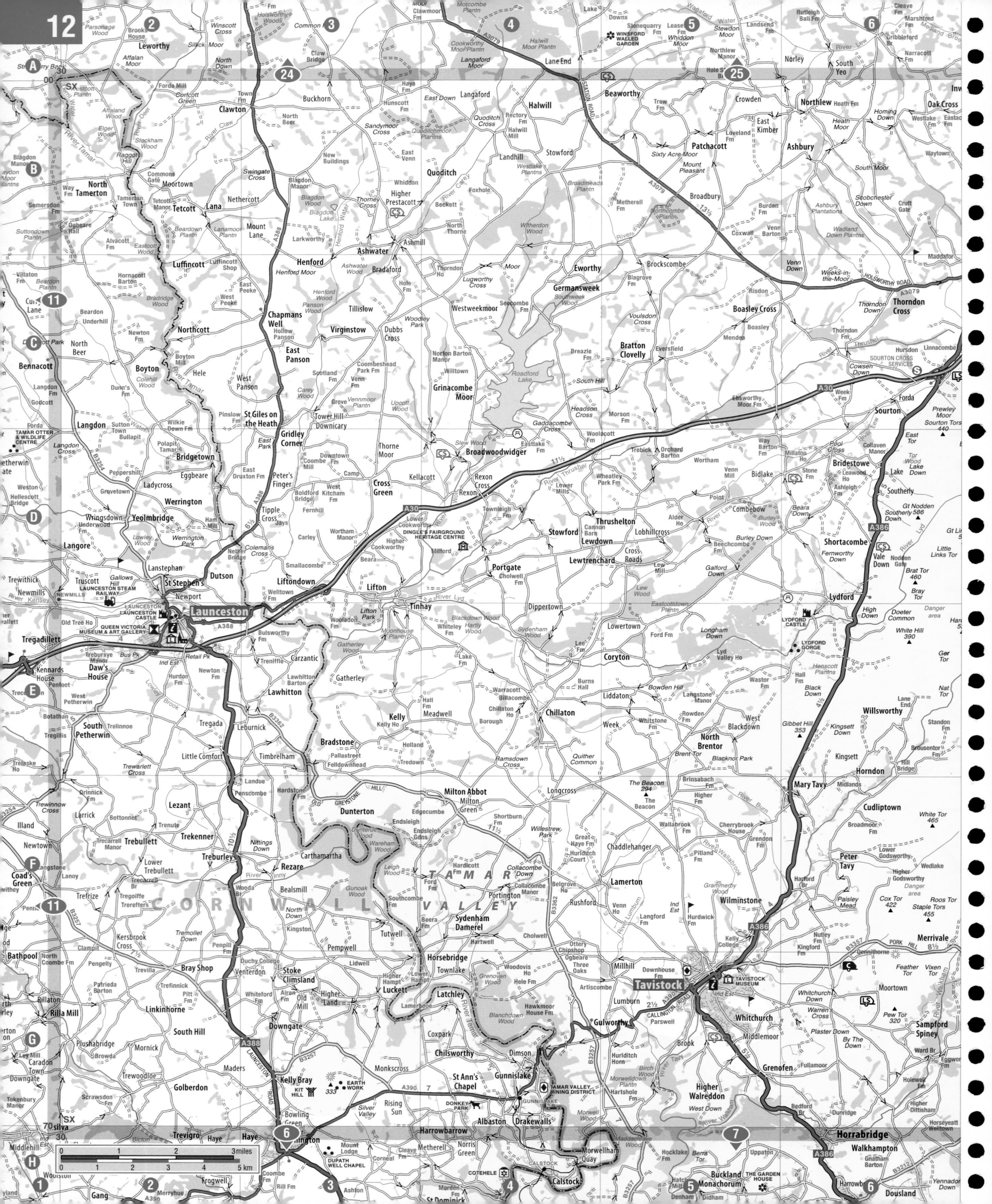

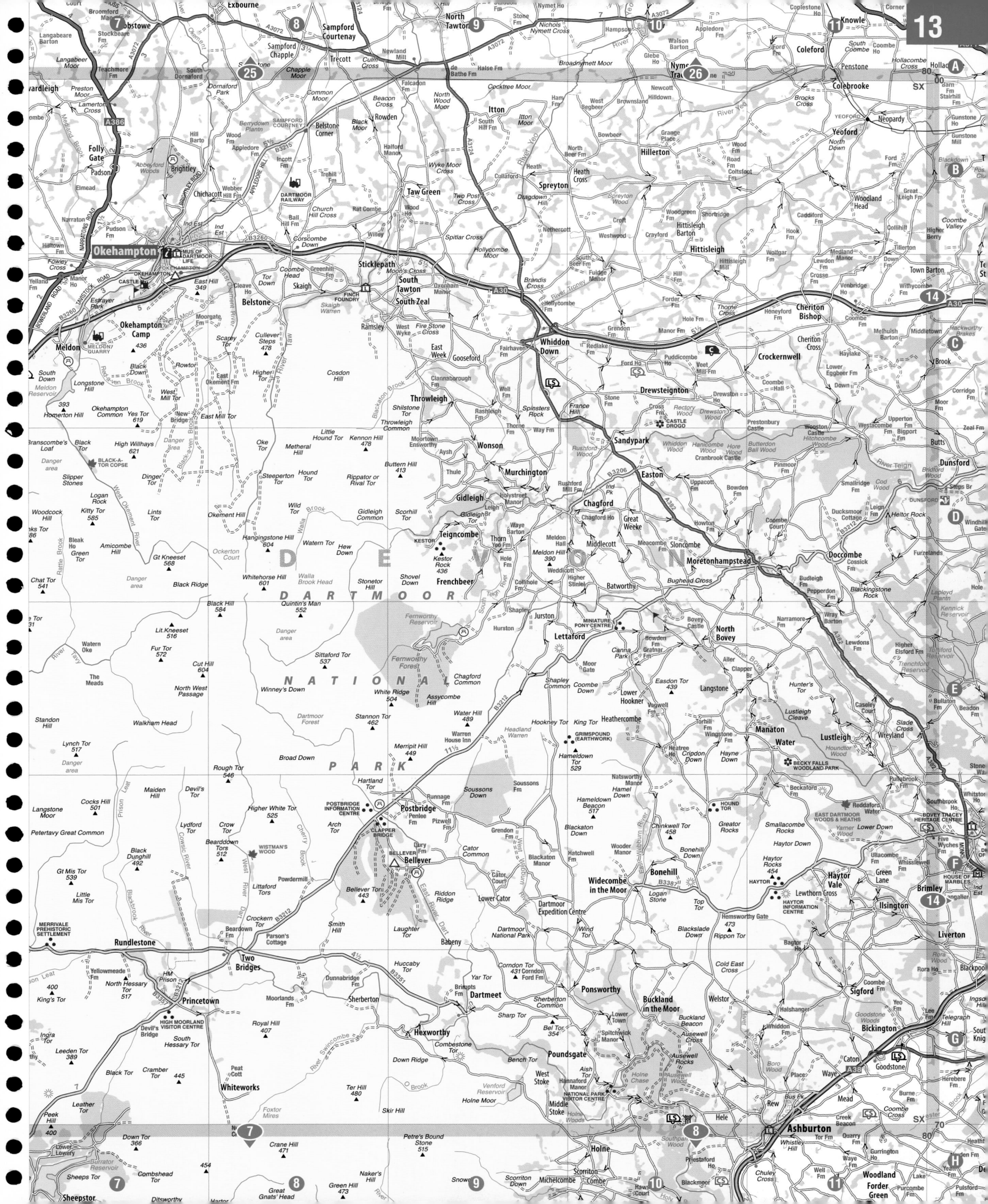

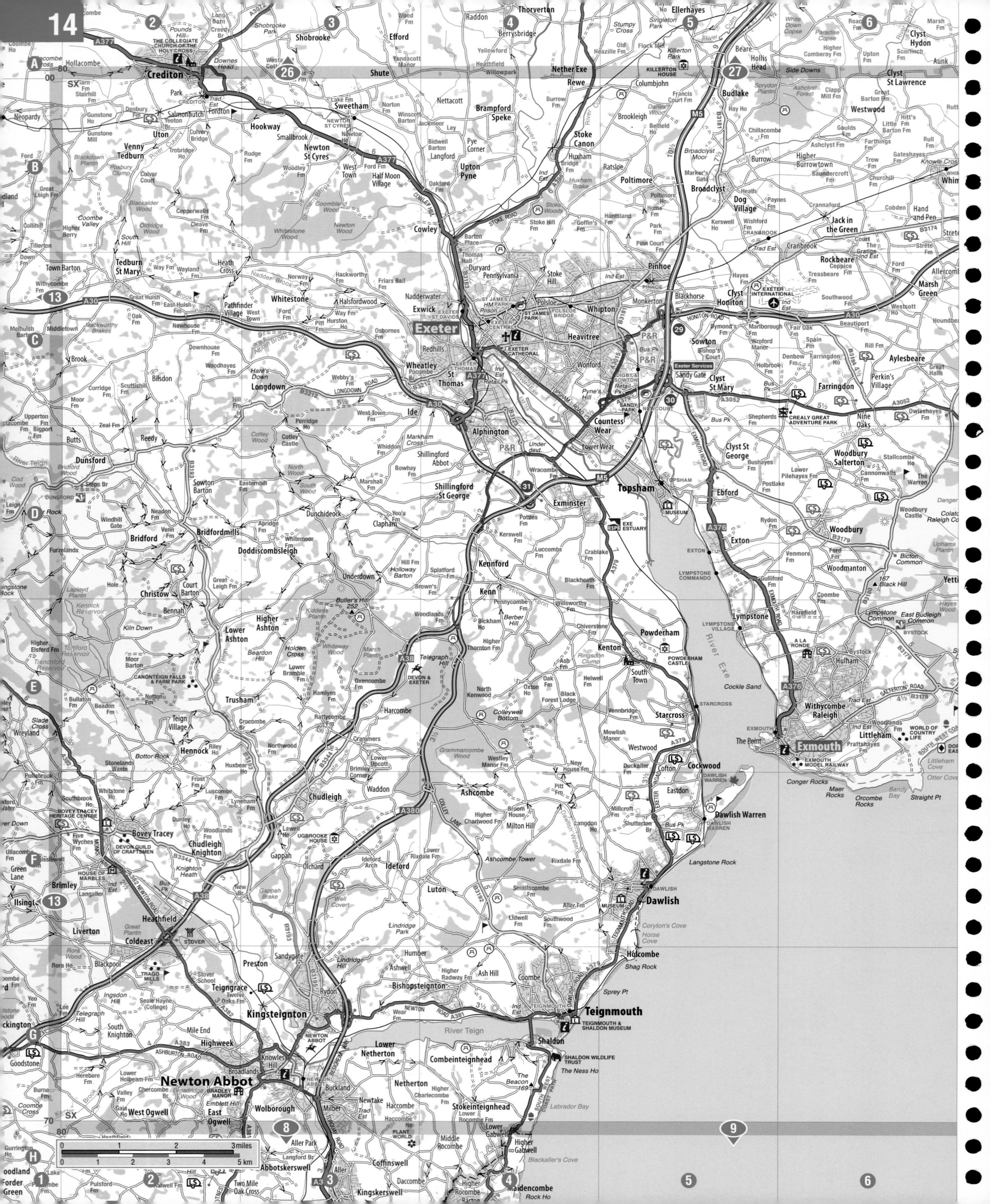

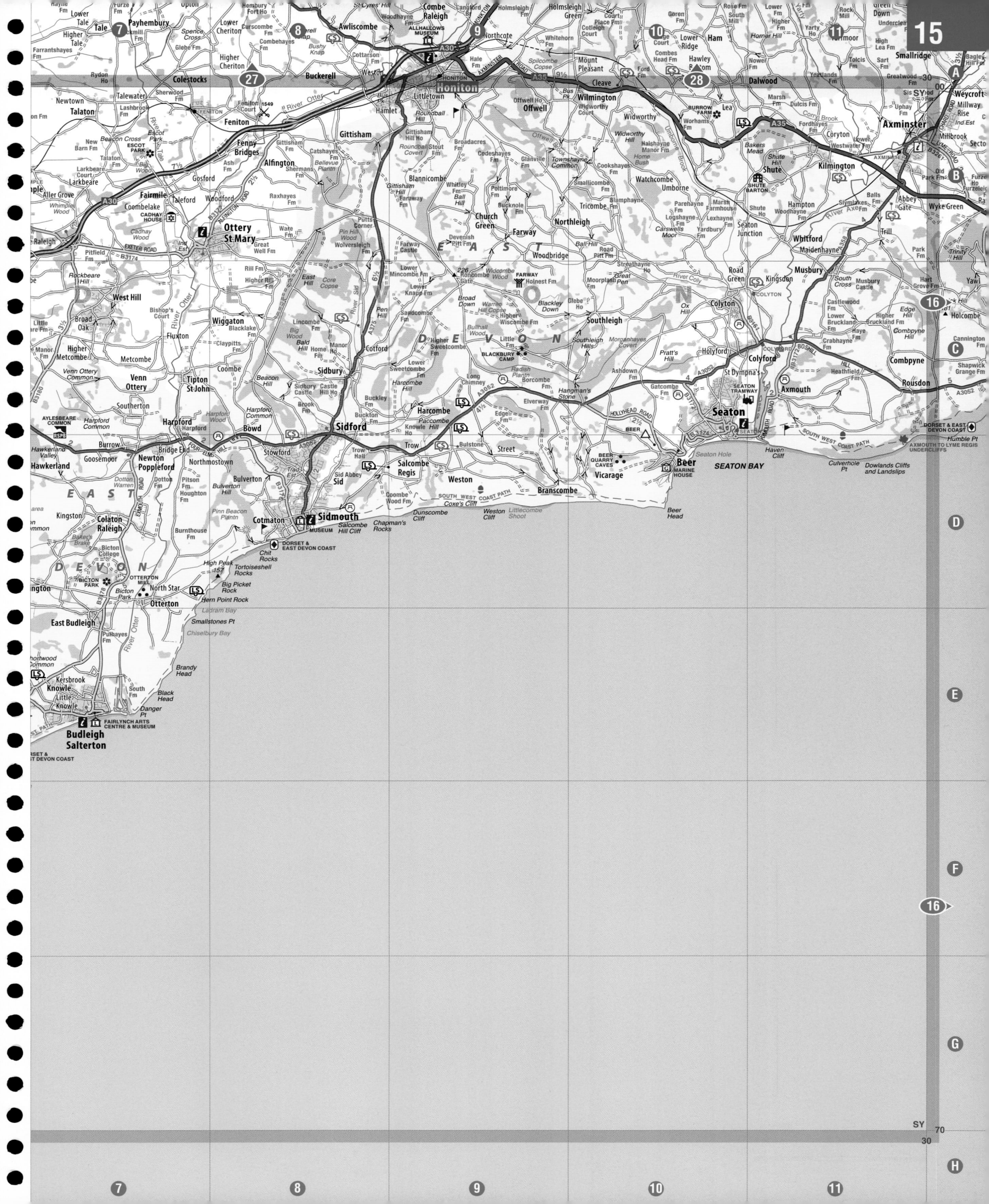

L Y M E

B A Y

DORSET

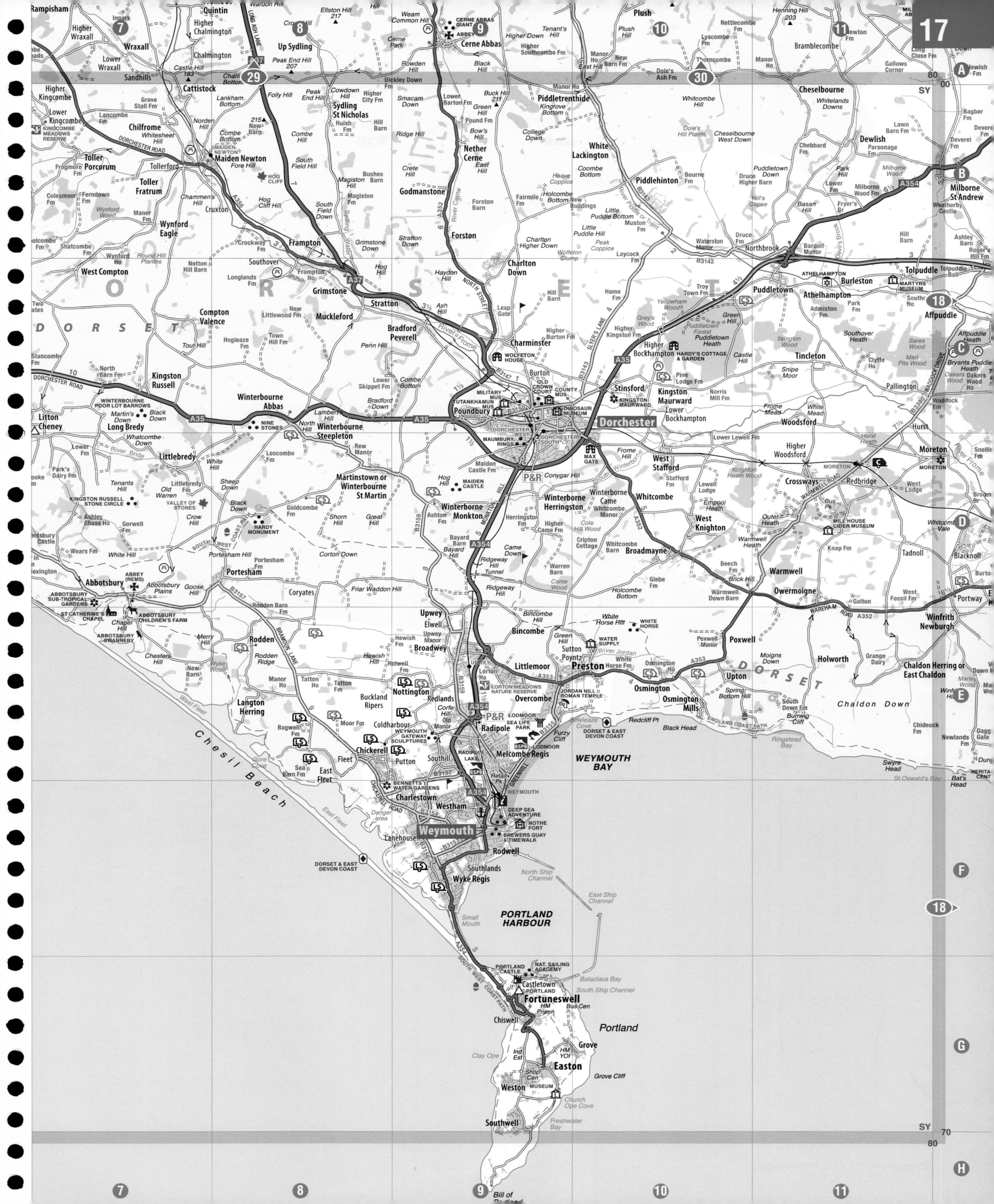

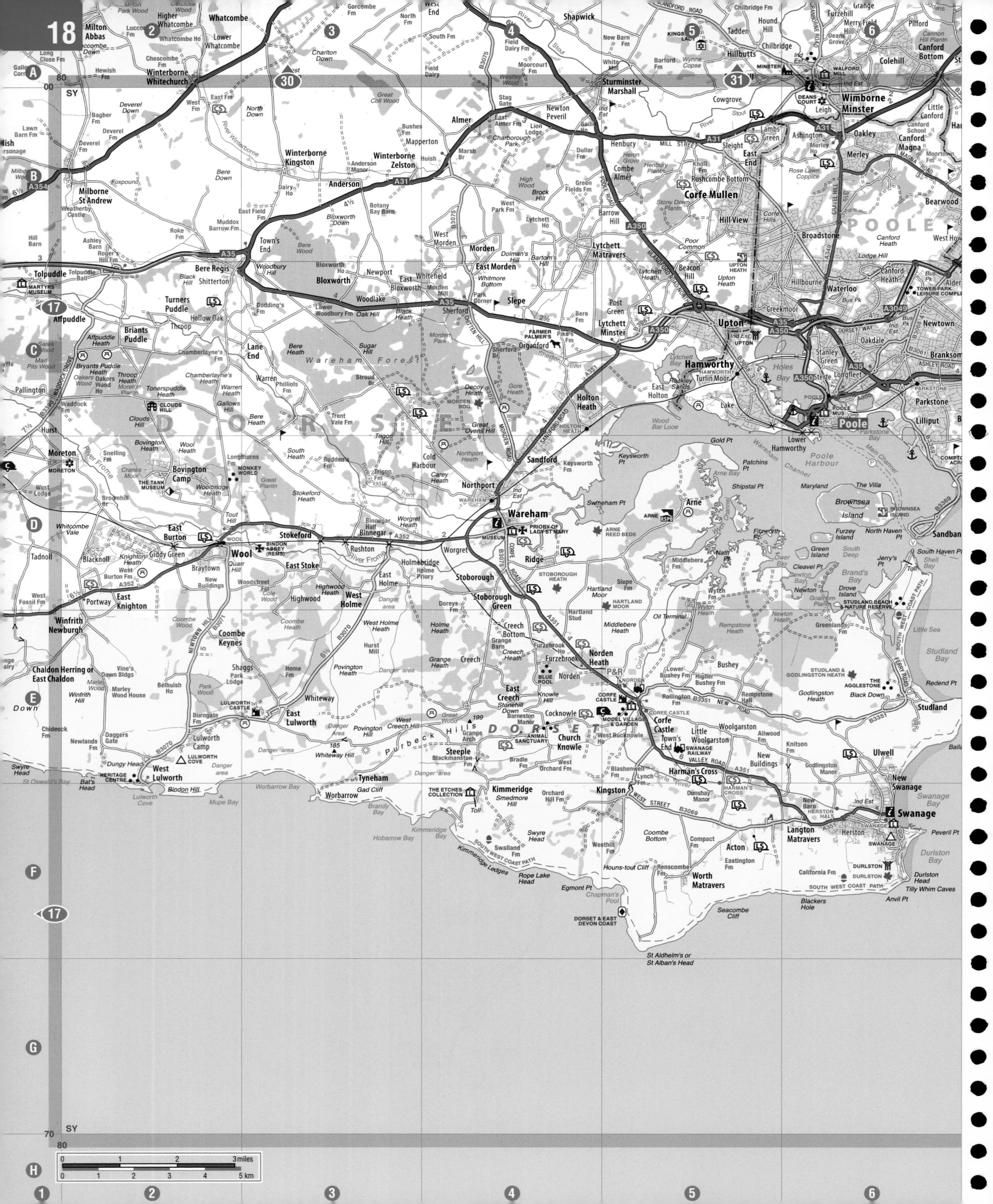

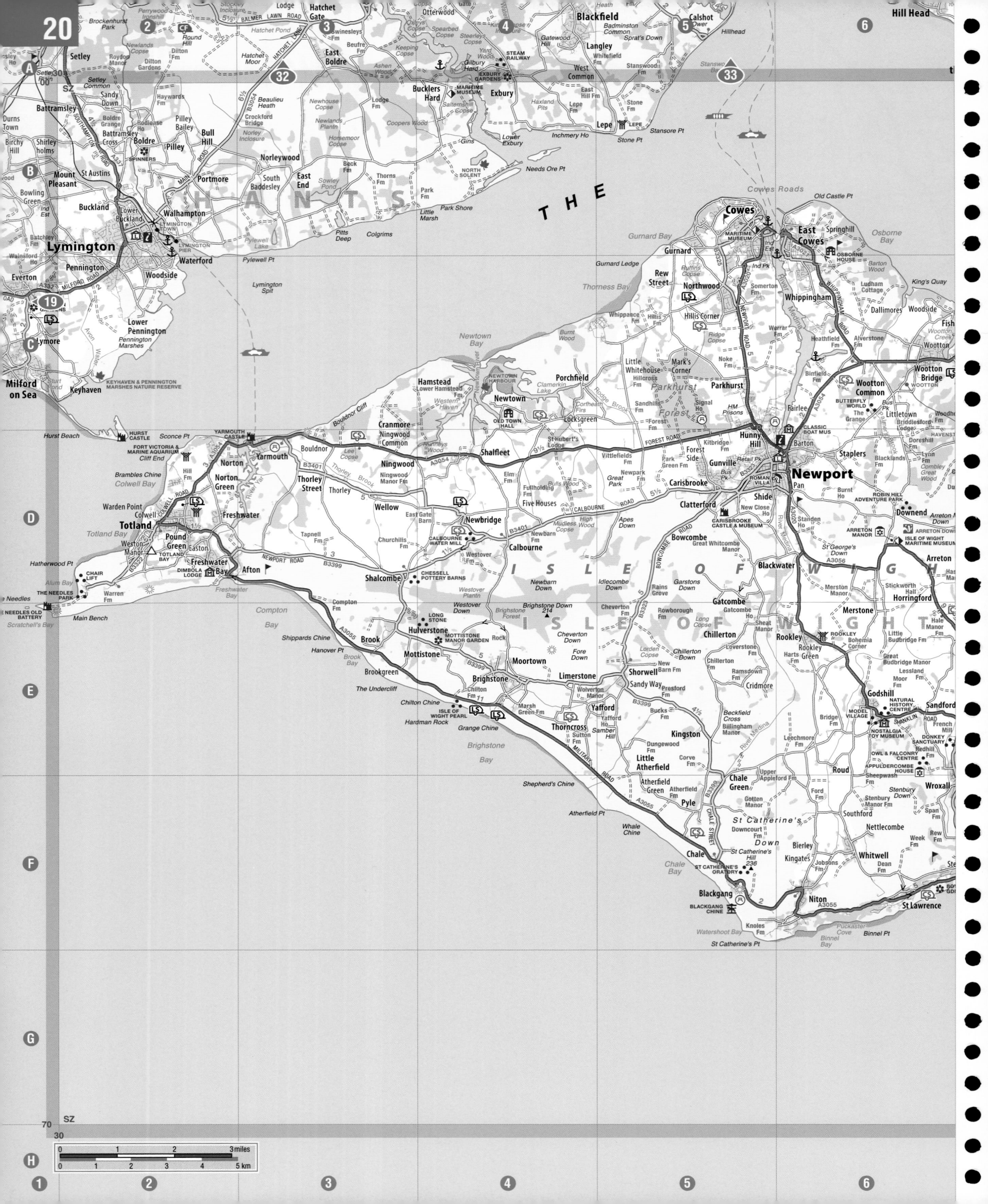

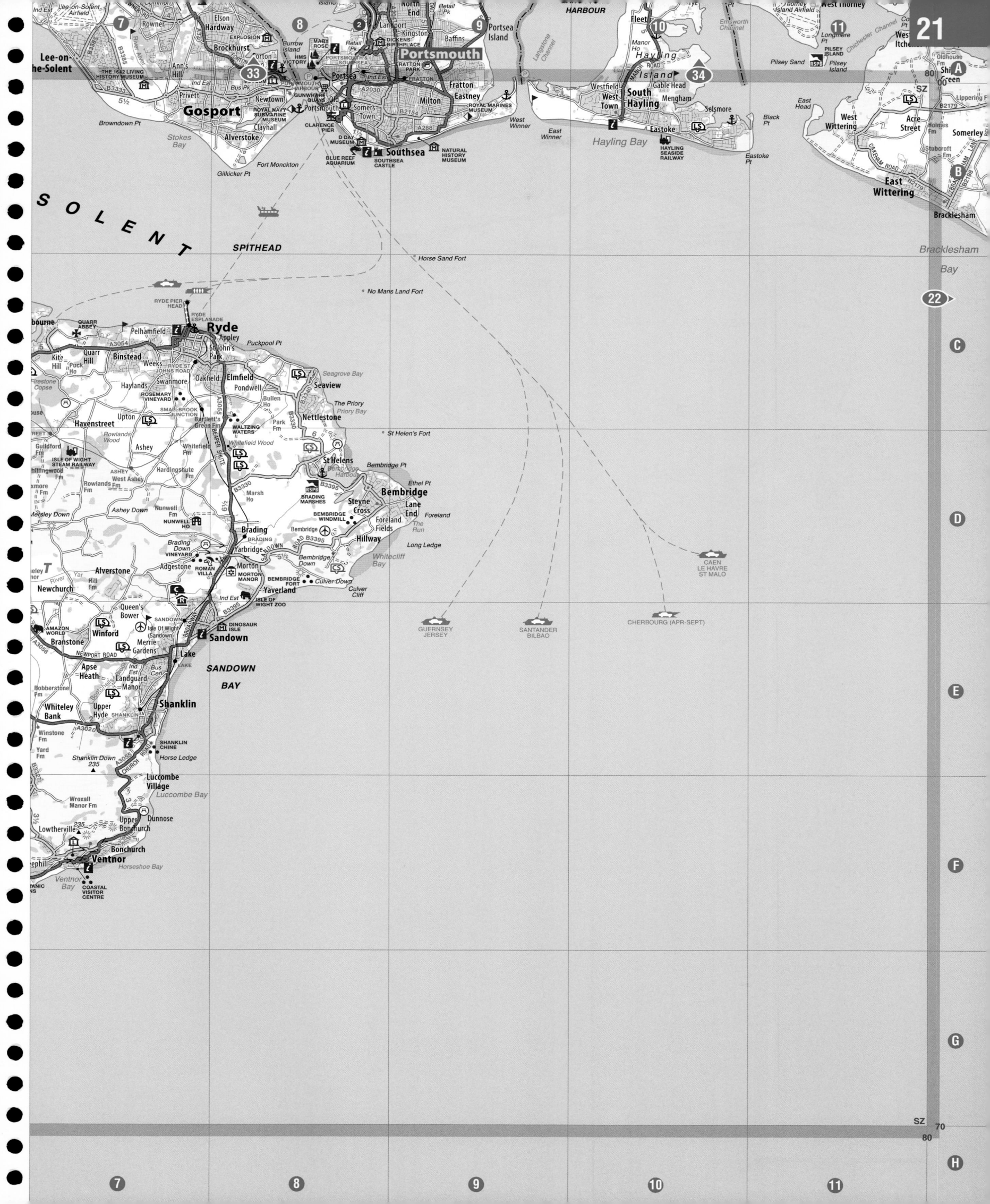

SOLENT

SPITHEAD

Horse Sand Fort

No Mans Land Fort

Bracklesham
Bay

CAEN
LE HAVRE
ST MALO

GUERNSEY
JERSEY

SANTANDER
BILBAO

CHERBOURG (APR-SEPT)

SANDOWN
BAY

HARBOUR

Lee-on-
the-Solent

Gosport

Portsmouth

Southsea

Hayling
Island

South
Hayling

Eastoke

Hayling Bay

West
Wittering

East
Wittering

Bracklesham

Ryde

Seaview

Nettlestone

St Helens

Bembridge

Lane
End

Brading

Yarbridge

Sandown

Lake

Shanklin

Luccombe
Village

Bonchurch

Ventnor

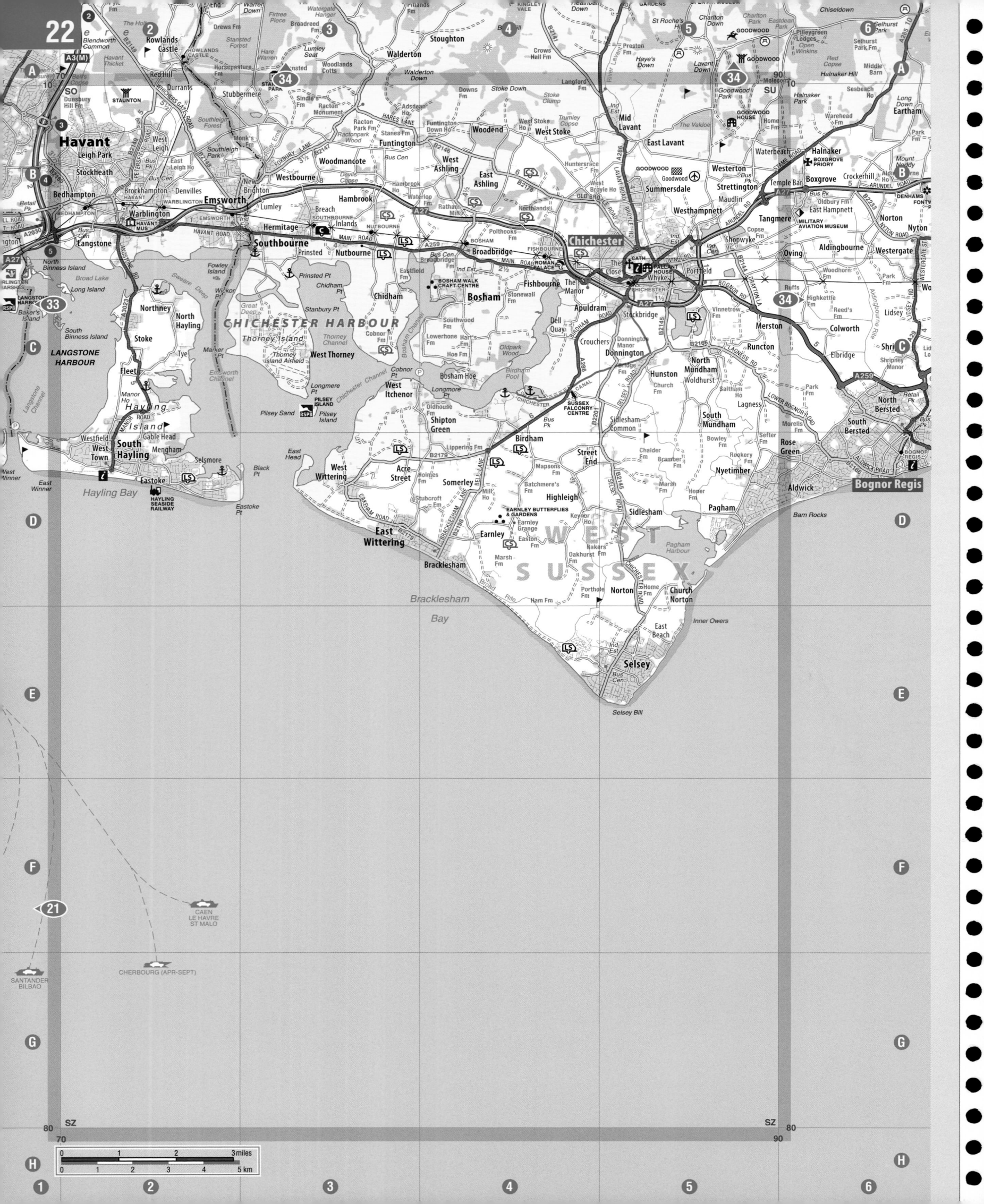

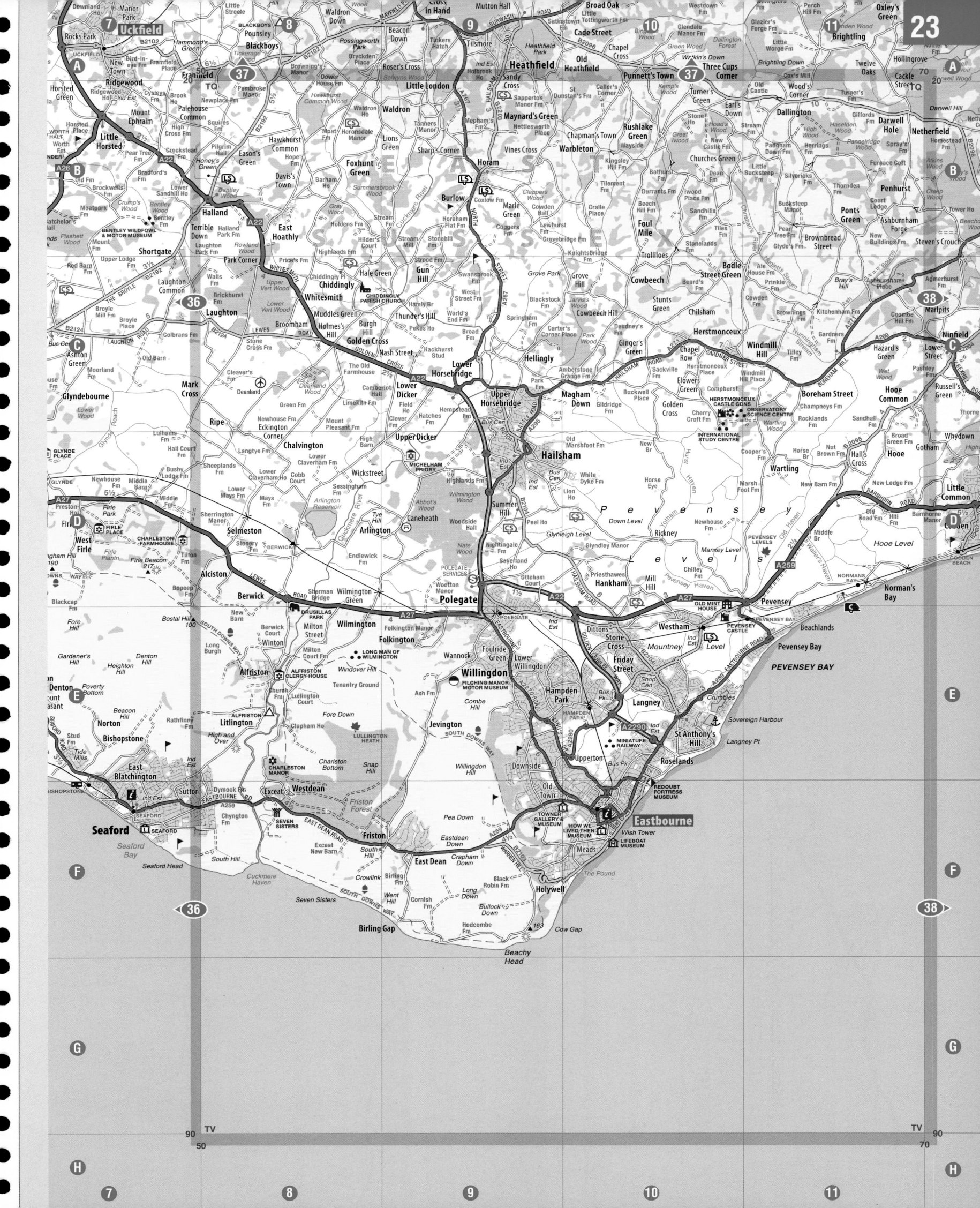

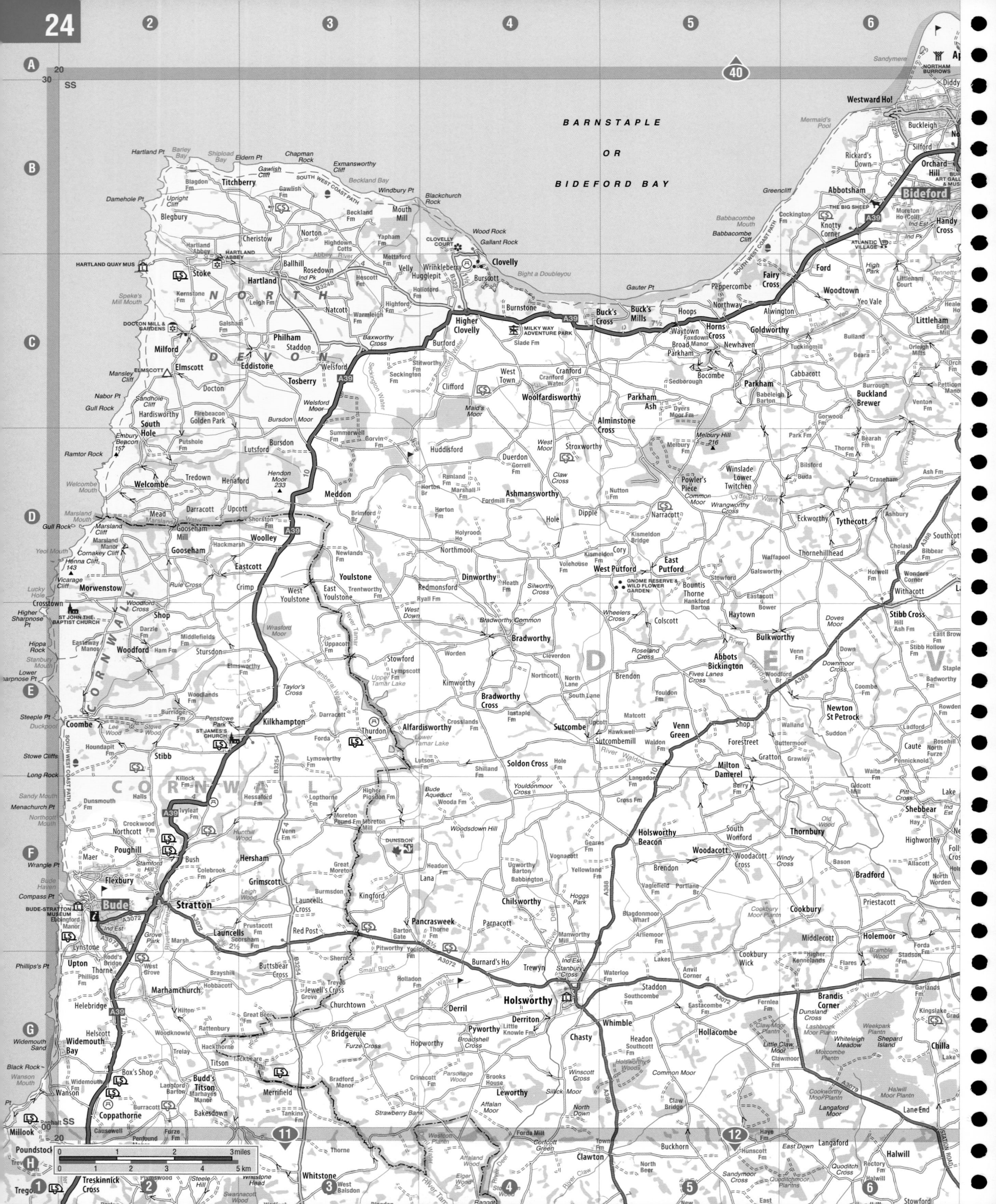

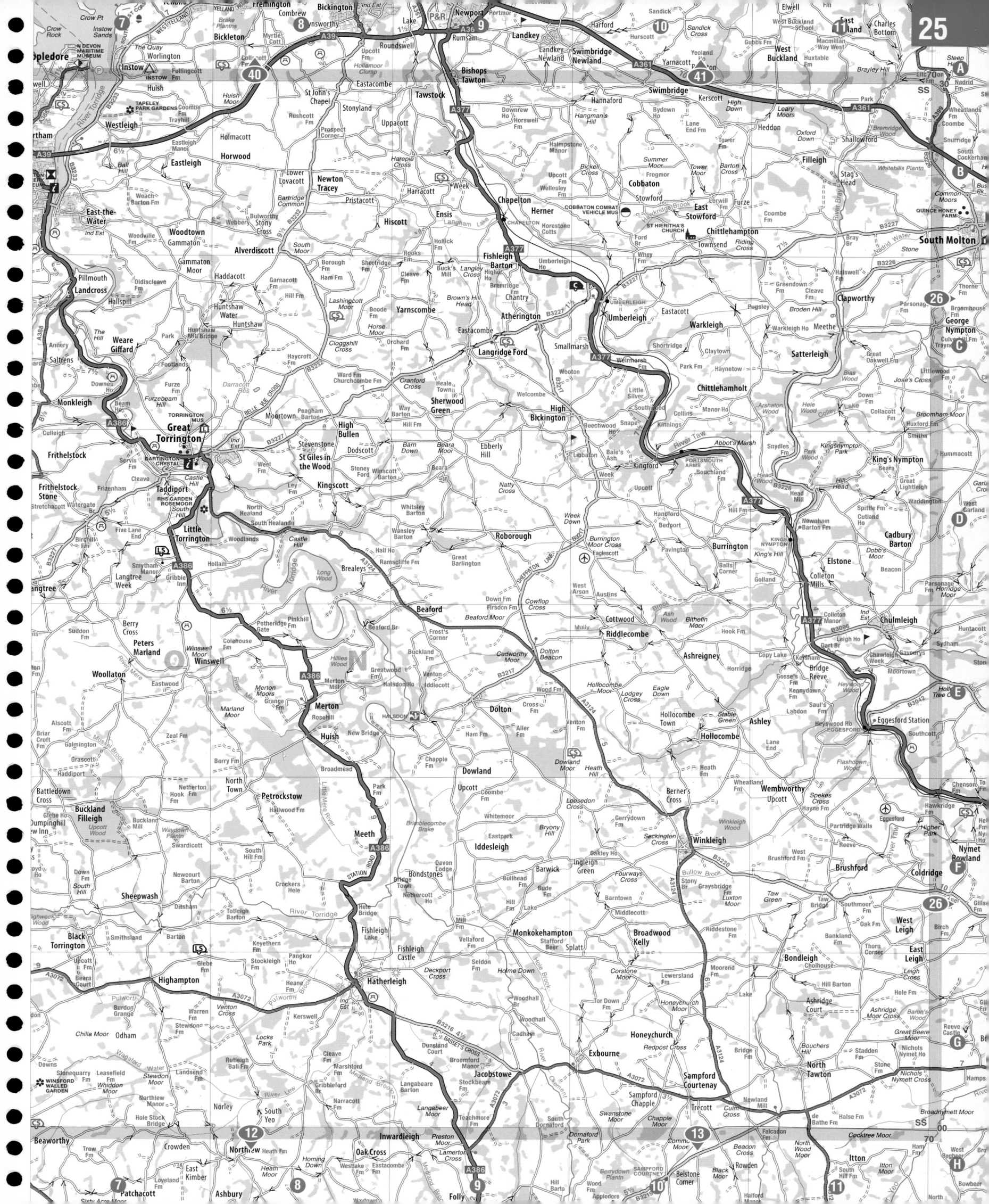

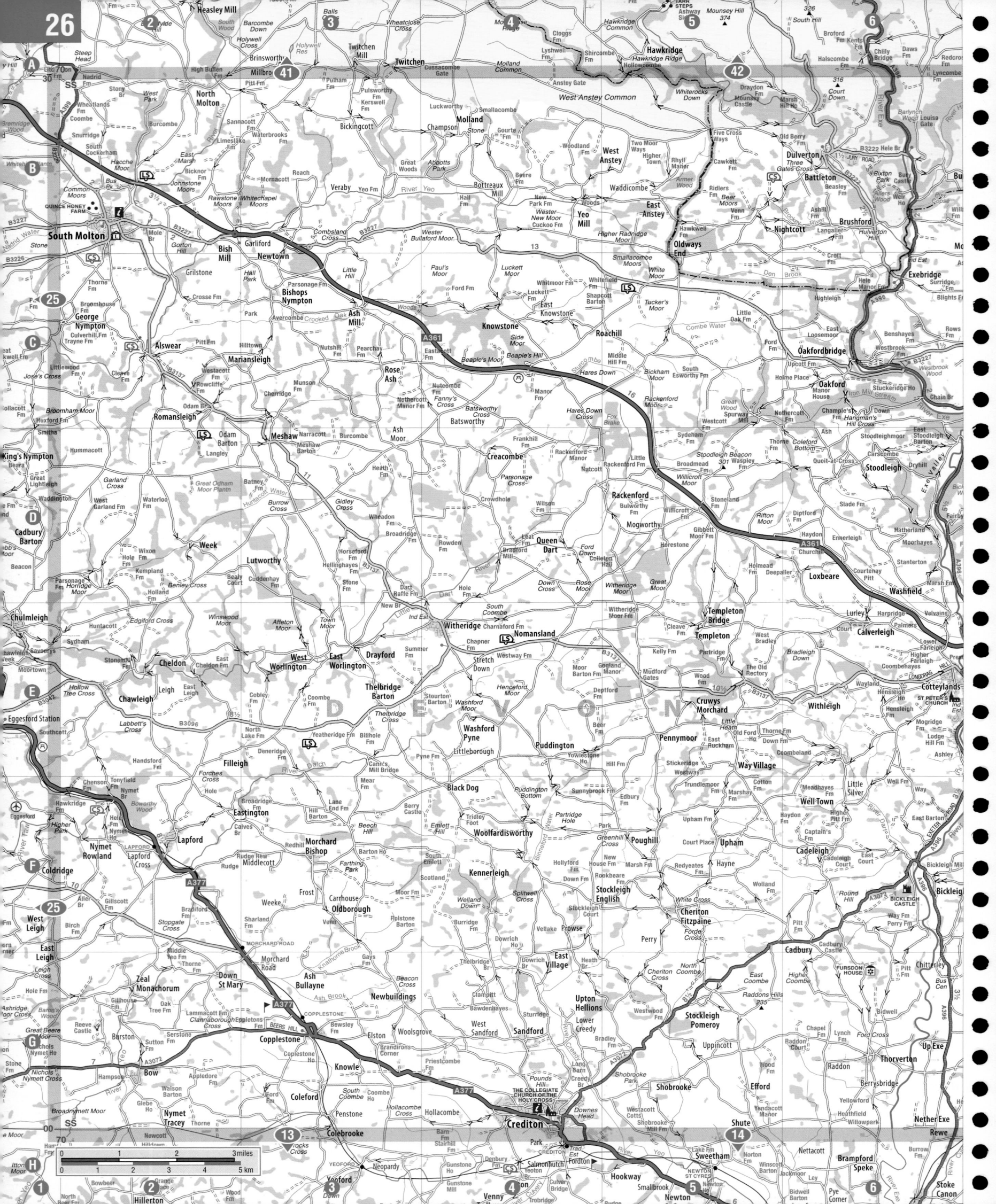

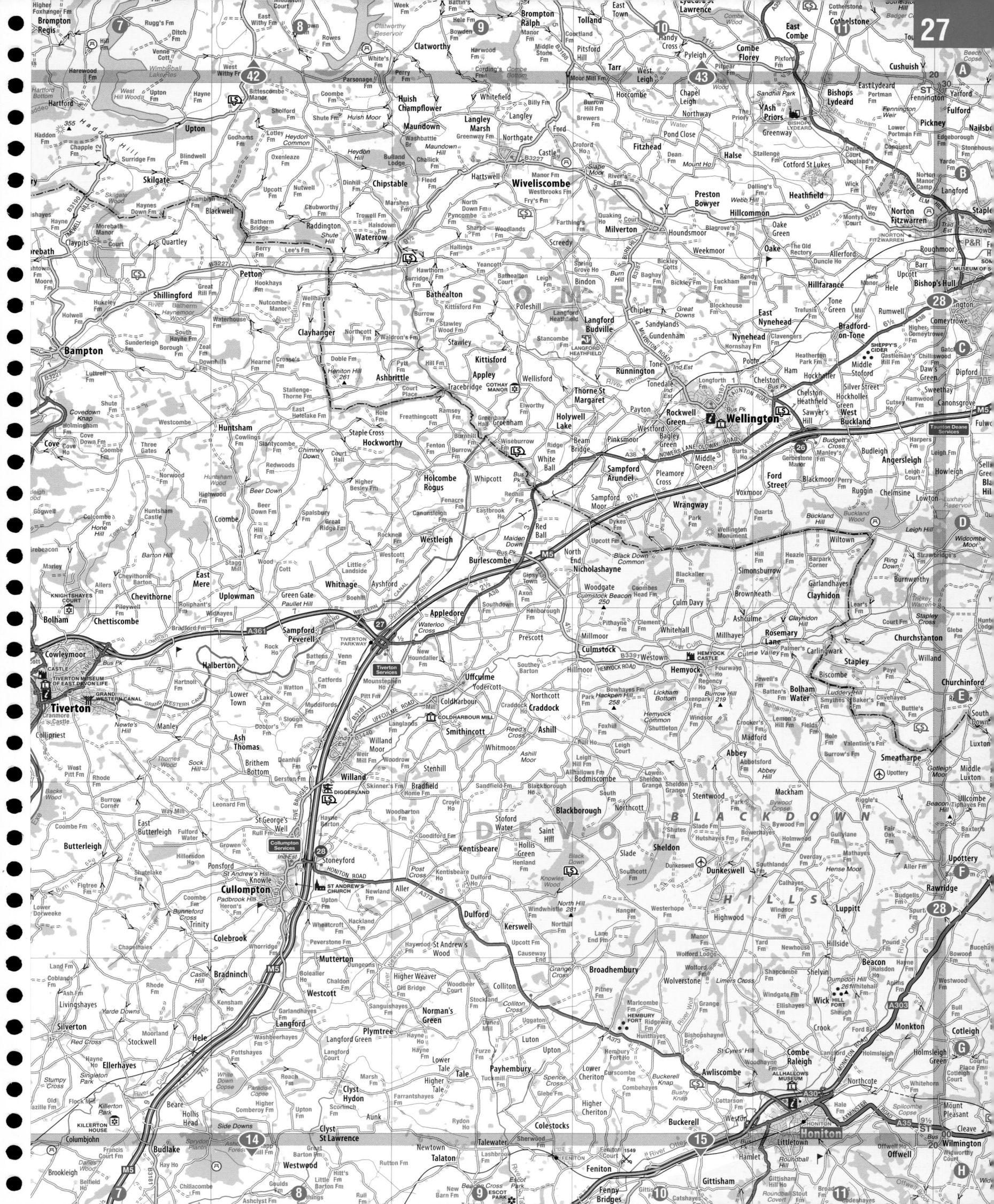

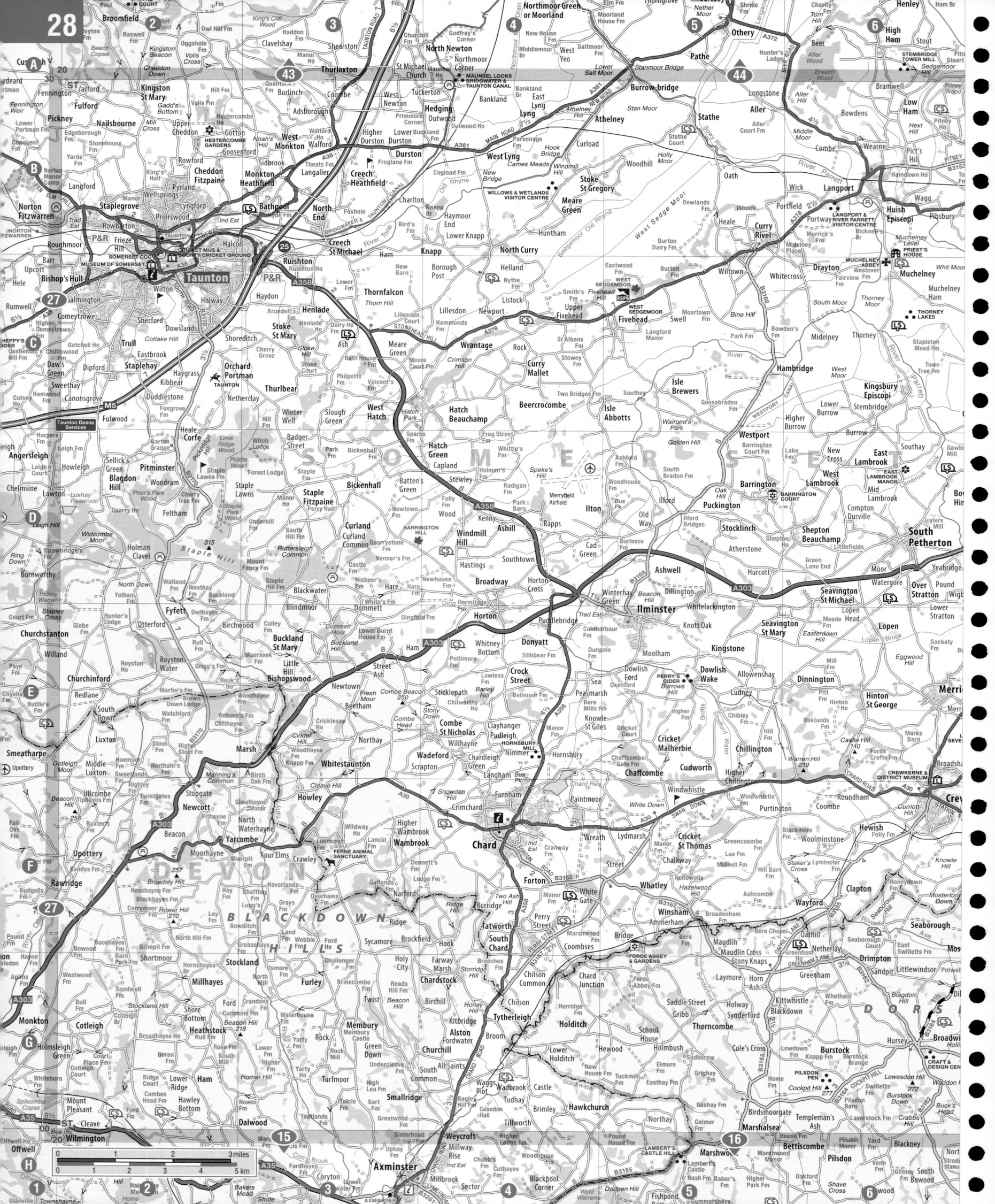

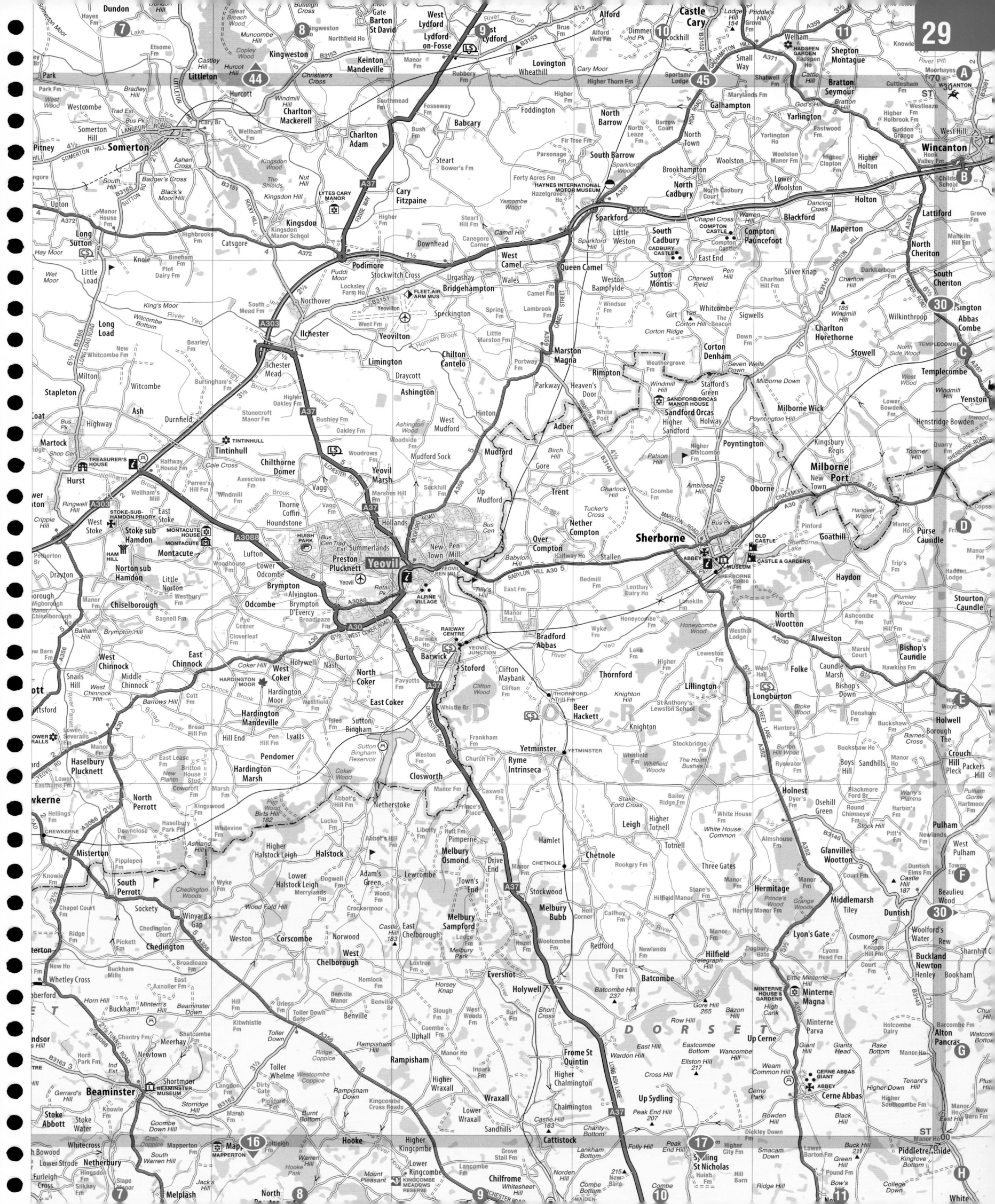

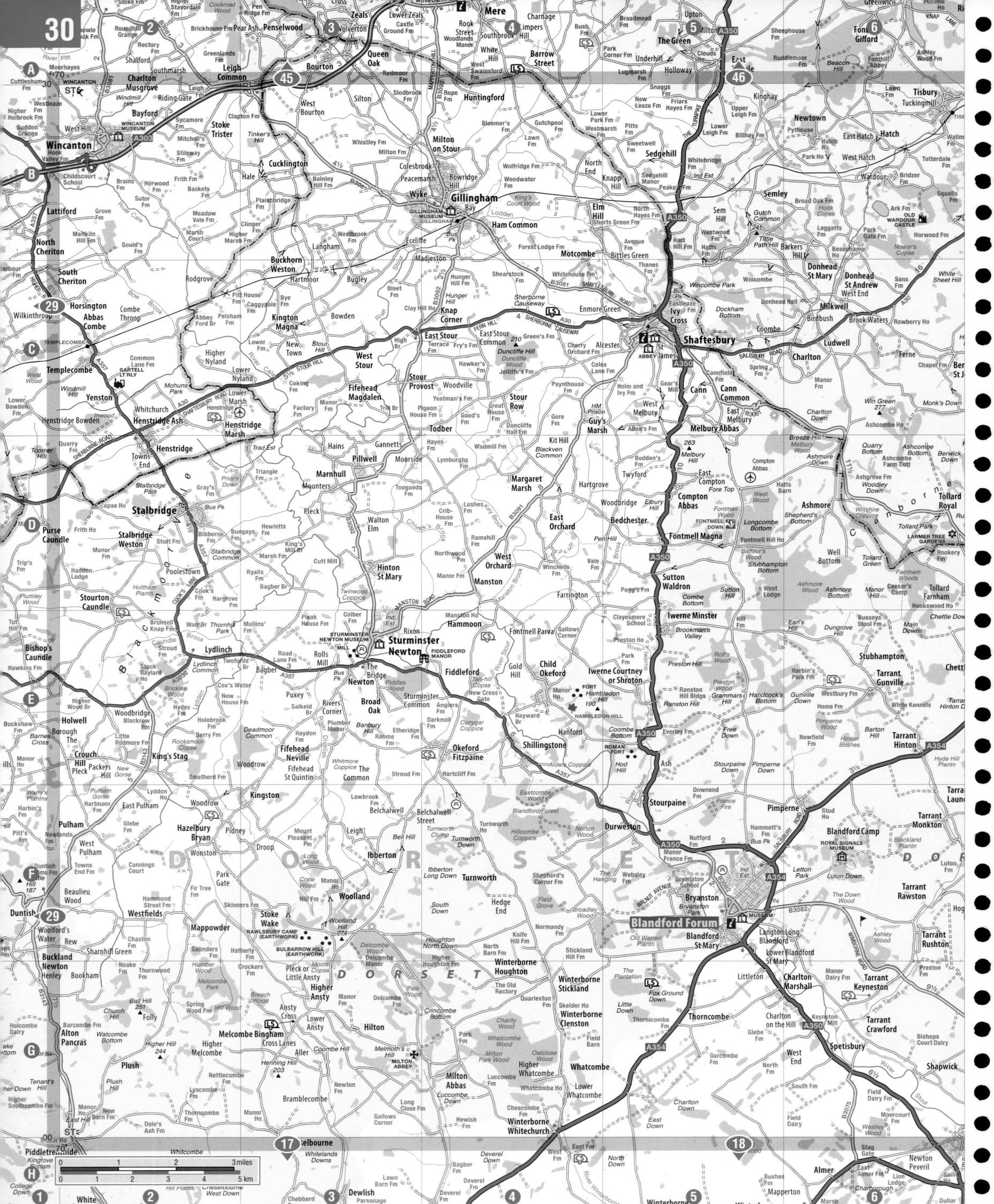

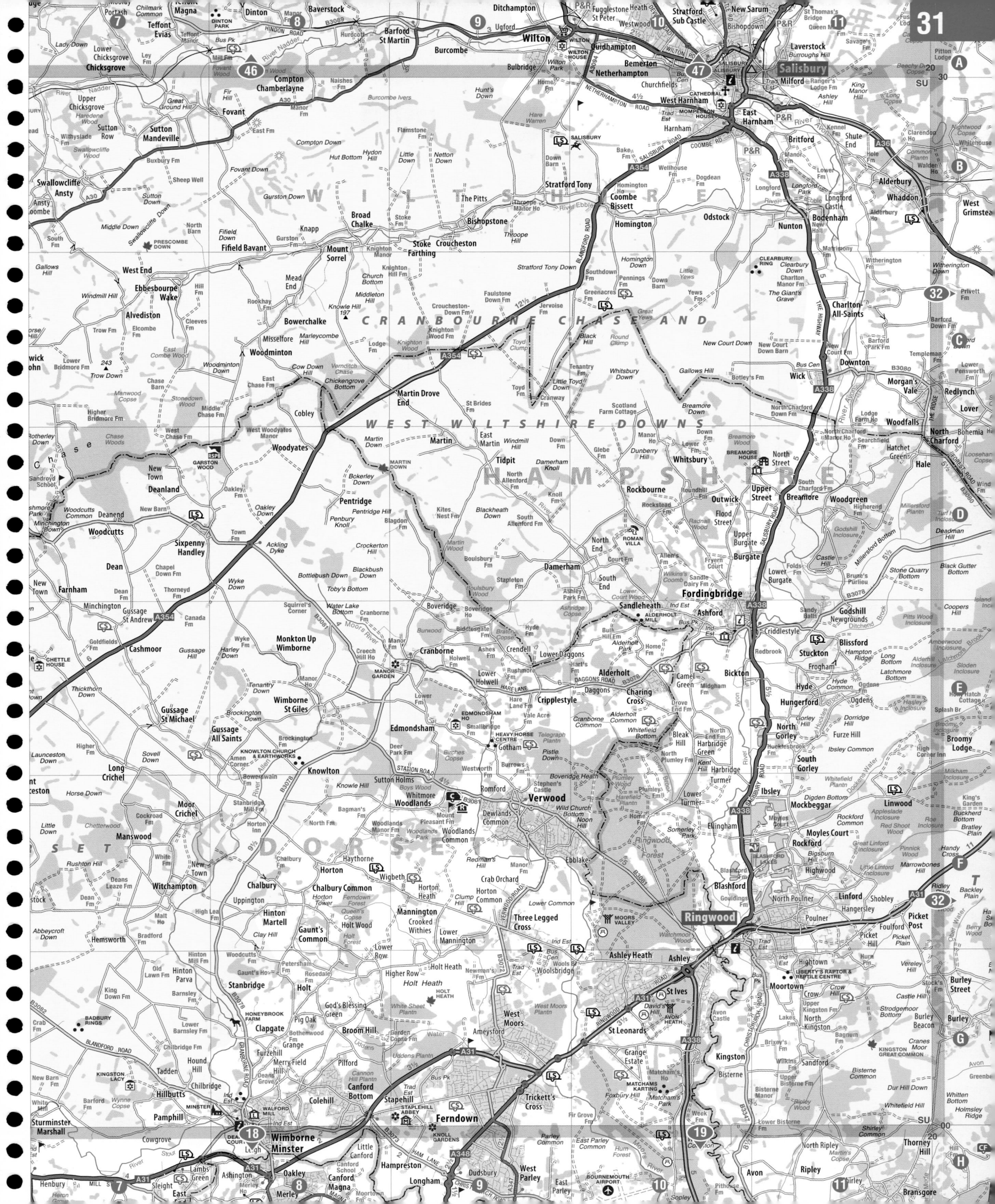

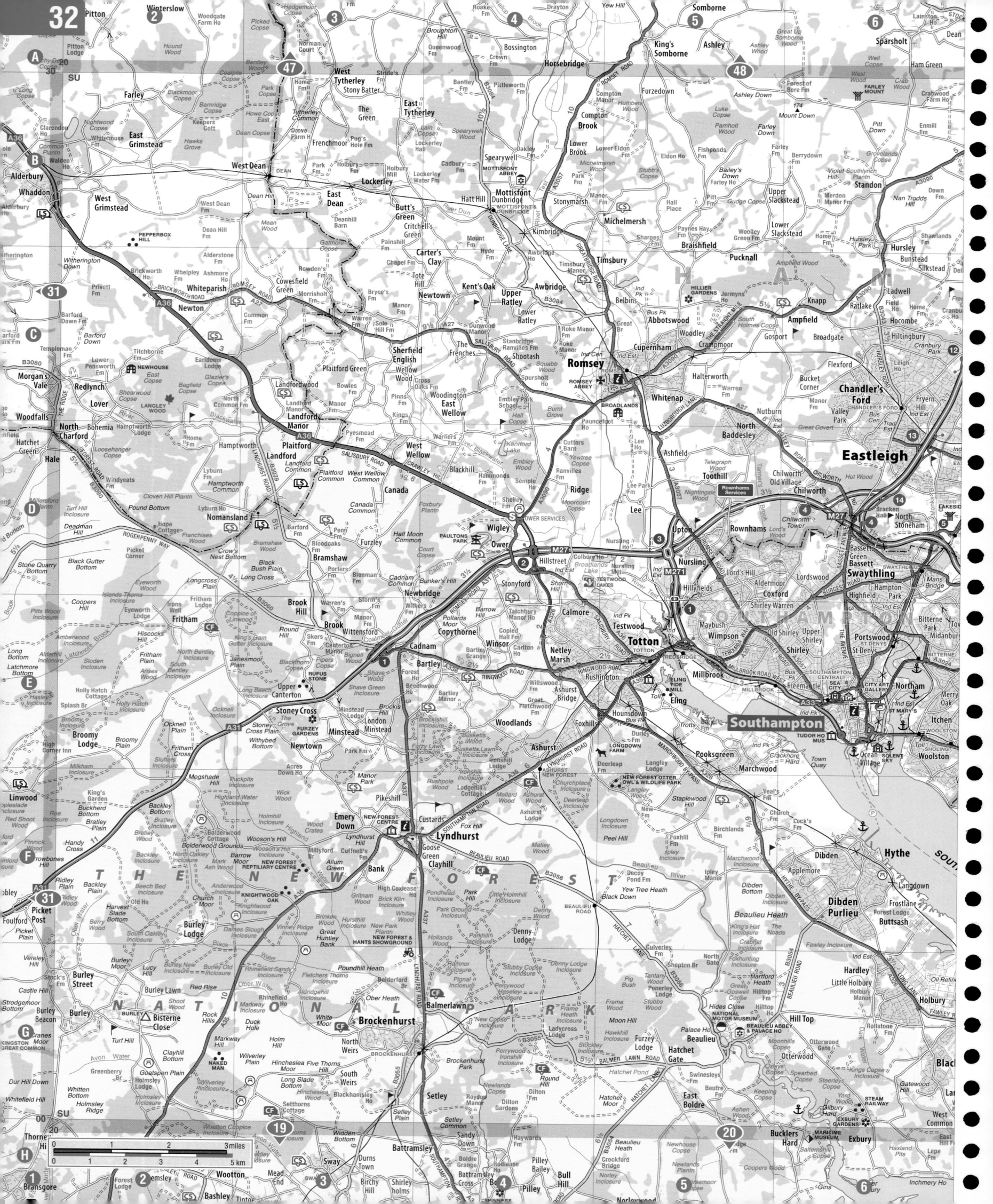

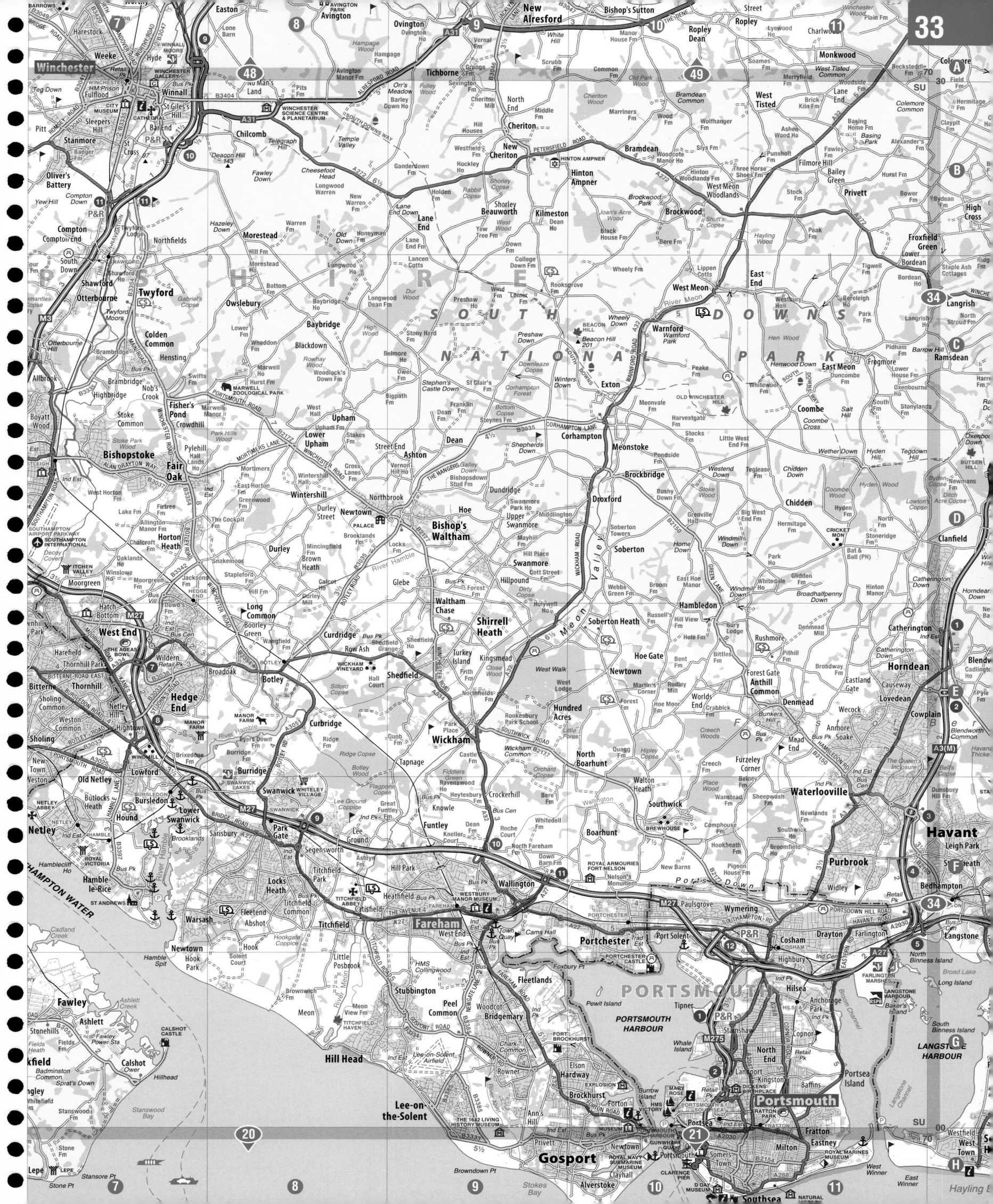

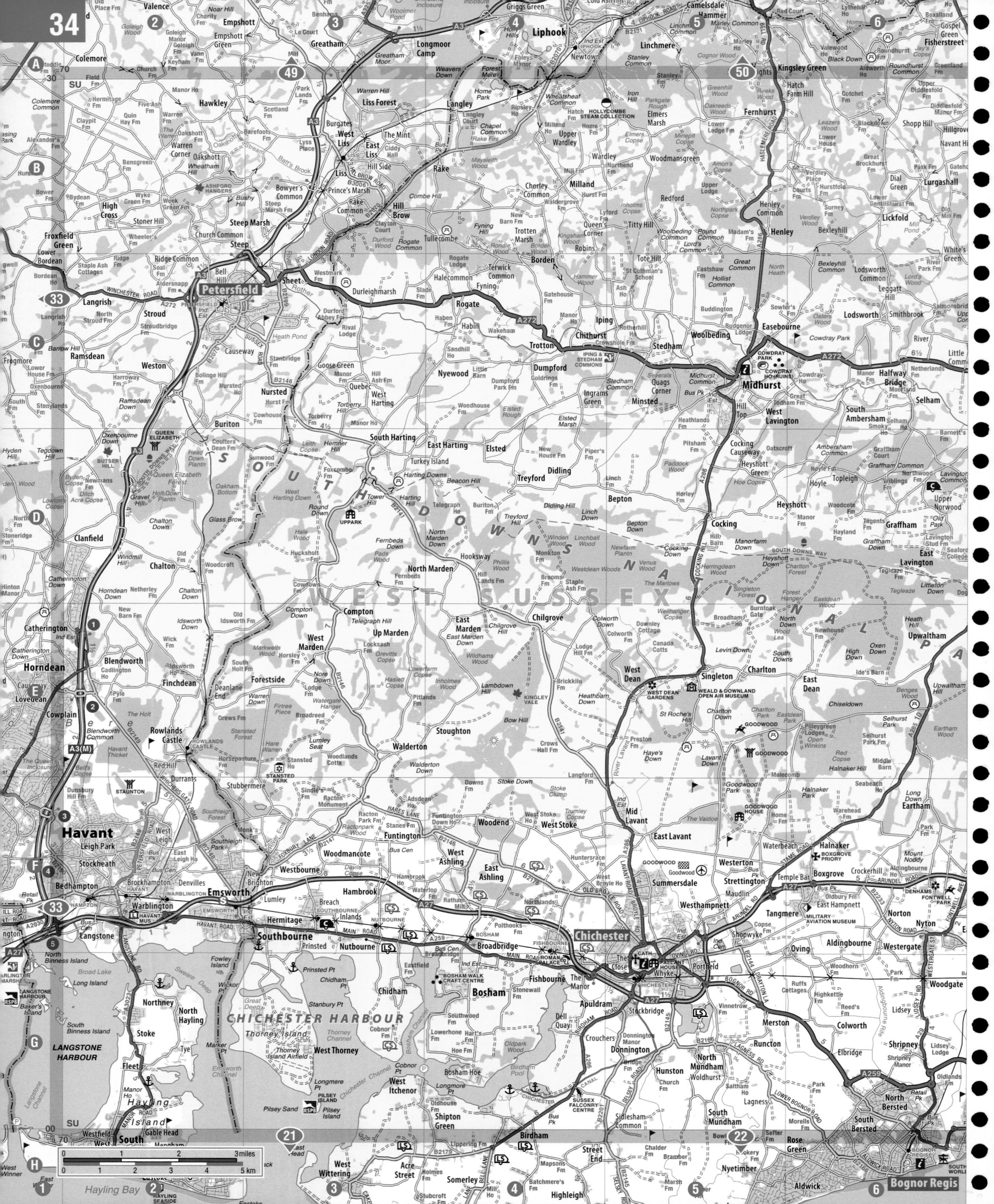

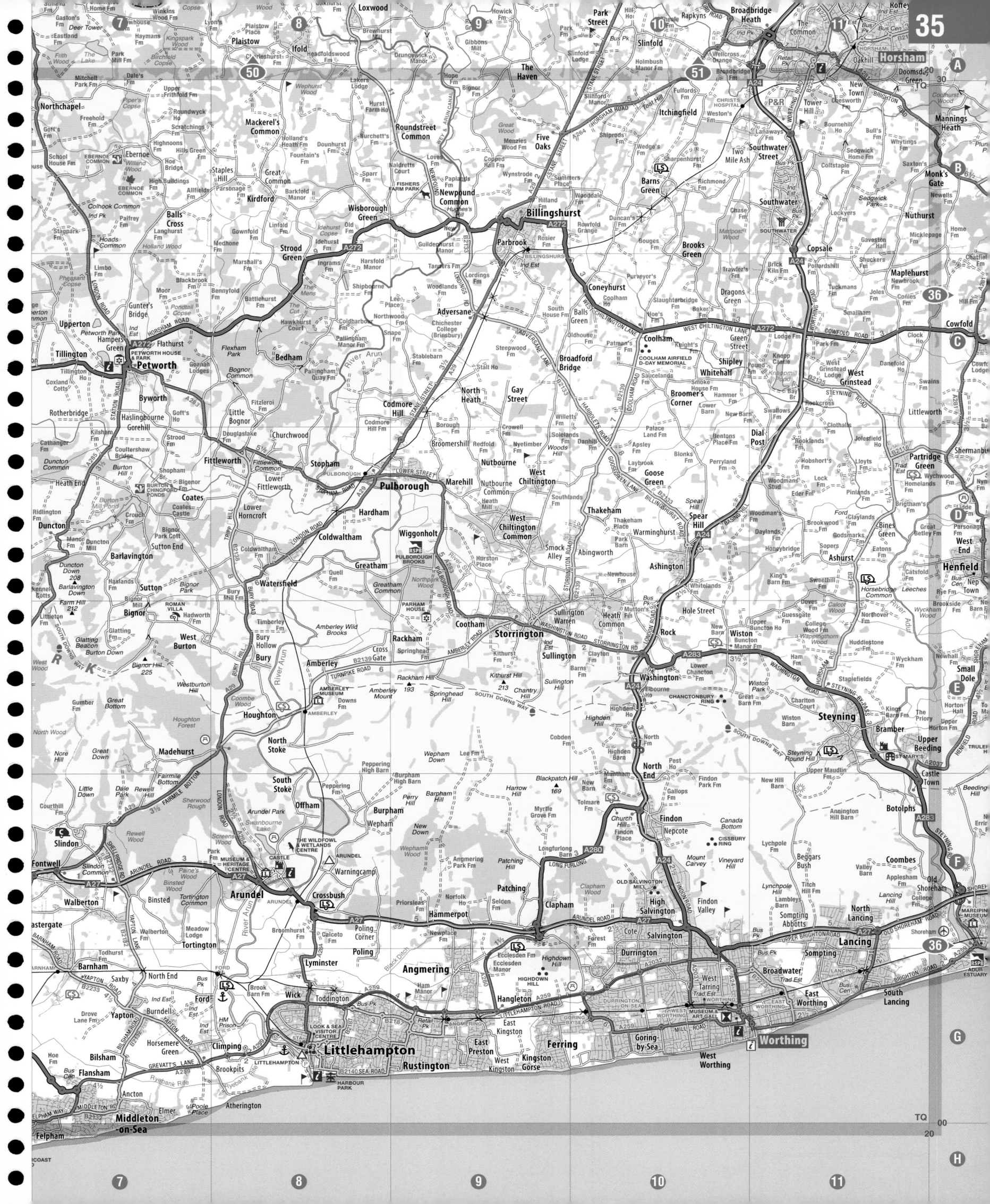

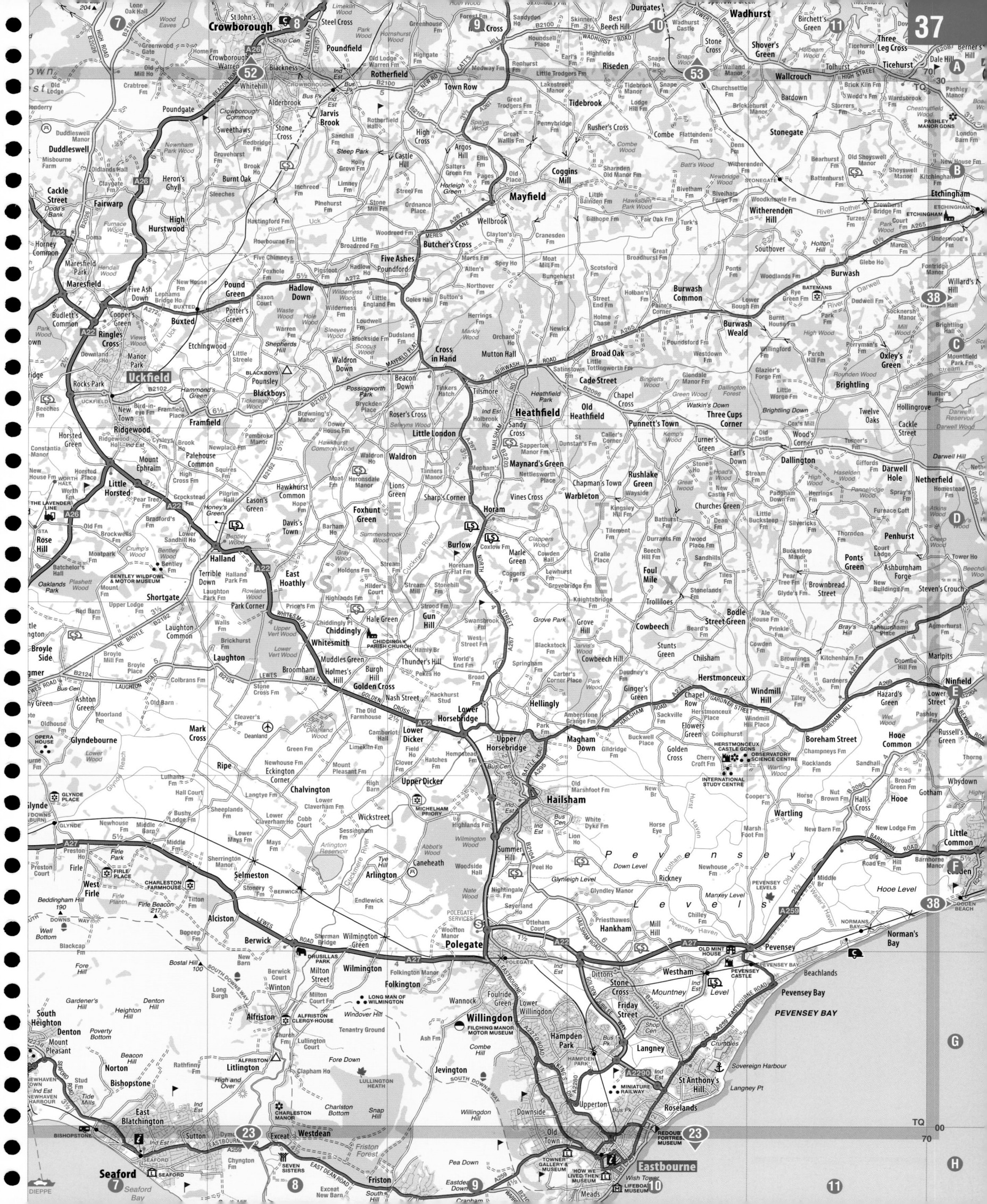

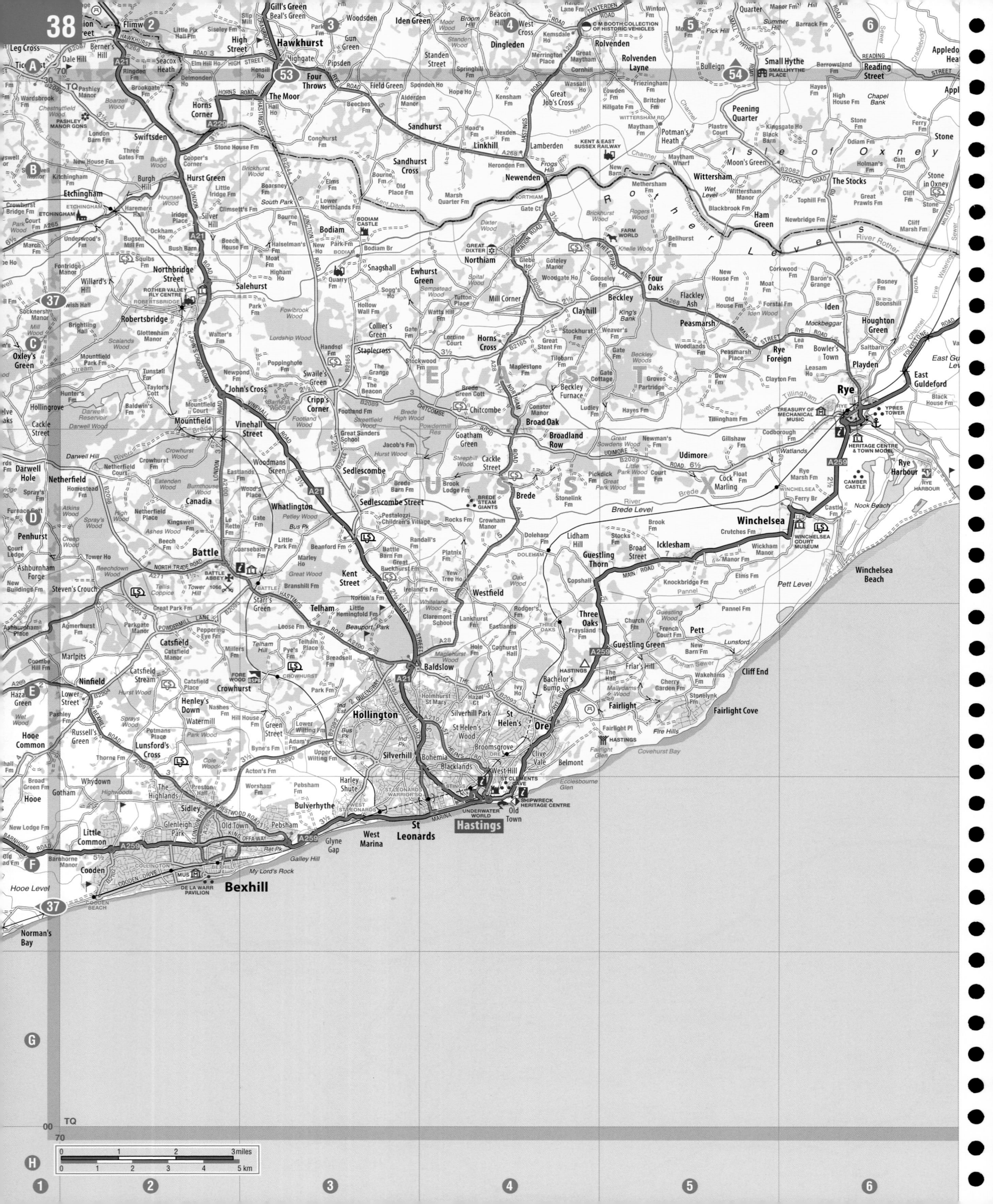

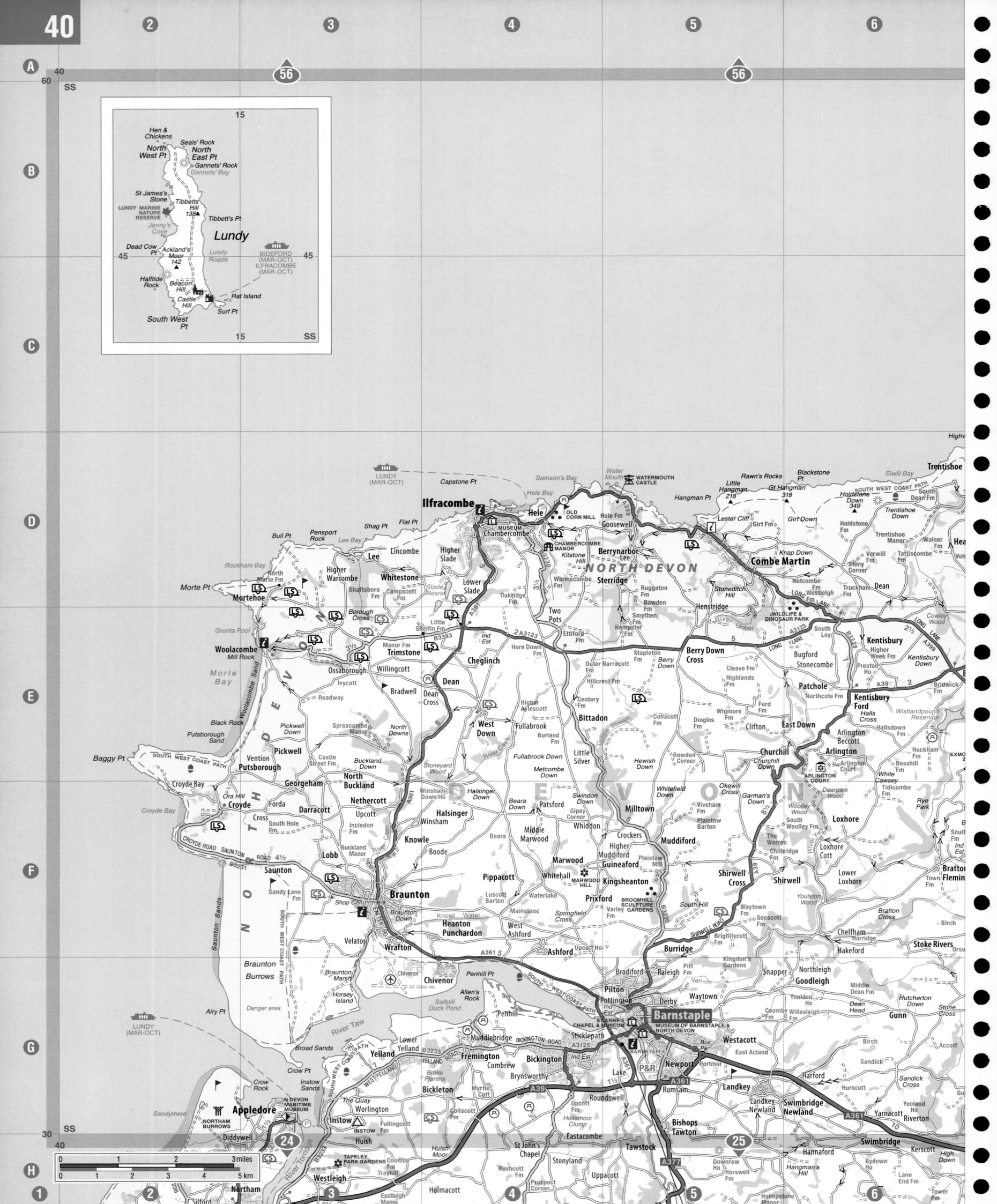

Lundy

Hen & Chickens
North West Pt
Seals' Rock
North East Pt
Gannets' Rock
Gannets' Bay
St James's Stone
Tibbetts Hill 132
LUNDY MARINE NATURE RESERVE
Jenny's Cove
Tibbett's Pt
Dead Cow Pt
Ackland's Moor 142
Lundy Roads
BIDEFORD (MAR-OCT) ILFRACOMBE (MAR-OCT)
Halftide Rock
Beacon Hill
Castle Hill
Rat Island
South West Pt
Surf Pt

Trentishoe
Elwill Bay
LUNDY (MAR-OCT)
Capstone Pt
Samson's Bay
Water Mouth
WATERMOUTH CASTLE
Little Hangman 218
Gt Hangman 318
Rawn's Rocks
Blackstone Pt
Holdstone Down 349
SOUTH WEST COAST PATH
Ilfracombe
Hele Bay
Hele
OLD CORN MILL
Hole Fm
Hangman Pt
Hangman
Trentishoe Down
Pensport Rock
Shag Pt
Flat Pt
MUSEUM Chambercombe
Goosewell
Lester Cliff
Girt Fm
Girl Down
Knap Down
Holdstone
Bull Pt
Lee Bay
Higher Slade
CHAMBERCOMBE MANOR
Kitstone Hill
Berrynarbor
Lee
Combe Martin
Verwill Hill
Stony Corner
Trentishoe Manor
Walner
Hea
Lee
Lincombe
NORTH DEVON
Rockham Bay
North Morte Fm
Higher Warcombe
Whitestone
Lower Slade
Warmscombe
Sterridge
Ruggaton
Bowden Fm
Smythen Fm
Henstridge
Stoneditch Hill
Nutcombe
Higher Westleigh
Truckham Fm
Dean
Cowley Wood
Morte Pt
Mortehoe
Shaftsboro
Campscott Fm
Slade Resrs
Oakridge
Two Pots
WILDLIFE & DINOSAUR PARK
South Ley
Kentisbury
Higher Week Fm
Kentisbury Down
Borough Cross
Little Shelfin Fm
B3343
Ind Est
2 A3123
Hore Down Fm
Hampster Fm
Ettiford Fm
Berry Down Cross
Stapleton
Berry Down
Cleave Fm
Bugford
Stonecombe
Preston Ho
Grunta Pool
Woolacombe
Mill Rock
Manor Fm
Trimstone
Willingcott
Cheglinch
Outer Narracott
Patchole
Northcote Fm
Kentisbury Ford
Halls Cross
Hallsdown
Bridwick
Morte Bay
Ossaborough
Ivycott
Dean
Dean Cross
Higher Aylescott
Century Fm
Highlands Fm
Ford Fm
A39
Clifton
East Down
Wistlandpound Reservoir
Black Rock
Roadway
Bradwell
West Down
Bittadon
Collacott Fm
Dingles Fm
Wigmore Fm
Churchill
Arlington Beccott
Huckham Fm
Besshill
Exmo
Putsborough Sand
Pickwell Down
Spreacombe Manor
North Downs
Fullabrook
Burland Fm
Little Silver
Bowden Corner
Churchill Down
Arlington
ARLINGTON COURT
White Cawsey
Tidicombe
Baggy Pt
SOUTH WEST COAST PATH
Vention
Pickwell
Castle Street Fm
Buckland Down
Fullabrook Down
Metcombe Fm
Hewish Down
Okewill Cross
Garman's Down
Woolley Wood
Deerpark Wood
Rye Park
Croyde Bay
Putsborough
North Buckland
Stoneyard Wood
Swindon Down
Whitefield Down
Viveham Fm
The Warren
Chilbridge
Loxhore
South
Ind
Est
Croyde Bay
Ora Hill
Forda
Darracott
Nethercott
Upcott Fm
Halsinger Down Ho
Beara Down
Patsford
Gipsy Corner
Milltown
Plaistow Barton
South Woolley Fm
Loxhore Cott
Croyde
Cross
South Hole Fm
Incledon Fm
Halsinger
Winsham
Whiddon
Crockers
Muddiford
Higher Muddiford
Plaistow Mill
Loxhore
Lower Loxhore
CROYDE ROAD
SAUNTON ROAD 4½
Lobb
Buckland Manor
Knowle
Boode
Middle Marwood
Marwood
Guineaford
Shirwell Cross
Shirwell
Bratton Fleming
Saunton
Sandy Lane
Shop Cen
Pippacott
Beara
MARWOOD HILL
Whitehall
Luscott Barton
Waterlake
Prixford
Kingsheanton
BROOMHILL SCULPTURE GARDENS
Varley Fm
South Hill
Waytown
Youlston Wood
Bratton Cross
Birch
Braunton
EXETER
Braunton Down
Knowl Water
Mainstone
Springfield Cross
Velator
Wrafton
Heanton Punchardon
West Ashford
Ashford
Upcott Ho
Brightlycott
Sepscott Fm
Chelfham
Horridge
Stoke Rivers
Orsw
Braunton Burrows
SOUTH WEST COAST PATH
A361
Braunton Marsh
Chivenor
Penhill Pt
Bradiford
Raleigh
Kingdon's Gardens
Snapper
Goodleigh
Northleigh
Middle Dean Fm
Hutcherton Down
Stone Cross
Airy Pt
Danger area
Horsey Island
Allen's Rock
Penhill
Saltpill Duck Pond
Pilton
Pottington
Ind
Derby
Waytown
Youlden Fm
Coombe Willesleigh
Dean Head
LUNDY (MAR-OCT)
River Taw
Braunton
ST ANNE'S CHAPEL & MUSEUM
Barnstaple
MUSEUM OF BARNSTAPLE & NORTH DEVON
Westacott
Gunn
Broad Sands
Lower Yelland
B3233
Muddlebridge
BICKINGTON ROAD
Sticklepath
A3125
Bus Pk
East Acland
Birch
Sandick
Accott
Sandymere
NORTHAM BURROWS
Crow Rock
Crow Pt
Instow Sands
Yelland
YELLAND ROAD
Fremington
Combrew
Bickington
Ind Est
Lake
P&R
Newport
Portmor
Harford
Hurscott
Sandick Cross
Appledore
N DEVON MARITIME MUSEUM
Instow
Bickleton
Myrtle Cott
Brynsworthy
A39
A361
Rumsam
Landkey Newland
Landkey
Swimbridge Newland
A361
Yarnacott
Yeoland
Riverton
Diddywell
The Quay
Worlington
Collacott Fm
Upcott
Roundswell
Hollamoor Clump
Bishops Tawton
Swimbridge
Kerscott
High Down
Westleigh
Huish
Fullingcott
Instow
Eastacombe
St John's Chapel
Hamiston
Stonyland
Tawstock
Downrew Ho
A377
Hannaford
Bydown Ho
Lane End Fm
TAPELEY PARK GARDENS
Coombe Fm
Trayhill
Rushcott
Uppacott
Horswell Fm
Hangman's Hill

0 1 2 3 miles
0 1 2 3 4 5 km

Northam
Silford
Westleigh
River Torridge
Hulsh Moor
Prospect Corner
Holmacott
Hampstone Manor
Tower Fm

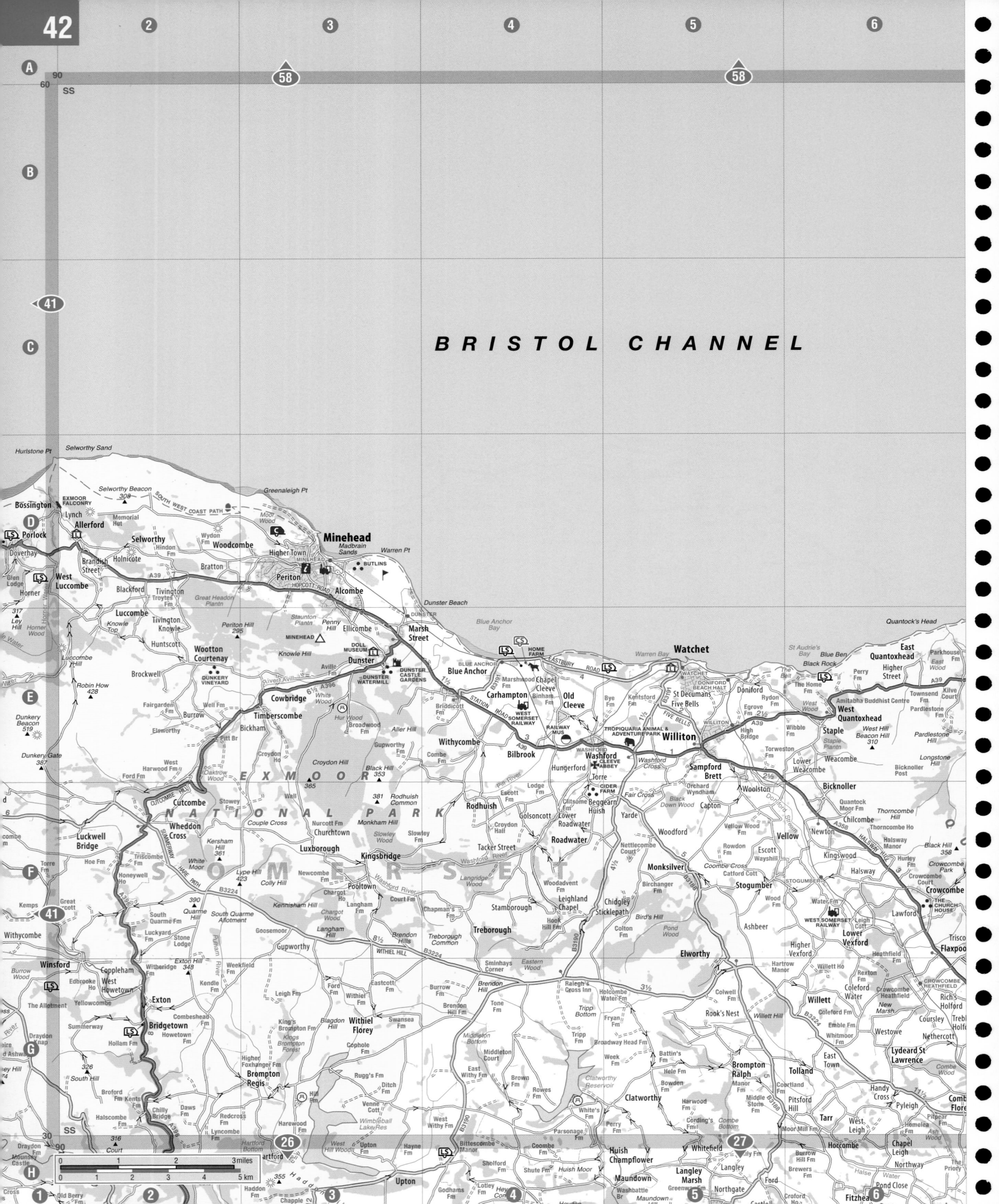

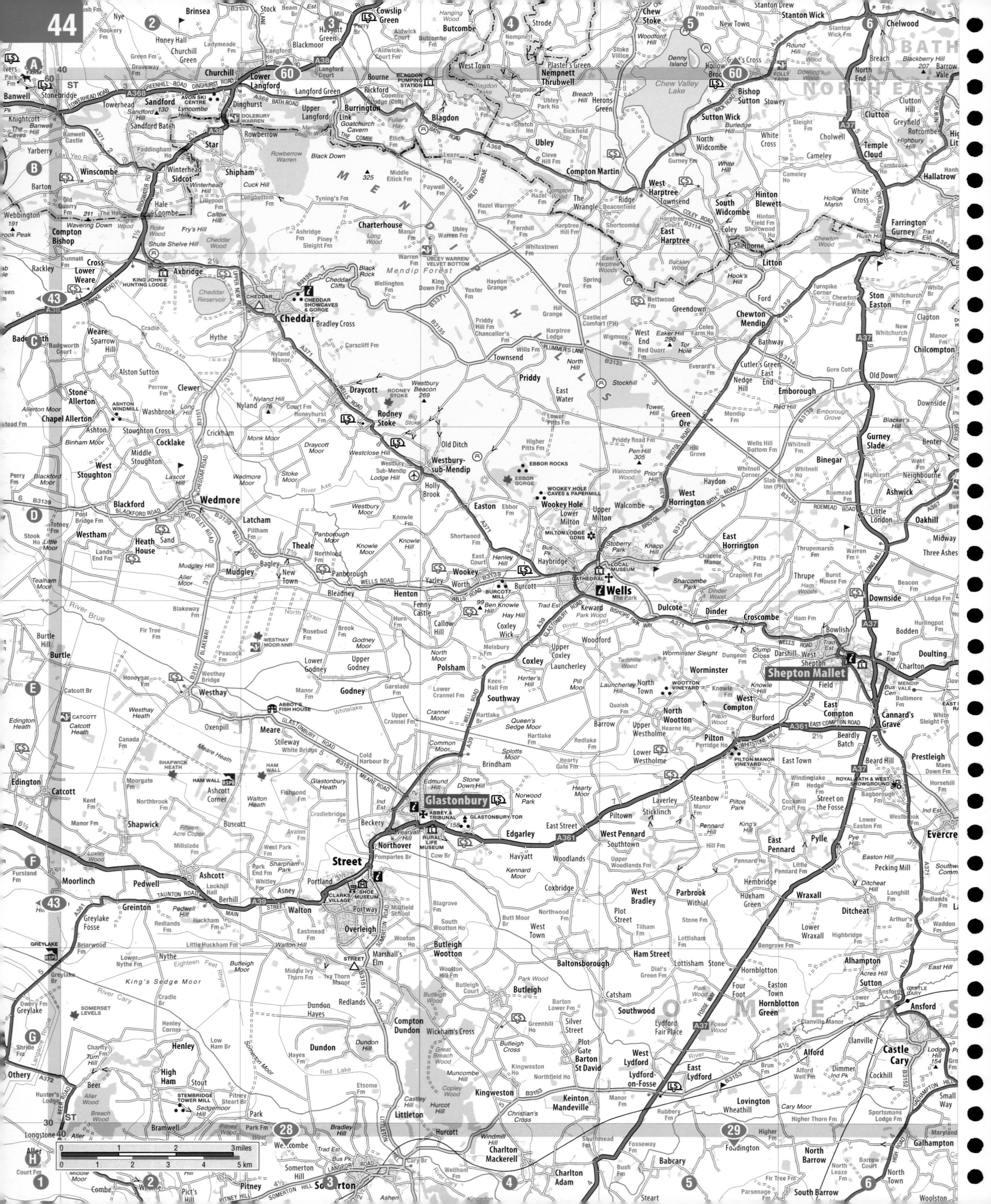

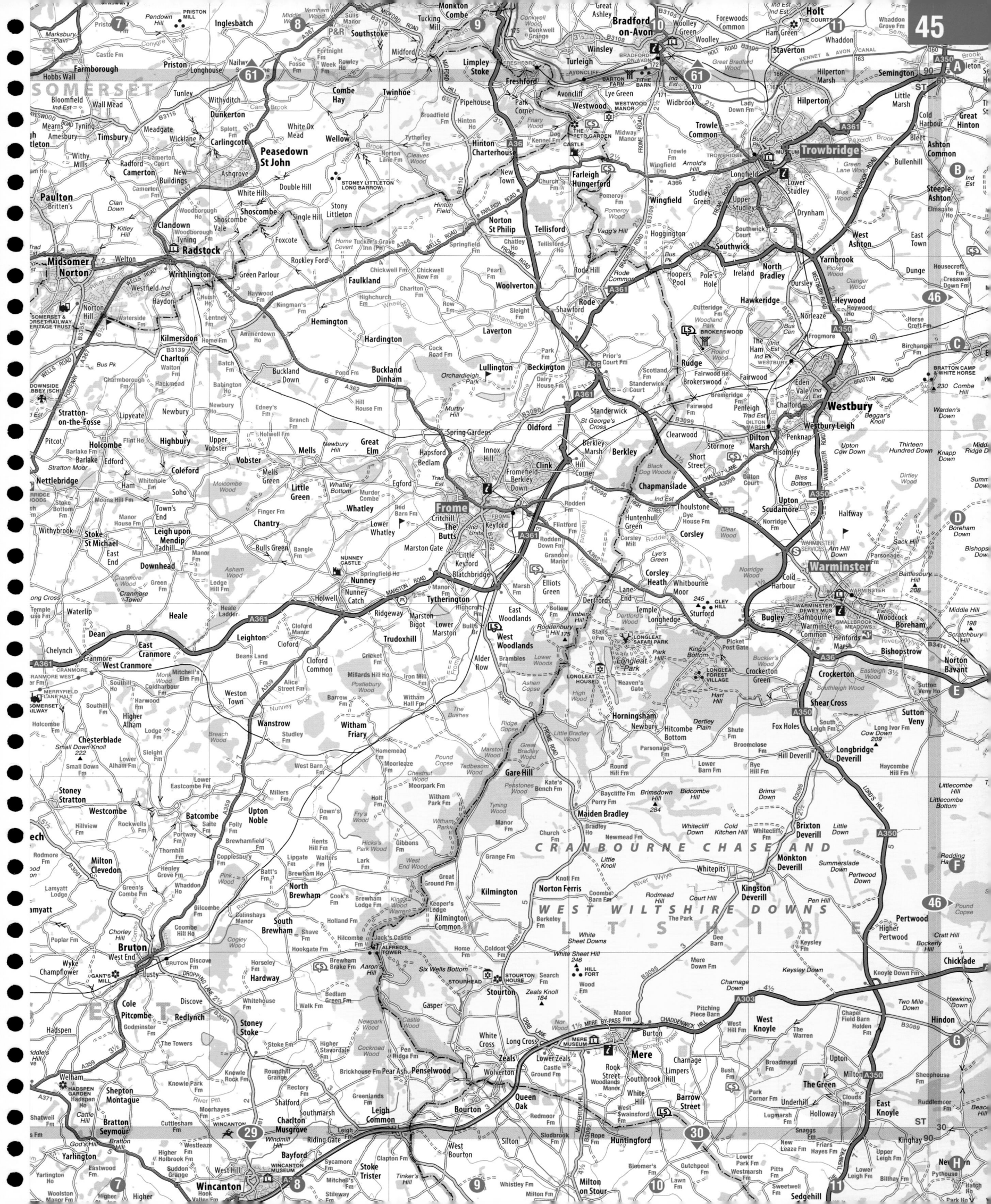

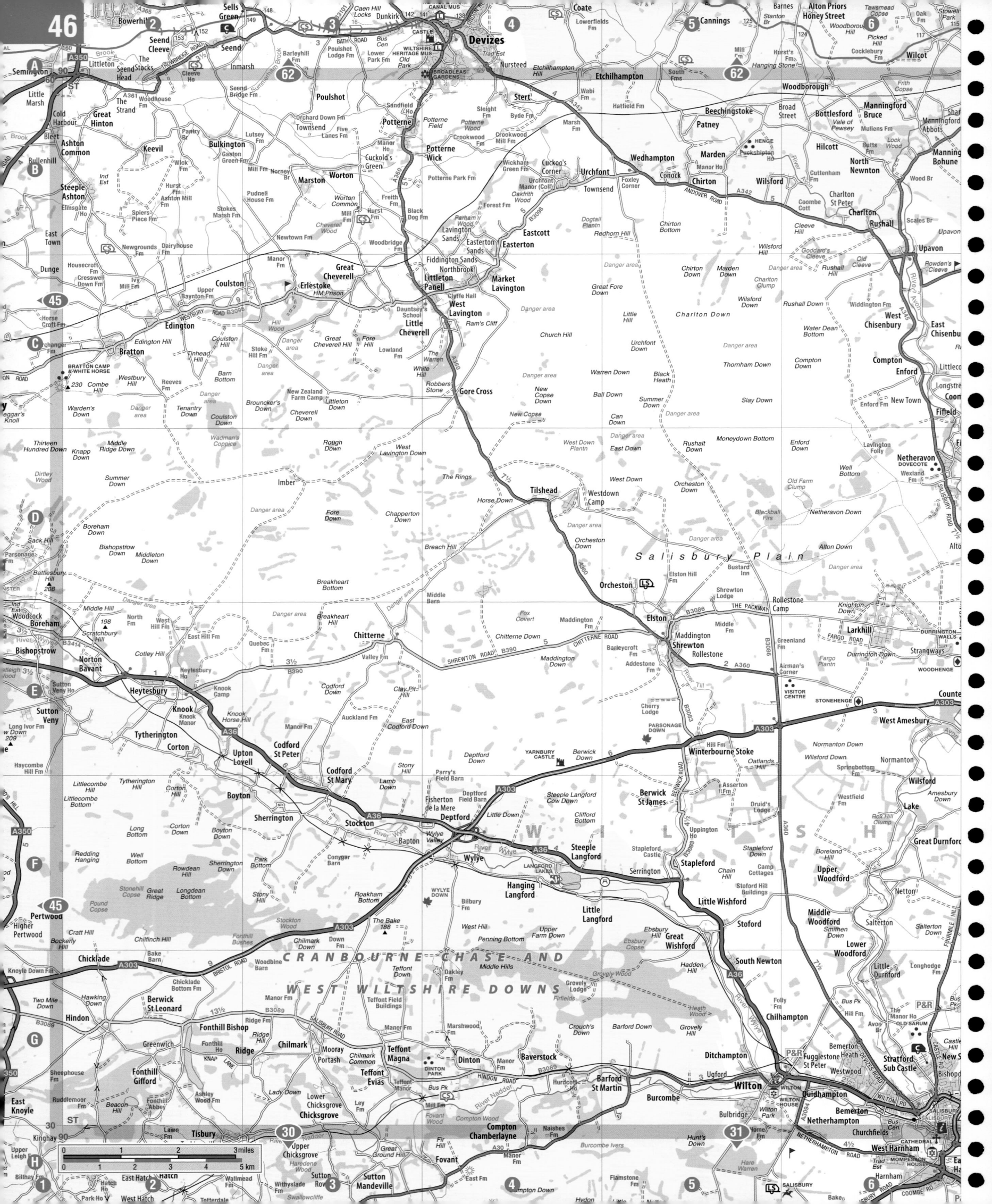

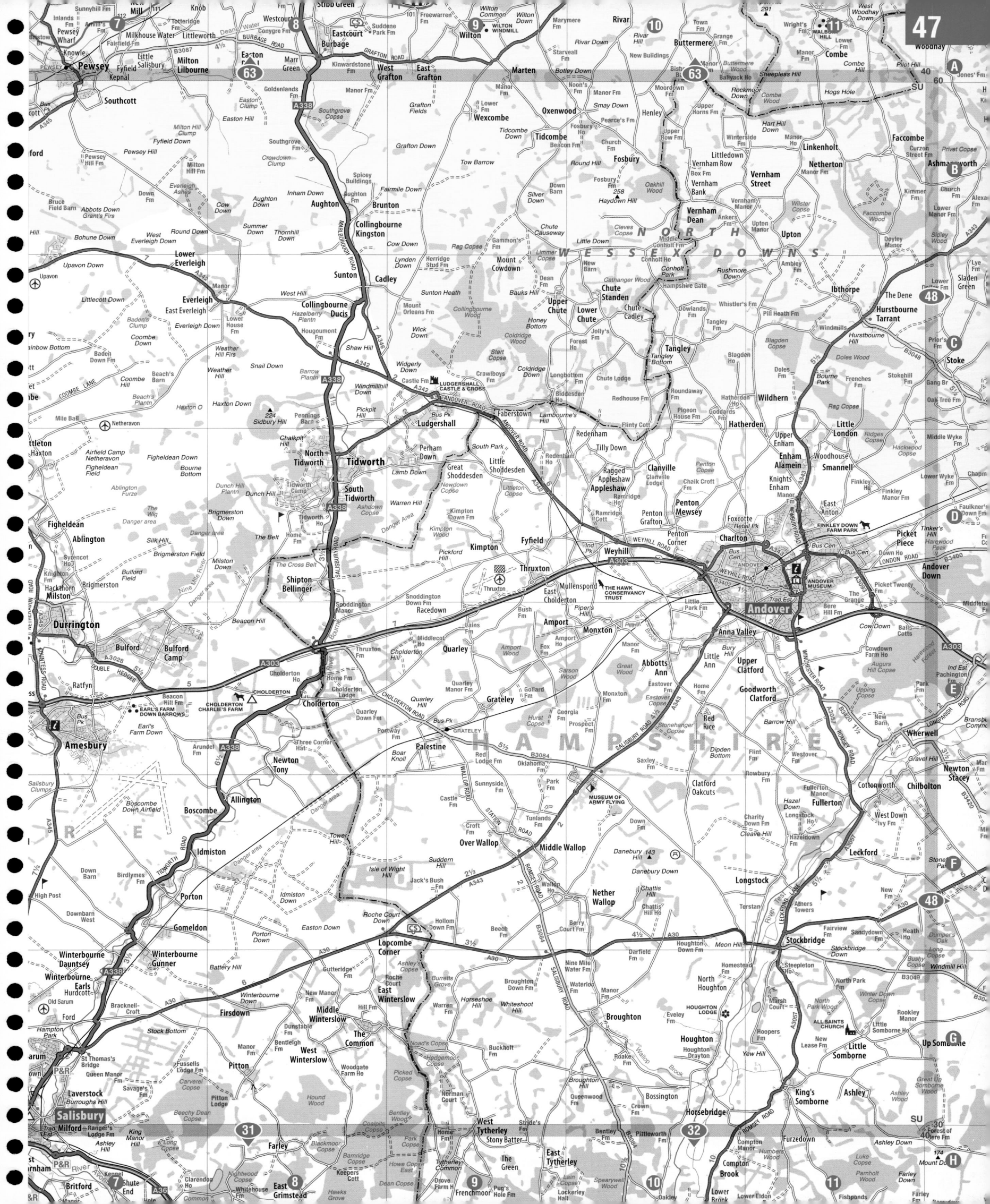

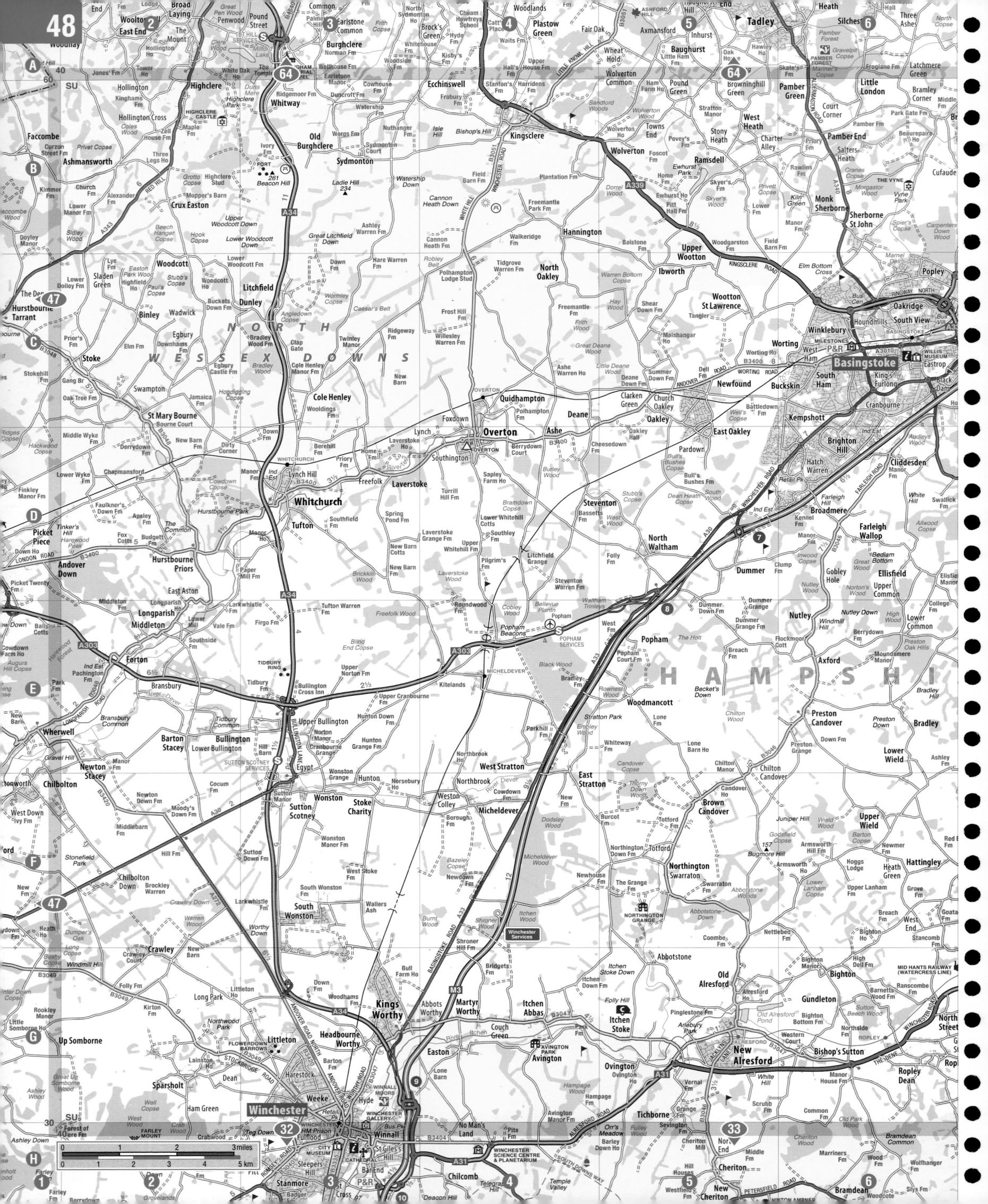

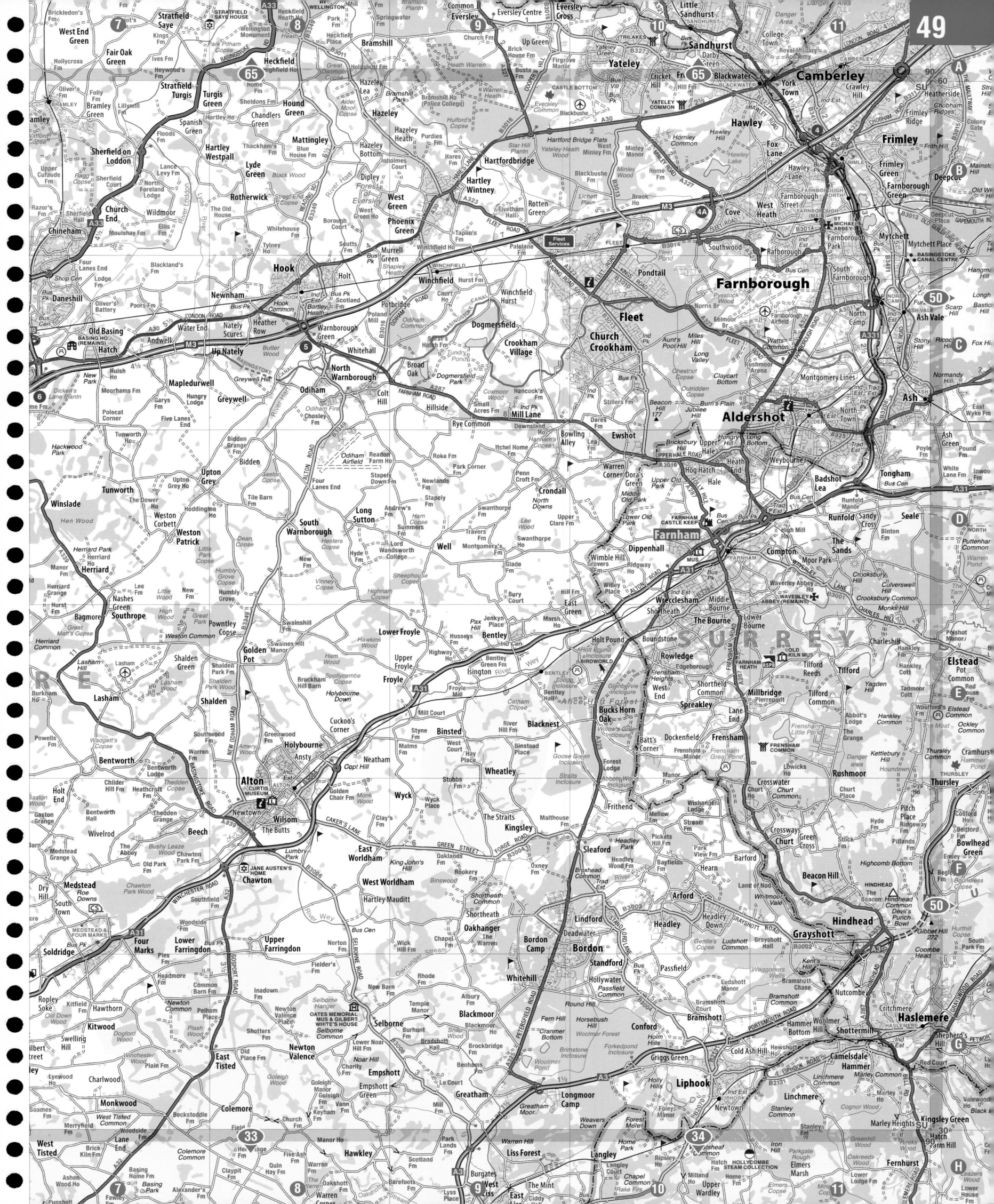

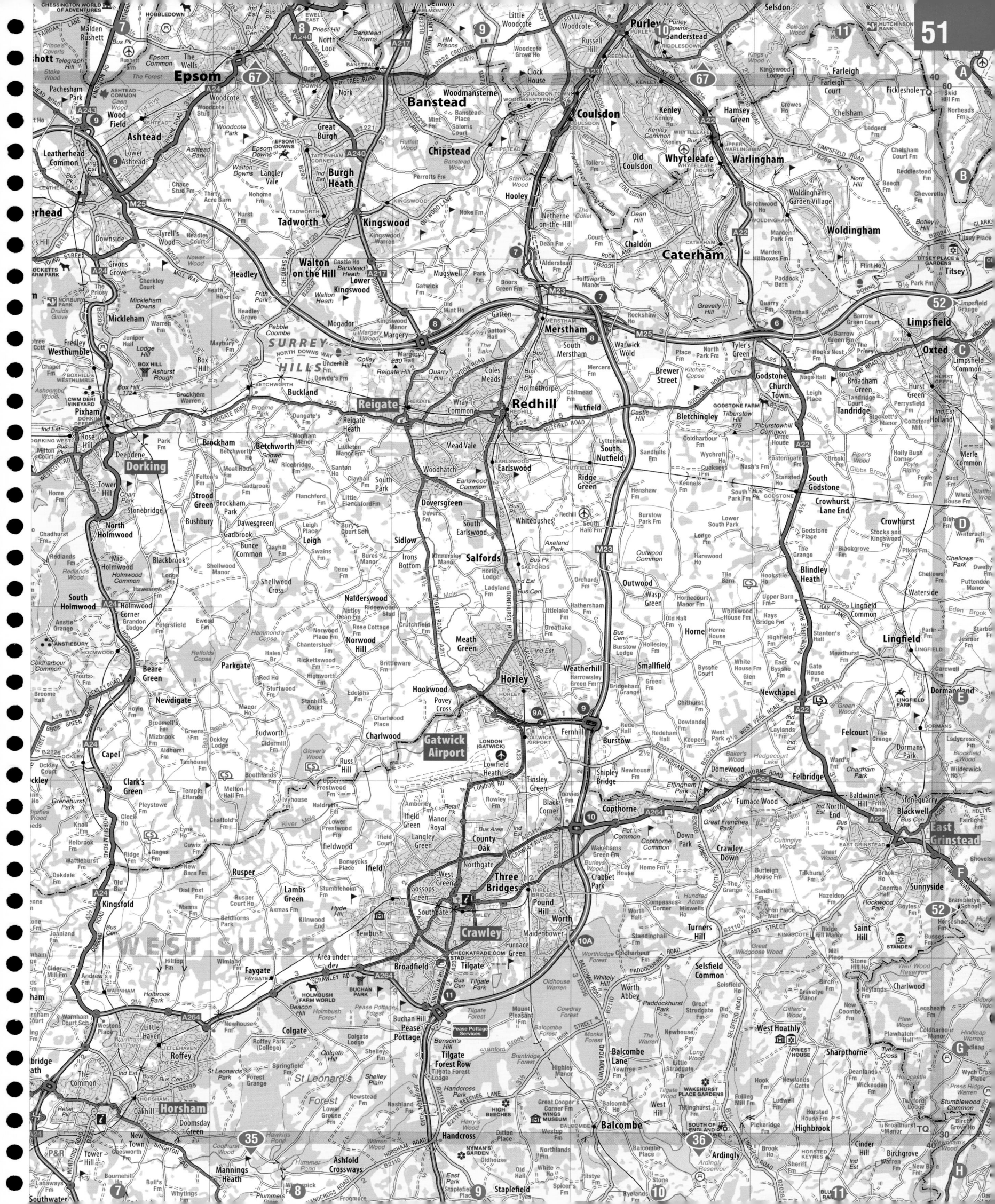

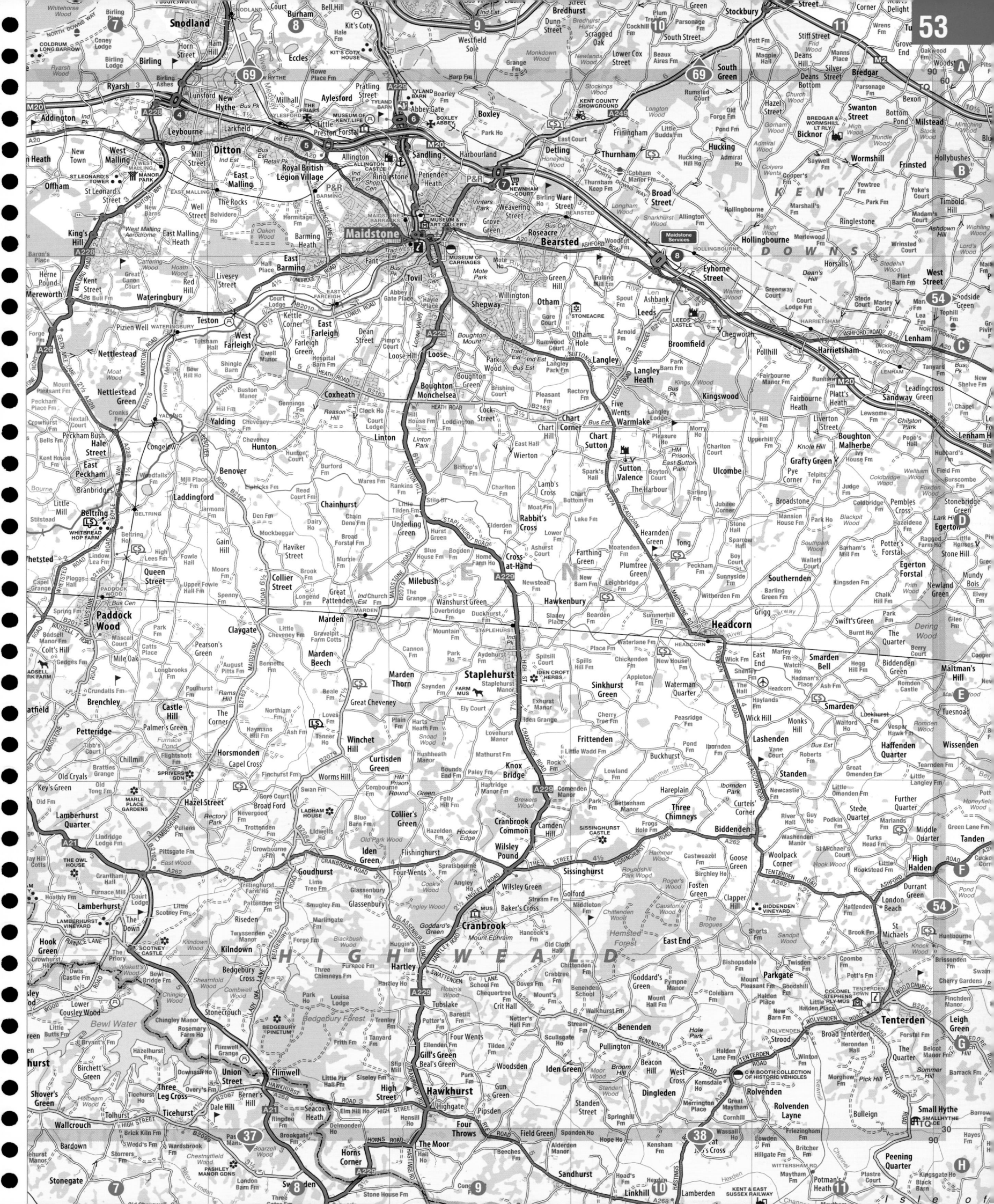

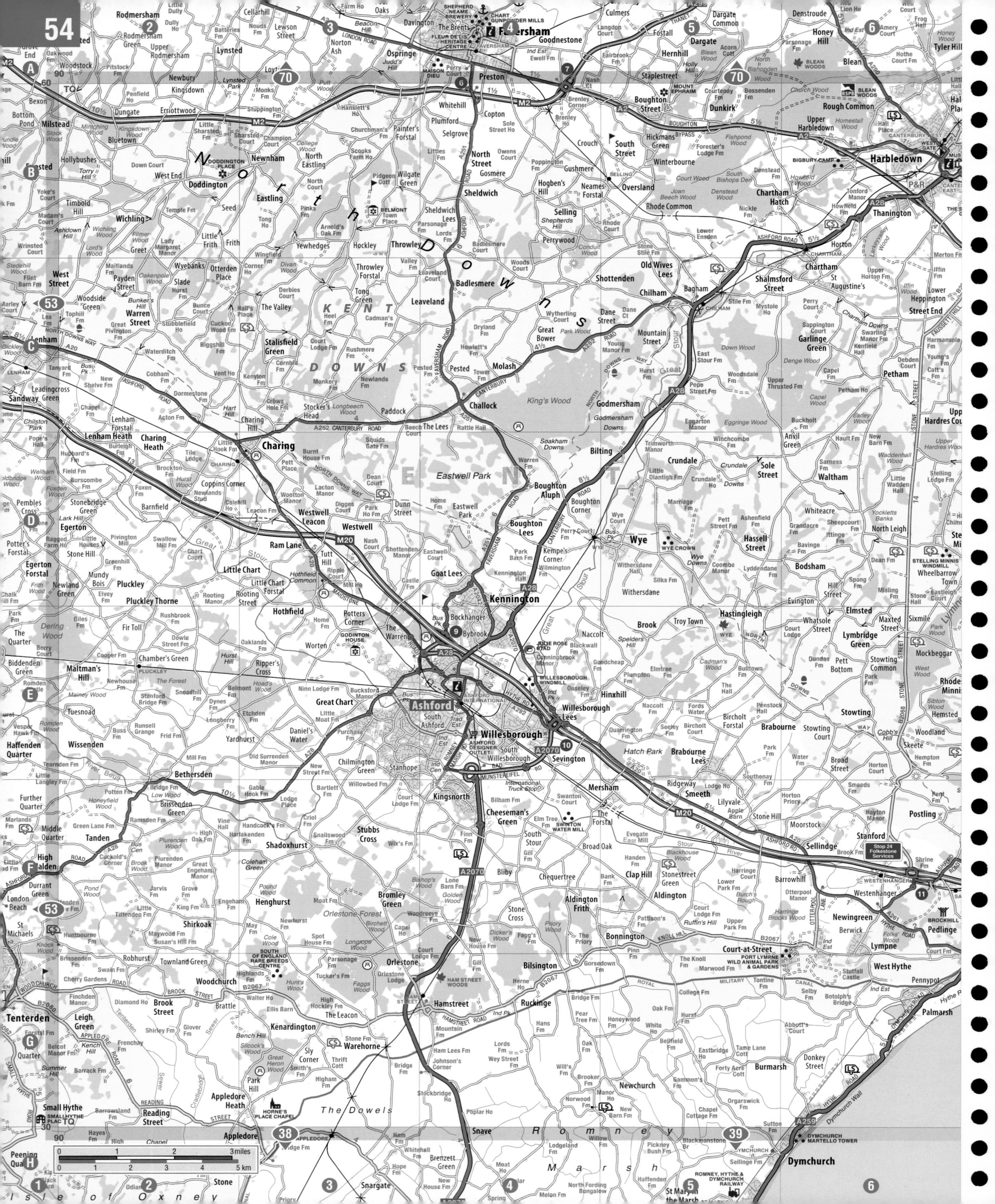

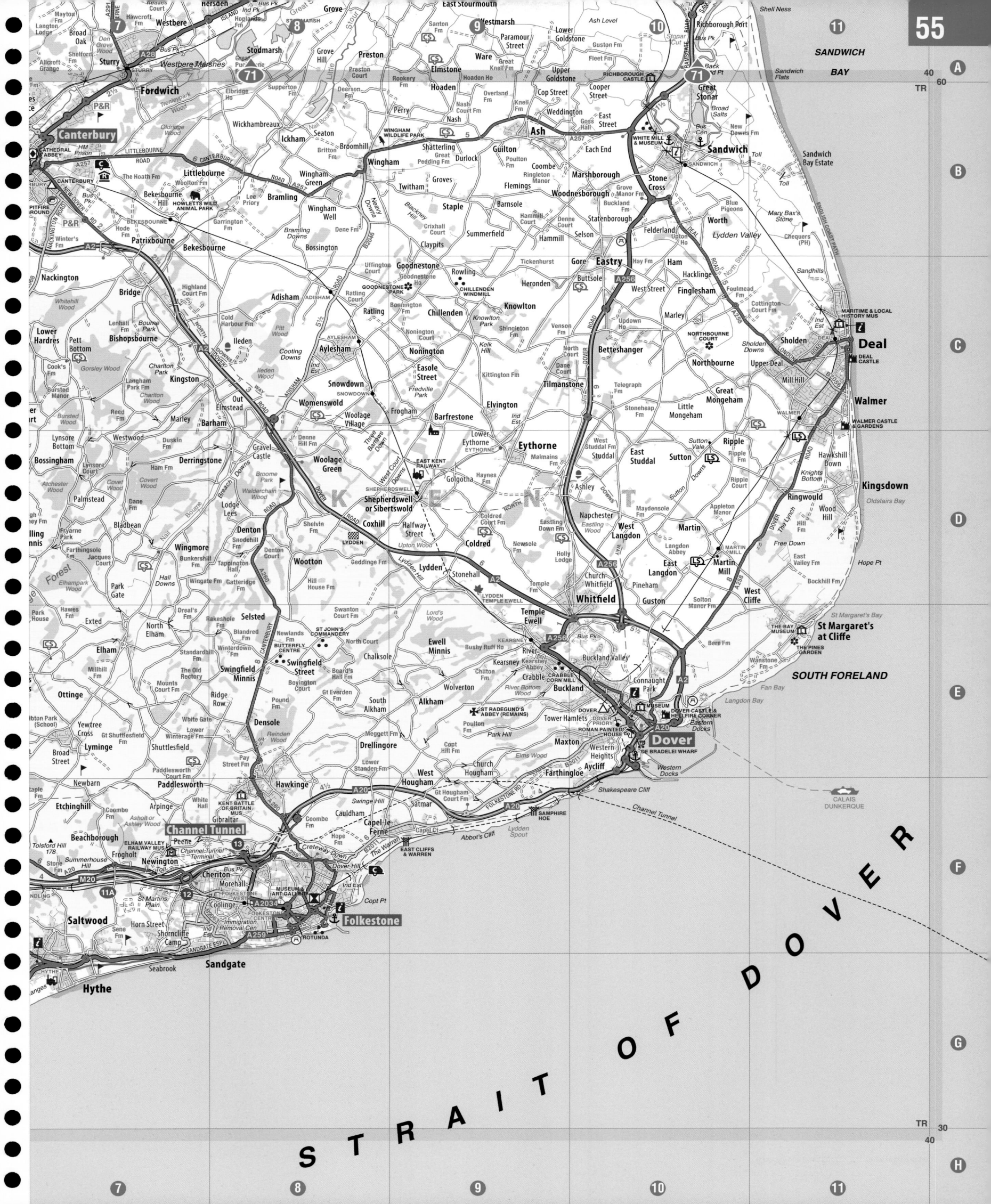

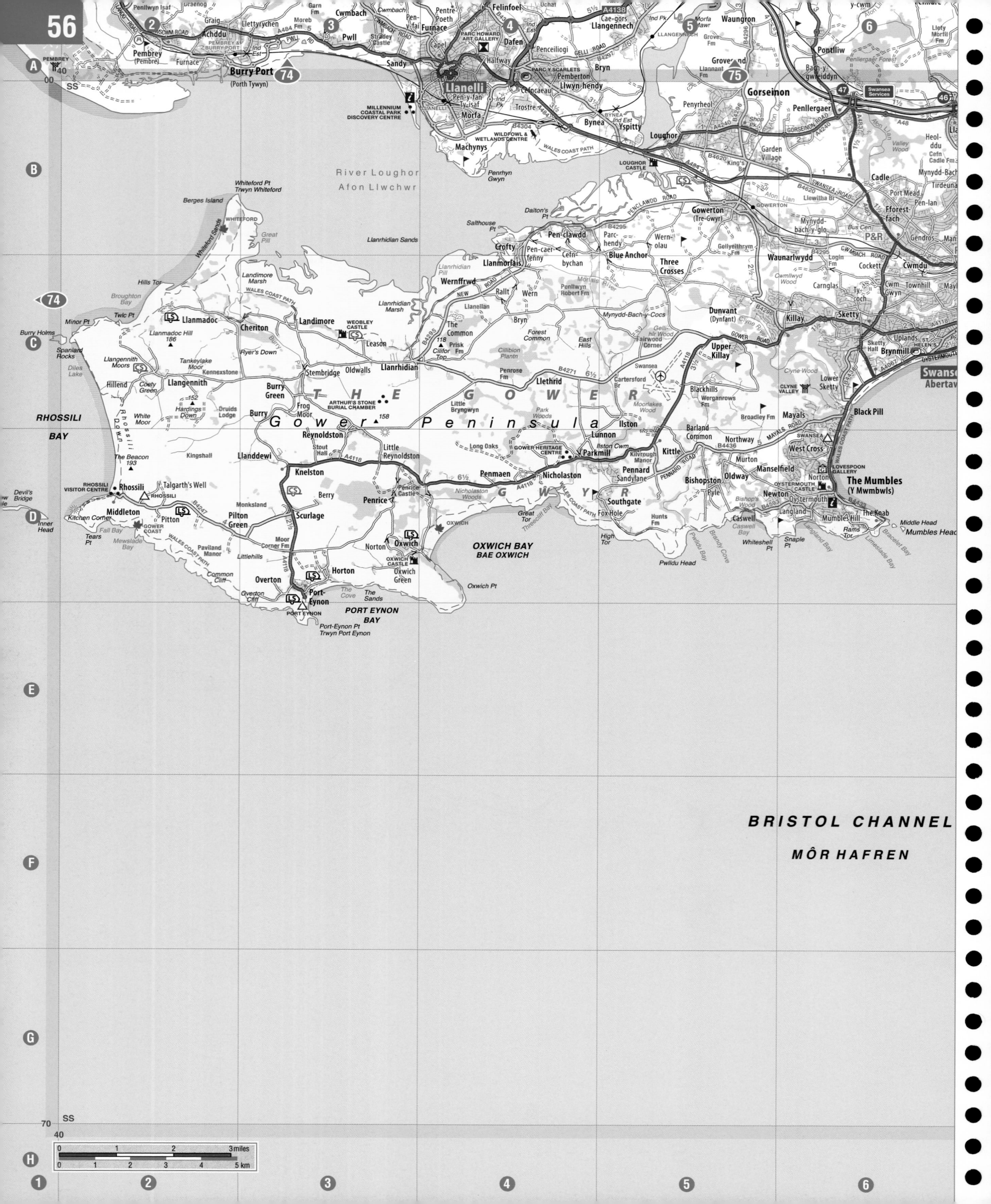

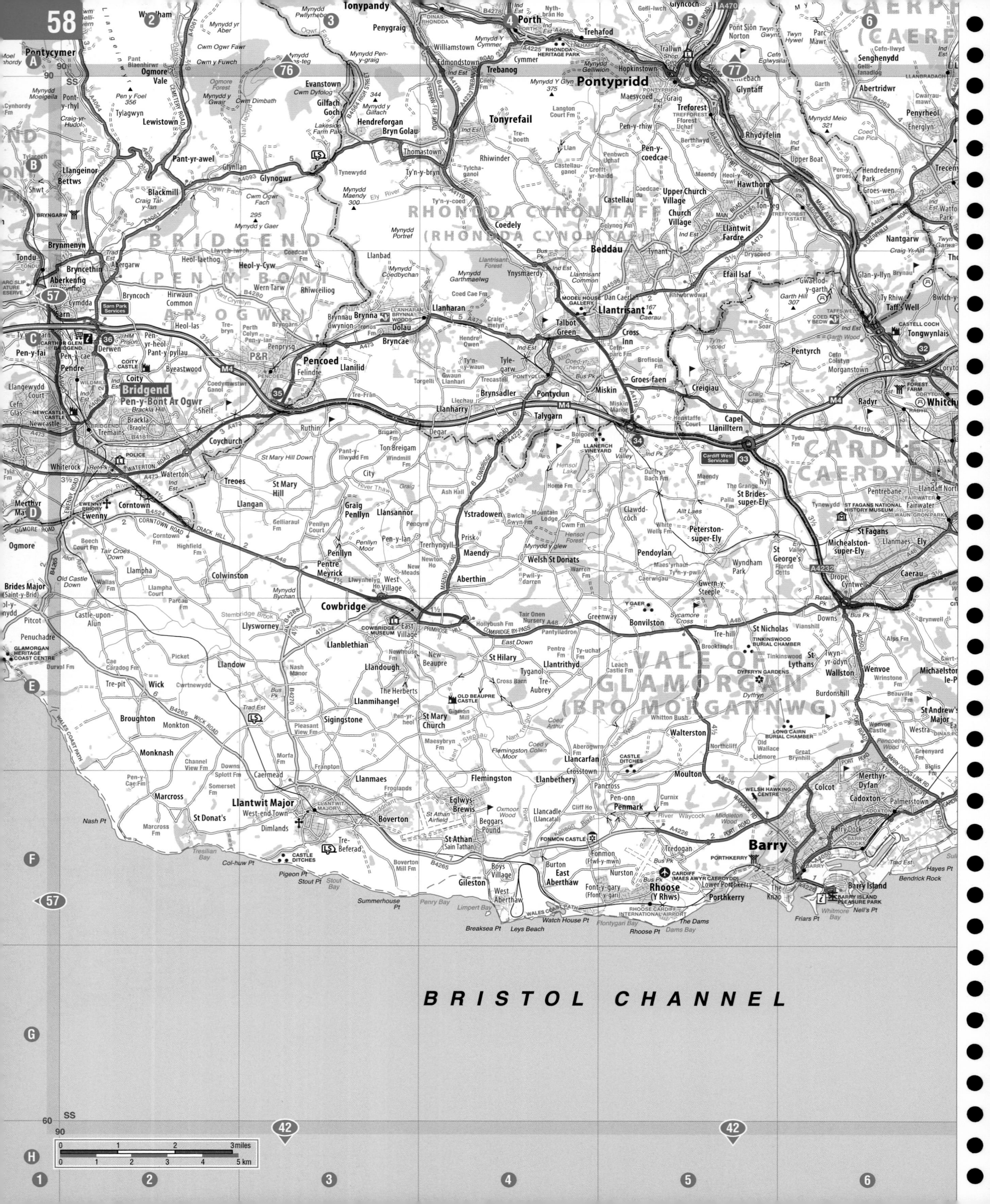

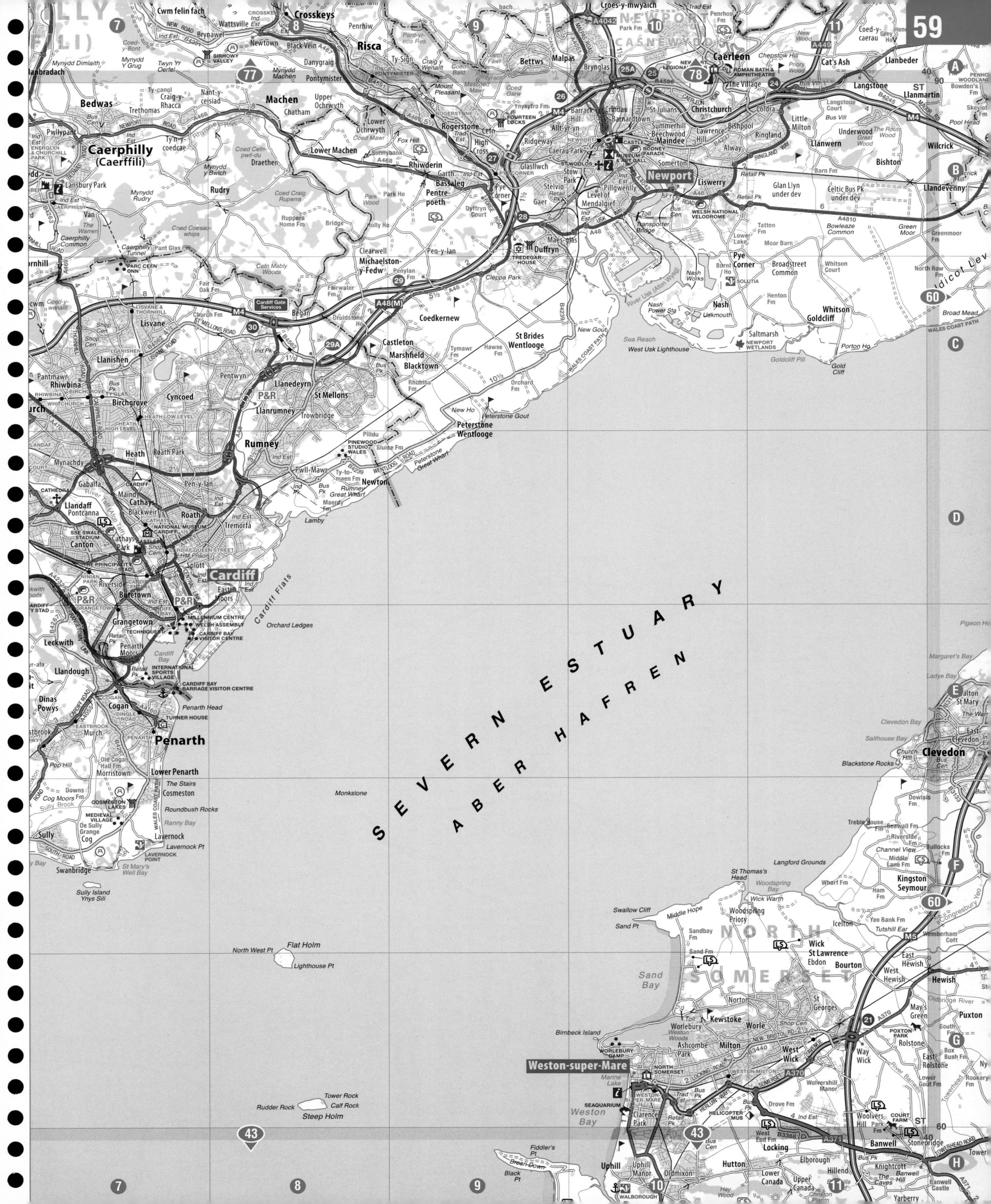

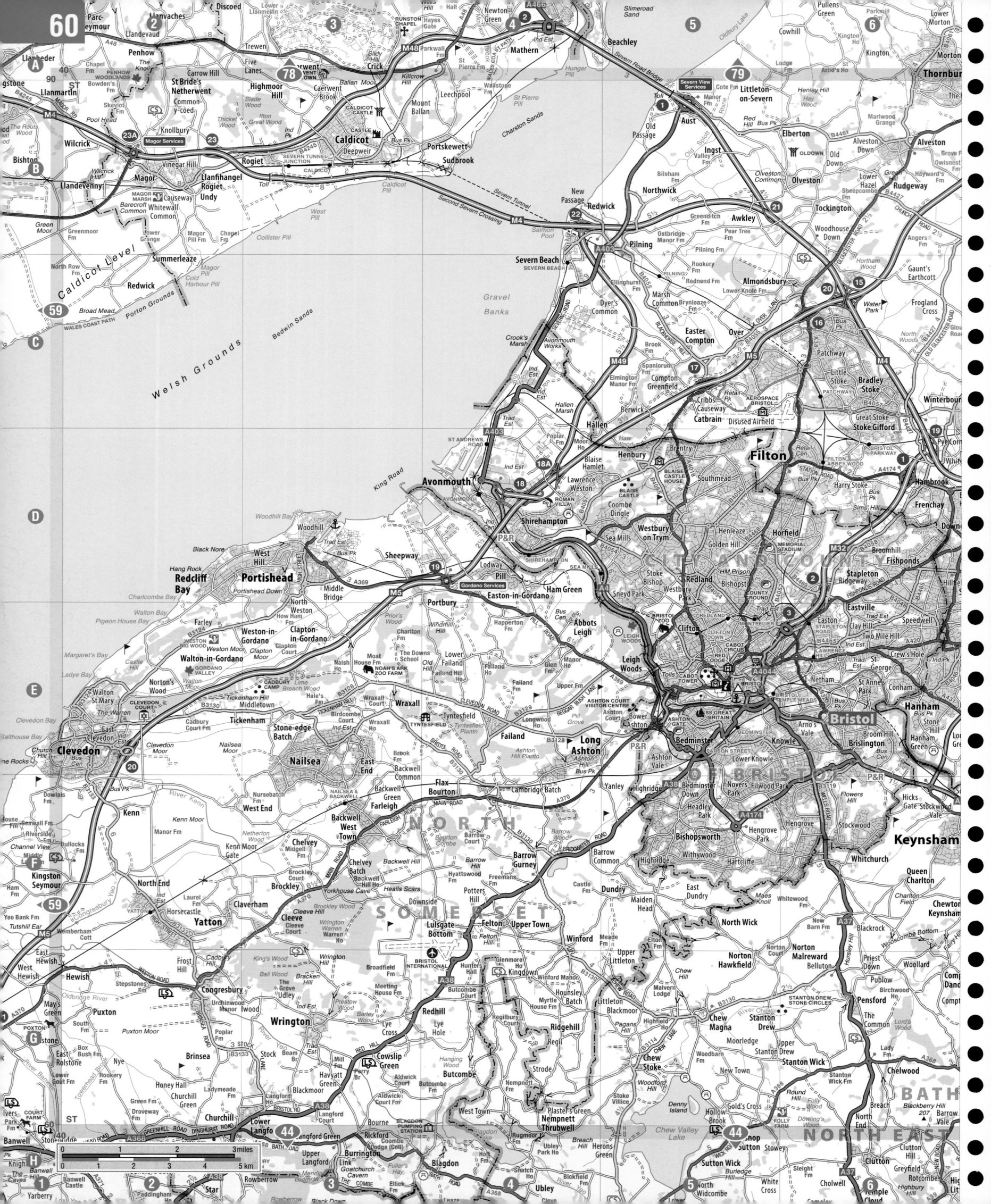

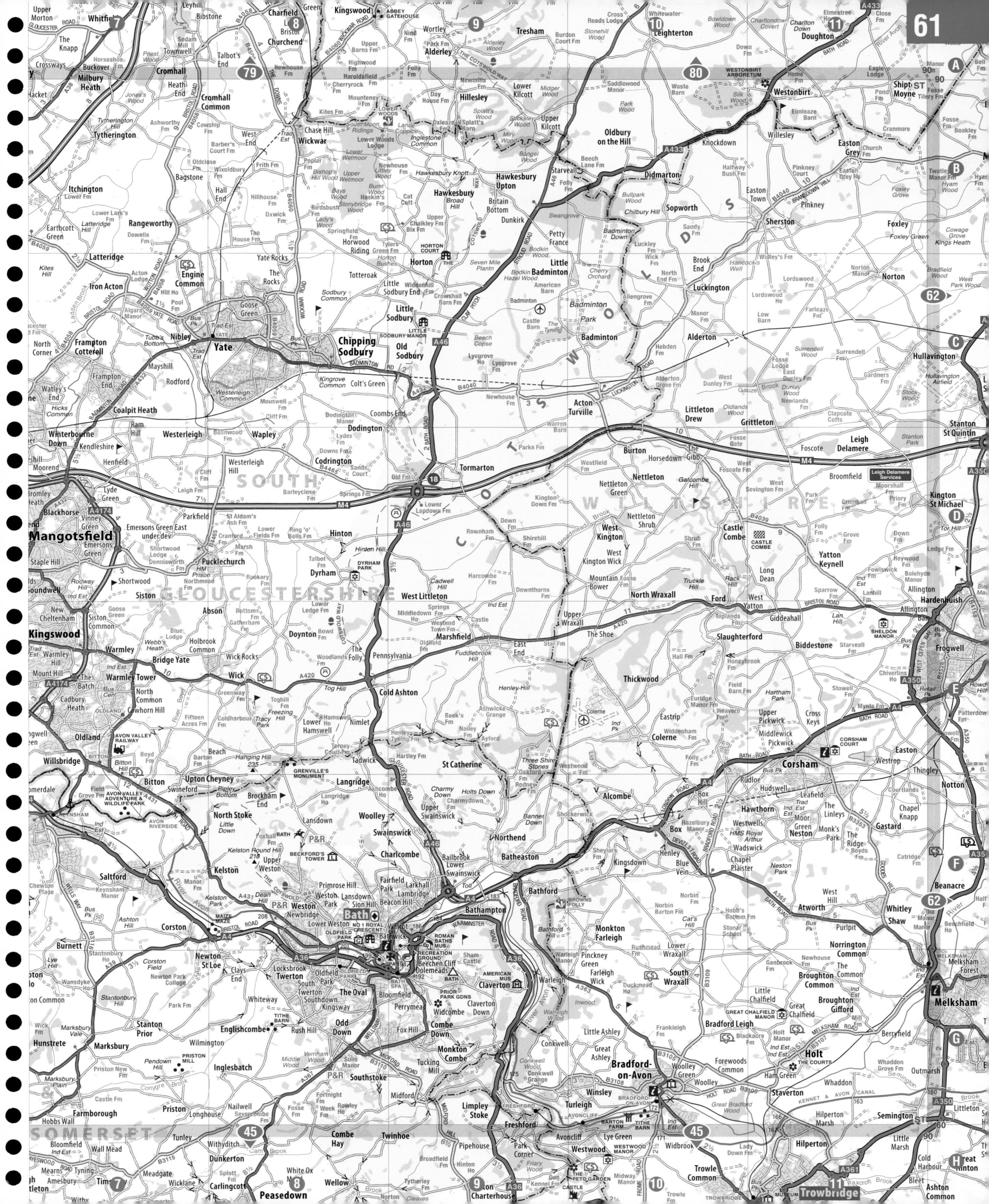

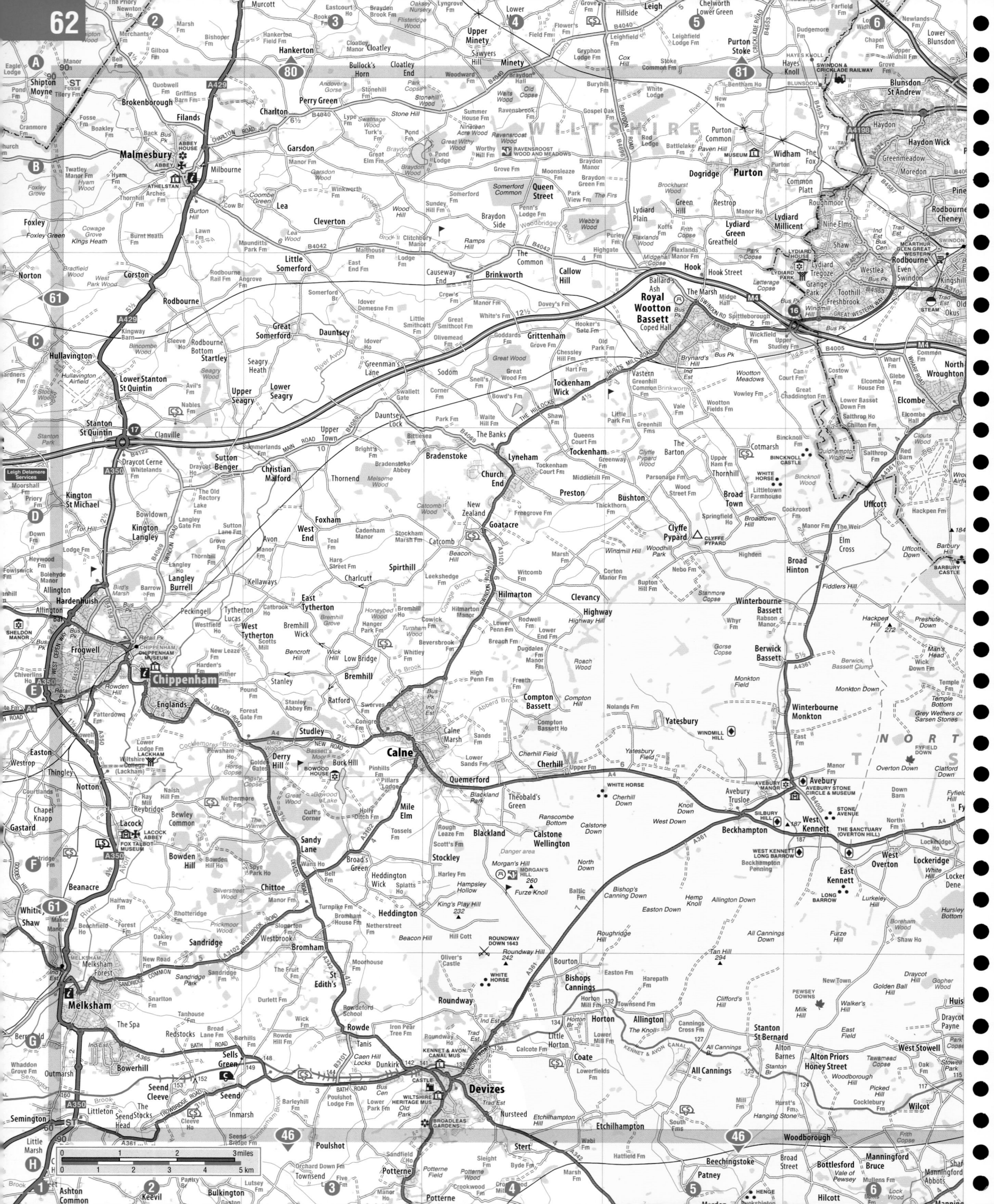

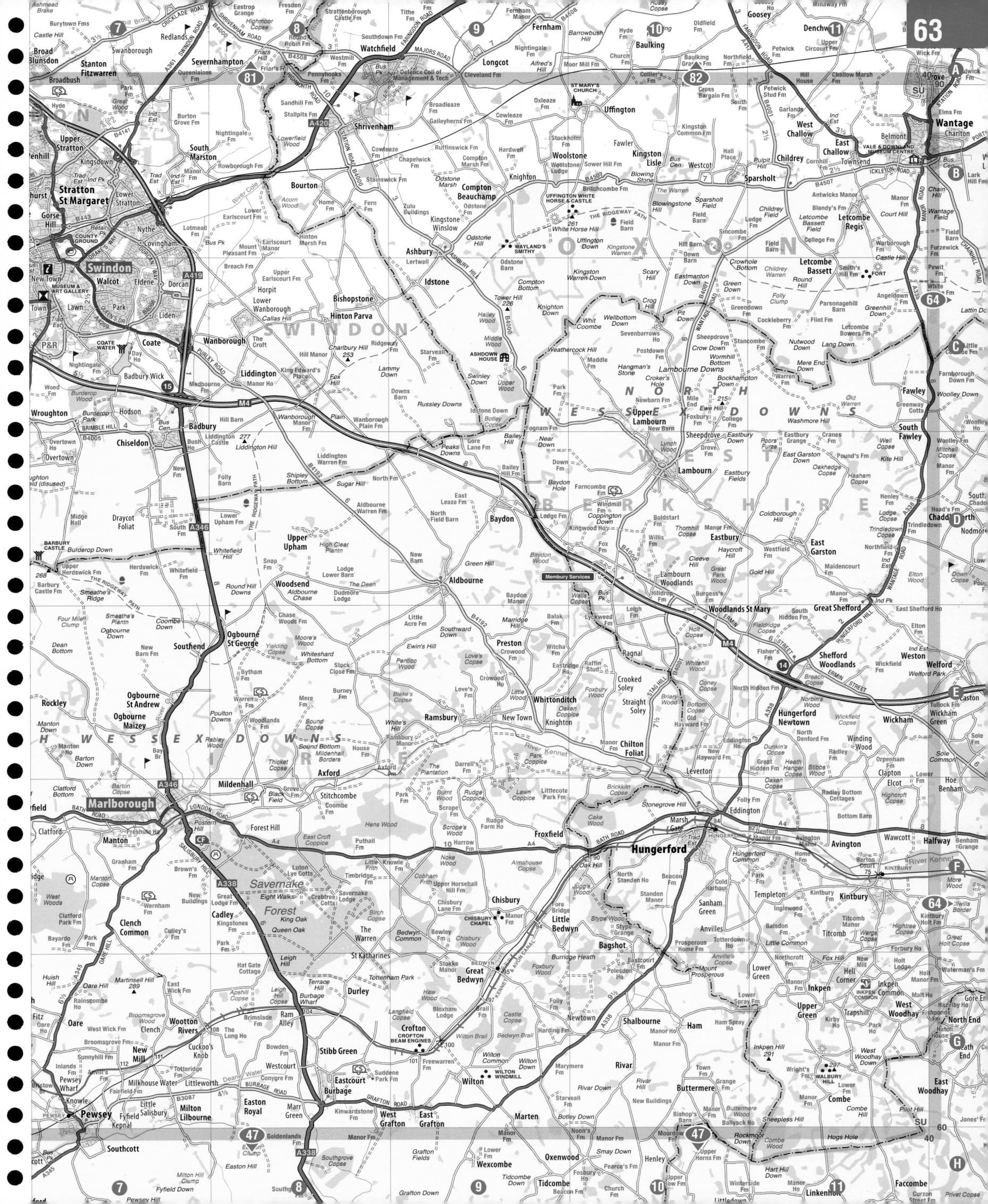

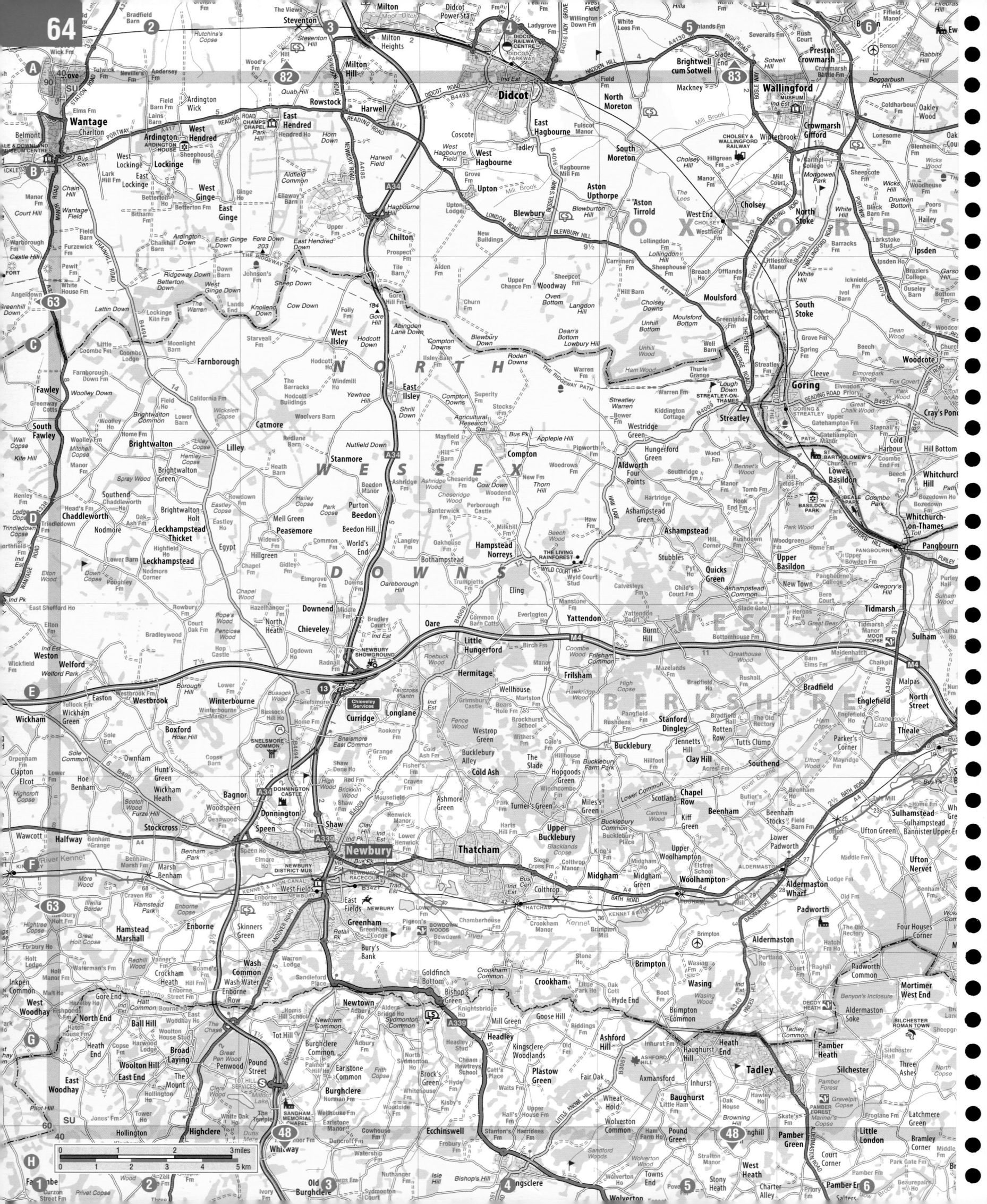

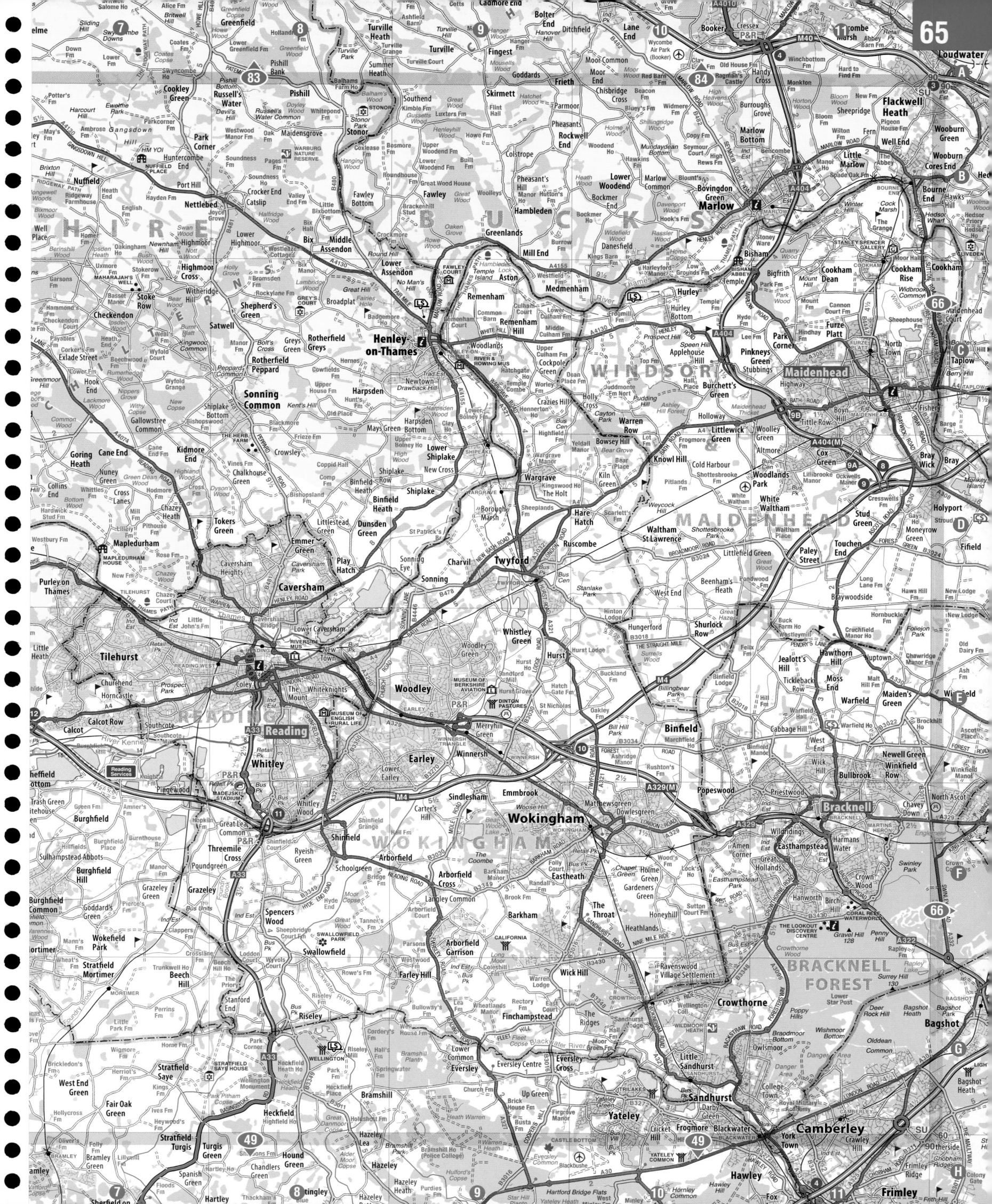

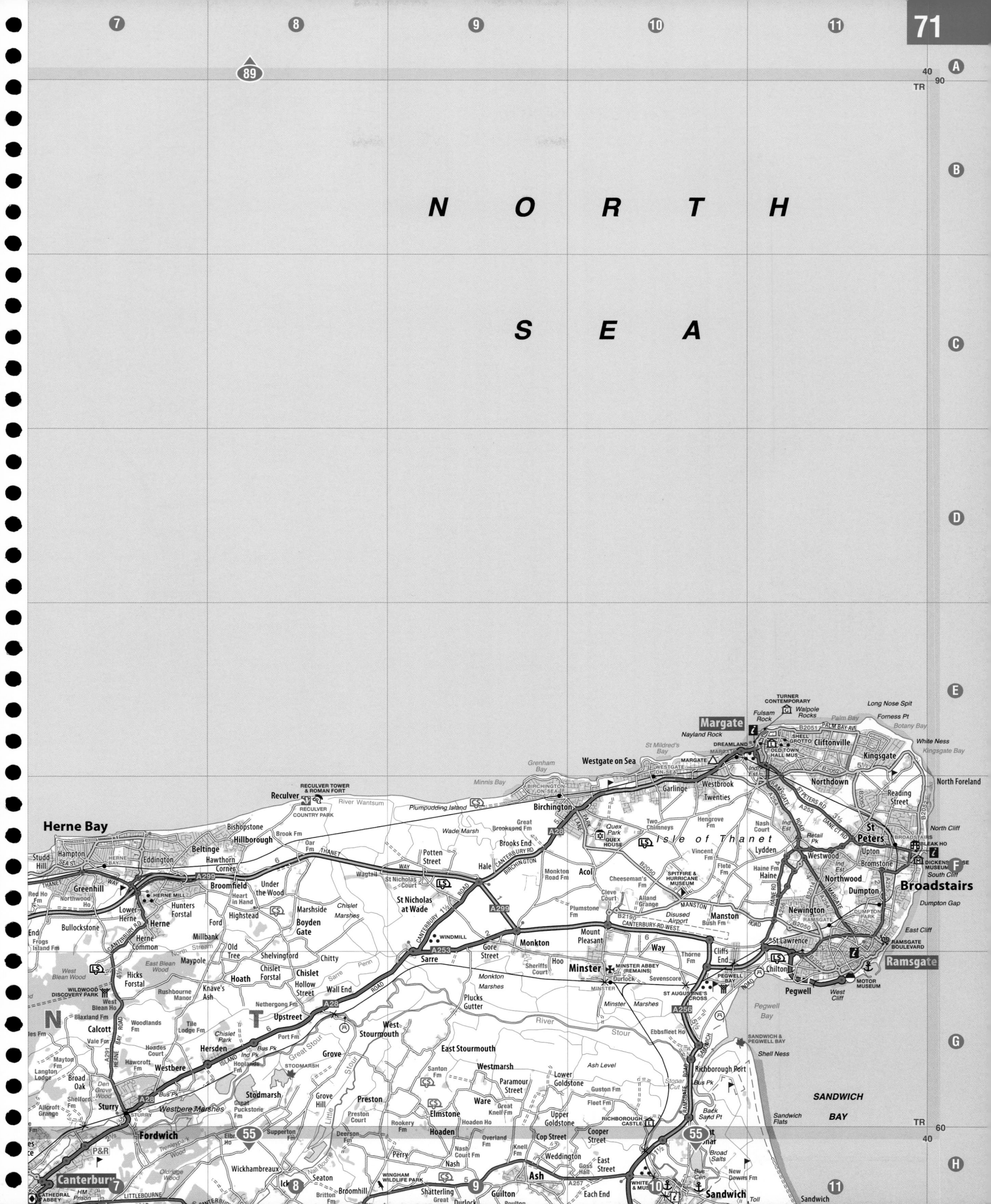

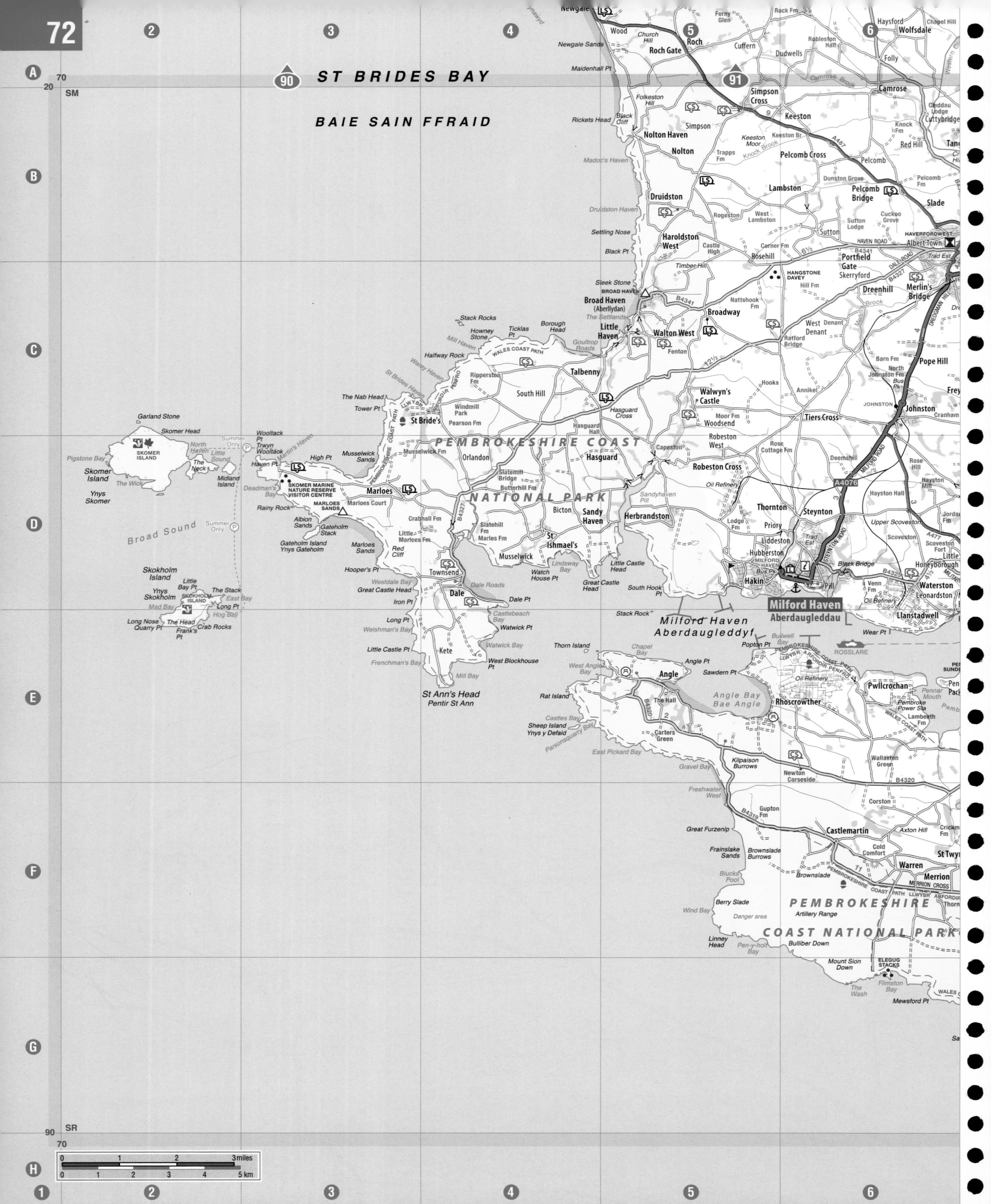

ST BRIDES BAY

BAIE SAIN FFRAID

A
70
20
SM

B

C

D

E

F

G

H

PEMBROKESHIRE COAST

NATIONAL PARK

PEMBROKESHIRE

COAST NATIONAL PARK

90
70
SR

0   1   2   3miles
0   1   2   3   4   5 km

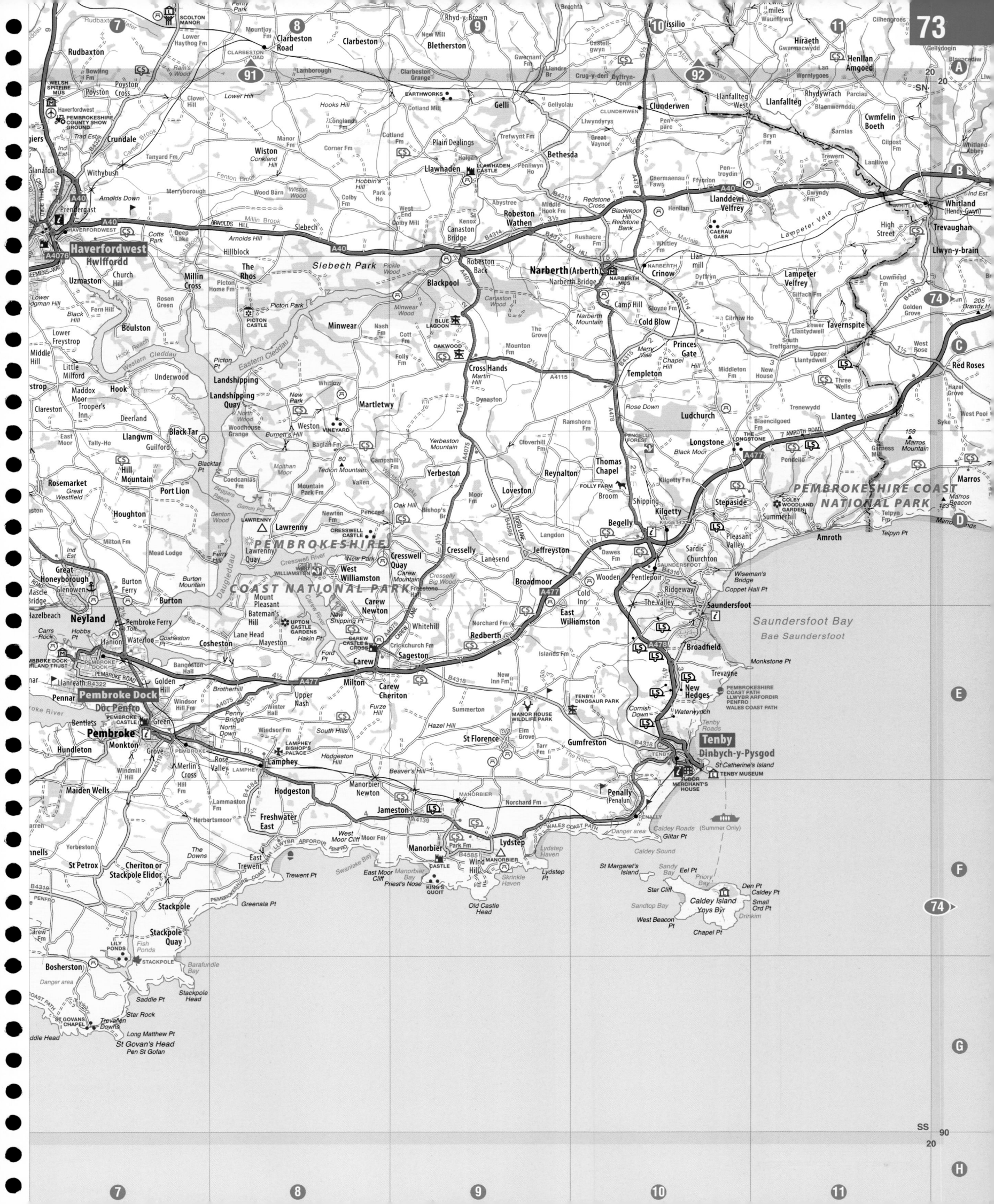

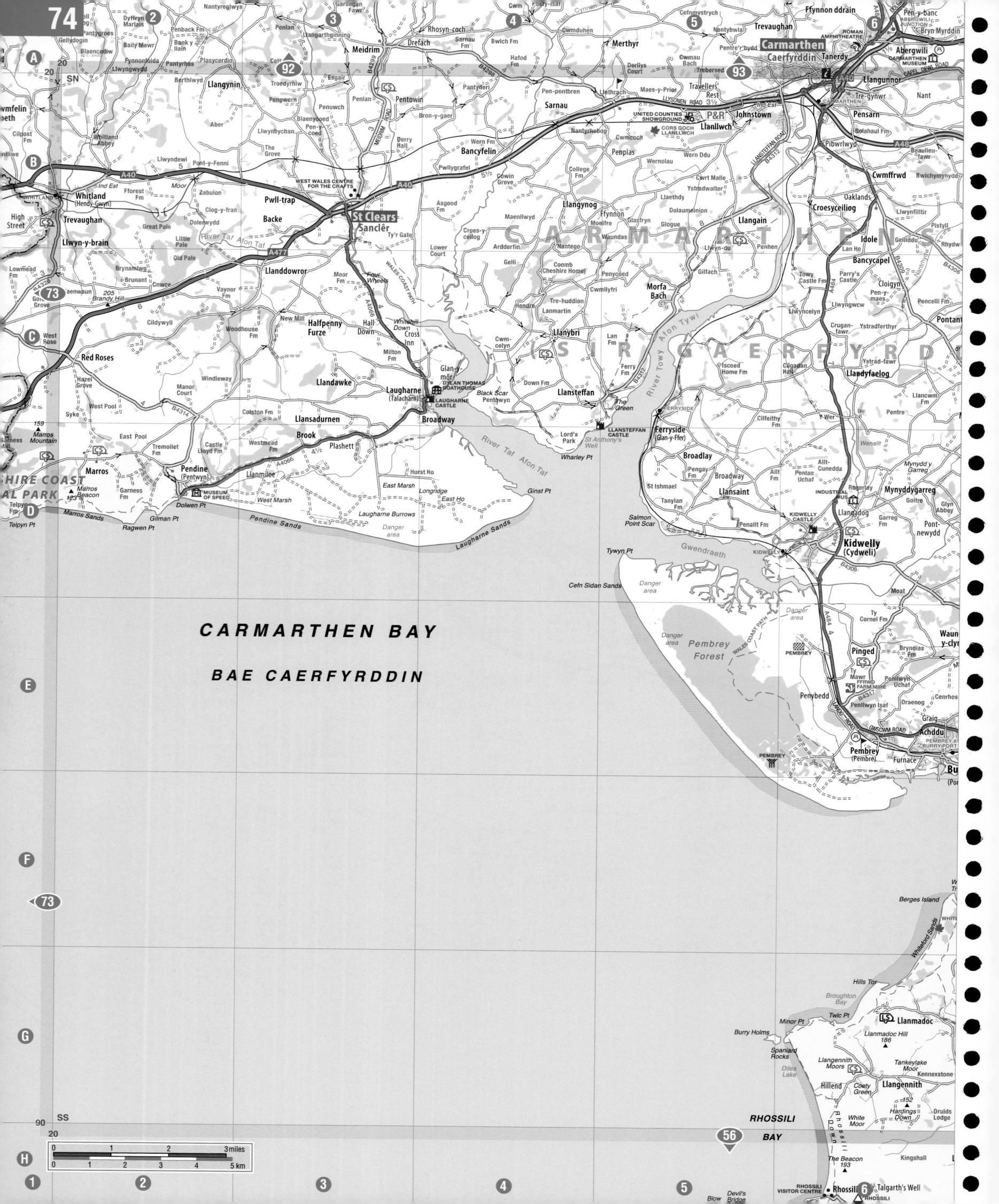

CARMARTHEN BAY

BAE CAERFYRDDIN

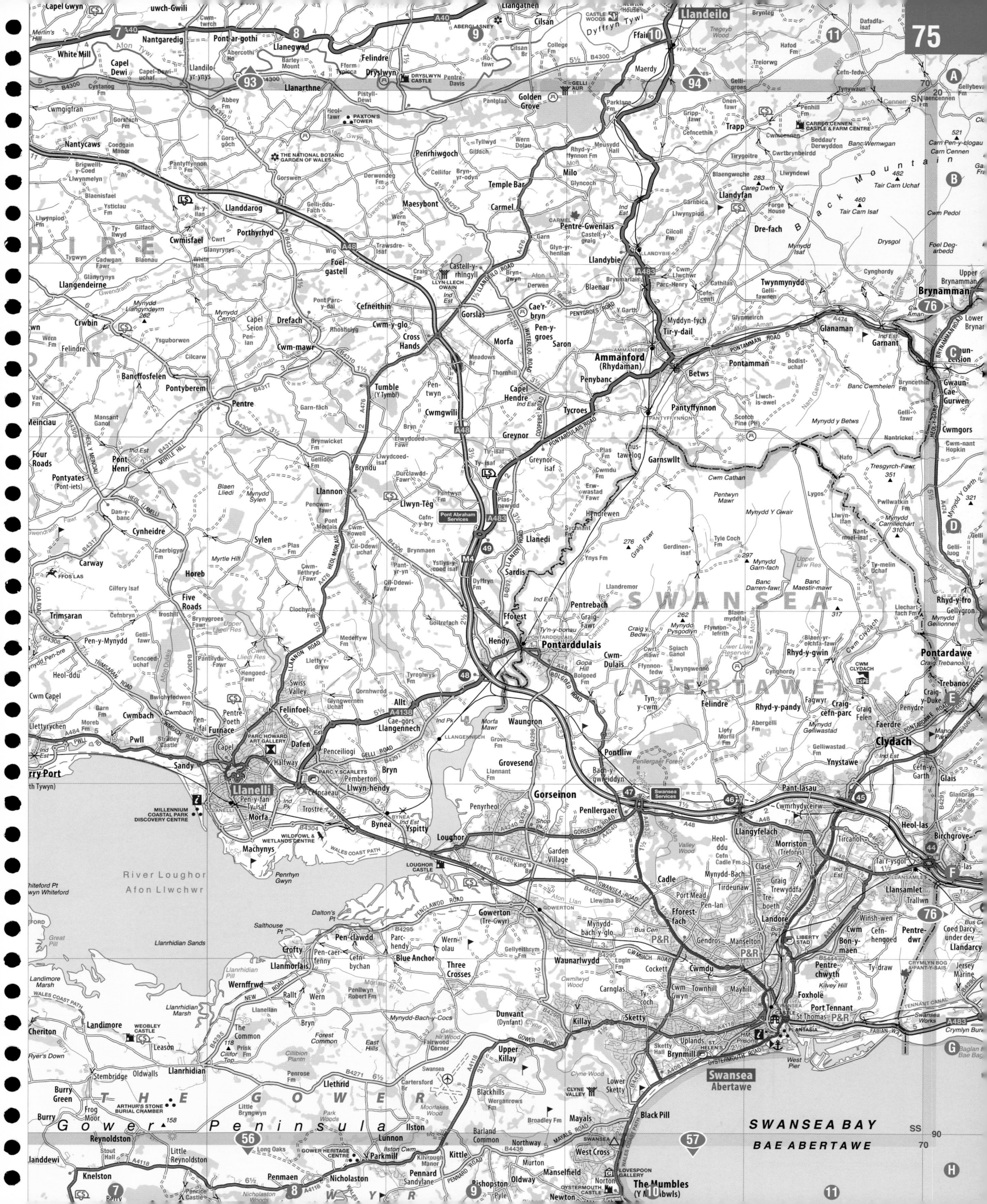

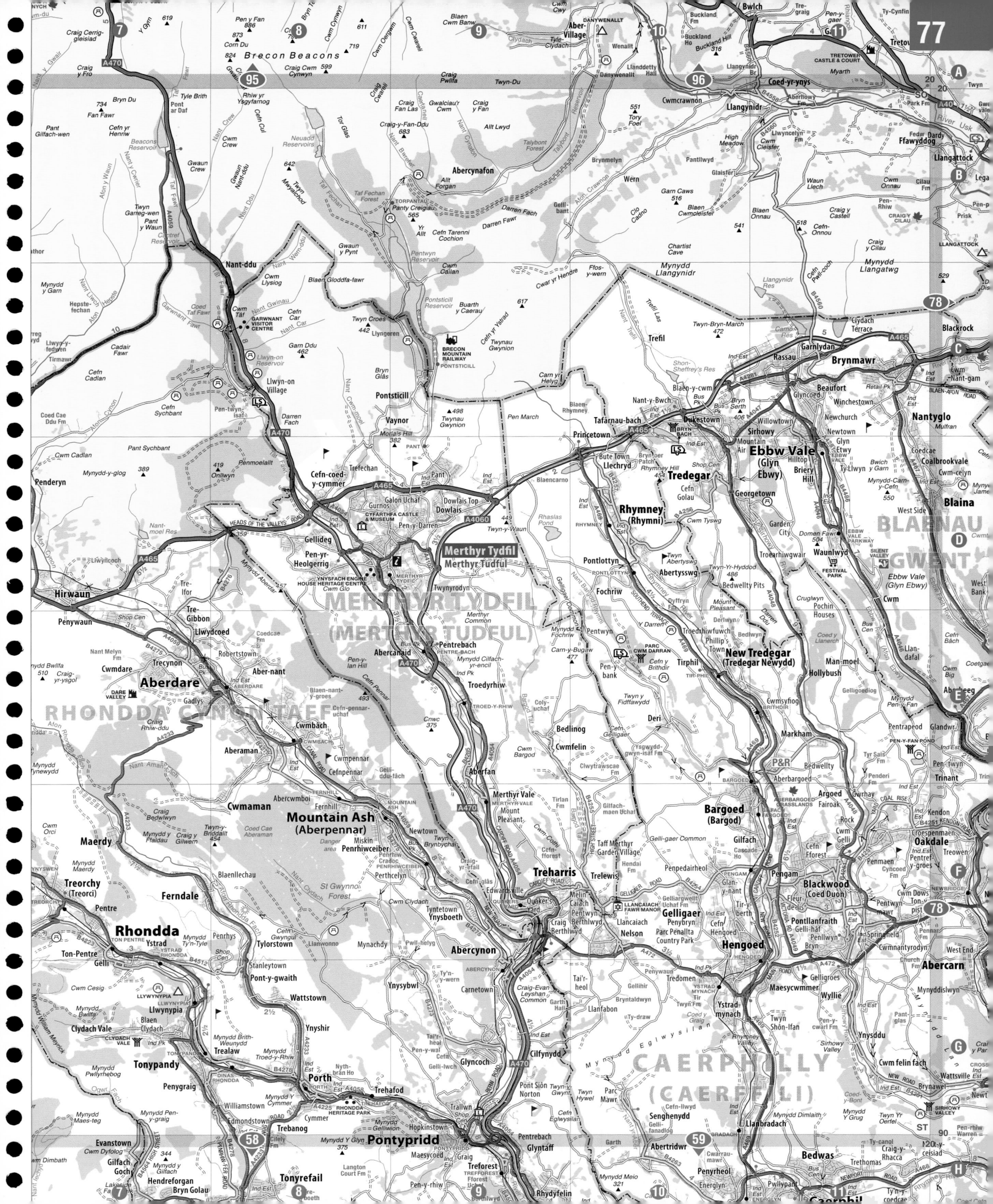

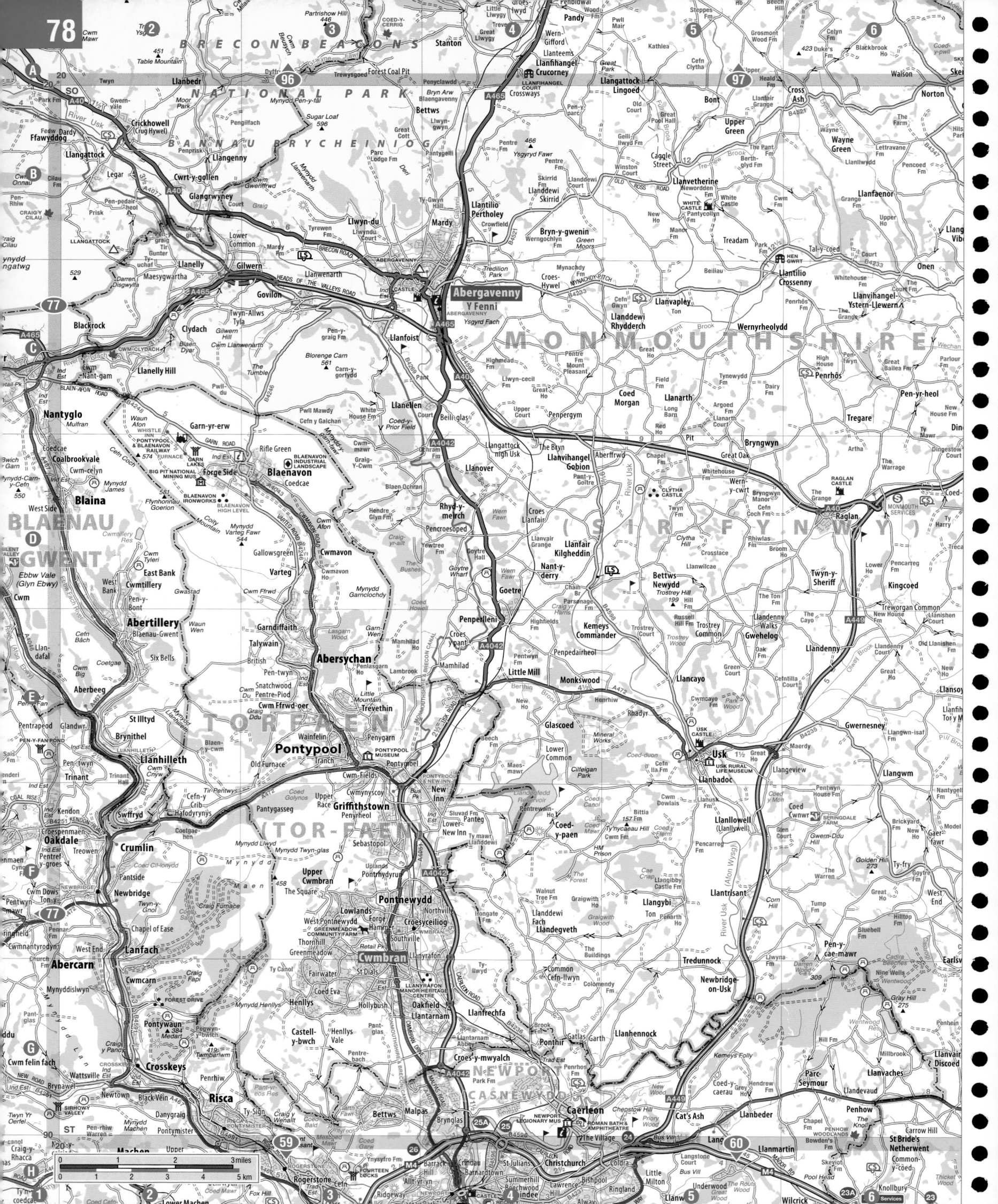

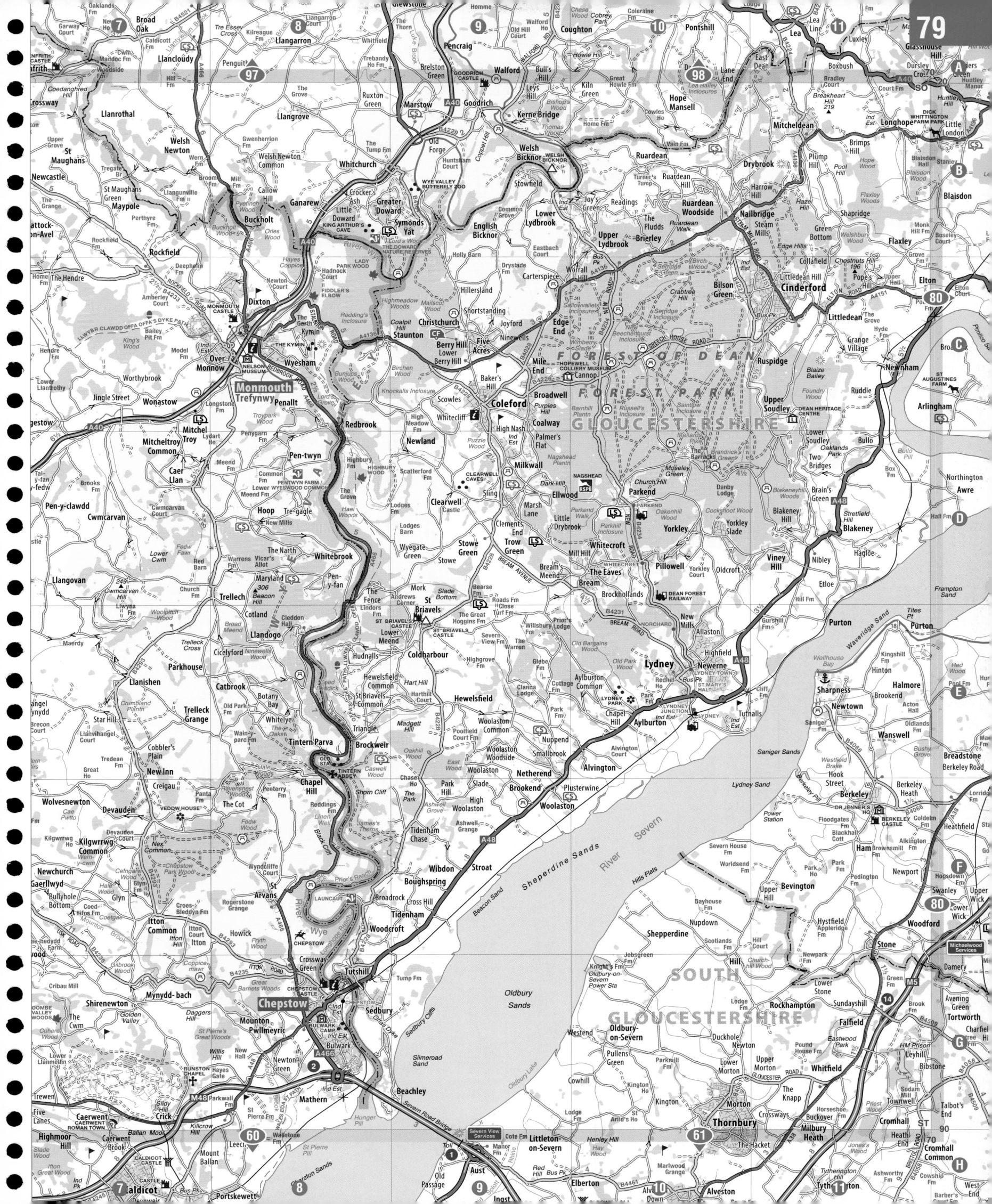

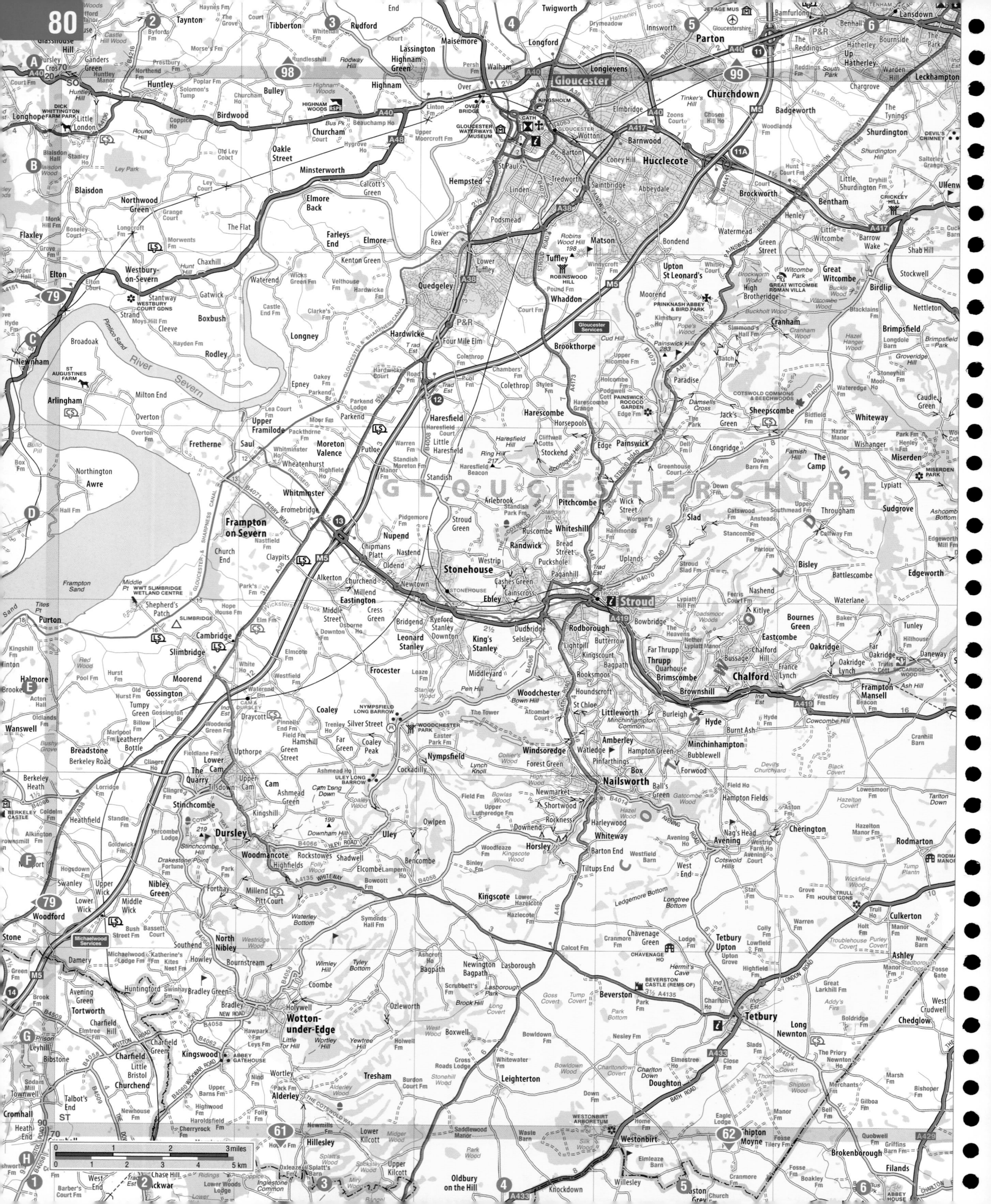

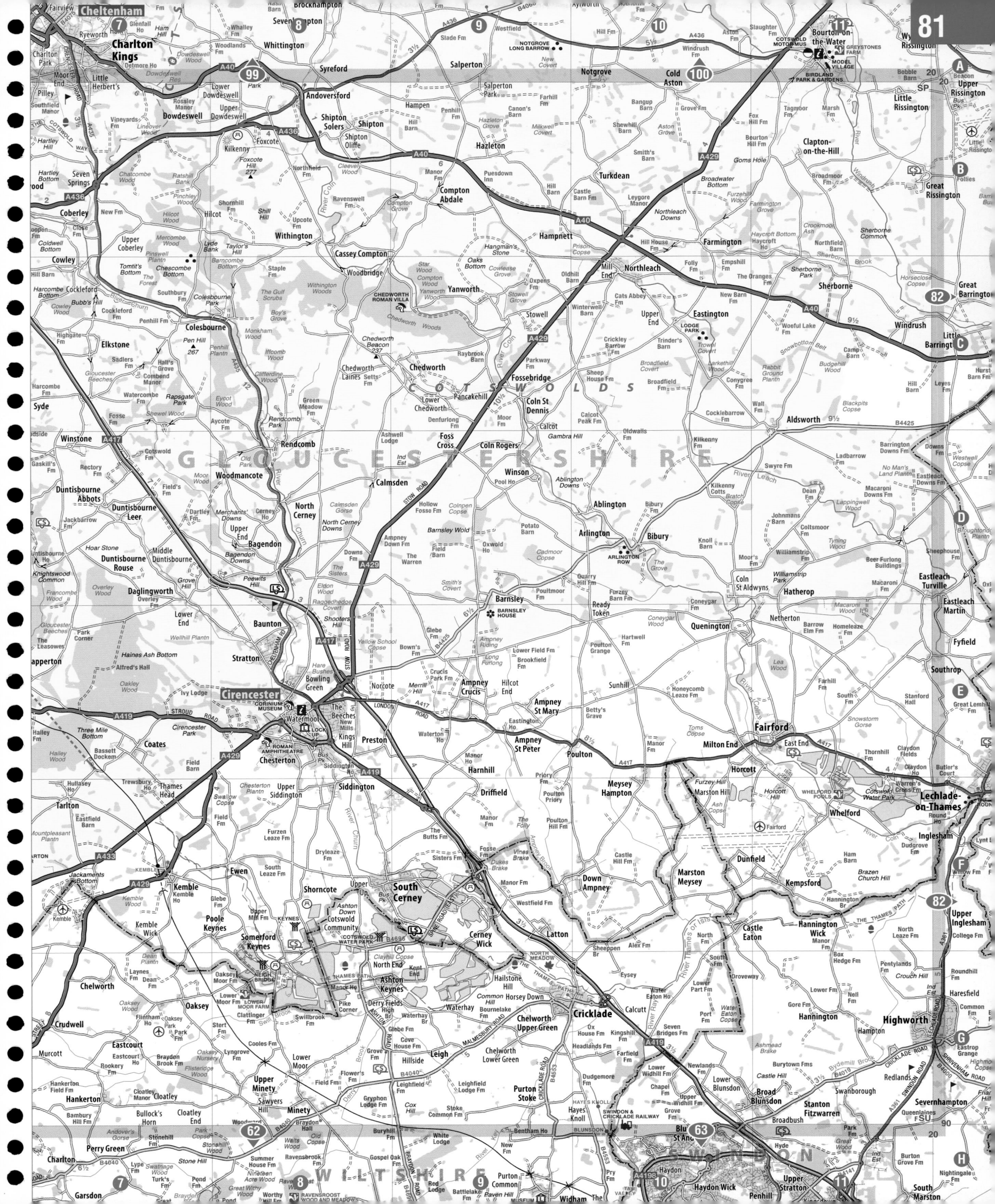

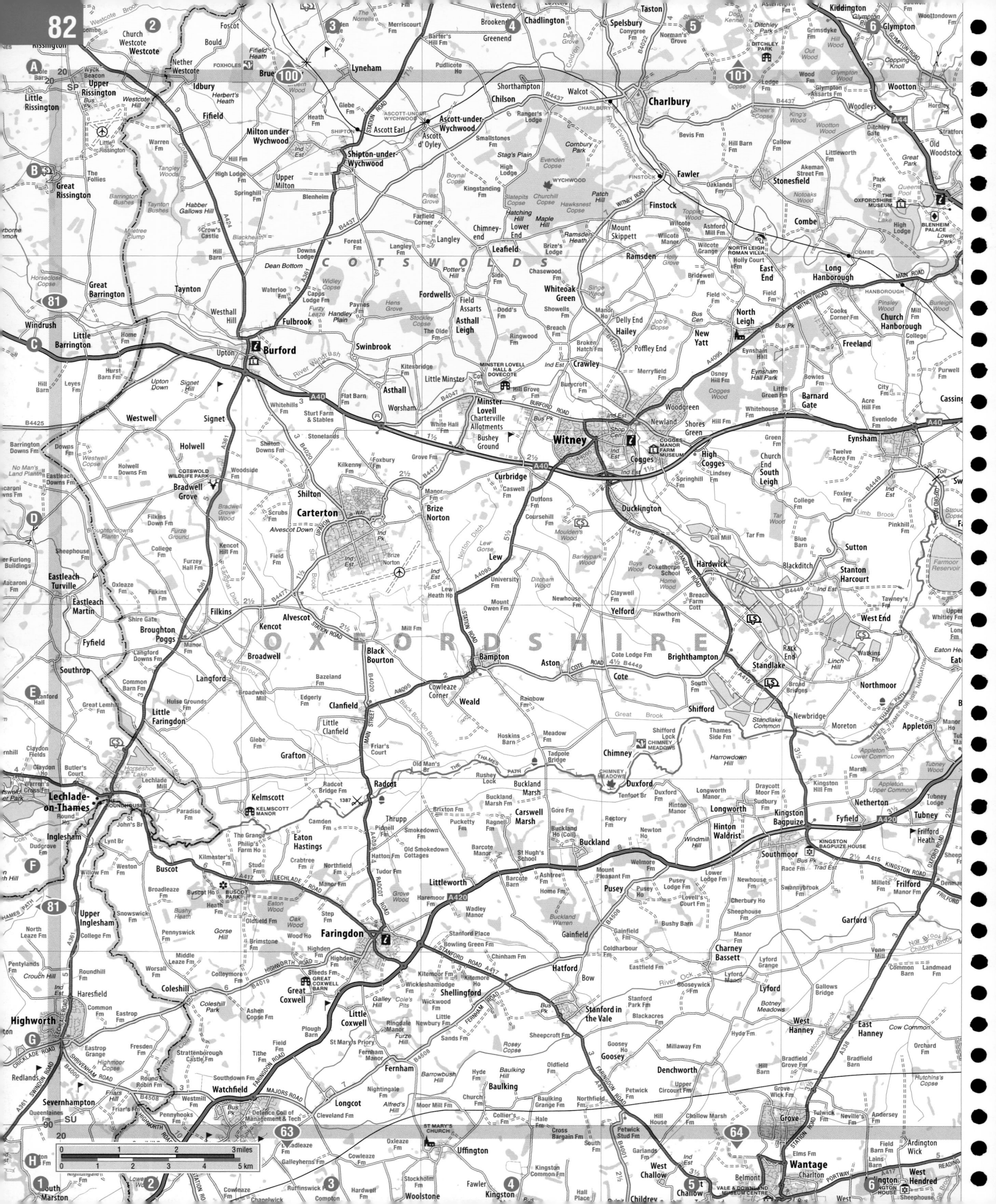

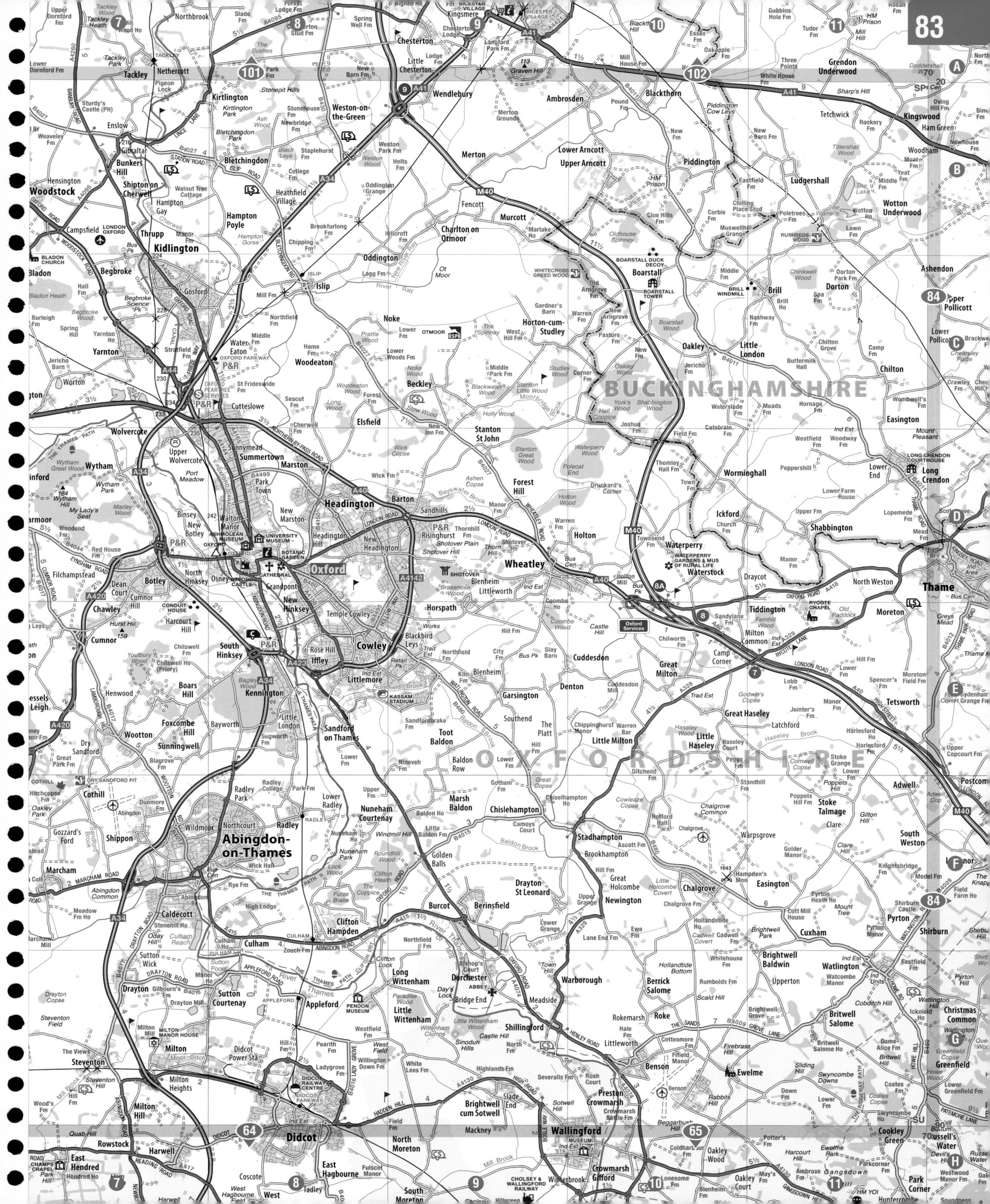

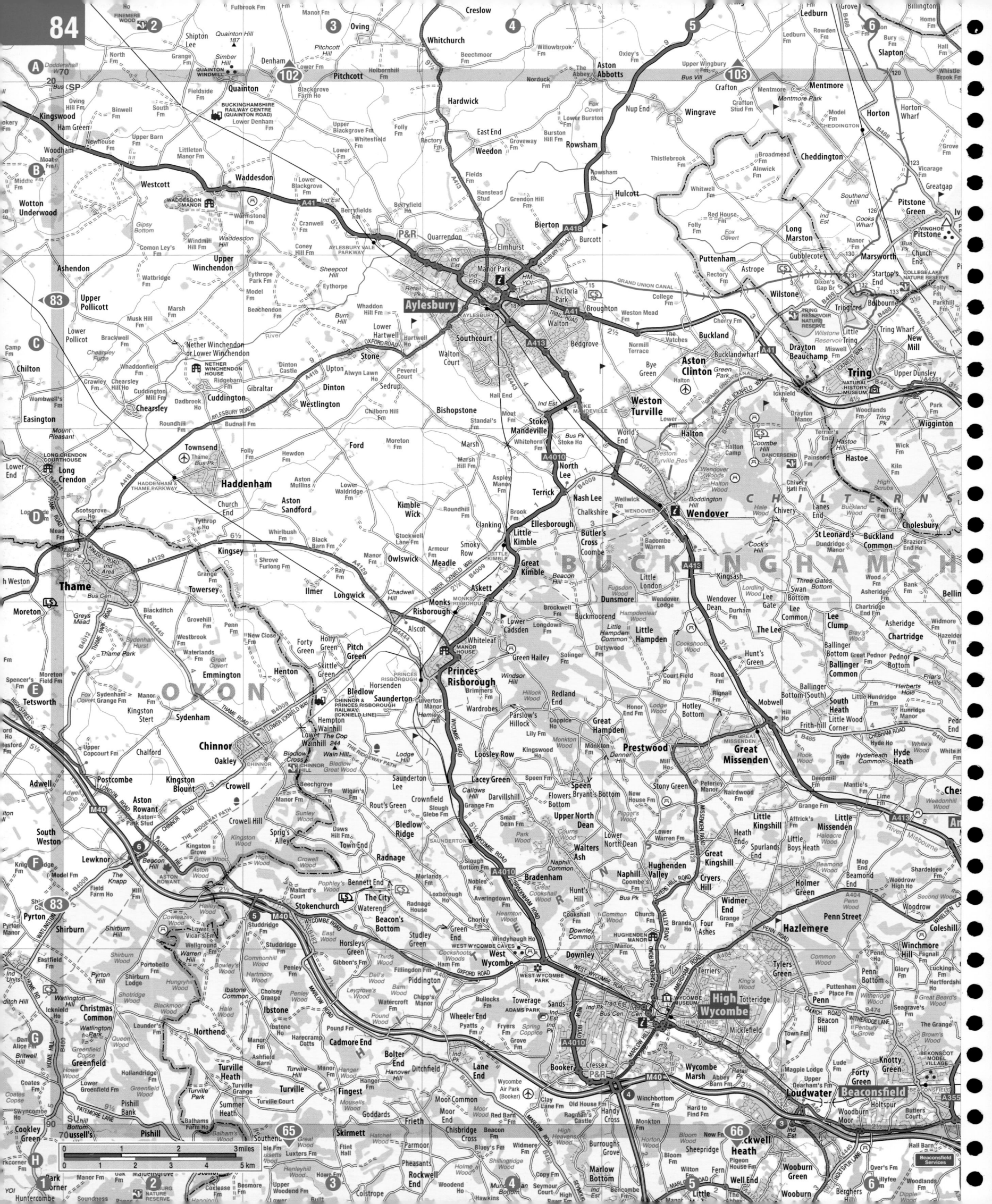

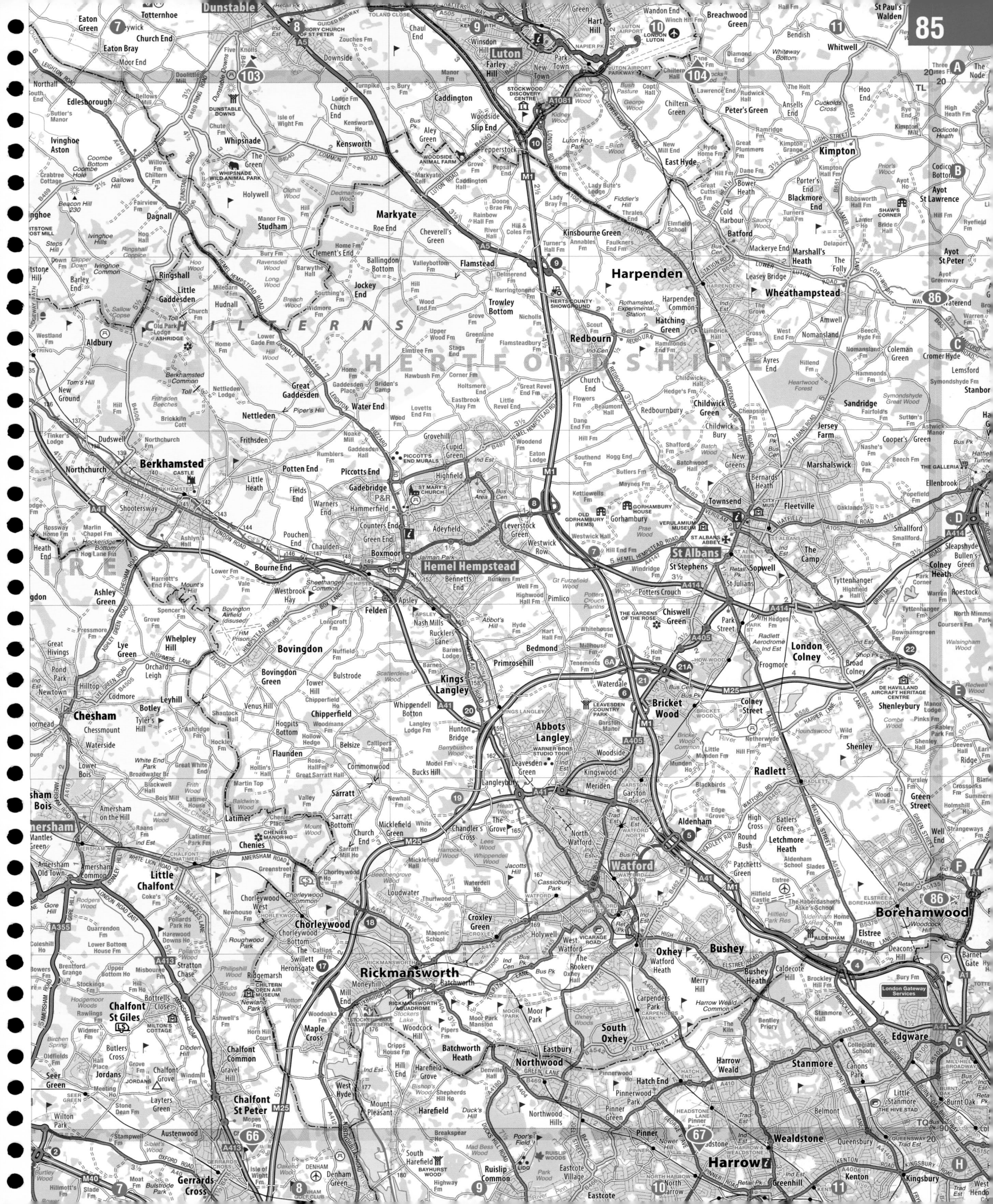

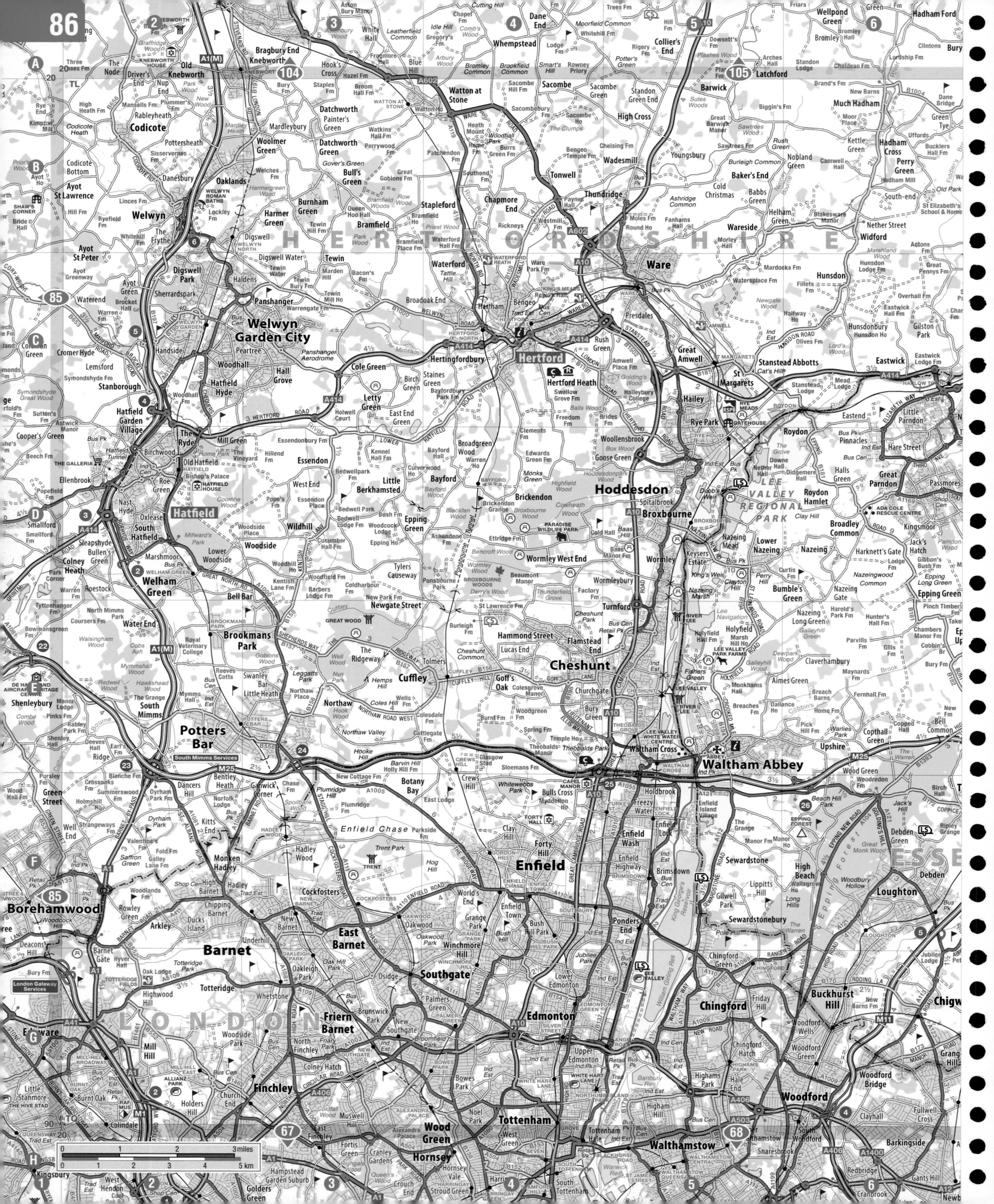

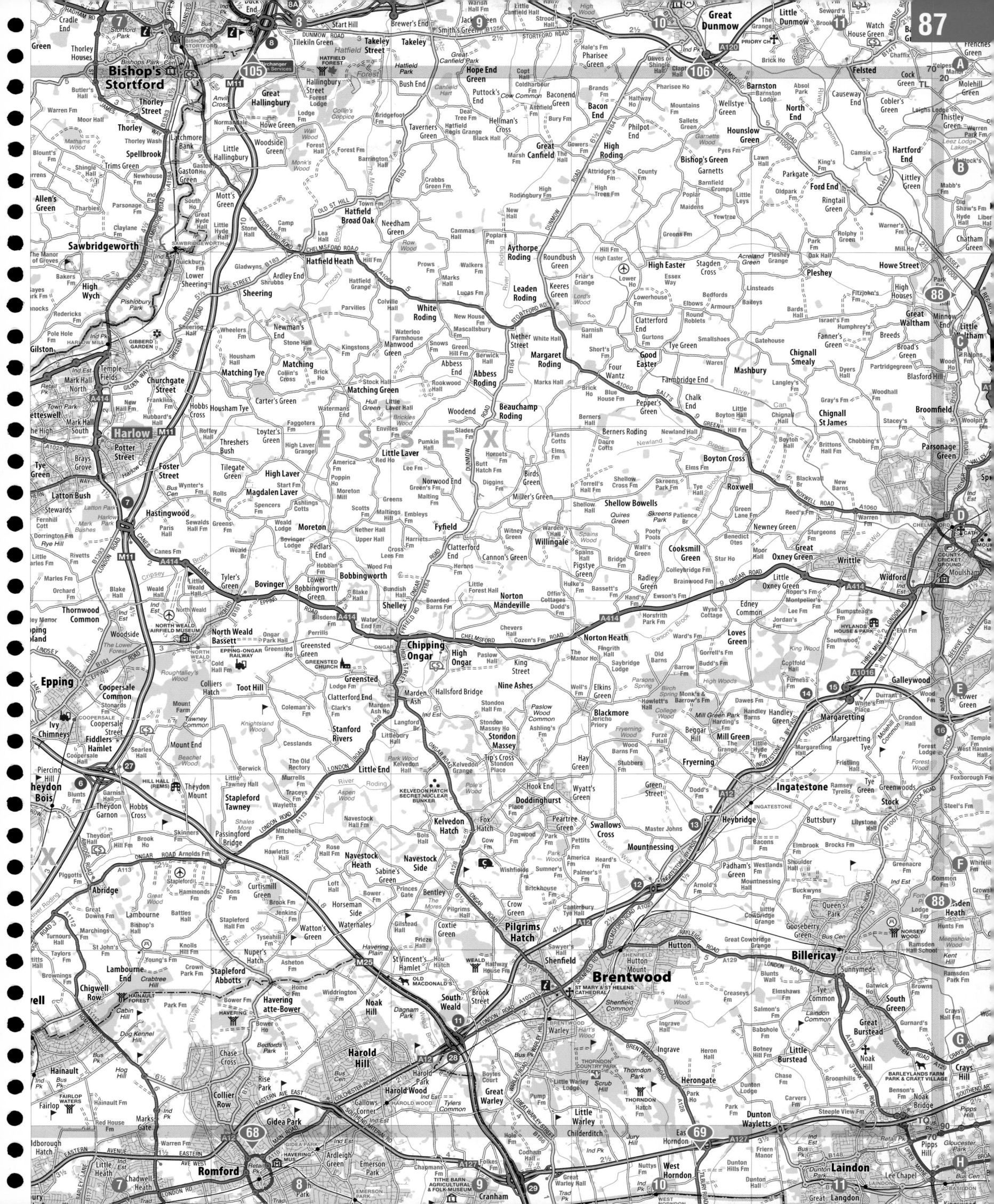

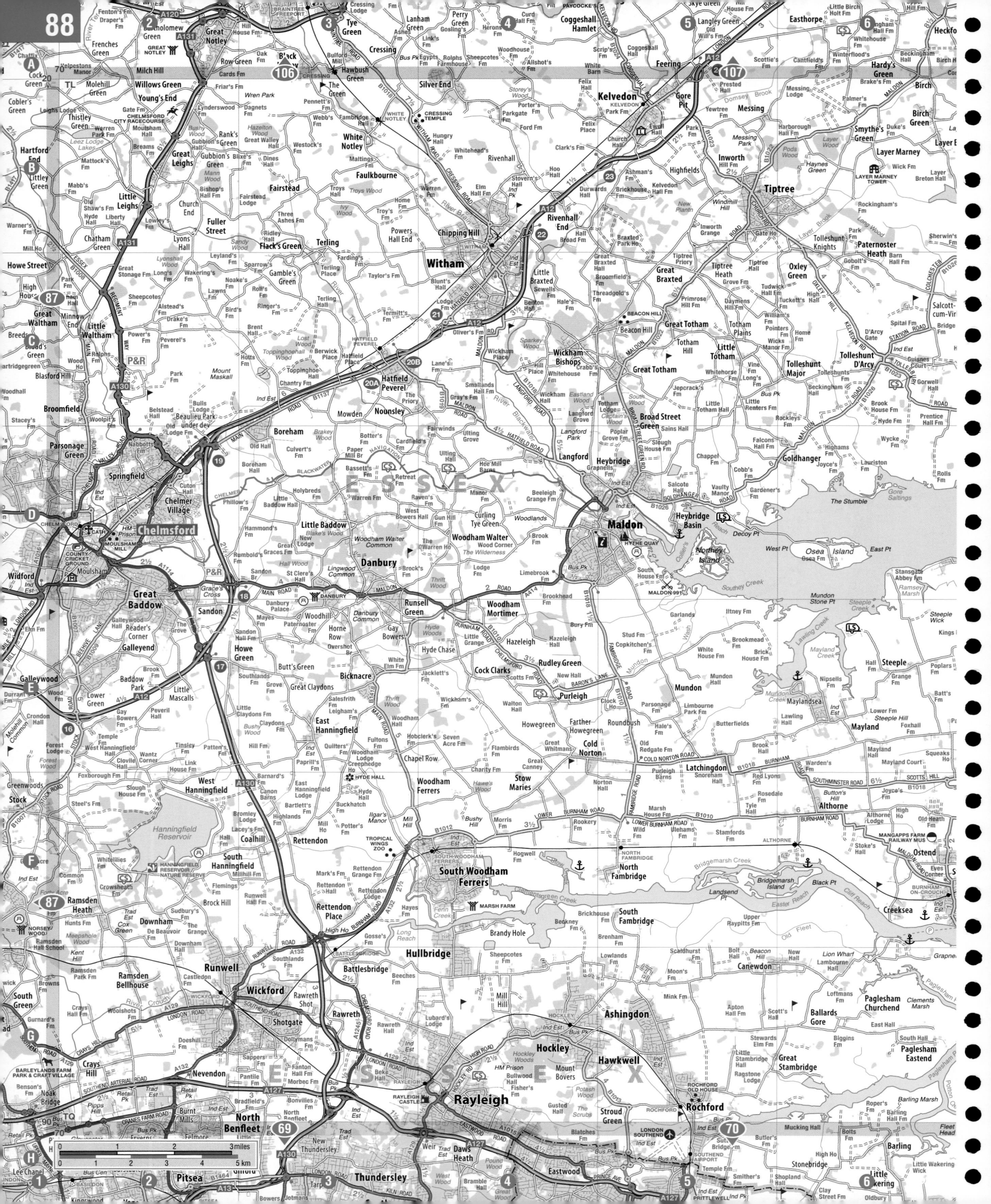

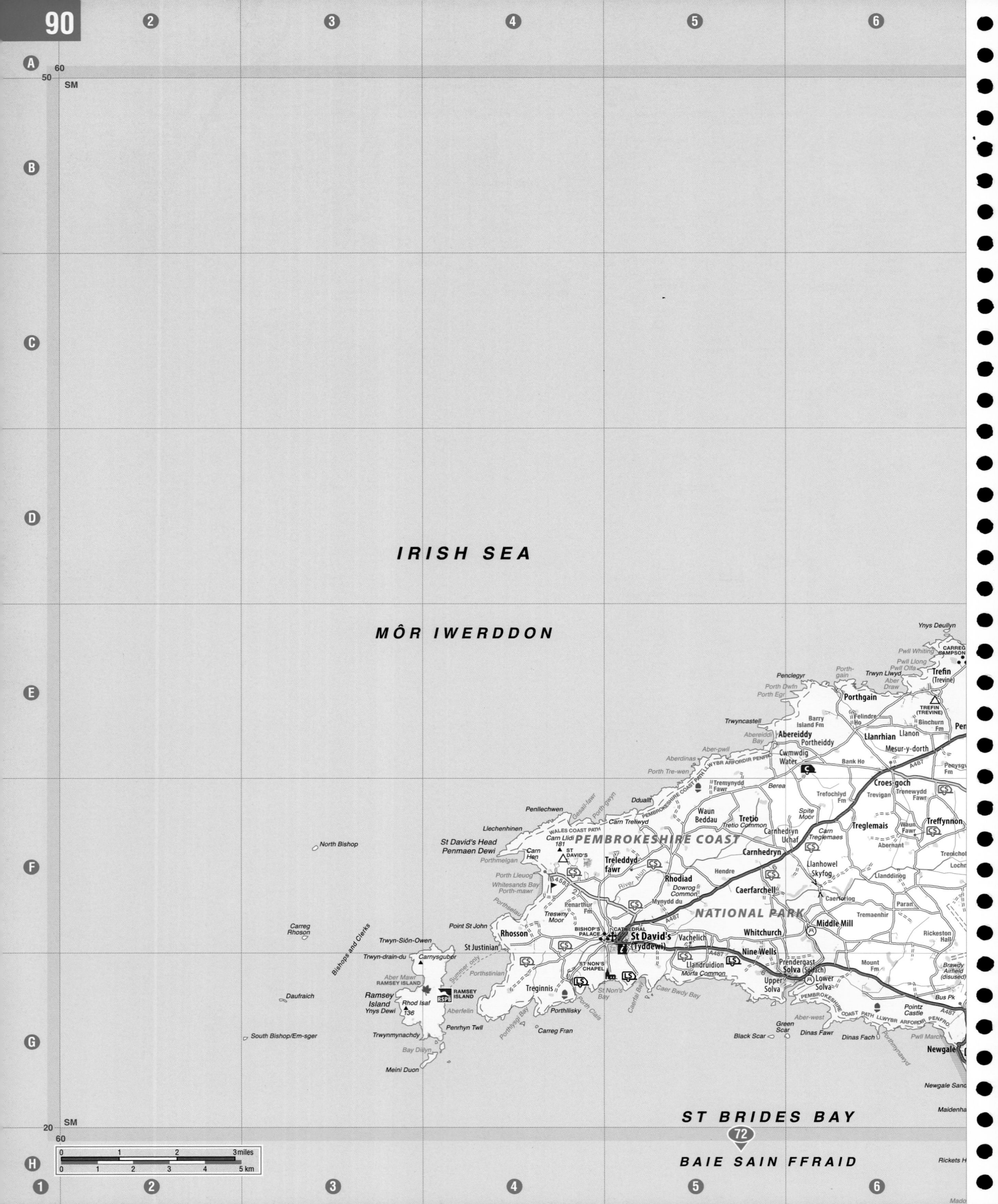

IRISH SEA

MÔR IWERDDON

North Bishop

Bishops and Clerks

Carreg
Rhoson

Daufraich

South Bishop/Em-sger

Ynys Deullyn

CARREG
SAMPSON
Pwll Whiting
Penclegyr
Porth-
Pwll Llong
gain
Pwll Olfa
Trwyn Llwyd
Trefin
Porth Dwfn
Aber
(Trevine)
Porth Egr
Draw
TREFIN
(TREVINE)
Porthgain
Twryncastell
Barry
Felindre
Binchurn
Island Fm
Ho
Fm
Pen-
Abereiddi
Abereiddy
Porthelddy
Llanon
Bay
Llanrhian
Penysgw
Aber-pwll
Cwmwdig
Mesur-y-dorth
Abordinas
Water
A487
Bank Ho
Croes-goch
Porth Tre-wen
Berea
Trefochlyd
Trevigan
Trenewydd
Fm
Fawr
Tremynydd
Dduallt
Fawr
Waun
Treffynnon
Penllechwen
Carn Treliwyd
Beddau
Tretio
Llechenhinen
WALES COAST PATH
Tretio Common
Carn
Treglemais
Carn Llidi
Carnhedryn
Treglemais
Spite
Treglemais
St David's Head
181
ST
PEMBROKESHIRE COAST
Uchaf
Moor
Waun
Penmaen Dewi
DAVID'S
Carnhedryn
Abernant
Fawr
Porthmelgan
Carn
Treleddyd
Llanhowel
Hen
fawr
Skyfog
Tremichol
Porth Lleuog
Rhodiad
Carnhedryn
Llanddinio
Lochr
Whitesands Bay
B4583
River Alun
Hendre
Porth-mawr
Dowrog
Caerfarchell
Paran
Common
Tremaenhir
Penarthur
Mynydd du
Fm
CATHEDRAL
NATIONAL PARK
Treswny
Middle Mill
Point St John
Moor
Rickeston
BISHOP'S
Whitchurch
Hall
Rhosson
PALACE
St Justinian
St David's
Vachelich
Trwyn-Siôn-Owen
(Tyddewi)
Nine Wells
Brawdy
Trwyn-drain-du
Carnysgubor
ST NON'S
Llandruidion
Prendergast
Airfield
CHAPEL
Mount
(disused)
Aber Mawr
Summer only
Morfa Common
Solva
Fm
RAMSEY ISLAND
Porthstinian
(Solfach)
Upper
RSPB
RAMSEY
Treginnis
Solva
Lower
Bus Pk
Ramsey
ISLAND
Solva
Island
Rhod Isaf
Aberfelin
PEMBROKESHIRE
Pointz
A487
Ynys Dewi
136
Porth Clais
Caer Bwdy Bay
Castle
Penrhyn Twll
Porthlysky
Green
Aber-west
COAST PATH LLWYBR ARFORD
PENFRO
Scar
Trwynmynachdy
Black Scar
Dinas Fawr
Pwll March
Carreg Fran
Dinas Fach
Newgale
Bay Dillyn
Meini Duon
Newgale Sand

ST BRIDES BAY

72

BAIE SAIN FFRAID

Rickets H

Maidenha

Mado

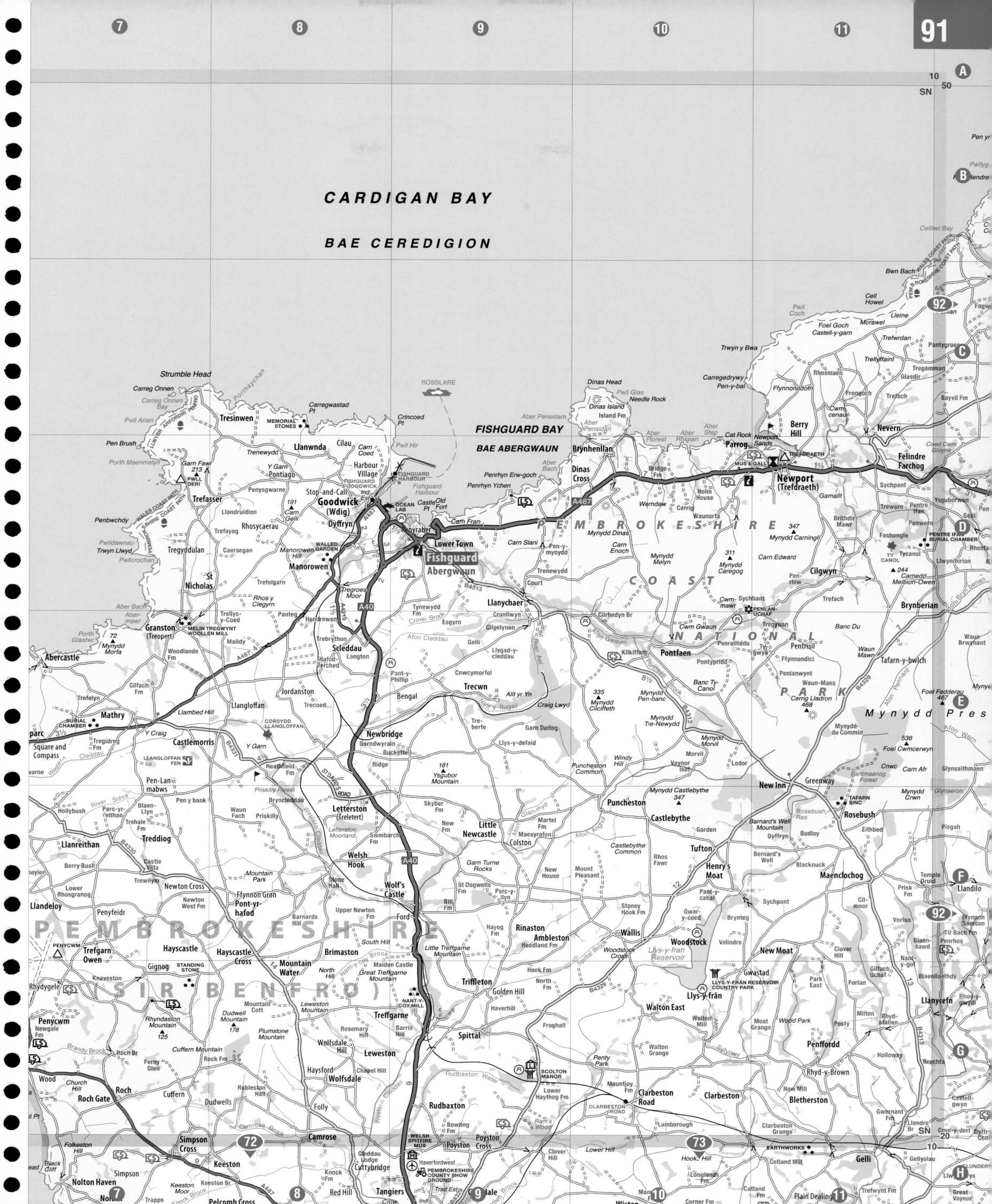

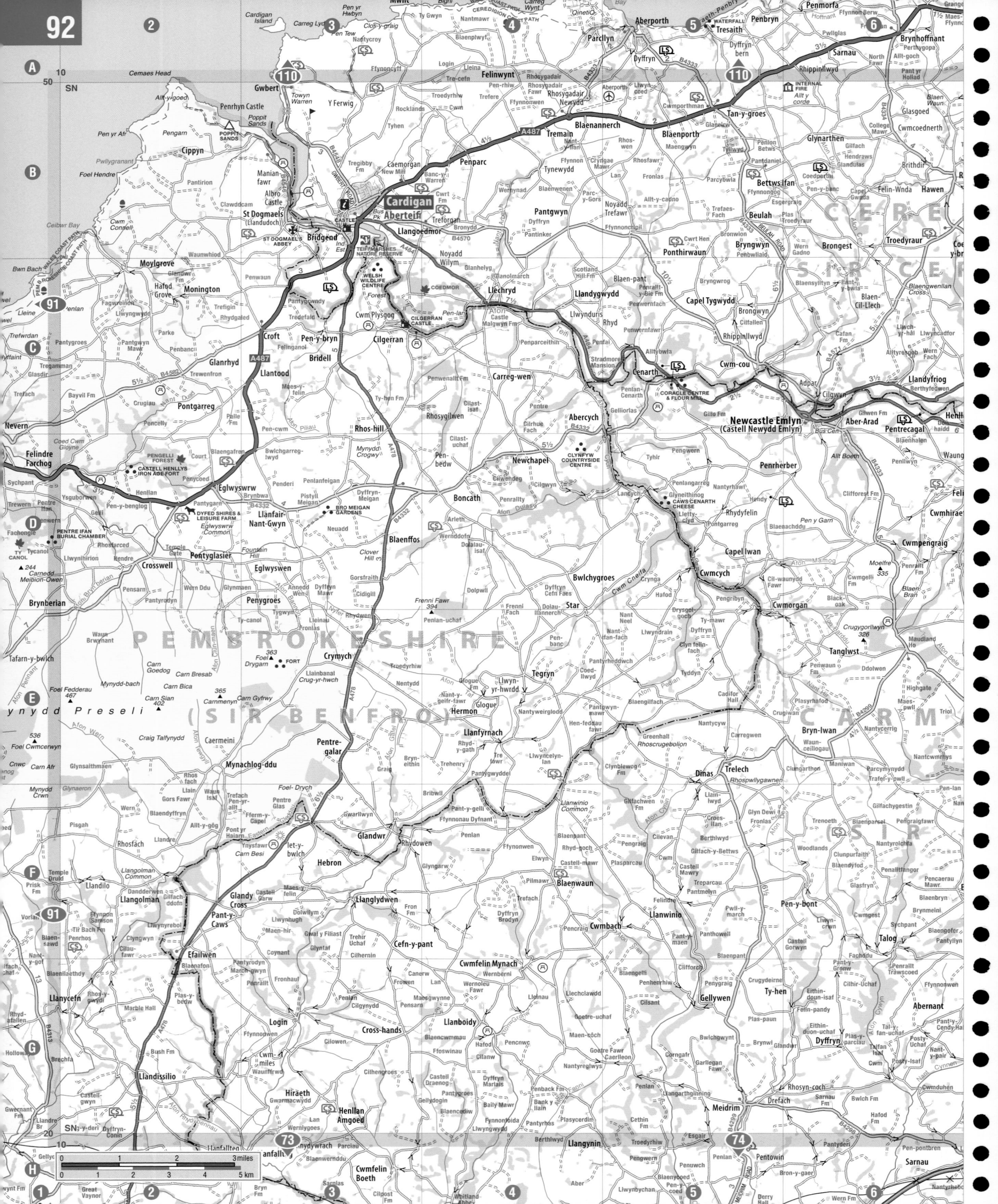

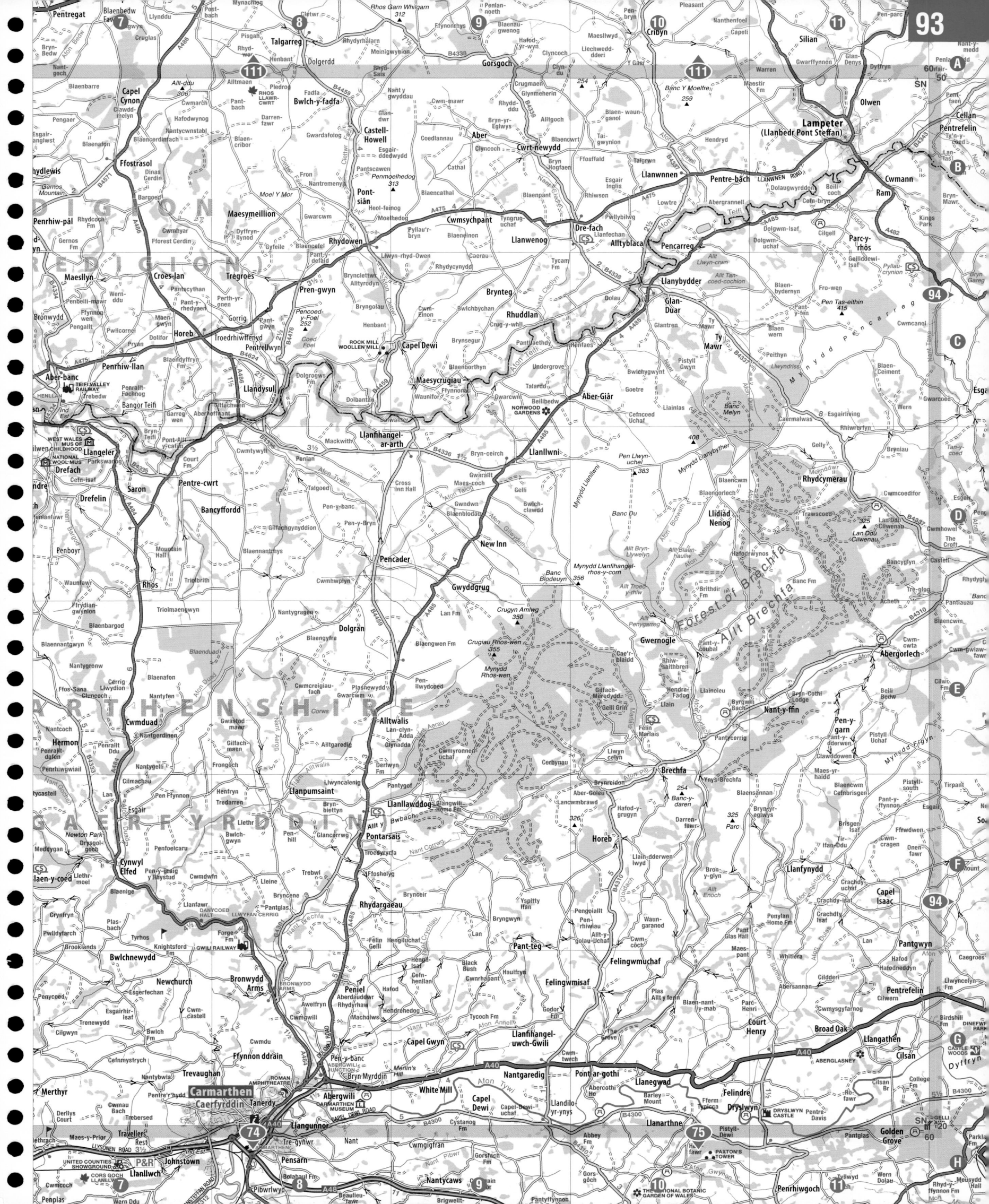

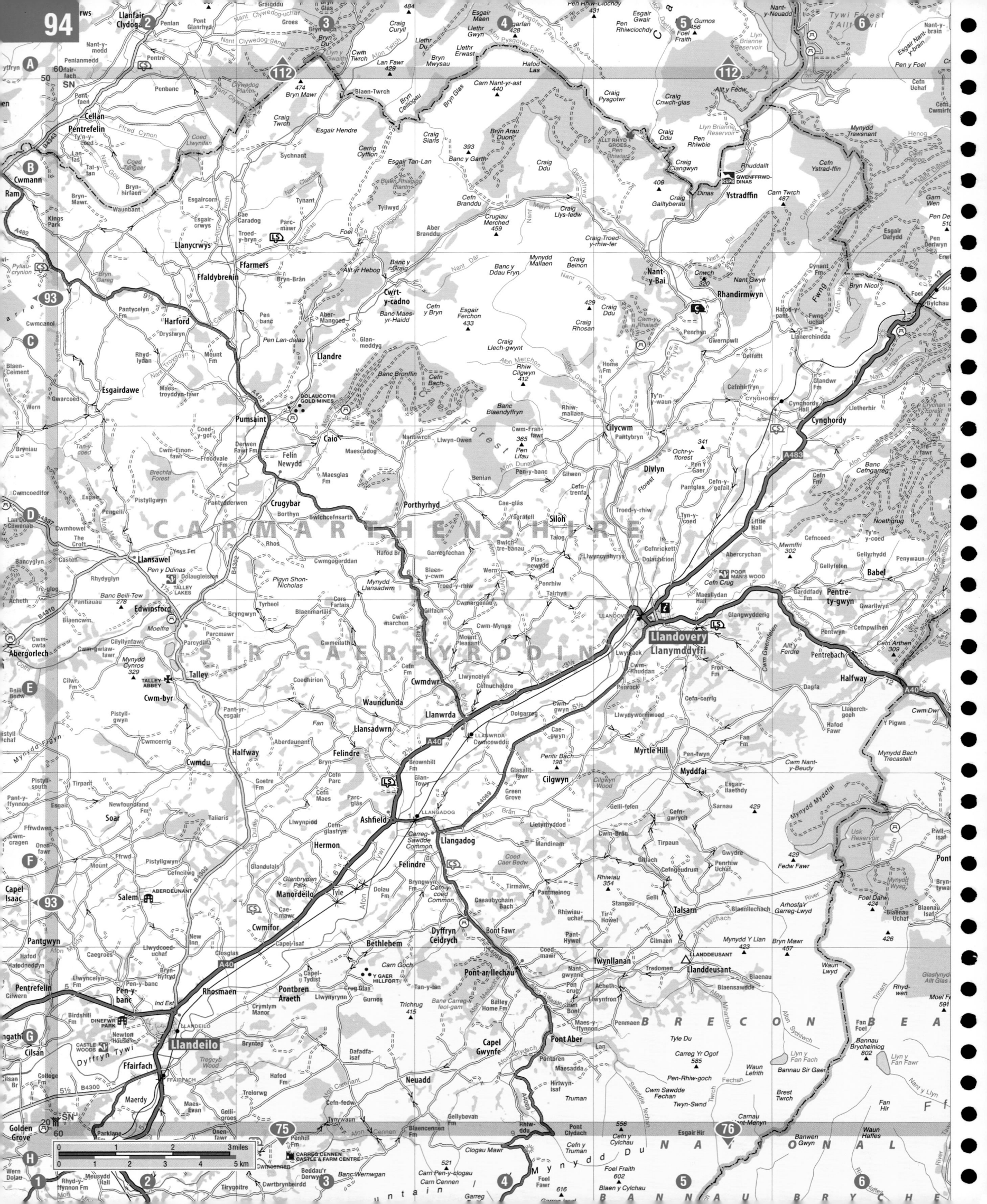

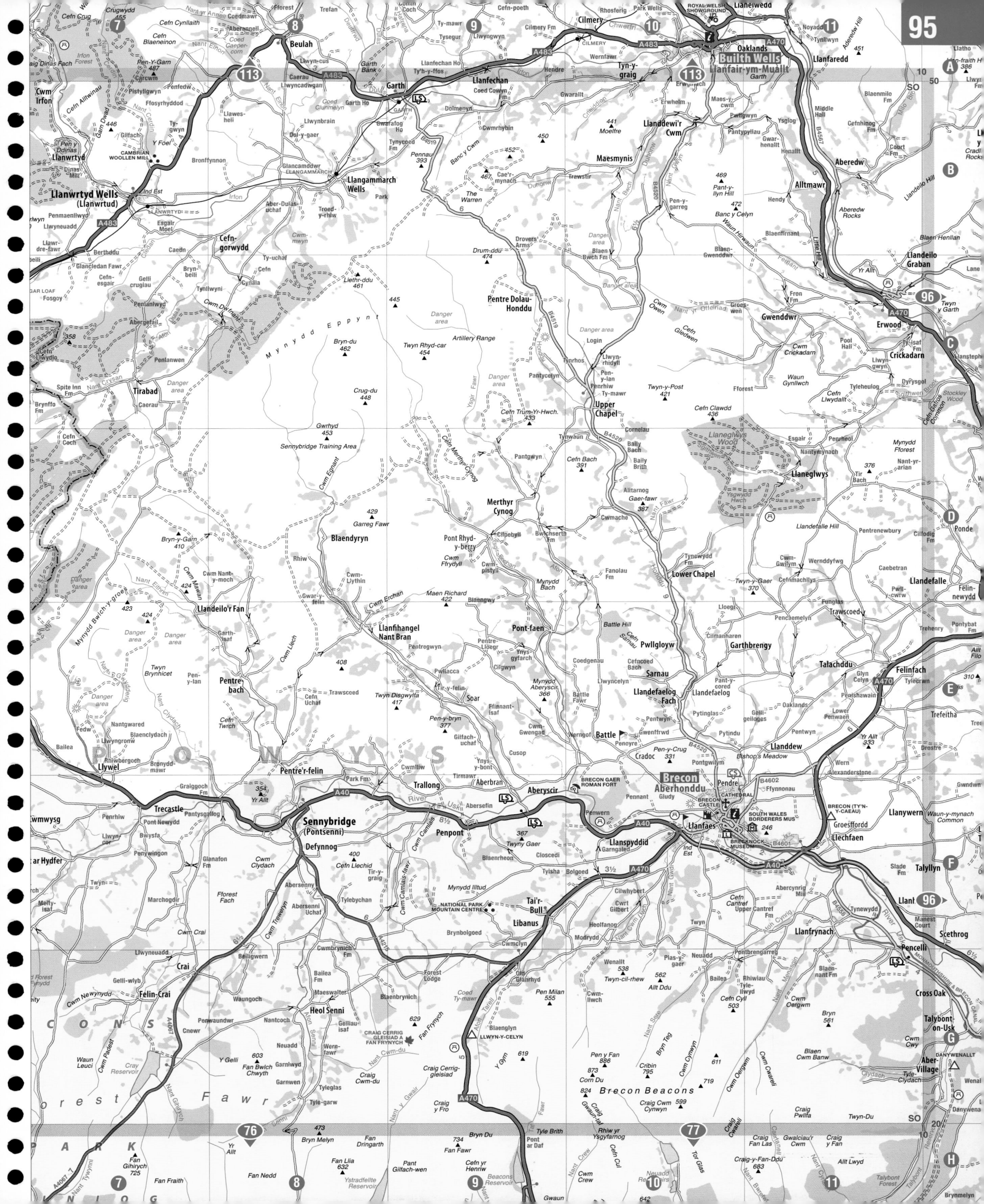

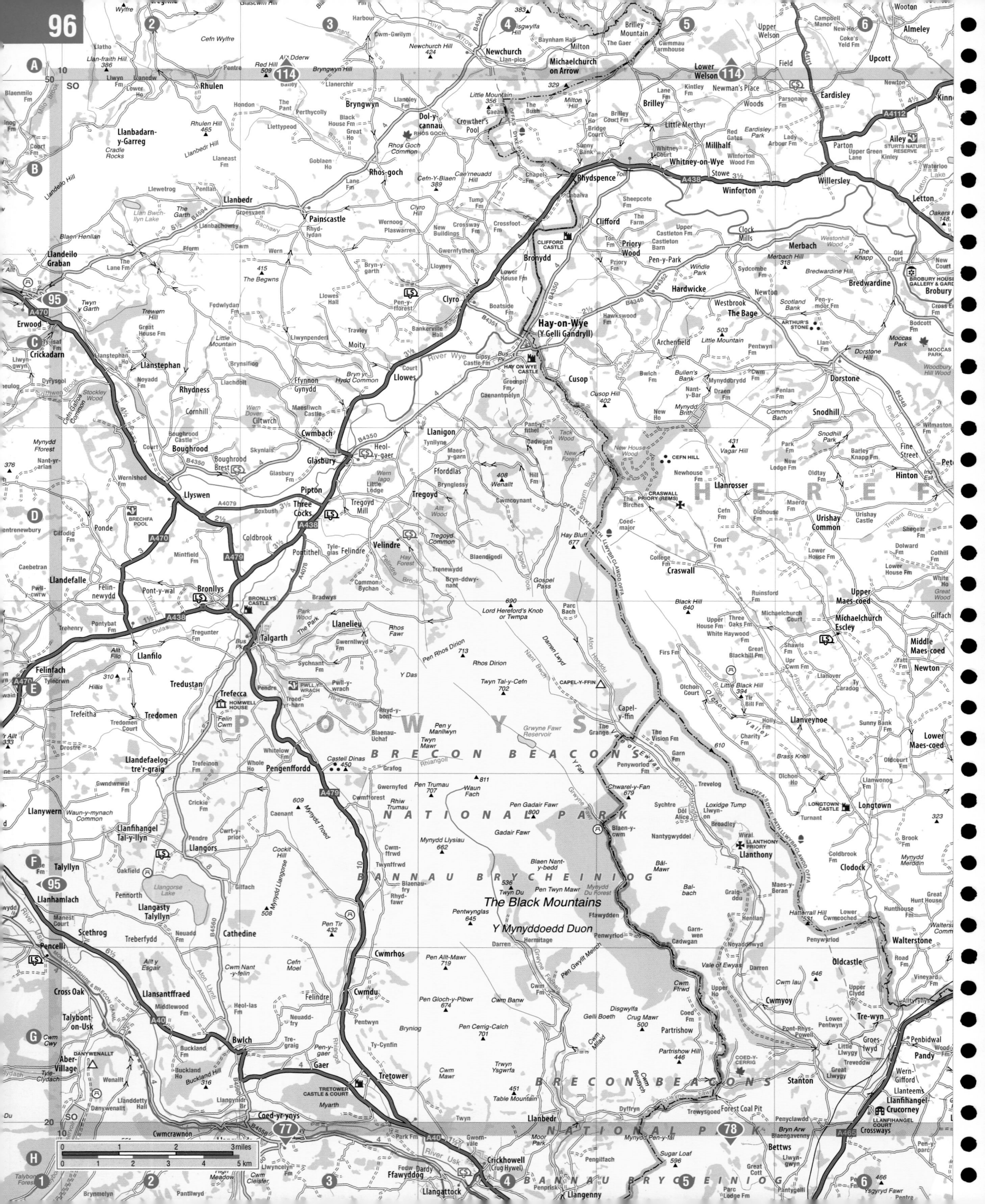

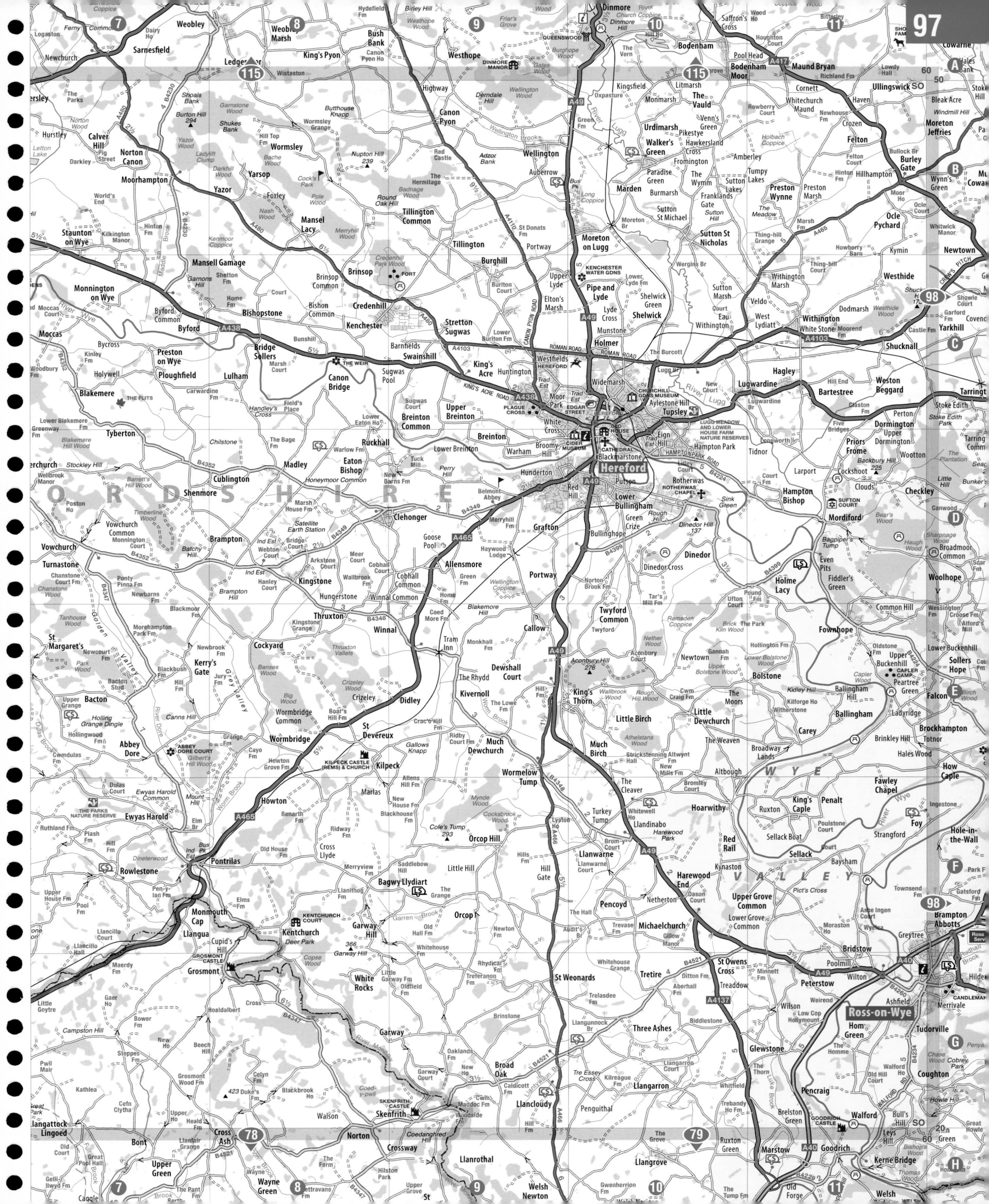

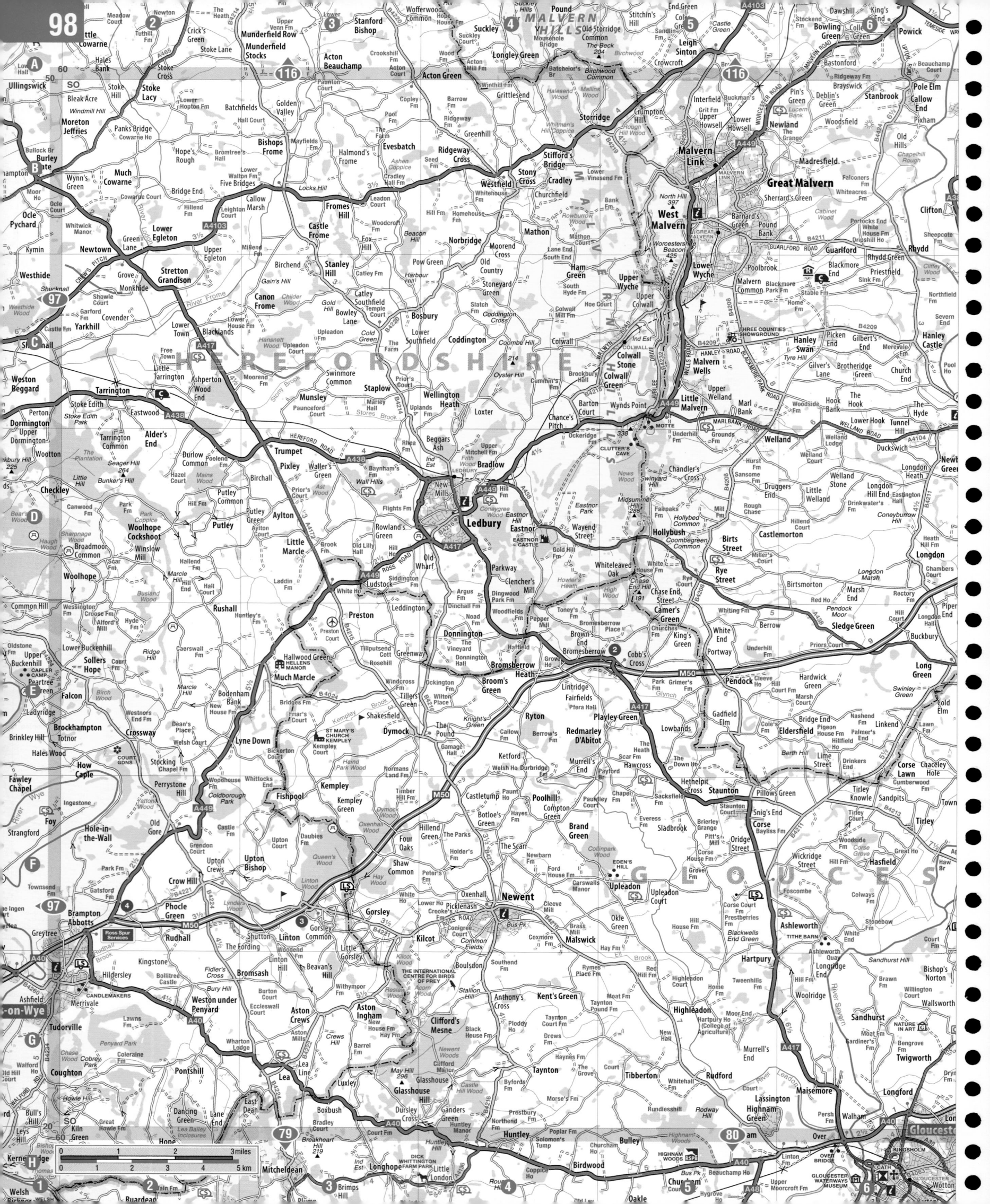

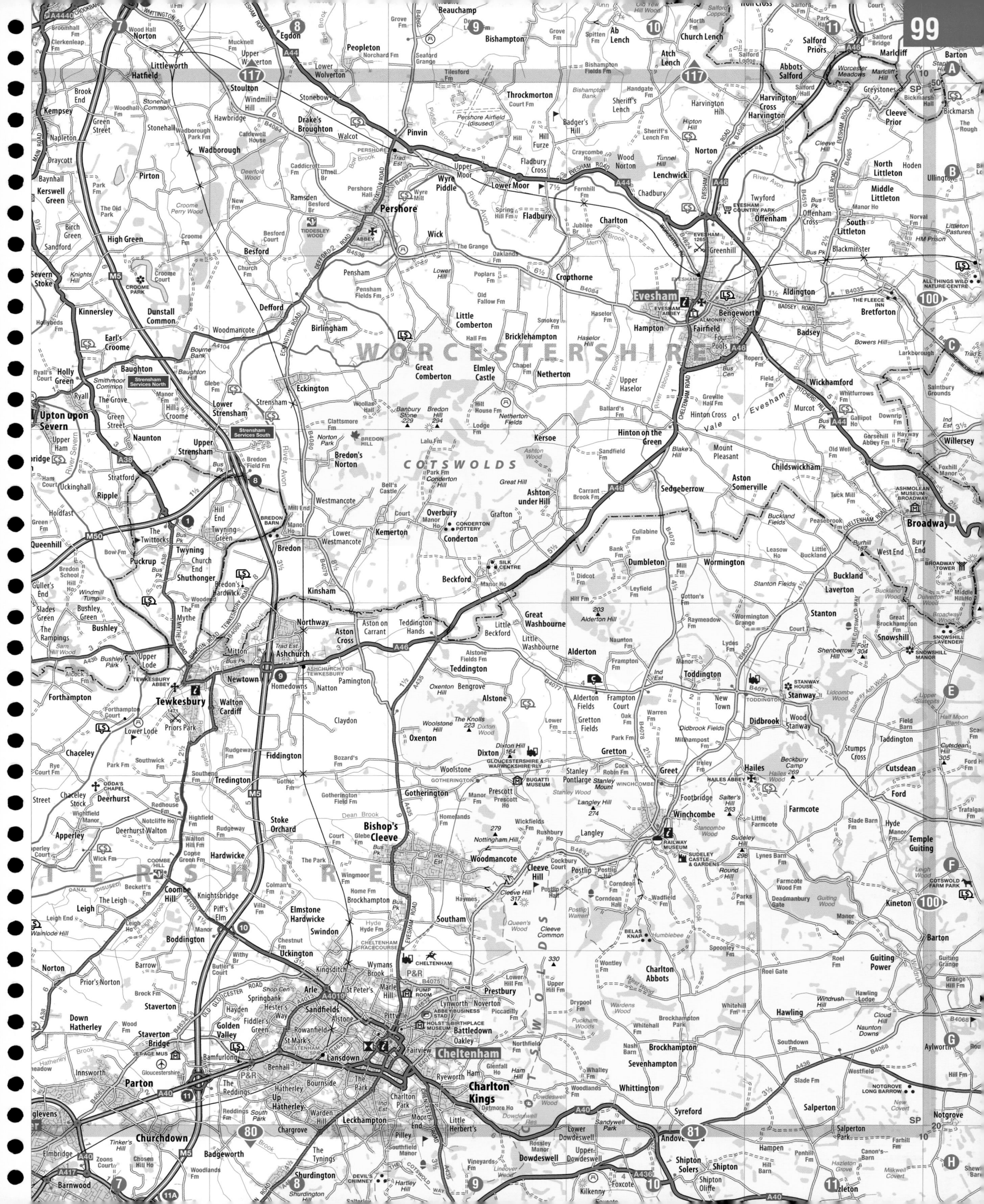

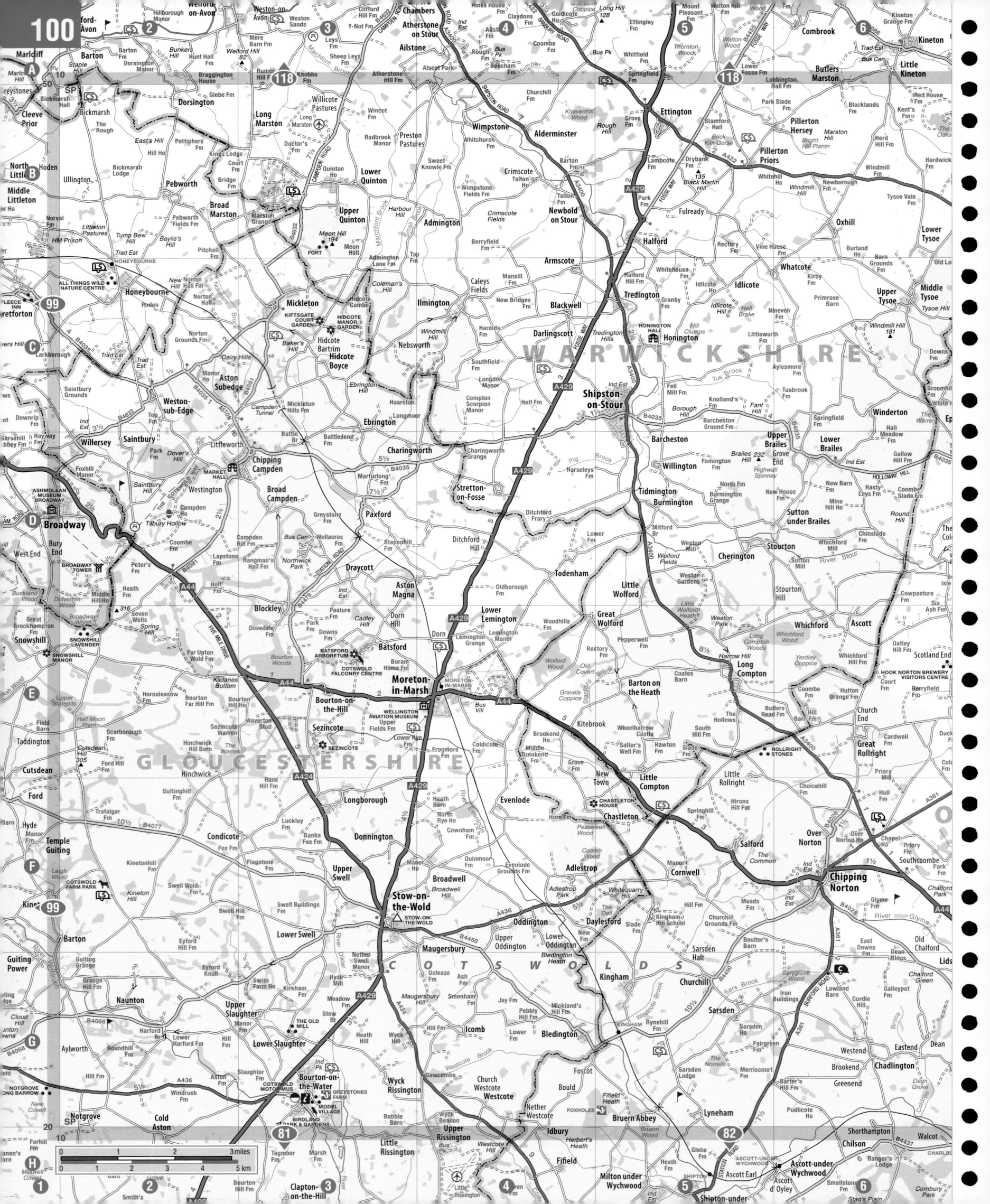

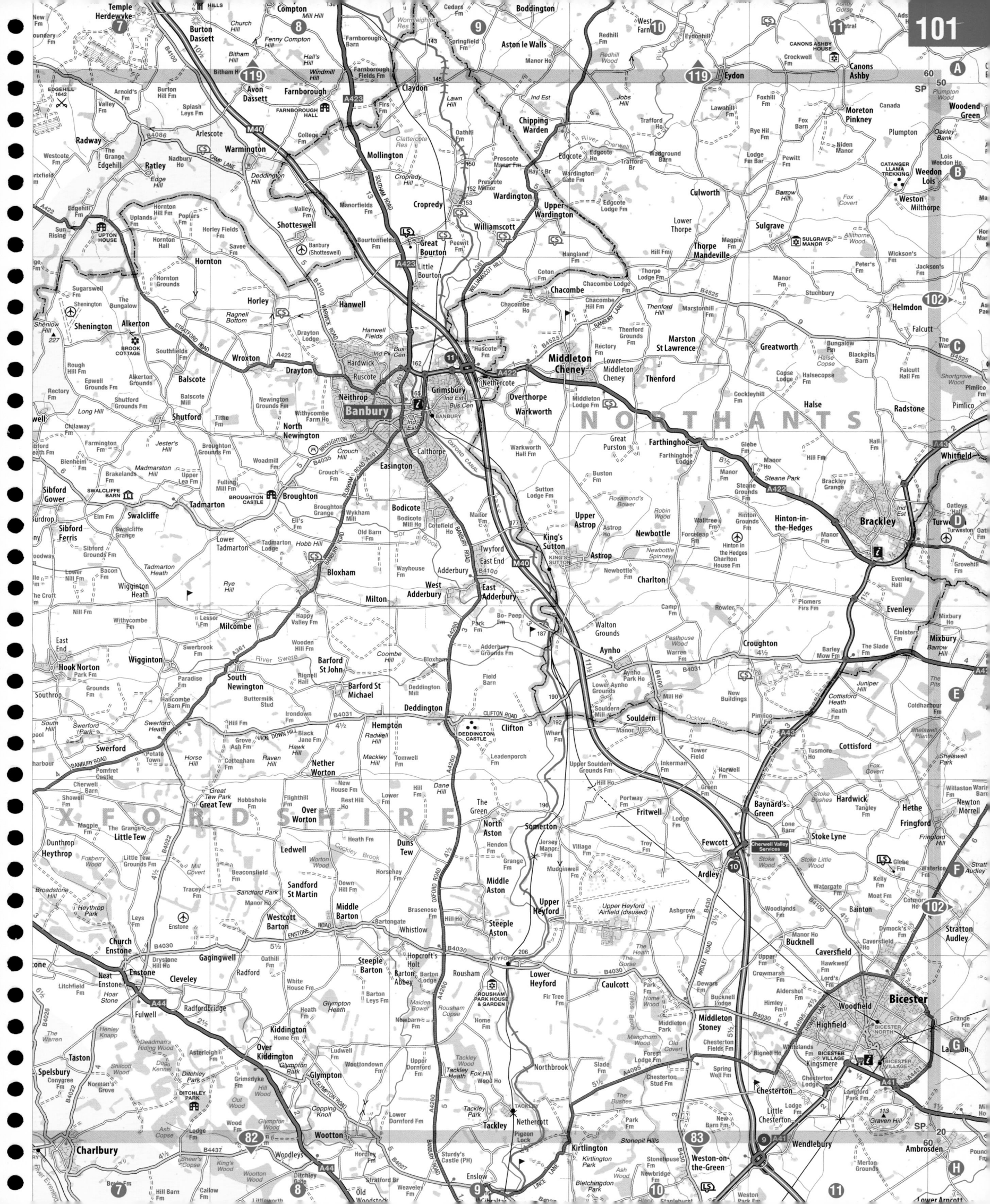

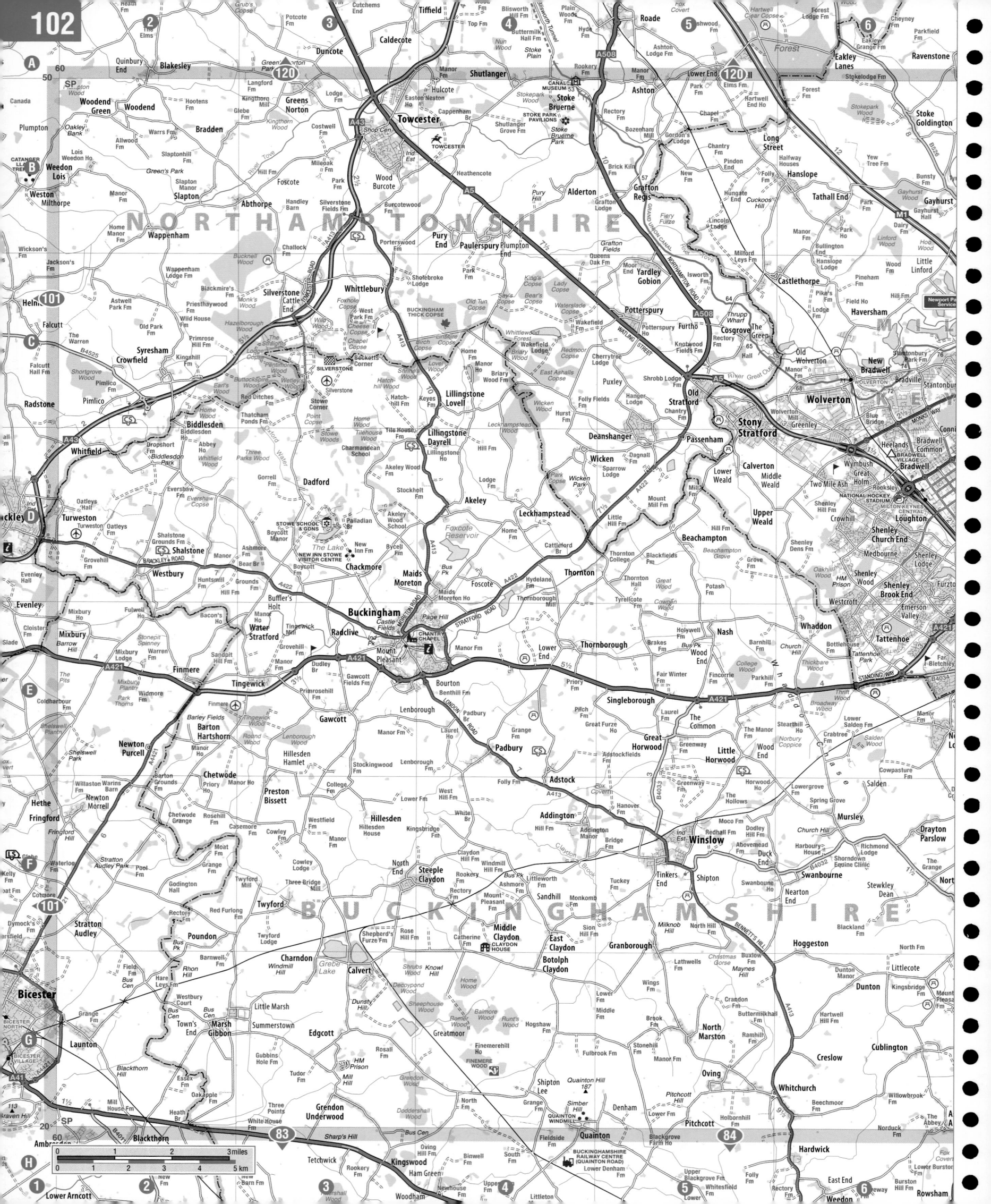

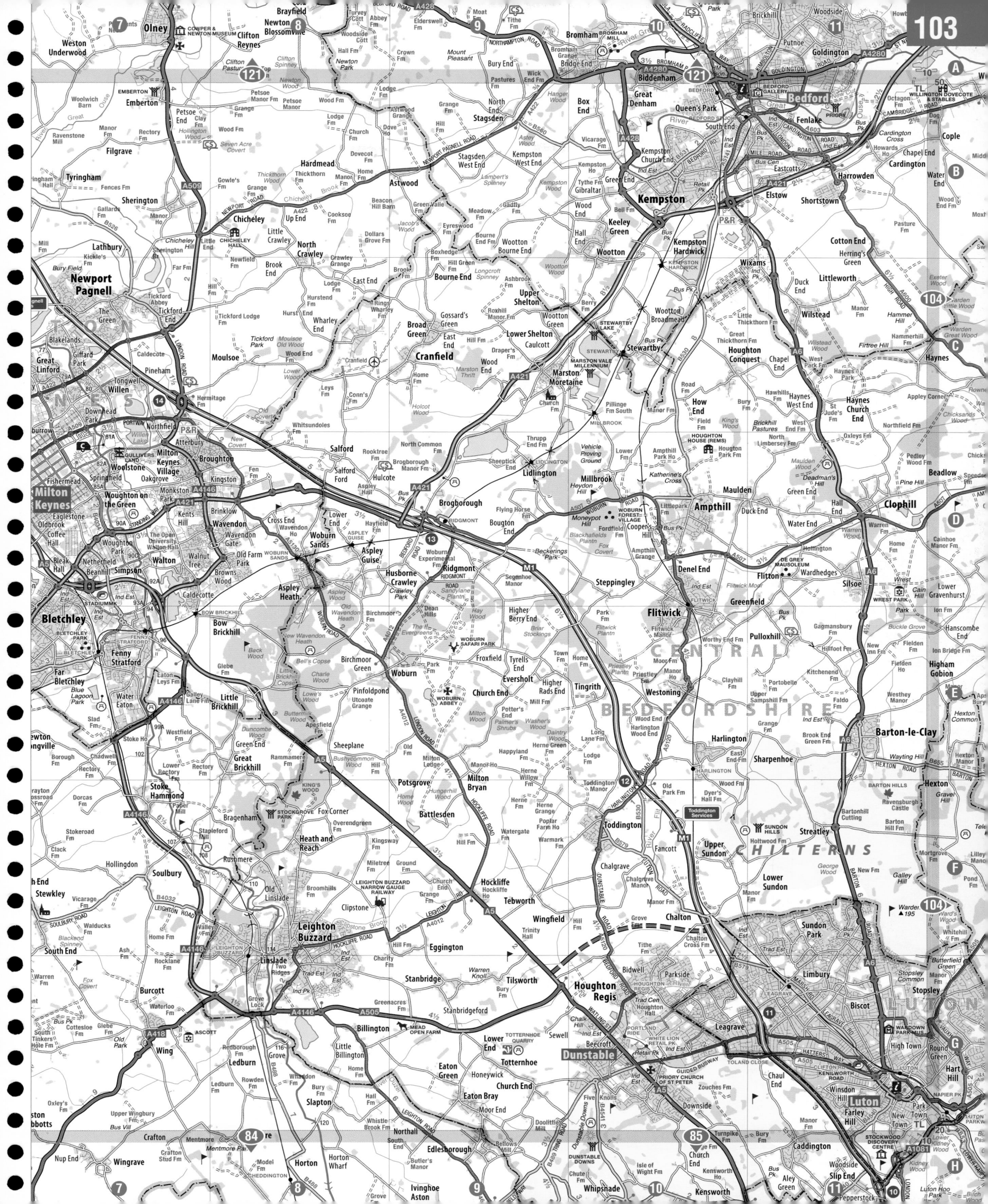

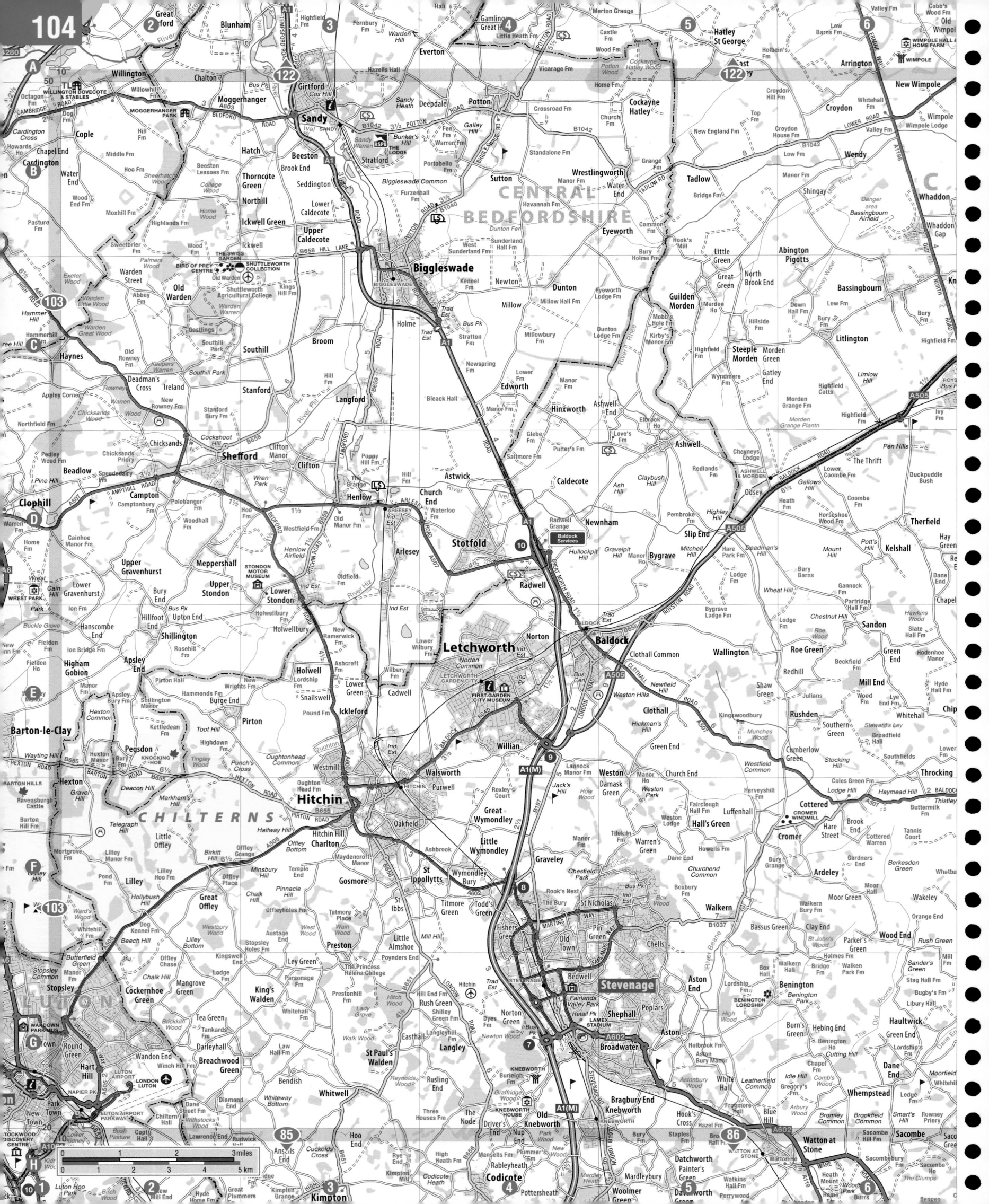

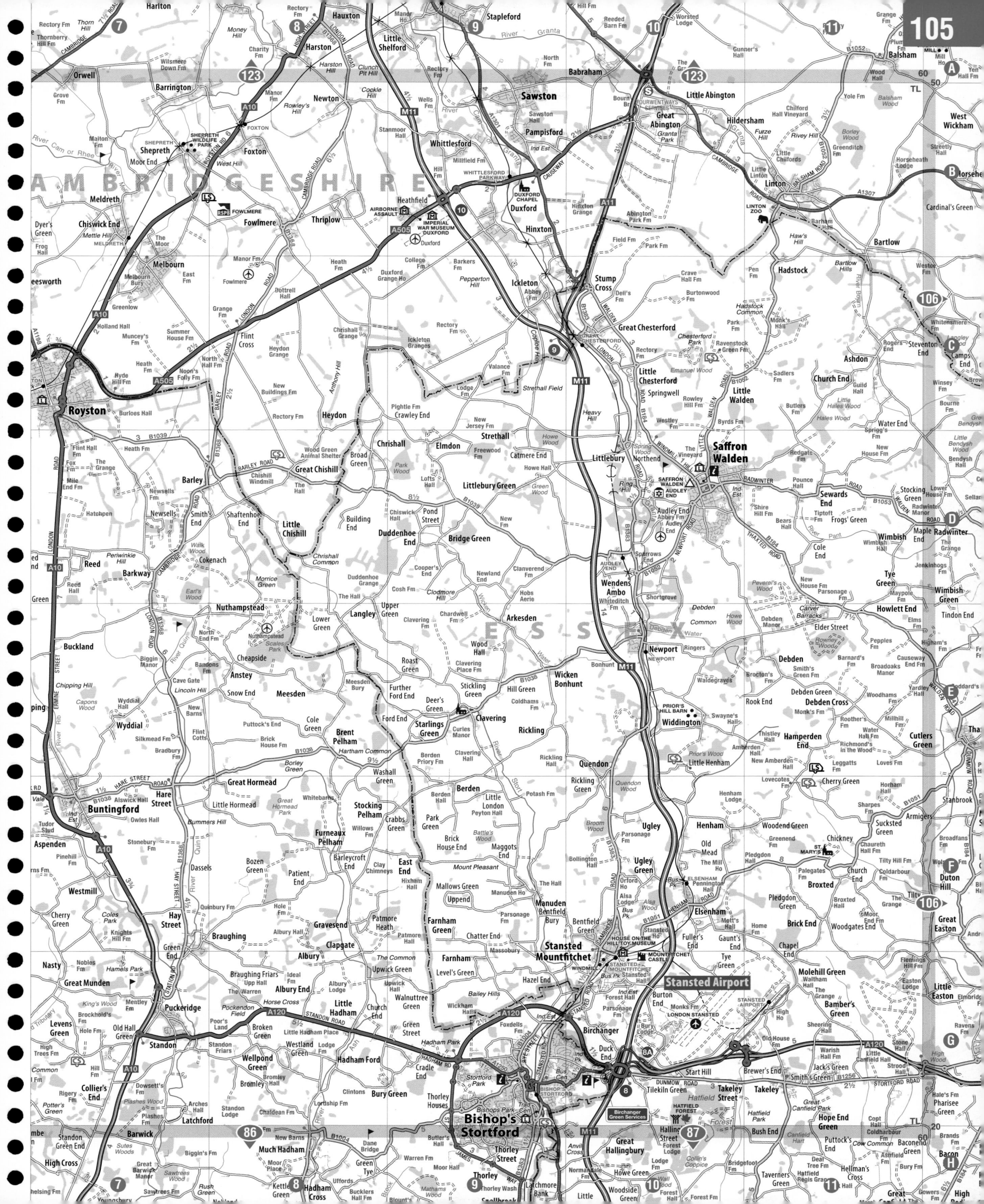

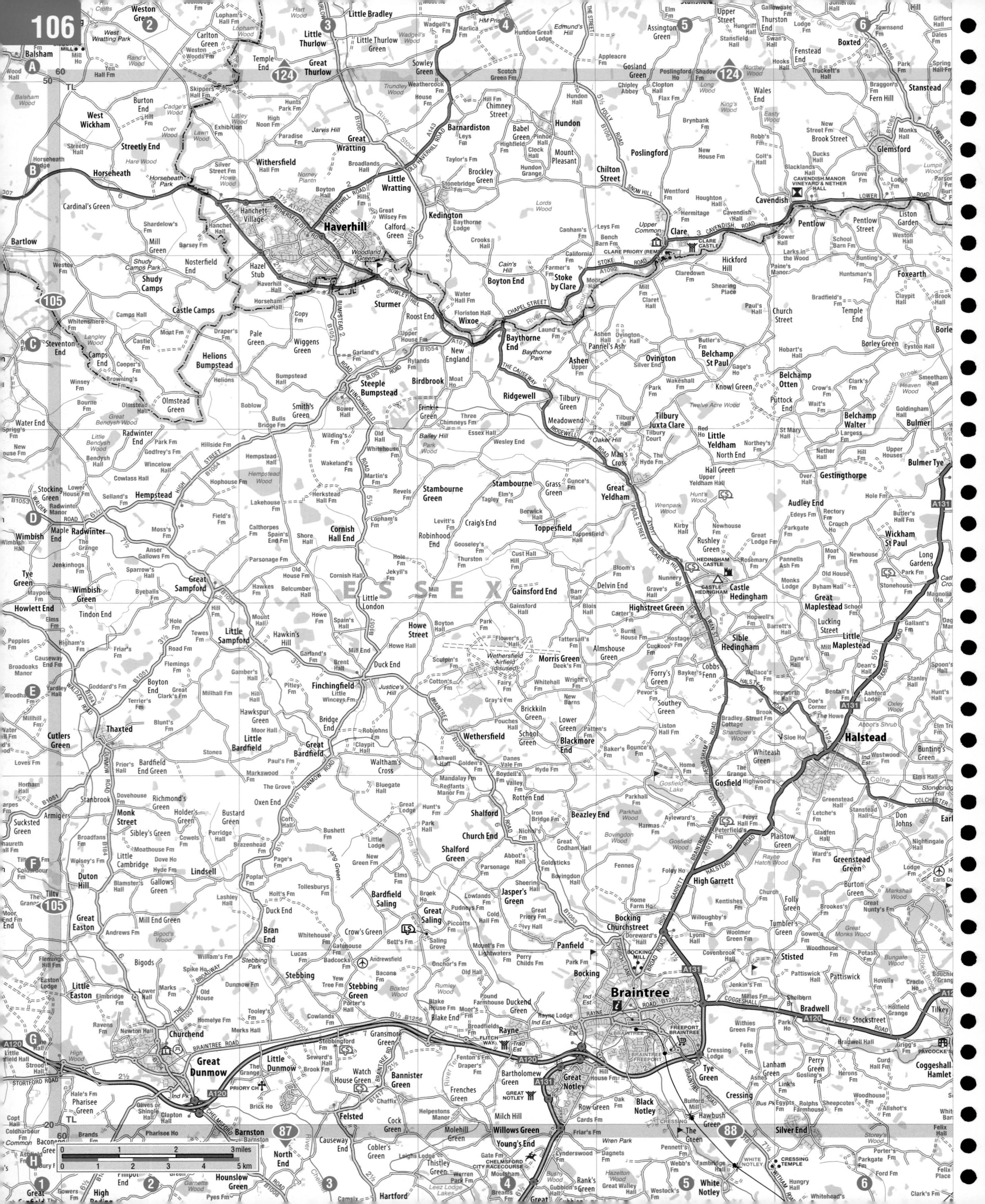

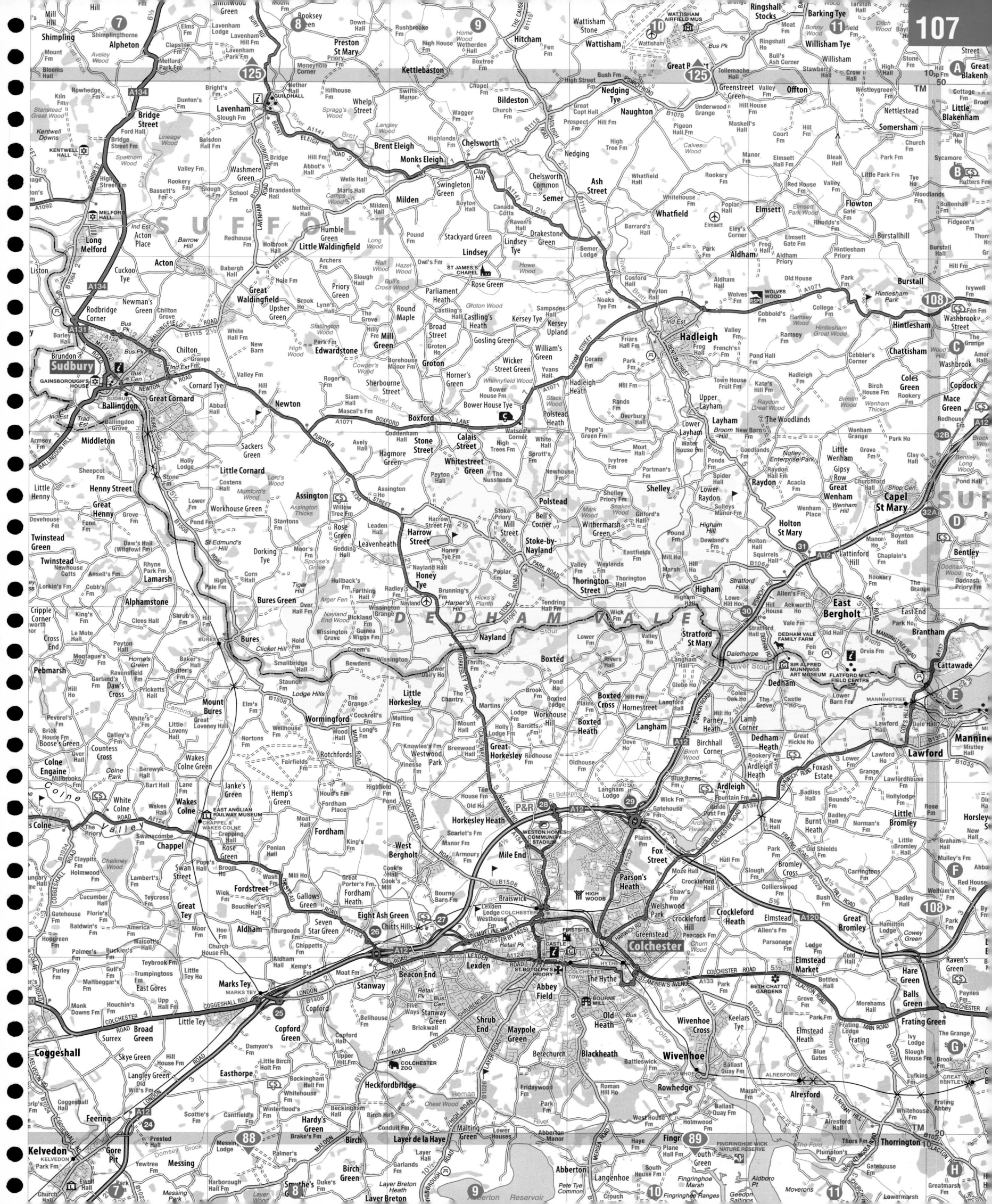

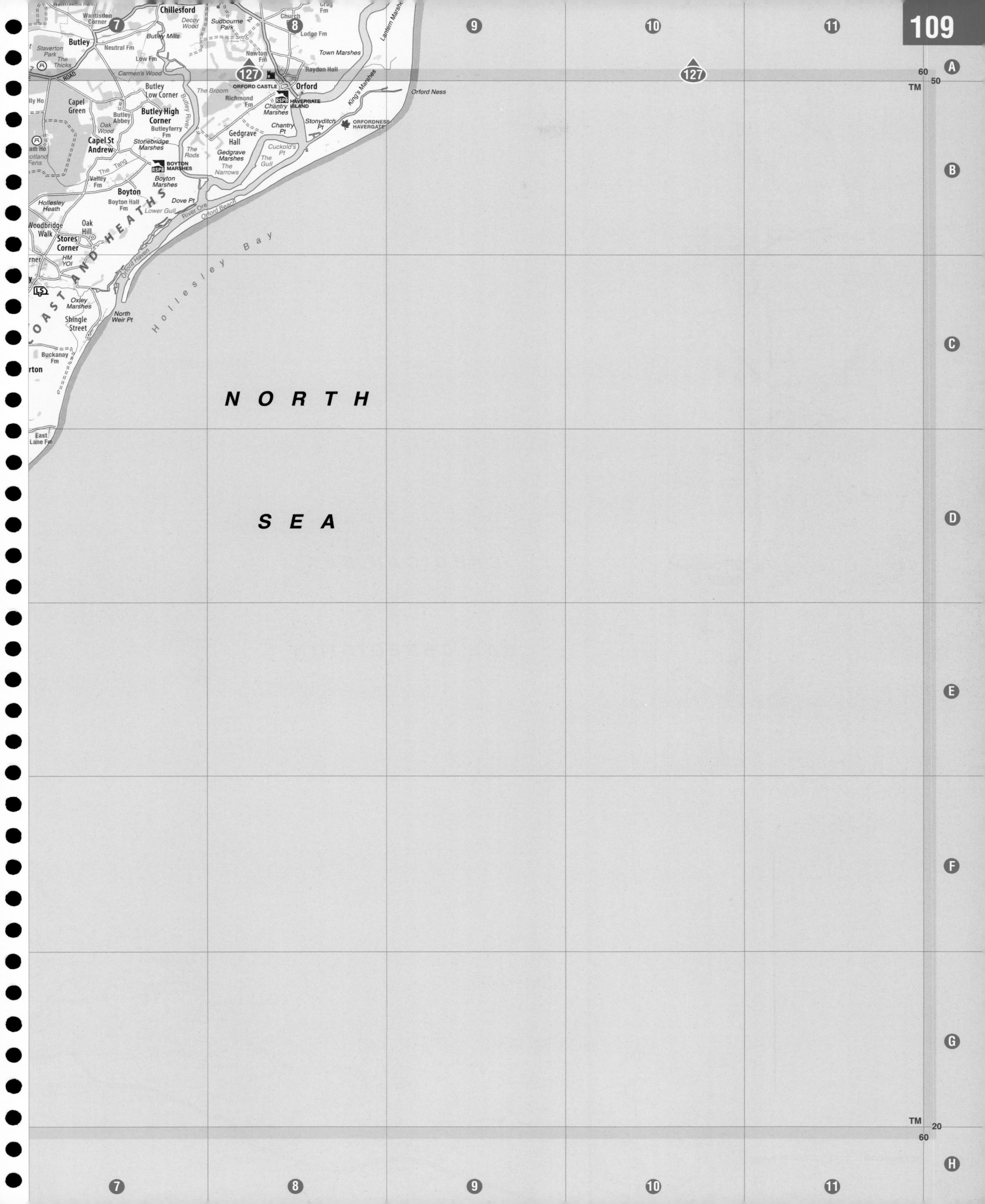

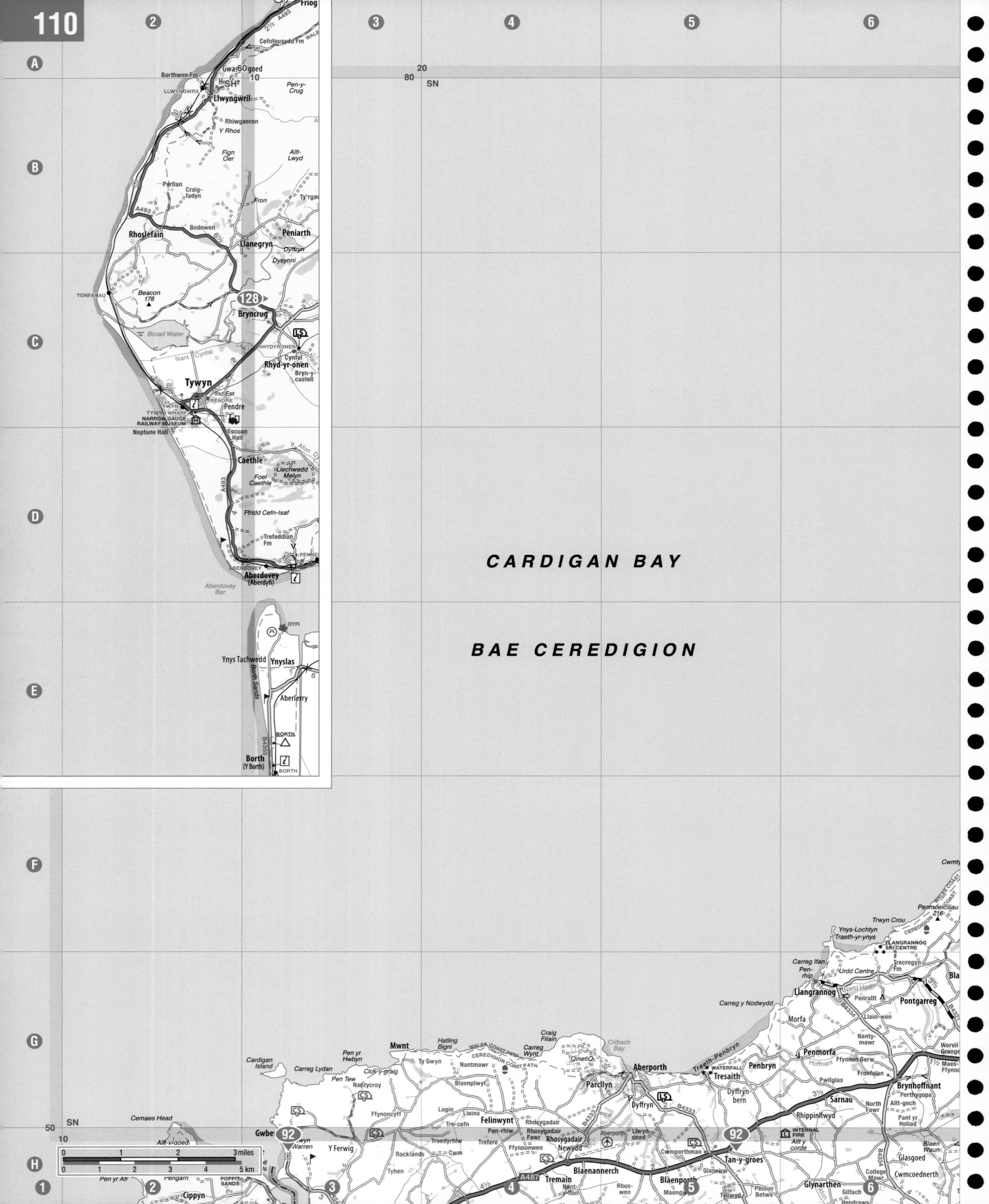

CARDIGAN BAY

BAE CEREDIGION

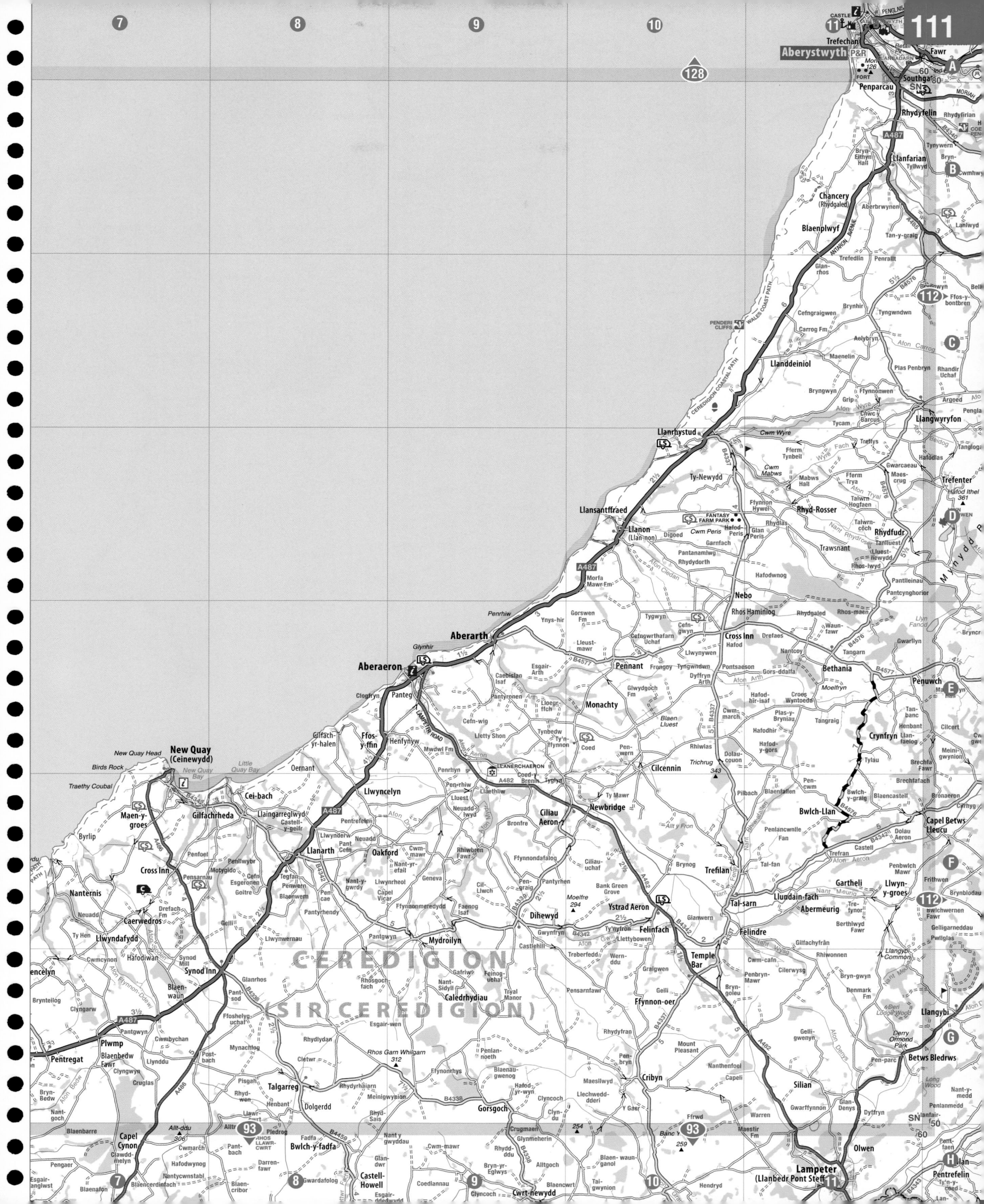

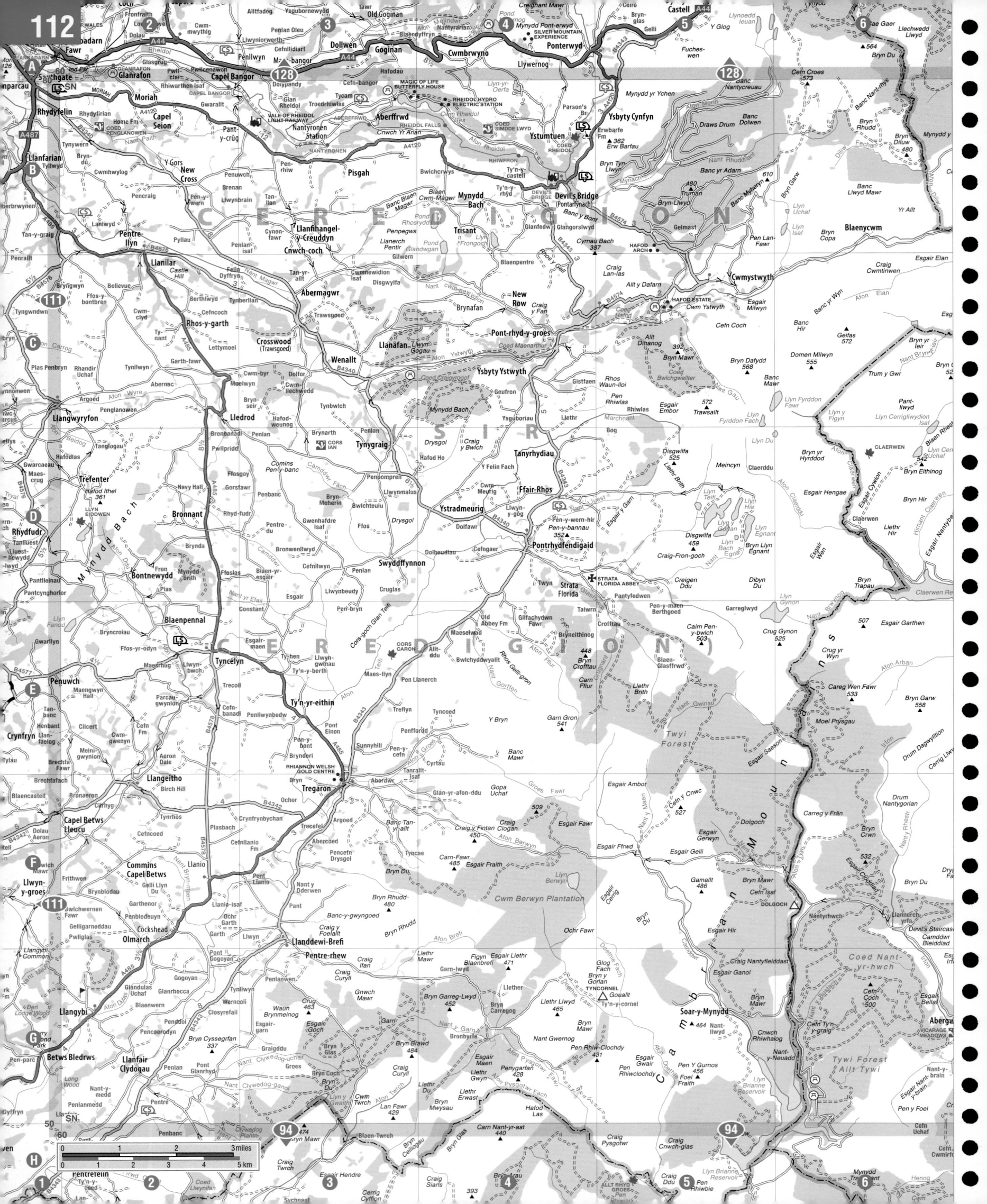

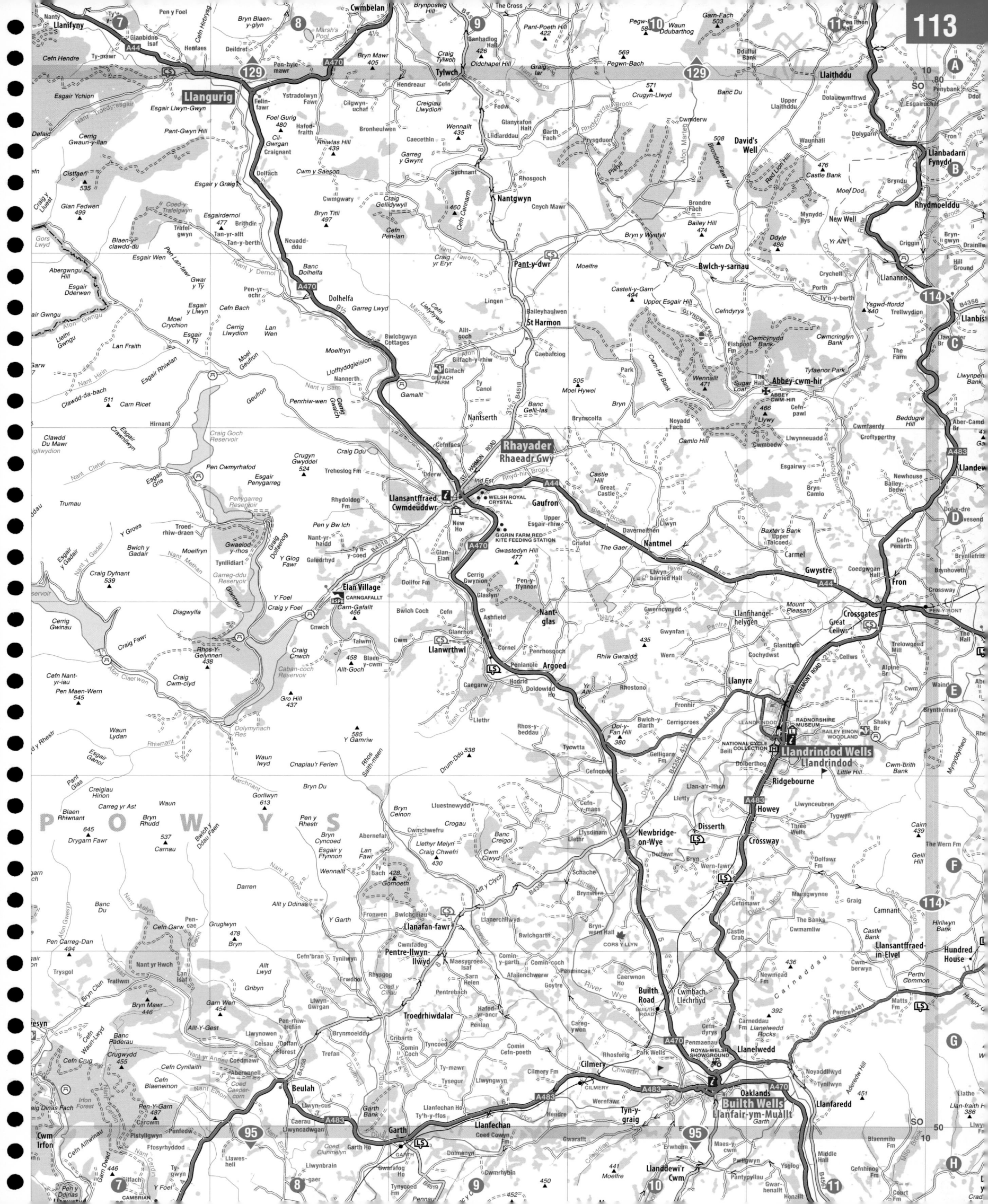

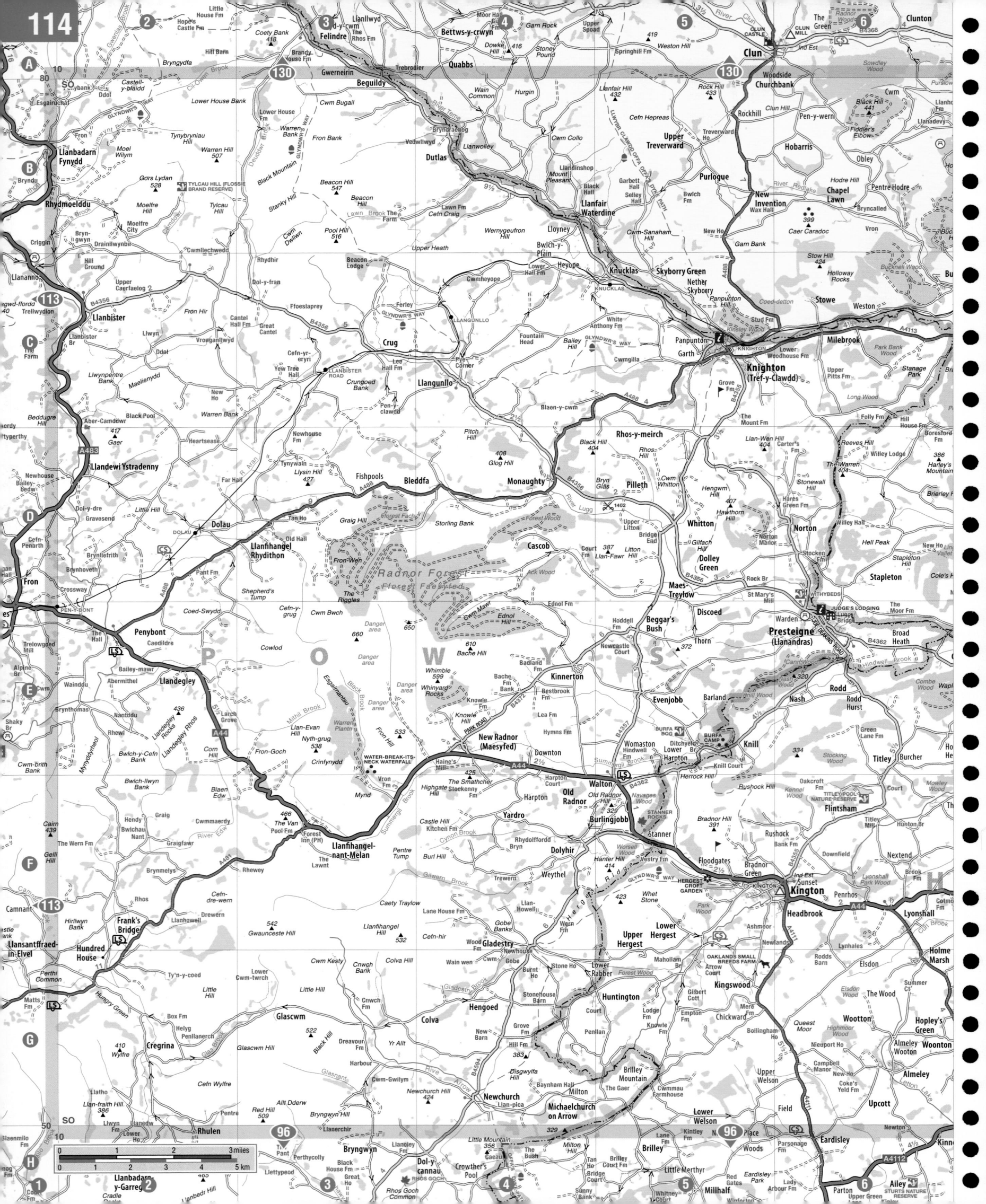

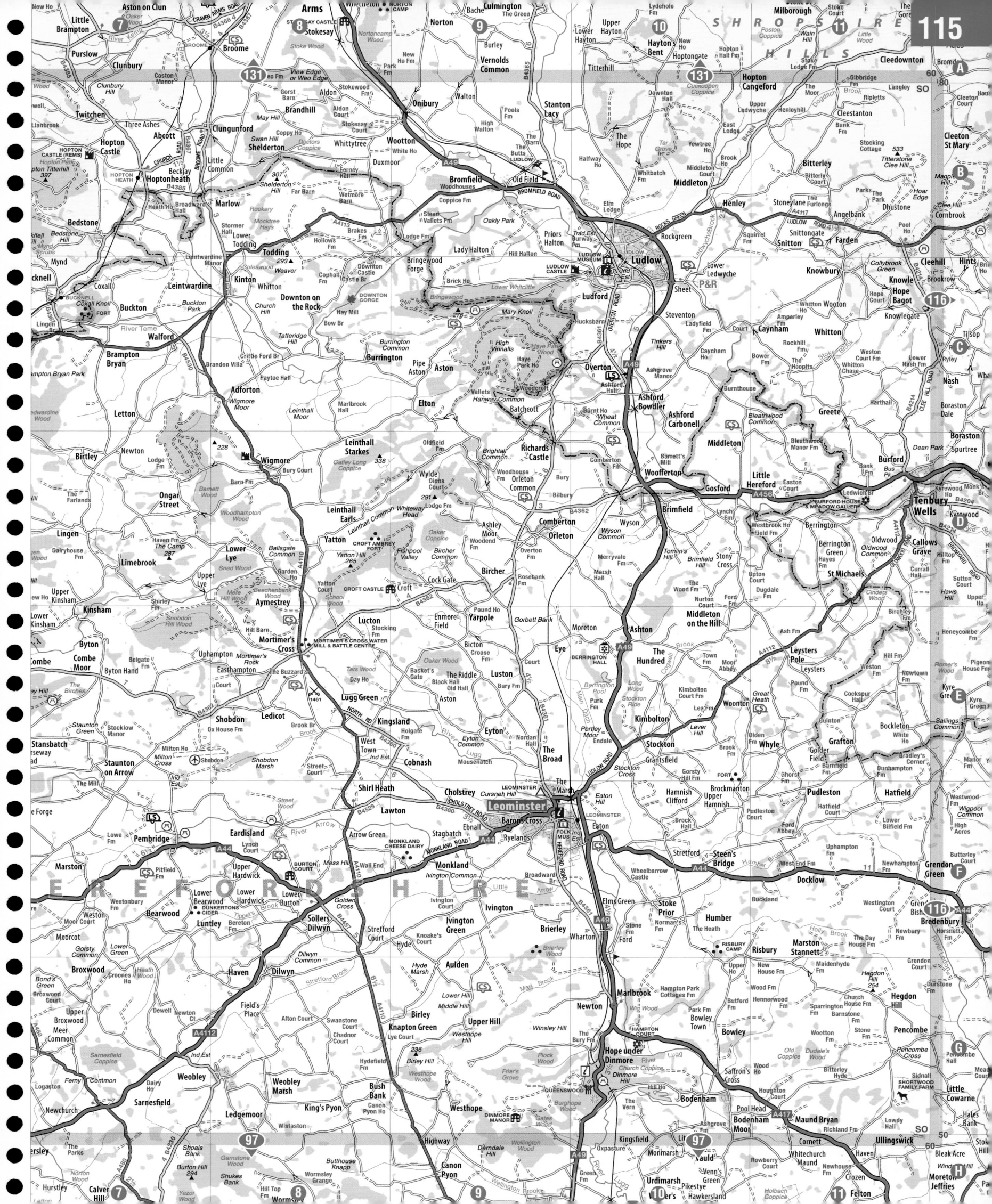

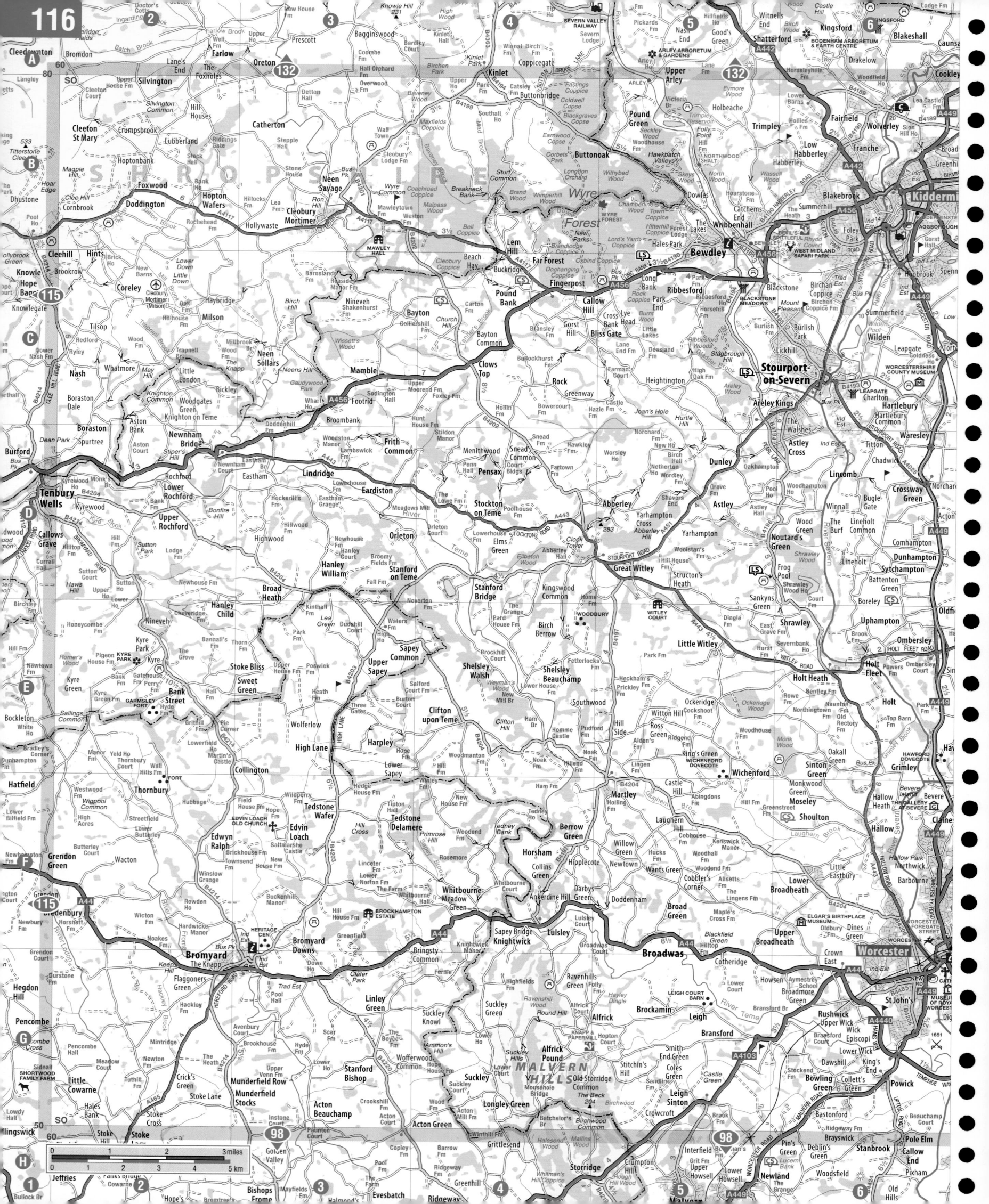

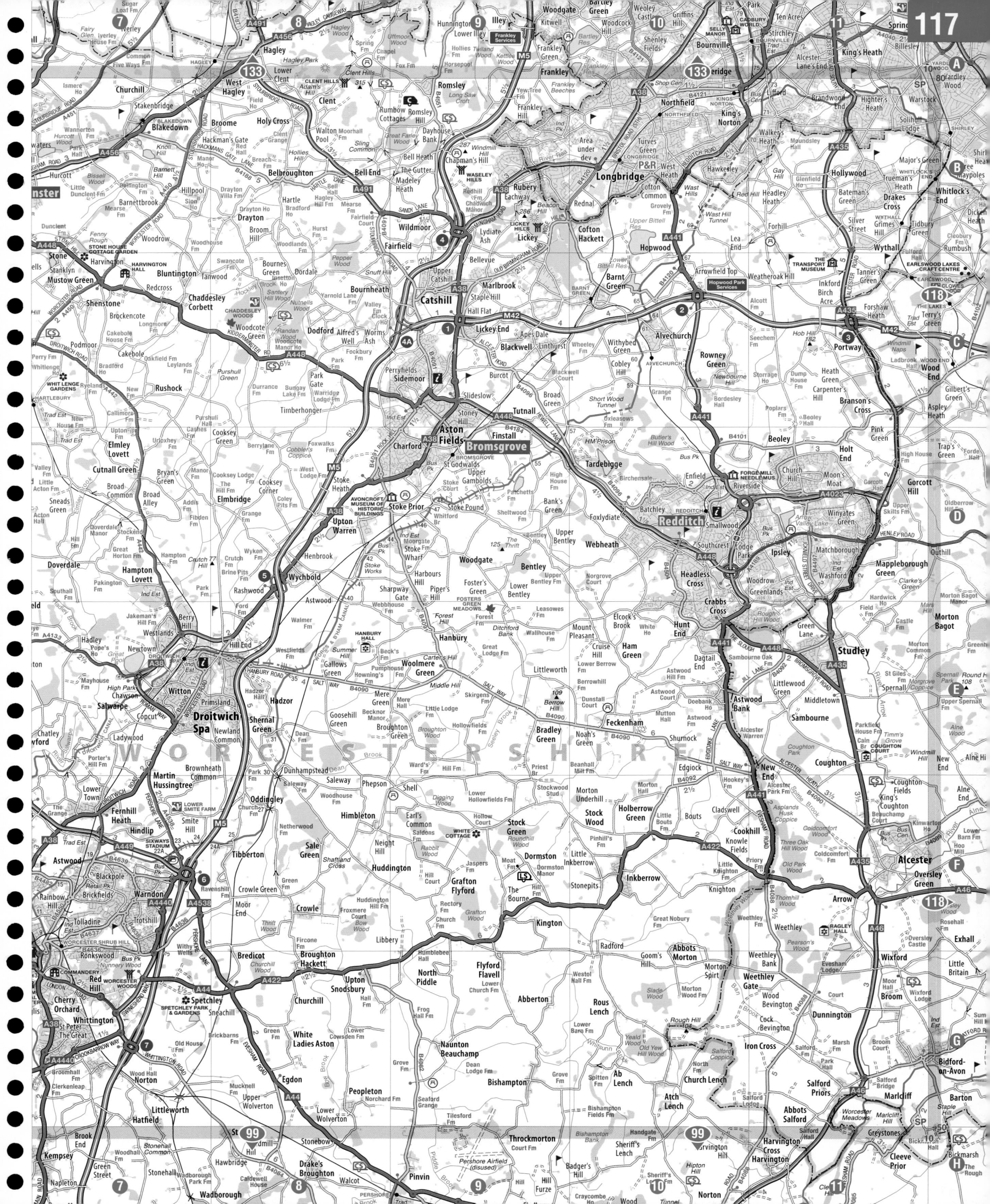

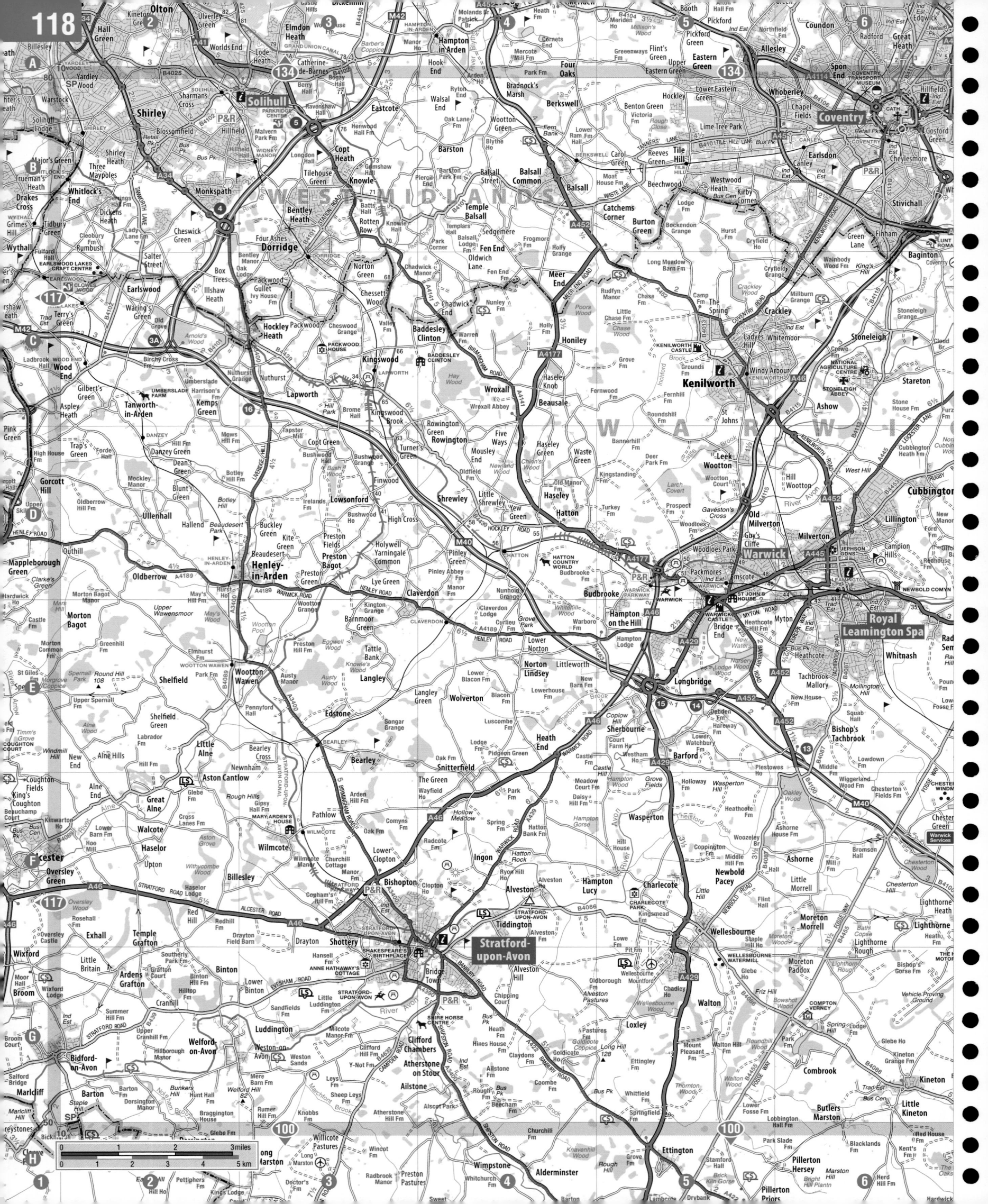

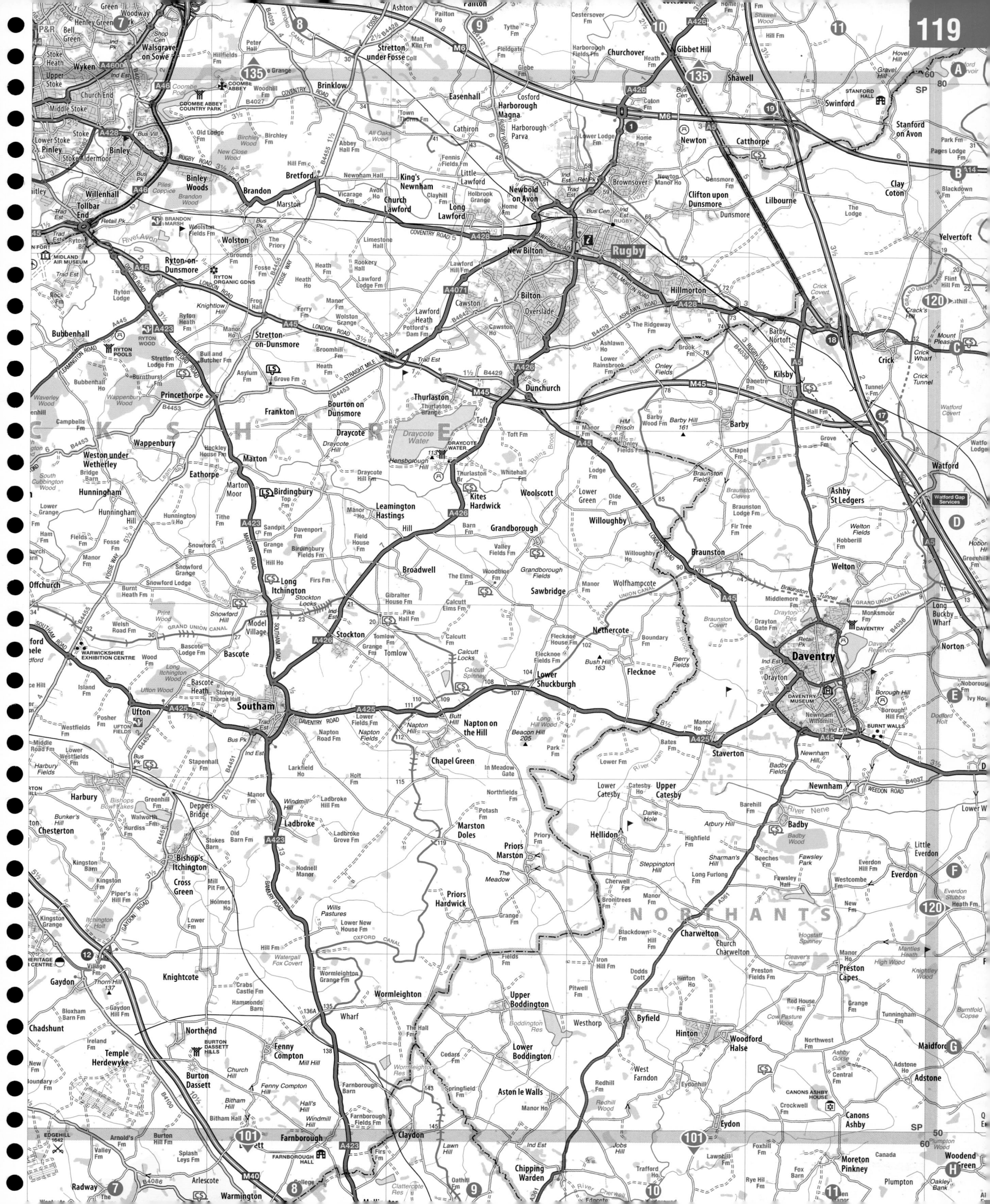

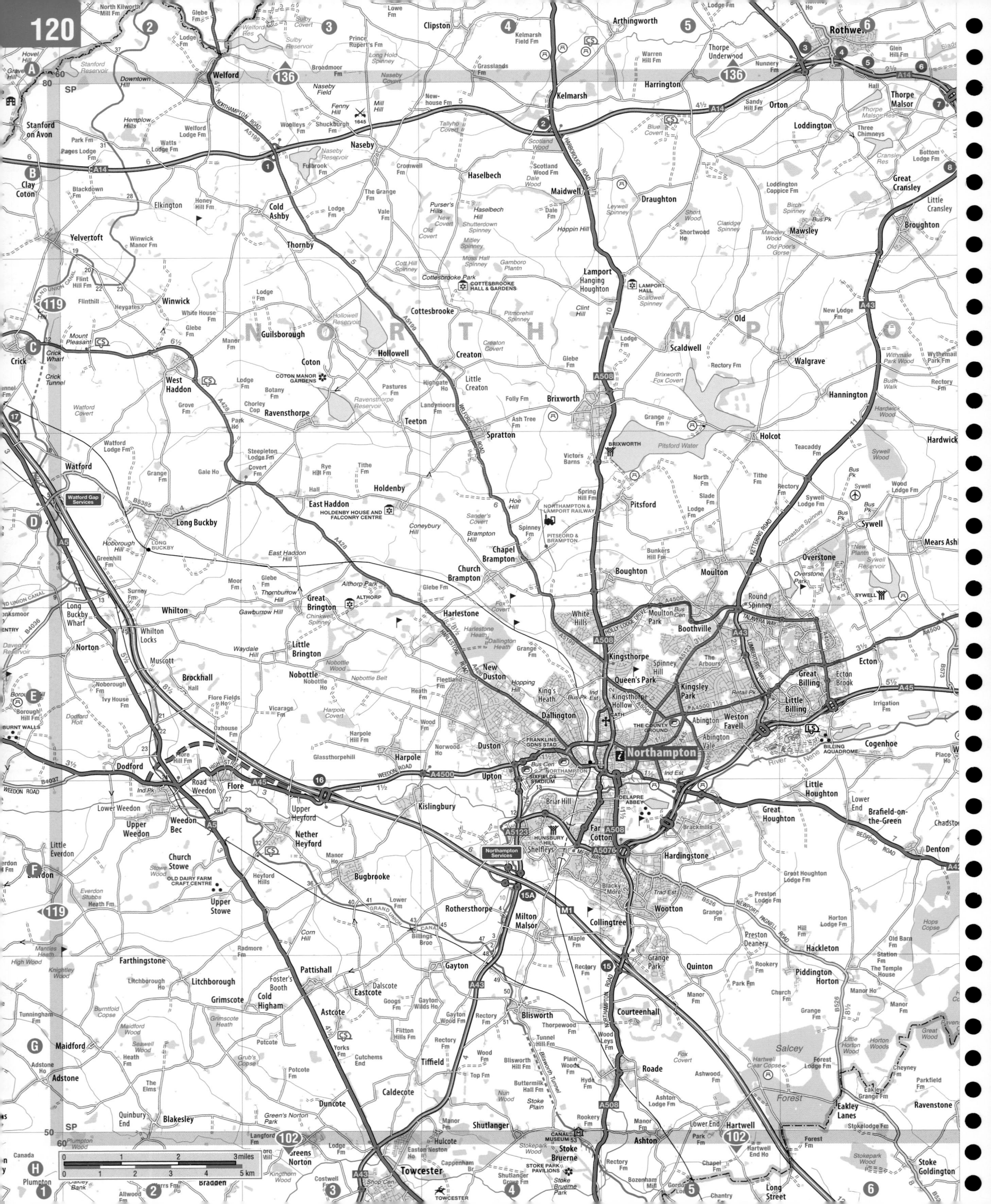

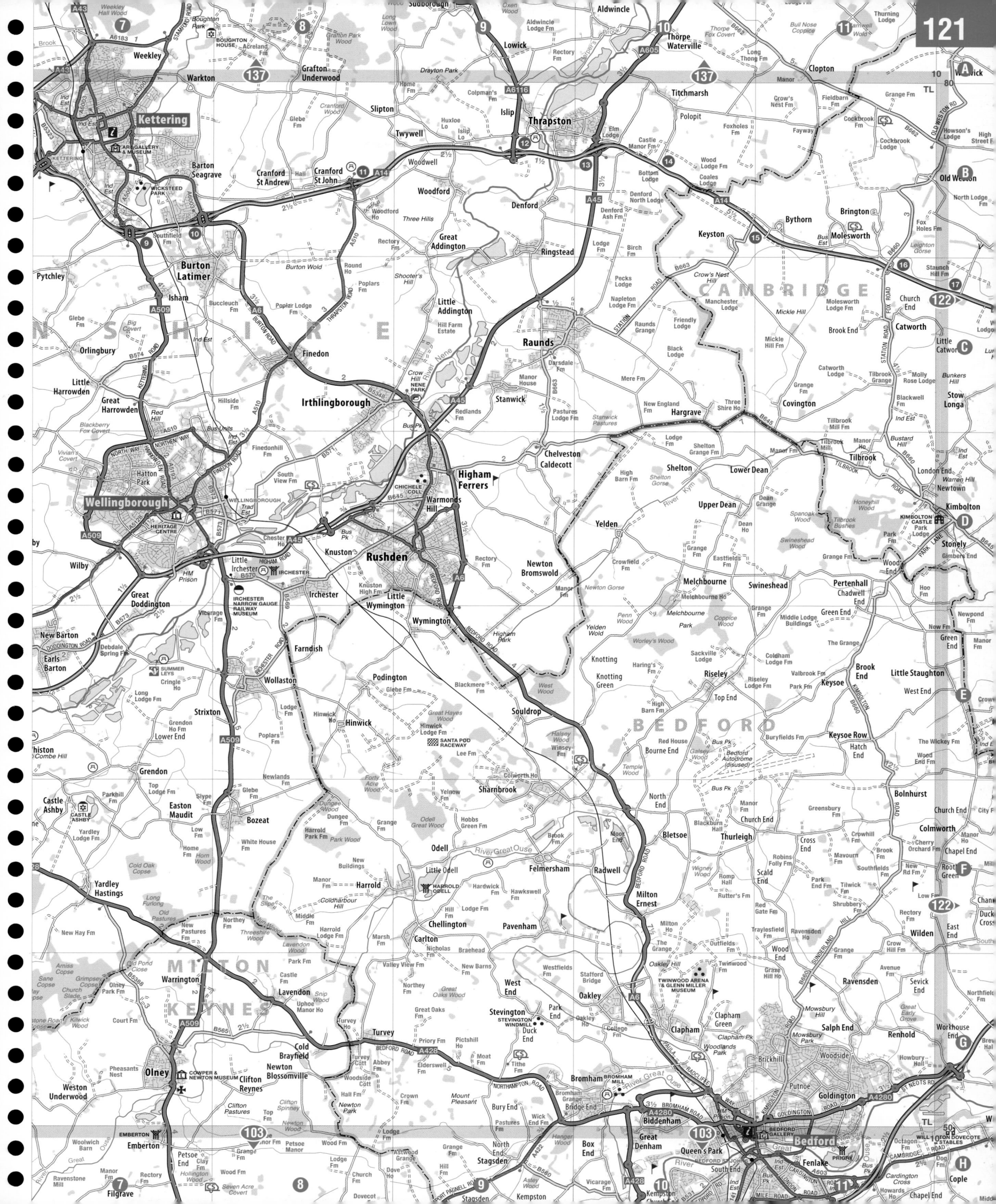

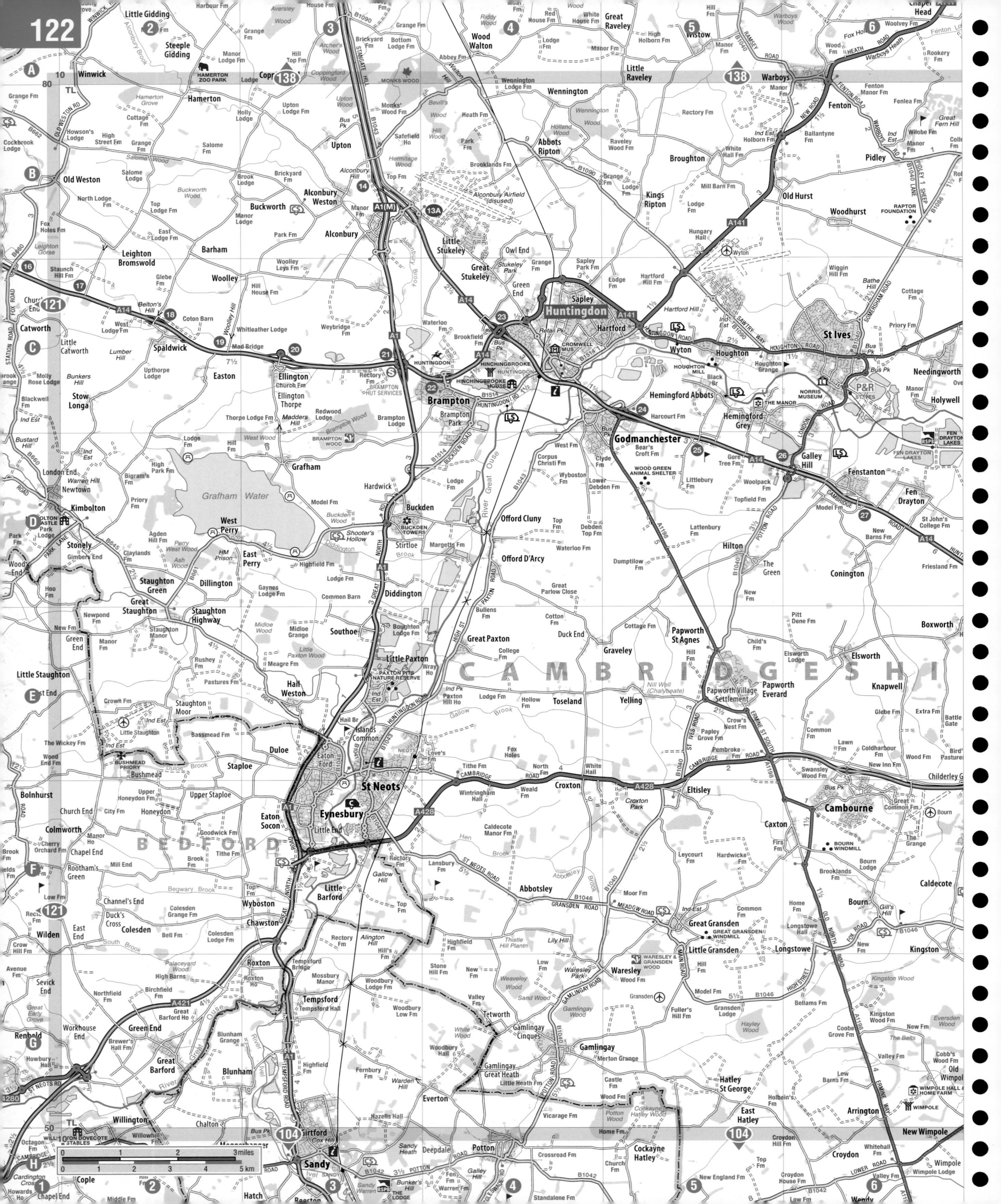

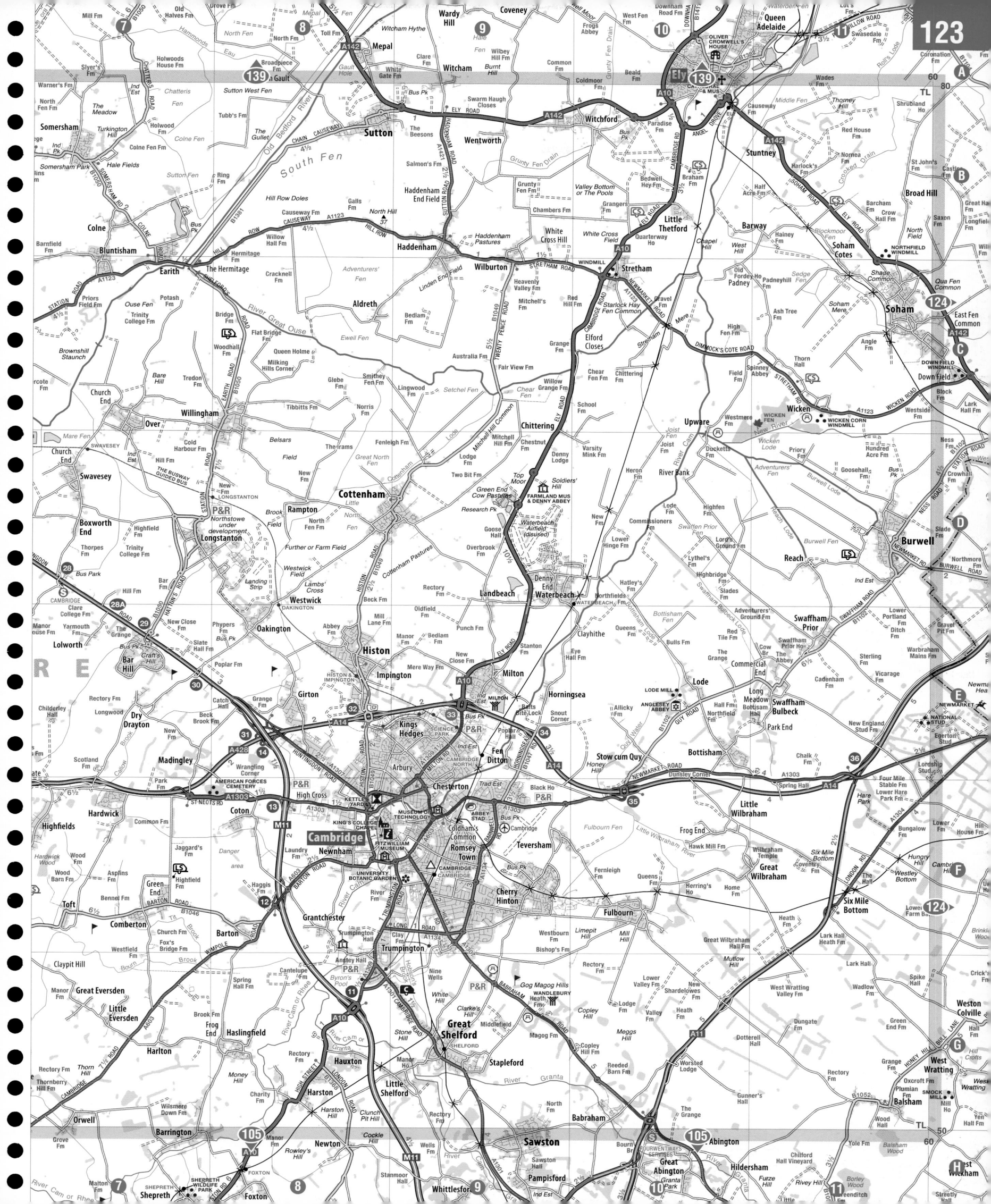

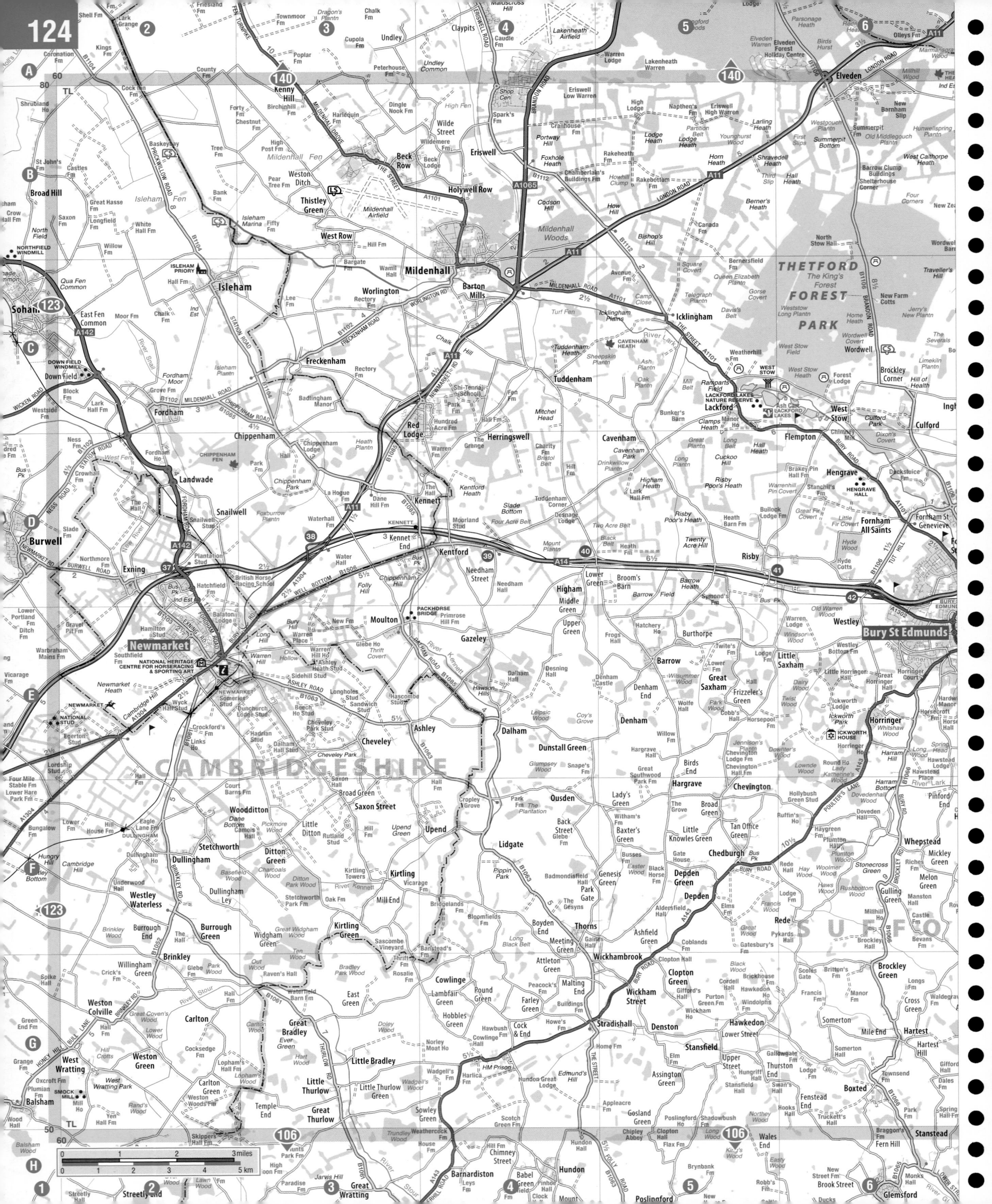

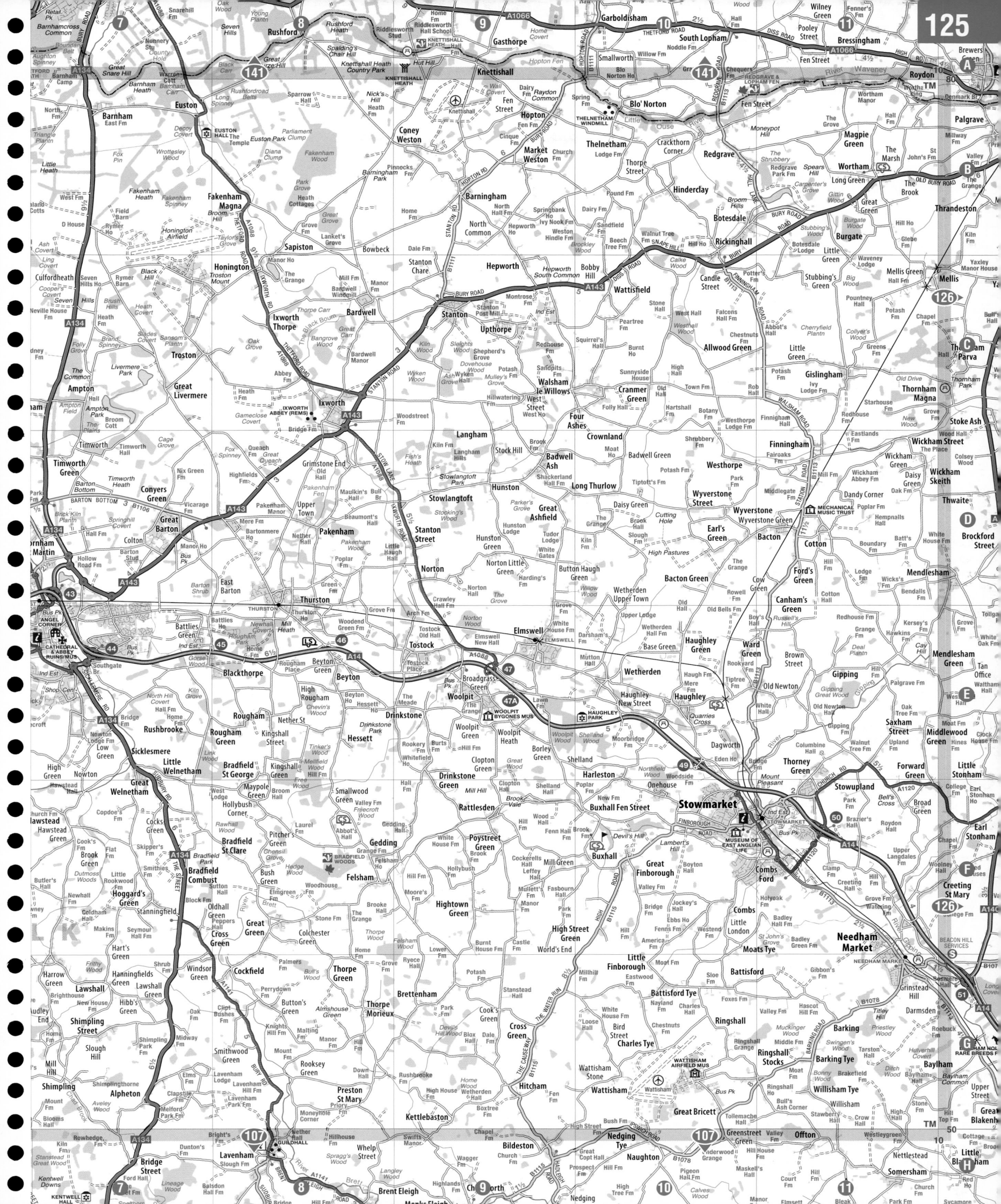

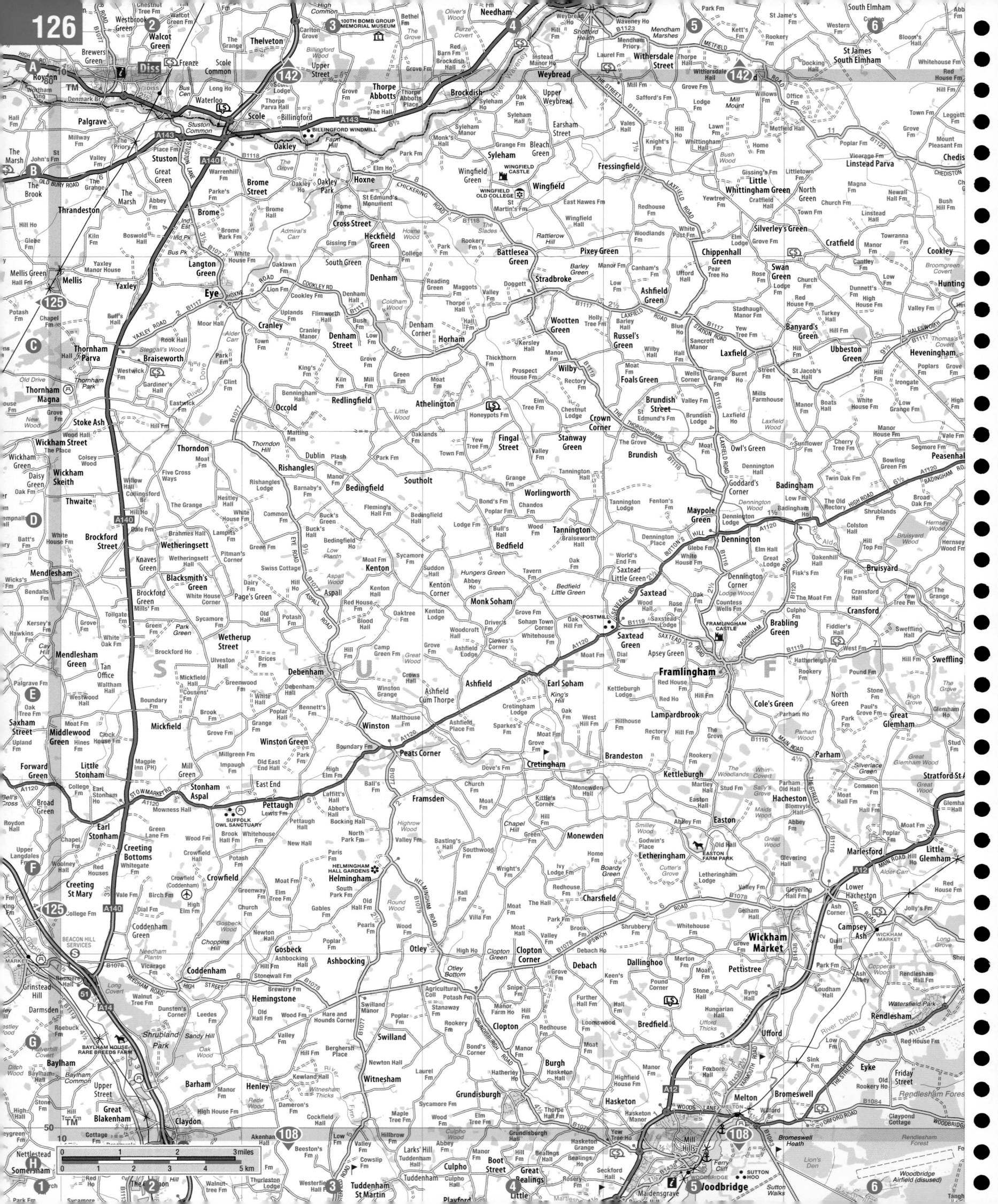

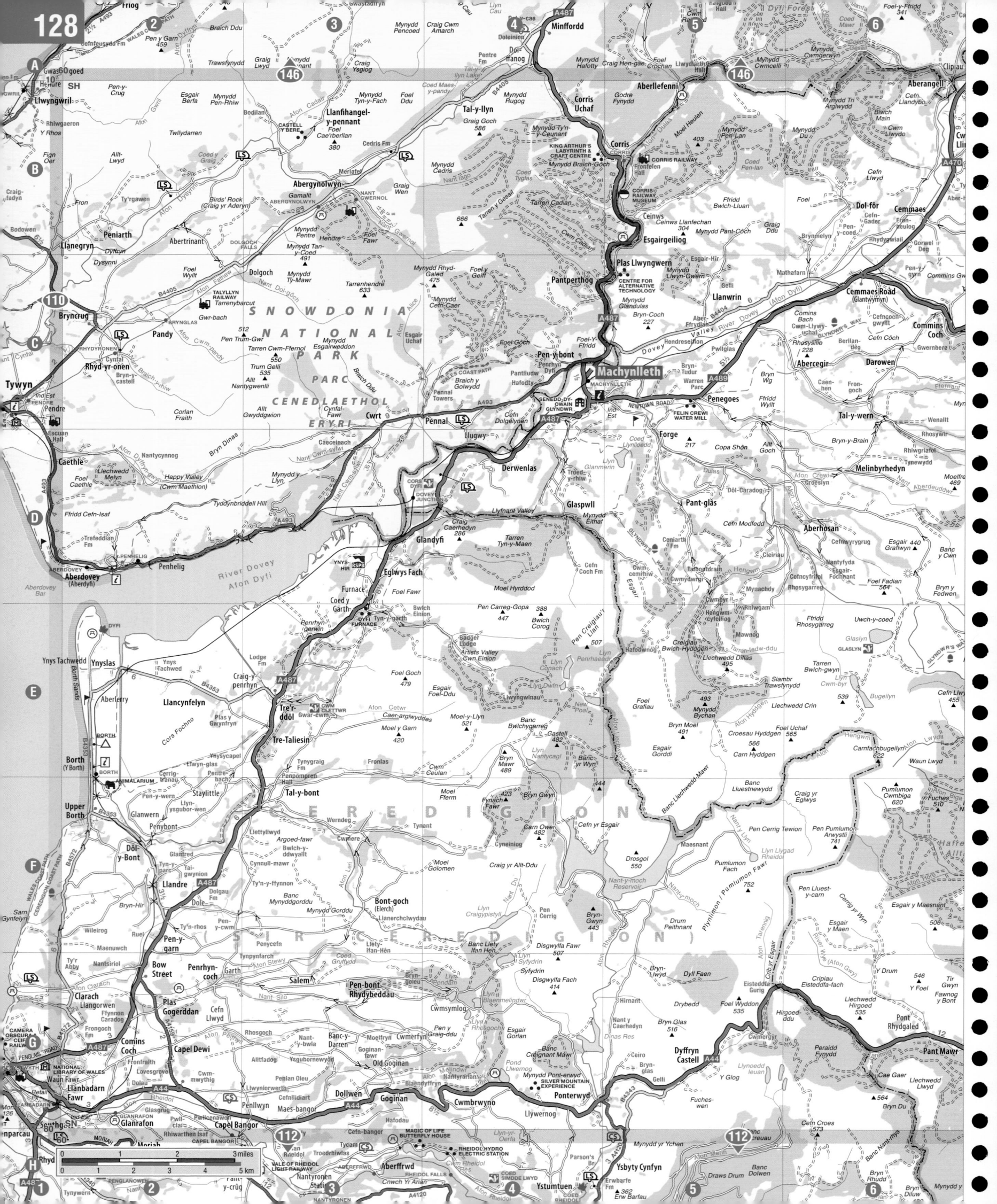

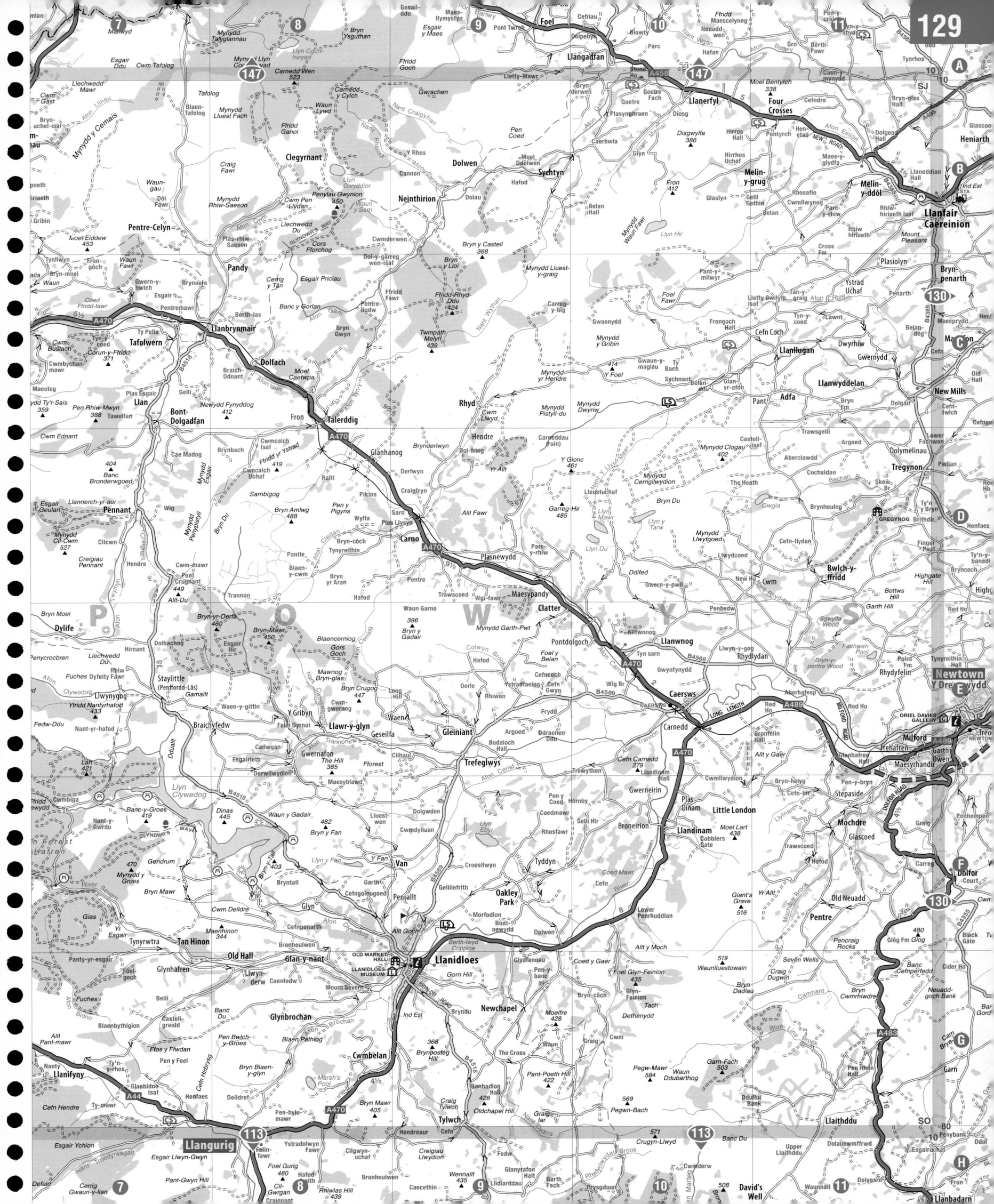

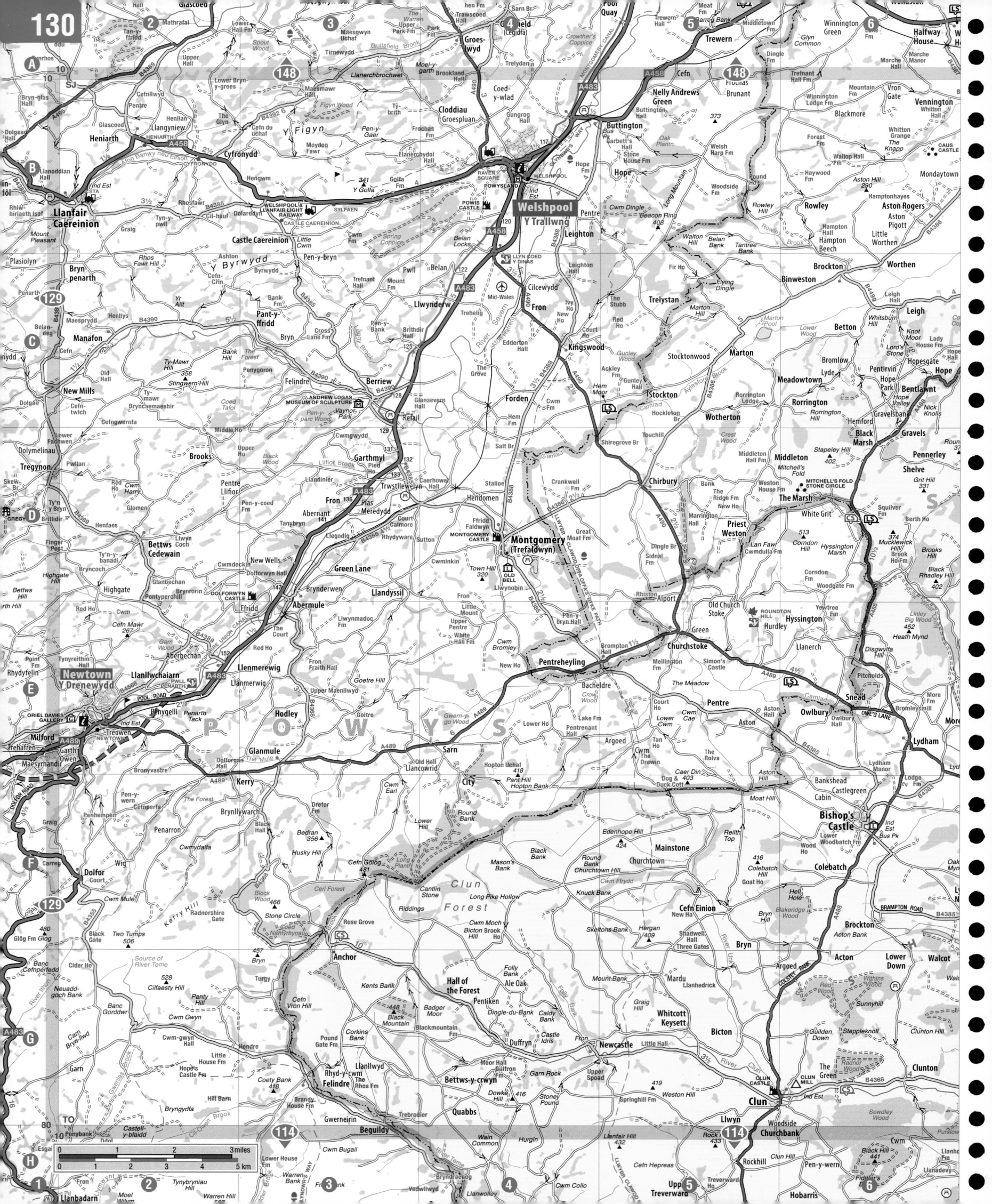

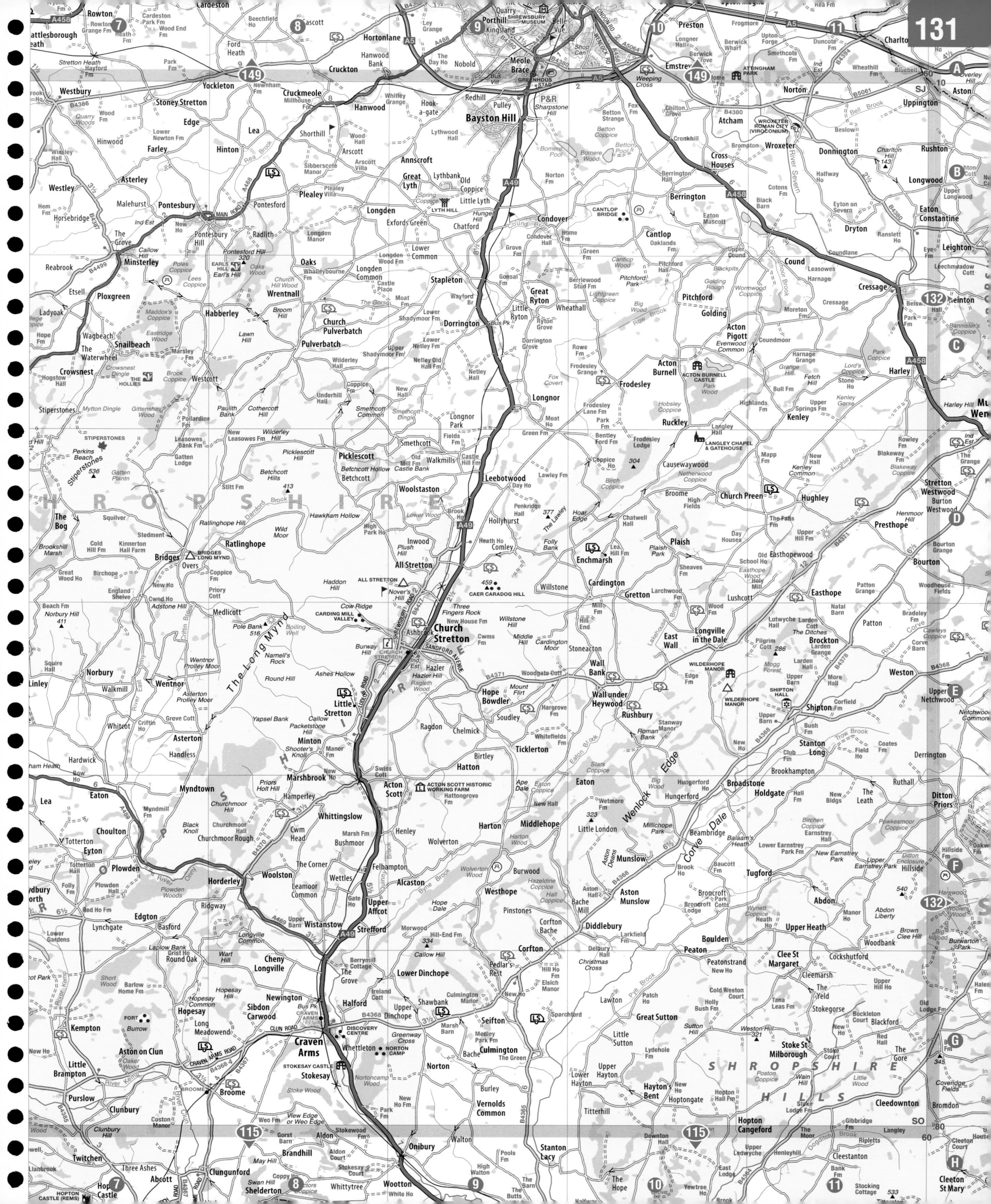

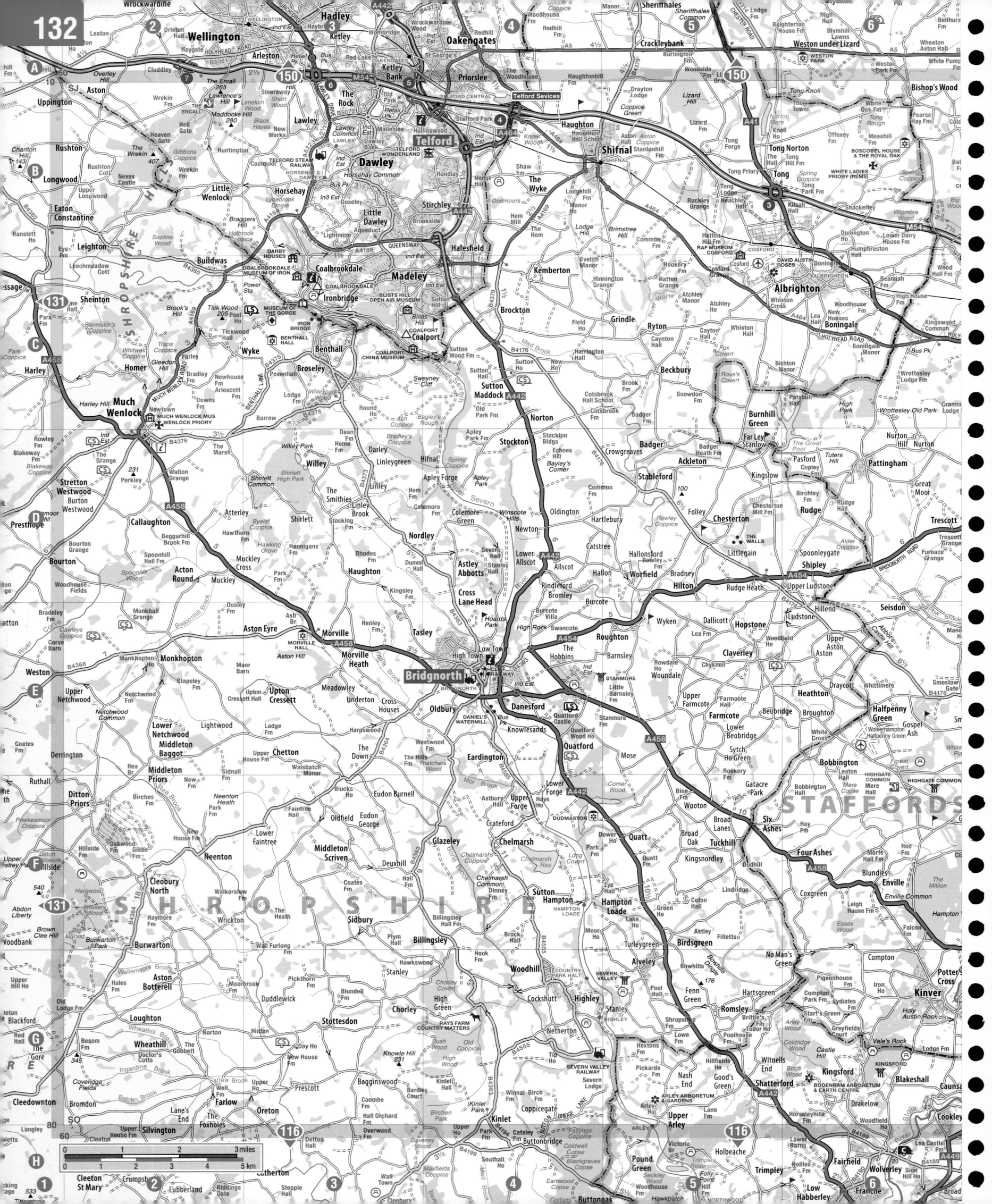

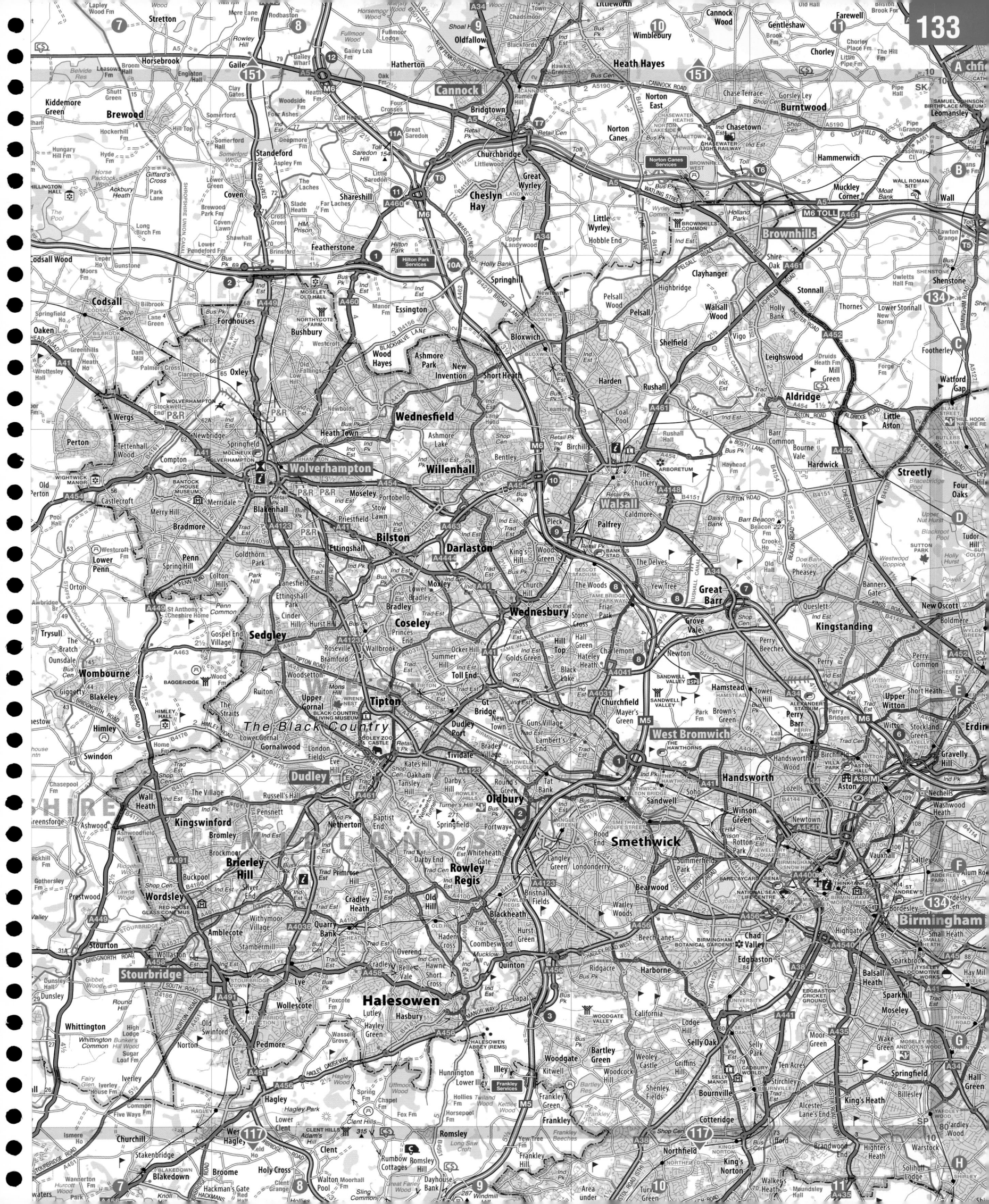

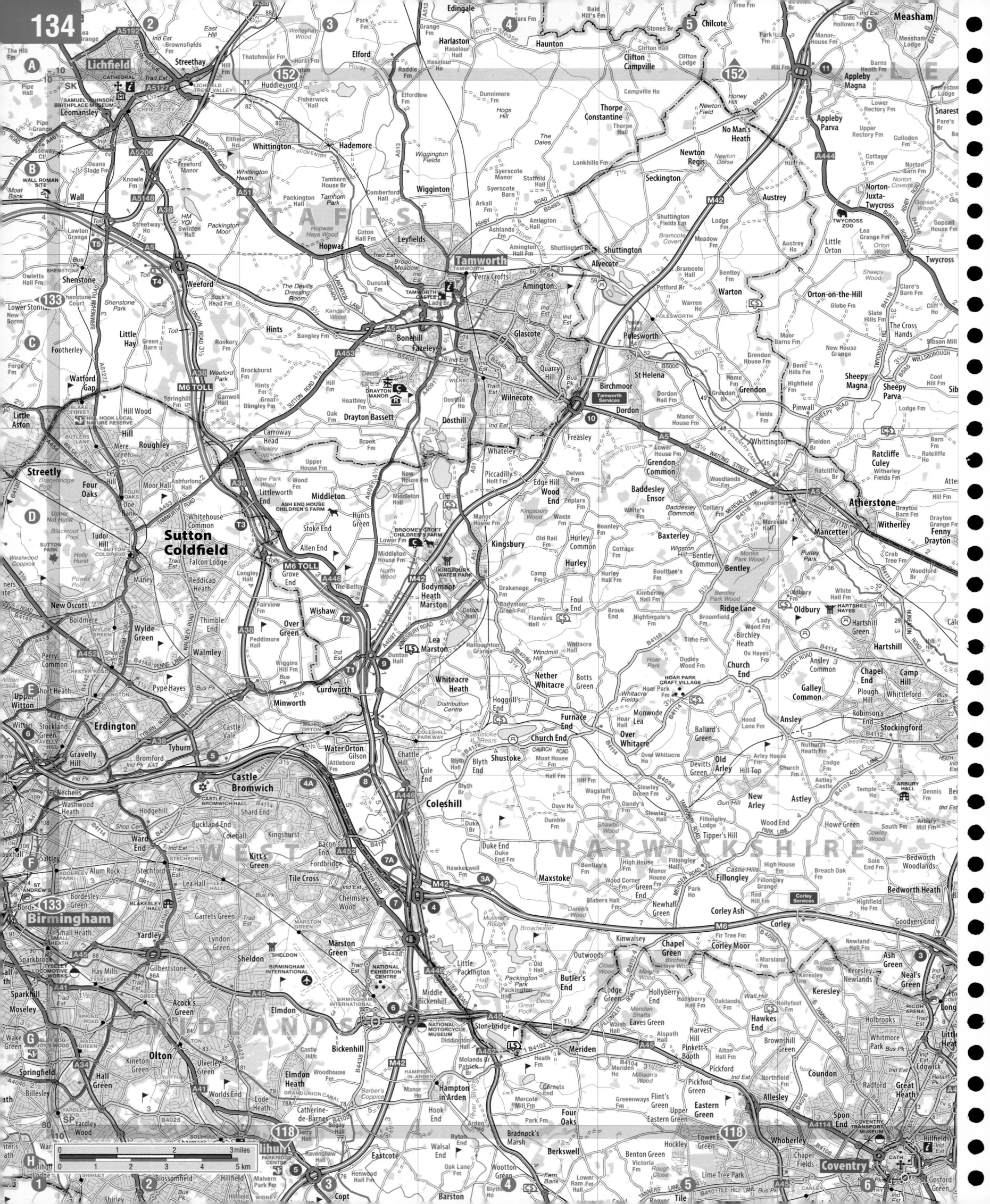

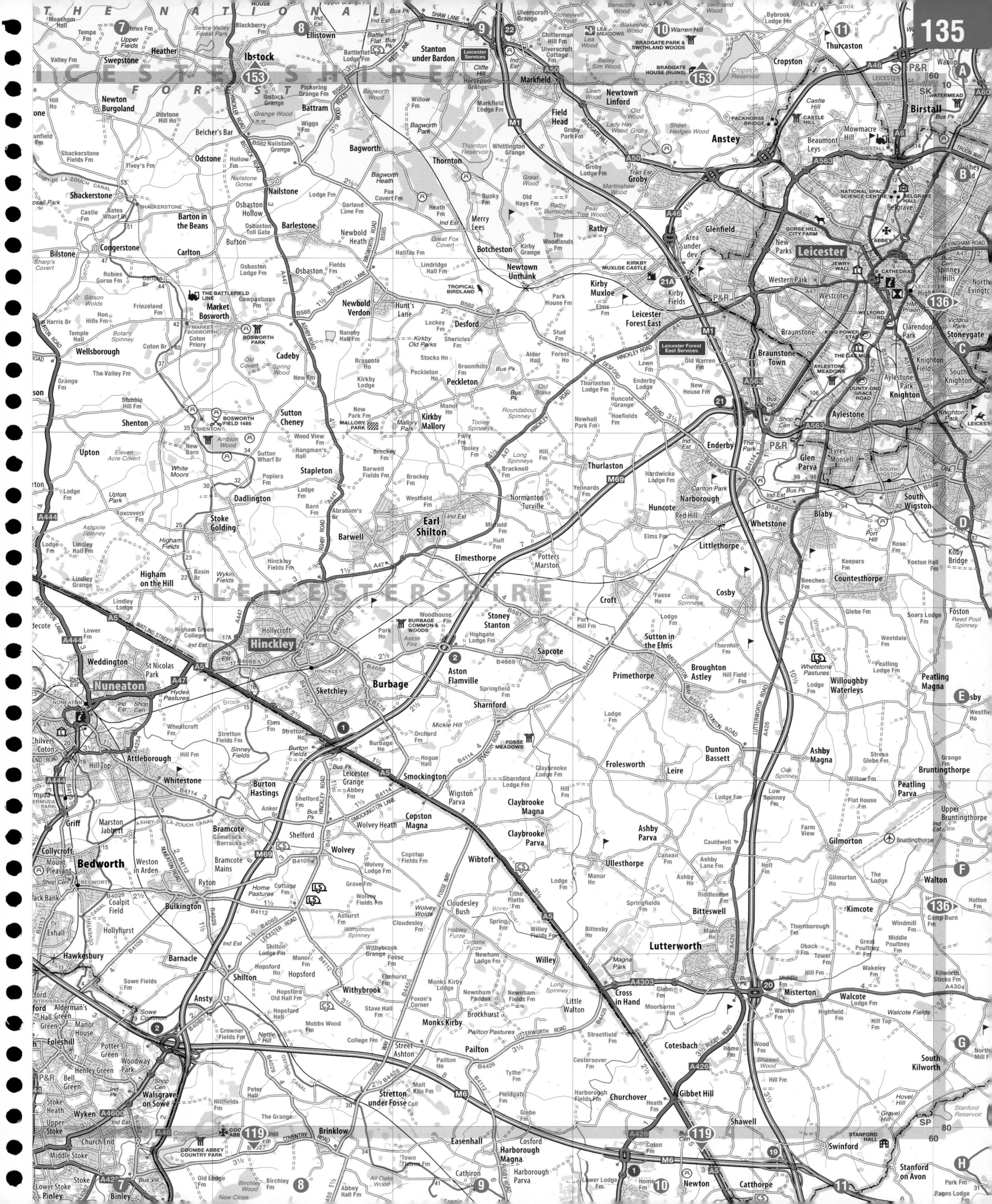

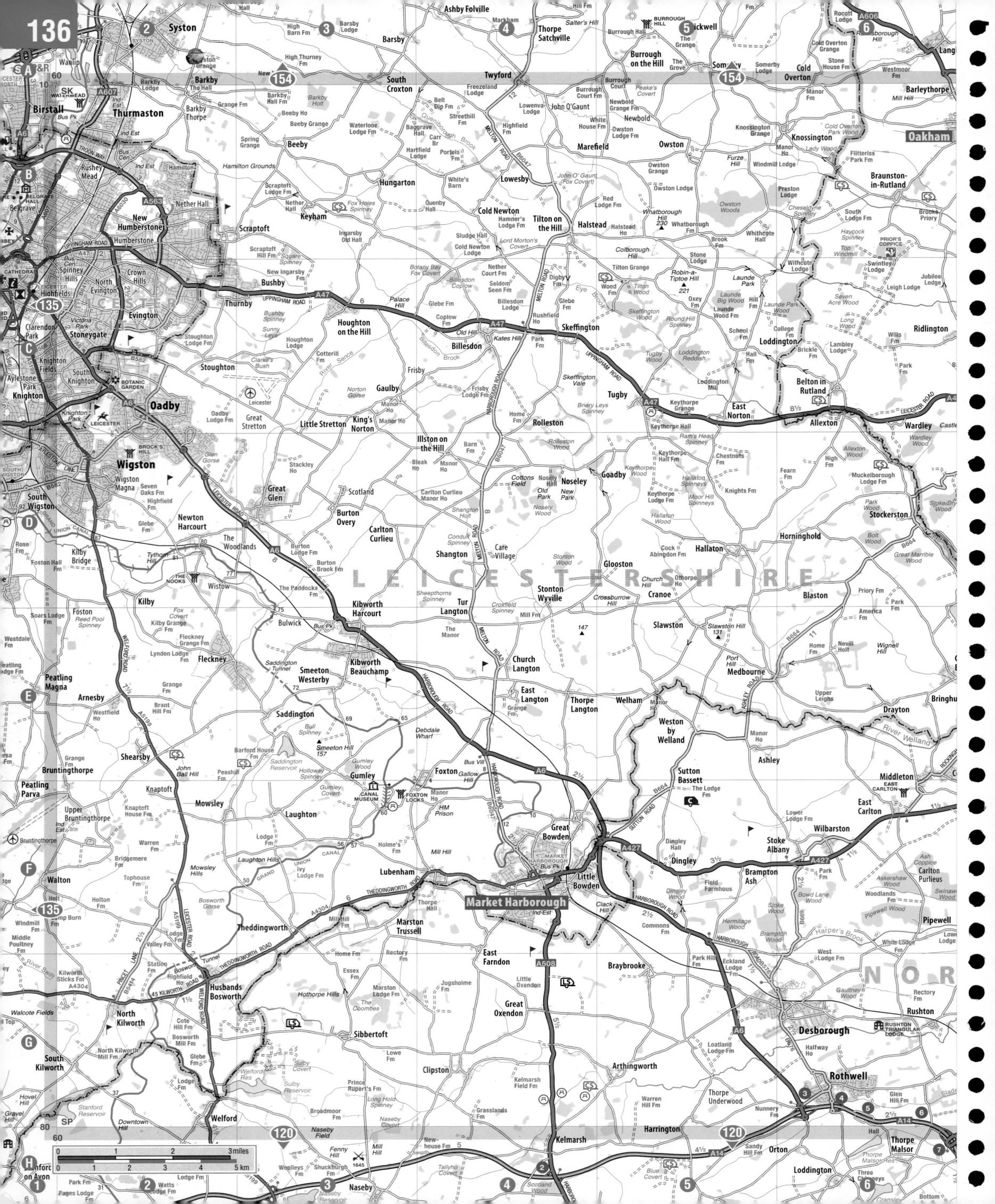

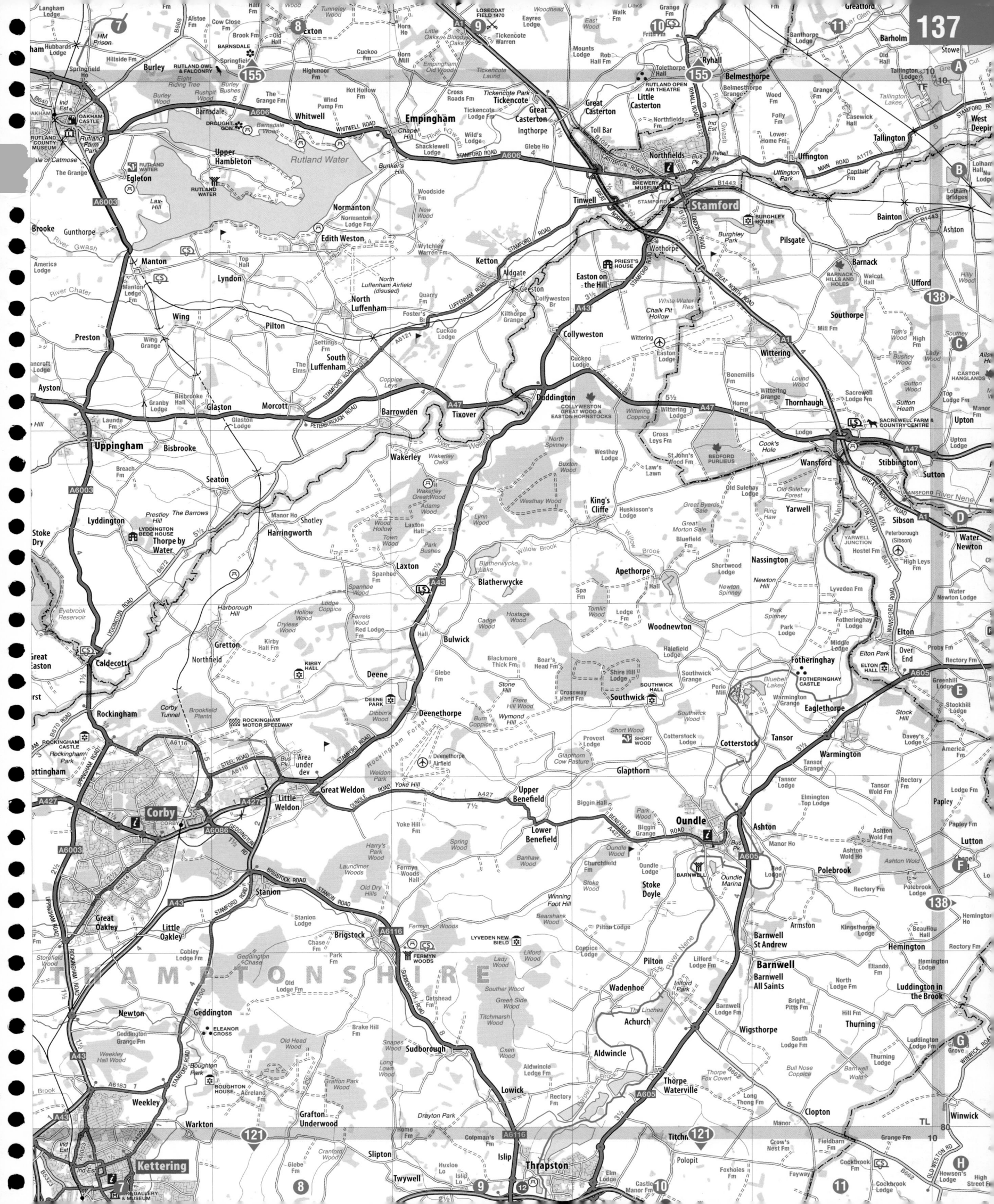

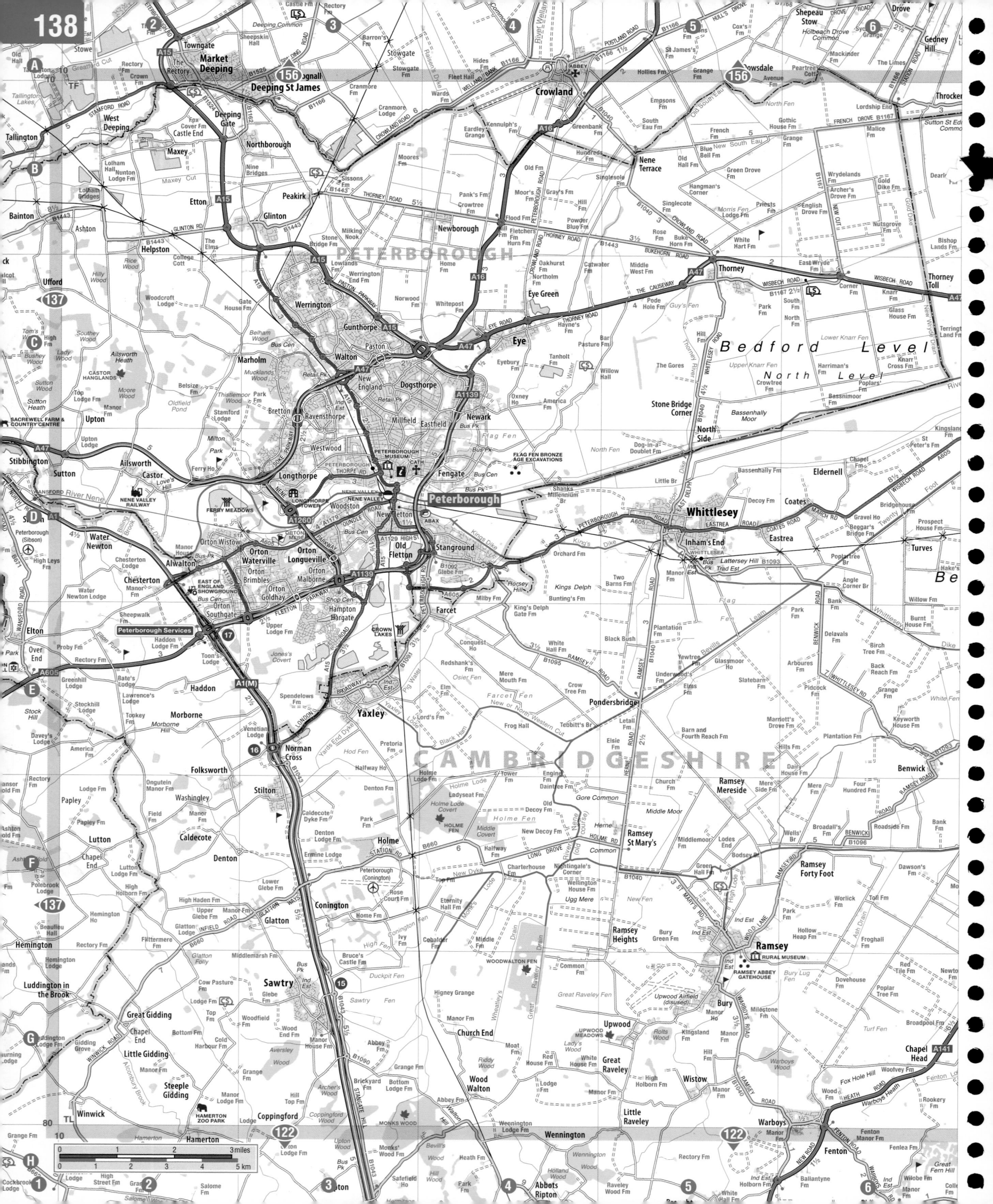

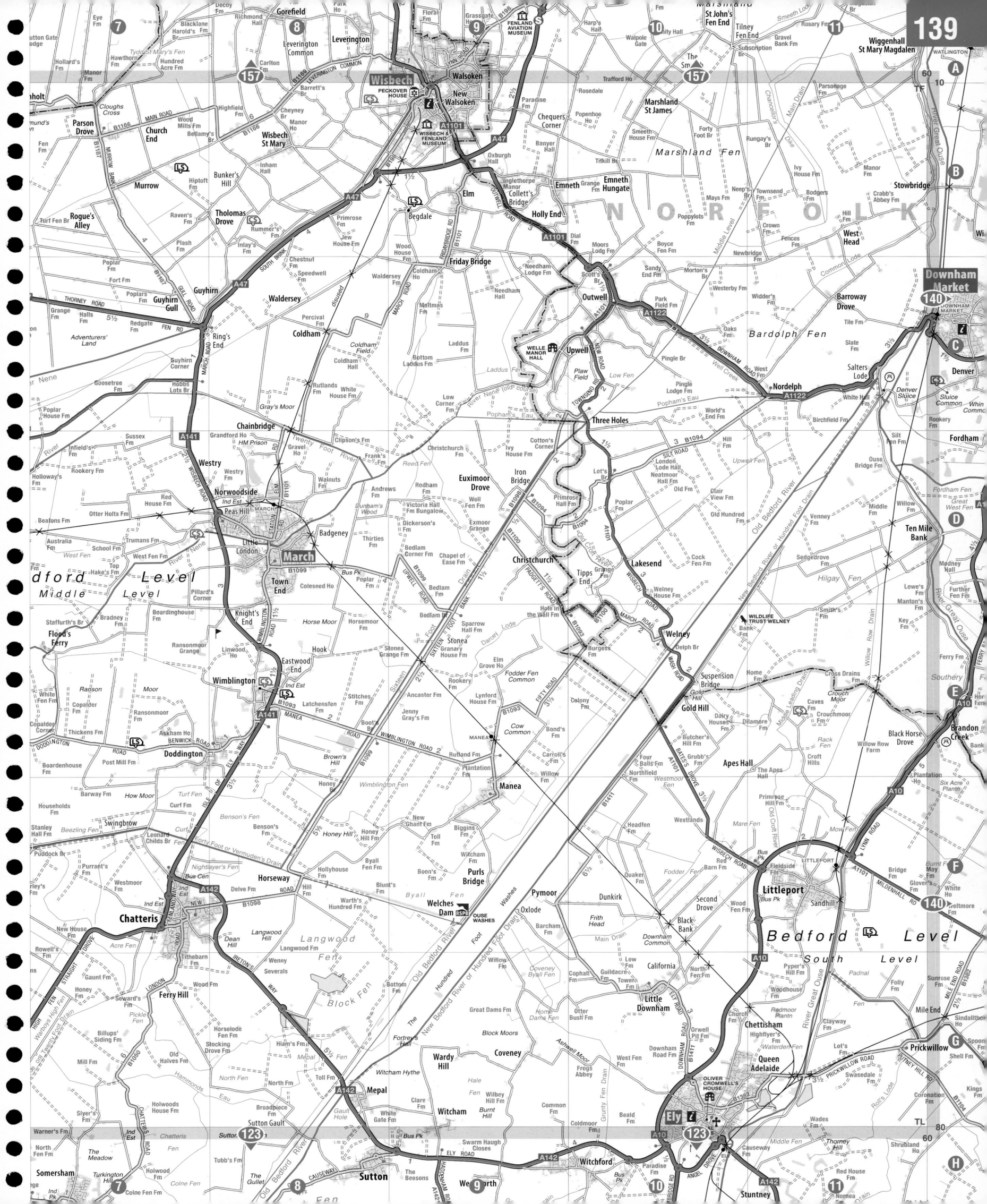

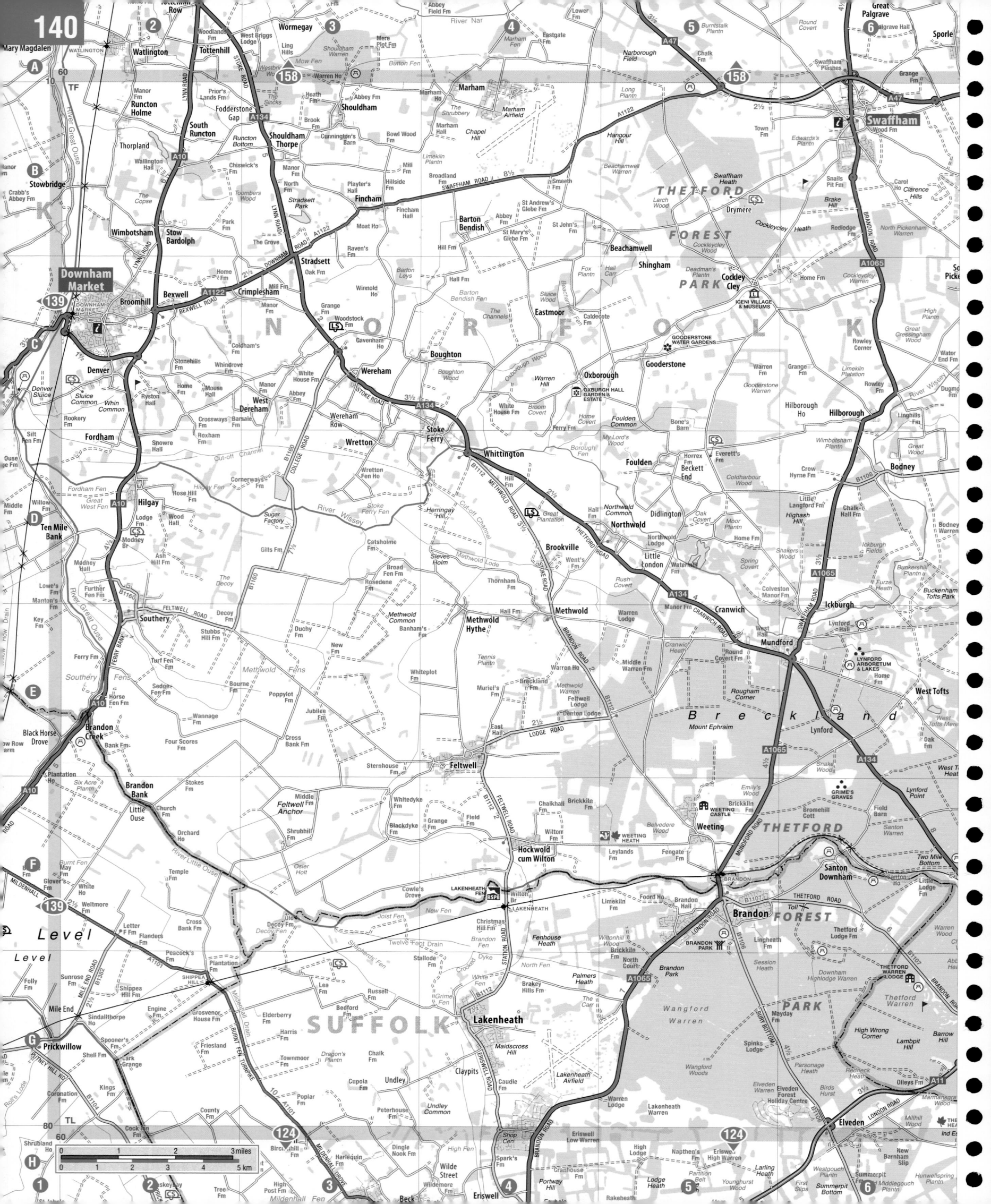

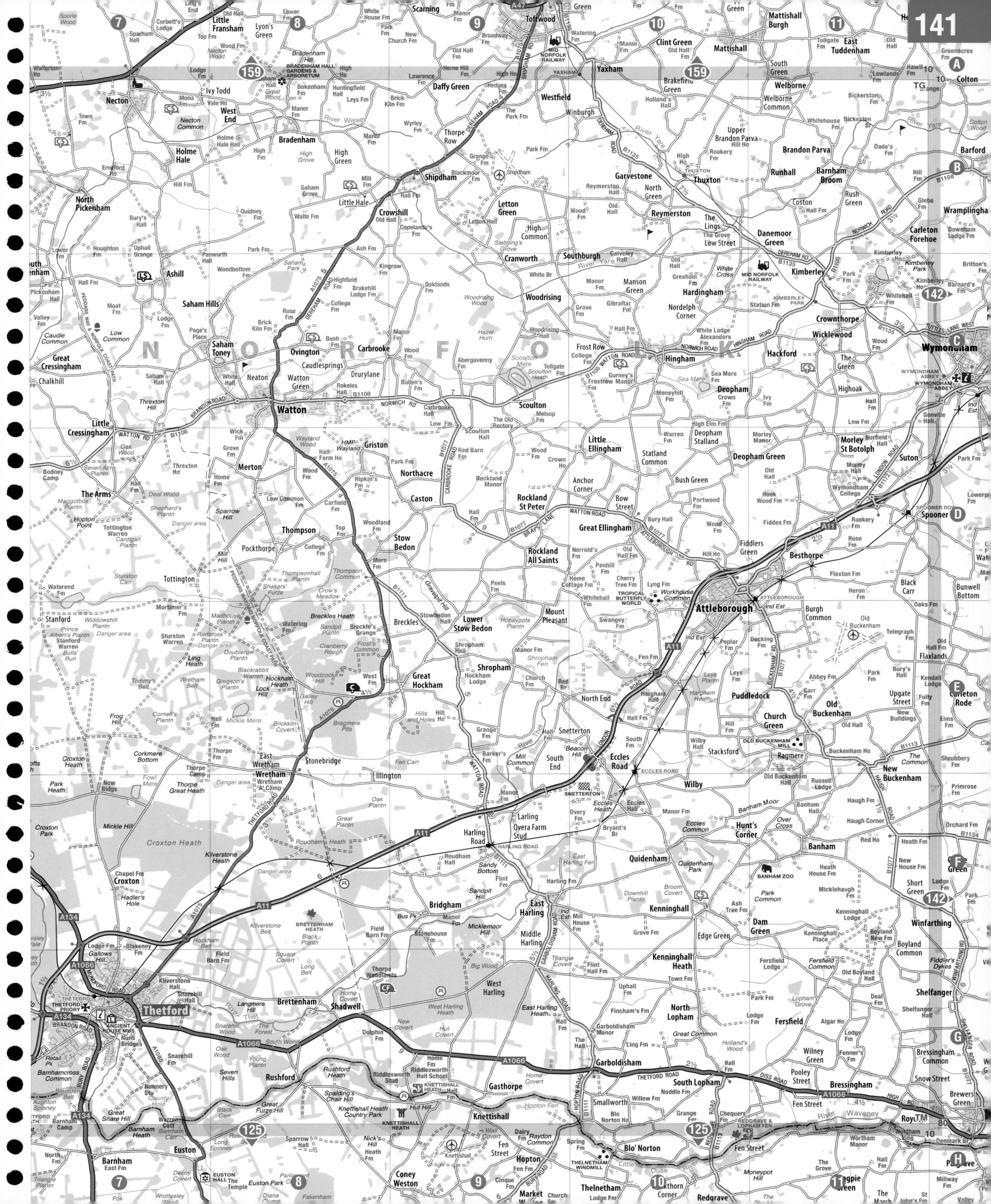

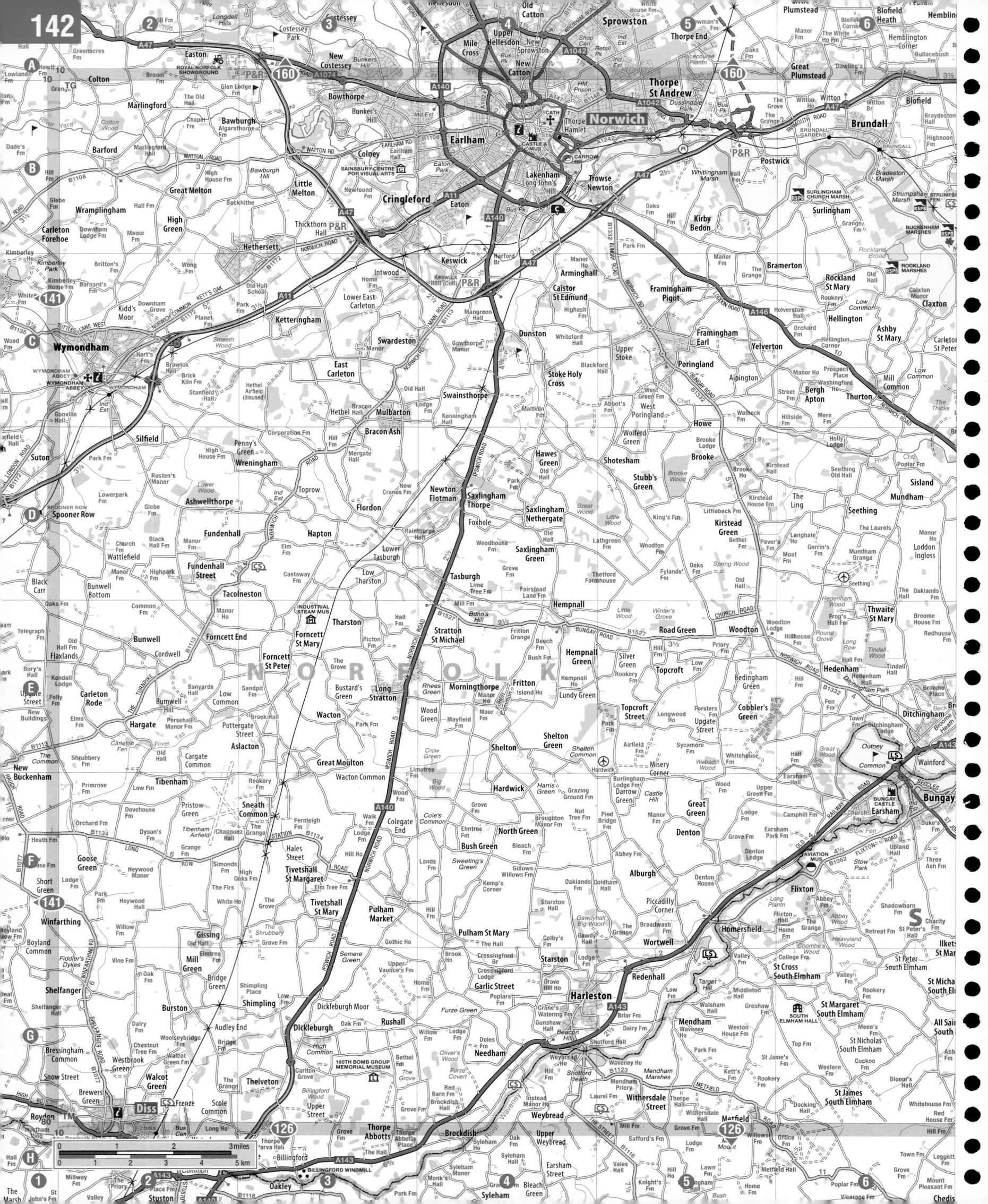

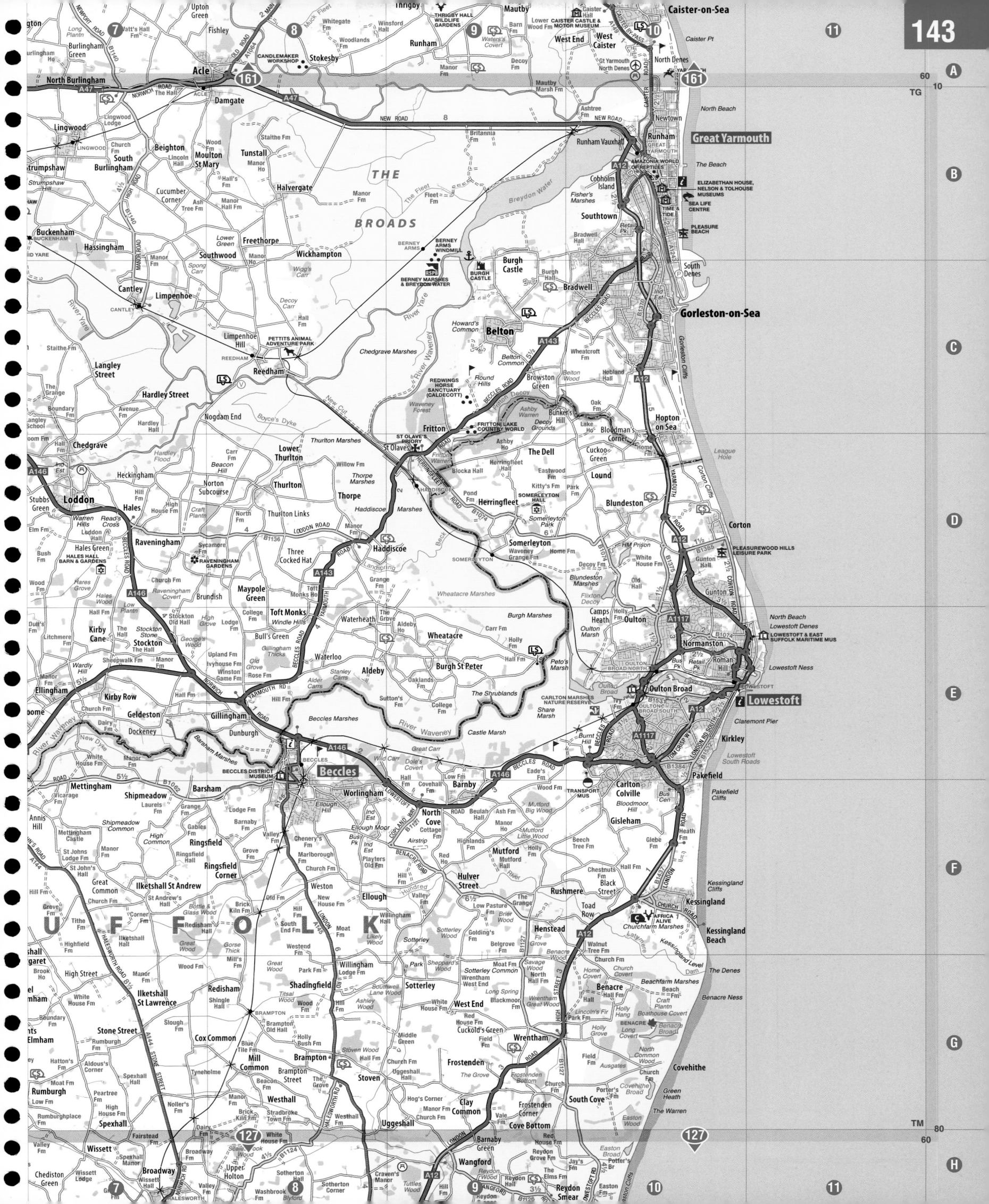

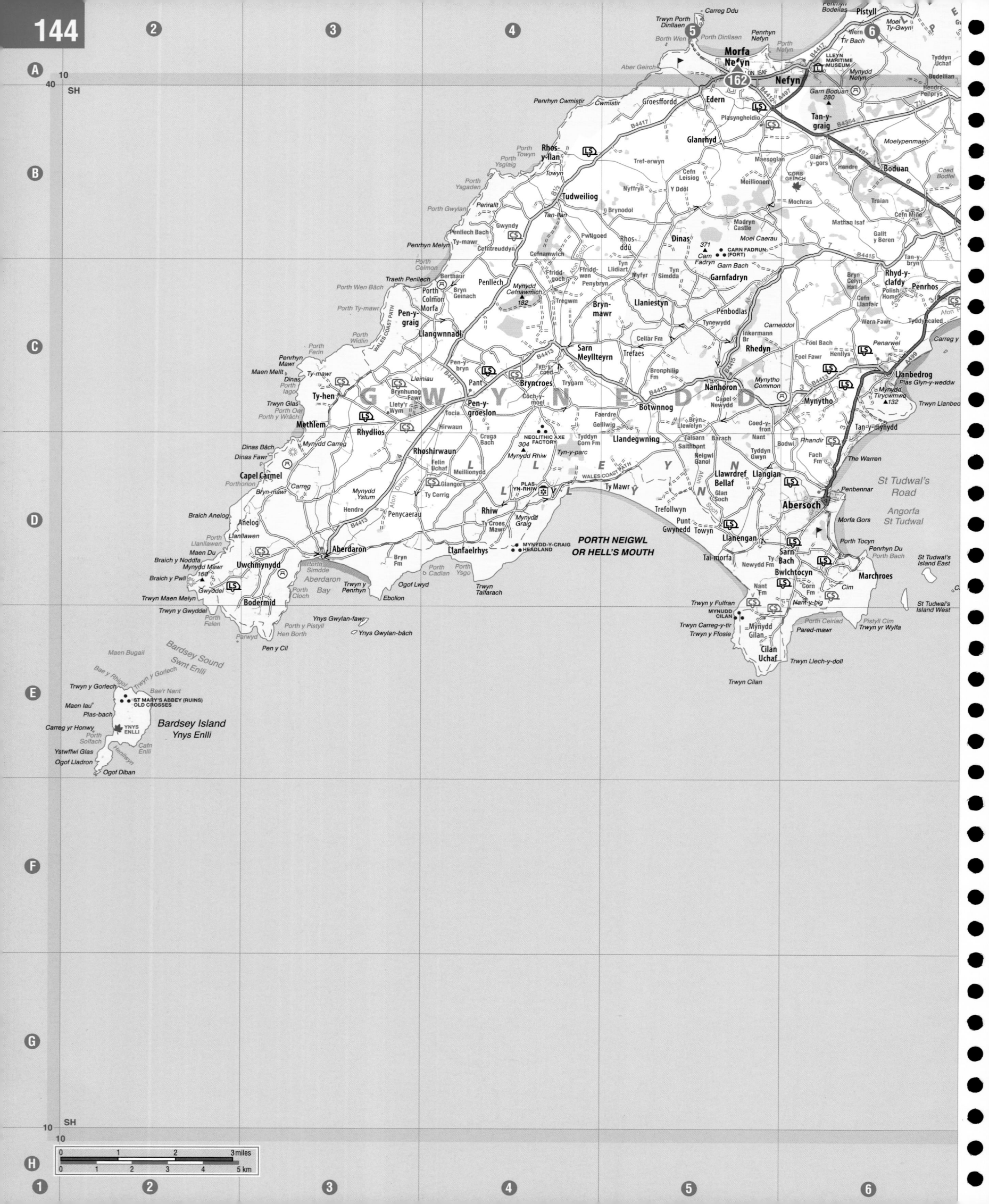

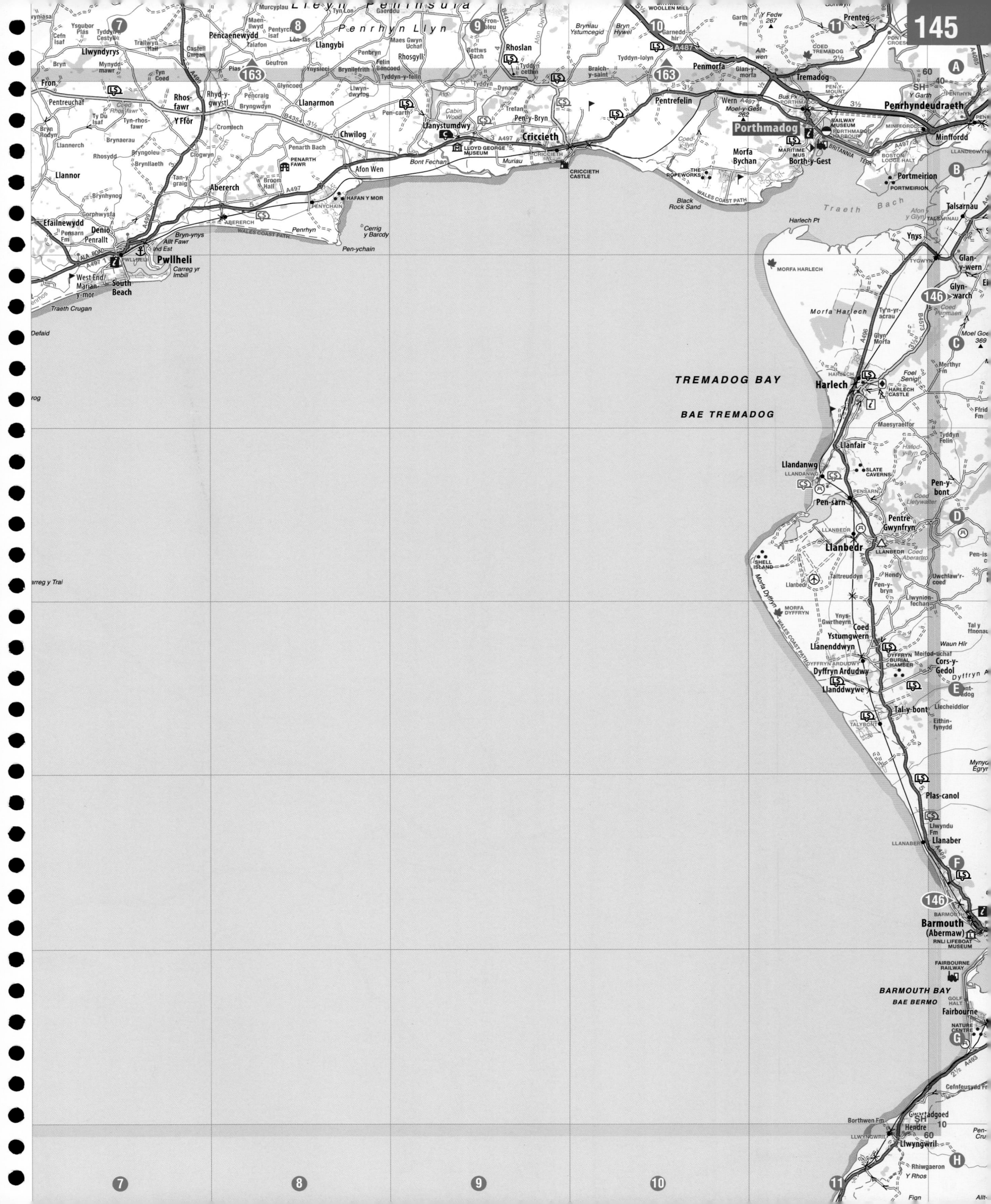

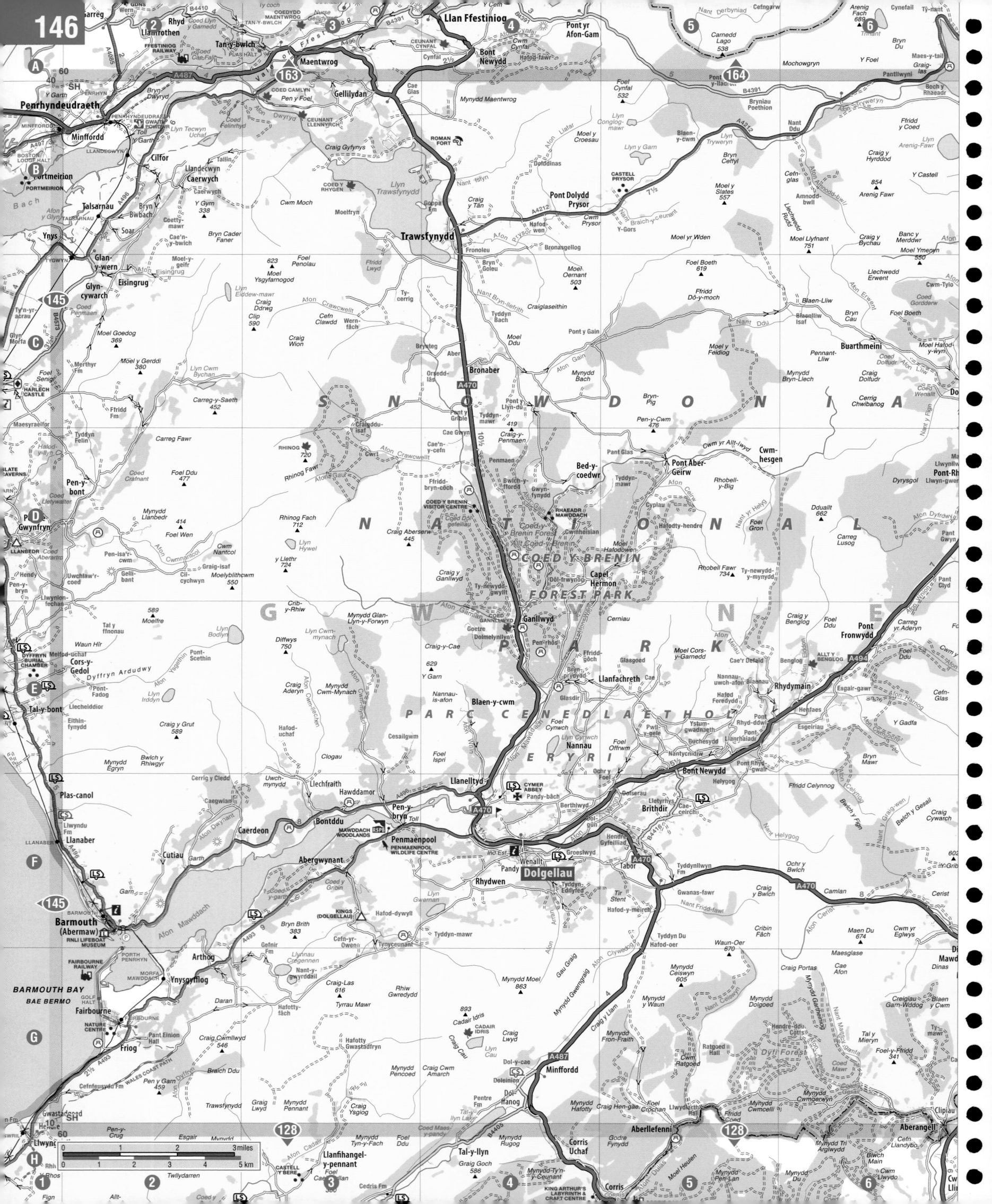

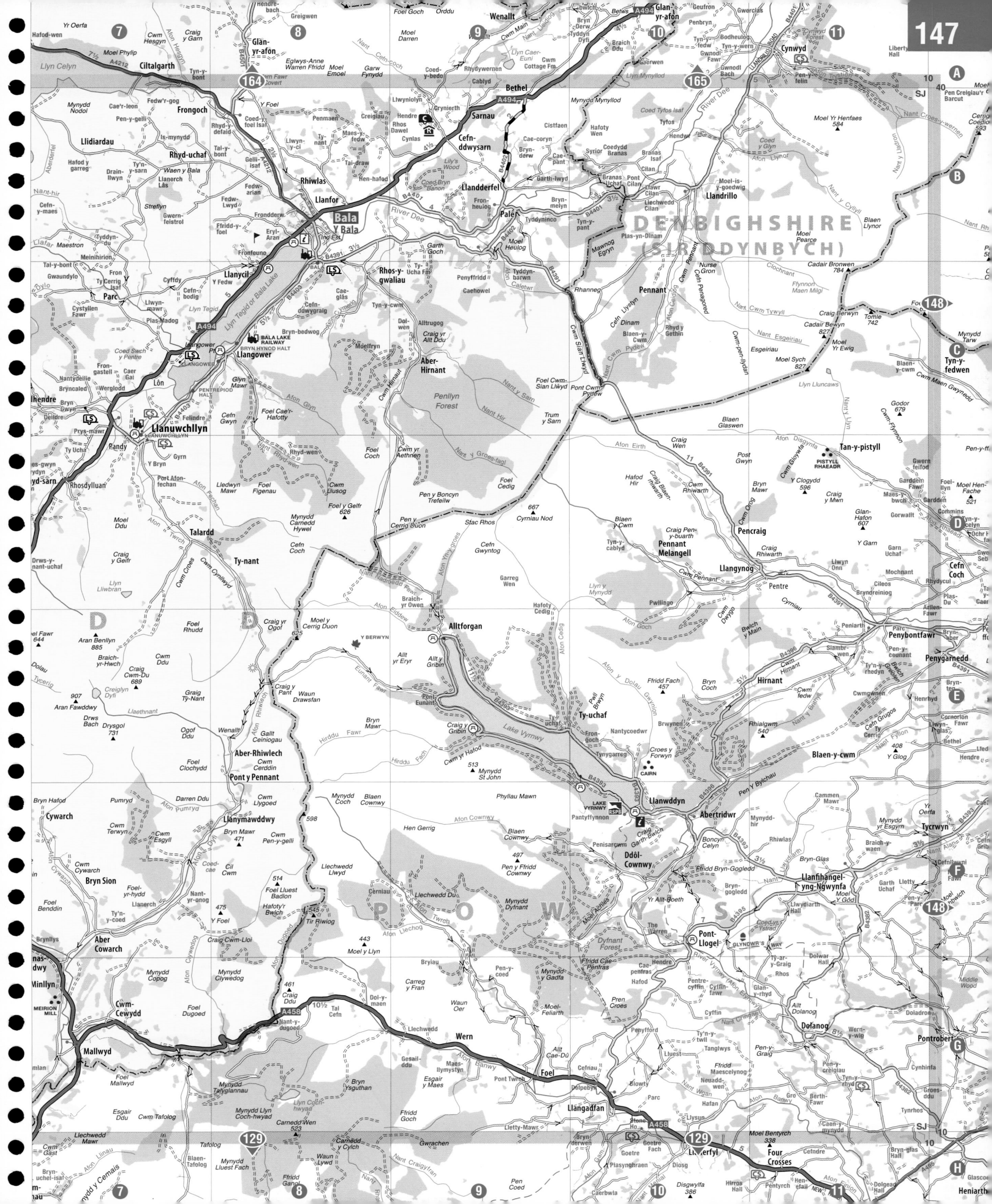

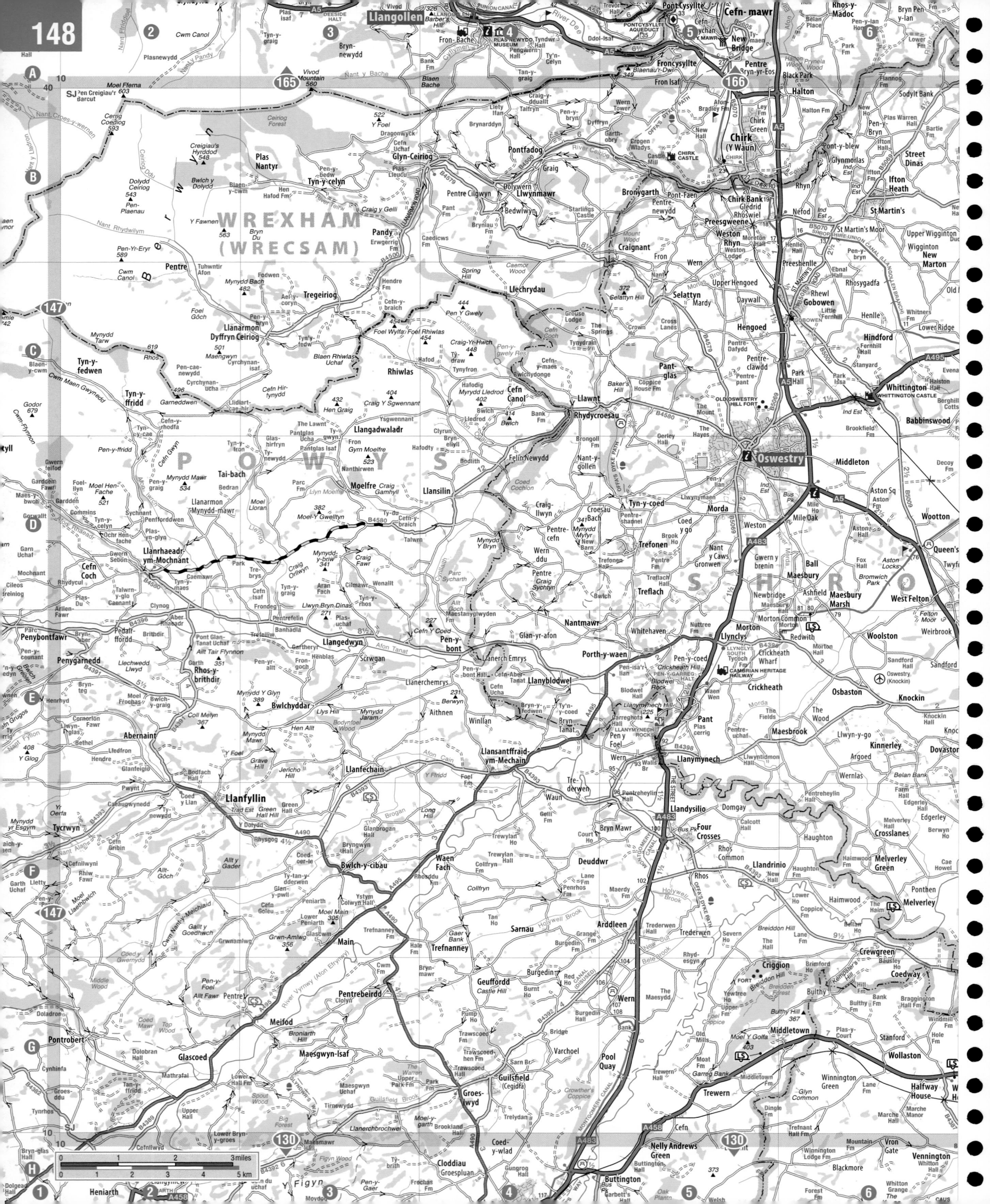

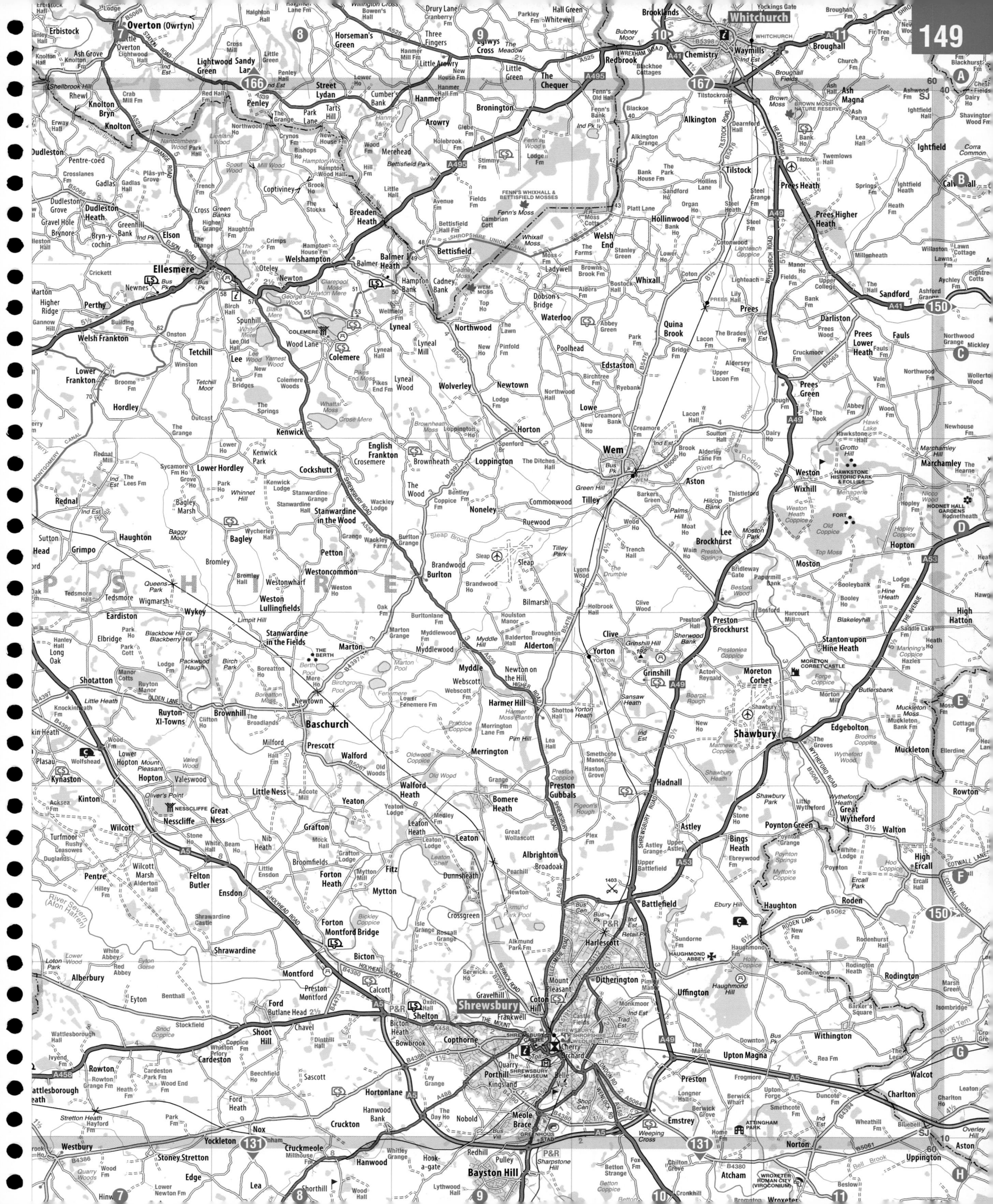

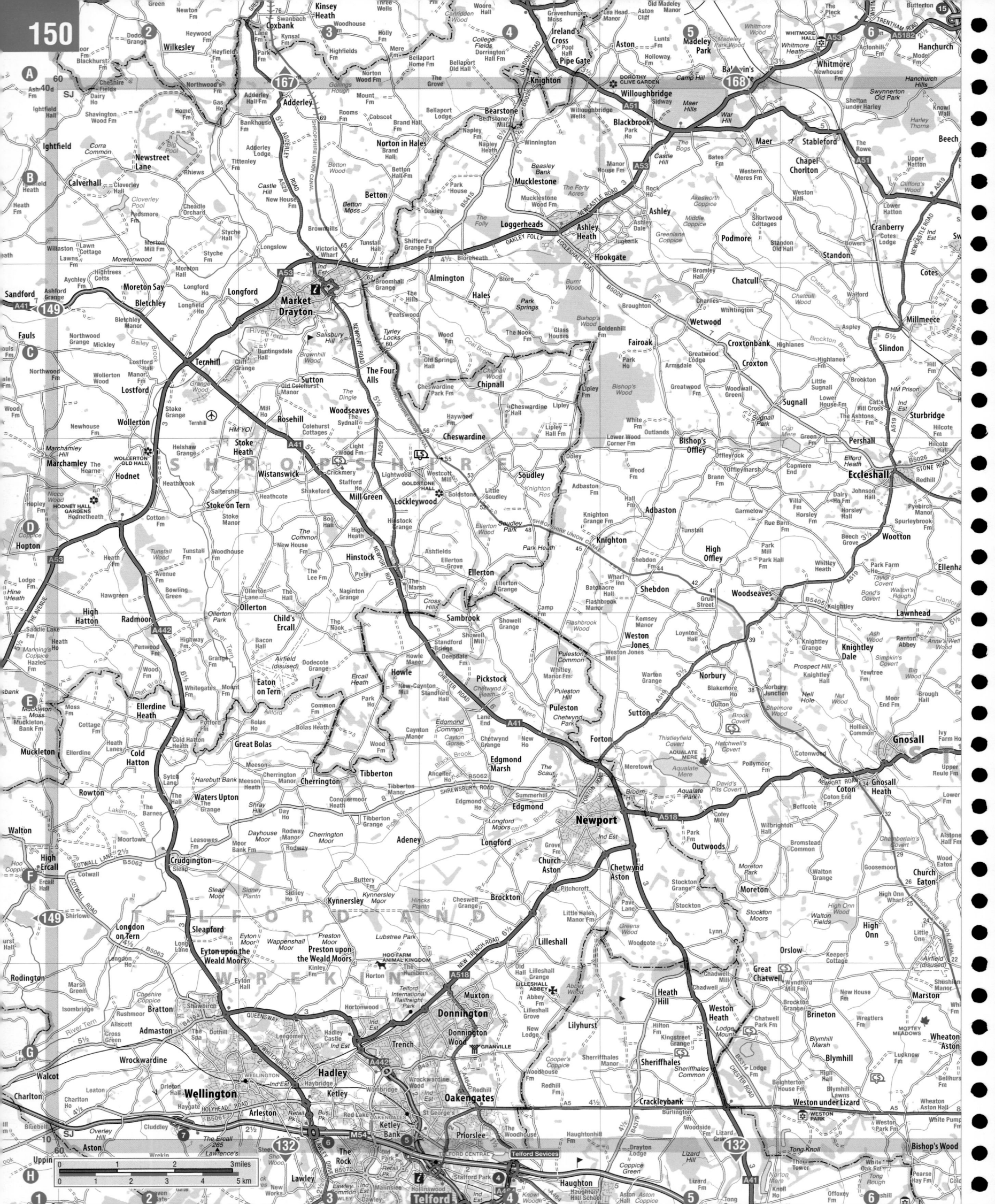

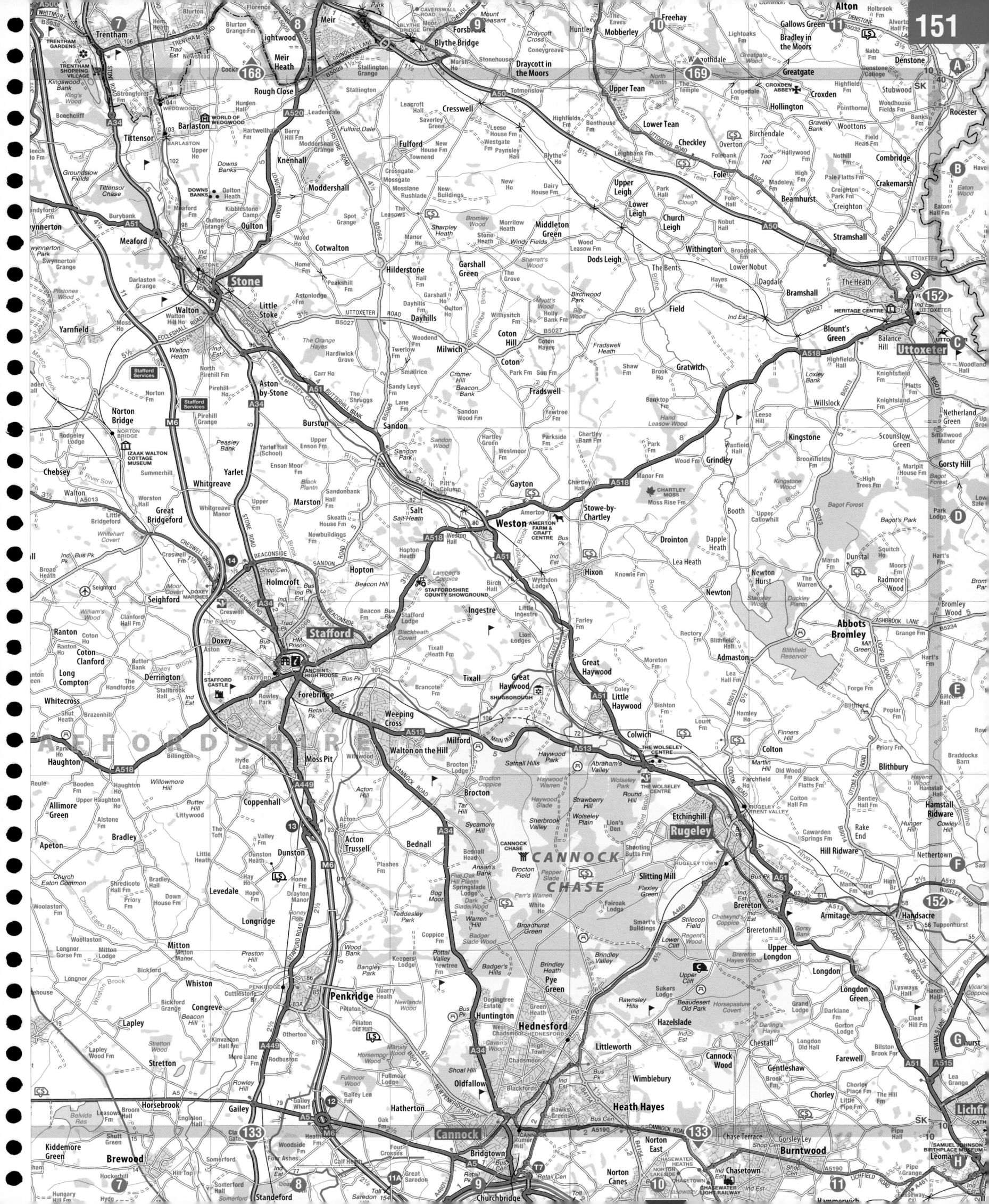

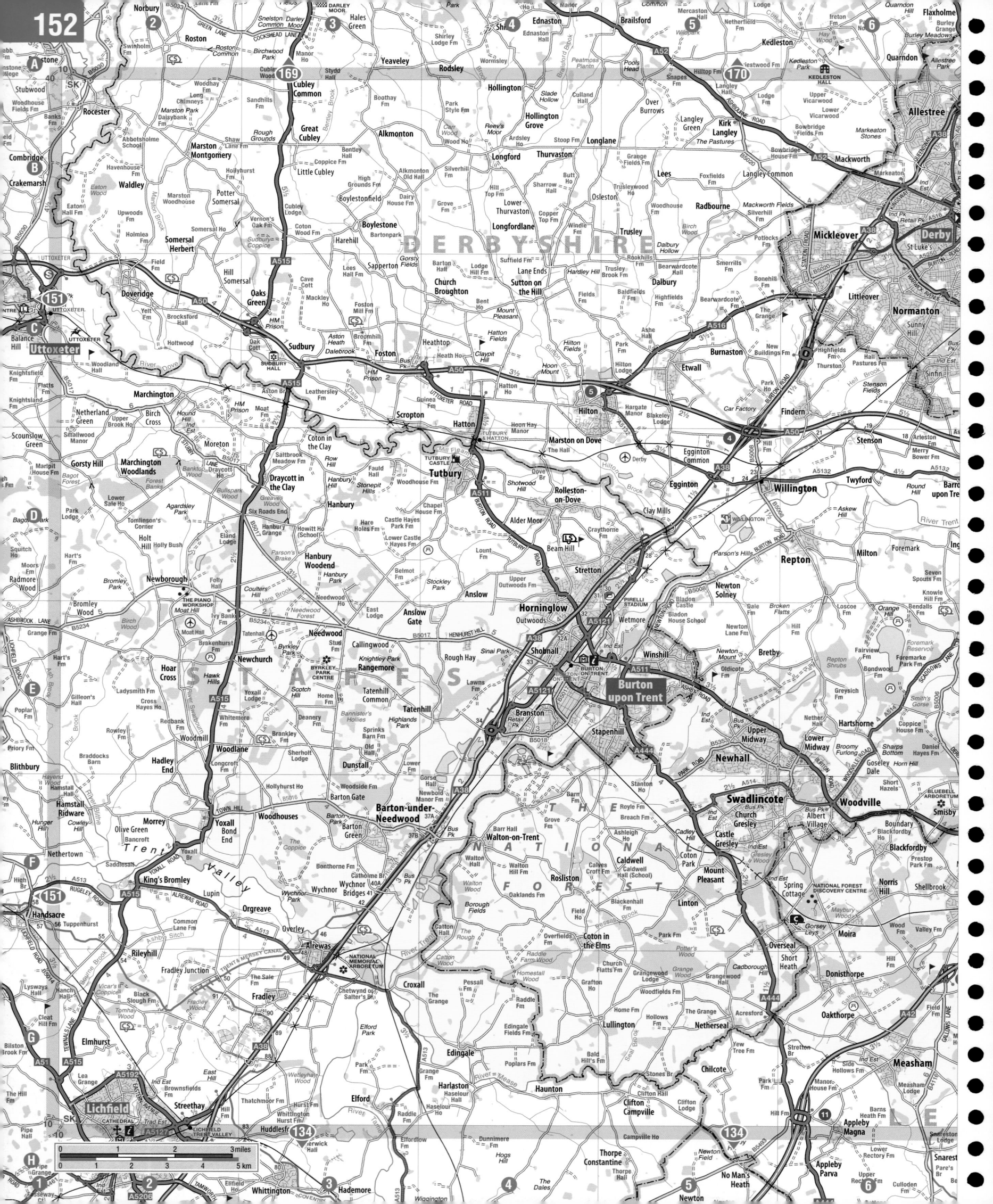

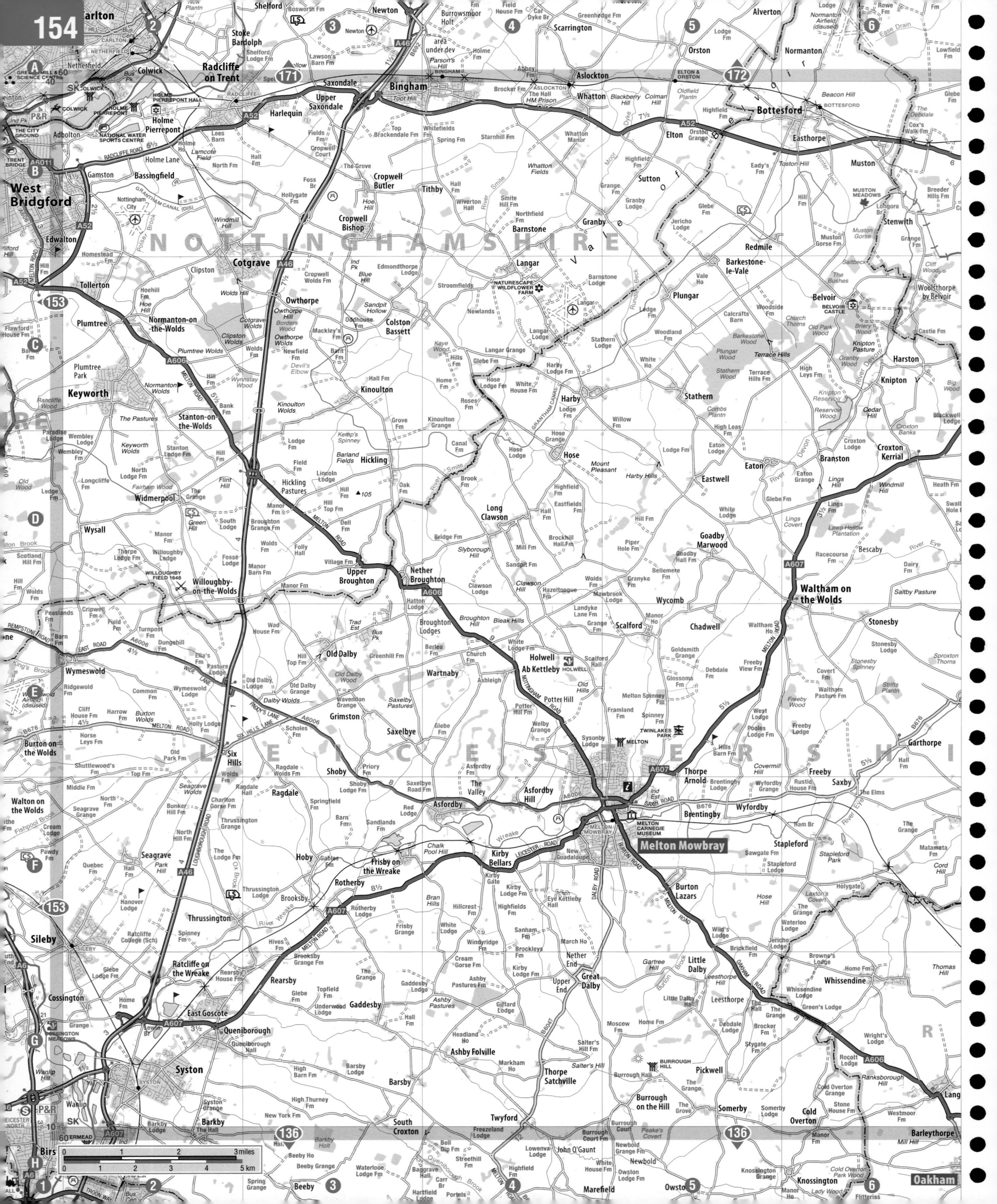

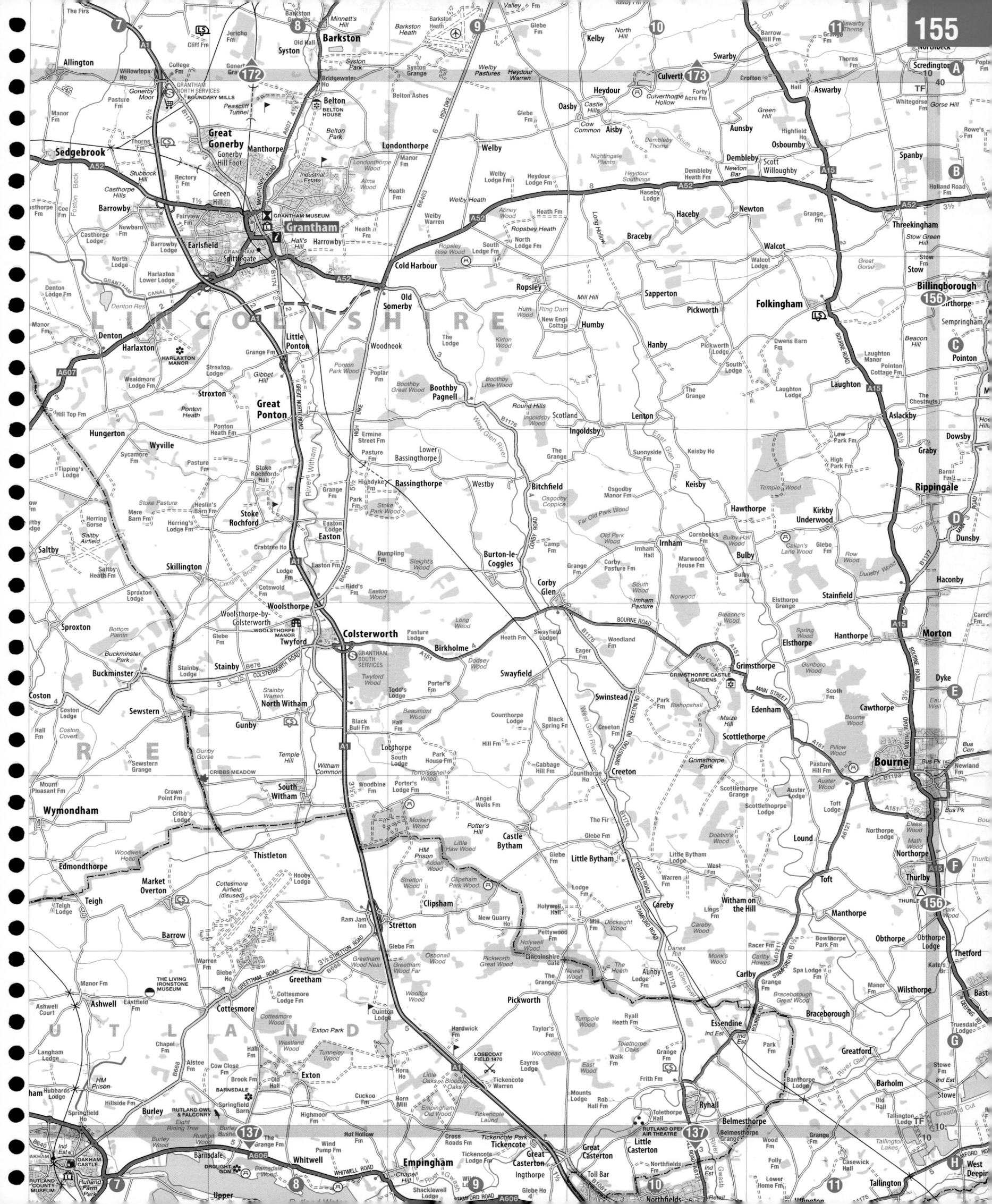

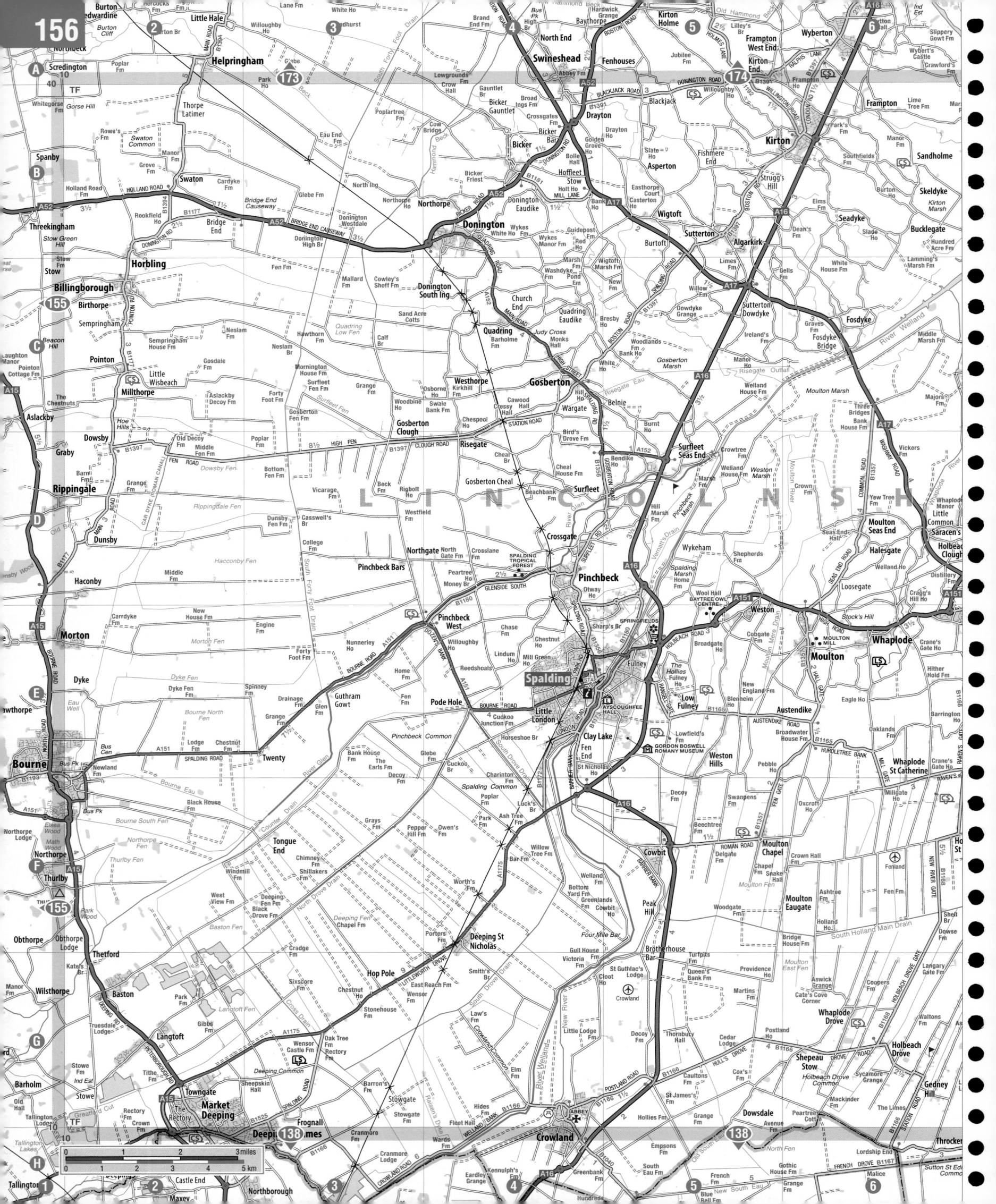

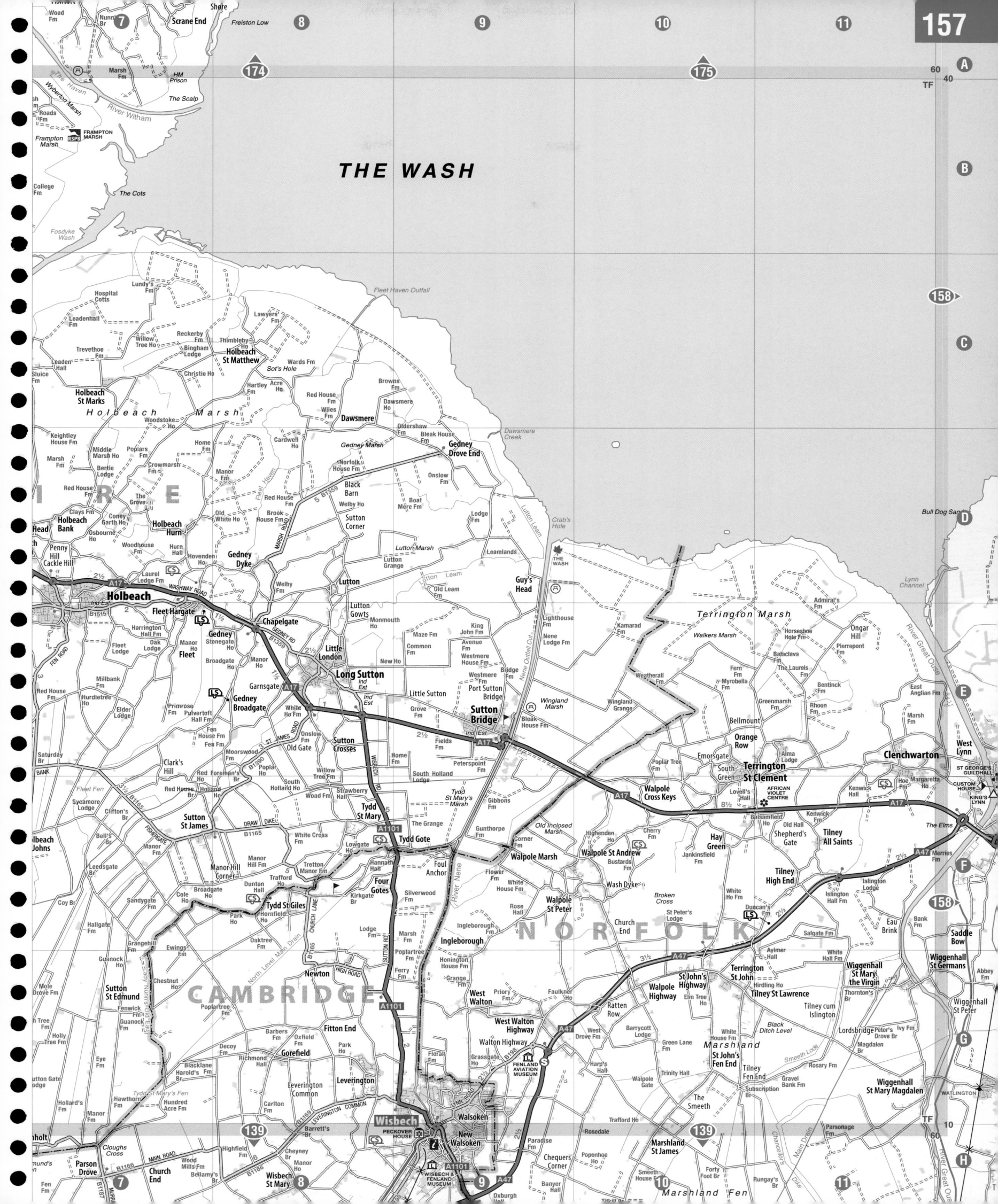

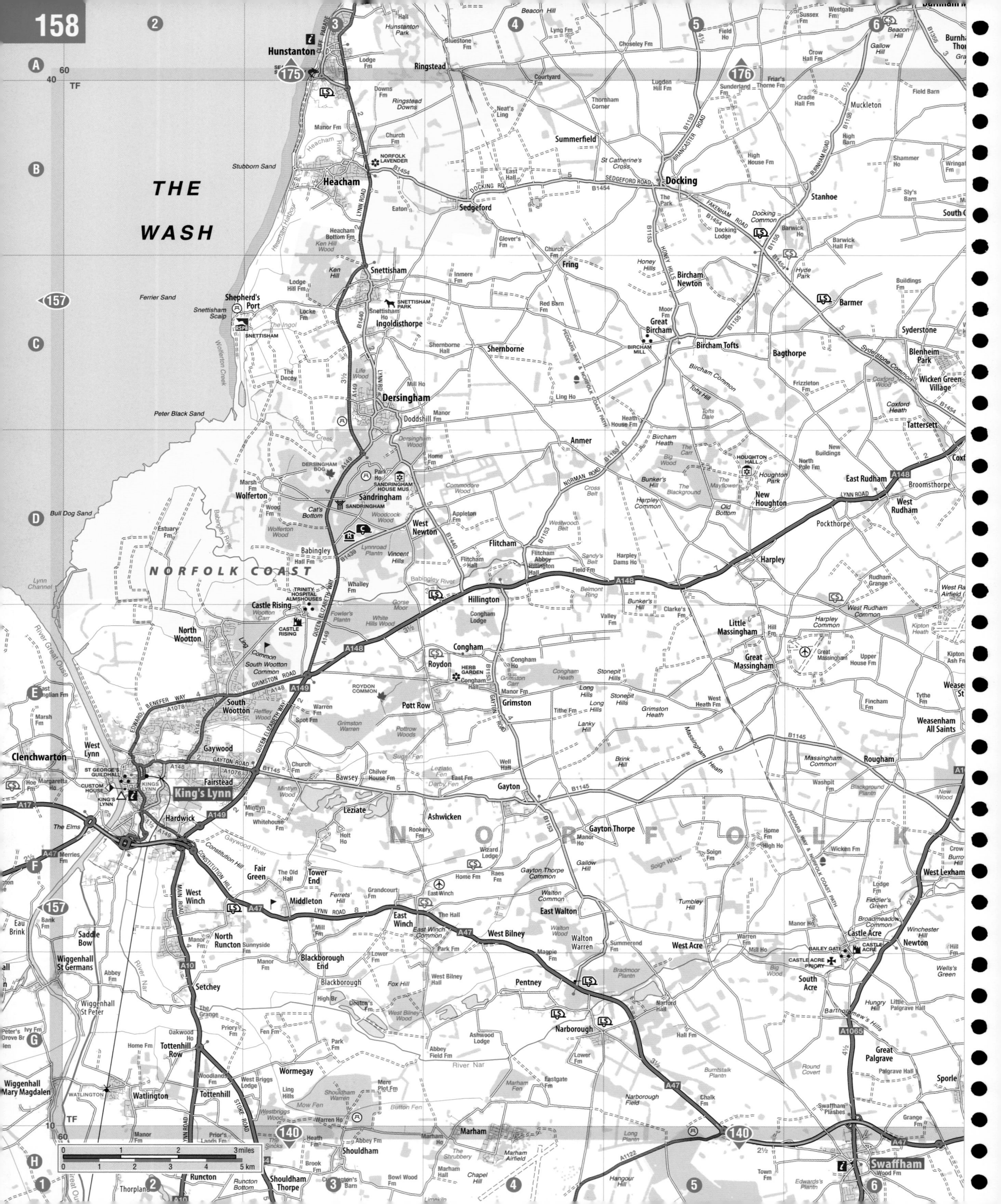

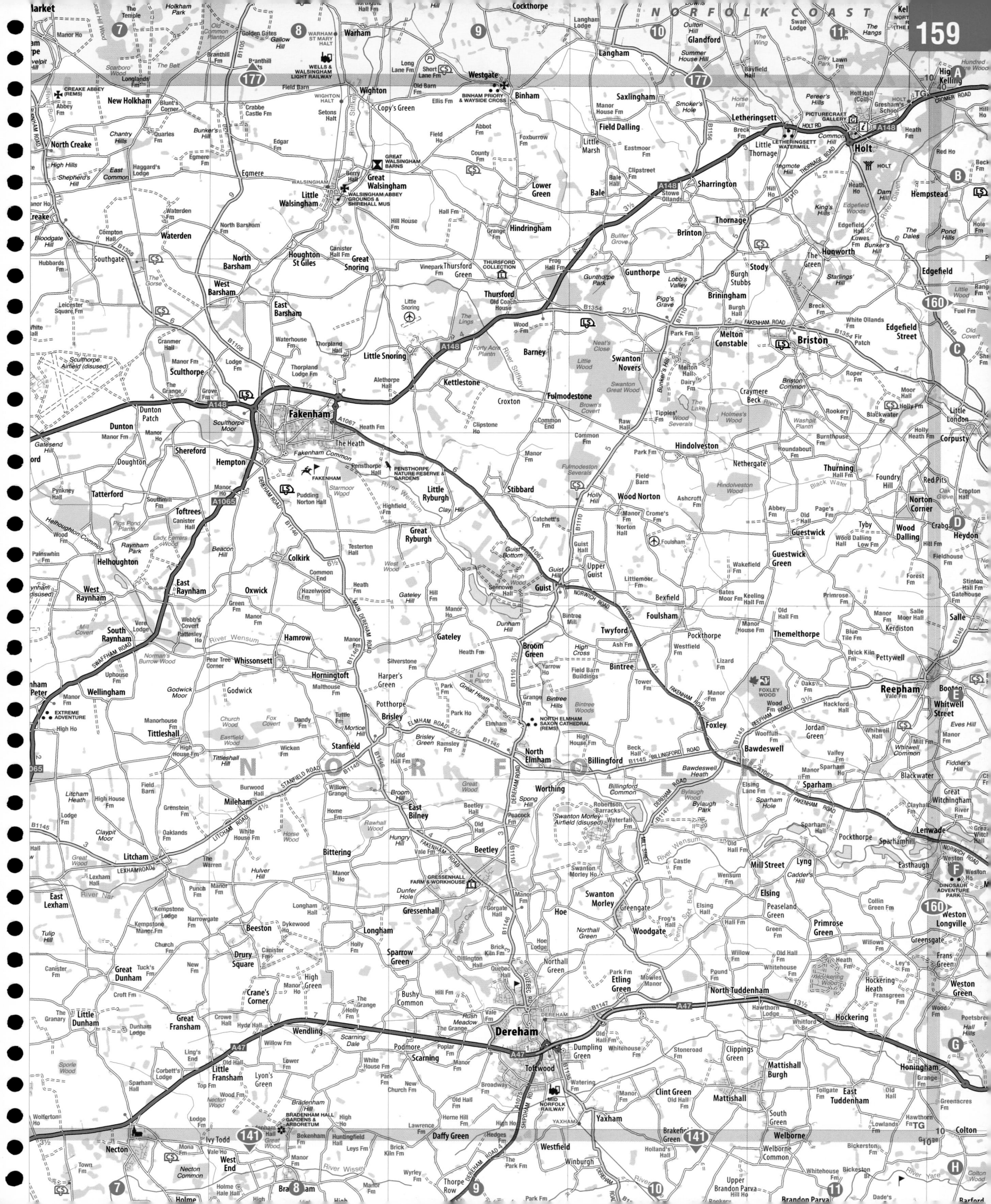

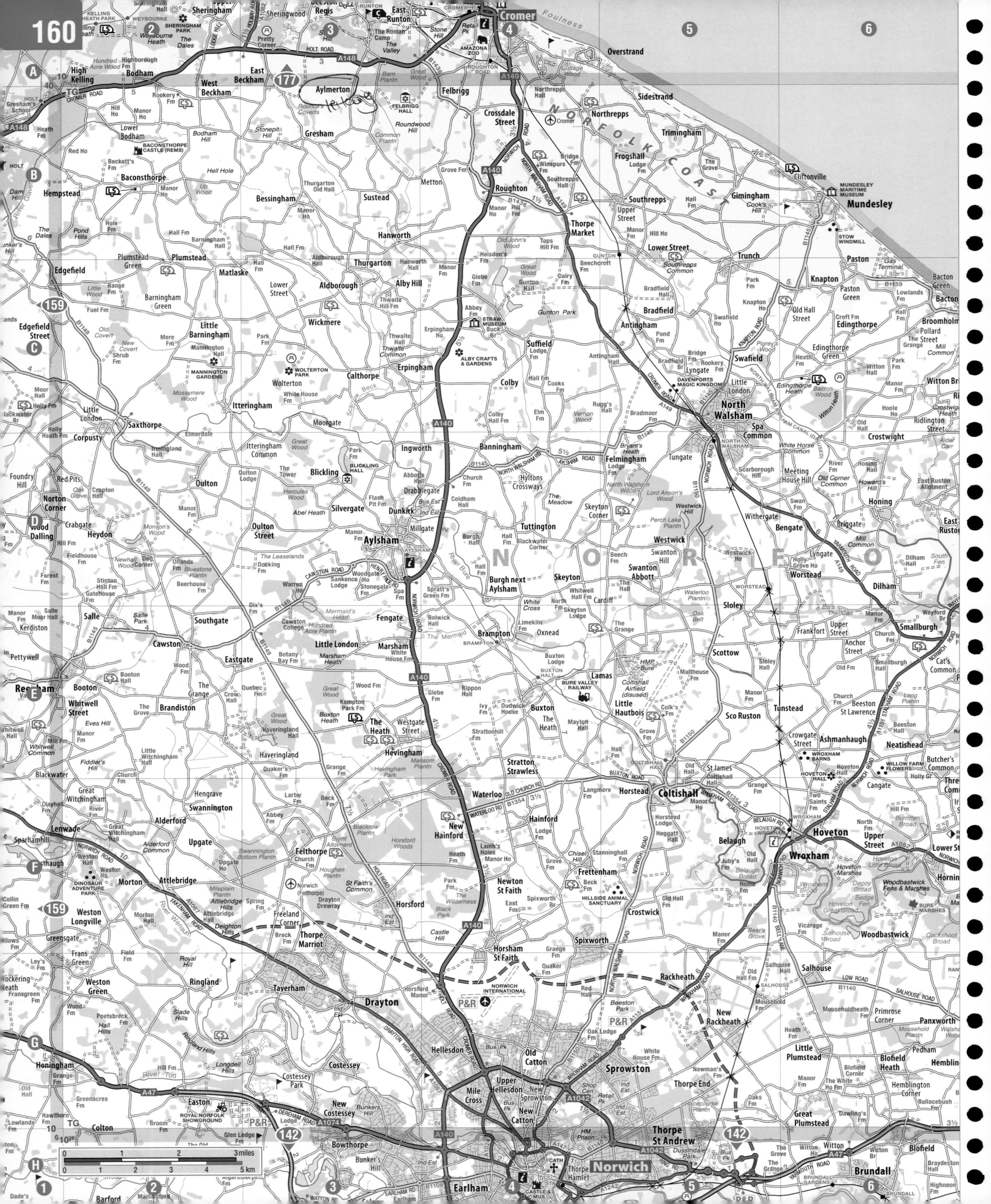

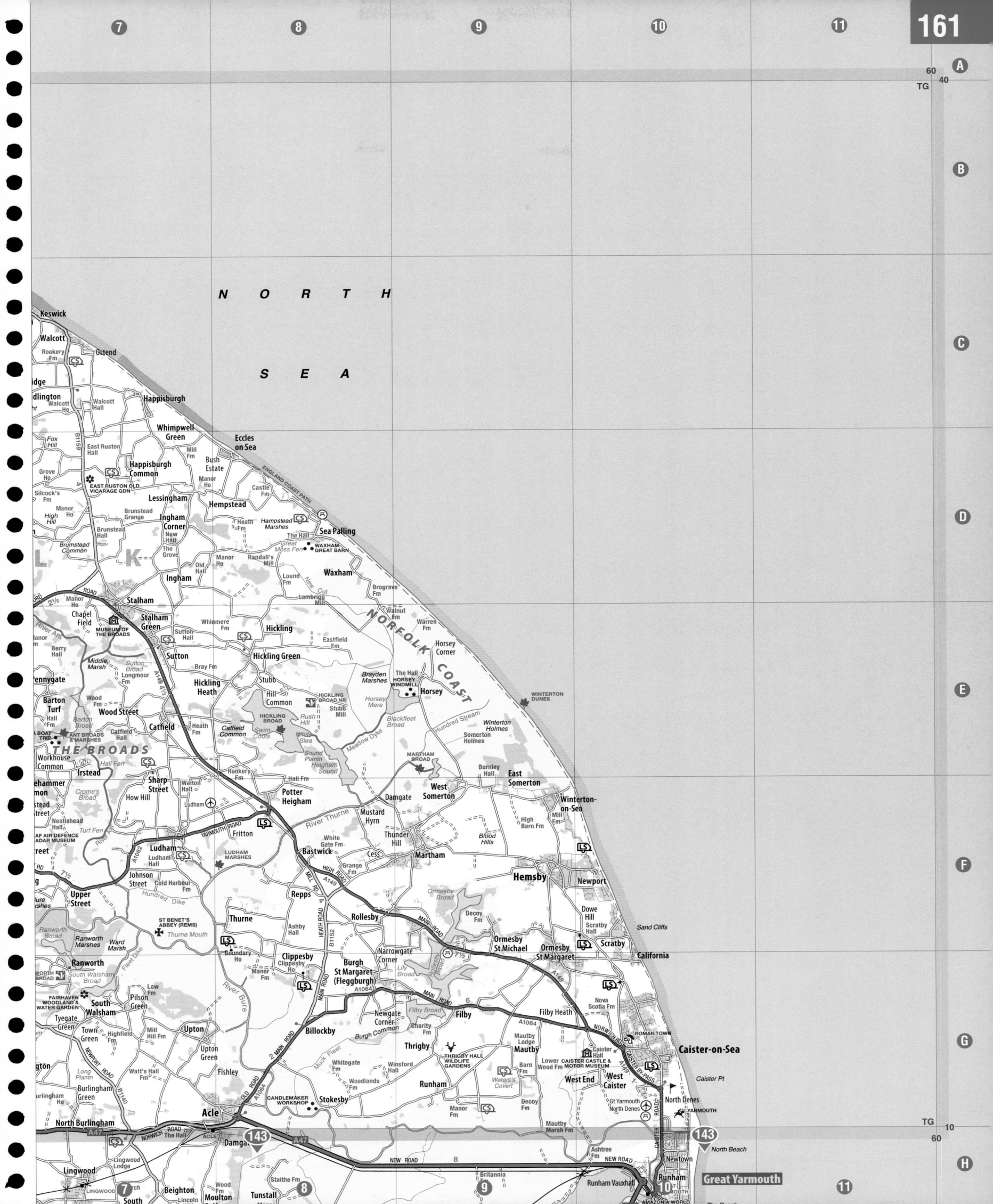

A
60
40
TG

B

N O R T H

Keswick
Walcott
Rookery
Fm
Ostend
C
idge
dlington
Walcott
Ho
Walcott
Hall

S E A

Happisburgh
Fox
Hill
East Ruston
Hall
Whimpwell
Green
Eccles
on Sea
Grove
Ho
Mill
Fm
Bush
Estate
Silcock's
Fm
Happisburgh
Common
EAST RUSTON OLD
VICARAGE GDN
Manor
Ho
Castle
Fm
ENGLAND COAST PATH
Manor
High
Hill
Brunstead
Grange
Lessingham
Hempstead
Hampstead
Marshes
D
Brunstead
Hall
Ingham
Corner
New
Hall
Heath
Fm
The Hall
Sea Palling
Brunstead
Common
The
Grove
Old
Hall
Manor
Ho
Randall's
Mill
Great
Moss Fen
WAXHAM
GREAT BARN
L   K
Ingham
Waxham
 D ROAD
Manor
Ho
2½
Stalham
Lound
Fm
New
Cut
Brograve
Fm
Lambrigg
Mill
Chapel
Field
Stalham
Green
Whimmere
Hickling
Eastfield
Fm
Walnut
Fm
NORFOLK COAST
anor
Berry
Hall
MUSEUM
OF THE BROADS
Sutton
Hall
Warren
Fm
River Ant
Sutton
Hickling Green
Horsey
Corner
ennygate
Middle
Marsh
Sutton
Broad
Longmoor
Bray Fn
Stubb
Brayden
Marshes
The Hall
HORSEY
WINDMILL
Horsey
E
Barton
Turf
Hall
Wood
Fm
Hickling
Heath
Hill
Common
HICKLING
BROAD NR
Stubb
Mill
WINTERTON
DUNES
Wood Street
HICKLING
BROAD
Horsey
Mere
Rush
Hill
White
Slea
Catfield
Heath
Fm
Catfield
Common
Swim
Coots
Blackfleet
Broad
Winterton
Holmes
BOAT
TREE
Barton
Broad
Catfield
Hall
Sound
Slea
Meadow Dyke
Hundred Stream
Somerton
Holmes
THE BROADS
Workhouse
Common
Hall Fen
Sound
Plantn
Heigham
Sound
MARTHAM
BROAD
Burnley
Hall
East
Somerton
ehammer
mon
Irstead
Crome's
Broad
Sharp
Street
Walton
Hall
Rookery
Fm
Hall Fm
West
Somerton
Winterton-
on-Sea
stead
reet
Neatishead
Hall
How Hill
Ludham
Potter
Heigham
Damgate
High
Barn Fm
Turf Fen
River Thurne
Mustard
Hyrn
F
RAF AIR DEFENCE
RADAR MUSEUM
Fritton
White
Gate Fm
Cess
Thunder
Hill
Blood
Hills
reet
Ludham
YARMOUTH ROAD
Grange
Fm
Martham
7½
Ludham
Hall
LUDHAM
MARSHES
Bastwick
Hemsby
Newport
Upper
Street
Johnson
Street
Cold Harbour
Repps
RD
Hundred Dike
MILL RD
A149
Ormesby
Broad
Decoy
Fm
Dowe
Hill
Scratby
Hall
ure
rshes
St BENET'S
ABBEY (REMS)
Thurne
Ashby
Hall
Rollesby
Sand Cliffs
Ranworth
Broad
Ward Marsh
Thurne Mouth
HEATH ROAD
Narrowgate
Corner
R   7½
Ormesby
St Michael
Scratby
Ranworth
Ranworth
Marshes
Boundary
Ho
Clippesby
Clippesby
Ho
MAIN ROAD
B1152
Ormesby
St Margaret
California
RWORTH
BROAD
South Walsham
Broad
Manor
Fm
Burgh
St Margaret
(Fleggburgh)
Lily
Broad
A149
Nova
Scotia Fm
FAIRHAVEN
WOODLAND &
WATER GARDEN
South
Walsham
Pilson
Green
MAIN ROAD
A1064
Newgate
Corner
Filby Broad
6
Filby
NORWICH
ROAD
Tyegate
Green
Town
Green
Highfield
Low
Fm
Mill
Hill Fm
River Bure
Charity
Fm
Filby Heath
ROMAN TOWN
Upton
Upton
Green
Billockby
Burgh
Common
Thrigby
THRIGBY HALL
WILDLIFE
GARDENS
Mautby
Lodge
Fm
Mautby
A1064
Caister
Hall
Lower CAISTER CASTLE &
Wood Fm MOTOR MUSEUM
Caister-on-Sea
G
gton
Long
Plantn
NEWPORT
ROAD
2 MAIN ROAD
Muck Fleet
Whitegate
Fm
Winsford
Hall
Barn
Fm
West End
West
Caister
Caister Pt
Burlingham
Green
B1140
Watt's
Hall
Fm
Fishley
OLD ROAD
Woodlands
Runham
Waters's
Covert
Decoy
Fm
North Denes
Gt Yarmouth
North Denes
North Beach
North Burlingham
A47
Acle
CANDLEMAKER
WORKSHOP
Stokesby
Manor
Fm
Mautby
Marsh Fm
GT YARMOUTH
TG
10
60
Lingwood
NORWICH ROAD
The Hall
ACLE
Damga
143
A47
Ashtree
Fm
NEW ROAD
CAISTER ROAD
Newtown
143
H
Lingwood
Lodge
NEW ROAD
8
Britannia
Runham Vauxhall
Runham
10
Great Yarmouth
11
South
Beighton
Lincoln
Wood
Fm
Tunstall
Staithe Fm
Moulton
AMAZONIA WORLD
7
8
9

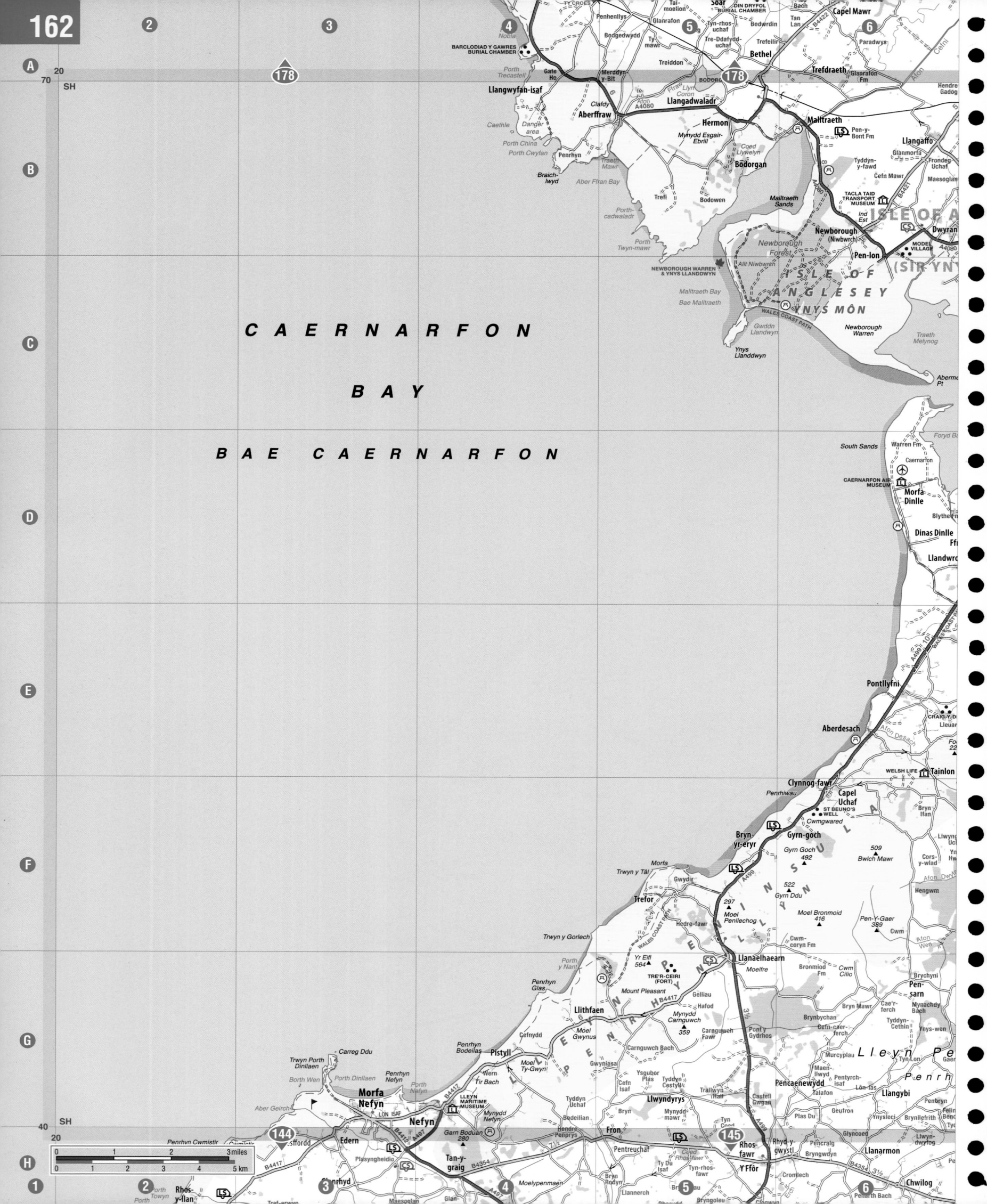

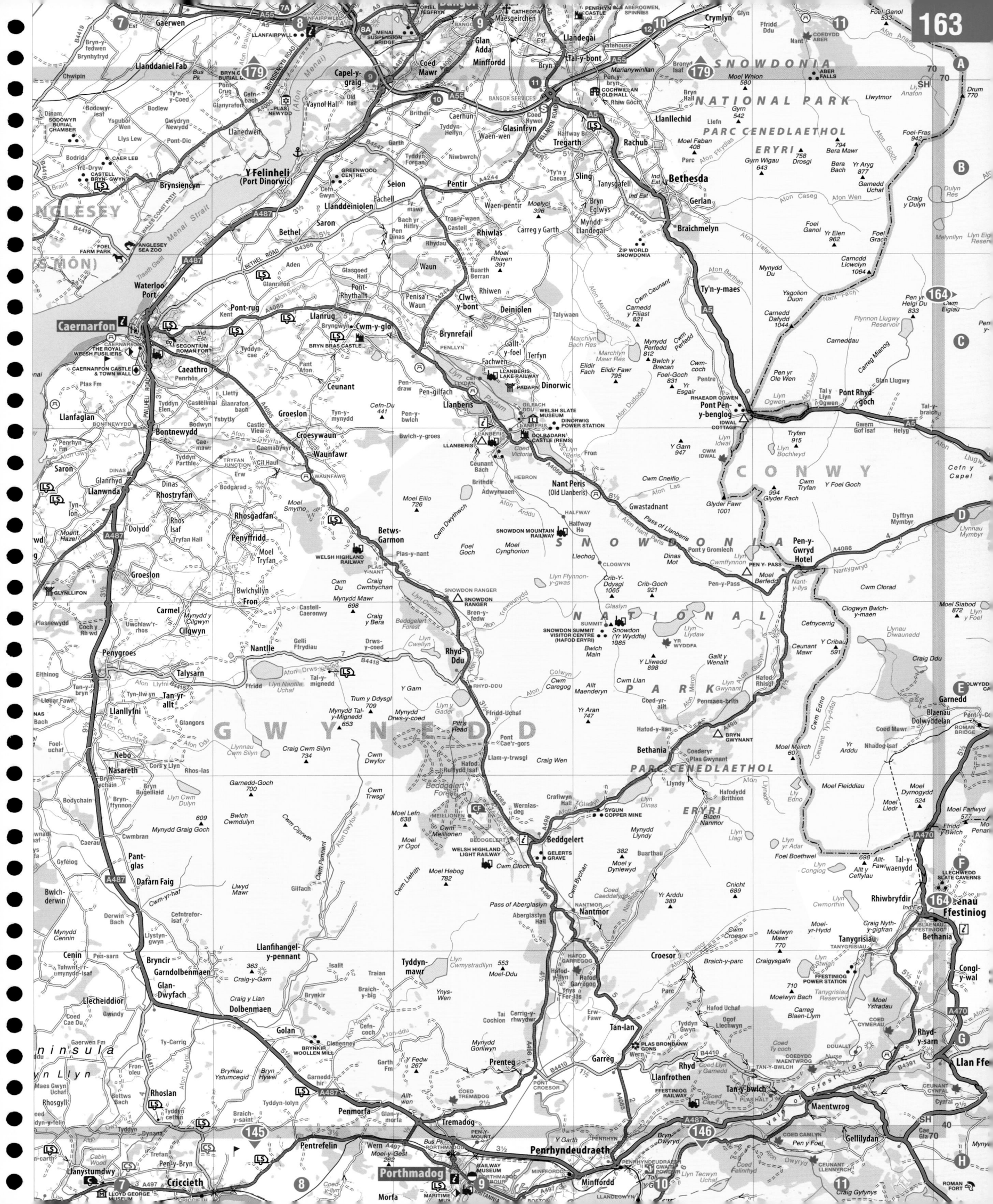

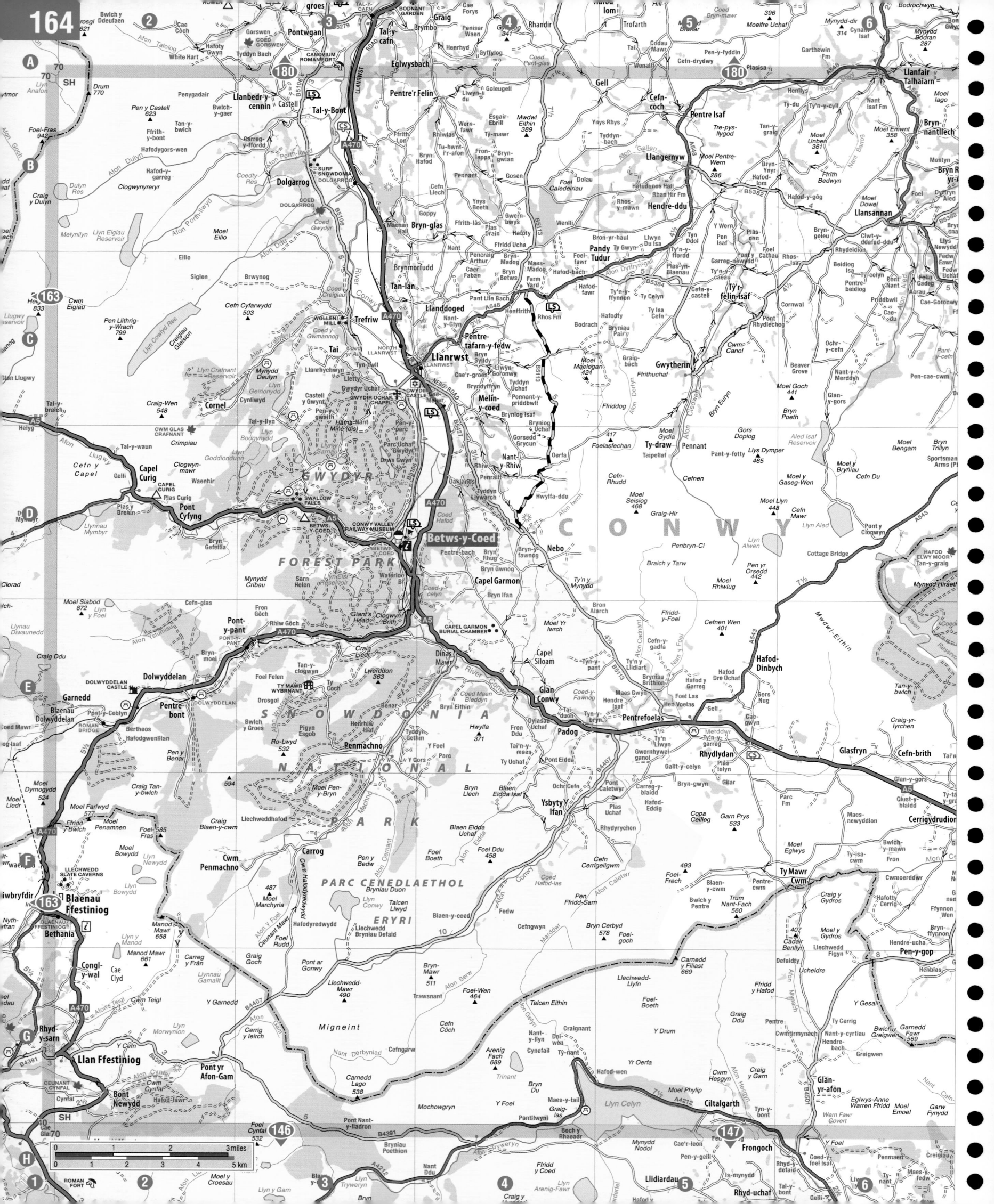

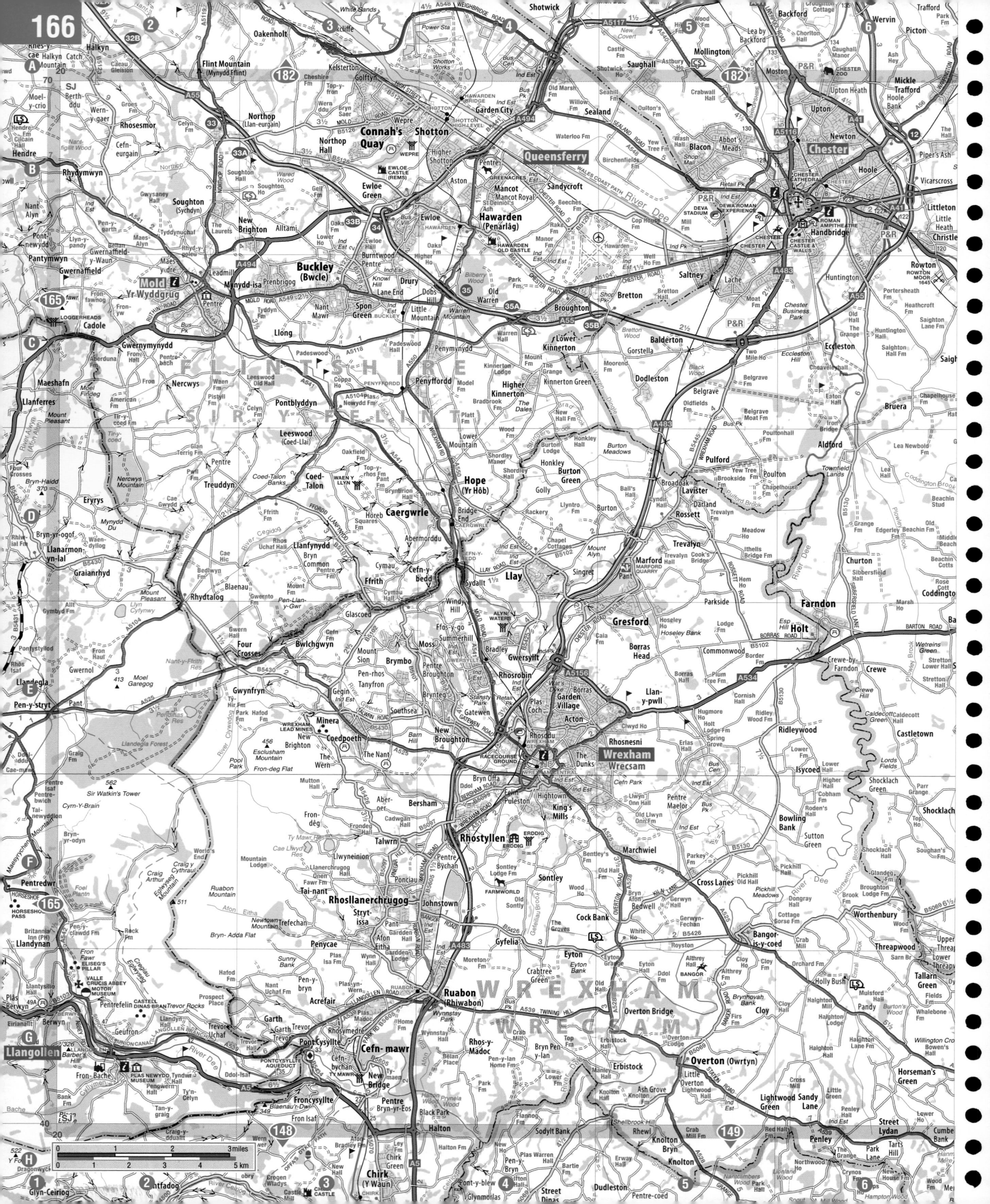

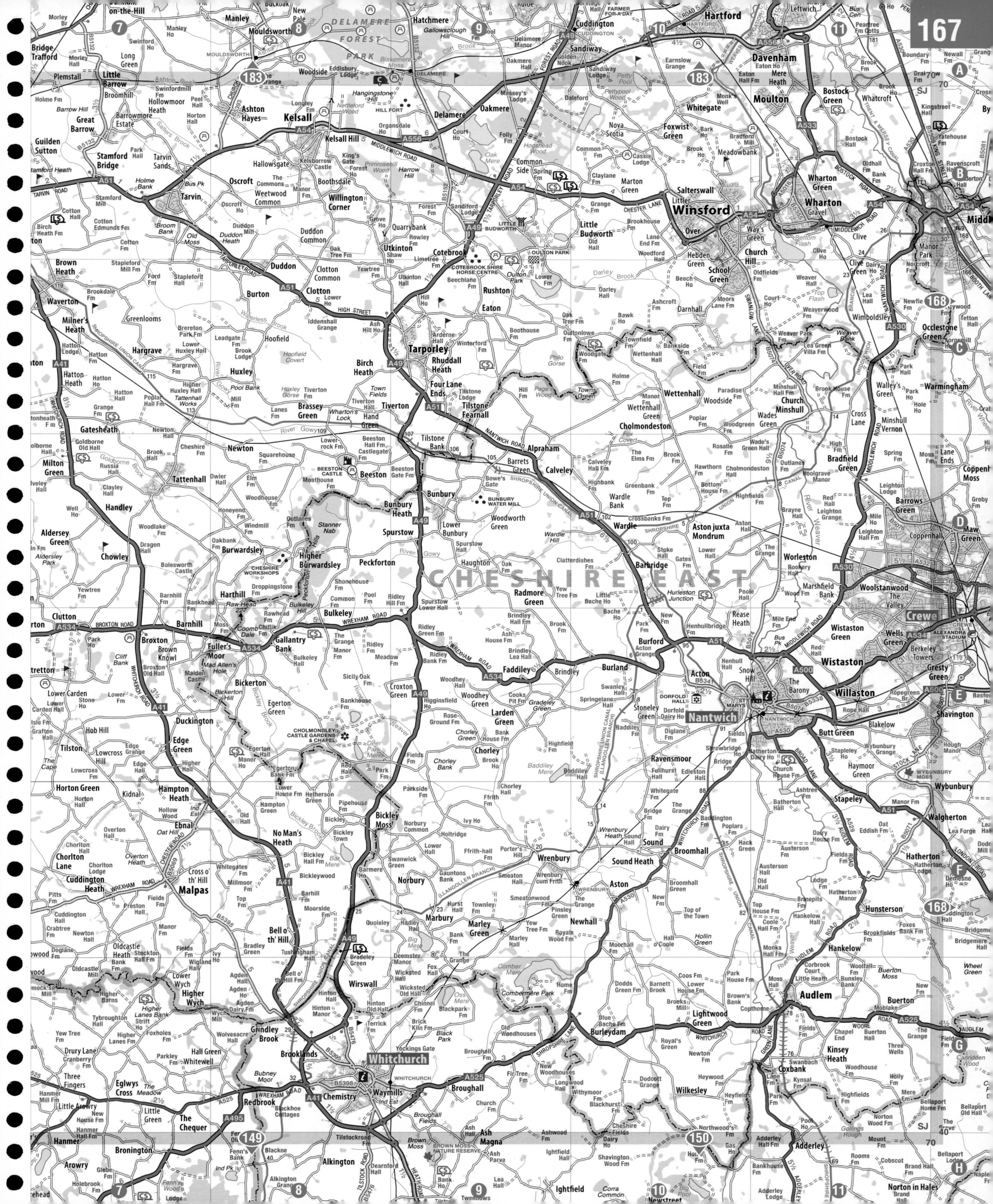

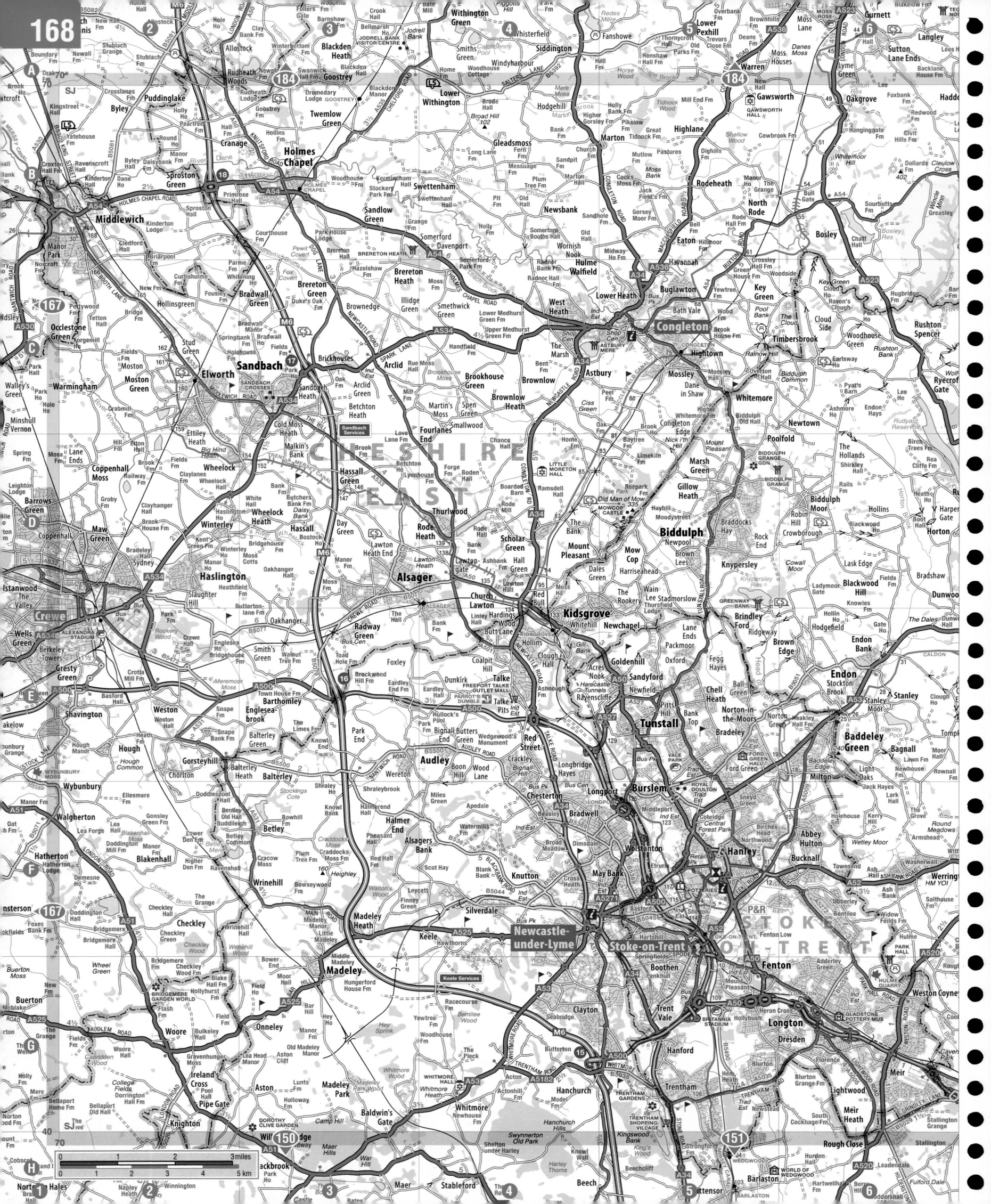

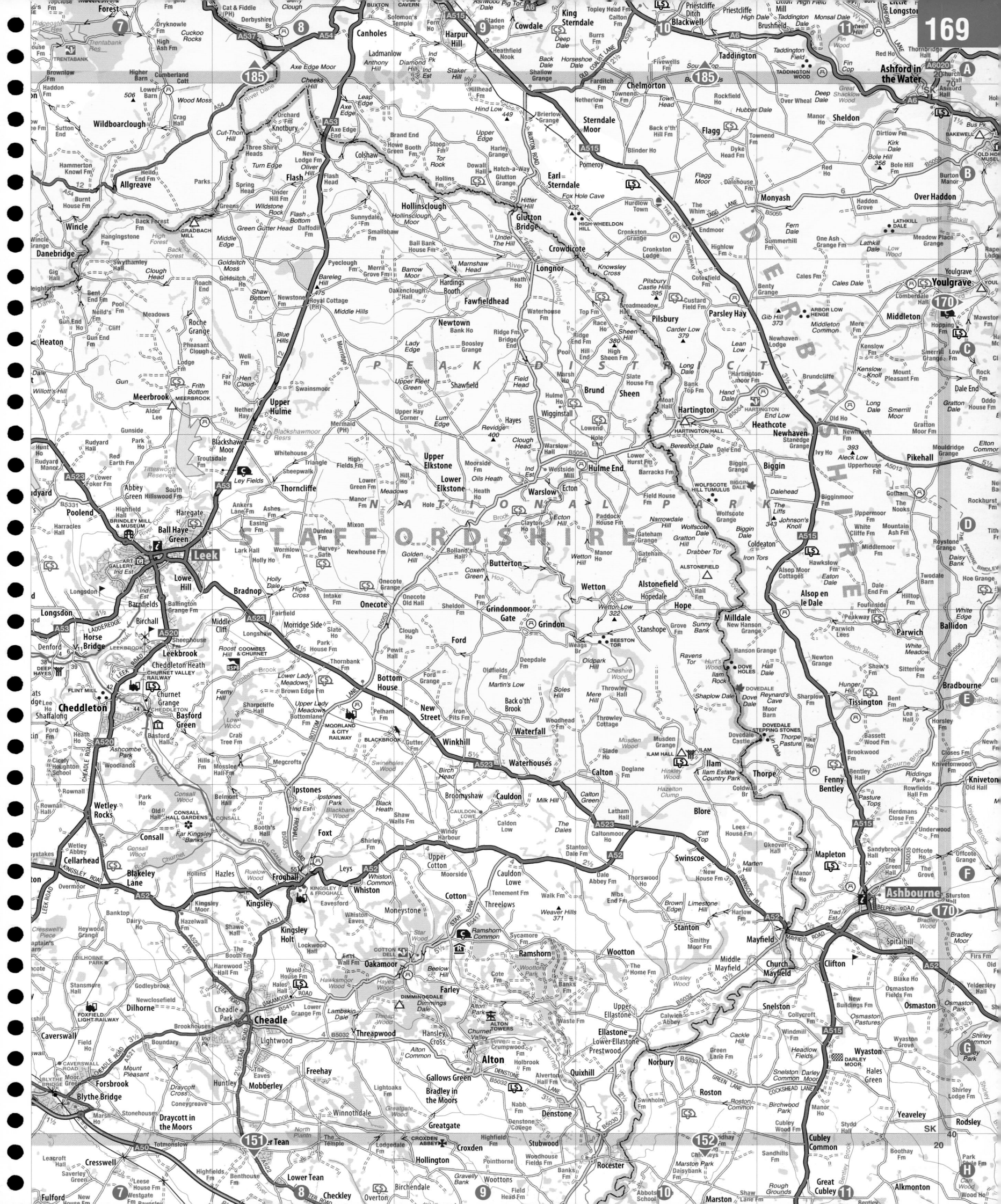

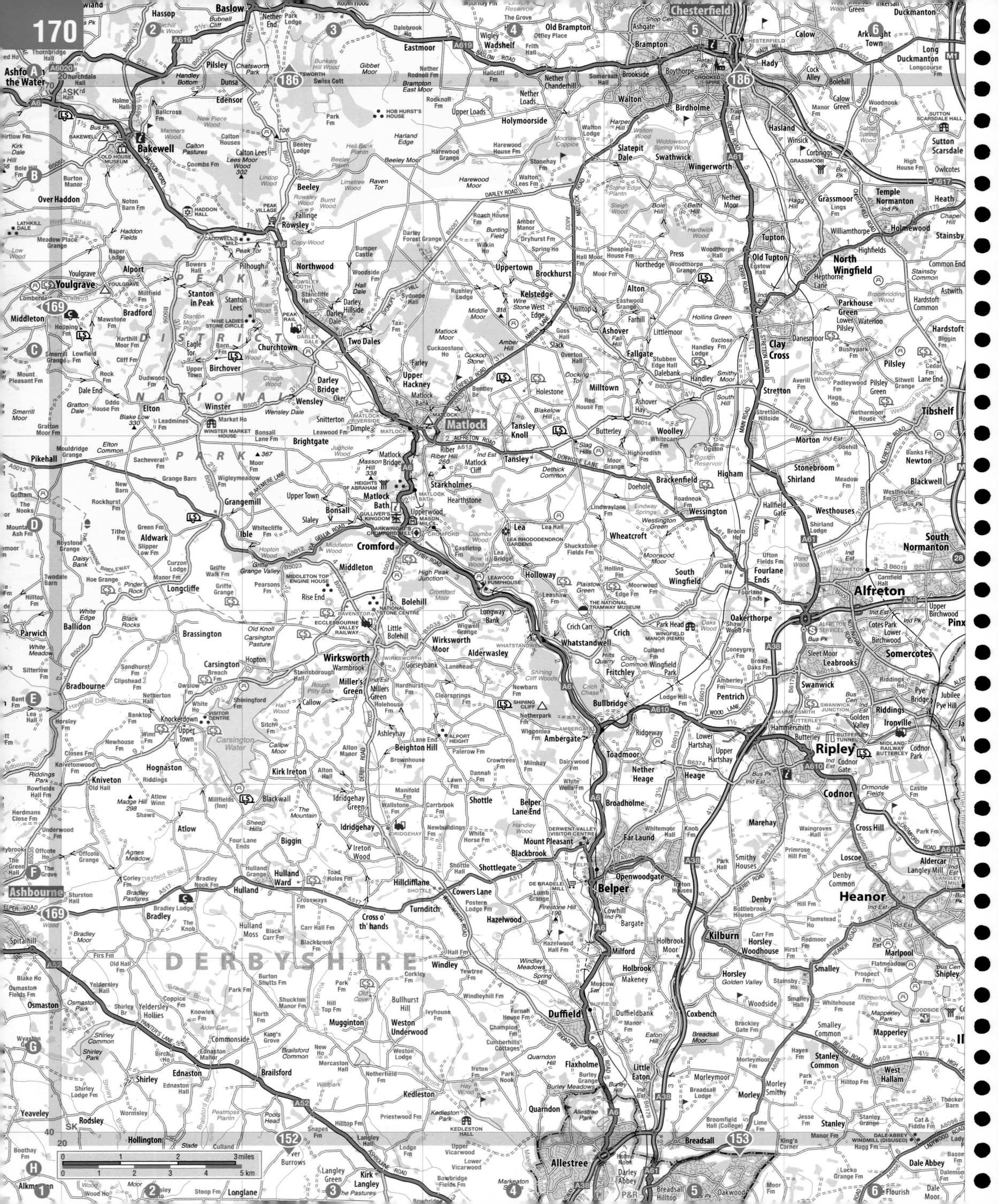

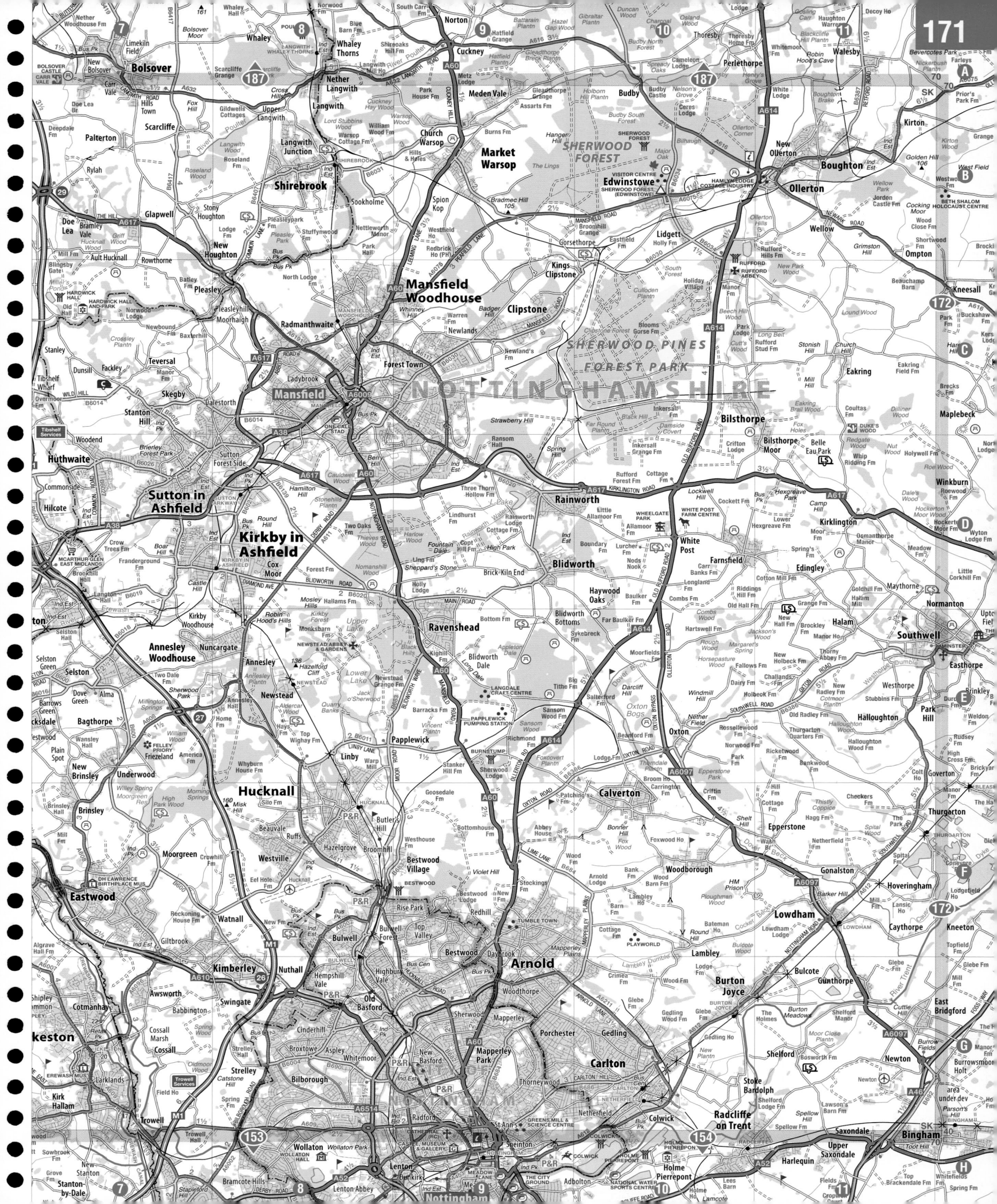

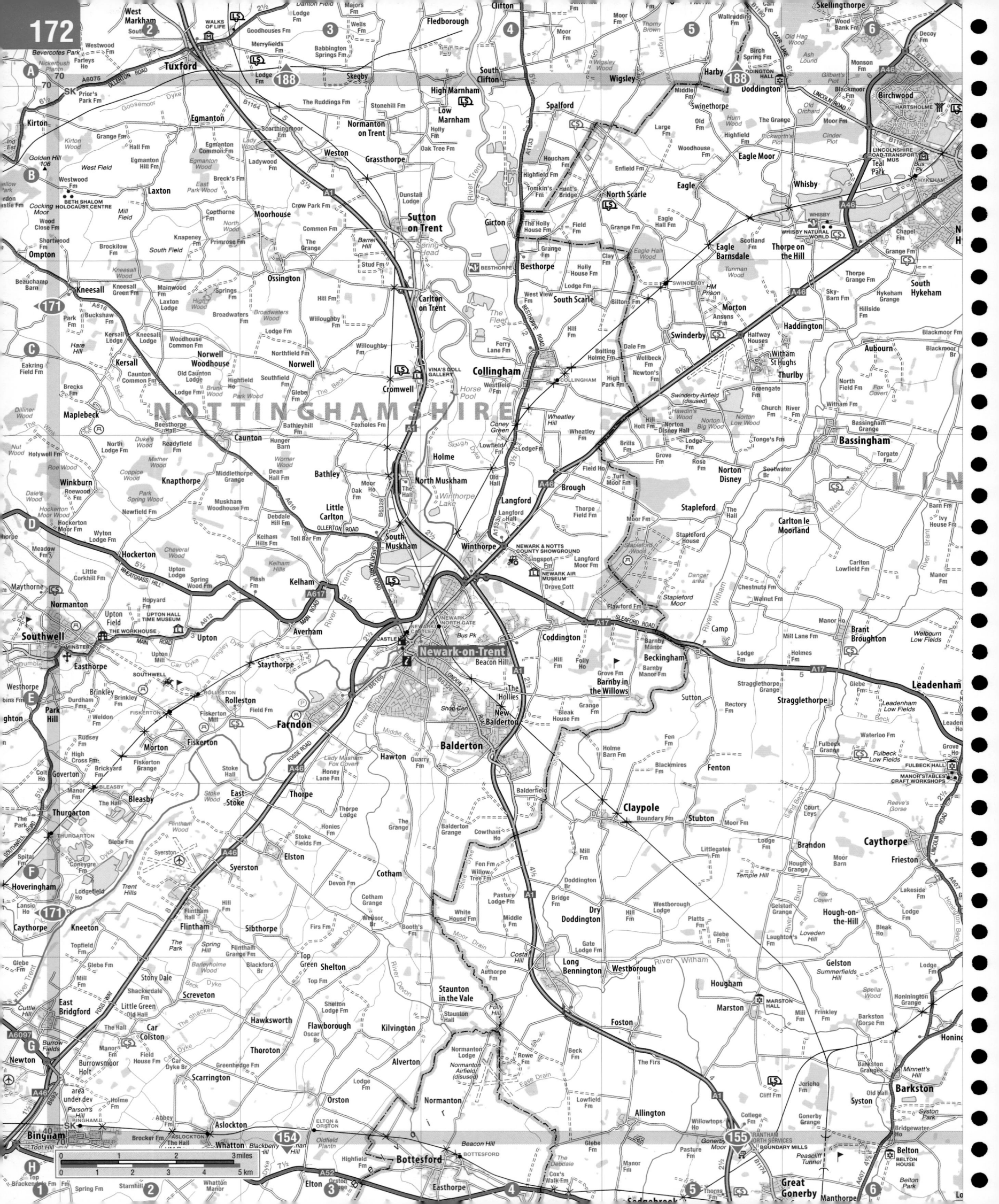

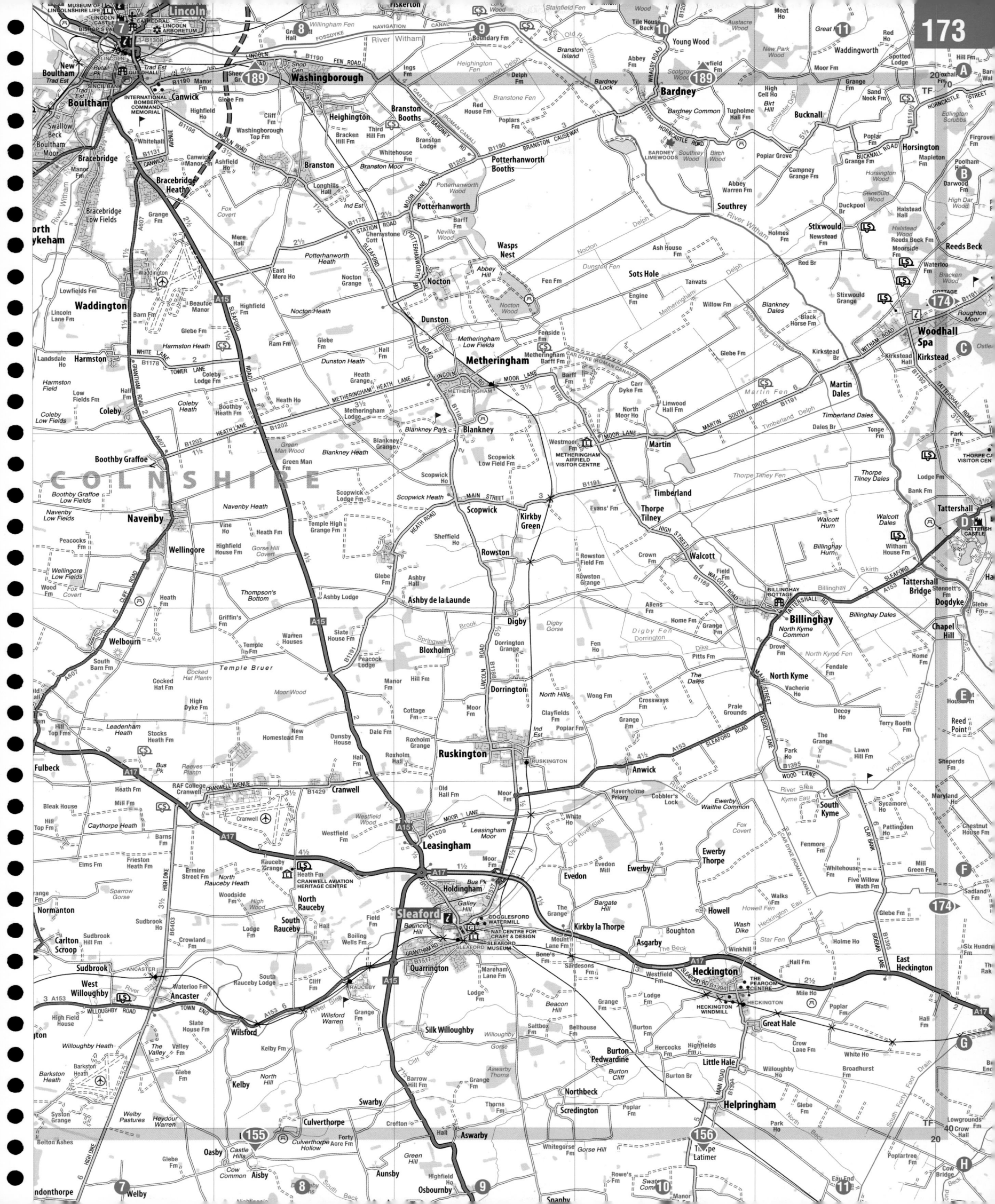

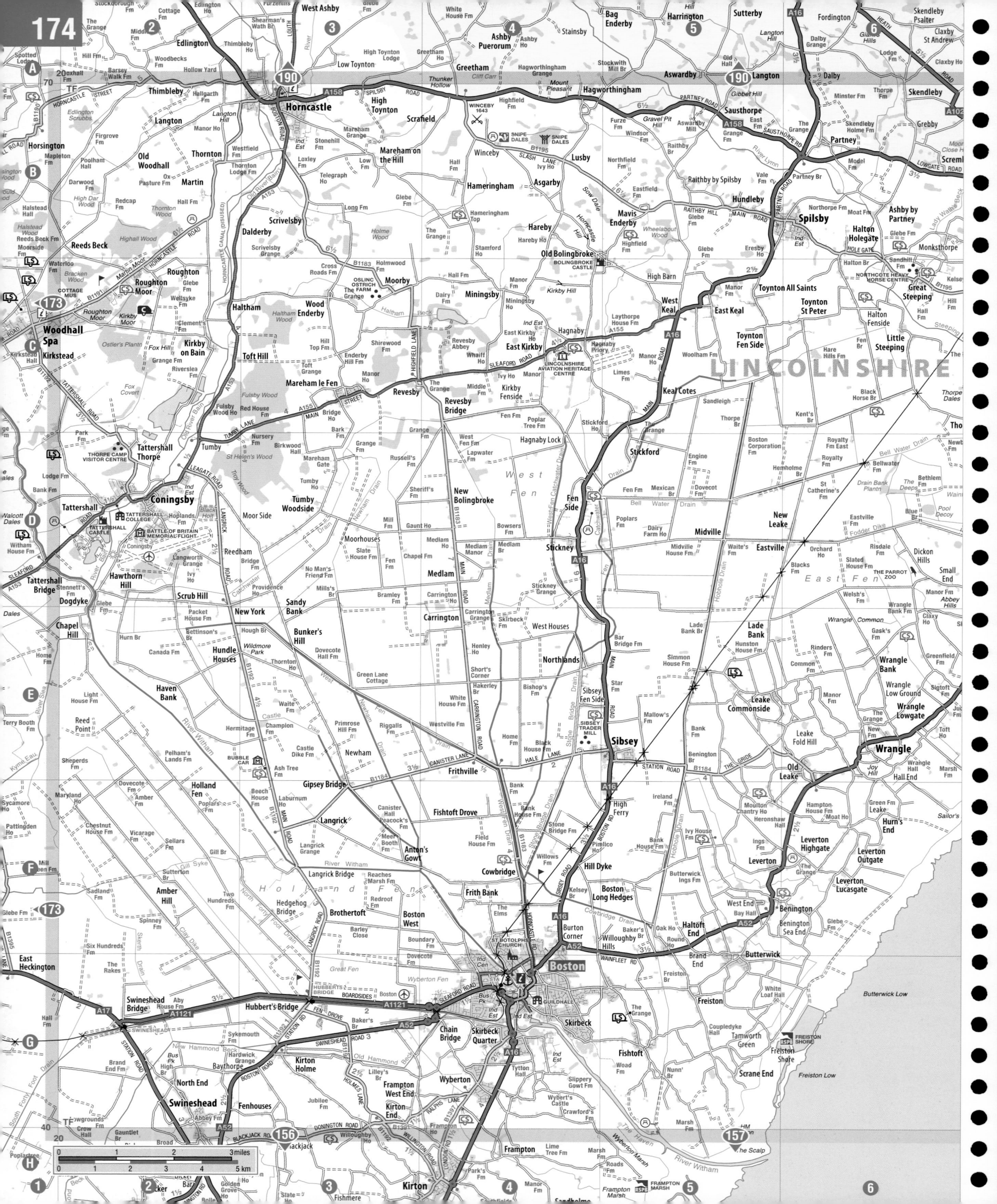

Willoughby

B1196

Listoft
Hogsthorpe

Chapel St Leonards

Poplar
Fm

7

8

9

10

11

A

191

191

70
70
TF

Claxby

Burlands Beck

Willoughby
High

A52

Sloothby

Welton
Low

Welton
High Wood

Hasthorpe

Howlet
Ho

Slackholme
End

Hope
Fm

Beeches
Fm

SKEGNESS ROAD

HARDY'S
ANIMAL FARM

Hogsbeck
Ho

Thwaite
Hall

Highfield Fm

BAKER'S LANE

Candlesby
Hill Rookery

Welton
le Marsh

Boothby
Hall

Habertoft

Addlethorpe

Ingoldmells

B

FANTASY ISLAND

Ingoldmells Pt

Candlesby

Boothby
Grange

Orby
Drn

Whitehouse
Fm

Corner
Fm

Manor
Fm

FUNCOAST
WORLD

Gunby

GUNBY HALL

Orby

Elmtree
Ho

Field Fm

3½

Fir Tree Fm

Teapot
Hall

Field
House Fm

A158

Home Fm

Ashington
End

Seathorne
Winthorpe

Glebe Fm

The Grange

Moat
House Fm

Elmstead
Fm

Willow
Lodge

Black
House Fm

Hunger
Hill

Burgh
le Marsh

Mill Hill

ROMAN BANK

A52

Bratoft

BURGH LE MARSH
WINDMILL

SKEGNESS ROAD

3½

South View

Firsby

9½

Moat
Fm

Bratoft
Corner

A158

Irby in the
Marsh

End House
Fm

Lloyd's Fm

Croft End

Middlemarsh
Fm

THE VILLAGE
CHURCH FARM

BURGH LINCOLN ROAD

Skegness

NATURELAND
SEAL SANCTUARY

B1195

Catchwater Drain

Grove
House Fm

Rookery Fm

WAINFLEET ROAD

SKEGNESS

THE LIFEBOAT
STATION MUSEUM

River

The Hundreds

Rivulet Ho

Church
Fm

Marsh
Fm

A52

C

Croft

5½

Oak Br

Croft Marsh

Croft
Grange

Seacroft

Thorpe
Culvert

THORPE
CULVERT

Lymn
Bank Fm

Poplar
Fm

CROFT BANK

Bank Ho

Kitchen's
Yard

Clough
House Fm

Bramble Hills

Thorpe St Peter

WAINFLEET

Crown Fm

Croft
Ho

New Yard
Fm

Wainfleet
Clough

Cow Bank Drain

rpe Fendykes

bridge

Wainfleet Common

Crow's
Br

New
England

White
House Fm

Steeping River

GIBRALTAR
POINT

Wainfleet
Bank

MAGDALEN
MUSEUM

WAINFLEET

Wainfleet
All Saints

Merrifield's

Marsh Farm
East

GIBRALTAR
POINT

White Cross
Clough

et St Mary Fen

BOSTON ROAD

Wainfleet Tofts

Wainfleet St Mary

GIBRALTAR
POINT NNR

D

Decoy
Fm

Pepperthorpe
Hall

Toft
House Fm

Outmarsh
Yard

Gibraltar Point

Decoy Wood

Ivy
Ho

Hall
Fm

Wainfleet
Harbour

Avenue
Fm

Friskney
Eaudyke

Wainfleet
Sand

Inner Knock

Friskney

New Marsh

Fold
Hill

urlmore
Ho

MAIN ROAD

E

Friskney Tofts

Greens
Marsh

Friskney Flats

A52

8

Whitehouse
Fm

egate

East
Toft Fm

Toftbouse
Fm

The Horseshoe

F

Home

Wrangle Flats

Gore Pt

HOLME
DUNES

HOLME BIRD
OBSERVATORY

NORFOLK COAST PATH

Holme next
the Sea

Old Hunstanton

PEDDARS WAY

Manor
Ho

G

St Edmund's Pt

4½

THE WASH

Hunstanton

Lodge
Fm

Ringstead

CLIFF PARADE

Hunstanton
Park

TF
40
70

SEA LIFE
SANCTUARY

Downs
Fm

Ringstead
Downs

157

158

H

Manor Fm

Church

7

8

9

10

11

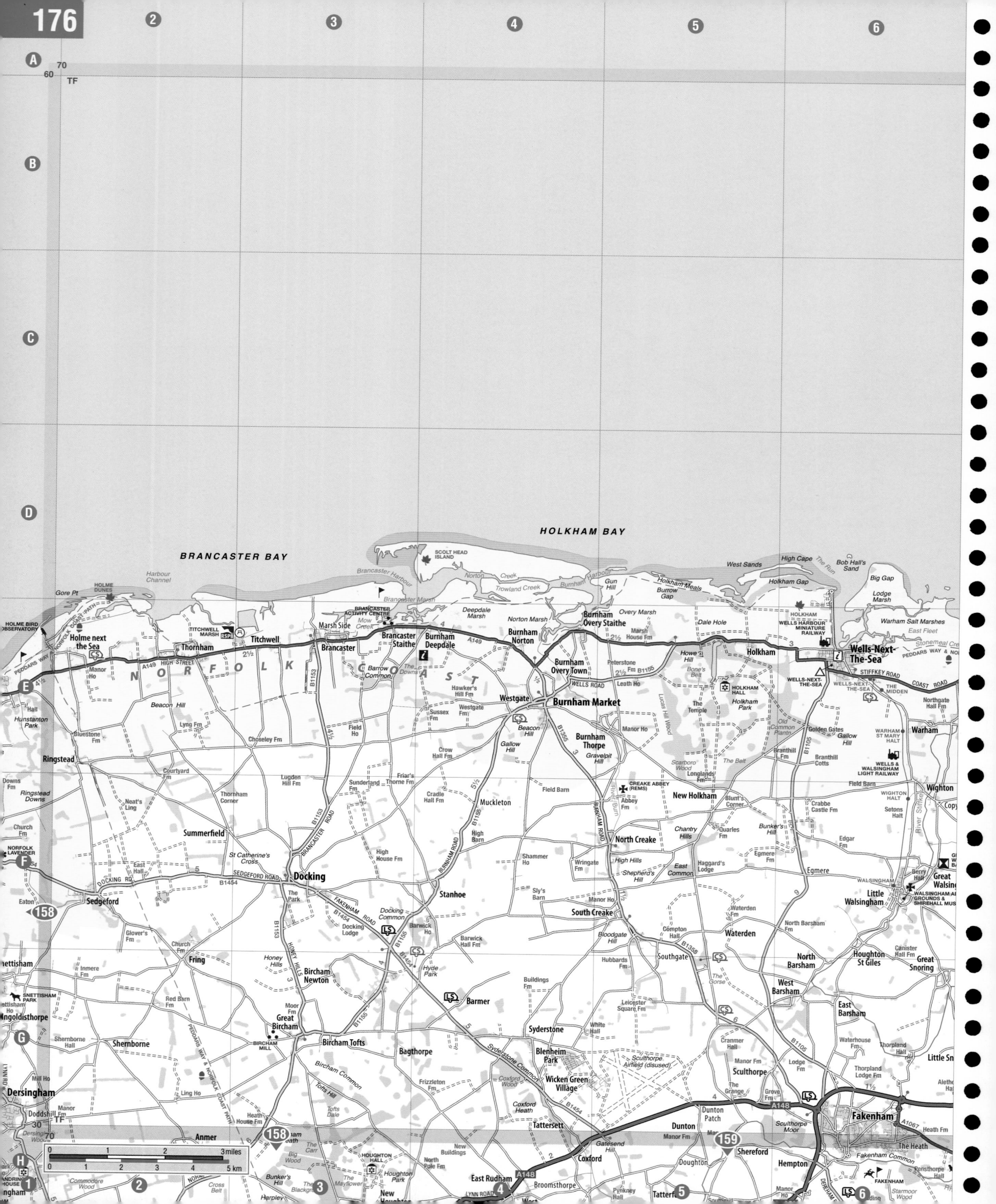

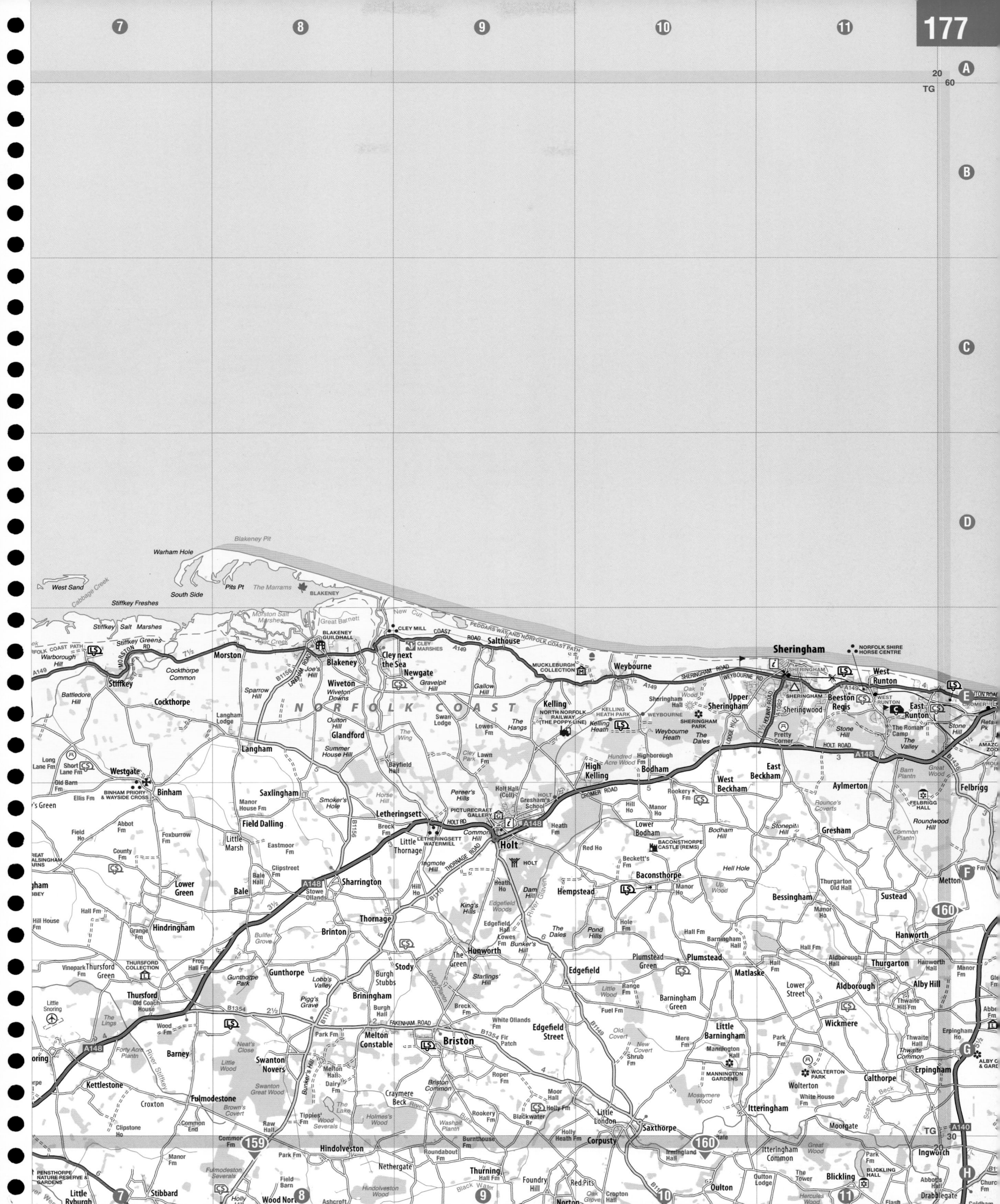

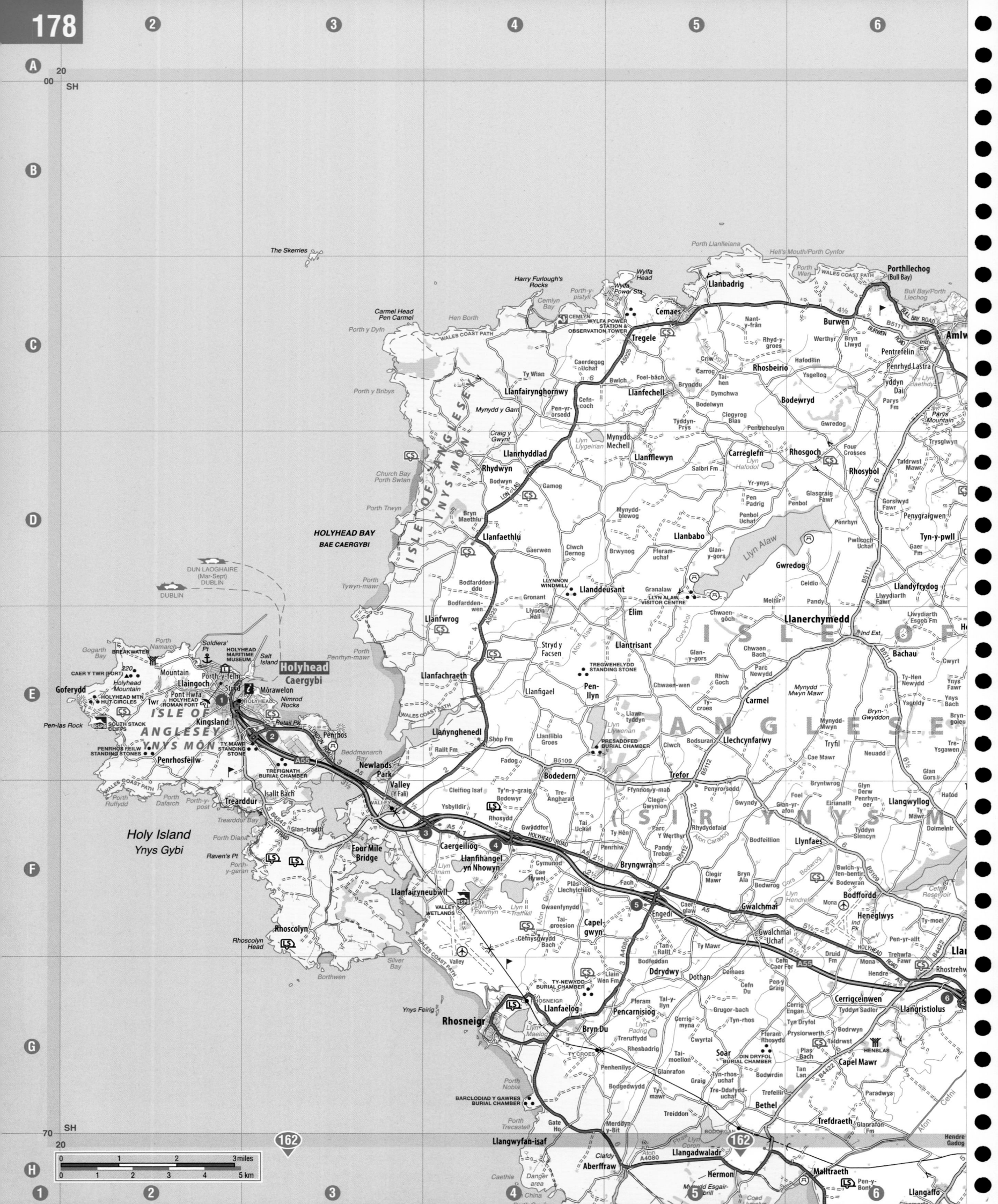

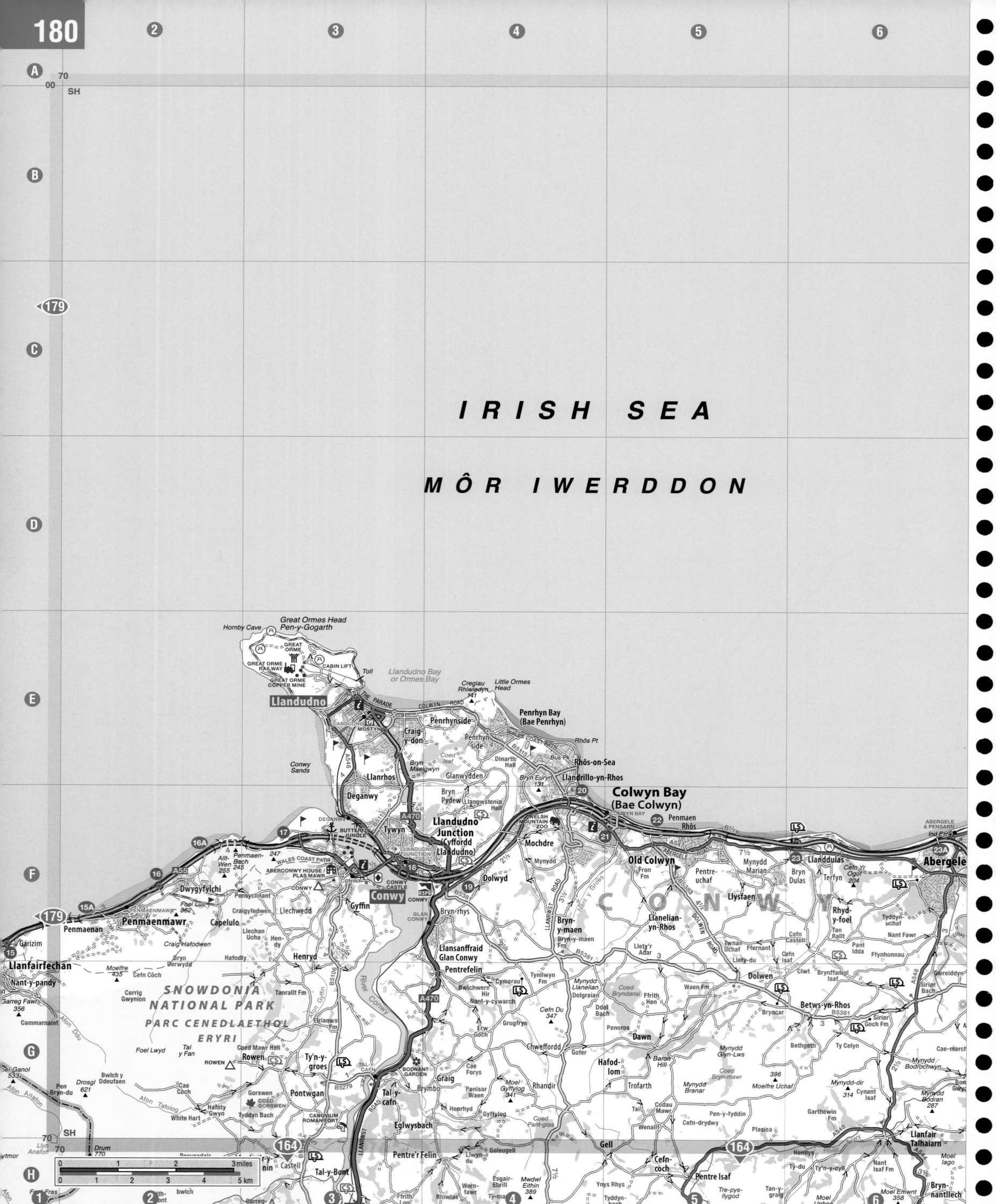

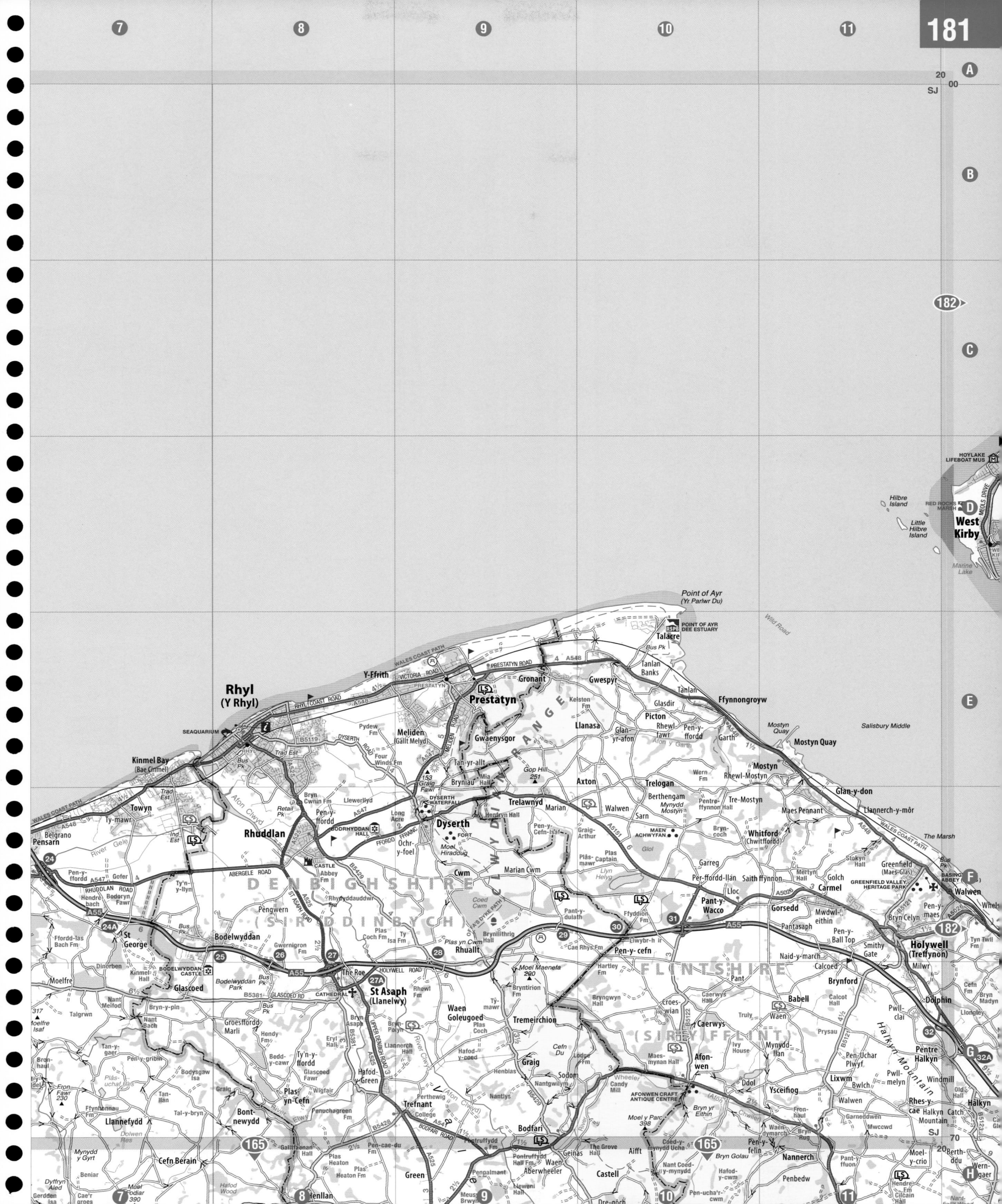

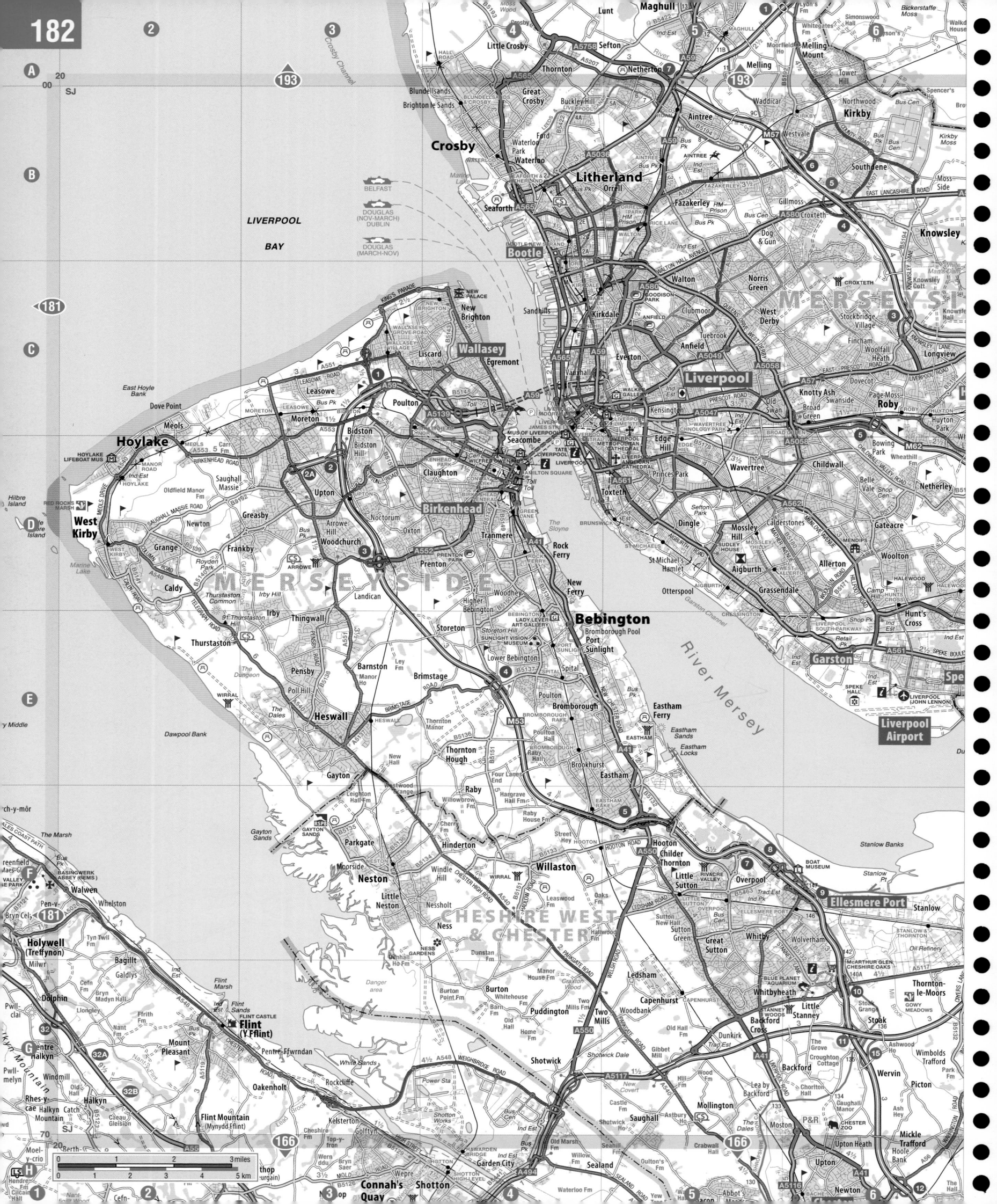

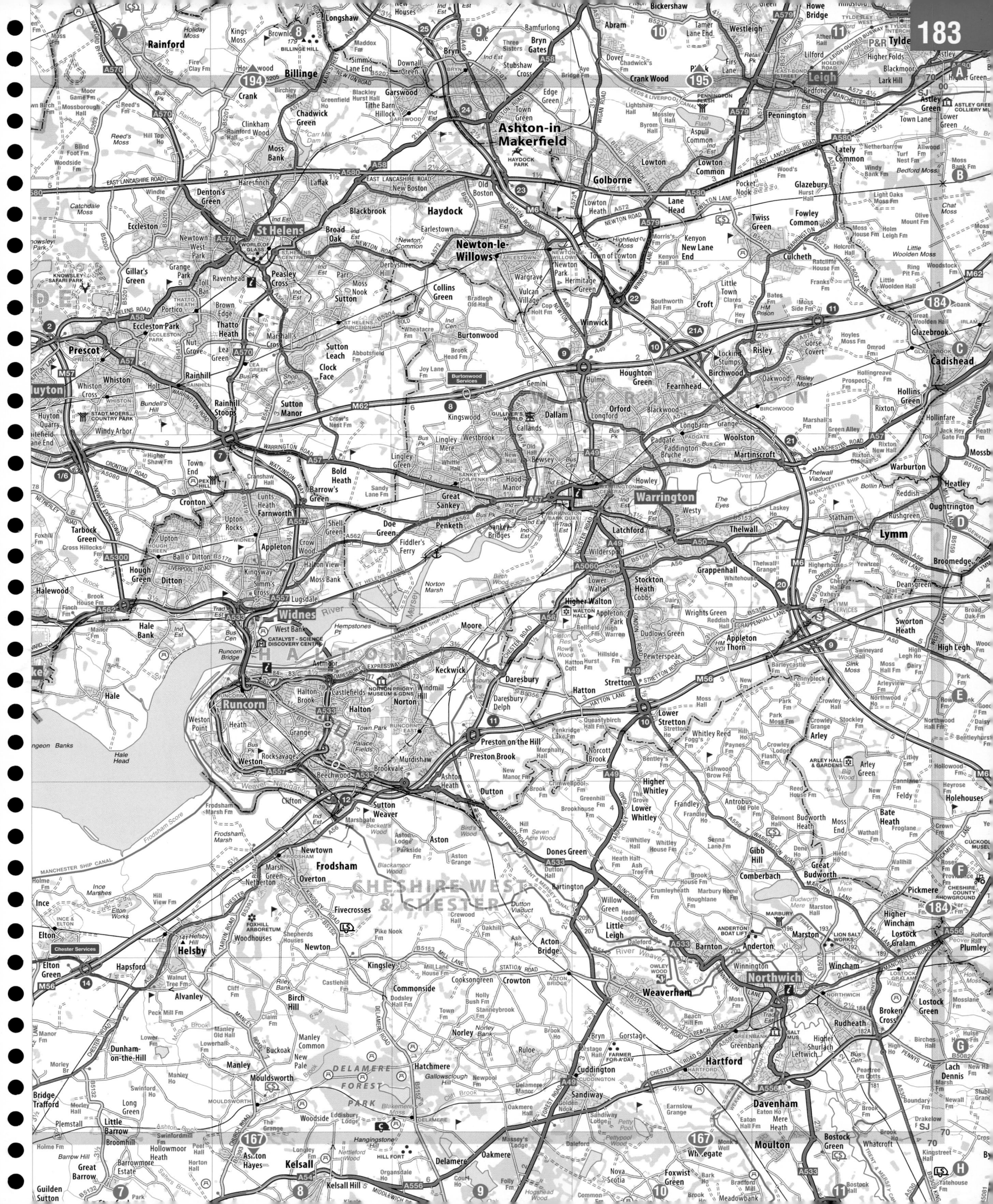

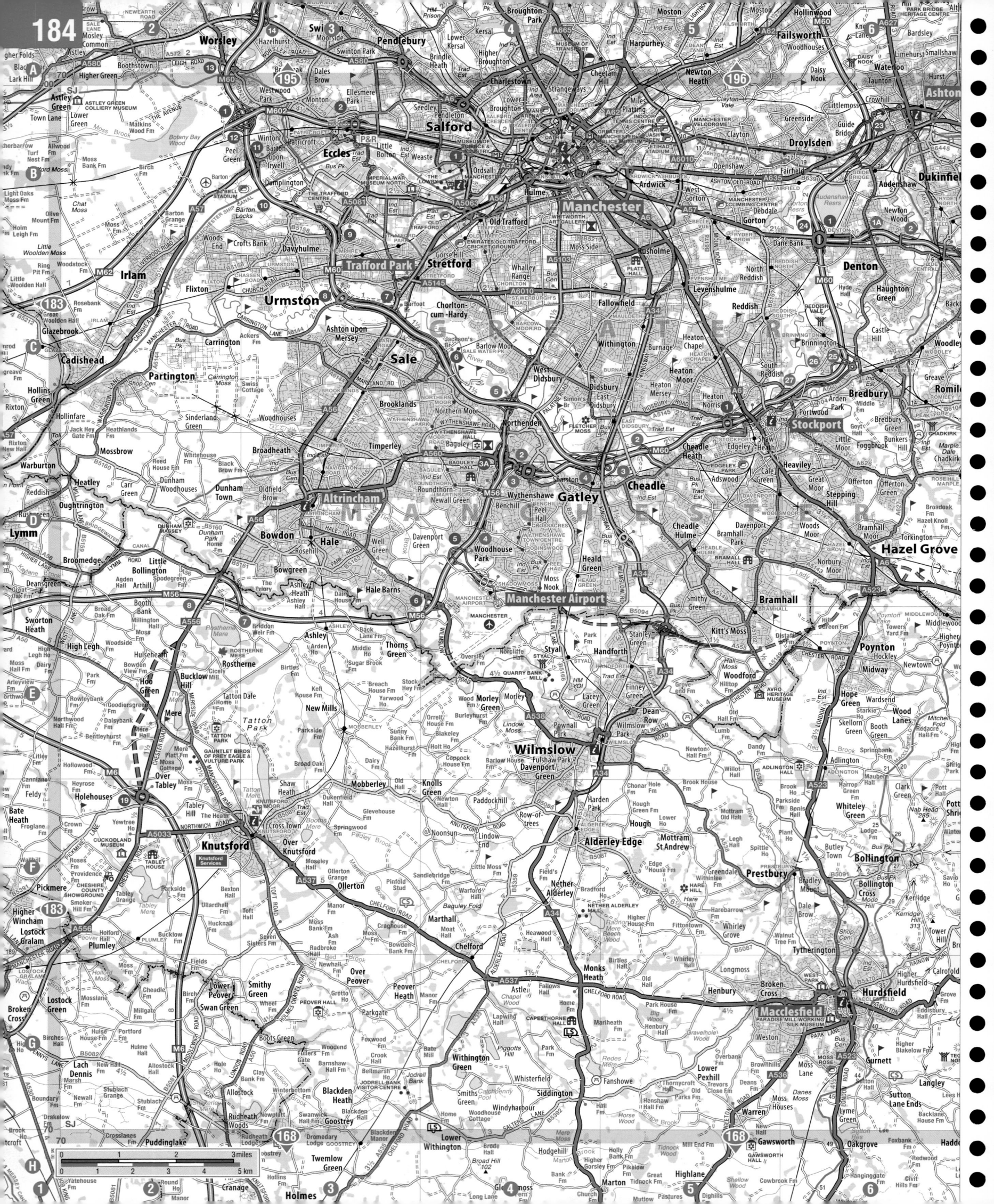

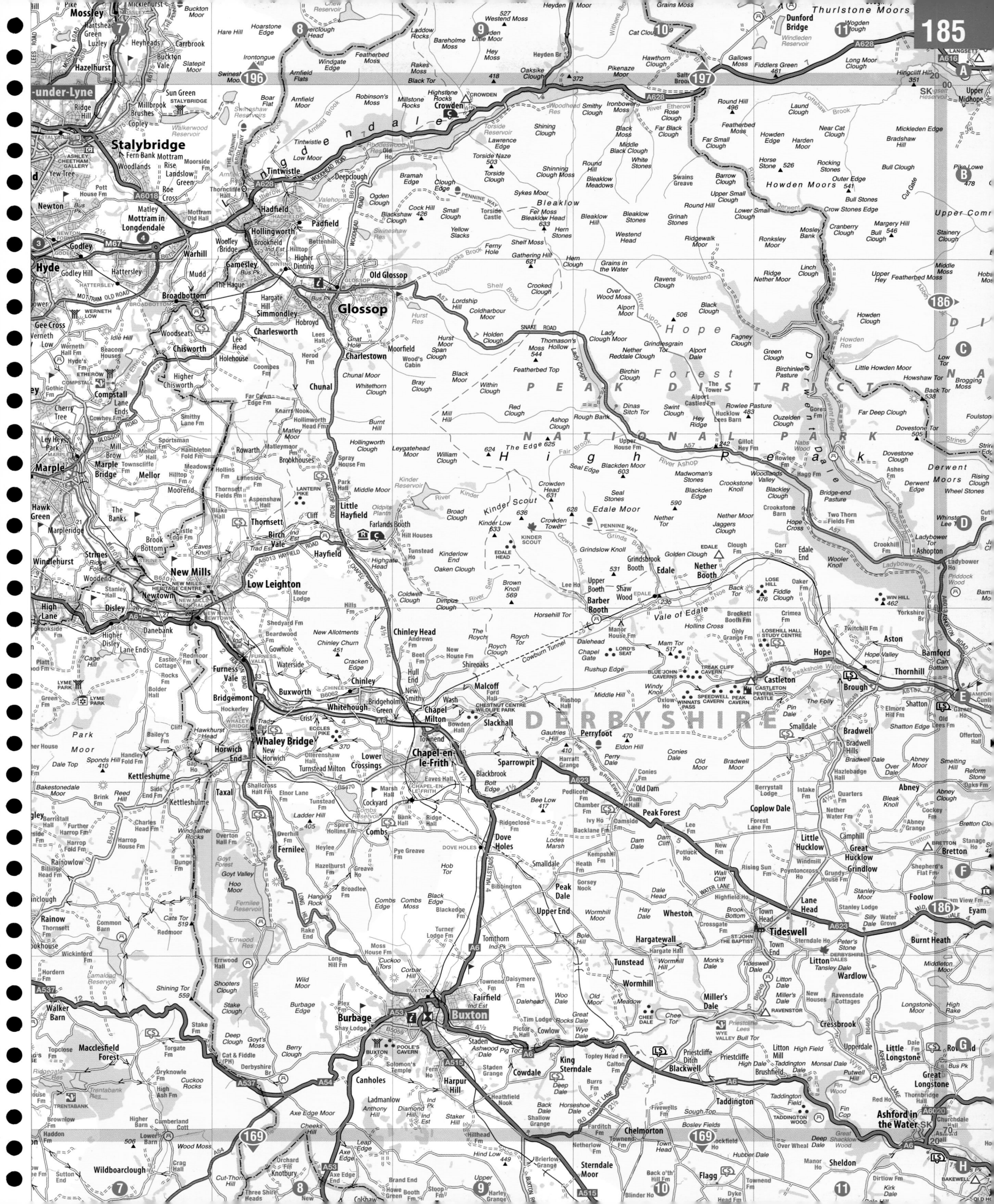

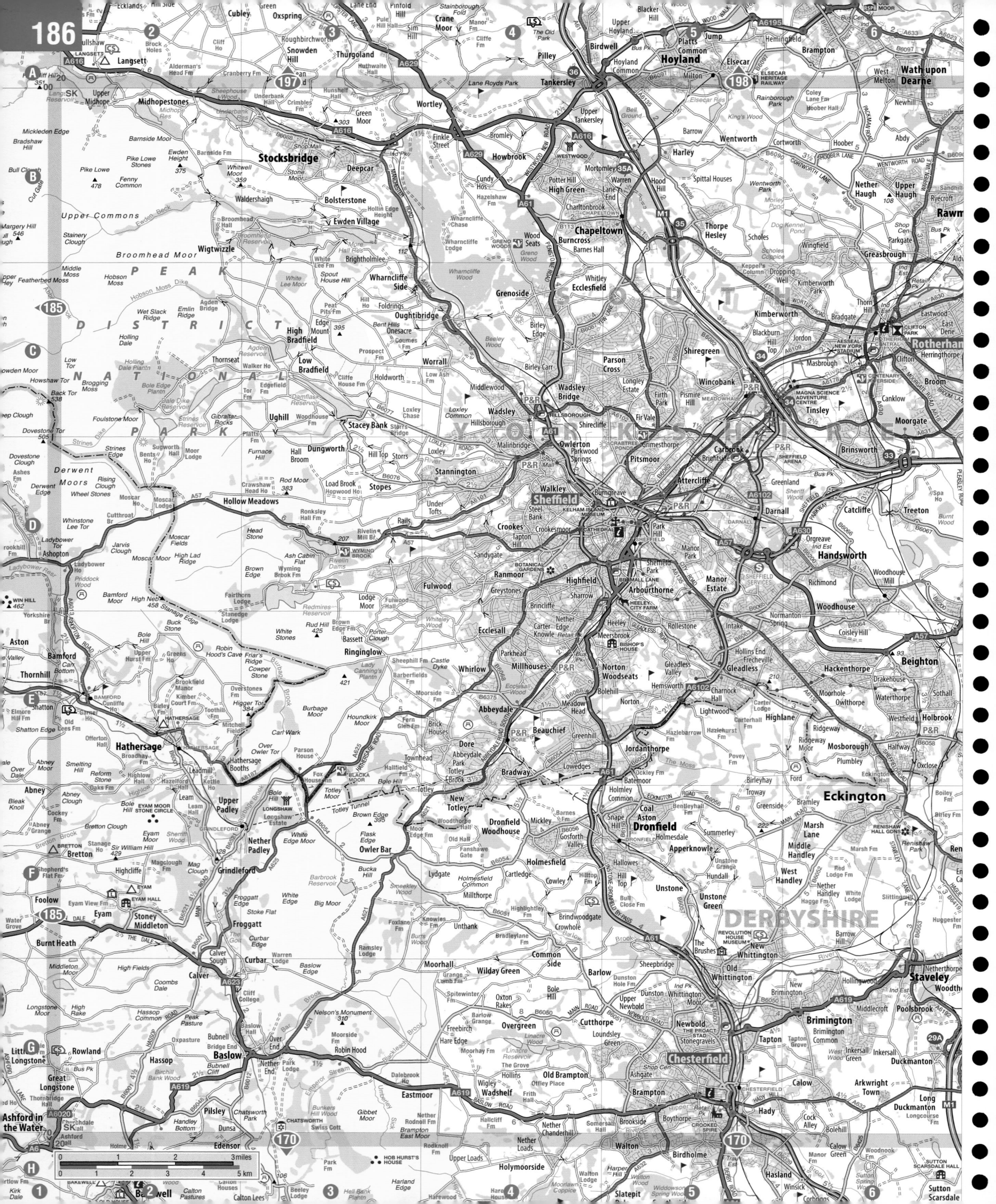

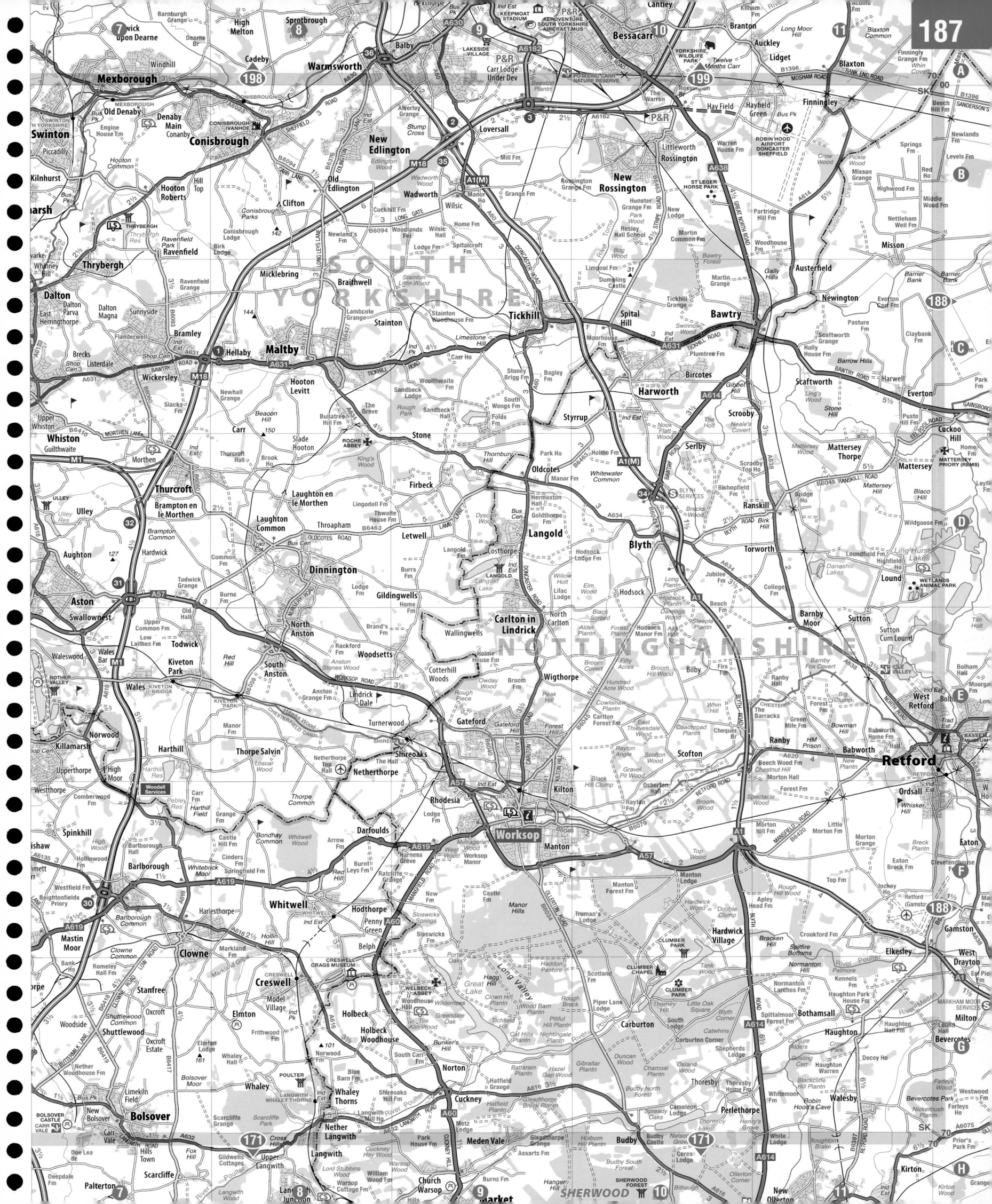

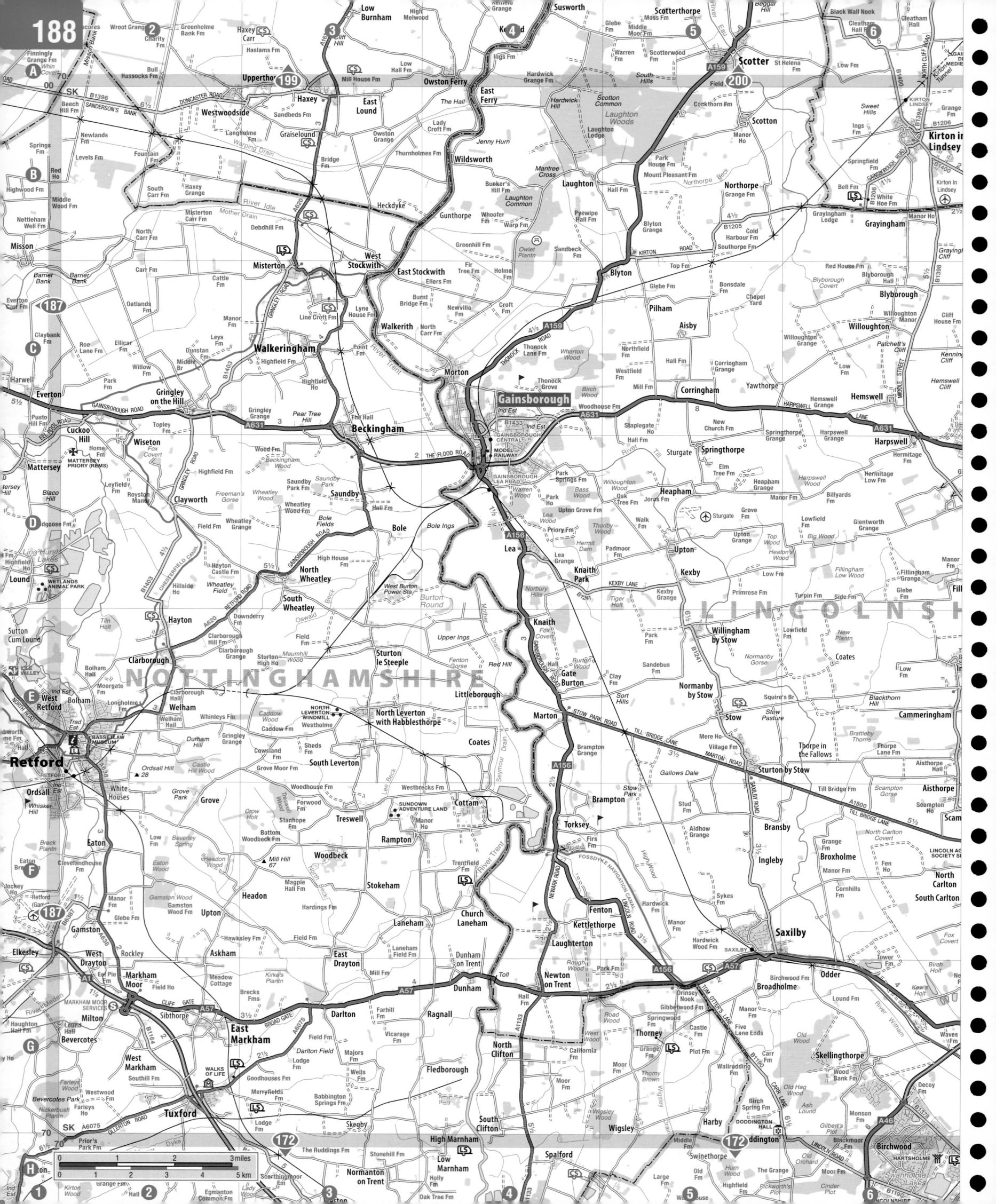

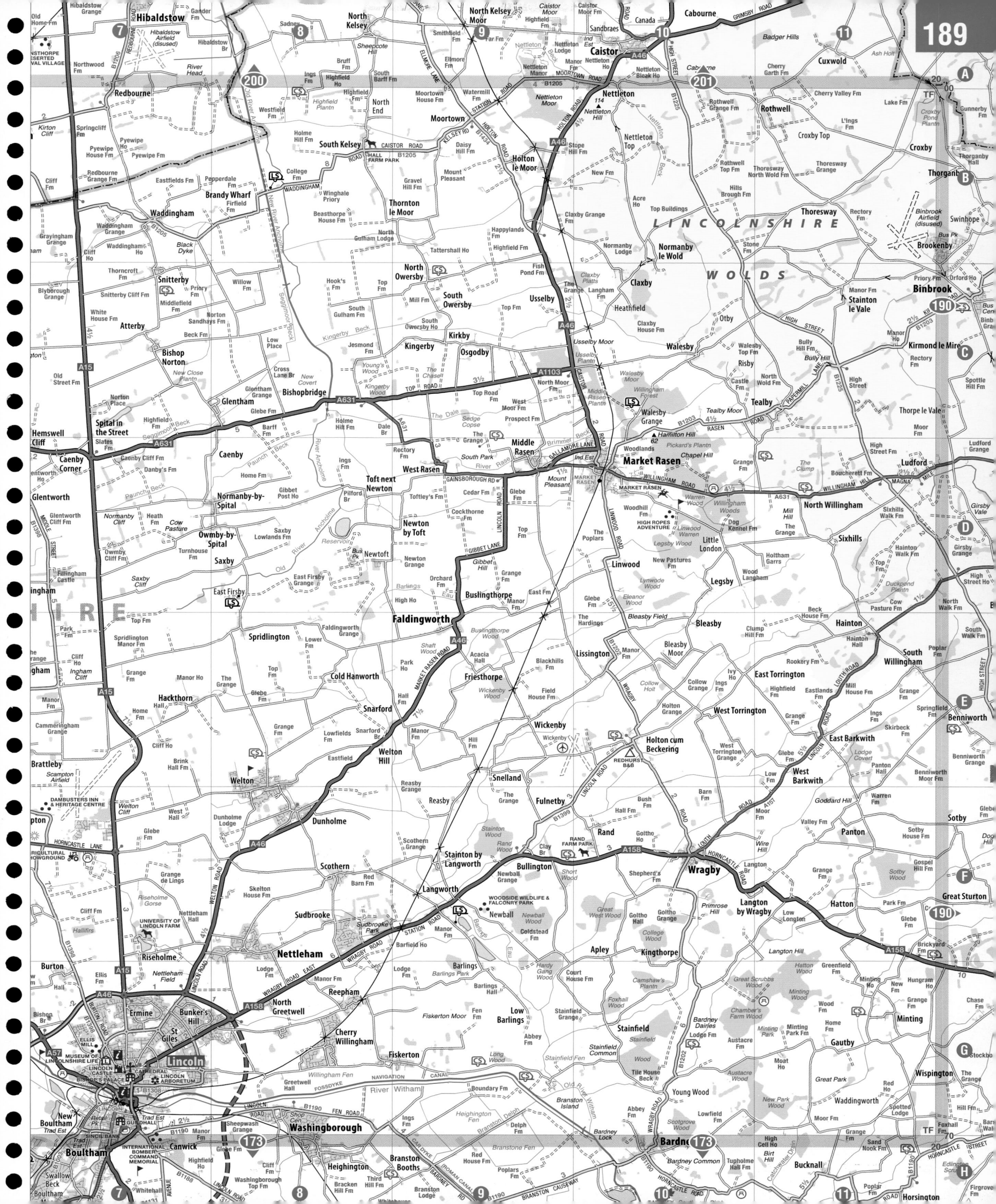

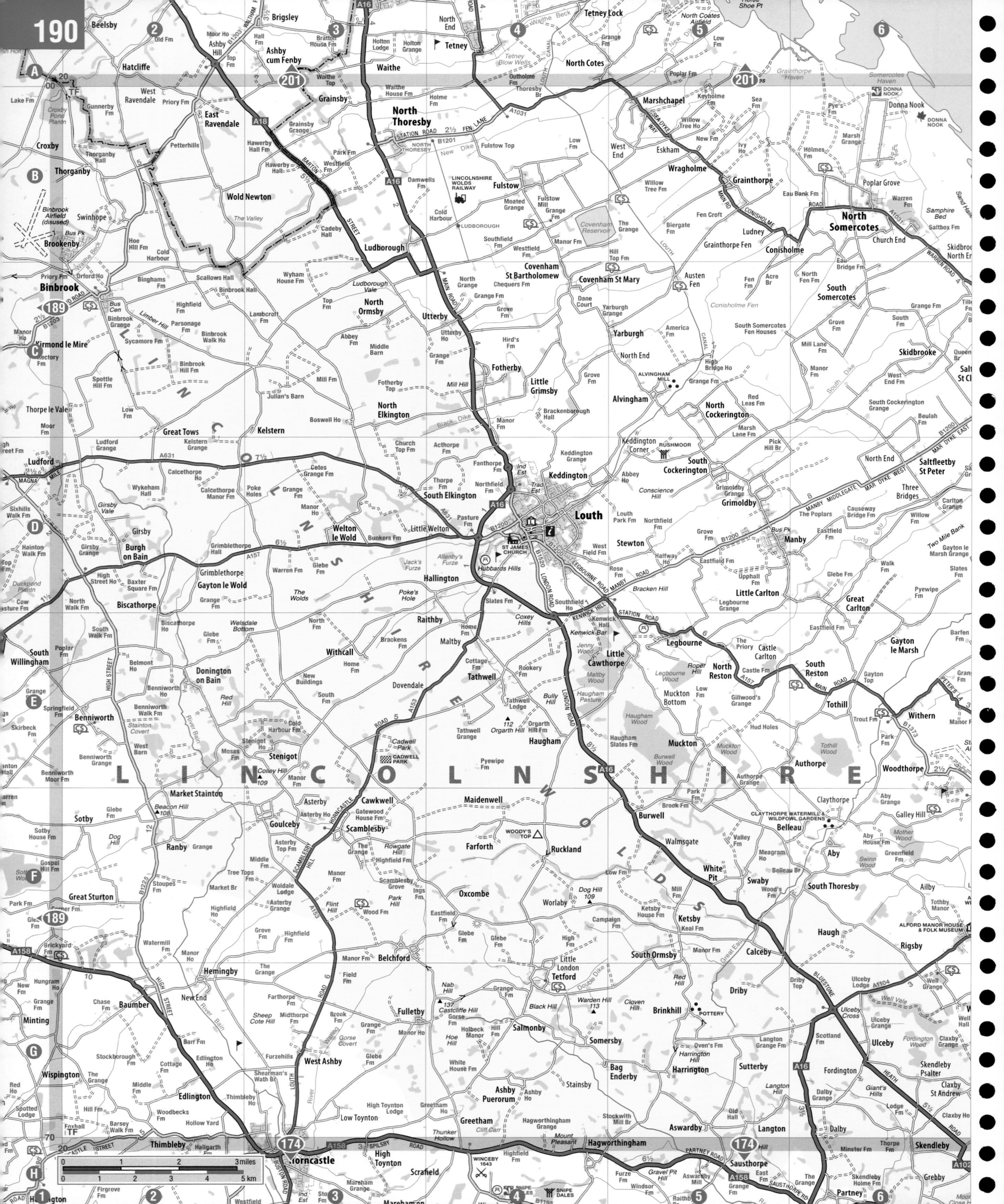

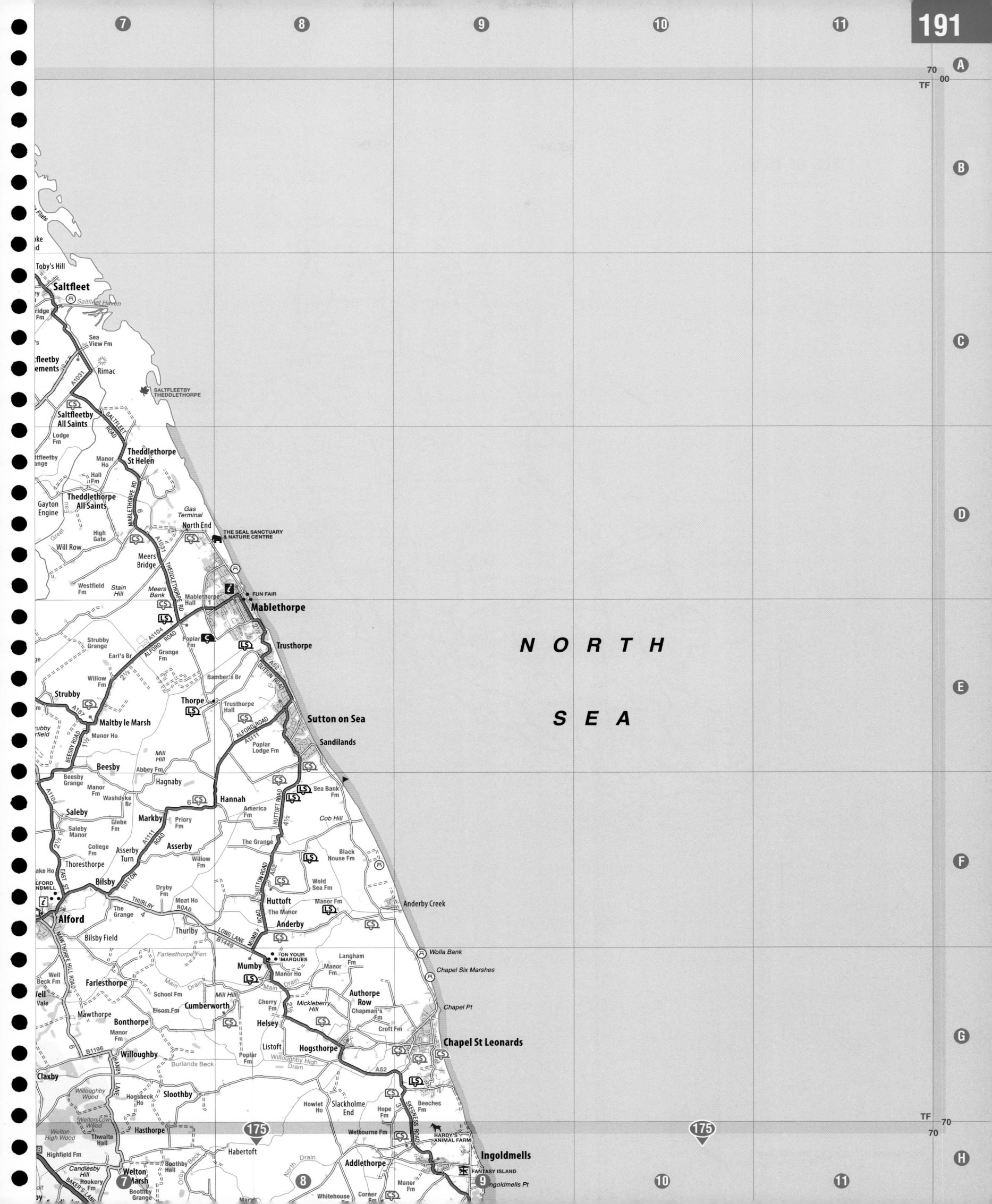

NORTH

SEA

Saltfleet
Toby's Hill
Saltfleet Haven
Sea View Fm
Rimac
fleetby ements
A1031
SALTFLEETBY THEDDLETHORPE
Saltfleetby All Saints
Lodge Fm
Manor Ho
Theddlethorpe St Helen
Hall
Gayton Engine
Theddlethorpe All Saints
Gas Terminal
North End
THE SEAL SANCTUARY & NATURE CENTRE
Will Row
High Gate
Meers Bridge
Westfield Fm
Stain Hill
Meers Bank
Mablethorpe Hall
FUN FAIR
Strubby Grange
Earl's Br
Poplar Fm
Mablethorpe
Grange Fm
Trusthorpe
Willow Fm
2½
Bamber's Br
Strubby
Thorpe
Trusthorpe Hall
Maltby le Marsh
Manor Ho
Sutton on Sea
Sandilands
Beesby
Mill Hill
Poplar Lodge Fm
Beesby Grange
Abbey Fm
Manor Fm
Hagnaby
Washdyke Br
Hannah
Sea Bank Fm
Saleby
Glebe Fm
America Fm
Cob Hill
Saleby Manor
Markby
Priory Fm
College Fm
Asserby Turn
Asserby
The Grange
Black House Fm
Thoresthorpe
Willow Fm
Bilsby
Dryby Fm
Moat Ho
Wold Sea Fm
Manor Fm
The Grange
Huttoft
The Manor
Anderby Creek
Alford
Anderby
Bilsby Field
Thurlby
LONG LANE
B1448
Wolla Bank
Farlesthorpe Fen
Langham Fm
Well Beck Fm
ON YOUR MARQUES
Mumby
Manor Ho
Chapel Six Marshes
Farlesthorpe
School Fm
Main Drain
Well Vale
Mawthorpe
Cumberworth
Mill Hill
Elsom Fm
Cherry Fm
Mickleberry Hill
Authorpe Row
Chapman's Fm
Chapel Pt
Bonthorpe
Manor Fm
Helsey
Croft Fm
Chapel St Leonards
Willoughby
Listoft
Hogsthorpe
B1196
Poplar Fm
Willoughby High Drain
A52
Claxby
Burlands Beck
Willoughby Wood
Sloothby
Hogsbeck Ho
Howlet Ho
Slackholme End
Hope Fm
Beeches Fm
Welton Cow Wilod
Hasthorpe
175
Welbourne Fm
175
HARDY'S ANIMAL FARM
Welton High Wood
Thwaite Hall
Highfield Fm
Boothby Hall
Habertoft
North Drain
Ingoldmells
Candlesby Hill
Welton Marsh
Rookery Fm
Addlethorpe
FANTASY ISLAND
Ingoldmells Pt
Boothby Grange
Manor Fm
Whitehouse
Corner Fm

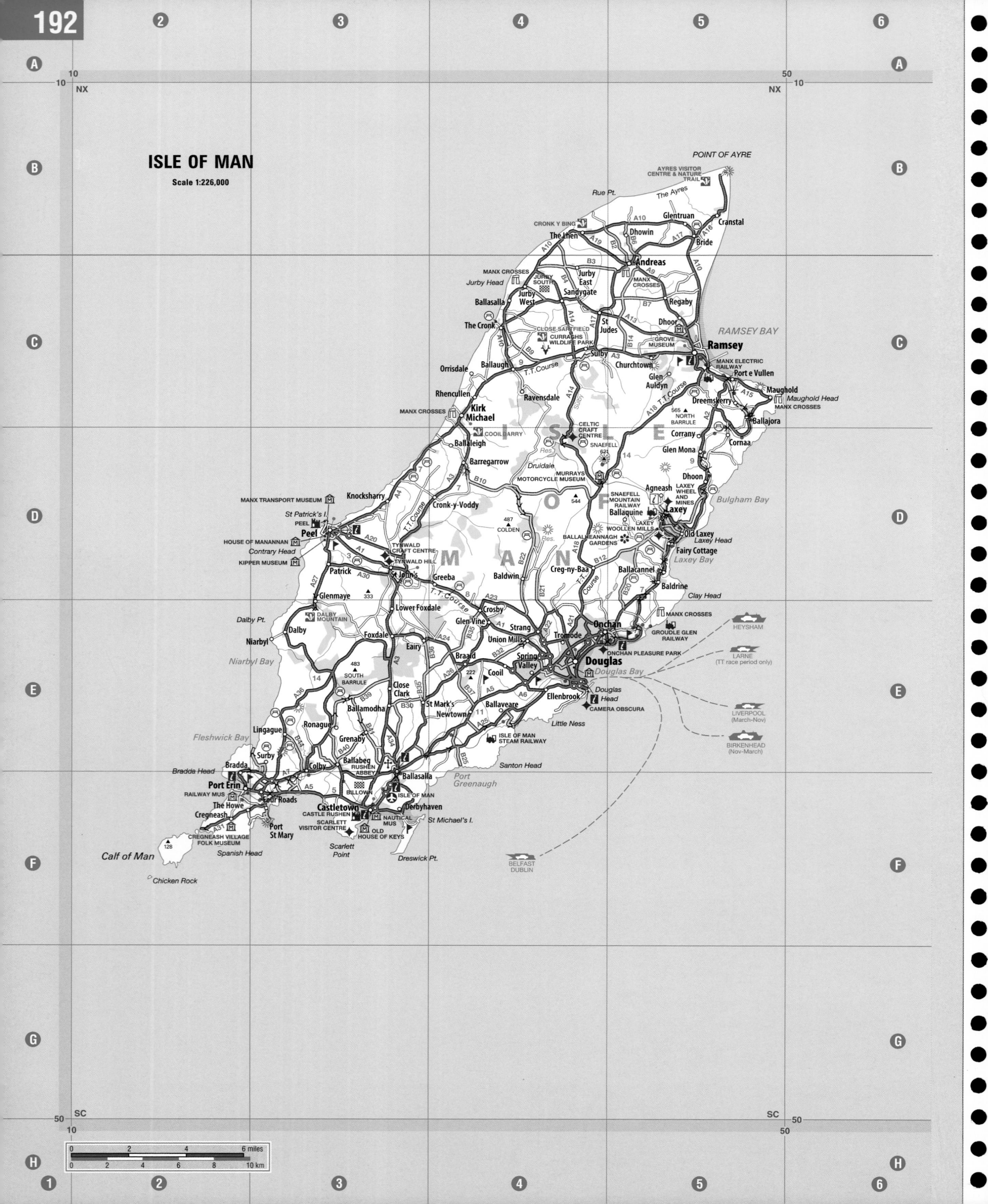

ISLE OF MAN

Scale 1:226,000

POINT OF AYRE

AYRES VISITOR
CENTRE & NATURE
TRAIL

Rue Pt.

The Ayres

CRONK Y BING   Glentruan
The Lhen   Dhowin   Cranstal
                                Bride
           Andreas
MANX CROSSES   Jurby
Jurby Head   SOUTH   East   Regaby
         Jurby Sandygate
         West   MANX
Ballasalla   CROSSES
                         Dhoor
The Cronk   St   RAMSEY BAY
         CLOSE SARTFIELD Judes   GROVE
         CURRAGHS   MUSEUM
         WILDLIFE PARK   Ramsey
Orrisdale Ballaugh   Sulby   MANX ELECTRIC
                Churchtown   RAILWAY
                           Glen   Port e Vullen
Rhencullen   Auldyn   Maughold
                                Dreemskerry Maughold Head
MANX CROSSES   Kirk   Ravensdale   MANX CROSSES
         Michael   565 ▲   Ballajora
                    CELTIC NORTH
                    CRAFT BARRULE   Cornaa
         COOIL DARRY CENTRE
              Snaefell Corrany   Glen Mona
Ballaleigh   621▲   14
         Barregarrow Druidale   Dhoon
MANX TRANSPORT MUSEUM MURRAYS   Agneash LAXEY
         Cronk-y-Voddy MOTORCYCLE MUSEUM 544   WHEEL
Knocksharry   SNAEFELL Ballaquine AND MINES
         St Patrick's I.   MOUNTAIN   Laxey   Bulgham Bay
PEEL   487▲ RAILWAY   LAXEY
HOUSE OF MANANNAN COLDEN   WOOLLEN MILLS
Contrary Head   Peel   BALLALHEANNAGH Old Laxey
KIPPER MUSEUM   GARDENS   Laxey Head
         Patrick TYNWALD   Creg-ny-Baa Fairy Cottage
         CRAFT CENTRE Baldwin   Laxey Bay
         TYNWALD HILL   Ballacannel
St John's Greeba   Baldrine
Glenmaye   333▲   Clay Head
         Lower Foxdale Crosby   MANX CROSSES
Dalby Pt. DALBY   Glen Vine Strang   GROUDLE GLEN
         MOUNTAIN   Onchan   RAILWAY   HEYSHAM
Niarbyl Dalby Foxdale Union Mills Tromode
                     Braaid   ONCHAN PLEASURE PARK LARNE
Niarbyl Bay Eairy   Spring   (TT race period only)
         483▲   222   Valley Douglas
         SOUTH   Cooil   Douglas Bay
         BARRULE Close   Douglas
         14   Clark   Head LIVERPOOL
Lingague Ronague   St Mark's Ballaveare Ellenbrook CAMERA OBSCURA (March-Nov)
Fleshwick Bay   Ballamodha Newtown   11   Little Ness
         Grenaby   Santon Head BIRKENHEAD
Surby Bradda Colby Ballabeg   ISLE OF MAN   (Nov-March)
Bradda Head   RUSHEN   STEAM RAILWAY
         ABBEY   Ballasalla
Port Erin   BILLOWN   Port
RAILWAY MUS Four Roads   Greenaugh
The Howe Castletown   Derbyhaven
Cregneash SCARLETT CASTLE RUSHEN NAUTICAL
         VISITOR Port OLD   MUS   St Michael's I.
CREGNEASH VILLAGE CENTRE St Mary HOUSE OF KEYS
FOLK MUSEUM   Scarlett   Dreswick Pt.
Calf of Man   Spanish Head Point   BELFAST
                           DUBLIN
° Chicken Rock

0   2   4   6 miles
0 2 4 6 8 10 km

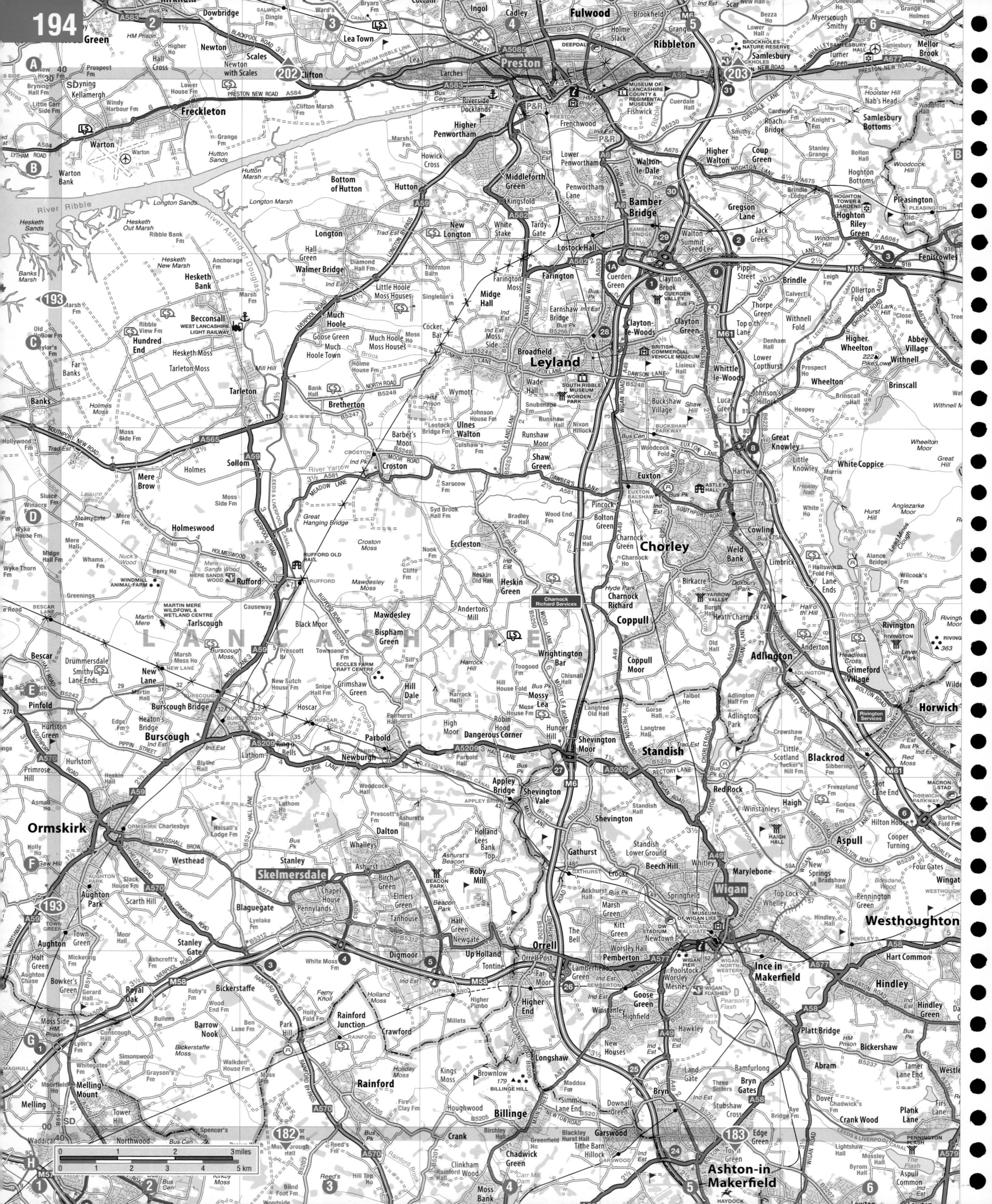

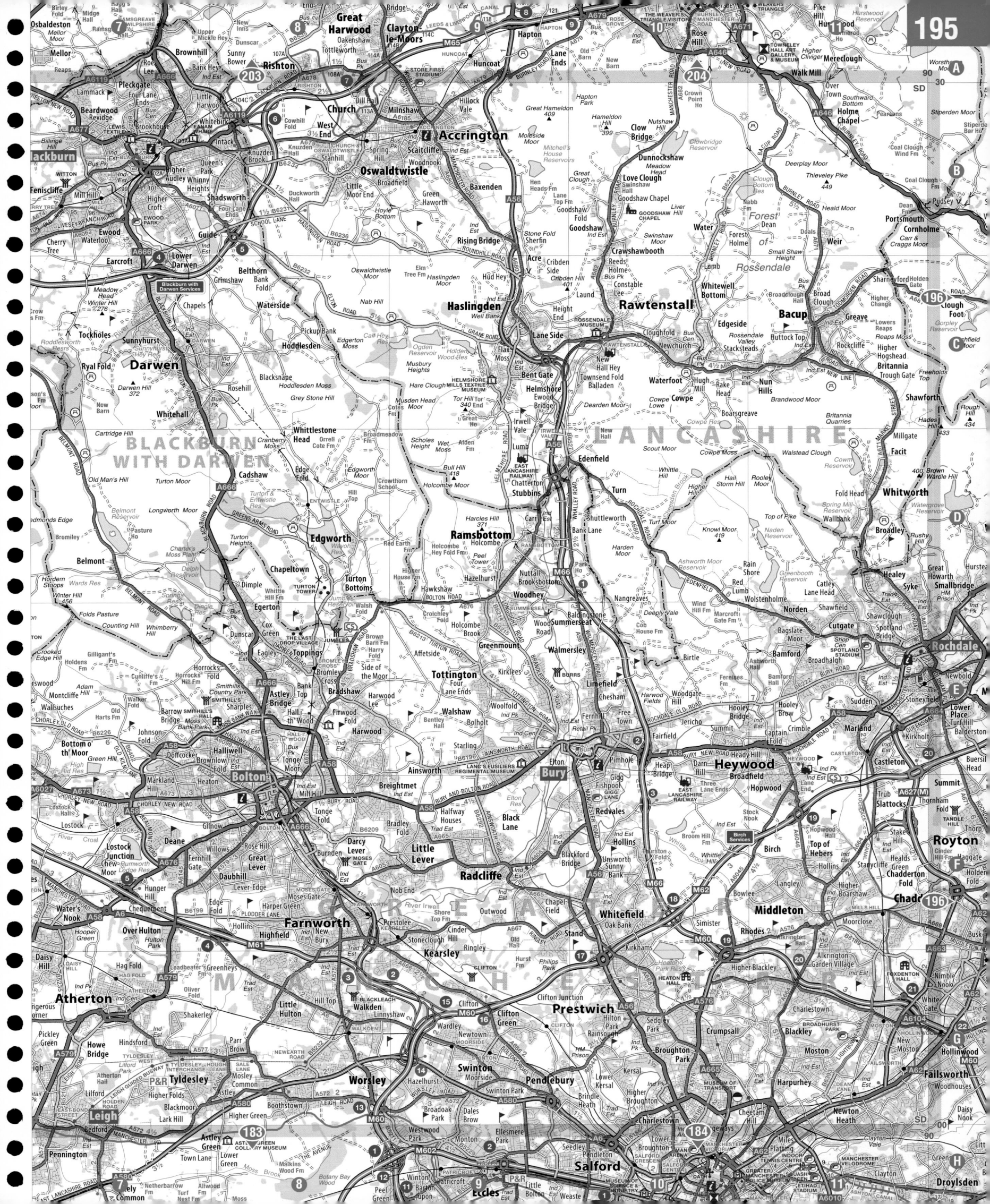

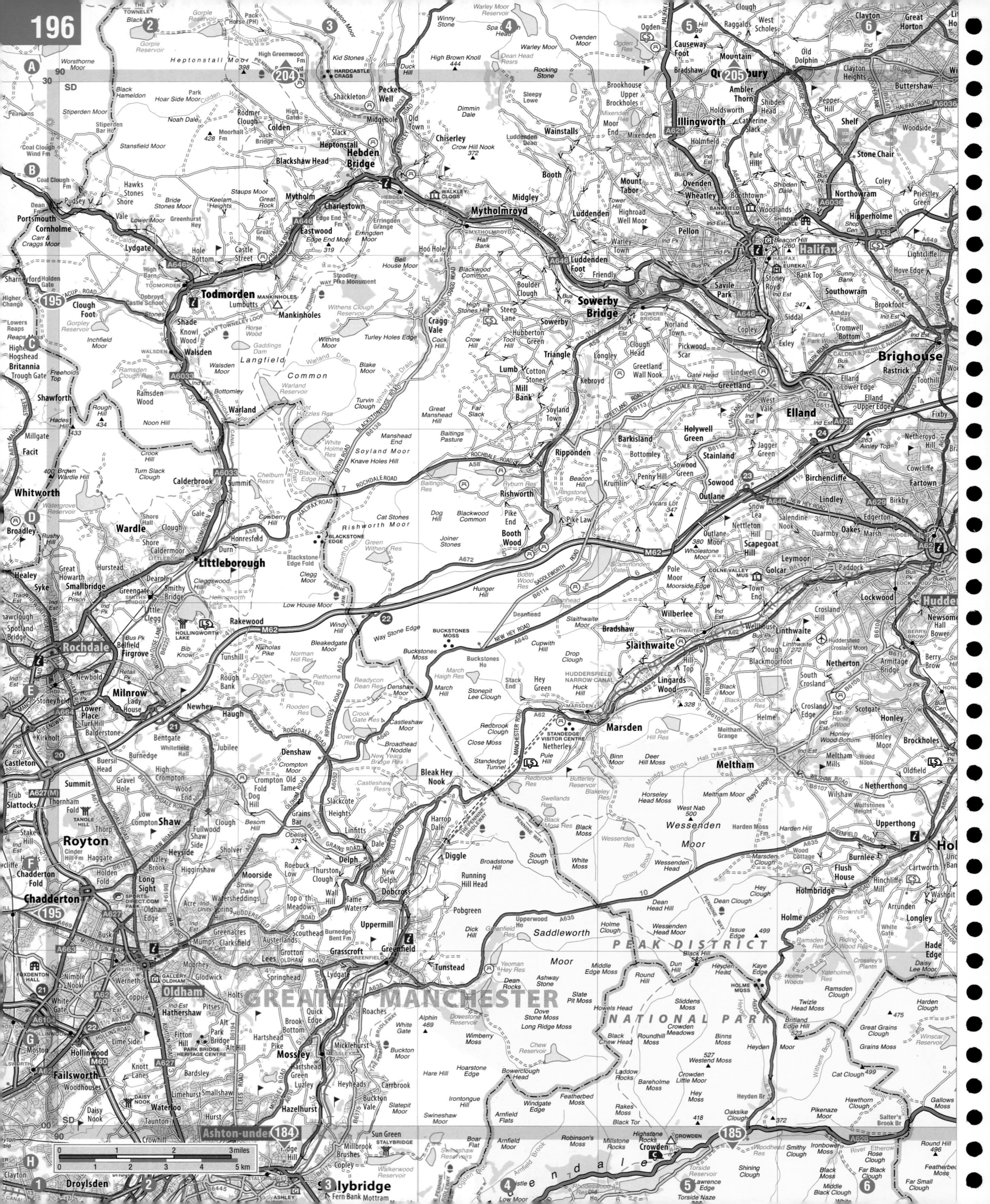

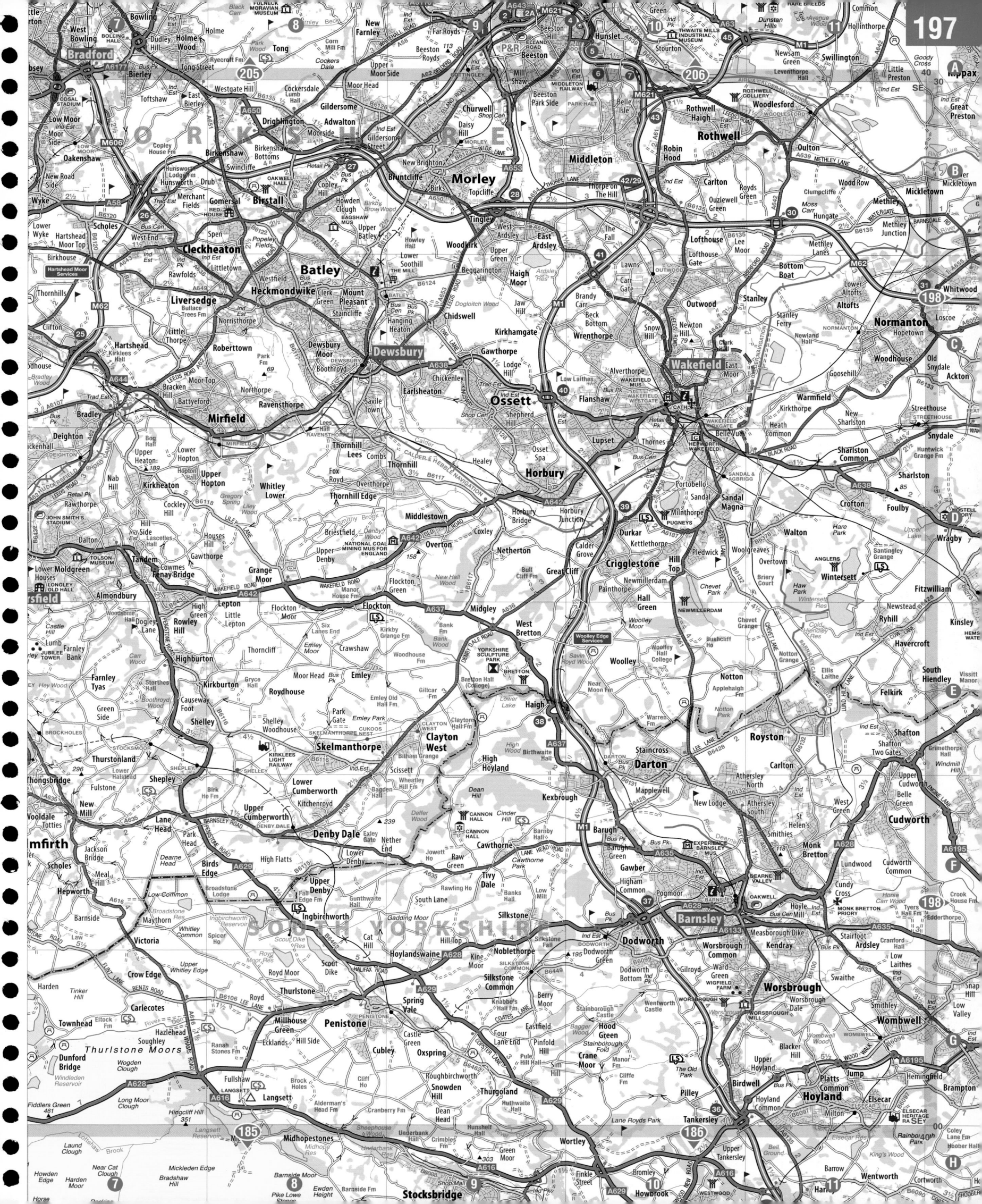

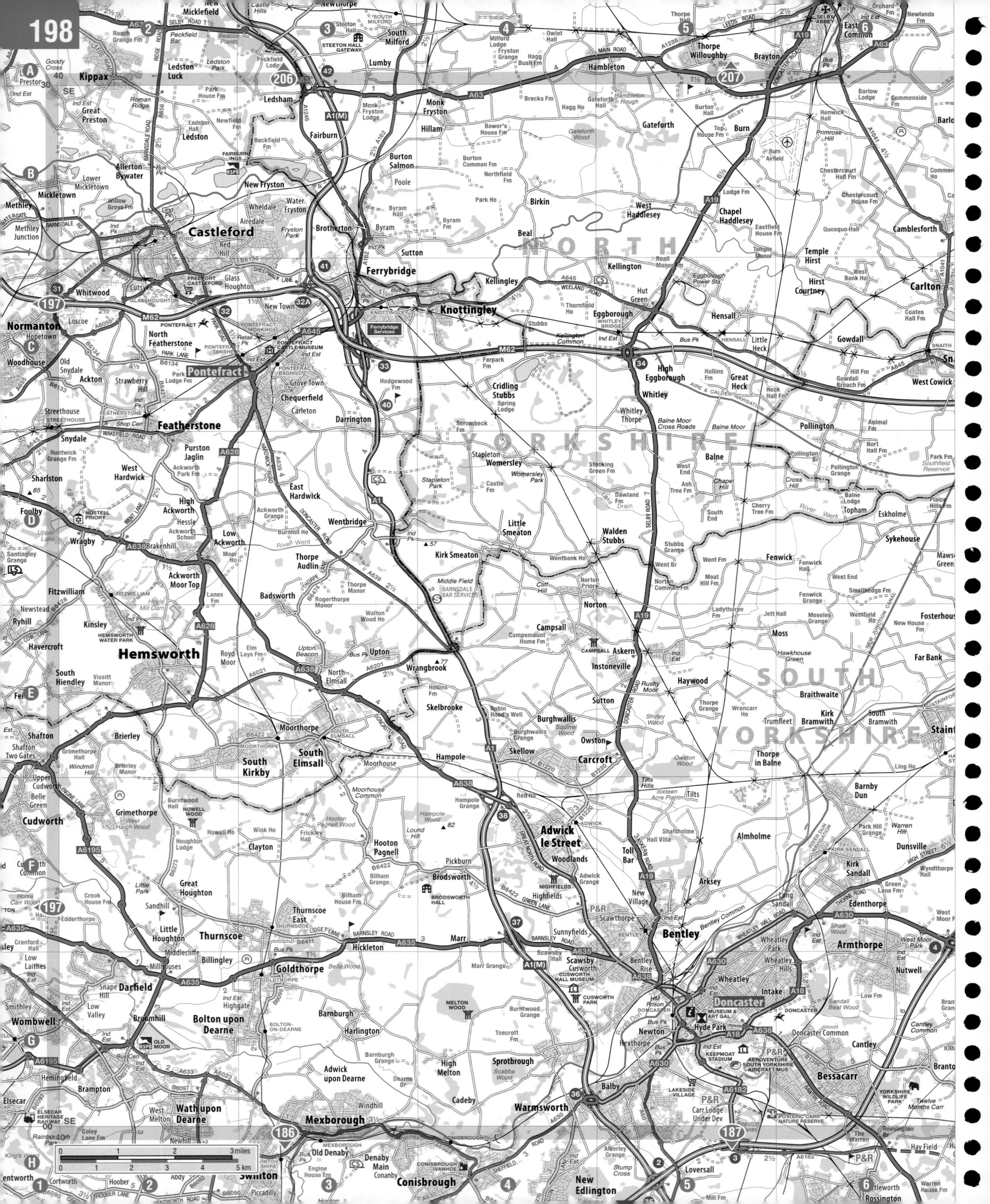

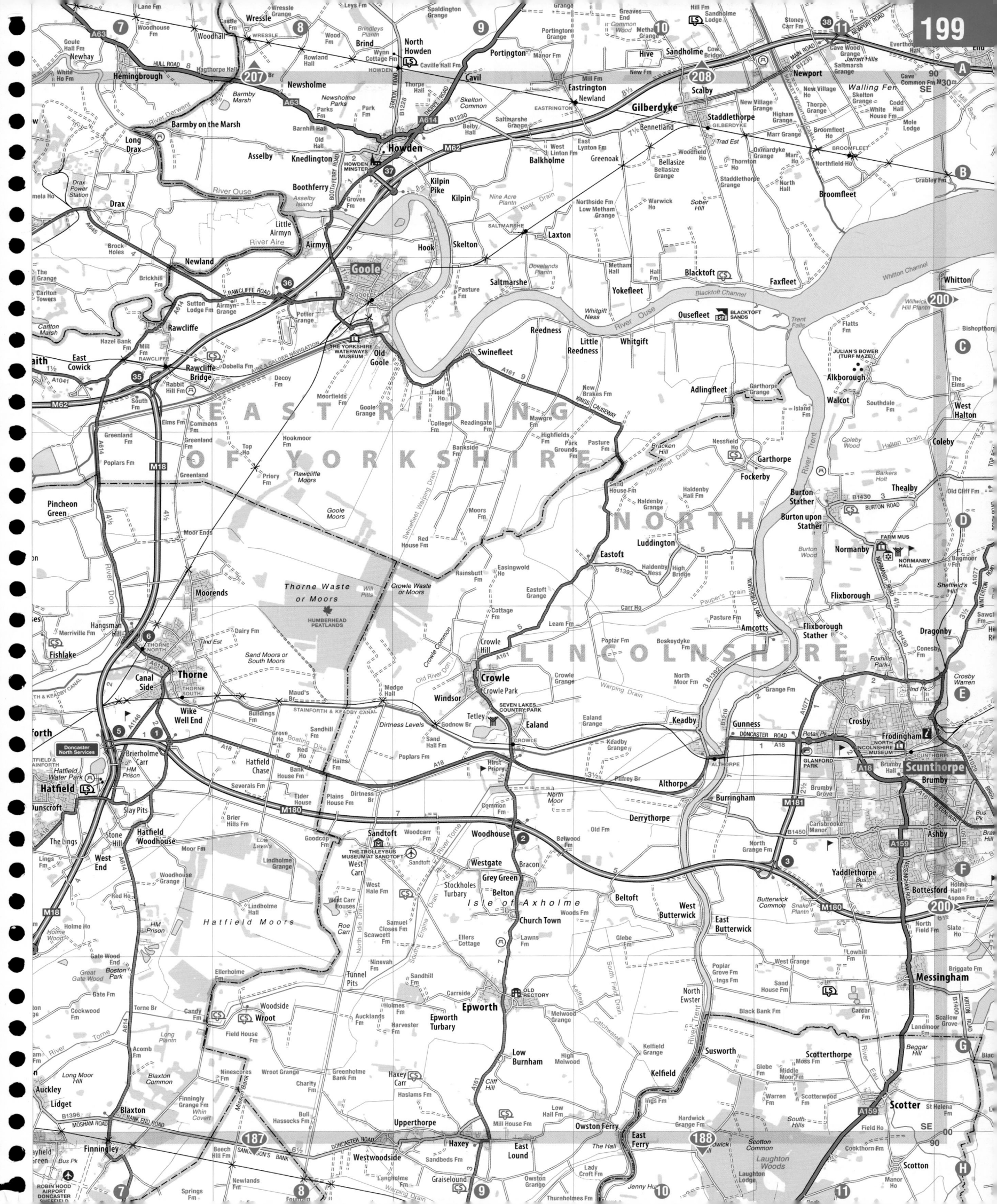

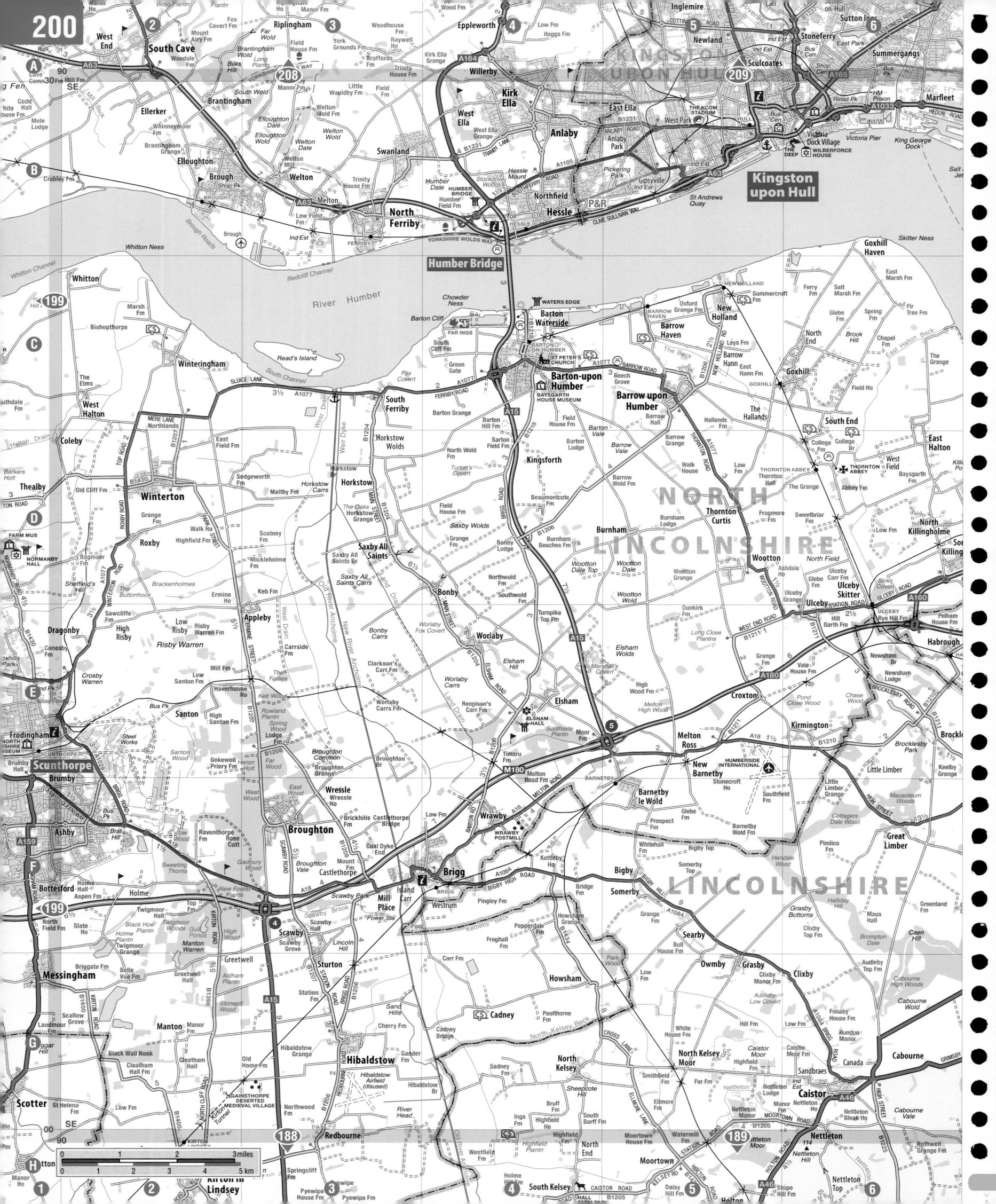

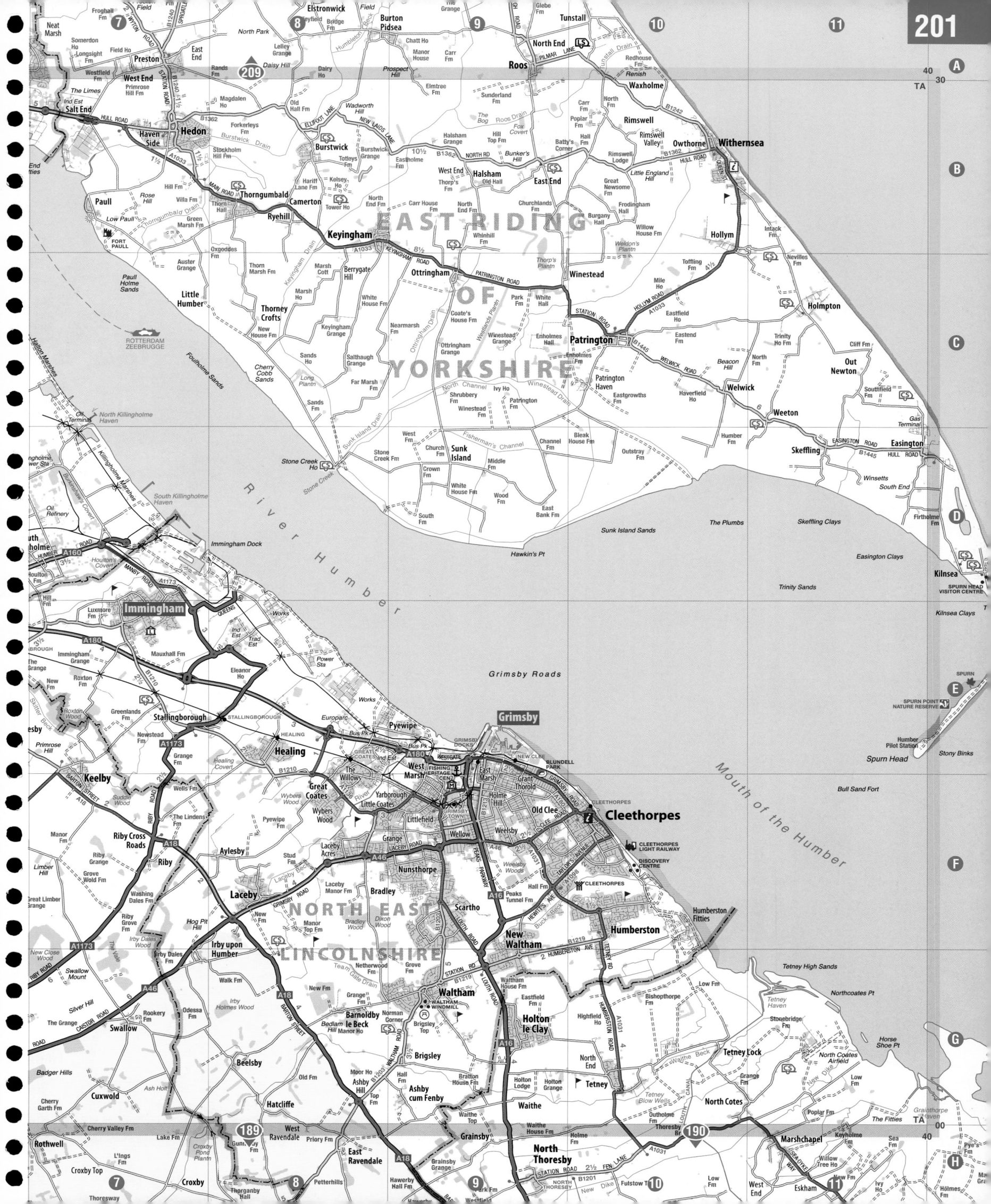

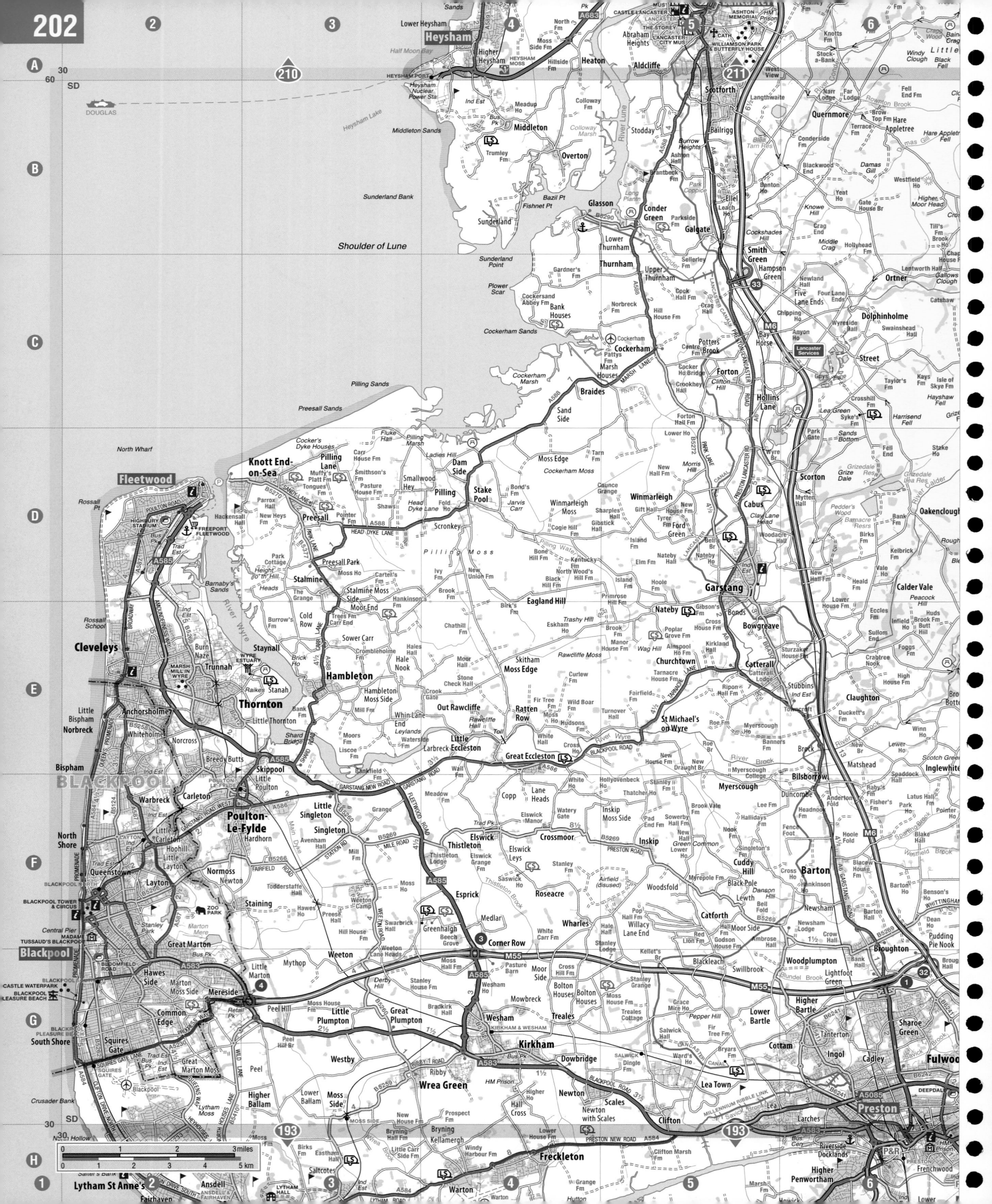

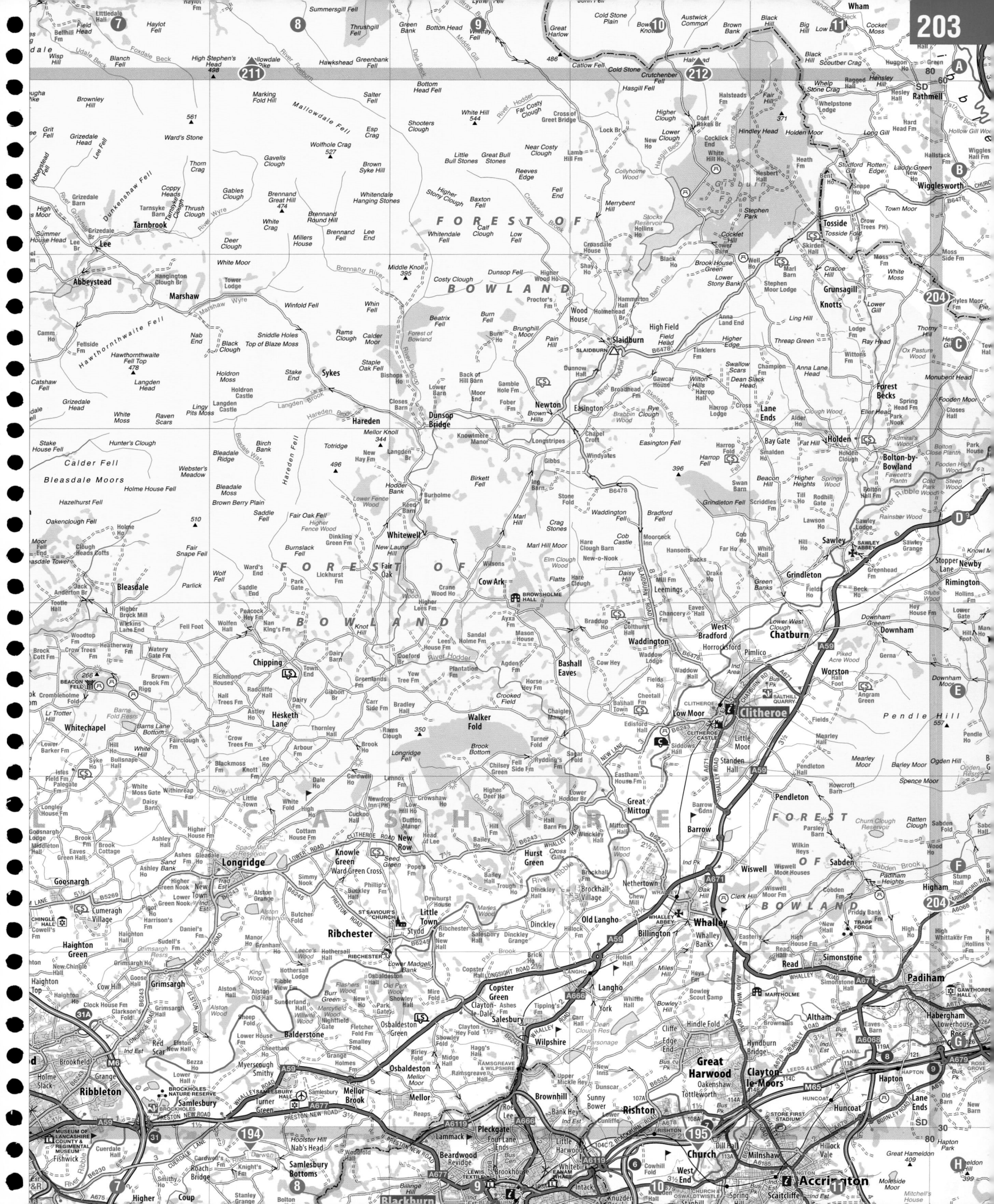

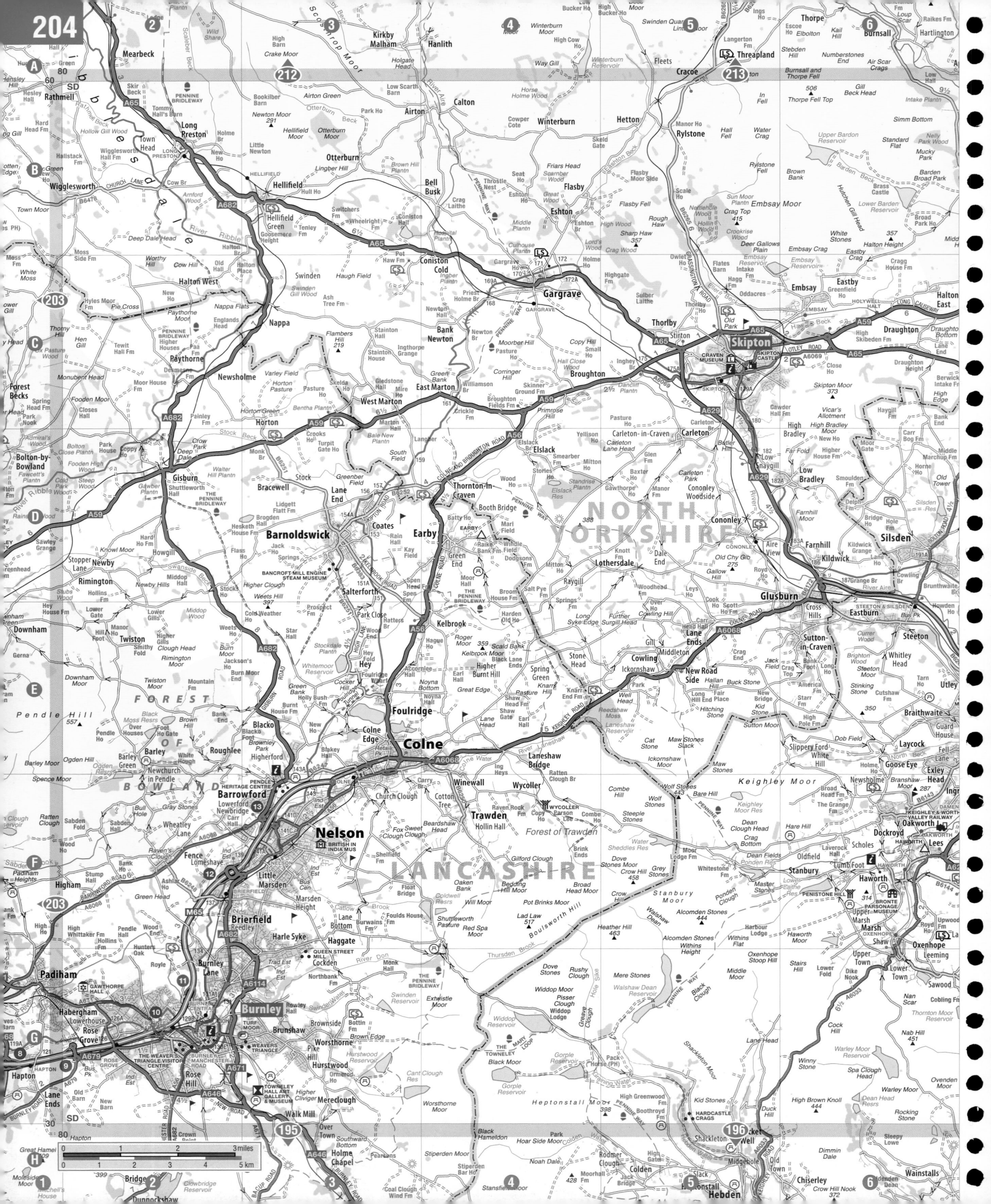

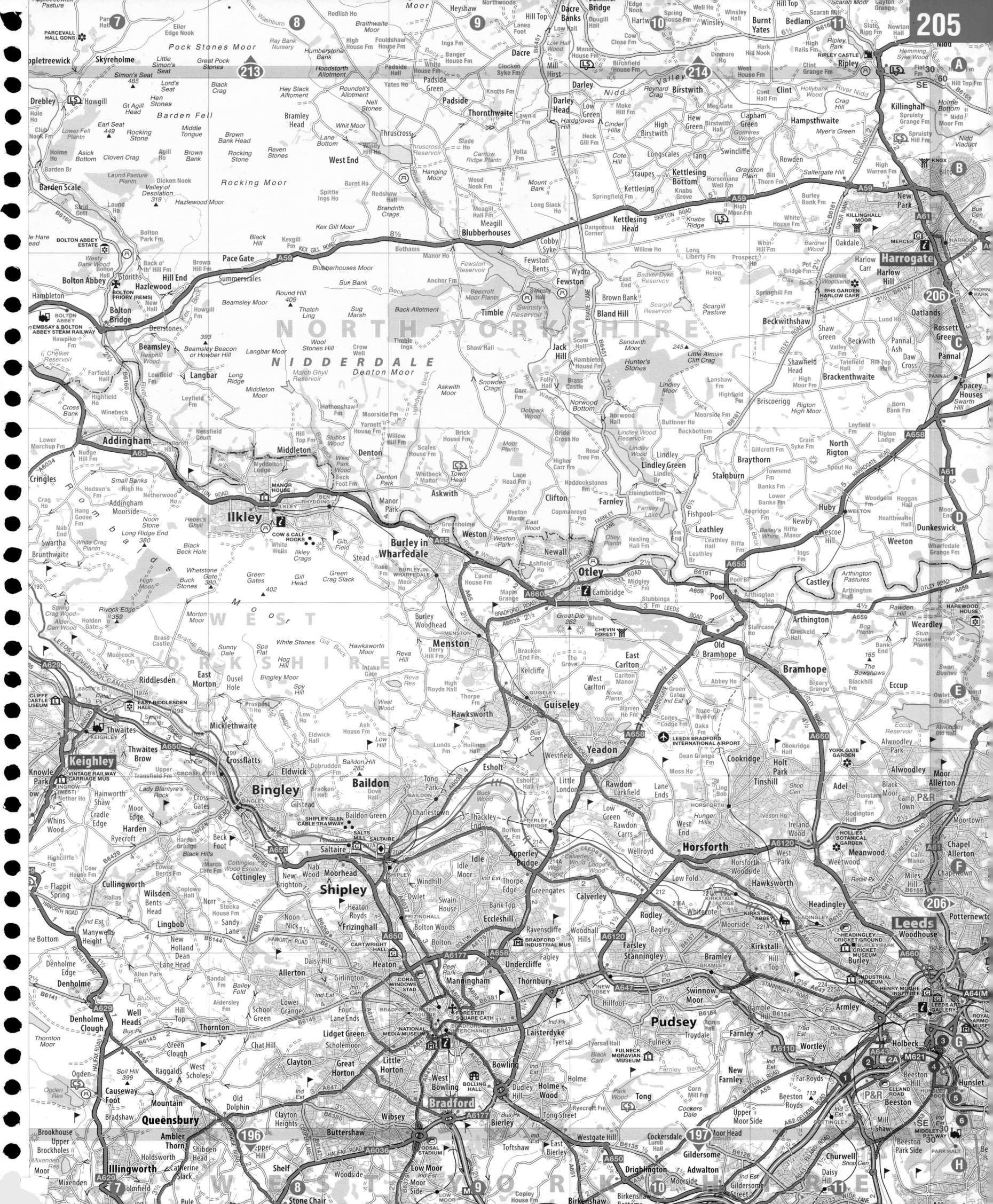

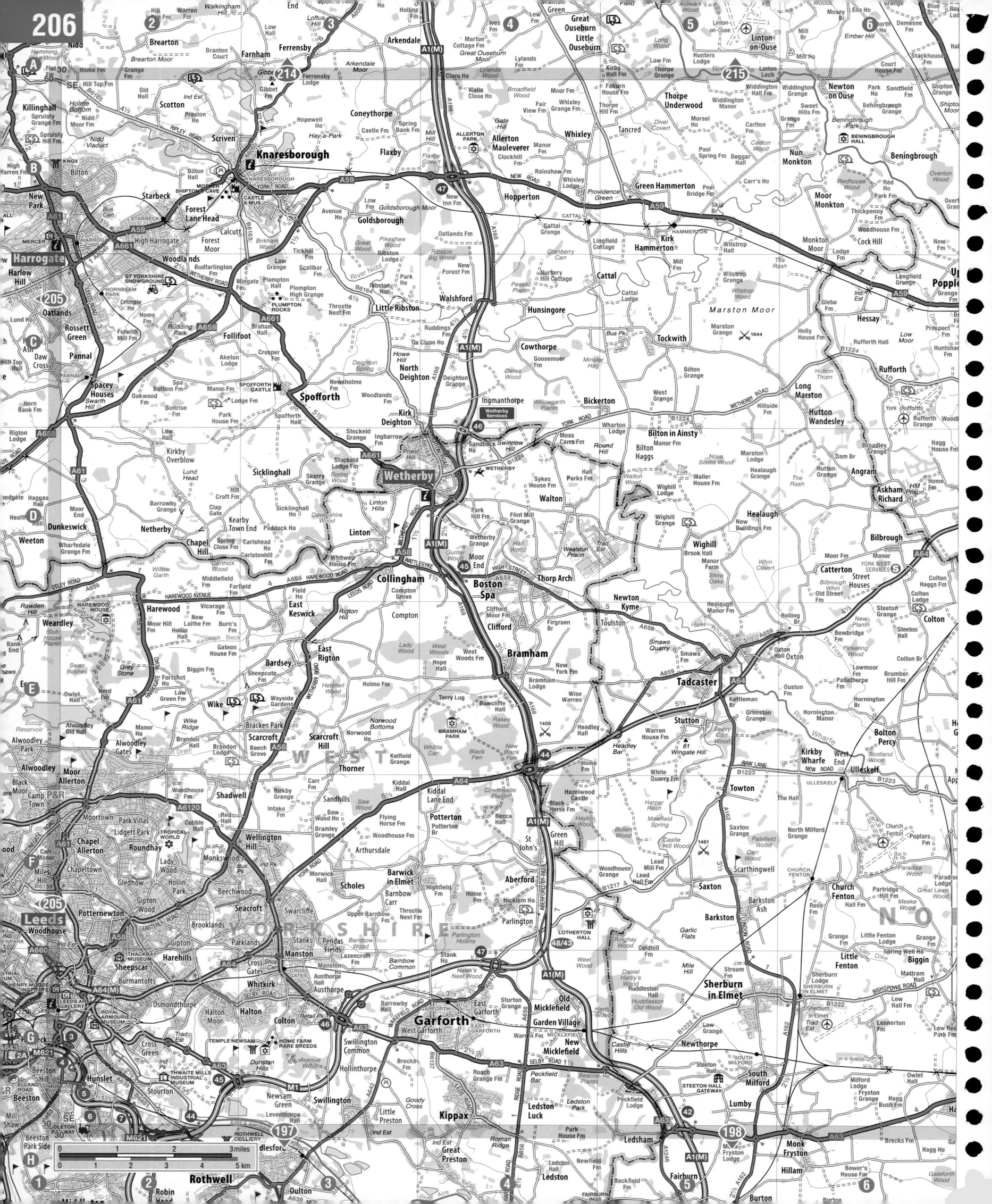

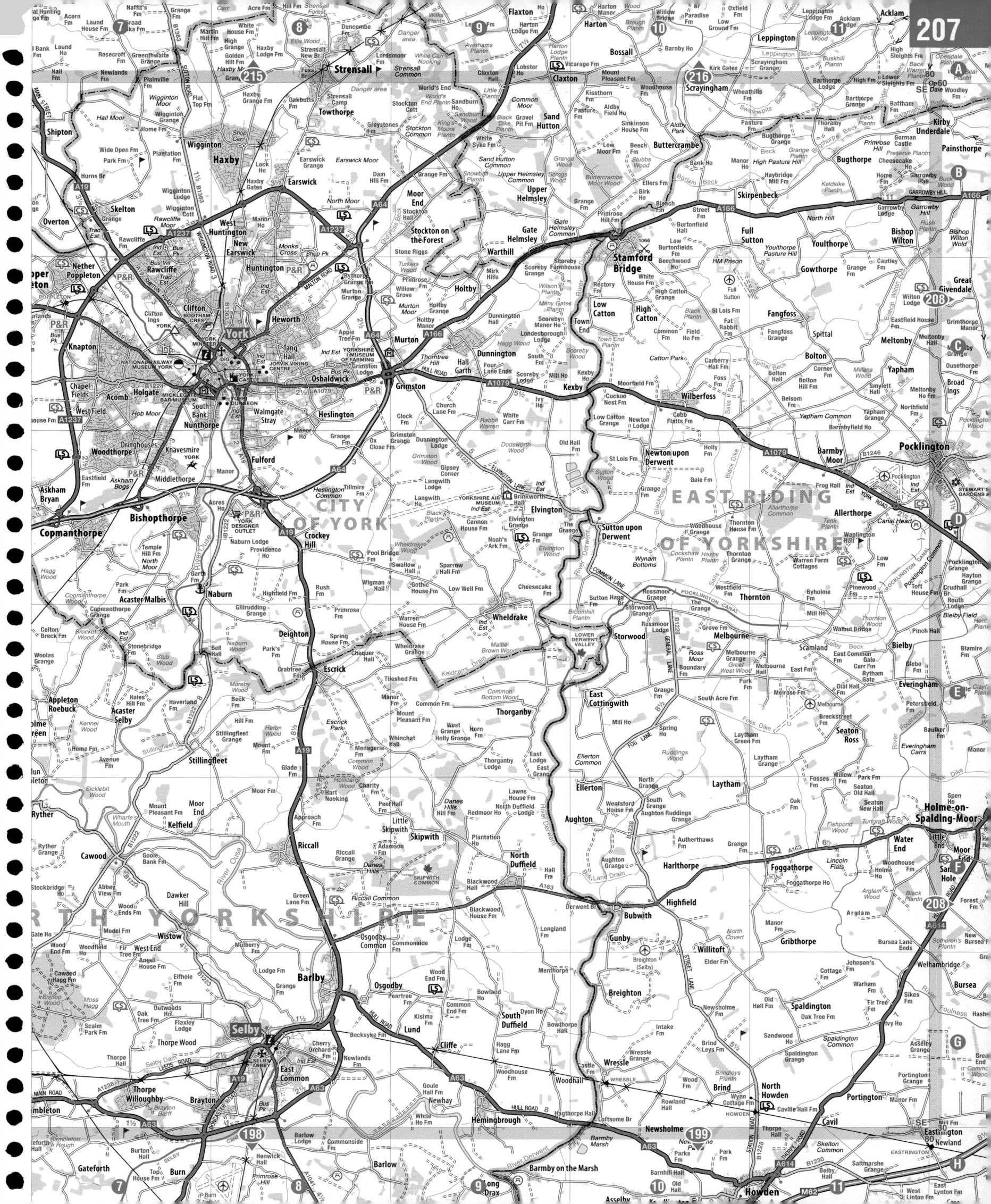

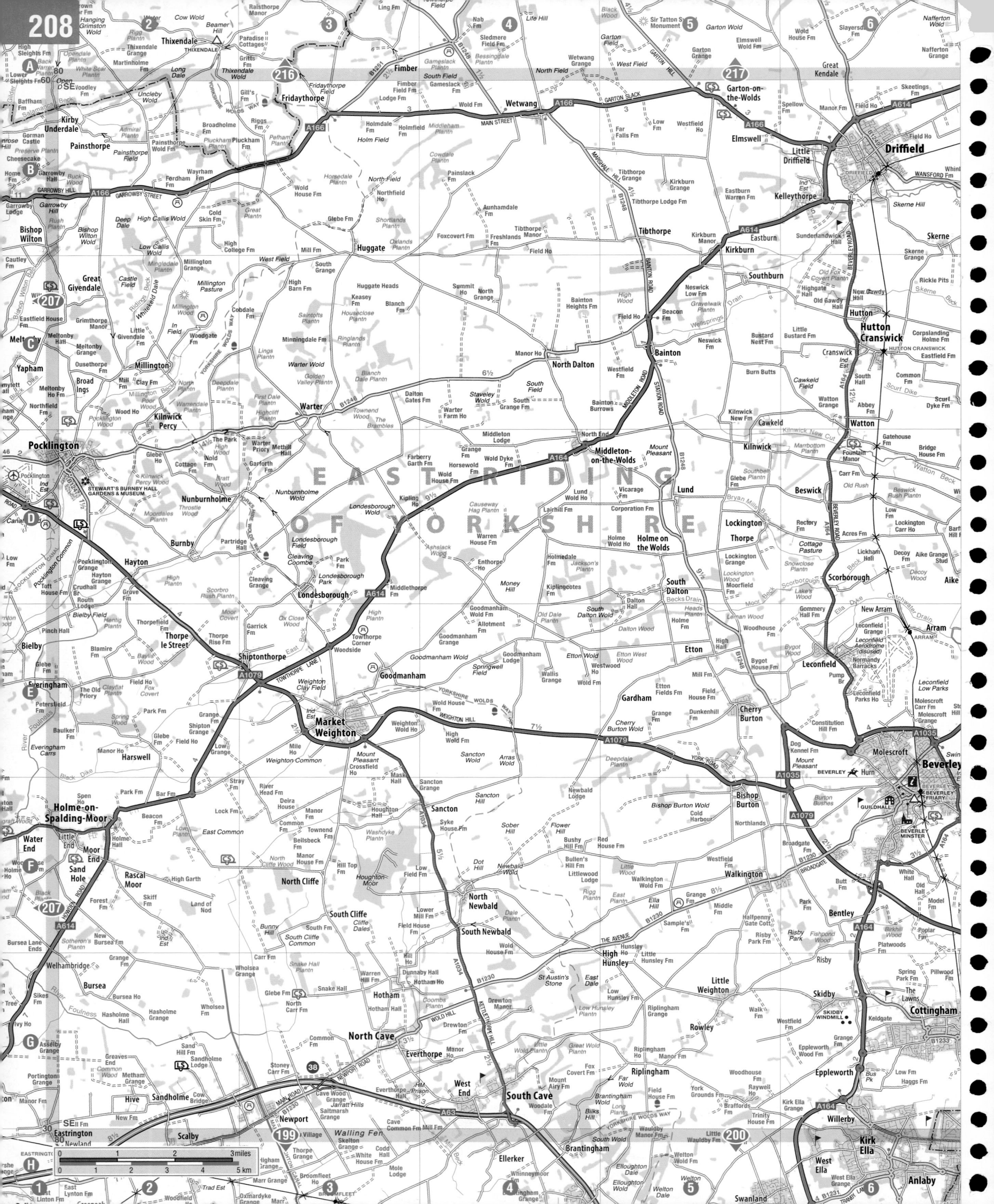

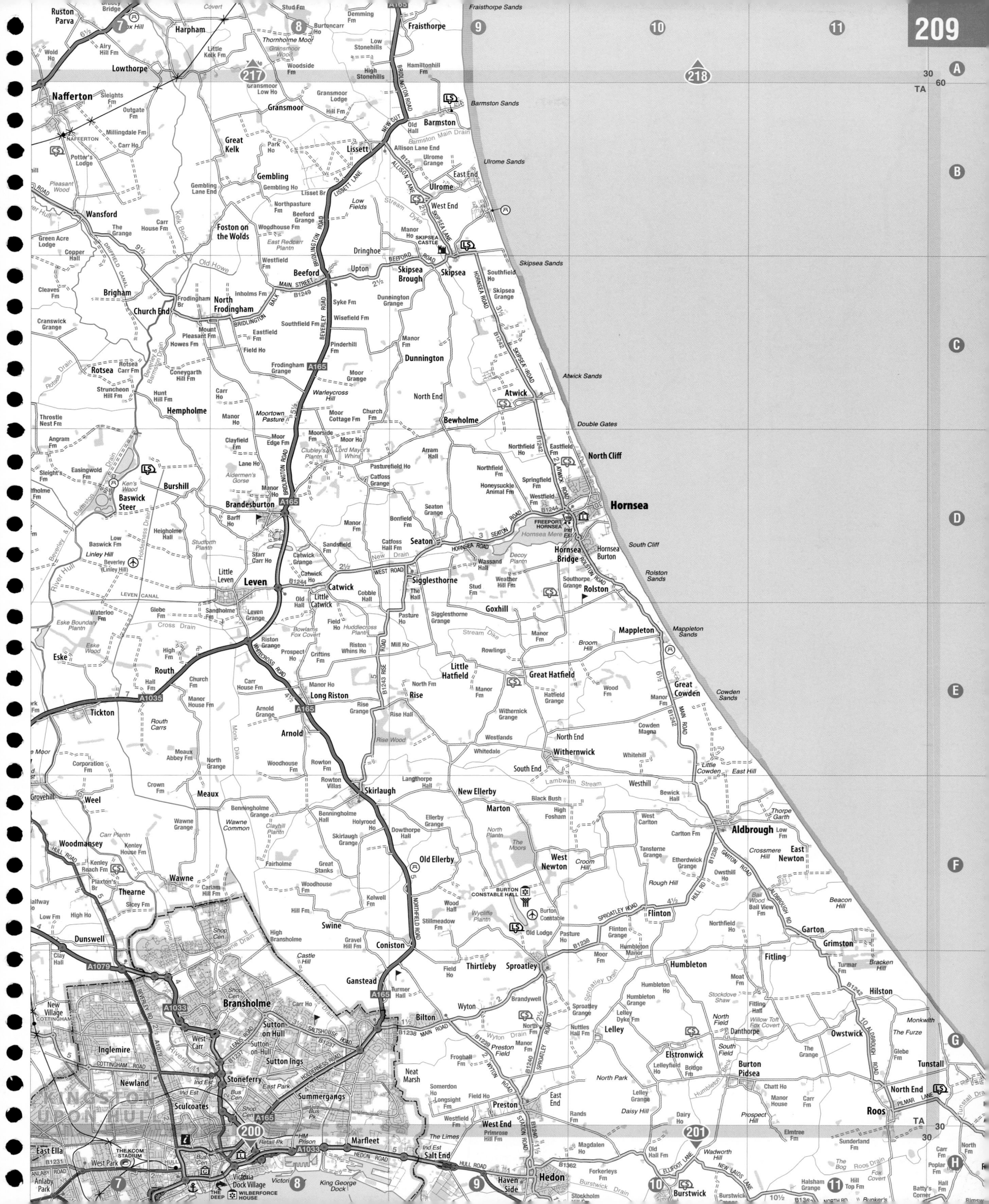

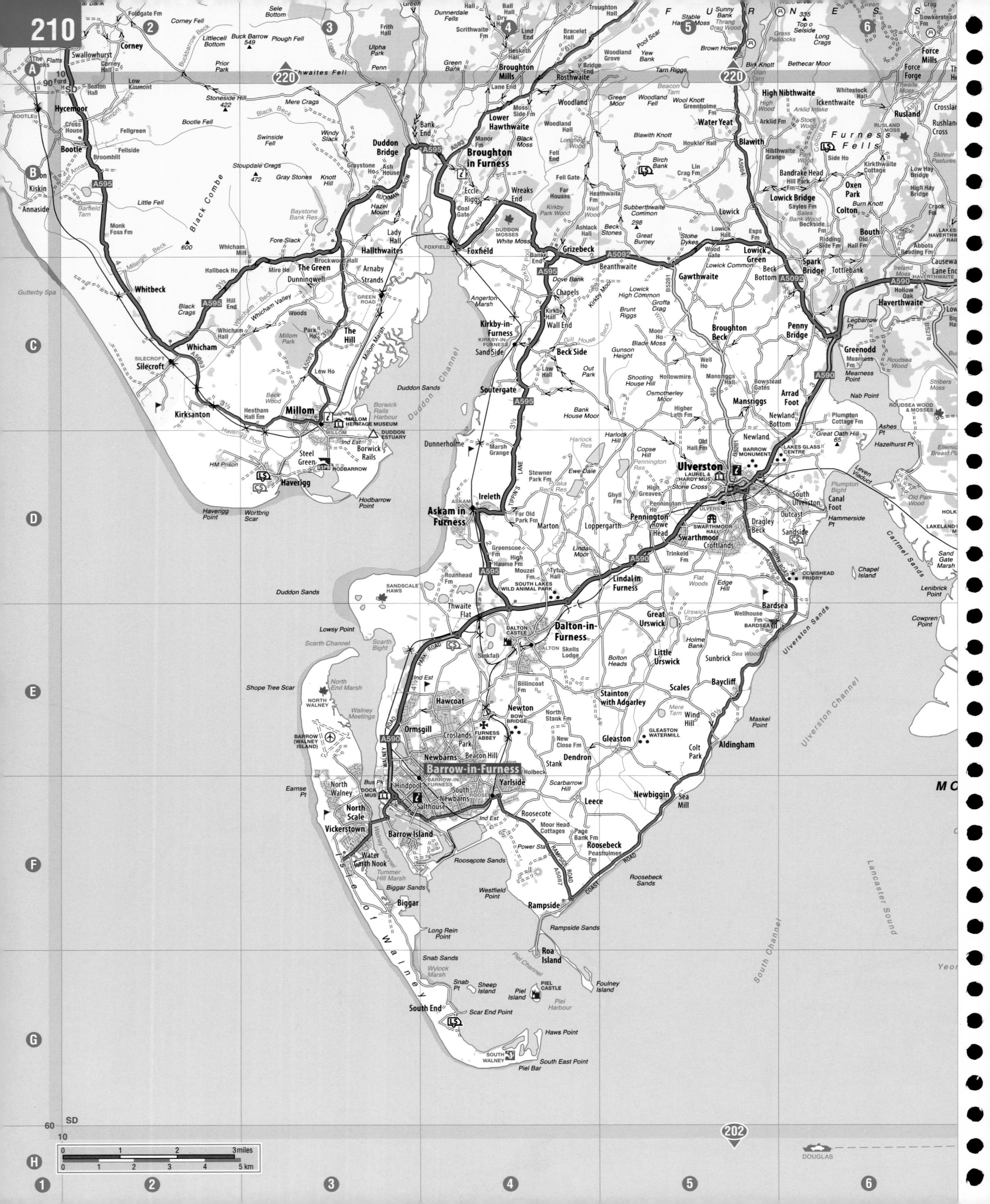

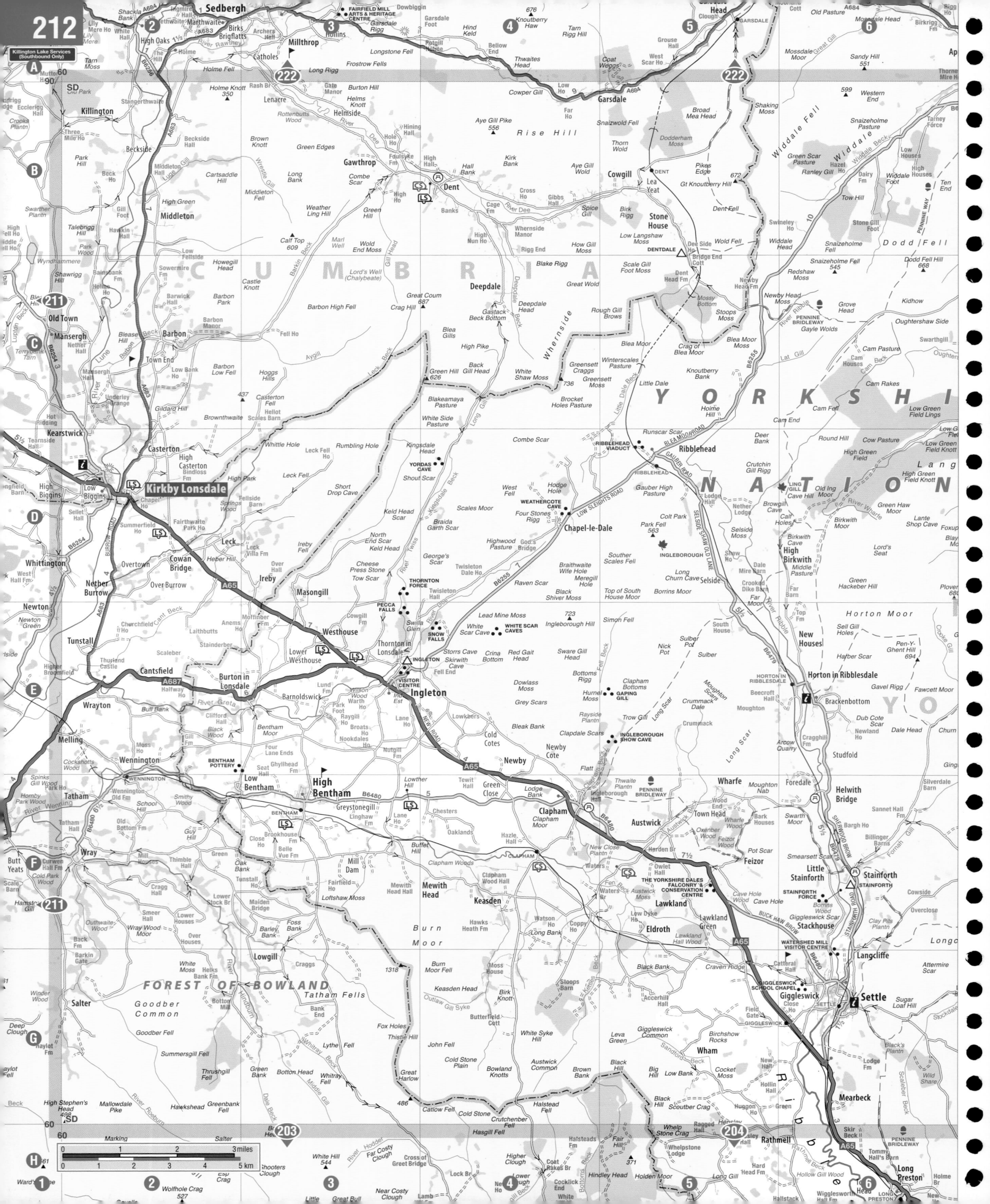

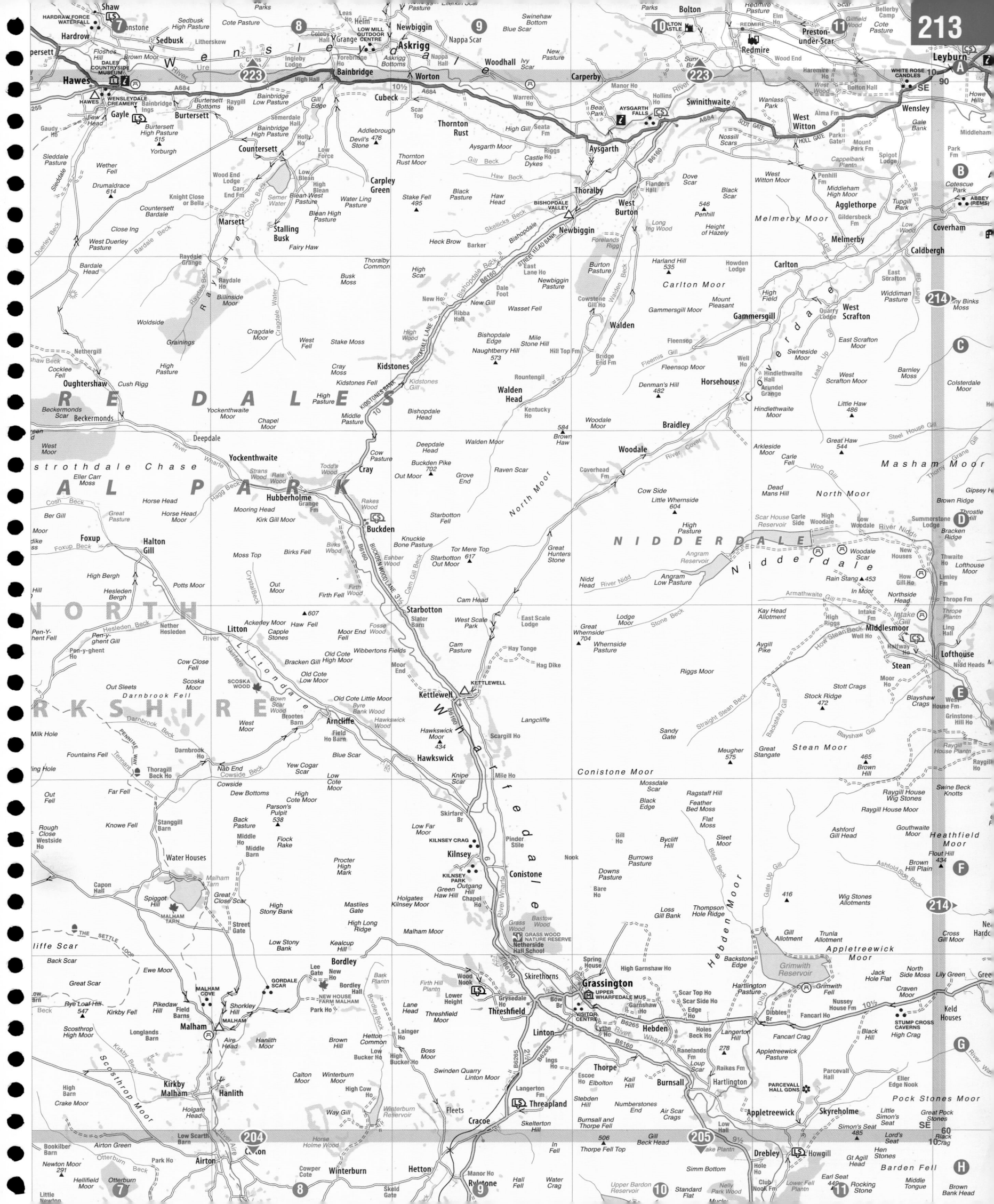

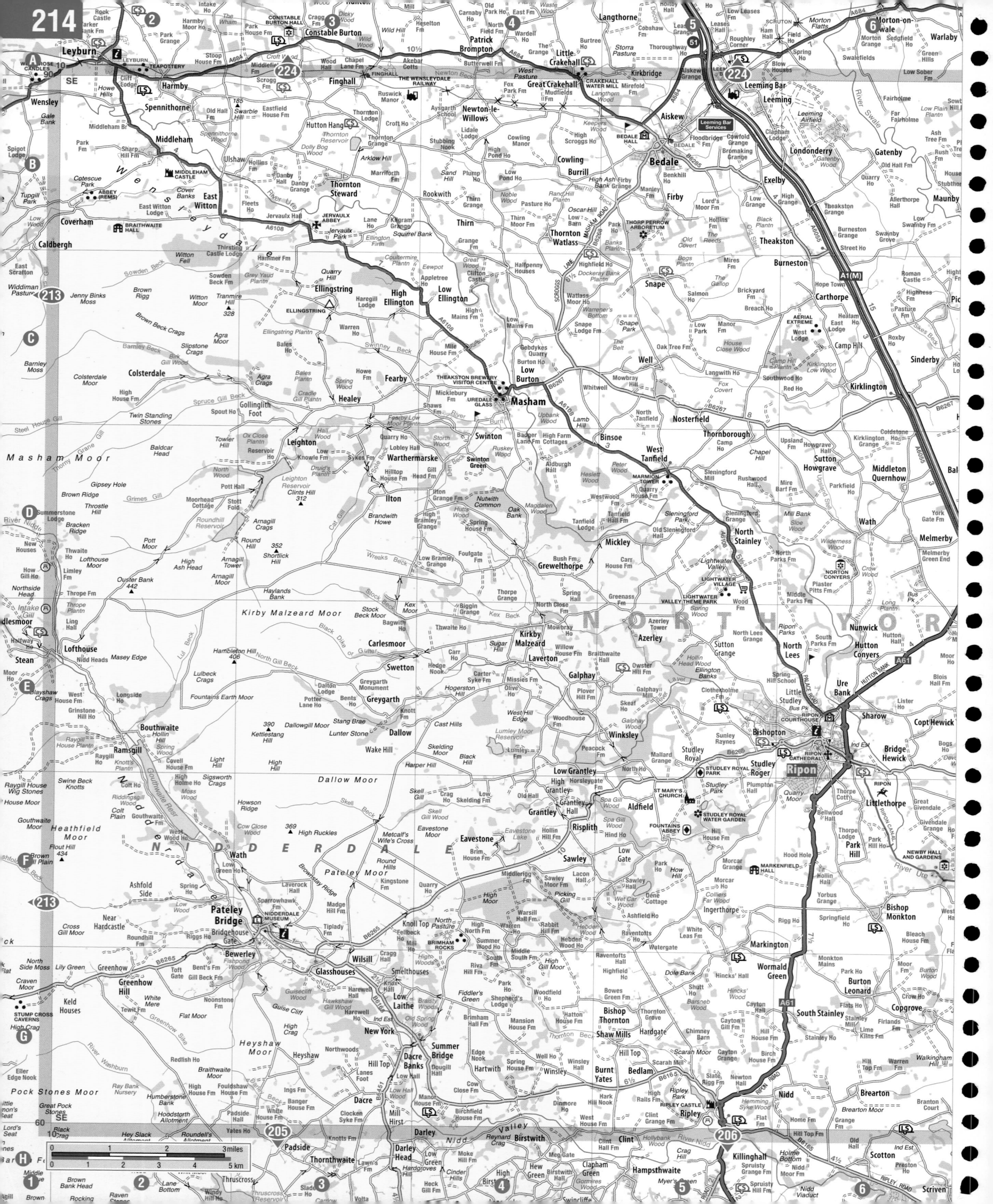

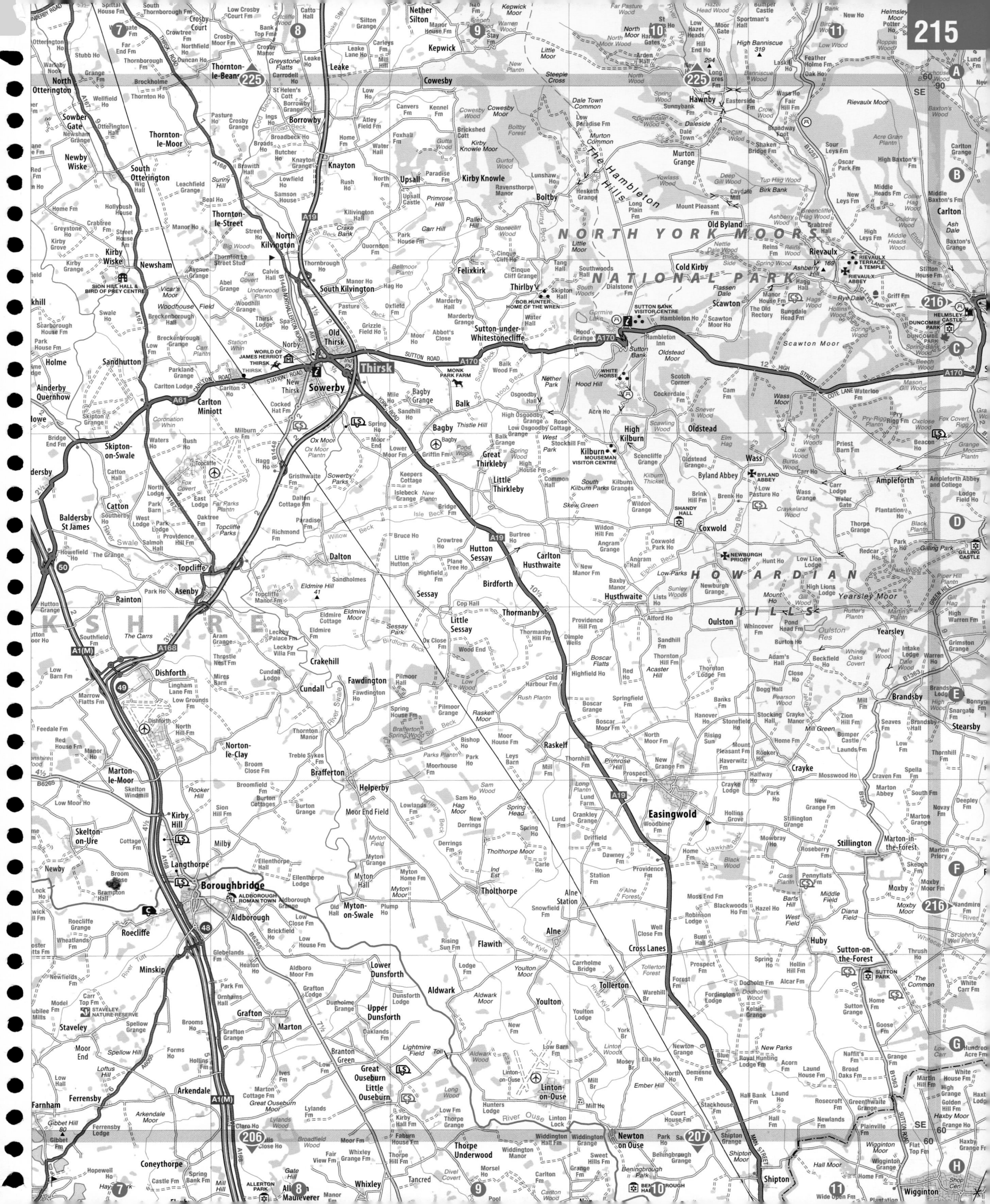

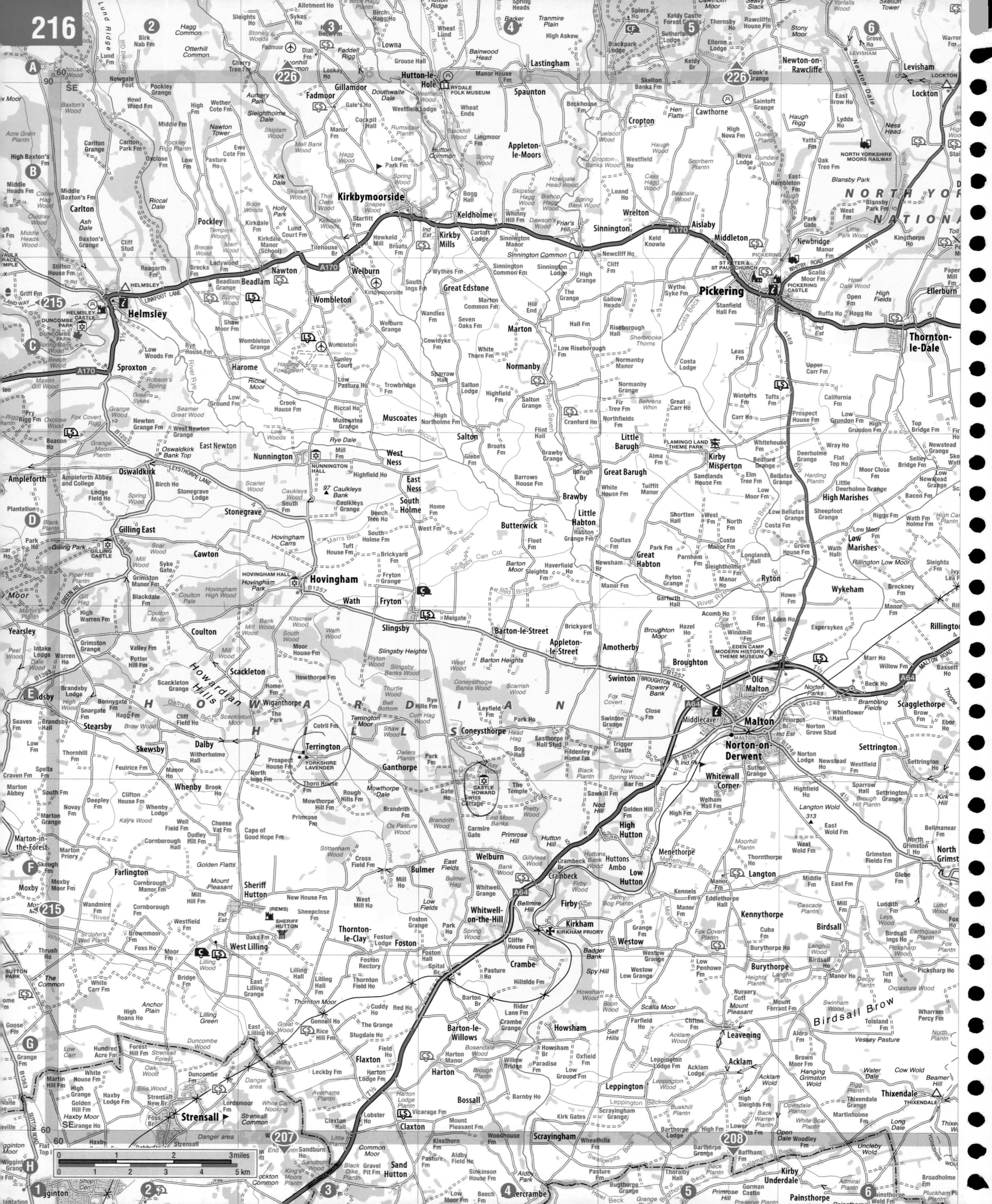

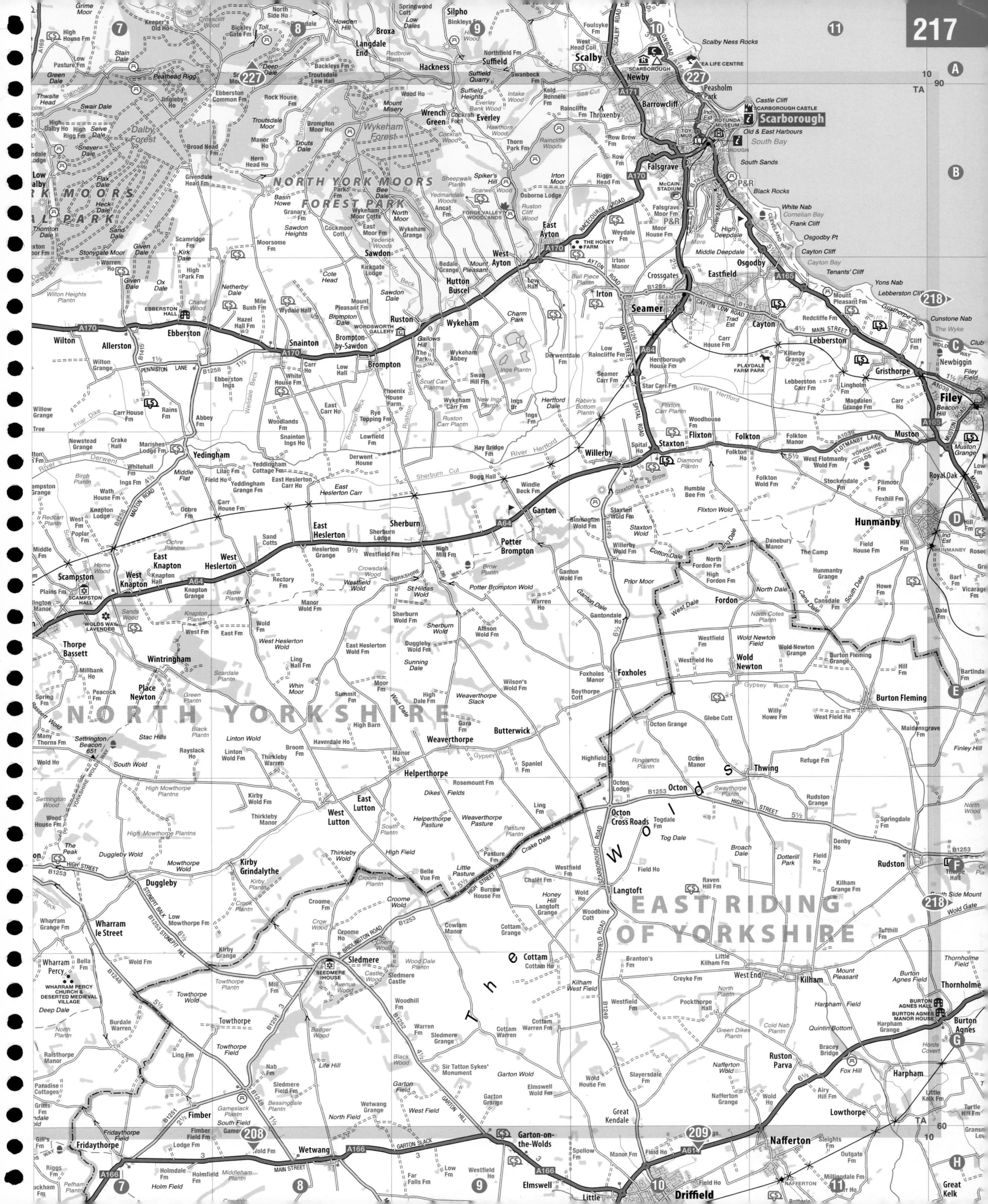

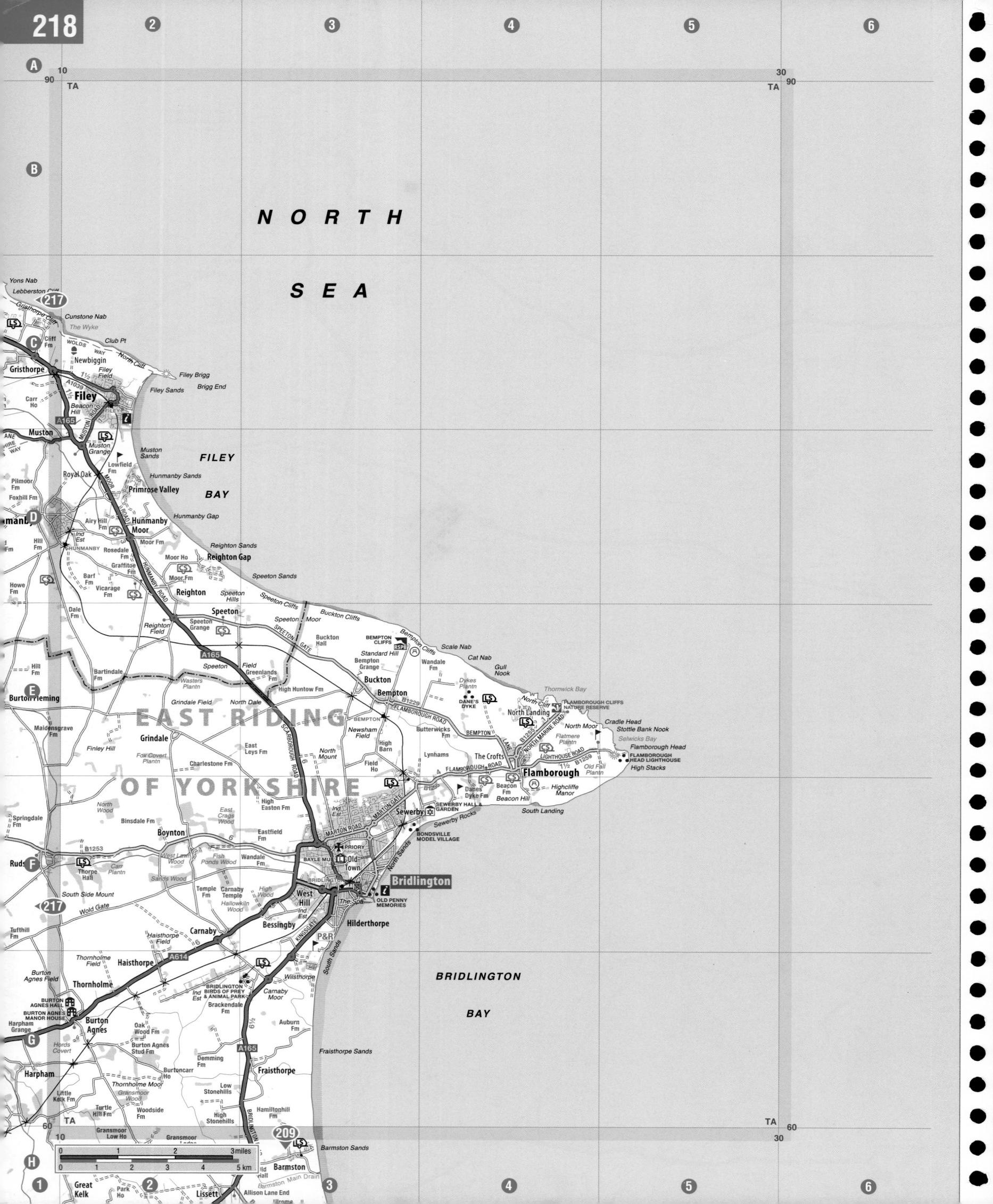

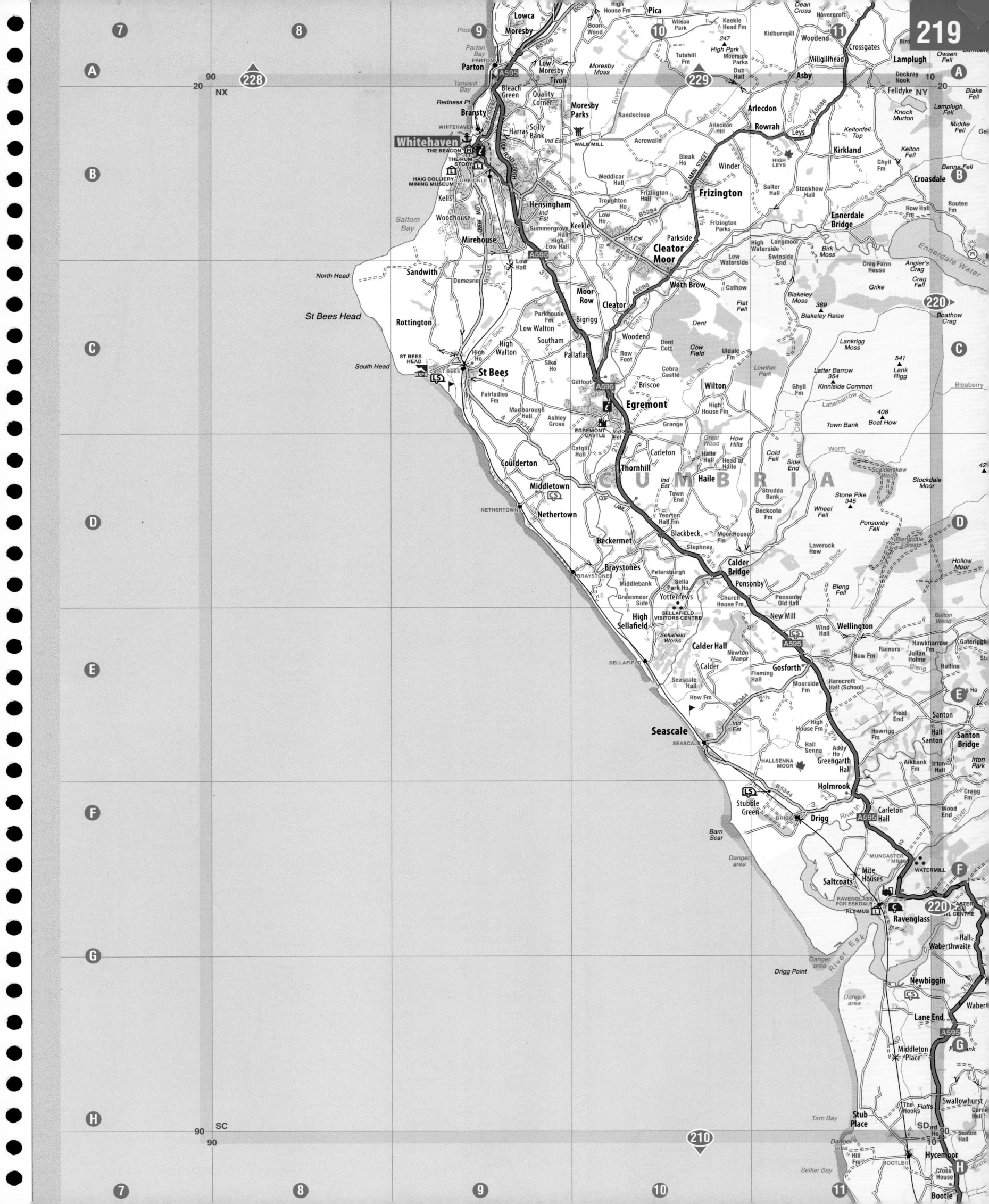

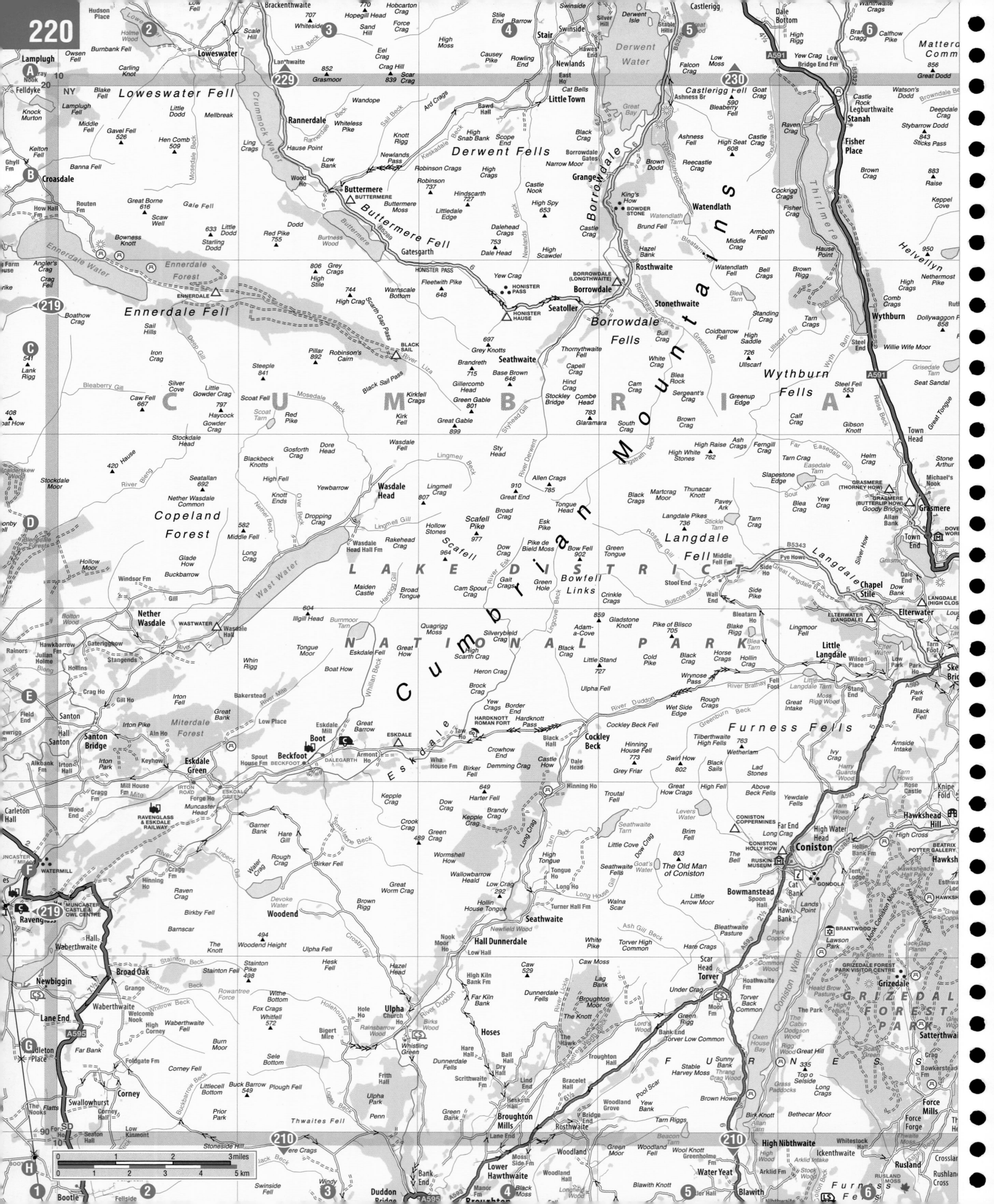

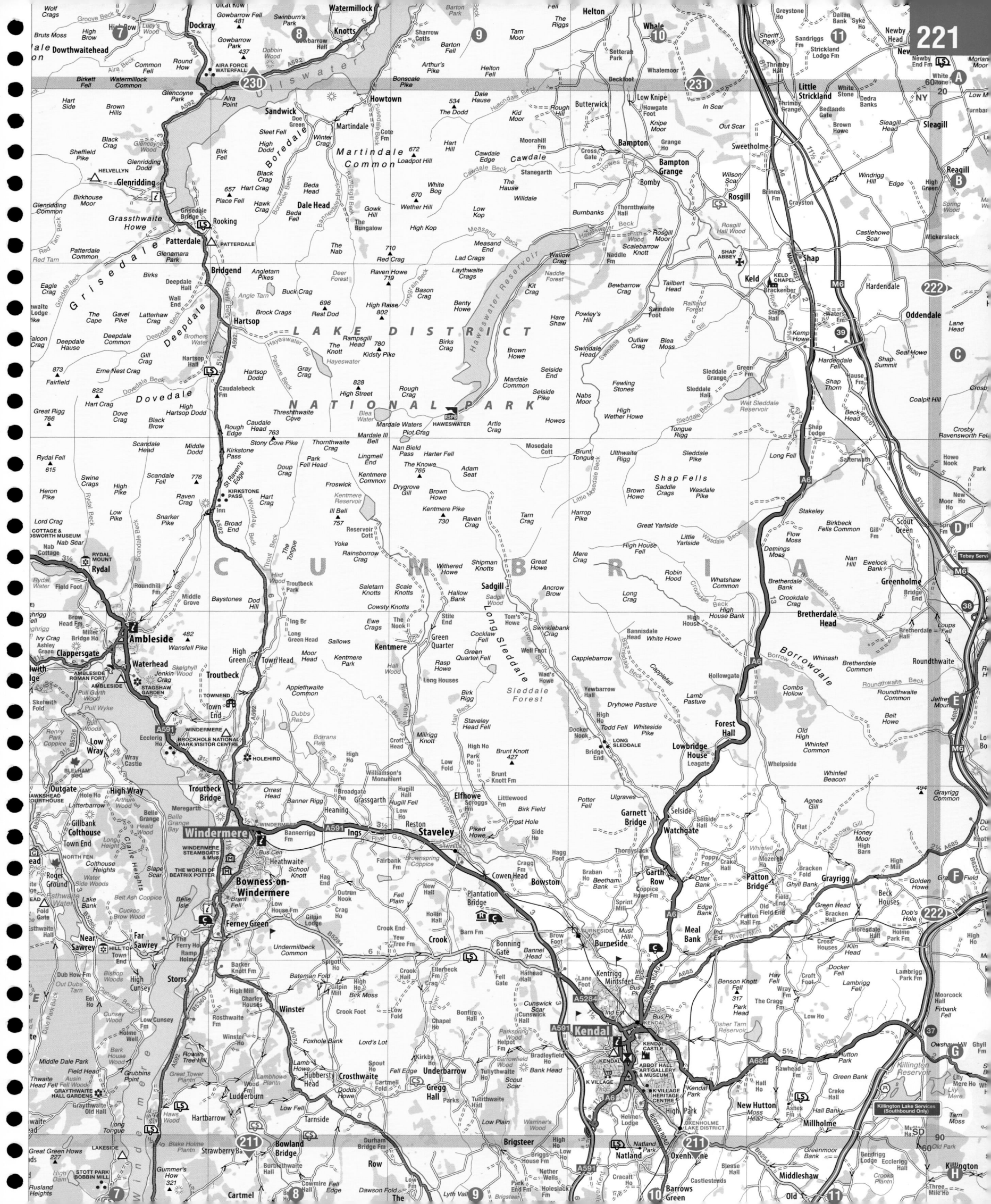

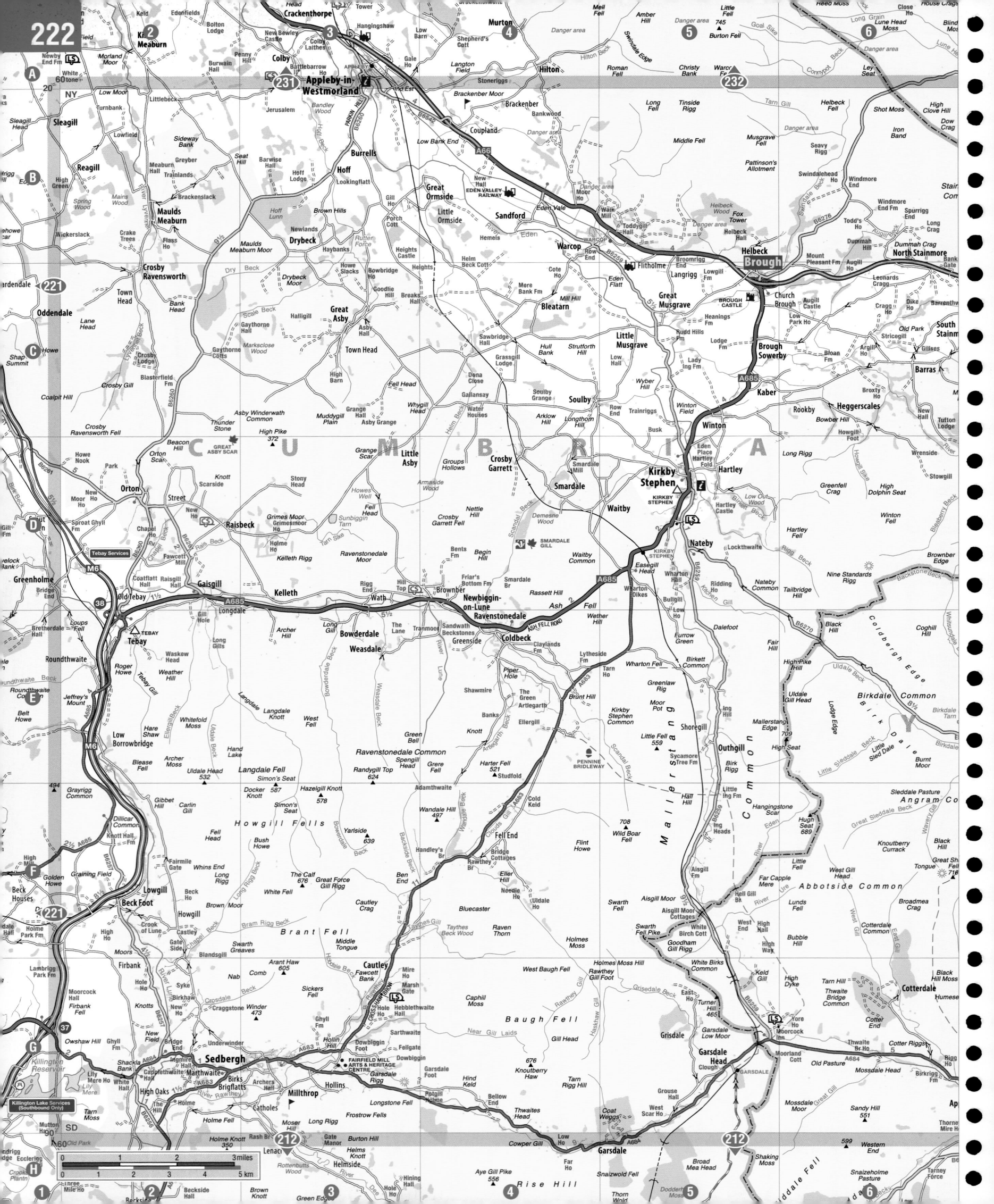

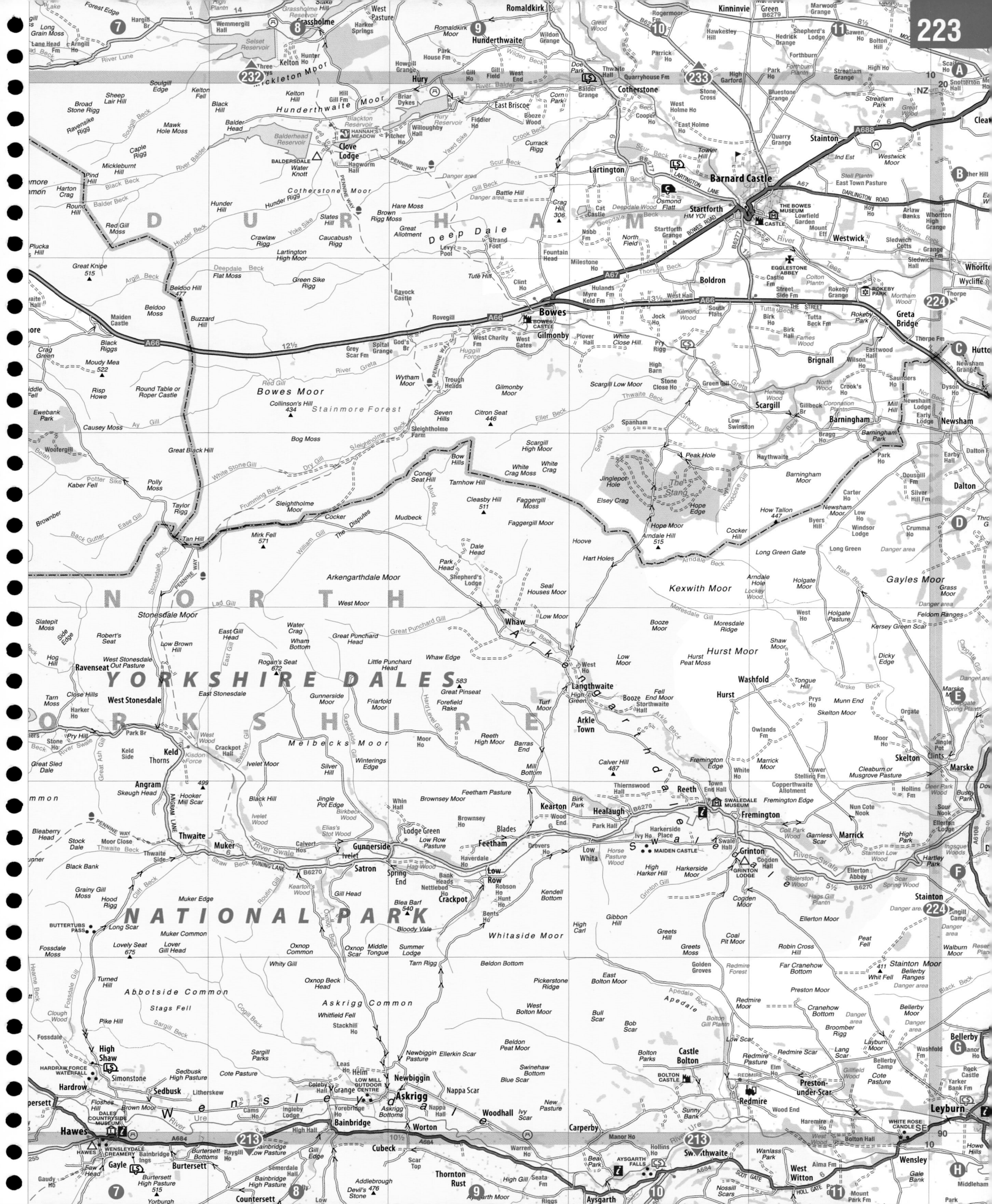

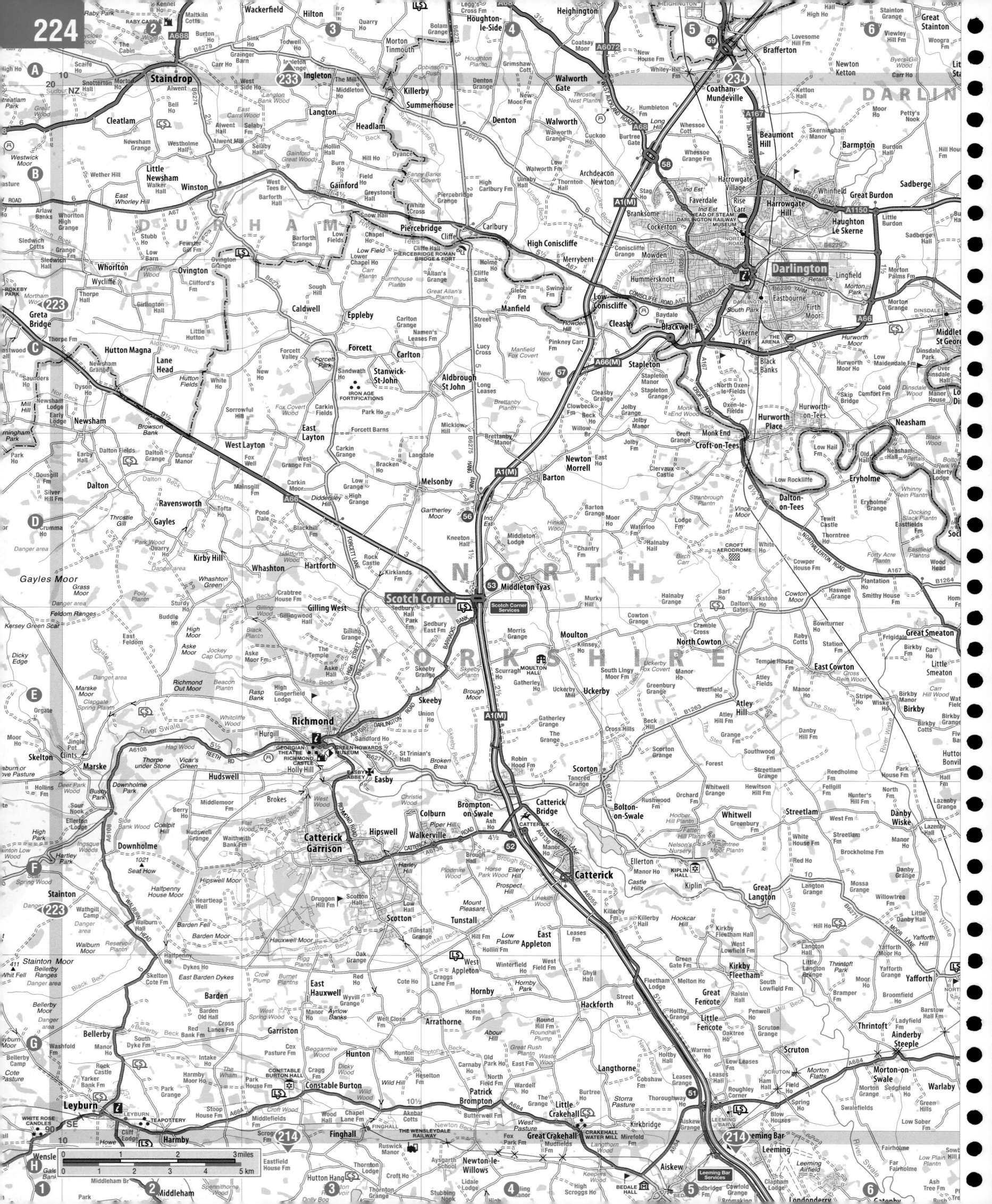

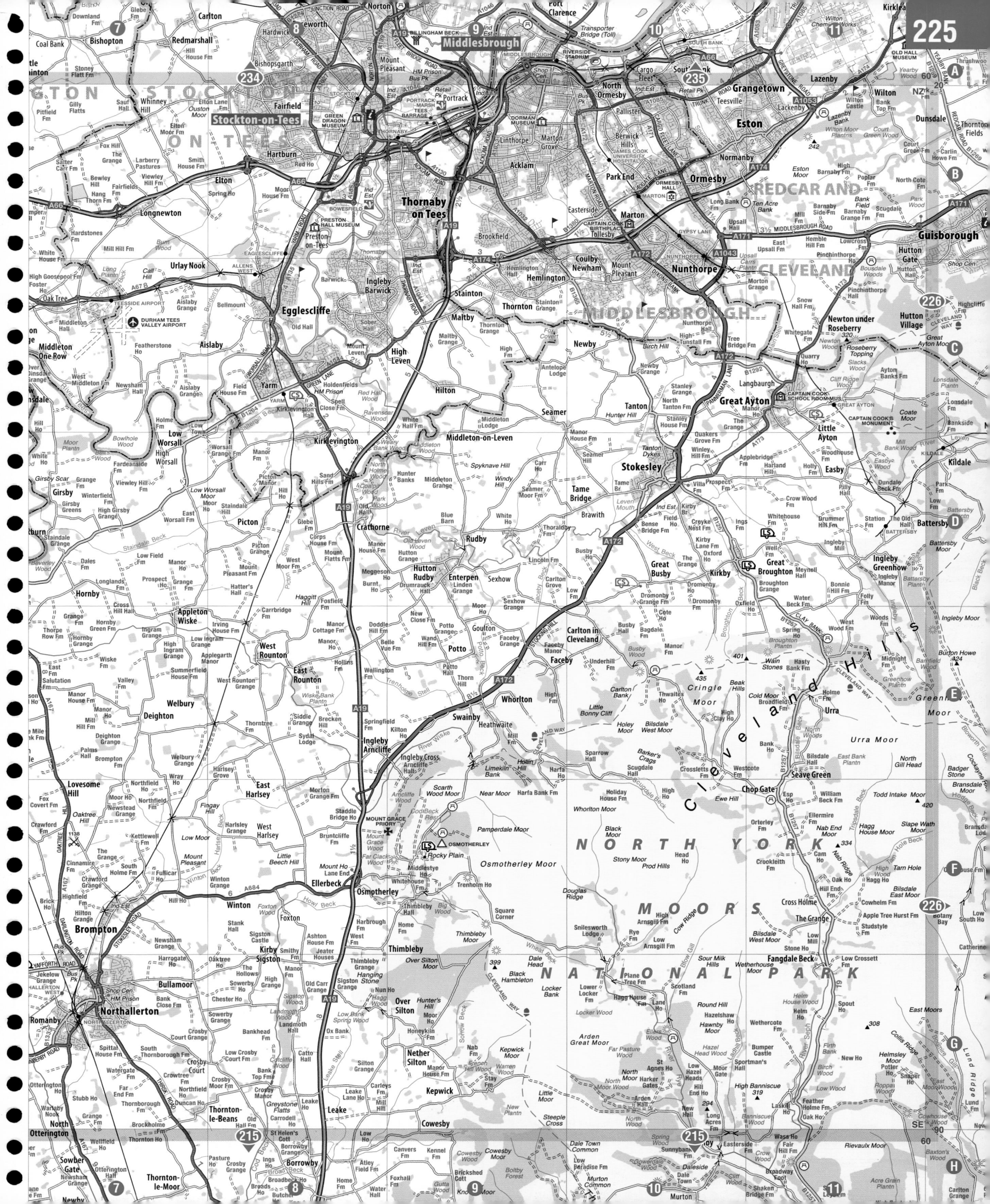

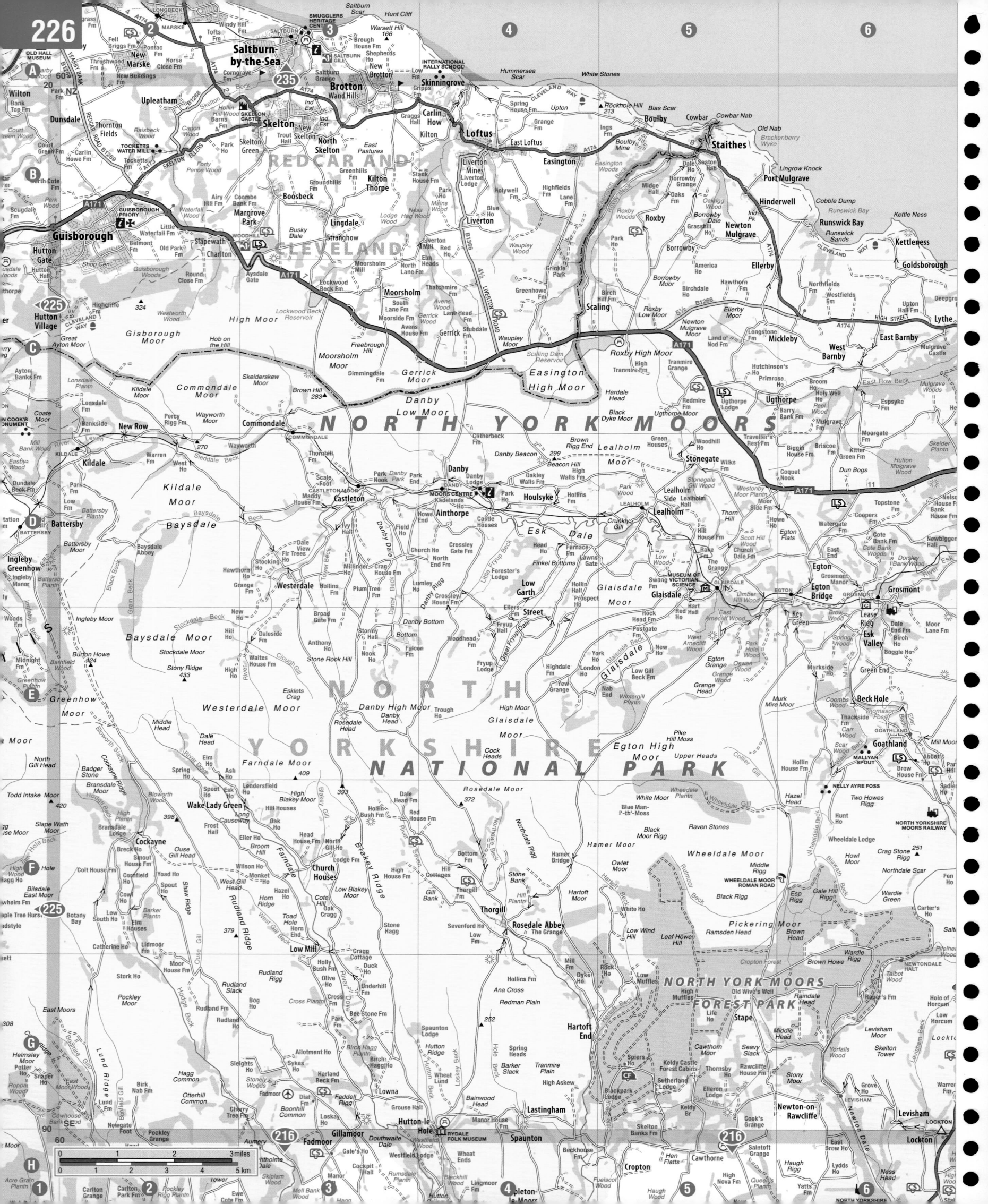

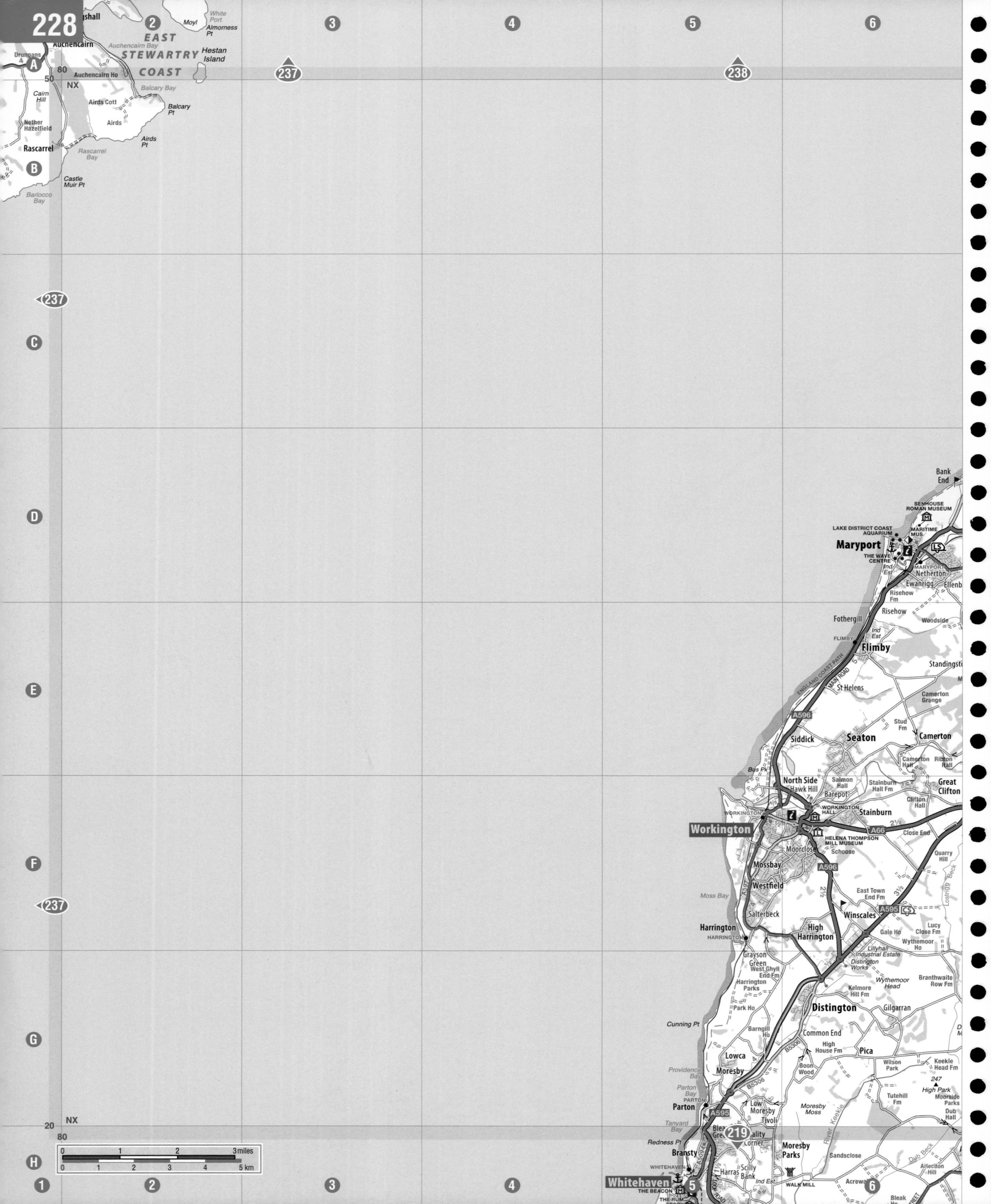

EAST STEWARTRY COAST

Moyl
White Port
Almorness Pt

Drungans

Auchencairn
Auchencairn Bay
Hestan Island

A

80
50
NX
Auchencairn Ho

Cairn Hill

Airds Cott
Balcary Bay

Nether Hazelfield
Airds
Balcary Pt

Rascarrel
Airds Pt

B
Rascarrel Bay
Castle Muir Pt

Barlocco Bay

237

C

Bank End

SENHOUSE ROMAN MUSEUM

D
LAKE DISTRICT COAST AQUARIUM
MARITIME MUS.

Maryport
THE WAVE CENTRE
MARYPORT Ind Est
Netherton
Ewanrigg
Ellenb

Risehow Fm

Fothergill
Risehow
Woodside
Ind Est
FLIMBY

Flimby
Standingsto

St Helens
Camerton Grange

E
A596
Stud Fm

Siddick
Seaton
Camerton

Camerton Hall
Ribton Hall

Bus Pk
North Side
Salmon Hall
Stainburn Hall Fm
Great Clifton

Hawk Hill
Barepot
Clifton Hall

WORKINGTON HALL
Stainburn
Close End

Workington
HELENA THOMPSON MILL MUSEUM
Schoose
A66 2½

Moorclose
Quarry Hill

F
Mossbay
A596
East Town End Fm
Losting Beck

Westfield
2½

Moss Bay
Salterbeck
Winscales
A595
Lucy Close Fm

Harrington
High Harrington
Gale Ho
Wythemoor Ho

HARRINGTON
Lillyhall Industrial Estate
Distington Works
Wythemoor Head
Branthwaite Row Fm

Grayson Green
West Ghyll End Fm
Kelmore Hill Fm

Harrington Parks

Park Ho
Distington
Gilgarran

Cunning Pt
Barngill
Common End
High House Fm

G
Lowca
Boon Wood
Wilson Park
Pica
Keekle Head Fm

Providence Bay
Moresby
247
High Park
Tutehill Fm
Moorside Parks

Parton Bay
PARTON
Moresby Moss
Dub Hall

Parton
A595
Low Moresby
Tivoli

Tanyard Bay
Ble Gre ality
219
Corner
Moresby Parks
Sandsclose

Redness Pt

H
0   1   2   3miles
0 1 2 3 4 5 km

20
NX
80

Bransty
WHITEHAVEN
Harras Bank
Scilly Banks
WALK MILL
Acrewo

Whitehaven
THE BEACON
THE RUM
Ind Est

1   2   3   4   5   6

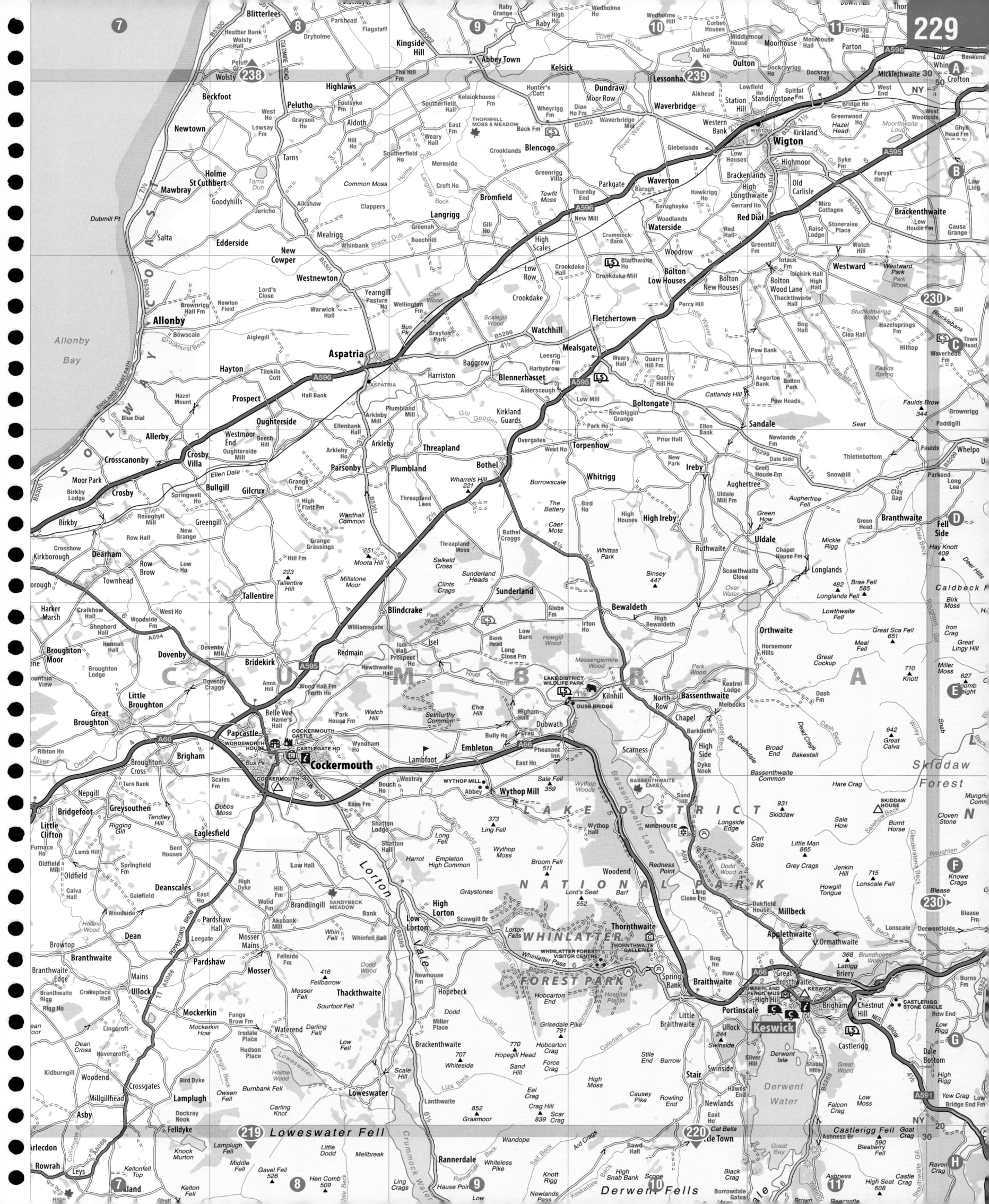

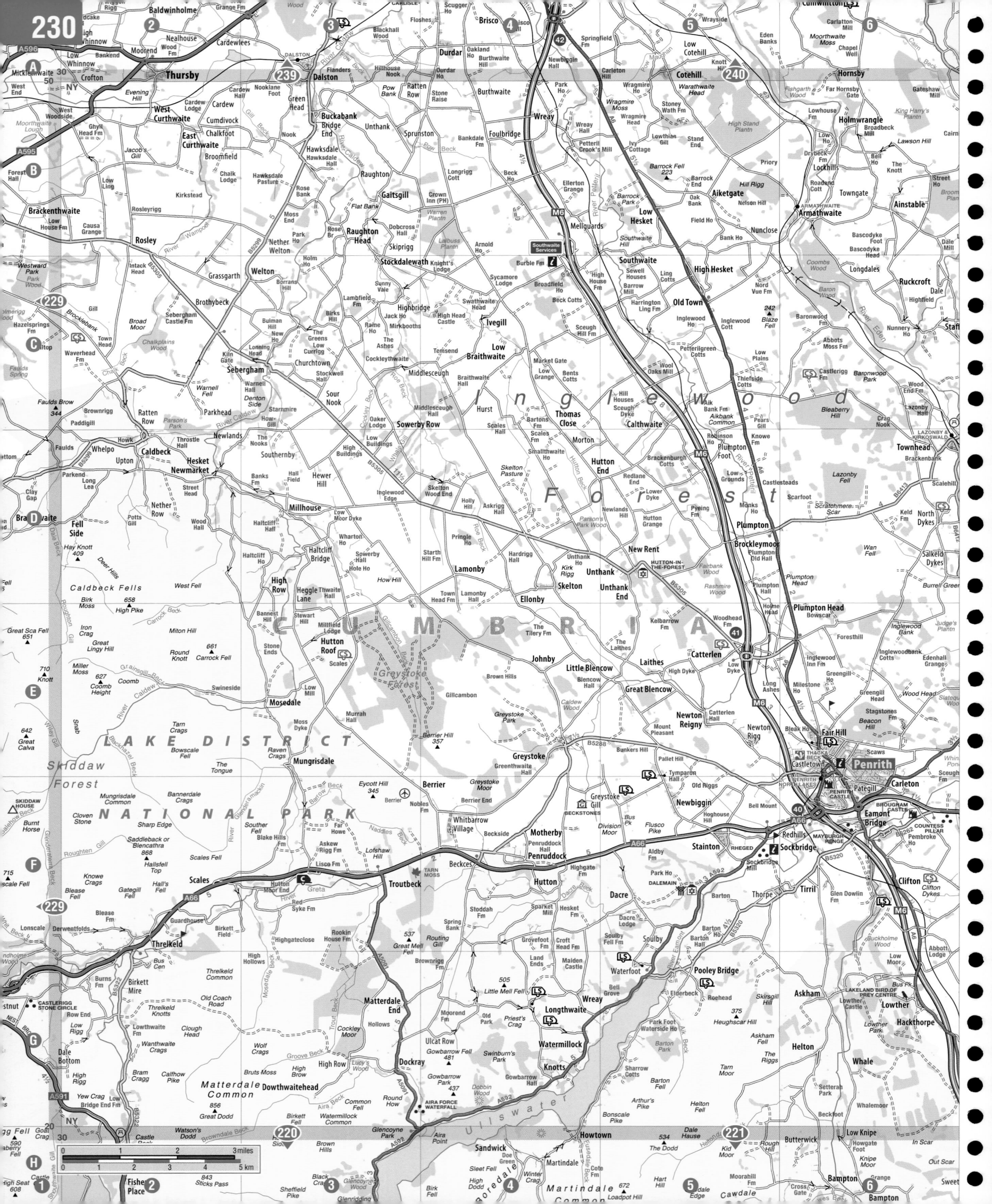

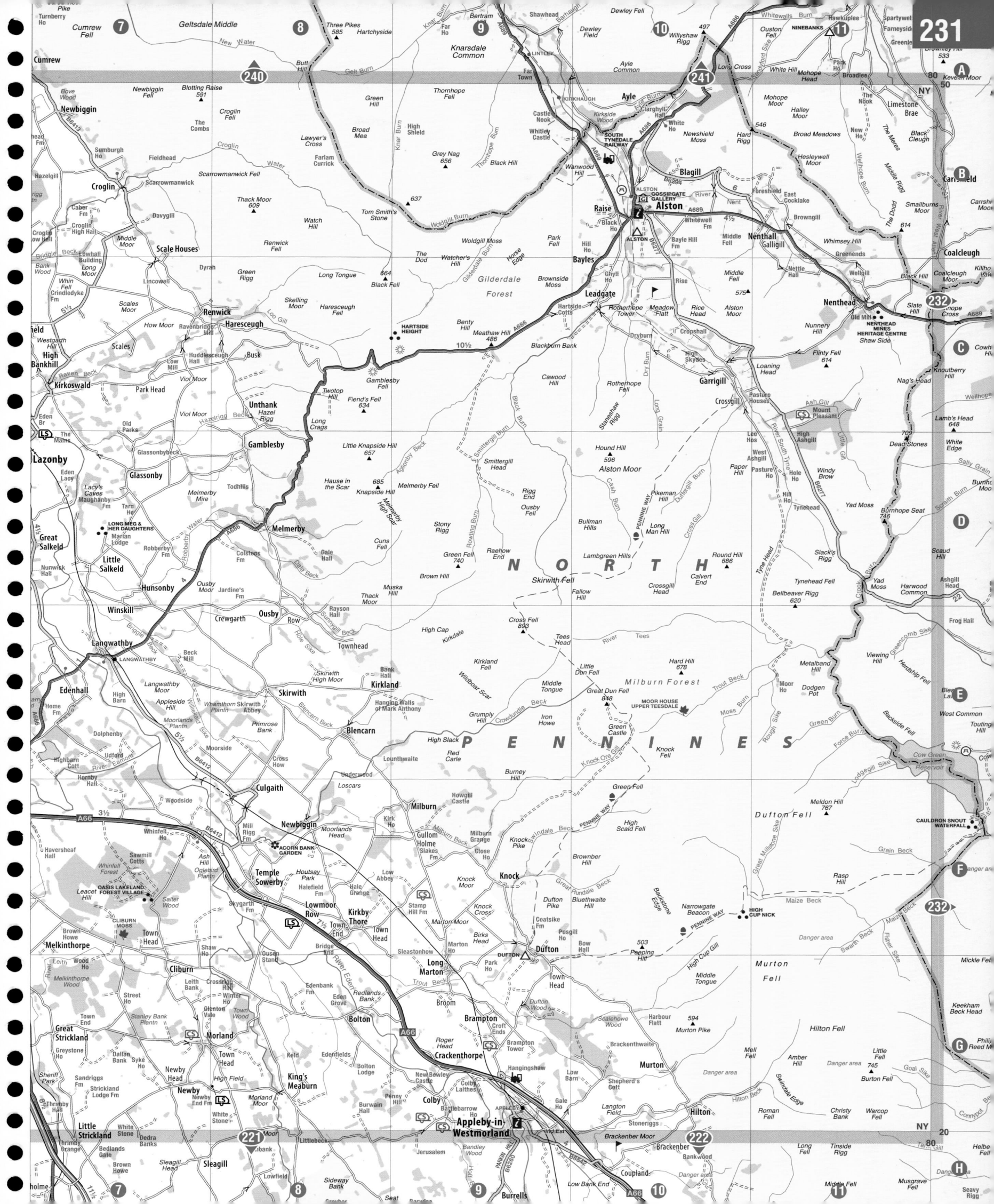

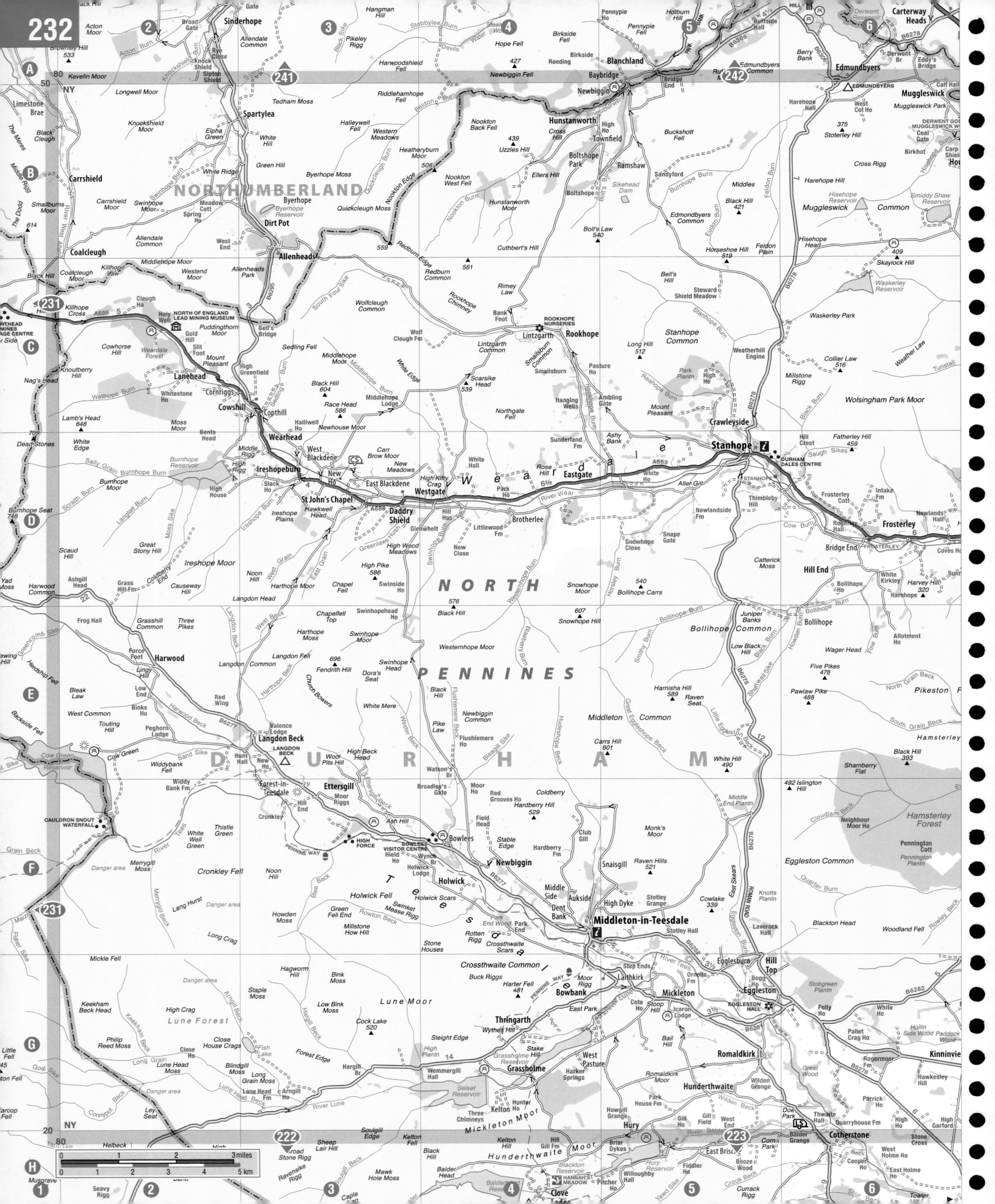

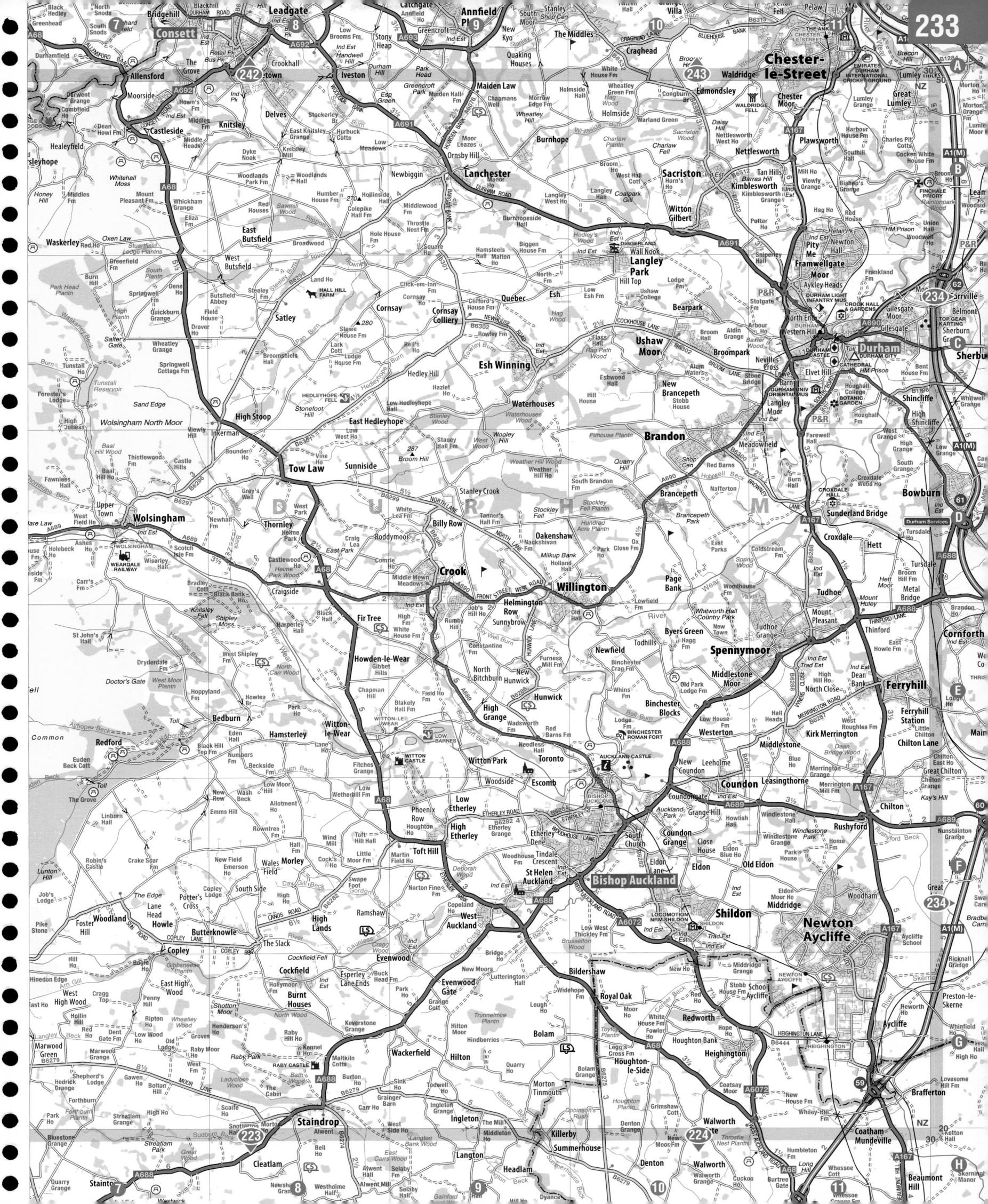

NORTH SEA

TEES BAY

Bran Sands

Coatham Sands

West Scar   Salt Scar

Redcar Rocks   The Flashes

Grangetown Works

COATHAM MARSH   Coatham

Warrenby

BRITISH STEEL REDCAR   Westfield   Redcar Racecourse   Mill Howle

Redcar

Dormanstown

Scanbeck Howle

Marske-by-the-Sea

Stone Gap

Kirkleatham

Grewgrass Fm   LONGBECK   MARSKE   Windy Hill Fm

Yearby   Fell Briggs Fm   Tofts Fm   SMUGGLERS HERITAGE CENTRE   Saltburn Scar   Hunt Cliff

Wilton Chemical Works   Pontac Fm   **Saltburn-by-the-Sea**   Brough House Fm   Warsett Hill 166

OLD HALL MUSEUM   New Marske   Horse Close Fm   Corngrave Fm   SALTBURN GILL   Saltburn Grange   Shepherds Ho   INTERNATIONAL RALLY SCHOOL

Throwshwood   New Buildings   New Brotton   New Brotton   Low   Hummersea Scar   White Stones

Lazenby   225   Upleatham   B1268   A174   **Brotton**   Wand Hills   Gripps   Skinningrove   226   WAY

ngetown   Wilton   Park Fm Top Fm   Hollin   Ind Est   Carlin   Spring House Fm   Upton   Rockhole Hill 213   Bias Scar

ton   Lackenby   GREYSTONE ROAD   Lazenby Bank   Dunsdale   Thornton Fields   Raisbeck Wood   SKELTON CASTLE   New   Ind Est   How   Kilton   Grange Fm   Ings Fm   Cowbar   Cowbar Nab

242   Wilton Moor Plantns   Court Green Wood   TOCKET WATER MI   Capon Wood   **Skelton**   Trout Hall   Skelton Green   **Loftus**   East Loftus   Boulby Mine   Old Nab

7   8   Carlin   Park Ho   Skelton   East Pastures   9   10   11   **Staithes**   Brackenberry Wyke

NZ 80 50

NZ 20 80

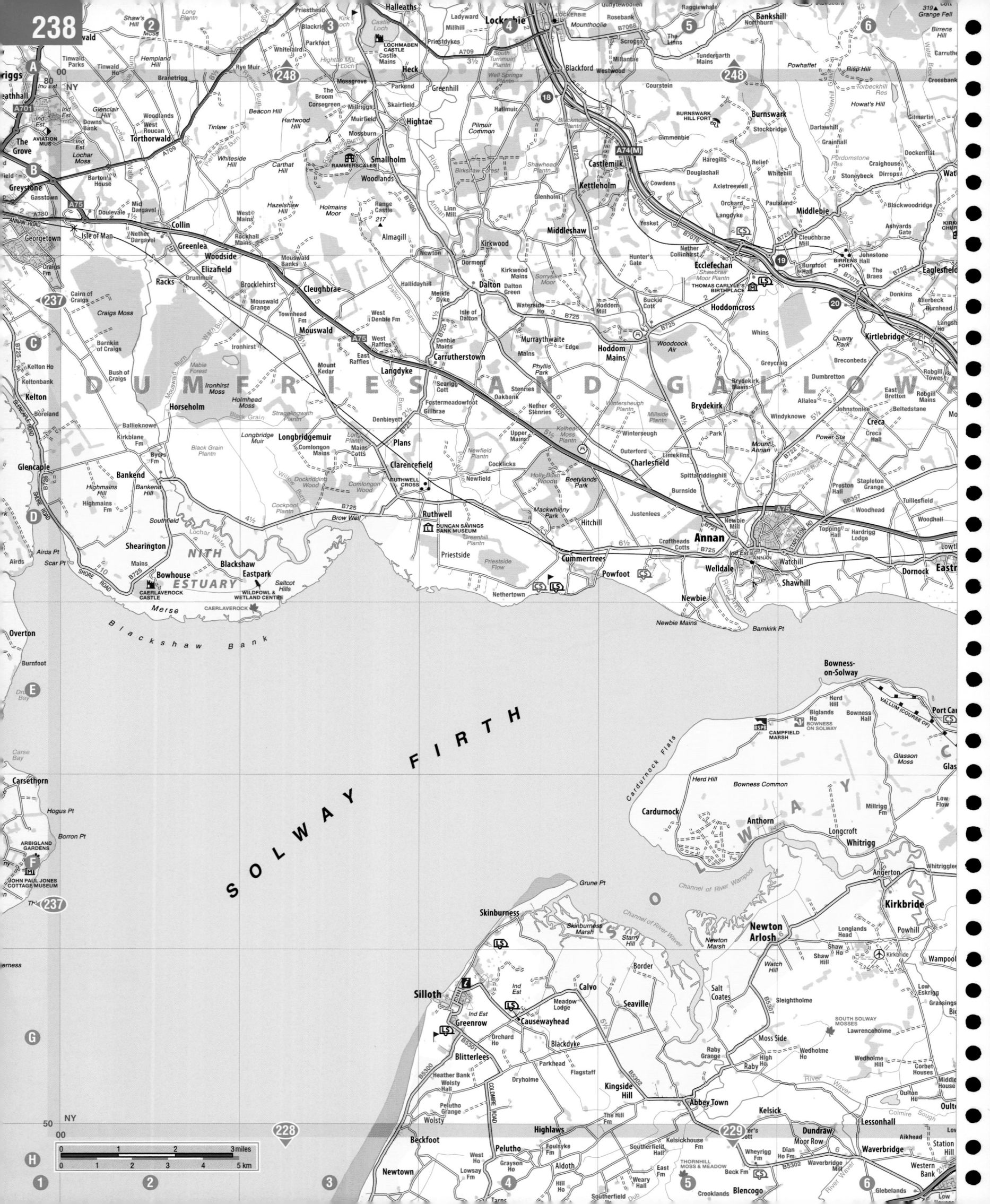

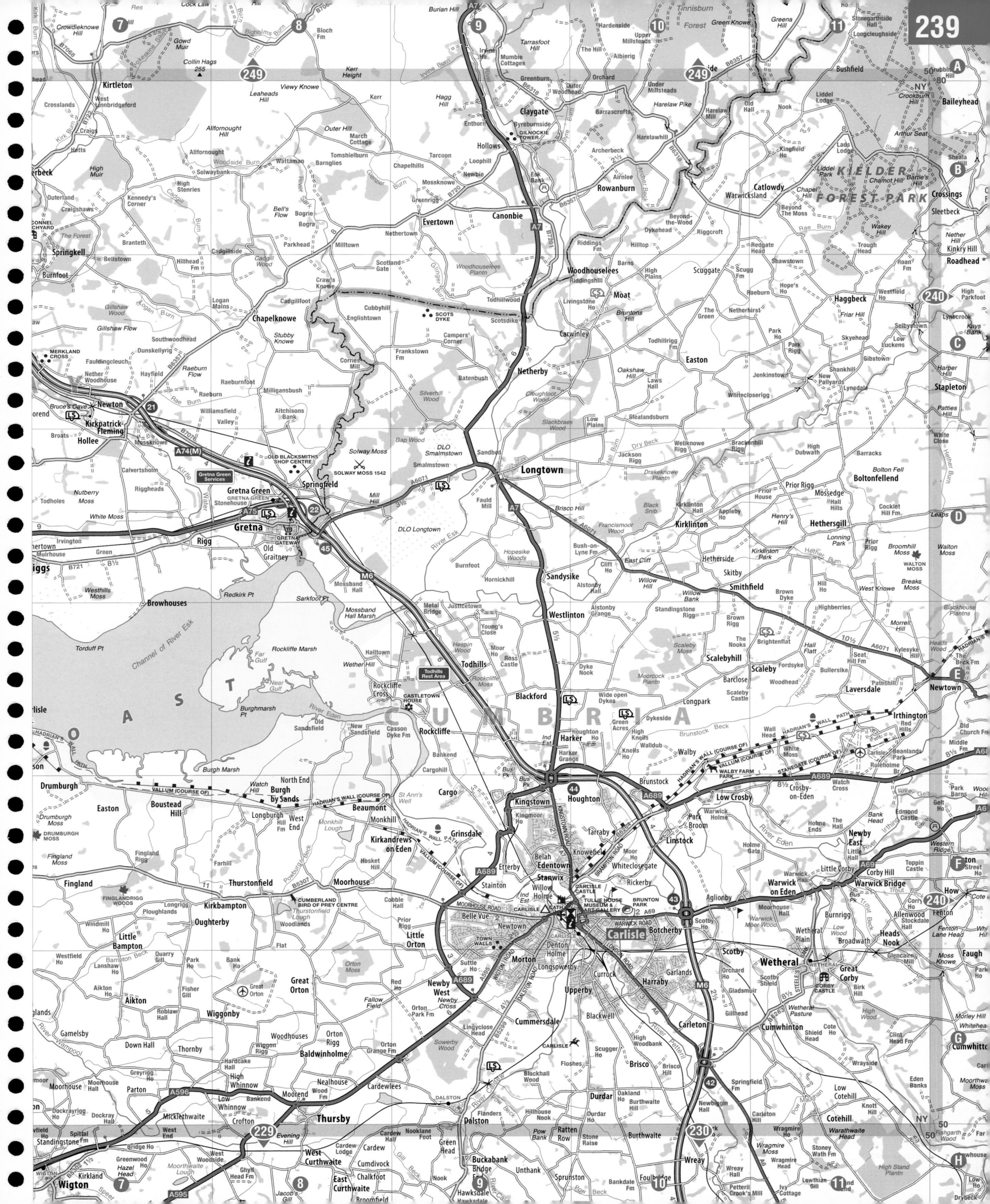

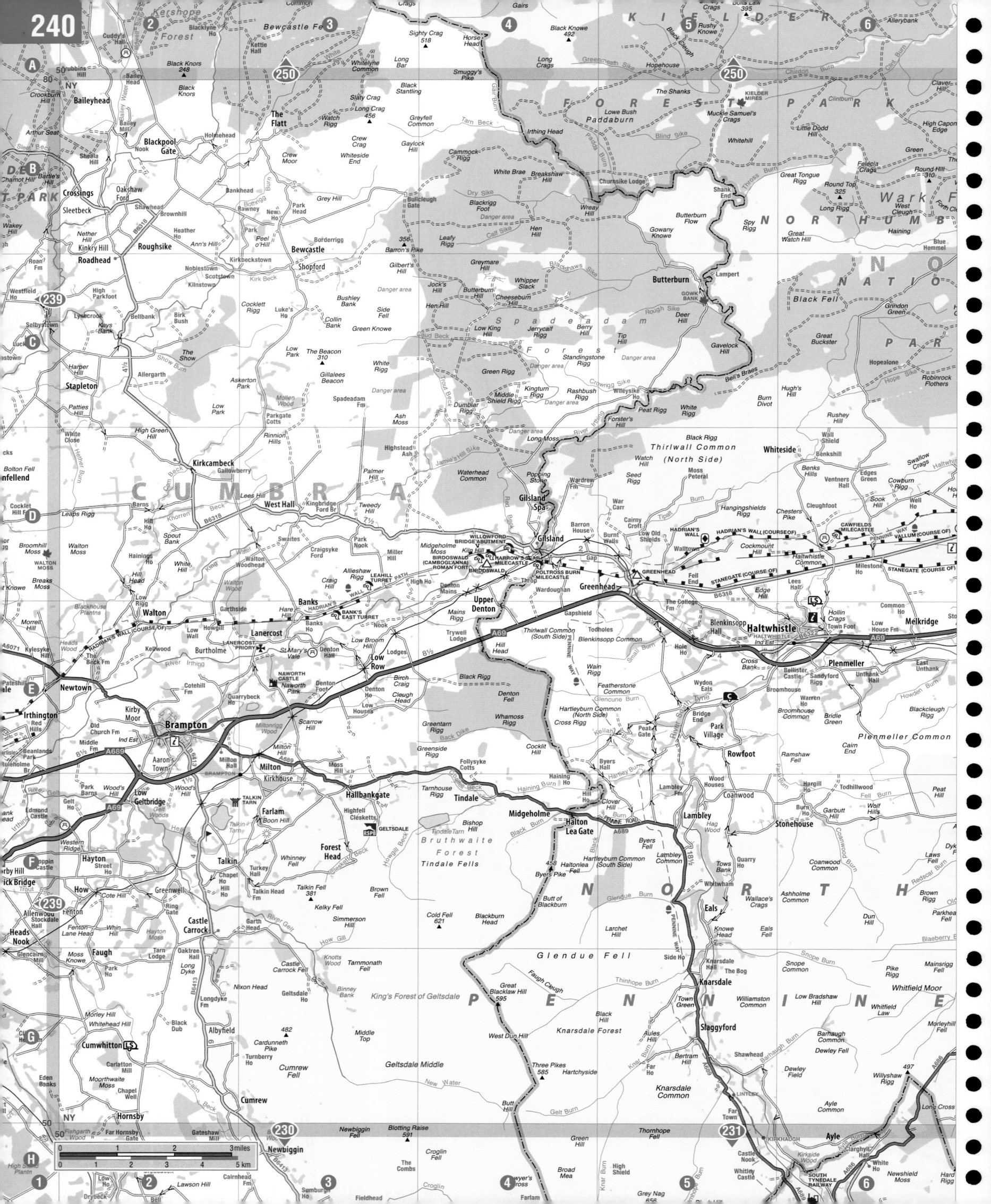

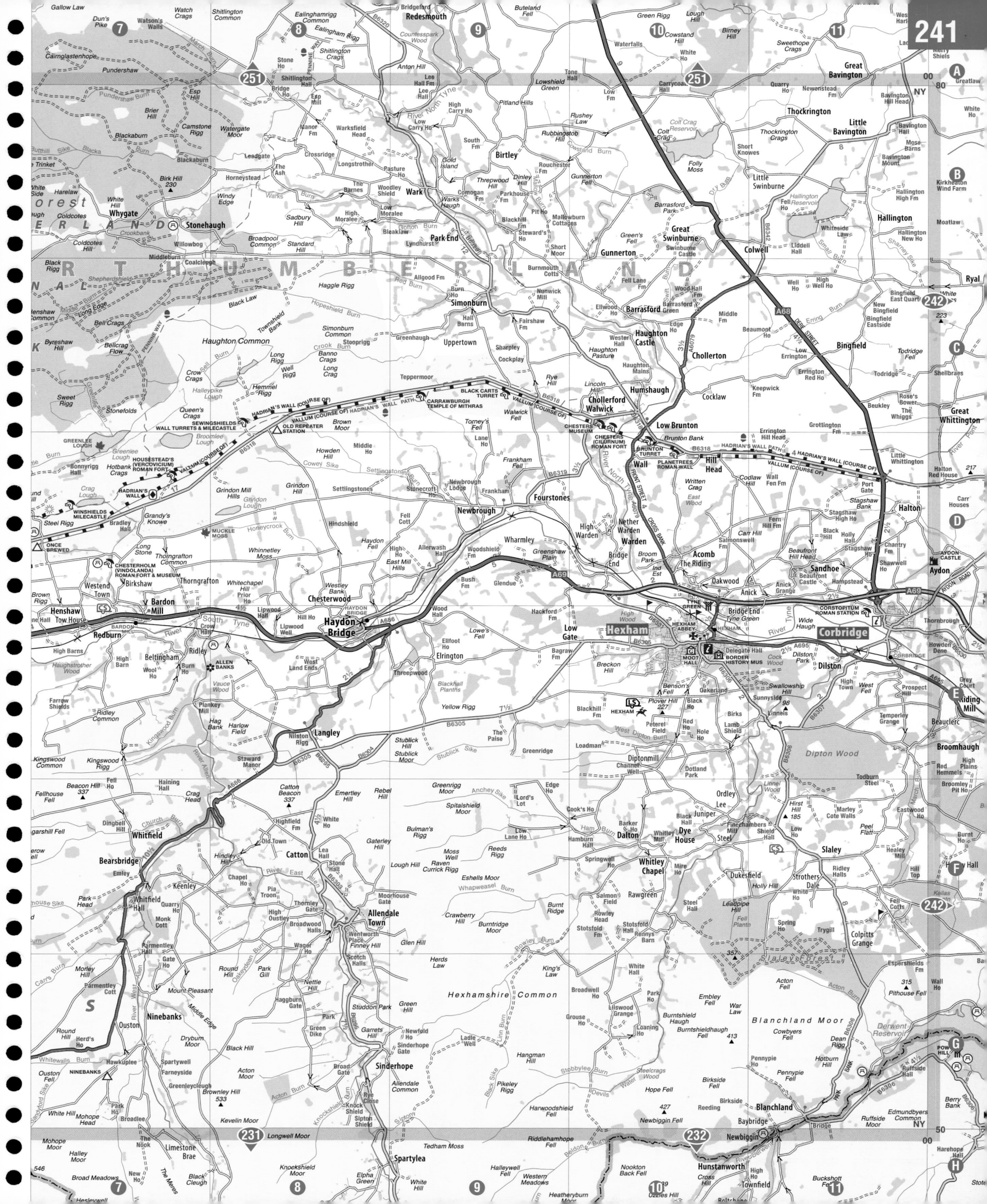

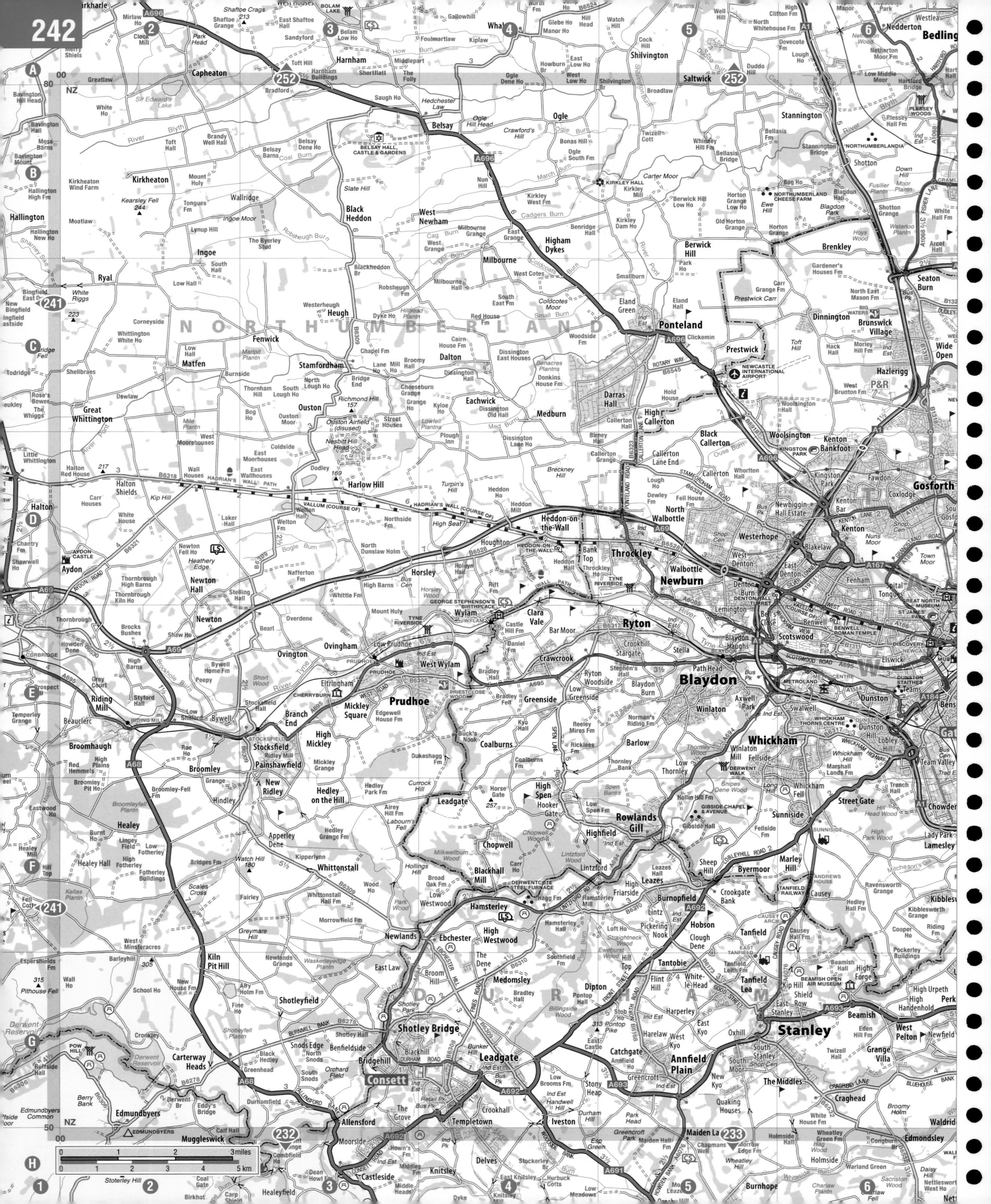

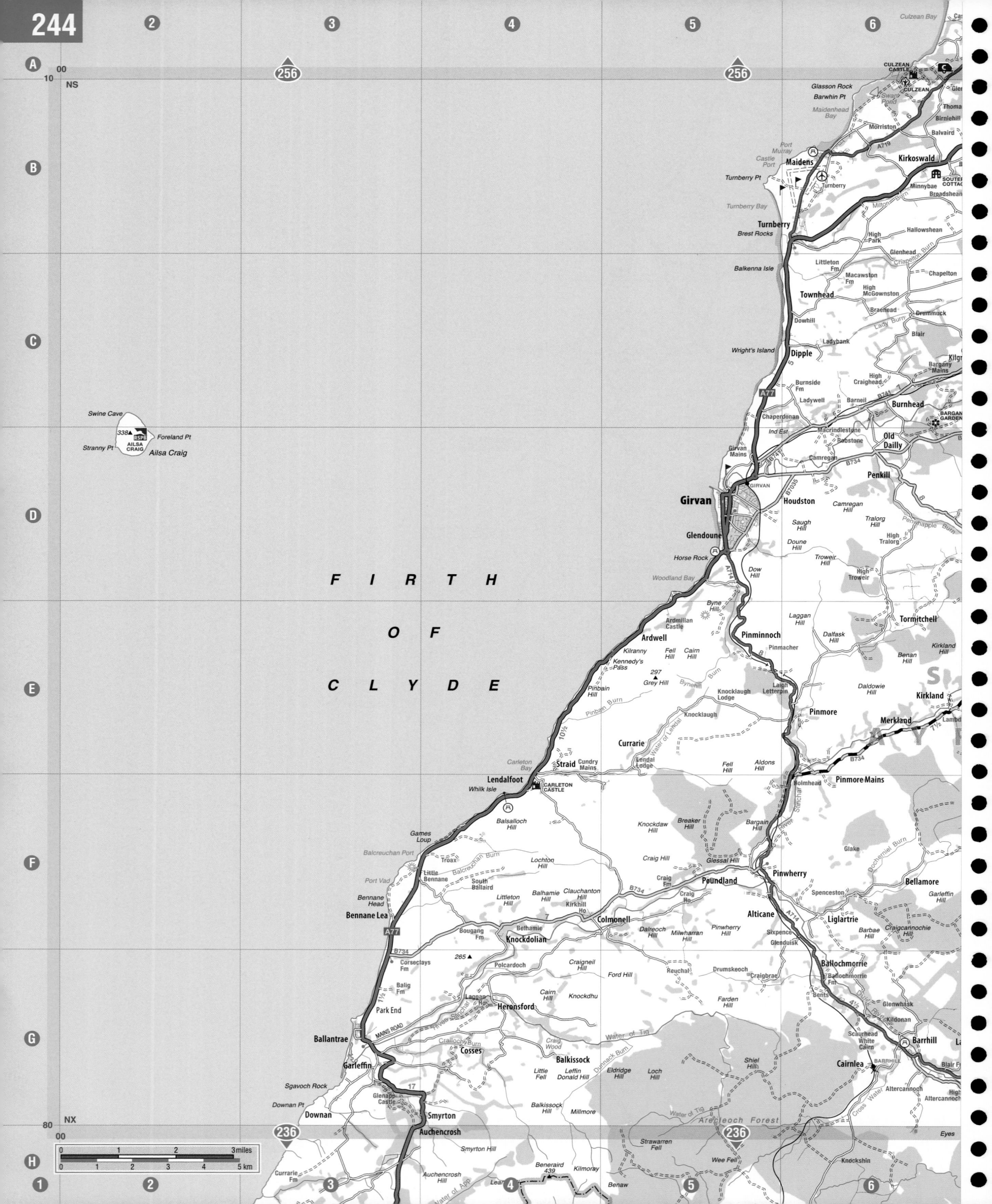

FIRTH
OF
CLYDE

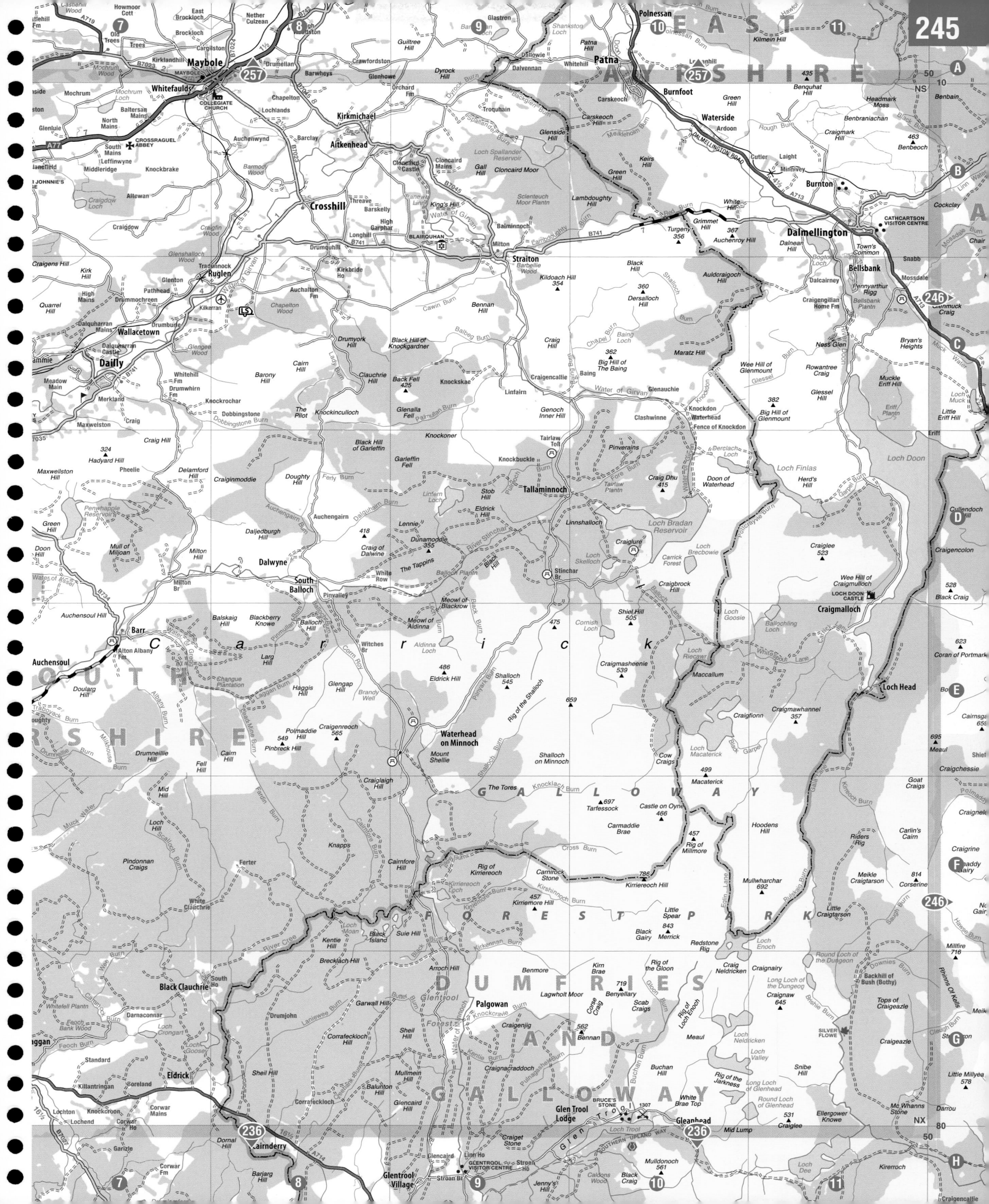

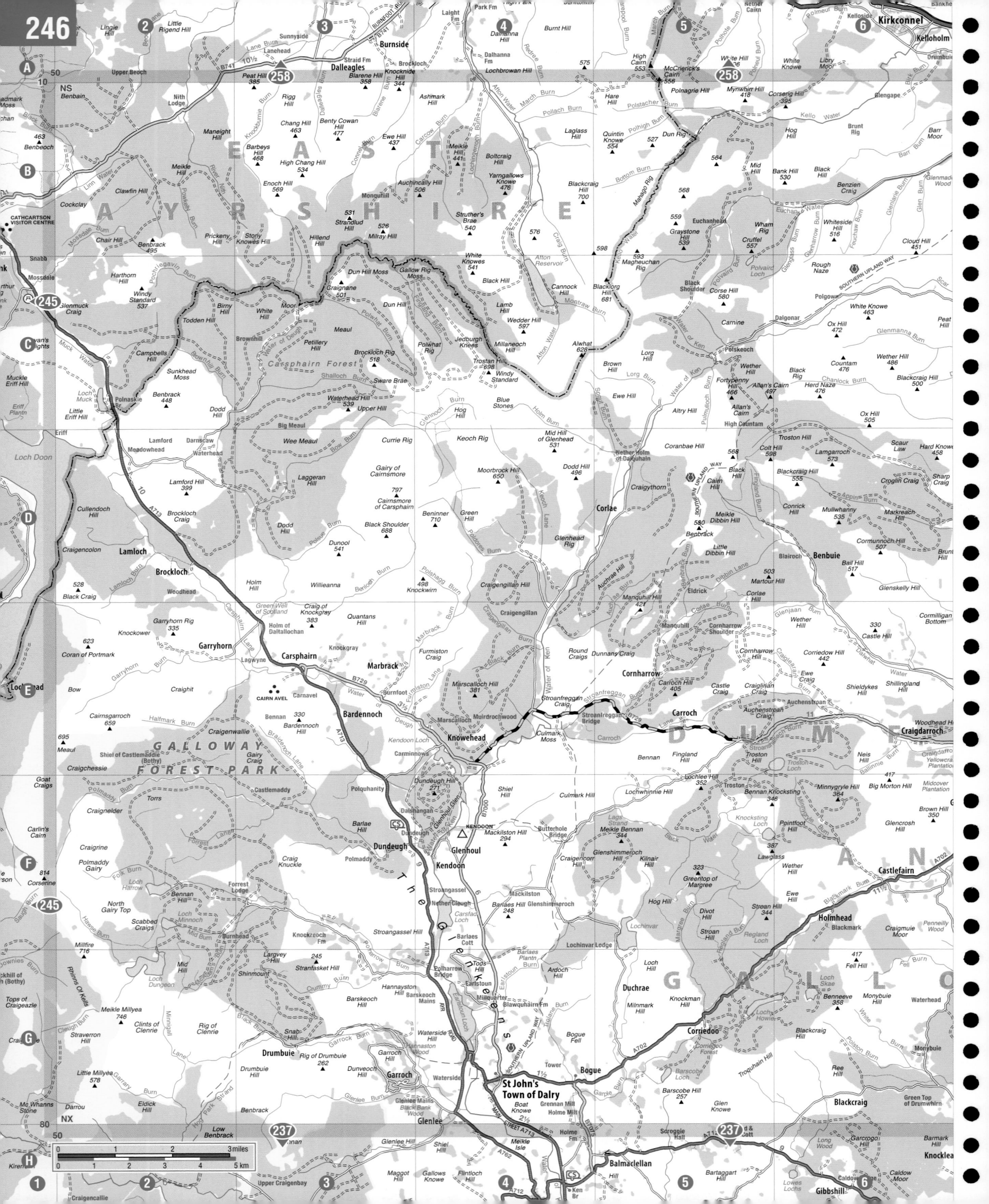

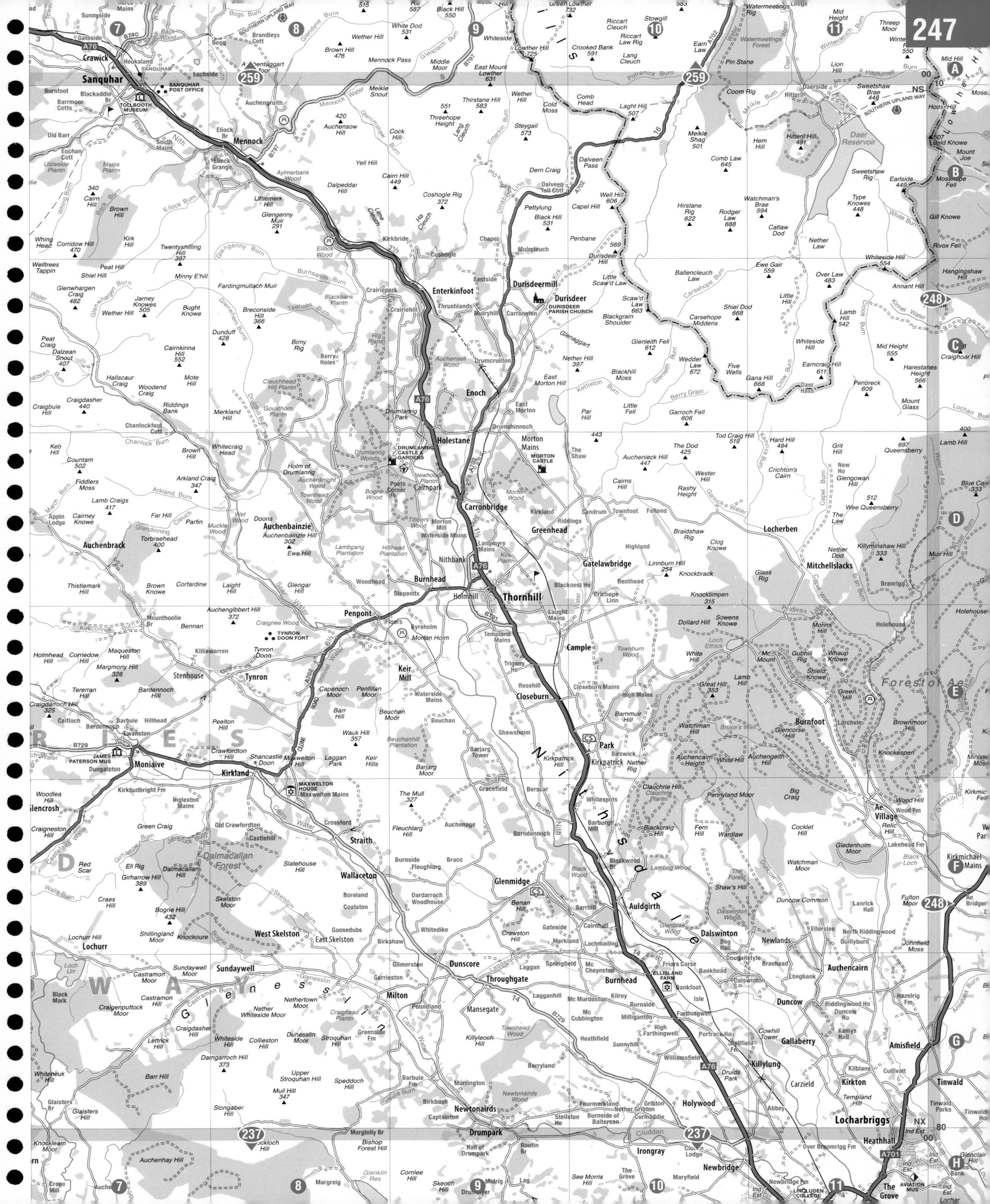

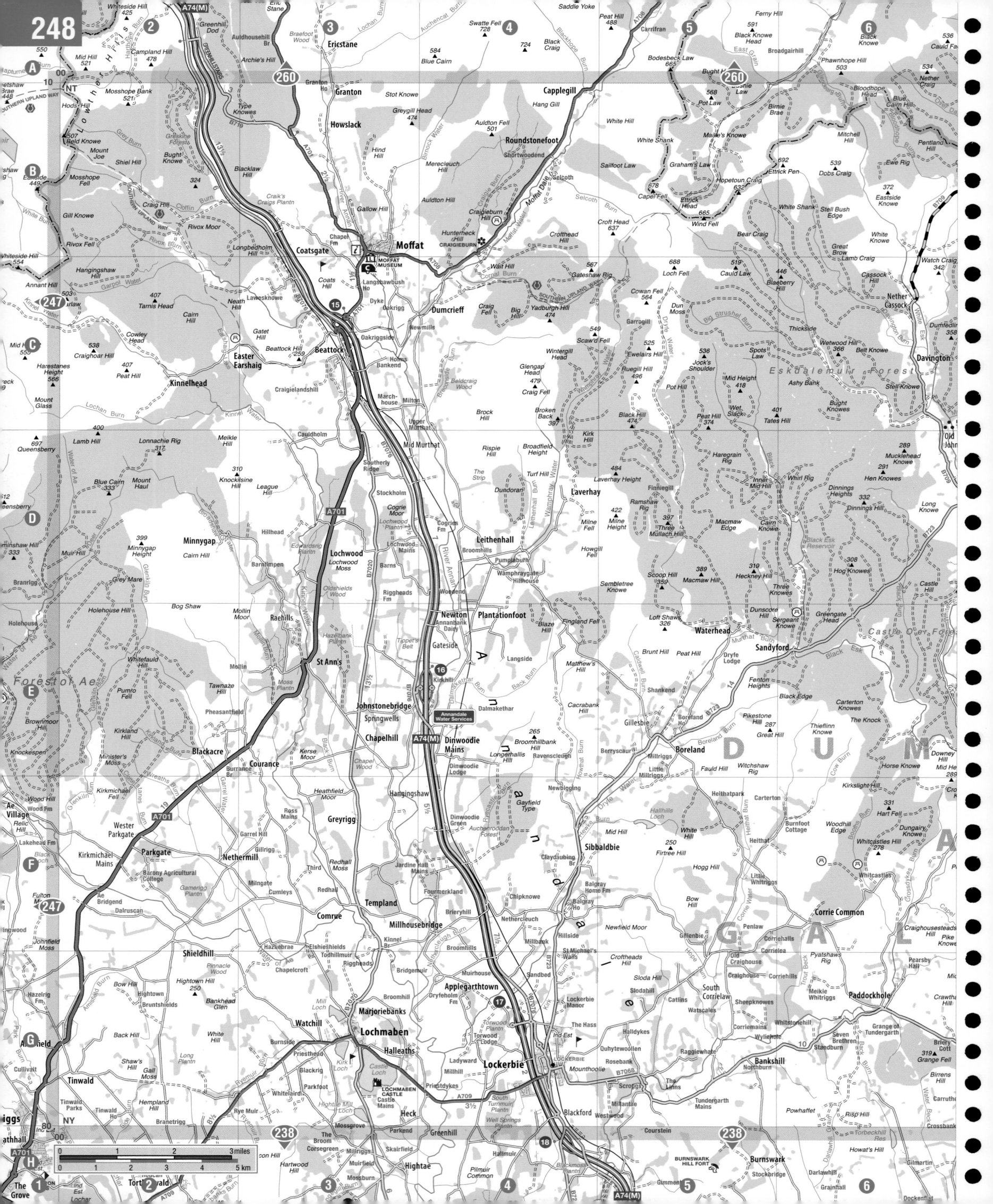

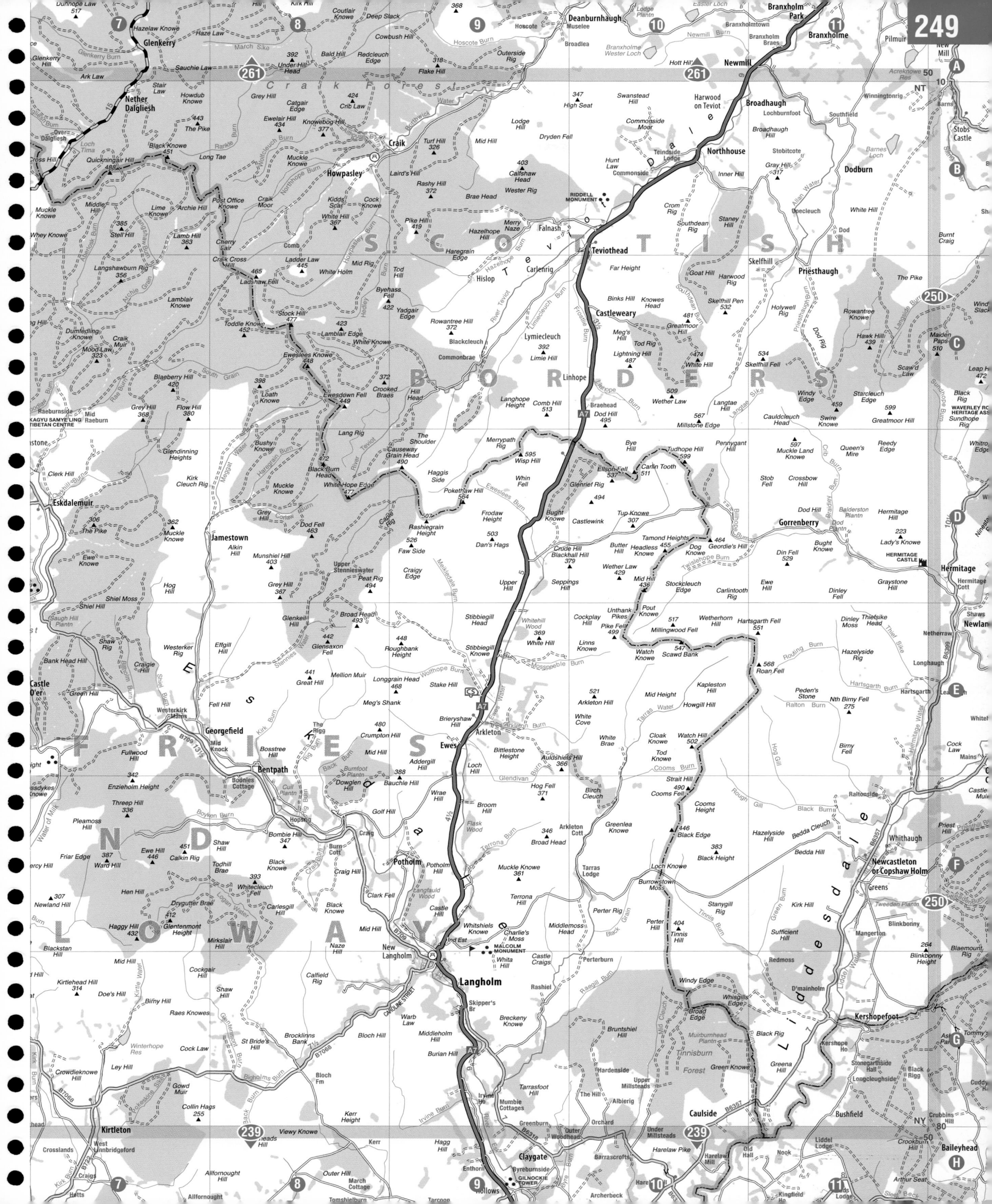

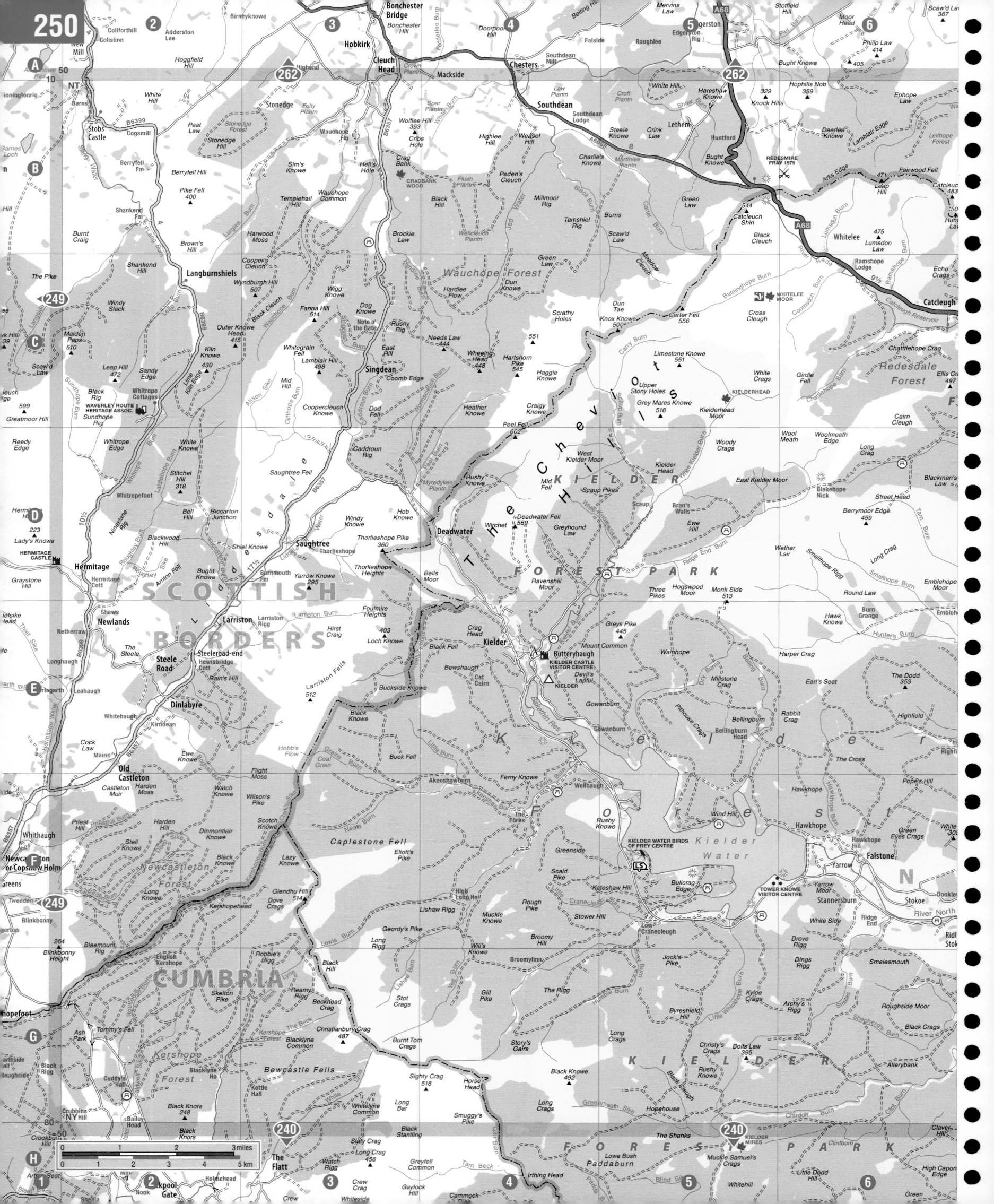

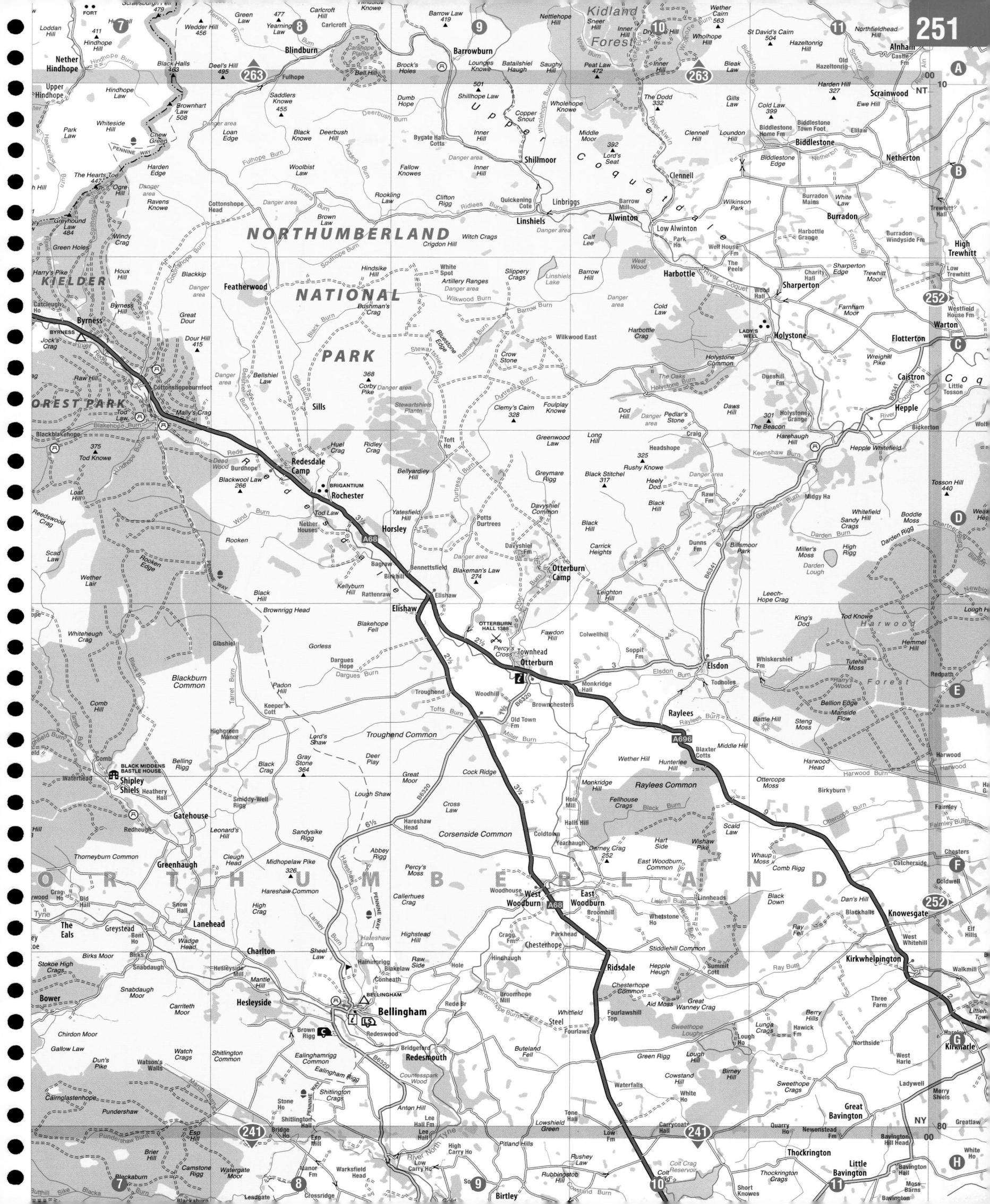

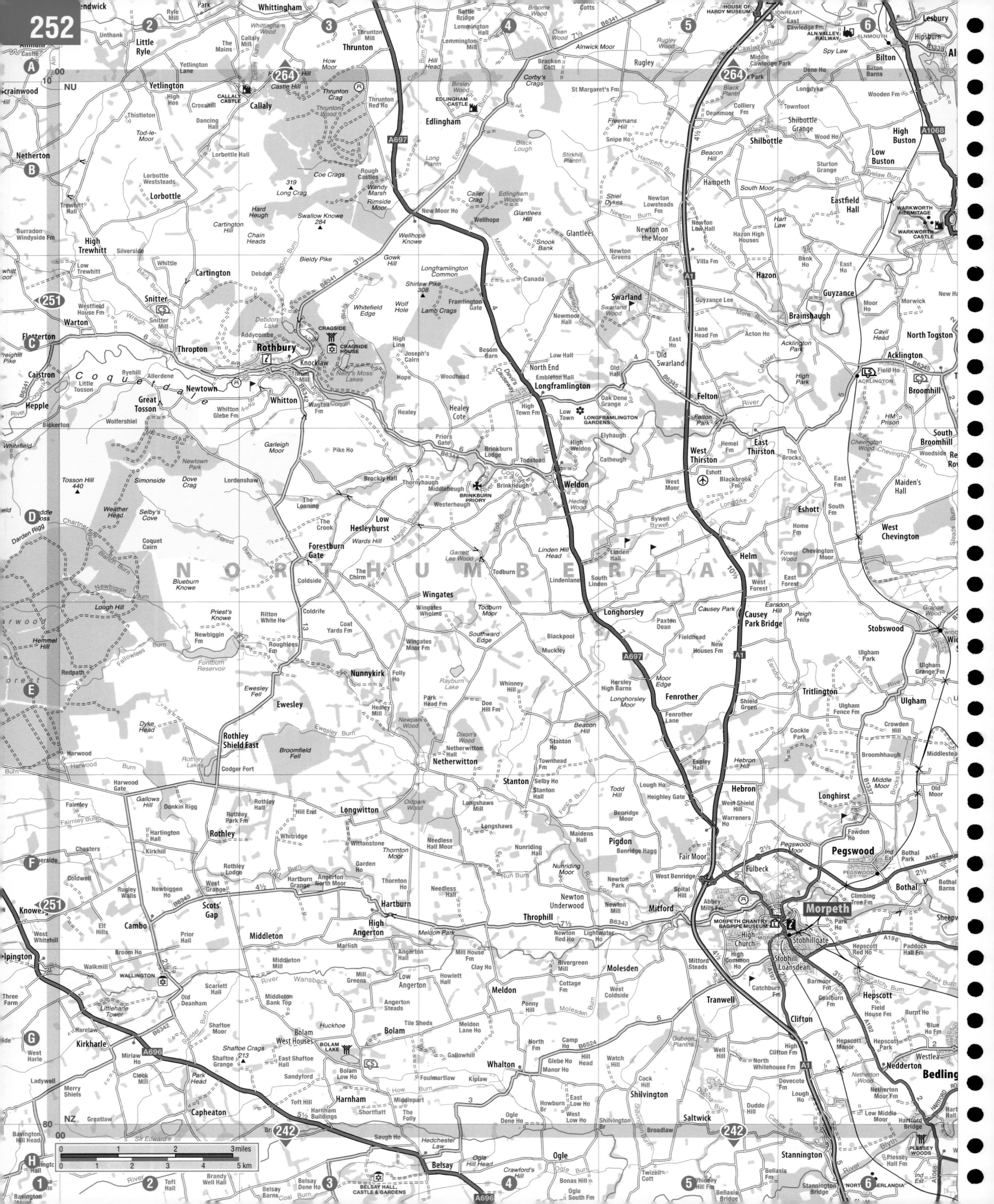

50
10
NU

A

B

C

N O R T H

S E A

D

E

F

G

NZ 80
50

H

Alnmouth
Alnmouth
Bay
265
265

Marden Rocks

Birling
Warkworth
Warkworth
Harbour
BEAL BANK
Pan
Pt
Wellhaugh
Pt
Coquet
Island
Gloster
Hill
Amble
B6345
Moorhouse
Fm
High Hauxley
Togston
Hall
Radcliffe
Low Hauxley
HAUXLEY
Togston
A1068
Barns
Togston
East Fm
B1330
ogston
Danger
area
Ladyburn
Lake
nd
Est
Hadston
DRURIDGE
BAY
B1330
w
Druridge
Bay
Whitefield
Ho
Chibburn
Fm
High Chibburn
2½
Widdrington
Hemscott Hill
B1337
A1068
RINGTON
ddrington
Station
Highthorn
Cresswell
Warkworthlane
Cott
LINTON LANE
North
nton Fm
Hagg
House
Ellington
Cresswell
Home Fm
Linton
Lynemouth
ds
East
Moor Fm
Potland
Fm
Works
QUEEN
ELIZABETH II
Woodhorn
WOODHORN
COLLIERY MUS
A189
WOODHORN
CHURCH MUS
Bus Cen
A196
Woodbridge
A197
Ashington
Hirst
North
Seaton
Newbiggin-by-the-Sea
Newbiggin Bay
River
WANSBECK
wash
Wansbeck
North Seaton
Colliery
Stakeford
West
Sleekburn
STAKEFORD LANE
Guide Post
Scotland
Gate
Bomarsund
Bus Cen
Cambois
A1147
Choppington
East
Sleekburn
A189
Bedlington
Station
Mount
Pleasant Fm
North Blyth
B1331 STEAD
COWPEN ROAD
A193
Bebside
Cowpen
ton
Humford
Mill
A189
B1331
HORTON ROAD
2½
Blyth
Isabella
Pit
B1329
East
Hartford
Low
Horton Fm
Newsh
243
243
South
Beach
est Hartford
Fm
A192
New Delaval
Laverock
Hall
A1061
South
Newsham
SOUTH NEWSHAM ROAD
Gloucester
Lodge Fm
Shankhouse
7
LAVEROCK HALL ROAD
Meggie's
Burn
8
Lysdon
Fn
Stickley Fm
Ind Est

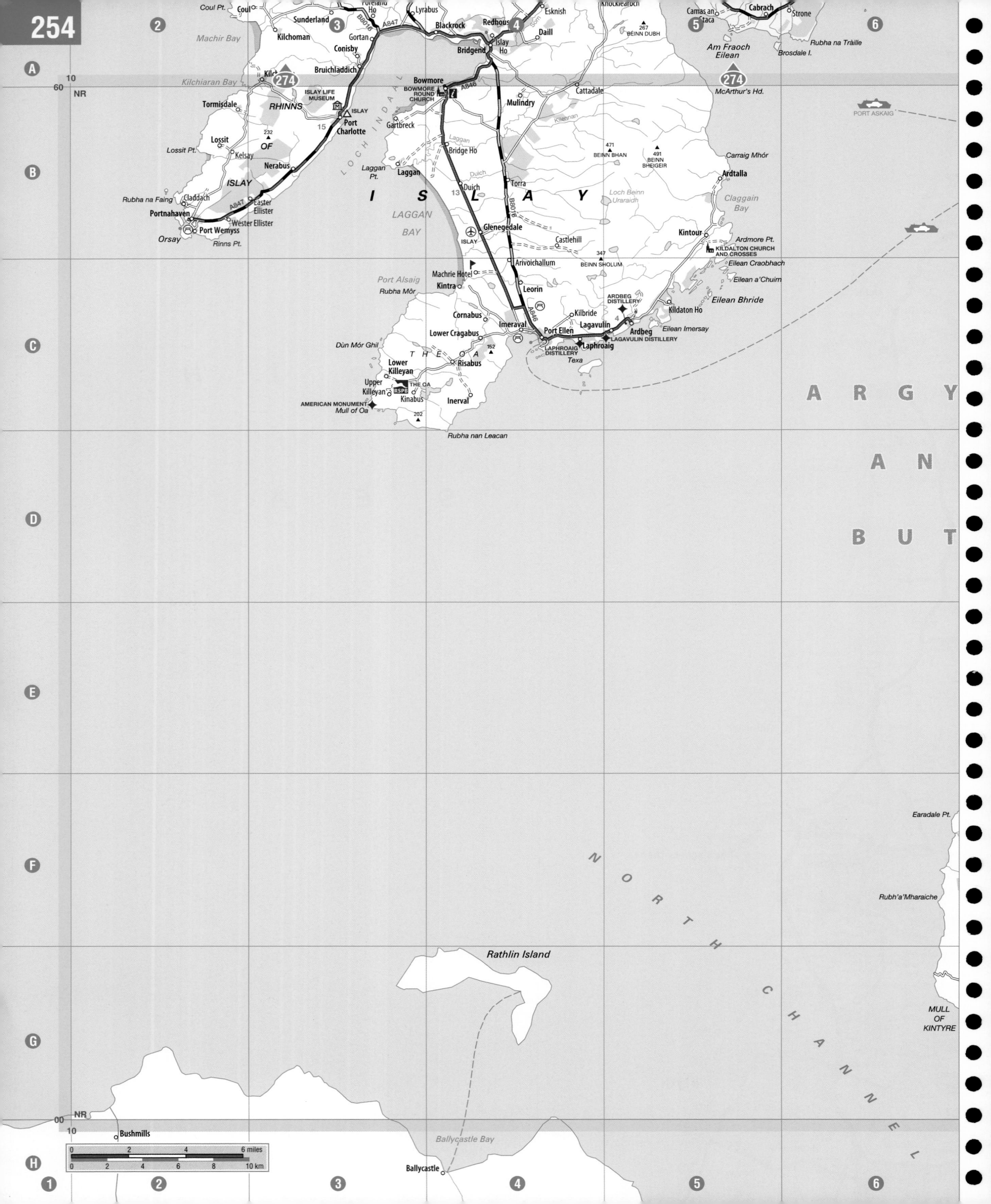

Coul Pt.
Coul
Lyrabus
Esknish
Knocklearoch
Camas an
Staca
Cabrach
Strone

Sunderland
Kilchoman
Conisby
Gortan
Blackrock
Redhouse
Daill
Beinn Dubh
Am Fraoch
Eilean
Rubha na Tràille
Brosdale I.

A
10
60
NR

Kilchiaran Bay
Kil
274
Bruichladdich
Bridgend
Islay
Ho
Bowmore
274
McArthur's Hd.

PORT ASKAIG

Tormisdale
RHINNS
ISLAY LIFE
MUSEUM
ISLAY
Port
Charlotte
BOWMORE ROUND
CHURCH
A846
Mulindry
Cattadale

15
Gartbreck
Kilennan

Lossit
Lossit Pt.
OF
Kelsay
Nerabus
Bridge Ho
Laggan
Duich
Torra
BEINN BHAN
BEINN
BHEIGEIR
Carraig Mhór

B
Rubha na Faing
Claddach
Easter
Ellister
ISLAY
Laggan
Pt.
Laggan
I S L A Y
Duich
B8016
Loch Beinn
Uraraidh
Ardtalla
Claggain
Bay

Portnahaven
Port Wemyss
Wester Ellister
A847

Orsay
Rinns Pt.
LAGGAN
BAY
ISLAY
Glenegedale
Castlehill
Kintour
Ardmore Pt.

Port Alsaig
Rubha Mór
Machrie Hotel
Kintra
Arivoichallum
BEINN SHOLUM
347
KILDALTON CHURCH
AND CROSSES
Eilean Craobhach
Eilean a'Chuirn

Leorin
Eilean Bhride

C
Dùn Mór Ghil
Cornabus
Lower Cragabus
Imeraval
Kilbride
ARDBEG
DISTILLERY
Kildaton Ho
Eilean Imersay

THE O A
152
Lower
Killeyan
Risabus
Port Ellen
Lagavulin
Ardbeg
LAGAVULIN DISTILLERY
Texa

A R G Y

Upper
Killeyan
RSPB
THE OA
Kinabus
Inerval
LAPHROAIG
DISTILLERY
Laphroaig

AMERICAN MONUMENT
Mull of Oa
202
Rubha nan Leacan

D

A N

B U T

E
Earadale Pt.

F
N
O
R
T
H
Rubh'a'Mharaiche

G
Rathlin Island
C
H
A
N
MULL
OF
KINTYRE

00
NR
10
Bushmills

H
0   2   4   6 miles
0   2   4   6   8   10 km
Ballycastle
Ballycastle Bay
N
E
L

1   **2**   **3**   **4**   **5**   **6**

NS

Maol Donn
368 ▲

Port nam
Balach

Glenshant
Hill

Merkland

Glen Rosa

Creag
Rosa

Torr
Breac

Merkland Pt
Wine Port

Merkland
Wood

Glenrosa

BRODICK
CASTLE

BRODICK
Cladach
Old Quay

ISLE OF ARRAN
HERITAGE MUSEUM

ARDROSSAN

Glen Shurig

THE STRING

Brodick

Gaolthe

Glen Ormidale

Strathwhillan

Corriegills Pt

Sgiath
Bhàn

Fairy
Glen

North
Corriegills

Knoc
breac

Cnoc
Dubh

Meall
Buidhe

Dun
Dubh

South
Corriegills

Clauchland
Hills

Clauchlands
Fm

Clauchlands Pt

Kerr's
Port

Hamilton Isle

Màrgnaheglish

Clauchlands

Isle
of

Arran

Benlister Glen

Benlister Burn

Blairbeg

Lamlash

The Ross
▲ 311

Monamore
Br

Monamore
Glen

Cordon

Gortonallister

White Pt

Mullach
Beag

Holy Island

314
▲
Mullach Mòr

Pillar Rock Pt

Cnoc
Dubh

Urie
Loch

The Knowe
Fm

Auchencairn

Kingscross
Pt

Kingscross

Invein

Knockenkelly

Sandbraes

Glas
Choirein

Allt Dhepin

Borrach

Allt Garbh

North Kiscadale

Cnoc
Donn

Cnoc an
Fheidh

Cnoc Mòr

South Kiscadale

Whiting Bay

GLENASHDALE
FALLS

Glenashdale Burn

Largymore

Auchareoch

NORTH

AYRSHIRE

Torr
Mhòr

Kilmory Water

Cnoc
Craobhach

Cnoc na
Garbad

Cnoc na
Comhairle

Largybeg

Largymeanoch

Largybeg Pt

Port na
Gaillin

Torr a'
Bheannain

Levencorroch
Hill

Margenaish
Fm

Dippin Head

Dippin

Southbank

East
Bennan

Levencorroch

West
Bennan

Auchenhew

Drumla

Porta
Leacach

Kildonan

STRUEY
ROCKS

Port a'Ghillie
Ghlais

Porta Buidhe

Port
Dearg

Bennan Head

Sound of Pladda

Pladda

FIRTH

OF

CLYDE

Ardrossan

BRODICK
CAMPBELTOWN
(May-Sept)

Saltcoats

ARDROSSAN
HARBOUR

ARDROSSAN
TOWN

South Bay

NORTH AYRSHIRE
MUSEUM

Outer
Nebbock

Dun

Broad Craig

Culzean Bay

CULZEAN
CASTLE

CULZEAN

Glasson Rock

Barwhin Pt

Swan
Pond

Maidenhead
Bay

Morriston

Birniehill

Thomas

Balvaird

0   1   2   3miles
0 1 2 3 4 5 km

NS

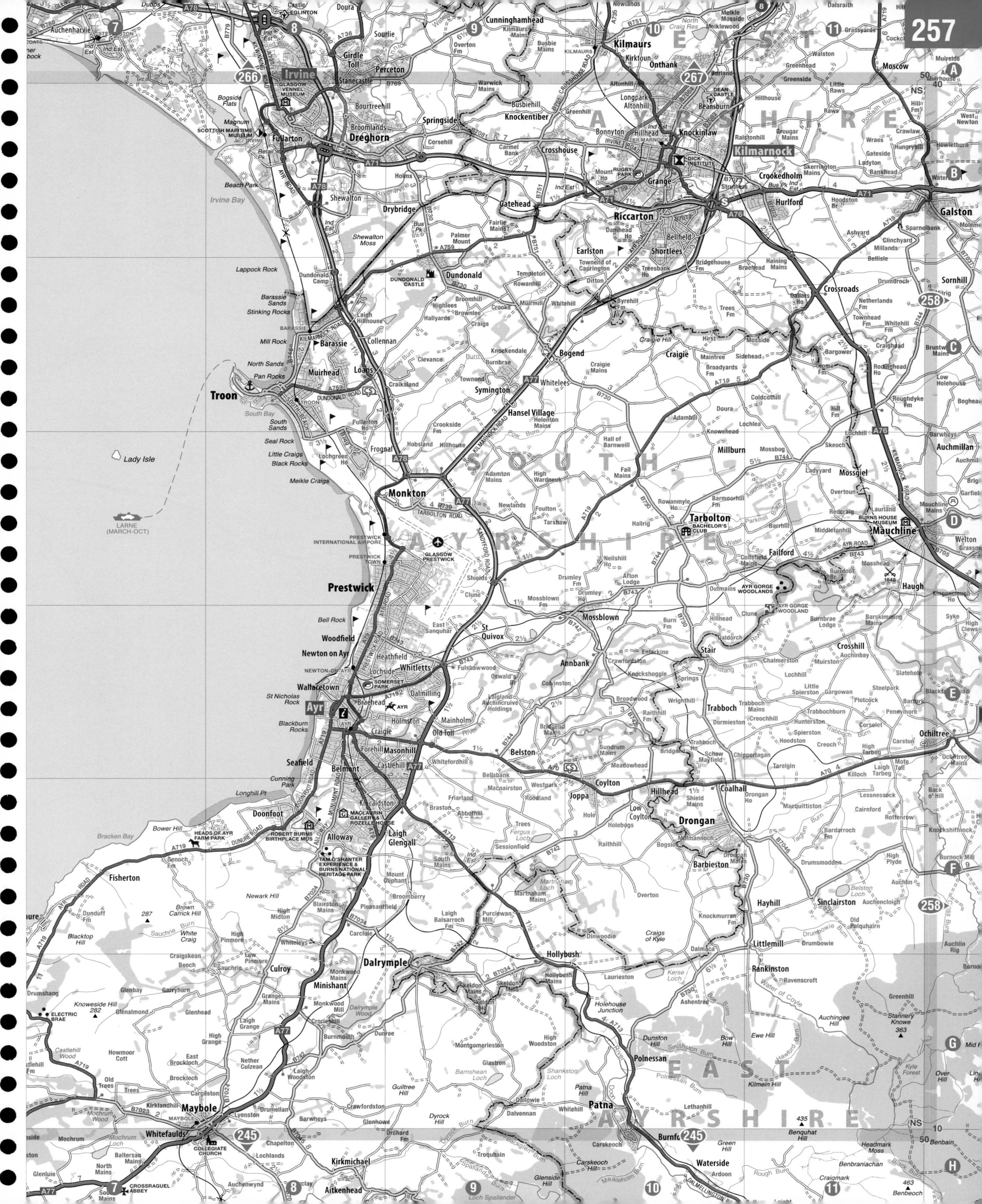

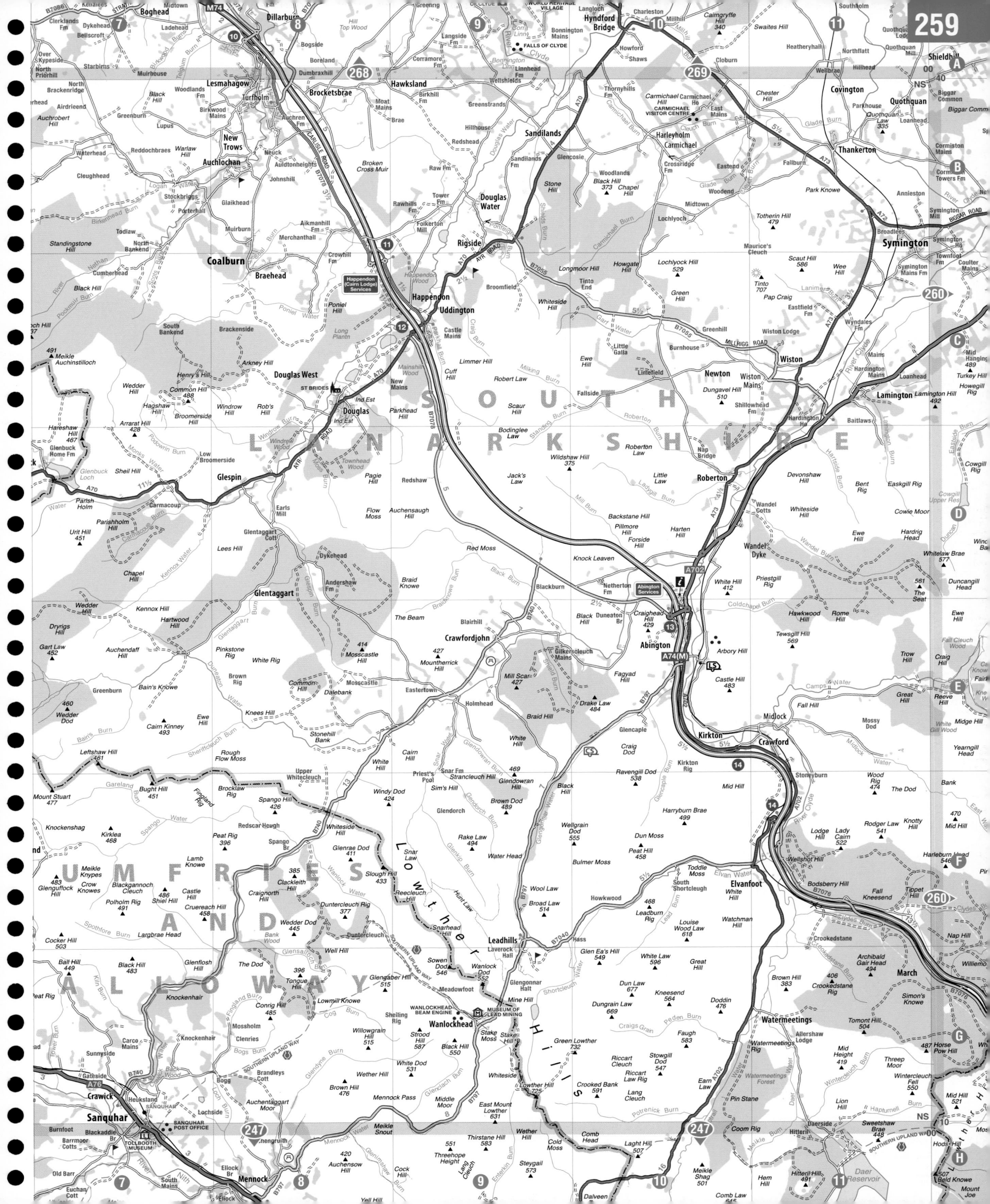

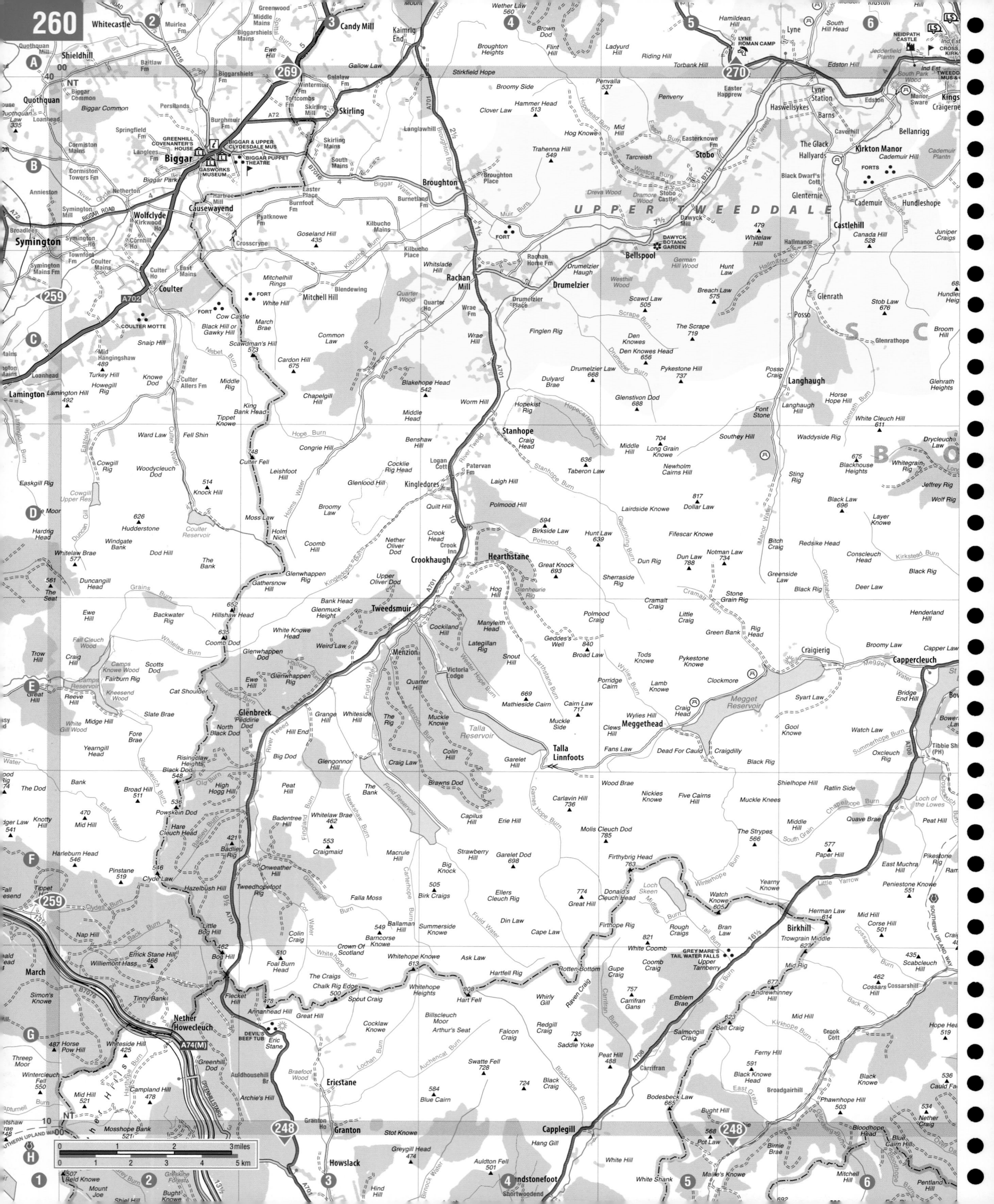

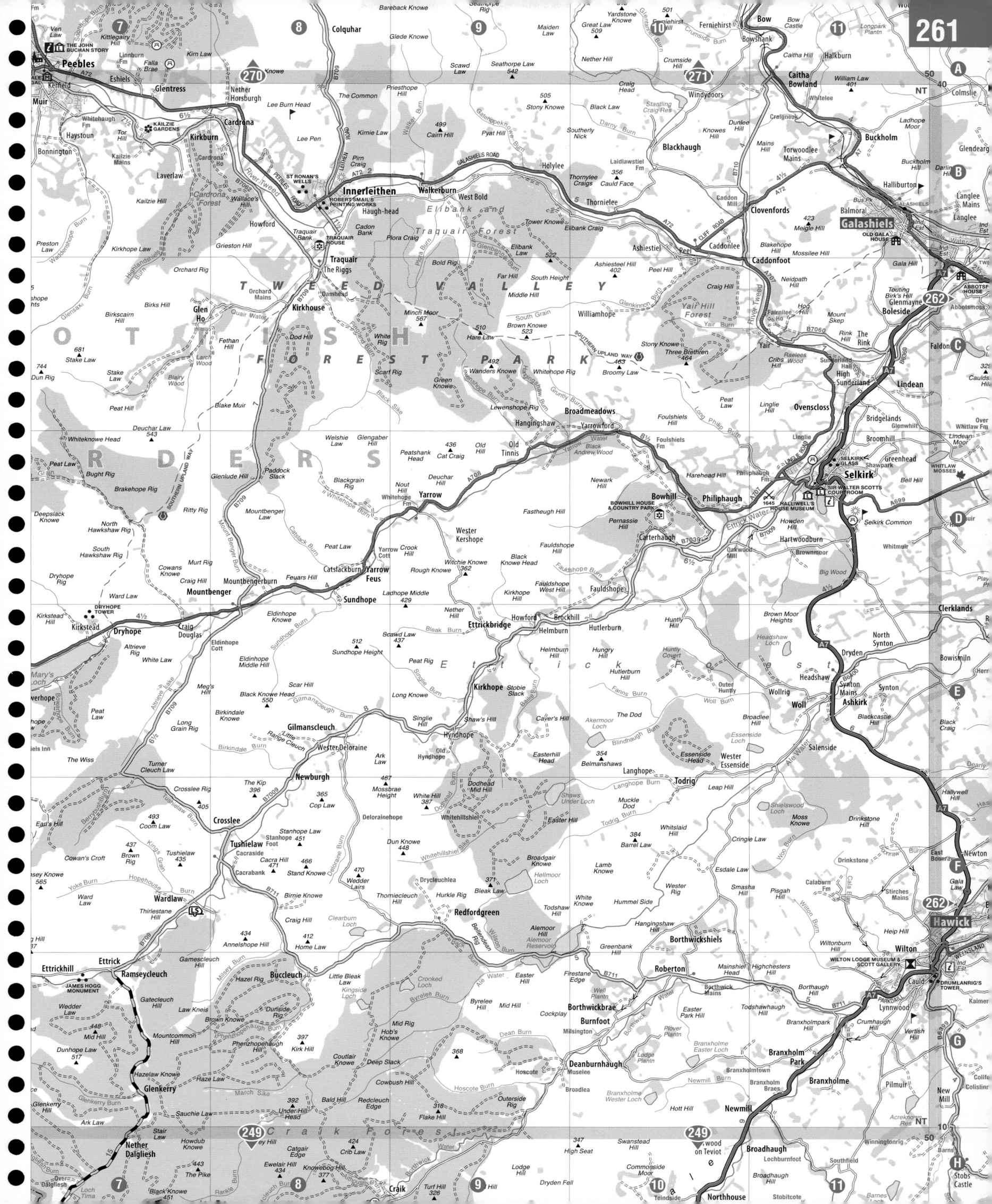

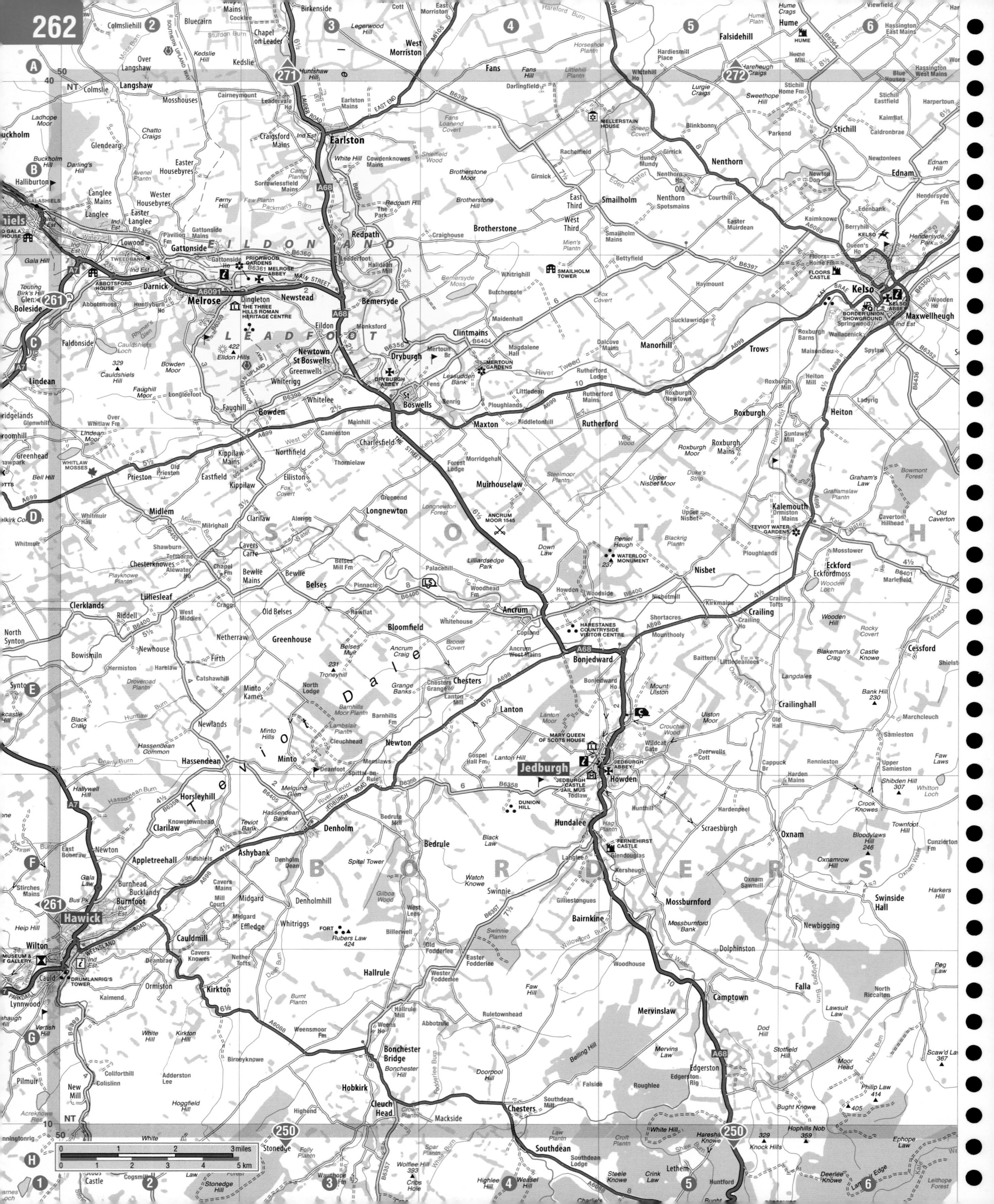

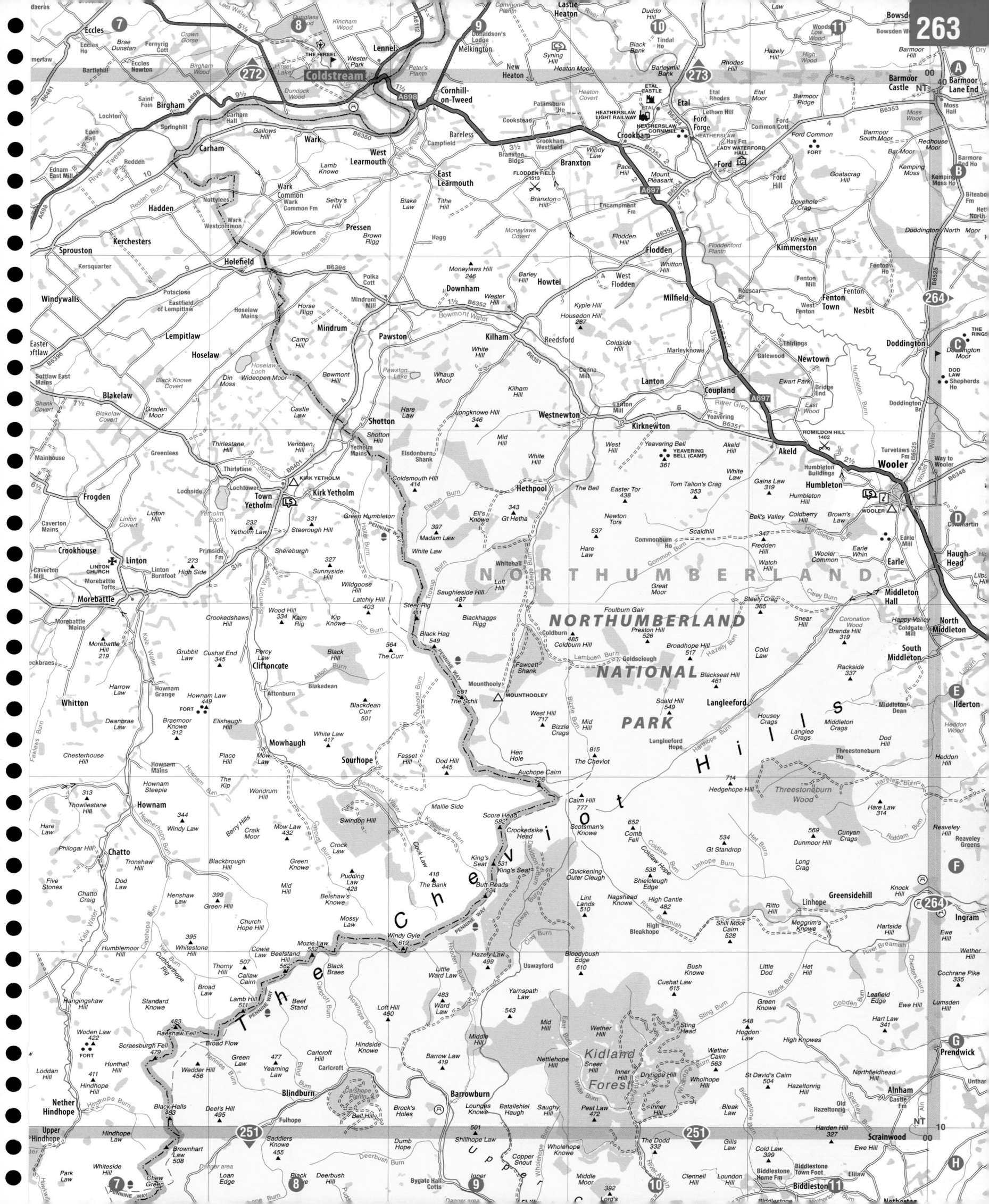

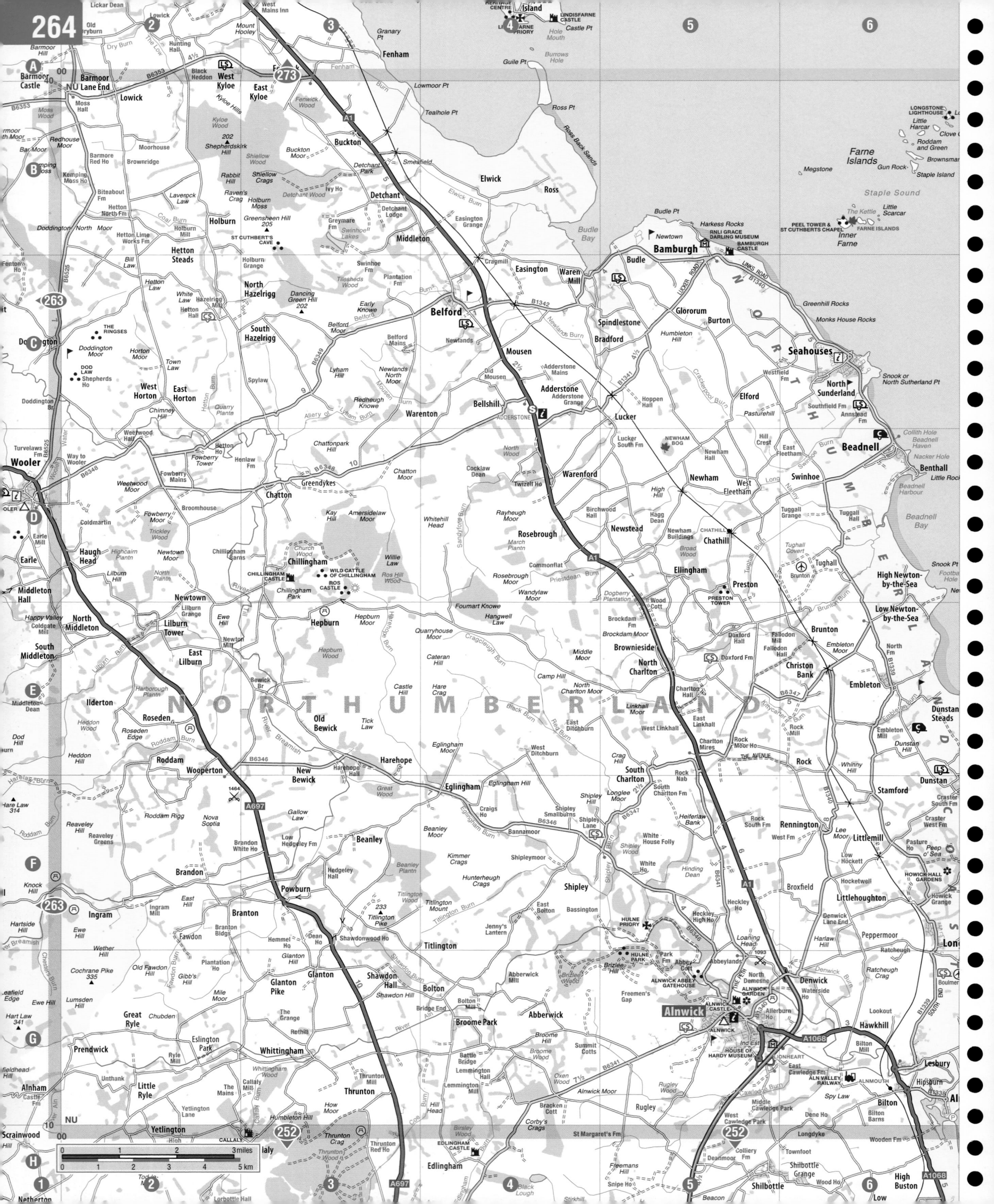

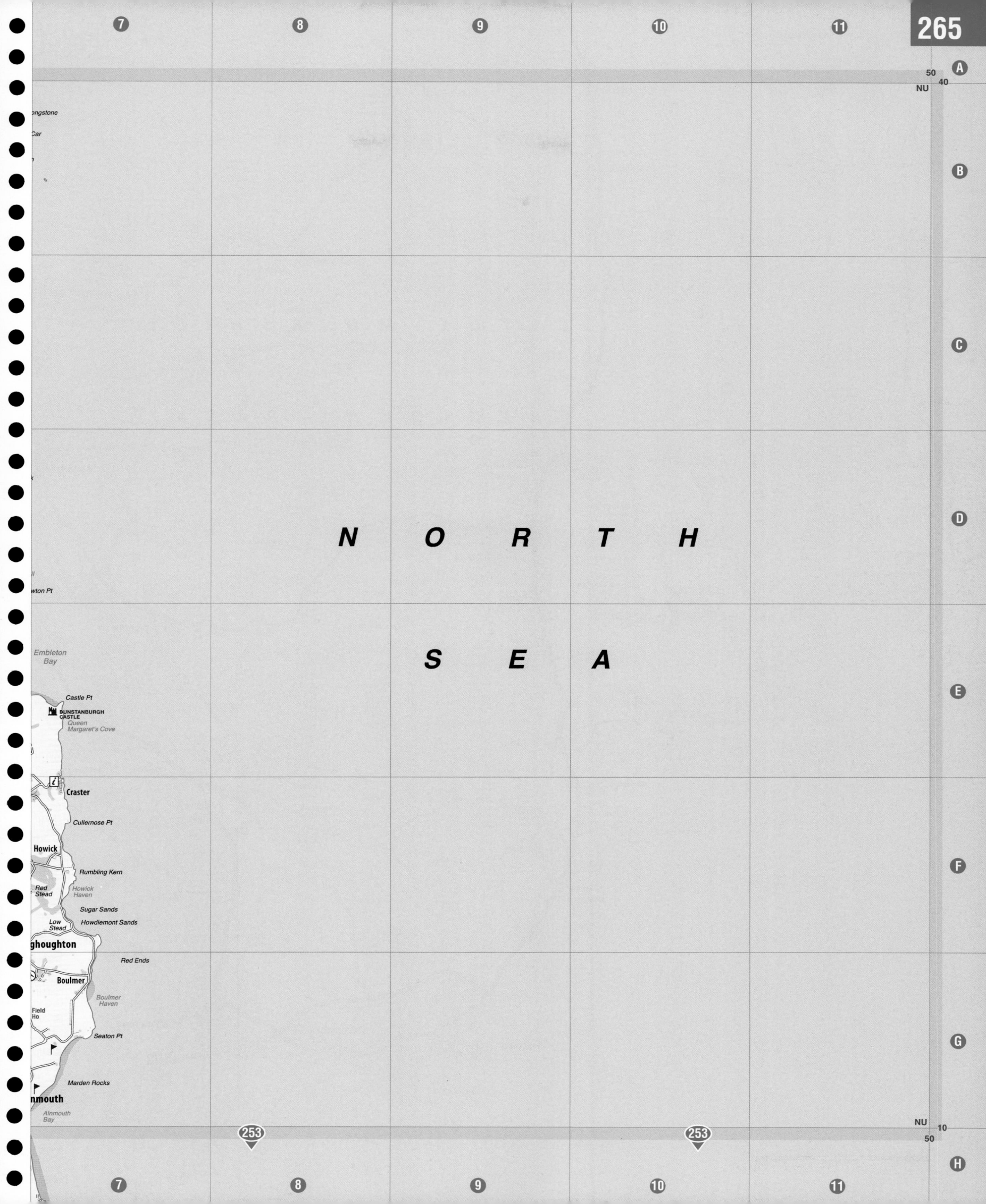

N O R T H

S E A

Longstone

Car

wton Pt

Embleton
Bay

Castle Pt

DUNSTANBURGH
CASTLE
Queen
Margaret's Cove

Craster

Cullernose Pt

Howick

Rumbling Kern

Red
Stead

Howick
Haven

Sugar Sands

Low
Stead

Howdiemont Sands

ghoughton

Red Ends

Boulmer

Boulmer
Haven

Field
Ho

Seaton Pt

Marden Rocks

nmouth

Alnmouth
Bay

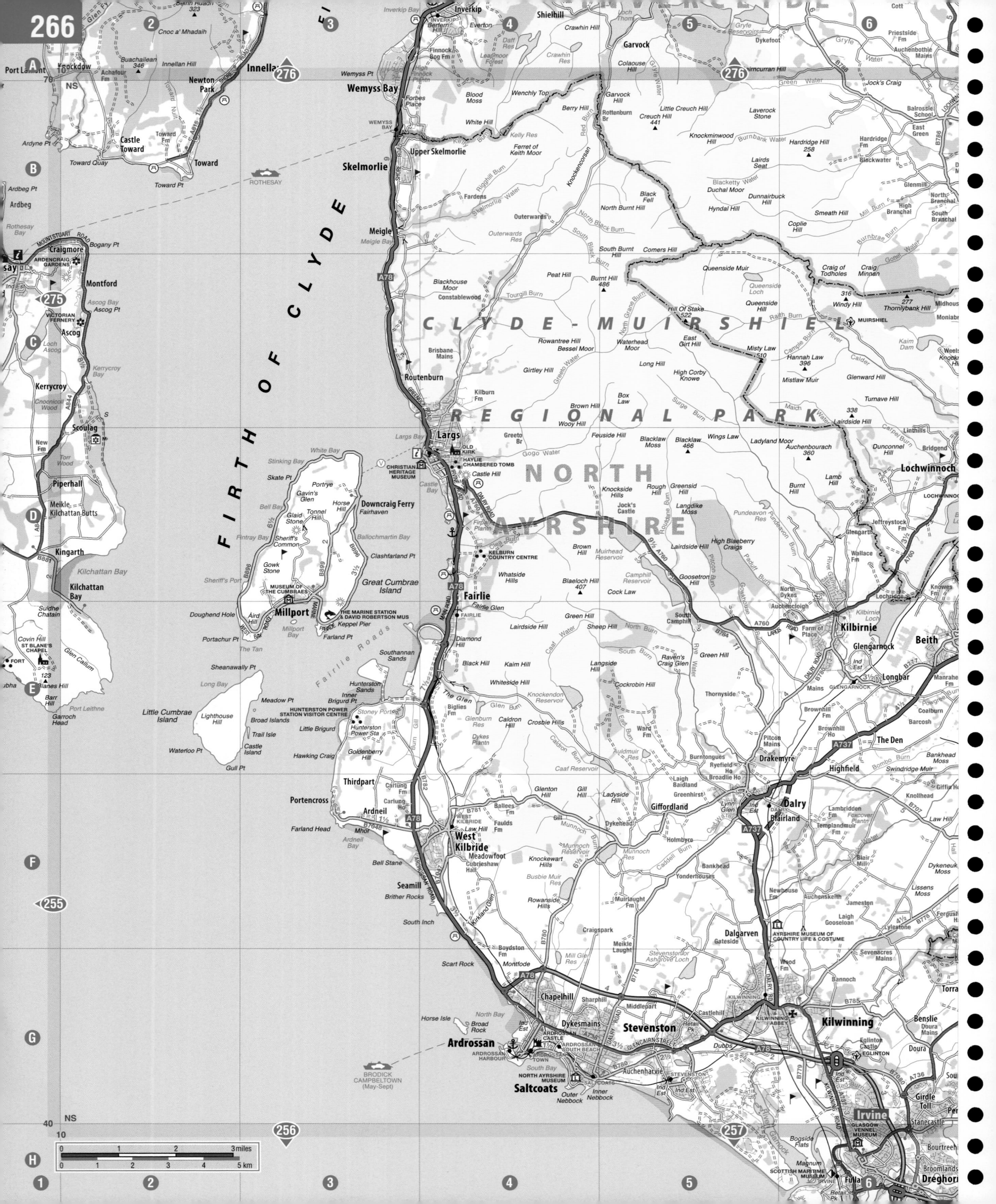

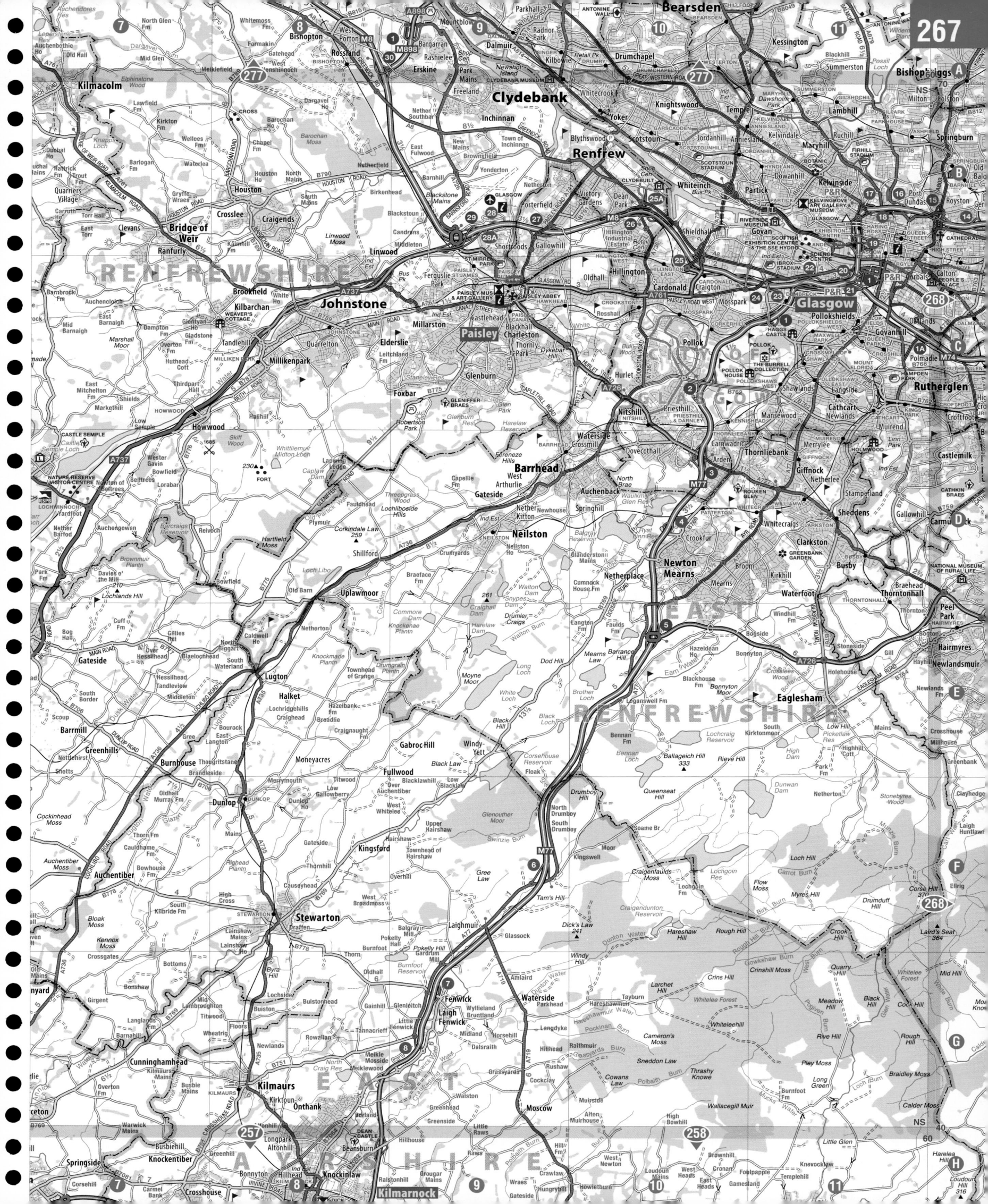

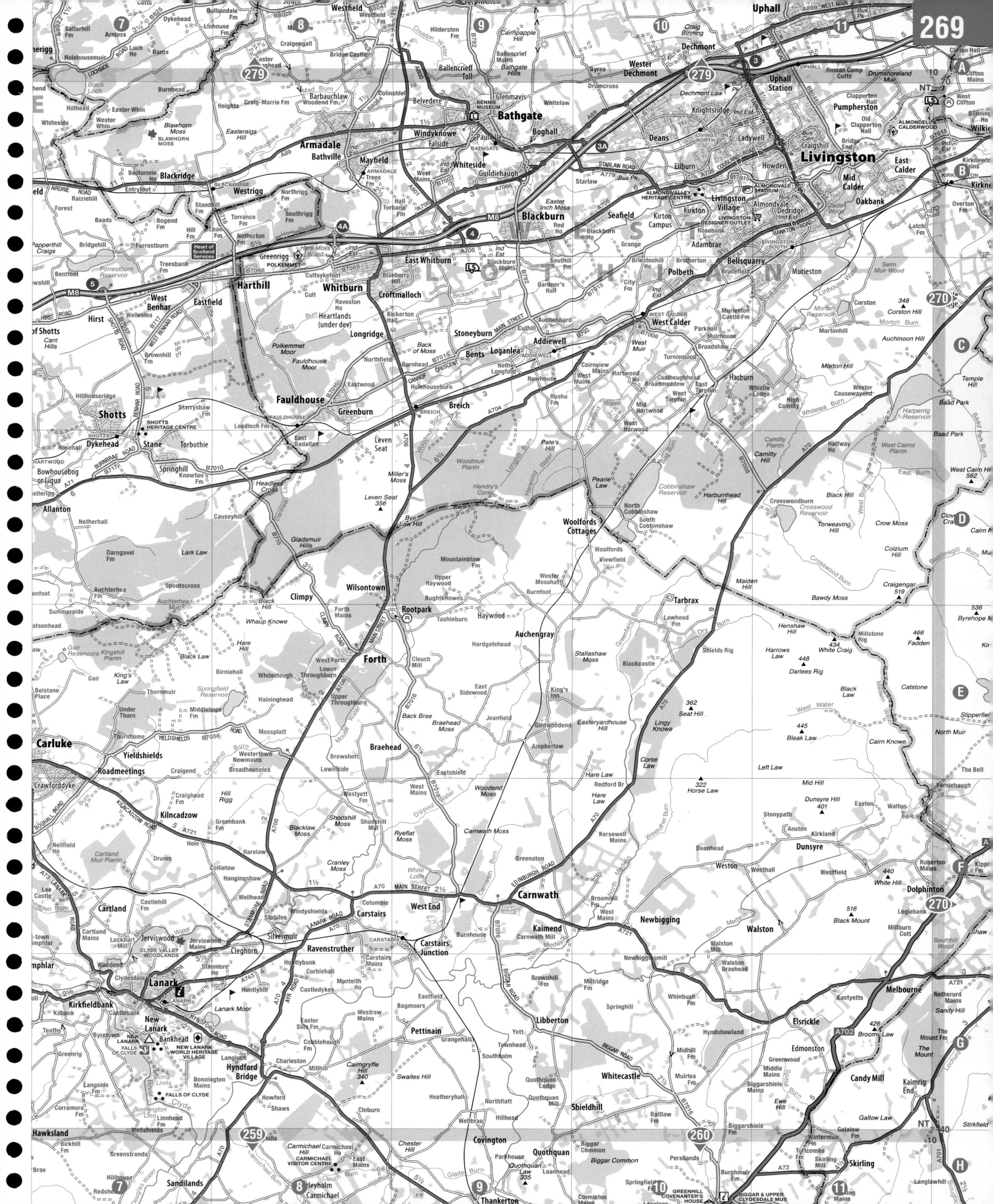

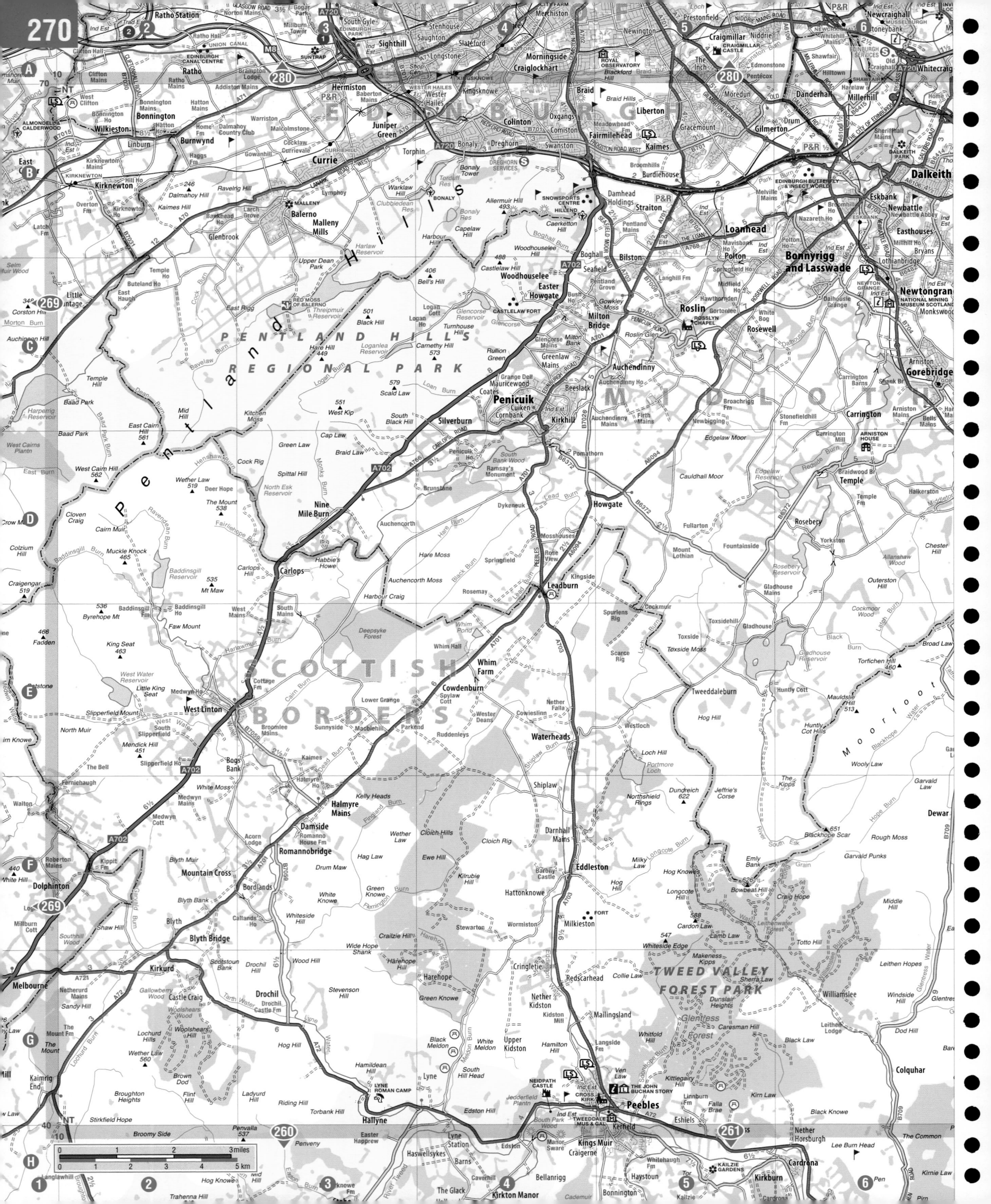

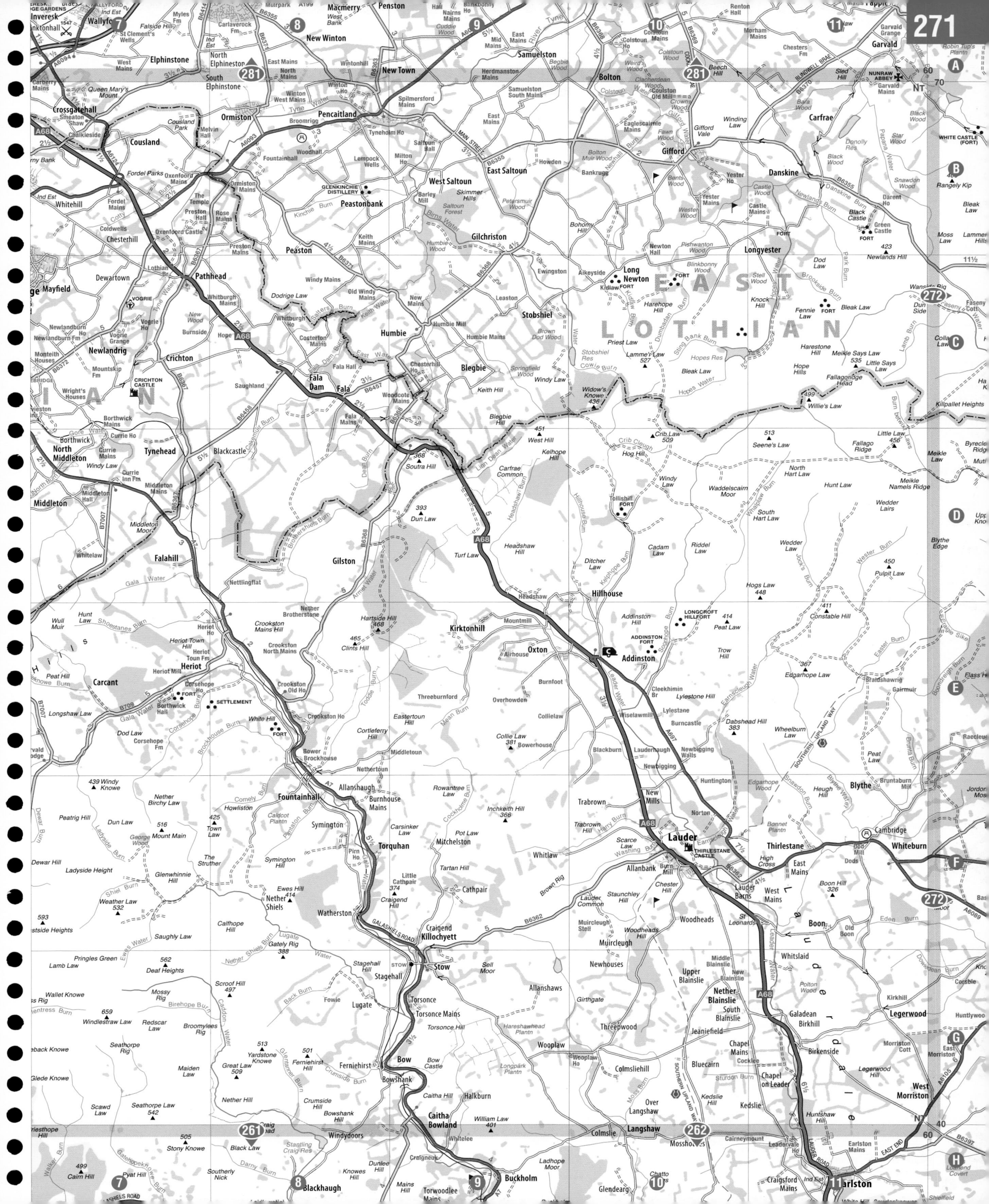

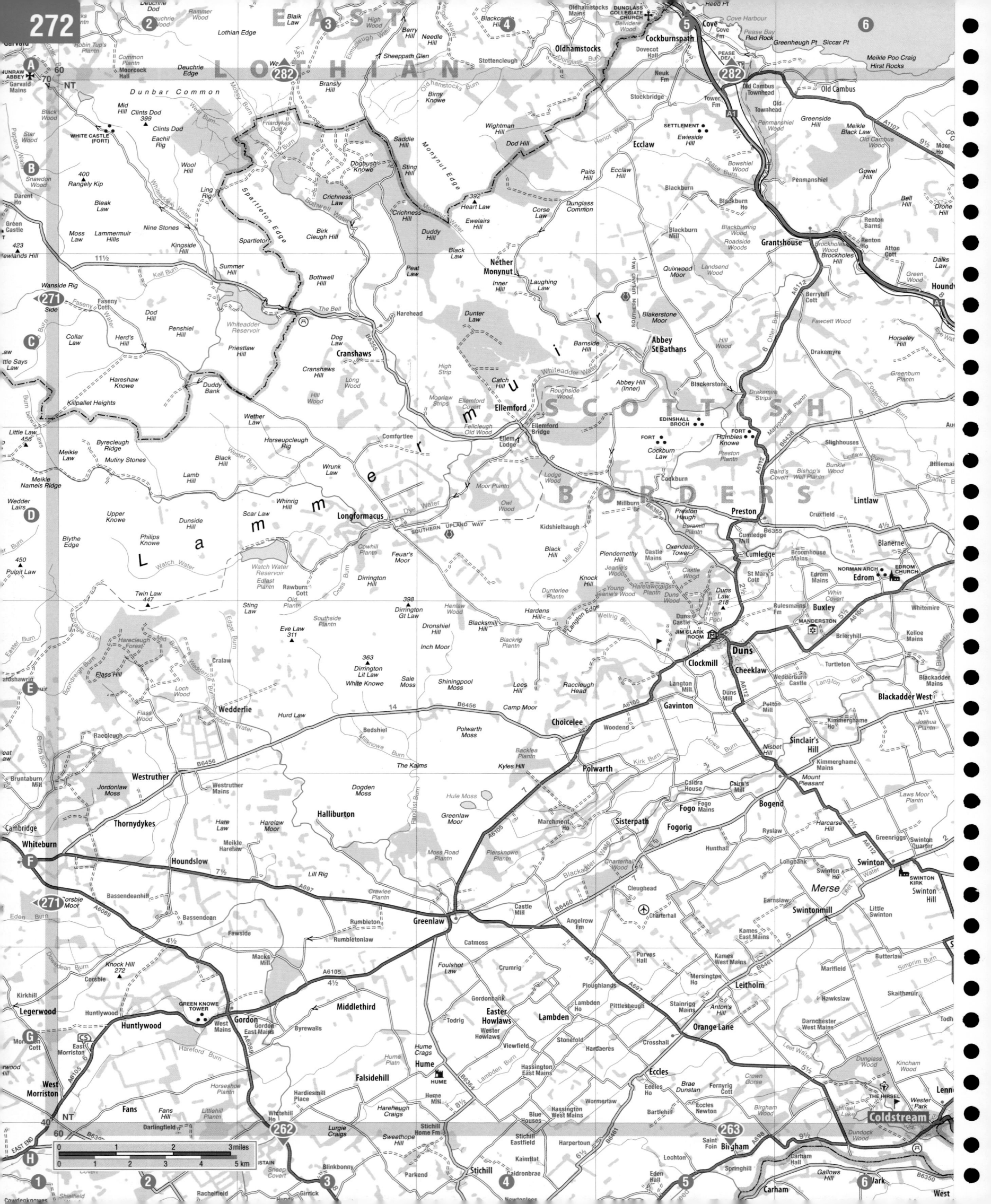

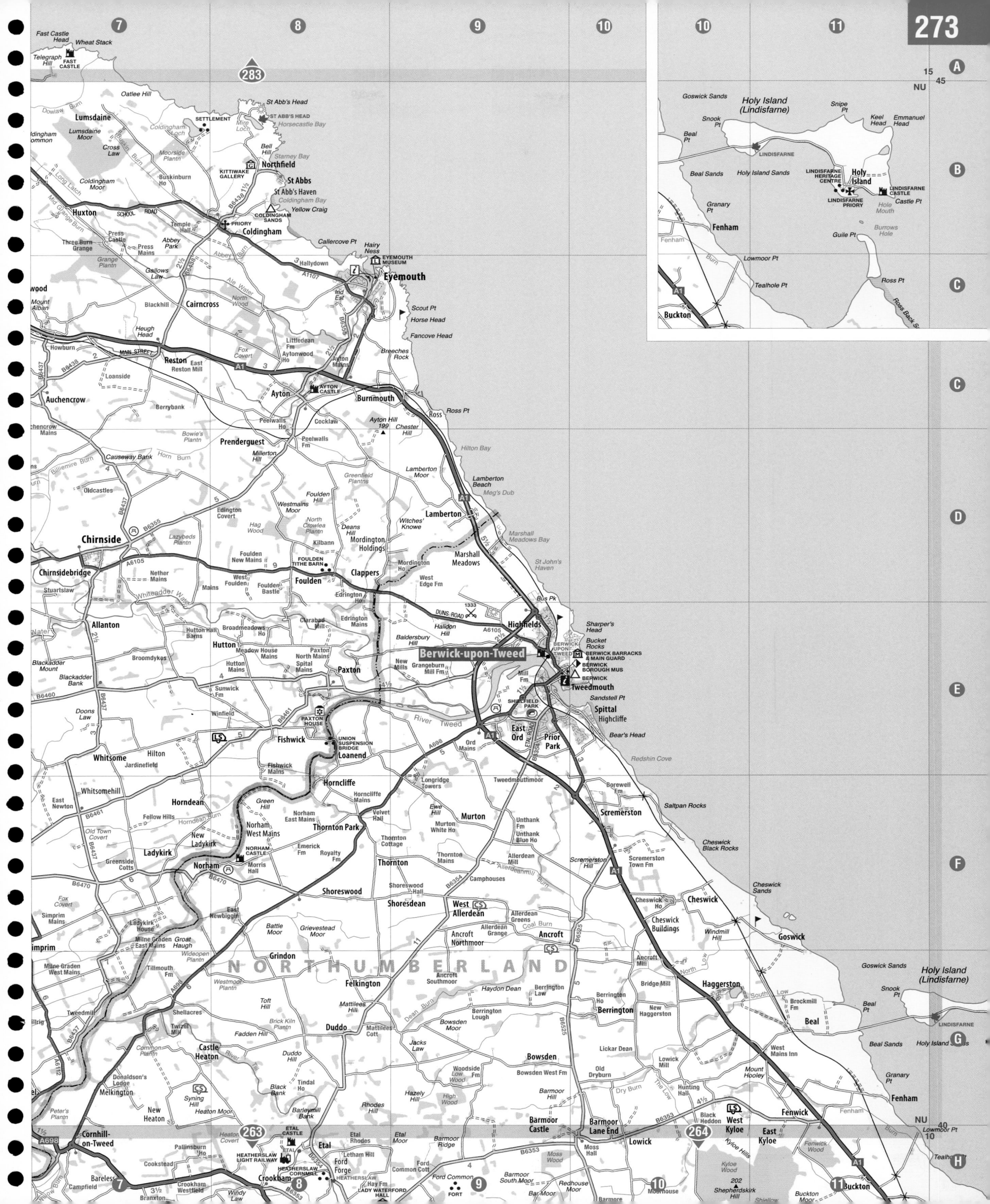

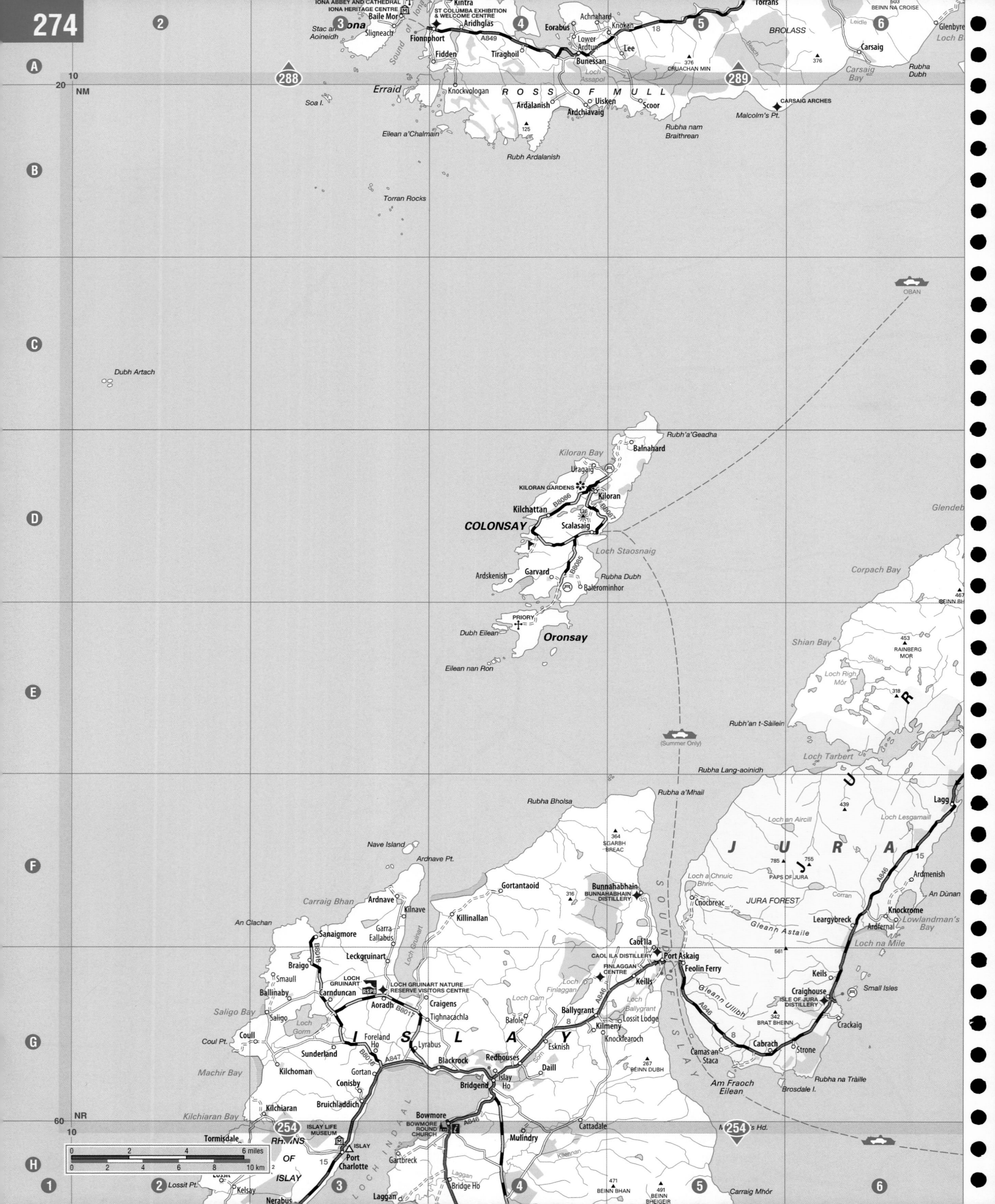

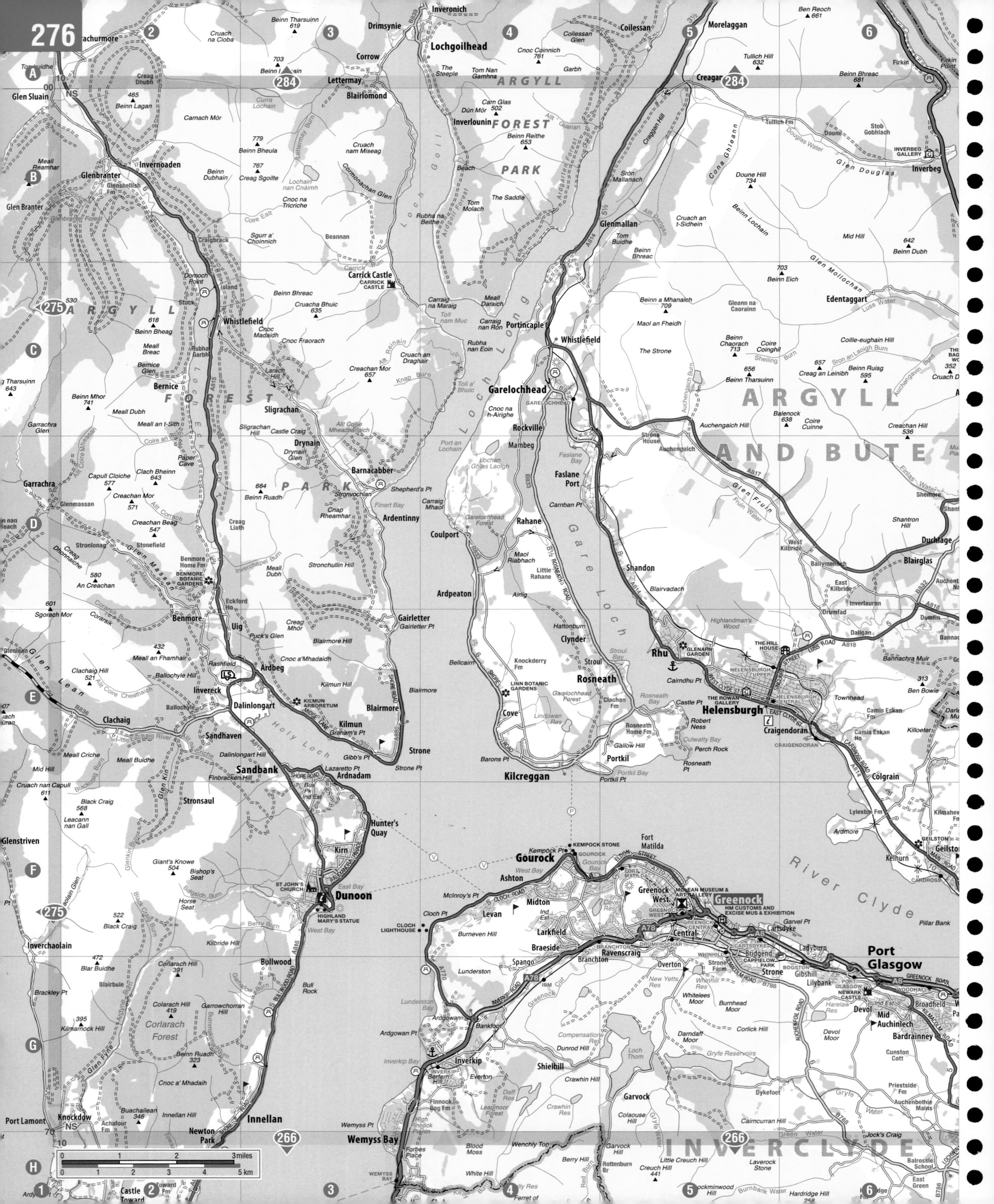

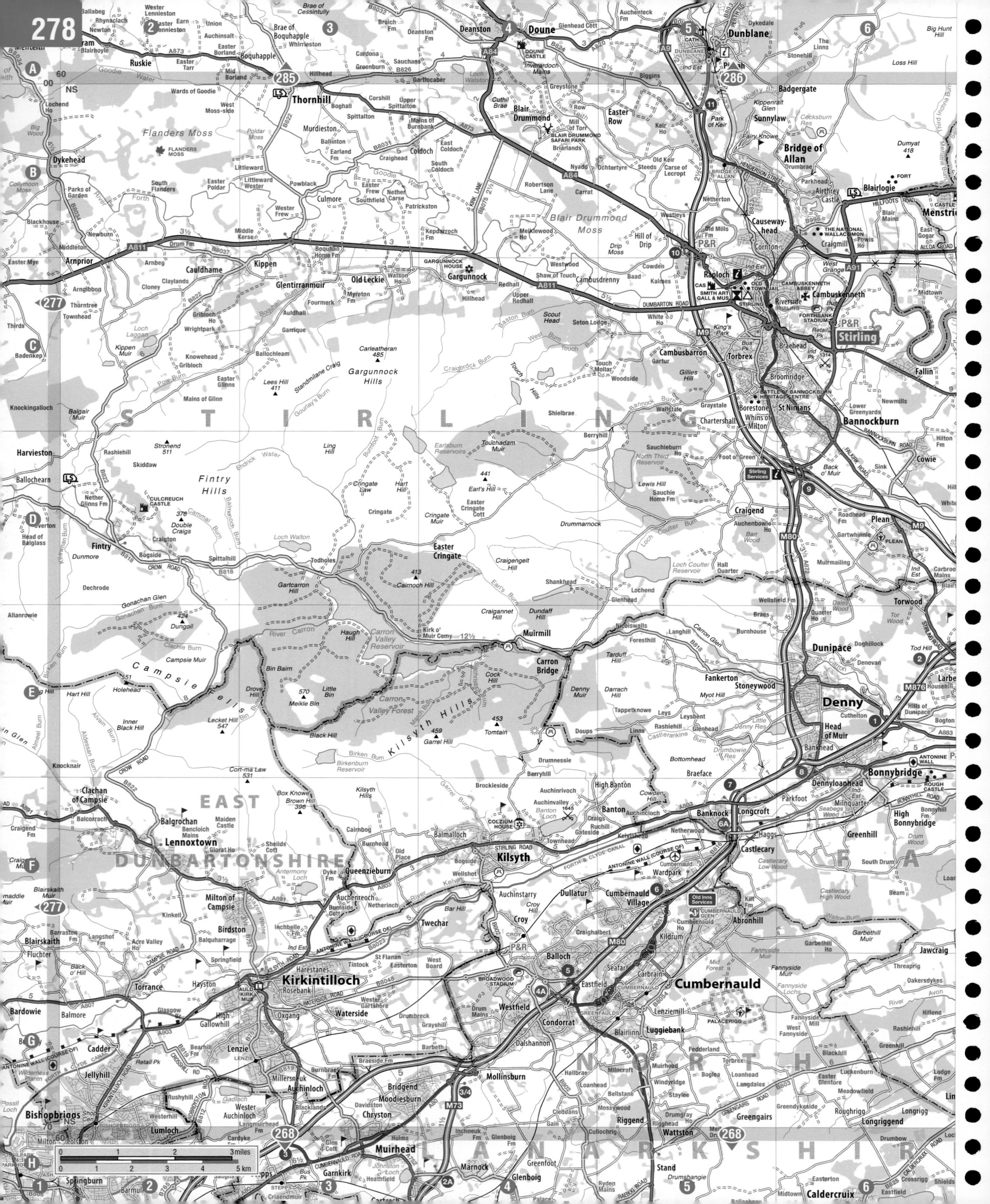

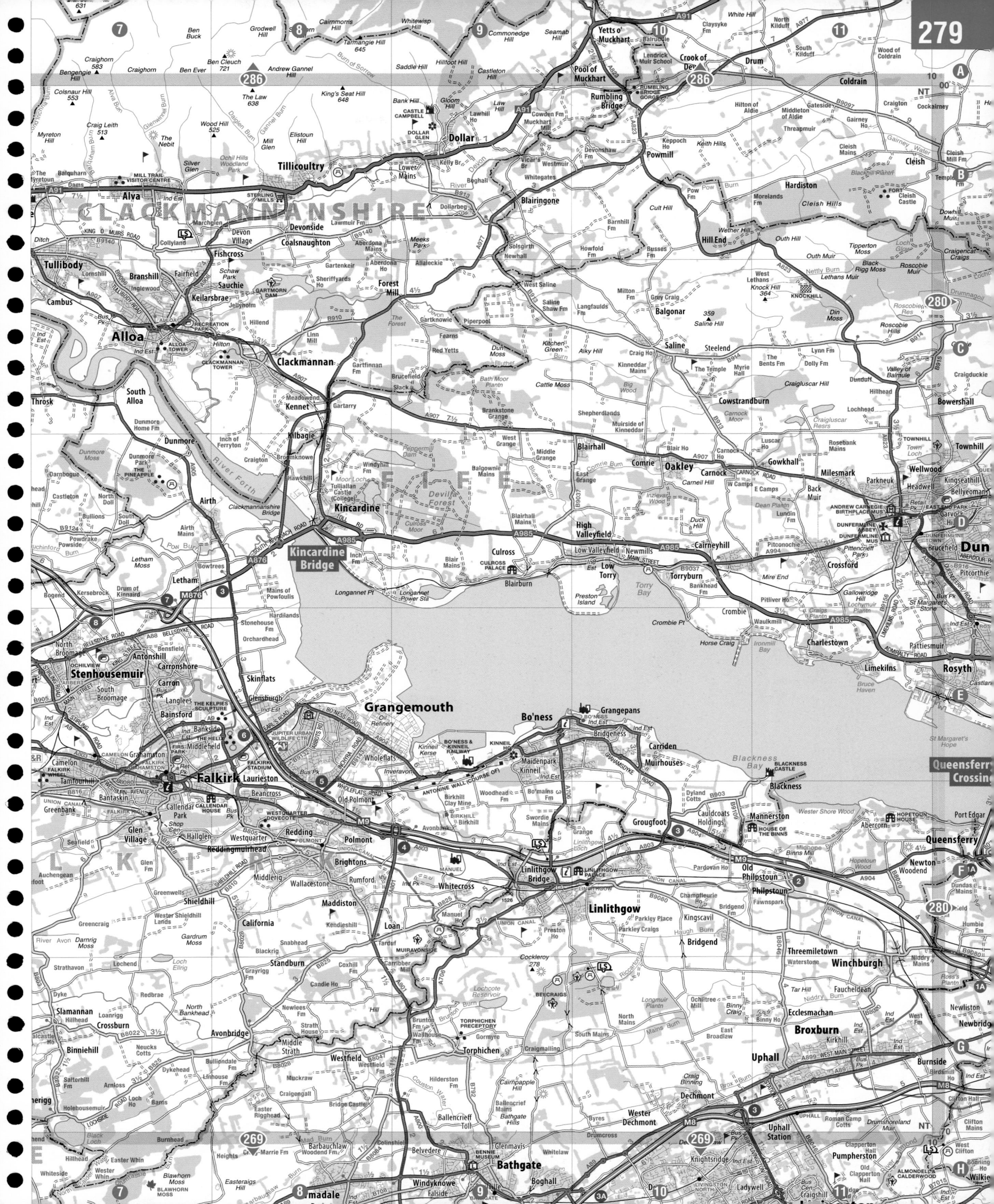

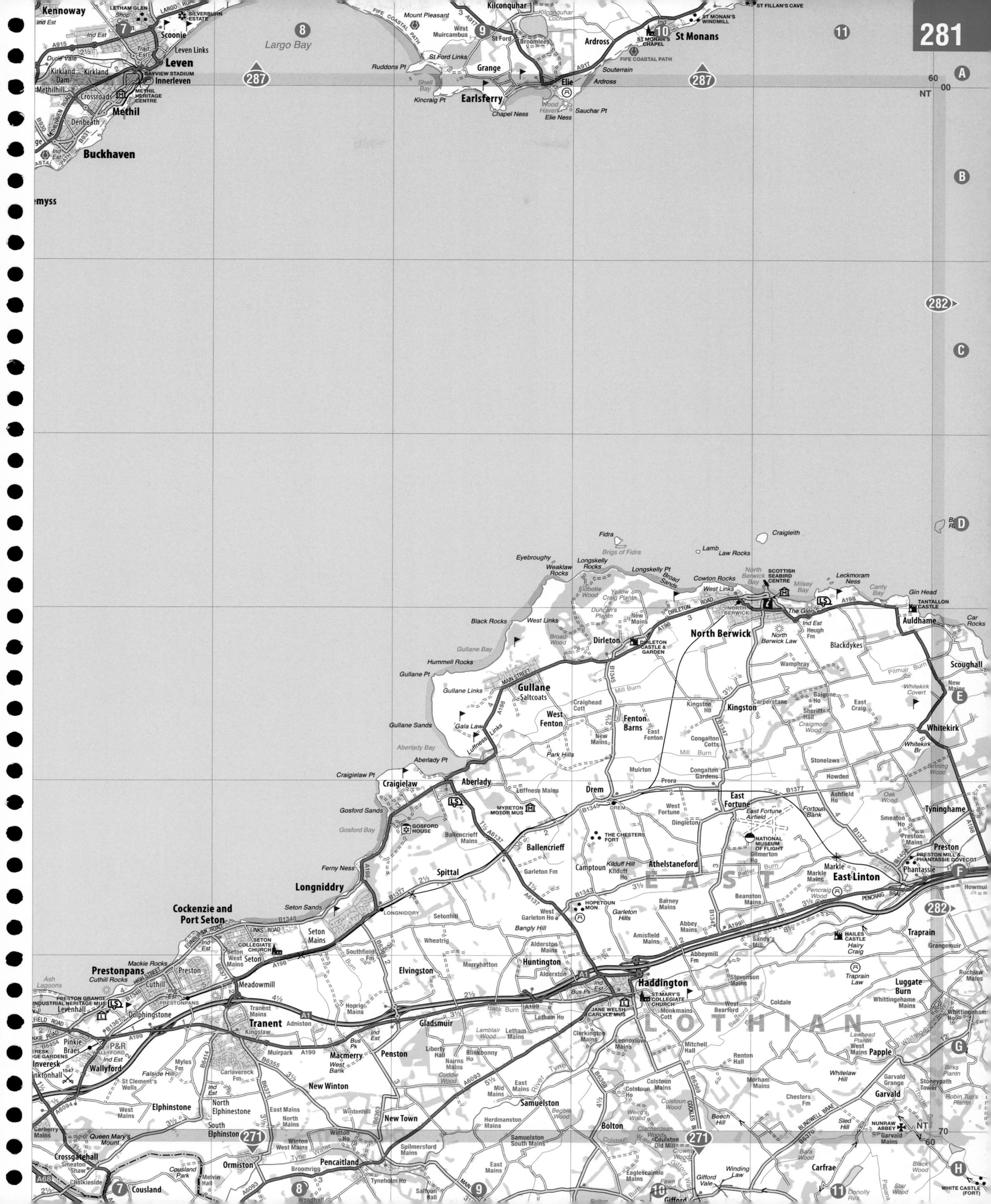

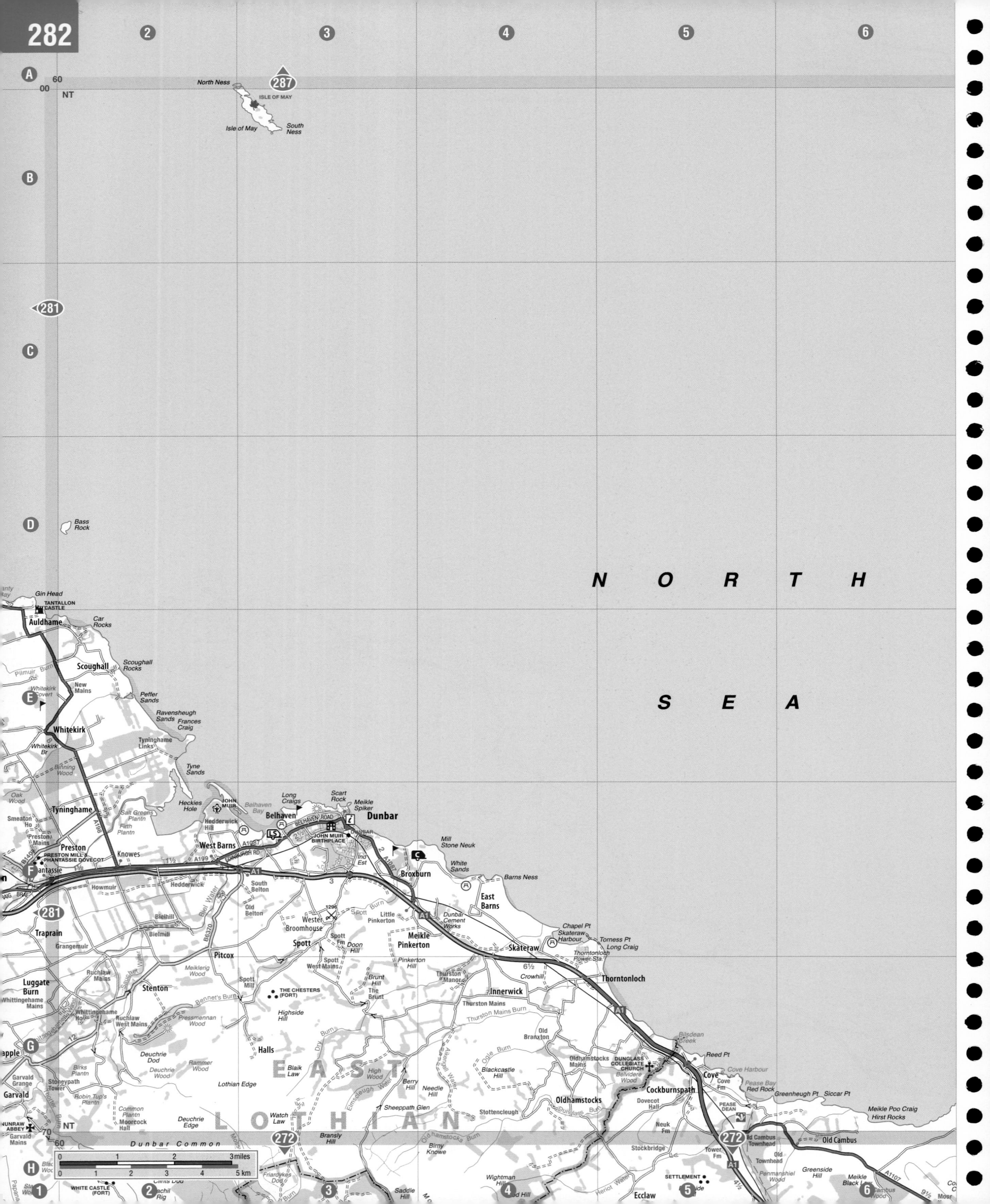

NORTH

SEA

Bass
Rock

Gin Head
TANTALLON
CASTLE
Auldhame

Car
Rocks

Scoughall
Scoughall
Rocks

Whitekirk
Covert
New Mains
Peffer
Sands

Ravensheugh
Sands
Frances
Craig

Whitekirk

Whitekirk
Br.

Tyninghame
Links

Binning
Wood

Tyne
Sands

Smeaton
Ho
Oak
Wood

Tyninghame
Salt Greens
Plantn
Fifth
Plantn

Heckies
Hole

JOHN
MUIR

Belhaven
Bay

Long Craigs

Scart
Rock

Meikle
Spiker

Preston
Mains
Preston

Knowes

Hedderwick
Hill

Belhaven
BELHAVEN ROAD
Dunbar

Mill
Stone Neuk

PRESTON MILL &
PHANTASSIE DOVECOT
Phantassie

Howmuir

Hedderwick

West Barns
A1087

2½

JOHN MUIR
BIRTHPLACE

Ind
Est

White
Sands

Knowes

1½

A199
EDINBURGH RD

A1

South
Belton

Old Belton

Spott
Burn

Broxburn

Barns Ness

East
Barns

281

Traprain

Grangemuir

Bielhill

Bielmill

1296

Wester
Broomhouse

Little
Pinkerton

Dunbar
Cement
Works

Chapel Pt
Skateraw
Harbour

Torness Pt
Long Craig

Pitcox

Meiklerig
Wood

Spott
Fm
Doon
Hill

Meikle
Pinkerton

Thornloch
Power Sta.

Ruchlaw
Mains

Stenton

Spott

Spott
Mill

Spott
West Mains

Pinkerton
Hill

6½

Skateraw

Luggate
Burn

Whittingehame
Mains

Whittingehame
Ho

Ruchlaw
West Mains

Pressmennan
Wood

THE CHESTERS
(FORT)

Bennet's Burn

Highside
Hill

Brunt
Hill
The
Brunt

Thurston
Manor

Thurston Mains

Crowhill

Innerwick

Thornlonloch

Birks
Plantn

Deuchrie
Dod

Deuchrie
Wood

Rammer
Wood

Halls

Blaik
Law

High
Wood

Dry Burn

Thurston Mains Burn

Berry
Hill

Needle
Hill

Old
Branxton

Ogle Burn

Bilsdean
Creek

Reed Pt

Cove Harbour

G
apple

Garvald
Grange

Garvald

Stoneypath
Tower

Robin Tup's
Plantn

Common
Plantn

12

Lothian Edge

Watch
Law

Blackcastle
Hill

Oldhamstocks
Mains

DUNGLASS
COLLEGIATE
CHURCH

Belvidere
Wood

Cove
Cove
Fm

Greenheugh Pt
Siccar Pt

NUNRAW
ABBEY

Garvald
Mains

Moorock
Hall

Deuchrie
Edge

EAST

High
Hill

Sheeppath Glen

Stottencleugh

Oldhamstocks

Cockburnspath

Dovecot
Hall

Dunglass

PEASE
DEAN

Red Rock

Meikle Poo Craig
Hirst Rocks

LOTHIAN

Dunbar Common

Bransly
Hill

Birny
Knowe

Old
Townhead

Tower
Fm

Old Cambus
Townhead

Old
Townhead

Old Cambus

Greenside
Hill
Meikle
Black Law

Blak
Wo

Wightman
Hill

Saddle
Hill

Heriot Water

SETTLEMENT

Ecclaw

Penmanshiel
Wood

Cove
C

0   1   2   3miles
0   1   2   3   4   5 km

A
10
NT 00
B
C
D
E
F
G
NT 70
10
H

Lumsdaine

Fast Castle
Head Wheat Stack
Telegraph
Hill FAST
CASTLE
Oatlee Hill
Dowlaw Burn

St Abb's Head
SETTLEMENT Mire
Loch ST ABB'S HEAD
Horsecastle Bay

Lumsdaine
Moor

Coldingham
Loch

Bell
Hill

dingham
ommon

Cross
Law

Moorside

273

273

7 8 9 10 11

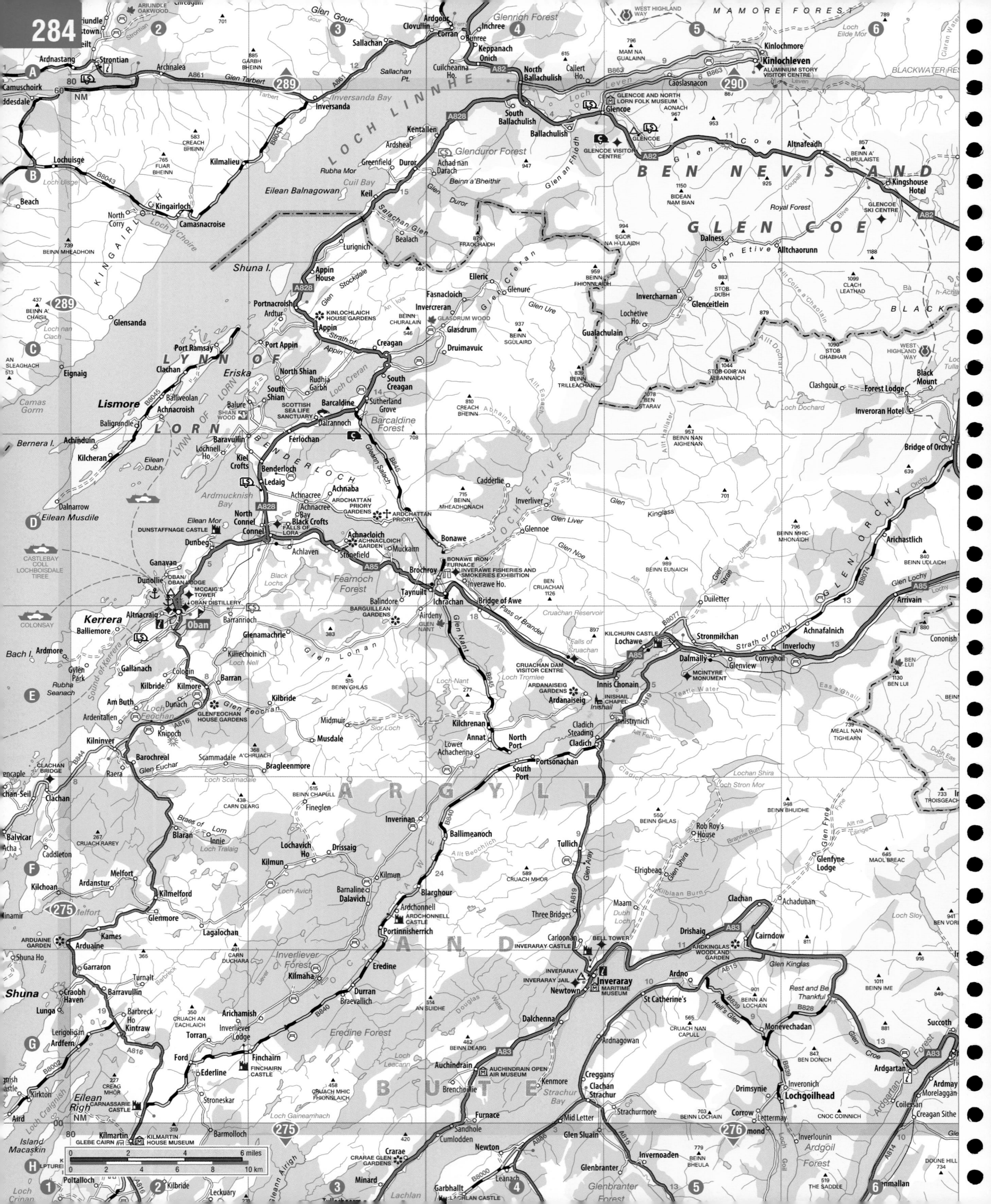

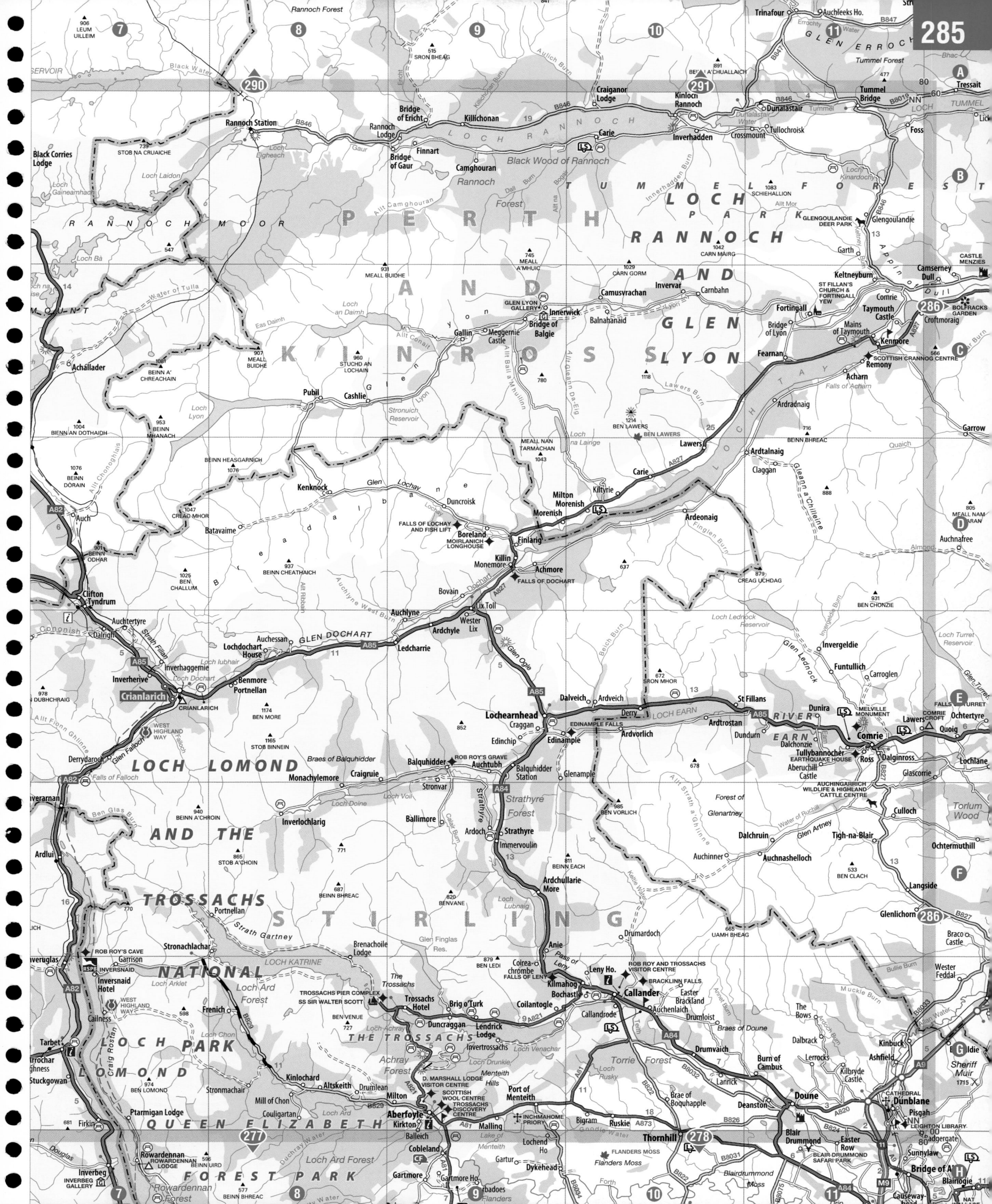

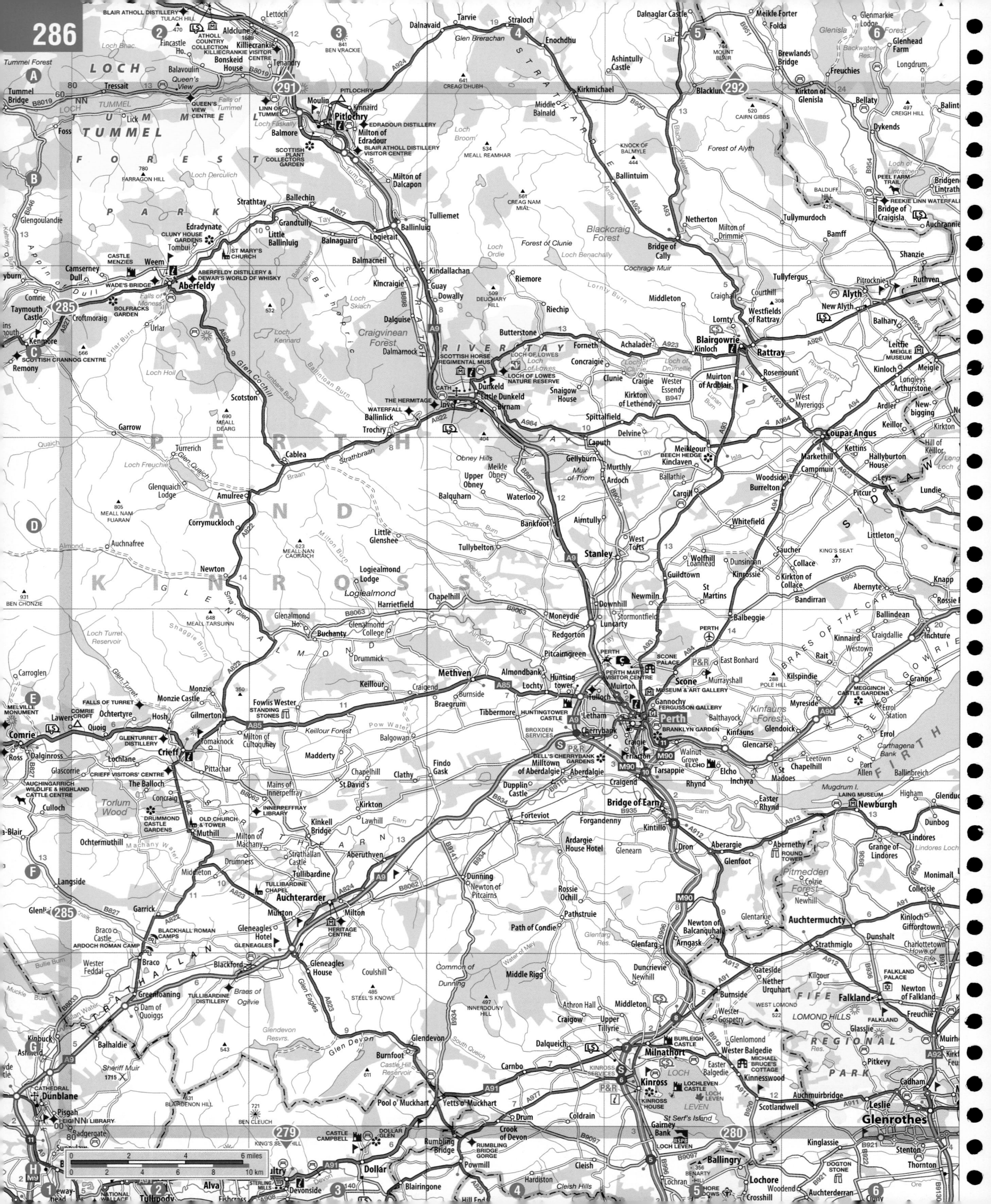

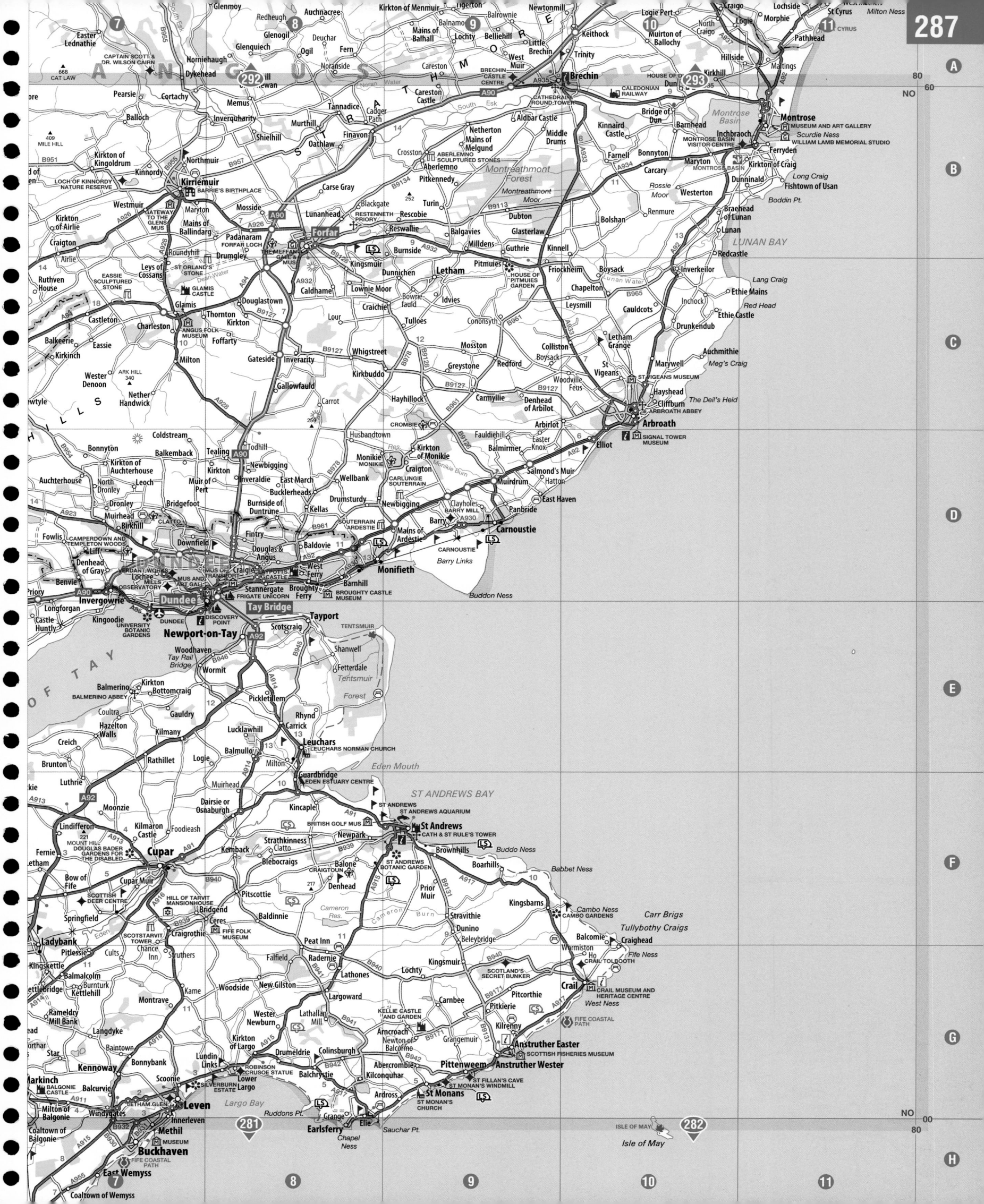

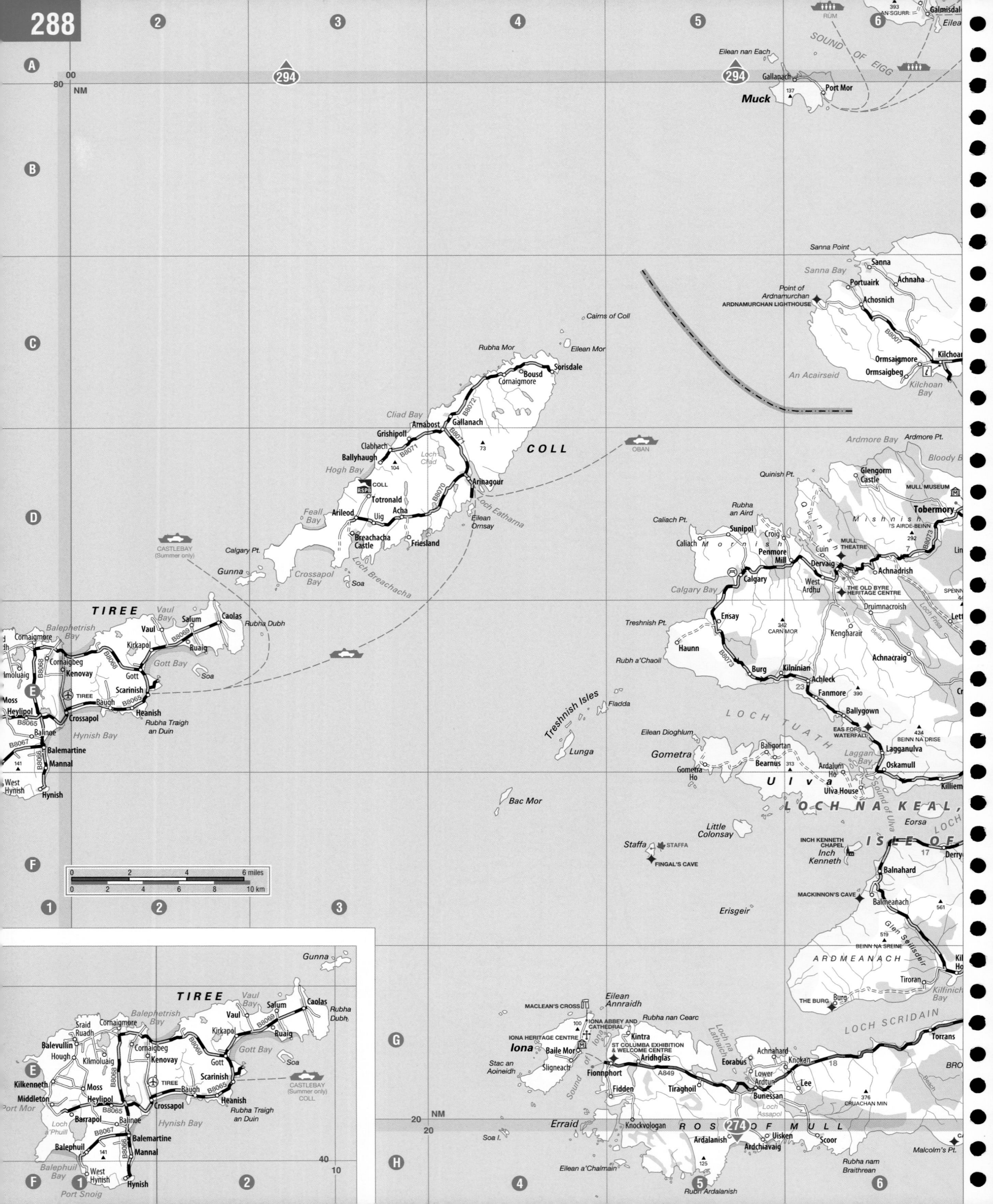

A

B

C

D

E

F

G

H

1

2

3

4

5

6

Muck

Eilean nan Each

SOUND OF EIGG

RUM

AN SGURR

393

Galmisdale

Eilea

Gallanach

Port Mor

137

Sanna Point

Sanna Bay

Sanna

Achnaha

Portuairk

Achosnich

Point of
Ardnamurchan
ARDNAMURCHAN LIGHTHOUSE

An Acairseid

Ormsaigmore

Ormsaigbeg

Kilchoan

Kilchoan
Bay

B8007

Cairns of Coll

Rubha Mor

Eilean Mor

Bousd

Sorisdale

Cornaigmore

COLL

OBAN

Gallanach

Arnabost

B8072

Grishipoll

Clabhach

B8071

B8071

Ballyhaugh

Loch
Chad

73

Hogh Bay

104

RSPB

COLL

Totronald

Arileod

Uig

Acha

B8070

Arinagour

Loch Eatharna

Feall
Bay

Breachacha
Castle

Friesland

Eilean
Ornsay

Calgary Pt.

Gunna

Crossapol
Bay

Loch Breachacha

Soa

Ardmore Bay

Ardmore Pt.

Quinish Pt.

Glengorm
Castle

Bloody B

MULL MUSEUM

Caliach Pt.

Rubha
an Aird

Mishnish

S AIRDE-BEINN

292

Tobermory

Sunipol

Croig

Caliach

Mornish

Cuin

MULL
THEATRE

7

Calgary

Penmore
Mill

Dervaig

Achnadrish

Calgary Bay

West
Ardhu

THE OLD BYRE
HERITAGE CENTRE

Druimnacroish

Loch Frisa

Lett

SPEINN

44

Treshnish Pt.

Ensay

342

CARN MOR

Kengharair

Achnacraig

Rubh a'Chaoil

Haunn

B8073

Burg

Kilninian

Achleck

Fanmore

390

23

Treshnish Isles

Fladda

Eilean Dioghlum

LOCH
TUATH

Ballygown

EAS FORS
WATERFALL

424

BEINN NA DRISE

Lunga

Gometra

Baligortan

Bearnus

313

Ardalum
Ho

Laggan
Bay

Lagganulva

Oskamull

Ulva
House

Ulva

Killiem

Bac Mor

LOCH NA KEAL

Eorsa

LOCH

ISLE OF

Little
Colonsay

Staffa

STAFFA

INCH KENNETH
CHAPEL

Inch
Kenneth

Derry

17

FINGAL'S CAVE

ARDMEANACH

561

Balnahard

MACKINNON'S CAVE

Balmeanach

Glen Seilisdeir

BEINN NA SREINE

519

Kil
Ho

Erisgeir

Tiroran

THE BURG

Burg

Kilfinich
Bay

LOCH SCRIDAIN

MACLEAN'S CROSS

Eilean
Annraidh

Rubha nan Cearc

Loch na
Lathaich

Torrans

IONA HERITAGE CENTRE

IONA ABBEY AND
CATHEDRAL

100

Iona

Baile Mor

ST COLUMBA EXHIBITION
& WELCOME CENTRE

Aridhglas

Achnahard

Knokan

18

Stac an
Aoineidh

Slighneach

Eorabus

BRO

Fionnphort

A849

Lower
Ardtun

Lee

Fidden

Tiraghoil

Bunessan

Loch
Assapol

376

CRUACHAN MIN

Erraid

20

NM

Knockvologan

ROSS OF MULL

274

Soa I.

Ardalanish

Uisken

Scoor

Ardchiavaig

Rubha nam
Braithrean

Malcolm's Pt.

Eilean a'Chalmain

125

Rubh Ardalanish

TIREE

Balephetrish
Bay

Vaul
Bay

Salum

Caolas

Rubha Dubh

Cornaigmore

Vaul

Cornaigbeg

Kirkapol

B8069

Kenovay

Ruaig

Imoluaig

B8068

Gott

Gott Bay

Soa

Moss

TIREE

Scarinish

CASTLEBAY
(Summer only)

Heylipol

Baugh

B8065

Balinoe

Crossapol

Heanish

B8067

Balemartine

Rubha Traig
an Duin

141

Hynish Bay

Mannal

West
Hynish

B8066

Hynish

CASTLEBAY
(Summer only)

Gunna

TIREE

Balephetrish
Bay

Vaul
Bay

Salum

Caolas

Rubha
Dubh

Sraid
Ruadh

Cornaigmore

Vaul

Balevullin

Hough

Kilmoluaig

Cornaigbeg

Kirkapol

B8069

Kenovay

Ruaig

Kilkenneth

Moss

Gott

Gott Bay

Soa

Middleton

Heylipol

TIREE

Scarinish

CASTLEBAY
(Summer only)

COLL

Port Mor

Loch
a'Phuill

B8068

Barrapol

Balinoe

Crossapol

Heanish

B8067

Balemartine

Rubha Traig
an Duin

141

Hynish Bay

Balephuil

B8066

Mannal

Balephuil
Bay

West
Hynish

Port Snoig

Hynish

0   2   4   6 miles

0 2 4 6 8 10 km

00

80

NM

294

294

20

20

40

10

NM

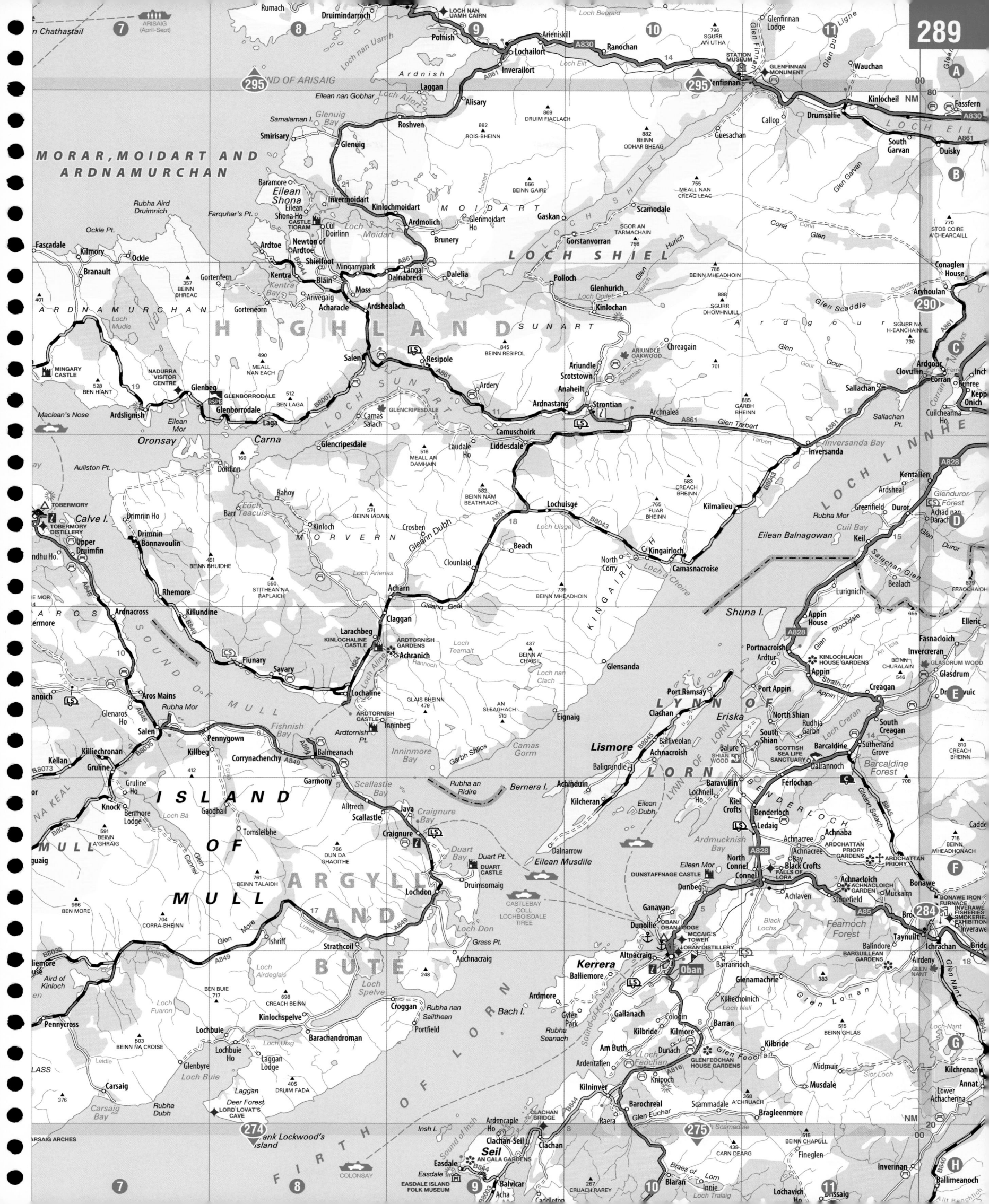

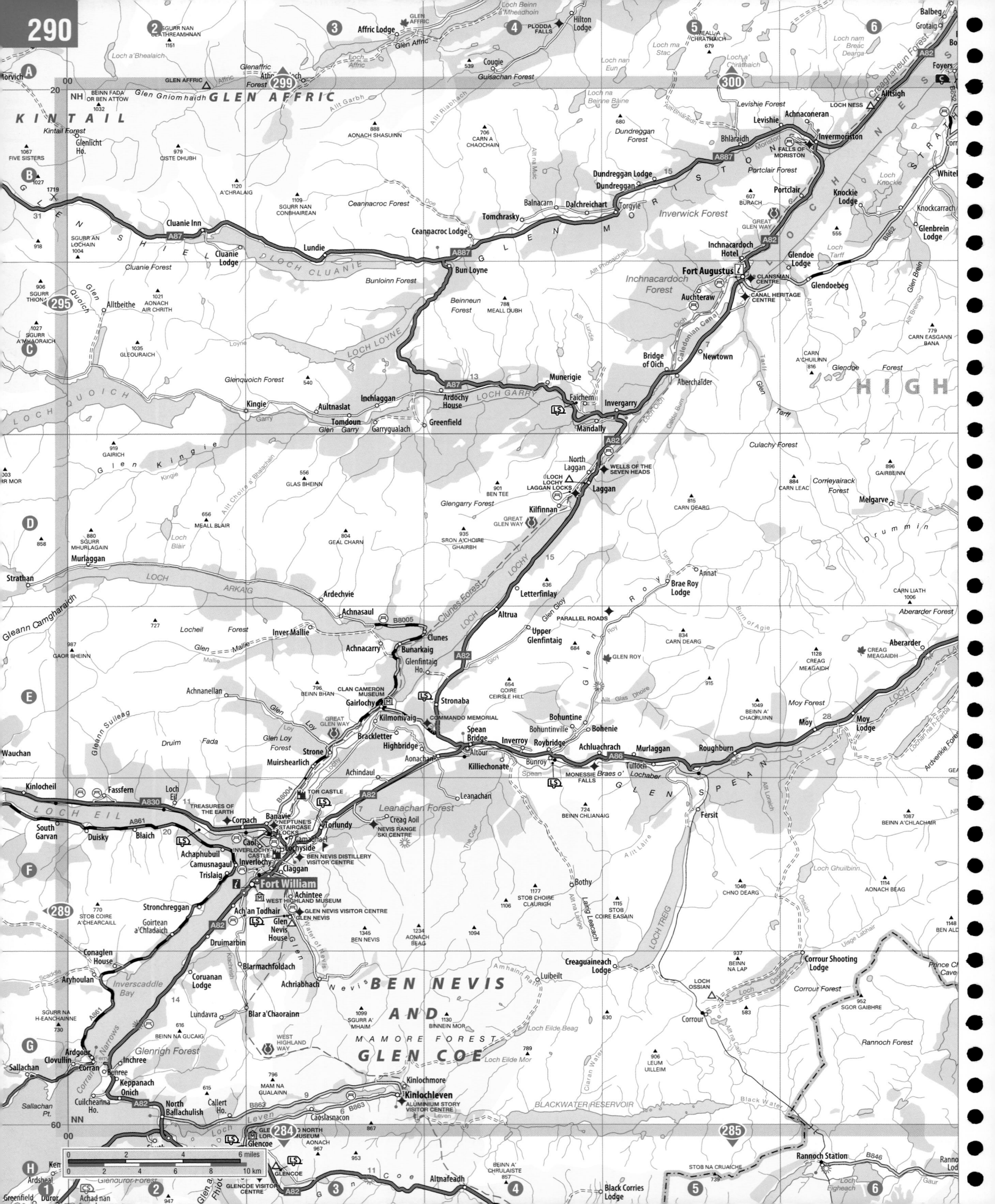

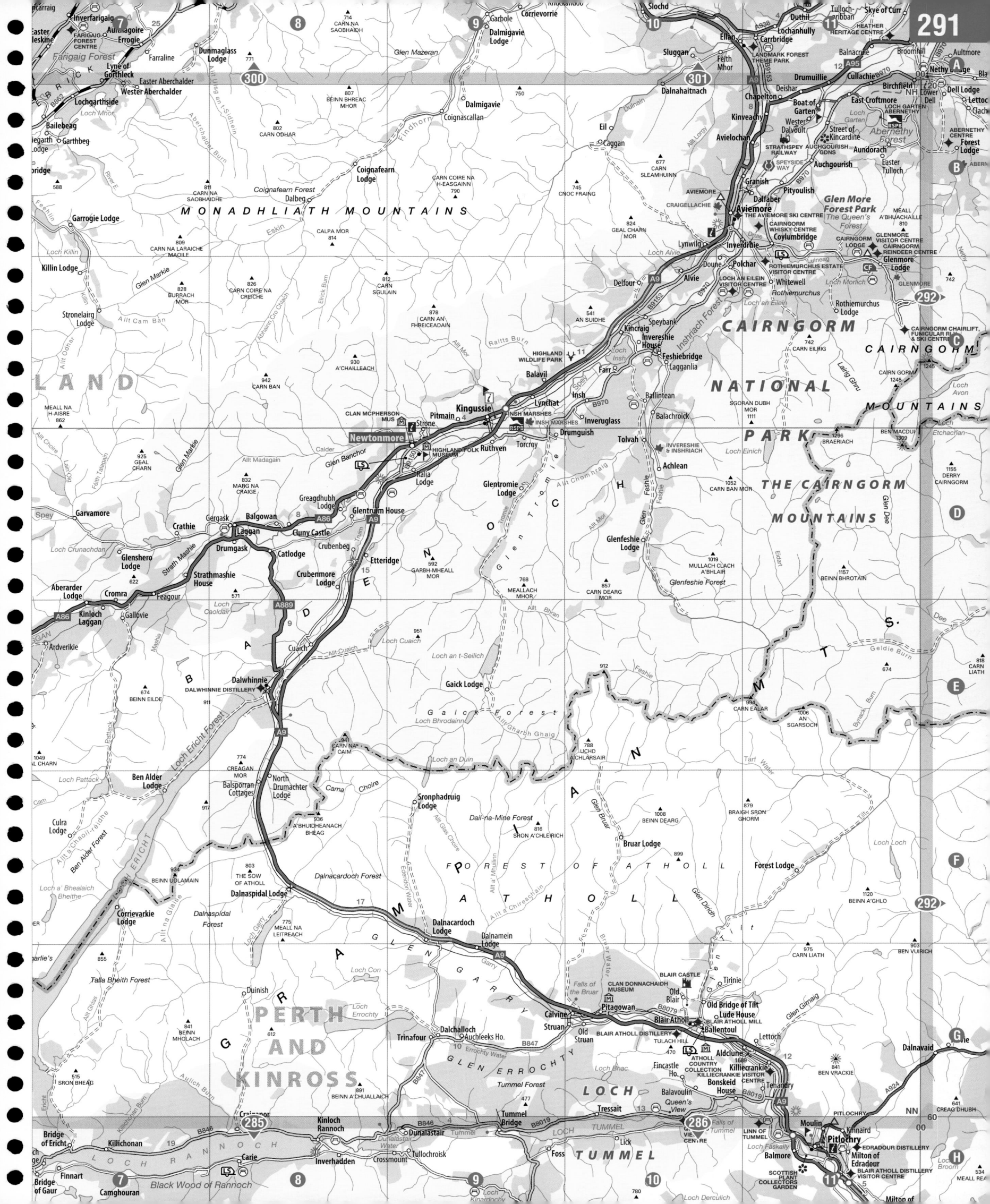

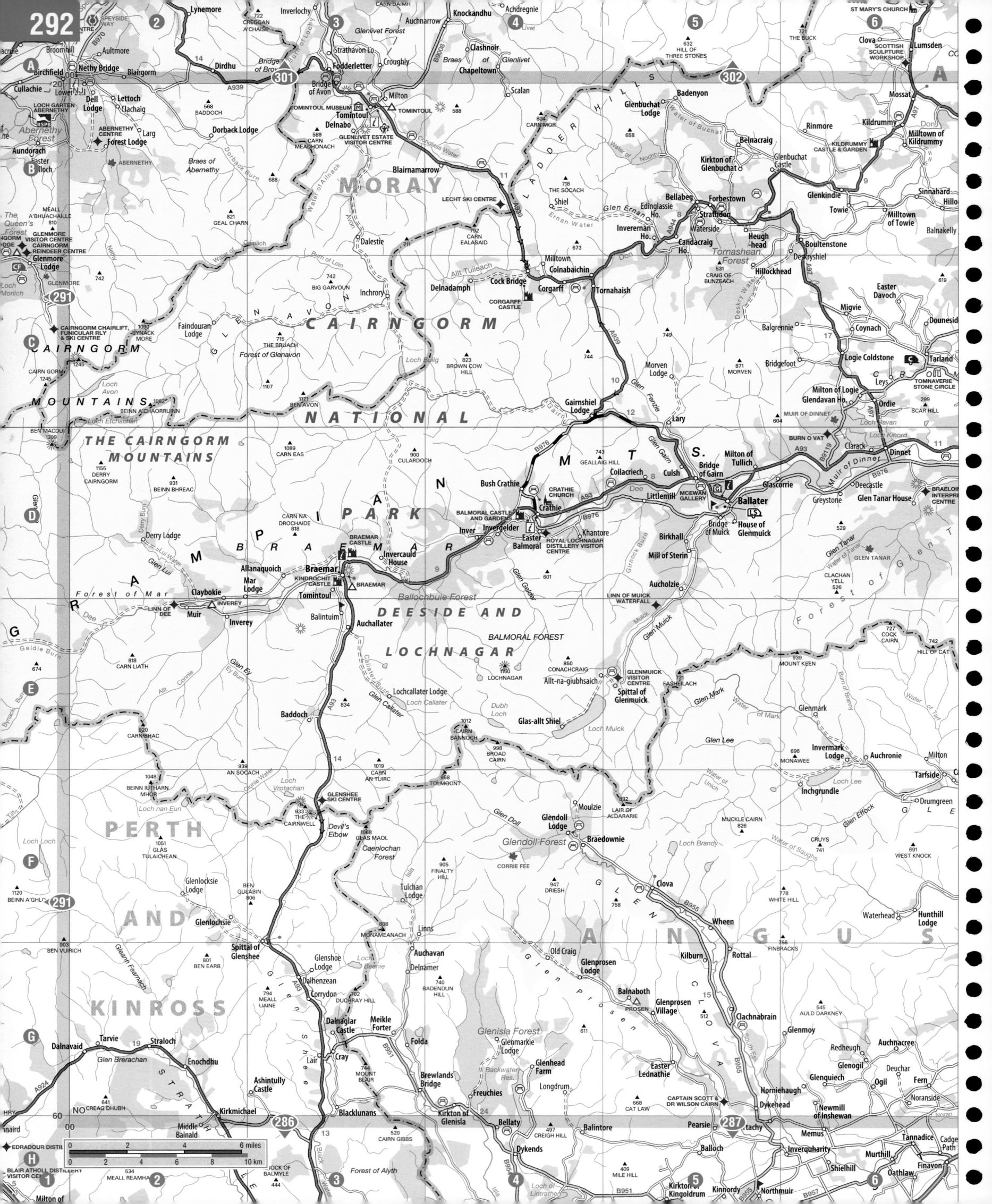

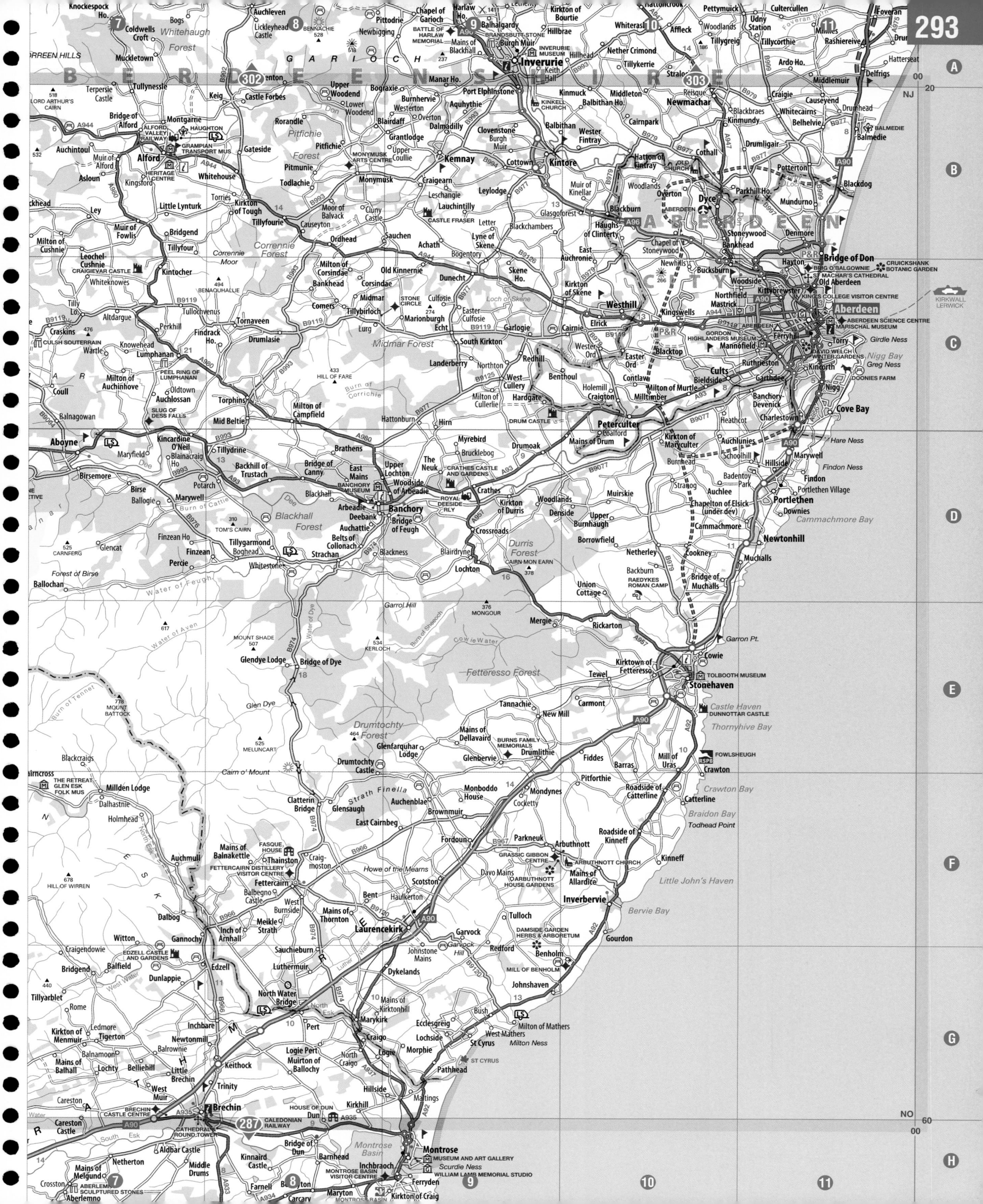

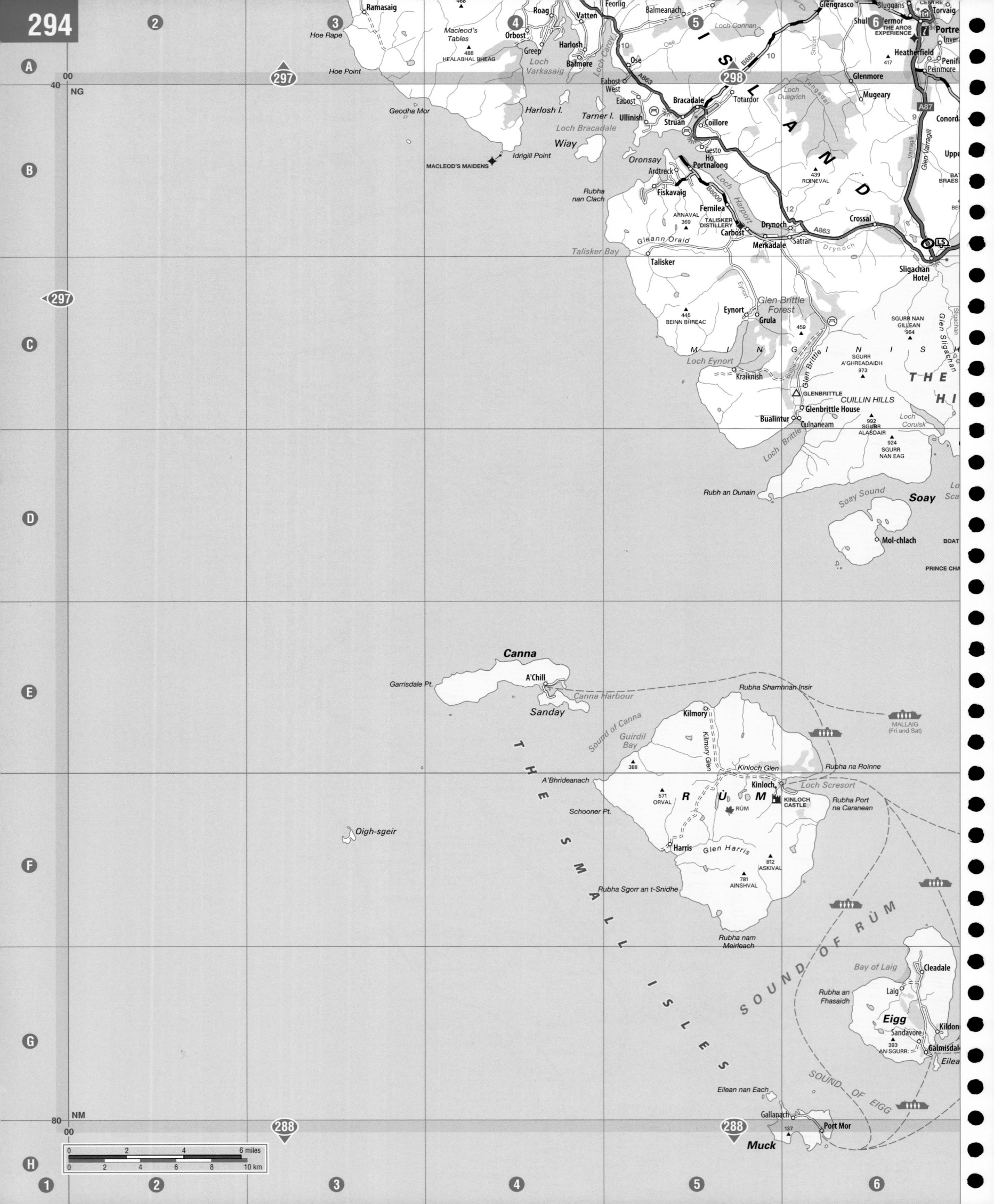

Ramasaig
Roag
Vatten
Feorlig
Balmeanach
Glengrasco
Sluggans
Torvaig
Portree
THE AROS EXPERIENCE
Inver

Hoe Rape
Macleod's Tables
Orbost
Greep
Harlosh
Ose
Loch Connan
10
10
Shul
Penmore
Heatherfield
Penif

HEALABHAL BHEAG
488
Balmore
Loch Varkasaig
Loch Caroy
I S L A N D
Glenmore
417
Peinmore

A
00
40
Hoe Point
Eabost West
Eabost
Bracadale
Totardor
Loch Duagrich
Mugeary
Conord

NG
Geodha Mor
Harlosh I.
Tarner I.
Ullinish
Struan
Coillore
Tangadal
A87
9

Wiay
Loch Bracadale
Gesto
Ho
Portnalong
439
ROINEVAL
BAT
BRAES
BE

297
MACLEOD'S MAIDENS
Idrigill Point
Oronsay
Ardtreck
Fiskavaig
Fernilea
ARNAVAL 369
TALISKER DISTILLERY
Carbost
Drynoch
A863
Crossal

B
Rubha nan Clach
Loch Harport
Merkadale
Satran
Drynoch

Talisker Bay
Talisker
Eynort
Glen Brittle Forest
Sligachan Hotel

297
445 BEINN BHREAC
Grula
459
SGURR NAN GILLEAN 964
Glen Sligachan

C
M I N G I N I S
Loch Eynort
Kraiknish
SGURR A'GHREADAIDH 973
THE HI

GLENBRITTLE
CUILLIN HILLS
Bualintur
Glenbrittle House
992 SGURR ALASDAIR
Loch Coruisk

924 SGURR NAN EAG
Culnaneam

Rubh an Dunain
Soay Sound
Soay
Lo Sca

D
Mol-chlach
BOAT

PRINCE CHA

Canna
A'Chill
Garrisdale Pt.
Canna Harbour
Rubha Shamhnan Insir
MALLAIG (Fri and Sat)

E
Sanday
Sound of Canna
Kilmory
Guirdil Bay
Kilmory Glen

Oigh-sgeir
A'Bhrideanach
388
Kinloch Glen
Kinloch
Loch Scresort
Rubha na Roinne

571 ORVAL
R Ù M
RÙM
KINLOCH CASTLE
Rubha Port na Caranean

T H E
Schooner Pt.
Harris
Glen Harris
812 ASKIVAL

F
Rubha Sgorr an t-Snidhe
781 AINSHVAL

S M A L L I S L E S
Rubha nam Meirleach
SOUND OF RÙM

Bay of Laig
Cleadale

Rubha an Fhasaidh
Laig
Eigg
Kildon

G
Sandavore
393 AN SGURR
Galmisdale
Eilea

Eilean nan Each
SOUND OF EIGG

80
NM
Gallanach
Port Mor

00
288
288
137

H
0 2 4 6 miles
0 2 4 6 8 10 km
Muck

1   2   3   4   5   6

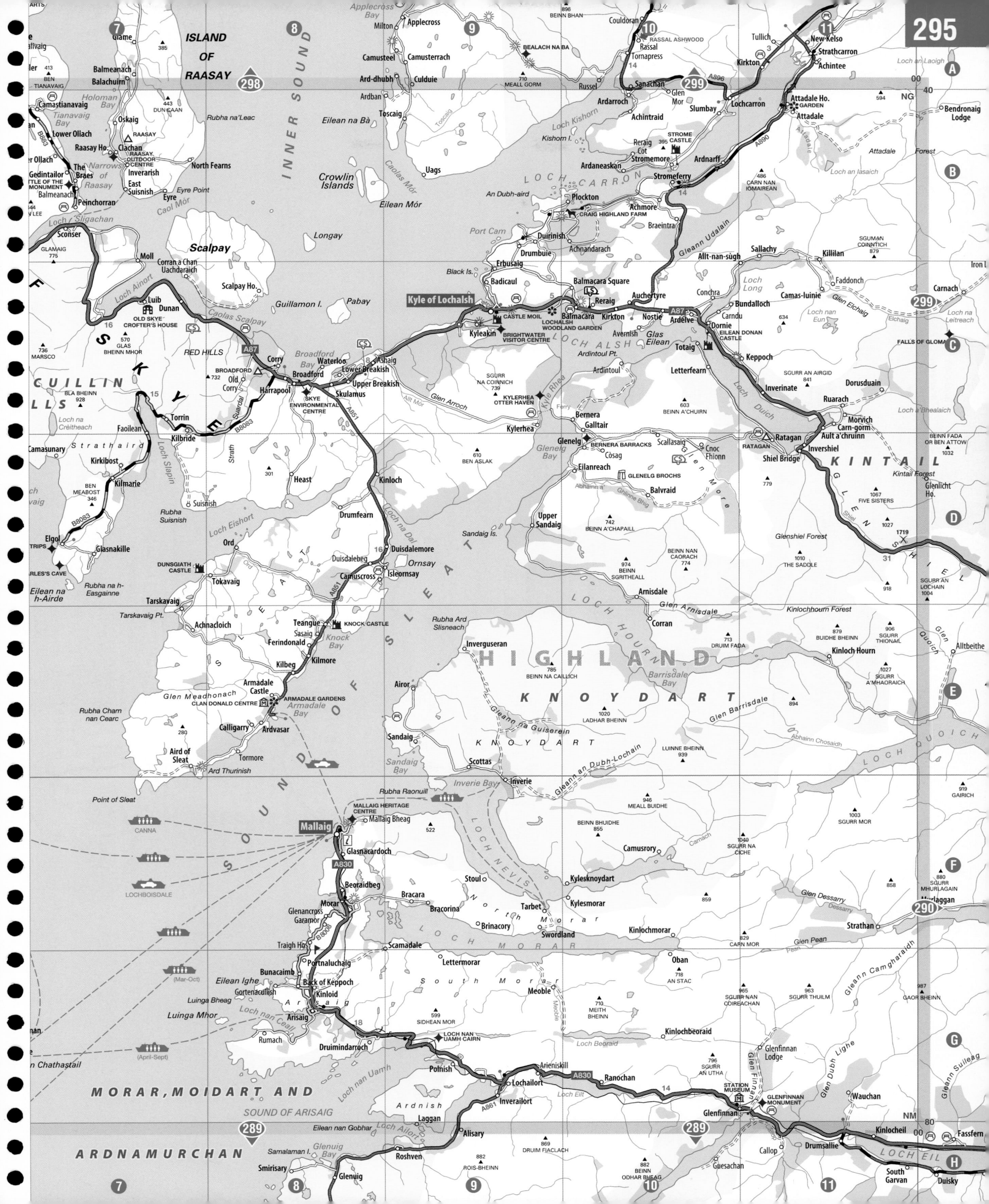

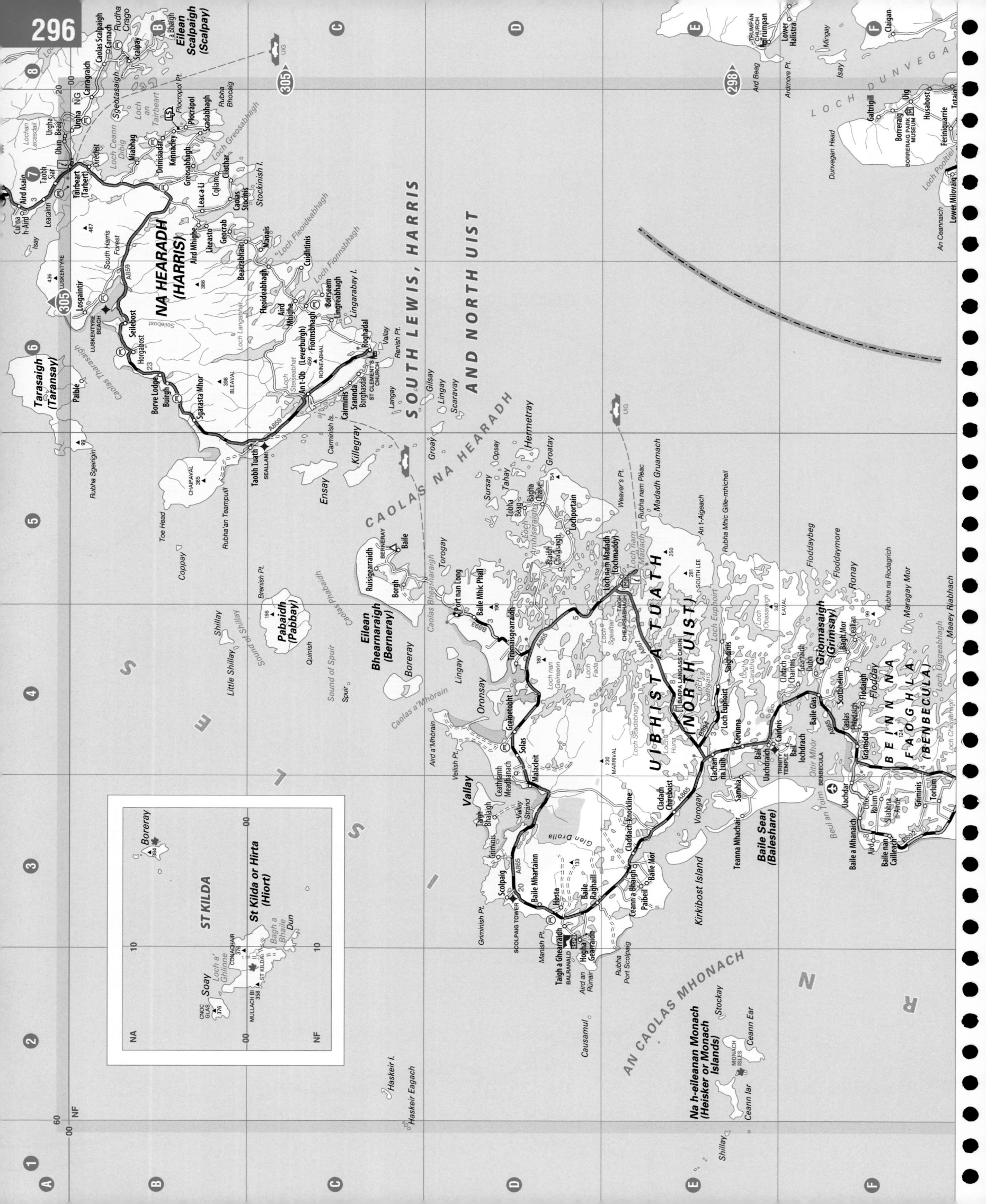

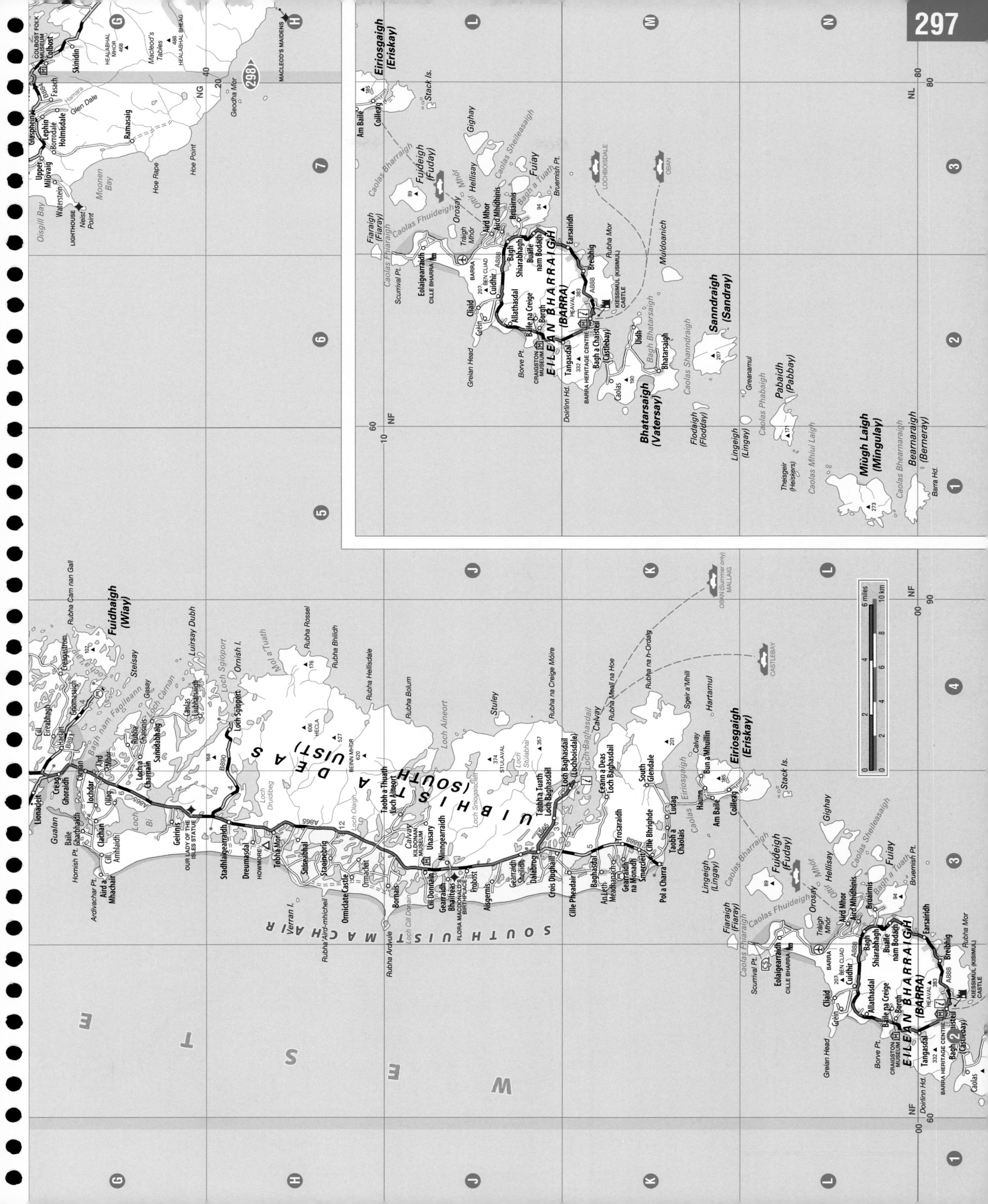

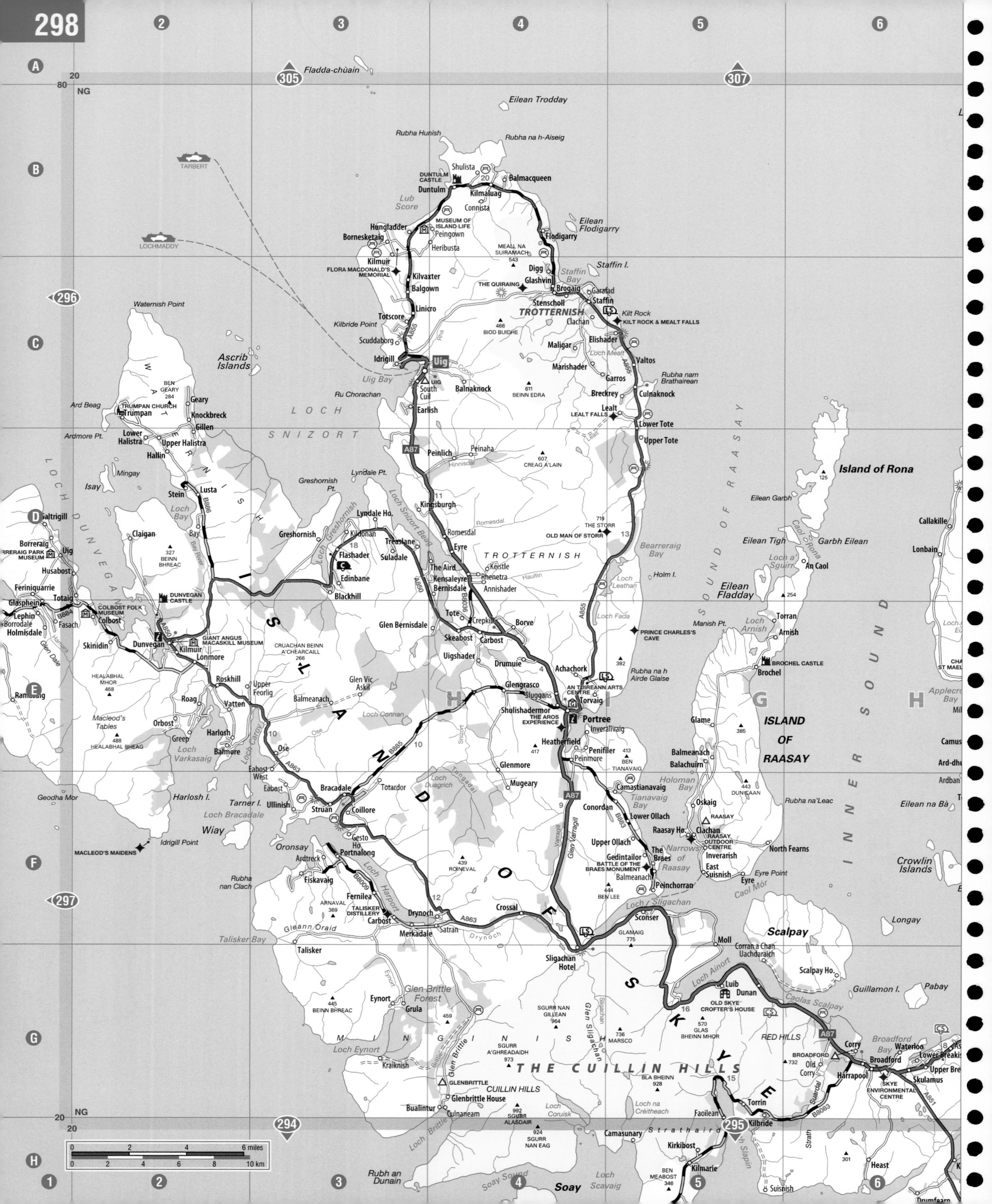

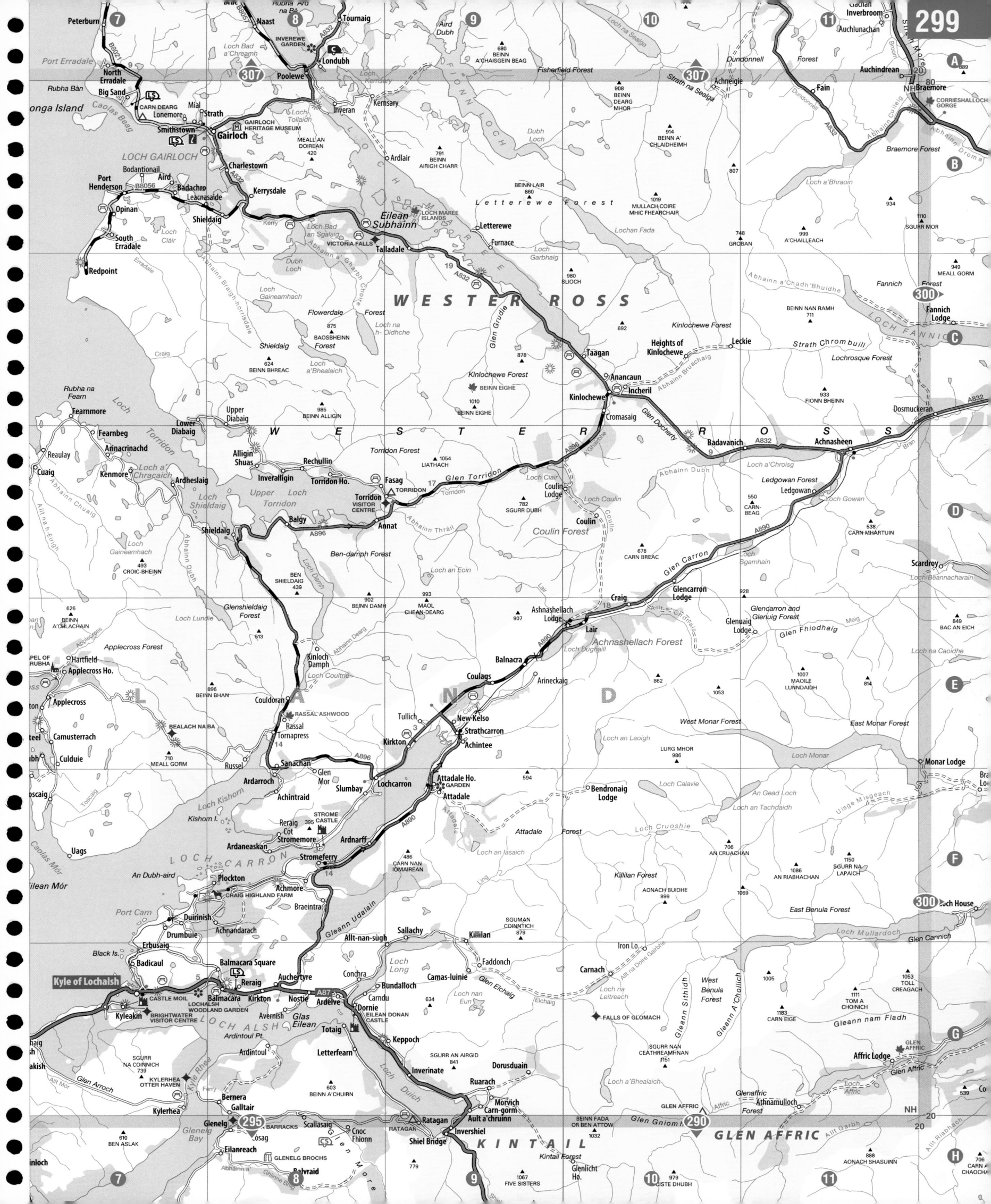

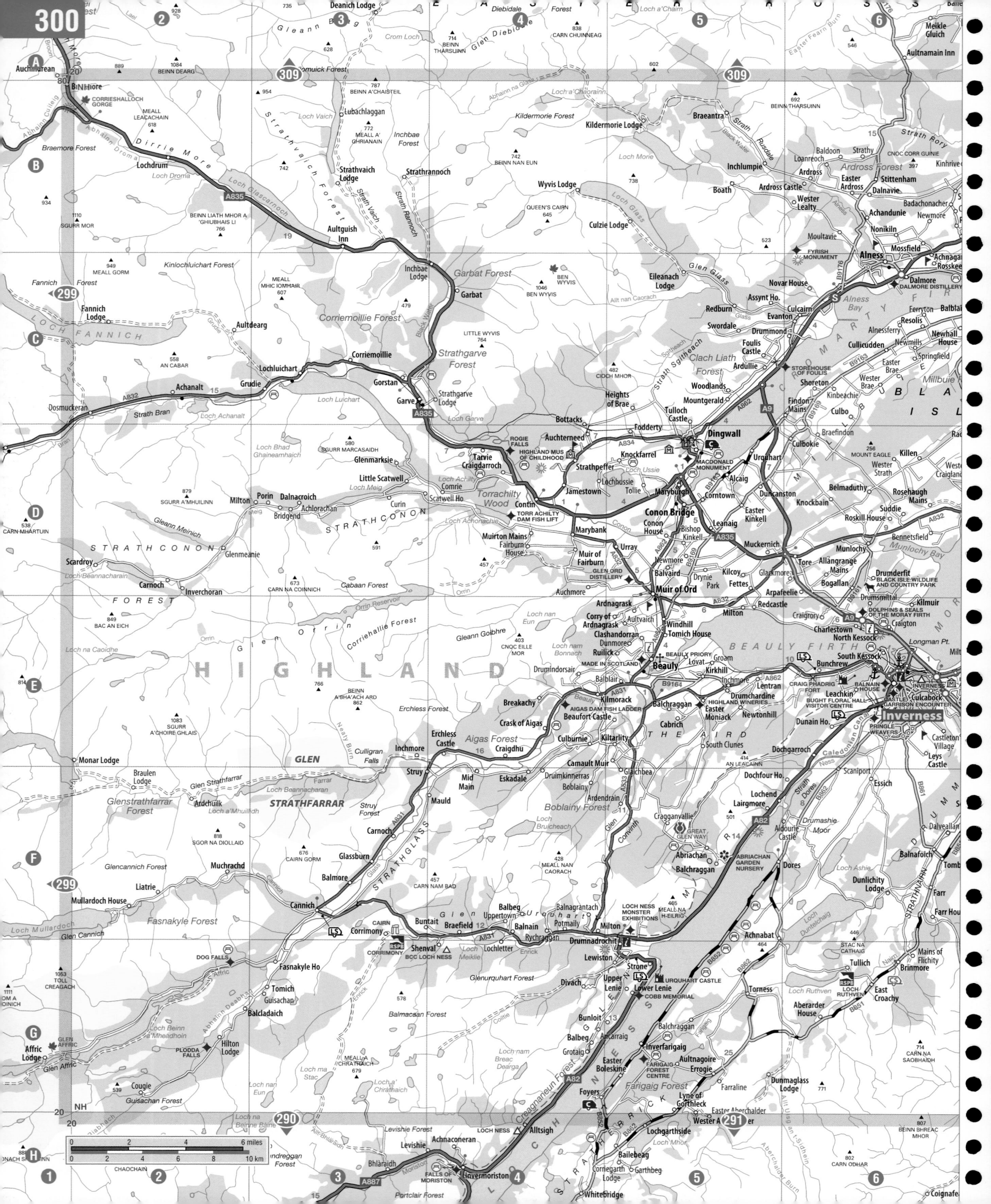

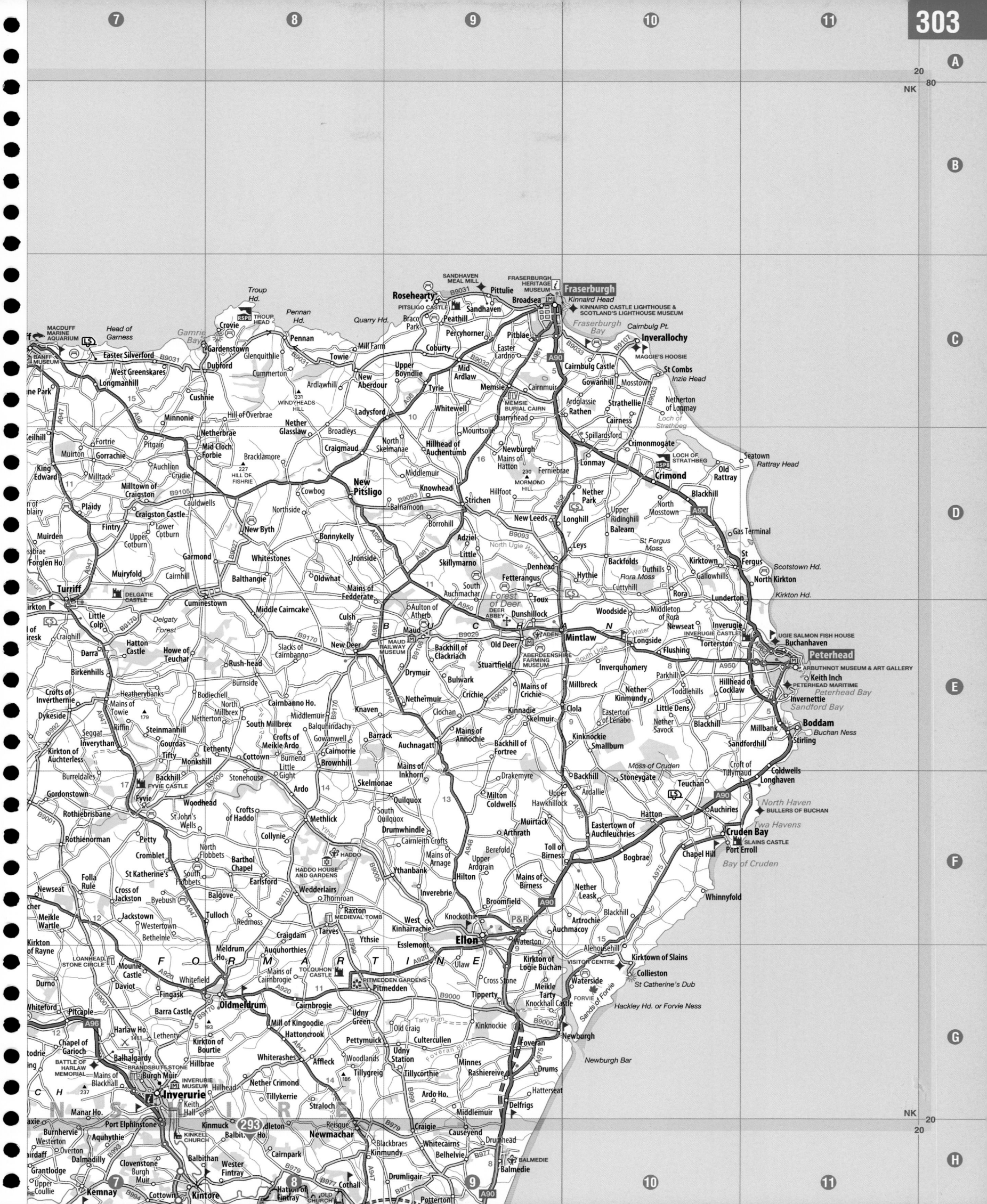

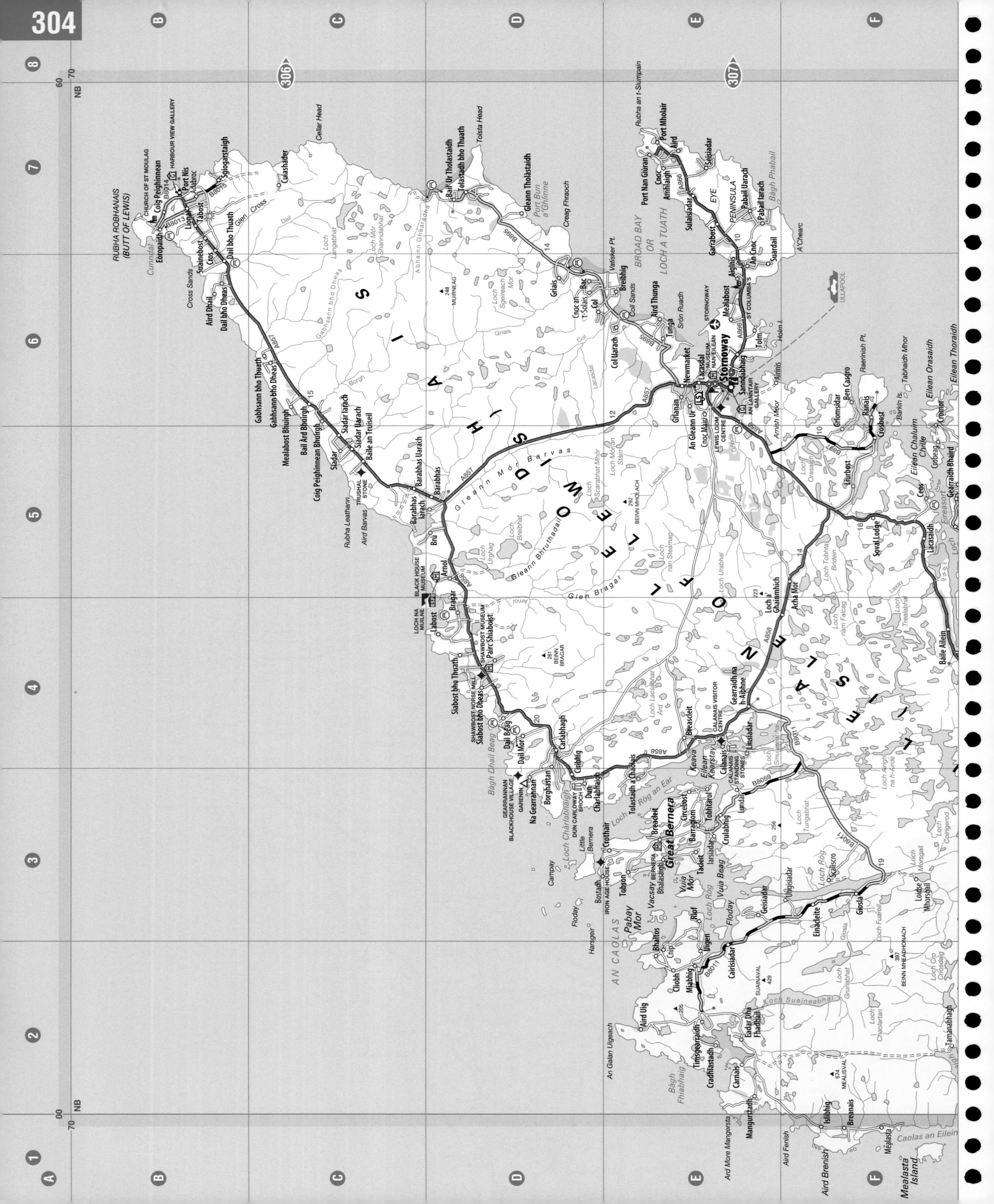

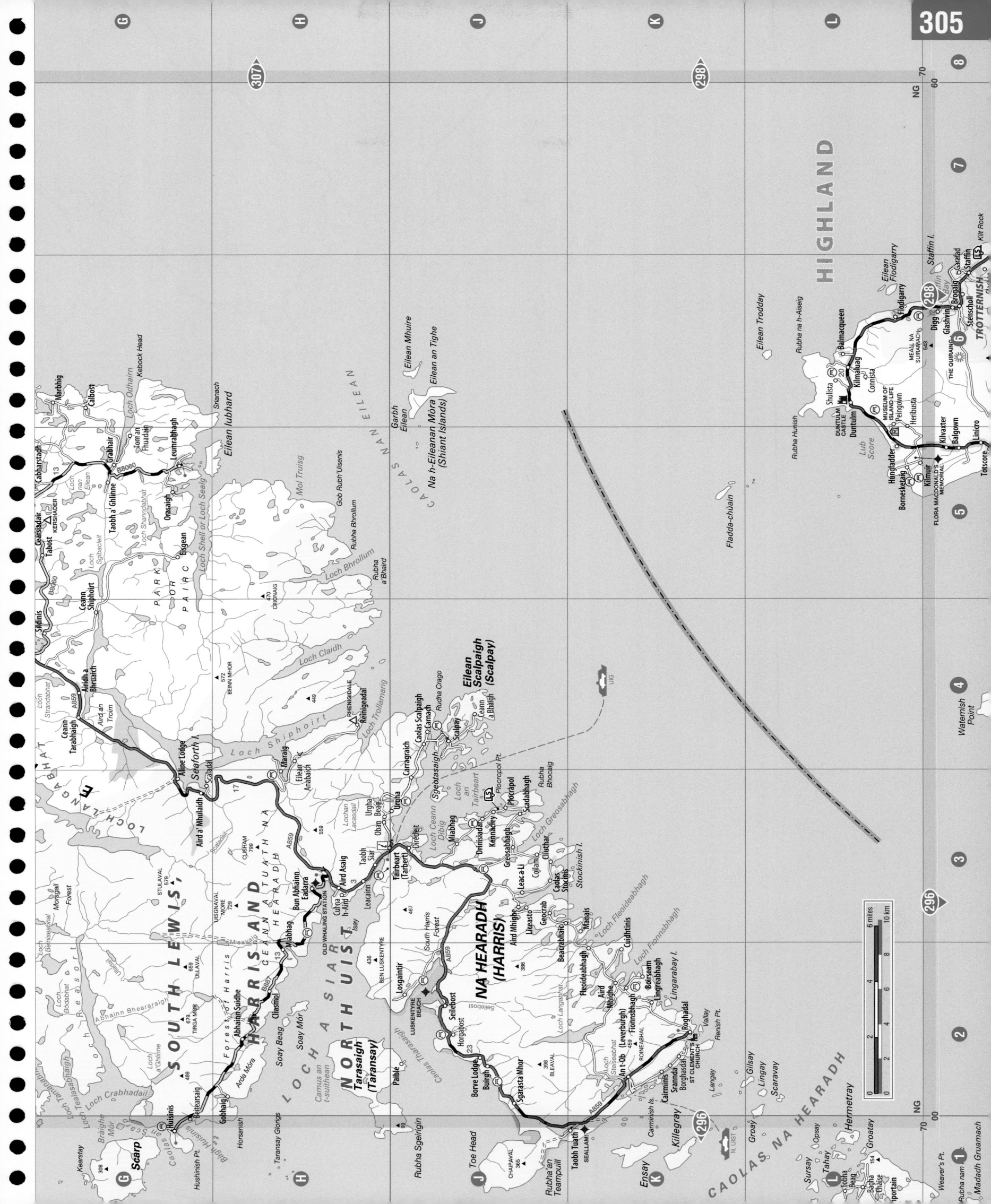

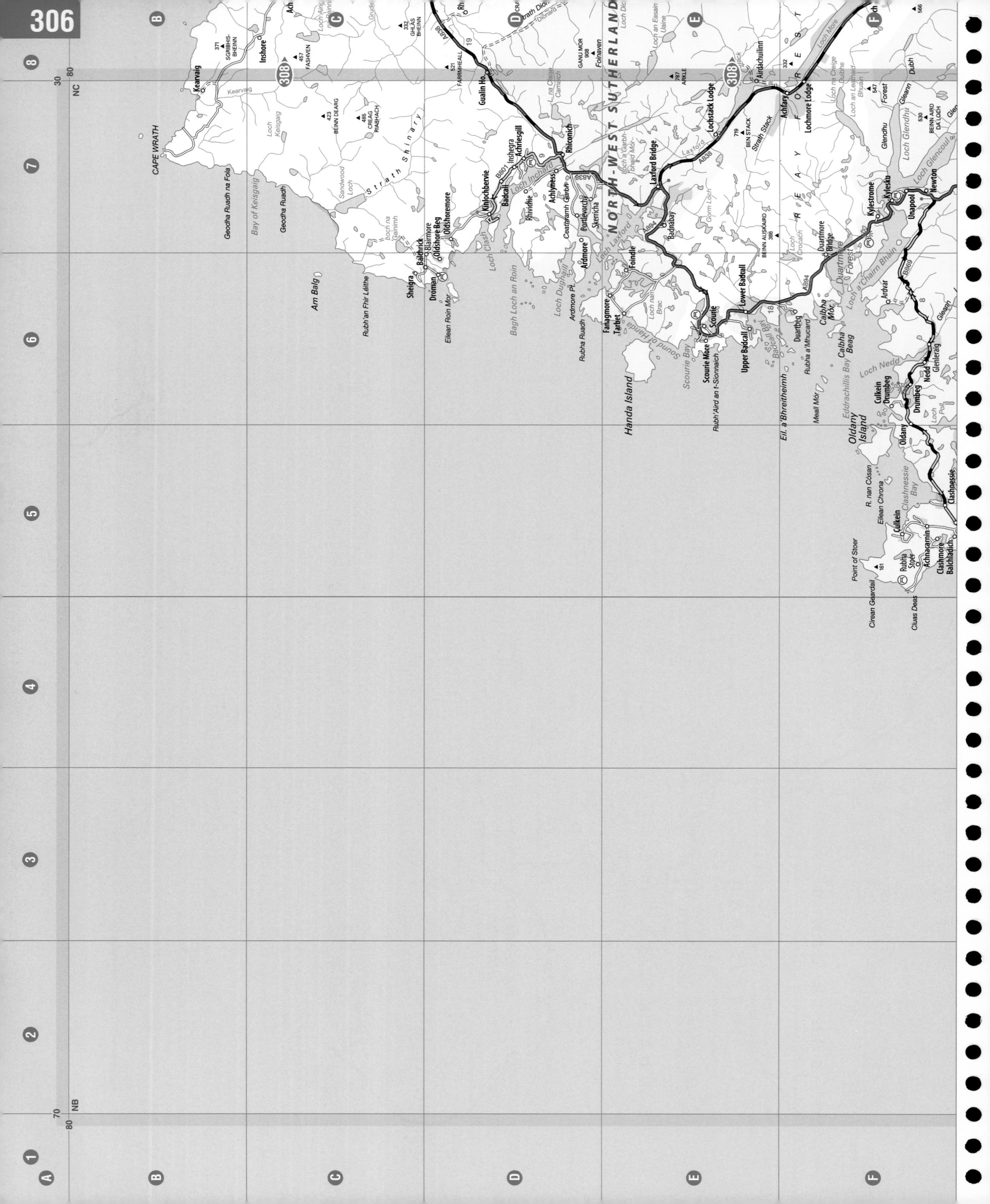

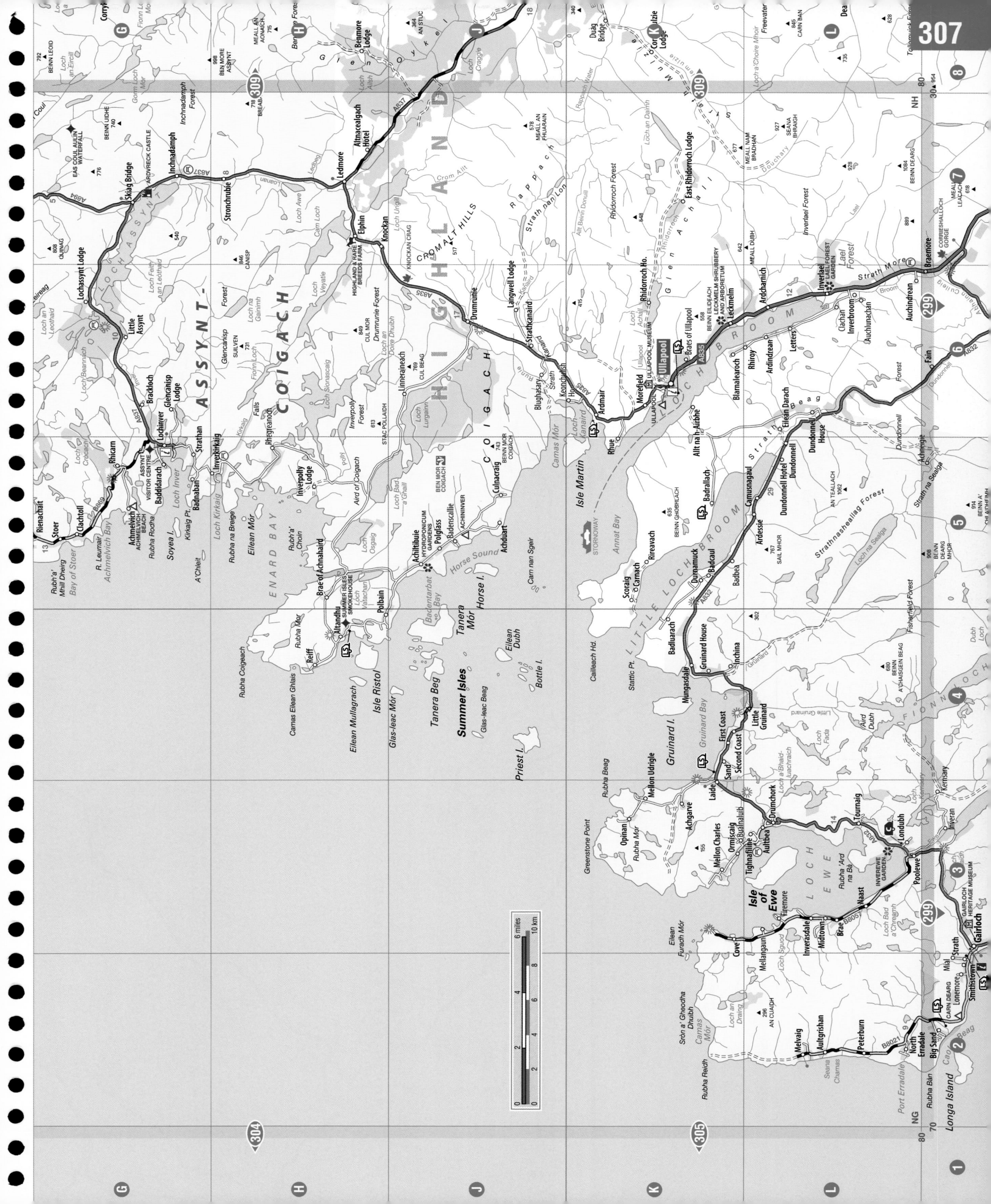

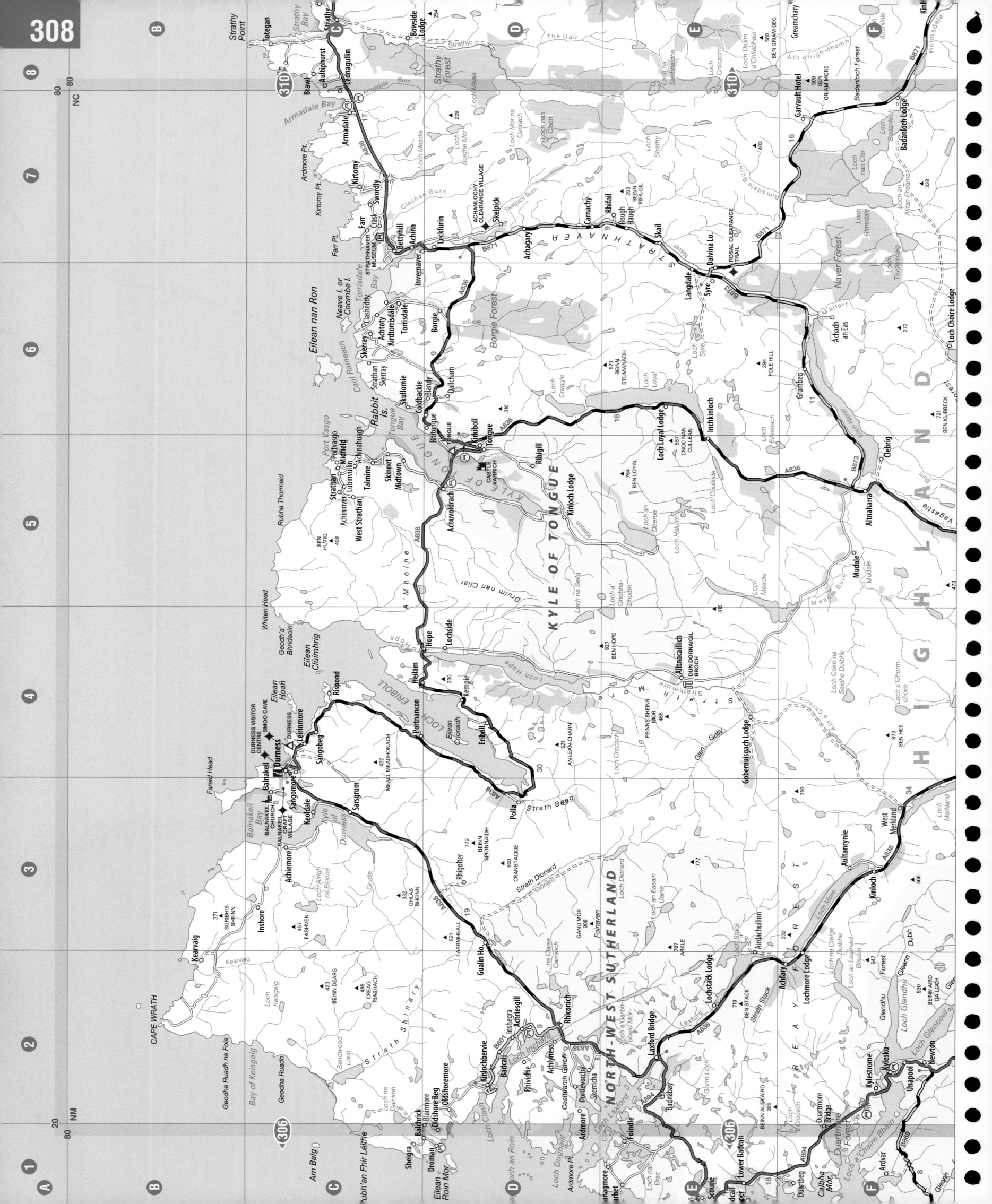

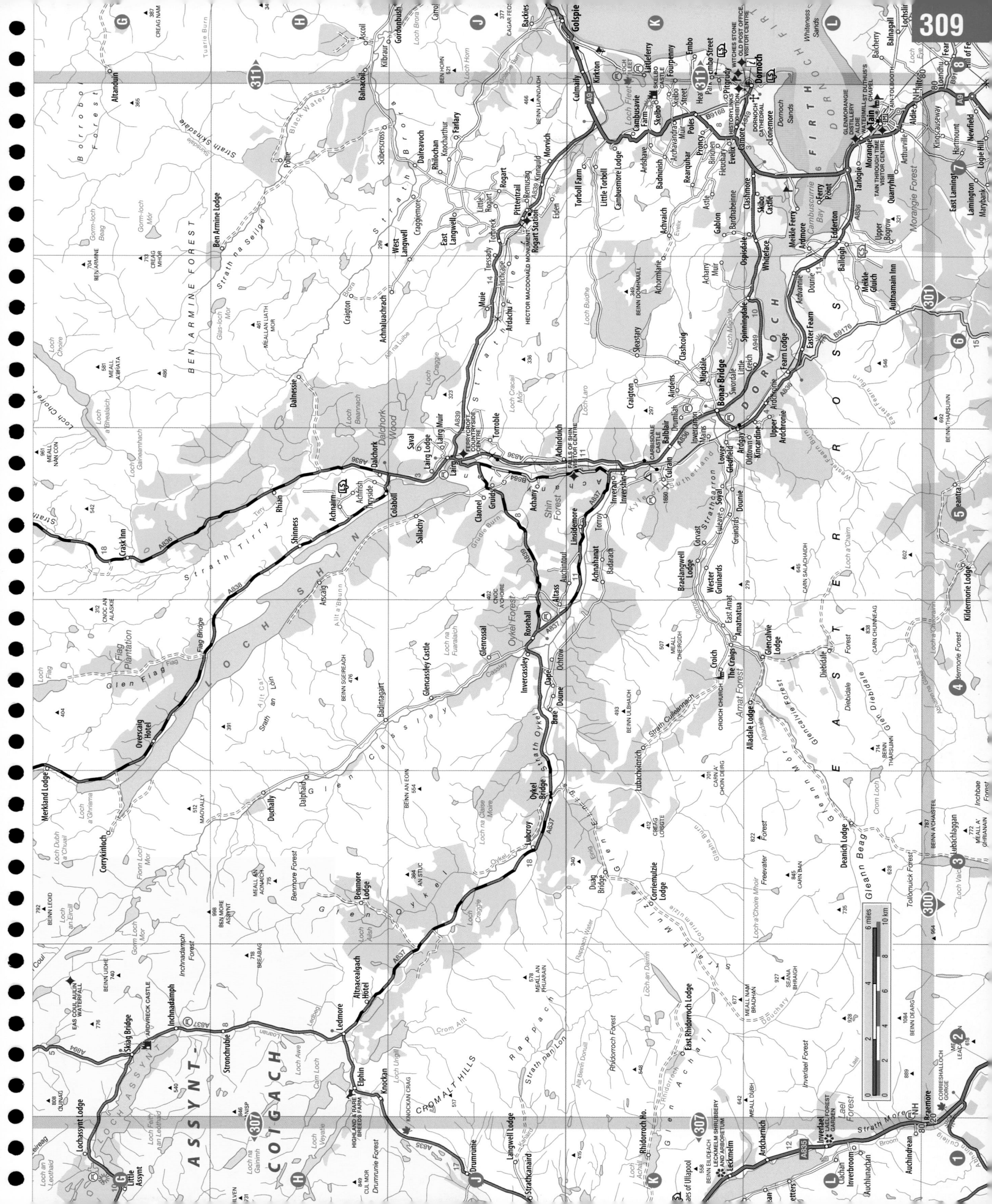

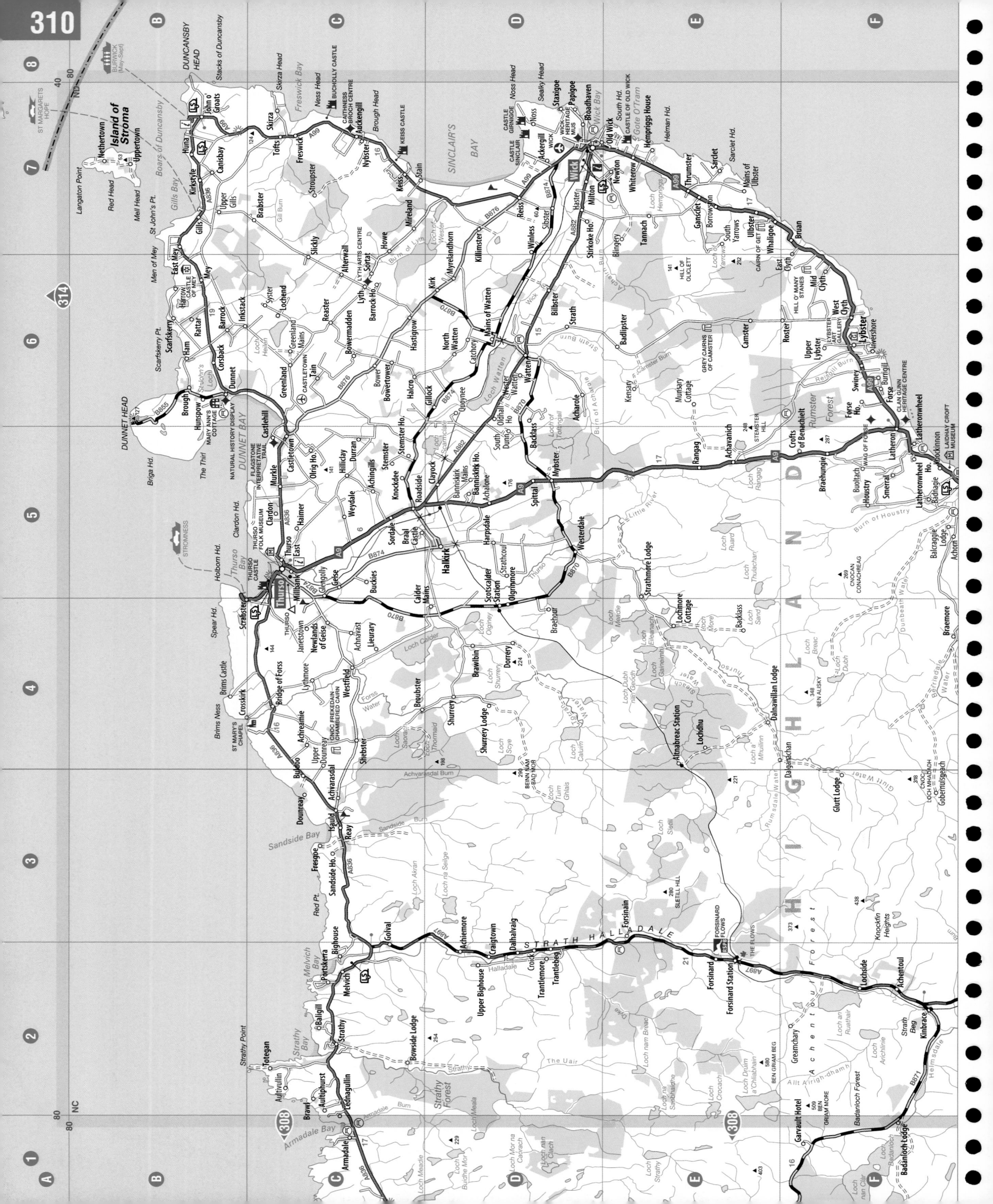

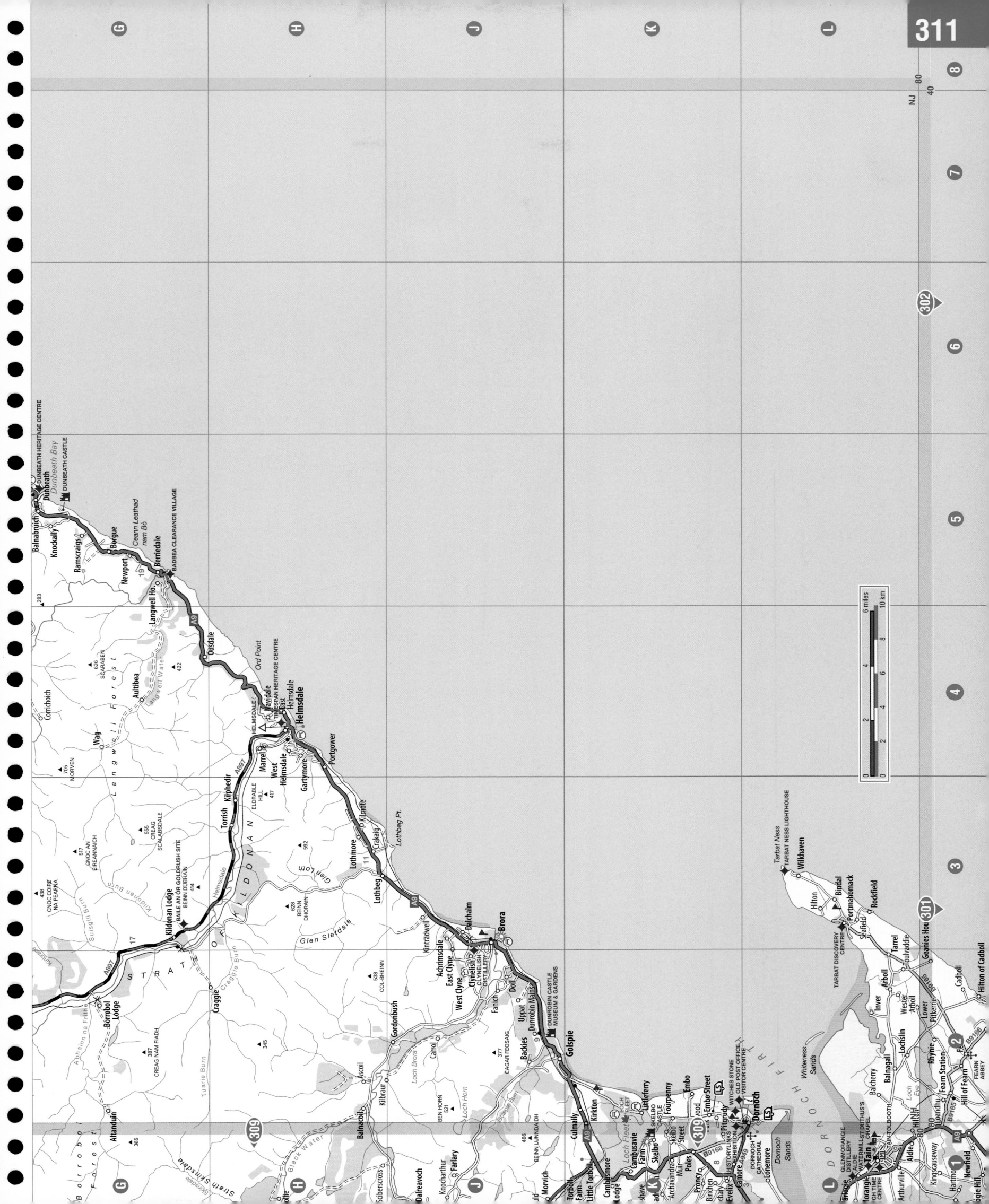

G   H   J   K   L

NJ 80 40

8
7
6
5
4
3
2
1

302
301
309

DUNBEATH HERITAGE CENTRE
Dunbeath
DUNBEATH CASTLE
Dunbeath Bay

Balnabruich
Knockally
Ramscraigs
Borgue
Newport
Ceann Leathad nam Bò
Berriedale
BADBEA CLEARANCE VILLAGE
283
Langwell Ho.
Ousdale
Ord Point
A9

626
SCARABEN
422
Corrichoich
Auttbea
Langwell Water
Langwell Forest
Wag
705
MORVEN
HELMSDALE
TIMESPAN HERITAGE CENTRE
Navidale
Helmsdale
Helmsdale
Portgower
A897
Marrel
West Helmsdale
Gartymore
ELDRABLE HILL 417
Kilphedir
517
CNOC AN ÉIREANNACH
Torrish
555 CREAG SCALAISDALE
592
Kinbrace Burn
Iothmore
11
Crakaig
Kinlofte
Lothbeg Pt.
Glen Loth
438 CNOC COIRE NA PEARNA
Kildonan Lodge
BAILE AN ÒR GOLDRUSH SITE
BENN DUBHÀIN 414
Helmsdale
Lothbeg
Lothmore
628 BEINN DHORAIN
A9
Dalchalm
Brora
17
Kintradwell
Glen Sletdale
Suisgill Burn
Kildonan Burn
STRATH OF KILDONAN
Achrimsdale
East Clyne
Clynelish
CLYNELISH DISTILLERY
West Clyne
538 COL-BHEINN
Fanich
Doll
Uppat
DUNROBIN CASTLE MUSEUM & GARDENS
9
Borrobol Lodge
Abhainn na Frithe
Craggie
Craggie Burn
345
Carrol
Gordonbush
377 CAGAR FEOSAIG
Backies
Golspie
Altanduin
365
Borrobol Forest
387 CREAG NAM FIADH
Dalreavoch
Knockarthur
Farlary
Ascoll
Kilbraur
Balnacoil
Black Water
Loch Brora
BEN HORN 521
Loch Horn
466 BENN LUNNDAIDH
Carrol
Culmaily
Kirkton
Sciberscross
Strath Skinsdale
Strath Brora
A839
Loch Fleet
Skelbo Farm
Skelbo Castle
Skelbo
Poles
Cambusmore Lodge
Torboll Farm
Little Torboll
Morvich
LITTLE TORBOLL
Proncy
Birichen
Evelix
B9168
DORNOCH CATHEDRAL
Clonemore
HISTORYLINKS
Pitgrudy
WITCHES STONE
OLD POST OFFICE
VISITOR CENTRE
Embo Street
Embo
Fourpenny
Littleferry
LOCH FLEET
Dornoch
Dornoch Sands

DORNOCH FIRTH
Whiteness Sands

Tarbat Ness
TARBAT NESS LIGHTHOUSE
Wilkhaven
Hilton
Balintore
Portmahomack
Rockfield
Seafield
TARBAT DISCOVERY CENTRE
Tarrel
Arboll
Wester Arboll
Inver
Lower Pitkerrie
Balchery
Geanies Hou
Hilton of Cadboll
Cadboll
Loch Eye
B9165
Rhynie
FEARN ABBEY
Fearn Station
Hill of Fearn
Lochslin
Balnagall
Fulvaddie

TAIN
TAIN TOLBOOTH
Aldie
GLENMORANGIE DISTILLERY
WESTER FEARN
HIGH TIME CENTRE
Kingscauseway
Newfield
Morangie
Arthurville
Knockbreck
B9175

6 miles
10 km
8
6
4
2
0
0   2   4   6

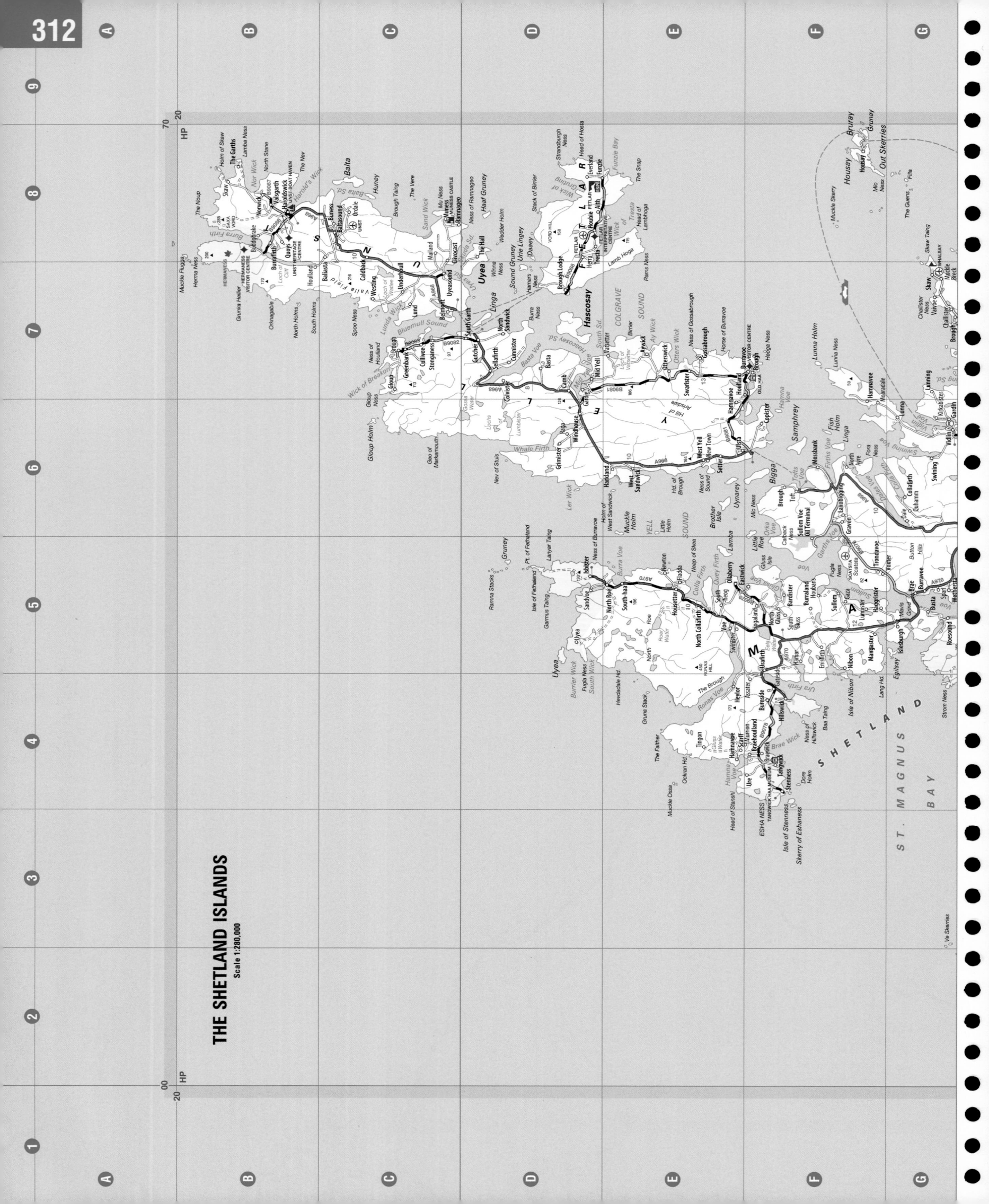

THE SHETLAND ISLANDS

Scale 1:280,000

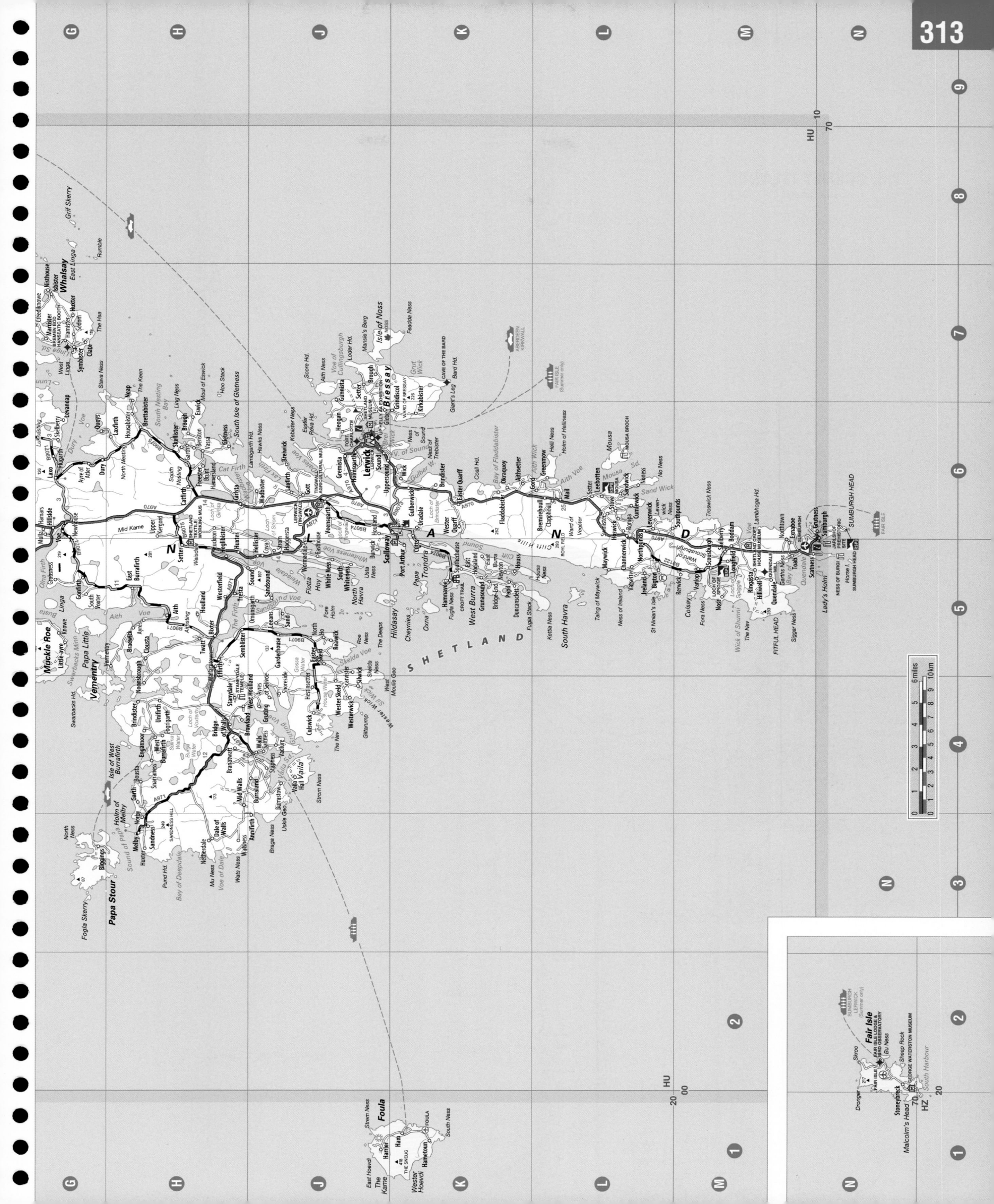

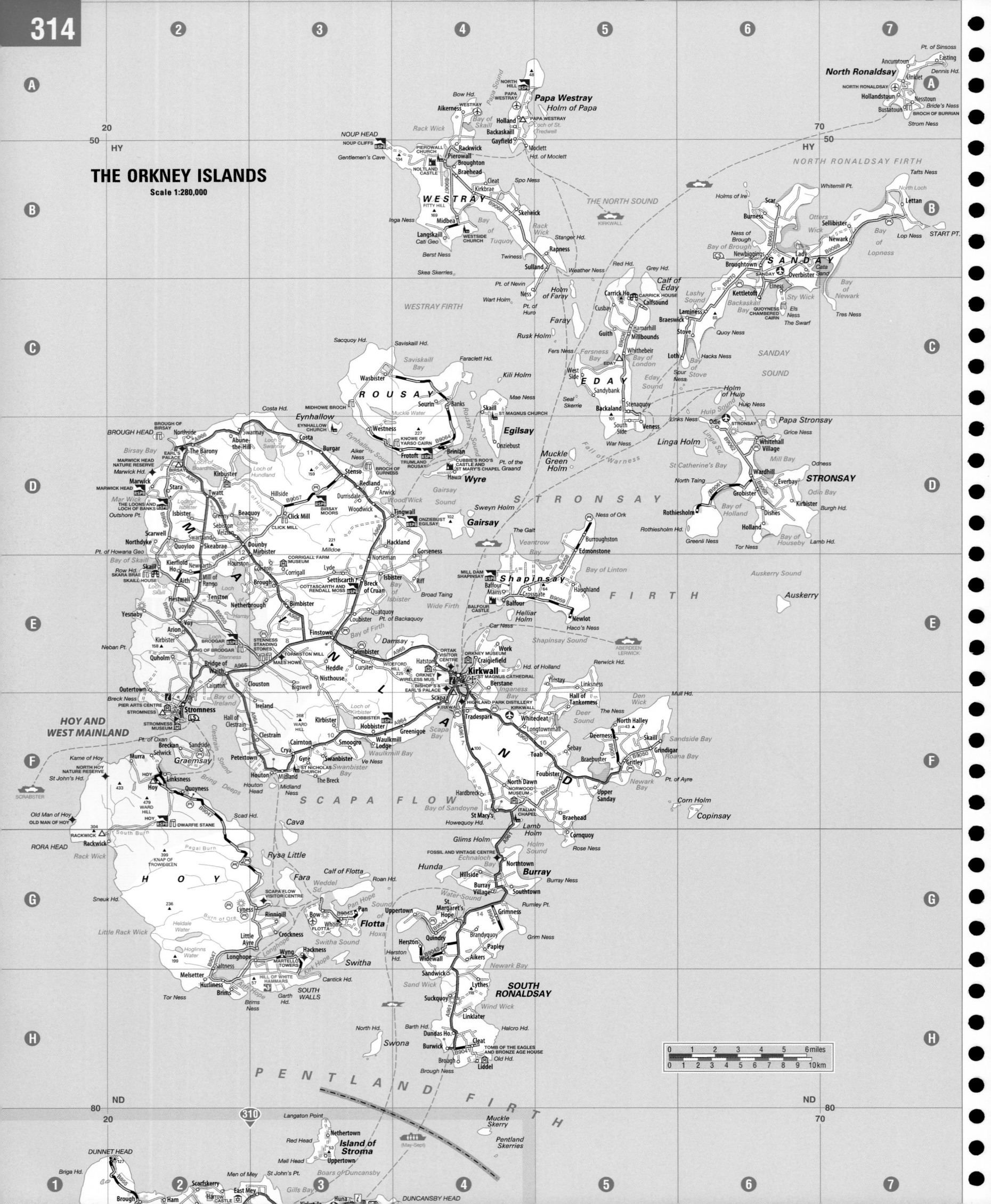

THE ORKNEY ISLANDS

Scale 1:280,000

North Ronaldsay

Papa Westray

WESTRAY

SANDAY

ROUSAY

EDAY

Egilsay

Wyre

STRONSAY

Gairsay

Shapinsay

Papa Stronsay

Linga Holm

KIRKWALL

M A I N L A N D

Stromness

HOY AND
WEST MAINLAND

HOY

SCAPA FLOW

SOUTH RONALDSAY

Burray

Flotta

SOUTH WALLS

PENTLAND FIRTH

Island of Stroma

DUNNET HEAD

DUNCANSBY HEAD

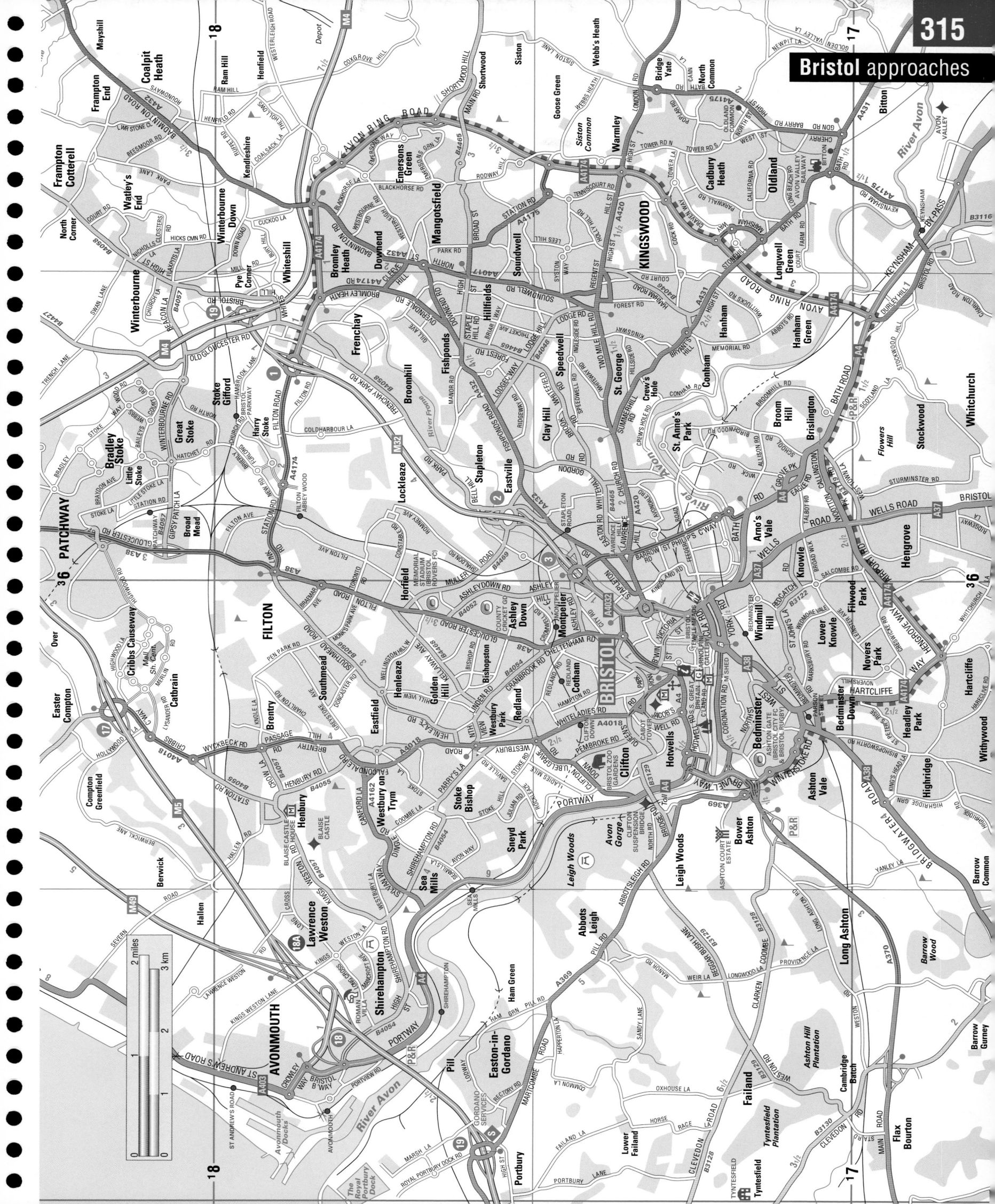

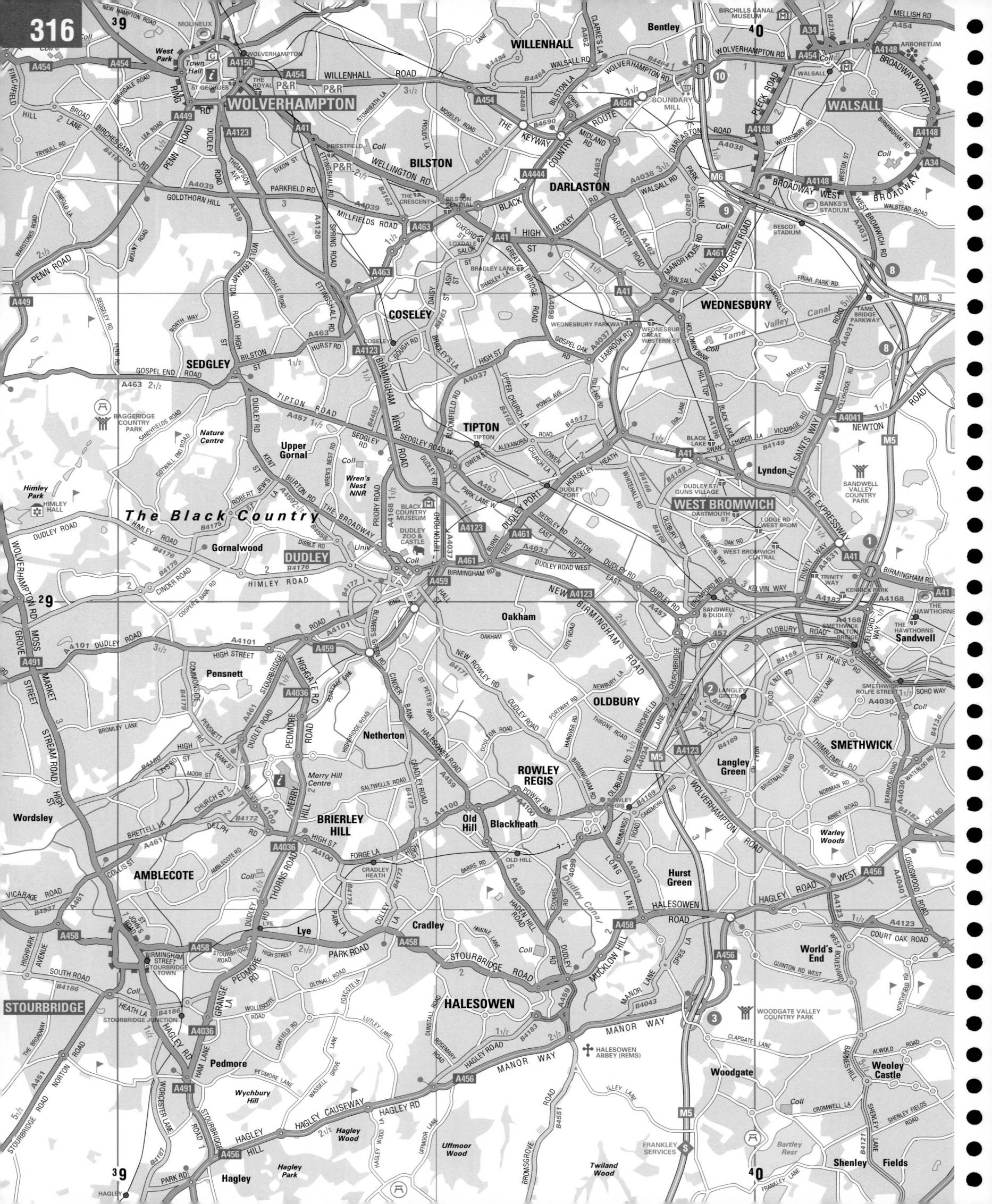

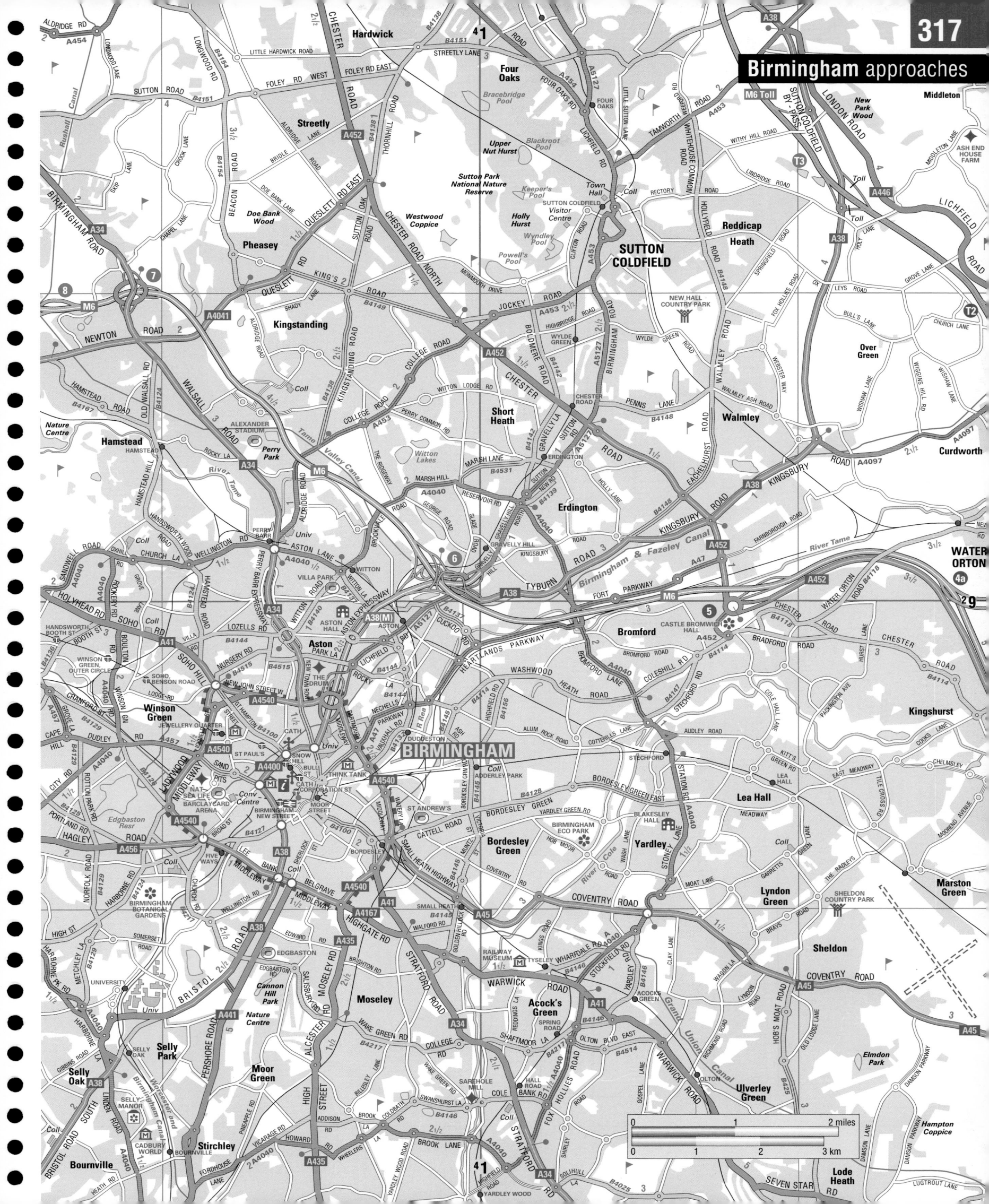

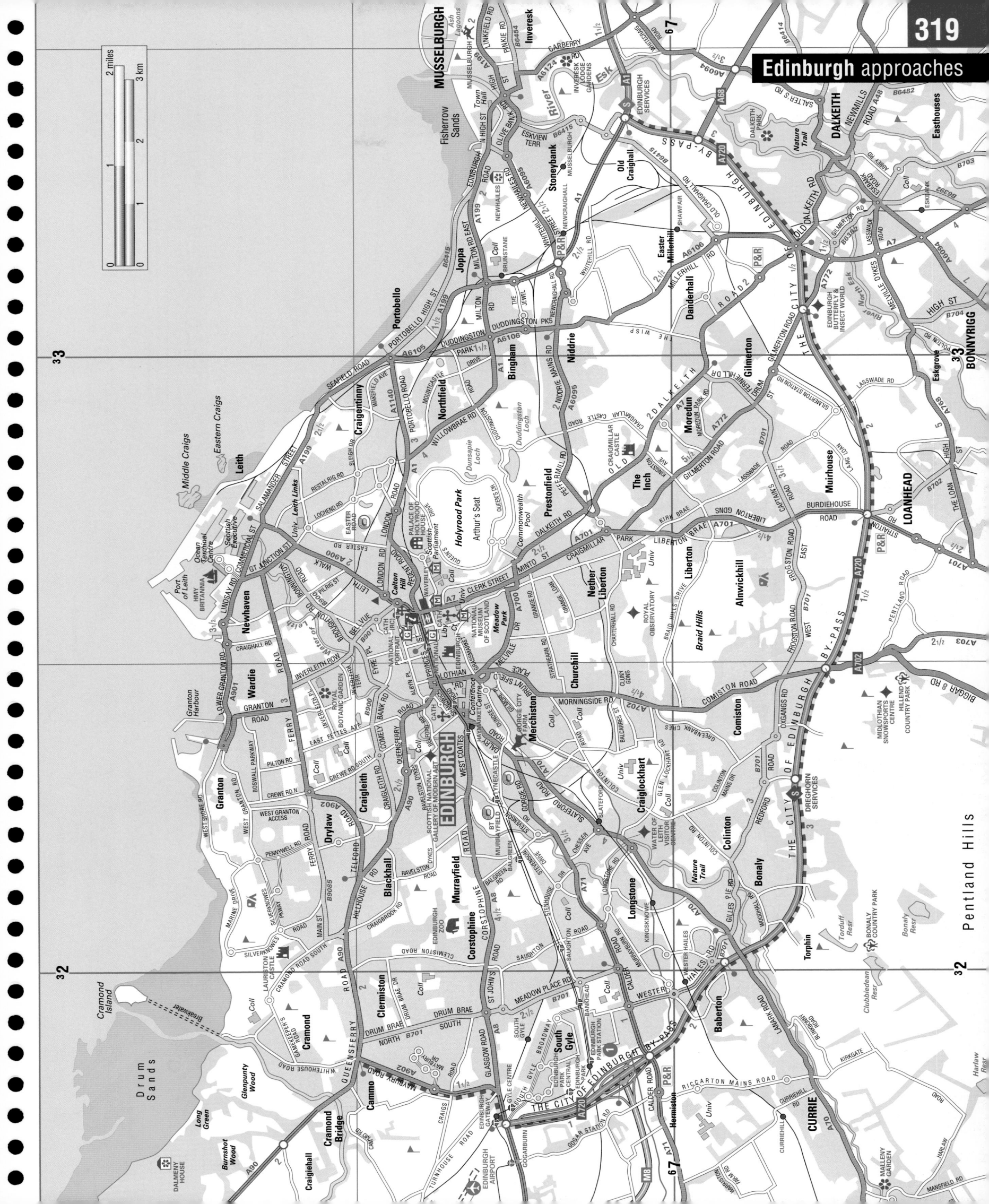

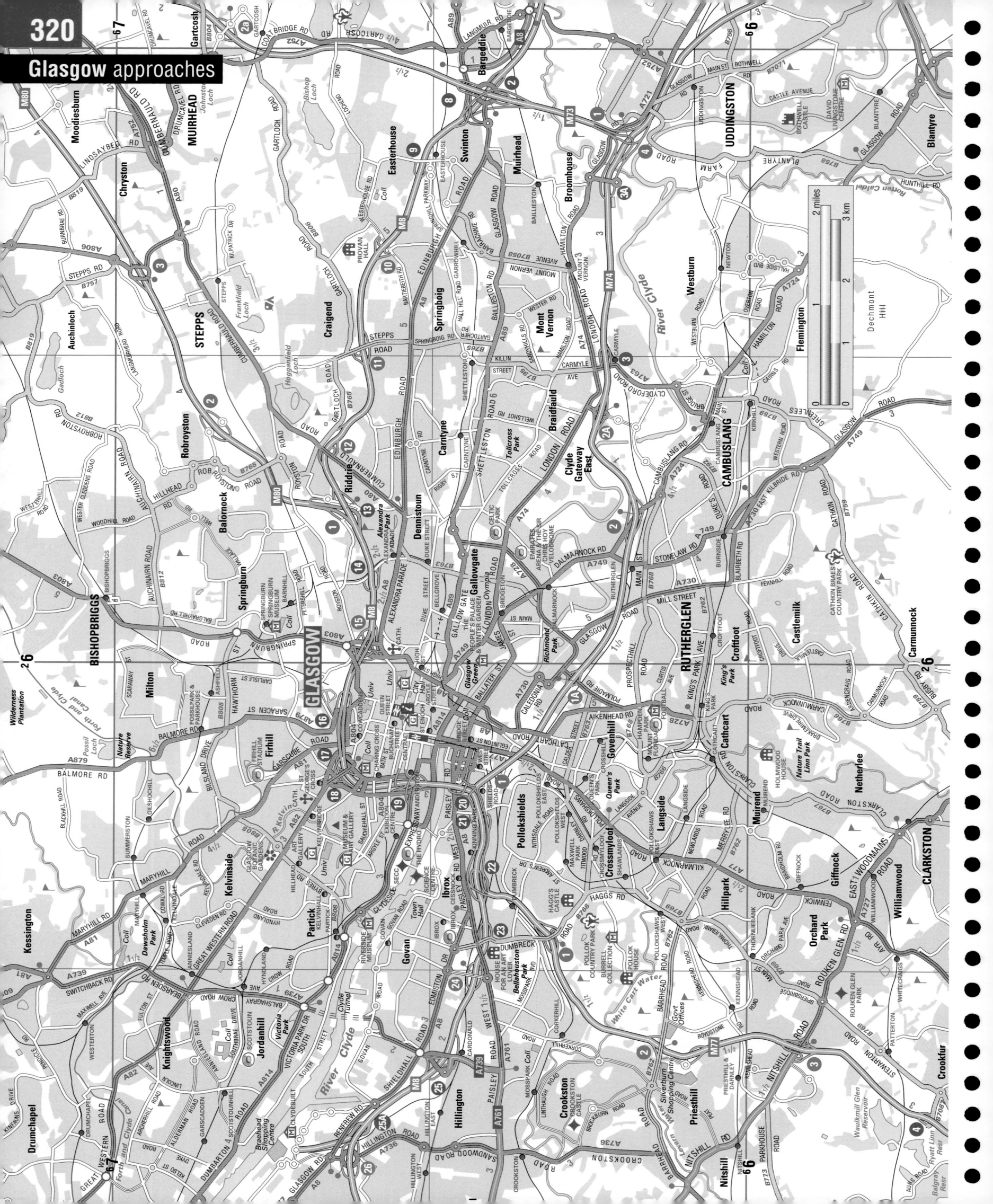

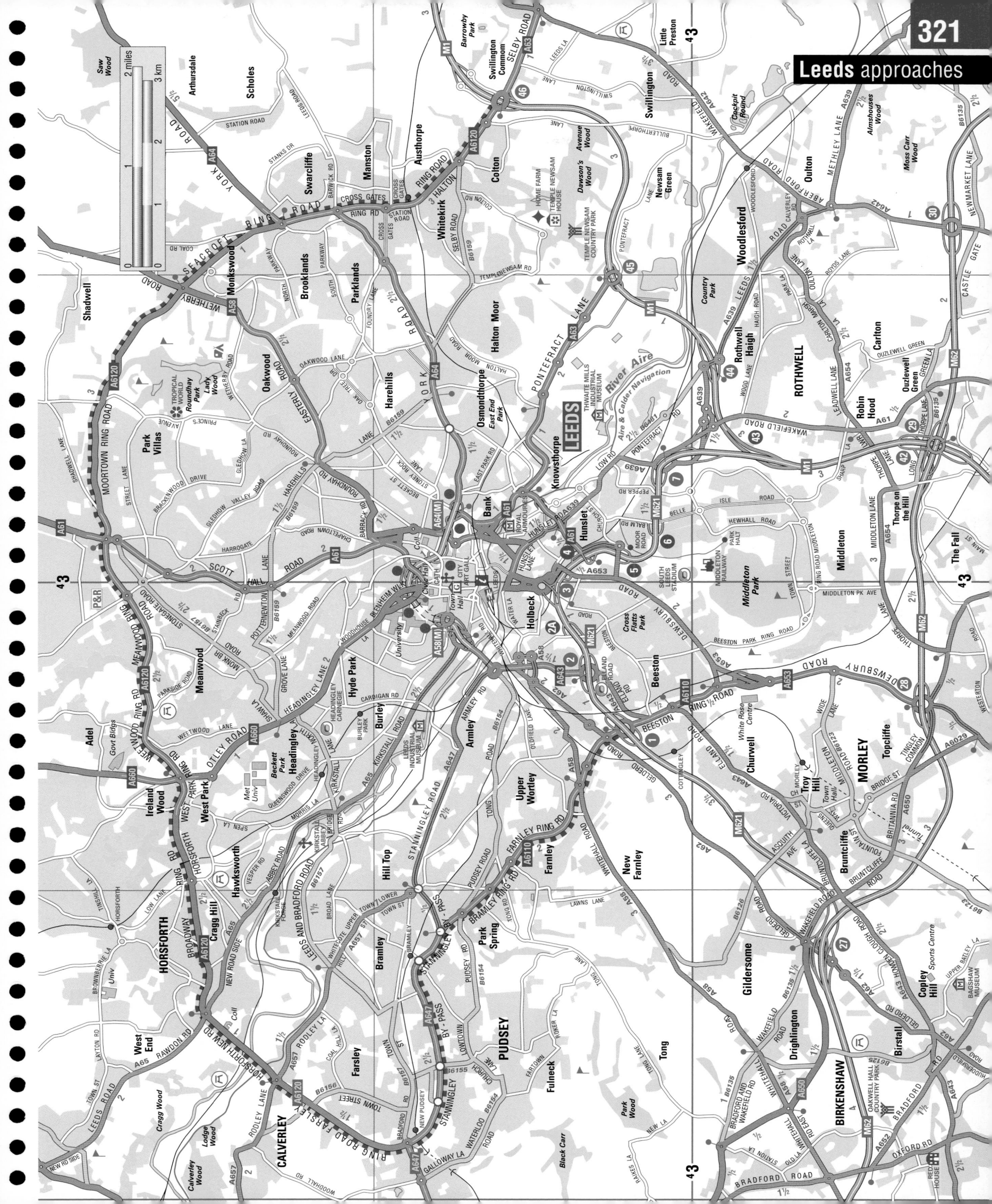

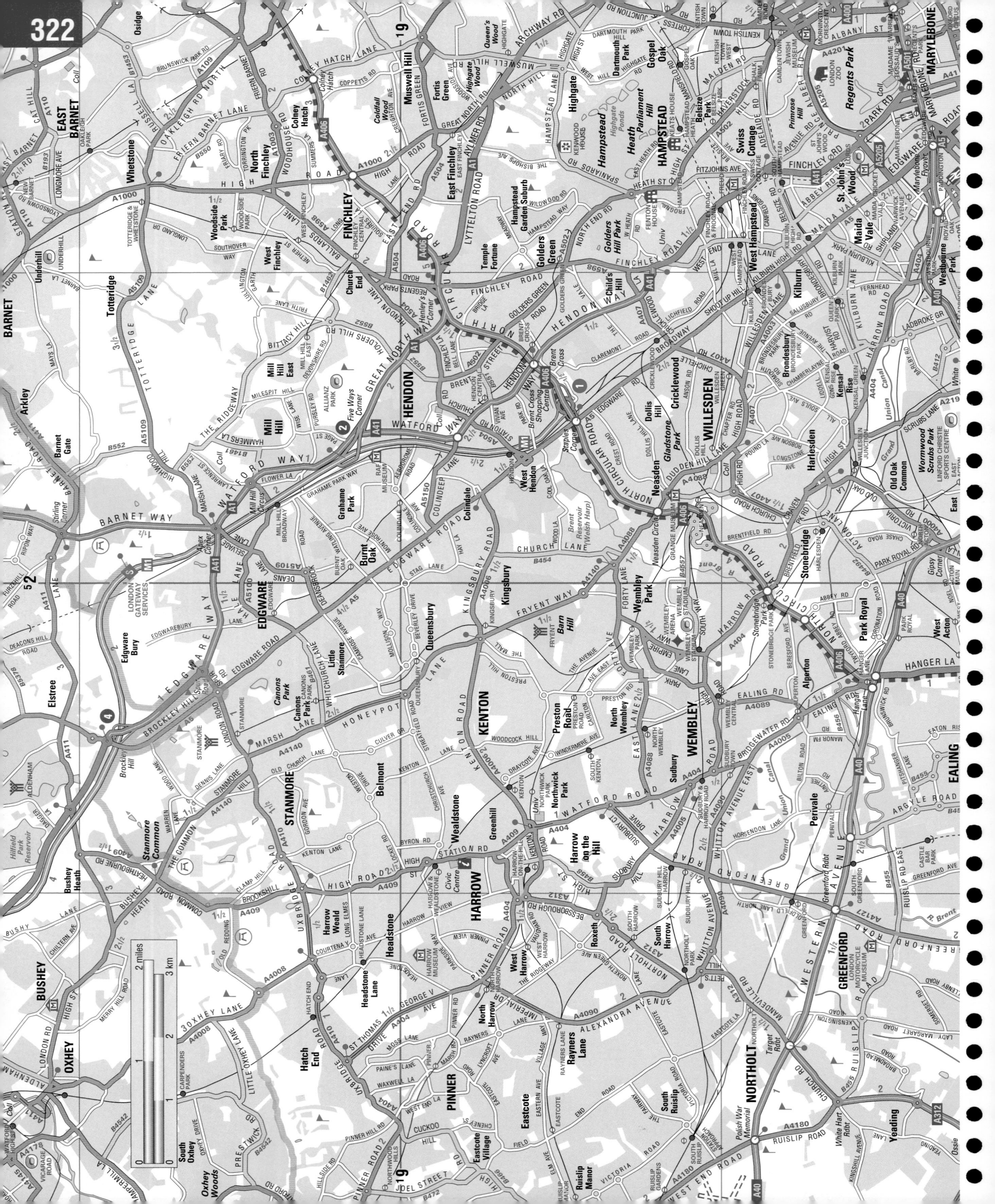

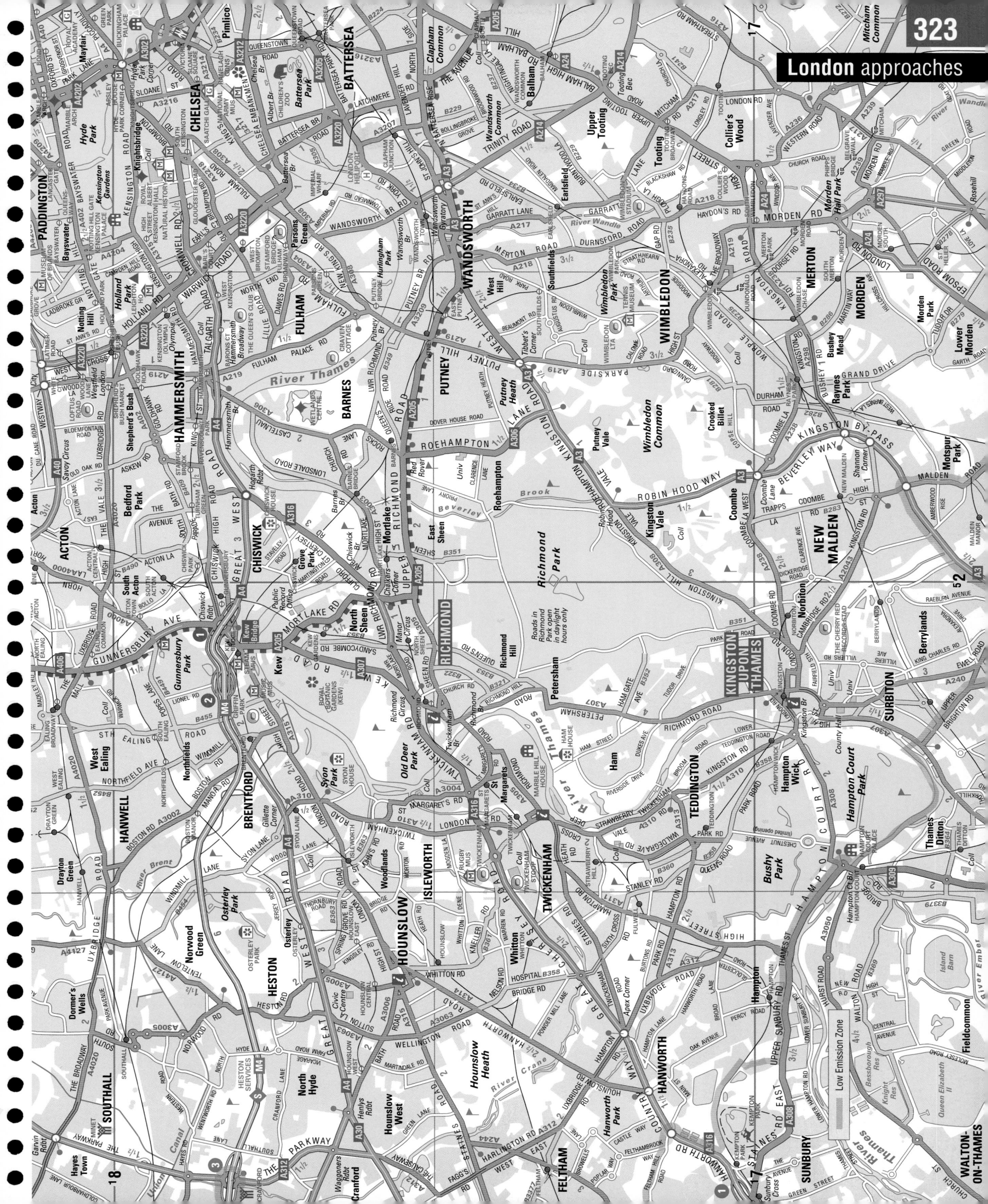

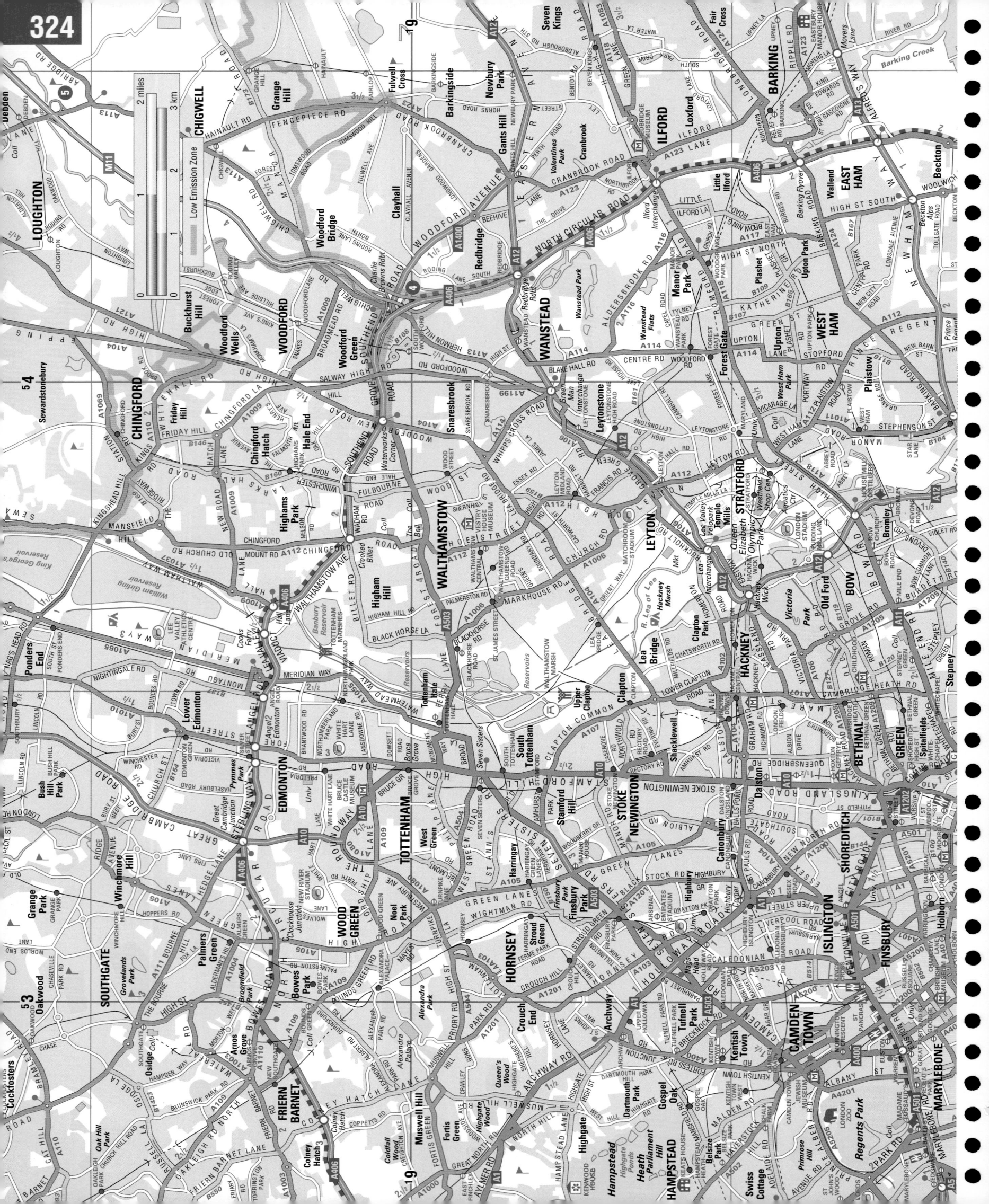

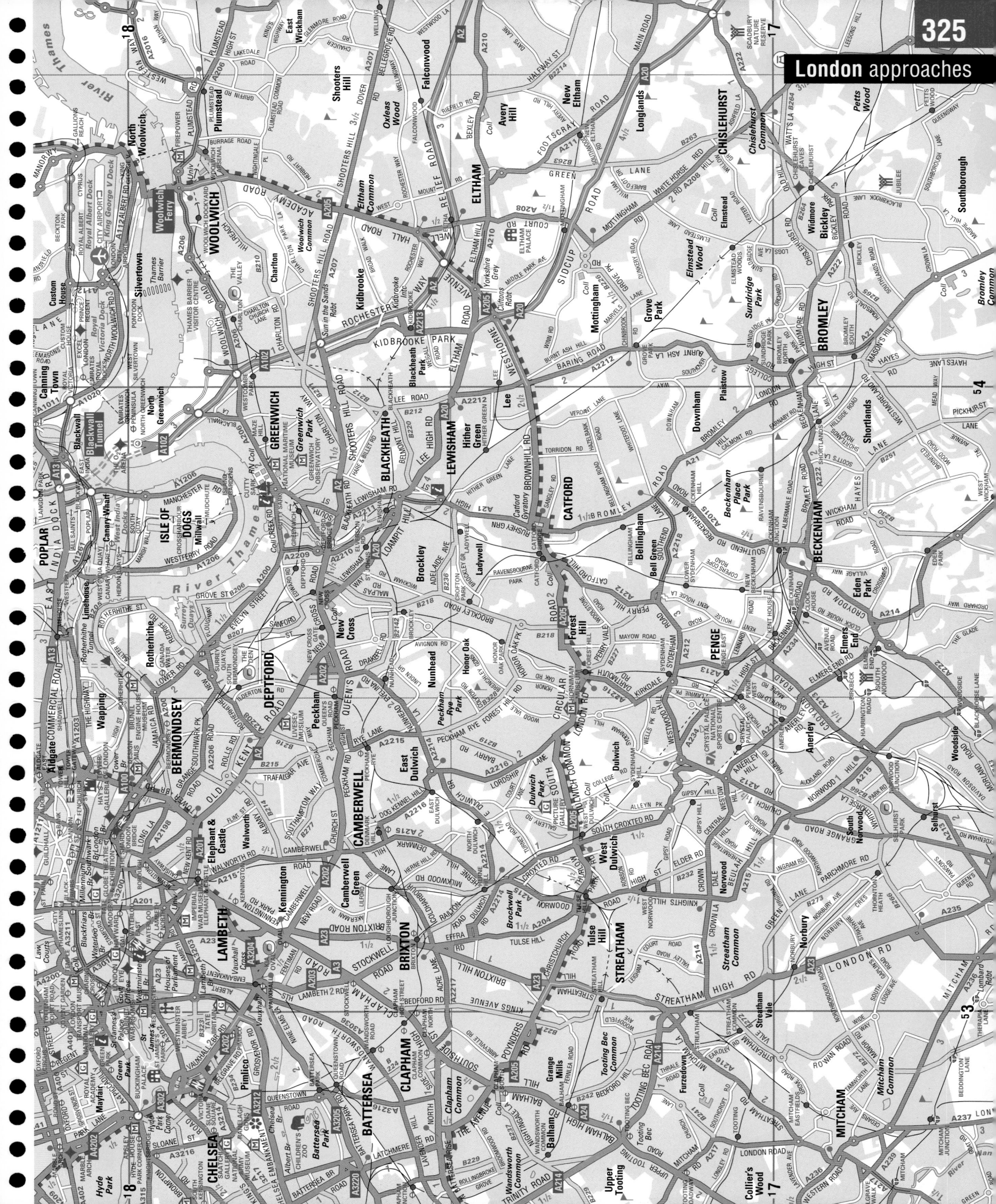

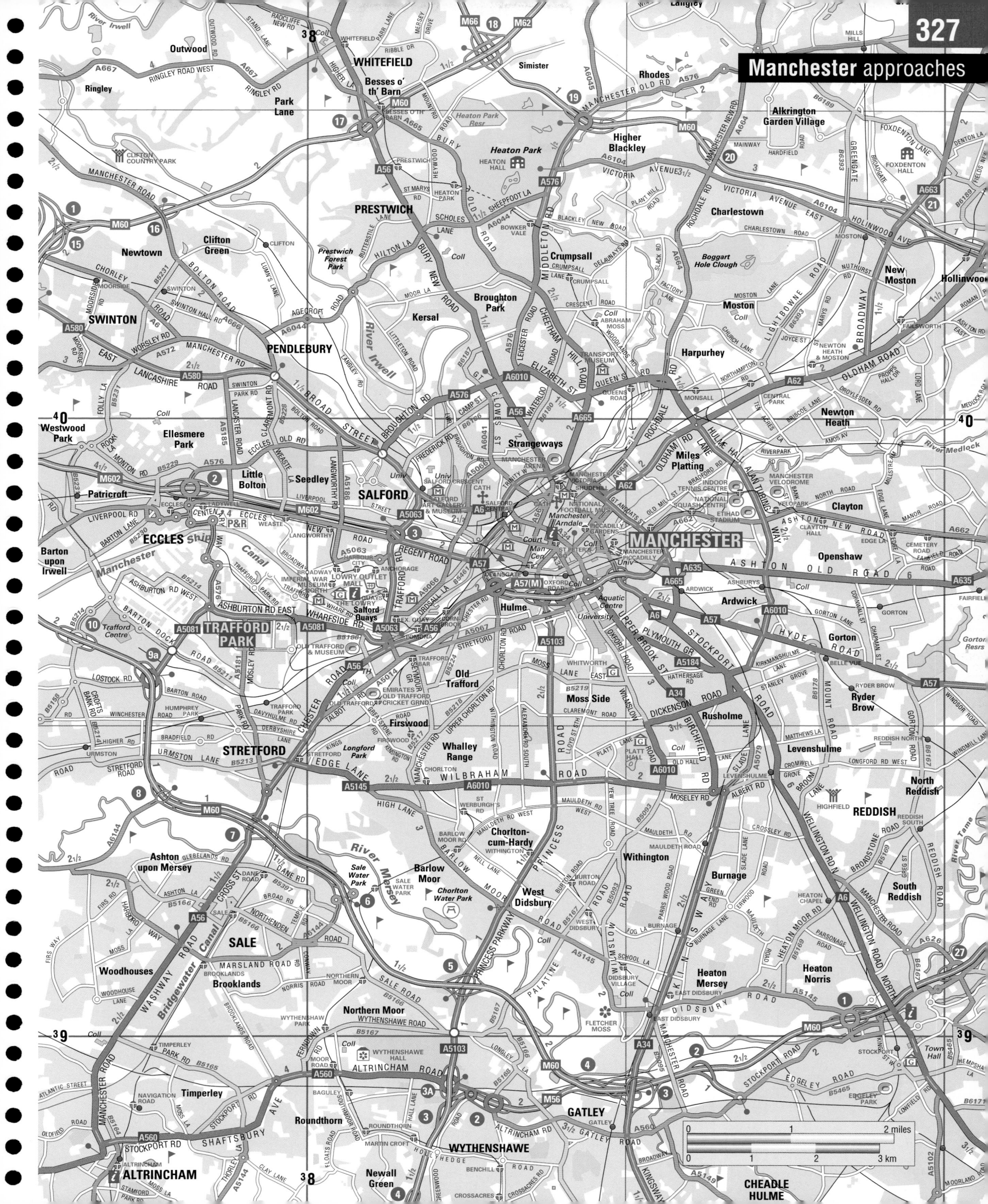

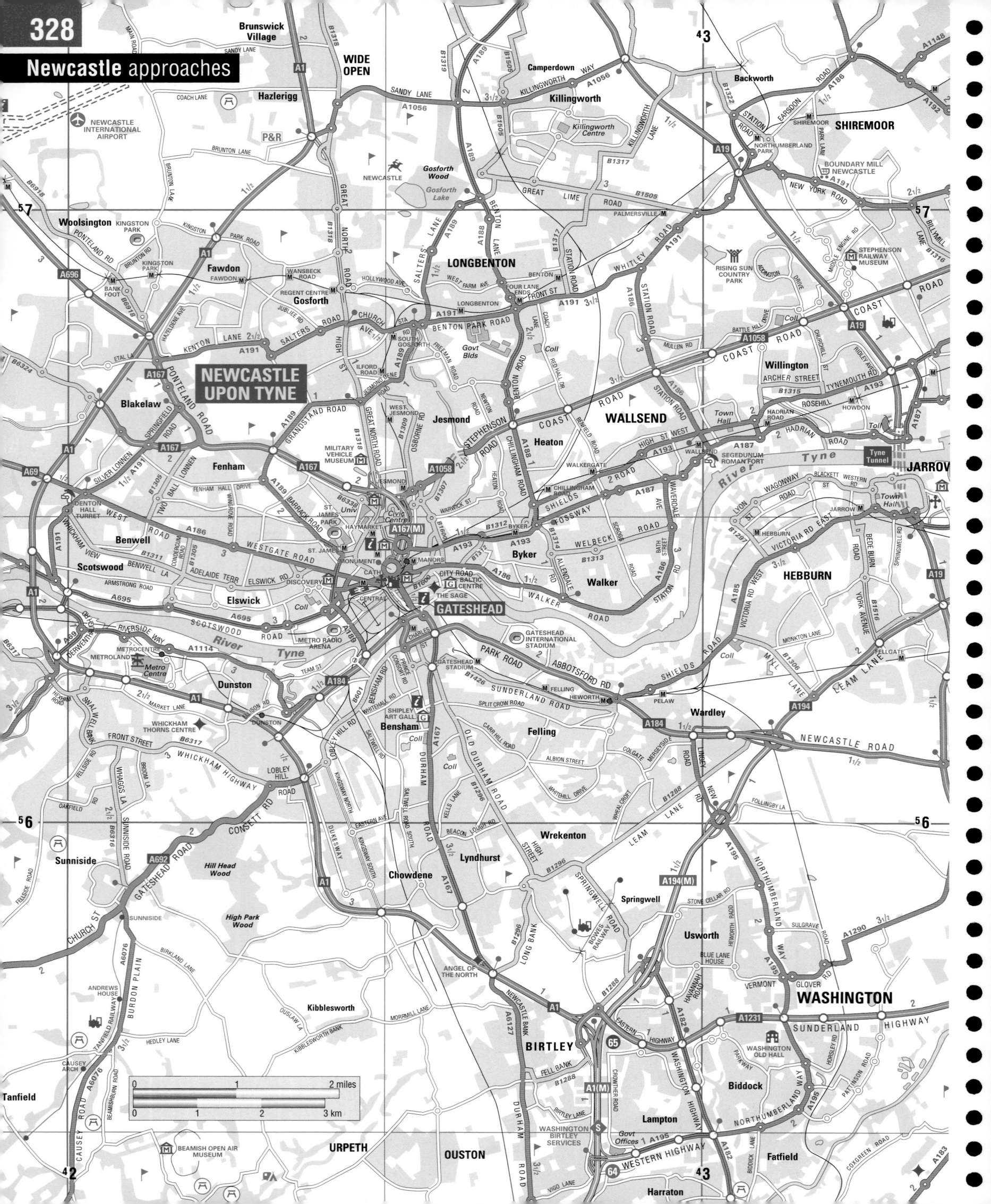

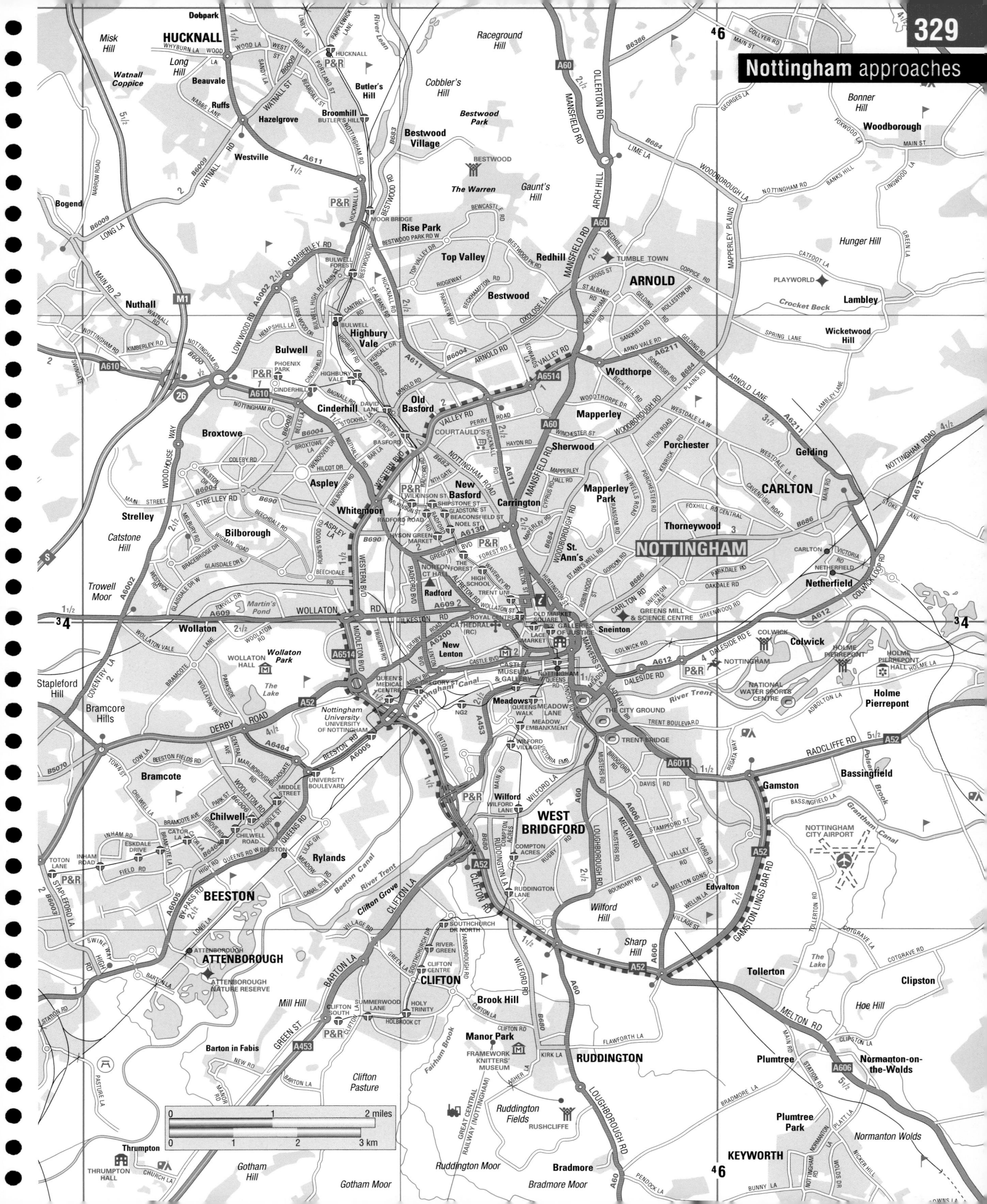

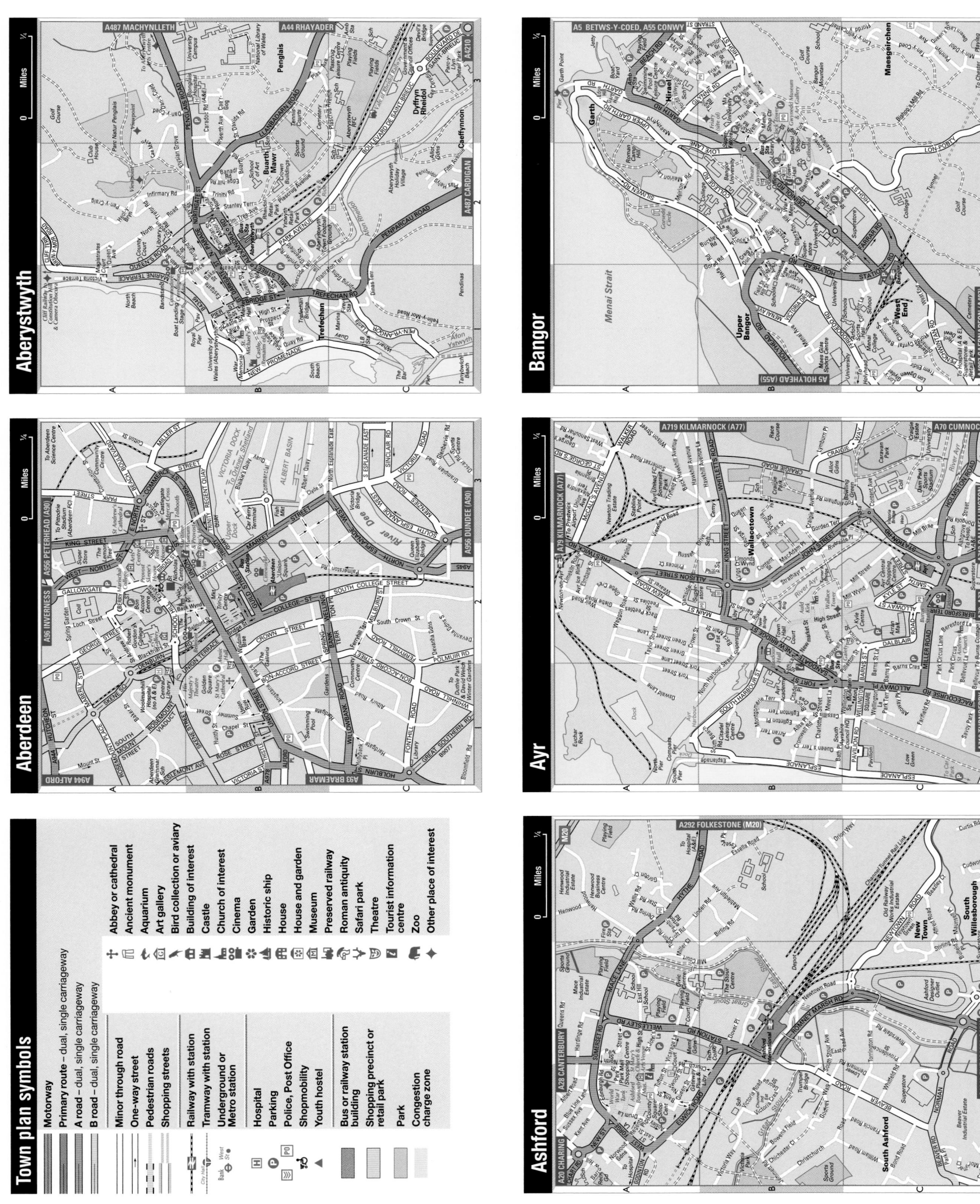

Aberystwyth

Bangor

Aberdeen

Ayr

Town plan symbols

Motorway
Primary route – dual, single carriageway
A road – dual, single carriageway
B road – dual, single carriageway
Minor through road
One-way street
Pedestrian roads
Shopping streets
Railway with station
Tramway with station
Underground or Metro station
Hospital
Parking
Police, Post Office
Shopmobility
Youth hostel
Bus or railway station building
Shopping precinct or retail park
Park
Congestion charge zone

Abbey or cathedral
Ancient monument
Aquarium
Art gallery
Bird collection or aviary
Building of interest
Castle
Church of interest
Cinema
Garden
Historic ship
House
House and garden
Museum
Preserved railway
Roman antiquity
Safari park
Theatre
Tourist information centre
Zoo
Other place of interest

Ashford

Berwick-upon-Tweed

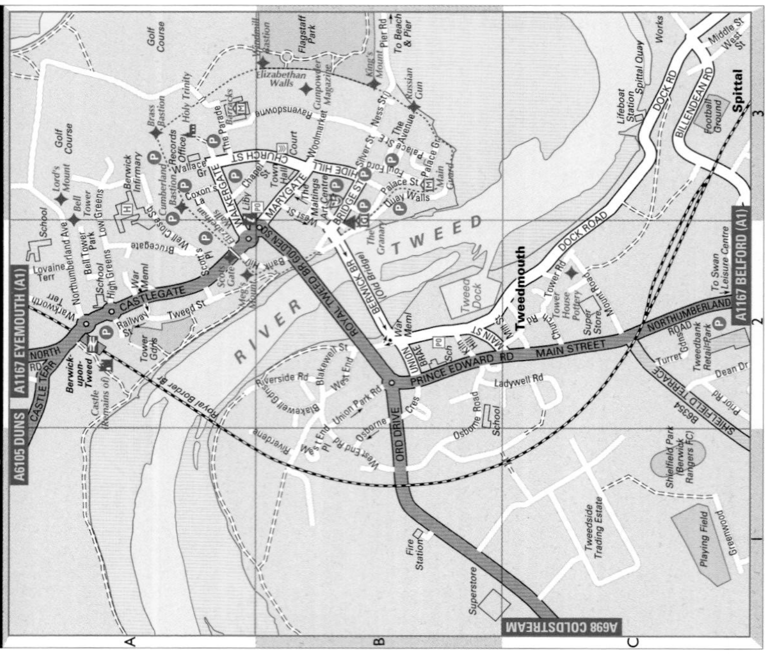

Bath

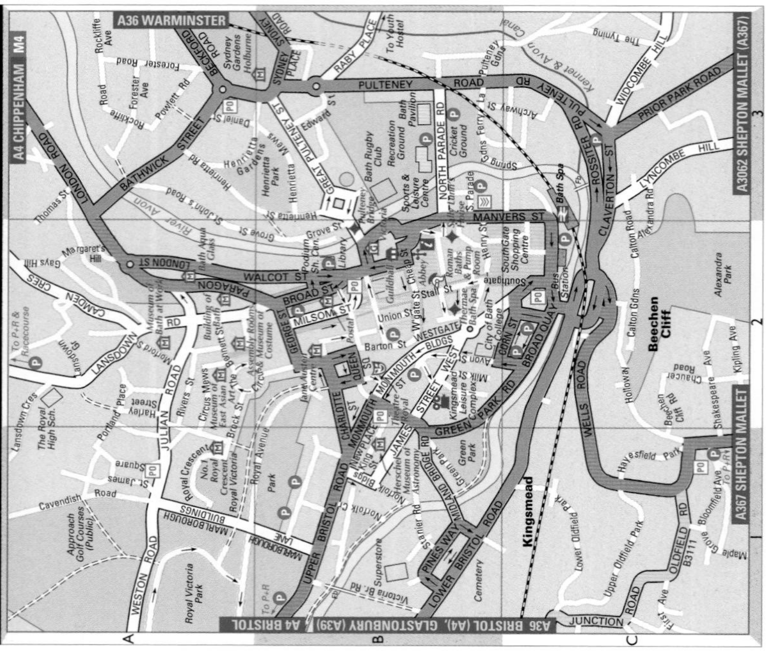

Barrow-in-Furness

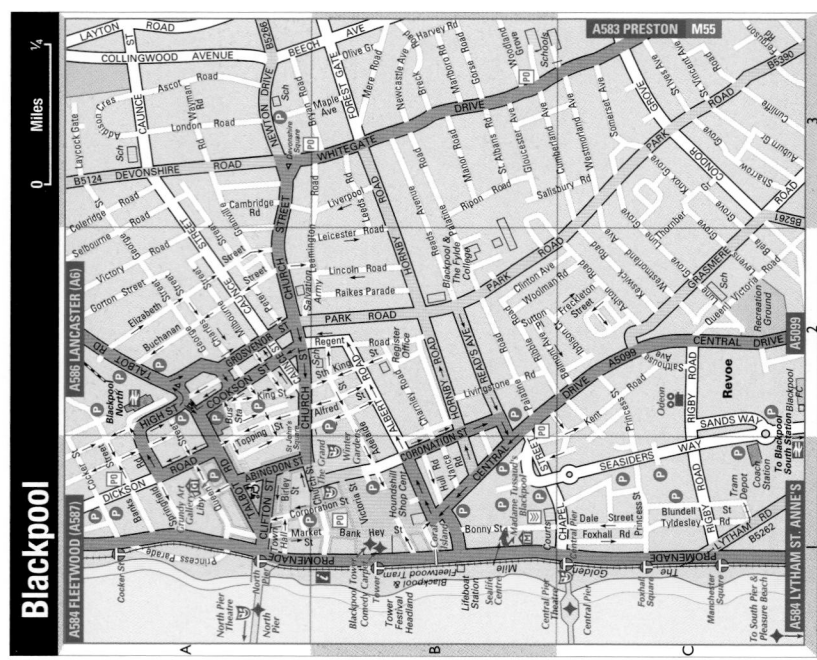

Blackpool

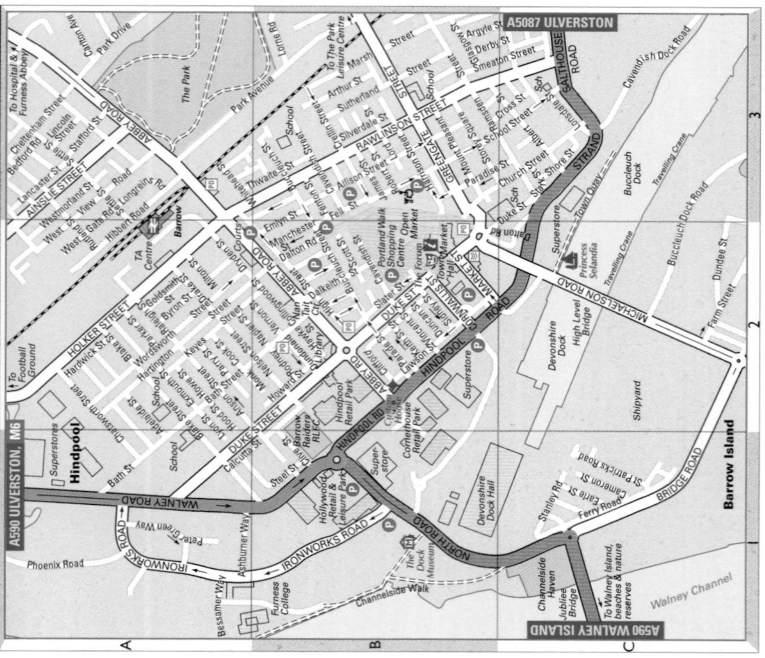

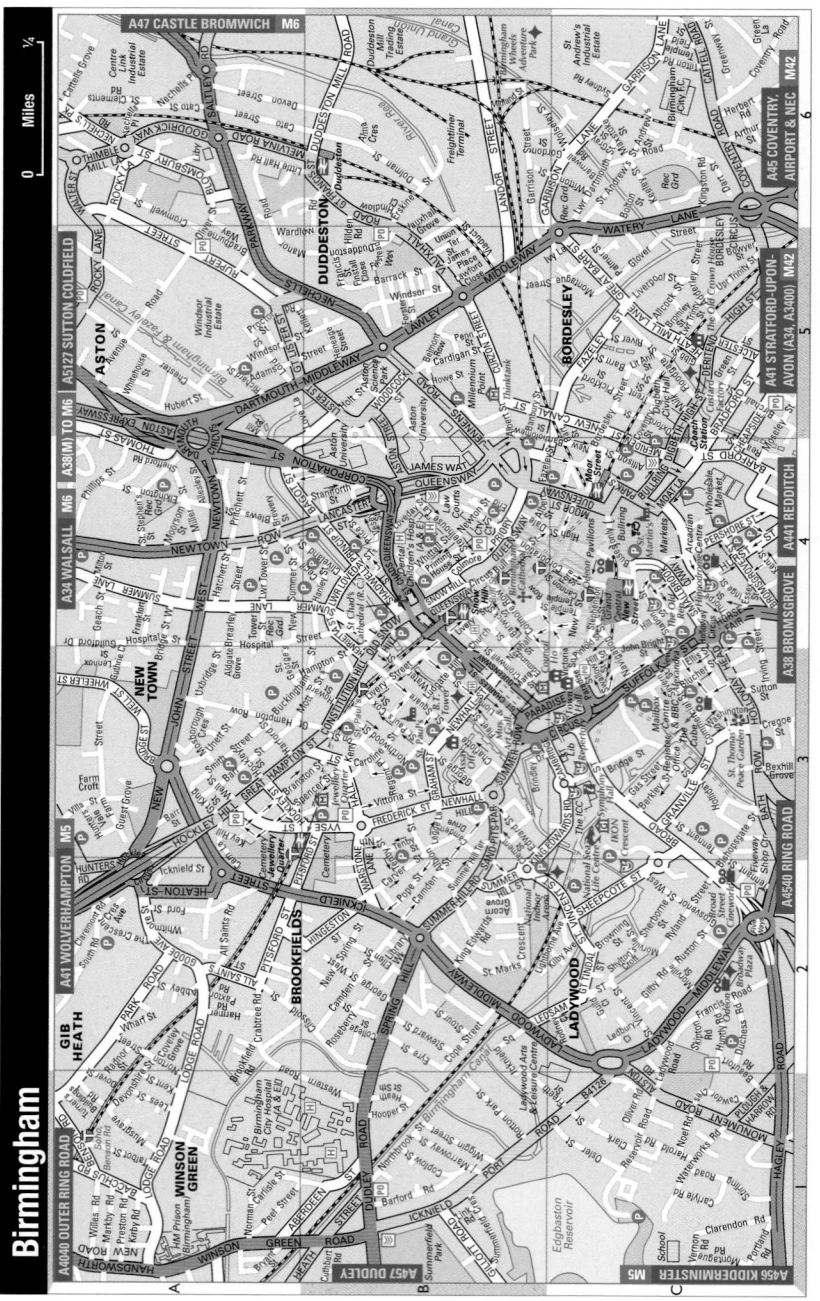

Birmingham

Brighton

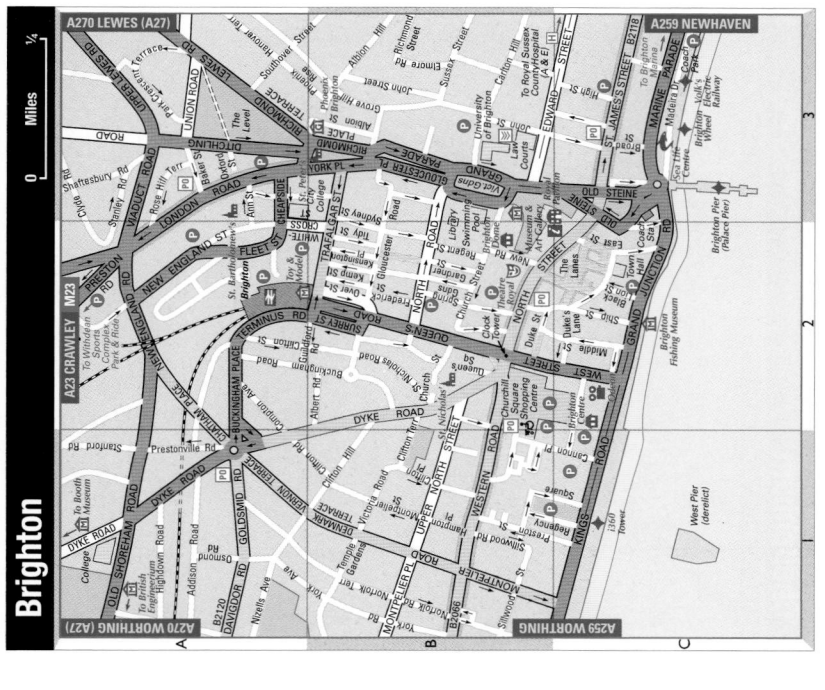

Bury St Edmunds

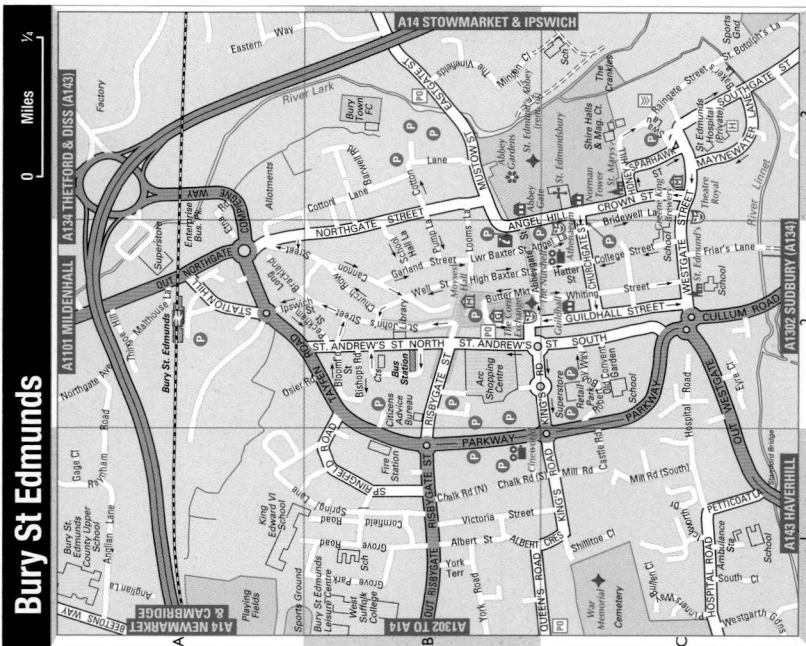

Bradford

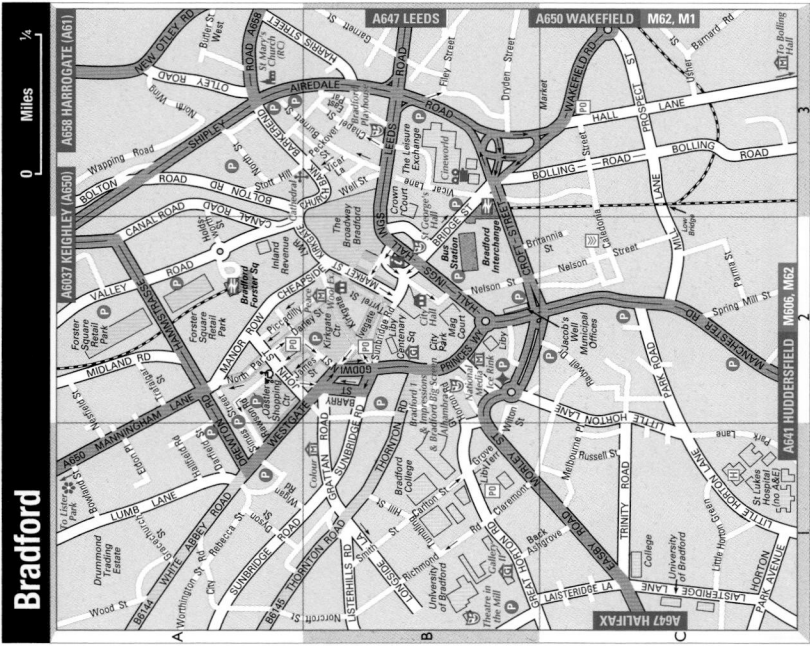

Bournemouth

Bristol

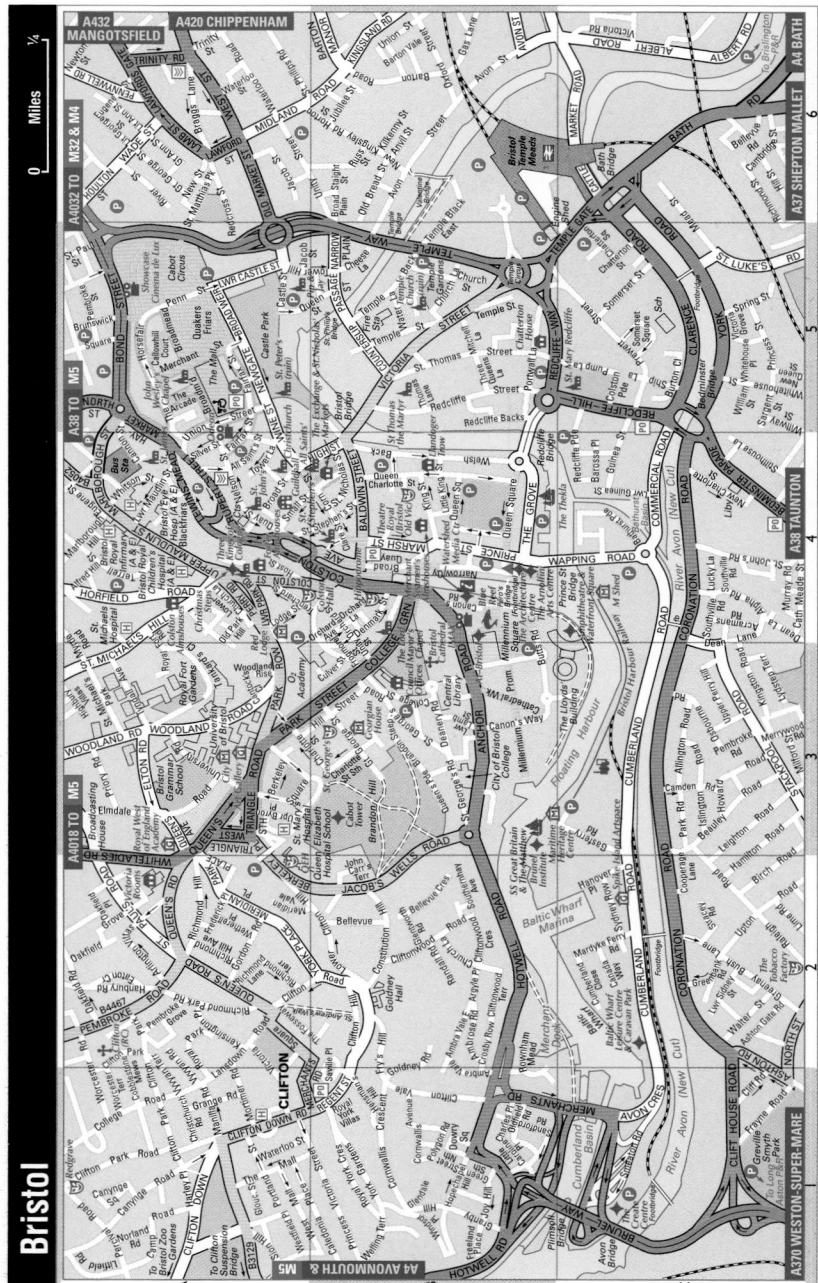

Cardiff / Caerdydd

Cheltenham

Canterbury

Chelmsford

Cambridge

Carlisle

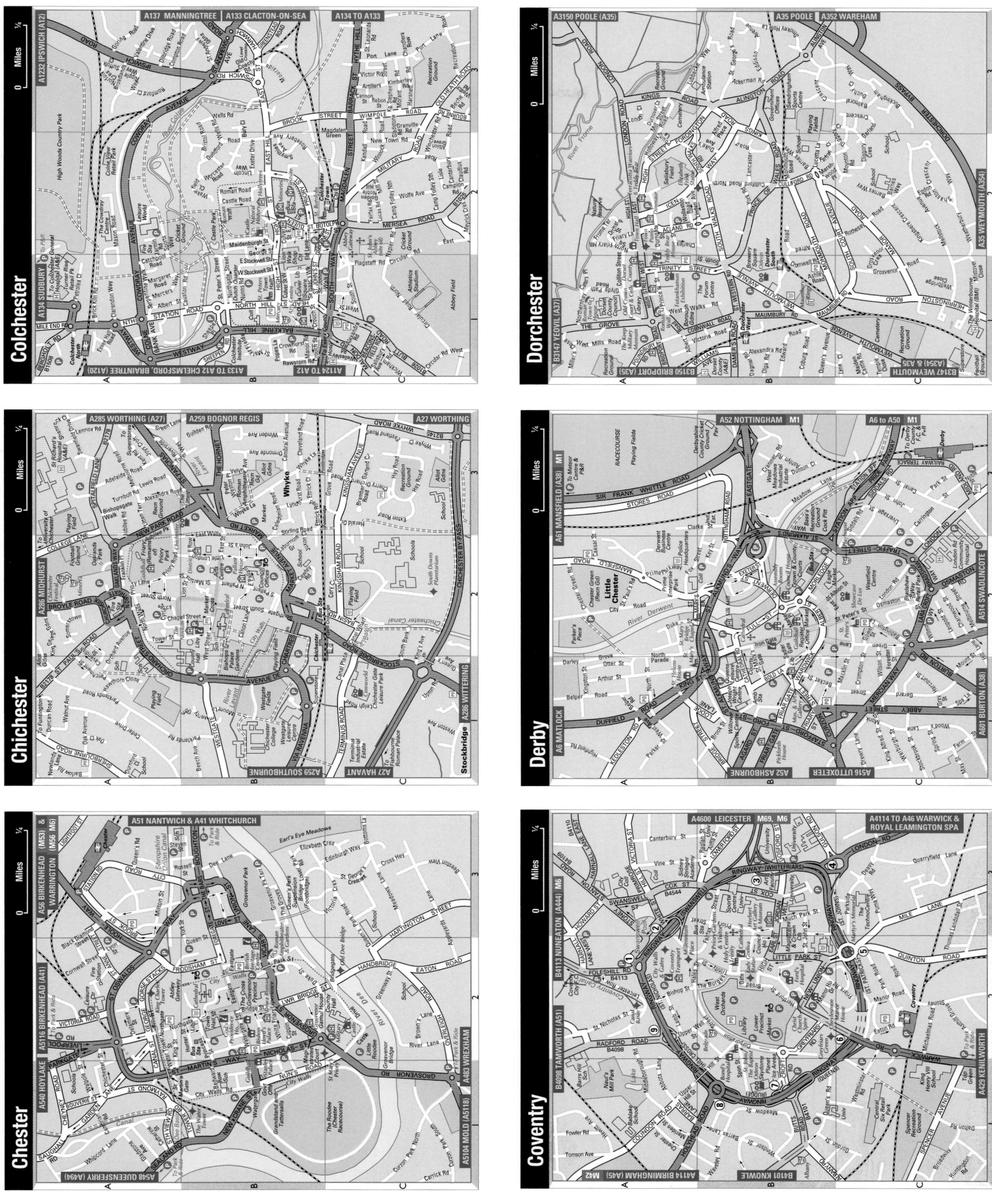

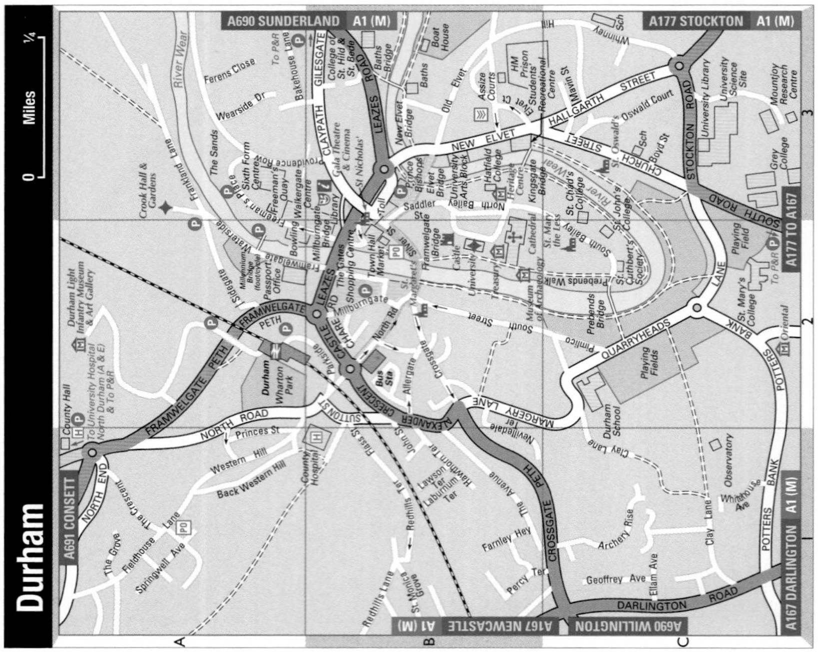

Durham

Exeter

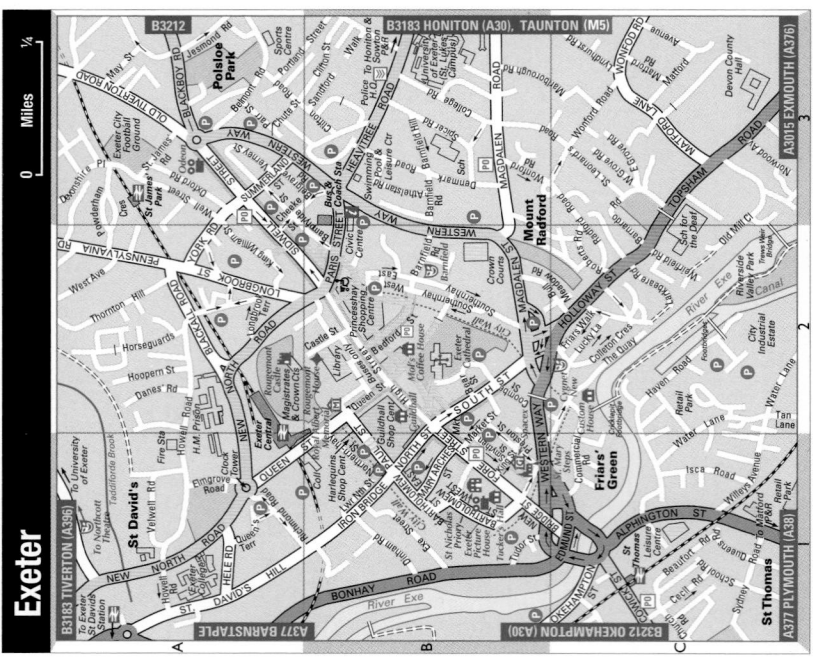

Dundee

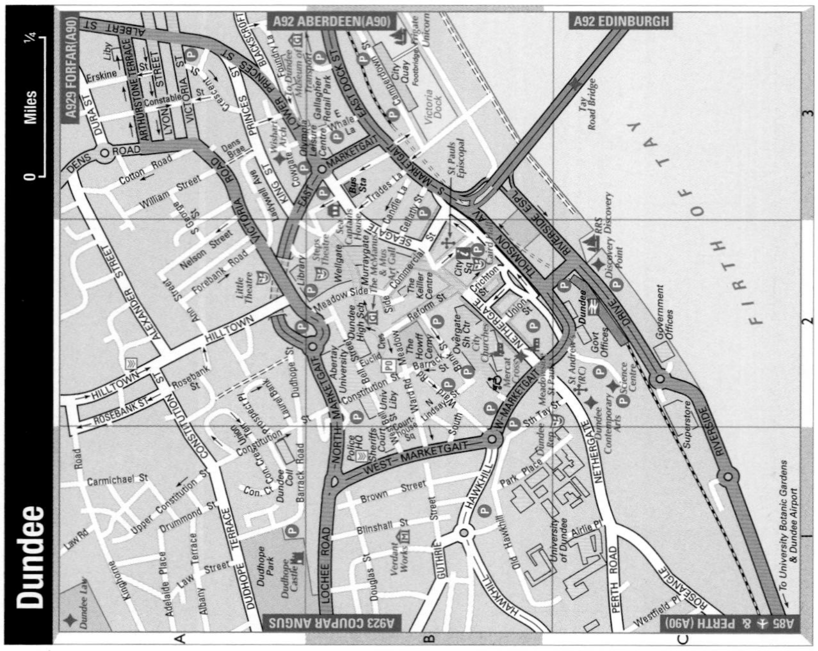

Dumfries

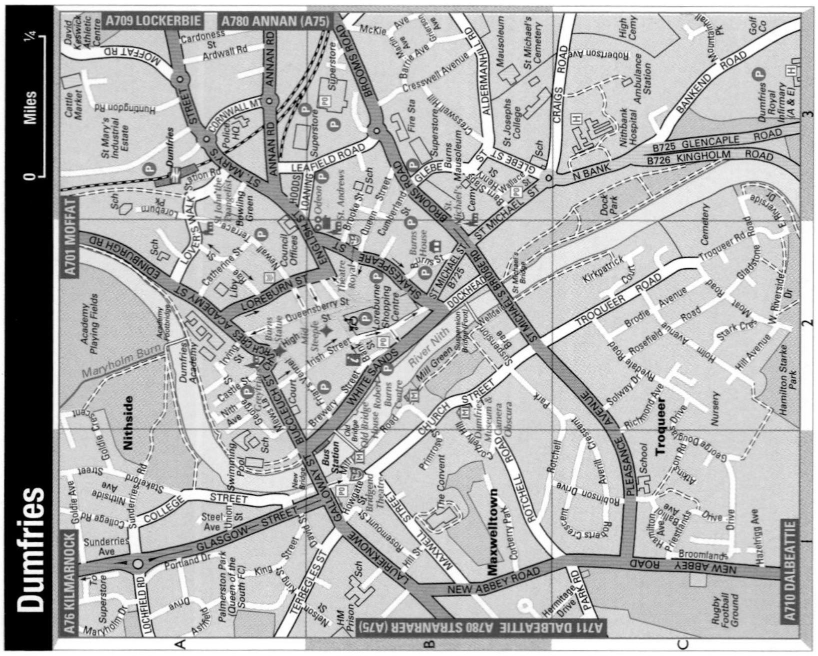

Edinburgh

Fort William page 290 • **Glasgow** page 267 • **Gloucester** page 80 • **Grimsby** page 201 • **Hanley (Stoke-on-Trent)** page 168

337

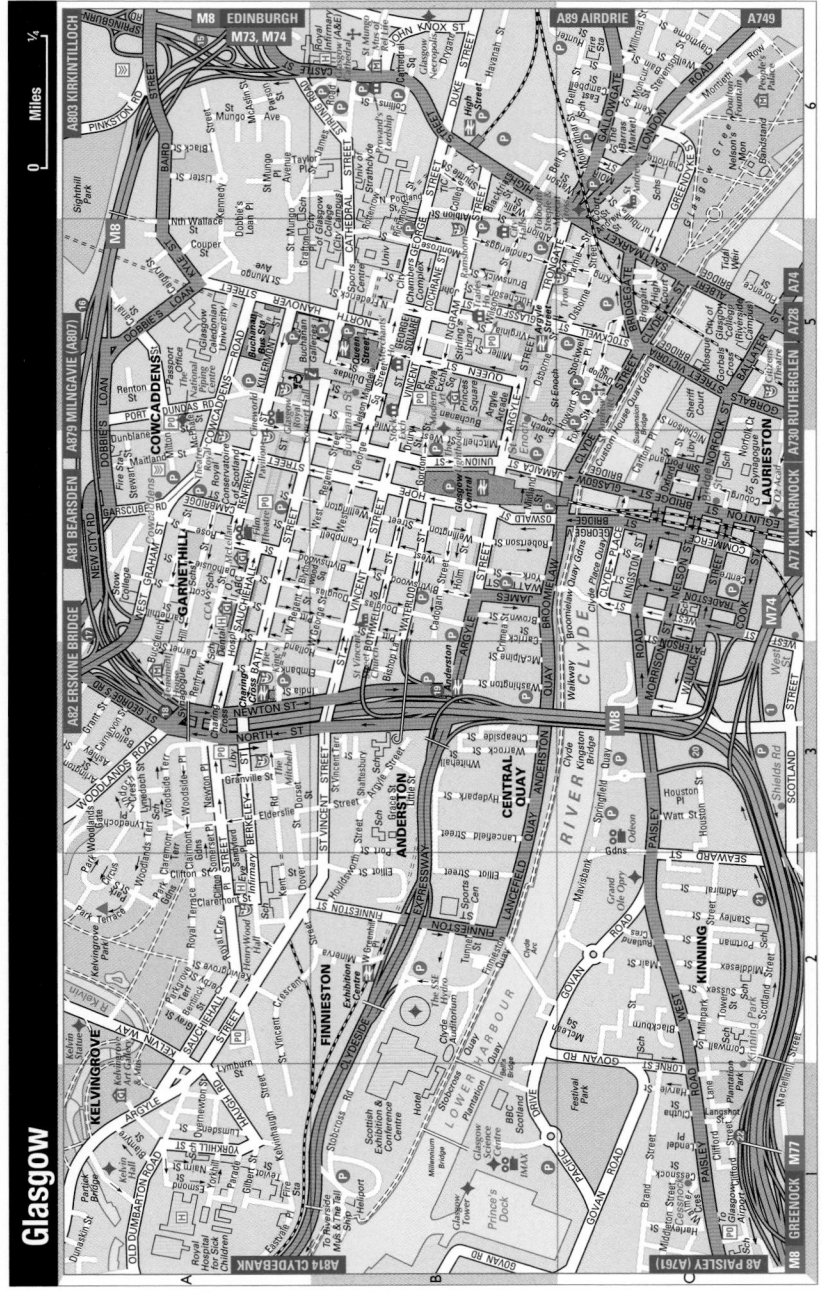

Glasgow

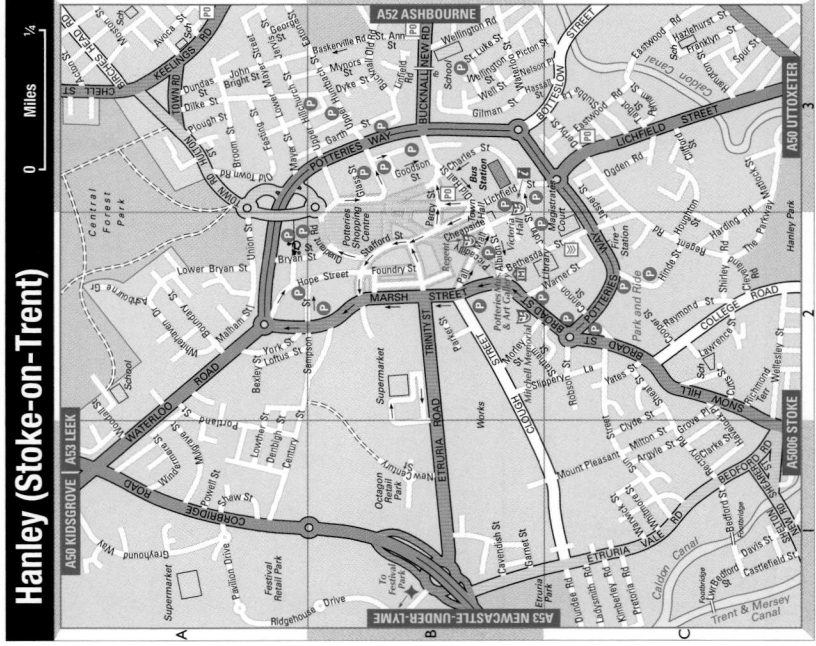

Hanley (Stoke-on-Trent)

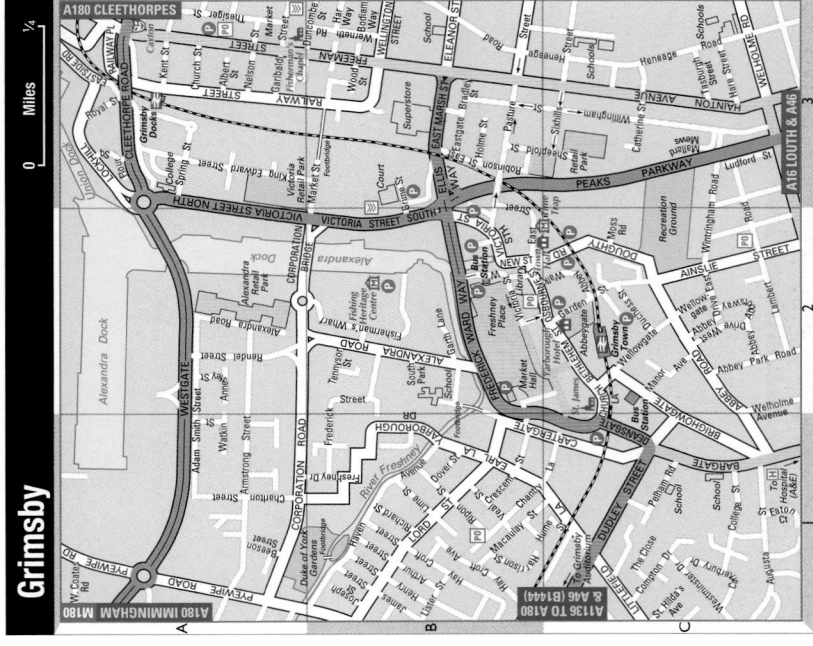

Grimsby

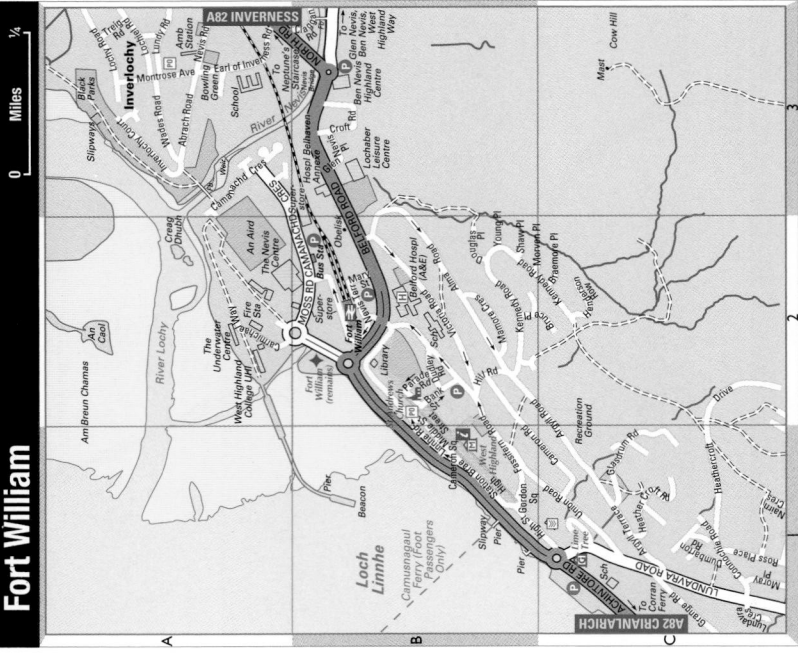

Fort William

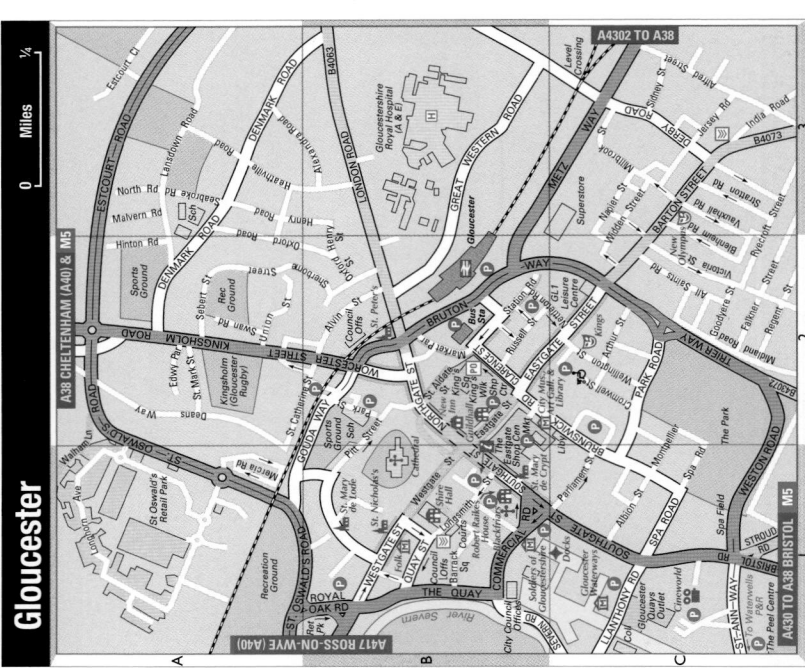

Gloucester

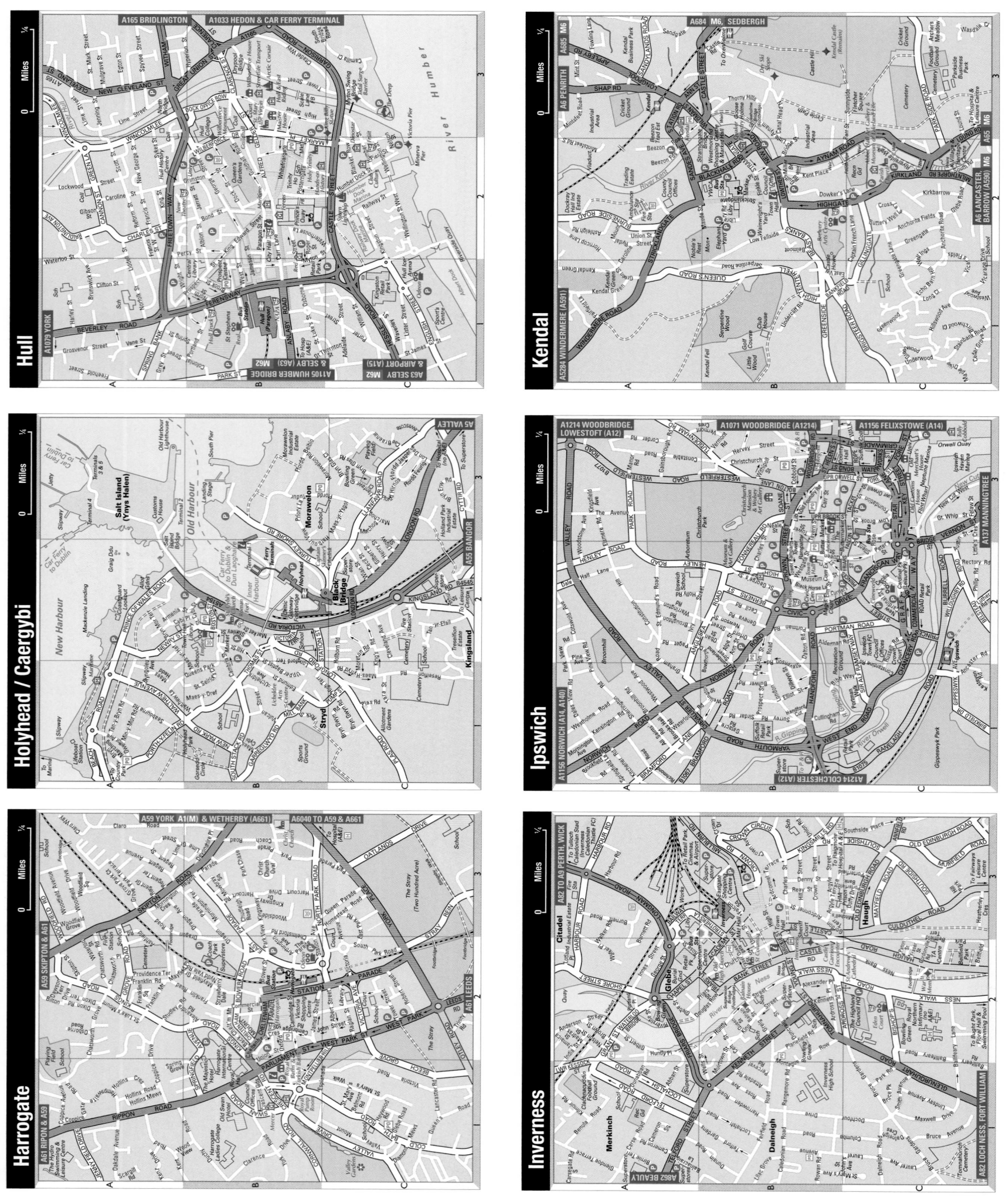

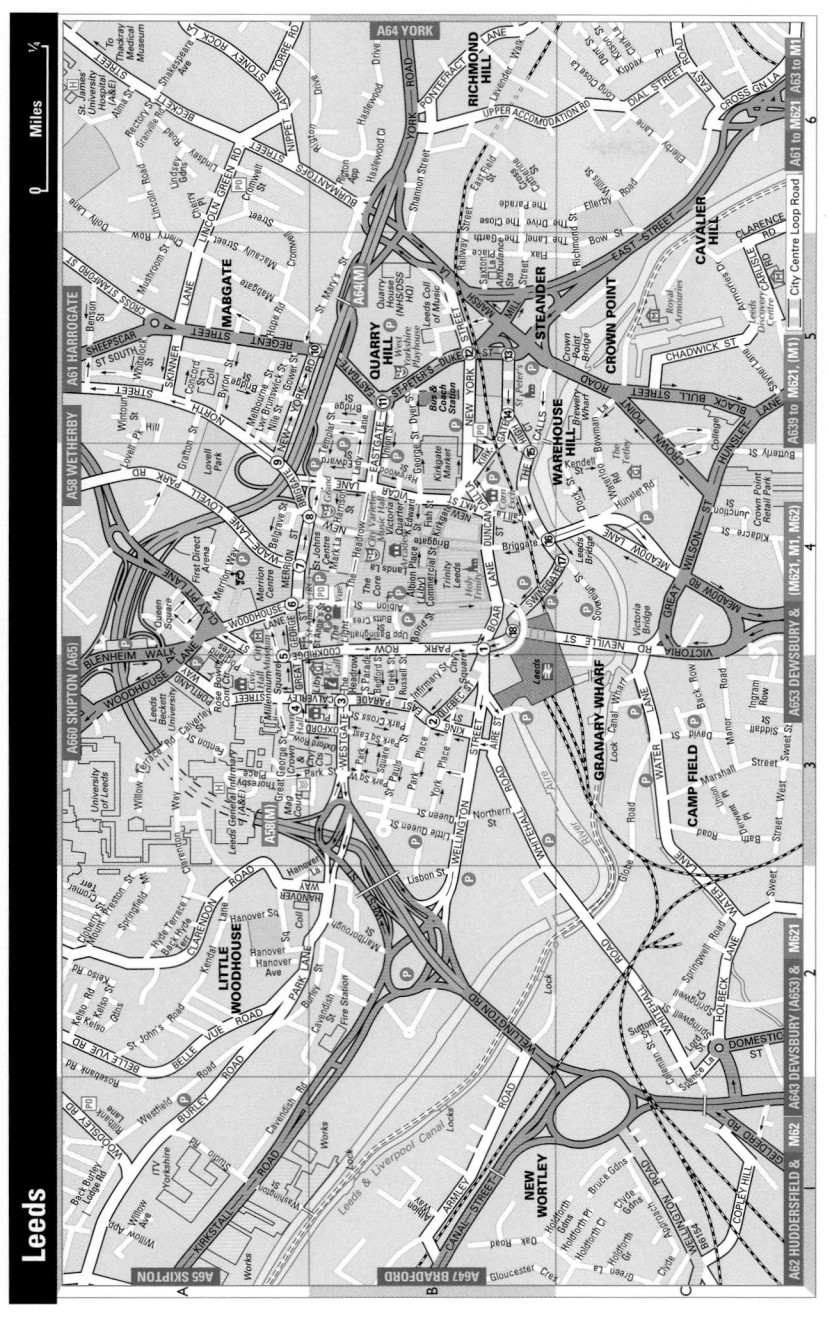

Leeds

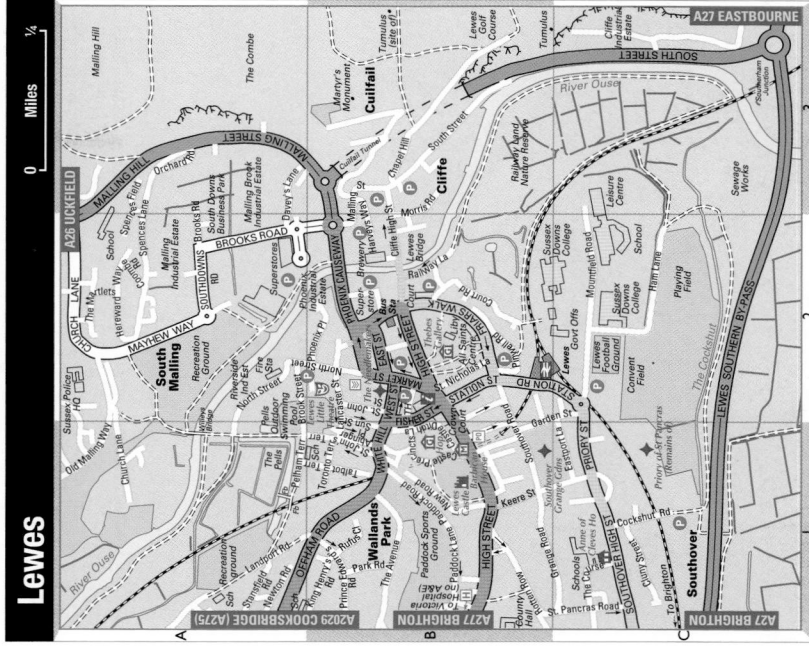

Lewes

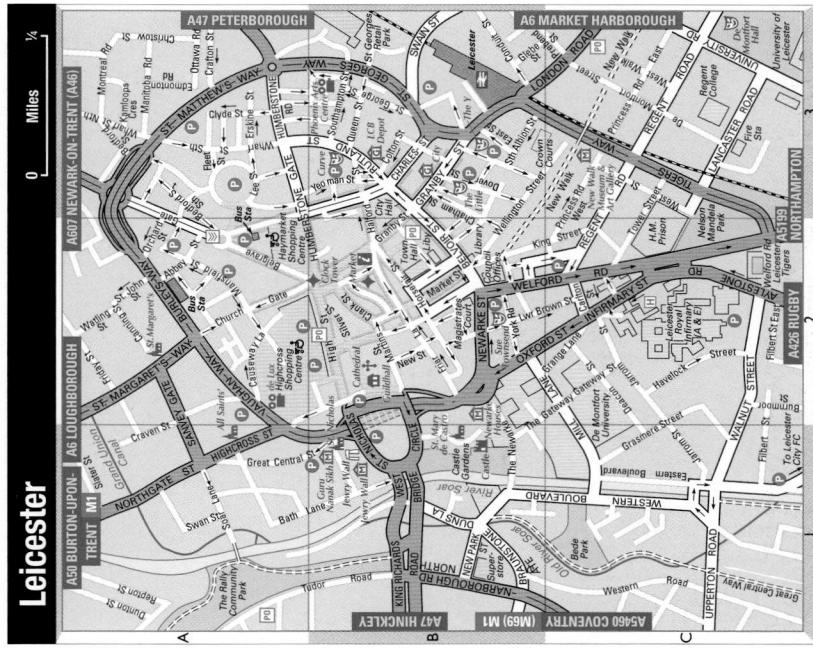

Leicester

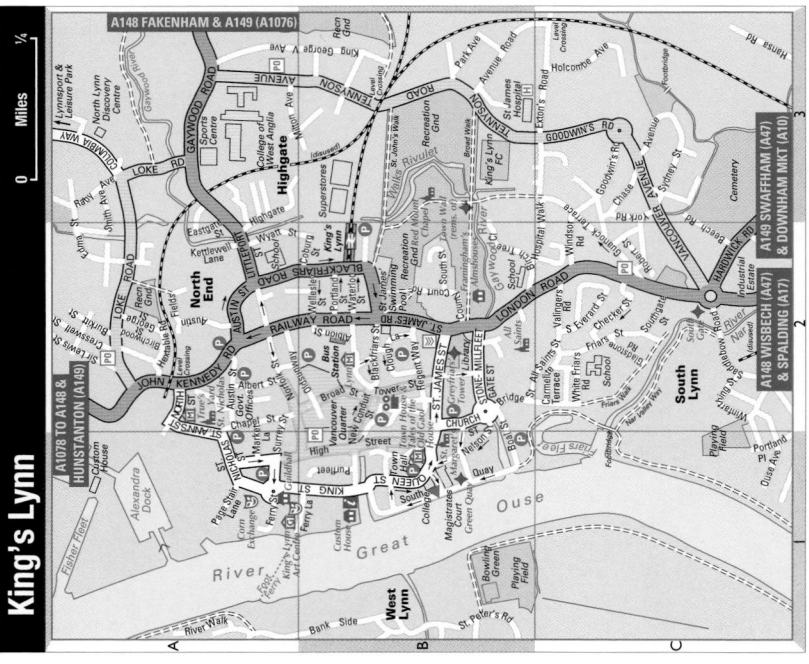

King's Lynn

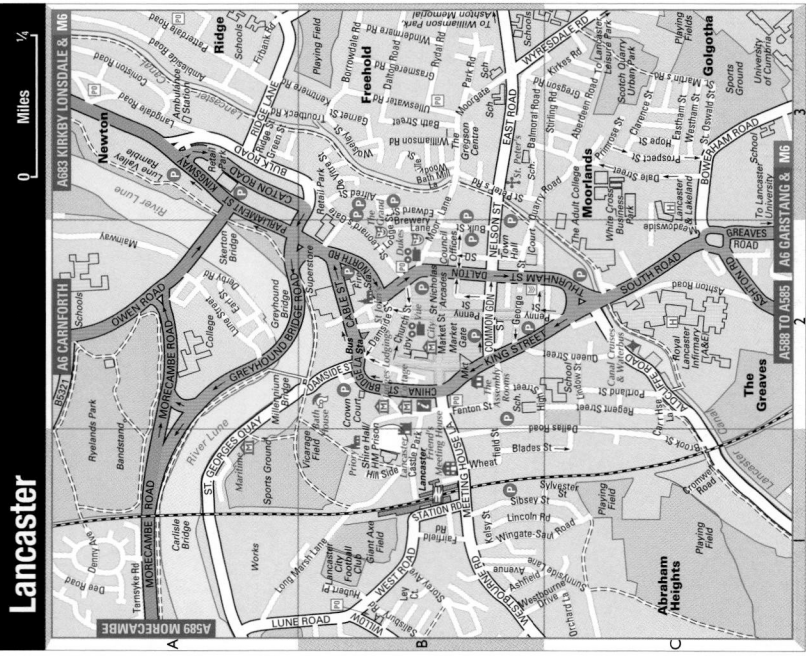

Lancaster

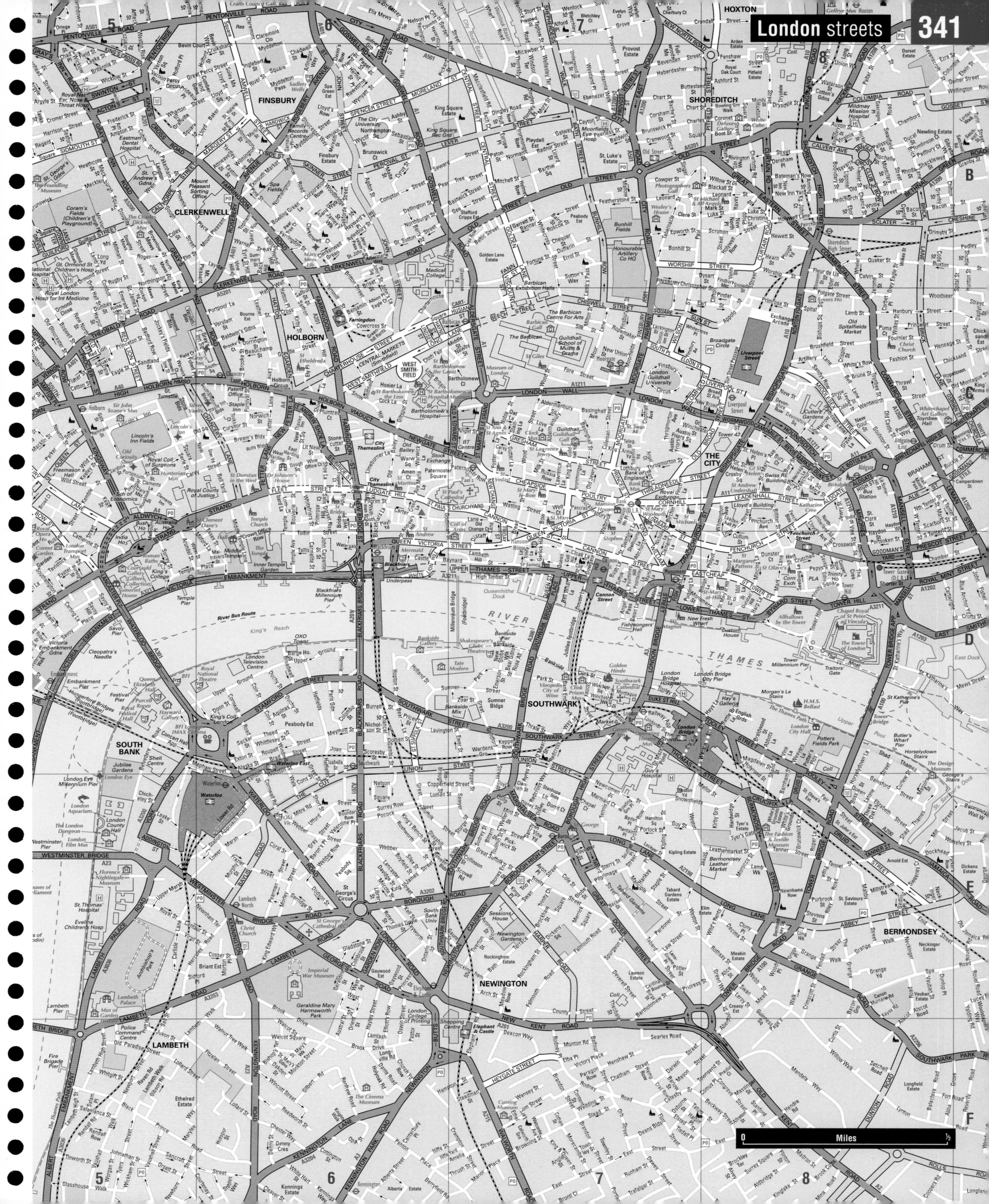

Manchester

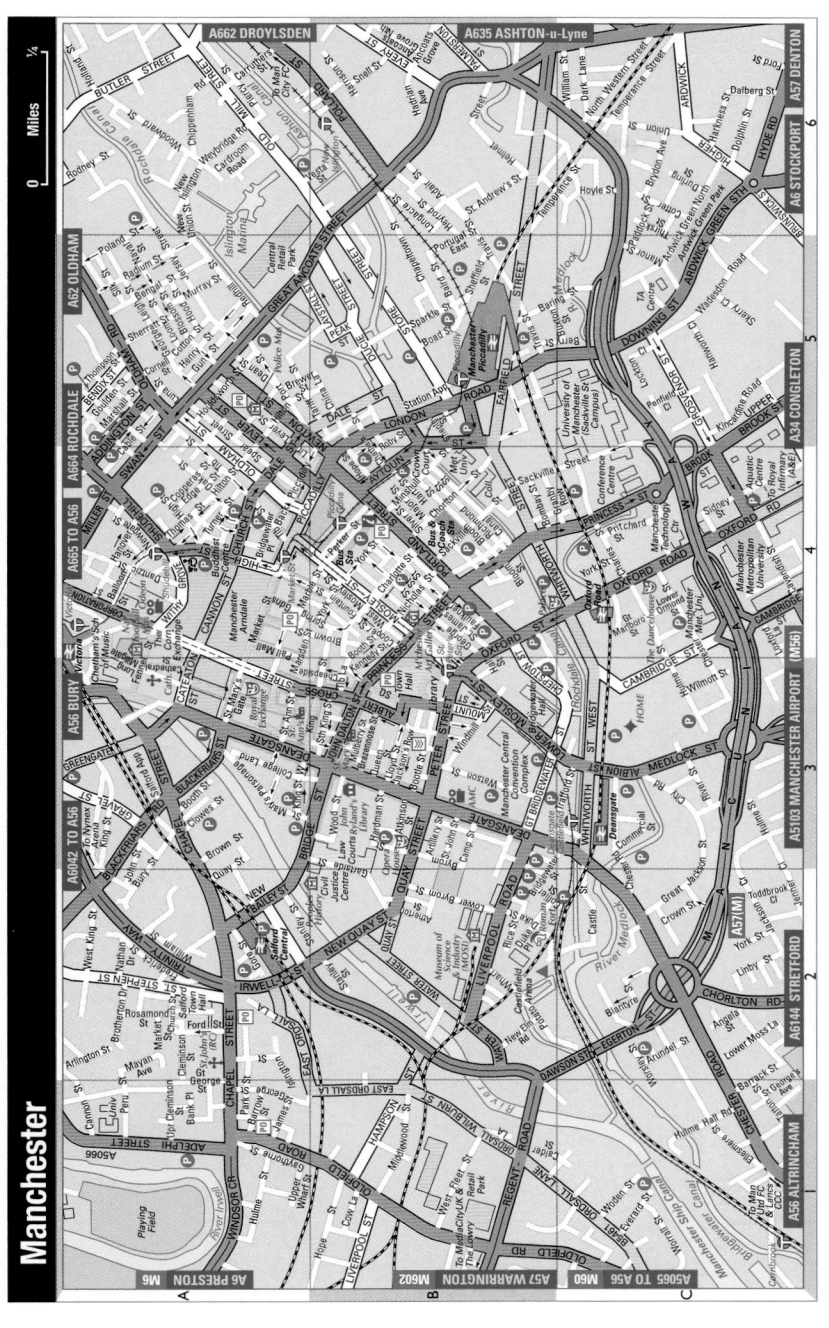

Middlesbrough

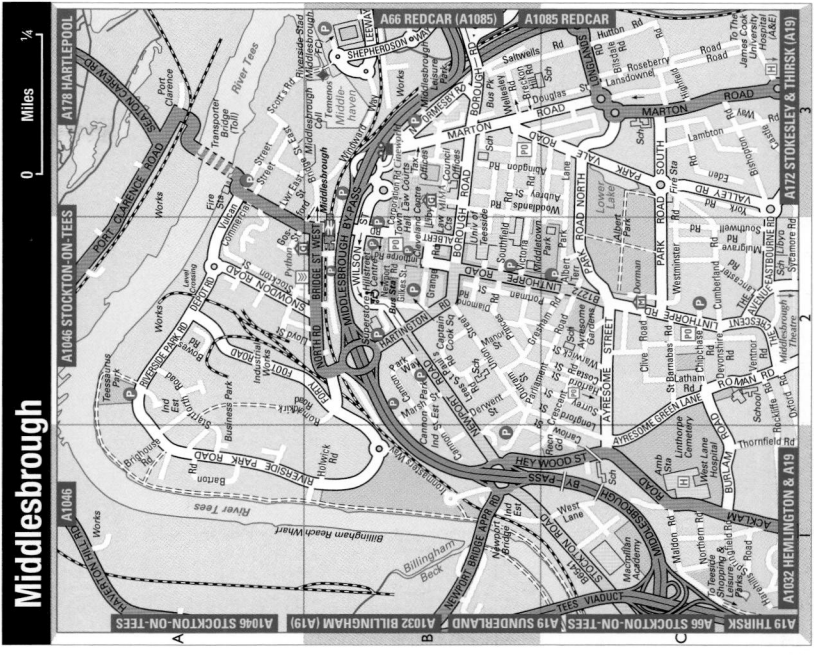

Merthyr Tydfil / Merthyr Tudful

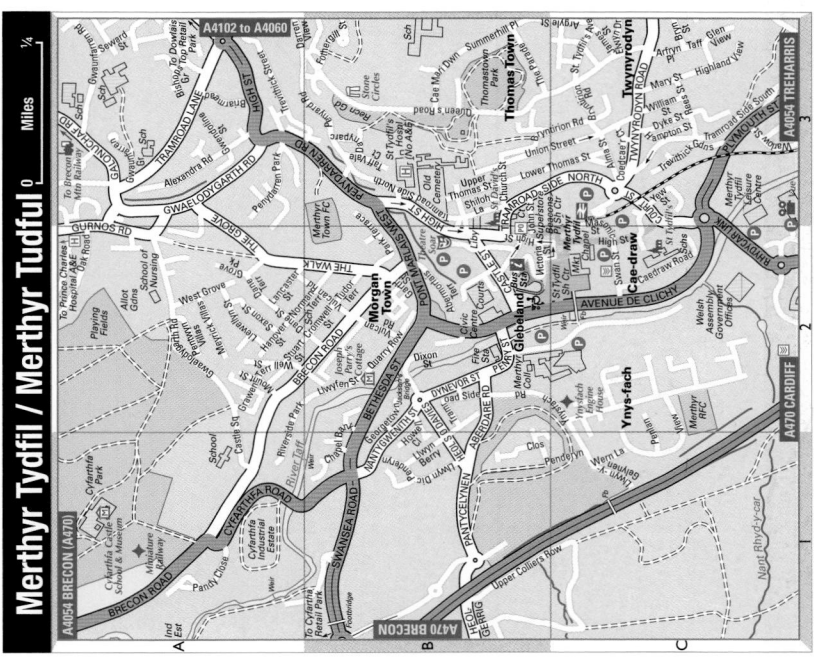

Macclesfield

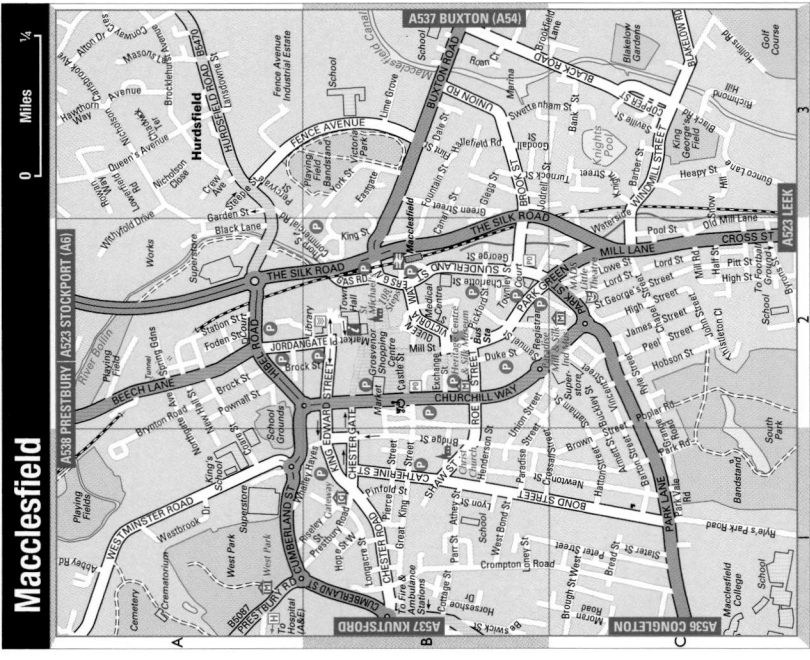

Maidstone

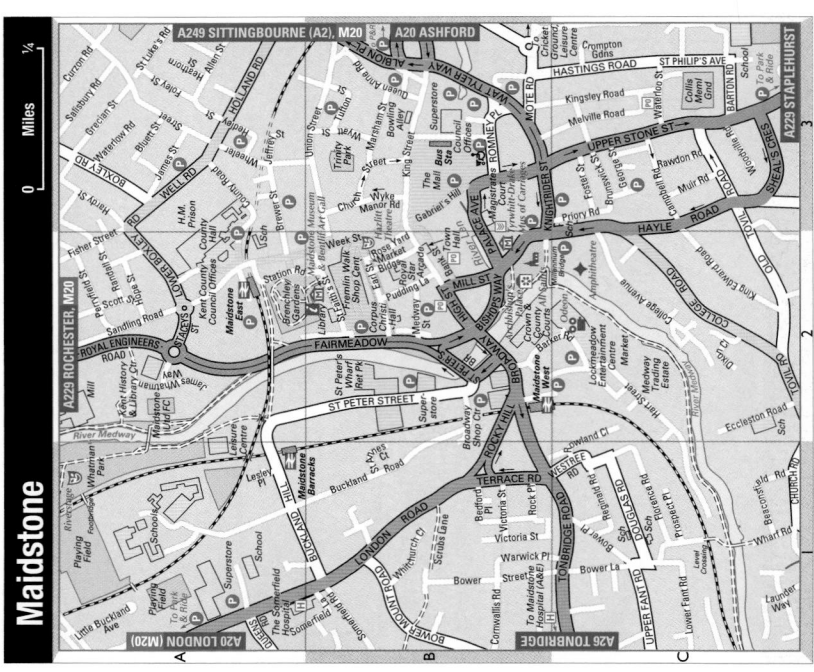

Norwich page 142 • **Nottingham** page 153 • **Oban** page 289 • **Oxford** page 83 • **Perth** page 286 • **Peterborough** page 138

345

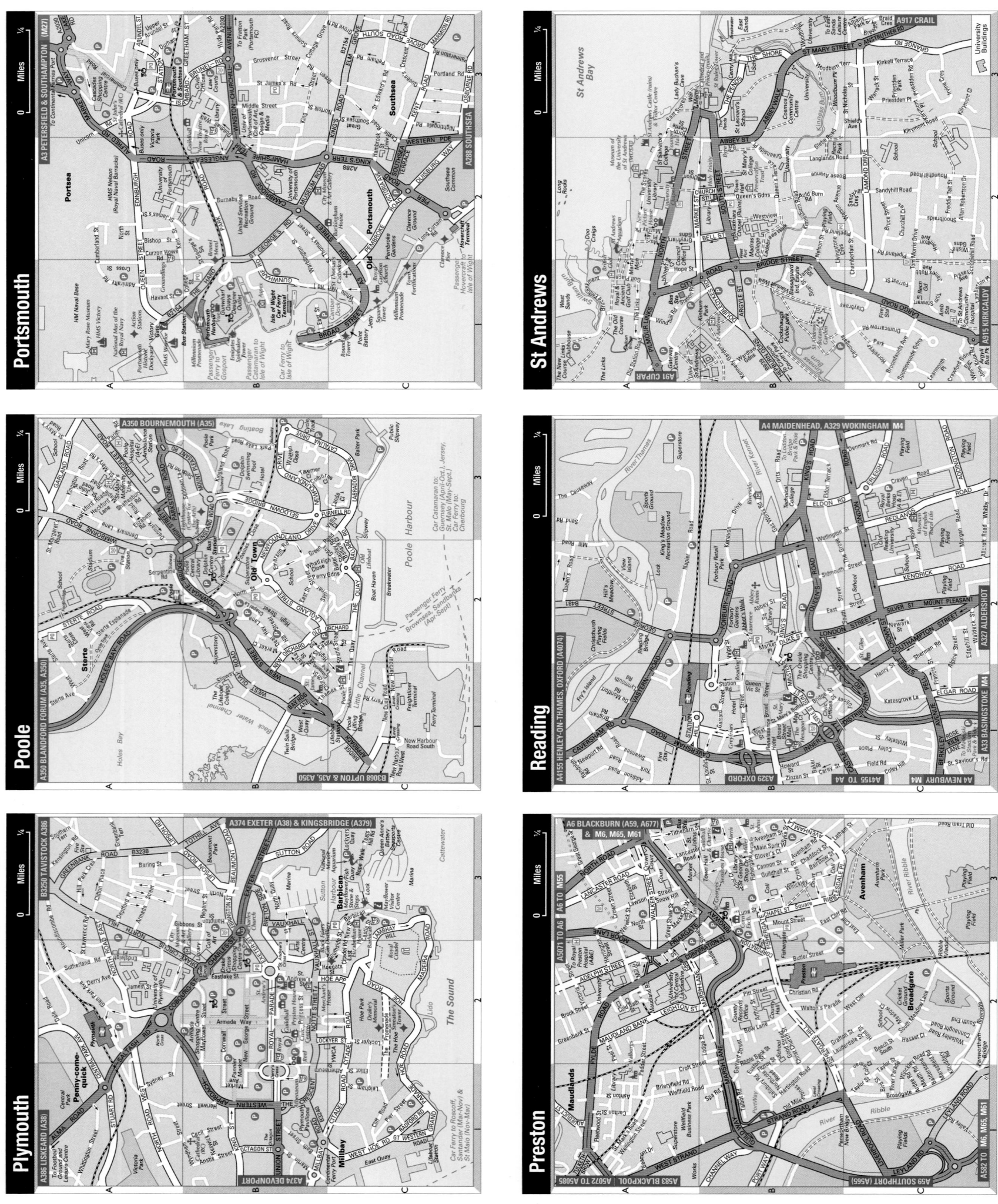

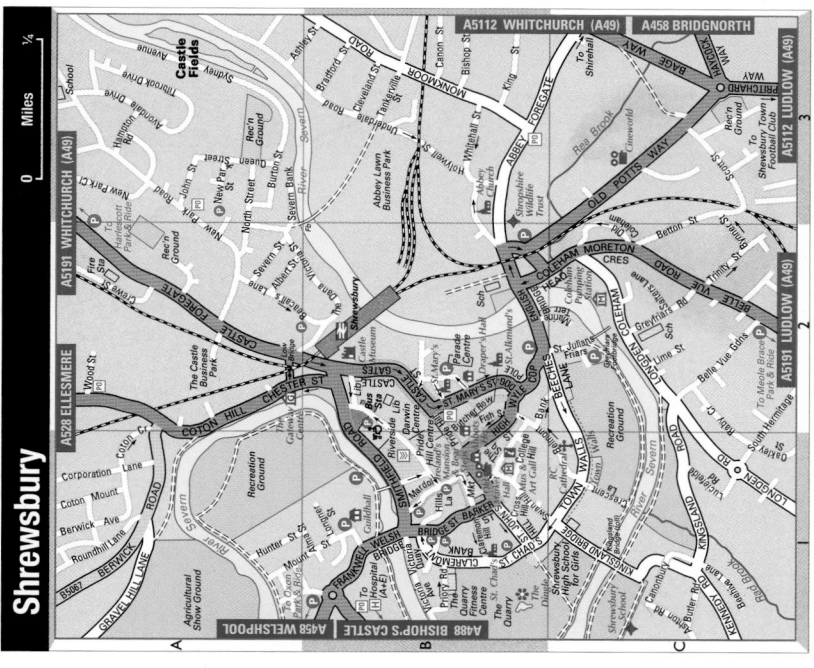

Shrewsbury

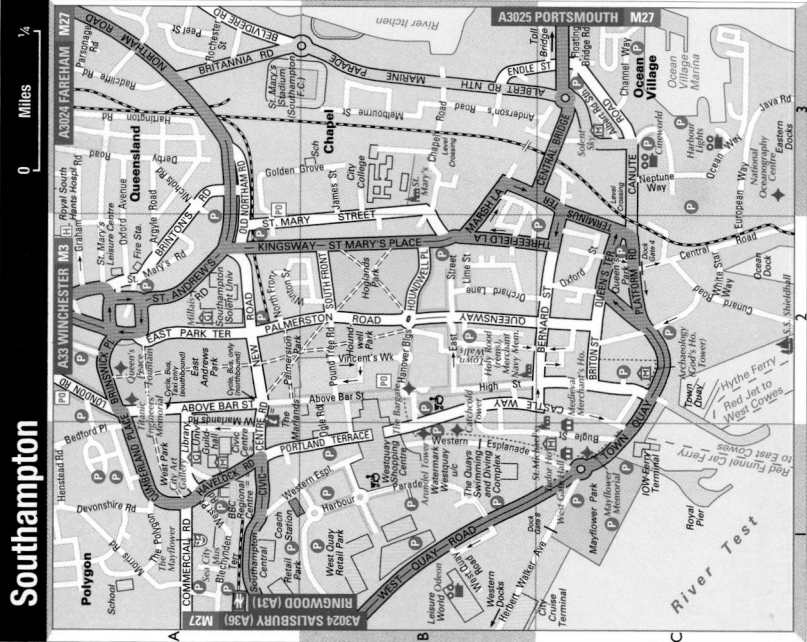

Southampton

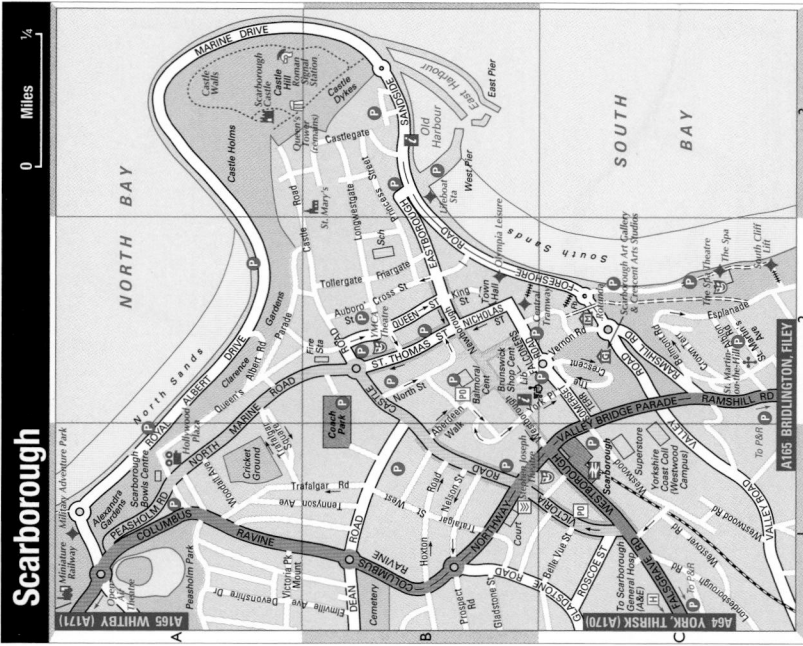

Scarborough

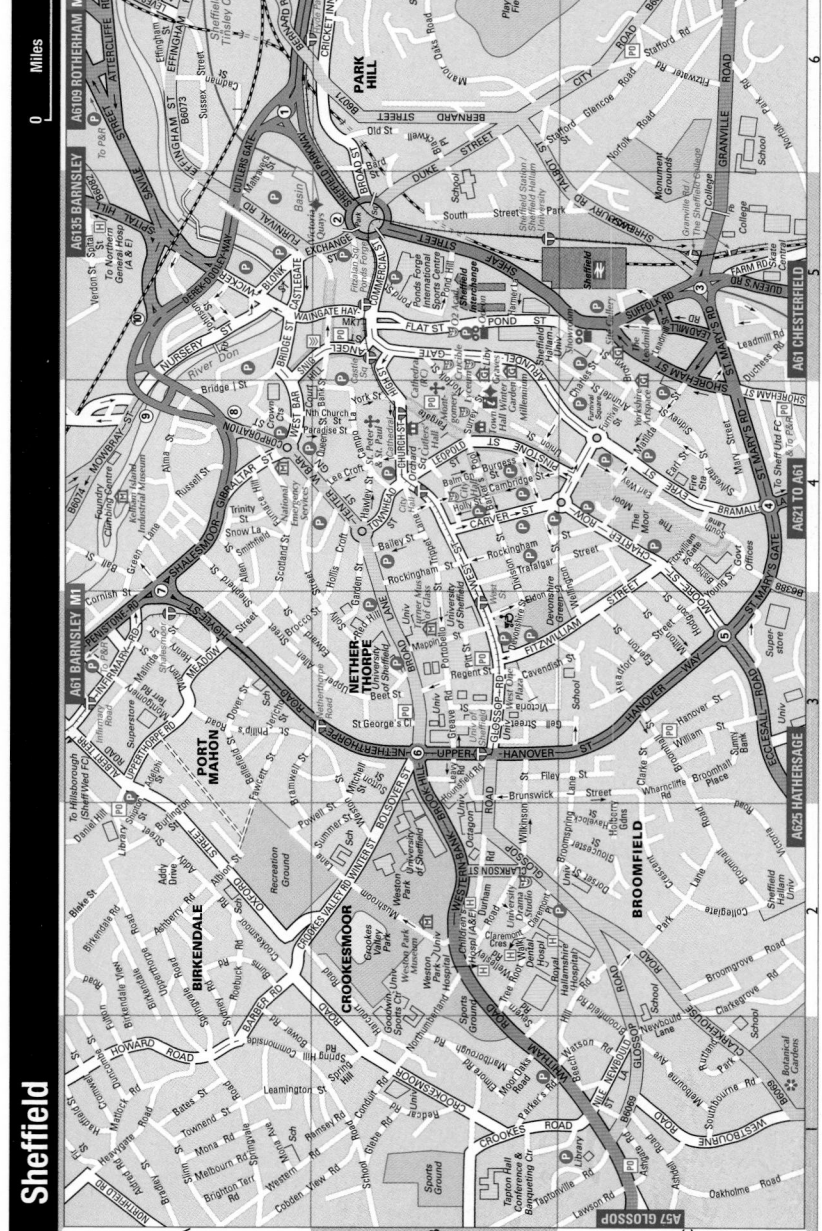

Sheffield

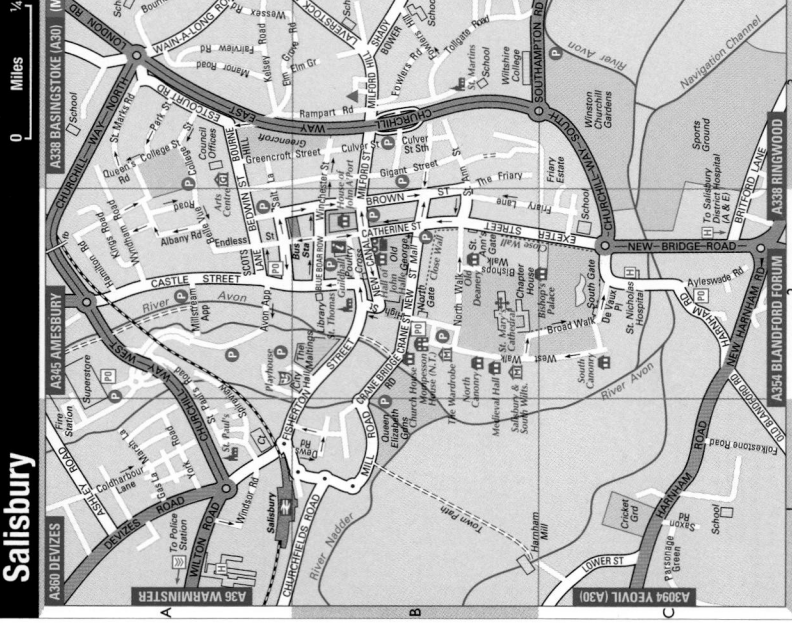

Salisbury

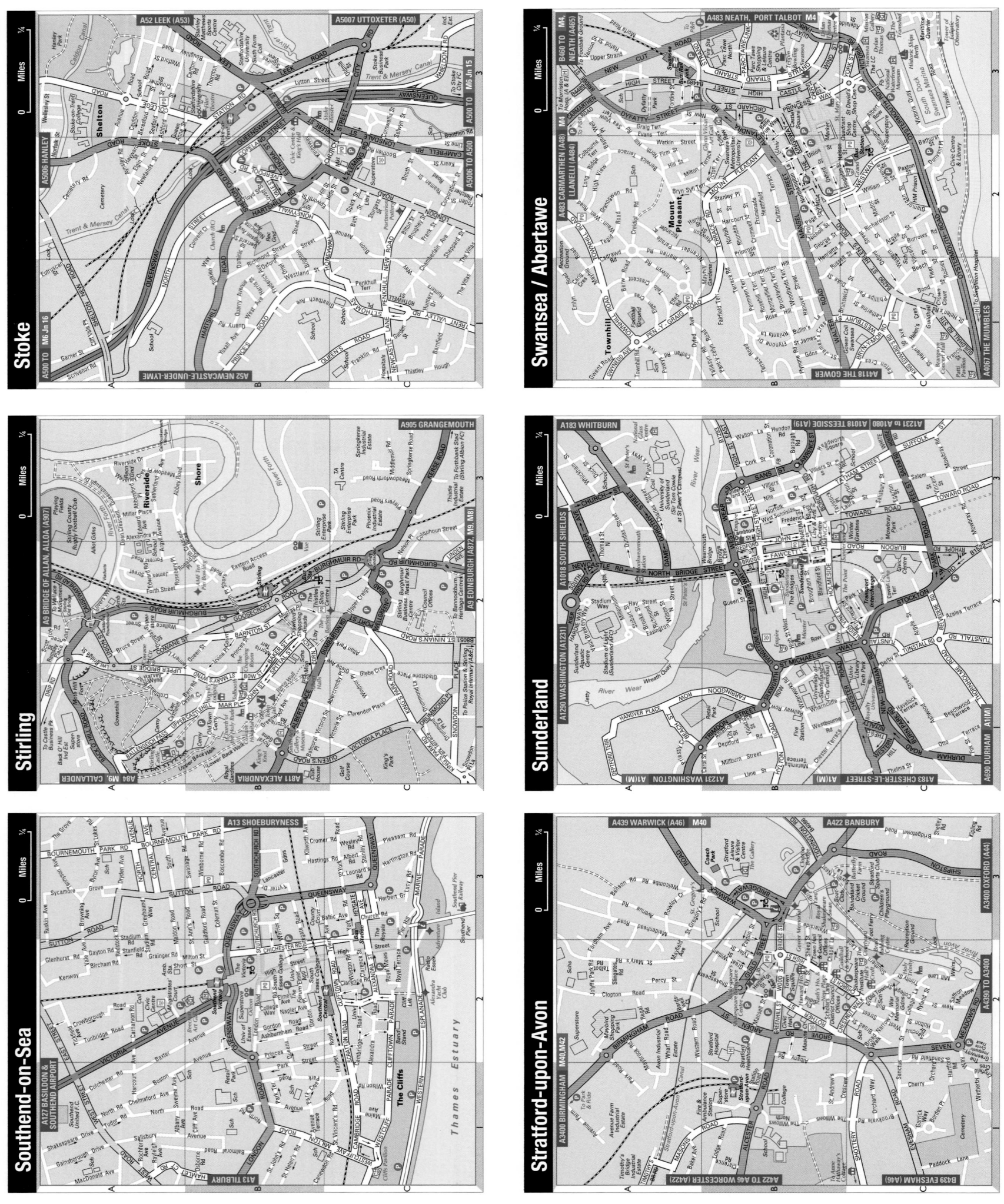

Stoke

Swansea / Abertawe

Stirling

Sunderland

Southend-on-Sea

Stratford-upon-Avon

Swindon page 63 • **Taunton** page 28 • **Telford** page 132 • **Torquay** page 9 • **Truro** page 4 • **Wick** page 310

349

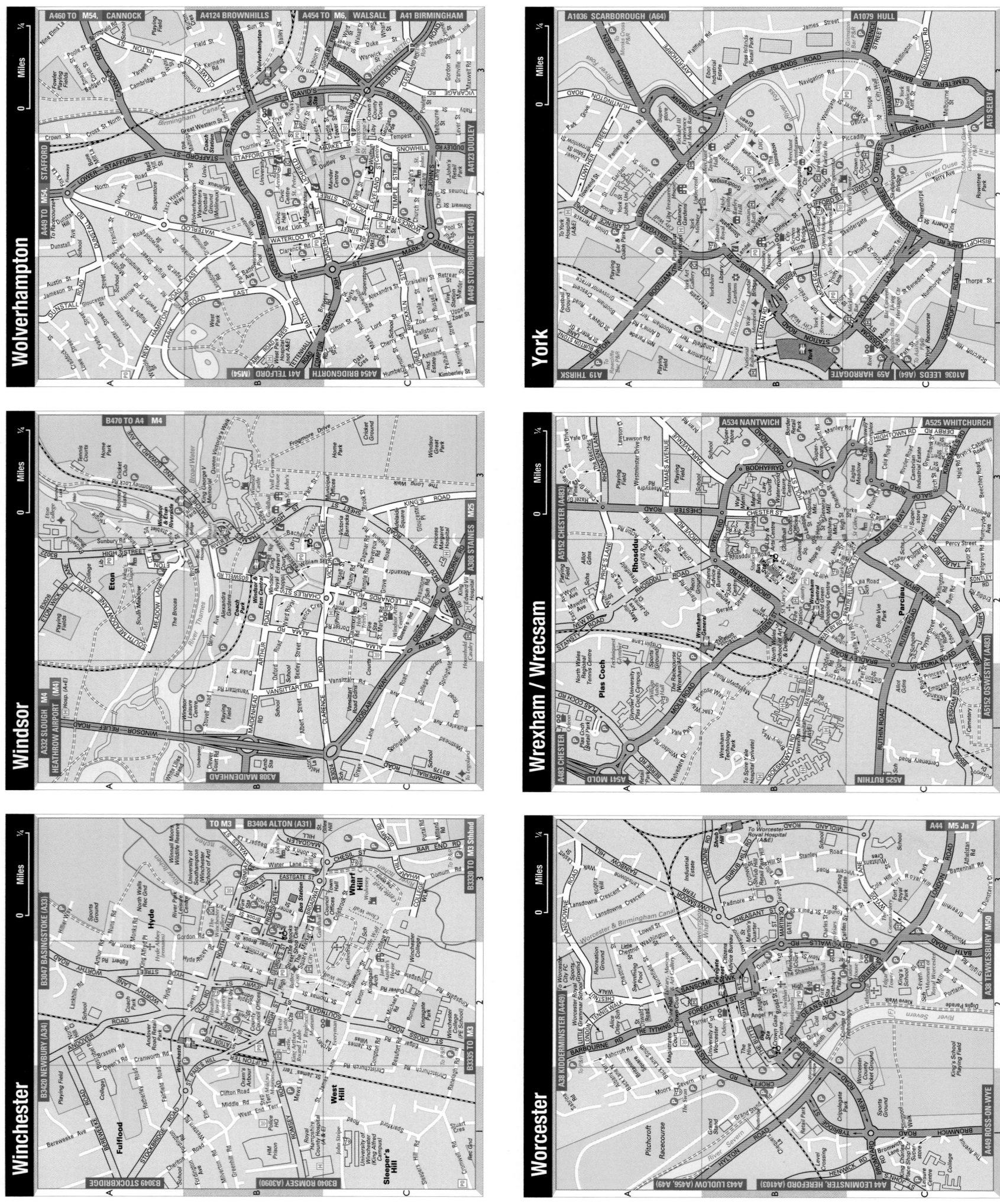

Aberdeen • Aberystwyth • Ashford • Ayr • Bangor • Barrow-in-Furness • Bath • Berwick-upon-Tweed • Birmingham 351

Town plan indexes

Aberdeen 331

Aberdeen ≥ B2
Aberdeen Grammar School A1
Academy, The B2
Albert Basin B3
Albert Quay B3
Albury Rd C1
Alford Pl B1
Art Gallery A2
Arts Centre A2
Back Wynd A2
Baker St A1
Beach Blvd A3
Belmont B2
Belmont St B2
Berry St A2
Blackfriars St A2
Blaikie's Quay B3
Bloomfield Rd C1
Bon Accord Centre A2
Bon-Accord St B1/C1
Bridge St B2
Broad St A2
Bus Station B2
Car Ferry Terminal B3
Castlegate A3
Central Library A1
Chapel St B1
Cineworld B2
Clyde St B3
College A2
College St B2
Commerce St A3
Commercial Quay B3
Community Ctr A3/C1
Constitution St A3
Cotton St A3
Crown St B2
Denburn Rd A2
Devanha Gdns C2
Devanha Gdns South C2
East North St A3
Esslemont Ave A1
Ferryhill Rd C2
Ferryhill Terr C2
Fish Market B3
Fonthill Rd C1
Galleria, The B1
Gallowgate A2
George St A2
Glenbervie Rd C3
Golden Sq B1
Grampian Rd C3
Great Southern Rd C1
Guild St B2
Hardgate B1/C1
His Majesty's Theatre A1
Holburn St C1
Hollybank Pl C1
Huntly St B1
Hutcheon St A1
Information Ctr B2
John St A2
Justice St A3
King St A2
Langstane Pl B1
Lemon Tree, The A2
Library C1
Loch St A2
Maberly St A1
Marischal College A2
Maritime Museum & Provost Ross's Ho B2
Market B2
Market St B2/B3
Menzies Rd C3
Mercat Cross ✦ A3
Millburn St C2
Miller St A3
Mount St A1
Music Hall B1
North Esp East C3
North Esp West C2
Oscar Rd C3
Palmerston Rd C2
Park St A3
Police Station A2
Polmuir Rd C2
Post Office A1/A2/A3/B1/C3
Provost Skene's Ho A2
Queen Elizabeth Br C1
Queen St A2
Regent Quay B3
Regent Road B3
Robert Gordon's Coll A2
Rose St B1
Rosemount Pl A1
Rosemount Viaduct A1
St Andrew St A2
St Andrew's Cath ✝ A3
St Mary's Cathedral ✝ B1
St Nicholas Centre A2
St Nicholas St A2
School Hill A2
Sinclair Rd C3
Skene Sq A1
Skene St B1
South College St C2
South Crown St C2
South Esp East C3
South Esp West C3
South Mount St A1
Sports Centre C3
Spring Garden A2
Springbank Terr C2
Summer St B1
Superstore A2
Swimming Pool B1
Thistle St B1
Tolbooth A3
Town House A2
Trinity Centre B2
Trinity Quay B3
Union Row B1
Union Square B2
Union St B1/B2
Upper Dock B3
Upper Kirkgate A2
Victoria Bridge C3
Victoria Dock B3
Victoria Rd C3
Victoria St B2
Virginia St A3
Vue B2
Wellington Pl B2
West North St A2
Whinhill Rd C1
Willowbank Rd C1
Windmill Brae B2
Woolmanhill Hospl A1

Aberystwyth 331

Aberystwyth Holiday Village C2
Aberystwyth RFC C3
Aberystwyth Sta ≥ B2
Aberystwyth Town Football Ground B2
Alexandra Rd B2
Ambulance Station C3
Baker St B1
Banadl Rd B2
Bandstand A1
Bar, The C1
Bath St A2
Boat Landing Stage A1
Bvd de Saint-Brieuc C3
Bridge St B1
Bronglais Hospital B3
Bryn-y-Mor Rd A2
Buarth Rd B2
Bus Station B2
Cae Ceredig C3
Cae Melyn A2
Cae'r-Gog B3
Cambrian St B2
Caradoc Rd B3
Caravan Site C2
Castle (Remains of) B1
Castle St B1
Cemetery B3
Ceredigion Mus A1
Chalybeate St B1
Cliff Terr A2
Club House A2
Commodore A1
County Court A2
Crown Buildings B2
Dan-y-Coed A3
Dinas Terr C1
Eastgate B1
Edge-hill Rd B2
Elm Tree Ave B2
Elysian Gr A2
Felin-y-Mor Rd C1
Fifth Ave C2
Fire Station C1
Glanrafon Terr B1
Glyndwr Rd B2
Golf Course A3
Government & Council Offices C3
Gray's Inn Rd B1
Great Darkgate St B1
Greenfield St B2
Heol-y-Bryn A2
High St B1
Infirmary Rd A2
Information Ctr B1
Iorwerth Ave B3
King St B1
Lauraplace B1
Library A2
Library A2
Lifeboat Station C1
Llanbadarn Rd B3
Loveden Rd A2
Magistrates Court A1
Marina C1
Marine Terr A1
Market Hall B1
Mill St B1
Moor La B2
National Library of Wales B3
New Promenade B1
New St B1
North Beach A1
North Parade B2
North Rd A2
Northgate St B2
Parc Natur Penglais A3
Parc-y-Llyn Retail Pk C3
Park & Ride B2
Park Ave B2
Pavillion B1
Pen-y-Craig A2
Pen-yr-angor C1
Pendinas C1
Penglais Rd B3
Penrheidol C2
Pier St B1
Plas Ave B3
Plas Helyg C2
Plascrug Ave B2/C3
Plascrug Leisure Ctr C3
Police Station C2
Poplar Row B2
Portland Rd B2
Portland St A2
Post Office B1/B3
Powell St B1
Prospect St B1
Quay Rd B1
Queen St B1
Queen's Ave A2
Queen's Rd A2
Rheidol Retail Park B2
Riverside Terr B1
St Davids Rd B3
St Michael's B1
School of Art B2
Seaview Pl B1
South Beach B1
South Rd B1
Sports Ground B2
Spring Gdns C1
Stanley Terr B2
Superstore B2/C3
Swimming Pool & Leisure Centre C3
Tanybwlch Beach C1
Tennis Courts B3
Terrace Rd B1
Trefechan Bridge B1
Trefechan Rd C2
Trefor Rd A2
Trinity Rd B2
University Campus B3
University of Wales (Aberystwyth) B1
Vale of Rheidol Railway C3
Vaynor St B2
Victoria Terr A1
Viewpoint ✦ A2
Viewpoint ✦ A3
War Memorial B1
Wharf Quay C1
Y Lanfa C1
Ystwyth Retail Park B2

Ashford 331

Albert Rd A1
Alfred Rd C3
Apsley St A1
Ashford Borough Museum A1
Ashford Designer Outlet C2
Ashford International Station ≥ B2
Bank St A1
Barrowhill Gdns A1
Beaver Industrial Est C1
Beaver Rd C1
Beazley Ct C3
Birling Rd B3
Blue Line La A1
Bond Rd C1
Bowens Field B1
Bulleid Pl C2
Cade Rd C1
Chart Rd A1
Chichester Cl B1
Christchurch Rd B1
Chunnel Ind Est B1
Church Rd A1
Civic Centre A2
County Square Sh Ctr A1
Court A1
Court A2
Croft Rd A3
Cudworth Rd C3
Curtis Rd C3
Dering Rd A3
Dover Pl B2
Drum La A1
East Hill A2
East St A1
Eastmead Ave B2
Edinburgh Rd A1
Elwick Rd A1
Essella Pk B3
Essella Rd B3
Fire Sta A3
Forge La A1
Francis Rd C1
George St B1
Godfrey Walk B1
Gordon Cl A3
Hardinge Rd A2
Henwood A3
Henwood Bsns Ctr A3
Henwood Ind Est A3
High St A2
Hythe Rd A3
Information Ctr A1
Jemmett Rd B1
Kent Ave A1
Library A1
Linden Rd B3
Lower Denmark Rd C1
Mabledon Ave B3
Mace Industrial Est A2
Mace La A2
Maunsell Pl C3
Memorial Gdns A2
Mill Ct A2
Miller Cl A2
Mortimer Cl C1
New St A1
Newtown Green C3
Newtown Rd B2/C3
Norman Rd C1
North St A2
Norwood Gdns A1
Norwood St A1
Old Railway Works Industrial Estate C3
Orion Way C3
Pk Mall Shopping Ctr A1
Park Pl C1
Park St A1/A2
Pemberton Rd A3
Police Station A1
Post Office A1/A3
Providence St C2
Queen St A1
Queens Rd A2
Regents Pl A1
Riversdale Rd C2
Romney Marsh Rd B2
St John's La A2
St Mary's Church & Arts Venue A1
Somerset Rd A2
South Stour Ave B2
Star Rd A3
Station Rd B2
Stirling Rd C2
Stour Centre, The B2
Sussex Ave A1
Tannery La A2
Technical College B2
Torrington Rd C2
Trumper Bridge B1
Tufton Rd A3
Tufton St A1
Vicarage La A2
Victoria Cres B1
Victoria Park B1
Victoria Rd B1
Victoria Way B1
Wallis Rd A3
Wellesley Rd A2
West St A1
Whitfeld Rd C1
William Rd C1
World War I Tank ✦ A1

Ayr 331

Ailsa Pl B1
Alexandra Terr A3
Allison St B2
Alloway Pk C1
Alloway Pl C1
Alloway St C2
Arran Mall C2
Arran Terr B1
Arthur St B2
Ashgrove St C2
Auld Brig B2
Auld Kirk B2
Ayr ≥ C2
Ayr Academy B1
Ayr Central Sh Ctr C2
Ayr Harbour A1
Ayr Ice Rink A2
Ayr United FC A3
Back Hawkhill Ave A3
Back Main St B2
Back Peebles St A2
Barns Cres C1
Barns Pk C1
Barns St C1
Barns Street La C1
Bath Pl B1
Bellevue Cres C1
Bellevue La C1
Beresford La C2
Beresford Terr C2
Boswell Pk B2
Britannia Pl A3
Bruce Cres B1
Burns Statue ✦ C2
Bus Sta B1
Carrick St C2
Cassillis St B1
Cathcart St B1
Charlotte St B1
Citadel Leisure Ctr B1
Citadel Pl B1
Compass Pier A1
Content Ave C3
Content St B2
Craigie Ave B3
Craigie Rd B3
Craigie Way B3
Cromwell Rd B1
Crown St A2
Dalblair Rd C2
Dam Park Sports Stadium C3
Damside A2
Dongola Rd C3
Eglinton Pl B1
Eglinton Terr B1
Elba St B2
Elmbank St A2
Esplanade B1
Euchar Rock A1
Farifield Rd C1
Fort St B1
Fothringham Rd C3
Fullarton St C1
Gaiety C2
Garden St B2
George St B2
George's Ave A3
Glebe Cres A2
Glebe Rd A2
Gorden Terr B3
Green St A2
Green Street La A2
Hawkhill Ave A3
Hawkhill Avenue La B3
High St B2
Holmston Rd C3
Information Ctr B1
James St B3
John St B2
King St B2
Kings Ct B2
Kyle Centre C2
Kyle St C2
Library B2
Limekiln Rd A2
Limonds Wynd B2
Loudoun Hall B2
Lymburn Pl B3
Macadam Pl B2
Main St B2
Mcadam's Monument C1
Mccall's Ave A3
Mews La B1
Mill Brae C3
Mill St C2
Mill Wynd C2
Miller Rd C1
Montgomerie Terr B1
New Bridge B2
New Bridge St B2
New Rd A2
Newmarket St B2
Newton-on-Ayr Station ≥ A2
North Harbour St B1
North Pier A1
Odeon C2
Oswald La A1
Park Circus C1
Park Circus La C1
Park Terr C1
Pavilion Rd C1
Peebles St A2
Philip Sq B2
Police Station B2
Post Office A2/B2
Prestwick Rd B1
Princes Ct A2
Queen St B3
Queen's Terr B1
Racecourse Rd C1
River St B2
Riverside Pl B2
Russell Dr A2
St Andrews Church C2
St George's Rd A3
Sandgate B1
Savoy Park C1
Smith St C2
Somerset Rd A3
South Beach Rd B1
South Harbour St B1
South Pier A1
Station Rd C2
Strathayr Pl B2
Superstore A2/B2
Taylor St A2
Town Hall B2
Tryfield Pl A3
Turner's Bridge B2
Union Ave A3
Victoria Bridge C3
Victoria St B3
Viewfield Rd A3
Virginia Gdns A2
Waggon Rd A2
Walker Rd A3
Wallace Tower ✦ B2
Weaver St A2
Weir Rd A2
Wellington La C1
Wellington Sq C1
West Sanouhar Rd A3
Whitletts Rd B3
Wilson St A3
York St A1
York Street La B1

Bangor 331

Abbey Rd C2
Albert St B1
Ambrose St A3
Ambulance Station A3
Arfon Sports Hall C1
Ashley Rd B3
Bangor Mountain B3
Bangor Station ≥ C1
Bangor University B2
Beach Rd A3
Belmont St C1
Bishop's Mill Rd C3
Boat Yard A3
Brick St B3
Buckley Rd B2
Bus Station B3
Caellepa B2
Caernarfon Rd C1
Cathedral ✝ B2
Cemetery C1
Clarence St C1
Clock Tower ✦ B3
College B2/C2
College La B2
College Rd B2
Convent La C1
Council Offices B2
Craig y Don Rd B2
Crescent, The B2
Dean St B3
Deiniol Rd B2
Deiniol Shopping Ctr B2
Deiniol St B2
Edge Hill A3
Euston Rd C1
Fairview Rd A3
Farrar Rd C2
Ffordd Cynfal C1
Ffordd Islwyn A3
Ffordd y Castell C3
Ffriddoedd Rd B1
Field St B1
Fountain St A3
Friars Ave B3
Friars Rd B3
Friary (Site of) ✦ B3
Gardd Deman C1
Garth Hill A3
Garth Point A3
Garth Rd A3
Glanrafon B2
Glanrafon Hill B2
Glynne Rd B3
Golf Course B3
Golf Course C2
Gorad Rd B1
Gorsedd Circle A2
Gwern Las C3
Gwynedd Museum & Art Gallery B2
Heol Dewi C1
High St B3/C2
Hill St B1
Holyhead Rd B1
Hwfa Rd B1
Information Ctr B2
James St B3
Library B2
Llys Emrys A3
Lon Ogwen C1
Lon-Pobty C2
Lon-y-Felin C3
Lon-y-Glyder C1
Love La B2
Lower Penrallt Rd B2
Lower St B2
Maes Glas Sports Ctr B1
Maes-y-Dref B3
Maeshyfryd A3
Meirion La A2
Meirion Rd A2
Menai Ave B1
Menai College C1
Menai Shopping Ctr B3
Min-y-Ddol C3
Minafon B2
Mount St B3
Orme Rd A3
Parc Victoria B1
Penchwintan Rd C1
Penlon Gr B3
Penrhyn Ave C3
Pier ✦ A3
Police Station B2
Post Office B2/B3/C1/C3
Prince's Rd B2
Queen's Ave C3
Sackville Rd B2
St Paul's St B2
Seion Rd A3
Seiriol Rd A3
Siliwen Rd A2
Snowdon View B1
Station Rd C1
Strand St B3
Superstore B3/C2
Swimming Pool and Leisure Centre A3
Tan-y-Coed C3
Tegid Rd B3
Temple Rd B2
Theatr Gwynedd B2
Totton Rd A3
Town Hall B2
Treflan B2
Trem Elidir C1
Upper Garth Rd A3
Victoria Ave B1
Victoria Dr B1
Victoria St B1
Vron St B2
Well St B3
West End C1
William St B3
York Pl B3

Barrow-in-Furness 332

Abbey Rd A3/B2
Adelaide St A2
Ainslie St A3
Albert St C3
Allison St B3
Anson St A2
Argyle St B3
Arthur St B3
Ashburner Way A1
Barrow Raiders RLFC B1
Barrow Station ≥ A2
Bath St A1/B2
Bedford Rd A3
Bessamer Way A1
Blake St A1/A2
Bridge Rd C1
Buccleuch Dock C3
Buccleuch Dock Rd C2/C3
Buccleuch St B2/B3
Byron St A2
Calcutta St A1
Cameron St C1
Carlton Ave A3
Cavendish Dock Rd C3
Cavendish St B2/B3
Channelside Haven C1
Channelside Walk B1
Chatsworth St A2
Cheltenham St A3
Church St C3
Clifford St B2
Clive St B1
Collingwood St B2
Cook St A2
Cornerhouse Retail Park B2
Cornwallis St B2
Courts A2
Crellin St B3
Cross St C3
Custom House ✦ B2
Dalkeith St B2
Dalton Rd B2/C2
Derby St B3
Devonshire Dock C2
Devonshire Dock Hall B1
Dock Museum, The B1
Drake St A2
Dryden St A2
Duke St A1/B2/C3
Duncan St B2
Dundee St C2
Dundonald St B2
Earle St C1
Emlyn St B2
Exmouth St A2
Farm St C2
Fell St B3
Fenton St B3
Ferry Rd C1
Forum, The B2
Furness College B1
Glasgow St B3
Goldsmith St A2
Greengate St B3
Hardwick St A2
Harrison St B3
Hartington St A2
Hawke St B2
Hibbert Rd A2
High Level Bridge C2
High St B2
Hindpool Rd B2
Hindpool Retail Park B2
Holker St A2
Hollywood Retail & Leisure Pk B1
Hood St A2
Howard St B2
Howe St A2
Information Ctr B2
Ironworks Rd A1/B1
James St B3
Jubliee Bridge C1
Keith St B2
Keyes St A2
Lancaster St A3
Lawson St B2
Library B2
Lincoln St A3
Longreins Rd A3
Lonsdale St C3
Lord St B3
Lorne Rd B3
Lyon St A2
Manchester St B2
Market B2
Market St B2
Marsh St B3
Michaelson Rd C2
Milton St A2
Monk St B2
Mount Pleasant B3
Nan Tait Centre B2
Napier St B2
Nelson St B2
North Rd B1
Open Market B2
Parade St B2
Paradise St B3
Park Ave A3
Park Dr A3
Park, The A3
Parker St A2
Parry St A2
Peter Green Way A1
Phoenix Rd A1
Police Station B2
Portland Walk Sh Ctr B2
Post Office A3/B2
Princess Selandia C2
Raleigh St A2
Ramsden St B3
Rawlinson St B3
Robert St B3
Rodney St B2
Rutland St A2
St Patricks Rd C1
Salthouse Rd C3
School St B3
Scott St B2
Settle St A3
Shore St C3
Sidney St B2
Silverdale St B3
Slater St B2
Smeaton St B3
Stafford St A3
Stanley Rd C1
Stark St C3
Steel St B1
Storey Sq B3
Strand C3
Superstore A1/B1/C3
Sutherland St B3
TA Centre A2
Thwaite St B3
Town Hall B2
Town Quay C3
Vernon St B2
Vincent St B2
Walney Rd A1
West Gate Rd A2
West View Rd A3
Westmorland St A3
Whitehead St A3
Wordsworth St A2

Bath 332

Alexandra Park C2
Alexandra Rd C2
Approach Golf Courses (Public) A1
Archway St C3
Assembly Rooms & Mus of Costume A2
Avon St B2
Barton St B2
Bath Abbey ✝ B2
Bath Aqua Glass A2
Bath City College B2
Bath Pavilion B3
Bath Rugby Club B3
Bath Spa Station ≥ C3
Bathwick St A3
Beckford Road A3
Beechen Cliff Rd C2
Bennett St A2
Bloomfield Ave C1
Broad Quay C2
Broad St B2
Brock St A1
Building of Bath Museum A2
Bus Station C2
Calton Gdns C2
Calton Rd C2
Camden Cr A2
Cavendish Rd A1
Cemetery B1
Charlotte St B2
Chaucer Rd C2
Cheap St B2
Circus Mews A2
Claverton St C2
Corn St C2
Cricket Ground B3
Daniel St A3
Edward St B3
Ferry La B3
First Ave C1
Forester Ave A3
Forester Rd A3
Gays Hill A2
George St B2
Great Pulteney St B3
Green Park B1
Green Park Rd B2
Grove St B2
Guildhall B2
Harley St A2
Hayesfield Park C1
Henrietta Gdns A3
Henrietta Mews B3
Henrietta Park B3
Henrietta Rd A3
Henrietta St B3
Henry St B2
Herschel Museum of Astronomy B1
Holburne Museum B3
Holloway C2
Information Ctr B2
James St West B1/B2
Jane Austen Ctr B2
Julian Rd A1
Junction Rd C1
Kingsmead Leisure Complex B2
Kipling Ave C2
Lansdown Cr A1
Lansdown Gr A2
Lansdown Rd A2
Library B2
London Rd A3
London St A2
Lower Bristol Rd B1
Lower Oldfield Park C1
Lyncombe Hill C3
Manvers St B3
Maple Gr C1
Margaret's Hill A2
Marlborough Bldgs A1
Marlborough La B1
Midland Bridge Rd B1
Milk St B2
Milsom St B2
Monmouth St B2
Morford St A2
Museum of Bath at Work A2
Museum of East Asian Art A2
New King St B1
No 1 Royal Cresc A1
Norfolk Bldgs B1
Norfolk Cr B1
North Parade Rd B3
Oldfield Rd C1
Paragon A2
Pines Way B1
Podium Shopping Ctr B2
Police Station B3
Portland Pl A2
Post Office A1/A3/B2/C1/C2
Postal Museum B2
Powlett Rd A3
Prior Park Rd C3
Pulteney Bridge ✦ B2
Pulteney Gdns B3
Pulteney Rd B3/C3
Queen Sq B2
Raby Pl B3
Recreation Ground B3
Rivers St A2
Rockliffe Ave A3
Rockliffe Rd A3
Roman Baths & Pump Room B2
Rossiter Rd C3
Royal Ave A1
Royal Cr A1
Royal High School, The A2
Royal Victoria Park A1
St James Sq A1
St John's Rd A3
Sally Lunn's House ✦ B2
Shakespeare Ave C2
South Pde B3
SouthGate Sh Ctr C2
Sports & Leisure Ctr B3
Spring Gdns C3
Stall St B2
Stanier Rd B1
Superstore B1
Sydney Gdns A3
Sydney Pl B3
Sydney Rd B3
Theatre Royal B2
Thermae Bath Spa ✦ B2
Thomas St A3
Tyning, The C3
Union St B2
Upper Bristol Rd B1
Upper Oldfield Park C1
Victoria Art Gallery B2
Victoria Bridge Rd B1
Walcot St B2
Wells Rd C1
Westgate Buildings B2
Westgate St B2
Weston Rd A1
Widcombe Hill C3

Berwick-upon-Tweed 332

Avenue, The B3
Bank Hill B2
Barracks A3
Bell Tower ✦ A3
Bell Tower Pk A2
Berwick Br B2
Berwick Infirmary A3
Berwick-upon-Tweed ≥ A2
Billendean Rd C3
Blakewell Gdns B2
Blakewell St B2
Brass Bastion ✦ A3
Bridge St B3
Brucegate St A2
Castle (Remains of) A2
Castle Terr A2
Castlegate A2
Chapel St A3
Church Rd C2
Church St B3
Court B3
Coxon's La A3
Cumberland Bastion ✦ A3
Dean Dr C2
Dock Rd C2/C3
Elizabethan Walls A2/B3
Fire Station B1
Flagstaff Park B3
Football Ground C3
Foul Ford B3
Golden Sq B2
Golf Course A3
Granary, The ✦ B3
Greenwood C1
Gunpowder Magazine ✦ B3
Hide Hill B3
High Greens A2
Holy Trinity A3
Information Ctr A2
Kiln Hill B2
King's Mount ✦ B3
Ladywell Rd C2
Library A3
Lifeboat Station C3
Lord's Mount ✦ A3
Lovaine Terr A2
Low Greens A3
Main Guard B3
Main St B2/C2
Maltings Art Ctr, The B3
Marygate B3
Meg's Mount ✦ A2
Middle St C3
Mill St C2
Mount Rd C2
Museum B3
Ness St B3
North Rd A2
Northumberland Ave A2
Northumberland Rd C2
Ord Dr B1
Osborne Cr B2
Osborne Rd B1
Palace Gr B3
Palace St B3
Palace St East B3
Parade, The A3
Pier Rd B3
Playing Field C1
Police Station B3
Post Office B2/B3
Prince Edward Rd B2
Prior Rd C2
Quay Walls B3
Railway St A2
Ravensdowne B3
Records Office A3
Riverdene B1
Riverside Rd B2
Royal Border Br A2
Royal Tweed Br B2
Russian Gun ✦ B3
Scots Gate ✦ A2
Scott's Pl A2
Shielfield Park (Berwick Rangers FC) C1
Shielfield Terr C2
Silver St B3
Spittal Quay C3
Superstore B1/C1/C2
Tower Gdns A2
Tower Ho Pottery ✦ C2
Tower Rd C2
Town Hall B3
Turret Gdns C2
Tweedbank Retail Pk C2
Tweed Dock B2
Tweed St A2
Tweedside Trading Estate C1
Union Brae B2
Union Park Rd B2
Walkergate A3
Wallace Gr A3
War Memorial A2
War Memorial B2
Warkworth Terr A2
Well Close Sq A2
West End B2
West End Pl B1
West End Rd B1
West St B3
West St C3
Windmill Bastion ✦ B3
Woolmarket B3
Works C3

Birmingham 332

Abbey St A2
Aberdeen St A1
Acorn Gr B2
Adams St A5
Adderley St C5
Albert St B4/B5
Albion St B2
Alcester St C5
Aldgate Gr A3
All Saint's St A2
All Saints Rd A2
Allcock St C5
Allesley St A4
Allison St C4
Alma Cr B6
Alston Rd C1

Arcadian Centre C4
Arthur St C6
Assay Office B3
Aston Expressway A5
Aston Science Park B5
Aston St B4
Aston University B4/B5
Avenue Rd A5
Bacchus Rd A1
Bagot St B4
Banbury St B5
Barford Rd B1
Barford St C4
Barn St C5
Barnwell Rd C6
Barr St A3
Barrack St B5
Bartholomew St C4
Barwick St B4
Bath Row C3
Beaufort Rd C1
Belmont Row B5
Benson Rd A1
Berkley St C3
Bexhill Gr C3
Birchall St C5
Birmingham City FC C6
Birmingham City Hospital (A&E) A1
Birmingham Wheels Adventure Pk ✦ B6
Bishopsgate St C3
Blews St A4
Bloomsbury St A6
Blucher St C3
Bordesley St C4
Bowyer St C5
Bradburne Way A5
Bradford St C5
Branston St A3
Brearley St A4
Brewery St A4
Bridge St A3
Bridge St C3
Bridge St West A4
Brindley Dr B3
Broad St C3
Broad St Cineworld C2
Broadway Plaza ✦ C2
Bromley St C5
Bromsgrove St C4
Brookfield Rd A2
Browning St C2
Bryant St A1
BT Tower ✦ B3
Buckingham St A3
Bull St B4
Bull St B4
Bullring C4
Cambridge St C3
Camden Dr B3
Camden St B2
Cannon St C4
Cardigan St B5
Carlisle St A1
Carlyle Rd C1
Caroline St B3
Carver St B2
Cato St A6
Cattell Rd C6
Cattells Gr A6
Cawdor Cr C1
Cecil St B4
Cemetery A2/B2
Cemetery La A2
Centre Link Industrial Estate A6
Charlotte St B3
Cheapside C4
Chester St A5
Children's Hospital (A&E) B4
Church St B4
Claremont Rd A2
Clarendon Rd C1
Clark St C1
Clement St B3
Clissold St B2
Cliveland St B4
Coach Station C5
College St B2
Colmore Circus B4
Colmore Row B4
Commercial St C3
Constitution Hill B3
Convention Ctr, The C3
Cope St B2
Coplow St B1
Corporation St C4
Corporation St B4
Council House B3
County Court B4
Coveley Gr A2
Coventry Rd C6
Coventry St C5
Cox St B3
Crabtree Rd A2
Cregoe St C3
Crescent Ave A2
Crescent Theatre C3
Crescent, The A2
Cromwell St A6
Cromwell St B3
Cube, The C3
Curzon St B5
Custard Factory ✦ C5
Cuthbert Rd B1
Dale End B4
Dart St C6
Dartmouth Circus A4
Dartmouth Middleway A5
Dental Hospital B4
Deritend C5
Devon St A6
Devonshire St A1
Digbeth Civic Hall C5
Digbeth High St C4
Dolman St B6
Dover St A1
Duchess Rd C2
Duddeston B6
Duddeston Manor Rd B5
Duddeston Mill Rd B6
Duddeston Mill Trading Estate B6
Dudley Rd B1
Edmund St B3
Edward St B3
Elkington St A4
Ellen St B2
Ellis St C3
Erskine St B6
Essex St C4
Eyre St B2
Farm Croft A3
Farm St A3
Fazeley St B4/C5
Felstead Way B5
Finstall Cl B5
Five Ways C2
Fiveway Shopping Ctr C2
Fleet St B3
Floodgate St C5
Ford St A2
Fore St C4
Forster St B5
Francis Rd C2
Francis St B5
Frankfort St A4
Frederick St B3
Freeth St C1
Freightliner Terminal B6
Garrison La C6
Garrison St B6
Gas St C3
Geach St A4
George St B3
George St West B2
Gibb St C5
Gilby Rd C2
Gillott Rd B1
Glover St C5
Goode Ave A2
Goodrick Way A6
Gordon St B6
Graham St B3
Grand Central C4
Granville St C3
Gray St C6
Great Barr St C5
Great Charles St B3
Great Francis St B6
Great Hampton Row A3
Great Hampton St A3
Great King St A3
Great Lister St A5
Great Tindal St C2
Green La C6
Green St C5
Greenway St C6
Grosvenor St West C2
Guest Gr A3
Guild Cl C2
Guildford Dr A4
Guthrie Cl A3
Hagley Rd C1
Hall St B3
Hampton St A3
Handsworth New Rd A1
Hanley St B4
Harford St A3
Harmer Rd A2
Harold Rd C1
Hatchett St A4
Heath Mill La C5
Heath St B1
Heath St South B1
Heaton St A2
Heneage St B5
Henrietta St B4
Herbert Rd C6
High St C4
High St C5
Hilden Rd B5
Hill St C3/C4
Hindlow Cl B6
Hingeston St B2
Hippodrome Theatre C4
HM Prison A1
Hockley Circus A2
Hockley Hill A3
Hockley St A3
Holliday St C3
Holloway Circus C4
Holloway Head C3
Holt St B5
Hooper St B1
Horse Fair C4
Hospital St A4
Howard St B3
Howe St B5
Hubert St A5
Hunters Rd A2
Hunters Vale A3
Huntly Rd C2
Hurst St C4
Icknield Port Rd B1
Icknield Sq B2
Icknield St A2/B2
IKON C3
Information Ctr C4
Inge St C4
Irving St C3
Ivy La C5
James Watt Queensway B4
Jennens Rd B5
Jewellery Quarter A3
Jewellery Quarter Museum B3
John Bright St C4
Keeley St C6
Kellett Rd B5
Kent St C4
Kenyon St B3
Key Hill A3
Kilby Ave C2
King Edwards Rd B2
King Edwards Rd C3
Kingston Rd C6
Kirby Rd A1
Ladywood Arts & Leisure Ctr B1
Ladywood Middleway C2/C3
Ladywood Rd C1
Lancaster St B4
Landor St B6
Law Courts B4
Lawford Cl B5
Lawley Middleway B5
Ledbury Cl C2
Ledsam St B2
Lees St A1
Legge La B3
Lennox St A3
Library A6/C3
Library Walk B2
Lighthorne Ave B2
Link Rd B1
Lionel St B3
Lister St B5
Little Ann St C5
Little Hall Rd A6
Liverpool St C5
Livery St B3/B4
Lodge Rd A1
Lord St A5
Love La A5
Loveday St B4
Lower Dartmouth St C6
Lower Loveday St B4
Lower Tower St A4
Lower Trinity St C5
Ludgate Hill B3
Mailbox Centre & BBC C3
Margaret St B3
Markby Rd A1
Marroway St B1
Maxstoke St C6
Melvina Rd A6
Meriden St C4
Metropolitan (RC) + B4
Midland St B6
Milk St C5
Mill St A5
Millennium Point B5
Miller St A4
Milton St A4
Moat La C4
Montague Rd C1
Montague St C5
Monument Rd C1
Moor St Queensway C4
Moor Street C4
Moorsom St A4
Morville St C2
Mosborough Cr A3
Moseley St C4
Mott St B3
Mus & Art Gallery B3
Musgrave Rd A1
National Indoor Arena C2
National Sea Life Centre C3
Navigation St C3
Nechell's Park Rd A6
Nechells Parkway B5
Nechells Pl A6
New Alexandra C3
New Bartholomew St C4
New Canal St C5
New John St West A3
New Spring St B2
New St C4
New Street C4
New Summer St A4
New Town Row A4
Newhall Hill B3
Newhall St B3
Newton St B4
Newtown A4
Noel Rd C1
Norman St A1
Northbrook St B1
Northwood St B3
Norton St A2
Odeon C2
Old Crown House C5
Old Rep Theatre, The C4
Old Snow Hill B4
Oliver Rd C1
Oliver St A5
Osler St C1
Oxford St C5
Palmer St C5
Paradise Circus C3
Paradise St C3
Park Rd A2
Park St C4
Pavilions C4
Paxton Rd A2
Peel St A1
Penn St B5
Pershore St C4
Phillips St A4
Pickford St C5
Pinfold St C4
Pitsford St A2
Plough & Harrow Rd C1
Police Station A4/B1/B4/C2/C4
Pope St B2
Portland Rd C1
Post Office A3/A5/B1/B3/B4/B5/C2/C3/C5
Preston Rd A1
Price St B4
Princip St B4
Printing House St B4
Priory Queensway B4
Pritchett St A4
Proctor St A5
Queensway B3
Radnor St A2
Rea St C4
Regent Pl B3
Register Office C3
Repertory Theatre C3
Reservoir Rd C1
Richard St A5
River St C5
Rocky La A5/A6
Rodney Cl C2
Roseberry St B2
Rotton Park St B1
Rupert St A5
Ruston St C2
Ryland St C2
St Andrew's Ind Est C6
St Andrew's Rd C6
St Andrew's St C6
St Bolton St C6
St Chads Queensway B4
St Clements Rd A6
St George's St A3
St James Pl B5
St Marks Cr B2
St Martin's C4
St Paul's B3
St Paul's B3
St Paul's Sq B3
St Philip's + B4
St Stephen's St A4
St Thomas' Peace Garden C3
St Vincent St C2
Saltley Rd A6
Sand Pits Pde B3
Severn St C3
Shadwell St B4
Sheepcote St C2
Shefford Rd A4
Sherborne St C2
Shylton's Croft C2
Skipton Rd C2
Smallbrook Queensway C4
Smith St A3
Snow Hill B4
Snow Hill Queensway B4
Soho, Benson Rd A1
South Rd A2
Spencer St B3
Spring Hill B2
Staniforth St B4
Station St C4
Steelhouse La B4
Stephenson St C4
Steward St B2
Stirling Rd C1
Stour St B2
Suffolk St C3
Summer Hill Rd B2
Summer Hill St B2
Summer Hill Terr B2
Summer La A4
Summer Row B3
Summerfield Cr B1
Summerfield Park B1
Sutton St C3
Swallow St C3
Sydney Rd C6
Symphony Hall C3
Talbot St A1
Temple Row C4
Temple St C4
Templefield St C6
Tenby St B3
Tenby St North B2
Tennant St C2/C3
Thimble Mill La A6
Thinktank (Science & Discovery) B5
Thomas St A4
Thorpe St C4
Tilton Rd C6
Tower St A4
Town Hall C3
Trent St C5
Turner's Buildings A1
Unett St A3
Union Terr B5
Upper Trinity St C5
Uxbridge St A3
Vauxhall Gr B5
Vauxhall Rd B5
Vernon Rd C1
Vesey St B4
Viaduct St B5
Victoria Sq C3
Villa St A3
Vittoria St B3
Vyse St B3
Walter St A6
Wardlow Rd A5
Warstone La B2
Washington St C3
Water St B3
Waterworks Rd C1
Watery La C5
Well St A3
Western Rd B1
Wharf St A2
Wheeler St A3
Whitehouse St A5
Whitmore St A2
Whittall St B4
Wholesale Market C4
Wiggin St B1
Willes Rd A1
Windsor Ind Est A5
Windsor St A5
Windsor St B5
Winson Green Rd A1
Witton St C6
Wolseley St C6
Woodcock St B5

Blackpool 332

Abingdon St A1
Addison Cr A3
Adelaide St B1
Albert Rd B2
Alfred St B2
Ascot Rd A3
Ashton Rd C2
Auburn Gr C3
Bank Hey St B1
Banks St A1
Beech Ave A3
Bela Gr C2
Belmont Ave B2
Birley St A1
Blackpool & Fleetwood Tram B1
Blackpool & the Fylde College B2
Blackpool FC C2
Blackpool North A2
Blackpool Tower ✦ B1
Blundell St C1
Bonny St B1
Breck Rd B3
Bryan Rd A3
Buchanan St A2
Bus Station A2
Cambridge Rd A3
Caunce St A2/A3
Central Dr B1/C2
Central Pier ✦ C1
Central Pier C1
Central Pier Theatre C1
Chapel St C1
Charles St A2
Charnley Rd B2
Church St A1/A2
Clinton Ave B2
Coach Station A2/C1
Cocker St A1
Cocker St A1
Coleridge Rd A3
Collingwood Ave A3
Comedy Carpet ✦ B1
Condor Gr C3
Cookson St A2
Coronation St B1
Corporation St A1
Courts B1
Cumberland Ave B3
Cunliffe Rd C3
Dale St C1
Devonshire Rd A3
Devonshire Sq A3
Dickson Rd A1
Elizabeth St A2
Ferguson Rd C3
Forest Gate B3
Foxhall Rd C1
Foxhall Sq C1
Freckleton St C2
George St A2
Gloucester Ave B3
Golden Mile, The C1
Gorse Rd B3
Gorton St A2
Grand Theatre, The B1
Granville Rd A2
Grasmere Rd C2
Grosvenor St A2
Grundy Art Gallery A1
Harvey Rd B3
Hornby Rd B2
Houndshill Sh Ctr B1
Hull Rd B1
Ibbison Ct C2
Information Ctr A1
Kent Rd C2
Keswick Rd C2
King St A2
Knox Gr C3
Laycock Gate A3
Layton Rd A3
Leamington Rd B2
Leeds Rd B3
Leicester Rd B2
Levens Gr C2
Library A1
Lifeboat Station B1
Lincoln Rd B2
Liverpool Rd B3
Livingstone Rd B2
London Rd A3
Lune Gr C2
Lytham Rd C1
Madame Tussaud's Blackpool B1
Manchester Sq C1
Manor Rd B3
Maple Ave B3
Market St A1
Marlboro Rd B3
Mere Rd B3
Milbourne St A2
Newcastle Ave B3
Newton Dr A3
North Pier ✦ A1
North Pier A1
North Pier Theatre A1
Odeon C2
Olive Gr B3
Palatine Rd B2
Park Rd B2/C3
Peter St A2
Police Station B1
Post Office A1/A3/B1/B2/B3
Princess Pde A1
Princess St C1/C2
Promenade A1/C1
Queen St A1
Queen Victoria Rd C2
Raikes Parade B2
Reads Ave B2
Regent Rd B2
Register Office B2
Ribble Rd B2
Rigby Rd C1/C2
Ripon Rd B3
St Albans Rd B3
St Ives Ave C3
St John's Square A1
St Vincent Ave C3
Salisbury Rd B3
Salthouse Ave C2
Salvation Army Centre A2
Sands Way C2
Sealife Centre B1
Seasiders Way C1
Selbourne Rd A2
Sharrow Gr C3
Somerset Ave C3
South King St B2
Springfield Rd A1
Sutton Pl B2
Talbot Rd A1/A2
Thornber Gr C2
Topping St A1
Tower B1
Town Hall A1
Tram Depot C1
Tyldesley Rd C1
Vance Rd B1
Victoria St B1
Victory Rd A2
Wayman Rd A3
Westmorland Ave C2/C3
Whitegate Dr B3
Winter Gardens Theatre B1
Woodland Gr B3
Woolman Rd B2

Bournemouth 333

Ascham Rd A3
Avenue Rd B1
Ave Shopping Centre B1
Bath Rd C2
Beach Office C2
Beacon Rd C1
Beechey Rd A3
Bodorgan Rd B1
Bourne Ave B1
Bournemouth A3
Bournemouth & Poole College B3
Bournemouth Balloon ✦ C2
Bournemouth Int Ctr C1
Bournemouth Pier C2
Bournemouth Sta B3
Braidley Rd A1
Cavendish Place A2
Cavendish Rd A2
Central Drive A1
Central Gdns B1
Christchurch Rd B3
Cliff Lift C1/C3
Coach House Pl A3
Coach Station A3
Commercial Rd B1
Cotlands Rd B3
Courts B3
Cranborne Rd C1
Cricket Ground A2
Cumnor Rd B2
Dean Park A2
Dean Park Cr B2
Dean Park Rd A2
Durrant Rd B1
East Overcliff Dr C3
Exeter Cr C1
Exeter La C2
Exeter Rd C1
Gervis Place B1
Gervis Rd B3
Glen Fern Rd B2
Golf Club B1
Grove Rd B3
Hinton Rd C2
Holdenhurst Rd B3
Horseshoe Common B2
Information Ctr B2
Lansdowne B3
Lansdowne Rd A2
Lorne Park Rd B2
Lower Gdns B1/C2
Madeira Rd B2
Methuen Rd A3
Meyrick Park A1
Meyrick Rd B3
Milton Rd A2
Nuffield Health Bournemouth Hospital (private) A2
Oceanarium C2
Odeon Cinema C2
Old Christchurch Rd B2
Ophir Rd A3
Oxford Rd B3
Park Rd A3
Parsonage Rd B2
Pavilion C2
Pier Approach C2
Pier Theatre C2
Police Station A3/B3
Portchester Rd A3
Post Office B1/B3
Priory Rd C1
Quadrant, The B2
Recreation Ground A1
Richmond Gardens Shopping Centre B2
Richmond Hill Rd B1
Russell Cotes Art Gallery & Museum C2
Russell Cotes Rd C2
St Anthony's Rd A1
St Michael's Rd C1
St Paul's A3
St Paul's La B3
St Paul's Rd A3
St Peter's B2
St Peter's B2
St Peter's Rd B2
St Stephen's Rd B1/B2
St Swithun's B3
St Swithun's Rd B3
St Swithun's Rd South B3
St Valerie Rd A2
St Winifred's Rd A2
Square, The B1
Stafford Rd B3
Terrace Rd B1
Town Hall B1
Tregonwell Rd C1
Triangle, The B1
Trinity Rd B2
Undercliff Drive C3
Upper Hinton Rd B2
Upper Terr Rd C1
Wellington Rd A2/A3
Wessex Way A3/B1/B2
West Cliff Promenade C1
West Hill Rd C1
West Undercliff Promenade C1
Westover Rd B2
Wimborne Rd A2
Wootton Mount B2
Wychwood Dr A1
Yelverton Rd B2
York Rd B3
Zig-Zag Walks C1/C3

Bradford 333

Alhambra B2
Back Ashgrove B1
Barkerend Rd A3
Barnard Rd C3
Barry St B2
Bolling Rd C3
Bolton Rd A3
Bowland St A1
Bradford 1 B2
Bradford College B1
Bradford Forster Square A2
Bradford Interchange B3
Bradford Playhouse B3
Bridge St B2
Britannia St B2
Broadway Bradford, The B2
Burnett St B3
Bus Station B2
Butler St West A3
Caledonia St C2
Canal Rd A2
Carlton St B1
Cathedral + A3
Centenary Sq B2
Chapel St B3
Cheapside A2
Church Bank B3
Cineworld B3
City Hall B2
City Rd A1
Claremont B1
Colour Museum B1
Croft St B2
Crown Court B3
Darfield St A1
Darley St A2
Drewton Rd A1
Drummond Trading Estate A1
Dryden St B3
Dyson St A1
Easby Rd C1
East Parade B3
Eldon Pl A1
Filey St B3
Forster Square Retail Park A2
Gallery II B1
Garnett St B3
Godwin St B2
Gracechurch St A1
Grattan Rd B1
Great Horton Rd B1/B2
Grove Terr B1
Hall Ings B2
Hall La C3
Hallfield Rd A1
Hammstrasse A2
Harris St B3
Holdsworth St A2
Ice Rink ✦ B2
Impressions B2
Information Ctr B2
Inland Revenue A2
Ivegate B2
Jacob's Well Municipal Offices B2
James St A2
John St A2
Kirkgate B2
Kirkgate Centre B2
Laisteridge La C1
Leeds Rd B3
Leisure Exchange, The B3
Library B1/B2
Listerhills Rd B1
Little Horton Gn C1
Little Horton La C1
Longside La B1
Lower Kirkgate B2
Lumb La A1
Magistrates Court B2
Manchester Rd C2
Manningham La A1
Manor Row A2
Market C3
Market St B2
Melbourne Place C1
Midland Rd A2
Mill La C2
Morley St B1
National Media B2
Nelson St B2/C2
Nesfield St A2
New Otley Rd A3
Norcroft St B1
North Parade A2
North St A3
North Wing A3
Oastler Shopping Ctr A2
Otley Rd A3
Park Ave C1
Park La C1
Park Rd C2
Parma St C2
Peace Museum B2
Peckover St B3
Piccadilly A2
Police Station C2
Post Office A2/B1/B2/C3
Princes Way B2
Prospect St C3
Radwell Drive C2
Rawson Rd A1
Rebecca St A1
Richmond Rd B1
Russell St C1
St George's Hall B2
St Lukes Hospital C1
St Mary's A3
Shipley Airedale Rd A3/B3
Shopmobility A2
Simes St A1
Smith St B1
Spring Mill St C2
Stott Hill A3
Sunbridge Rd A1/B1/B2
Theatre in the Mill B1
Thornton Rd A1/B1
Trafalgar St A2
Trinity Rd C1
Tumbling Hill St B1
Tyrrel St B2
Univ of Bradford B1/C1
Usher St C3
Valley Rd A2
Vicar La B3
Wakefield Rd C3
Wapping Rd A3
Well St B3
Westgate A1
White Abbey Rd A1
Wigan Rd A1
Wilton St B1
Wood St A1
Wool Exchange B2
Worthington St A1

Brighton 333

Addison Rd A1
Albert Rd B2
Albion Hill B3
Albion St B3
Ann St A3
Baker St A3
Black Lion St C2
Brighton A2
Brighton Centre C2
Brighton Fishing Museum C2
Brighton Pier (Palace Pier) ✦ C3
Brighton Wheel ✦ C3
Broad St C3
Buckingham Pl A2
Buckingham Rd B2
Cannon Pl C1
Carlton Hill B3
Chatham Pl A1
Cheapside A3
Church St B2
Churchill Square Shopping Centre B2
Clifton Hill B1
Clifton Pl B1
Clifton Rd B1
Clifton St A2
Clifton Terr B1
Clock Tower B2
Clyde Rd A3
Coach Park C3
Coach Station C3
Compton Ave A2
Davigdor Rd A1
Denmark Terr B1
Ditchling Rd A3
Dome B2
Duke St B2
Duke's La C2
Dyke Rd A1/B2
East St C2
Edward St B3
Elmore Rd B3
Fleet St A2
Frederick St B2
Gardner St B2
Gloucester Pl B3
Gloucester Rd B2
Goldsmid Rd A1
Grand Junction Rd C2
Grand Pde B3
Grove Hill B3
Guildford St A2
Hampton Pl B1
Hanover Terr A3
High St C3
Highdown Rd A1
i360 Tower ✦ C1
Information Ctr C2
John St B3
Kemp St B2
Kensington Pl B2
Kings Rd C1
Lanes, The C2
Law Courts B3
Lewes Rd A3
Library B2
London Rd A3
Madeira Dr C3
Marine Pde C3
Middle St C2
Montpelier Pl B1
Montpelier Rd B1
Montpelier St B1
Mus & Art Gallery B3
New England Rd A2
New England St A2
New Rd B2
Nizells Ave A1
Norfolk Rd B1
Norfolk Terr B1
North Rd B2
North St B2
Odeon C2
Old Shoreham Rd A1
Old Steine C3
Osmond Rd A1
Over St B2
Oxford St A3
Park Crescent Terr A3
Phoenix Brighton B3
Phoenix Rise A3
Police Station B3
Post Office A1/A3/B2/C3
Preston Rd A2
Preston St B1
Prestonville Rd A1
Queen's Rd B2
Queen's Sq B2
Regency Sq C1
Regent St B2
Richmond Pl B3
Richmond St B3
Richmond Terr A3
Rose Hill Terr A3
Royal Pavilion B2
St Bartholomew's A3
St James's St C3
St Nicholas Rd B2
St Nicholas' B2
St Peter's A3
Sea Life Centre C3
Shaftesbury Rd A3
Ship St C2
Sillwood Rd B1
Sillwood St B1
Southover St A3
Spring Gdns B2
Stanford Rd A1
Stanley Rd A3
Surrey St B2
Sussex St B3
Swimming Pool B3
Sydney St B3
Temple Gdns B1
Terminus Rd A2
Theatre Royal B2
Tidy St B2
Town Hall C2
Toy & Model Mus A2
Trafalgar St B2
Union Rd A3
University of Brighton B3
Upper Lewes Rd A3
Upper North St B1
Viaduct Rd A3
Victoria Gdns B3
Victoria Rd B1
Volk's Electric Railway C3
West Pier (derelict) C1
West St C2
Western Rd B1
Whitecross St B2
York Ave B1
York Pl B3
York Rd B1

Bristol 333

Acramans Rd C4
Albert Rd C6
Alfred Hill A4
All Saint's St A4
All Saints' B4
Allington Rd C3
Alpha Rd C4
Ambra Vale B1
Ambra Vale East B2
Ambrose Rd B2
Amphitheatre & Waterfront Sq ✦ C4
Anchor Rd B3
Anvil St B6
Arcade, The A5
Architecture Centre, The ✦ B4
Argyle Pl B2
Arlington Villas A2
Arnolfini Arts Centre, The ✦ B4
Art Gallery A3
Ashton Gate Rd C2
Ashton Rd C1
At-Bristol ✦ B3
Avon Bridge C1
Avon Cr C1
Avon St B6
Baldwin St B4
Baltic Wharf C2
Baltic Wharf Leisure Ctr & Caravan Pk ✦ C2
Baltic Wharf Marina C2
Barossa Pl C4
Barton Manor B6
Barton Rd B6
Barton Vale B6
Bath Rd C6
Bathurst Basin C4
Bathurst Parade C4
Beauley Rd C3
Bedminster Bridge C5
Bedminster Parade C4
Bellevue B2
Bellevue Cr B2
Bellevue Rd C6
Berkeley Pl A2
Berkeley Sq A3
Birch Rd C2
Blackfriars A4
Bond St A5
Braggs La A6
Brandon Hill B3
Brandon Steep B3
Bristol Bridge B5
Bristol Cath (CE) + B3

Court B2
Court St B2
Crosby St B2
Crown St C2
Currock Rd C2
Dacre Rd A1
Dale St C1
Denton St C1
Devonshire Walk A1
Duke's Rd A2
East Dale St C1
East Norfolk St C1
Eden Bridge A2
Edward St B3
Elm St B1
English St B2
Fire Station A2
Fisher St A1
Flower St B3
Freer St C1
Fusehill St B3
Georgian Way A2
Gloucester Rd C3
Golf Course A2
Graham St C1
Grey St B3
Guildhall Museum 🏛 A2
Halfey's La B3
Hardwicke Circus A2
Hart St B3
Hewson St C2
Howard Pl A3
Howe St B3
Information Ctr ℹ A2
James St B2
Junction St B1
King St B2
Lancaster St B2
Lanes Shopping Centre, The B2
Laser Quest ✦ B2
Library A2/B1
Lime St B1
Lindisfarne St C3
Linton St B3
Lismore Pl A3
Lismore St B3
London Rd C3
Lonsdale Rd B2
Lord St C3
Lorne Cres B1
Lorne St B1
Lowther St B2
Madford Retail Park B1
Magistrates' Ct A2
Market Hall A2
Mary St B2
Memorial Bridge A3
Metcalfe St C1
Milbourne St B1
Myddleton St B3
Nelson St C1
Norfolk St C1
Old Fire Sta, The 🎭 A2
Old Town Hall A2
Oswald St C3
Peter St A2
Petteril St B3
Pools Swimming & Health Ctr, The B2
Portland Pl B2
Portland Sq B2
Post Office 📮 A2/B2/B3/C1/C3
Princess St C2
Pugin St B1
Red Bank Terr C2
Regent St C3
Richardson St C1
Rickerby Park A3
Rickergate A2
River St B3
Rome St C2
Rydal St B3
Shopmobility A2
St Cuthbert's ⛪ B2
St Cuthbert's La B2
St James' Park C1
St James' Rd C1
St Nicholas Gate Retail Park C3
St Nicholas St C3
Sands Centre, The A2
Scotch St A2
Shaddongate B1
Sheffield St B1
South Henry St B3
South John St C2
South St B3
Spencer St B2
Strand Rd A2
Superstore B1
Sybil St B3
Tait St B2
Thomas St B1
Thomson St C3
Trafalgar St C1
Trinity Leisure Centre A2
Tullie Ho Museum 🏛 A1
Tyne St C3
University of Cumbria B3
Viaduct Estate Rd B1
Victoria Pl A2
Victoria Viaduct B2
Vue 🎦 B2
Warwick Rd B2
Warwick Sq B3
Water St B2
West Walls B1
Westmorland St C1

Chelmsford 334

Anchor St C1
Anglia Ruskin Univ A2
Arbour La A3
Baddow Rd B2/C3
Baker St C1
Barrack Sq B2
Bellmead B2
Bishop Hall La A2
Bishop Rd A2
Bond St B2
Boswells Dr B3
Bouverie Rd C2
Bradford St C1
Braemar Ave C1
Brook St A2
Broomfield Rd A1
Burns Cres C2
Bus Station B1
Can Bridge Way B2
Cedar Ave A1
Cedar Ave West A1
Cemetery A1
Cemetery A2
Cemetery C1
Central Park B1
Chelmsford ✝ B2
Chelmsford ⇌ A1
Chichester Dr A3
Chinery Cl A3
Civic Centre A1
Civic Theatre 🎭 B1
College C1
Cottage Pl A2
County Cricket Gd B2
County Hall B2
Coval Ave B1
Coval La B1
Coval Wells B1
Crown Court B2
Duke St B2
Elm Rd C1
Elms Dr A1
Essex Record Office, The B3
Fairfield Rd B1
Falcons Mead B1
George St C2
Glebe Rd A1
Godfrey's Mews C2
Goldlay Ave C3
Goldlay Rd C2
Grove Rd C2
Hall St C2
Hamlet Rd C2
Hart St C1
Henry Rd A2
High Bridge Rd B2
High Chelmer Sh Ctr B2
High St B2
Hill Cres B3
Hill Rd B3
Hill Rd Sth B3
Hillview Rd A3
HM Prison A3
Hoffmans Way A2
Hospital Ⓗ B2
Lady La C2
Langdale Gdns C3
Legg St B2
Library B2
Lionfield Terr A3
Lower Anchor St C1
Lynmouth Ave C2
Lynmouth Gdns C3
Magistrates Court B2
Maltese Rd A1
Manor Rd C2
Marconi Rd A2
Market B2
Market Rd B2
Marlborough Rd C1
Meadows Sh Ctr, The B2
Meadowside A3
Mews Ct C2
Mildmay Rd C2
Moulsham Dr C2
Moulsham Mill ✦ C3
Moulsham St C1/C2
Navigation Rd B3
New London Rd B2/C1
New St A2/B2
New Writtle St C1
Nursery Rd C2
Orchard St C2
Odeon 🎦 B2
Park Rd B1
Parker Rd C2
Parklands Dr A3
Parkway A1/B1/B2
Police Station 🚓 A2
Post Office 📮 B2/C2
Primrose Hill A1
Prykes Dr B1
Queen St C1
Queen's Rd B3
Railway St A1
Rainsford Rd A1
Ransomes Way A2
Rectory La A2
Regina Rd A2
Riverside Ice & Leisure Centre B2
Riverside Retail Park A3
Rosebery Rd C2
Rothesay Ave C1
St John's Rd C2
Sandringham Pl B3
Seymour St B1
Shrublands Cl B3
Southborough Rd C1
Springfield Basin B3
Springfield Rd A3/B2/B3
Stapleford Cl C1
Superstore B2
Swiss Ave A1
Telford Pl A3
Tindal St B2
Townfield St A1
Trinity Rd B3
University B1
Upper Bridge Rd C1
Upper Roman Rd C2
Van Dieman's Rd C3
Viaduct Rd B1
Vicarage Rd C1
Victoria Rd A2
Victoria Rd South B2
Vincents Rd C2
Waterloo La B2
Weight Rd B3
Westfield Ave A1
Wharf Rd B3
Writtle Rd C1
YMCA A2
York Rd C1

Cheltenham 334

Albert Rd A3
Albion St B3
All Saints Rd B3
Ambrose St B2
Andover Rd C1
Art Gallery & Mus 🏛 B2
Axiom Centre 🏛 B3
Back Montpellier Terr C2
Bandstand ✦ C2
Bath Pde B2
Bath Rd C2
Bays Hill Rd C1
Beechwood Sh Ctr B3
Bennington St B2
Berkeley St B3
Brewery, The A2
Brunswick St South A2
Bus Station B2
CAB B2
Carlton St B3
Central Cross Road A3
Cheltenham College C2
Cheltenham FC A3
Cheltenham General (A&E) Ⓗ C3
Christchurch Rd B1
Cineworld 🎦 A2
Clarence Rd A2
Clarence Sq A2
Clarence St B2
Cleeveland St A1
Coach Park A2
College Baths Road C3
College Rd C2
Colletts Dr A1
Corpus St C3
Devonshire St A2
Douro Rd B1
Duke St B3
Dunalley Pde A2
Dunalley St A2
Everyman 🎭 B2
Evesham Rd A3
Fairview Rd B3
Fairview St B3
Fire Station C3
Folly La A2
Gloucester Rd A1
Grosvenor St B3
Grove St A1
Gustav Holst 🏛 A3
Hanover St A2
Hatherley St C1
Henrietta St A2
Hewlett Rd B3
High St B2/B3
Hudson St A2
Imperial Gdns C2
Imperial La B2
Imperial Sq C2
Information Ctr ℹ B2
Keynsham Rd C3
King St A2
Knapp Rd B2
Ladies College ⌂ B2
Lansdown Cr C1
Lansdown Rd C1
Leighton Rd B3
Library B2
London Rd C3
Lypiatt Rd C1
Malvern Rd B1
Manser St A2
Market St A1
Marle Hill Pde A2
Marle Hill Rd A2
Millbrook St A1
Milsom St A2
Montpellier Gdns C2
Montpellier Gr C2
Montpellier Pde C2
Montpellier Spa Rd C2
Montpellier St C1
Montpellier Terr C2
Montpellier Walk C2
New St B2
North Pl B2
Old Bath Rd C3
Oriel Rd B2
Overton Park Rd B1
Overton Rd B1
Oxford St C3
Parabola Rd B1
Park Pl C1
Park St A1
Pittville Circus A3
Pittville Cr A3
Pittville Lawn A3
Pittville Park A2
Playhouse 🎭 B2
Police Station 🚓 B1/C1
Portland St B3
Post Office 📮 B2/C2
Prestbury Rd A3
Prince's Rd C1
Priory St B3
Promenade B2
Queen St A1
Recreation Ground A2
Regent Arcade B2
Regent St B2
Rodney Rd B2
Royal Cr B2
Royal Wells Rd B2
St George's Pl B2
St Georges Rd B1
St Gregory's ⛪ B2
St James St B3
St John's Ave B3
St Luke's Rd C2
St Margarets Rd A2
St Mary's ⛪ B2
St Matthew's ⛪ B2
St Paul's La A2
St Paul's Rd A2
St Paul's St A2
St Stephen's Rd C1
Sandford Lido C3
Sandford Mill Road C3
Sandford Park C3
Sandford Rd C2
Selkirk St A3
Sherborne Pl B3
Sherborne St B3
Suffolk Pde C2
Suffolk Rd C1
Suffolk Sq C1
Sun St A1
Swindon Rd B2
Sydenham Villas Rd C3
Tewkesbury Rd A1
The Courtyard B1
Thirlstaine Rd C2
Tivoli Rd C1
Tivoli St C1
Town Hall & Theatre 🎭 B2
Townsend St A1
Trafalgar St C2
Union St B3
Univ of Gloucestershire (Francis Cl Hall) A2
Univ of Gloucestershire (Hardwick) A1
Victoria Pl B3
Victoria St A2
Vittoria Walk C2
Wel Pl B2
Wellesley Rd A2
Wellington Rd A3
Wellington Sq A3
Wellington St B2
West Drive A3
Western Rd B1
Winchcombe St B3
Winston Churchill Memorial Gardens ✿ A1

Chester 335

Abbey Gateway A2
Appleyards La C3
Bars, The B3
Bedward Row B1
Beeston View C3
Bishop Lloyd's Pal ⌂ B2
Black Diamond St A2
Bottoms La C3
Boughton B3
Bouverie St A1
Bridge St B2
Bridgegate C2
British Heritage Ctr 🏛 B2
Brook St A3
Brown's La C2
Bus Station B2
Cambrian Rd A1
Canal St A2
Carrick Rd C1
Castle 🏰 C2
Castle Dr C2
Cathedral ✝ B2
Catherine St A1
Chester ⇌ A3
Cheyney Rd A1
Chichester St A1
City Rd A3
City Walls B1/B2
City Walls Rd B1
Cornwall St A2
County Hall C2
Cross Hey C3
Cross, The B2
Cuppin St B2
Curzon Park North C1
Curzon Park South C1
Dee Basin A1
Dee La B3
Delamere St A2
Dewa Roman Experience 🏛 B2
Duke St B2
Eastgate B2
Eastgate St B2
Eaton Rd C2
Edinburgh Way C3
Elizabeth Cr B3
Fire Station A2
Foregate St B2
Frodsham St B2
Gamul House B2
Garden La A1
George St A2
Gladstone Ave A1
God's Providence House ⌂ B2
Gorse Stacks A2
Greenway St C2
Grosvenor Bridge C1
Grosvenor Mus 🏛 B2
Grosvenor Park B3
Grosvenor Park Terr C1
Grosvenor Precinct B2
Grosvenor St B2
Groves Rd B3
Groves, The B3
Guildhall Museum 🏛 B1
Handbridge C2
Hartington St C3
Hoole Way A2
Hunter St B2
Information Ctr ℹ B2
King Charles' Tower ✦ A2
King St A2
Leisure Centre A2
Library B2
Lightfoot St A3
Little Roodee C2
Liverpool Rd A2
Love St B3
Lower Bridge St B2
Lower Park Rd B3
Lyon St A2
Magistrates Court B2
Meadows La C3
Meadows, The B3
Military Museum 🏛 C2
Milton St A3
New Crane St B1
Nicholas St B2
Northgate A2
Northgate St A2
Nun's Rd B1
Old Dee Bridge ✦ C2
Overleigh Rd C2
Park St B2
Police Station 🚓 B2
Post Office 📮 A2/A3/B2
Princess St B2
Queen St B2
Queen's Park Rd C3
Queen's Rd A3
Race Course B1
Raymond St A1
River La C2
Roman Amphitheatre & Gardens 🏟 B2
Roodee (Chester Racecourse), The B1
Russell St A3
St Anne St A2
St George's Cr C3
St Martin's Gate A1
St Martin's Way B1
St Mary's Priory ✦ B2
St Oswalds Way A2
Saughall Rd A1
Sealand Rd A1
South View Rd A1
Stanley Palace ⌂ B1
Station Rd A3
Steven St A3
Tower Rd B1
Town Hall B2
Union St B3
Vicar's La B2
Victoria Cr C3
Victoria Rd A2
Walpole St A1
Water Tower St A1
Water Tower, The ✦ B1
Watergate B1
Watergate St B2
Whipcord La A1
White Friars B2
York St B3

Chichester 335

Adelaide Rd A3
Alexandra Rd A3
Arts Centre B2
Ave de Chartres B1/B2
Barlow Rd A1
Basin Rd C2
Beech Ave B1
Bishops Pal Gardens B2
Bishopsgate Walk A3
Bramber Rd C3
Broyle Rd A2
Bus Station B2
Caledonian Rd B3
Cambrai Ave B3
Canal Pl C1
Canal Wharf C2
Canon La B2
Cathedral ✝ B2
Cavendish St A1
Cawley Rd B2
Cedar Dr A1
Chapel St A2
Cherry Orchard Rd C3
Chichester ⇌ B2
Chichester By-Pass C2/C3
Chichester Coll B1
Chichester Cinema 🎦 B3
Chichester Festival 🎭 A2
Chichester Gate L Pk C1
Churchside A2
Cineworld 🎦 C1
City Walls B2
Cleveland Rd B3
College La A2
Cory Cl C2
Council Offices B2
County Hall B2
District 🏛 B2
Duncan Rd A1
Durnford Cl A1
East Pallant B2
East Row B2
East St B2
East Walls B3
Eastland Rd C3
Ettrick Cl B3
Ettrick Rd B3
Exton Rd C3
Fire Station A2
Football Ground A2
Franklin Pl A2
Friary (Rems of) A2
Garland Cl C3
Green La A3
Grove Rd C3
Guilden Rd B3
Guildhall 🏛 A2
Hawthorn Cl A1
Hay Rd C3
Henty Gdns B1
Herald Dr C3
Hornet, The B3
Information Ctr ℹ B2
John's St B2
Joys Croft A3
Jubilee Pk A3
Jubilee Rd A3
Juxon Cl B2
Kent Rd A3
King George Gdns A2
King's Ave C2
Kingsham Ave C3
Kingsham Rd C2
Laburnum Gr B2
Leigh Rd C1
Lennox Rd A3
Lewis Rd A3
Library B2
Lion St B2
Litten Terr A3
Litten, The A3
Little London B2
Lyndhurst Rd B3
Market B3
Market Ave B2
Market Cross B2
Market Rd B3
Melbourne Rd A3
Minerva 🎭 A2
Mount La B1
New Park Rd A3
Newlands La A1
North Pallant B2
North St A2
North Walls A2
Northgate A2
Novium, The B2
Oak Ave A1
Oak Cl A1
Oaklands Park A2
Oaklands Way A2
Orchard Ave A1
Orchard St A1
Ormonde Ave B3
Pallant House 🏛 B2
Parchment St A1
Parklands Rd A1/B1
Peter Weston Pl B3
Police Station 🚓 C2
Post Office 📮 A1/B2/C3
Priory La A2
Priory Park A2
Priory Rd A2
Queen's Ave C1
Riverside A3
Roman Amphitheatre B3
St Cyriacs A2
St Martins' St B2
St Pancras A3
St Paul's Rd A2
St Richard's Hospital (A&E) Ⓗ A3
Shamrock Cl A3
Sherbourne Rd A1
Somerstown A2
South Bank C2
South Downs Planetarium ✦ C2
South Pallant B2
South St B2
Southgate B2
Spitalfield La A3
Stirling Rd B3
Stockbridge Rd C1/C2
Swanfield Dr A3
Terminus Ind Est C1
Tower St A2
Tozer Way A3
Turnbull Rd A3
Upton Rd C1
Velyn Ave B3
Via Ravenna B1
Walnut Ave A1
West St B2
Westgate B1
Westgate Fields B1
Westgate Leisure Ctr B1
Weston Ave C1
Whyke Cl C3
Whyke La B3
Whyke Rd C3
Winden Ave B3

Colchester 335

Abbey Gateway ✝ C2
Albert St A1
Albion Grove C2
Alexandra Rd C1
Artillery St C3
Arts Centre 🏛 B1
Balkerne Hill B1
Barrack St C3
Beaconsfield Rd C1
Beche Rd C3
Bergholt Rd A1
Bourne Rd C3
Brick Kiln Rd A1
Bristol Rd B2
Broadlands Way A3
Brook St B3
Bury Cl B2
Bus Sta B2
Butt Rd C1
Camp Folley North C2
Camp Folley South C2
Campion Rd C2
Cannon St C3
Canterbury Rd C2
Castle 🏰 B2
Castle Park B2
Castle Rd B2
Catchpool Rd A1
Causton Rd B1
Chandlers Row C3
Circular Rd East C2
Circular Rd North C1
Circular Rd West C1
Clarendon Way A1
Claudius Rd C2
Colchester ⇌ A1
Colchester Camp Abbey Field C1
Colchester Institute B1
Colchester Town ⇌ C2
Colne Bank Ave A1
Colne View Retail Park A2
Compton Rd A3
Cowdray Ave A1/A2
Cowdray Centre, The A2
Crouch St B1
Crowhurst Rd B1
Culver Square Sh Ctr B1
Culver St East B2
Culver St West B1
Dilbridge Rd A3
East Hill B2
East St B3
East Stockwell St B1
Eld La B1
Essex Hall Rd A1
Exeter Dr B2
Fairfax Rd C2
Fire Station A2
Firstsite 🏛 B2
Flagstaff Rd C1
George St B2
Gladstone Rd C2
Golden Noble Hill C2
Goring Rd A3
Granville Rd C3
Greenstead Rd B3
Guildford Rd B2
Harsnett Rd C3
Harwich Rd B3
Head St B1
High St B1/B2
High Woods Country Park A2
Hollytrees 🏛 B2
Hythe Hill C3
Information Ctr ℹ B2
Ipswich Rd A3
Jarmin Rd A2
Kendall Rd C2
Kimberley Rd C3
King Stephen Rd C3
Leisure World A2
Library B1
Lincoln Way B2
Lion Walk Sh Ctr B1
Lisle Rd C2
Lucas Rd C2
Magdalen Green C3
Magdalen St C2
Maidenburgh St B2
Maldon Rd C1
Manor Rd B1
Margaret Rd A1
Mason Rd A2
Mercers Way A1
Mercury 🎭 B1
Mersea Rd C2
Meyrick Cr C2
Mile End Rd A1
Military Rd C2
Mill St C2
Minories 🏛 B2
Moorside B3
Morant Rd C3
Napier Rd C2
Natural History 🏛 B2
New Town Rd C2
Norfolk Cr A3
North Hill B1
North Station Rd A1
Northgate St B1
Nunns Rd B1
Odeon 🎦 B1
Old Coach Rd B3
Old Heath Rd C3
Osborne St B2
Petrolea Cl A1
Police Station 🚓 C1
Popes La B1
Port La C3
Post Office 📮 B2/C1
Priory St B2
Queen St B2
Rawstorn Rd B1
Rebon St C3
Recreation Rd C3
Ripple Way A3
Roman Rd B2
Roman Wall B2
Romford Cl A3
Rosebery Ave B2
St Andrews Ave B3
St Andrews Gdns B3
St Botolph St B2
St Botolphs ⛪ B2
St John's Abbey (site of) ✝ C2
St John's St B1
St Johns Walk Sh Ctr B1
St Leonards Rd C3
St Marys Fields B1
St Peter's St B1
St Peters ⛪ B1
Salisbury Ave C1
Serpentine Walk A1
Sheepen Pl B1
Sheepen Rd B1
Sir Isaac's Walk B1
Smythies Ave B2
South St C1
South Way C1
Sports Way A2
Suffolk Cl A3
Town Hall B1
Turner Rise Retail Pk A1
Valentine Dr A3
Victor Rd C3
Wakefield Cl B2
Wellesley Rd C1
Wells Rd B2/B3
West St C1
West Stockwell St B1
Weston Rd C3
Westway A1
Wickham Rd C1
Wimpole Rd C3
Winchester Rd C2
Winnock Rd C2
Wolfe Ave C2
Worcester Rd B2

Coventry 335

Abbots La A1
Albany 🎭 B1
Albany Rd B1
Alma St B3
Art Faculty B3
Asthill Grove C2
Bablake School A1
Barras La A1/B1
Barrs Hill School A1
Belgrade 🎭 B2
Bishop St A2
Bond's Hospital ⌂ B1
Broad Gate B2
Broadway C1
Burges, The B2
Bus Station A3
Butts Radial B1
Canal Basin ✦ A2
Canterbury St A3
Cathedral ✝ B3
Central Six Retail Pk C1
Chester St A1
Cheylesmore Manor House ⌂ B2
Christ Church Spire ✦ B2
City Coll A3
City Walls & Gates ✦ A2
Corporation St B2
Council House B2
Coundon Rd A1
Coventry Station ⇌ C2
Coventry Transport Museum 🏛 A2
Cox St A3
Croft Rd B1
Dalton Rd C1
Deasy Rd C3
Earl St B2
Eaton Rd C2
Fairfax St B2
Foleshill Rd A2
Ford's Hospital ⌂ B2
Fowler Rd A1
Friars Rd C2
Gordon St C1
Gosford St B3
Greyfriars Green ✦ B2
Greyfriars Rd B2
Gulson Rd B3
Hales St A2
Harnall Lane East A3
Harnall Lane West A2
Herbert Art Gallery & Museum 🏛 B3
Hertford St B2
Hewitt Ave A1
High St B2
Hill St B1
Holy Trinity ⛪ B2
Holyhead Rd A1
Howard St A3
Huntingdon Rd C1
Information Ctr ℹ B2
Jordan Well B3
King Henry VIII Sch C1
Lady Godiva Statue ✦ B2
Lamb St A2
Leicester Row A2
Library B2
Little Park St B2
London Rd C3
Lower Ford St B3
Lower Prec Shop Ctr B2
Magistrates & Crown Courts B2
Manor House Drive B2
Manor Rd C2
Market B2
Martyr's Memorial ✦ C2
Meadow St B1
Meriden St A1
Michaelmas Rd C2
Middleborough Rd A1
Mile La C3
Millennium Place ✦ A2
Much Park St B3
Naul's Mill Park A1
New Union B2
Odeon 🎦 B1
Park Rd C2
Parkside C3
Planet Ice Arena B1
Post Office 📮 B2/C2
Primrose Hill St A3
Priory Gardens & Visitor Centre B2
Priory St B3
Puma Way C3
Quarryfield La C3
Queen's Rd B1
Quinton Rd C2
Radford Rd A2
Raglan St B3
Ringway (Hill Cross) A1
Ringway (Queens) B1
Ringway (Rudge) B1
Ringway (St Johns) B3
Ringway (St Nicholas) A2
Ringway (St Patricks) C2
Ringway (Swanswell) A2
Ringway (Whitefriars) B3
St John St B2
St John the Baptist ⛪ B2
St Nicholas St A2
Sidney Stringer Acad A3
Skydome B1
Spencer Ave C1
Spencer Rec Gnd C1
Spon St B1
Sports Centre B3
Stoney Rd C2
Stoney Stanton Rd A3
Swanswell Pool A3
Technocentre, The C3
Thomas Landsdail St C2
Tomson Ave A1
Top Green C1
Trinity St B2
University B3
University Sports Ctr B3
Upper Hill St A1
Upper Well St A2
Victoria St A3
Vine St A3
Warwick Rd C2
Waveley Rd B1
West Orchards Sh Ctr B2
Westminster Rd C1
White St A3
Windsor St B1

Derby 335

Abbey St C1
Agard St B1
Albert St B2
Albion St B2
Ambulance Station B1
Arthur St A1
Ashlyn Rd B3
Assembly Rooms 🏛 B2
Babington La C2
Becket St B1
Belper Rd A1
Bold La B1
Bradshaw Way C2
Bradshaw Way Ret Pk C2
Bridge St B1
Brook St B1
Burton Rd C1
Bus Station B2
Caesar St A2
Canal St C3
Carrington St C3
Cathedral ✝ B2
Cathedral Rd B1
Charnwood St C2
Chester Green Rd A2
City Rd A2
Clarke St A3
Cock Pitt B3
Council House 🏛 B2
Courts B1
Cranmer Rd B3
Crompton St C1
Crown & County Courts B2
Curzon St B1
Darley Grove A1
Derby ⇌ C3
Derbyshire County Cricket Ground B3
Derwent Bsns Centre A2
Derwent St B2
Drewry La C1
Duffield Rd A1
Duke St A2
Dunton Cl B3
Eagle Market C2
East St B2
Eastgate B3
Exeter St B2
Farm St C1
Ford St B1
Forester St C1
Fox St A2
Friar Gate B1
Friary St B1
Full St B2
Gerard St C1
Gower St C2
Green La C2
Grey St C1
Guildhall 🏛 B2
Harcourt St C1
Highfield Rd A1
Hill La C2
Information Ctr ℹ B2
Iron Gate B2
John St C3
Joseph Wright Centre B1
Kedleston Rd A1
Key St B2
King Alfred St C1
King St A1
Kingston St A1
Lara Croft Way C2
Leopold St C2
Library B1
Liversage St C3
Lodge La B1
London Rd C2
London Rd Community Hospital Ⓗ C2
Macklin St C1
Mansfield Rd A2
Market B2
Market Pl B2
May St C1
Meadow La B3
Melbourne St C2
Mercian Way C1
Midland Rd C3
Monk St C1
Morledge B2
Mount St C1
Mus & Art Gallery 🏛 B1
Noble St C3
North Parade A1
North St A1
Nottingham Rd B3
Osmaston Rd C2
Otter St A1
Park St C3
Parker St A1
Pickfords House 🏛 B1
Playhouse 🎭 C2
Police HQ 🚓 A2
Police Station 🚓 B2
Post Office 📮 A1/A2/B1/C2/C3
Pride Parkway C3
Prime Enterprise Park A2
Prime Parkway A2
Queens Leisure Centre B1
Racecourse A3
Railway Terr C3
Register Office B2

School for the Deaf . . .C2
School Rd C1
Sidwell St B1
Smythen St B1
South St C2
Southernhay East B2
Southernhay West B2
Spacex Gallery B1
Spicer Rd B3
Sports Centre A3
Summerland St A1
Swimming Pool &
  Leisure Ctr. B2
Sydney Rd C1
Tan La B1
Thornton Hill C1
Topsham Rd C3
Tucker's Hall B1
Tudor St B2
University of Exeter
  (St Luke's Campus) . .A1
Velwell Rd A1
Verney St A3
Water La C1/C2
Weirfield Rd C2
Well St A2
West Ave A2
West Grove Rd. C1
Western Way . . .A3/B1/B2
Willeys Ave C1
Wonford Rd B3/C3
York Rd B1

Fort William   337

Abrach Rd C2
Achintore Rd. C1
Alma Rd C2
Am Breun Chamas B2
Ambulance Station A3
An Aird A2
Argyll Rd C2
Argyll Terr C1
Bank St B2
Belford Hospital B2
Ben Nevis Highland
  Centre B3
Black Parks A3
Braemore Pl C2
Bruce Pl C2
Bus Station B2
Camanachd Cr . . .A3/B2
Cameron Rd C1
Cameron Sq B1
Carmichael Way A2
Claggan Rd C1
Connochie Rd C1
Cow Hill C3
Creag Dhubh B3
Croft Rd B3
Douglas Pl B2
Dudley Rd B2
Dumbarton Rd C1
Earl of Inverness Rd. . . .A3
Fassifern Rd B2
Fire Station B2
Fort William ≋ B2
Fort William
  (Remains) ✦ B2
Glasdrum Rd C1
Glen Nevis Pl B3
Gordon Sq B1
Grange Rd C1
Heathercroft Rd C1
Heather Croft Rd C1
Henderson Row A1
High St B1
Hill Rd C2
Hospital Belhaven
  Annexe A3
Information Ctr ⓘ A3
Inverlochy Ct. A3
Kennedy Rd B2/C2
Library B2
Lime Tree Gallery ✦ . .C1
Linnhe Rd. B1
Lochaber Leisure Ctr. . . .B3
Lochiel Rd A3
Lochy Rd A3
Lundavra Cres. C1
Lundavra Rd C1
Lundy Rd A2
Mamore Cr. B2
Mary St. B2
Middle St A3
Montrose Ave A1
Moray Pl C1
Morven Pl C2
Moss Rd B2
Nairn Cres A1
Nevis Bridge B3
Nevis Centre, The. B3
Nevis Rd A3
Nevis Terr B3
North Rd. B3
Obelisk B2
Parade Rd C2
Police Station ⧉ C1
Post Office ⊠ A3/B2
Ross Pl C1
St Andrews ⛪ B2
Shaw Pl C1
Station Brae B3
Superstore B1
Treig Rd A2
Underwater Ctr, The . .A2
Union Rd C1
Victoria Rd. C2
Wades Rd A3
West Highland ⧉ B1
West Highland College
  UHI A1
Young Pl B2

Glasgow   337

Admiral St C2
Albert Bridge C5
Albion St B5
Anderston ≋ B3

Anderston Quay B3
Argyle Arcade B5
Argyle
  St. A1/A2/B3/B4/B5
Argyle Street ≋ B5
Arlington St A3
Arts Centre ⧉ B3
Ashley St A3
Bain St C6
Baird St A6
Baliol St A3
Ballater St C5
Barras (Market), The . .C6
Bath St A3
BBC Scotland B1
Bell St C6
Bell's Bridge B1
Bentinck St A2
Berkeley St A3
Bishop La. B3
Black St A6
Blackburn St C2
Blackfriars St B6
Blantyre St A1
Blythswood Sq A4
Blythswood St B4
Bothwell St B4
Brand St C1
Breadalbane St A2
Bridge St ≋ C4
Bridge St ⓜ C4
Bridgegate C5
Briggait C5
Broomielaw. B3
Broomielaw Quay
  Gdns. B3
Brown St B4
Brunswick St B5
Buccleuch St. A3
Buchanan Bus Station . .A5
Buchanan Galleries A5
Buchanan St B5
Buchanan St ⓜ B5
Cadogan St B4
Caledonian University . .A5
Calgary St A5
Cambridge St A4
Canal St A4
Candleriggs B5
Carlton Pl. C5
Carnarvon St A3
Carrick St B4
Castle St B6
Cathedral Sq B6
Cathedral St B5
Ctr for Contemporary
  Arts ⧉ A4
Centre St C4
Cessnock ⓜ C1
Cessnock St C1
Charing Cross ≋ A3
Cheapside St. B3
Cineworld ♦ A5
Citizens' Theatre ⧉ . . .C5
City Chambers
  Complex. B5
City Halls ⧉ B5
City of Glasgow Coll
  (City Campus) B5
City of Glasgow Coll
  (Riverside Campus) . .C5
Clairmont Gdns. A3
Claremont St. A2
Claremont Terr A2
Claythorne St C6
Cleveland St A3
Clifford La C1
Clifford St C1
Clifton Pl A3
Clifton St A2
Clutha St C1
Clyde Arc B2
Clyde Auditorium B2
Clyde Pl C4
Clyde Place Quay C4
Clyde St C5
Clyde Walkway C1
Clydeside Expressway . .B2
Coburg St C4
Cochrane St B5
College St B6
Collins St B6
Commerce St C4
Cook St C4
Cornwall St C2
Couper St. A5
Cowcaddens ⓜ A4
Cowcaddens Rd A4
Crimea St B3
Custom Ho Quay Gdns .C4
Dalhousie St A4
Dental Hospital Ⓗ A4
Derby St. A2
Dobbie's Loan. A4/A5
Dobbie's Loan Pl. A5
Dorset St A3
Douglas St B4
Doulton Fountain ✦ . .C6
Dover St A2
Drury St B4
Drygate B6
Duke St. B6
Dunaskin St A1
Dunblane St A4
Dundas St B5
Dunlop St. C5
East Campbell St C6
Eastvale Pl A1
Eglinton St C4
Elderslie St A3
Elliot St B2
Elmbank St A3
Esmond St A1
Exhibition Centre ≋ . . .B2
Eye Infirmary Ⓗ A2
Festival Park C1
Film Theatre ⧉ A4
Finnieston Quay B1
Finnieston St. B2

Fire Station C6
Florence St C5
Fox St C5
Gallowgate C6
Garnet St A3
Garnethill St A4
Garscube Rd A4
George Sq B5
George St B5
George V Bridge. C4
Gilbert St A1
Glasgow Bridge C4
Glasgow Cathedral † . .B6
Glasgow Central ≋ B5
Glasgow Green C6
Glasgow Necropolis ✦ B6
Glasgow Royal
  Concert Hall ⧉ A5
Glasgow Science
  Centre ✦ B1
Glasgow Tower ✦ B1
Glassford St B5
Glebe St A6
Gorbals Cross C5
Gorbals St C5
Gordon St B4
Govan Rd B1/C1/C2
Grace St B3
Grafton Pl A5
Grand Ole Opry ✦ C2
Grant St A3
Granville St A3
Gray St A2
Greendyke St C6
Grey Eagle St. B7
Harley St C1
Harvie St C1
Haugh Rd A1
Havannah St B6
Heliport B1
Henry Wood Hall ⧉ . . .A3
High Court. C5
High St B6
High Street ≋ B6
Hill St A3
Holland St A3
Holm St B4
Hope St A5
Houldsworth St B2
Houston Pl C3
Houston St C3
Howard St C5
Hunter St C6
Hutcheson St B5
Hydepark St B3
Imax Cinema ▦ B1
India St A3
Ingram St B5
Jamaica St B4
James Watt St B4
John Knox St B6
John St B5
Kelvin Hall ♦ A1
Kelvin Statue ✦ A2
Kelvin Way A2
Kelvingrove Art Gallery &
  Museum ⧉ A1
Kelvingrove Park A2
Kelvinhaugh St A1
Kennedy St A6
Kent Rd A2
Killermont St A5
King St B5
King's, The ⧉ A3
Kingston Bridge C3
Kingston St C4
Kinning Park ⓜ C2
Kyle St A5
Lancefield Quay B2
Lancefield St B3
Langshot St C1
Lendel Pl C1
Lighthouse, The ✦. . . .B4
Lister St A5
Little St B3
London Rd C6
Lorne St C1
Lower Harbour C1
Lumsden St A1
Lymburn St A1
Lyndoch Cr A3
Lyndoch Pl. A3
Lyndoch St A3
Maclellan St C1
Mair St C2
Maitland St A4
Mansell St C7
Mavisbank Gdns C2
Mcalpine St B3
Mcaslin St A6
Mclean Sq. C2
McLellan Gallery ⧉ . . .A4
McPhater St A4
Middlesex St C2
Middleton St C1
Midland St B4
Miller St B5
Millennium Bridge. B1
Millroad St C6
Milnpark St C2
Milton St A4
Minerva St A2
Mitchell Library, The. . . .A3
Mitchell St West B4
Mitchell Theatre,
  The ⧉ A3
Modern Art Gallery ⧉ .B5
Moir St C6
Molendinar St C6
Moncur St C6
Montieth Row C6
Montrose St B5
Morrison St C3
Mosque C5
Nairn St A1
National Piping Centre,
  The ✦ A5

Nelson Mandela Sq B5
Nelson St C4
Nelson's Monument C6
New City Rd A4
Newton Pl A3
Newton St A3
Nicholson St C4
Nile St B5
Norfolk Court C4
Norfolk St C4
North Frederick St B5
North Hanover St B5
North Portland St. B6
North St A3
North Wallace St A5
O2 ABC A4
O2 Academy ✦ C4
Odeon ▦ A4
Old Dumbarton Rd. A1
Osborne St B5/C5
Oswald St B4
Overnewton St A1
Oxford St C4
Pacific Dr. B1
Paisley Rd C3
Paisley Rd West C1
Park Circus A2
Park Gdns A2
Park St South A2
Park Terr A2
Parkgrove Terr A2
Parnie St C5
Parson St A6
Partick Bridge A1
Passport Office ✦ A3
Pavilion Theatre ⧉ A4
Pembroke St A3
People's Palace ⧉ C6
Pinkston Rd A6
Pitt St A4/B4
Plantation Park C1
Plantation Quay B1
Police Station A4/A6
Port Dundas Rd. A5
Port St A2
Portman St C2
Prince's Dock B1
Princes Sq B5
Provand's Lordship ⧉ B6
Queen St B5
Queen Street ≋ B5
Ramshorn ⧉ B5
Renfrew St. A3/A4
Renton St. A5
Richmond St B5
Robertson St B4
Rose St A4
Rottenrow. B5
Royal Concert Hall ⧉ . .A5
Royal Conservatoire
  of Scotland A4
Royal Cr A2
Royal Exchange Sq. B5
Royal Highland Fusiliers
  Museum ⧉ A3
Royal Hospital For Sick
  Children ⧉ A1
Royal Infirmary Ⓗ B6
Royal Terr A2
Rutland Cr C2
St Andrew's ⛪ C6
St Andrew's (RC) † C5
St Andrew's St C5
St Enoch ⓜ B5
St Enoch Shopping Ctr B5
St Enoch Sq B4
St George's Rd A3
St James Rd B6
St Kent St C6
St Mungo Ave A5/A6
St Mungo Museum of
  Religious Life ⧉ B6
St Mungo Pl. A6
St Vincent Cr A2
St Vincent Pl B5
St Vincent St. B3/B4
St Vincent Street
  Church ⧉ B4
St Vincent Terr B3
Saltmarket C5
Sandyford Pl A3
Sauchiehall St. A2/A4
School of Art A4
Sclater St. B7
Scotland St C2
Scott St A4
Scottish Exhibition &
  Conference Centre ≋ .B1
Seaward St C2
Shaftesbury St B3
Sheriff Court. C5
Shields Rd ⓜ C3
Shopmobility A5
Shuttle St B6
Sighthill Park A6
Somerset Pl. A2
South Portland St. C4
Springburn Rd A6
Springfield Quay C3
SSE Hydro The ⧉ B2
Stanley St. C2
Stevenson St C6
Stewart St A4
Stirling Rd B6
Stirling's Library B5
Stobcross Quay. B1
Stobcross Rd. B1
Stock Exchange ⧉ B5
Stockwell Pl C5
Stockwell St B5
Stow College A4
Sussex St C2
Synagogues A3/C4
Taylor Pl A5
Tenement House ⧉ A3
Teviot St A1
Theatre Royal ⧉ A5
Tolbooth Steeple & C5
Mercat Cross ✦ C5
Tower St C2

Trades House ⧉ B5
Tradeston St C4
Transport Museum ⧉ . .A1
Tron ⧉ C5
Trongate B5
Tunnel St B2
Turnbull St C5
Union St B4
Univ of Strathclyde B6
Victoria Bridge C5
Virginia St B5
Wallace St C3
Walls St B6
Walmer Cr C1
Warrock St B3
Washington St B3
Waterloo St B4
Watson St B6
Watt St C2
Wellington St. B4
West Campbell St B4
West George St B4
West Graham St A4
West Greenhill Pl B2
West Regent St A4
West Regent St. B4
West St ⓜ C4
West St C4
Whitehall St B3
Wilkes St C7
Wilson St B5
Woodlands Gate A3
Woodlands Rd. A3
Woodlands Terr A2
Woodside Pl A3
Woodside Terr A3
York St B4
Yorkhill Pde. A1
Yorkhill St A1

Gloucester   337

Albion St C1
Alexandra Rd. B3
Alfred St C3
All Saints Rd C2
Alvin St B2
Arthur St C2
Barrack Square . . . .
Barton St C2
Blackfriars † B1
Blenheim Rd C2
Bristol Rd C1
Brunswick Rd B2
Bruton Way B2
Bus Station B2
Cineworld C1
City Council Offices B1
City Mus, Art Gallery &
  Library ⧉ B2
Clarence St B2
Commercial Rd. B1
Council Offices. B1
Courts B1
Cromwell St C2
Deans Way A2
Denmark Rd A3
Derby Rd C3
Docks ✦ C1
Eastgate St B2
Eastgate, The B1
Edwy Pde A2
Estcourt Cl. A3
Estcourt Rd. A3
Falkner St C2
Folk Museum ⧉ B1
GL1 Leisure Centre C2
Gloucester Cath † B1
Gloucester Quays
  Outlet. C1
Gloucester Station ≋ . .B2
Gloucester
  Waterways ⧉ C1
Gloucestershire Royal
  Hospital (A&E) Ⓗ . . .A3
Goodyere St C2
Gouda Way A1
Great Western Rd. B3
Guildhall ⧉ B2
Heathville Rd. A3
Henry Rd A3
Henry St B2
Hinton Rd. A2
India Rd C3
Information Ctr ⓘ B1
Jersey Rd C3
King's B1
King's Walk Sh Ctr B2
Kingsholm
  (Gloucester Rugby) . .A2
Kingsholm Rd A2
Lansdown Rd A3
Library B2
Llanthony Rd C1
London Rd A2
Longhorn Ave A1
Longsmith St B1
Malvern Rd A3
Market B2
Market Pde B2
Mercia Rd A2
Metz Way C3
Midland Rd. C2
Millbrook St C3
Montpellier C1
Napier St C3
Nettleton Rd B2
New Inn ⧉ B2
New Olympus ⧉ C2
North Rd. A3
Northgate St B2
Oxford Rd A3
Oxford St C2
Pk & Ride Gloucester . . .A1
Park Rd C2
Park, The C2
Parliament St C1
Peel Centre, The. C1
Pitt St B1

Police Station B1/C3
Post Office ⊠ B1
Quay St B1
Quay, The. B1
Recreation Gd A1/A2
Regent St C2
Robert Raikes Ho ⧉ . . .B1
Royal Oak Rd B1
Russell St B2
Ryecroft St. C2
St Aldate St B2
St Ann Way C1
St Catherine St A2
St Mark St A2
St Mary de Crypt ⛪ . . .B1
St Mary de Lode ⛪ B1
St Nicholas's ⛪ B1
St Oswald's Rd A1
St Oswald's Retail Pk. . .A1
St Peter's ⛪ B2
Seabroke Rd A3
Sebert St A2
Severn Rd C1
Sherborne St. B2
Shire Hall ⧉ B1
Sidney St C3
Soldiers of
  Gloucestershire ⧉ . . .B1
Southgate St B1/C1
Spa Field B1
Spa Rd C1
Sports Ground . . .A2/B2
Station Rd B2
Stratton Rd C3
Stroud Rd. C1
Superstore A1
Swan Rd A2
Trier Way C1/C2
Union St A2
Vauxhall Rd C3
Victoria St C2
Walham Lane A1
Wellington St C2
Westgate Retail Park. . .B1
Westgate St B1
Weston Rd C1
Widden St C2
Worcester St B2

Grimsby   337

Abbey Drive East C2
Abbey Drive West C2
Abbey Park Rd. C2
Abbey Rd C2
Abbey Walk C2
Abbeygate Sh Ctr B2
Abbotsway. C2
Adam Smith St . . .A1/A2
Ainslie St C1
Albert St A3
Alexandra Dock . . .A2/B2
Alexandra Retail Park .A2
Annesley St B1
Armstrong St A1
Arthur St B1
Augusta St C1
Bargate C1
Beeson St A1
Bethlehem St C2
Bodiam Way B3
Bradley St B3
Brighowgate C1/C2
Bus Station B2/C2
Canterbury Dr. C1
Cartergate. B1/C1
Catherine St C2
Caxton St A3
Chantry La B1
Charlton St A1
Church La C2
Church St A3
Cleethorpe Rd A3
Close, The C1
College A1
College St C1
Compton Dr. C1
Corporation Bridge A2
Corporation Rd. A1
Court B3
Crescent St B1
Deansgate C1
Doughty Rd C2
Dover St. C1
Duchess St C2
Dudley St. C2
Duke of York Gardens .B1
Duncombe St B3
Earl La B3
East Marsh St B3
East St B2
Eastgate. B1
Eastside Rd A3
Eaton Ct C1
Eleanor St B3
Ellis Way A1
Fisherman's Chapel ⛪ A3
Fisherman's Wharf C1
Fishing Heritage
  Centre ⧉ B2
Flour Sq A3
Frederick St B3
Frederick Ward Way . . .B2
Freeman St A3/B3
Freshney Dr. B1
Freshney Pl. B2
Garden St C2
Garibaldi St A3
Garth La B2
Grime St B3
Grimsby Docks Sta ≋ . .A3
Grimsby Town Sta ≋ . .C2
Hainton Ave C2
Har Way A3
Hare St C2
Harrison St B1
Haven Ave C1
Hay Croft Ave B1
Hay Croft St B1

Heneage Rd B3/C3
Henry St B3
Holme St B3
Hume St C1
James St B1
Joseph St B3
Kent St A3
King Edward St B1
Lambert Rd C2
Library B2
Lime St B1
Lister St B3
Littlefield La C1
Lockhill B1
Lord St C2
Ludford St B3
Macaulay St B1
Mallard Mews C3
Manor Ave C2
Market B2
Market Hall B2
Market St. B3
Moss Rd C2
Nelson St A3
New St B2
Osbourne St B2
Pasture St B3
Peaks Parkway C3
Pelham Rd C3
Police Station ⧉ A3
Post Office ⊠ . .B1/B2/C2
Pyewipe Rd A1
Railway Pl A3
Railway St C3
Recreation Ground C2
Rendel St A2
Retail Park. B2
Richard St B3
Ripon St C1
Robinson St East. B3
Royal St A3
St Hilda's Ave C1
St James B2
Sheepfold St B3/C3
Sixhills St. C2
South Park. C1
Spring St A3
Superstore B3
Tasburgh St A3
Tennyson St B2
Thesiger St C2
Time Trap ⧉ B2
Town Hall ⧉ B2
Veal St B1
Victoria Retail Park . . .A3
Victoria St North A2
Victoria St South B2
Victoria St West C2
Watkin St A1
Welholme Ave. C2
Welholme Rd. C2
Wellington St B3
Wellowgate C2
Werneth Rd C2
West Coates Rd. A1
Westgate. A2
Westminster Dr C1
Willingham St C2
Wintringham Rd. C2
Wood St B3
Yarborough Dr B1
Yarborough Hotel ⧉ . .C2

Hanley   337

Acton St A3
Albion St B2
Argyle St C1
Ashbourne Gr A2
Avoca St A3
Baskerville Rd. B3
Bedford Rd C1
Bedford St B3
Bethesda St B2
Bexley St A2
Birches Head Rd A3
Botteslow St C3
Boundary St A1
Broad St C2
Brockfield Rd B3
Broom St A3
Bryan St. B2
Bucknall New Rd B3
Bucknall Old Rd B3
Bus Station B3
Cannon St C2
Castlefield St C1
Cavendish St A1
Central Forest Pk. A2
Charles St B3
Cheapside B2
Chell St A3
Clarke St C1
Cleveland Rd C2
Clifford St C3
Clough St B2
Clyde St C1
College Rd C2
Cooper St C2
Corbridge Rd. A1
Cutts St C2
Davis St C1
Denbigh St A1
Derby St C3
Dilke St A3
Dundas St A3
Dundee Rd C1
Dyke St B3
Eastwood Rd B3
Eaton St A3
Etruria Park. B1
Etruria Rd B1
Etruria Vale Rd C1
Festing St A3
Festival Retail Park . . .A1
Fire Station C3
Foundry St B2
Franklin St C3
Garnet St A3
Garth St. B3
George St A3

Gilman St B3
Glass St B3
Goodson St B3
Greyhound Way A1
Grove Pl C1
Hampton St C3
Hanley Park C2
Hanley Park C2
Harding Rd C1
Hassall St B3
Havelock Pl A3
Hazlehurst St C1
Hinde St C2
Hope St. B2
Houghton St A3
Hulton St A2
Information Ctr ⓘ B3
Jasper St C1
Jervis St A3
John Bright St B2
John St B2
Keelings Rd A3
Kimberley Rd C1
Ladysmith Rd C1
Lawrence St C2
Leek Rd C2
Library B2
Lichfield St C3
Linfield Rd B2
Loftus St C2
Lower Bedford St C1
Lower Bryan St A2
Lower Mayer St A3
Lowther St A1
Magistrates Court C2
Malham St A3
Marsh St B2
Matlock St A3
Mayer St A3
Milton St C1
Mitchell Memorial
  Theatre ⧉ B2
Morley St C2
Moston St A3
Mount Pleasant C1
Mulgrave St A2
Mynors St B3
Nelson Pl C1
New Century St A1
Octagon Retail Park. . . .A1
Ogden Rd C3
Old Hall St B3
Old Town Rd A3
Pall Mall B2
Palmerston St C2
Park and Ride B2
Parker St B2
Parkway, The A1
Pavilion Dr A1
Pelham St C3
Percy St B2
Piccadilly. B2
Picton St B3
Plough St. A3
Police Station ⧉ B3
Portland St A1
Post Office ⊠ . .A3/B3/C3
Potteries Museum &
  Art Gallery ⧉ B2
Potteries Sh Ctr B2
Potteries Way C2
Powell St A1
Pretoria Rd C1
Quadrant Rd B2
Ranelagh St C2
Raymond St C1
Rectory Rd C1
Regent Rd C2
Regent Theatre ⧉ B2
Richmond Terr C2
Ridgehouse Dr A1
Robson St C2
St Ann St B3
St Luke St B3
Sampson St B2
Shaw St A1
Sheaf St C2
Shearer St C1
Shelton New Rd C1
Shirley Rd C2
Slippery La B2
Snow Hill C2
Spur St C1
Stafford St B2
Statham St B2
Stubbs La C3
Sun St C1
Supermarket A1/B2
Talbot St C1
Town Hall B2
Town Rd B3
Trinity St B2
Union St A2
Upper Hillchurch St A3
Upper Huntbach St B3
Victoria Hall
  Theatre ⧉ B3
Warner St. C2
Warwick St C1
Waterloo Rd A1
Waterloo St. B3
Well St A2
Wellesley St C1
Wellington Rd C3
Wellington St C3
Whitehaven Dr A2
Whitmore St C1
Windermere St A1
Woodall St A1
Yates St C2
York St A2

Harrogate   338

Albert St. C2
Alexandra Rd. B2
Arthington Ave B2
Ashfield Rd A2
Back Cheltenham
  Mount B2

Beech Grove C1
Belmont Rd C1
Bilton Dr A2
Bower Rd B2
Bower St B2
Bus Station B2
Cambridge Rd. B1
Cambridge St B2
Cemetery A2
Chatsworth Grove A2
Chatsworth Pl A2
Chatsworth Rd. A2
Chelmsford Rd B3
Cheltenham Cr B2
Cheltenham Mt B2
Cheltenham Pde. B2
Christ Church B3
Christ Church Oval B3
Chudleigh Rd B3
Clarence Dr B1
Claro Rd A3
Claro Way. A3
Coach Park B2
Coach Rd B3
Cold Bath Rd C1
Commercial St B2
Coppice Ave A1
Coppice Dr. A1
Coppice Gate. A1
Cornwall Rd B1
Council Offices. B1
Court C3
Crescent Gdns B1
Crescent Rd B1
Dawson Terr A2
Devonshire Pl B3
Diamond Mews A2
Dixon Rd A2
Dixon Terr A2
Dragon Ave B3
Dragon Parade B2
Dragon Rd B2
Duchy Rd B1
East Parade B2
East Park Rd C3
Esplanade B1
Fire Station A2
Franklin Mount A2
Franklin Rd B2
Franklin Square A2
Glebe Rd. C1
Grove Park Ct A3
Grove Park Terr A3
Grove Rd A2
Hampswaite Rd A1
Harcourt Dr. B3
Harcourt Rd. B3
Harrogate ≋ B2
Harrogate Int Ctr B1
Harrogate Ladies Coll . .B1
Harrogate Theatre ⧉ . .B2
Heywood Rd C1
Hollins Cr A1
Hollins Mews A1
Hollins Rd A1
Homestead Rd B3
Hydro Leisure Ctr, The A1
Information Ctr ⓘ B1
James St B2
Jenny Field Dr A1
John St B2
Kent Dr A1
Kent Rd A1
Kings Rd A2
Kingsway B3
Kingsway Dr B3
Lancaster Rd C1
Leeds Rd C2
Lime Grove B3
Lime St A3
Mayfield Grove B2
Mayfield Pl A2
Mercer ⧉ B1
Montpellier Hill C1
Mornington Cr A3
Mornington Terr. A3
Mowbray Sq B3
North Park Rd B3
Nydd Vale Rd B2
Oakdale Ave A1
Oatlands Dr C3
Odeon ▦ B2
Osborne Rd A2
Otley Rd C1
Oxford St B2
Parade, The. B2
Park Chase B3
Park Parade B3
Park View. B2
Parliament St B1
Police Station ⧉ C1
Post Office ⊠ B2/C1
Providence Terr A2
Queen Parade B3
Queen's Rd C1
Raglan St C2
Regent Ave A3
Regent Grove A3
Regent Parade A3
Regent St A3
Regent Terr A3
Rippon Rd A1
Robert St C2
Royal Baths &
  Turkish Baths ⧉ B1
Royal Pump Room ⧉ . .B1
St Luke's Mount A2
St Mary's Ave C1
St Mary's Walk C1
Scargill Rd. A1
Skipton Rd A3
Skipton St A3
Slingsby Walk C3
South Park Rd C2
Spring Grove A1
Springfield Ave. B1
Station Ave B2
Station Parade B2
Strawberry Dale A2
Stray Rein C3

Holyhead • Hull • Inverness • Ipswich • Kendal • King's Lynn • Lancaster • Leeds 357

Stray, The C2/C3
Studley Rd A2
Superstore B2
Swan Rd B1
Tower St C2
Trinity Rd C2
Union St B2
Valley Dr C1
Valley Gardens C1
Valley Mount C1
Victoria Ave C2
Victoria Rd C1
Victoria Shopping Ctr B2
Waterloo St A2
West Park C2
West Park St C2
Wood View A1
Woodfield Ave A3
Woodfield Dr A3
Woodfield Grove A3
Woodfield Rd A3
Woodfield Square A3
Woodside B3
York Pl C3
York Rd B1

Holyhead Caergybi 338

Armenia St A2
Arthur St C2
Beach Rd A1
Boston St B2
Bowling Green C3
Bryn Erw Rd C3
Bryn Glas Cl C3
Bryn Glas Rd C3
Bryn Gwyn Rd C1
Bryn Marchog A1
Bryn Mor Terr A2
Bryngoleu Ave A1
Cae Braenar C3
Cambria St B1
Captain Skinner's Obelisk B2
Cecil St C2
Celtic Gateway Footbridge B2
Cemetery C1/C2
Cleveland Ave C2
Coastguard Lookout A2
Court B2
Customs House A3
Cybi Pl A2
Cyttir Rd C3
Edmund St B1
Empire B2
Ferry Terminals B2
Ffordd Beibio B3
Ffordd Feurig C3
Ffordd Hirnos C3
Ffordd Jasper C3
Ffordd Tudur B3
Fire Station C2
Garreglwyd Rd B1
Gilbert St C2
Gorsedd Circle B1
Gwelfor Ave A1
Harbour View B3
Henry St C2
High Terr C1
Hill St B2
Holborn Rd C2
Holland Park Ind Est C3
Holyhead Park B1
Holyhead Station A2
Information Ctr B2
King's Rd C2
Kingsland Rd C2
Lewascote C3
Library B2
Lifeboat Station A1
Llanfawr Cl C3
Llanfawr Rd C3
Lligwy St C2
Lon Deg C3
London Rd C3
Longford Rd B1
Longford Terr B1
Maes Cybi B1
Maes Hedd A1
Maes-Hyfryd Rd C1
Maes-y-Dref B1
Maes-yr-Haf A2/B1
Maes-yr-Ysgol C3
Marchog C3
Marina A1
Maritime Museum A1
Market B2
Market St B2
Mill Bank B1
Min-y-Mor Rd A1
Morawelon Ind Est B3
Morawelon Rd B3
Moreton Rd C1
New Park Rd B1
Newry St A2
Old Harbour Lighthouse A3
Plas Rd C1
Police Station B2
Porth-y-Felin Rd A1
Post Office A1/B2/B3
Prince of Wales Rd A2
Priory La B3
Pump St C1
Queens Park B1
Reseifion Rd C1
Rock St B1
Roman Fort B2
St Cybi St B2
St Cybi's Church B2
St Seiriol's Cl B1
Salt Island Bridge A2
Seabourne Rd A1
South Stack Rd B1
Sports Ground B1
Stanley St B2
Station St B2
Superstore C2
Tan-y-Bryn Rd A1
Tan-yr-Efail C2
Tara St C1
Thomas St B1
Town Hall A2
Treseifion Estate C2
Turkey Shore Rd B2
Ucheldre Arts Ctr B1
Ucheldre Ave B1
Upper Baptist St B1
Victoria Rd B2
Victoria Terr B2
Vulcan St B1
Walthew Ave A1
Walthew La A1
Wian St C2

Hull 338

Adelaide St C1
Albert Dock C1
Albion St B2
Alfred Gelder St B2
Anlaby Rd B1
Arctic Corsair B3
Beverley Rd A1
Blanket Row C2
Bond St B2
Bridlington Ave A2
Brook St B1
Brunswick Ave A1
Bus Station B1
Camilla Cl C3
Cannon St A2
Caroline St A2
Carr La B2
Castle St C2
Central Library B1
Charles St A2
Citadel Way B3
City Hall B2
City Hall Theatre B2
Clarence St B3
Cleveland St A3
Clifton St A1
Club Culture C2
Colonial St B1
Court B2
Deep, The C3
Dinostar C2
Dock Office Row B3
Dock St B2
Drypool Bridge B3
Egton St A3
English St C1
Ferens Gallery B2
Ferensway B1
Francis St A2
Francis St West A2
Freehold St A1
Freetown Way A2
Früit Theatre C2
Garrison Rd B3
George St B2
Gibson St A2
Great Thornton St B1
Great Union St A3
Green La A2
Grey St A1
Grimston St B2
Grosvenor St A1
Guildhall B2
Guildhall Rd B2
Hands-on History B2
Harley St A1
Hessle Rd C1
High St B3
Holy Trinity B2
Hull (Paragon) Sta B1
Hull & East Riding Museum B3
Hull Ice Arena C1
Hull College B3
Hull History Centre A2
Hull Truck Theatre B1
Humber Dock Marina C2
Humber Dock St C2
Humber St C2
Hyperion St A3
Information Ctr B2
Jameson St B1
Jarratt St B2
Jenning St A3
King Billy Statue C2
King Edward St B2
King St A2
Kingston Retail Park C1
Kingston St C2
Liddell St A1
Lime St A3
Lister St C1
Lockwood St A2
Maister House B3
Maritime Museum B2
Market B2
Market Place B2
Minerva Pier C2
Mulgrave St A3
Myton Swing Bridge C3
Myton St B1
NAPA (Northern Acad of Performing Arts) B1
Nelson St C2
New Cleveland St A3
New George St A2
New Theatre A2
Norfolk St A1
North Bridge A3
North St B1
Odeon C1
Old Harbour C3
Osborne St B1
Paragon St B2
Park St B1
Percy St A2
Pier St C2
Police Station B2
Porter St C1
Portland St B1
Post Office B1/B2
Posterngate B2
Prince's Quay B2
Prospect Centre B1
Prospect St B1
Queen's Gdns B2
Railway Dock Marina C2
Railway St C2
Real B1
Red Gallery B1
Reform St A2
Retail Park B1
Riverside Quay C2
Roper St B2
St James St C1
St Luke's St B1
St Mark St A3
St Mary the Virgin B3
St Stephens Sh Ctr B1
Scale Lane Footbridge B3
Scott St A2
South Bridge Rd B3
Sport's Centre C1
Spring Bank A1
Spring St B1
Spurn Lightship C2
Spyvee St A3
Streetlife Transport Museum B3
Sykes St A2
Tidal Surge Barrier C3
Tower St B3
Trinity House B2
University B2
Vane St A1
Victoria Pier C2
Waterhouse La B2
Waterloo St A1
Waverley St C1
Wellington St C2
Wellington St West C2
West St B1
Whitefriargate B2
Wilberforce Dr B2
Wilberforce House B3
Wilberforce Monument B3
William St C1
Wincolmlee A3
Witham A3
Wright St A1

Inverness 338

Abban St A1
Academy St B2
Alexander Pl B2
Anderson St A2
Annfield Rd C3
Ardconnel St B3
Ardconnel Terr B3
Ardross Pl B2
Ardross St B2
Argyle St B3
Argyle Terr B3
Attadale Rd B1
Ballifeary La C2
Ballifeary Rd C1/C2
Balnacraig La A1
Balnain House B2
Balnain St B2
Bank St B2
Bellfield Park C2
Bellfield Terr C3
Benula Rd A1
Birnie Terr A1
Bishop's Rd C2
Bowling Green A2
Bowling Green B2
Bowling Green C2
Bridge St B2
Brown St A2
Bruce Ave C1
Bruce Gdns C1
Bruce Pk C1
Burial Ground A2
Burnett Rd A3
Bus Station B3
Caledonian Rd B1
Cameron Rd A1
Cameron Sq A1
Carse Rd A1
Carsegate Rd Sth A1
Castle Garrison Encounter B2
Castle Rd B2
Castle St B3
Celt St B2
Chapel St A2
Charles St B3
Church St B2
Clachnacuddin Football Ground A1
Columba Rd B1/C1
Crown Ave B3
Crown Circus B3
Crown Dr B3
Crown Rd B3
Crown St B3
Culduthel Rd C3
Dalneigh Cres C1
Dalneigh Rd C1
Denny St B3
Dochfour Dr B1/C1
Douglas Row B2
Duffy Dr C3
Dunabban Rd A1
Dunain Rd B1
Duncraig St B2
Eastgate Shopping Ctr B3
Eden Court C2
Fairfield Rd B1
Falcon Sq B3
Fire Station A3
Fraser St B2
Fraser St C2
Friars' Bridge A2
Friars' La B2
Friars' St A2
George St A2
Gilbert St A2
Glebe St A2
Glendoe Terr A1
Glenurquhart Rd C1
Gordon Terr B3
Gordonville Rd C2
Grant St A2
Greig St B2
Harbour Rd A3
Harrowden Rd B1
Haugh Rd C2
Heatherley Cres C3
High St B3
Highland Council HQ, The C2
Hill Park C3
Hill St B3
HM Prison B3
Huntly Pl A2
Huntly St B2
India St A2
Industrial Estate A3
Information Ctr B2
Innes St A2
Inverness B3
Inverness High School B1
Inverness Museum B2
Jamaica St A2
Kenneth St B2
Kilmuir Rd A1
King St B2
Kingsmills Rd B3
Laurel Ave B1/C1
Library A3
Lilac Gr B1
Lindsay Ave C1
Lochalsh Rd A1/B1
Longman Rd A3
Lotland Pl A2
Lower Kessock St A1
Madras St A2
Market Hall B3
Maxwell Dr C1
Mayfield Rd C3
Millburn Rd B3
Mitchell's La C3
Montague Row B2
Muirfield Rd C3
Muirtown St B1
Nelson St A2
Ness Bank C2
Ness Bridge B2
Ness Walk B2/C2
Old Edinburgh Rd C3
Old High Church B2
Park Rd C1
Paton St C2
Perceval Rd B1
Planefield Rd B2
Police Station A3
Porterfield Bank C3
Porterfield Rd C3
Portland Pl A2
Post Office A2/B1/B2
Queen St B2
Queensgate B2
Railway Terr A3
Rangemore Rd B1
Reay St B3
Riverside St A2
Rose St A2
Ross Ave B1
Rowan Rd B1
Royal Northern Infirmary C2
St Andrew's Cath C2
St Columba B2
St John's Ave C1
St Mary's Ave C1
Sheriff Court B3
Shore St A2
Smith Ave C1
Southside Pl C3
Southside Rd C3
Spectrum Centre B2
Strothers La B3
Superstore A1/B2
TA Centre C2
Telford Gdns B1
Telford Rd A1
Telford St A1
Tomnahurich Cemetery C1
Tomnahurich St B2
Town Hall B3
Union Rd B3
Union St B3
Walker Pl A2
Walker Rd A3
War Memorial C2
Waterloo Bridge A2
Wells St B1
Young St B2

Ipswich 338

Alderman Rd B2
All Saints' Rd A1
Alpe St B2
Ancaster Rd C1
Ancient House B3
Anglesea Rd B2
Ann St B2
Arboretum A2
Austin St C2
Avenue, The A3
Belstead Rd C2
Berners St B2
Bibb Way B1
Birkfield Dr C1
Black Horse La B2
Bolton La B3
Bond St C3
Bowthorpe Cl B2
Bramford La A1
Bramford Rd A1
Bridge St C2
Brookfield Rd A1
Brooks Hall Rd A1
Broomhill A2
Broomhill Rd A1
Broughton Rd A2
Bulwer Rd B1
Burrell Rd C2
Butter Market B2
Buttermarket Shopping Centre, The B3
Cardinal Park L Park C2
Carr St B3
Cecil Rd B2
Cecilia St C2
Chancery Rd C2
Charles St B2
Chevallier St A1
Christchurch Mansion & Wolsey Art Gallery B3
Christchurch Park A3
Christchurch St B3
Cineworld C2
Civic Centre B2
Civic Dr B2
Clarkson St B1
Cobbold St B3
Commercial Rd C2
Constable Rd A3
Constantine Rd C1
Constitution Hill A2
Corder Rd A3
Corn Exchange B2
Cotswold Ave A2
Council Offices C2
County Hall B3
Crown Court C2
Crown St B2
Cullingham Rd B1
Cumberland St B2
Curriers La B2
Dale Hall La A2
Dales View Rd A1
Dalton Rd B2
Dillwyn St B1
Elliot St B1
Elm St B2
Elsmere Rd A3
Falcon St C2
Felaw St C3
Flint Wharf C3
Fonnereau Rd B2
Fore St C3
Foundation St C3
Franciscan Way C2
Friars St C2
Gainsborough Rd A3
Gatacre Rd B1
Geneva Rd B2
Gippeswyk Ave C1
Gippeswyk Park C1
Grafton Way C2
Graham Rd A1
Great Whip St C3
Grimwade St C3
Handford Cut B1
Handford Rd B1
Henley Rd A2
Hervey St B3
High St B2
Holly Rd A2
Information Ctr B3
Ipswich Haven Marina C3
Ipswich School A2
Ipswich Station C2
Ipswich Town FC (Portman Road) C2
Ivry St A2
Kensington Rd A1
Kesteven Rd C1
Key St C3
Kingsfield Ave A3
Kitchener Rd A1
Little's Cr C2
London Rd B1
Low Brook St C3
Lower Orwell St C3
Luther Rd C2
Magistrates Court B2
Manor Rd A3
Mornington Ave A1
Mus & Art Gallery B2
Museum St B2
Neale St B3
New Cardinal St C2
New Cut East C3
New Cut West C3
New Wolsey B2
Newson St B2
Norwich Rd A1/B1
Oban St B2
Old Customs House C3
Old Foundry Rd B3
Old Merchant's Ho C3
Orford St B2
Paget Rd A2
Park Rd A3
Park View Rd A2
Peter's St C2
Philip Rd C2
Pine Ave A2
Pine View Rd A2
Police Station B2
Portman Rd B2
Portman Walk C1
Post Office B2/B3
Princes St C2
Prospect St B1
Queen St B2
Ranelagh Rd C1
Recreation Ground B1
Rectory Rd C2
Regent Theatre B3
Retail Park C1
Retail Park C2
Richmond Rd A1
Rope Walk C3
Rose La C2
Russell Rd C2
St Edmund's Rd A2
St George's St B2
St Helen's St B3
Sherrington Rd A1
Silent St C2
Sir Alf Ramsey Way C1
Sirdar Rd B1
Soane St B3
Springfield La A1
Star La C3
Stevenson Rd B1
Suffolk College C3
Suffolk Retail Park B1
Superstore B1
Surrey Rd B1
Tacket St C3
Tavern St B3
Tolly Cobbold Mus C3
Tower Ramparts B2
Tower Ramparts Shopping Centre B2
Tower St B3
Town Hall B2
Tuddenham Rd A3
University C3
Upper Brook St B3
Upper Orwell St B3
Valley Rd A2
Vermont Cr B3
Vermont Rd B3
Vernon St C3
Warrington Rd A2
Waterloo Rd A1
Waterworks St C3
Wellington St B1
West End Rd B1
Westerfield Rd A3
Westgate St B2
Westholme Rd A1
Westwood Ave A1
Willoughby Rd C2
Withipoll St B3
Woodbridge Rd B3
Woodstone Ave A3
Yarmouth Rd B1

Kendal 338

Abbot Hall Art Gallery & Museum of Lakeland Life C2
Ambulance Station A2
Anchorite Fields C2
Anchorite Rd C2
Ann St A3
Appleby Rd A3
Archers Meadow C3
Ashleigh Rd A2
Aynam Rd B2
Bankfield Rd B1
Beast Banks B2
Beezon Fields A2
Beezon Rd A2
Beezon Trad Est A3
Belmont B2
Birchwood Cl C1
Blackhall Rd B2
Brewery Arts Ctr B2
Bridge St B2
Brigsteer Rd C1
Burneside Rd A2
Bus Station B2
Buttery Well La C2
Canal Head North B3
Captain French La C2
Caroline St A2
Castle Hill B3
Castle Howe B2
Castle Rd B3
Castle St A3/B3
Cedar Gr C1
Council Offices B2
County Council Offices A2
Cricket Ground A3
Cricket Ground C3
Cross La C2
Dockray Hall Ind Est A2
Dowker's La B2
Dry Ski Slope B3
East View B1
Echo Barn Hill C1
Elephant Yard B2
Fairfield La A1
Finkle St B2
Fire Station A2
Fletcher Square C3
Football Ground C3
Fowling La A3
Gillinggate C2
Glebe Rd C2
Golf Course B1
Goose Holme B3
Gooseholme Bridge B3
Green St A1
Greengate C2
Greengate La C1/C2
Greenside B1
Greenwood C1
Gulfs Rd B2
High Tenterfell B1
Highgate B2
Hillswood Ave C1
Horncop La A2
Information Ctr A2
K Village and Heritage Centre C2
Kendal A3
Kendal Business Park A3
Kendal Castle (Remains) B3
Kendal Fell B1
Kendal Green A1
Kendal Station A3
Kent Pl B2
Kirkbarrow C2
Kirkland C2
Library B2
Library Rd B2
Little Aynam B3
Little Wood B1
Long Cl C1
Longpool A3
Lound Rd C3
Lound St C3
Low Fellside B2
Lowther St B2
Maple Dr C1
Market Pl B2
Maude St B2
Miller Bridge B2
Milnthorpe Rd C2
Mint St A3
Mintsfeet Rd A3
Mintsfeet Rd South A2
New Rd B2
Noble's Rest B2
Parish Church C2
Park Side Rd C3
Parkside Bsns Park C3
Parr St B3
Police Station A2
Post Office A3/B2
Quaker Tapestry B2
Queen's Rd B1
Riverside Walk C2
Rydal Mount A2
Sandes Ave A2
Sandgate A3
Sandylands Rd A3
Serpentine Rd B1
Serpentine Wood B1
Shap Rd A3
South Rd C2
Stainbank Rd C1
Station Rd A3
Stramongate B2
Stramongate Bridge B2
Stricklandgate A2/B2
Sunnyside C3
Thorny Hills B3
Town Hall B2
Undercliff Rd B1
Underwood C1
Union St A2
Vicar's Fields C2
Vicarage Dr C1/C2
Wainwright's Yard B2
Wasdale Cl C3
Well Ings C2
Westmorland Shopping Ctr & Market Hall B2
Westwood Ave C1
Wildman St A3
Windermere Rd A1
YHA B2
YWCA B2

King's Lynn 339

Albert St A2
Albion St B2
All Saints B2
All Saints St B2
Austin Fields A2
Austin St A2
Avenue Rd B3
Bank Side B1
Beech Rd C2
Birch Tree Cl B2
Birchwood St A2
Blackfriars Rd B2
Blackfriars St B2
Boal St B1
Bridge St B2
Broad St B2
Broad Walk B3
Burkitt St A2
Bus Station A2
Carmelite Terr C2
Chapel St A2
Chase Ave C3
Checker St C2
Church St B2
Clough La B2
Coburg St B2
College of West Anglia A3
Columbia Way A3
Corn Exchange A1
County Court Rd B2
Cresswell St A2
Custom House A1
Eastgate St A2
Edma St A2
Exton's Rd C3
Ferry La B1
Ferry St A1
Framingham's Almshouses B2
Friars St C2
Friars Walk C2
Gaywood Rd A3
George St A2
Gladstone Rd C2
Goodwin's Rd C3
Green Quay B1
Greyfriars' Tower B2
Guanock Terr C2
Guildhall A1
Hansa Rd C3
Hardwick Rd C2
Hextable Rd A2
High St B1
Holcombe Ave C3
Hospital Walk C2
Information Ctr B1
John Kennedy Rd A2
Kettlewell Lane A2
King George V Ave B3
King St B1
King's Lynn Art Ctr A1
King's Lynn FC B3
King's Lynn Station B2
Library B2
Littleport St A2
Loke Rd A2
London Rd B2
Lynn Museum B2
Magistrates Court B1
Majestic B2
Market La A1
Millfleet B2
Milton Ave A3
Nar Valley Walk C2
Nelson St B1
New Conduit St B2
Norfolk St A2
North Lynn Discovery Centre A3
North St A2
Oldsunway B2
Ouse Ave C1
Page Stair Lane A1
Park Ave B3
Police Station B2
Portland Pl C1
Portland St B2
Post Office A3/C2
Purfleet B1
Queen St B1
Raby Ave A3
Railway Rd A2
Red Mount Chapel B3
Regent Way B2
River Walk A1
Robert St C2
Saddlebow Rd C2
St Ann's St A1
St James St B2
St James' Rd B2
St James' Swimming Pool B2
St John's Walk B3
St Margaret's B1
St Nicholas A2
St Nicholas St A1
St Peter's Rd B1
Sir Lewis St A2
Smith Ave A3
South Everard St C2
South Gate C2
South Quay B1
South St B2
Southgate St C2
Stonegate St B2
Surrey St A1
Sydney St C3
Tennyson Ave B3
Tennyson Rd B3
Tower St B2
Town Hall B1
Town Ho & Tales of the Old Gaol Ho B1
Town Wall (Remains) B3
True's Yard Mus A2
Valingers Rd C2
Vancouver Ave C2
Vancouver Quarter B2
Waterloo St B2
Wellesley St B2
White Friars Rd C2
Windsor Rd C2
Winfarthing St C2
Wyatt St A2
York Rd C3

Lancaster 339

Aberdeen Rd C3
Adult College, The C3
Aldcliffe Rd C2
Alfred St B3
Ambleside Rd A3
Ambulance Sta A3
Ashfield Ave B1
Ashton Rd C2
Assembly Rooms, The B2
Balmoral Rd B3
Bath House B2
Bath Mill La B3
Bath St B3
Blades St B1
Borrowdale Rd B3
Bowerham Rd C3
Brewery La B2
Bridge La B2
Brook St C2
Bulk Rd A3
Bulk St B2
Bus Station B2
Cable St B2
Canal Cruises & Waterbus C2
Carlisle Bridge A1
Carr House La C2
Castle B1
Castle Park B1
Caton Rd A3
China St B2
Church St B2
City Museum B2
Clarence St C3
Common Gdn St B2
Coniston Rd A3
Cottage Museum B2
Council Offices B2
Court B2
Cromwell Rd C1
Crown Court B1
Dale St C3
Dallas Rd B1/C1
Dalton Rd B3
Dalton Sq B2
Damside St B2
De Vitre St B3
Dee Rd A1
Denny Ave A1
Derby Rd A2
Dukes B2
Earl St A2
East Rd B3
Eastham St C3
Edward St B3
Fairfield Rd B1
Fenton St B2
Firbank Rd A3
Fire Station B2
Friend's Meeting House B1
Garnet St B3
George St B2
Giant Axe Field B1
Grand, The B2
Grasmere Rd B3
Greaves Rd C2
Green St A3
Gregson Centre, The B3
Gregson Rd C3
Greyhound Bridge A2
Greyhound Bridge Rd A2
High St B2
Hill Side B1
Hope St C3
Hubert Pl B1
Information Ctr B2
Judges Lodgings B2
Kelsy St B1
Kentmere Rd B3
King St B2
Kingsway A3
Kirkes Rd C3
Lancaster & Lakeland C3
Lancaster City Football Club B1
Lancaster Station B1
Langdale Rd A3
Ley Ct B1
Library B2
Lincoln Rd B1
Lindow St C2
Lodge St B2
Long Marsh La B1
Lune Rd A1
Lune St A2
Lune Valley Ramble A3
Mainway A2
Maritime Museum A1
Mkt Gate Shopping Centre B2
Market St B2
Meadowside C2
Meeting House La B1
Millennium Bridge A2
Moor La B2
Moorgate B3
Morecambe Rd A1/A2
Nelson St B2
North Rd B2
Orchard La C1
Owen Rd A2
Park Rd B3
Parliament St A3
Patterdale Rd A3
Penny St B2
Police Station B2
Portland St C2
Post Office A3/B1/B2/B3/C3
Primrose St C3
Priory B1
Prospect St C3
Quarry Rd B3
Queen St C2
Regent St C2
Ridge La A3
Ridge St A3
Royal Lancaster Infirmary (A&E) C2
Rydal Rd B3
Ryelands Park A1
St Georges Quay A1
St John's B2
St Leonard's Gate B2
St Martin's Rd C3
St Nicholas Arcades Shopping Centre B2
St Oswald St C3
St Peter's B3
St Peter's Rd B3
Salisbury Rd B1
Scotch Quarry Urban Park C3
Shire Hall/HM Prison B1
Sibsey St B1
Skerton Bridge A2
South Rd C2
Station Rd B1
Stirling Rd C3
Storey Ave B1
Sunnyside La C1
Sylvester St C1
Tarnsyke Rd A1
Thurnham St C2
Town Hall B2
Troutbeck Rd B3
Ulleswater Rd B3
University of Cumbria C3
Vicarage Field B1
Vue B2
West Rd B1
Westbourne Dr C1
Westbourne Rd B1
Westham St C3
Wheatfield St B1
White Cross Bsns Pk C2
Williamson Rd B3
Willow La B1
Windermere Rd B3
Wingate-Saul Rd B1
Wolseley St B3
Woodville St B3
Wyresdale Rd C3

Leeds 339

Aire St B3
Albion Pl B4
Albion St B4
Albion Way B1
Alma St A6
Ambulance Sta B5
Arcades B4
Armley Rd B1
Back Burley Lodge Rd A1
Back Hyde Terr A2
Back Row C3
Bath Rd C3
Beckett St A6
Bedford St B3
Belgrave St A4
Belle Vue Rd A2
Benson St A5

358 Leicester • Lewes • Lincoln • Liverpool

Black Bull St C5
Blenheim Walk A3
Boar La B4
Bond St B4
Bow St C5
Bowman La C4
Brewery C4
Brewery Wharf C5
Bridge St A5/B5
Briggate B4
Bruce Gdns C1
Burley Rd A1
Burley St B1
Burmantofs St B6
Bus & Coach Station B5
Butterly St C4
Butts Cr B4
Byron St A5
Call La B4
Calls, The B5
Calverley St A3/B3
Canal St B1
Canal Wharf C3
Carlisle Rd C5
Cavendish Rd A1
Cavendish St A2
Chadwick St C5
Cherry Pl A6
Cherry Row A5
City Museum A4
City Varieties Music Hall B4
City Sq B3
Civic Hall A3
Clarence Road C5
Clarendon Rd A2
Clarendon Way A3
Clark La C6
Clay Pit La A4
Cloberry St A2
Close, The B6
Clyde Approach C1
Clyde Gdns C1
Coleman St C2
Commercial St B4
Concord St A5
Cookridge St A4
Copley Hill C1
Core, The B4
Corn Exchange B4
Cromer Terr A2
Cromwell St A5
Cross Catherine St B6
Cross Green La C6
Cross Stamford St A5
Crown & County Courts A3
Crown Point Bridge C5
Crown Point Rd C4
Crown Point Retail Pk C4
David St C3
Dent St C6
Derwent Pl C3
Dial St C6
Dock St C4
Dolly La A6
Domestic St C2
Drive, The B6
Duke St B5
Duncan St B4
Dyer St B5
East Field St B6
East Pde B3
East St C5
Eastgate B5
Easy Rd C6
Edward St B4
Ellerby La C6
Ellerby Rd C6
Fenton St A3
Fire Station B2
First Direct Arena A4
Fish St B4
Flax Pl B5
Garth, The B5
Gelderd Rd C1
George St B4
Globe Rd C2
Gloucester Cr B1
Gower St A5
Grafton St A4
Grand Theatre B4
Granville Rd A6
Great George St A3
Great Wilson St C4
Greek St B3
Green La C1
Hanover Ave A2
Hanover La A2
Hanover Sq A2
Hanover Way A2
Harewood St B4
Harrison St B4
Haslewood Cl B6
Haslewood Drive B6
Headrow, The B3/B4
High Court B5
Holbeck La C2
Holdforth Cl C1
Holdforth Gdns B1
Holdforth Gr C1
Holdforth Pl C1
Holy Trinity B4
Hope Rd A5
Hunslet La C4
Hunslet Rd C4
Hyde Terr A2
Infirmary St B3
Information Ctr B3
Ingram Row C3
ITV Yorkshire A1
Junction St C4
Kelso Gdns A2
Kelso Rd A2
Kelso St A2
Kendal La A2
Kendell St C4
Kidacre St C4
King Edward St B4
King St B3
Kippax Pl C6
Kirkgate B4
Kirkgate Market B4
Kirkstall Rd A1
Kitson St C6
Lady La B4
Lands La B4
Lane, The B5
Lavender Walk B6
Leeds Art Gallery B3
Leeds Beckett Univ A3
Leeds Bridge C4
Leeds Coll of Music B5
Leeds Discovery Centre C5
Leeds General Infirmary (A&E) A3
Leeds Station B3
Library B3/B4
Light, The B4
Lincoln Green Rd A6
Lincoln Rd A6
Lindsey Gdns A6
Lindsey Rd A6
Lisbon St B3
Little Queen St B3
Long Close La C6
Lord St C2
Lovell Park A4
Lovell Park Hill A4
Lovell Park Rd A4
Lower Brunswick St A5
Mabgate A5
Macauly St A5
Magistrates Court A3
Manor Rd C3
Mark La B4
Marlborough St B2
Marsh La B5
Marshall St C3
Meadow La C4
Meadow Rd C4
Melbourne St A5
Merrion Centre A4
Merrion St A4
Merrion Way A4
Mill St B5
Millennium Sq A3
Mount Preston St A2
Mushroom St A5
Neville St C4
New Briggate A4/B4
New Market St B4
New York Rd A5
New York St B5
Nile St A5
Nippet La A6
North St A4
Northern St B3
Oak Rd B1
Oxford Pl B3
Oxford Row A3
Parade, The B6
Park Cross St B3
Park La A2
Park Pl B3
Park Row B4
Park Sq B3
Park Sq East B3
Park Sq West B3
Park St B3
Police Station A3
Pontefract La B6
Portland Cr A3
Portland Way A3
Post Office B4/B5
Quarry House (NHS/DSS Headquarters) B5
Quebec St B3
Queen St B3
Railway St B5
Rectory St A6
Regent St A5
Richmond St C5
Rigton Approach B6
Rigton Dr B6
Rillbank La A1
Rosebank Rd A1
Rose Bowl Conference Centre A3
Royal Armouries C5
Russell St B3
St Anne's Cath (RC) A4
St Anne's St B4
St James' Hospital A6
St John's Rd A2
St Johns Centre B4
St Mary's St B5
St Pauls St B3
St Peter's B5
Saxton La B5
Sayner La C5
Shakespeare Ave A6
Shannon St B6
Sheepscar St South A5
Siddall St C3
Skinner La A5
South Pde B3
Sovereign St C4
Spence La C2
Springfield Mount A2
Springwell Ct C2
Springwell Rd C2
Springwell St C2
Stoney Rock La A6
Studio Rd A1
Sutton St C2
Sweet St C3
Sweet St West C3
Swinegate B4
Templar St B5
Tetley, The C4
Thoresby Pl A3
Torre Rd A6
Town Hall A3
Union Pl C3
Union St B5
University of Leeds A3
Upper Accomodation Rd B6
Upper Basinghall St B4
Vicar La B4
Victoria Bridge C4
Victoria Quarter B4
Victoria Rd C4
Vue B4
Wade La A4
Washington St A1
Water La C3
Waterloo Rd C4
Wellington Rd B2/C1
Wellington St B3
West St B2
West Yorkshire Playhouse B5
Westfield Rd A1
Westgate B3
Whitehall Rd B3/C2
Whitelock St A5
Willis St C6
Willow Approach A1
Willow Ave A1
Willow Terrace Rd A3
Wintoun St A5
Woodhouse La A3/A4
Woodsley Rd A1
York Pl B3
York Rd B6

Leicester 339

Abbey St A2
All Saints' A1
Aylestone Rd C2
Bath La A1
Bede Park C1
Bedford St A3
Bedford St South A3
Belgrave Gate A2
Belvoir St B2
Braunstone Gate B1
Burleys Way A2
Burnmoor St C2
Bus Station A2
Canning St A2
Carlton St C2
Castle B1
Castle Gardens B1
Cathedral B2
Causeway La A2
Charles St B3
Chatham St B2
Christow St A3
Church Gate A2
City Gallery B3
City Hall B3
Clank St B2
Clock Tower B2
Clyde St A3
Colton St B3
Conduit St B3
Crafton St A3
Craven St A1
Crown Courts B3
Curve B3
De Lux A2
De Montfort Hall C3
De Montfort St C3
De Montfort Univ C1
Deacon St C2
Dover St B3
Duns La B1
Dunton St A1
East St B3
Eastern Boulevard C1
Edmonton Rd A3
Erskine St A3
Filbert St C1
Filbert St East C2
Fire Station C3
Fleet St A3
Friar La B2
Friday St A2
Gateway St C2
Gateway, The C2
Glebe St B3
Granby St B3
Grange La C2
Grasmere St C1
Great Central St A1
Guildhall B2
Guru Nanak Sikh Museum B1
Halford St B2
Havelock St C2
Haymarket Sh Ctr A2
High St A2
Highcross Sh Ctr A2
Highcross St A1
HM Prison C2
Horsefair St B2
Humberstone Gate B2
Humberstone Rd A3
Infirmary St C2
Information Ctr B2
Jarrom St C2
Jewry Wall B1
Kamloops Cr A3
King Richards Rd B1
King St B2
Lancaster Rd C3
LCB Depot B3
Lee St A3
Leicester Royal Infirmary (A&E) C2
Leicester Station B3
Library B2
London Rd C3
Lower Brown St B2
Magistrates Court B2
Manitoba Rd A3
Mansfield St A2
Market B2
Market St B2
Mill La C2
Montreal Rd A3
Narborough Rd North B1
Nelson Mandela Park C2
New Park St B1
New St B2
New Walk C3
New Walk Museum & Art Gallery C3
Newarke Houses B2
Newarke St B2
Newarke, The B1
Northgate St A1
Orchard St A2
Ottawa Rd A3
Oxford St C2
Phoenix Arts Ctr B3
Police Station A3
Post Office A1/B2/C3
Prebend St C3
Princess Rd East C3
Princess Rd West C3
Queen St B3
Rally Com Park, The A2
Regent College C3
Regent Rd C2/C3
Repton St A1
Rutland St B3
St Georges Retail Pk B3
St George St B3
St Georges Way B3
St John St A2
St Margaret's A2
St Margaret's Way A2
St Martins B2
St Mary de Castro B1
St Matthew's Way A3
St Nicholas B1
St Nicholas Circle B1
Sanvey Gate A2
Silver St B2
Slater St A1
Soar La A1
South Albion St B3
Southampton St B3
Sue Townsend Theatre B3
Swain St B3
Swan St A1
Tigers Way C3
Tower St C3
Town Hall B2
Tudor Rd B1
University of Leicester C3
University Rd C3
Upper Brown St B2
Upperton Rd C1
Vaughan Way A2
Walnut St C2
Watling St A2
Welford Rd B2
Welford Rd Leicester Tigers C2
Wellington St B2
West Bridge B1
West St C3
West Walk C3
Western Boulevard C1
Western Rd C1
Wharf St North A3
Wharf St South A3
Y Theatre, The B3
Yeoman St B3
York Rd B2

Lewes 339

Abinger Pl B1
All Saints Centre B2
Anne of Cleves Ho C1
Avenue, The B1
Barbican Ho Mus B1
Brewery B2
Brook St A2
Brooks Rd A2
Bus Station B2
Castle Ditch La B1
Castle Precincts B1
Chapel Hill B3
Church La A1/A2
Cliffe High St B2
Cliffe Industrial Est C3
Cluny St C1
Cockshut Rd C1
Convent Field C2
Coombe Rd A2
County Hall B1
Course, The C1
Court B2
Court Rd B2
Crown Court B2
Cuilfail Tunnel B3
Davey's La A3
East St B2
Eastport La C1
Fire Station A2
Fisher St B2
Friars Walk B2
Garden St B1
Government Offices C2
Grange Rd B1
Ham La C2
Harveys Way B2
Hereward Way A2
High St B1/B2
Hop Gallery B2
Information Ctr B2
Keere St B1
King Henry's Rd B1
Lancaster St B2
Landport Rd A1
Leisure Centre C3
Lewes Bridge B2
Lewes Castle B1
Lewes Football Gd C2
Lewes Golf Course B3
Lewes Southern By-Pass C2
Lewes Station B2
Library B2
Malling Brook Ind Est A3
Malling Hill A3
Malling Ind Est A2
Malling St A3/B3
Market St B2
Martlets, The A2
Martyr's Monument B3
Mayhew Way A2
Morris Rd B3
Mountfield Rd C2
Needlemakers, The B2
New Rd B1
Newton Rd A1
North St A2/B2
Offham Rd B1
Old Malling Way A1
Orchard Rd A3
Paddock La B1
Paddock Rd B1
Paddock Sports Gd B1
Park Rd B1
Pelham Terr A1
Pells Outdoor Swimming Pool A1
Pells, The A1
Phoenix Causeway B2
Phoenix Ind Est B2
Phoenix Pl B2
Pinwell Rd B2
Police Station B2
Post Office A2/B1/B2/C1
Prince Edward's Rd B1
Priory of St Pancras (remains of) C1
Priory St C1
Railway La B2
Railway Land Nature Reserve B3
Rotten Row B1
Riverside Ind Est A2
Rufus Cl B1
St John St B1
St John's Terr B1
St Nicholas La B2
St Pancras Rd C1
Sewage Works C3
South Downs Bsns Pk A3
South St B3/C3
Southdowns Rd A2
Southerham Junction C3
Southover Grange Gdns B1
Southover High St C1
Southover Rd B1
Spences Field A3
Spences La A2
Stansfield Rd A1
Station Rd B2
Station St B2
Sun St B1
Superstore A2/B2
Sussex Downs Coll C2
Sussex Police HQ A2
Talbot Terr B1
Thebes Gallery B2
Toronto Terr B1
Town Hall B2
West St B2
White Hill B1
Willeys Bridge A1

Lincoln 342

Alexandra Terr B1
Anchor St C1
Arboretum B3
Arboretum Ave B3
Avenue, The B1
Baggholme Rd B3
Bailgate A2
Beaumont Fee B1
Brayford Way C1
Brayford Wharf East C1
Brayford Wharf North B1
Bruce Rd A2
Burton Rd A1
Bus Station (City) C2
Canwick Rd C2
Cardinal's Hat B2
Carline Rd B1
Castle B1
Castle St A1
Cathedral B2
Cathedral St B2
Cecil St A2
Chapel La A2
Cheviot St B3
Church La A2
City Hall B1
Clasketgate B2
Clayton Sports Gd A3
Coach Park C2
Collection, The B2
County Hospl (A&E) B3
County Office B1
Courts C1
Croft St B2
Cross St C2
Crown Courts B1
Curle Ave A3
Danesgate B2
Drill Hall B2
Drury La B1
East Bight A2
East Gate A2
Eastcliff Rd B3
Eastgate B2
Egerton Rd A3
Ellis Windmill A1
Engine Shed, The C1
Environment Agency C2
Exchequer Gate B2
Firth Rd C1
Flaxengate B2
Florence St B3
George St C3
Good La A2
Gray St A1
Great Northern Terr C3
Great Northern Terrace Industrial Estate C3
Greetwell Rd B3
Greetwellgate B3
Grove, The A3
Haffenden Rd A2
High St B2/C1
HM Prison A3
Hospital (Private) A2
Hungate B2
James St A2
Jews House & Ct B2
Kesteven St C2
Langworthgate A2
Lawn, The B1
Lee Rd A3
Library B2
Lincoln Central Sta C2
Lincoln College B2
Lincolnshire Life/Royal Lincolnshire Regiment Museum A1
Lindum Rd B2
Lindum Sports Gd A3
Lindum Terr B3
Mainwaring Rd A3
Manor Rd A2
Market C2
Massey Rd A3
Medieval Bishop's Palace B2
Mildmay St A1
Mill Rd A1
Millman Rd B3
Minster Yard B2
Monks Rd B3
Montague St B2
Mount St A1
Nettleham Rd A2
Newland B1
Newport A2
Newport Arch A2
Newport Cemetery A2
Northgate A2
Odeon C1
Orchard St B1
Oxford St C2
Park St B1
Pelham Bridge C2
Pelham St C2
Police Station B1
Portland St C2
Post Office A1/B3/C2
Potter Gate B2
Priory Gate B2
Queensway A3
Rasen La A1
Ropewalk C1
Rosemary La B2
St Anne's Rd B3
St Benedict's C1
St Giles Ave A3
St Mark's Sh Ctr C1
St Marks St C1
St Mary-Le-Wigford C1
St Mary's St C2
St Nicholas St A2
St Swithin's B2
Saltergate C1
Saxon St A1
Sch of Art & Design B2
Sewell Rd B3
Silver St B2
Sincil St C2
Spital St A2
Spring Hill B1
Stamp End C3
Steep Hill B2
Stonebow & Guildhall C2
Stonefield Ave A2
Tentercroft St C1
Theatre Royal B2
Tritton Rd C1
Tritton Retail Park C1
Union Rd B1
University of Lincoln C1
Upper Lindum St B3
Upper Long Leys Rd A1
Usher B2
Vere St A2
Victoria St B1
Victoria Terr B1
Vine St B3
Wake St A1
Waldeck St A1
Waterside North C2
Waterside Sh Ctr C2
Waterside South C2
West Pde B1
Westgate A2
Wigford Way C1
Williamson St A2
Wilson St A1
Winn St B3
Wragby Rd A3
Yarborough Rd A1

Liverpool 342

Abercromby Sq C5
Acc Liverpool C2
Addison St A3
Adelaide Rd B6
Ainsworth St B4
Albany Rd B6
Albert Dock C2
Albert Edward Rd B6
Angela St C6
Anson St B4
Argyle St C3
Arrad St C4
Ashton St B5
Audley St A4
Back Leeds St A2
Basnett St B3
Bath St A1
Beacon, The B3
Beatles Story C2
Beckwith St C3
Bedford Close C5
Bedford St North C5
Bedford St South C5
Benson St C4
Berry St C4
Birkett St A4
Bixteth St B2
Blackburne Place C4
Bluecoat B3
Bold Place C4
Bold St C4
Bolton St B3
Bridport St B4
Bronte St B4
Brook St A1
Brownlow Hill B4/B5
Brownlow St B5
Brunswick Rd A5
Brunswick St B1
Bus Station C2
Butler Cr A6
Byrom St A3
Caledonia St C4
Cambridge St C5
Camden St A4
Canada Blvd B1
Canning Dock C2
Canterbury St A4
Cardwell St C6
Carver St A4
Cases St B3
Castle St B2
Catherine St C5
Cavern Club B3
Central Library A3
Central Station B3
Chapel St B2
Charlotte St B3
Chatham Place C6
Chatham St C5
Cheapside B2
Chestnut St C5
Christian St A3
Church St B3
Churchill Way North A3
Churchill Way South B3
Clarence St B4
Coach Station A4
Cobden St A5
Cockspur St A2
College St C3
College St North A5
College St South A5
Colquitt St C4
Comus St A3
Concert St C3
Connaught Rd B6
Cook St B2
Copperas Hill B4
Cornwallis St C3
Covent Garden A4
Craven St A4
Cropper St B3
Crown St B5/C6
Cumberland St B2
Cunard Building B1
Dale St B2
Dansie St B4
Daulby St B5
Dawson St B3
Derby Sq B2
Drury La B2
Duckinfield St B4
Duke St C3
Earle St A2
East St A2
Eaton St A2
Edgar St A3
Edge La B6
Edinburgh Rd A6
Edmund St B2
Elizabeth St B5
Elliot St B3
Empire Theatre B4
Empress Rd B6
Epstein Theatre B3
Epworth St A5
Erskine St A5
Everyman Theatre C5
Exchange St East B2
FACT C4
Falkland St A5
Falkner St C5/C6
Farnworth St A6
Fenwick St B2
Fielding St A6
Fire Sta A4
Fleet St C3
Fraser St A4
Freemasons Row A2
Gardner Row A3
Gascoyne St A2
George Pier Head C1
George St B2
Gibraltar Road A1
Gilbert St C3
Gildart St A4
Gill St B4
Goree B2
Gower St C2
Gradwell St C3
Great Crosshall St A3
Great George St C4
Great Howard St A1
Great Newton St B4
Greek St B4
Green La B4
Greenside A5
Greetham St C3
Gregson St A5
Grenville St C3
Grinfield St C6
Grove St C5
Guelph St A6
Hackins Hey B2
Haigh St A4
Hall La B6
Hanover St B3
Harbord St C6
Hardman St C4
Harker St A4
Hart St B4
Hatton Garden A2
Hawke St B4
Helsby St B6
Henry St C3
Highfield St A2
Highgate St B6
Hilbre St B4
HM Customs & Excise National Museum C2
Hope Place C4
Hope St C4
Hope University A5
Houghton St B3
Hunter St A3
Hutchinson St A6
Information Ctr B4/C2
Institute for the Performing Arts C4
Int Slavery C2
Irvine St B6
Irwell St B2
Islington A4
James St B2
James St Station B2
Jenkinson St A4
John Moores Univ A2/A3/A4/B4/C4
Johnson St A3
Jubilee Drive B6
Kempston St A4
Kensington A6
Kensington Gdns B6
Kensington St A6
Kent St C3
King Edward St A1
Kinglake St B6
Knight St C4
Lace St A3
Langsdale St A4
Law Courts C2
Leece St C4
Leeds St A2
Leopold Rd B6
Lime St B3
Lime St Station B4
Little Woolton St B5
Liver St C2
Liverpool Landing Stage B1
Liverpool Institute for Performing Arts C4
Liverpool ONE C2
Liverpool Wheel, The C2
London Rd A4/B4
Lord Nelson St B4
Lord St B2
Lovat St B4
Low Hill A5
Low Wood St A6
Lydia Ann St C3
Mansfield St A4
Marmaduke St B6
Marsden St A6
Martensen St B6
Marybone A3
Maryland St C4
Mason St B6
Mathew St B2
May St B4
Melville Place C6
Merseyside Maritime Museum C2
Metquarter B3
Metropolitan Cathedral (RC) B5
Midghall St A2
Molyneux Rd A6
Moor Place B4
Moorfields B2
Moorfields Station B2
Moss St A5
Mount Pleasant B4/B5
Mount St C4
Mount Vernon B6
Mulberry St C5
Municipal Buildings B2
Mus of Liverpool C2
Myrtle Gdns C6
Myrtle St C5
Naylor St A2
Nelson St C4
New Islington A4
New Quay B1
Newington St C3
North John St B2
North St A3
North View B6
Norton St A4
O2 Academy B4
Oakes St B5
Odeon B4
Old Hall St A1
Old Leeds St A2
Oldham Place C4
Oldham St C4
Olive St C6
Open Eye Gallery C3
Oriel St A2
Ormond St B2
Orphan St C6
Overbury St C6
Overton St B6
Oxford St C5
Paisley St A1
Pall Mall A2
Paradise St C3
Park La C3
Parker St B3
Parr St C3
Peach St B5
Pembroke Place B4
Pembroke St B5
Philharmonic Hall C5
Pickop St A2
Pilgrim St C4
Pitt St C3
Playhouse Theatre B3
Pleasant St B4
Police HQ C2
Police Sta A4/A6/B4
Pomona St B4
Port of Liverpool Building B2
Post Office A2/A4/A5/B2/B3/B4/C4
Pownall St C2
Prescot St A5
Preston St B3
Princes Dock A1
Princes Gdns A2
Princes Jetty A1
Princes Pde B1
Princes St B2
Pythian St A6
Queen Square Bus Station B3
Queensland St C6
Queensway Tunnel (Docks exit) B1
Queensway Tunnel (Entrance) B3
Radio City B2
Ranelagh St B3
Redcross St B2
Renfrew St B6
Renshaw St B4
Richmond Row A4
Richmond St B3
Rigby St A2
Roberts St A1
Rock St B4
Rodney St C4
Rokeby St A4
Romily St A6
Roscoe La C4
Roscoe St C4
Rose Hill A3
Royal Ct Theatre B3
Royal Liver Building B1
Royal Liverpool Hospital (A&E) B5
Royal Mail St B4
Rumford Place B2
Rumford St B2
Russell St B4
St Andrew St B4
St Anne St A4
St Georges Hall B3
St John's Centre B3
St John's Gdns B3
St John's La B3
St Joseph's Cr A4
St Minishull St B5
St Nicholas Place B1
St Paul's Sq A2
St Vincent Way B4
Salisbury St A4
Salthouse Dock C2
Salthouse Quay C2
Sandon St C5
Saxony Rd B6
Schomberg St A6
School La B2
Seel St C3
Seymour St B4
Shaw St A5
Shopmobility C2
Sidney Place C6
Sir Thomas St B3
Skelhorne St B4
Slater St C3
Smithdown La B6
Soho Sq A4
Soho St A4
South John St B2
Springfield A4
Stafford St A4
Standish St A3
Stanley St B2
Strand St C2
Strand, The B2
Suffolk St C3
Tabley St C3
Tarleton St B3
Tate Gallery C2
Teck St B6
Temple St B2
Tithebarn St B2
Town Hall B2
Traffic Police HQ C6
Trowbridge St B4
Trueman St A3
Union St B2
Unity Theatre C4
University C5
University of Liverpool B5
Upper Baker St A6
Upper Duke St C4
Upper Frederick St C3
Vauxhall Rd A2
Vernon St B2
Victoria Gallery & Museum B5
Victoria St B2
Vine St C5
Wakefield St A4
Walker Art Gallery A3
Walker St A6
Wapping C2
Water St B1/B2
Waterloo Rd A1
Wavertree Rd B6
West Derby Rd A6
West Derby St B5
Western Approaches War Museum B2
Whitechapel B3
Whitley Gdns A5
William Brown St B3
William Henry St A4
Williamson Sq B3
Williamson St B3
Williamson's Tunnels Heritage Centre C6
Women's Hospital C6
Wood St B3
World Museum, Liverpool A3
York St C3

Llandudno 342

Abbey Pl B1
Abbey Rd B1
Adelphi St B3
Alexandra Rd C2
Anglesey Rd A1
Argyll Rd B3
Arvon Ave A2
Atlee Cl C3
Augusta St B3
Back Madoc St B2
Bodafon St B3
Bodhyfryd Rd A2
Bodnant Cr C3
Bodnant Rd C3
Bridge Rd C2
Bryniau Rd C1
Builder St B3
Builder St West C2
Cabin Lift A2
Camera Obscura ✦ A3
Caroline Rd B2
Chapel St A2
Charlton St B3
Church Cr C1
Church Walks A2
Claremont Rd B2
Clement Ave A2
Clifton Rd B2
Clonmel St B3
Coach Station B3
Conway Rd B3
Council St West C3
Cricket and Rec Gd B2
Cwlach Rd A2
Cwlach St A1
Cwm Howard La C3
Cwm Pl C3
Cwm Rd C3
Dale Rd C1
Deganwy Ave B2
Denness Pl C2
Dinas Rd C2
Dolydd B1
Erol Pl B2
Ewloe Dr C3
Fairways C2
Ffordd Dewi C3
Ffordd Dulyn C2
Ffordd Dwyfor C3
Ffordd Elisabeth C3
Ffordd Gwynedd C3
Ffordd Las C3
Ffordd Morfa C3
Ffordd Penrhyn C3
Ffordd Tudno C3
Ffordd yr Orsedd C3
Ffordd Ysbyty C2
Fire & Ambulance Sta B3
Garage St B3
George St A2
Gloddaeth Ave B1
Gloddaeth St B2
Gogarth Rd B1
Great Orme Mines ✦ A1
Great Ormes Rd B1
Great Orme Tramway ✦ A1
Happy Valley A2
Happy Valley Rd A3
Haulfre Gardens ✿ A1
Herkomer Cr C1
Hill Terr A2
Home Front Mus 🏛 B2
Hospice B1
Howard Rd B3
Information Ctr ℹ B2
Invalids' Walk B1
James St B2
Jubilee St B3
King's Ave C2
King's Rd C2
Knowles Rd C2
Lees Rd C2
Library B2
Lifeboat Station B2
Llandudno 🏛 A2
Llandudno (A&E) Ⓗ C2
Llandudno Station ≹ B3
Llandudno Town Football Ground C2
Llewelyn Ave A2
Lloyd St B2
Lloyd St West B1
Llwynon Rd A1
Llys Maelgwn B1
Madoc St B2
Maelgwn Rd B2
Maes-y-Cwm C3
Maes-y-Orsedd C3
Maesdu Bridge C2
Maesdu Rd C2/C3
Marian Pl C2
Marian Rd C2
Marine Drive (Toll) A3
Market Hall A2
Market St A2
Miniature Golf Course A1
Morfa Rd B1
Mostyn 🏛 B3
Mostyn Broadway B3
Mostyn St B3
Mowbray Rd C2
New St A2
Norman Rd B3
North Parade A2
North Wales Golf Links C1
Old Bank Gallery 🏛 A2
Old Rd A2
Oval, The B1
Oxford Rd B3
Parade, The B3
Parc Llandudno Retail Park B3
Pier ✦ A3
Plas Rd A2
Police Station ▣ B3
Post Office ✉ B3
Promenade A3
Pyllau Rd A1
Rectory La A2
Rhuddlan Ave C3
St Andrew's Ave B2
St Andrew's Pl B2
St Beuno's Rd A1
St David's Pl B2
St David's Rd B2
St George's Pl A3
St Mary's Rd B2
St Seriol's Rd B2
Salisbury Pass B1
Salisbury Rd B2
Somerset St B3
South Parade A2
Stephen St B3
TA Centre B3
Tabor Hill A2
Town Hall B2
Trinity Ave B1
Trinity Cres C1
Trinity Sq B3
Tudno St A2
Ty-Coch Rd A2
Ty-Gwyn Rd A1/A2
Ty'n-y-Coed Rd A1
Vaughan St B3
Victoria Shopping Ctr B3
Victoria 🚋 A2
War Memorial ✦ A2
Werny Wylan C3
West Parade B1
Whiston Pass A2
Winllan Ave C2
Wyddfyd Rd A2
York Rd A2

Llanelli 342

Alban Rd B3
Albert St B1
Als St B3
Amos St C1
Andrew St A3
Ann St C2
Annesley St B2
Arfryn Ave A3
Avenue Cilfig, The A2
Belvedere Rd A1
Bigyn Park Terr C3
Bigyn Rd C3
Bond Ave C3
Brettenham St A1
Bridge St B2
Bryn Pl C1
Bryn Rd C1
Bryn Terr C1
Bryn-More Rd C1
Brynhyfryd Rd A2
Brynmelyn Ave A3
Brynmor Rd B1
Burry St C1
Bus Station B2
Caersalem Terr C2
Cambrian St C1
Caswell St C3
Cedric St B3
Cemetery A2
Chapman St A1
Charles Terr C2
Church St B2
Clos Caer Elms A1
Clos Sant Paul C2
Coastal Link Rd B1/C1
Coldstream St B2
Coleshill Terr B1
College Hill B3
College Sq B3
Copperworks Rd C2
Coronation Rd C3
Corporation Ave A3
Council Offices B2
Court B2
Cowell St B2
Cradock St C2
Craig Ave C3
Cricket Ground A1
Derwent St A1
Dillwyn St C2
Druce St C1
Eastgate Leisure Complex ✦ B2
Elizabeth St B2
Emma St C2
Erw Rd B1
Felinfoel Rd A2
Fire Station A3
Firth Rd C3
Fron Terr C3
Furnace Rugby Football Ground A1
Gelli-On B2
George St C2
Gilbert Cres A2
Gilbert Rd A2
Glanmor Rd C2
Glanmor Terr C2
Glasfryn Terr A3
Glenalla Rd B3
Glevering St B3
Goring Rd A2
Gorsedd Circle ⊓ A2
Grant St C3
Graveyard C2
Great Western Cl C2
Greenway St B1
Hall St B2
Harries Ave A2
Hedley Terr A2
Heol Elli B3
Heol Goffa A3
Heol Nant-y-Felin A3
Heol Siloh B2
Hick St C2
High St C1
Indoor Bowls Centre B1
Inkerman St B2
Island Pl B2
James St B3
John St B2
King George Ave B3
Lake View Cl A2
Lakefield Pl C1
Lakefield Rd C1
Langland Rd C3
Leisure Centre B1
Library B2
Llanelli House 🏛 B2
Llanelli Parish Church ⛪ B2
Llanelli Station ≹ C2
Llewellyn St C2
Lliedi Cres A3
Lloyd St B2
Llys Alys B3
Llys Fran A3
Llysnewedd C1
Long Row A3
Maes Gors C2
Maesyrhaf A3
Mansel St C3
Marblehall Rd B3
Marborough Rd A2
Margam St C3
Marged St C2
Marine St C1
Mariners, The C1
Market B2
Market St B2
Marsh St C2
Martin Rd C3
Miles St A1
Mill La A3/B2
Mincing La B2
Murray St B2
Myn y Mor B1
Nathan St C1
Nelson Terr C1
Nevill St C2
New Dock Rd C2
New Rd A1
New Zealand St A1
Odeon 🎬 B2
Old Lodge C2
Old Rd A2
Paddock St C2
Palace Ave B3
Parc Howard A2
Parc Howard Museum & Art Gallery 🏛🏛 A2
Park Cres B1
Park St B2
Parkview Terr B1
Pemberton St C2
Pembrey Rd A1
Peoples Park B1
Police Station ▣ B2
Post Office ✉ B2/C2
Pottery Pl B3
Pottery St B3
Princess St B1
Prospect Pl A2
Pryce St A1
Queen Mary's Walk C3
Queen Victoria Rd C1
Raby St B1
Railway Terr C2
Ralph St B2
Ralph Terr C1
Regalia Terr B3
Rhydyrafon A3
Richard St B2
Robinson St B2
Roland Ave A1
Russell St C3
St David's Cl C1
St Elli Shopping Ctr B2
St Margaret's Dr A1
Spowart Ave A1
Station Rd B2/C2
Stepney Pl B2
Stepney St B2
Stewart St A1
Stradey Park Ave A1
Sunny Hill A2
Superstore A2
Swansea Rd A3
Talbot St C3
Temple St B3
Theatr Elli 🎬🎭 B2
Thomas St A2
Tinopolos TV Studios ✦ B2
Toft Pl A3
Town Hall B2
Traeth Ffordd C1
Trinity Rd C3
Trinity Terr C2
Tunnel Rd B3
Tyisha Rd C3
Union Blgs A2
Upper Robinson St B2
Vauxhall Rd B2
Walter's Rd B3
Waun Lanyrafon B2
Waun Rd A3
Wern Rd B3
West End A2
Y Bwthyn C3
Zion Row B3

London 340

Abbey Orchard St E4
Abbey St E8
Abchurch La D7
Abingdon St E5
Achilles Way D3
Acton St B5
Addington St E5
Air St D4
Albany St B3
Albemarle St D4
Albert Embankment F5
Alberta St F6
Aldenham St A4
Alderney St F3
Aldersgate St C7
Aldford St D3
Aldgate ⊖ C8
Aldgate High St C8
Aldwych C5
Allsop Pl B2
Alscot Rd E8
Amwell St B6
Andrew Borde St C4
Angel ⊖ A6
Appold St C8
Argyle Sq B5
Argyle St B5
Argyll St C4
Arnold Circus B8
Artillery La C8
Artillery Row E4
Ashbridge St B2
Association of Photographers Gallery 🏛 B7
Baker St ⊖ B2
Baker St B2
Balaclava Rd F8
Balcombe St B2
Baldwin's Gdns C6
Balfour St F7
Baltic St B7
Bank ⊖ C7
Bank Museum 🏛 C7
Bank of England C7
Bankside D7
Bankside Gallery 🏛 D6
Banner St B7
Barbican ≹⊖ C7
Barbican Centre for Arts, The C7
Barbican Gallery 🏛 C7
Basil St E2
Bastwick St B7
Bateman's Row B8
Bath St B7
Bath Terr E7
Bayley St C4
Baylis Rd E6
Bayswater Rd D2
Beak St D4
Beauchamp Pl E2
Bedford Row C5
Bedford Sq C4
Bedford St D5
Bedford Way B4
Beech St C7
Belgrave Pl E3
Belgrave Rd F4
Belgrave Sq E3
Bell La C8
Belvedere Rd E5
Berkeley Sq D3
Berkeley St D3
Bermondsey St E8
Bernard St B5
Berners Pl C4
Berners St C4
Berwick St C4
Bessborough St F4
Bethnal Green Rd B8
Bevenden St B7
Bevis Marks C8
BFI (British Film Institute) 🎬 D5
BFI London IMAX Cinema 🎬 D6
Bidborough St B5
Binney St C3
Birdcage Walk E4
Bishopsgate C8
Black Prince Rd F5
Blackfriars ≹⊖ D6
Blackfriars Bridge D6
Blackfriars Rd E6
Blandford St C2
Blomfield St C7
Bloomsbury St C4
Bloomsbury Way C5
Bolton St D3
Bond St ⊖ C3
Borough ⊖ E7
Borough High St E7
Borough Rd E6
Boswell St C5
Bourne St F3
Bow St C5
Bowling Green La B6
Brad St D6
Brandon St F7
Bressenden Pl E4
Brewer St D4
Brick St D3
Bridge St E5
Britannia Walk B7
British Film Institute (BFI) 🎬 D5
British Library 🏛 B4
British Museum 🏛 C5
Britton St B6
Broad Sanctuary E4
Broadley St C2
Broadway E4
Brompton Rd E2
Brompton Sq E2
Brook Dr F6
Brook St D3
Brown St C2
Brunswick Pl B7
Brunswick Sh Ctr, The B5
Brunswick Sq B5
Brushfield St C8
Bruton St D3
Bryanston St C2
BT Centre C7
Buckingham Gate E4
Buckingham Palace 🏰 E4
Buckingham Pal Rd F3
Bunhill Row B7
Byward St D8
Cabinet War Rooms & Churchill Museum 🏛 E4
Cadogan La E3
Cadogan Pl E2
Cadogan Sq F2
Cadogan St F2
Cale St F2
Caledonian Rd A5
Calshot St A5
Calthorpe St B5
Calvert Ave B8
Cambridge Circus C4
Cambridge Sq C2
Cambridge St F3
Camomile St C8
Cannon St D7
Cannon St ≹⊖ D7
Capland St B1
Carey St C5
Carlisle La E5
Carlisle Pl E4
Carlton House Terr D4
Carmelite St D6
Carnaby St C4
Carter La C6
Carthusian St C7
Cartwright Gdns B5
Castle Baynard St D6
Cavendish Pl C3
Cavendish Sq C3
Caxton Hall E4
Caxton St E4
Central St B7
Chalton St B4
Chancery Lane ⊖ C6
Chapel St C2
Chapel St E3
Charing Cross ≹⊖ D5
Charing Cross Rd C4
Charles II St D4
Charles Sq B7
Charles St D3
Charlotte Rd B8
Charlotte St C4
Chart St B7
Charterhouse Sq C6
Charterhouse St C6
Chatham St F7
Cheapside C7
Chenies St C4
Chesham St E3
Chester Sq F3
Chester Way F6
Chesterfield Hill D3
Cheval Pl E2
Chiltern St C3
Chiswell St C7
Church St B2
City Garden Row A6
City Rd B7
City Thameslink ≹ C6
City University, The B6
Claremont Sq A6
Clarendon St F3
Clarges St D3
Clerkenwell Cl B6
Clerkenwell Green B6
Clerkenwell Rd B6
Cleveland St C4
Clifford St D4
Clink Prison Mus 🏛 D7
Cliveden Pl F3
Clock Museum 🏛 C7
Club Row B8
Cockspur St D4
Coleman St C7
Columbia Rd B8
Commercial Rd C9
Commercial St C8
Compton St B6
Conduit St D3
Congreve St F8
Connaught Sq C2
Connaught St C2
Constitution Hill E3
Copperfield St E6
Coptic St C5
Cornhill C7
Cornwall Rd D6
Coronet St B8
County St E7
Courtauld Gallery 🏛 D5
Courtenay St F6
Covent Garden ⊖ D5
Covent Garden ✦ D5
Cowcross St C6
Cowper St B7
Crampton St F7
Cranbourn St D4
Craven St D5
Crawford Pl C2
Crawford St C2
Creechurch La C8
Cricket Museum 🏛 B1
Cromer St B5
Cromwell Rd F1
Crosby Row E7
Crucifix La E8
Cumberland Gate D2
Cumberland St F3
Cumberland Terr A3
Cuming Mus 🏛 F7
Curtain Rd B8
Curzon St D3
Cut, The E6
D'arblay St C4
Dante Rd F6
Davies St C3
Dean St C4
Deluxe Gallery 🏛 B8
Denbigh Pl F4
Denmark St C4
Dering St C3
Devonshire St C3
Diana, Princess of Wales Memorial Garden ✦ D1
Diana, Princess of Wales Memorial Walk E4
Dingley Rd B7
Dorset St C2
Doughty St B5
Douglas St F4
Dover St D3
Downing St E5
Draycott Avenue F2
Draycott Pl F2
Druid St E8
Drummond St B4
Drury La C5
Drysdale St B8
Duchess St C3
Dufferin St B7
Duke of Wellington Pl E3
Duke St C3/D3
Duke St Hill D7
Duke's Pl C8
Duncannon St D5
Dunton Rd F8
East Rd B7
East St F7
Eastcastle St C4
Eastcheap D8
Eastman Dental Hospital Ⓗ B5
Eaton Gate F3
Eaton Pl E3
Eaton Sq E3
Eaton Terr F3
Ebury Bridge F3
Ebury Bridge Rd F3
Eccleston Bridge F3
Eccleston Sq F3
Eccleston St E3
Edgware Rd C2
Edgware Rd ⊖ C2
Egerton Gdns E2
Eldon St C7
Elephant & Castle ≹ F7
Elephant and Castle ≹⊖ E6
Elephant Rd F7
Elizabeth Bridge F3
Elizabeth St F3
Elm Tree Rd B1
Elystan Pl F2
Elystan St F2
Embankment ⊖ D5
Endell St C5
Endsleigh Pl B4
Enid St E8
Ennismore Gdns E2
Erasmus St F4
Euston ≹⊖ B4
Euston Rd B4
Euston Square ⊖ B4
Evelina Children's Hospital E5
Eversholt St A4
Exhibition Rd E1
Exmouth Market B6
Fair St E8
Falmouth Rd E7
Fann St B7
Farringdon ≹⊖ C6
Farringdon Rd C6
Farringdon St C6
Featherstone St B7
Fenchurch St D8
Fenchurch St ≹ D8
Fetter La C6
Finsbury Circus C7
Finsbury Pavement C7
Finsbury Sq B7
Fitzalan St F6
Fitzmaurice Pl D3
Fleet St C6
Fleming Laboratory Museum 🏛 C1
Floral St D5
Florence Nightingale Museum 🏛 E5
Folgate St C8
Fore St C7
Foster La C7
Francis St F4
Frazier St E6
Freemason's Hall C5
Friday St C7
Fulham Rd F1
Gainsford St E8
Garden Row E6
Gee St B7
Geological Mus 🏛 E1
George Row E9
George St C2
Gerrard St D4
Gibson Rd F5
Giltspur St C6
Glasshouse St D4
Glasshouse Walk F5
Gloucester Pl C2
Gloucester Sq C1
Gloucester St F4
Golden Hinde ⛵ D7
Golden La B7
Golden Sq D4
Goodge St ⊖ C4
Goodge St C4
Gordon Hospital Ⓗ F4
Gordon Sq B4
Goswell Rd B6
Gough St B5
Goulston St C8
Gower St B4
Gracechurch St D7
Grafton Way B4
Graham Terr F3
Grange Rd E8
Grange Walk E8
Gray's Inn Rd B5
Great College St E5
Great Cumberland Pl C2
Great Dover St E7
Great Eastern St B8
Great Guildford St D7
Great Marlborough St C4
Great Ormond St B5
Great Ormond St Children's Hospl Ⓗ B5
Great Percy St B5
Great Peter St E4
Great Portland St ⊖ B3
Great Portland St C3
Great Queen St C5
Great Russell St C4
Great Scotland Yd D5
Great Smith St E4
Great Suffolk St D6/E6
Great Titchfield St C4
Great Tower St D8
Great Windmill St D4
Greek St C4
Green Park ⊖ D4
Green St D3
Greencoat Pl F4
Gresham St C7
Greville St B5/C6
Greycoat Hosp Sch E4
Greycoat Pl E4
Grosvenor Cres E3
Grosvenor Gdns E3
Grosvenor Pl E3
Grosvenor Sq D3
Grosvenor St D3
Grove End Rd B1
Guards Museum and Chapel 🏛 E4
Guildhall Art Gallery 🏛 C7
Guilford St B5
Guy's Hospital Ⓗ D7
Haberdasher St B7
Hackney Rd B8
Half Moon St D3
Halkin St E3
Hall Pl B1
Hall St B6
Hallam St C3
Hamilton Cl B1
Hampstead Rd B4
Hanover Sq C3
Hans Cres E2
Hans Rd E2
Hanway St C4
Hardwick St B6
Harewood Ave B2
Harley St C3
Harper Rd E7
Harrington Rd F1
Harrison St B5
Harrowby St C2
Hasker St F2
Hastings St B5
Hatfields D6
Hay's Galleria D8
Hay's Mews D3
Hayles St F6
Haymarket D4
Hayne St C6
Hayward Gallery 🏛 D5
Helmet Row B7
Herbrand St B5
Hercules Rd E5
Hertford St D3
Heygate St F7
High Holborn C5
Hill St D3
HMS Belfast ⛵ D8
Hobart Pl E3
Holborn ⊖ C5
Holborn C6
Holborn Viaduct C6
Holland St D6
Holmes Mus 🏛 B2
Holywell La B8
Horse Guards' Rd D4
Horseferry Rd F4
Houndsditch C8
Houses of Parliament 🏛 E5
Howland St C4
Hoxton Sq B8
Hoxton St B8
Hugh St F3
Hunter St B5
Hunterian Mus 🏛 C5
Hyde Park D2
Hyde Park Cnr ⊖ E3
Hyde Park Cres C2
Hyde Park St C2
Imperial Coll London E1
Imperial College Rd E1
Imperial War Mus 🏛 E6
Inner Circle B3
Institute of Archaeology (London Univ) B3
Ironmonger Row B7
Jacob St E9
Jamaica Rd E8
James St C3
James St D5
Jermyn St D4
Jockey's Fields C5
John Carpenter St D6
John Fisher St D9
John Islip St F4
John St B5
Johnathan St F5
Judd St B5
Kennings Way F6
Kennington ⊖ F6
Kennington La F6
Kennington Park Rd E6/F6
Kensington Gardens D1
Kensington Gore E1
Kensington Rd E1
Keyworth St E6
King Charles St E5
King St D5
King William St C7
King's College London D5
King's Cross ≹ A5
King's Cross Rd B5
King's Cross St Pancras ⊖ A5
King's Rd F2
Kingley St C4
Kingsland Rd B8
Kingsway C5
Kinnerton St E3
Kipling St E7
Knightsbridge ⊖ E2
Lamb St C8
Lamb's Conduit St C5
Lambeth Bridge F5
Lambeth High St F5
Lambeth North ⊖ E6
Lambeth Palace 🏰 E5
Lambeth Palace Rd E5
Lambeth Rd E6
Lambeth Walk F5
Lancaster Gate ⊖ D1
Lancaster Pl D5
Lancaster St E6
Lancaster Terr D1
Langham Pl C3
Lant St E7
Leadenhall St C8
Leake St E5
Leather La C6
Leathermarket St E8
Leicester Sq ⊖ D4
Leicester St D4
Leonard St B7
Leroy St E8
Lever St B7
Lexington St D4
Lidlington Pl A4
Lime St D8
Lincoln's Inn Fields C5
Lindsey St C6
Lisle St D4
Lisson Gr B1
Lisson St C2
Liverpool St C8
Liverpool St ≹⊖ C8
Lloyd Baker St B6
Lloyd Sq B6
Lodge Rd B2
Lollard St F6
Lombard St C7
London Aquarium 🐟 E5
London Bridge ≹⊖ D7
London Bridge Hospital Ⓗ D7
London City Hall 🏛 D8
London Dungeon 🏛 E5
London Film Mus ✦ E5
London Guildhall Univ C7
London Rd E6
London St C1
London Transport Museum 🏛 D5
London Wall C7
London-Eye ✦ E5
Long Acre D5
Long La C6
Long La E7
Longford St B3
Lord's Cricket Gd (MCC & Middlesex CCC) B1
Lower Belgrave St E3
Lower Grosvenor Pl E3
Lower Marsh E6
Lower Sloane St F3
Lower Thames St D7
Lowndes St E3
Ludgate Circus C6
Ludgate Hill C6
Luxborough St C3
Lyall St E3
Macclesfield Rd B7
Madame Tussaud's ✦ B3
Maddox St D3
Malet St C4
Mall, The E4
Maltby St E8
Manchester Sq C3
Manchester St C3
Manciple St E7
Mandela Way F8
Mandeville Pl C3
Mansell St D8
Mansion House 🏛 C7
Mansion House ⊖ D7
Maple St C4
Marble Arch ⊖ C2
Marble Arch D2
Marchmont St B5
Margaret St C4
Margery St B6
Mark La D8
Marlborough Rd D4
Marshall St C4
Marshalsea Rd E7
Marsham St E4
Marylebone ≹⊖ B2
Marylebone High St C3
Marylebone La C3
Marylebone Rd B3/C2
Marylebone St C3
Mecklenburgh Sq B5
Middle Temple La C6
Middlesex St (Petticoat La) C8
Midland Rd A4
Millbank F5
Milner St F2
Minories C8
Monck St E4
Monkton St F6
Monmouth St C5
Montagu Pl C2
Montagu Sq C2
Montagu St C5
Montague Pl C4
Montpelier St E2
Montpelier Walk E2
Monument ⊖ D7
Monument St D7
Monument, The ✦ D7
Moor La C7
Moorfields C7
Moorfields Eye Hospital Ⓗ B7
Moorgate C7
Moorgate ≹⊖ C7
Moreland St B6
Morley St E6
Mortimer St C4
Mossop St F2
Mount Pleasant B6
Mount St D3
Murray Gr A7
Mus of Gdn History 🏛 E5
Museum of London 🏛 C7
Museum St C5
Myddelton Sq B6
Myddelton St B6
National Gallery 🏛 D4
National Hospital Ⓗ B5
National Portrait Gallery 🏛 D4
Natural History Museum 🏛 E1
Neal St C5
Nelson's Column ✦ D5
Neville St F1
New Bond St C3/D3
New Bridge St C6
New Cavendish St C3
New Change C7
New Fetter La C6
New Inn Yard B8
New Kent Rd F7
New North Rd A7
New Oxford St C4
New Scotland Yard E4
New Sq C5
Newburn St F5
Newgate St C6
Newington Butts F6
Newington Cswy E7
Newton St C5
Nile St B7
Noble St C7
Noel St C4
Norfolk Cres C2
Norfolk Sq C1
North Audley St D3
North Carriage Dr D2
North Cres C4
North Ride D2
North Row D3
North Wharf Rd C1
Northampton Sq B6
Northington St B5
Northumberland Ave D5
Norton Folgate C8
Nottingham Pl C3
Old Bailey C6
Old Broad St C7
Old Brompton Rd F1
Old Compton St C4
Old County Hall E5
Old Gloucester St C5
Old Jamaica Rd E9
Old Kent Rd F8
Old King Edward St C7
Old Marylebone Rd C2
Old Montague St C9
Old Nichol St B8
Old Paradise St F5
Old Spitalfields Mkt C8
Old St B7
Old St ≹⊖ B7
Old Vic 🎭 E6
Onslow Gdns F1
Onslow Sq F1
Ontario St E6
Open Air Theatre 🎭 B3
Operating Theatre Museum 🏛 D7
Orange St D4
Orchard St C3
Ossulston St A4
Outer Circle B2
Ovington Sq E2
Oxford Circus ⊖ C4
Oxford St C3/C4
Paddington ≹⊖ C1
Paddington Green Hospital Ⓗ C1
Paddington St C3
Page's Walk E8
Palace St E4
Pall Mall D4
Pall Mall East D4
Pancras Rd A5
Panton St D4
Paris Gdn D6
Park Cres B3
Park La D2
Park Rd B2
Park St D3
Park St D7
Parker St C5
Parliament Sq E5
Parliament St E5
Paternoster Sq C6
Paul St B7
Pear Tree St B6
Pelham Cres F2
Pelham St F1
Penfold St C2
Penton Pl F6
Penton Rise B5
Penton St A6
Pentonville Rd A5/A6
Percival St B6
Petticoat La (Middlesex St) C8
Petty France E4
Phoenix Pl B5
Phoenix Rd A4
Photo Gallery 🏛 D4
Piccadilly D3
Piccadilly Circus ⊖ D4
Pilgrimage St E7
Pimlico ⊖ F4
Pimlico Rd F3
Pitfield St B8
Pollock's Toy Mus 🏛 C4
Polygon Rd A4
Pont St E2
Porchester Pl C2
Portland Pl C3
Portman Mews C3
Portman Sq C3
Portman St C2
Portugal St C5
Poultry C7
Praed St C1
Primrose St C8
Prince Consort Rd E1

360 Luton • Macclesfield • Maidstone • Manchester

Prince's Gdns E1
Princes St C7
Procter St C5
Provost St B7
Quaker St B8
Queen Anne St C3
Queen Elizabeth Hall D5
Queen Elizabeth St E8
Queen Sq B5
Queen St D7
Queen Street Pl D7
Queen Victoria St D6
Queens Gallery E4
Queensberry Pl F1
Quilter St B9
Radnor St B7
Rathbone Pl C4
Rawlings St F2
Rawstorne St B6
Red Lion Sq C5
Red Lion St C5
Redchurch St B8
Redcross Way D7
Reedworth St F6
Regency St F4
Regent Sq B5
Regent St C4
Regent's Park B3
Richmond Terr E5
Ridgmount St C4
Riley Rd E8
Rivington St B8
Robert St B3
Rochester Row F4
Rockingham St E7
Rodney Rd F7
Rolls Rd F8
Ropemaker St C7
Rosebery Ave B6
Rossmore Rd B2
Rothsay St E8
Rotten Row E2
Roupell St D6
Royal Acad of Arts D4
Royal Academy of Dramatic Art B4
Royal Acad of Music B3
Royal Albert Hall E1
Royal Artillery Memorial ✦ E2
Royal Brompton Hospital F1, F2
Royal Coll of Nursing C3
Royal Coll of Surgeons C5
Royal Festival Hall D5
Royal London Hospital for Integrated Medicine C5
Royal Marsden Hospital F1
Royal National Theatre D6
Royal National Throat, Nose and Ear Hospital B5
Royal Opera House D5
Rushworth St E6
Russell Sq B4
Russell Square ⊖ B5
Rutland Gate E2
Sackville St D4
Sadlers Wells B6
Saffron Hill C6
St Alban's St D4
St Andrew St C6
St Barnabas St F3
St Bartholomew's Hospital C6
St Botolph St C8
St Bride St C6
St George's Circus E6
St George's Dr F4
St George's Rd E6
St George's Sq F4
St Giles High St C4
St James's Palace D4
St James's Park ⊖ E4
St James's St D4
St John St B6
St John's Wood Rd B1
St Margaret St E5
St Mark's Hosp B6
St Martin's La D5
St Martin's Le Grand C7
St Mary Axe C8
St Mary's Hosp C1
St Pancras Int ⇌ A5
St Paul's ⊖ C7
St Paul's Cath ✝ C7
St Paul's Churchyard C6
St Thomas St D7
St Thomas' Hosp E5
Sale Pl C2
Sancroft St F5
Savile Row D4
Savoy Pl D5
Savoy St D5
School of Hygiene & Tropical Medicine C4
Science Mus E1
Scrutton St B8
Sekforde St B6
Serpentine Gallery E1
Serpentine Rd D2
Seven Dials C5
Seward St B6
Seymour Pl C2
Seymour St C2
Shad Thames D8/E8
Shaftesbury Ave D4
Shakespeare's Globe Theatre D7
Shepherd Market D3
Sherwood St D4
Shoe La C6
Shoreditch High St B8
Shoreditch High St ⊖ B8
Shorts Gdns C5
Shouldham St C2
Sidmouth St B5
Silk St C7
Sir John Soane's Museum C5
Skinner St B6
Sloane Ave F2
Sloane Sq F2
Sloane Square ⊖ F3
Sloane St E2
Snow Hill C6
Soho Sq C4
Somerset House D5
South Audley St D3
South Carriage Dr E2
South Eaton Pl F3
South Kensington ⊖ F1
South Molton St C3
South Parade F1
South Pl C7
South St D3
South Terr F2
South Wharf Rd C1
Southampton Row C5
Southampton St D5
Southwark ⊖ D6
Southwark Bridge D7
Southwark Bridge Rd D7
Southwark Cath ✝ D7
Southwark Park Rd F8
Southwark St D7
Spa Rd E8
Speakers' Corner D2
Spencer St B6
Spital Sq C8
Spring St C1
Stamford St D6
Stanhope St B4
Stanhope Terr D1
Stephenson Way B4
Stock Exchange C6
Stoney St D7
Strand C5
Strathearn Pl D2
Stratton St D3
Sumner St D6
Sussex Gdns C1
Sussex Pl C1
Sussex Sq D1
Sussex St F3
Sutton's Way B7
Swan St E7
Swanfield St B8
Swinton St B5
Sydney Pl F1
Sydney St F2
Tabard St E7
Tabernacle St B7
Tachbrook St F4
Tanner St E8
Tate Britain F5
Tate Modern D7
Tavistock Pl B5
Tavistock Sq B4
Tea & Coffee Mus D7
Temple ⊖ D6
Temple Ave D6
Temple Pl D5
Terminus Pl E3
Thayer St C3
Theobald's Rd C5
Thorney St F5
Threadneedle St C7
Throgmorton St C7
Thurloe Pl F1
Thurloe Sq F2
Tonbridge St B5
Tooley St D8
Torrington Pl B4
Tothill St E4
Tottenham Court Rd B4
Tottenham Ct Rd ⊖ C4
Tottenham St C4
Tower Bridge ✦ D8
Tower Bridge App D8
Tower Bridge Rd E8
Tower Hill D8
Tower Hill ⊖ D8
Tower of London, The D8
Toynbee St C8
Trafalgar Square D4
Trinity Sq D8
Trinity St E7
Trocadero Centre D4
Tudor St D6
Turin St B9
Turnmill St C6
Tyers St F5
Ufford St E6
Union St D6
Univ Coll Hospl B4
University of London C4
Univ of Westminster C3
University St B4
Upper Belgrave St E3
Upper Berkeley St C2
Upper Brook St D3
Upper Grosvenor St D3
Upper Ground D6
Upper Montague St C2
Upper St Martin's La D5
Upper Thames St D7
Upper Wimpole St C3
Upper Woburn Pl B4
Vauxhall Bridge Rd F4
Vauxhall St F5
Vere St C3
Vernon Pl C5
Vestry St B7
Victoria ⇌⊖ E3
Victoria and Albert Museum E1
Victoria Coach Sta F3
Victoria Embankment D5
Victoria Place Sh Ctr F3
Victoria St E4
Villiers St D5
Vincent Sq F4
Vinopolis City of Wine D7
Virginia Rd B8
Wakley St B6
Walbrook C7
Walcot Sq F6
Wallace Collection C3
Walnut Tree Walk F6
Walton St F2
Walworth Rd F7
Wardour St C4/D4
Warner St B6
Warren St ⊖ B4
Warren St B4
Warwick Sq F4
Warwick Way F3
Waterloo ⇌⊖ E6
Waterloo Bridge D5
Waterloo East ⇌ D6
Waterloo Rd E6
Watling St C7
Webber St E6
Welbeck St C3
Wellington Arch ✦ E3
Wellington Mus E3
Wellington Rd B2
Wellington Row B9
Wells St C4
Wenlock St A7
Wentworth St C8
West Carriage Dr D2
West Smithfield C6
West Sq E6
Westbourne St D1
Westbourne Terr C1
Westminster ⊖ E5
Westminster Abbey ✝ E5
Westminster Bridge E5
Westminster Bridge Rd E6
Westminster Cathedral (RC) ✝ E4
Westminster City Hall E4
Westminster Hall E5
Weston St E7
Weymouth St C3
Wharf Rd A7
Wharton St B5
Whitcomb St D4
White Cube B8
White Lion Hill D6
White Lion St A6
Whitechapel Rd C9
Whitecross St B7
Whitefriars St C6
Whitehall D5
Whitehall Pl D5
Wigmore Hall C3
Wigmore St C3
William IV St D5
Willow Walk F8
Wilmington Sq B6
Wilson St C7
Wilton Cres E3
Wilton Rd F4
Wimpole St C3
Winchester St F3
Wincott St F6
Windmill Walk D6
Woburn Pl B5
Woburn Sq B4
Wood St C7
Woodbridge St B6
Wootton St D6
Wormwood St C8
Worship St B7
Wren St B5
Wynyatt St B6
York Rd E5
York St C2
York Terrace East B3
York Terrace West B3
York Way A5

Luton 342
Adelaide St B1
Albert Rd C2
Alma St B2
Alton Rd C3
Anthony Gdns C1
Arthur St C2
Ashburnham Rd B1
Ashton Rd C2
Avondale Rd A1
Back St A2
Bailey St C3
Baker St C2
Biscot Rd A1
Bolton Rd B3
Boyle Cl A2
Brantwood Rd B1
Bretts Mead C1
Bridge St B2
Brook St A1
Brunswick St A3
Burr St A3
Bury Park Rd A1
Bute St B2
Buxton Rd B2
Cambridge St C3
Cardiff Grove B1
Cardiff Rd B1
Cardigan St A2
Castle St B2/C2
Chapel St C2
Charles St A3
Chase St C2
Cheapside B2
Chequer St C3
Chiltern Rise C1
Church St B2/B3
Cinema A2
Cobden St A3
Collingdon St A1
Community Centre C3
Concorde Ave A3
Corncastle Rd C1
Cowper St C2
Crawley Green Rd B3
Crawley Rd A1
Crescent Rd A3
Crescent Rise A3
Cromwell Rd A1
Cross St A2
Cross Way, The C1
Crown Court B2
Cumberland St B2
Cutenhoe Rd C3
Dallow Rd B1
Downs Rd B1
Dudley St A2
Duke St A2
Dumfries St B1
Dunstable Place B2
Dunstable Rd A1/B1
Edward St A3
Elizabeth St C2
Essex Cl C3
Farley Hill C1
Farley Lodge C1
Flowers Way B2
Francis St A1
Frederick St A2
Galaxy L Complex A2
George St B2
George St West B2
Gordon St B2
Grove Rd B1
Guildford St A2
Haddon Rd A3
Harcourt St C2
Hart Hill Drive A3
Hart Hill Lane A3
Hartley Rd A3
Hastings St B2
Hat Factory, The B2
Hatters Way A1
Havelock Rd A2
Hibbert St C2
High Town Rd A3
Highbury Rd A1
Hightown Community Sports & Arts Centre A3
Hillary Cres C1
Hillborough Rd C1
Hitchin Rd A3
Holly St C2
Holm C1
Hucklesby Way A2
Hunts Cl C1
Information Ctr B2
Inkerman St A2
John St B2
Jubilee St A3
Kelvin Cl C2
King St B2
Kingsland Rd C3
Larches, The A2
Latimer Rd C2
Lawn Gdns C2
Lea Rd B3
Library B2
Library Rd B2
Liverpool Rd B1
London Rd C2
Luton Station ⇌ A2
Lyndhurst Rd B1
Magistrates Court B2
Mall, The B2
Manchester St B2
Manor Rd B3
May St C3
Meyrick Ave C1
Midland Rd A2
Mill St A2
Milton Rd B1
Moor St A1
Moor, The A1
Moorland Gdns A2
Moulton Rise A3
Museum & Art Gallery A2
Napier Rd B1
New Bedford Rd A1
New Town St C2
North St A3
Old Bedford Rd A2
Old Orchard C2
Osbourne Rd C3
Oxen Rd A3
Park Sq B2
Park St B3/C3
Park St West B2
Park Viaduct B3
Parkland Drive C1
Police Station B1
Pomfret Ave A3
Pondwicks Rd B3
Post Office A1/A2/B2/C3
Power Court B3
Princess St B1
Red Rails C1
Regent St B2
Reginald St A2
Rothesay Rd B1
Russell Rise C1
Russell St C1
St Ann's Rd B3
St George's B2
St George's Square B2
St Mary's B3
St Marys Rd B3
St Paul's Rd C2
St Saviour's Cres C1
Salisbury Rd B1
Seymour Ave C3
Seymour Rd C3
Silver St B2
South Rd C2
Stanley St B1
Station Rd A2
Stockwood Cres C2
Stockwood Park C1
Strathmore Ave C2
Stuart St B2
Studley Rd A1
Surrey St C3
Sutherland Place C1
Tavistock St C2
Taylor St A3
Telford Way A1
Tennyson Rd C2
Tenzing Grove C1
Thistle Rd B3
Town Hall B2
Townsley Cl C2
UK Centre for Carnival Arts ✦ B3
Union St B2
Univ of Bedfordshire B3
Upper George St B2
Vicarage St B3
Villa Rd A2
Waldeck Rd A1
Wellington St B1/B2
Wenlock St A2
Whitby Rd A1
Whitehill Ave C1
William St A2
Wilsden Ave C1
Windmill Rd B3
Windsor St C2
Winsdon Rd B1
York St A3

Macclesfield 343
108 Steps B2
Abbey Rd A1
Alton Dr A3
Armett St C1
Athey St B1
Bank St C3
Barber St C3
Barton St C1
Beech La A2
Beswick St B1
Black La A2
Black Rd C3
Blakelow Gardens C3
Blakelow Rd C3
Bond St B1/C1
Bread St C1
Bridge St B1
Brock St A2
Brocklehurst Ave A3
Brook St B3
Brookfield La B3
Brough St West C1
Brown St C1
Brynton Rd A2
Buckley St C2
Bus Station B2
Buxton Rd B3
Byrons St C2
Canal St B3
Carlsbrook Ave A3
Castle St B2
Catherine St B1
Cemetery A1
Chadwick Terr A3
Chapel St C2
Charlotte St B2
Chester Rd B1
Chestergate B1
Christ Church B1
Churchill Way B2
Coare St A1
Commercial Rd B2
Conway Cres A3
Copper St C3
Cottage St B1
Court B2
Court B2
Crematorium A1
Crew Ave A3
Crompton Rd B1/C1
Cross St C2
Crossall St C1
Cumberland St A1/B1
Dale St B3
Duke St B2
Eastgate B3
Exchange St B2
Fence Ave B3
Fence Ave Ind Est A3
Flint St B3
Foden St A2
Fountain St B3
Garden St A3
Gas Rd B2
Gateway Gallery ✦ B1
George St B2
Glegg St B3
Golf Course C3
Goodall St B3
Grange Rd C1
Great King St B1
Green St B3
Grosvenor Sh Ctr B2
Gunco La C3
Half St C2
Hallefield Rd B3
Hatton St C1
Hawthorn Way A3
Heapy St C3
Henderson St B1
Heritage Centre & Silk Museum B2
Hibel Rd A2
High St C2
Hobson St C2
Hollins Rd A3
Hope St West B1
Horseshoe Dr B1
Hurdsfield Rd A3
Information Ctr B2
James St C2
Jodrell St B3
John St C2
Jordangate A2
King Edward St B2
King George's Field C3
King St B2
King's School A1
Knight Pool C3
Knight St C3
Lansdowne St A3
Library B2
Lime Gr B3
Loney St B1
Longacre St B1
Lord St C2
Lowe St C2
Lowerfield Rd A3
Lyon St B1
Macclesfield College C1
Macclesfield Sta ⇌ B2
MADS Little Theatre C2
Marina B3
Market B2
Market Pl B2
Masons La A3
Mill La C2
Mill Rd C2
Mill St B2
Moran Rd C1
New Hall St A2
Newton St C1
Nicholson Ave A3
Nicholson Cl A3
Northgate Ave A2
Old Mill La C2
Paradise Mill C2
Paradise St B1
Park Green B2
Park La C1
Park Rd C1
Park St C2
Park Vale Rd C1
Parr St B1
Peel St C2
Percyvale St A3
Peter St C1
Pickford St B2
Pierce St B1
Pinfold St B1
Pitt St C2
Police Station B2
Pool St C2
Poplar Rd C2
Post Office B2
Pownall St A2
Prestbury Rd A1/B1
Queen Victoria St B2
Queen's Ave A3
Registrar B2
Richmond Hill C3
Riseley St B1
Roan Ct B3
Roe St B2
Rowan Way A3
Ryle St C2
Ryle's Park Rd C1
St George's St C2
St Michael's B2
Samuel St B2
Saville St C3
Shaw St B1
Silk Rd, The A2/B2
Slater St C1
Snow Hill C3
South Park C1
Spring Gdns A2
Statham St C2
Station St A2
Steeple St A3
Sunderland St B2
Superstore A1/A2/C2
Swettenham St B3
Thistleton Cl C2
Thorp St B2
Town Hall B2
Townley St B2
Turnock St C3
Union Rd B3
Union St B2
Victoria Park B3
Vincent St C2
Waters Green B2
Waterside C2
West Bond St B1
West Park A1
West Park Museum A1
Westbrook Dr A1
Westminster Rd A1
Whalley Hayes B1
Windmill St C3
Withyfold Dr A2
York St B3

Maidstone 343
Albion Pl B3
All Saints B2
Allen St A3
Amphitheatre ✦ C2
Archbishop's Pal B2
Bank St B2
Barker Rd C2
Barton Rd C3
Beaconsfield Rd C1
Bedford Pl B1
Bishops Way B2
Bluett St A3
Bower La C1
Bower Mount Rd B1
Bower Pl C1
Bower St B1
Bowling Alley B3
Boxley Rd A3
Brenchley Gardens A2
Brewer St A3
Broadway B2
Broadway Sh Ctr B2
Brunswick St C3
Buckland Hill A1
Buckland Rd B1
Bus Station B3
Campbell Rd C3
Church Rd C1
Church St B3
Cinema C2
College Ave C2
College Rd C2
Collis Memorial Gdn C3
Cornwallis Rd B1
Corpus Christi Hall B2
Council Offices B3
County Hall A2
County Rd A3
Crompton Gdns C3
Crown & County Courts B2
Curzon Rd A3
Dixon Cl C2
Douglas Rd C1
Earl St B2
Eccleston Rd C2
Fairmeadow B2
Fisher St A2
Florence Rd C1
Foley St A3
Foster St C3
Fremlin Walk Sh Ctr B2
Gabriel's Hill B3
George St C3
Grecian St A3
Hardy St A3
Hart St C2
Hastings Rd C3
Hayle Rd C3
Hazlitt Theatre B2
Heathorn St A3
Hedley St A3
High St B2
HM Prison A3
Holland Rd A3
Hope St A2
Information Ctr B2
James St A3
James Whatman Way A2
Jeffrey St A3
Kent County Council Offices A2
Kent History & Library Centre A2
King Edward Rd C2
King St B3
Kingsley Rd C3
Knightrider St B3
Launder Way C1
Leisure Ctr A1
Lesley Pl A1
Library B2
Little Buckland Ave A1
Lockmeadow Leisure Complex C2
London Rd B1
Lower Boxley Rd A2
Lower Fant Rd C1
Magistrates Court B3
Maidstone Barracks Station ⇌ A1
Maidstone East Sta ⇌ A2
Maidstone Museum & Bentlif Art Gall B2
Maidstone Utd FC A2
Maidstone West Sta ⇌ B2
Mall, The B3
Market C2
Market Buildings B2
Marsham St B3
Medway St B2
Medway Trading Est C2
Melville Rd C3
Mill St B2
Millennium Bridge C2
Mote Rd B3
Muir Rd C3
Old Tovil Rd C2
Palace Ave B3
Perryfield St A2
Police Station B3
Post Office B2/C3
Priory Rd C3
Prospect Pl C1
Pudding La B2
Queen Anne Rd B3
Queens Rd A1
Randall St A2
Rawdon Rd C3
Reginald Rd C1
Riverstage A1
Rock Pl B1
Rocky Hill B1
Romney Pl B3
Rose Yard B2
Rowland Cl C1
Royal Engineers' Rd A2
Royal Star Arcade B2
St Annes Ct B1
St Faith's St B2
St Luke's Rd A3
St Peter St B2
St Peter's Br B2
St Peter's Wharf Retail Park B2
St Philip's Ave C3
Salisbury Rd A3
Sandling Rd A2
Scott St A2
Scrubs La B1
Sheal's Cres C3
Somerfield Hospital, The A1
Somerfield La B1
Somerfield Rd B1
Staceys St A2
Station Rd A2
Superstore A1/B2/B3
Terrace Rd B1
Tonbridge Rd C1
Tovil Rd C2
Town Hall B2
Trinity Park B3
Tufton St B3
Tyrwhitt-Drake Mus of Carriages B2
Union St B3
Upper Fant Rd C1
Upper Stone St C3
Victoria St B1
Warwick Pl B1
Wat Tyler Way B3
Waterloo St C3
Waterlow Rd A3
Week St B2
Well Rd A3
Westree Rd C1
Wharf Rd C1
Whatman Park A1
Wheeler St A3
Whitchurch Cl B1
Woodville Rd C3
Wyatt St B3
Wyke Manor Rd B3

Manchester 343
Adair St B6
Addington St A5
Adelphi St A1
Albert Sq B3
Albion St C3
AMC Great Northern B3
Ancoats Gr B6
Ancoats Gr North B6
Angela St C2
Aquatic Centre C4
Ardwick Green North C5
Ardwick Green Park C5
Ardwick Green South C5
Arlington St A2
Artillery St B3
Arundel St C2
Atherton St B2
Atkinson St B3
Aytoun St B4
Back Piccadilly A4
Baird St B5
Balloon St A4
Bank Pl A1
Baring St B5
Barrack St C1
Barrow St A1
Bendix St A5
Bengal St A5
Berry St C5
Blackfriars Rd A3
Blackfriars St A3
Blantyre St C2
Bloom St B4
Blossom St A5
Boad St B5
Bombay St B4
Booth St A3
Booth St B4
Bootle St B3
Brazennose St B3
Brewer St A5
Bridge St A3
Bridgewater Hall B3
Bridgewater Pl A4
Bridgewater St B2
Brook St C4
Brotherton Dr A2
Brown St A3
Brown St B4
Brunswick St C6
Brydon Ave C6
Buddhist Centre A4
Bury St A2
Bus & Coach Station B4
Bus Station B4
Butler St A6
Buxton St C5
Byrom St B3
Cable St A5
Calder St B1
Cambridge St C3/C4
Camp St B3
Canal St B4
Cannon St A1
Cannon St A4
Cardroom Rd A6
Carruthers St A6
Castle St C2
Castlefield Arena B2
Cateaton St A3
Cathedral ✝ A3
Cathedral St A3
Cavendish St C4
Central Retail Pk A5
Chapel St A1/A3
Chapeltown St B5
Charles St C4
Charlotte St B4
Chatham St B4
Cheapside A3
Chepstow St B3
Chester Rd C1/C2
Chester St C4
Chetham's Sch of Music A3
China La B5
Chippenham Rd A6
Chorlton Rd C2
Chorlton St B4
Church St A2
Church St A4
City Park A4
City Rd C3
Civil Justice Centre B2
Cleminson St A2
Clowes St A3
College Land A3
Collier St A2
Commercial St C3
Conference Centre C4
Cooper St B4
Copperas St A4
Corn Exchange, The A4
Cornbrook C1
Cornell St A5
Corporation St A4
Cotter St C6
Cotton St A5
Cow La B1
Cross St B3
Crown Court B4
Crown St C2
Dalberg St C6
Dale St A4/B5
Dancehouse, The C4
Dantzic St A4
Dark La C6
Dawson St C2
Dean St A5
Deansgate A3/B3
Deansgate Castlefield C3
Deansgate Station ⇌ C3
Dolphin St C6
Downing St C5
Ducie St B5
Duke Pl B2
Duke St B2
Durling St C6
East Ordsall La A2/B1
Edge St A4
Egerton St C2
Ellesmere St C1
Everard St C1
Every St B6
Fairfield St B5
Faulkner St B4
Fennel St A3
Ford St A2
Ford St C6
Fountain St B4
Frederick St A2
Gartside St B2
Gaythorne St A1
George Leigh St A5
George St A1
George St B4
Gore St A2
Goulden St A5
Granby Row B4
Gravel St A3
Great Ancoats St A5
Great Bridgewater St B3
Great George St A1
Great Jackson St C2
Great Marlborough St C4
Greengate A3
Grosvenor St C5
Gun St A5
Hadrian Ave B6
Hall St B3
Hampson St B1
Hanover St A4
Hanworth Cl C5
Hardman St B3
Harkness St C6
Harrison St B6
Hart St B4
Helmet St B6
Henry St A5
Heyrod St B6
High St A4
Higher Ardwick C6
Hilton St A4/A5
Holland St A6
HOME ✦ C3
Hood St A5
Hope St B1
Hope St B4
Houldsworth St A5
Hoyle St C6
Hulme Hall Rd C1
Hulme St A1
Hulme St C3
Hyde Rd C6
Information Ctr B4
Irwell St A2
Islington St A2
Jackson Cr C2
Jackson's Row B3
James St A1
Jenner Cl C2
Jersey St A5
John Dalton St B3
John Ryland's Liby B3
John St A2
Kennedy St B3
Kincardine Rd C5
King St A3
King St West A3
Law Courts B3
Laystall St B5
Lever St A5
Library B3
Linby St C2
Little Lever St A4
Liverpool Rd B2
Liverpool St B1
Lloyd St B3
Lockton Cl C5
London Rd B5
Long Millgate A3
Longacre St B6
Loom St A5
Lower Byrom St B2
Lower Mosley St B3
Lower Moss La C2
Lower Ormond St C4
Loxford La C4
Luna St A5
Major St B4
Manchester Arndale A4
Manchester Art Gallery B4
Manchester Central Convention Complex B3
Manchester Metropolitan University B4/C4
Manchester Piccadilly Station ⇌ B5
Manchester Technology Centre C4
Mancunian Way C3
Manor St C5
Marble St A4
Market St A2
Market St A4
Market St A4
Marsden St A3
Marshall St A5
Mayan Ave A2
Medlock St C3
Middlewood St B1
Miller St A4
Minshull St B4
Mosley St A4
Mount St B3

Mulberry St B3
Murray St A5
Museum of Science & Industry (MOSI) B2
Nathan Dr A2
National Football Museum A4
Naval St A5
New Bailey St A2
New Elm Rd B2
New Islington A6
New Islington Sta B6
New Quay St B2
New Union St A6
Newgate St A4
Newton St A5
Nicholas St B4
North Western St C6
Oak St A4
Odeon A4
Old Mill St A6
Oldfield Rd A1/C1
Oldham Rd A5
Oldham St A4
Opera House B3
Ordsall La C1
Oxford Rd C4
Oxford Rd C4
Oxford St B4
Paddock St C6
Palace Theatre B4
Pall Mall A3
Palmerston St B6
Park St A1
Parker St B4
Peak St B5
Penfield Cl C5
Peoples' History Museum B2
Peru St A1
Peter St B3
Piccadilly A4
Piccadilly B5
Piccadilly Gdns B4
Piercy St A6
Poland St A5
Police Museum A5
Police Station B3/B5
Pollard St B6
Port St A5
Portland St B4
Portugal St East B5
Post Office A1/A2/A4/A5/B3/B4
Potato Wharf B2
Princess St B3/C4
Pritchard St C4
Quay St A2
Quay St B2
Queen St B3
Radium St A5
Redhill St A5
Regent Rd B1
Retail Park A5
Rice St B2
Richmond St B4
River St C3
Roby St B5
Rodney St A6
Roman Fort B2
Rosamond St A2
Royal Exchange A3
Sackville St B4
St Andrew's St B6
St Ann St A3
St Ann's A3
St George's Ave C1
St James St B4
St John St B3
St John's Cath (RC) A2
St Mary's B3
St Mary's Gate A3
St Mary's Parsonage A3
St Peter's Sq B3
St Stephen St A2
Salford Approach A3
Salford Central A2
Sheffield St B5
Shepley St B5
Sherratt St A5
Shopmobility A4
Shudehill A4
Shudehill A4
Sidney St C4
Silk St A5
Silver St B4
Skerry Cl C5
Snell St B6
South King St B3
Sparkle St B5
Spear St A4
Spring Gdns A4
Stanley St A2/B2
Station Approach B5
Store St B5
Swan St A4
Tariff St B5
Tatton St C1
Temperance St B6/C6
Thirsk St C6
Thomas St A4
Thompson St A5
Tib La B3
Tib St A4
Town Hall (Manchester) B3
Town Hall (Salford) A2
Trafford St C3
Travis St B5
Trinity Way A2
Turner St A4
Union St C6
University of Manchester (Sackville Street Campus) C5
University of Salford A1
Upper Brook St C5
Upper Cleminson St A1
Upper Wharf St A1
Vesta St B6
Victoria A4
Victoria Station A4
Wadeson Rd C5
Water St B2
Watson St B3
West Fleet St B1
West King St A2
West Mosley St B4
Weybridge Rd A6
Whitworth St B4
Whitworth St West C3
Wilburn St B1
William St A2
William St C6
Wilmott St C3
Windmill St B3
Windsor Cr A1
Withy Gr A4
Woden St C1
Wood St B3
Woodward St A6
Worrall St C1
Worsley St C2
York St B4
York St C2
York St C4

Merthyr Tydfil

Merthyr Tudful 343

Aberdare Rd B2
Abermorlais Terr B2
Alexandra Rd A3
Alma St C3
Arfryn Pl C3
Argyle St C3
Avenue De Clichy C2
Beacons Place Sh Ctr C2
Bethesda St B2
Bishops Gr A3
Brecon Rd A1/B2
Briarmead A3
Bryn St C3
Bryntirion Rd B3/C3
Bus Station B2
Cae Mari Dwn B3
Caedraw Rd C2
Castle Sq A1
Castle St B2
Chapel C2
Chapel Bank B1
Church St B3
Civic Centre B2
Clos Penderyn B1
Coedcae'r Ct C3
Court B3
Court St C3
Courts B2
Cromwell St B2
Cyfarthfa Castle School and Museum A1
Cyfarthfa Ind Est A1
Cyfarthfa Park A1
Cyfarthfa Rd A1
Dane St A2
Dane Terr A2
Danyparc B3
Darren View A3
Dixon St B2
Dyke St C3
Dynevor St B2
Elwyn Dr C3
Fire Station B2
Fothergill St B3
Galonuchaf Rd A3
Garth St B2
Georgetown B2
Grawen Terr A2
Grove Pk A2
Grove, The A2
Gurnos Rd A2
Gwaelodygarth Rd A2/A3
Gwaunfarren Gr A3
Gwaunfarren Rd A3
Gwendoline St A3
Hampton St C3
Hanover St A2
Heol S O Davies B1
Heol-Gerrig B1
High St A3/B2/B3/C2
Highland View C3
Howell Cl B1
Information Ctr B2
Jackson's Bridge B2
James St C3
John St B3
Joseph Parry's Cott B2
Lancaster St A2
Library B2
Llewellyn St A2
Llwyfen St B2
Llwyn Berry B1
Llwyn Dic Penderyn B1
Llwyn-y-Gelynen C1
Lower Thomas St B3
Market C2
Mary St C3
Masonic St C2
Merthyr College B2
Merthyr RFC C2
Merthyr Town FC B3
Merthyr Tydfil Leisure Centre C3
Merthyr Tydfil Sta C3
Meyrick Villas A2
Miniature Railway A1
Mount St A2
Nantygwenith St B1
Norman Terr B2
Oak Rd A2
Old Cemetery B3
Pandy Cl A1
Pantycelynen B1
Parade, The B3
Park Terr B2
Penlan View C2
Penry St B2
Pentwyn Villas A2
Penyard Rd B3
Penydarren Park A3
Penydarren Rd B3
Plymouth St C3
Police Station C2
Pont Marlais West B2
Post Office B2
Quarry Row B2
Queen's Rd B3
Rees St C3
Rhydycar Link C2
Riverside Park A1
St David's B3
St Tydfil's C2
St Tydfil's Ave C3
St Tydfil's Hospital (No A+E) B3
St Tydfil's Square Shopping Centre C2
Saxon St A2
School of Nursing A2
Seward St A3
Shiloh La B3
Stone Circles B1
Stuart St A2
Summerhill Pl B3
Superstore B3
Swan St C2
Swansea Rd B1
Taff Glen View C3
Taff Vale Ct B3
Theatre Soar B2
Thomastown Park B3
Tramroad La A3
Tramroad Side B2
Tramroad Side North B3
Tramroad Side South C3
Trevithick Gdns C3
Trevithick St A3
Tudor Terr B2
Twynyrodyn Rd C3
Union St B3
Upper Colliers Row B1
Upper Thomas St B3
Victoria St B2
Vue C3
Vulcan Rd B2
Walk, The B2
Warlow St C3
Well St A2
Welsh Assembly Government Offices C2
Wern La C1
West Gr A2
William St C3
Yew St C3
Ynysfach Engine Ho C2
Ynysfach Rd C2

Middlesbrough 343

Abingdon Rd C3
Acklam Rd C1
Albert Park C2
Albert Rd B2
Albert Terr C2
Ambulance Station C1
Aubrey St C3
Avenue, The C2
Ayresome Gdns C2
Ayresome Green La C1
Ayresome St C2
Barton Rd A1
Bilsdale Rd C3
Bishopton Rd C3
Borough Rd B2/B3
Bowes Rd A2
Breckon Hill Rd B3
Bridge St East B3
Bridge St West B2
Brighouse Rd A1
Burlam Rd C1
Bus Station B2
Cannon Park B1
Cannon Park Way B2
Cannon St B1
Captain Cook Sq B2
Carlow St C1
Castle Way C3
Chipchase Rd C2
Cineworld B3
Cleveland Centre B2
Clive Rd C2
Commercial St A2
Corporation Rd B2
Costa St C2
Council Offices B3
Crescent Rd C2
Crescent, The C2
Cumberland Rd C2
Depot Rd A2
Derwent St B2
Devonshire Rd C2
Diamond Rd B2
Dorman Museum C2
Douglas St B3
Eastbourne Rd C2
Eden Rd C3
Fire Sta A3
Forty Foot Rd A2
Gilkes St B2
Gosford St A2
Grange Rd B2
Gresham Rd B2
Harehills Rd C1
Harford St C2
Hartington Rd B2
Haverton Hill Rd A1
Hey Wood St B1
Highfield Rd C3
Hillstreet Centre B2
Holwick Rd B1
Hutton Rd C3
Ironmasters Way B1
Lambton Rd C3
Lancaster Rd C2
Lansdowne Rd C3
Latham Rd C2
Law Courts B2/B3
Lees Rd B2
Leeway B3
Library B2/C2
Linthorpe Cemetery C1
Linthorpe Rd B2
Lloyd St B2
Longford St C2
Longlands Rd C3
Lower East St A3
Lower Lake C3
Macmillan Academy C1
Maldon Rd C1
Manor St B2
Marsh St B2
Marton Rd B3
Middlehaven B3
Middlesbrough By-Pass B2/C1
Middlesbrough Coll B3
Middlesbrough Leisure Park B3
Middlesbrough Sta B2
Middletown Park C2
MIMA B3
Mulgrave Rd C2
Newport Bridge B1
Newport Bridge Approach Rd B1
Newport Rd B2
North Ormesby Rd B3
North Rd B2
Northern Rd C1
Outram St B2
Oxford Rd C2
Park La C2
Park Rd North C2
Park Rd South C2
Park Vale Rd C3
Parliament Rd B1
Police Station A2
Port Clarence Rd A3
Portman St B2
Post Office B3/C1/C2
Princes Rd B2
Python A2
Riverside Park Rd A1
Riverside Stadium (Middlesbrough FC) B3
Rockliffe Rd C2
Romaldkirk Rd B1
Roman Rd C2
Roseberry Rd C3
St Barnabas' Rd C2
St Paul's Rd B2
Saltwells Rd B3
Scott's Rd A3
Seaton Carew Rd A3
Shepherdson Way B3
Shopmobility B2
Snowdon Rd A2
South West Ironmasters Park B1
Southfield Rd B2
Southwell Rd C2
Springfield Rd C1
Startforth Rd A2
Stockton Rd C1
Stockton St A2
Superstore B2
Surrey St C2
Sycamore Rd C2
Tax Offices B3
Tees Viaduct C1
Teessaurus Park A2
Teesside Tertiary Coll C3
Temenos B3
Thornfield Rd C1
Town Hall B2
Transporter Bridge (Toll) A3
Union St B2
University of Teesside B2
Upper Lake C2
Valley Rd C3
Ventnor Rd C2
Victoria Rd B2
Vulcan St A2
Warwick St C2
Wellesley Rd B3
West La B1
West Lane Hospital C1
Westminster Rd C2
Wilson St B2
Windward Way B3
Woodlands Rd B2
York Rd C3

Milton Keynes 344

Abbey Way A1
Arbrook Ave B1
Armourer Dr A3
Arncliffe Dr A1
Avebury C2
Avebury Blvd C2
Bankfield B3
Bayard Ave A2
Belvedere A2
Bishopstone A1
Blundells Rd A1
Boundary, The C3
Boycott Ave C2
Bradwell Comm Blvd B1
Bradwell Rd C1
Bramble Ave A2
Brearley Ave C2
Breckland A1
Brill Place B1
Burnham Dr B1
Bus Station C1
Campbell Park B3
Cantle Ave A3
Central Retail Park C1
Century Ave C2
Chaffron Way C3
Childs Way C1
Christ the Cornerstone B2
Cineworld B2
Civic Offices B2
Cleavers Ave B2
Colesbourne Dr A3
Conniburrow Blvd B2
County Court B2
Currier Dr A2
Dansteed Way A2/A3/B1
Deltic Ave B1
Downs Barn A2
Downs Barn Blvd A3
Eaglestone C3
Eelbrook Ave B1
Elder Gate B1
Evans Gate C2
Fairford Cr A3
Falcon Ave B3
Fennel Dr A2
Fishermead Blvd C3
Food Centre B3
Fulwoods Dr C3
Glazier Dr A2
Glovers La A1
Grafton Gate C1
Grafton St A1/C2
Gurnards Ave B3
Harrier Dr C3
Ibstone Ave B1
Information Centre B2
Langcliffe Dr A1
Leisure Centre C3
Leisure Plaza C1
Leys Rd C1
Library B2
Linford Wood A2
Marlborough Gate B3
Marlborough St A2/B3
Mercers Dr A1
Midsummer C2
Midsummer Blvd B2
Milton Keynes Central C1
Milton Keynes Hospital (A&E) C3
Monks Way A1
Mullen Ave A3
Mullion Pl C3
Neath Hill A3
North Elder C1
North Grafton B1
North Overgate A3
North Row B2
North Saxon B2
North Secklow B2
North Skeldon A3
North Witan B1
Oakley Gdns A3
Oldbrook Blvd C2
Open-Air Theatre B3
Overgate A3
Overstreet A3
Patriot Dr B1
Pencarrow Pl B3
Penryn Ave B3
Perran Ave C3
Pitcher La C1
Place Retail Park, The C1
Police Station B2
Portway B2
Post Office A2/B2/B3
Precedent Dr B1
Quinton Dr B1
Ramsons Ave B2
Retail Park C2
Rockingham Dr A2
Rooksley B1
Saxon Gate B2
Saxon St A1/C3
Secklow Gate B2
Shackleton Pl C2
Shopmobility B2
Silbury Blvd B2
Skeldon A3
South Enmore B3
South Grafton C2
South Row C2
South Saxon C2
South Secklow B3
South Witan C2
Springfield B3
Stanton Wood A1
Stantonbury A1
Stantonbury Leisure Centre A1
Strudwick Dr C2
Sunrise Parkway A2
Theatre & Art Gallery B3
theCentre:mk B2
Tolcarne Ave C3
Tourist Information Centre B3
Towan Ave C3
Trueman Pl C2
Vauxhall A1
Winterhill Retail Park C2
Witan Gate B2
X-Scape B3

Newcastle upon Tyne 344

Albert St B3
Argyle St B3
Back New Bridge St B3
BALTIC Centre for Contemporary Art C3
Barker St A3
Barrack Rd B1
Bath La B1
Bessie Surtees Ho C2
Bigg Market C2
Biscuit Factory B3
Black Gate C2
Blackett St B2
Blandford Sq C1
Boating Lake A1
Boyd St B3
Brandling Park A2
Bus Station B2
Buxton St B3
Byron St A3
Camden St B2
Castle Keep C2
Central C1
Central Library B2
Central Motorway B2
Chester St A3
City Hall B2
City Rd B3/C3
City Walls C1
Civic Centre A2
Claremont Rd A1
Clarence St B3
Clarence Walk B3
Clayton St C1/B1
Clayton St West C1
Close, The C2
Coach Station C1
College St B2
Collingwood St C2
Copland Terr B3
Coppice Way B3
Corporation St B1
Courts C3
Crawhall Rd B3
Dean St C2
Dental Hospital A1
Dinsdale Pl A3
Dinsdale Rd A3
Discovery C1
Doncaster Rd A3
Durant Rd B2
Eldon Garden Shopping Centre B1
Eldon Sq B1
Ellison Pl B2
Empire B1
Eskdale Terr A2
Eslington Terr A1
Exhibition Park A1
Falconar St B3
Fenkle St C1
Forth Banks C1
Forth St C1
Gallowgate B1
Gate, The B1
Gateshead Millennium Bridge C3
Gibson St B3
Goldspink La A3
Grainger Market B2
Grainger St B2
Grantham Rd A3
Granville Rd A3
Great North Children's Hospital A1
Great North Mus:Hancock A2
Grey St B2
Groat Market C2
Guildhall C2
Hancock St A2
Hanover St C2
Hatton Gallery A1
Hawks Rd C3
Haymarket B2
Heber St B1
Helmsley Rd A3
High Bridge B2
High Level Bridge C2
Hillgate C3
Howard St B3
Hutton Terr A3
Information Ctr C3
intu Eldon Square Shopping Centre B2
Jesmond A2
Jesmond Rd A2/A3
John Dobson St B2
John George Joicey Museum C2
Jubilee Rd B3
Kelvin Gr A3
Kensington Terr A2
Laing Gallery B2
Lambton Rd A2
Leazes Cr B1
Leazes La B1
Leazes Park B1
Leazes Park Rd B1
Leazes Terr B1
Library A2
Live C2
Low Friar St C1
Manor Chare C2
Manors B2
Manors Station B2
Market St B2
Melbourne St B2
Mill Rd C3
Monument B2
Monument Mall Shopping Centre B2
Morpeth St A2
Mosley St C2
Napier St A3
New Bridge St B2/B3
Newcastle Central Station C1
Newcastle University A1
Newgate Shopping Ctr C1
Newgate St B1
Newington Rd A3
Northern Design Ctr C3
Northern Stage Theatre A2
Northumberland Rd B2
Northumberland St B2
Northumbria Univ A2
Northwest Radial Rd A1
O2 Academy C1
Oakwellgate C3
Open Univ C3
Orchard St C2
Osborne Rd A2
Osborne Terr A3
Pandon C3
Pandon Bank B3
Park Terr A1
Percy St B1
Pilgrim St B2
Pipewellgate C2
Pitt St B1
Plummer Tower A2
Police Station B2
Portland Rd A3/B3
Portland Terr A3
Post Office B1/B2
Pottery La C1
Prudhoe Pl B1
Prudhoe St B1
Quayside C2
Queen Elizabeth II Bridge C2
Queen Victoria Rd A1
Richardson Rd A1
Ridley Pl B2
Rock Terr B3
Rosedale Terr A3
Royal Victoria Infirmary A1
Sage Gateshead C3
St Andrew's St B1
St James B1
St James' Blvd C1
St James' Park (Newcastle Utd FC) B1
St Mary's Heritage Centre C3
St Mary's (RC) C1
St Mary's Place B2
St Nicholas C2
St Nicholas St C2
St Thomas' St B1
Sandyford Rd A2/A3
Science Park B2
Shield St B3
Shieldfield B3
Shopmobility B1
Side, The C2
Simpson Terr B3
South Shore Rd C3
South St C1
Starbeck Ave A3
Stepney Rd B3
Stoddart St B3
Stowell St B1
Strawberry Pl B1
Swing Bridge C2
Temple St C1
Terrace Pl B1
Theatre Royal B2
Times Sq C1
Tower St B3
Trinity House C2
Tyne Bridge C2
Tyne Bridges C2
Tyne Theatre & Opera Ho C1
Tyneside B2
Victoria Sq A2
Warwick St A3
Waterloo St C1
Wellington St B1
Westgate Rd C1/C2
Windsor Terr A2
Worswick St B2
Wretham Pl B3

Newport

Casnewydd 344

Albert Terr B1
Allt-yr-Yn Ave A1
Alma St C2
Ambulance Station C3
Bailey St B2
Barrack Hill A2
Bath St A3
Bedford Rd B3
Belle Vue La C1
Belle Vue Park C1
Bishop St A3
Blewitt St B1
Bolt Cl C3
Bolt St C3
Bond St A2
Bosworth Dr A1
Bridge St B1
Bristol St A3
Bryngwyn Rd B1
Brynhyfryd Ave C1
Brynhyfryd Rd C1
Bus Station B2
Caerau Cres C1
Caerau Rd B1
Caerleon Rd A3
Capel Cres C2
Cardiff Rd C2
Caroline St B3
Castle (Remains) A2
Cedar Rd A3
Charles St B2
Charlotte Dr C2
Chepstow Rd A3
Church Rd A3
Cineworld B2
Civic Centre B1
Clarence Pl A2
Clifton Pl B1
Clifton Rd C1
Clyffard Cres B1
Clytha Park Rd B1
Clytha Sq C2
Coldra Rd C1
Collier St A3
Colne St B3
Comfrey Cl A1
Commercial Rd C3
Commercial St B2
Corelli St A3
Corn St B2
Corporation Rd B3
Coulson Cl C2
County Court A2
Courts A1
Courts B1
Crawford St A3
Cyril St B3
Dean St A3
Devon Pl B1
Dewsland Park Rd C2
Dolman B2
Dolphin St C3
East Dock Rd C3
East St B1
East Usk Rd A3
Ebbw Vale Wharf A3
Emlyn St B2
Enterprise Way C3
Eton Rd B3
Evans St A2
Factory Rd A2
Fields Rd B1
Francis Dr C2
Frederick St C3
Friars Rd C1
Friars Walk B2
Gaer La C1
George St C3
George Street Bridge C3
Godfrey Rd B1
Gold Tops B1
Gore St A3
Gorsedd Circle C1
Grafton Rd A3
Graham St B1
Granville St C3
Harlequin Dr A1
Harrow Rd B3
Herbert Rd A3
Herbert Walk C2
Hereford St A3
High St B2
Hill St B2
Hoskins St A2
Information Ctr B2
Ivor St B2
Jones St B1
Junction Rd A3
Keynshaw Ave C2
King St C2
Kingsway B2
Kingsway Centre B2
Ledbury Dr A2
Library A3
Library, Museum & Art Gallery B2
Liverpool Wharf B3
Llanthewy Rd B1
Llanvair Rd A3
Locke St A2
Lower Dock St C3
Lucas St A2
Manchester St A3
Market B2
Marlborough Rd B3
Mellon St C3
Mill St A2
Morgan St A3
Mountjoy Rd C2
Newport Bridge A2
Newport Ctr B2
Newport RFC B3
Newport Station B2
North St B2
Oakfield Rd B1
Park Sq C2
Police Station A3/C2
Post Office B2/C3
Power St A1
Prince St A3
Pugsley St A2
Queen St C2
Queen's Cl A1
Queen's Hill A1
Queen's Hill Cres A1
Queensway B2
Railway St B2
Riverfront Theatre & Arts Centre, The B2
Riverside A3
Rodney Rd B2
Royal Gwent (A&E) C2
Rudry St A3
Rugby Rd B3
Ruperra La C3
Ruperra St C3
St Edmund St B1
St Mark's Cres A1
St Mary St B1
St Vincent Rd A3
St Woolos C2
St Woolos General (no A&E) C1
St Woolos Rd B1
School La B2
Serpentine Rd B1
Shaftesbury Park A2
Sheaf La A3
Skinner St B2
Sorrel Dr A1
South Market St C3
Spencer Rd B1
Stow Hill B2/C1/C2
Stow Park Ave C1
Stow Park Dr C1
TA Centre A1
Talbot St B2
Tennis Club A1
Tregare St A3
Trostrey St A3
Tunnel Terr B1
Turner St A3
Univ of Wales Newport City Campus B3
Upper Dock St B2
Usk St A3
Usk Way B3/C3
Victoria Cr B1
War Memorial A3
Waterloo Rd C1
West St B1
Wharves B2
Wheeler St A2
Whitby Pl A3
Windsor Terr B1
York Pl C1

Newquay 344

Agar Rd B2
Alma Pl B1
Ambulance Station B2
Anthony Rd C1
Atlantic Hotel A1
Bank St B1
Barrowfields A3
Bay View Terr B2
Beach Rd B1
Beachfield Ave B1
Beacon Rd A1
Belmont Pl A1
Berry Rd B2
Blue Reef Aquarium B1
Boating Lake C2
Bus Station B1
Chapel Hill B1
Chester Rd A3
Cheviot Rd C1/C2
Chichester Cres C2
Chynance Dr C1
Chyverton Cl C1
Cliff Rd B2
Coach Park B2
Colvreath Rd A3
Council Offices B1
Crantock St B1
Crescent, The B1
Criggar Rocks A3
Dale Cl C3
Dale Rd C3
Dane Rd A1
East St B2
Edgcumbe Ave B3
Edgcumbe Gdns B3
Eliot Gdns B3
Elm Cl C3
Ennor's Rd B1
Fernhill Rd B1
Fire Station B1
Fore St B1
Gannel Rd C2
Golf Driving Range B3
Gover La B1
Great Western Beach A2
Grosvenor Ave B2
Harbour A1
Hawkins Rd C2
Headleigh Rd B2
Hilgrove Rd A3/B3
Holywell Rd B3
Hope Terr B1
Huer's House, The A1
Information Ctr B1
Island Cres B2
Jubilee St B1
Kew Cl C3
Killacourt Cove A2
King Edward Cres A1
Lanhenvor Ave B2
Library B1
Lifeboat Station A1
Linden Ave C2
Listry Rd C2
Lusty Glaze Beach A3
Lusty Glaze Rd A3
Manor Rd B1
Marcus Hill B2
Mayfield Rd B2
Meadowside C3
Mellanvrane La C2
Michell Ave B2
Miniature Golf Course C3
Miniature Railway B3
Mount Wise B1
Mowhay Cl C3
Narrowcliff A3
Newquay B2
Newquay Hospital (no A&E) B2
Newquay Town Football Ground B1
Newquay Zoo B3
North Pier A1
North Quay Hill A1
Oakleigh Terr B2
Pargolla Rd B2
Pendragon Cres C3
Pengannel Cl C1
Penina Ave C3
Police Sta & Courts B2
Post Office B1/B2
Quarry Park Rd B3
Rawley La C2
Reeds Way B1
Robartes Rd B2
St Anne's Rd A3
St Aubyn Cres B3
St George's Rd B1
St John's Rd B1
St Mary's Rd B1
St Michael's B1
St Michael's Rd B1
St Thomas' Rd B2
Seymour Ave B2
South Pier A1
South Quay Hill A1
Sweet Briar Cres C3
Sydney Rd A1
Tolcarne Beach A2
Tolcarne Point A2
Tolcarne Rd B2
Tor Rd B2
Towan Beach A1
Towan Blystra Rd B3
Tower Rd A1
Trebarwith Cres B2
Tredour Rd C2
Treforda Rd C3
Tregoss Rd B3
Tregunnel Hill B1/C1
Tregunnel Saltings C1
Trelawney Rd B2
Treloggan La C3
Treloggan Rd C3
Trembath Cres C1
Trenance Ave B2
Trenance Gardens B2
Trenance La C2
Trenance Leisure Pk B3
Trenance Rd B2
Trenarth Rd B2

362 Newtown • Northampton • Norwich • Nottingham • Oban • Oxford • Perth • Peterborough

Treninnick Hill C3
Tretherras Rd B3
Trethewey Way C1
Trevemper Rd C2
Tunnels Through Time B1
Ulalia Rd B3
Vivian Cl B2
Waterworld B3
Whitegate Rd B3
Wych Hazel Way C3

Newtown
Y Drenewydd 344

Ash Cl A3
Back La B2
Baptist Chapel B2
Barn La A2
Bear Lanes Sh Ctr B2
Beech Cl A2
Beechwood Dr A2
Brimmon Cl C2
Brimmon Rd C2
Broad St B2
Bryn Bank A1
Bryn Cl A1
Bryn Gdns A1
Bryn House A1
Bryn La A1/A2
Bryn Meadows A2
Bryn St A1
Bryn, The A1
Brynglais Ave A2
Brynglais Cl A2
Bus Station B2
Byrnwood Dr A1
Cambrian Bridge B3
Cambrian Gdns B2
Cambrian Way B2
Canal Rd A3
Castle Mound B2
Cedewain C1
Cefnaire C2
Cefnaire Coppice C2
Ceiriog C2
Cemetery A3
Church (Remains of) B2
Churchill Dr A3
Cledan B3
Colwyn B3
Commercial St A2
Council Offices B1
Crescent St A1
Cwm Llanfair A2
Dinas B2
Dolafon Rd B3
Dolerw Park B1
Dolfor Rd C1
Eirianell C1
Fairfield Dr A2
Ffordd Croesawdy B2
Fire Station C1
Frankwell St A2
Frolic St B2
Fron La A1
Garden La A2
Gas St B2
Glyndwr C1
Golwgydre La B2
Gorsedd Circle B1
Great Brimmon Farm C3
Hafren C1
Halfpenny Bridge B2
High St B2
Hillside Ave A3
Hoel Treowen C2
Information Ctr B2
Kerry Rd B3
Ladywell Shopping Ctr B2
Library B1
Llanfair Rd A2
Llanidloes Rd C1
Llys Ifor A2
Lon Cerddyn B1
Lon Helyg C1
Lonesome La A3
Long Bridge A2
Lower Canal Rd B3
Maldwyn Leisure Ctr C1
Market B2
Market St B2
Milford Rd B1
Mill Cl B2
Miniature Railway B1
Montgomery County Infirmary A2
Mwyn Fynydd A3
New Church St B2
New Rd B2
Newtown Football Gd B1
Newtown Station B2
Oak Tree Ave A3
Old Kerry Rd B2
Oldbarn La A2
Oriel Davies Gallery B2
Park Cl B1
Park La B1
Park St B2
Park, The B1
Parklands B1
Pavillion Ct C1
Plantation La C1
Police Station B1
Pont Brynfedw A2
Pool Rd B3
Poplar Rd A3
Post Office B2
Powys C1
Powys Theatre A2
Pryce Jones Stores & Museum B2
Quaker Meeting Ho B1
Regent B2
Robert Owen House B1
Robert Owen Mus B2
Rugby Club A3
St David's B2
School La A2
Sheaf St B3
Short Bridge St B2
Stone St B2
Superstore B3/C1
Sycamore Dr A2
Textile Museum A2
Town Hall B2
Union St A2
Upper Brimmon C3
Vastre Industrial Est B3
War Memorial B2
WHSmith Museum B2
Wynfields C1
Y Ffrydd A3

Northampton 344

78 Derngate B3
Abington Sq B3
Abington St B3
Alcombe St A3
All Saints' B2
Ambush St B1
Angel St B2
Arundel St A2
Ash St A2
Auctioneers Way C2
Bailiff St A2
Barrack Rd A2
Beaconsfield Terr A3
Becketts Park C3
Becketts Park Marina C3
Bedford Rd B3
Billing Rd B3
Brecon St A1
Brewery C2
Bridge St C2
Broad St B2
Burns St A3
Bus Station B2
Campbell St A2
Castle (Site of) B2
Castle St B2
Cattle Market Rd C2
Central Museum & Art Gallery B2
Charles St A3
Cheyne Walk B3
Church La A2
Clare St A3
Cloutsham St A3
College St B2
Colwyn Rd A3
Cotton End C2
Countess Rd A1
County Hall B2
Court A2
Craven St A3
Crown & County Courts B3
Denmark Rd B3
Derngate B3
Derngate & Royal Theatres B3
Doddridge Church B2
Drapery, The B2
Duke St A3
Dunster St A3
Earl St A3
Euston Rd C2
Fire Station A3
Foot Meadow B2
Gladstone Rd A1
Gold St B2
Grafton St A2
Gray St A3
Green St B1
Greenwood Rd B1
Greyfriars B2
Grosvenor Centre B2
Grove Rd A3
Guildhall B2
Hampton St A2
Harding Terr A2
Hazelwood Rd B3
Herbert St B2
Hervey St A3
Hester St A2
Holy Sepulchre A2
Hood St A3
Horse Market B2
Hunter St A3
Information Ctr B1
Kettering Rd A3
Kingswell St B2
Lady's La B2
Leicester St A2
Leslie Rd A2
Library B3
Lorne Rd A2
Lorry Park A1
Louise Rd A2
Lower Harding St A2
Lower Hester St A2
Lower Mounts B3
Lower Priory St A2
Main Rd C1
Marefair B2
Market Sq B2
Marlboro Rd B1
Marriott St A2
Military Rd A3
Mounts Baths Leisure Centre A3
Nene Valley Retail Pk C1
New South Bridge Rd C2
Northampton General Hospital (A&E) B3
Northampton Sta B1
Northcote St A2
Nunn Mills Rd C3
Old Towcester Rd C2
Overstone Rd A3
Peacock Pl B2
Pembroke Rd A1
Penn Court C2
Police Station B3
Post Office A1/A2/B3/C2
Quorn Way A2
Ransome Rd C3
Regent Sq A2
Ridings, The B3
Robert St A2
St Andrew's Rd B1
St Andrew's St A2
St Edmund's Rd B3
St George's St A2
St Giles B3
St Giles St B3
St Giles' Terr B3
St James Park Rd B1
St James Rd B1
St James Retail Park C1
St James' Mill Rd B1
St James' Mill Rd East C1
St Leonard's Rd C2
St Mary's St B2
St Michael's Rd A3
St Peter's B2
St Peter's Square Shopping Precinct B2
St Peter's Way B2
Salisbury St A2
Scarletwell St B2
Semilong Rd A2
Sheep St B2
Sol Central (Leisure Centre) B2
Somerset St A3
South Bridge C2
Southfield Ave C2
Spencer Bridge Rd A1
Spencer Rd A3
Spring Gdns B3
Spring La B2
Swan St B3
TA Centre A3
Tanner St B2
Tintern Ave A1
Towcester Rd C2
Upper Bath St B2
Upper Mounts A2
Victoria Park A1
Victoria Promenade B2
Victoria Rd B3
Victoria St A2
Wellingborough Rd B3
West Bridge B1
York Rd B3

Norwich 345

Albion Way C3
All Saints Green C2
Anchor St A3
Anglia Sq A2
Argyle St C3
Arts Centre B1
Ashby St C2
Assembly House B1
Bank Plain B2
Barker St A1
Barn Rd A1
Barrack St A3
Ber St C2
Bethel St B1
Bishop Bridge A3
Bishopbridge Rd A3
Bishopgate A3
Blackfriars St A2
Botolph St A2
Bracondale C3
Brazen Gate C2
Bridewell B2
Brunswick Rd C1
Bull Close Rd A2
Bus Station C2
Calvert St A2
Cannell Green A3
Carrow Rd C3
Castle & Museum B2
Castle Mall B2
Castle Meadow B2
Cathedral B2
Cathedral Retail Park A1
Cattlemarket St B2
Chantry Rd C1
Chapel Loke C2
Chapelfield East B1
Chapelfield Gdns B1
Chapelfield North B1
Chapelfield Rd B1
City Hall B1
City Rd C2
City Wall C1/C3
Close, The B3
Colegate A2
Coslany St B1
Cow Hill B1
Cow Tower A3
Cowgate A2
Crown & Magistrates' Courts A2
Dragon Hall Heritage Centre C3
Duke St A1
Edward St A2
Elm Hill B2
Erpingham Gate B2
Fire Station B1
Fishergate A2
Forum, The B1
Foundry Bridge B3
Fye Bridge A2
Garden St C2
Gas Hill B3
Gentlemans Walk B2
Grapes Hill B1
Great Hospl Halls, The A3
Grove Ave C1
Grove Rd C1
Guildhall B1
Gurney Rd A3
Hall Rd C2
Heathgate A3
Heigham St A1
Horn's La C2
Information Ctr B1
intu Chapelfield C1
Ipswich Rd C1
James Stuart Gdns B3
King Edward VI School B2
King St B2
King St C3
Koblenz Ave C3
Library B1
London St B2
Lower Cl B3
Lower Clarence Rd B3
Maddermarket B1
Magdalen St A2
Mariners La C2
Market B2
Market Ave B2
Mountergate B3
Mousehold St A3
Newmarket Rd C1
Norfolk St C1
Norwich City FC C3
Norwich Gallery B2
Norwich Station B3
Oak St A1
Palace St A2
Pitt St A1
Playhouse B2
Police Station A3
Post Office A2/B2/C2
Pottergate B1
Prince of Wales Rd B2
Princes St B2
Pull's Ferry B3
Puppet Theatre A2
Queen St B2
Queens Rd C2
RC Cathedral B1
Recorder Rd B3
Riverside Entertainment Centre C3
Riverside Leisure Ctr C3
Riverside Rd B3
Riverside Retail Park C3
Rosary Rd B3
Rose La B2
Rouen Rd C2
Royal Norfolk Regimental Mus B2
St Andrews St B2
St Augustines St A1
St Benedicts St B1
St Ethelbert's Gate B2
St Faiths La B3
St Georges St A2
St Giles St B1
St James Cl A3
St Julians C2
St Leonards Rd B3
St Martin's La A1
St Peter Mancroft B2
St Peters St B1
St Stephens Rd C1
St Stephens St C1
Shopmobility C1
Silver Rd A2
Silver St A2
Southwell Rd C2
St. Andrew's & Blackfriars' Hall B2
Strangers' Hall B1
Superstore C2
Surrey St C2
Sussex St A1
Theatre Royal B1
Theatre St B1
Thorn La C2
Thorpe Rd B3
Tombland B2
Union St C1
Vauxhall St B1
Victoria St C1
Walpole St B1
Waterfront, The C3
Wensum St A2
Wessex St C1
Westwick St A1
Wherry Rd C3
Whitefriars A2
Willow La B1
Yacht Station B3

Nottingham 345

Abbotsford Dr A3
Addison St A1
Albert Hall B1
Alfred St South A3
Alfreton Rd B1
All Saints Rd A1
Annesley Gr A2
Arboretum A1
Arboretum St A1
Arthur St A1
Arts Theatre B3
Ashforth St A3
Balmoral Rd A1
Barker Gate B3
Bath St B3
BBC Nottingham C3
Belgrave Rooms B1
Bellar Gate B3
Belward St B3
Blue Bell Hill Rd B3
Brewhouse Yard C2
Broad Marsh Bus Sta C2
Broad St B3
Brook St B3
Burns St A1
Burton St B2
Bus Station A2
Canal St C2
Carlton St B3
Carrington St C2
Castle C2
Castle Blvd C1
Castle Gate C2
Castle Meadow Rd C1
Castle Mdw Retail Pk C1
Castle Museum & Gallery C2
Castle Rd C2
Castle Wharf C2
Cavendish Rd East C1
Cemetery B1
Chaucer St B1
Cheapside B2
Church Rd A3
City Link C3
City of Caves C2
Clarendon St B1
Cliff Rd C3
Clumber Rd East C1
Clumber St B2
College St B1
Collin St C2
Conway Cl A2
Council House B2
Cranbrook St B3
Cranmer St A2
Cromwell St B1
Curzon St B3
Derby Rd B1
Dryden St A2
Exchange Ctr, The B2
Fishpond Dr C1
Fletcher Gate B3
Forest Rd East A1
Forest Rd West A1
Friar La C2
Galleries of Justice C3
Gedling Gr A1
Gedling St B3
George St B3
Gill St A2
Glasshouse St B2
Goldsmith St B2
Goose Gate B3
Great Freeman St A2
Guildhall B2
Hamilton Dr C1
Hampden St A1
Heathcote St B3
High Pavement C3
High School A1
Holles Cr C1
Hope Dr C1
Hungerhill Rd A3
Huntingdon Dr C1
Huntingdon St A2
Information Ctr B2
Instow Rise A3
International Com Ctr A2
intu Broadmarsh C2
intu Victoria Centre B2
Kent St B3
King St B2
Lace Centre, The C2
Lace Market B3
Lace Mkt Theatre C3
Lamartine St B3
Leisure Ctr C3
Lenton Rd C1
Lewis Cl A3
Lincoln St B2
London Rd C3
Long Row B2
Low Pavement C2
Lower Parliament St B3
Magistrates' Court C2
Maid Marian Way B2
Mansfield Rd A2/B2
Middle Hill C2
Milton St B2
Mount St B2
National Ice Centre C3
Newcastle Dr B1
Newstead Gr A2
North Sherwood St A2
Nottingham Arena C3
Nottingham Station C3
Nottingham Trent University A2/B2
Old Market Square B2
Oliver St A1
Park Dr C1
Park Row C1
Park Terr B1
Park Valley C1
Park, The C1
Peas Hill Rd A3
Peel St A1
Pelham St B2
Peveril Dr C1
Plantagenet St A3
Playhouse Theatre B1
Plumptre St C3
Police Station B1/B2
Poplar St C3
Portland Rd B1
Post Office B2
Queen's Rd C3
Raleigh St A1
Regent St B1
Rick St B3
Robin Hood St B3
Robin Hood Statue C2
Ropewalk, The B1
Royal Centre B2
Royal Children Inn C2
Royal Concert Hall B2
St Ann's Hill Rd A2
St Ann's Way A2
St Ann's Well Rd A3
St Barnabas B1
St James' St B2
St Mark's St B3
St Mary's Gdn of Rest B3
St Mary's Gate B3
St Nicholas C2
St Peter's C2
St Peter's Gate B2
Salutation Inn C2
Shakespeare St B2
Shelton St A2
Shopmobility A2
South Pde B2
South Rd C1
South Sherwood St B2
Station St C3
Station Street C3
Stoney St B3
Talbot St B1
Tattershall Dr C1
Tennis Dr B1
Tennyson St A1
Theatre Royal B2
Trent St C3
Trent University B2
Union Rd B3
Upper Parliament St B2
Victoria Leisure Ctr B3
Victoria Park B3
Victoria St B2
Walter St A1
Warser Gate B3
Watkin St A2
Waverley St A1
Wheeler Gate B2
Wilford Rd C2
Wilford St C2
Willoughby House C2
Wollaton St B1
Woodborough Rd A2
Woolpack La B3
Ye Old Trip to Jerusalem C2
York St A2

Oban 345

Aird's Cres B2
Albany St B2
Albert La A2
Albert Rd A2
Alma Cres B1
Ambulance Station C2
Angus Terr C3
Ardconnel Rd A2
Ardconnel Terr B2
Argyll Sq B2
Argyll St B2
Atlantis Leisure Ctr A2
Bayview Rd A1
Benvoullin Rd A2
Bowling Green A2
Breadalbane St A2
Bus Station B2
Campbell St B2
College B2
Colonsay Terr C3
Columba Building B2
Combie St B2
Corran Brae A1
Corran Esplanade A1/A2
Corran Halls, The A2
Court B2
Crannaig-a-Mhinisteir B1
Crannog La C2
Croft Ave A2
Dalintart Dr C3
Dalriach Rd A2
Distillery B2
Drummore Rd C2
Duncraggan Rd A2
Dunollie Rd A2
Dunuaran Rd B1
Feochan Gr C3
Ferry Terminal B1
Gallanach Rd B1
George St A2
Glencruitten Dr C3
Glencruitten Rd B3
Glenmore Rd C1
Glenshellach Rd C1
Glenshellach Terr B2
Hazeldean Cres A3
High St B2
Highland Theatre Cinema, The A2
Hill St B2
Industrial Estate C2
Information Ctr B2
Islay Rd C3
Jacob's Ladder B2
Jura Rd C3
Knipoch Pl C3
Laurel Cres A2
Laurel Rd A2/A3
Library B1
Lifeboat Station B1
Lighthouse Pier B1
Lismore Cres A2
Lochavullin Dr B2
Lochavullin Rd C2
Lochside St B2
Longsdale Cres A3
Longsdale Rd A2/A3
Longsdale Terr A3
Lunga Rd C3
Lynn Rd C2
Market St B2
McCaig Rd C3
McCaig's Tower A2
Mill La C2
Miller Rd C2
Millpark Ave C2
Millpark Rd C2
Mossfield Ave B3
Mossfield Dr B3
Mossfield Stadium B3
Nant Dr C3
Nelson Rd C2
North Pier B2
Nursery La A2
Oban B2
Police Station B2
Polvinister Rd B3
Post Office A2/B2
Pulpit Dr C1
Pulpit Hill C1
Pulpit Hill Viewpoint B1
Quarry Rd C2
Queen's Park Pl B2
Railway Quay B1
Rockfield Rd B2
St Columba's A1
St John's A2
Scalpay Terr C3
Shore St B1
Shuna Terr C3
Sinclair Dr C2
Soroba Rd B2/C2
South Pier B1
Stevenson St B2
Tweedale St B2
Ulva Rd C2
Villa Rd B1
War & Peace A2

Oxford 345

Adelaide St A1
Albert St A1
All Souls (Coll) B2
Ashmolean Mus B2
Balliol (Coll) B2
Banbury Rd A2
Bate Collection of Musical Instruments C2
Beaumont St B1
Becket St B1
Blackhall Rd A2
Blue Boar St B2
Bodleian Library B2
Botanic Garden B3
Brasenose (Coll) B2
Brewer St C2
Broad St B2
Burton-Taylor Theatre B2
Bus Station B1
Canal St A1
Cardigan St A1
Carfax Tower B2
Castle B1
Castle St B1
Catte St B2
Cemetery C1
Christ Church (Coll) B2
Christ Church Cath C2
Christ Church Mdw C2
Clarendon Centre B2
Coach & Lorry Park C1
College B3
Coll of Further Ed C1
Cornmarket St B2
Corpus Christi (Coll) B2
County Hall B1
Covered Market B2
Cowley Pl C3
Cranham St A1
Cranham Terr A1
Cricket Ground B1
Crown & County Courts C2
Deer Park B3
Exeter (Coll) B2
Folly Bridge C2
George St B1
Great Clarendon St A1
Hart St A1
Hertford (Coll) B2
High St B3
Hollybush Row B1
Holywell St B2
Hythe Bridge St B1
Ice Rink C1
Information Ctr B2
Jericho St A1
Jesus (Coll) B2
Jowett Walk B3
Juxon St A1
Keble (Coll) A2
Keble Rd A2
Library B2
Linacre (Coll) A3
Lincoln (Coll) B2
Little Clarendon St A1
Longwall St B3
Magdalen (Coll) B3
Magdalen Bridge B2
Magdalen St B2
Magistrate's Court C2
Manchester (Coll) B2
Manor Rd B3
Mansfield (Coll) A2
Mansfield Rd A3
Market B1
Marlborough Rd C2
Martyrs' Memorial B2
Merton (Coll) B3
Merton Field B3
Merton St B2
Mus of Modern Art B2
Museum of Oxford B2
Museum Rd A2
New College (Coll) B3
New Inn Hall St B2
New Rd B1
New Theatre B2
Norfolk St C1
Nuffield (Coll) B1
Observatory A1
Observatory St A1
Odeon B1/B2
Old Fire Station B1
Old Greyfriars St C2
Oriel (Coll) B2
Oxford Station B1
Oxford University Research Centres A1
Oxpens Rd C1
Paradise Sq C1
Paradise St B1
Park End St B1
Parks Rd A2/B2
Pembroke (Coll) C2
Phoenix A1
Picture Gallery C2
Plantation Rd A1
Playhouse B2
Police Station C2
Post Office A1/B2
Pusey St B1
Queen's (Coll) B3
Queen's La B3
Radcliffe Camera B2
Rewley Rd B1
Richmond Rd A1
Rose La B3
Ruskin (Coll) B1
Said Business School B1
St Aldates C2
St Anne's (Coll) A1
St Antony's (Coll) A1
St Bernard's Rd A1
St Catherine's (Coll) B3
St Cross Building A3
St Cross Rd A3
St Edmund Hall (Coll) B3
St Giles St A2
St Hilda's (Coll) C3
St John St B2
St John's (Coll) B2
St Mary the Virgin B2
St Michael at the Northgate B2
St Peter's (Coll) B1
St Thomas St B1
Science Area A2
Science Museum B2
Sheldonian Theatre B2
Somerville (Coll) A1
South Parks Rd A2
Speedwell St C2
Sports Ground C3
Thames St C2
Town Hall B2
Trinity (Coll) B2
Turl St B2
University Coll (Coll) B3
Univ Mus & Pitt Rivers Mus A2
University Parks A2
Wadham (Coll) B2
Walton Cr A1
Walton St A1
Western Rd C2
Westgate Sh Ctr B2
Woodstock Rd A1
Worcester (Coll) B1

Perth 345

AK Bell Library B2
Abbot Cres C1
Abbot St C1
Albany Terr A1
Albert Monument A3
Alexandra St B2
Atholl St A2
Balhousie Ave A2
Balhousie Castle Black Watch Museum A2
Balhousie St A2
Ballantine Pl A1
Barossa Pl A2
Barossa St A2
Barrack St A2
Bell's Sports Centre A2
Bellwood B3
Blair St B1
Burn Park C1
Bus Station B2
Caledonian Rd B2
Canal Cres B2
Canal St B3
Cavendish Ave C1
Charles St B2
Charlotte Pl A2
Charlotte St A3
Church St A1
City Hall B3
Club House C3
Clyde Pl C1
Commercial St A3
Concert Hall B3
Council Chambers B3
County Pl B2
Court B3
Craigie Pl C2
Crieff Rd A1
Croft Park C2
Cross St B2
Darnhall Cres C1
Darnhall Dr C1
Dewars Centre B1
Dundee Rd B3
Dunkeld Rd A1
Earl's Dykes B1
Edinburgh Rd C3
Elibank St B1
Fair Maid's House A3
Fergusson B3
Feus Rd A1
Fire Station A1
Fitness Centre B3
Foundry La A2
Friar St C1
George St B3
Glamis Pl C1
Glasgow Rd B1
Glenearn Rd C2
Glover St B1/C1
Golf Course A2
Gowrie St A3
Gray St B1
Graybank Rd B1
Greyfriars Burial Grnd B3
Hay St A2
High St B2/B3
Hotel B2
Inchaffray St A1
Industrial/Retail Park B1
Information Ctr B2
Isla Rd A3
James St B2
Keir St A3
King Edward St B3
King James VI Golf Course C3
King St B2
Kings Pl C2
Kinnoull Aisle 'Tower' B3
Kinnoull Causeway B2
Kinnoull St B2
Knowelea Pl C1
Knowelea Terr C1
Ladeside Bsns Centre A1
Leisure Pool B1
Leonard St B2
Lickley St B2
Lochie Brae A3
Long Causeway A1
Low St A2
Main St A3
Marshall Pl C3
Melville St A2
Mill St B3
Milne St B2
Murray Cres C1
Murray St B2
Needless Rd C1
New Rd B2
North Inch A3
North Methven St A2
Park Pl C1
Perth B2
Perth Bridge A3
Perth Business Park B1
Perth Museum & Art Gallery B3
Perth Station C2
Pickletulllum Rd B1
Pitheavlis Cres C1
Playhouse B2
Police Station A2
Pomarium St B2
Post Office B2/C2
Princes St B3
Priory Pl C2
Queen St C1
Queen's Bridge B3
Riggs Rd B1
Riverside B3
Riverside Park B3
Rodney Park B3
Rose Terr A2
St Catherine's Rd A1/A2
St Catherines Ret Pk A1
St John St B3
St John's Kirk B3
St John's Shopping Centre B2
St Leonards Bridge C2
St Ninians Cath A2
Scott Monument C2
Scott St B2
Sheriff Court B3
Shore Rd C3
Skate Park C3
South Inch C2
South Inch Bsns Ctr C3
South Inch Park C2
South Inch View C2
South Methven St B2
South St B3
South William St B2
Stables, The A1
Stanners, The B3
Stormont St A2
Strathmore St A3
Stuart Ave C1
Superstore B1/B2
Tay St B3
Union La A2
Victoria St B2
Watergate B3
Wellshill Cemetery A1
West Bridge St A3
West Mill St B2
Whitefriers Cres B1
Whitefriers St B1
Wilson St C1
Windsor Terr C1
Woodside Cres C1
York Pl B2
Young St C1

Peterborough 345

ABAX Stadium (Peterborough United) C2
Athletics Arena B3
Bishop's Palace B2
Bishop's Rd B2/B3
Boongate A3
Bourges Boulevard A1
Bourges Retail Pk B1/B2
Bridge House (Council Offices) C2
Bridge St B2
Bright St A1
Broadway A2
Broadway A2
Brook St A2
Burghley Rd A2
Bus Station B2
Cavendish St A3
Charles St A3
Church St B2
Church Walk A2
Cobden Ave A1
Cobden St A1
Cowgate B2
Craig St A2
Crawthorne Rd A2
Cromwell Rd A1
Dickens St A3
Eastfield Rd A3
Eastgate B3
Fire Station A1
Fletton Ave C2
Frank Perkins Parkway C3
Geneva St A2
George St C1
Gladstone St A1
Glebe Rd C2
Gloucester Rd C3
Granby St B3
Grove St C1
Guildhall B2
Hadrians Ct C3

Plymouth • Poole • Portsmouth • Preston • Reading • St Andrews • Salisbury • Scarborough 363

Hawksbill Way C2
Henry St A2
Hereward Cross (Sh) B2
Hereward Rd B3
Information Ctr B2
Jubilee St C1
Kent Rd B1
Key Theatre C2
Kirkwood Cl B1
Lea Gdns B1
Library A2
Lincoln Rd A2
London Rd C2
Long Causeway B2
Lower Bridge St C2
Magistrates Court B2
Manor House St A2
Mayor's Walk A1
Midland Rd A1
Monument St A2
Morris St A3
Mus & Art Gallery B2
Nene Valley Railway C1
New Rd A2
New Rd C1
Northminster A2
Old Customs House C2
Oundle Rd C1
Padholme Rd A3
Palmerston Rd C1
Park Rd A2
Passport Office B2
Peterborough Nene Valley C1
Peterborough Sta B1
Police Station B2
Post Office A3/B1/B2/B3/C1
Priestgate B2
Queen's Walk C2
Queensgate Centre B2
Railworld C1
Regional Swimming & Fitness Centre B3
River La B1
Rivergate Sh Ctr B2
Riverside Mead C3
Russell St A1
St John's B2
St John's St A3
St Marks St A2
St Peter's B2
St Peter's Rd B2
Saxon Rd A3
Spital Bridge A1
Stagshaw Dr C3
Star Rd B3
Thorpe Lea Rd B1
Thorpe Rd B1
Thorpe's Lea Rd B1
Tower St A2
Town Hall B2
Viersen Platz B2
Vineyard Rd B3
Wake Rd B3
Wellington St A3
Wentworth St B2
Westgate B2
Whalley St A3
Wharf Rd C1
Whitsed St A3
YMCA A3

Plymouth 346

Alma Rd A1
Anstis St B1
Armada Shop Ctr B2
Armada St A3
Armada Way B2
Arts Centre B2
Athenaeum B1
Athenaeum St C1
Barbican C3
Barbican C3
Baring St A3
Bath St B1
Beaumont Park B3
Beaumont Rd B3
Black Friars Gin Distillery C2
Breton Side B3
Castle St C3
Cathedral (RC) B1
Cecil St B1
Central Park A1
Central Park Ave A2
Charles Church B3
Charles Cross B3
Charles St B2
Citadel Rd C2
Citadel Rd East C2
City Museum & Art Gallery B2
Civic Centre B2
Cliff Rd C1
Clifton Pl A3
Cobourg St A2
College of Art B2
Continental Ferry Port B1
Cornwall St B2
Crescent, The B1
Dale Rd A2
Deptford Pl A3
Derry Ave A2
Derry's Cross B1
Drake Circus B2
Drake Circus Sh Ctr B2
Drake's Memorial C2
Eastlake St B2
Ebrington St B3
Elizabethan House C3
Elliot St C1
Endsleigh Pl A2
Exeter St B3
Fire Station A3
Fish Quay C3
Gibbons St A3
Glen Park Ave A2
Grand Pde C1
Great Western Rd C1
Greenbank Rd A3
Greenbank Terr A3
Guildhall B2
Hampton St B3
Harwell St B1
Hill Park Cr A3
Hoe Approach B2
Hoe Rd C2
Hoe, The C2
Hoegate St C2
Houndiscombe Rd A2
Information Ctr C3
James St A2
Kensington Rd A3
King St B1
Lambhay Hill C3
Leigham St C1
Library B2
Lipson Rd A3/B3
Lockyer St C2
Lockyers Quay C3
Madeira Rd C2
Marina B3
Market Ave B1
Martin St B1
Mayflower St B2
Mayflower Stone and Steps C3
Mayflower Visitor Centre C3
Merchant's House B2
Millbay Rd B1
National Marine Aquarium C3
Neswick St B1
New George St B2
New St C3
North Cross A2
North Hill A3
North Quay B2
North Rd East A2
North Rd West A1
North St B3
Notte St B2
Octagon, The B1
Octagon St B1
Pannier Market B1
Pennycomequick A1
Pier St C1
Plymouth Pavilions B1
Plymouth Station A2
Police Station B3
Post Office C2
Princess St B2
Promenade, The C2
Prysten House B2
Queen Anne's Battery Seasports Centre C3
Radford Rd C1
Reel B2
Regent St B3
Rope Walk C3
Royal Citadel C2
Royal Pde B2
Royal Theatre B2
St Andrew's B2
St Andrew's Cross B2
St Andrew's St B2
St Lawrence Rd A2
Saltash Rd A2
Shopmobility B2
Smeaton's Tower C2
Southern Terr A3
Southside St C2
Stuart Rd A1
Sutherland Rd A2
Sutton Rd B3
Sydney St A1
Teats Hill Rd C3
Tothill Ave B3
Union St B1
Univ of Plymouth A2
Vauxhall St B2/3
Victoria Park A1
West Hoe Rd C1
Western Approach B1
Whittington St A1
Wyndham St B1
YMCA B2
YWCA C2

Poole 346

Ambulance Station A3
Baiater Gdns C2
Baiter Park C3
Ballard Cl C2
Ballard Rd C2
Bay Hog La B1
Bridge Approach C1
Bus Station B2
Castle St B2
Catalina Dr B3
Chapel La B2
Church St B1
Cinnamon La B1
Colborne Cl B3
Dear Hay La B2
Denmark La A3
Denmark Rd A3
Dolphin Ctr B2
East St B2
Elizabeth Rd A3
Emerson Rd B2
Ferry Rd C1
Ferry Terminal C1
Fire Station A2
Freightliner Terminal C1
Furnell Rd B3
Garland Rd A3
Green Rd B2
Heckford La A3
Heckford Rd A3
High St B2
High St North A3
Hill St B2
Holes Bay Rd A1
Hospital (A&E) A3
Information Ctr C2
Kingland Rd B3
Kingston Rd A3
Labrador Dr C3
Lagland St B2
Lander Cl C3
Lifeboat College, The B2
Lighthouse – Poole Centre for the Arts B3
Longfleet Rd A3
Maple Rd A3
Market Cl B2
Market St B2
Mount Pleasant Rd B3
New Harbour Rd C1
New Harbour Rd South C1
New Harbour Rd West C1
New Orchard B1
New Quay Rd C1
New St B2
Newfoundland Dr B2
North St B2
Old Lifeboat C2
Old Orchard B2
Parish Rd A3
Park Lake Rd B3
Parkstone Rd A3
Perry Gdns B2
Pitwines Cl B2
Police Station A2
Poole Central Library B2
Poole Lifting Bridge C1
Poole Park B2
Poole Station A2
Poole Museum C1
Post Office A2/B2
Quay, The C2
St John's Rd A3
St Margaret's Rd A2
St Mary's Maternity Unit A3
St Mary's Rd A3
Seldown Bridge B3
Seldown La B3
Seldown Rd B3
Serpentine Rd A2
Shaftesbury Rd A3
Skinner St B2
Slipway B1
Stanley Rd C2
Sterte Ave A2
Sterte Ave West A1
Sterte Cl A2
Sterte Esplanade A2
Sterte Rd A2
Strand St C2
Swimming Pool B3
Taverner Cl B3
Thames St B1
Towngate Bridge B2
Twin Sails Bridge B1
Vallis Cl C3
Waldren Cl B3
West Quay B1
West Quay Rd B1
West St B1
West View Rd A2
Whatleigh Cl B2
Wimborne Rd A3

Portsmouth 346

Action Stations C1
Admiralty Rd A1
Alfred Rd A2
Anglesea Rd A2
Arundel St B3
Aspex B1
Bishop St A2
Broad St C1
Buckingham House C2
Burnaby Rd B2
Bus Station B1
Camber Dock C1
Cambridge Rd B2
Car Ferry to Isle of Wight B1
Cascades Sh Ctr A3
Castle Rd C3
City Museum & Art Gallery B2
Civic Offices B3
Clarence Pier C2
College St B1
Commercial Rd A3
Cottage Gr B3
Cross St A1
Cumberland St A2
Duisburg Way C2
Durham St A3
East St B1
Edinburgh Rd A2
Elm Gr C3
Emirates Spinnaker Tower B1
Great Southsea St C3
Green Rd B3
Greetham St B3
Grosvenor St B3
Groundlings A2
Grove Rd North C3
Grove Rd South C3
Guildhall B3
Guildhall Walk B3
Gunwharf Quays Designer Outlet B1
Gunwharf Rd B1
Hambrook St C2
Hampshire Terr B2
Hanover St A1
Hard, The B1
High St C2
HM Naval Base A1
HMS Nelson (Royal Naval Barracks) A2
HMS Victory A1
HMS Warrior A1
Hovercraft Terminal C2
Hyde Park Rd B3
Information Ctr A1/B3
Isambard Brunel Rd B3
Isle of Wight Car Ferry Terminal B1
Kent Rd C3
Kent St A2
King St B3
King's Rd C3
King's Terr C2
Lake Rd A3
Law Courts B3
Library B3
Long Curtain Rd C2
Market Way A3
Marmion Rd C3
Mary Rose Museum A1
Middle St B3
Millennium Prom B1/C1
Museum Rd B2
National Museum of the Royal Navy A1
Naval Recreation Gd C2
Nightingale Rd C3
Norfolk St B3
North St A2
Osborne Rd C3
Park Rd B2
Passenger Catamaran to Isle of Wight B1
Passenger Ferry to Gosport B1
Pelham Rd C3
Pembroke Gdns C2
Pier Rd C2
Point Battery C1
Police Station B3
Portsmouth & Southsea A3
Portsmouth Harbour B1
Portsmouth Historic Dockyard A1
Post Office A3/B1/B3
Queen St A1
Queen's Cr C3
Round Tower C1
Royal Garrison Church C1
St Edward's Rd C3
St George's Rd B2
St George's Sq B1
St George's Way B2
St James's Rd B3
St James's St A2
St John's Cath (RC) A3
St Thomas's Cath C1
St Thomas's St B2
Shopmobility A3/B1
Somers Rd B3
Southsea Common C2
Southsea Terr C2
Square Tower C1
Station St A3
Town Fortifications C1
Unicorn Rd A2
United Services Recreation Ground B2
University of Portsmouth A2/B2
Univ of Portsmouth – Coll of Art, Design & Media B3
Upper Arundel St A3
Victoria Ave C2
Victoria Park A2
Victory Gate A1
Vue B1
Warblington St B1
Western Pde C2
White Hart Rd C1
Winston Churchill Ave B3

Preston 346

Adelphi St A2
Anchor Ct B3
Aqueduct St A1
Ardee Rd C1
Arthur St B2
Ashton St A1
Avenham La B3
Avenham Park C3
Avenham Rd B3
Avenham St B3
Bairstow St B3
Balderstone Rd C1
Beamont Dr A1
Beech St South C2
Bird St C1
Bow La B2
Brieryfield Rd A1
Broadgate C1
Brook St A2
Bus Station A3
Butler St B2
Cannon St B3
Carlton St A1
Chaddock St B3
Channel Way B1
Chapel St B3
Christ Church St B2
Christian Rd B2
Cold Bath St A2
Coleman Ct C1
Connaught Rd C2
Corn Exchange B3
Corporation St A2/B2
County Hall B2
County Records Office B2
Court A3
Court B3
Cricket Ground C2
Croft St A1
Cross St B3
Crown Court A3
Crown St A3
East Cliff C3
East Cliff Rd B3
Edward St A2
Elizabeth St A3
Euston St B1
Fishergate B2/B3
Fishergate Hill B2
Fishergate Sh Ctr B2
Fitzroy St B1
Fleetwood St A1
Friargate A3
Fylde Rd A1/A2
Gerrard St B2
Glover's Ct B3
Good St B2
Grafton St B2
Great George St A3
Great Shaw St A3
Greenbank St A2
Guild Way B1
Guildhall & Charter B3
Guildhall St B3
Harrington St A2
Harris Museum B3
Hartington Rd B1
Hasset Cl C2
Heatley St B2
Hind St C2
Information Ctr B3
Kilruddery Rd C1
Lancaster Rd A3/B3
Latham St B3
Lauderdale St C2
Lawson St A3
Leighton St A2
Leyland Rd C1
Library A1
Library B3
Liverpool Rd C1
Lodge St B2
Lune St B3
Main Sprit West B3
Maresfield Rd C1
Market St West A3
Marsh La B1/B2
Maudland Bank A2
Maudland Rd A2
Meadow Ct C2
Meath Rd C1
Mill Hill A2
Miller Arcade B3
Miller Park C3
Moor La A3
Mount St B3
North Rd A3
North St A3
Northcote Rd B1
Old Milestones B1
Old Tram Rd C3
Pedder St A1/A2
Peel St A2
Penwortham Bridge C2
Penwortham New Bridge C1
Pitt St B2
Playhouse A3
Police Station A3
Port Way B1
Post Office B3
Preston Station B2
Ribble Bank St B2
Ribble Viaduct C2
Ribblesdale Pl B3
Ringway B3
River Parade C1
Riverside C2
St George's Sh Ctr B3
St Georges B3
St Johns B3
St Johns Shopping Ctr A3
St Mark's Rd A1
St Walburges A1
Salisbury Rd B1
Sessions House B3
Snow Hill A3
South End C2
South Meadow La C2
Spa Rd B1
Sports Ground C2
Strand Rd B1
Syke St B3
Talbot Rd B1
Taylor St C1
Tithebarn St A3
Town Hall B3
Tulketh Brow A1
University of Central Lancashire A2
Valley Rd C1
Victoria St A2
Walker St A3
Walton's Parade B2
Warwick St A3
Wellfield Bsns Park A1
Wellfield Rd A1
Wellington St A1
West Cliff C2
West Strand A1
Winckley Rd C1
Winckley Square B3
Wolseley Rd C2

Reading 346

Abbey Ruins B2
Abbey Sq B2
Abbey St B2
Abbot's Walk B2
Acacia Rd C2
Addington Rd C3
Addison Rd A1
Allcroft Rd C3
Alpine St C2
Baker St B1
Berkeley Ave C1
Bridge St B1
Brigham Rd A1
Broad St B1
Broad Street Mall B1
Carey St B1
Castle Hill C1
Castle St B1
Causeway, The A3
Caversham Rd A1
Christchurch Playing Fields A2
Civic Offices B1
Coley Hill C1
Coley Pl C1
Craven Rd C3
Crown St C2
De Montfort Rd A1
Denmark Rd C3
Duke St B2
East St B2
Edgehill St C2
Eldon Rd B3
Eldon Terr B3
Elgar Rd C1
Erleigh Rd C3
Field Rd C1
Fire Station A1
Fobney St B1
Forbury Gdns B2
Forbury Rd B2
Forbury Retail Park B2
Francis St C1
Friar St B1
Garrard St B1
Gas Works Rd B3
George St A2
Great Knollys St B1
Greyfriars B1
Grove, The B2
Gun St B1
Henry St C1
Hexagon Theatre, The B1
Hill's Meadow A2
Howard St B1
Information Ctr B1
Inner Distribution Rd B1
Katesgrove La C1
Kenavon Dr B2
Kendrick Rd C2
King's Meadow Rec Gd A2
King's Rd B2
Library B2
London Rd C3
London St B2
Lynmouth Rd A1
Magistrate's Court B1
Market Pl B2
Mill La B2
Mill Rd A2
Minster St B1
Morgan Rd C3
Mount Pleasant C2
Museum of English Rural Life C3
Napier Rd A2
Newark St C2
Newport Rd A1
Old Reading Univ C3
Oracle Shopping Centre, The B1
Orts Rd B3
Pell St C1
Police Station B1
Post Office B2
Queen Victoria St B1
Queen's Rd A2
Queen's Rd B2
Randolph Rd A1
Reading Bridge A2
Reading Station A1
Redlands Rd C3
Renaissance Hotel B1
Riverside Museum B3
Rose Kiln La C1
Royal Berks Hospital (A&E) C3
St Giles C2
St Laurence B2
St Mary's B1
St Mary's Butts B1
St Saviour's Rd C1
Send Rd A3
Sherman Rd C2
Sidmouth St B2
Silver St C2
South St B2
Southampton St C2
Station Hill A1
Station Rd B1
Superstore A3
Swansea Rd A1
Technical College B3
Valpy St B2
Vastern Rd A1
Vue B2
Waldeck St C2
Watlington St B3
West St B1
Whitby Dr C3
Wolseley St C1
York Rd A1
Zinzan St B1

St Andrews 346

Abbey St B2
Abbey Walk B3
Abbotsford Cres A1
Albany Pk C3
Allan Robertson Dr C2
Ambulance Station C1
Anstruther Rd C3
Argyle St B1
Argyll Business Park C1
Auld Burn Rd B2
Bassaguard Ind Est B1
Bell St B2
Blackfriars Chapel (Ruins) B2
Boase Ave B2
Braid Cres C3
Brewster Pl C3
Bridge St B1
British Golf Mus A1
Broomfaulds Ave C1
Bruce Embankment A1
Bruce St C2
Bus Station A1
Byre B2
Canongate C1
Cathedral and Priory (Ruins) B3
Cemetery B3
Chamberlain St C1
Church St B2
Churchill Cres C2
City Rd A1
Claybraes C1
Cockshaugh Public Park B1
Cosmos Com Centre B3
Council Office A2
Crawford Gdns C1
Doubledykes Rd B1
Drumcarrow Rd C1
East Sands B3
East Scores A3
Fire Station C1
Forrest St C1
Fraser Ave C1
Freddie Tait St C2
Gateway Centre A1
Glebe Rd B2
Golf Pl A1
Grange Rd C3
Greenside Pl B2
Greyfriars Gdns A2
Hamilton Ave C2
Hepburn Gdns B1
Holy Trinity B2
Horseleys Park C1
Information Ctr B2
Irvine Cres C3
James Robb Ave C1
James St B1
John Knox Rd C1
Kennedy Gdns B1
Kilrymont Cl C3
Kilrymont Pl C3
Kilrymont Rd C3
Kinburn Park B1
Kinkell Terr C3
Kinnesburn Rd B2
Ladebraes Walk B2
Lady Buchan's Cave A3
Lamberton Pl C1
Lamond Dr C2
Langlands Rd B2
Largo Rd C1
Learmonth Pl C1
Library B2
Links Clubhouse A1
Links, The A1
Livingstone Cres B2
Long Rocks A2
Madras College B2
Market St A2
Martyr's Monument A1
Murray Pk A2
Murray Pl A2
Mus of the University of St Andrews (MUSA) A2
Nelson St B2
New Course, The A1
New Picture House A2
North Castle St A3
North St A2
Old Course, The A1
Old Station Rd A1
Pends, The B3
Pilmour Links A1
Pipeland Rd B2/C2
Police Station A2/C1
Post Office B2
Preservation Trust B2
Priestden Pk C3
Priestden Pl C3
Priestden Rd C3
Queen's Gdns B2
Queen's Terr B2
Roundhill Rd C2
Royal & Ancient Golf Club A1
St Andrews B1
St Andrews Aquarium A2
St Andrews Botanic Garden B1
St Andrews Castle (Ruins) & Visitor Centre A2
St Leonard's School B3
St Mary St B3
St Mary's College B2
St Nicholas St C3
St Rules Tower B3
St Salvator's College A2
Sandyhill Cres C2
Sandyhill Rd C2
Scooniehill Rd C2
Scores, The A2
Shields Ave C3
Shoolbraids C2
Shore, The B3
Sloan St B1
South St B2
Spottiswoode Gdns C1
Station Rd A1
Swilcen Bridge A1
Tom Morris Dr C2
Tom Stewart La C1
Town Hall B2
Union St A2
University Chapel A2
University Library A2
Univ of St Andrews A1
Viaduct Walk B1
War Memorial A3
Wardlaw Gdns B1
Warrack St C3
Watson Ave B2
West Port B2
West Sands A1
Westview B2
Windmill Rd A1
Winram Pl C1
Wishart Gdns C2
Woodburn Pk B3
Woodburn Pl B3
Woodburn Terr B3
Younger Hall A2

Salisbury 347

Albany Rd A2
Arts Centre A3
Ashley Rd A1
Avon Approach A2
Ayleswade Rd C2
Bedwin St A2
Belle Vue A2
Bishop's Palace C2
Bishops Walk B2
Blue Boar Row B2
Bourne Ave A3
Bourne Hill A3
Britford La C2
Broad Walk C2
Brown St B2
Bus Station B2
Castle St A2
Catherine St B2
Chapter House B2
Church House B2
Churchfields Rd B1
Churchill Way East B3
Churchill Way North A3
Churchill Way South C2
Churchill Way West A1
City Hall B2
Close Wall B2
Coldharbour La A1
College St A3
Council Offices A3
Court A1
Crane Bridge Rd B2
Crane St B2
Cricket Ground C1
Culver St South B3
De Vaux Pl C2
Devizes Rd A1
Dews Rd B1
Elm Grove B3
Elm Grove Rd A3
Endless St A2
Estcourt Rd A3
Exeter St C2
Fairview Rd A3
Fire Station A1
Fisherton St A1
Folkestone Rd C1
Fowlers Hill B3
Fowlers Rd B3
Friary Estate C3
Friary La B2
Friary, The B3
Gas La A1
Gigant St B3
Greencroft B3
Greencroft St A3
Guildhall B2
Hall of John Halle B2
Hamilton Rd A2
Harnham Mill B1
Harnham Rd C1/C2
High St B2
Hospital A1
Ho of John A'Port B2
Information Ctr B2
Kelsey Rd A3
King's Rd A2
Laverstock Rd B3
Library B2
London Rd A3
Lower St C1
Maltings, The B2
Manor Rd A3
Marsh La A1
Medieval Hall B2
Milford Hill B3
Milford St B3
Mill Rd B1
Millstream Approach A2
Mompesson House (NT) B2
New Bridge Rd C2
New Canal B2
New Harnham Rd C2
New St B2
North Canonry B2
North Gate B2
North Walk B2
Old Blandford Rd C1
Old Deanery B2
Old George Hall B2
Park St A3
Parsonage Green C1
Playhouse Theatre A2
Post Office A2/B2/C2
Poultry Cross B2
Queen Elizabeth Gdns B1
Queen's Rd A3
Rampart Rd B3
St Ann St B3
St Ann's Gate B2
St Marks Rd A3
St Martins B3
St Mary's Cathedral B2
St Nicholas Hospl C2
St Paul's A1
St Paul's Rd A1
St Thomas B2
Salisbury & South Wiltshire Museum B2
Salisbury Station A1
Salt La A3
Saxon Rd C1
Scots La A2
Shady Bower B3
South Canonry C2
South Gate C2
Southampton Rd B2
Spire View A1
Sports Ground C3
Tollgate Rd B3
Town Path B1
Wain-a-Long Rd A3
Wardrobe, The B2
Wessex Rd A3
West Walk C2
Wilton Rd A1
Wiltshire College B3
Winchester St B3
Windsor Rd A1
Winston Churchill Gdns C3
Wyndham Rd A2
YHA B3
York Rd A1

Scarborough 347

Aberdeen Walk B2
Albert Rd A2
Albion Rd C2
Alexandra Gardens A1
Auborough St B2
Balmoral Ctr B2
Belle Vue St C1
Belmont Rd C2
Brunswick Shop Ctr B2
Castle Dykes B3
Castle Hill A3
Castle Holms A3
Castle Rd B2
Castle Walls A3
Castlegate B3
Cemetery B1
Central Tramway B2
Clarence Gardens A2
Coach Park B1
Columbus Ravine A1
Court B1
Crescent, The C2
Cricket Ground A1
Cross St B2
Crown Terr C2
Dean Rd B1
Devonshire Dr A1
East Harbour B3
East Pier B3
Eastborough B2
Elmville Ave B1
Esplanade C2
Falconers Rd B2
Falsgrave Rd C1
Fire Station B2
Foreshore Rd B2
Friargate B2
Gladstone Rd B1
Gladstone St B1
Hollywood Plaza A1
Hoxton Rd B1
Information Ctr B2/B3
King St B2
Library B2
Lifeboat Station B3
Londesborough Rd C1
Longwestgate B3
Marine Dr A3
Military Adventure Pk A1
Miniature Railway A1
Nelson St B1
Newborough B2
Nicolas St B2
North Marine Rd A1
North St B2
Northway B1
Old Harbour B3
Olympia Leisure B2
Peasholm Park A1
Peasholm Rd A1
Police Station B1
Post Office B2/C1
Princess St B3
Prospect Rd B1
Queen St B2
Queen's Parade A2
Queen's Tower (Remains) A3
Ramshill Rd C2
Roman Signal Sta A3
Roscoe St C1
Rotunda Museum C2
Royal Albert Dr A2
St Martin-on-the-Hill C2
St Martin's Ave C2
St Mary's B3
St Thomas St B2
Sandside B3
Scarborough C1
Scarborough Art Gallery and Crescent Art Studios C2
Scarborough Bowls Centre A1
Scarborough Castle A3
Shopmobility C2
Somerset Terr C2
South Cliff Lift C2
Spa Theatre, The C2
Spa, The C2
Stephen Joseph Theatre B1
Tennyson Ave B1
Tollergate B2
Town Hall B2
Trafalgar Rd B1
Trafalgar Square A1
Trafalgar St West B1
Valley Bridge Parade C2
Valley Rd C1
Vernon Rd C2
Victoria Park Mount A1
Victoria Rd B1
West Pier B3
Westborough C1
Westover Rd C1
Westwood C1
Woodall Ave A1
YMCA Theatre B2
York Pl B2
Yorkshire Coast College (Westwood Campus) C1

364 Sheffield • Shrewsbury • Southampton • Southend-on-Sea • Stirling • Stoke • Stratford-upon-Avon

Sheffield 347

Addy Dr A2
Addy St A2
Adelphi St A3
Albert Terrace Rd A3
Albion St A2
Aldred Rd A1
Allen St A4
Alma St A4
Angel St B5
Arundel Gate B5
Arundel St C4
Ashberry Rd A2
Ashdell Rd C1
Ashgate Rd C1
Athletics Centre B2
Attercliffe Rd A6
Bailey St B4
Ball St A4
Balm Green B4
Bank St B4
Barber Rd A2
Bard St B5
Barker's Pool B4
Bates St A1
Beech Hill Rd C1
Beet St B3
Bellefield St A3
Bernard Rd A6
Bernard St B6
Birkendale A2
Birkendale Rd A2
Birkendale View A1
Bishop St C4
Blackwell Pl B6
Blake St A2
Blonk St A5
Bolsover St B2
Botanical Gdns C1
Bower Rd A1
Bradley St A1
Bramall La C4
Bramwell St A3
Bridge St A4/A5
Brighton Terrace Rd A1
Broad La B3
Broad St B6
Brocco St A3
Brook Hill B3
Broomfield Rd C1
Broomgrove Rd C2
Broomhall Pl C3
Broomhall Rd C2
Broomhall St C3
Broomspring La C2
Brown St C5
Brunswick St B3
Burgess St B4
Burlington St A2
Burns Rd A2
Cadman St A6
Cambridge St B4
Campo La B4
Carver St B4
Castle Square B5
Castlegate A5
Cathedral B4
Cathedral (RC) B4
Cavendish St B3
Charles St C4
Charter Row C4
Children's Hospital (A&E) B2
Church St B4
City Hall B4
City Hall B4
City Rd C6
Claremont Cr B2
Claremont Pl B2
Clarke St C3
Clarkegrove Rd C2
Clarkehouse Rd C1
Clarkson St B2
Cobden View Rd A1
Collegiate Cr C2
Commercial St B5
Commonside A1
Conduit Rd B1
Cornish St A3
Corporation St A4
Court B4
Cricket Inn Rd B6
Cromwell St A1
Crookes Rd B1
Crookes Valley Park B2
Crookes Valley Rd B2
Crookesmoor Rd A2
Crown Court A4
Crucible Theatre B5
Cutlers' Hall B4
Cutlers Gate A6
Daniel Hill A2
Dental Hospital B2
Derek Dooley Way A5
Devonshire Green B3
Devonshire St B3
Division St B4
Dorset St C2
Dover St A3
Duchess Rd C5
Duke St B5
Duncombe St A1
Durham Rd B2
Earl St C4
Earl Way C4
Ecclesall Rd C3
Edward St B3
Effingham Rd A6
Effingham St A6
Egerton St C3
Eldon St B3
Elmore Rd B1
Exchange St B5
Eyre St C4
Fargate B4
Farm Rd C5
Fawcett St A3
Filey St B3
Fir St A1
Fire Station C4
Fitzalan Sq/ Ponds Forge B5
Fitzwater Rd C6
Fitzwilliam Gate C4
Fitzwilliam St B3
Flat St B5
Foley St A6
Foundry Climbing Ctr A4
Fulton Rd A1
Furnace Hill A4
Furnival Rd A5
Furnival Sq C4
Furnival St C4
Garden St B3
Gell St B3
Gibraltar St A4
Glebe Rd B1
Glencoe Rd C6
Glossop Rd B2/B3/C1
Gloucester St C2
Government Offices C4
Granville Rd C6
Granville Rd / The Sheffield College C5
Graves Gallery B5
Greave Rd B3
Green La A4
Hadfield St A1
Hanover St C3
Hanover Way C3
Harcourt Rd B1
Harmer La B5
Havelock St C2
Hawley St B4
Haymarket B5
Headford St C3
Heavygate Rd A1
Henry St A3
High St B4
Hodgson St C3
Holberry Gdns C2
Hollis Croft B4
Holly St B4
Hounsfield Rd B3
Howard Rd A1
Hoyle St A3
Hyde Park A6
Infirmary Rd A3
Infirmary Rd A3
Information Ctr B4
Jericho St A3
Johnson St A5
Kelham Island Industrial Museum A4
Lawson Rd C1
Leadmill Rd C5
Leadmill St C5
Leadmill, The C5
Leamington St A1
Leavy Rd B3
Lee Croft B4
Leopold St B4
Leveson St A6
Library A2/B5/C1
Lyceum Theatre B5
Malinda St A3
Maltravers St A5
Manor Oaks Rd B6
Mappin St B3
Marlborough Rd B1
Mary St C4
Matilda St C4
Matlock Rd A1
Meadow St A3
Melbourn Rd A1
Melbourne Ave C1
Millennium Galleries B5
Milton St C3
Mitchell St B3
Mona Ave A1
Mona Rd A1
Montgomery Terr Rd A3
Montgomery Theatre B4
Monument Grounds C6
Moor Oaks Rd B1
Moor, The C4
Moor, The C4
Moore St C3
Mowbray St A4
Mushroom La B2
National Emergency Service A4
Netherthorpe Rd B3
Netherthorpe Rd B3
Newbould La C1
Nile St C1
Norfolk Park Rd C6
Norfolk Rd C6
Norfolk St B4
North Church St B4
Northfield Rd A1
Northumberland Rd B1
Nursery St A5
O2 Academy B5
Oakholme Rd C1
Octagon B2
Odeon B5
Old St B6
Orchard Square B4
Oxford St A2
Paradise St B4
Park La C2
Park Sq B5
Parker's Rd B1
Pearson Building (Univ) C2
Penistone Rd A3
Pinstone St B4
Pitt St B3
Police Station B5
Pond Hill B5
Pond St B5
Ponds Forge Int Sports Ctr B5
Portobello St B3
Post Office A2/B3/B4/ B5/C1/C3/C4/C6
Powell St A2
Queen St B4
Queen's Rd C5
Ramsey Rd B1
Red Hill B3
Redcar Rd B1
Regent St B3
Rockingham St B4
Roebuck Rd A2
Royal Hallamshire Hospital C2
Russell St A4
Rutland Park C1
St George's Cl B3
St Mary's Gate C3
St Mary's Rd C4/C5
St Peter & St Paul Cathedral B4
St Philip's Rd A3
Savile St A5
School Rd B1
Scotland St A4
Severn Rd B1
Shalesmoor A4
Shalesmoor A3
Sheaf St B5
Sheffield Hallam Univ B5
Sheffield Ice Sports Ctr – Skate Central C5
Sheffield Interchange B5
Sheffield Parkway A6
Sheffield Station C5
Sheffield Sta/ Sheffield Hallam Univ B5
Sheffield University B2
Shepherd St A3
Shipton St A2
Shopmobility B3
Shoreham St C4
Showroom C5
Shrewsbury Rd C5
Sidney St C4
Site Gallery C5
Slinn St A1
Smithfield A4
Snig Hill A5
Snow La A4
Solly St B3
South La C4
South Street Park B5
Southbourne Rd C1
Spital Hill A5
Spital St A5
Spring Hill B1
Spring Hill Rd B1
Springvale Rd A1
Stafford Rd C6
Stafford St B6
Suffolk Rd C5
Summer St B2
Sunny Bank C3
Superstore A3/C3
Surrey St B4
Sussex St A6
Sutton St B3
Sydney Rd A2
Sylvester St C4
Talbot St B5
Tapton Hall Conference & Banqueting Ctr B1
Taptonville Rd B1
Tenter St B4
Town Hall B4
Townend St A1
Townhead St B4
Trafalgar St B4
Tree Root Walk B2
Trinity St A4
Trippet La B4
Turner Mus of Glass B3
Union St B4
Univ Drama Studio B2
Univ of Sheffield B3
Upper Allen St A3
Upper Hanover St B3
Upperthorpe Rd A2/A3
Verdon St A5
Victoria Quays B5
Victoria Rd C2
Victoria St B3
Waingate B5
Watery St A3
Watson Rd C1
Wellesley Rd B2
Wellington St C3
West Bar A4
West Bar Green A4
West One Plaza B3
West St B3
West St B4
Westbourne Rd C1
Western Bank B2
Western Rd A1
Weston Park B2
Weston Park Hospl B2
Weston Park Mus B2
Weston St B2
Wharncliffe Rd C3
Whitham Rd B1
Wicker A5
Wilkinson St B2
William St C3
Winter Garden B4
Winter St B2
York St B4
Yorkshire Artspace C5
Young St C4

Shrewsbury 347

Abbey Church B3
Abbey Foregate B3
Abbey Lawn Bsns Park B3
Abbots House B2
Agricultural Show Gd A1
Albert St A2
Alma St B1
Ashley St A3
Ashton Rd C1
Avondale Dr A3
Bage Way C3
Barker St B1
Beacall's La A2
Beeches La C2
Beehive La C1
Belle Vue Gdns C2
Belle Vue Rd C2
Belmont Bank C1
Berwick Ave A1
Berwick Rd A1
Betton St C2
Bishop St B3
Bradford St B3
Bridge St B1
Burton St A3
Bus Station B2
Butcher Row B2
Butler Rd C1
Bynner St C2
Canon St B3
Canonbury C1
Castle Bsns Park, The A2
Castle Foregate A2
Castle Gates B2
Castle Museum B2
Castle St B2
Cathedral (RC) C1
Chester St A2
Cineworld C3
Claremont Bank B1
Claremont Hill B1
Cleveland St B3
Coleham Head B2
Coleham Pumping Station C2
College Hill B1
Corporation La A1
Coton Cres A1
Coton Hill A2
Coton Mount A1
Crescent La C1
Crewe St A2
Cross Hill B1
Dana, The B2
Darwin Centre B2
Dingle, The B1
Dogpole B2
Draper's Hall B2
English Bridge B2
Fish St B2
Frankwell B1
Gateway Ctr, The A2
Gravel Hill La A1
Greyfriars Rd C2
Guildhall B1
Hampton Rd A3
Haycock Way C3
High St B1
Hills La B1
Holywell St B3
Hunter St A1
Information Ctr B1
Ireland's Mansion & Bear Steps B1
John St A3
Kennedy Rd C1
King St B3
Kingsland Bridge C1
Kingsland Bridge (toll) C1
Kingsland Rd C1
Library B2
Lime St C2
Longden Coleham C2
Longden Rd C1
Longner St B1
Luciefelde Rd C1
Mardol B1
Marine Terr C2
Market B1
Monkmoor Rd B3
Moreton Cr C2
Mount St A1
New Park Cl A3
New Park Rd A2
New Park St A3
North St A2
Oakley St C1
Old Coleham C2
Old Market Hall B1
Old Potts Way C3
Parade Centre B2
Police Station B1
Post Office A2/B1/B2/B3
Pride Hill B1
Pride Hill Centre B1
Priory Rd B1
Pritchard Way C3
Quarry, The B1
Queen St A3
Raby Cr C2
Rad Brook C1
Rea Brook C3
Riverside B1
Roundhill La A1
St Alkmund's B2
St Chad's B1
St Chad's Terr B1
St John's Hill B1
St Julians Friars C2
St Mary's B2
St Mary's St B2
Salters La C2
Scott St C3
Severn Bank A3
Severn St A2
Shrewsbury B2
Shrewsbury High School for Girls C1
Shrewsbury Mus & Art Gall B1
Shrewsbury School C1
Shropshire Wildlife Trust B3
Smithfield Rd B1
South Hermitage C1
Square, The B1
Swan Hill B1
Sydney Ave A3
Tankerville St B3
Tilbrook Dr A3
Town Walls C1
Trinity St C2
Underdale Rd B3
Victoria Ave B1
Victoria Quay B1
Victoria St B2
Welsh Bridge B1
Whitehall St B3
Wood St A2
Wyle Cop B2

Southampton 347

Above Bar St A2
Albert Rd North B3
Albert Rd South C3
Anderson's Rd B3
Archaeology Mus (God's Ho Tower) C2
Argyle Rd A2
Arundel Tower B1
Bargate, The B2
BBC Regional Centre A1
Bedford Pl A1
Belvidere Rd A3
Bernard St C2
Blechynden Terr A1
Brinton's Rd A2
bristol A3
Britannia Rd A3
Briton St C2
Brunswick Pl A2
Bugle St C1
Canute Rd C3
Castle Way C2
Catchcold Tower B1
Central Bridge C3
Central Rd C2
Channel Way C3
Chapel Rd B3
Cineworld C3
City Art Gallery A1
City College B3
City Cruise Terminal C1
Civic Centre A1
Civic Centre Rd A1
Coach Station B1
Commercial Rd A1
Cumberland Pl A1
Cunard Rd C2
Derby Rd A3
Devonshire Rd A1
Dock Gate 4 C2
Dock Gate 8 B1
East Andrews Park A2
East Park Terr A2
East St B2
Endle St B3
European Way C2
Fire Station A2
Floating Bridge Rd C3
Golden Gr A3
Graham Rd A2
Guildhall A1
Hanover Bldgs B2
Harbour Lights C3
Harbour Pde B1
Hartington Rd A3
Havelock Rd A1
Henstead Rd A1
Herbert Walker Ave B1
High St B2
Hoglands Park B2
Holy Rood (Rems), Merchant Navy Memorial B2
Houndwell Park B2
Houndwell Pl B2
Hythe Ferry C2
Information Ctr A1
Isle of Wight Ferry Terminal C1
James St B3
Java Rd C2
Kingsway A2
Leisure World B1
Library A1
Lime St B2
London Rd A2
Marine Pde B3
Marlands Shop Ctr, The A1
Marsh La B2
Mayflower Meml C1
Mayflower Park C1
Mayflower Theatre, The A1
Medieval Merchant's House C1
Melbourne St B3
Millais A2
Morris Rd A1
National Oceanography Centre C3
Neptune Way C3
New Rd A2
Nichols Rd A3
North Front A2
Northam Rd A3
Ocean Dock C2
Ocean Village Marina C3
Ocean Way C3
Odeon B1
Ogle Rd B1
Old Northam Rd A2
Orchard La B2
Oxford Ave A2
Oxford St C2
Palmerston Park A2
Palmerston Rd A2
Parsonage Rd A3
Peel St A3
Platform Rd C2
Polygon, The A1
Portland Terr B1
Post Office A2/A3/B2
Pound Tree Rd B2
Quays Swimming & Diving Complex, The B1
Queen's Park C2
Queen's Peace Fountain A2
Queen's Terr C2
Queensway B2
Radcliffe Rd A3
Rochester St A3
Royal Pier C1
Royal South Hants Hospital A2
St Andrew's Rd A2
St Mary St A2
St Mary's Leisure Ctr A2
St Mary's Pl B2
St Mary's Rd A2
St Mary's Stadium (Southampton FC) A3
St Michael's C1
Sea City Mus A1
Solent Sky C3
South Front B2
Southampton Central Station A1
Southampton Solent University A2
SS Shieldhall C2
Terminus Terr C2
Threefield La B2
Titanic Engineers' Memorial A2
Town Quay C1
Town Walls B2
Tudor House C1
Vincent's Walk B2
West Gate Hall C1
West Marlands Rd A1
West Park A1
West Park Rd A1
West Quay Rd B1
West Quay Retail Park B1
Western Esplanade B1
Westquay Shop Ctr B1
White Star Way C2
Winton St A2

Southend-on-Sea 348

Adventure Island C3
Albany Ave A1
Albert Rd C3
Alexandra Rd C2
Alexandra St C2
Alexandra Yacht Club C2
Ashburnham Rd B2
Ave Rd B1
Avenue Terr B1
Balmoral Rd B1
Baltic Ave B3
Baxter Ave A2/B2
Beecroft Art Gallery B2
Bircham Rd A2
Boscombe Rd B3
Boston Ave A1/B2
Bournemouth Park Rd A3
Browning Ave A3
Bus Station C3
Byron Ave A3
Cambridge Rd C1/C2
Canewdon Rd B1
Carnarvon Rd A2
Central Ave A3
Chelmsford Ave A1
Chichester Rd B2
Church Rd C3
Civic Centre A2
Clarence Rd C2
Clarence St C2
Cliff Ave B1
Cliffs Pavilion C1
Clifftown Parade C2
Clifftown Rd C2
Colchester Rd A1
Coleman St B3
College Way B2
County Court B3
Cromer Rd B3
Crowborough Rd A2
Dryden Ave A3
East St A2
Elmer App B2
Elmer Ave B2
Forum, The B2
Gainsborough Dr A1
Gayton Rd A2
Glenhurst Rd A2
Gordon Pl B2
Gordon Rd B2
Grainger Rd A2
Greyhound Way A3
Grove, The A3
Guildford Rd B3
Hamlet Ct Rd B1
Hamlet Rd C1
Harcourt Ave A1
Hartington Rd C3
Hastings Rd B3
Herbert Gr C3
Heygate Ave C3
High St B2/C2
Information Ctr C3
Kenway A2
Kilworth Ave B3
Lancaster Gdns B3
London Rd B1
Lucy Rd C3
MacDonald Ave A1
Magistrates' Court A2
Maine Ave C1
Maldon Rd A2
Marine Parade C3
Milton Rd B1
Milton St B2
Napier Ave B2
North Ave A3
North Rd A1/B1
Odeon B2
Osborne Rd B1
Park Cres B1
Park Rd B1
Park St B1
Park Terr B1
Pier Hill C3
Pleasant Rd C3
Police Station A2
Post Office B2/B3
Princes St B2
Queens Rd B2
Queensway B2/B3/C3
Radio Essex C2
Rayleigh Ave A1
Redstock Rd A2
Rochford Ave A1
Royal Mews C2
Royal Terr C2
Royals Shopping Centre, The C3
Ruskin Ave A3
St Ann's Rd B3
St Helen's Rd B1
St John's Rd B1
St Leonard's Rd C3
St Lukes Rd A3
St Vincent's Rd C1
Salisbury Ave A1/B1
Scratton Rd C2
Shakespeare Dr A1
Shopmobility B2
Short St A2
South Ave A3
South Essex College B2
Southchurch Rd B3
Southend Central B2
Southend Pier Railway C3
Southend United FC A1
Southend Victoria B2
Stadium Rd A2
Stanfield Rd A2
Stanley Rd C3
Sutton Rd A3/B3
Swanage Rd B3
Sweyne Ave A1
Sycamore Gr A3
Tennyson Ave A3
Tickfield Ave A2
Tudor Rd A1
Tunbridge Rd A2
Tylers Ave B3
Tyrrel Dr B3
Univ of Essex B2/C2
Vale Ave A2
Victoria Ave A2
Victoria Sh Ctr, The B2
Warrior Sq B3
Wesley Rd C3
West Rd A1
West St A1
Westcliff Ave C1
Westcliff Parade C1
Western Esplanade C1
Weston Rd C2
Whitegate Rd B3
Wilson Rd C1
Wimborne Rd B3
York Rd C3

Stirling 348

Abbey Rd A3
Abbotsford Pl A3
Abercromby Pl C1
Albert Halls B1
Albert Pl B1
Alexandra Pl A3
Allan Park C2
Ambulance Station A2
AMF Ten Pin Bowling B2
Argyll Ave A3
Argyll's Lodging B1
Back O' Hill Ind Est A1
Back O' Hill Rd A1
Baker St B2
Ballengeich Pass A1
Balmoral Pl B1
Barn Rd B1
Barnton St B2
Bastion, The C2
Bow St B1
Bruce St A2
Burghmuir Retail Pk C2
Burghmuir Rd A2/B2/C2
Bus Station B2
Cambuskenneth Bridge A3
Castle Ct B1
Causewayhead Rd A2
Cemetery A1
Changing Room, The B1
Church of the Holy Rude B1
Clarendon Pl C1
Club House B1
Colquhoun St C3
Corn Exchange B2
Council Offices C2
Court B2
Cowane Ctr A2
Cowane St A2
Cowane's Hospital B1
Crawford Sh Arc B2
Crofthead Rd A1
Dean Cres A3
Douglas St A2
Drip Rd A1
Drummond La C1
Drummond Pl C1
Drummond Pl La C1
Dumbarton Rd C2
Eastern Access Rd B2
Edward Ave A3
Edward Rd A2
Forrest Rd A2
Fort A1
Forth Cres B2
Forth St A2
Gladstone Pl C1
Glebe Ave C1
Glebe Cres C1
Golf Course C1
Goosecroft Rd B2
Gowanhill A1
Greenwood Ave B1
Harvey Wynd A1
Information Ctr B1
Irvine Pl B2
James St A2
John St B1
Kerse Rd C3
King's Knot B1
King's Park C1
King's Park Rd C1
Laurencecroft Rd A2
Leisure Pool B2
Library B2
Linden Ave C2
Lovers Wk A2
Lower Back Walk B1
Lower Bridge St A2
Lower Castlehill A1
Mar Pl B1
Meadow Pl A3
Meadowforth Rd C3
Middlemuir Rd C3
Millar Pl A3
Morris Terr B2
Mote Hill A1
Murray Pl B2
Nelson Pl C2
Old Town Cemetery B1
Old Town Jail B1
Park Terr C1
Phoenix Industrial Est C3
Players Rd C3
Port St C2
Post Office B2
Princes St B2
Queen St B2
Queen's Rd B1
Queenshaugh Dr A3
Ramsay Pl A2
Riverside Dr A3
Ronald Pl A1
Rosebery Pl A2
Royal Gardens B1
Royal Gdns B1
St Mary's Wynd B1
St Ninian's Rd C2
Scott St A2
Seaforth Pl B2
Shore Rd B2
Smith Art Gallery & Museum B1
Snowdon Pl C1
Snowdon Pl La C1
Spittal St B2
Springkerse Ind Est C3
Springkerse Rd C3
Stirling Bsns Centre C2
Stirling Castle A1
Stirling County Rugby Football Club A3
Stirling Enterprise Pk B3
Stirling Old Bridge A2
Stirling Station B2
Superstore A1/A2
Sutherland Ave A3
TA Centre C3
Tannery La A2
Thistle Industrial Est C3
Thistles Sh Ctr, The B2
Tolbooth B1
Town Wall B1
Union St A2
Upper Back Walk B1
Upper Bridge St A1
Upper Castlehill B1
Upper Craigs C2
Victoria Pl C1
Victoria Rd B1
Victoria Sq B1/C1
Vue B2
Wallace St A2
Waverley Cres A3
Wellgreen Rd C2
Windsor Pl C1
YHA B1

Stoke 348

Ashford St A3
Avenue Rd A3
Aynsley Rd A2
Barnfield C1
Bath St C2
Beresford St A3
Bilton St C2
Boon Ave C2
Booth St C2
Boothen Rd C2/C3
Boughey St C2
Boughley Rd B3
Brighton St B1
Campbell Rd C2
Carlton Rd B3
Cauldon Rd A3
Cemetery A2
Cemetery Rd A2
Chamberlain Ave C1
Church (RC) B2
Church St C2
City Rd C3
Civic Centre & King's Hall B3
Cliff Vale Pk A1
College Rd A3
Convent Cl B2
Copeland St B2
Cornwallis St C3
Corporation St C2
Crowther St A3
Dominic St B1
Elenora St B2
Elgin St B2
Epworth St A3
Etruscan St A1
Film Theatre B3
Fleming Rd C2
Fletcher Rd C2
Floyd St B2
Foden St C2
Frank St C2
Franklin Rd C1
Frederick Ave B1
Garden St C1
Garner St A1
Gerrard St B2
Glebe St B3
Greatbach Ave B1
Hanley Park A3
Harris St B1
Hartshill Rd B1
Hayward St A2
Hide St B2
Higson Ave B2
Hill St B2
Honeywall B2
Hunters Dr C1
Hunters Way C1
Keary St C2
Kingsway B2
Leek Rd B3
Library C2
Lime St C2
Liverpool Rd B2
London Rd C2
Lonsdale St C2
Lovatt St B2
Lytton St B3
Market C2
Newcastle La C1
Newlands St A2
Norfolk St A2
North St A1/B2
Northcote Ave B2
Oldmill St C3
Oriel St B1
Oxford St B1
Penkhull New Rd C1
Penkhull St C1
Police Station C2
Portmeirion Pottery C2
Post Office A3
Prince's Rd B1
Pump St B2
Quarry Ave B1
Quarry Rd B1
Queen Anne St A3
Queen's Rd C1
Queensway A1/B2/C3
Richmond St B1
Rothwell St C1
St Peter's B3
St Thomas Pl C1
Scrivenor Rd A1
Seaford St A3
Selwyn St C3
Shelton New Rd A1
Shelton Old Rd B2
Sheppard St C2
Sixth Form College B3
Spark St C2
Spencer Rd B3
Spode St C2
Squires View B3
Staffordshire Univ B3
Stanley Matthews Sports Centre B3
Station Rd B3
Stoke Business Park C3
Stoke Rd A2
Stoke-on-Trent College A3
Stoke-on-Trent Station B3
Sturgess St C2
Thistley Hough C1
Thornton Rd B3
Tolkien Way B1
Trent Valley Rd C1
Vale St B2
Villas, The C1
Watford St A3
Wellesley St A3
West Ave B1
Westland St B1
Yeaman St C2
Yoxall Ave B1

Stratford-upon-Avon 348

Albany Rd B1
Alcester Rd B1
Ambulance Station B1
Arden St B2
Avenue Farm A1
Ave Farm Ind Est A1
Avenue Rd A3
Avon Industrial Est A2
Baker Ave A1
Bandstand C3
Benson Rd A3
Birmingham Rd A2
Boat Club B3
Borden Pl C1
Brass Rubbing Ctr C2
Bridge St B2
Bridgetown Rd C3
Bridgeway B3
Broad St C2
Broad Walk C2
Brookvale Rd C1
Bull St C2
Butterfly Farm C3
Cemetery C1
Chapel La B2
Cherry Orchard C1
Chestnut Walk B2
Children's Playground C3
Church St C2
Civic Hall B2

Clarence Rd B1
Clopton Bridge ✦ B3
Clopton Rd A2
College B1
College La C2
College St C2
Com Sports Centre B1
Council Offices (District) B2
Courtyard, The C2
Cox's Yard ✦ B3
Cricket Ground C3
Ely Gdns B2
Ely St B2
Evesham Rd C1
Fire Station B1
Foot Ferry C3
Fordham Ave A2
Gallery, The B3
Garrick Way C1
Gower Memorial ✦ B3
Great William St B2
Greenhill St B2
Greenway, The C2
Grove Rd B2
Guild St B2
Guildhall & School B2
Hall's Croft C2
Hartford Rd C1
Harvard House B2
Henley St B2
High St B2
Holton St C2
Holy Trinity C2
Information Ctr B3
Jolyffe Park Rd A2
Kipling Rd C3
Library B2
Lodge Rd B1
Maidenhead Rd A3
Mansell St B2
Masons Court B2
Masons Rd A1
Maybird Shopping Pk A2
Maybrook Rd A1
Mayfield Ave A2
Meer St B2
Mill La C2
Moat House Hotel B3
Narrow La C2
Nash's House and New Place B2
New St C2
Old Town C2
Orchard Way C1
Paddock La C1
Park Rd A1
Payton St B2
Percy St A2
Police Station B2
Post Office B2
Recreation Ground C2
Regal Road A2
Rother St B2
Rowley Cr A3
Royal Shakespeare Theatre B3
Ryland St C2
Saffron Meadow C2
St Andrew's Cr B1
St Gregory's A3
St Gregory's Rd A3
St Mary's Rd A2
Sanctus Dr C2
Sanctus St C1
Sandfield Rd C2
Scholars La B2
Seven Meadows Rd C2
Shakespeare Ctr ✦ B2
Shakespeare Institute C2
Shakespeare St B2
Shakespeare's Birthplace ✦ B2
Sheep St B2
Shelley Rd C3
Shipston Rd C3
Shottery Rd C1
Slingates Rd A2
Southern La C2
Station Rd B1
Stratford Healthcare B2
Stratford Hospital B2
Stratford Leisure & Visitor Centre B3
Stratford Sports Club B1
Stratford-upon-Avon Station B1
Swan Theatre B3
Swan's Nest La B3
Talbot Rd A2
Tiddington Rd B3
Timothy's Bridge Industrial Estate A1
Timothy's Bridge Rd A1
Town Hall & Council Offices B2
Town Sq B2
Trinity St C2
Tyler St B2
War Memorial Gdns B3
Warwick Rd B3
Waterside B3
Welcombe Rd A3
West St C2
Western Rd A2
Wharf Rd A2
Willows North, The B1
Willows, The B1
Wood St B2

Sunderland 348

Albion Pl C2
Alliance Pl B1
Argyle St C2
Ashwood St C1
Athenaeum St B2
Azalea Terr C2
Beach St A1
Bedford St B2
Beechwood Terr C1
Belvedere Rd C2
Blandford St B2
Borough Rd B3
Bridge Cr B2
Bridge St B2
Bridges, The B2
Brooke St A2
Brougham St B2
Burdon Rd C2
Burn Park C1
Burn Park Rd C1
Burn Park Tech Park C1
Carol St B1
Charles St A3
Chester Rd C1
Chester Terr B1
Church St A3
Civic Centre C2
Cork St B3
Coronation St B3
Cowan Terr C2
Dame Dorothy St A2
Deptford Rd B1
Deptford Terr A1
Derby St C2
Derwent St C2
Dock St A3
Dundas St A2
Durham Rd C1
Easington St A2
Egerton St C3
Empire B3
Empire Theatre B2
Farringdon Row B1
Fawcett St B2
Fire Station B1
Fox St C1
Foyle St B3
Frederick St B3
Hanover Pl A1
Havelock Terr C1
Hay St A2
Headworth Sq B3
Hendon Rd B3
High St East B3
High St West B2/B3
Holmeside B2
Hylton Rd B1
Information Ctr B2
John St B3
Kier Hardie Way A2
Lambton St B3
Laura St C3
Lawrence St B3
Library & Arts Centre B3
Lily St B1
Lime St B1
Livingstone Rd B2
Low Row B2
Matamba Terr B1
Millburn St B1
Millennium Way A2
Minster B2
Monkwearmouth Station Museum A2
Mowbray Park C3
Mowbray Rd C3
Murton St C3
National Glass Ctr ✦ A3
New Durham Rd C1
Newcastle Rd A2
Nile St B3
Norfolk St B3
North Bridge St A2
Northern Gallery for Contemporary Art B3
Otto Terr C1
Park La C2
Park Lane C2
Park Rd C2
Paul's Rd B3
Peel St C3
Police Station B2
Priestly Cr A1
Queen St B2
Railway Row B1
Retail Park B1
Richmond St A2
Roker Ave A2
Royalty Theatre C1
Royalty, The C1
Ryhope Rd C2
St Mary's Way B2
St Michael's Way B2
St Peter's A3
St Peter's A2
St Peter's Way A3
St Vincent St C3
Salem Rd C3
Salem St C3
Salisbury St C3
Sans St B3
Shopmobility B2
Silkworth Row B1
Southwick Rd A2
Stadium of Light (Sunderland AFC) A2
Stadium Way A2
Stobart St A2
Stockton Rd C2
Suffolk St C3
Sunderland B2
Sunderland Aquatic Centre A2
Sunderland Mus B3
Sunderland St B3
Sunderland Station B2
Tatham St C3
Tavistock Pl B3
Thelma St C1
Thomas St North A2
Thornholme Rd C1
Toward Rd C3
Transport Interchange C2
Trimdon St Way B1
Tunstall Rd C2
University C1
University Library C1
University of Sunderland (City Campus) B1
University of Sunderland (Sir Tom Cowle at St Peter's Campus) A3
Vaux Brewery Way A2
Villiers St B3
Villiers St South B3
Vine Pl C2
Violet St B1
Walton La B3
Waterworks Rd B1
Wearmouth Bridge B2
West Sunniside B3
West Wear St B3
Westbourne Rd B1
Western Hill C1
Wharncliffe B1
Whickham St A3
White House Rd C3
Wilson St North A2
Winter Gdns C3
Wreath Quay A1

Swansea Abertawe 348

Adelaide St C3
Albert Row C3
Alexandra Rd B3
Argyle St C1
Baptist Well Pl A2
Beach St C1
Belle Vue Way B3
Berw Rd A1
Berwick Terr A2
Bond St C1
Brangwyn Concert Hall C1
Bridge St A3
Brooklands Terr B1
Brunswick St C1
Bryn-Syfi Terr A2
Bryn-y-Mor Rd C1
Bullins La B1
Burrows Rd C1
Bus Station C2
Bus/Rail link A3
Cadfan Rd A1
Cadrawd Rd A1
Caer St B3
Carig Cr A1
Carlton Terr B2
Carmarthen Rd A3
Castle Square B3
Castle St B3
Catherine St C1
Cinema C3
Civic Centre & Library C2
Clarence St C2
Colbourne Terr A2
Constitution Hill B1
Court B3
Creidiol Rd A2
Cromwell St B2
Crown Courts C1
Duke St B1
Dunvant Pl C2
Dyfatty Park A3
Dyfatty St A3
Dyfed Ave A1
Dylan Thomas Ctr ✦ B3
Dylan Thomas Theatre C3
Eaton Cr C1
Eigen Cr A1
Elfed Rd A1
Emlyn Rd A1
Evans Terr A3
Fairfield Terr B1
Ffynone Dr B1
Ffynone Rd B1
Fire Station B3
Firm St A2
Fleet St C1
Francis St C1
Fullers Row B2
George St B2
Glamorgan St C2
Glynn Vivian Art Gall B3
Gower Coll Swansea C1
Graig Terr A3
Grand Theatre C3
Granogwen Rd A2
Guildhall C1
Guildhall Rd South C1
Gwent Rd A1
Gwynedd Ave A1
Hafod St A3
Hanover St B1
Harcourt St B2
Harries St A2
Heathfield B2
Henrietta St B2
Hewson St B2
High St A3/B3
High View A2
Hill St A2
Historic Ships Berth C3
HM Prison C2
Information Ctr C2
Islwyn Rd A1
King Edward's Rd C1
Kingsway, The B2
LC, The C3
Long Ridge A2
Madoc St C2
Mansel St B2
Maritime Quarter C3
Market B3
Mayhill Gdns B1
Mayhill Rd A1
Milton Terr A2
Mission Gallery C3
Montpellier Terr B1
Morfa Rd A3
Mount Pleasant B2
National Waterfront Museum C3
Nelson St C2
New Cut Rd A3
New St A3
Nicander Pde A2
Nicander Pl A2
Nicholl St B2
Norfolk St B2
North Hill Rd A2
Northampton La B2
Orchard St B3
Oxford St B2
Oystermouth Rd C1
Page St B2
Pant-y-Celyn Rd B1
Parc Tawe Link B3
Parc Tawe North B3
Parc Tawe Sh & Leisure Centre B3
Patti Pavilion C1
Paxton St C2
Pen-y-Graig Rd A1
Penmaen Terr B1
Phillips Pde C1
Picton Terr B2
Plantasia B3
Police Station B2
Post Office A1/A2/C1/C2
Powys Ave A1
Primrose St B2
Princess Way B3
Promenade B2
Pryder Gdns A1
Quadrant Shop Ctr C2
Quay Park B3
Rhianfa La B1
Rhondda St B2
Richardson St C2
Rodney St C1
Rose Hill B1
Rosehill Terr B1
Russell St B1
St David's Shop Ctr C3
St Helen's Ave C1
St Helen's Cr C1
St Helen's Rd C1
St James Gdns B1
St James's Cr B1
St Mary's B3
Sea View Terr A3
Singleton St C2
South Dock C3
Stanley Pl B2
Strand B3
Swansea Castle B3
Swansea Metropolitan University B2
Swansea Museum C3
Swansea Station A3
Taliesyn Rd B1
Tan y Marian Rd A1
Tegid Rd A2
Teilo Cr A1
Tenpin Bowling ✦ B3
Terrace Rd B1/B2
Tontine St A3
Tower of Ecliptic Observatory ✦ C3
Townhill Rd A1
Tramshed, The C3
Trawler Rd C3
Union St B2
Upper Strand A3
Vernon St A3
Victoria Quay C3
Victoria Rd B3
Vincent St C1
Walter Rd B1
Watkin St A2
Waun-Wen Rd A2
Wellington St C2
Westbury St C1
Western St C1
Westway C2
William St C2
Wind St B3
Woodlands Terr B1
YMCA B2
York St C3

Swindon 349

Albert St C3
Albion St C1
Alfred St A2
Alvescot Rd C3
Art Gallery & Mus C3
Ashford Rd C1
Aylesbury St A2
Bath Rd C2
Bathampton St B1
Bathurst Rd B3
Beatrice St A2
Beckhampton St B3
Bowood Rd C1
Bristol St B1
Broad St A3
Brunel Arcade B2
Brunel Plaza B2
Brunswick St C2
Bus Station B2
Cambria Bridge Rd B1
Cambria Place B1
Canal Walk B2
Carfax St B2
Carr St B1
Cemetery C1/C3
Chandler Cl C3
Chapel C1
Chester St B1
Christ Church C3
Church Place B1
Cirencester Way A3
Clarence St B2
Clifton St C1
Cockleberry A2
Colbourne A3
Colbourne St A3
College St B2
Commercial Rd B2
Corporation St A2
Council Offices B3
County Rd A3
Courts B2
Cricket Ground A3
Cricklade Street C3
Crombey St B1/C2
Cross St C2
Curtis St B1
Deacon St C1
Designer Outlet (Great Western) B1
Dixon St C2
Dover St C2
Dowling St C2
Drove Rd C3
Dryden St C1
Durham St C3
East St B1
Eastcott Hill C2
Eastcott Rd C2
Edgeware Rd B2
Edmund St C2
Elmina Rd A3
Emlyn Square B1
Euclid St B3
Exeter St B1
Fairview C1
Faringdon Rd B1
Farnsby St B1
Fire Station B3
Fleet St B2
Fleming Way B2/B3
Florence St A2
Gladstone St A3
Gooch St A2
Graham St A3
Great Western Way A1/A2
Groundwell Rd B3
Hawksworth Way A1
Haydon St A2
Henry St B2
Hillside Ave C1
Holbrook Way B2
Hunt St C3
Hydro B1
Hythe Rd C2
Information Ctr B2
Joseph St C1
Kent Rd C2
King William St C2
Kingshill Rd C1
Lansdown Rd C2
Lawn, The C3
Leicester St B3
Library B2
Lincoln St B3
Little London C3
London St B1
Magic B3
Maidstone Rd C2
Manchester Rd A3
Maxwell St B1
Milford St B2
Milton Rd B1
Morse St C2
National Monuments Record Centre B1
Newcastle St B3
Newcombe Drive A1
Newcombe Trading Estate A1
Newhall St C2
North St C2
North Star A1
North Star Ave A1
Northampton St B3
Nurseries, The C1
Oasis Leisure Centre A1
Ocotal Way A3
Okus Rd C1
Old Town C3
Oxford St B1
Parade, The B2
Park Lane B1
Park Lane B1
Park, The B1
Pembroke St C2
Plymouth St B3
Polaris House A2
Polaris Way A2
Police Station B2
Ponting St A2
Post Office B1/B2/C1/C3
Poulton St A3
Princes St B2
Prospect Hill C2
Prospect Place C2
Queen St B2
Queen's Park C3
Radnor St C1
Read St C1
Reading St B1
Regent St B2
Retail Park A2/A3/B3
Rosebery St A3
St Mark's B1
Salisbury St A3
Savernake St C2
Shelley St C1
Sheppard St B1
South St C2
Southampton St B3
Spring Gardens B3
Stafford Street C2
Stanier St C2
Station Road A2
STEAM B1
Swindon College A2
Swindon Rd C2
Swindon Station A2
Swindon Town Football Club A3
T A Centre B1
Tennyson St B1
Theobald St B1
Town Hall B2
Transfer Bridges A3
Union St C2
Upham Rd C3
Victoria Rd C3
Walcot Rd B3
War Memorial ✦ B2
Wells St B3
Western St C2
Westmorland Rd B3
Whalebridge B2
Whitehead St C1
Whitehouse Rd A2
William St C1
Wood St C3
Wyvern Theatre & Arts Centre B2
York Rd B3

Taunton 349

Addison Gr A1
Albemarle Rd A1
Alfred St B3
Alma St C2
Avenue, The A1
Bath Pl C1
Belvedere Rd A1
Billet St B2
Billetfield C2
Birch Gr A1
Brewhouse Theatre B2
Bridge St B1
Bridgwater & Taunton Canal A2
Broadlands Rd C1
Burton Pl C1
Bus Station B1
Canal Rd A2
Cann St C1
Canon St B2
Castle B1
Castle St B1
Cheddon Rd A2
Chip Lane A1
Clarence St B1
Cleveland St B1
Clifton Terr A2
Coleridge Cres C3
Compass Hill C1
Compton Cl A2
Corporation St B1
Council Offices A1
County Walk Sh Ctr C2
Courtyard B2
Cranmer Rd B2
Crescent, The C1
Critchard Way B3
Cyril St A1
Deller's Wharf B1
Duke St B2
East Reach B3
East St B3
Eastbourne Rd B2
Eastleigh Rd C3
Eaton Cres A2
Elm Gr A1
Elms Cl A1
Fons George C1
Fore St B2
Fowler St A1
French Weir Rec Grd B1
Geoffrey Farrant Wk A2
Gray's Almshouses B2
Grays Rd B3
Greenway Ave A1
Guildford Pl C1
Hammet St B2
Haydon Rd B3
Heavitree Way A2
Herbert St A1
High St C2
Holway Ave C3
Hugo St B3
Huish's Almshouses B2
Hurdle Way C2
Information Ctr C2
Jubilee St A1
King's College C3
Kings Cl C3
Laburnum St B2
Lambrook Rd B3
Lansdowne Rd A3
Leslie Ave A1
Leycroft Rd B3
Library C2
Linden Gr A1
Magdalene St B2
Magistrates Court B1
Malvern Terr A2
Market House B2
Mary St C2
Middle St B2
Midford Rd B3
Mitre Court B3
Mount Nebo C1
Mount St C2
Mount, The C2
Mountway C2
Mus of Somerset B1
North St B2
Northern Inner Distributor Rd A1
Northfield Ave B1
Northfield Rd B1
Northleigh Rd C3
Obridge Allotments A3
Obridge Lane A3
Obridge Rd A3
Obridge Viaduct A3
Old Mkt Shopping Ctr C2
Osborne Way C1
Park St C1
Paul St C2
Plais St A2
Playing Field C3
Police Station C1
Portland St B1
Post Office B1/B2/C1
Priorswood Ind Est A3
Priorswood Rd A2
Priory Ave B2
Priory Bridge Rd B2
Priory Fields Retail Pk A3
Priory Park A2
Priory Way A3
Queen St B3
Railway St A1
Records Office A2
Recreation Grd A1
Riverside Place B2
St Augustine St B2
St George's C2
St Georges Sq C2
St James B2
St James St B2
St John's C1
St John's Rd B1
St Josephs Field C2
St Mary Magdalene's B2
Samuels Ct A1
Shire Hall & Law Courts C1
Somerset County Cricket Ground B2
Somerset County Hall C1
Somerset Cricket B2
South Rd C3
South St C3
Staplegrove Rd B1
Station Rd A1
Stephen St B2
Swimming Pool A1
Tancred St B2
Tauntfield Cl C3
Taunton Dean Cricket Club C2
Taunton Station A2
Thomas St A1
Toneway A3
Tower St B1
Trevor Smith Pl C3
Trinity Bsns Centre C3
Trinity Rd C3
Trinity St B3
Trull Rd C1
Tudor House B2
Upper High St C1
Venture Way A3
Victoria Gate B3
Victoria Park B3
Victoria St B3
Viney St B3
Vivary Park C2
Vivary Rd C1
War Memorial ✦ C1
Wellesley St A2
Wheatley Cres A3
Whitehall A1
Wilfred Rd B3
William St A1
Wilton Church C1
Wilton Cl C1
Wilton Gr C1
Wilton St C1
Winchester St B2
Winters Field B2
Wood St B1
Yarde Pl B1

Telford 349

Alma Ave C1
Amphitheatre C2
Bowling Alley B2
Brandsfarm Way C3
Brunel Rd B1
Bus Station B2
Buxton Rd C1
Central Park A2
Civic Offices B2
Coach Central B2
Coachwell Cl B1
Colliers Way A1
Courts B2
Dale Acre Way B3
Darliston C3
Deepdale B3
Deercote B2
Dinthill C3
Doddington C3
Dodmoor Grange C3
Downemead B3
Duffryn B3
Dunsheath B3
Euston Way A3
Eyton Mound C1
Eyton Rd C1
Forgegate A2
Grange Central B2
Hall Park Way B1
Hinkshay Rd C2
Hollinsworth Rd A2
Holyhead Rd A3
Housing Trust A1
Ice Rink B2
Information Ctr B2
Ironmasters Way A2
Job Centre B1
Land Registry B1
Lawn Central B2
Lawnswood C1
Library B2
Malinsgate B1
Matlock Ave C1
Moor Rd C1
Mount Rd C1
NFU Offices B1
Odeon B2
Park Lane A1
Police Station B2
Priorslee Ave A3
Queen Elizabeth Ave C3
Queen Elizabeth Way B1
Queensway A2/B3
Rampart Way A2
Randlay Ave C3
Randlay Wood C3
Rhodes Ave C1
Royal Way B1
St Leonards Rd B1
St Quentin Gate B2
Shifnal Rd A3
Sixth Ave A1
Southwater One (SW1) B2
Southwater Way B1
Spout Lane C1
Spout Mound B1
Spout Way C1
Stafford Court B3
Stafford Park B3
Stirchley Ave C3
Stone Row C1
Telford Bridge Ret Pk A1
Telford Central Sta A3
Telford Centre, The B2
Telford Forge Sh Pk A1
Telford Hornets RFC C2
Telford Int Ctr C2
Telford Way A2
Third Ave A2
Town Park C2
Town Park Visitor Ctr B2
Walker House B2
Wellswood Ave A2
West Centre Way B1
Withywood Drive C1
Woodhouse Central B2
Yates Way A1

Torquay 349

Abbey Rd B2
Alexandra Rd A2
Alpine Rd B3
Ash Hill Rd A2
Babbacombe Rd B3
Bampfylde Rd B1
Barton Rd A1
Beacon Quay C2
Belgrave Rd A1/B1
Belmont Rd A3
Berea Rd A3
Braddons Hill Rd East B3
Brewery Park A3
Bronshill Rd A2
Castle Circus A2
Castle Rd A2
Cavern Rd A3
Central B2
Chatsworth Rd A2
Chestnut Ave B1
Church St A1
Civic Offices A2
Coach Station A1
Corbyn Head C1
Croft Hill B1
Croft Rd B1
Daddyhole Plain C3
East St A1
Egerton Rd A3
Ellacombe Church Rd A3
Ellacombe Rd A2
Falkland Rd B1
Fleet St B2
Fleet Walk Sh Ctr B2
Grafton Rd B3
Haldon Pier C2
Hatfield Rd A2
Highbury Rd A2
Higher Warberry Rd A3
Hillesdon Rd B3
Hollywood Bowl C3
Hoxton Rd A3
Hunsdon Rd B3
Information Ctr B2
Inner Harbour C3
Kenwyn Rd A3
King's Drive, The B1
Laburnum St A1
Law Courts A2
Library A2
Lime Ave B1
Living Coasts C3
Lower Warberry Rd B3
Lucius St B1
Lymington Rd A1
Magdalene Rd A1
Marina C2
Market Forum, The B2
Market St B2
Meadfoot Lane C3
Meadfoot Rd C3
Melville St B2
Middle Warberry Rd B3
Mill Lane A1
Montpellier Rd B3
Morgan Ave A1
Museum Rd B3
Newton Rd A1
Oakhill Rd A1
Outer Harbour C2
Parkhill Rd C3
Pavilion Shopping Ctr C2
Pimlico B2
Police Station A1
Post Office A1/B2
Princes Rd A3
Princes Rd East A3
Princes Rd West A3
Princess Gdns C2
Princess Pier C2
Princess Theatre C2
Rathmore Rd B1
Recreation Grd B1
Riviera Int Ctr B1
Rock End Ave C3
Rock Rd B2
Rock Walk B2
Rosehill Rd A3
St Efride's Rd A1
St John's B3
St Luke's Rd B2
St Luke's Rd North B2
St Luke's Rd South B2
St Marychurch Rd A2
Scarborough Rd B1
Shedden Hill B2
South Pier C2
South St A1
Spanish Barn B1
Stitchill Rd B3
Strand B3
Sutherland Rd B3
Teignmouth Rd A1
Temperance St B2
Terrace, The B3
Thurlow Rd A1
Tor Bay B1
Tor Church Rd A1
Tor Hill Rd A1
Torbay Rd B2
Torquay Museum B3
Torquay Station C1
Torre Abbey Mansion B1
Torre Abbey Meadows B1
Torre Abbey Sands B1
Torwood Gdns B3
Torwood St C3
Town Hall A2
Union Square A2
Union St A1
Upton Hill A2
Upton Park A1
Upton Rd A1
Vanehill Rd C3
Vansittart Rd A1
Vaughan Parade C2
Victoria Parade C3
Victoria Rd A2
Warberry Rd West B2
Warren Rd B2
Windsor Rd A2/A3
Woodville Rd A3

Truro 349

Adelaide Ter B1
Agar Rd B3
Arch Hill C2
Arundell Pl C2
Avenue, The A3
Avondale Rd B1
Back Quay B3
Barrack La C3
Barton Meadow A1
Benson Rd A2
Bishops Cl A2
Bosvean Gdns B1
Bosvigo Gardens B1
Bosvigo La A1
Bosvigo Rd B2
Broad St A3
Burley Cl C3
Bus Station B3
Calenick St B2
Campfield Hill B3
Carclew St B3
Carew Rd A2
Carey Park B2
Carlyon Rd A2
Carvoza Rd A3
Castle St B2
Cathedral View A2
Chainwalk Dr A2
Chapel Hill B1
Charles St B2
City Hall B3
City Rd B2
Coinage Hall B3
Comprigney Hill A1
Coosebean La A1
Copes Gdns A2
County Hall B1
Courtney Rd A2
Crescent Rd B1
Crescent Rise B1
Crescent, The B1
Daniell Court C2
Daniell Rd C2
Daniell St C2
Daubuz Cl A2
Dobbs La B1
Edward St B2
Eliot Rd A2
Elm Court A3
Enys Cl A1
Enys Rd A1
Fairmantle St B3
Falmouth Rd C2
Ferris Town B2
Fire Station B1
Frances St B2
George St B2
Green Cl C2
Green La C1
Grenville Rd A2
Hall For Cornwall B3
Hendra Rd A2
Hendra Vean A1
High Cross B3
Higher Newham La C3
Higher Trehaverne A2
Hillcrest Ave B1
Hospital B2
Hunkin Cl A2
Hurland Rd C3
Infirmary Hill B2
James Pl B3
Kenwyn Church Rd A1
Kenwyn Hill A1
Kenwyn Rd A2
Kenwyn St B2
Kerris Gdns A1
King St B3
Leats, The B2
Lemon Quay B3
Lemon St Gallery B3
Library B1/B3
Malpas Rd B3
Market
Memorial Gdns B3
Merrifield Close B1
Mitchell Hill A3
Moresk Cl A3
Moresk Rd A3
Morlaix Ave C3
Nancemere Rd A3

Newham Bsns Park C3
Newham
Industrial Est. C3
Newham Rd C3
Northfield Dr. C3
Oak Way A3
Old County Hall B1
Pal's Terr A3
Park View C3
Pendarves Rd A2
Plaza Cinema B3
Police Station B3
Post Office B2/B3
Prince's St B3
Pydar St A2
Quay St B3
Redannick Cres C2
Redannick La B2
Richard Lander
Monument C2
Richmond Hill B1
River St B2
Rosedale Rd A2
Royal Cornwall Mus B2
St Aubyn Rd C3
St Clement St B3
St George's Rd A1
School La C2
Spires, The A2
Station Rd B1
Stokes Rd A2
Strangways Terr C3
Tabernacle St B3
Trehaverne La A2
Tremayne Rd A2
Treseder's Gdns A3
Treworder Rd B1
Treyew Rd B1
Truro Cathedral B3
Truro Harbour Office B3
Truro Station B3
Union St B2
Upper School La C2
Victoria Gdns B2
Waterfall Gdns B2

Wick 349

Ackergill Cres A2
Ackergill St A2
Albert St C2
Ambulance Station A2
Argyle Sq C2
Assembly Rooms C2
Bank Row C2
Bankhead B1
Barons Well B2
Barrogill St C2
Bay View B3
Bexley Terr C3
Bignold Park C2
Bowling Green C2
Breadalbane Terr C2
Bridge of Wick B1
Bridge St B2
Brown Pl C2
Burn St B2
Bus Station B1
Caithness General
Hospital (A&E) B1
Cliff Rd B1
Coach Rd B2
Coastguard Station C2
Corner Cres B3
Coronation St C1
Council Offices B2
Court B2
Crane Rock C3
Dempster St C2
Dunnet Ave A2
Fire Station B2
Francis St C1
George St A1
Girnigoe St B2
Glamis Rd B2
Gowrie Pl B1
Grant St C2
Green Rd B2
Gunns Terr B3
Harbour Quay B2
Harbour Rd C3
Harbour Terr C2
Harrow Hill C2
Henrietta St A2/B2
Heritage Museum C2
High St B2
Hill Ave A2
Hillhead Rd B3
Hood St C1
Huddart St C2
Kenneth St C1
Kinnaird St C2
Kirk Hill B1
Langwell Cres B3
Leishman Ave B3
Leith Walk A2
Library B2
Lifeboat Station C3
Lighthouse C3
Lindsay Dr B3
Lindsay Pl B3
Loch St C2
Louisburgh St B2
Lower Dunbar St C2
Macleay La B1
Macleod Rd B3
MacRae St C2
Martha Terr B2
Miller Ave B1
Miller La B1
Moray St C2
Mowat Pl B3
Murchison St C3
Newton Ave C1
Newton Rd C1
Nicolson St C3
North Highland Coll B2
North River Pier B3
Northcote St C2
Owen Pl A2
Police Station B1
Port Dunbar B3
Post Office B2/C2
Pulteney Distillery C2
River St B2
Robert St A1
Rutherford St C2
St John's Episcopal C2
Sandigoe Rd B3
Scalesburn B3
Seaforth Ave C1
Shore La B2
Shore, The B2
Sinclair Dr B3
Sinclair Terr C2
Smith Terr C3
South Pier C3
South Quay C3
South Rd C1
South River Pier B3
Station Rd B1
Superstore A1/B1
Swimming Pool B2
Telford St B2
Thurso Rd B1
Thurso St B1
Town Hall B2
Union St B2
Upper Dunbar St C2
Vansittart St C3
Victoria Pl B2
War Memorial A1
Well of Cairndhuna C3
Wellington Ave C3
Wellington St C3
West Banks Ave C1
West Banks Terr C1
West Park C1
Whitehorse Park B2
Wick Harbour Bridge B2
Wick Industrial Estate A2
Wick Parish Church B1
Wick Station B1
Williamson St B2
Willowbank B2

Winchester 350

Andover Rd A2
Andover Rd Retail Pk A2
Archery La C2
Arthur Rd A2
Bar End Rd C3
Beaufort Rd C2
Beggar's La B3
Bereweeke Ave A1
Bereweeke Rd A1
Boscobel Rd A2
Brassey Rd A2
Broadway B3
Brooks Shopping
Centre, The B3
Bus Station B3
Butter Cross B2
Canon St C2
Castle Wall C2/C3
Castle, King Arthur's
Round Table B2
Cathedral C2
Cheriton Rd A1
Chesil St C3
Chesil Theatre C3
Christchurch Rd C1
City Mill B3
City Museum B2
City Rd B2
Clifton Rd B1
Clifton Terr B2
Close Wall C2/C3
Coach Park A2
Colebrook St C3
College St C2
College Walk C3
Compton Rd C2
Council Offices C3
County Council
Offices B2
Cranworth Rd A2
Cromwell Rd C1
Culver Rd C2
Domum Rd C3
Durngate Pl B3
Eastgate St B3
Edgar Rd C2
Egbert Rd A2
Elm Rd B1
Everyman C2
Fairfield Rd A1
Fire Station B3
Fordington Ave B1
Fordington Rd A1
Friarsgate B3
Gordon Rd B3
Greenhill Rd B1
Guildhall B3
Hatherley Rd A1
High St B2
Hillier Way A3
HM Prison B1
Hyde Abbey
(Remains) A2
Hyde Abbey Rd B2
Hyde Cl A2
Hyde St A2
Information Ctr B3
Jane Austen's Ho C2
Jewry St B2
John Stripe Theatre C1
King Alfred Pl A2
Kingsgate Arch C2
Kingsgate Park C2
Kingsgate Rd C2
Kingsgate St C2
Lankhills Rd A2
Law Courts B2
Library B2
Lower Brook St B3
Magdalen Hill B3
Market La B2
Mews La B1
Middle Brook St B3
Middle Rd B1
Military Museums B2
Milland Rd C3
Milverton Rd B1
Monks Rd A3
North Hill Cl A2
North Walls B2
North Walls Rec Gnd A3
Nuns Rd A3
Oram's Arbour B1
Owen's Rd A2
Parchment St B2
Park & Ride C3
Park Ave B3
Playing Field A1
Police HQ B1
Police Station B3
Portal Rd C3
Post Office B2/C1
Quarry Rd C3
Ranelagh Rd C1
Regiment Museum B2
River Park Leisure Ctr B3
Romans' Rd C2
Romsey Rd B1
Royal Hampshire County
Hospital (A&E) B1
St Cross Rd C2
St George's St B2
St Giles Hill C3
St James Villas C2
St James' La B1
St James' Terr B1
St John's B3
St John's St B3
St Michael's Rd C2
St Paul's Hill B1
St Peter St B2
St Swithun St C2
St Thomas St C2
Saxon Rd A2
School of Art B3
Sleepers Hill Rd C1
Southgate St B2
Sparkford Rd C1
Square, The B2
Staple Gdns B2
Station Rd B2
Step Terr B1
Stockbridge Rd A1
Stuart Cres C1
Sussex St B2
Swan Lane B2
Tanner St B3
Theatre Royal B2
Tower St B2
Town Hall C3
Union St B3
Univ of Southampton
(Winchester School
of Art) B3
University of Winchester
(King Alfred Campus) C1
Upper Brook St B2
Wales St B3
Water Lane B3
Weirs, The C3
West End Terr B1
Western Rd B1
Westgate B2
Wharf Hill C3
Winchester College C2
Winchester Gallery,
The B3
Winchester Station A2
Winnall Moors Wildlife
Reserve A3
Wolvesey Castle C3
Worthy Lane A2
Worthy Rd A2

Windsor 350

Adelaide Sq C3
Albany Rd C2
Albert St B1
Alexandra Gdns B2
Alexandra Rd C2
Alma Rd B2
Ambulance Station B1
Arthur Rd B2
Bachelors Acre B3
Barry Ave B2
Beaumont Rd C2
Bexley St B1
Boat House B2
Brocas St B2
Brocas, The A2
Brook St C3
Bulkeley Ave C1
Castle Hill B3
Charles St B2
Claremont Rd C2
Clarence Cr B2
Clarence Rd B1
Clewer Court Rd B1
Coach Park B2
College Cr C1
Courts C2
Cricket Club A3
Cricket Ground C3
Dagmar Rd C2
Datchet Rd B3
Devereux Rd C2
Dorset Rd C2
Duke St B1
Elm Rd C1
Eton College A3
Eton Ct A2
Eton Sq A2
Eton Wick Rd A2
Farm Yard B3
Fire Station C2
Frances Rd C2
Frogmore Dr B3
Gloucester Pl C3
Goslar Way C1
Goswell Hill B2
Goswell Rd B2
Green La C1
Grove Rd C2
Guildhall B3
Helena Rd C2
Helston La B1
High St A2/B3
Holy Trinity C2
Home Park, The A3/C3
Hospital (Private) C2
Household Cavalry C2
Imperial Rd C1
Information Ctr B2/B3
Keats La A2
King Edward Ct B2
King Edward VII Ave A3
King Edward VII
Hospital C2
King George V Meml B3
King Stable St A2
King's Rd C3
Library C2
Long Walk, The C3
Maidenhead Rd B1
Meadow La A2
Municipal Offices C3
Nell Gwynne's Ho B3
Osborne Rd C2
Oxford Rd B1
Park St B3
Peascod St B2
Police Station C2
Post Office A2
Princess Margaret
Hospital C2
Queen Victoria's Walk B3
Queen's Rd C2
River St B2
Romney Island A3
Romney Lock A3
Romney Lock Rd A3
Russell St C2
St John's B3
St John's Chapel A2
St Leonards Rd C2
St Mark's Rd C2
Sheet St C3
South Meadow A2
South Meadow La A2
Springfield Rd C1
Stovell Rd B1
Sunbury Rd A3
Tangier La A2
Tangier St A3
Temple Rd C2
Thames St B3
Theatre Royal B3
Trinity Pl C2
Vansittart Rd B1/C1
Vansittart Rd Gdns C1
Victoria Barracks C2
Victoria St C2
Ward Royal B2
Westmead C1
White Lilies Island A1
William St B2
Windsor & Eton
Central B2
Windsor & Eton
Riverside A3
Windsor Arts Ctr C2
Windsor Bridge B3
Windsor Castle B3
Windsor Great Park C3
Windsor Leisure Ctr B1
Windsor Relief Rd A1
Windsor Royal Sh B2
York Ave C1
York Rd C1

Wolverhampton 350

Albion St B3
Alexandra St C1
Arena B2
Arts Gallery B2
Ashland St C1
Austin St A1
Badger Dr A3
Bailey St B3
Bath Ave B1
Bath Rd B1
Bell St C2
Berry St B3
Bilston Rd C3
Bilston St C3
Birmingham Canal A3
Bone Mill La A2
Brewery Rd B1
Bright St A1
Burton Cres B3
Bus Station B3
Cambridge St A3
Camp St B2
Cannock Rd A3
Castle St C2
Chapel Ash C1
Cherry St C1
Chester St A1
Church La C2
Church St C2
Civic Centre B2
Civic Hall B2
Clarence Rd B2
Cleveland St C2
Clifton St C1
Coach Station B2
Compton Rd B1
Corn Hill B3
Coven St A3
Craddock St A1
Cross St North A2
Crown & County
Courts C3
Crown St A2
Culwell St B3
Dale St C1
Darlington St C1
Devon Rd A1
Drummond St B2
Dudley Rd C2
Dudley St B2
Duke St C3
Dunkley St B1
Dunstall Ave A2
Dunstall Hill A2
Dunstall Rd A1/A2
Evans St A1
Fawdry St A1
Field St B3
Fire Station C1
Fiveways A2
Fowler Playing Fields A3
Fox's La A2
Francis St A2
Fryer St B3
Gloucester St A1
Gordon St C3
Graiseley St C1
Grand B3
Granville St C3
Great Brickkiln St C1
Great Hampton St A1
Great Western St A2
Grimstone St B3
Harrow St A1
Hilton St A3
Horseley Fields C3
Humber Rd C1
Jack Hayward Way A2
Jameson St A1
Jenner St C3
Kennedy Rd B3
Kimberley St C1
King St B2
Laburnum St C1
Lansdowne Rd B1
Leicester St A1
Lever St C3
Library C3
Lichfield St B2
Light House B3
Little's La B3
Lock St B3
Lord St C1
Lowe St A1
Lower Stafford St A2
Maltings, The B2
Mander Centre C2
Mander St C1
Market C2
Market St B2
Maxwell Rd C3
Melbourne St C3
Merridale St C1
Middlecross C3
Molineux St B2
Mostyn St A1
New Hampton Rd East A1
Nine Elms La A3
North Rd A2
Oaks Cres C1
Oxley St A2
Paget St A1
Park Ave B1
Park Road East A1
Park Road West B1
Paul St C2
Pelham St C1
Penn Rd C2
Piper's Row B3
Pitt St C2
Police Station C2
Pool St C2
Poole St A3
Post Office
A1/B2/B2/C2
Powlett St C3
Queen St B2
Raby St C3
Railway Dr B3
Red Hill St A2
Red Lion St B2
Retreat St C1
Ring Rd B2
Royal, The C3
Rugby St A1
Russell St C1
St Andrew's B1
St David's B3
St George's C3
St George's Pde C2
St James St C3
St John's C2
St John's C2
St John's Retail Park C2
St John's Square C2
St Mark's C1
St Marks Rd C1
St Marks St C1
St Patrick's B2
St Peter's B2
St Peter's B2
Salisbury St C1
Salop St C2
School St C2
Sherwood St A2
Smestow St A3
Snowhill C2
Springfield Rd A3
Stafford St B2
Staveley Rd A1
Steelhouse La C3
Stephenson St C1
Stewart St C2
Sun St B3
Tempest St C2
Temple St C2
Tettenhall Rd B1
Thomas St C2
Thornley St B2
Tower St C2
University B2
Upper Zoar St C1
Vicarage Rd C3
Victoria St C2
Walpole St A1
Walsall St C3
Ward St C3
Warwick St C3
Water St A3
Waterloo Rd B2
Wednesfield Rd B3
West Park (not A&E) B1
West Park Swimming
Pool B1
Wharf St C3
Whitmore Hill B2
Wolverhampton B3
Wolverhampton St
George's C2
Wolverhampton
Wanderers Football
Gnd (Molineux) B2
Worcester St C2
Wulfrun Centre C2
Yarwell Cl A3
York St C3
Zoar St C1

Worcester 350

Albany Terr A1
Alice Otley School A2
Angel Pl B2
Angel St B2
Ashcroft Rd A2
Athelstan Rd C3
Avenue, The C1
Back Lane North A1
Back Lane South A1
Barbourne Rd A2
Bath Rd C2
Battenhall Rd C3
Bridge St B2
Britannia Sq A1
Broad St B2
Bromwich La C1
Bromwich Rd C1
Bromyard Rd C1
Bus Station B2
Butts, The B2
Carden St B3
Castle St A2
Cathedral C2
Cathedral Plaza B2
Charles St B3
Chequers La B1
Chestnut St A2
Chestnut Walk A2
Citizens' Advice
Bureau B2
City Walls Rd B2
Cole Hill C3
College of Technology B2
College St C2
Commandery, The C3
Cripplegate Park B1
Croft Rd B1
Cromwell St B3
Cross, The B2
CrownGate Ctr B2
Deansway B2
Diglis Pde C2
Diglis Rd C2
Edgar Tower C2
Farrier St A2
Fire Station B2
Foregate St B2
Foregate Street B2
Fort Royal Hill C3
Fort Royal Park C3
Foundry St B3
Friar St C2
George St B3
Grand Stand Rd B1
Greenhill C3
Greyfriars B2
Guildhall B2
Henwick Rd B1
High St B2
Hill St B3
Hive, The B2
Huntingdon Hall B2
Hylton Rd B1
Information Ctr B2
King Charles Place
Shopping Centre C1
King's School C2
King's School
Playing Field C2
Kleve Walk C2
Lansdowne Cr A3
Lansdowne Rd A3
Lansdowne Walk A3
Laslett St A3
Leisure Centre A3
Library, Museum &
Art Gallery A2
Little Chestnut St A2
Little London A2
London Rd C3
Lowell St A3
Lowesmoor B2
Lowesmoor Terr A3
Lowesmoor Wharf A3
Magistrates Court A2
Midland Rd B3
Mill St C2
Moors Severn Terr A1
Museum of Royal
Worcester C2
New Rd C1
New St B2
Northfield St A2
Odeon B2
Padmore St B3
Park St C3
Pheasant St B3
Pitchcroft
Racecourse A1
Police Station A2
Portland St C2
Post Office B2
Quay St B2
Queen St B2
Rainbow Hill A3
Recreation Ground A2
Reindeer Court B2
Rogers Hill A3
Sabrina Rd A1
St Dunstan's Cr C3
St John's C1
St Martin's Gate B3
St Martin's Quarter B3
St Oswald's Rd A2
St Paul's St B3
St Swithin's Church B2
St Wulstans Cr C3
Sansome Walk A2
Severn St C2
Shambles, The B2
Shaw St B2
Shire Hall Crown Ct A2
Shrub Hill B3
Shrub Hill Rd B3
Shrub Hill Retail Park B3
Slingpool Walk C1
South Quay B2
Southfield St A2
Sports Ground A2/C1
Stanley Rd B3
Swan, The A1
Swimming Pool A2
Tallow Hill B3
Tennis Walk A2
Tolladine Rd B3
Tudor House B2
Tybridge St B1
Tything, The A2
Univ of Worcester B2
Vincent Rd B3
Vue C2
Washington St A3
Woolhope Rd C3
Worcester Bridge B2
Worcester County
Cricket Ground C1
Worcester Royal
Grammar School A2
Wylds La C3

Wrexham
Wrecsam 350

Abbot St B2
Acton Rd A3
Albert St C3
Alexandra Rd C1
Aran Rd A3
Barnfield C3
Bath Rd C2
Beeches, The A3
Beechley Rd C3
Belgrave Rd C2
Belle Vue Park C2
Belle Vue Rd C2
Belvedere Dr A1
Bennion's Rd C3
Berse Rd A1
Bersham Rd C1
Birch St C3
Bodhyfryd B3
Border Retail Park B3
Bradley Rd C2
Bright St B1
Bron-y-Nant B1
Brook St C2
Bryn-y-Cabanau Rd C3
Bury St C3
Bus Station B2
Butchers Market B3
Caia Rd C3
Cambrian Ind Est C3
Caxton Pl B2
Cemetery C1
Centenary Rd C1
Chapel St C2
Charles St B3
Chester Rd A3
Chester St B3
Cilcen Gr A3
Citizens Advice
Bureau B2
Cobden Rd B1
Council Offices B3
County B2
Crescent Rd B3
Crispin La A2
Croesnewyth Rd B1
Cross St A2
Cunliffe St A2
Derby Rd C3
Dolydd Rd B1
Duke St B2
Eagles Meadow C3
Earle St C2
East Ave A2
Edward St C2
Egerton St B2
Empress Rd C1
Erddig Rd C2
Fairy Rd C2
Fire Station B2
Foster Rd A3
Foxwood Dr C1
Garden Rd A2
General Market B3
Gerald St B2
Gibson St C1
Glynd?r University Plas
Coch Campus A1
Greenbank St C3
Greenfield A2
Grosvenor Rd B2
Grove Park B2
Grove Park Rd B3
Grove Rd A3
Guildhall B2
Haig Rd C3
Hampden Rd C2
Hazel Gr A3
Henblas St B3
High St B3
Hightown Rd C3
Hill St B2
Holt Rd B3
Holt St B3
Hope St B2
Huntroyde Ave C3
Information Ctr B3
Island Green Sh Ctr B2
Job Centre B2
Jubilee Rd B2
King St B2
Kingsmills Rd C3
Lambpit St B3
Law Courts B3
Lawson Cl A3
Lawson Rd A3
Lea Rd C2
Library & Arts Centre B2
Lilac Way B1
Llys David Lord B1
Lorne St A2
Maesgwyn Rd B1
Maesydre Rd A3
Manley Rd B3
Market St B3
Mawddy Ave A2
Mayville Ave A2
Memorial Gallery B2
Memorial Hall B3
Mold Rd A1
Mount St C3
Neville Cres A3
New Rd A2
North Wales Regional
Tennis Centre A1
North Wales School of
Art & Design B2
Oak Dr A3
Park Ave A3
Park St A2
Peel St C1
Pen y Bryn C2
Pentre Felin C2
Penymaes Ave A3
Peoples Market B3
Percy St C2
Pines, The A3
Plas Coch Rd A1
Plas Coch Retail Park A1
Police Station B3
Poplar Rd C2
Post Office
A2/B2/C2/C3
Powell Rd B3
Poyser St C2
Price's La A2
Primose Way B1
Princess St C1
Queen St B3
Queens Sq B2
Regent St B2
Rhosddu Rd A2/B2
Rhosnesni La A3
Rivulet Rd C3
Ruabon Rd C2
Ruthin Rd C1/C2
St Giles C3
St Giles Way C3
St James Ct A2
St Mary's B2
Salisbury Rd C3
Salop Rd C3
Sontley Rd C2
Spring Rd A2
Stanley St C3
Stansty Rd A2
Station Approach B2
Studio B2
Talbot Rd C2
Techniquest
Glyndŵr A2
Town Hill C2
Trevor St C2
Trinity St B2
Tuttle St C3
Vale Park A1
Vernon St B2
Vicarage Hill B2
Victoria Rd C2
Walnut St A2
War Memorial B3
Waterworld
Leisure Centre B3
Watery Rd B1/B2
Wellington Rd C2
Westminster Dr A3
William Aston Hall A1
Windsor Rd A1
Wrecsam
Wrexham AFC A1
Wrexham Central B2
Wrexham General B2
Wrexham Maelor
Hospital (A&E) B1
Wrexham Technology
Park B1
Wynn Ave A2
Yale College B3
Yale Gr A3
Yorke St C3

York 350

Aldwark B2
Barbican Rd C3
Bar Convent Living
Heritage Ctr C1
Barley Hall B2
Bishopgate St C2
Bishopthorpe Rd C2
Blossom St C1
Bootham A1
Bootham Cr A1
Bootham Terr A1
Bridge St B2
Brook St A2
Brownlow St A2
Burton Stone La A1
Castle Museum C2
Castlegate B2
Cemetery Rd C3
Cherry St C2
City Screen B2
City Wall A2/B1/C3
Clarence St A2
Clementhorpe C2
Clifford St B2
Clifford's Tower B2
Clifton A1
Coach park A2
Coney St B2
Coppergate Ctr B2
Cromwell Rd C2
Crown Court C2
Davygate B2
Deanery Gdns A2
DIG B2
Ebor Industrial Estate B3
Fairfax House B2
Fishergate C3
Foss Islands Rd B3
Foss Islands Retail Pk B3
Fossbank A3
Garden St A2
George St C3
Gillygate A2
Goodramgate B2
Grand Opera House B2
Grosvenor Terr A1
Guildhall B2
Hallfield Rd A3
Heslington Rd C3
Heworth Green A3
Holy Trinity B2
Hope St C3
Huntington Rd A3
Information Ctr B2
James St B3
Jorvik Viking Ctr B2
Kent St C3
Lawrence St C3
Layerthorpe A3
Leeman Rd B1
Lendal B2
Lendal Bridge B1
Library A2/B1
Longfield Terr A1
Lord Mayor's Walk A2
Lower Eldon St A2
Lowther St A2
Mansion House B2
Margaret St C3
Marygate A1
Melbourne St C3
Merchant Adventurers'
Hall B2
Merchant Taylors'
Hall B2
Micklegate B1
Micklegate Bar C1
Monkgate A2
Moss St C1
Museum Gdns B1
Museum St B1
National Railway
Museum B1
Navigation Rd B3
Newton Terr C2
North Pde A1
North St B2
Nunnery La C1
Nunthorpe Rd C1
Ouse Bridge B2
Paragon St C3
Park Gr A3
Park St C1
Parliament St B2
Peasholme Green B3
Penley's Grove St A2
Piccadilly B2
Police Station B2
Post Office B1/B2/C3
Priory St B1
Purey Cust Nuffield
Hospital, The A2
Queen Anne's Rd A1
Reel C1
Regimental Mus B2
Richard III Experience
at Monk Bar A2
Roman Bath B2
Rowntree Park C2
St Andrewgate B2
St Benedict Rd C1
St John St A2
St Olave's Rd A1
St Peter's Gr A1
St Saviourgate B2
Scarcroft Hill C1
Scarcroft Rd C1
Shambles, The B2
Shopmobility B2
Skeldergate C2
Skeldergate Bridge C2
Station Rd B1
Stonebow, The B2
Stonegate B2
Superstore A3
Sycamore Terr A1
Terry Ave C2
Theatre Royal B2
Thorpe St C1
Toft Green B1
Tower St C2
Townend St A2
Treasurer's House A2
Trinity La B1
Undercroft Mus A2
Union Terr A2
Victor St C2
Vine St C2
Walmgate B3
War Memorial B1
Wellington St C3
York Art Gallery A1
York Barbican C3
York Brewery B1
York Dungeon, The B2
York Minster A2
York St John Uni A2
York Station B1

367

Index to road maps of Britain

Abbreviations used in the index

Aberdeen	**Aberdeen City**
Aberds	**Aberdeenshire**
Ald	**Alderney**
Anglesey	**Isle of Anglesey**
Angus	**Angus**
Argyll	**Argyll and Bute**
Bath	**Bath and North East Somerset**
Bedford	**Bedford**
Bl Gwent	**Blaenau Gwent**
Blackburn	**Blackburn with Darwen**
Blackpool	**Blackpool**
Bmouth	**Bournemouth**
Borders	**Scottish Borders**
Brack	**Bracknell**
Bridgend	**Bridgend**
Brighton	**City of Brighton and Hove**
Bristol	**City and County of Bristol**
Bucks	**Buckinghamshire**
C Beds	**Central Bedfordshire**
Caerph	**Caerphilly**
Cambs	**Cambridgeshire**
Cardiff	**Cardiff**
Carms	**Carmarthenshire**
Ceredig	**Ceredigion**
Ches E	**Cheshire East**
Ches W	**Cheshire West and Chester**
Clack	**Clackmannanshire**
Conwy	**Conwy**
Corn	**Cornwall**
Cumb	**Cumbria**
Darl	**Darlington**
Denb	**Denbighshire**
Derby	**City of Derby**
Derbys	**Derbyshire**
Devon	**Devon**
Dorset	**Dorset**
Dumfries	**Dumfries and Galloway**
Dundee	**Dundee City**
Durham	**Durham**
E Ayrs	**East Ayrshire**
E Dunb	**East Dunbartonshire**
E Loth	**East Lothian**
E Renf	**East Renfrewshire**
E Sus	**East Sussex**
E Yorks	**East Riding of Yorkshire**
Edin	**City of Edinburgh**
Essex	**Essex**
Falk	**Falkirk**
Fife	**Fife**
Flint	**Flintshire**
Glasgow	**City of Glasgow**
Glos	**Gloucestershire**
Gtr Man	**Greater Manchester**
Gwyn	**Gwynedd**
Halton	**Halton**
Hants	**Hampshire**
Hereford	**Herefordshire**
Herts	**Hertfordshire**
Highld	**Highland**
Hrtlpl	**Hartlepool**
Hull	**Hull**
IoM	**Isle of Man**
IoW	**Isle of Wight**
Invclyd	**Inverclyde**
Kent	**Kent**
Lancs	**Lancashire**
Leicester	**City of Leicester**
Leics	**Leicestershire**
Lincs	**Lincolnshire**
London	**Greater London**
Luton	**Luton**
M Keynes	**Milton Keynes**
M Tydf	**Merthyr Tydfil**
Mbro	**Middlesbrough**
Medway	**Medway**
Mers	**Merseyside**
Midloth	**Midlothian**
Mon	**Monmouthshire**
Moray	**Moray**
N Ayrs	**North Ayrshire**
N Lincs	**North Lincolnshire**
N Lanark	**North Lanarkshire**
N Som	**North Somerset**
N Yorks	**North Yorkshire**
NE Lincs	**North East Lincolnshire**
Neath	**Neath Port Talbot**
Newport	**City and County of Newport**
Norf	**Norfolk**
Northants	**Northamptonshire**
Northumb	**Northumberland**
Nottingham	**City of Nottingham**
Notts	**Nottinghamshire**
Orkney	**Orkney**
Oxon	**Oxfordshire**
Pboro	**Peterborough**
Pembs	**Pembrokeshire**
Perth	**Perth and Kinross**
Plym	**Plymouth**
Poole	**Poole**
Powys	**Powys**
Ptsmth	**Portsmouth**
Reading	**Reading**
Redcar	**Redcar and Cleveland**
Renfs	**Renfrewshire**
Rhondda	**Rhondda Cynon Taff**
Rutland	**Rutland**
S Ayrs	**South Ayrshire**
S Glos	**South Gloucestershire**
S Lanark	**South Lanarkshire**
S Yorks	**South Yorkshire**
Scilly	**Scilly**
Shetland	**Shetland**
Shrops	**Shropshire**
Slough	**Slough**
Som	**Somerset**
Soton	**Southampton**
Staffs	**Staffordshire**
Southend	**Southend-on-Sea**
Stirling	**Stirling**
Stockton	**Stockton-on-Tees**
Stoke	**Stoke-on-Trent**
Suff	**Suffolk**
Sur	**Surrey**
Swansea	**Swansea**
Swindon	**Swindon**
T&W	**Tyne and Wear**
Telford	**Telford & Wrekin**
Thurrock	**Thurrock**
Torbay	**Torbay**
Torf	**Torfaen**
V Glam	**The Vale of Glamorgan**
W Berks	**West Berkshire**
W Dunb	**West Dunbartonshire**
W Isles	**Western Isles**
W Loth	**West Lothian**
W Mid	**West Midlands**
W Sus	**West Sussex**
W Yorks	**West Yorkshire**
Warks	**Warwickshire**
Warr	**Warrington**
Wilts	**Wiltshire**
Windsor	**Windsor and Maidenhead**
Wokingham	**Wokingham**
Worcs	**Worcestershire**
Wrex	**Wrexham**
York	**City of York**

How to use the index

Example **Blatherwycke** Northants **137** D9

- grid square
- page number
- county or unitary authority

Aar–Ald

A

Aaron's Hill Sur 50 E3
Aaron's Town Cumb 240 E2
Abbas Combe Som 30 C2
Abberley Worcs 116 D5
Abberton Essex 89 B8
Worcs 117 G9
Abberwick
Northumb 264 G4
Abbess End Essex 87 C9
Abbess Roding Essex 87 C9
Abbey Devon 27 E10
Abbeycwmhir
Powys 113 C11
Abbey-cwm-hir
Powys 113 C11
Abbeydale Glos 80 B5
S Yorks 186 E4
Abbeydale Park
S Yorks 186 E4
Abbey Dore Hereford 97 E7
Abbey Field Essex 107 G9
Abbey Gate Kent 53 B9
Abbey Green
Shrops 149 C10
Staffs 169 D7
Abbey Hey Gtr Man 184 B5
Abbeyhill Edin 280 G5
Abbey Hulton Stoke 168 F6
Abbey Mead Sur 66 F4
Abbey St Bathans
Borders 272 C5
Abbeystead Lancs 203 C7
Abbey Town Cumb 238 G5
Abbey Village Lancs 194 C6
Abbey Wood London 68 D3
Abbots Bickington
Devon 24 E5
Abbots Bromley
Staffs 151 E11
Abbotsbury Dorset 17 D7
Abbotsford W Sus 36 C4
Abbotsham Devon 24 B6
Abbotskerswell Devon 9 B7
Abbots Langley Herts 85 E9
Abbotsleigh Devon 8 F6
Abbots Leigh N Som 60 E4
Abbotsley Cambs 122 F4
Abbot's Meads
Ches W 166 B5
Abbots Morton
Worcs 117 F10
Abbots Ripton
Cambs 122 B4
Abbots Salford
Warks 117 G11
Abbotstone Hants 48 G5
Abbotswood Hants 32 C5
Sur 50 C4
Abbots Worthy Hants 48 G3
Abbotts Ann Hants 47 E10
Abcott Shrops 115 B7
Abdon Shrops 131 F11
Abdy S Yorks 186 B6
Aber Ceredig 93 B9
Aberaeron Ceredig 111 E9
Aberaman Rhondda 77 E8
Aberangell Gwyn 146 G6
Aber-Arad Carms 92 D6
Aberarder Highld 290 E6
Aberarder House
Highld 300 G6
Aberarder Lodge
Highld 291 E7
Aberargie Perth 286 F5
Aberarth Ceredig 111 E9
Aberavon Neath 57 C8
Aber-banc Ceredig 93 C7
Aberbargoed
Caerph 77 E11
Aberbechan Powys 130 E2
Aberbeeg Bl Gwent 78 E2
Aberbran Powys 95 F9
Abercanaid M Tydf 77 E9
Abercarn Caerph 78 G2
Abercastle Pembs 91 E7
Abercegir Powys 128 C6
Aberchalder Highld 290 C5
Aberchirder Aberds 302 D6
Abercorn W Loth 279 F11
Aber Cowarch Gwyn 147 F7
Abercraf Powys 76 C4
Abercregan Neath 57 B11
Abercrombie Fife 287 G9
Abercwmboi Rhondda 77 F8
Abercych Pembs 92 C4
Abercynafon Powys 77 B9
Abercynffig / Aberkenfig
Bridgend 57 E11
Abercynon Rhondda 77 F9
Aberdalgie Perth 286 E4
Aberdâr / Aberdare
Rhondda 77 E7
Aberdare / Aberdâr
Rhondda 77 E7
Aberdaron Gwyn 144 D3
Aberdeen
Aberdeen 293 C11
Aberdesach Gwyn 162 E6
Aberdour Fife 280 D3
Aberdovey / Aberdyfi
Gwyn 128 D2
Aberdulais Neath 76 E3
Aberdyfi / Aberdovey
Gwyn 128 D2
Aberedw Powys 95 B11
Abereiddy Pembs 90 E5
Abererch Gwyn 145 B7
Aberfan M Tydf 77 E9
Aberfeldy Perth 286 C2
Aberffraw Anglesey 162 B5
Aberffrwd Ceredig 112 B3
Mon 78 D5
Aberford W Yorks 206 F4
Aberfoyle Stirl 285 G9
Abergarw Bridgend 58 C2
Abergarwed Neath 76 E4
Abergavenny Mon 78 C3
Abergele Conwy 180 F6
Aber-Giâr Carms 93 C10
Abergorlech Carms 93 E11
Abergwaun / Fishguard
Pembs 91 D9
Abergwesyn Powys 113 G7
Abergwili Carms 93 G8
Abergwynant Gwyn 146 F3
Abergwynfi Neath 57 B11
Aber-gwynfi Neath 57 B11
Abergwyngregyn
Gwyn 179 G11
Abergynolwyn Gwyn 128 B3
Aber-Hirnant Gwyn 147 C9
Aberhosan Powys 128 D6
Aberkenfig / Abercynffig
Bridgend 57 E11
Aberlady E Loth 281 E9
Aberlemno Angus 287 B9
Aberlerry Ceredig 128 E2
Aberllefenni Gwyn 128 B5
Aberllydan / Broad Haven Pembs 72 C5
Aberllynfi / Three Cocks
Powys 96 D3
Abermagwr Ceredig 112 C3
Abermaw / Barmouth
Gwyn 146 F2
Abermeurig
Ceredig 111 F11
Aber miwl / Abermule
Powys 130 E3
Abermorddu Flint 166 D4
Abermule / Aber-miwl
Powys 130 E3
Abernaint Powys 148 E2
Abernant Carms 92 G6
Powys 130 D3
Aber-nant Rhondda 77 E8
Abernethy Perth 286 F5
Abernyte Perth 286 D6
Aber-oer Wrex 166 F3
Aberogwr / Ogmore by Sea V Glam 57 F11
Aberpennar / Mountain Ash Rhondda 77 F8
Aberporth Ceredig 110 G5
Aber-Rhiwlech
Gwyn 147 E8
Aberriw / Berriew
Powys 130 C3
Abersoch Gwyn 144 D6
Abersychan Torf 78 E3
Abertawe / Swansea
Swansea 56 C6
Aberteifi / Cardigan
Ceredig 92 B3
Aberthin V Glam 58 D4
Abertillery Bl Gwent 78 E2
Abertridwr Caerph 58 B6
Powys 147 F10
Abertrinant Gwyn 128 B2
Abertysswg Caerph 77 D10
Aberuchill Castle
Perth 285 E11
Aberuthven Perth 286 F3
Aber-Village Powys 96 G2
Aberyscir Powys 95 F9
Aberystwyth
Ceredig 111 A11
Abhainn Suidhe
W Isles 305 H2
Abingdon-on-Thames
Oxon 83 F7
Abinger Common
Sur 50 D6
Abinger Hammer
Sur 50 D5
Abington Northants 120 E5
S Lnrk 259 E10
Abington Pigotts
Cambs 104 C6
Abington Vale
Northants 120 E5
Abingworth W Sus 35 D10
Ab Kettleby Leics 154 E4
Ab Lench Worcs 117 G10
Ablington Glos 81 D10
Wilts 47 D7
Abney Derbys 185 F11
Aboyne Aberds 293 D7
Abraham Heights
Lancs 211 G9
Abram Gtr Man 194 G6
Abriachan Highld 300 F5
Abridge Essex 87 F7
Abronhill N Lnrk 278 F5
Abshot Hants 33 F8
Abson S Glos 61 E8
Abthorpe Northants 102 B2
Abune-the-Hill
Orkney 314 D2
Aby Lincs 190 F6
Acaster Malbis York 207 D7
Acaster Selby
N Yorks 207 E7
Accrington Lancs 195 B9
Acha Argyll 275 B8
Argyll 288 D3
Achabraid Argyll 275 E9
Achachork Highld 298 E4
Achadh an Eas
Highld 308 F6
Achad nan Darach
Highld 284 B4
Achadunan Argyll 284 F5
Achafolla Argyll 275 B8
Achagary Highld 308 D7
Achaglass Argyll 255 C8
Achahoish Argyll 275 F8
Achalader Perth 286 C5
Achallader Argyll 285 C7
Achalone Highld 310 D5
Acha Mor W Isles 304 F5
Achanalt Highld 300 C2
Achanamara Argyll 275 E8
Achandunie Highld 300 B6
Achanelid Argyll 275 E11
Ach'an Todhair
Highld 290 F2
Achany Highld 309 J5
Achaphubuil Highld 290 F2
Acharacle Highld 289 C8
Acharn Highld 289 D9
Perth 285 C11
Acharole Highld 310 D6
Acharossan Argyll 275 F10
Acharry Muir Highld 309 K6
Achath Aberds 293 B9
Achavanich Highld 310 E5
Achavelgin Highld 301 D9
Achavraat Highld 301 E9
Achddu Carms 74 E6
Achdregnie Moray 302 G2
Achduart Highld 307 J5
Achentoul Highld 310 F2
Achfary Highld 306 F7
Achfrish Highld 309 H5
Achgarve Highld 307 K3
Achiemore Highld 308 C3
Highld 310 D2
A'Chill Highld 294 E4
Achiltibuie Highld 307 J5
Achina Highld 308 C7
Achinahuagh Highld 308 C5
Achindaul Highld 290 E3
Achindown Highld 301 E8
Achinduich Highld 309 J5
Achinduin Argyll 289 F10
Achingills Highld 310 C5
Achininver Highld 308 C5
Achintee Highld 290 F3
Highld 299 E9
Achintraid Highld 295 B10
Achlaven Argyll 289 F11
Achlean Highld 291 D10
Achleck Argyll 288 E6
Achlorachan Highld 300 D3
Achluachrach
Highld 290 E4
Achlyness Highld 306 D7
Achmelvich Highld 307 G5
Achmore Highld 295 B10
Stirl 285 D9
Achnaba Argyll 275 E10
Argyll 289 F11
Achnabat Highld 300 F5
Achnabreck Argyll 275 D9
Achnacarnin Highld 306 F5
Achnacarry Highld 290 E3
Achnacloich Argyll 289 F11
Highld 295 E7
Achnaconeran
Highld 290 B6
Achnacraig Argyll 288 E6
Achnacree Argyll 289 F11
Achnacree Bay
Argyll 289 F11
Achnacroish Argyll 289 E10
Achnadrish Argyll 288 D6
Achnafalnich Argyll 284 E6
Achnagarron Highld 300 C6
Achnaha Highld 288 C6
Achnahanat Highld 309 K5
Achnahannet Highld 301 G9
Achnahard Argyll 288 G5
Achnairn Highld 309 H5
Achnaluachrach
Highld 309 J6
Achnandarach
Highld 295 B10
Achnanellan Highld 290 E2
Achnasaul Highld 290 E3
Achnasheen
Highld 299 D11
Achnashelloch
Argyll 275 D9
Achnavast Highld 310 C4
Achneigie Highld 299 B10
Achormlarie Highld 309 K6
Achorn Highld 310 F5
Achosnich Highld 288 C6
Achranich Highld 289 E9
Achreamie Highld 310 C4
Achriabhach Highld 290 G3
Achriesgill Highld 306 D7
Achrimsdale Highld 311 J3
Achtoty Highld 308 C6
Achurch Northants 137 G10
Achuvoldrach
Highld 308 D5
Achvaich Highld 309 K7
Achvarasdal Highld 310 C3
Ackenthwaite
Cumb 211 C10
Ackergill Highld 310 D7
Acklam Mbro 225 B9
N Yorks 216 G5
Ackleton Shrops 132 D5
Acklington
Northumb 252 C6
Ackton W Yorks 198 C2
Ackworth Moor Top
W Yorks 198 D2
Acle Norf 161 G8
Acock's Green
W Mid 134 G2
Acol Kent 71 F10
Acomb Northumb 241 D10
York 207 C7
Acre Gtr Man 196 F2
Lancs 195 C9
Acrefair Wrex 166 G3
Acres Nook Staffs 168 E4
Acre Street W Sus 21 B11
Acton Ches E 167 E10
Dorset 18 F5
London 67 C8
Shrops 130 G6
Staffs 168 G4
Suff 107 C7
Worcs 116 D6
Wrex 166 E4
Acton Beauchamp
Hereford 116 G3
Acton Bridge
Ches W 183 F9
Acton Burnell
Shrops 131 C10
Acton Green
Hereford 116 G3
London 67 D8
Acton Pigott
Shrops 131 C10
Acton Place Suff 107 B7
Acton Reynald
Shrops 149 E10
Acton Round
Shrops 132 D2
Acton Scott Shrops 131 F9
Acton Trussell
Staffs 151 F8
Acton Turville
S Glos 61 C10
Adabroc W Isles 304 B7
Adambrae W Loth 269 A10
Adam's Green Dorset 29 F8
Adbaston Staffs 150 D5
Adber Dorset 29 C9
Adbolton Notts 154 B2
Adderbury Oxon 101 D9
Adderley Shrops 150 B3
Adderley Green
Stoke 168 G6
Adderstone
Northumb 264 C4
Addiewell W Loth 269 C9
Addingham
W Yorks 205 D7
Addingham Moorside
W Yorks 205 D7
Addington Bucks 102 F4
Corn 6 B5
Kent 53 B7
London 67 G11
Addinston Borders 271 E10
Addiscombe London 67 F10
Addlestone Sur 66 G5
Addlestonemoor Sur 66 F4
Addlethorpe Lincs 175 B8
Adel W Yorks 205 F11
Adeney Telford 150 F4
Adeyfield Herts 85 D9
Adfa Powys 129 C11
Adforton Hereford 115 C8
Adgestone IoW 21 D7
Adisham Kent 55 C8
Adlestrop Glos 100 F4
Adlingfleet
E Yorks 199 C10
Adlington Ches E 184 E6
Lancs 194 E6
Adlington Park
Lancs 194 E5
Admaston Staffs 151 E10
Telford 150 G2
Admington Warks 100 B4
Adpar Ceredig 92 C6
Adsborough Som 28 B3
Adscombe Som 43 F7
Adstock Bucks 102 E4
Adstone Northants 119 G11
Adswood Gtr Man 184 D5
Adversane W Sus 35 C9
Advie Highld 301 F11
Adwalton W Yorks 197 B8
Adwell Oxon 83 F11
Adwick le Street
S Yorks 198 F4
Adwick upon Dearne
S Yorks 198 G3
Adziel Aberds 303 D9
Ae Dumfries 247 F11
Ae Village Dumfries 247 F11
Affetside Gtr Man 195 E9
Affleck Aberds 303 G8
Affpuddle Dorset 18 C2
Affric Lodge
Highld 299 G11
Afon Eitha Wrex 166 F3
Afon-wen Flint 181 G10
Afon Wen Gwyn 145 B8
Afton IoW 20 D2
Agar Nook Leics 153 G9
Agbrigg W Yorks 197 D10
Aggborough Worcs 116 B6
Agglethorpe
N Yorks 213 B11
Aglionby Cumb 239 F10
Agneash IoM 192 D5
Aifft Denb 165 B10
Aigburth Mers 182 D5
Aiginis W Isles 304 E6
Aike E Yorks 209 D7
Aikenway Moray 302 E2
Aikerness Orkney 314 A4
Aikers Orkney 314 G4
Aiketgate Cumb 230 B5
Aikton Cumb 239 G7
Ailby Lincs 190 F6
Ailey Hereford 96 B6
Ailstone Warks 118 G4
Ailsworth Pboro 138 D2
Aimes Green Essex 86 E5
Ainderby Quernhow
N Yorks 215 C7
Ainderby Steeple
N Yorks 224 G6
Aingers Green
Essex 108 G2
Ainley Top W Yorks 196 D6
Ainsdale Mers 193 E10
Ainsdale-on-Sea
Mers 193 E9
Ainstable Cumb 230 B6
Ainsworth Gtr Man 195 E9
Ainthorpe N Yorks 226 D4
Aintree Mers 182 B5
Aird Argyll 275 C8
Dumfries 236 C2
Highld 299 B7
W Isles 296 F3
W Isles 304 E7
Airdachuilinn Highld 306 E7
Aird a Mhachair
W Isles 297 G3
Aird a' Mhulaidh
W Isles 305 G3
Aird Asaig W Isles 305 H3
Aird Dhail W Isles 304 B6
Airdens Highld 309 K6
Airdeny Argyll 289 G11
Aird Mhidhinis
W Isles 297 L3
Aird Mhighe
W Isles 296 C6
W Isles 305 J3
Aird Mhòr W Isles 297 G4
Aird Mhor W Isles 297 L3
Aird of Sleat Highld 295 E7
Airdrie N Lnrk 268 B5
Airds of Kells
Dumfries 237 B8
Aird Thunga
W Isles 304 E6
Airdtorrisdale
Highld 308 C6
Aird Uig W Isles 304 E2
Airedale W Yorks 198 B3
Aire View N Yorks 204 D5
Airidh a Bhruaich
W Isles 305 G4
Airieland Dumfries 237 D9
Airinis W Isles 304 E6
Airlie Angus 287 B7
Airlies Dumfries 236 D5
Airmyn E Yorks 199 B8
Airntully Perth 286 D4
Airor Highld 295 E9
Airth Falk 279 D7
Airthrey Castle Stirl 278 B6
Airton N Yorks 204 B4
Airyhassen Dumfries 236 E5
Airy Hill N Yorks 227 D7
Airyligg Dumfries 236 C4
Aisby Lincs 155 B10
Lincs 188 C5
Aisgernis W Isles 297 J3
Aish Devon 8 C3
Devon 8 D6
Aisholt Som 43 F7
Aiskew N Yorks 214 B5
Aislaby N Yorks 216 B5
N Yorks 227 D7
Stockton 225 C8
Aisthorpe Lincs 188 E6
Aith Orkney 314 E2
Shetland 312 D8
Shetland 313 H5
Aithnen Powys 148 E4
Aithsetter Shetland 313 K6
Aitkenhead S Ayrs 245 B8
Aitnoch Highld 301 F9
Akeld Northumb 263 D11
Akeley Bucks 102 D4
Akenham Suff 108 B2
Albany T&W 243 F7
Albaston Corn 12 G4
Alberbury Shrops 149 G7
Albert Town Pembs 72 B6
Albert Village Leics 152 F6
Albourne W Sus 36 D3
Albourne Green
W Sus 36 D3
Albrighton Shrops 132 C6
Shrops 149 F9
Albro Castle Ceredig 92 B3
Alburgh Norf 142 F5
Albury Herts 105 G8
Sur 50 D5
Albury End Herts 105 G8
Albury Heath Sur 50 D5
Albyfield Cumb 240 G2
Alby Hill Norf 160 C3
Alcaig Highld 300 D5
Alcaston Shrops 131 F9
Alcester Dorset 30 C5
Warks 117 F11
Alcester Lane's End
W Mid 133 G11
Alciston E Sus 23 D8
Alcombe Som 42 D3
Wilts 61 F10
Alconbury Cambs 122 B3
Alconbury Weston
Cambs 122 B3
Aldbar Castle Angus 287 B9
Aldborough Norf 160 C3
N Yorks 215 F8
Aldborough Hatch
London 68 B3
Aldbourne Wilts 63 D9
Aldbrough E Yorks 209 F10
Aldbrough St John
N Yorks 224 C4
Aldbury Herts 85 C7
Aldcliffe Lancs 211 G9
Aldclune Perth 291 G11
Aldeburgh Suff 127 F9
Aldeby Norf 143 E8
Aldenham Herts 85 F10
Alderbrook E Sus 37 B8
Alderbury Wilts 31 B11
Aldercar Derbys 170 F6
Alderford Norf 160 F2
Alder Forest
Gtr Man 184 B3
Alderholt Dorset 31 E10
Alderley Glos 80 G3
Alderley Edge
Ches E 184 F4
Alderman's Green
W Mid 135 G7
Aldermaston
W Berks 64 F5
Aldermaston Soke
W Berks 64 G6
Aldermaston Wharf
W Berks 64 F6
Alderminster Warks 100 B4

Warks 117 C11
Aspull Gtr Man 194 F6
Aspult Common
Gtr Man 183 B10
Assater Shetland 312 F4
Asselby E Yorks 199 B8
Asserby Lincs 191 F7
Asserby Turn Lincs 191 F7
Assington Suff 107 D8
Assington Green
Suff 124 G5
Assynt Ho Highld 300 C5
Astbury Ches E 168 C4
Astcote Northants 120 G3
Asterby Lincs 190 F3
Asterley Shrops 131 B7
Asterton Shrops 131 E7
Asthall Oxon 82 C3
Asthall Leigh Oxon 82 C4
Astle Ches E 184 G4
Highld 309 K7
Astley Gtr Man 195 G8
Shrops 149 F10
Warks 134 F6
Worcs 116 D5
Astley Abbotts
Shrops 132 D4
Astley Bridge
Gtr Man 195 E8
Astley Cross Worcs 116 D6
Astley Green
Gtr Man 184 B2
Astmoor Halton 183 E8
Aston Ches E 167 F10
Ches W 183 F9
Derbys 152 C3
Derbys 185 E11
Flint 166 B4
Hereford 115 C9
Hereford 115 E9
Herts 104 G5
Oxon 82 E4
Powys 130 E5
Shrops 132 E6
Shrops 149 D10
Staffs 151 E7
Staffs 168 G3
S Yorks 187 D7
Telford 132 B2
W Mid 133 F11
Wokingham 65 C9
Aston Abbotts
Bucks 102 G6
Aston Bank Worcs 116 C2
Aston Botterell
Shrops 132 G2
Aston-by-Stone
Staffs 151 C8
Aston Cantlow
Warks 118 F2
Aston Clinton Bucks 84 C5
Aston Crews
Hereford 98 G3
Aston Cross Glos 99 E8
Aston End Herts 104 G5
Aston Eyre Shrops 132 E3
Aston Fields Worcs 117 D9
Aston Flamville
Leics 135 E9
Aston Ingham
Hereford 98 G3
Aston juxta Mondrum
Ches E 167 D11
Aston le Walls
Northants 119 G9
Aston Magna Glos 100 D3
Aston Munslow
Shrops 131 F10
Aston on Carrant
Glos 99 E8
Aston on Clun
Shrops 131 G7
Aston-on-Trent
Derbys 153 D8
Aston Pigott Shrops 130 B6
Aston Rogers
Shrops 130 B6
Aston Rowant Oxon 84 F2
Aston Sandford
Bucks 84 D3
Aston Somerville
Worcs 99 D10
Aston Square
Shrops 148 D6
Aston Subedge
Glos 100 C2
Aston Tirrold Oxon 64 B5
Aston Upthorpe Oxon 64 B5
Astrop Northants 101 D10
Astrope Herts 84 C5
Astwick C Beds 104 D4
Astwith Derbys 170 C6
Astwood M Keynes 103 B9
Worcs 117 D8
Worcs 117 F7
Astwood Bank
Worcs 117 E10
Aswarby Lincs 173 G9
Aswardby Lincs 190 G5
Atcham Shrops 131 B10
Atch Lench Worcs 117 G10
Athelhampton
Dorset 17 C11
Athelington Suff 126 C4
Athelney Som 28 B4
Athelstaneford
E Loth 281 F10
Atherfield Green
IoW 20 F5
Atherington Devon 25 C9
W Sus 35 G8
Athersley North
S Yorks 197 F11
Athersley South
S Yorks 197 F11
Atherstone Som 28 D5
Warks 134 D6
Atherstone on Stour
Warks 118 G4
Atherton Gtr Man 195 G7
Athnamulloch
Highld 299 G11
Athron Hall Perth 286 G4
Atley Hill N Yorks 224 E5
Atlow Derbys 170 F2
Attadale Highld 295 B11
Attadale Ho Highld 295 B11
Attenborough
Notts 153 B10
Atterbury M Keynes 103 D7
Atterby Lincs 189 C7
Attercliffe S Yorks 186 D5
Atterley Shrops 132 D2
Atterton Leics 135 D7
Attleborough Norf 141 D10
Warks 135 E7
Attlebridge Norf 160 F2
Attleton Green Suff 124 G4
Atwick E Yorks 209 C9
Atworth Wilts 61 F11
Auberrow Hereford 97 B9
Aubourn Lincs 172 C6
Auch Argyll 285 D7
Auchagallon
N Ayrs 255 D9
Auchallater Aberds 292 E3
Auchareoch
N Ayrs 255 E10
Aucharnie Aberds 302 E6
Auchattie Aberds 293 D8
Auchavan Angus 292 G3
Auchbreck Moray 302 G2
Auchenback
E Renf 267 D10
Auchenbainzie
Dumfries 247 D8
Auchenblae Aberds 293 F9
Auchenbrack
Dumfries 247 D7
Auchenbreck Argyll 255 C8
Argyll 275 E11
Auchencairn
Dumfries 237 D9
Dumfries 247 G11
N Ayrs 256 D2
Auchencairn Ho
Dumfries 237 D10
Auchencar N Ayrs 255 D9
Auchencarroch
W Dunb 277 E8
Auchencrosh
S Ayrs 236 B3
Auchencrow
Borders 273 C7
Auchendinny
Midloth 270 C5
Auchengray S Lnrk 269 E9
Auchenhalrig Moray 302 C3
Auchenharvie
N Ayrs 266 G5
Auchenheath S Lnrk 268 G6
Auchenhew N Ayrs 256 E2
Auchenlaich Stirl 285 G10
Auchenleck
Dumfries 237 D9
Auchenlochan
Argyll 275 F10
Auchenmalg
Dumfries 236 D4
Auchenreoch
E Dunb 278 F3
Auchensoul S Ayrs 245 E7
Auchentibber S Lnrk 268 E3
Auchentiber N Ayrs 267 F7
Auchertyre Highld 295 C10
Auchessan Stirl 285 E8
Auchgourish
Highld 291 B11
Auchinairn E Dunb 268 B2
Auchindrain Argyll 284 G4
Auchindrean Highld 307 L6
Auchininna Aberds 302 E6
Auchinleck Dumfries 236 B6
E Ayrs 258 E3
Auchinloch N Lnrk 278 G3
Auchinner Perth 285 F10
Auchinraith S Lnrk 268 D3
Auchinroath Moray 302 D2
Auchinstarry N Lnrk 278 F4
Auchintoul Aberds 293 B7
Highld 309 K5
Auchiries Aberds 303 F10
Auchlee Aberds 293 D10
Auchleeks Ho Perth 291 G9
Auchleven Aberds 302 G6
Auchlinn Aberds 303 D7
Auchlochan S Lnrk 259 B8
Auchlossan Aberds 293 C7
Auchlunachan
Highld 307 L6
Auchlunies Aberds 293 D10
Auchlyne Stirl 285 E9
Auchmacoy Aberds 303 F9
Auchmair Moray 302 G3
Auchmantle
Dumfries 236 C3
Auchmenzie Aberds 302 G5
Auchmillan E Ayrs 258 D2
Auchmithie Angus 287 C10
Auchmore Highld 300 D4
Auchmuirbridge
Fife 286 G6
Auchmull Angus 293 F7
Auchnacraig Argyll 289 G9
Auchnacree Angus 292 G6
Auchnafree Perth 286 D2
Auchnagallin
Highld 301 F10
Auchnagarron
Argyll 275 E11
Auchnagatt Aberds 303 E9
Auchnaha Argyll 275 E10
Auchnahillin Highld 301 F7
Auchnarrow Moray 302 G2
Auchnashelloch
Perth 285 F11
Auchnotteroch
Dumfries 236 C1
Aucholzie Aberds 292 D5
Auchrannie Angus 286 B6
Auchroisk Highld 301 G10
Auchronie Angus 292 E6
Auchterarder Perth 286 F3
Auchteraw Highld 290 C5
Auchterderran Fife 280 B4
Auchterhouse
Angus 287 D7
Auchtermuchty Fife 286 F6
Auchterneed Highld 300 D4
Auchtertool Fife 280 C4
Auchtertyre Moray 301 D11
Stirl 285 E7
Auchtubh Stirl 285 E9
Auckengill Highld 310 C7
Auckley S Yorks 199 G7
Audenshaw
Gtr Man 184 B6
Audlem Ches E 167 G11
Audley Staffs 168 E3
Audley End Essex 105 D10
Essex 106 D6
Norf 142 G2
Suff 125 G7
Auds Aberds 302 C6
Aughertree Cumb 229 D11
Aughton E Yorks 207 F10
Lancs 193 F11
Lancs 211 F10
S Yorks 187 D7
Wilts 47 B8
Aughton Park Lancs 194 F2
Aukside Durham 232 F4
Auldearn Highld 301 D9
Aulden Hereford 115 G9
Auldgirth Dumfries 247 F10
Auldhame E Loth 281 E11
Auldhouse S Lnrk 268 E2
Auldtown of Carnoustie
Aberds 302 E6
Ault a'chruinn
Highld 295 C11
Aultanrynie Highld 308 F3
Aultbea Highld 307 L3
Aultdearg Highld 300 C2
Aultgrishan Highld 307 L2
Aultguish Inn Highld 300 B3
Ault Hucknall
Derbys 171 B7
Aultibea Highld 311 G4
Aultiphurst Highld 310 C2
Aultivullin Highld 310 C2
Aultmore Highld 301 G10
Moray 302 D4
Aultnagoire Highld 300 G5
Aultnamain Inn
Highld 309 L6
Aultnaslat Highld 290 C3
Aulton Aberds 302 G6
Aulton of Atherb
Aberds 303 E9
Aultvaich Highld 300 E5
Aunby Lincs 155 G10
Aundorach Highld 291 B11
Aunk Devon 27 G8
Aunsby Lincs 155 B10
Auquhorthies
Aberds 303 G8
Aust S Glos 60 B5
Austendike Lincs 156 E5
Austen Fen Lincs 190 C5
Austenwood Bucks 66 B3
Austerfield
S Yorks 187 C11
Austerlands
Gtr Man 196 F3
Austhorpe W Yorks 206 G3
Austrey Warks 134 B5
Austwick N Yorks 212 F5
Authorpe Lincs 190 E6
Authorpe Row Lincs 191 G8
Avebury Wilts 62 F6
Avebury Trusloe
Wilts 62 F5
Aveley Thurrock 68 C5
Avening Glos 80 F5
Avening Green
S Glos 80 G2
Averham Notts 172 E3
Avernish Highld 295 C10
Avery Hill London 68 E2
Aveton Gifford Devon 8 F3
Avielochan Highld 291 B11
Aviemore Highld 291 B10
Avington Hants 48 G4
W Berks 63 F11
Avoch Highld 301 D7
Avon Hants 19 B8
Wilts 62 D3
Avonbridge Falk 279 G8
Avoncliff Wilts 45 B10
Avon Dassett Warks 101 B8
Avonmouth Bristol 60 D4
Avonwick Devon 8 D4
Awbridge Hants 32 C4
Awhirk Dumfries 236 D2
Awkley S Glos 60 B5
Awliscombe Devon 27 G10
Awre Glos 80 D2
Awsworth Notts 171 G7
Axbridge Som 44 C2
Axford Hants 48 E6
Wilts 63 F8
Axmansford Hants 64 G5
Axminster Devon 15 B11
Axmouth Devon 15 C11
Axton Flint 181 E10
Axtown Devon 7 B10
Axwell Park T&W 242 E5
Aycliff Kent 55 E10
Aycliffe Durham 233 G11
Aydon Northumb 242 D2
Aykley Heads
Durham 233 C11
Aylburton Glos 79 E10
Aylburton Common
Glos 79 E10
Ayle Northumb 231 B10
Aylesbeare Devon 14 C6
Aylesbury Bucks 84 C4
Aylesby NE Lincs 201 F8
Aylesford Kent 53 B8
Aylesham Kent 55 C8
Aylestone Leicester 135 C11
Aylestone Hill
Hereford 97 C10
Aylestone Park
Leicester 135 C11
Aylmerton Norf 160 B3
Aylsham Norf 160 D3
Aylton Hereford 98 D3
Aylworth Glos 100 G2
Aymestrey Hereford 115 D8
Aynho Northants 101 E10
Ayot Green Herts 86 C2
Ayot St Lawrence
Herts 85 B11
Ayot St Peter Herts 86 B2
Ayr S Ayrs 257 E8
Ayre of Atler
Shetland 313 G6
Ayres Shetland 313 H5
Ayres End Herts 85 C11
Ayres of Selivoe
Shetland 313 J4
Ayres Quay T&W 243 F9
Aysgarth N Yorks 213 B10
Ayshford Devon 27 D8
Ayside Cumb 211 C7
Ayston Rutland 137 C7
Aythorpe Roding
Essex 87 B9
Ayton Borders 273 C8
T&W 243 F7
Ayton Castle
Borders 273 C8
Aywick Shetland 312 E7
Azerley N Yorks 214 E5

B

Babbacombe Torbay 9 B8
Babbington Notts 171 G7
Babbinswood
Shrops 148 C6
Babbs Green Herts 86 B5
Babcary Som 29 B9
Babel Carms 94 D6
Babel Green Suff 106 B4
Babell Flint 181 G11
Babeny Devon 13 F9
Babingley Norf 158 D3
Babraham Cambs 123 G10
Babworth Notts 187 E11
Bac W Isles 304 D6
Bachau Anglesey 178 E6
Bache Shrops 131 G9
Bacheldre Powys 130 E4
Bachelor's Bump
E Sus 38 E4
Bache Mill Shrops 131 F10
Bach-y-gwreiddyn
Swansea 75 E10
Backaland Orkney 314 C5
Backaskaill Orkney 314 A4
Backbarrow Cumb 211 C7
Backbower Gtr Man 185 C7
Backburn Aberds 293 D10
Backe Carms 74 B3
Backfolds Aberds 303 D10
Backford Ches W 182 G6
Backford Cross
Ches W 182 G5
Backhill Aberds 303 F7
Aberds 303 F10
Backhill of Clackriach
Aberds 303 E9
Backhill of Fortree
Aberds 303 E9
Backhill of Trustach
Aberds 293 D8
Backies Highld 311 J2
Backlass Highld 310 D6
Highld 310 E4
Back Muir Fife 279 D11
Back of Keppoch
Highld 295 G8
Back o' th' Brook
Staffs 169 E9
Back Rogerton
E Ayrs 258 E3
Back Street Suff 124 F4
Backwell N Som 60 F3
Backwell Common
N Som 60 F3
Backwell Green
N Som 60 F3
Backworth T&W 243 C8
Bacon End Essex 87 B10
Baconend Green
Essex 87 B10
Bacon's End W Mid 134 F3
Baconsthorpe Norf 160 B2
Bacton Hereford 97 E7
Norf 160 C6
Suff 125 D11
Bacton Green Norf 160 C6
Suff 125 D10
Bacup Lancs 195 C11
Badachonacher
Highld 300 B6
Badachro Highld 299 B7
Badanloch Lodge
Highld 308 F7
Badarach Highld 309 K5
Badavanich Highld 299 D11
Badbea Highld 307 K5
Badbury Swindon 63 C7
Badbury Wick
Swindon 63 C7
Badby Northants 119 F11
Badcall Highld 306 D7
Badcaul Highld 307 K5
Baddeley Edge
Stoke 168 E6
Baddeley Green
Stoke 168 E6
Baddesley Clinton
Warks 118 C4
Baddesley Ensor
Warks 134 D5
Baddidarach Highld 307 G5
Baddoch Aberds 292 E3
Baddock Highld 301 D7
Baddow Park Essex 88 E2
Badeach Moray 302 F2
Badenscallie Highld 307 J5
Badenscoth Aberds 303 F7
Badentoy Park
Aberds 293 D11
Badenyon Aberds 292 B5
Badgall Corn 11 D10
Badgeney Cambs 139 D8
Badger Shrops 132 D5
Badgergate Stirl 278 B5
Badger's Hill Worcs 99 B10
Badger's Mount Kent 68 G3
Badger Street Som 28 D3
Badgeworth Glos 80 B6
Badgworth Som 43 C11
Badharlick Corn 11 D11
Badicaul Highld 295 C9
Badingham Suff 126 D6
Badintagairt Highld 309 H4
Badlesmere Kent 54 C4
Badlipster Highld 310 E6
Badluarach Highld 307 K4
Badminton S Glos 61 C10
Badnaban Highld 307 G5
Badnabay Highld 306 E7
Badnagie Highld 310 F5
Badninish Highld 309 K7
Badrallach Highld 307 K5
Badsey Worcs 99 C11
Badshalloch
W Dunb 277 D9
Badshot Lea Sur 49 D11
Badsworth W Yorks 198 E3
Badwell Ash Suff 125 D9
Badwell Green
Suff 125 D10
Badworthy Devon 8 C3
Bae Cinmel/
Kinmel Bay Conwy 181 E7
Bae Colwyn/
Colwyn Bay Conwy 180 F4
Bae Penrhyn/
Penrhyn Bay Conwy 180 E4
Baffins Ptsmth 33 G11
Bagber Dorset 30 E3
Bagby N Yorks 215 C9
Bagby Grange
N Yorks 215 C9
Bag Enderby Lincs 190 G5
Bagendon Glos 81 D8
Bagginswood
Shrops 132 G3
Baggrow Cumb 229 C9
Bàgha Chàise
W Isles 296 D5
Bagh a Chaisteil
W Isles 297 M2
Bagham Kent 54 C5
Baghasdal W Isles 297 K3
Bagh Mor W Isles 296 F4
Bagh Shiarabhagh
W Isles 297 L3
Bagillt Flint 182 F2
Baginton Warks 118 C6
Baglan Neath 57 C8
Bagley Shrops 149 D8
Som 44 D3
W Yorks 205 F10
Bagley Green Som 27 D10
Bagley Marsh
Shrops 149 D7
Bagmore Hants 49 E7
Bagnall Staffs 168 E6
Bagnor W Berks 64 F3
Bagpath Glos 80 E5
Glos 80 G4
Bagshaw Derbys 185 E9
Bagshot Sur 66 G2
Wilts 63 F10
Bagshot Heath Sur 66 G2
Bagslate Moor
Gtr Man 195 E11
Bagstone S Glos 61 B7
Bagthorpe Norf 158 C5
Notts 171 E7
Baguley Gtr Man 184 D4
Bagworth Leics 135 B8
Bagwyllydiart
Hereford 97 F8
Bagwy Llydiart
Hereford 97 F8
Bail Àrd Bhuirgh
W Isles 304 C6
Bailbrook Bath 61 F9
Baildon W Yorks 205 F9
Baildon Green
W Yorks 205 F8
Baile W Isles 296 C5
Baile Ailein W Isles 304 F4
Baile a Mhanaich
W Isles 296 F3
Baile an Truiseil
W Isles 304 C5
Bailebeag Highld 291 B7
Baile Boidheach
Argyll 275 F8
Baile Gharbhaidh
W Isles 297 G3
Baile Glas W Isles 296 F4
Baile Mhartainn
W Isles 296 D3
Baile Mhic Phail
W Isles 296 D4
Baile Mor Argyll 288 G4
W Isles 296 E3
Baile na Creige
W Isles 297 L2
Baile nan Cailleach
W Isles 296 F3
Baile Raghaill
W Isles 296 D3
Bailey Green Hants 33 B11
Baileyhead Cumb 240 B2
Bailiesward Aberds 302 F4
Bailiff Bridge
W Yorks 196 C6
Baillieston Glasgow 268 C3
Bail' lochdrach
W Isles 296 F4
Bailrigg Lancs 202 B5
Bail Uachdraich
W Isles 296 E4
Bail' Ur Tholastaidh
W Isles 304 D7
Bainbridge N Yorks 223 G8
Bainsford Falk 279 E7
Bainshole Aberds 302 F6
Bainton E Yorks 208 C5
Oxon 101 F11
Pboro 137 B11
Baintown Fife 287 G7
Bairnkine Borders 262 F5
Baker's Cross Kent 53 F9
Bakers End Herts 86 B5
Baker's Hill Glos 79 C9
Baker Street
Thurrock 68 C6
Baker's Wood Bucks 66 B4
Bakesdown Corn 24 G2
Bakestone Moor
Derbys 187 F8
Bakewell Derbys 170 B2
Balachroick Highld 291 C10
Balachuirn Highld 298 E5
Balance Hill Staffs 151 C11
Balavil Highld 291 C9
Balavoulin Perth 291 G10
Bala/Y Bala Gwyn 147 B8
Balbeg Highld 300 F4
Highld 300 G4
Balbeggie Perth 286 E5
Balbegno Castle
Aberds 293 F8
Balbithan Aberds 293 B9
Balbithan Ho
Aberds 293 B10
Balblair Highld 300 E5
Highld 301 C7
Highld 309 K5
Balby S Yorks 198 G5
Balcherry Highld 311 L2
Balchladich Highld 306 F5
Balchraggan Highld 300 E5
Highld 300 F5
Highld 300 G5
Balchrick Highld 306 D6
Balchrystie Fife 287 G8
Balcladaich Highld 300 G2
Balcombe W Sus 51 G10
Balcombe Lane
W Sus 51 G10
Balcomie Fife 287 F10
Balcraggie Lodge
Highld 310 F5
Balcurvie Fife 287 G7
Baldersby N Yorks 215 D7
Baldersby St James
N Yorks 215 D7
Balderstone
Gtr Man 196 E2
Lancs 203 G8
Balderton Ches W 166 C5
Notts 172 E4
Baldhu Corn 4 G5
Baldingstone
Gtr Man 195 E10
Baldinnie Fife 287 F8
Baldock Herts 104 E4
Baldon Row Oxon 83 E9
Baldoon Highld 300 B6
Baldovie Dundee 287 D8
Baldrine IoM 192 D5
Baldslow E Sus 38 E3
Baldwin IoM 192 D4
Baldwinholme
Cumb 239 G8
Baldwin's Gate
Staffs 168 G3
Baldwins Hill W Sus 51 F11
Bale Norf 159 B10
Balearn Aberds 303 D10
Balemartine Argyll 288 E1
Balephuil Argyll 288 E1
Balerno Edin 270 B3
Balerominhor Argyll 274 D4
Balevullin Argyll 288 E1
Balfield Angus 293 G7
Balfour Orkney 314 E4
Balfour Mains
Orkney 314 E4
Balfron Stirl 277 D10
Balfron Station
Stirl 277 D10
Balgaveny Aberds 302 E6
Balgavies Angus 287 B9
Balgonar Fife 279 C10
Balgove Aberds 303 F8
Balgowan Highld 291 D8
Perth 286 E3
Balgown Highld 298 C3
Balgrennie Aberds 292 C6
Balgrochan E Dunb 278 F2
Balgy Highld 299 D8
Balhaldie Stirl 286 G2
Balhalgardy Aberds 303 G7
Balham London 67 E9
Balhary Perth 286 C6
Baliasta Shetland 312 C8
Baligill Highld 310 C2
Baligortan Argyll 288 E5
Baligrundle Argyll 289 E10
Balindore Argyll 289 F11
Balinoe Argyll 288 E1
Balintore Angus 286 B6
Highld 301 B8
Balintraid Highld 301 B7
Balintuim Aberds 292 E3
Balk N Yorks 215 C9
Balkeerie Angus 287 C7
Balkemback Angus 287 D7
Balk Field Notts 188 E2
Balkholme E Yorks 199 B9
Balkissock S Ayrs 244 G4
Ball Corn 10 G6
Shrops 148 D6
Ballabeg IoM 192 E3
Ballacannel IoM 192 D5
Ballachraggan
Moray 301 E11
Ballachrochin
Highld 301 F8
Ballachulish Highld 284 B4
Balladen Lancs 195 C10
Ballajora IoM 192 C5
Ballaleigh IoM 192 D4
Ballamodha IoM 192 E3
Ballantrae S Ayrs 244 G3
Ballaquine IoM 192 D5
Ballard's Ash Wilts 62 C5
Ballards Gore Essex 88 G6
Ballard's Green
Warks 134 E5
Ballasalla IoM 192 C4
IoM 192 E3
Ballater Aberds 292 D5
Ballathie Perth 286 D5
Ballaugh IoM 192 C4
Ballaveare IoM 192 E4
Ballcorach Moray 301 G11
Ballechin Perth 286 B3
Balleich Stirl 277 B10
Balleigh Highld 309 L7
Ballencrieff E Loth 281 F9
Ballencrieff Toll
W Loth 279 G9
Ballentoul Perth 291 G10
Ball Green Stoke 168 E5
Ball Haye Green
Staffs 169 D7
Ballhill Devon 24 C3
Ball Hill Hants 64 G2
Ballidon Derbys 170 E2
Balliekine N Ayrs 255 D9
Balliemore Argyll 275 E11
Argyll 289 G10
Ballikinrain Stirl 277 D11
Ballimeanoch Argyll 284 F4
Ballimore Argyll 275 E10
Stirl 285 F9
Ballinaby Argyll 274 G3
Ballinbreich Fife 286 E6
Ballindean Perth 286 E6
Ballingdon Suff 107 C7
Ballingdon Bottom
Herts 85 C8
Ballinger Bottom
Bucks 84 E6
Ballinger Bottom
(South) Bucks 84 E6
Ballinger Common
Bucks 84 E6
Ballingham Hereford 97 E11
Ballingham Hill
Hereford 97 E11
Ballingry Fife 280 B3
Ballinlick Perth 286 C3
Ballinluig Perth 286 B3
Ballintean Highld 291 C10
Ballintuim Perth 286 B5
Balliveolan Argyll 289 E10
Balloch Angus 287 B7
Highld 301 E7
N Lnrk 278 G4
W Dunb 277 E7
Ballochan Aberds 293 D7
Ballochearn Stirl 277 D11
Ballochford Moray 302 F3
Ballochmorrie
S Ayrs 244 G6
Ball o'Ditton Halton 183 D7
Ballogie Aberds 293 D7
Balls Cross W Sus 35 B7
Balls Green Essex 107 G11
E Sus 52 F3
W Sus 35 C10
Ball's Green Glos 80 F5
Balls Hill W Mid 133 E9
Ballygown Argyll 288 E6
Ballygrant Argyll 274 G4
Ballygroggan Argyll 255 F7
Ballyhaugh Argyll 288 D3
Balmacara Highld 295 C10
Balmacara Square
Highld 295 C10
Balmaclellan
Dumfries 237 B8
Balmacneil Perth 286 B3
Balmacqueen
Highld 298 B4
Balmae Dumfries 237 E8
Balmaha Stirl 277 C8
Balmalcolm Fife 287 G7
Balmalloch N Lnrk 278 F4
Balmeanach Argyll 288 F6
Argyll 289 E8
Highld 295 B7
Highld 298 E3
Highld 298 E5
Balmedie Aberds 293 B11
Balmer Shrops 149 C8
Balmer Heath
Shrops 149 C8
Balmerino Fife 287 E7
Balmerlawn Hants 32 G4
Balmesh Dumfries 236 D3
Balmichael N Ayrs 255 D10
Balminnoch
Dumfries 236 C4
Balmirmer Angus 287 D9
Balmoral Borders 261 B11
Balmore E Dunb 278 G2
Highld 298 E2
Highld 300 F3
Highld 301 E8
Perth 286 B3
Balmule Fife 280 D4
Balmullo Fife 287 E8
Balmungie Highld 301 D7
Balmurrie Dumfries 236 C4
Balnaboth Angus 292 G5
Balnabreich Moray 302 D3
Balnabruaich Highld 301 C7
Balnabruich Highld 311 G5
Balnacarn Highld 290 B4
Balnacoil Highld 311 H2
Balnacra Highld 299 E9
Balnacruie Highld 301 G9
Balnafoich Highld 300 F6
Balnagall Highld 311 L2
Balnagowan Aberds 293 C7
Balnagrantach
Highld 300 F4
Balnaguard Perth 286 B3
Balnahanaid Perth 285 C10
Balnahard Argyll 274 D5
Argyll 288 F6
Balnain Highld 300 F4
Balnakeil Highld 308 C3
Balnakelly Aberds 293 B7
Balnaknock Highld 298 C4
Balnamoon Aberds 303 D9
Angus 293 G7
Balnapaling Highld 301 C7
Balne N Yorks 198 D5
Balnoon Corn 2 B2
Balochroy Argyll 255 B8
Balole Argyll 274 G4
Balone Fife 287 F8
Balornock Glasgow 268 B2
Balquharn Perth 286 D4
Balquhidder Stirl 285 E9
Balquhidder Station
Stirl 285 E9
Balquhindachy
Aberds 303 E8
Balrownie Angus 293 G7
Balsall W Mid 118 B4
Balsall Common
W Mid 118 B4
Balsall Heath
W Mid 133 G11
Balsall Street
W Mid 118 B4
Balsam Cambs 123 G11
Balscote Oxon 101 C7
Balscott Oxon 101 C7
Balsham Cambs 123 G11
Balsporran Cottages
Highld 291 F8
Balstonia Thurrock 69 C7
Baltasound Shetland 312 C8
Balterley Staffs 168 E3
Balterley Green
Staffs 168 E3
Balterley Heath
Staffs 168 E2
Baltersan Dumfries 236 C6
Balthangie Aberds 303 D8
Balthayock Perth 286 E5
Baltonsborough Som 44 G4
Balure Argyll 289 E11
Balvaird Highld 300 D5
Balvenie Moray 302 E3
Balvicar Argyll 275 B8
Balvraid Highld 295 D10
Highld 301 F8
Balwest Corn 2 C3
Bamber Bridge
Lancs 194 B5
Bamber's Green
Essex 105 G11
Bamburgh Northumb 264 C5
Bamff Perth 286 B6
Bamford Derbys 186 E2
Gtr Man 195 E11
Bamfurlong Glos 99 G8
Gtr Man 194 G5
Bampton Cumb 221 B10
Devon 27 C7
Oxon 82 E4
Bampton Grange
Cumb 221 B10
Banavie Highld 290 F3
Banbury Oxon 101 C9
Bancffosfelen Carms 75 C7
Banchor Highld 301 E9
Banchory Aberds 293 D8
Banchory-Devenick
Aberds 293 C11
Bancycapel Carms 74 B6
Banc-y-Darren
Ceredig 128 G3
Bancyfelin Carms 74 B4
Bancyffordd Carms 93 D8
Bandirran Perth 286 D6
Bandonhill London 67 G9
Bandrake Head
Cumb 210 B6
Banff Aberds 302 C6
Bangor Gwyn 179 G9
Bangor is y coed /
Bangor on Dee
Wrex 166 F5
Bangor on Dee / Bangor-
is-y-coed Wrex 166 F5
Bangors Corn 11 B10
Bangor Teifi Ceredig 93 C7
Banham Norf 141 F11
Bank Hants 32 F3
Bankend Dumfries 238 D2
Bank End Cumb 210 B3
Cumb 228 D6
Bank Fold Blkburn 195 C8
Bankfoot Perth 286 D4
Bankglen E Ayrs 258 G4
Bankhead
Aberdeen 293 B10
Aberds 293 C8
Dumfries 236 C2
Falk 278 E6
S Lnrk 269 G7
Bank Hey Blkburn 203 G9
Bank Houses Lancs 202 C4
Bankland Som 28 B4
Bank Lane Gtr Man 195 D9
Bank Newton
N Yorks 204 C4
Banknock Falk 278 F5
Banks Cumb 240 E3
Lancs 193 C11
Orkney 314 C4
Bank's Green Worcs 117 D9
Bankshead Shrops 130 F6
Bankshill Dumfries 248 G5
Bankside Falk 279 E7
Bank Street Worcs 116 E2
Bank Top Gtr Man 195 E8
Lancs 194 F4
Stoke 168 E5
T&W 242 D4
W Yorks 196 C6
W Yorks 205 F9
Banners Gate
W Mid 133 D11
Banningham Norf 160 D4
Banniskirk Ho
Highld 310 D5
Banniskirk Mains
Highld 310 D5
Bannister Green
Essex 106 G3
Bannockburn Stirl 278 C5
Banns Corn 4 F4
Banstead Sur 51 B8
Bantam Grove
W Yorks 197 B9
Bantaskin Falk 279 F7
Bantham Devon 8 G3
Banton N Lnrk 278 F5
Banwell N Som 43 B11
Banyard's Green
Suff 126 C5
Bapchild Kent 70 G2
Baptist End W Mid 133 F8
Bapton Wilts 46 F3
Barabhas W Isles 304 D5
Barabhas Iarach
W Isles 304 D5
Barabhas Uarach
W Isles 304 C5
Barachandroman
Argyll 289 G8
Baramore Highld 289 B8
Barassie S Ayrs 257 C8
Baravullin Argyll 289 F10
Barbadoes Stirl 277 B11
Barbaraville Highld 301 B7
Barbauchlaw
W Loth 269 B8
Barber Booth
Derbys 185 E10
Barber Green Cumb 211 C7
Barber's Moor
Lancs 194 D3
Barbican Plym 7 E9
Barbieston S Ayrs 257 F10
Barbon Cumb 212 C2
Barbourne Worcs 116 F6

370 Bar–Ber

Barbreck Ho Argyll 275 C9
Barbridge Ches E 167 D10
Barbrook Devon 41 D8
Barby Northants 119 C10
Barby Nortoft Northants 119 C11
Barcaldine Argyll 289 E11
Barcelona Corn 6 E4
Barcheston Warks 100 D5
Barclose Cumb 239 E10
Barcombe E Sus 36 E6
Barcombe Cross E Sus 36 D6
Barcroft W Yorks 204 F6
Barden N Yorks 224 G2
Bardennoch Dumfries 246 E3
Barden Park Kent 52 D5
Barden Scale N Yorks 205 B7
Bardfield End Green Essex 106 E2
Bardfield Saling Essex 106 F3
Bardister Shetland 312 F5
Bardnabeinne Highld 309 K7
Bardney Lincs 173 B10
Bardon Leics 153 G8
Bardon Mill Northumb 241 E7
Bardowie E Dunb 277 G11
Bardown E Sus 37 B11
Bardrainney Invclyd 276 G6
Bardrishaig Argyll 275 B8
Bardsea Cumb 210 E6
Bardsey W Yorks 206 E3
Bardsley Gtr Man 196 G2
Bardwell Suff 125 C8
Bare Lancs 211 G9
Bare Ash Som 43 F9
Bareless Northumb 263 B9
Bar End Hants 33 B7
Barepot Cumb 228 F6
Bareppa Corn 3 D7
Barfad Argyll 275 G9
Dumfries 236 C5
Barford Norf 142 B2
Sur 49 F11
Warks 118 E5
Barford St John Oxon 101 E8
Barford St Martin Wilts 46 G5
Barford St Michael Oxon 101 E8
Barfrestone Kent 55 C9
Bargaly Dumfries 236 C6
Bargarran Renfs 277 G9
Bargate Derbys 170 F5
Bargeddie N Lnrk 268 C4
Bargoed Caerph 77 F10
Bargrennan Dumfries 236 B5
Barham Cambs 122 B2
Kent 55 C8
Suff 126 G2
Barharrow Dumfries 237 D8
Barhill Dumfries 237 C10
Bar Hill Cambs 123 E7
Staffs 168 G3
Barholm Dumfries 237 D7
Lincs 155 G11
Barkby Leics 136 B2
Barkby Thorpe Leics 136 B2
Barkers Green Shrops 149 D10
Barkers Hill Wilts 30 B6
Barkestone-le-Vale Leics 154 C5
Barkham Wokingham 65 F9
Barking London 68 C2
Suff 125 G11
Barkingside London 68 B2
Barking Tye Suff 125 G11
Barkisland W Yorks 196 D5
Barkla Shop Corn 4 E4
Barkston Lincs 172 G6
N Yorks 206 F5
Barkston Ash N Yorks 206 F5
Barkway Herts 105 D7
Barlake Som 45 D7
Barlanark Glasgow 268 C3
Barland Powys 114 E5
Barland Common Swansea 56 D5
Barlaston Staffs 151 B7
Barlavington W Sus 35 D7
Barlborough Derbys 187 F7
Barlby N Yorks 207 G8
Barlestone Leics 135 B8
Barley Herts 105 D7
Lancs 204 E2
Barleycroft End Herts 105 F8
Barley End Bucks 85 C7
Barley Green Lancs 204 E2
Barley Mow T&W 243 G7
Barleythorpe Rutland 136 B6
Barling Essex 70 B2
Barlings Lincs 189 G9
Barlow Derbys 186 G4
N Yorks 198 B6
T&W 242 E5
Barlow Moor Gtr Man 184 C4
Barmby Moor E Yorks 207 D11
Barmby on the Marsh E Yorks 199 B7
Barmer Norf 158 C6
Barming Heath Kent 53 B8
Barmolloch Argyll 275 D9
Bar Moor T&W 242 E4
Barmoor Castle Northumb 263 B11
Barmoor Lane End Northumb 264 B2
Barmouth / Abermaw Gwyn 146 F2
Barmpton Darl 224 B6
Barmston E Yorks 209 B9
T&W 243 F8
Barmulloch Glasgow 268 B2
Barnaby Green Suff 127 B9
Barnacabber Argyll 276 D3
Barnack Pboro 137 B11
Barnacle Warks 135 G7
Barnaline Argyll 275 B10
Barnard Castle Durham 223 B11
Barnard Gate Oxon 82 C6
Barnardiston Suff 106 B4
Barnard's Green Worcs 98 B5
Barnardtown Newport 59 B10
Barnbarroch Dumfries 237 D10
Barnbow Carr W Yorks 206 F3
Barnburgh S Yorks 198 G3
Barnby Suff 143 F9
Barnby Dun S Yorks 198 F6
Barnby in the Willows Notts 172 E5
Barnby Moor Notts 187 E11
Barncluith S Lnrk 268 E4
Barndennoch Dumfries 247 F9
Barne Barton Plym 7 D8
Barnehurst London 68 D4
Barnes Cray London 68 D4
Barnes Hall S Yorks 186 B4
Barnes Street Kent 52 D6
Barnet London 86 F2
Barnetby le Wold N Lincs 200 F5
Barnet Gate London 86 F2
Barnettbrook Worcs 117 B7
Barnett Brook Ches E 167 G10
Barney Norf 159 C9
Barnfield Kent 54 D2
Barnfields Hereford 97 C9
Staffs 169 D7
Barnham Suff 125 B7
W Sus 35 G7
Barnham Broom Norf 141 B11
Barnhead Angus 287 B10
Barnhill Ches W 167 E7
Dundee 287 D8
Moray 301 D11
Barnhills Dumfries 236 B1
Barningham Durham 223 C11
Suff 125 B9
Barningham Green Norf 160 C2
Barnmoor Green Warks 118 E3
Barnoldby le Beck NE Lincs 201 G8
Barnoldswick Lancs 204 D3
N Yorks 212 E3
Barns Borders 260 B6
Barnsbury London 67 C10
Barnsdale Rutland 137 B8
Barns Green W Sus 35 B10
Barnside W Yorks 197 F7
Barnsley Glos 81 D9
Shrops 132 E5
S Yorks 197 F10
Barnsole Kent 55 B9
Barnstaple Devon 40 G5
Barnston Essex 87 B10
Mers 182 E3
Barnstone Notts 154 B4
Barnt Green Worcs 117 C10
Barnton Ches W 183 F10
Edin 280 F3
Barnwell Northants 137 G10
Barnwell All Saints Northants 137 G10
Barnwell St Andrew Northants 137 F10
Barnwood Glos 80 B5
Barochreal Argyll 289 G10
Barons Cross Hereford 115 F9
Barr Highld 289 D8
S Ayrs 245 E7
Som 27 C11
Barra Castle Aberds 303 G7
Barrachan Dumfries 236 E5
Barrachnie Glasgow 268 C3
Barrack Aberds 303 E8
Barrack Hill Newport 59 B10
Barraer Dumfries 236 C5
Barraglom W Isles 304 E3
Barrahormid Argyll 275 E8
Barran Argyll 289 G10
Barranrioch Argyll 289 G10
Barrapol Argyll 288 E1
Barras Aberds 293 E10
Cumb 222 C6
Barrasford Northumb 241 C10
Barravullin Argyll 275 C9
Barr Common W Mid 133 D11
Barregarrow IoM 192 D4
Barrets Green Ches E 167 D9
Barrhead E Renf 267 D9
Barrhill S Ayrs 244 G6
Barrington Cambs 105 B7
Som 28 D5
Barripper Corn 2 B4
Barrmill N Ayrs 267 E7
Barrock Highld 310 B6
Barrock Ho Highld 310 C6
Barrow Glos 99 G7
Lancs 203 F10
Rutland 155 F7
Shrops 132 C3
Som 44 E5
Suff 124 E5
S Yorks 186 B5
Barroway Drove Norf 139 C11
Barrow Bridge Gtr Man 195 E7
Barrowburn Northumb 263 G9
Barrow Burn Northumb 263 G9
Barrowby Lincs 155 B7
Barrowcliff N Yorks 217 B10
Barrow Common N Som 60 F4
Barrowden Rutland 137 C8
Barrowford Lancs 204 F3
Barrow Green Kent 70 G3
Barrow Gurney N Som 60 F4
Barrow Hann N Lincs 200 C5
Barrow Haven N Lincs 200 C5
Barrowhill Kent 54 F6
Barrow Hill Derbys 186 F6
Dorset 18 B5
Barrow-in-Furness Cumb 210 F4
Barrow Island Cumb 210 F3
Barrowmore Estate Ches W 167 B7
Barrow Nook Lancs 194 G2
Barrows Green Ches E 167 D11
Cumb 211 B10
Notts 171 E7
Barrow's Green Mers 183 D8
Barrow Street Wilts 45 G10
Barrow upon Humber N Lincs 200 C5
Barrow upon Soar Leics 153 F11
Barrow upon Trent Derbys 153 D7
Barrow Vale Bath 60 G6
Barrow Wake Glos 80 B6
Barry Angus 287 D9
V Glam 58 F6
Barry Dock V Glam 58 F6
Barry Island V Glam 58 F6
Barsby Leics 154 G3
Barsham Suff 143 F7
Barshare E Ayrs 258 F3
Barstable Essex 69 B8
Barston W Mid 118 B4
Bartestree Hereford 97 C11
Barthol Chapel Aberds 303 F8
Bartholomew Green Essex 106 G4
Barthomley Ches E 168 E3
Bartington Ches W 183 F10
Bartley Hants 32 E4
Bartley Green W Mid 133 G10
Bartlow Cambs 105 B11
Barton Cambs 123 F8
Ches W 166 E6
Glos 80 B4
Glos 99 F11
IoW 20 D6
Lancs 193 F11
Lancs 202 F6
N Som 43 B11
N Yorks 224 D4
Oxon 83 D9
Torbay 9 B8
Warks 118 G2
Barton Abbey Oxon 101 G9
Barton Bendish Norf 140 B4
Barton Court Hereford 98 C4
Barton End Glos 80 F4
Barton Gate Devon 41 E7
Staffs 152 F3
Barton Green Staffs 152 F3
Barton Hartshorn Bucks 102 E2
Barton Hill Bristol 60 E6
N Yorks 216 G4
Barton in Fabis Notts 153 C10
Barton in the Beans Leics 135 B7
Barton-le-Clay C Beds 103 E11
Barton-le-Street N Yorks 216 E4
Barton-le-Willows N Yorks 216 G4
Barton Mills Suff 124 C4
Barton on Sea Hants 19 C10
Barton on the Heath Warks 100 E5
Barton St David Som 44 G4
Barton Seagrave Northants 121 B7
Bartonsham Hereford 97 D10
Barton Stacey Hants 48 E2
Barton Town Devon 41 E7
Barton Turf Norf 161 E7
Barton Turn Staffs 152 F4
Barton-under-Needwood Staffs 152 F3
Barton-upon-Humber N Lincs 200 C4
Barton Upon Irwell Gtr Man 184 B3
Barton Waterside N Lincs 200 C4
Barugh S Yorks 197 F10
Barugh Green S Yorks 197 F10
Barway Cambs 123 B10
Barwell Leics 135 D8
London 67 G7
Barwick Devon 25 F9
Herts 86 B5
Som 29 E9
Barwick in Elmet W Yorks 206 F3
Baschurch Shrops 149 E8
Bascote Warks 119 E8
Bascote Heath Warks 119 E7
Base Green Suff 125 E10
Basford Shrops 131 F7
Staffs 168 F5
Basford Green Staffs 169 E7
Bashall Eaves Lancs 203 E9
Bashley Hants 19 B10
Bashley Park Hants 19 B10
Basildon Essex 69 B8
Basingstoke Hants 48 C6
Baslow Derbys 186 G3
Bason Bridge Som 43 D10
Bassaleg Newport 59 B9
Bassenthwaite Cumb 229 E10
Bassett Soton 32 D6
S Yorks 186 E3
Bassett Green Soton 32 D6
Bassingbourn Cambs 104 C6
Bassingfield Notts 154 B2
Bassingham Lincs 172 C6
Bassingthorpe Lincs 155 D9
Bassus Green Herts 104 F6
Basta Shetland 312 D7
Basted Kent 52 B6
Baston Lincs 156 G2
Bastonford Worcs 116 G6
Bastwick Norf 161 F8
Baswich Staffs 151 E8
Baswick Steer E Yorks 209 D7
Batavaime Stirl 285 D8
Batch Som 43 B10
Batchcott Shrops 115 C9
Batchfields Hereford 98 B3
Batchley Worcs 117 D10
Batchworth Herts 85 G9
Batchworth Heath Herts 85 G9
Batcombe Dorset 29 G10
Som 45 F7
Bate Heath Ches E 183 F11
Bateman's Green Worcs 117 B11
Bateman's Hill Pembs 73 E8
Batemoor S Yorks 186 E5
Batford Herts 85 B10
Bath Bath 61 F8
Bathampton Bath 61 F9
Bathealton Som 27 C9
Batheaston Bath 61 F9
Bathford Bath 61 F9
Bathgate W Loth 269 B9
Bathley Notts 172 D3
Bathpool Corn 11 G11
Som 28 B3
Bath Side Essex 108 E5
Bath Vale Ches E 168 C5
Bathville W Loth 269 B8
Bathway Som 44 C5
Bathwick Bath 61 F9
Batlers Green Herts 85 F11
Batley W Yorks 197 C8
Batley Carr W Yorks 197 C8
Batsford Glos 100 E3
Batson Devon 9 G9
Batsworthy Devon 26 D4
Batten's Green Som 28 D3
Battenton Green Worcs 116 D6
Battersby N Yorks 225 D11
Battersea London 67 D9
Battisborough Cross Devon 7 F11
Battisford Suff 125 G11
Battisford Tye Suff 125 G10
Battle E Sus 38 D2
Powys 95 E10
Battledown Glos 99 G9
Battledown Cross Devon 25 F7
Battlefield Shrops 149 F10
Battle Hill T&W 243 D8
Battlesbridge Essex 88 G3
Battlescombe Glos 80 D6
Battlesden C Beds 103 F9
Battlesea Green Suff 126 B4
Battleton Som 26 B6
Battlies Green Suff 125 E7
Battram Leics 135 B8
Battramsley Hants 20 B2
Battramsley Cross Hants 20 B2
Batt's Corner Hants 49 E10
Battyeford W Yorks 197 C7
Batworthy Devon 13 D10
Bauds of Cullen Moray 302 C4
Baugh Argyll 288 E2
Baughton Worcs 99 C7
Baughurst Hants 48 B5
Baulking Oxon 82 G4
Baumber Lincs 190 G2
Baunton Glos 81 E8
Baverstock Wilts 46 G4
Bawburgh Norf 142 B3
Bawdeswell Norf 159 E10
Bawdrip Som 43 F10
Bawdsey Suff 108 C6
Bawsey Norf 158 F3
Bawtry S Yorks 187 C11
Baxenden Lancs 195 B9
Baxterley Warks 134 D5
Baxter's Green Suff 124 F5
Bay Dorset 30 B4
Highld 298 D2
Baybridge Hants 33 C8
Northumb 241 G11
Baycliff Cumb 210 E5
Baydon Wilts 63 D9
Bayford Herts 86 D4
Som 30 B2
Bay Gate Lancs 203 D11
Bay Horse Lancs 202 C5
Bayles Cumb 231 C10
Bayley's Hill Kent 52 C4
Baylham Suff 126 G2
Baylis Green Worcs 117 C11
Baynard's Green Oxon 101 F10
Baynhall Worcs 99 B7
Baysham Hereford 97 F11
Bayston Hill Shrops 131 B9
Bayswater London 67 C9
Baythorne End Essex 106 C4
Baythorpe Lincs 174 G2
Bayton Worcs 116 C3
Bayton Common Worcs 116 C4
Bay View Kent 70 E4
Bayworth Oxon 83 E8
Beach Highld 289 D9
S Glos 61 E8
Beachampton Bucks 102 D5
Beachamwell Norf 140 B5
Beachans Moray 301 E10
Beacharr Argyll 255 C7
Beachborough Kent 55 F7
Beach Hay Worcs 116 C4
Beachlands E Sus 23 E11
Beachley Glos 79 G9
Beacon Corn 2 B5
Devon 27 F11
Devon 28 F2
Beacon Down E Sus 37 C9
Beacon End Essex 107 G9
Beaconhill Northumb 243 B7
Beacon Hill Bath 61 F9
Bucks 84 G6
Cumb 210 E4
Dorset 18 C5
Essex 88 C5
Kent 53 G10
Notts 172 E4
Suff 108 B4
Sur 49 F11
Beacon Lough T&W 243 F7
Beacon's Bottom Bucks 84 F3
Beaconsfield Bucks 66 B2
Beaconside Staffs 151 E8
Beacrabhaic W Isles 305 J3
Beadlam N Yorks 216 C3
Beadlow C Beds 104 D2
Beadnell Northumb 264 D6
Beaford Devon 25 E9
Beal Northumb 273 G11
N Yorks 198 B4
Bealach Highld 289 D11
Bealach Maim Argyll 275 E10
Bealbury Corn 7 B7
Beal's Green Kent 53 G9
Bealsmill Corn 12 F3
Beambridge Shrops 131 F10
Beam Bridge Som 27 D10
Beam Hill Staffs 152 D4
Beamhurst Staffs 151 B11
Beamhurst Lane Staffs 151 B11
Beaminster Dorset 29 G7
Beamish Durham 242 G6
Beamond End Bucks 84 F6
Beamsley N Yorks 205 C7
Bean Kent 68 E5
Beanacre Wilts 62 F2
Beancross Falk 279 F8
Beanhill M Keynes 103 D7
Beanley Northumb 264 F3
Beansburn E Ayrs 257 B10
Beanthwaite Cumb 210 C4
Beaquoy Orkney 314 D3
Bear Cross Bmouth 19 B7
Beard Hill Som 44 E6
Beardly Batch Som 44 E6
Beardwood Blkburn 195 B7
Beare Devon 27 G7
Beare Green Sur 51 E7
Bearley Warks 118 E3
Bearley Cross Warks 118 E3
Bearnus Argyll 288 E5
Bearpark Durham 233 C10
Bearsbridge Northumb 241 F7
Bearsden E Dunb 277 G10
Bearsted Kent 53 B9
Bearstone Shrops 150 B4
Bearwood Hereford 115 F7
Poole 18 B6
W Mid 133 F10
Beasley Staffs 168 F4
Beattock Dumfries 248 C3
Beauchamp Roding Essex 87 C9
Beauchief S Yorks 186 E4
Beauclerc Northumb 242 E2
Beaudesert Warks 118 D3
Beaufort Bl Gwent 77 C11
Beaufort Castle Highld 300 E5
Beaulieu Hants 32 G5
Beaulieu Park Essex 88 C2
Beaulieu Wood Dorset 30 F2
Beauly Highld 300 E5
Beaumaris Anglesey 179 F10
Beaumont Cumb 239 F8
Essex 108 G3
Windsor 66 E3
Beaumont Hill Darl 224 B5
Beaumont Leys Leicester 135 B11
Beausale Warks 118 C4
Beauvale Notts 171 F8
Beauworth Hants 33 B9
Beavan's Hill Hereford 98 G3
Beaworthy Devon 12 B5
Beazley End Essex 106 F4
Bebington Mers 182 E4
Bebside Northumb 253 G7
Beccles Suff 143 E8
Becconsall Lancs 194 C2
Beck Bottom Cumb 210 C5
W Yorks 197 C10
Beckbury Shrops 132 C5
Beckces Cumb 230 F4
Beckenham London 67 F11
Beckermet Cumb 219 D10
Beckermonds N Yorks 213 C7
Beckery Som 44 F3
Beckett End Norf 140 D5
Beckfoot Cumb 220 E3
Cumb 229 B7
Beck Foot Cumb 222 F2
W Yorks 205 F8
Beckford Worcs 99 D9
Beckhampton Wilts 62 F5
Beck Head Cumb 211 C8
Beck Hole N Yorks 226 E6
Beck Houses Cumb 221 F11
Beckingham Lincs 172 E5
Notts 188 D3
Beckington Som 45 C10
Beckjay Shrops 115 B7
Beckley E Sus 38 C5
Hants 19 B10
Oxon 83 C9
Beckley Furnace E Sus 38 C4
Beck Row Suff 124 B3
Beckside Cumb 212 B2
Beck Side Cumb 210 C4
Cumb 211 C7
Beckton London 68 C2
Beckwith N Yorks 205 C11
Beckwithshaw N Yorks 205 C11
Becontree London 68 B3
Bedale N Yorks 214 B5
Bedburn Durham 233 E8
Bedchester Dorset 30 D5
Beddau Rhondda 58 B5
Beddgelert Gwyn 163 F9
Beddingham E Sus 36 F6
Beddington London 67 G10
Beddington Corner London 67 F9
Bedfield Suff 126 D4
Bedford Beds 121 G11
Gtr Man 183 B11
Bedford Park London 67 D8
Bedgebury Cross Kent 53 G8
Bedgrove Bucks 84 C4
Bedham W Sus 35 C8
Bedhampton Hants 22 B2
Bedingfield Suff 126 D3
Bedingham Green Norf 142 E5
Bedlam N Yorks 214 G5
Som 45 D9
Bedlam Street W Sus 36 D3
Bedlar's Green Essex 105 G10
Bedlington Northumb 253 G7
Bedlington Station Northumb 253 G7
Bedlinog M Tydf 77 E9
Bedminster Bristol 60 E5
Bedminster Down Bristol 60 F5
Bedmond Herts 85 E9
Bednall Staffs 151 F9
Bednall Head Staffs 151 F9
Bedrule Borders 262 F4
Bedstone Shrops 115 B7
Bedwas Caerph 59 B7
Bedwell Herts 104 G4
Wrex 166 F5
Bedwellty Caerph 77 E11
Bedwellty Pits Bl Gwent 77 D11
Bedwlwyn Wrex 148 B4
Bedworth Warks 135 F7
Bedworth Heath Warks 134 F6
Bedworth Woodlands Warks 134 F6
Bed-y-coedwr Gwyn 146 D4
Beeby Leics 136 B3
Beech Hants 49 F7
Staffs 151 B7
Beechcliff Staffs 151 B7
Beechcliffe W Yorks 205 E7
Beechen Cliff Bath 61 G9
Beech Hill Gtr Man 194 F5
W Berks 65 G7
Beechingstoke Wilts 46 B5
Beech Lanes W Mid 133 F10
Beechwood Halton 183 E8
Newport 59 B10
W Mid 118 B5
W Yorks 206 F2
Beecroft C Beds 103 G10
Beedon W Berks 64 D3
Beedon Hill W Berks 64 D3
Beeford E Yorks 209 C8
Beeley Derbys 170 B3
Beelsby NE Lincs 201 G8
Beenham W Berks 64 F5
Beenham's Heath Windsor 65 D10
Beenham Stocks W Berks 64 F5
Beeny Corn 11 C8
Beer Devon 15 D10
Som 44 G2
Beercrocombe Som 28 C4
Beer Hackett Dorset 29 E9
Beesands Devon 8 G6
Beesby Lincs 191 E7
Beeslack Midloth 270 C4
Beeson Devon 8 G6
Beeston C Beds 104 B3
Ches W 167 D8
Norf 159 F8
Notts 153 B10
W Yorks 205 G11
Beeston Hill W Yorks 205 G11
Beeston Park Side W Yorks 197 B9
Beeston Regis Norf 177 E11
Beeston Royds W Yorks 205 G11
Beeston St Lawrence Norf 160 E6
Beeswing Dumfries 237 C10
Beetham Cumb 211 D9
Som 28 E3
Beetley Norf 159 F9
Beffcote Staffs 150 F6
Began Cardiff 59 C8
Begbroke Oxon 83 C7
Begdale Cambs 139 B9
Begelly Pembs 73 D10
Beggar Hill Essex 87 E10
Beggarington Hill W Yorks 197 C9
Beggars Ash Hereford 98 D4
Beggars Bush W Sus 35 F11
Beggar's Bush Powys 114 E5
Beggars Pound V Glam 58 F4
Beggearn Huish Som 42 F4
Beguildy Powys 114 B3
Beighton Norf 143 B7
S Yorks 186 E6
Beighton Hill Derbys 170 E3
Beili-glas Mon 78 C4
Beitearsaig W Isles 305 G1
Beith N Ayrs 266 E6
Bekesbourne Kent 55 B7
Bekesbourne Hill Kent 55 B7
Belah Cumb 239 F9
Belan Powys 130 C4
Belaugh Norf 160 F5
Belbins Hants 32 C5
Belbroughton Worcs 117 B8
Belchalwell Dorset 30 F3
Belchalwell Street Dorset 30 F3
Belchamp Otten Essex 106 C6
Belchamp St Paul Essex 106 C5
Belchamp Walter Essex 106 C6
Belcher's Bar Leics 135 B8
Belchford Lincs 190 F3
Beleybridge Fife 287 F9
Belfield Gtr Man 196 E2
Belford Northumb 264 C4
Belgrano Conwy 181 F7
Belgrave Ches W 166 C5
Leicester 135 B11
Staffs 134 C4
Belgravia London 67 D9
Belhaven E Loth 282 F3
Belhelvie Aberds 293 B11
Belhinnie Aberds 302 G4
Bellabeg Aberds 292 B5
Bellamore S Ayrs 244 F6
Bellanoch Argyll 275 D8
Bellanrigg Borders 260 B6
Bellasize E Yorks 199 B10
Bellaty Angus 286 B6
Bell Bar Herts 86 D3
Bell Busk N Yorks 204 B4
Bell Common Essex 86 E6
Belleau Lincs 190 F6
Belle Eau Park Notts 171 D11
Belle Green S Yorks 197 F11
Bellehiglash Moray 301 F11
Belle Isle W Yorks 197 B10
Bell End Worcs 117 B8
Bellerby N Yorks 224 G2
Belle Vale Mers 182 D6
W Mid 133 G9
Bellever Devon 13 F9
Bellevue Worcs 117 C9
Belle Vue Cumb 229 E8
Cumb 239 F9
Gtr Man 184 B5
Shrops 149 G9
S Yorks 198 G5
W Yorks 197 D10
Bellfield E Ayrs 257 B10
Bellfields Sur 50 C3
Bell Green London 67 E11
W Mid 135 G7
Bell Heath Worcs 117 B9
Bell Hill Hants 34 C2
Belliehill Angus 293 G7
Bellingdon Bucks 84 D6
Bellingham London 67 E11
Northumb 251 G8
Bellmount Norf 157 E10
Belloch Argyll 255 D7
Bellochantuy Argyll 255 D7
Bell o' th' Hill Ches W 167 F8
Bellsbank E Ayrs 245 C11
Bell's Close T&W 242 E5
Bell's Corner Suff 107 D9
Bellshill N Lnrk 268 C4
Northumb 264 C4
Bellside N Lnrk 268 D6
Bellsmyre W Dunb 277 F8
Bellspool Borders 260 B5
Bellsquarry W Loth 269 C10
Bells Yew Green E Sus 52 F6
Belluton Bath 60 G6
Bellyeoman Fife 280 D2
Belmaduthy Highld 300 D6
Belmesthorpe Rutland 155 G10
Belmont Blkburn 195 D7
Durham 234 C2
E Sus 38 E4
Harrow 67 G9
Oxon 63 B11
S Ayrs 257 E8
Shetland 312 C7
Sutton 85 G11
Belnacraig Aberds 292 B5
Belnagarrow Moray 302 E3
Belnie Lincs 156 C5
Belowda Corn 5 C9
Belper Derbys 170 F4
Belper Lane End Derbys 170 F4
Belph Derbys 187 F8
Belsay Northumb 242 B4
Belses Borders 262 D3
Belsford Devon 8 D5
Belsize Herts 85 E8
Belstead Suff 108 C2
Belston S Ayrs 257 E9
Belstone Devon 13 C8
Belstone Corner Devon 13 B8
Belthorn Blkburn 195 C8
Beltinge Kent 71 F7
Beltingham Northumb 241 E7
Beltoft N Lincs 199 F10
Belton Leics 153 E8
Lincs 155 B8
N Lincs 199 F9
Norf 143 C9
Belton in Rutland Rutland 136 C6
Beltring Kent 53 D7
Belts of Collonach Aberds 293 D8
Belvedere London 68 D3
W Loth 269 B9
Belvoir Leics 154 C6
Bembridge IoW 21 D8
Bemersyde Borders 262 C3
Bemerton Wilts 46 G6
Bemerton Heath Wilts 46 G6
Bempton E Yorks 218 E3
Benacre Suff 143 G10
Ben Alder Lodge Highld 291 F7
Ben Armine Lodge Highld 309 H7
Benbuie Dumfries 246 D6
Ben Casgro W Isles 304 F6
Benchill Gtr Man 184 D4
Bencombe Glos 80 F3
Benderloch Argyll 289 F11
Bendish Herts 104 G3
Bendronaig Lodge Highld 299 F10
Benenden Kent 53 G10
Benfield Dumfries 236 C5
Benfieldside Durham 242 G3
Bengal Pembs 91 E9
Bengate Norf 160 D6
Bengeo Herts 86 C4
Bengeworth Worcs 99 C10
Bengrove Glos 99 E9
Benhall Glos 99 G8
Benhall Green Suff 127 E7
Benhall Street Suff 127 E7
Benhilton London 67 F9
Benholm Aberds 293 G10
Beningbrough N Yorks 206 B6
Benington Herts 104 G5
Lincs 174 F5
Benington Sea End Lincs 174 F6
Benllech Anglesey 179 E8
Benmore Argyll 276 E2
Stirl 285 E8
Benmore Lodge Argyll 289 F7
Highld 309 H3
Bennacott Corn 11 C11
Bennah Devon 14 E2
Bennan N Ayrs 255 E10
Bennane Lea S Ayrs 244 F3
Bennetland E Yorks 199 B10
Bennetsfield Highld 300 D6
Bennett End Bucks 84 F3
Bennetts End Herts 85 D9
Benniworth Lincs 190 E2
Benover Kent 53 D8
Ben Rhydding W Yorks 205 D8
Bensham T&W 242 E6
Benslie N Ayrs 266 G6
Benson Oxon 83 G10
Benston Shetland 313 H6
Bent Aberds 293 F8
Benter Som 44 D6
Bentfield Bury Essex 105 F9
Bentfield Green Essex 105 F10
Bentgate Gtr Man 196 E2
Bent Gate Lancs 195 C9
Benthall Northumb 264 D6
Shrops 132 C3
Bentham Glos 80 B6
Benthoul Aberdeen 293 C10
Bentilee Stoke 168 F6
Bentlass Pembs 73 E7
Bentlawnt Shrops 130 C6
Bentley Essex 87 F9
E Yorks 208 F6
Hants 49 E9
Suff 108 D2
S Yorks 198 F5
Warks 134 D5
W Mid 133 D9
Worcs 117 D9
Bentley Common Warks 134 D5
Bentley Heath Herts 86 F2
W Mid 118 B3
Bentley Rise S Yorks 198 G5
Benton Devon 41 F7
Benton Green W Mid 118 B5
Bentpath Dumfries 249 E8
Bents W Loth 269 C9
Bents Head W Yorks 205 F7
Bentwichen Devon 41 G8
Bentworth Hants 49 E7
Benvie Dundee 287 D7
Benville Dorset 29 G8
Benwell T&W 242 E6
Benwick Cambs 138 E6
Beobridge Shrops 132 E5
Beoley Worcs 117 D11
Beoraidbeg Highld 295 F8
Bepton W Sus 34 D5
Berden Essex 105 F9
Bere Alston Devon 7 B8
Berechurch Essex 107 G9
Bere Ferrers Devon 7 C9
Berefold Aberds 303 F9
Berepper Corn 2 E5
Bere Regis Dorset 18 C2
Bergh Apton Norf 142 C6
Berghers Hill Bucks 66 B2
Berhill Som 44 F2
Berinsfield Oxon 83 F9
Berkeley Glos 79 F11
Berkeley Heath Glos 79 F11

Berkeley Road Glos 80 E2
Berkeley Towers Ches E 167 E11
Berkhamsted Herts 85 D7
Berkley Som 45 D10
Berkley Down Som 45 D9
Berkley Marsh Som 45 D10
Berkswell W Mid 118 B4
Bermondsey London 67 D10
Bermuda Warks 135 F7
Bernards Heath Herts 85 D11
Bernera Highld 295 C10
Berner's Cross Devon 25 F10
Berner's Hill E Sus 53 G8
Berners Roding Essex 87 D10
Bernice Argyll 276 C2
Bernisdale Highld 298 D4
Berrick Salome Oxon 83 G10
Berriedale Highld 311 G5
Berrier Cumb 230 F3
Berriew / Aberriw Powys 130 C3
Berrington Northumb 273 G10
Shrops 131 B10
Worcs 115 D11
Berrington Green Worcs 115 D11
Berriowbridge Corn 11 F11
Berrow Som 43 C10
Worcs 98 E5
Berrow Green Worcs 116 F4
Berry Swansea 56 D3
Berry Brow W Yorks 196 E6
Berry Cross Devon 25 E7
Berry Down Cross Devon 40 E5
Berryfield Wilts 61 G11
Berrygate Hill E Yorks 201 C8
Berry Hill Glos 79 C9
Pembs 91 C11
Stoke 168 F6
Worcs 117 E7
Berryhillock Moray 302 C5
Berrylands London 67 F7
Berry Moor S Yorks 197 G9
Berrynarbor Devon 40 D5
Berry Pomeroy Devon 8 C6
Berrysbridge Devon 26 G6
Berry's Green London 52 B2
Bersham Wrex 166 F4
Berstane Orkney 314 E4
Berth-ddu Flint 166 B2
Berthengam Flint 181 F10
Berwick E Sus 23 D8
Kent 54 F6
S Glos 60 C5
Berwick Bassett Wilts 62 E5
Berwick Hill Northumb 242 B5
Berwick Hills Mbro 225 B10
Berwick St James Wilts 46 F5
Berwick St John Wilts 30 C6
Berwick St Leonard Wilts 46 G2
Berwick-upon-Tweed Northumb 273 E9
Berwick Wharf Shrops 149 G10
Berwyn Denb 165 G11
Bescaby Leics 154 D6
Bescar Lancs 193 E11
Bescot W Mid 133 D10
Besford Shrops 149 E11
Worcs 99 C8
Bessacarr S Yorks 198 G6
Bessels Green Kent 52 B4
Bessels Leigh Oxon 83 E7
Besses o' th' Barn Gtr Man 195 F10
Bessingby E Yorks 218 F3
Bessingham Norf 160 B3
Best Beech Hill E Sus 52 G6
Besthorpe Norf 141 D11
Notts 172 C4
Bestwood Nottingham 171 G9
Bestwood Village Notts 171 F9
Beswick E Yorks 208 D6
Gtr Man 184 B5
Betchcott Shrops 131 D8
Betchton Heath Ches E 168 C3
Betchworth Sur 51 D8
Bethania Ceredig 111 E11
Gwyn 163 E10
Gwyn 164 F2
Bethany Corn 6 D6
Bethel Anglesey 178 G5
Corn 5 E10
Gwyn 147 B9
Gwyn 163 B8
Bethelnie Aberds 303 F7
Bethersden Kent 54 E2
Bethesda Gwyn 163 B10
Pembs 73 B9
Bethlehem Carms 94 F3
Bethnal Green London 67 C10
Betley Staffs 168 F3
Betley Common Staffs 168 F2
Betsham Kent 68 E6
Betteshanger Kent 55 C10
Bettiscombe Dorset 16 B3
Bettisfield Wrex 149 B9
Betton Shrops 130 C6
Shrops 150 B3
Betton Strange Shrops 131 B10
Bettws Bridgend 58 B2
Mon 78 B3
Newport 78 G3
Bettws Cedewain Powys 130 D2
Bettws Gwerfil Goch Denb 165 F8
Bettws Ifan Ceredig 92 B6
Bettws Newydd Mon 78 D5
Bettws-y-crwyn Shrops 130 G4
Bettyhill Highld 308 C7
Betws Bridgend 57 D11
Carms 75 C10
Betws Bledrws Ceredig 111 G11
Betws-Garmon Gwyn 163 D8
Betws Ifan Ceredig 92 B6
Betws-y-Coed Conwy 164 D4
Betws-yn-Rhos Conwy 180 G6
Beulah Ceredig 92 B5
Powys 113 G8
Bevendean Brighton 36 F4
Bevercotes Notts 187 G11
Bevere Worcs 116 F6
Beverley E Yorks 208 F6
Beverston Glos 80 G5
Bevington Glos 79 F11
Bewaldeth Cumb 229 E10
Bewbush W Sus 51 F8
Bewcastle Cumb 240 C3
Bewdley Worcs 116 B5
Bewerley N Yorks 214 G3
Bewholme E Yorks 209 C9
Bewley Common Wilts 62 F2
Bewlie Borders 262 D3
Bewlie Mains Borders 262 D3
Bewsey Warr 183 D9
Bexfield Norf 159 D10
Bexhill E Sus 38 F2
Bexley London 68 E3
Bexleyheath London 68 D3
Bexleyhill W Sus 34 B6
Bexon Kent 53 B11
Bexwell Norf 140 C2
Beyton Suff 125 E8
Beyton Green Suff 125 E8
Bhalasaigh W Isles 304 E3
Bhaltos W Isles 304 E2
Bhatarsaigh W Isles 297 M2
Bhlàraidh Highld 290 B5
Bibstone S Glos 79 G11
Bibury Glos 81 D10
Bicester Oxon 101 G11
Bickenhall Som 28 D3
Bickenhill W Mid 134 G3
Bicker Lincs 156 B4
Bicker Bar Lincs 156 B4
Bicker Gauntlet Lincs 156 B4
Bickershaw Gtr Man 194 G6
Bickerstaffe Lancs 194 G2
Bickerton Ches E 167 E8
Devon 9 G11
N Yorks 206 C5
Northumb 251 C11
Bickford Staffs 151 G7
Bickham Som 42 E3
Bickingcott Devon 26 B3
Bickington Devon 13 G11
Devon 40 G4
Bickleigh Devon 7 C10
Devon 26 F6
Bickleton Devon 40 G4
Bickley Ches W 167 F8
London 68 F2
Worcs 116 C2
Bickley Moss Ches W 167 F8
Bickley Town Ches W 167 F8
Bickleywood Ches W 167 F8
Bickmarsh Warks 100 B2
Bicknacre Essex 88 E3
Bicknoller Som 42 F6
Bicknor Kent 53 B11
Bickton Hants 31 E11
Bicton Hereford 115 E9
Pembs 72 D4
Shrops 130 G5
Shrops 149 F8
Bicton Heath Shrops 149 G9
Bidborough Kent 52 E5
Bidden Hants 49 D8
Biddenden Kent 53 F11
Biddenden Green Kent 53 E11
Biddenham Beds 103 B10
Biddestone Wilts 61 E11
Biddick T&W 243 F8
Biddick Hall T&W 243 E9
Biddisham Som 43 C11
Biddlesden Bucks 102 C2
Biddlestone Northumb 251 B11
Biddulph Staffs 168 D5
Biddulph Moor Staffs 168 D6
Bideford Devon 25 B7
Bidford-on-Avon Warks 118 G2
Bidlake Devon 12 D5
Bidston Mers 182 C3
Bidston Hill Mers 182 D3
Bidwell C Beds 103 G10
Bielby E Yorks 207 E11
Bieldside Aberdeen 293 C10
Bierley IoW 20 F6
W Yorks 205 G9
Bierton Bucks 84 B4
Bigbury Devon 8 F3
Bigbury-on-Sea Devon 8 G3
Bigby Lincs 200 F5
Bigfrith Windsor 65 C11
Biggar Cumb 210 F3
S Lnrk 260 B2
Biggar Road N Lnrk 268 C5
Biggin Derbys 169 D11
Derbys 170 F3
N Yorks 206 F6
Thurrock 69 D7
Biggings Shetland 313 G3
Biggin Hill London 52 B2
Biggleswade C Beds 104 C3
Bighouse Highld 310 C2
Bighton Hants 48 G6
Biglands Cumb 239 G7
Big Mancot Flint 166 B4
Bignall End Staffs 168 E4
Bignor W Sus 35 E7
Bigods Essex 106 G2
Bigram Stirl 285 G10
Bigrigg Cumb 219 C10
Big Sand Highld 299 B7
Bigswell Orkney 314 E3
Bigton Shetland 313 L5
Bilberry Corn 5 C10
Bilborough Nottingham 171 G8
Bilbrook Som 42 E4
Staffs 133 C7
Bilbrough N Yorks 206 D6
Bilbster Highld 310 D6
Bilby Notts 187 E10
Bildershaw Durham 233 G10
Bildeston Suff 107 B9
Billacombe Plym 7 E10
Billacott Corn 11 C11
Billericay Essex 87 G11
Billesdon Leics 136 C4
Billesley Warks 118 F2
W Mid 133 G11
Billesley Common W Mid 133 G11
Billingborough Lincs 156 C2
Billinge Mers 194 G4
Billingford Norf 126 B3
Norf 159 E10
Billingham Stockton 234 G5
Billinghay Lincs 173 E11
Billingley S Yorks 198 G2
Billingshurst W Sus 35 B9
Billingsley Shrops 132 F4
Billington C Beds 103 G8
Lancs 203 F10
Staffs 151 E7
Billockby Norf 161 G8
Bill Quay T&W 243 E7
Billy Mill T&W 243 D8
Billy Row Durham 233 D9
Bilmarsh Shrops 149 D9
Bilsborrow Lancs 202 F6
Bilsby Lincs 191 F7
Bilsby Field Lincs 191 F7
Bilsdon Devon 14 C2
Bilsham W Sus 35 G7
Bilsington Kent 54 G4
Bilson Green Glos 79 C11
Bilsthorpe Notts 171 C10
Bilsthorpe Moor Notts 171 D11
Bilston Midloth 270 C5
W Mid 133 D9
Bilstone Leics 135 B7
Bilting Kent 54 D5
Bilton E Yorks 209 G9
Northumb 264 G6
N Yorks 206 B2
Warks 119 C9
Bilton Haggs N Yorks 206 D5
Bilton in Ainsty N Yorks 206 D5
Bimbister Orkney 314 E3
Binbrook Lincs 190 C2
Binchester Blocks Durham 233 E10
Bincombe Dorset 17 E9
Som 43 F7
Bindal Highld 311 L3
Bindon Som 27 C10
Binegar Som 44 D6
Bines Green W Sus 35 D11
Binfield Brack 65 E10
Binfield Heath Oxon 65 D8
Bingfield Northumb 241 C11
Bingham Edin 280 G6
Notts 154 B4
Bingley W Yorks 205 F8
Bings Heath Shrops 149 F10
Binham Norf 159 B9
Binley Hants 48 C2
W Mid 119 B7
Binley Woods Warks 119 B7
Binnegar Dorset 18 D3
Binniehill Falk 279 G7
Binscombe Sur 50 D3
Binsey Oxon 83 D7
Binsoe N Yorks 214 D4
Binstead Hants 49 E9
IoW 21 C7
Binsted Hants 49 E9
W Sus 35 F7
Binton Warks 118 G2
Bintree Norf 159 E10
Binweston Shrops 130 C6
Birch Essex 88 B6
Gtr Man 195 F11
Birch Acre Worcs 117 C11
Birchall Hereford 98 D3
Staffs 169 E7
Bircham Newton Norf 158 C5
Bircham Tofts Norf 158 C5
Birchan Coppice Worcs 116 C6
Birchanger Essex 105 G10
Birch Berrow Worcs 116 E4
Birchburn N Ayrs 255 E10
Birch Cross Staffs 152 C2
Birchden E Sus 52 F4
Birchencliffe W Yorks 196 D6
Birchend Hereford 98 C3
Birchendale Staffs 151 B11
Bircher Hereford 115 D9
Birches Green W Mid 134 E2
Birches Head Stoke 168 F5
Birchett's Green E Sus 53 G7
Birchfield Highld 301 G9
W Mid 133 E11
Birch Green Essex 88 B6
Herts 86 C3
Lancs 194 F3
Worcs 99 B7
Birchgrove Cardiff 59 D7
E Sus 36 B6
Swansea 57 B8
Birchhall Corner Essex 107 E10
Birch Heath Ches W 167 C8
Birch Hill Brack 65 F11
Ches W 183 G8
Birchill Devon 28 G4
Birchills W Mid 133 D10
Birchington Kent 71 F9
Birchley Heath Warks 134 E5
Birchmoor Warks 134 C5
Birchmoor Green C Beds 103 E8
Bircholt Forstal Kent 54 E5
Birchover Derbys 170 C2
Birch Vale Derbys 185 D8
Birchwood Herts 86 D2
Lincs 172 B6
Som 28 E2
Warr 183 C10
Birchy Hill Hants 19 B11
Bircotes Notts 187 C10
Birdbrook Essex 106 C4
Birdbush Wilts 30 C6
Birdfield Argyll 275 D10
Birdforth N Yorks 215 D9
Birdham W Sus 22 D4
Birdholme Derbys 170 B5
Birdingbury Warks 119 D8
Birdlip Glos 80 C6
Birdsall N Yorks 216 F6
Birds Edge W Yorks 197 F8
Birds End Suff 124 E5
Birdsgreen Shrops 132 F5
Birds Green Essex 87 D9
Birdsmoorgate Dorset 28 G5
Birdston E Dunb 278 F3
Bird Street Suff 125 G10
Birdwell S Yorks 197 G10
Birdwood Glos 80 B2
Birgham Borders 263 B7
Birichen Highld 309 K7
Birkacre Lancs 194 D5
Birkby Cumb 229 D7
N Yorks 224 E6
W Yorks 196 D6
Birkdale Mers 193 D10
Birkenbog Aberds 302 C5
Birkenhead Mers 182 D4
Birkenhills Aberds 303 E7
Birkenshaw N Lnrk 268 C3
S Lnrk 268 F5
W Yorks 197 B8
Birkenshaw Bottoms W Yorks 197 B8
Birkenside Borders 271 G11
Birkett Mire Cumb 230 G2
Birkhall Aberds 292 D5
Birkhill Angus 287 D7
Borders 260 F6
Borders 271 G11
Birkholme Lincs 155 E9
Birkhouse W Yorks 197 C7
Birkin N Yorks 198 B4
Birks Cumb 222 G3
W Yorks 197 B9
Birkshaw Northumb 241 D7
Birley Hereford 115 G9
Birley Carr S Yorks 186 C4
Birley Edge S Yorks 186 C4
Birleyhay Derbys 186 E5
Birling Kent 69 G7
Northumb 252 B6
Birling Gap E Sus 23 F9
Birlingham Worcs 99 C8
Birmingham W Mid 133 F11
Birnam Perth 286 C4
Birniehill S Lnrk 268 E2
Birse Aberds 293 D7
Birsemore Aberds 293 D7
Birstall Leics 135 B11
W Yorks 197 B8
Birstall Smithies W Yorks 197 B8
Birstwith N Yorks 205 B10
Birthorpe Lincs 156 C2
Birtle Gtr Man 195 E10
Birtley Hereford 115 D7
Northumb 241 B9
Shrops 131 E9
T&W 243 F7
Birtley Green Sur 50 E4
Birtsmorton Worcs 98 D6
Birts Street Worcs 98 D5
Bisbrooke Rutland 137 D7
Biscathorpe Lincs 190 D2
Biscombe Som 27 E11
Biscot Luton 103 G11
Biscovey Corn 5 E11
Bisham Windsor 65 C10
Bishampton Worcs 117 G9
Bish Mill Devon 26 B2
Bishon Common Hereford 97 C8
Bishop Auckland Durham 233 F10
Bishopbridge Lincs 189 C8
Bishopbriggs E Dunb 278 G2
Bishop Burton E Yorks 208 F5
Bishopdown Wilts 47 G7
Bishop Kinkell Highld 300 D5
Bishop Middleham Durham 234 E2
Bishopmill Moray 302 C2
Bishop Monkton N Yorks 214 F6
Bishop Norton Lincs 189 C7
Bishopsbourne Kent 55 C7
Bishops Cannings Wilts 62 G4
Bishop's Castle Shrops 130 F6
Bishop's Caundle Dorset 29 E11
Bishop's Cleeve Glos 99 F9
Bishop's Down Dorset 29 E11
Bishops Frome Hereford 98 B3
Bishopsgarth Stockton 234 G4
Bishopsgate Sur 66 E3
Bishops Green Essex 87 B5
Bishop's Green W Berks 64 G4
Bishop's Hull Som 28 C2
Bishop's Itchington Warks 119 F7
Bishops Lydeard Som 27 B11
Bishop's Norton Glos 98 G6
Bishops Nympton Devon 26 C3
Bishop's Offley Staffs 150 D5
Bishop's Quay Corn 2 D6
Bishop's Stortford Herts 105 G9
Bishop's Sutton Hants 48 G6
Bishop's Tachbrook Warks 118 E6
Bishops Tawton Devon 40 G5
Bishopsteignton Devon 14 G4
Bishopstoke Hants 33 D7
Bishopston Bristol 60 D5
Swansea 56 D5
Bishopstone Bucks 84 C4
E Sus 23 E7
Hereford 97 C8
Kent 71 F8
Swindon 63 C8
Wilts 31 B9
Bishopstrow Wilts 45 E11
Bishop Sutton Bath 44 B5
Bishop's Waltham Hants 33 D9
Bishopswood Som 28 E3
Bishop's Wood Staffs 132 B6
Bishopsworth Bristol 60 F5
Bishop Thornton N Yorks 214 G5
Bishopthorpe York 207 D7
Bishopton Darl 234 G3
Dumfries 236 E6
N Yorks 214 E6
Renfs 277 G8
Warks 118 F3
Bishopwearmouth T&W 243 F9
Bishop Wilton E Yorks 207 B11
Bishpool Newport 59 B10
Bishton Newport 59 B11
Staffs 151 E10
Bisley Glos 80 D6
Sur 50 B3
Bisley Camp Sur 50 B2
Bispham Blkpool 202 E2
Bispham Green Lancs 194 E3
Bissoe Corn 4 G5
Bissom Corn 3 C7
Bisterne Hants 31 G10
Bisterne Close Hants 32 G2
Bitchet Green Kent 52 C5
Bitchfield Lincs 155 D9
Bittadon Devon 40 E4
Bittaford Devon 8 D3
Bittering Norf 159 F8
Bitterley Shrops 115 B11
Bitterne Soton 33 E7
Bitterne Park Soton 32 E6
Bitterscote Staffs 134 C4
Bitteswell Leics 135 F10
Bittles Green Dorset 30 C5
Bitton S Glos 61 F7
Bix Oxon 65 B8
Bixter Shetland 313 H5
Blaby Leics 135 D11
Blackacre Dumfries 248 E2
Blackadder West Borders 272 E6
Blackawton Devon 8 E6
Black Bank Cambs 139 F10
Warks 135 F7
Black Banks Darl 224 C5
Black Barn Lincs 157 D8
Blackbeck Cumb 219 D10
Blackbird Leys Oxon 83 E9
Blackborough Devon 27 F9
Norf 158 G3
Blackborough End Norf 158 G3
Black Bourton Oxon 82 E3
Blackboys E Sus 37 C8
Blackbraes Aberds 293 B10
Blackbrook Derbys 170 F4
Derbys 185 E9
Mers 183 B8
Staffs 150 B5
Sur 51 D7
Blackburn Aberds 293 B10
Aberds 302 F5
Blkburn 195 B7
S Yorks 186 C5
W Loth 269 B9
Black Callerton T&W 242 D5
Black Carr Norf 141 D11
Blackcastle Midloth 271 D8
Blackchambers Aberds 293 B9
Black Clauchrie S Ayrs 245 G7
Black Corner W Sus 51 F9
Black Corries Lodge Highld 284 B6
Blackcraig Dumfries 246 G6
Blackcraigs Angus 293 E7
Black Crofts Argyll 289 F11
Black Cross Corn 5 C8
Black Dam Hants 48 C6
Blackden Heath Ches E 184 G3
Blackditch Oxon 82 D6
Blackdog Aberds 293 B11
Black Dog Devon 26 F4
Blackdown Dorset 28 G5
Hants 33 C8
Warks 118 D6
Blackdyke Cumb 238 G4
Blackdykes E Loth 281 E11
Blacker Hill S Yorks 197 G11
Blacketts Kent 70 F2
Blackfell T&W 243 F7
Blackfen London 68 E3
Blackfield Hants 32 G6
Blackford Cumb 239 E9
Dumfries 248 G4
Perth 286 G2
Shrops 131 G11
Som 29 B11
Som 42 D2
Som 44 D2
Blackford Bridge Gtr Man 195 F10
Blackfordby Leics 152 F6
Blackfords Staffs 151 G9
Blackgang IoW 20 F5
Blackgate Angus 287 B8
Blackhall Aberds 293 D8
Edin 280 G4
Renfs 267 C9
Blackhall Colliery Durham 234 D5
Blackhall Mill T&W 242 F4
Blackhall Rocks Durham 234 D5
Blackham E Sus 52 F3
Blackhaugh Borders 261 B10
Blackheath Essex 107 G10
London 67 D11
Suff 127 C8
Sur 50 D4
W Mid 133 F9
Blackheath Park London 68 D2
Black Heddon Northumb 242 B3
Blackhill Aberds 303 D10
Aberds 303 E10
Aberds 303 F10
Durham 242 G3
Hants 32 D4
Highld 298 D3
Black Hill W Yorks 204 E6
Blackhillock Moray 302 E4
Blackhills Highld 301 D9
Moray 302 D2
Swansea 56 C5
Blackhorse Devon 14 C5
S Glos 61 D7
Black Horse Drove Cambs 139 E11
Blackjack Lincs 156 B5
Black Lake W Mid 133 E9
Blackland Wilts 62 F4
Blacklands E Sus 38 E4
Hereford 98 C2
Black Lane Gtr Man 195 F9
Blacklaw Aberds 302 D6
Blackleach Lancs 202 G5
Blackley Gtr Man 195 G11
W Yorks 196 D6
Blacklunans Perth 292 G3
Black Marsh Shrops 130 D6
Blackmarstone Hereford 97 D10
Blackmill Bridgend 58 B2
Blackminster Worcs 99 C11
Blackmoor Bath 60 G5
Gtr Man 195 G7
Hants 49 G9
N Som 60 G3
Som 27 D11
Black Moor Lancs 194 E3
W Yorks 205 F11
Blackmoorfoot W Yorks 196 E5
Blackmoor Gate Devon 41 E7
Blackmore Essex 87 E10
Shrops 130 B6
Blackmore End Essex 106 E4
Herts 85 B11
Worcs 98 C6
Black Mount Argyll 284 C6
Blackness Aberds 293 D8
E Sus 52 G4
Falk 279 F11
Blacknest Hants 49 E9
Windsor 66 F3
Blacknoll Dorset 18 D2
Black Notley Essex 106 G5
Blacko Lancs 204 E3
Blackoe Shrops 149 B10
Blackpark Dumfries 236 C5
Black Park Wrex 166 G4
Black Pill Swansea 56 C6
Blackpole Worcs 117 F7
Black Pole Lancs 202 F5
Blackpool Blkpool 202 F2
Devon 7 E11
Devon 9 F7
Devon 14 G2
Pembs 73 C9
Blackpool Gate Cumb 240 B2
Blackridge W Loth 269 B7
Blackrock Argyll 274 G4
Bath 60 F6
Mon 78 C2
Black Rock Brighton 36 G4
Corn 2 C5
Blackrod Gtr Man 194 E6
Blackshaw Dumfries 238 D2
Blackshaw Head W Yorks 196 B3
Blackshaw Moor Staffs 169 D8
Blacksmith's Corner Suff 108 C2
Blacksmith's Green Suff 126 D2
Blacksnape Blkburn 195 C8
Blackstone Worcs 116 C5
W Sus 36 D2
Black Street Suff 143 F10
Black Tar Pembs 73 D7
Blackthorn Oxon 83 B10
Blackthorpe Suff 125 E8
Blacktoft E Yorks 199 C10
Blacktop Aberdeen 293 C10
Black Torrington Devon 25 F7
Blacktown Newport 59 C9
Black Vein Caerph 78 G2
Blackwall Derbys 170 F3
London 67 C11
Blackwall Tunnel London 67 C11
Blackwater Corn 4 F4
Dorset 19 B8
Hants 49 B11
IoW 20 D6
Norf 159 E11
Som 28 D3
Blackwaterfoot N Ayrs 255 E9
Blackwater Lodge Moray 302 G3
Blackweir Cardiff 59 D7
Blackwell Cumb 239 G10
Darl 224 C5
Derbys 170 D6
Derbys 185 G10
Devon 27 B8
Warks 100 C4
Worcs 117 C9
W Sus 51 F11
Blackwood Caerph 77 F11
S Lnrk 268 G5
Warr 183 C10
Blackwood Hill Staffs 168 D6
Blacon Ches W 166 B5
Bladbean Kent 55 D7
Blades N Yorks 223 F9
Bladnoch Dumfries 236 D6
Bladon Oxon 82 C6
Blaenannerch Ceredig 92 B4
Blaenau Carms 75 C10
Flint 166 D2
Blaenau Dolwyddelan Conwy 164 E2
Blaenau Ffestiniog Gwyn 164 F2
Blaenau-Gwent Bl Gwent 78 E2
Blaenavon Torf 78 D3
Blaenbedw Fawr Ceredig 111 G7
Blaencaerau Bridgend 57 C11
Blaencelyn Ceredig 111 G7
Blaen-Cil-Llech Ceredig 92 C6
Blaen Clydach Rhondda 77 G7
Blaencwm Rhondda 76 F6
Blaendulais / Seven Sisters Neath 76 D4
Blaendyryn Powys 95 D8
Blaenffos Pembs 92 D3
Blaengarw Bridgend 76 G6
Blaengwrach Neath 76 D5
Blaengwynfi Neath 57 B11
Blaen-gwynfi Neath 57 B11
Blaenllechau Rhondda 77 F8
Blaen-pant Ceredig 92 C5
Blaenpennal Ceredig 112 E2
Blaenplwyf Ceredig 111 B11
Blaenporth Ceredig 92 B5
Blaenrhondda Rhondda 76 E6
Blaenwaun Carms 92 F4
Blaen-waun Carms 92 F4
Blaen-y-coed Carms 92 F6
Blaenycwm Ceredig 112 B6
Blaen-y-cwm Bl Gwent 77 C10
Denb 147 C10
Gwyn 146 E4
Powys 147 E11
Blagdon N Som 44 B4
Torbay 9 C7
Blagdon Hill Som 28 D2
Blagill Cumb 231 B10
Blaguegate Lancs 194 F3
Blaich Highld 290 F2
Blain Highld 289 C8
Blaina Bl Gwent 78 D2
Blainacraig Ho Aberds 293 D7
Blair Fife 280 C6
Blair Atholl Perth 291 G10
Blairbeg N Ayrs 256 C2
Blairburn Fife 279 D9
Blairdaff Aberds 293 B8
Blair Drummond Stirl 278 B4
Blairdryne Aberds 293 D9
Blairglas Argyll 276 D6
Blairgorm Highld 301 G10
Blairgowrie Perth 286 C5
Blairhall Fife 279 D10
Blairhill N Lnrk 268 B4
Blairingone Perth 279 B9
Blairland N Ayrs 266 F6
Blairlinn N Lnrk 278 G5
Blairlogie Stirl 278 B6
Blairlomond Argyll 276 B3
Blairmore Argyll 276 E3
Highld 306 D6
Blairnamarrow Moray 292 B4
Blairquhosh Stirl 277 E10
Blair's Ferry Argyll 275 G10
Blairskaith E Dunb 277 F11
Blaisdon Glos 80 B2
Blaise Hamlet Bristol 60 D5
Blakebrook Worcs 116 B6
Blakedown Worcs 117 B7
Blake End Essex 106 G4
Blakelands M Keynes 103 C7
Blakelaw Borders 263 C7
T&W 242 D6
Blakeley Staffs 133 E7
Blakeley Lane Staffs 169 F7
Blakelow Ches E 167 E11
Blakemere Hereford 97 C7
Blakenall Heath W Mid 133 C10
Blakeney Glos 79 D11
Norf 177 E8
Blakenhall Ches E 168 F2
W Mid 133 D8
Blakeshall Worcs 132 G6
Blakesley Northants 120 G2
Blanchland Northumb 241 G11
Blandford Camp Dorset 30 F6
Blandford Forum Dorset 30 F5
Blandford St Mary Dorset 30 F5
Bland Hill N Yorks 205 C10
Blandy Highld 308 D6
Blanefield Stirl 277 F11
Blanerne Borders 272 D6
Blank Bank Staffs 168 F4
Blankney Lincs 173 C9
Blantyre S Lnrk 268 D3
Blar a'Chaorainn Highld 290 G3
Blaran Argyll 275 B9
Blarghour Argyll 275 B10
Blarmachfoldach Highld 290 G2
Blarnalearoch Highld 307 K6
Blasford Hill Essex 88 C2
Blashford Hants 31 F11
Blaston Leics 136 D6
Blatchbridge Som 45 D9
Blatherwycke Northants 137 D9
Blawith Cumb 210 B5
Blaxhall Suff 127 F7
Blaxton S Yorks 199 G7
Blaydon T&W 242 E5
Blaydon Burn T&W 242 E5
Blaydon Haughs T&W 242 E5
Bleach Green Cumb 219 B9
Suff 126 B4
Bleadney Som 44 D3
Bleadon N Som 43 B10
Bleak Acre Hereford 98 B2
Bleak Hall M Keynes 103 D7
Bleak Hey Nook Gtr Man 196 F4
Bleak Hill Hants 31 E10
Blean Kent 70 G6
Bleasby Lincs 189 E10
Notts 172 F2
Bleasby Moor Lincs 189 E10
Bleasdale Lancs 203 D7
Bleatarn Cumb 222 C4
Blebocraigs Fife 287 F8
Bleddfa Powys 114 D4
Bledington Glos 100 G4
Bledlow Bucks 84 E3
Bledlow Ridge Bucks 84 F3
Bleet Wilts 45 B11
Blegbie E Loth 271 C9
Blegbury Devon 24 B2
Blencarn Cumb 231 E8
Blencogo Cumb 229 B9
Blendworth Hants 34 E2
Blenheim Oxon 83 D9
Oxon 83 E9
Blenheim Park Norf 158 C6
Blenkinsopp Hall Northumb 240 E5
Blennerhasset Cumb 229 C9
Blervie Castle Moray 301 D10
Bletchingdon Oxon 83 B8
Bletchingley Sur 51 C10
Bletchley M Keynes 103 E7
Shrops 150 C2
Bletherston Pembs 91 G11
Bletsoe Beds 121 F10
Blewbury Oxon 64 B4
Bliby Kent 54 F4
Blickling Norf 160 D3
Blidworth Notts 171 D9
Blidworth Bottoms Notts 171 E9
Blidworth Dale Notts 171 E9
Blindburn Northumb 263 G8
Blindcrake Cumb 229 E8
Blindley Heath Sur 51 D11
Blindmoor Som 28 E3
Blingery Highld 310 E7
Blisland Corn 11 G8
Blissford Hants 31 E11
Bliss Gate Worcs 116 C4
Blisworth Northants 120 G4
Blithbury Staffs 151 E11
Blitterlees Cumb 238 G4
Blockley Glos 100 D3
Blofield Norf 142 B6
Blofield Heath Norf 160 G6
Blo' Norton Norf 125 B10
Bloodman's Corner Suff 143 D10
Bloomfield Bath 45 B7
Bath 61 G8
Borders 262 E3
W Mid 133 E9
Bloomsbury London 67 C10
Blore Staffs 150 C4
Staffs 169 F10
Bloreheath Staffs 150 B4
Blossomfield W Mid 118 B2
Blount's Green Staffs 151 C11
Blowick Mers 193 D11
Blowinghouse Corn 4 E4
Bloxham Oxon 101 D8
Bloxholm Lincs 173 E9
Bloxwich W Mid 133 C9
Bloxworth Dorset 18 C3
Blubberhouses N Yorks 205 B9
Blue Anchor Corn 5 D8
Som 42 E4
Swansea 56 B4
Bluebell Telford 149 G11
Blue Bell Hill Kent 69 G8

Bywell Northumb 242 E2
Byworth W Sus 35 C7

C

Cabbacott Devon 24 C6
Cabbage Hill Brack 65 E11
Cabharstadh W Isles 304 F5
Cabin Shrops 130 F6
Cablea Perth 286 D3
Cabourne Lincs 200 G6
Cabrach Argyll 274 G5
Moray 302 G3
Cabrich Highld 300 E5
Cabus Lancs 202 D5
Cackle Hill Lincs 157 D7
Cackleshaw W Yorks 204 F6
Cackle Street E Sus 23 B11
E Sus 37 B7
E Sus 38 D4
Cadbury Devon 26 G6
Cadbury Barton Devon 25 D11
Cadbury Heath S Glos 61 E7
Cadder E Dunb 278 G2
Cadderlie Argyll 284 D4
Caddington C Beds 85 B9
Caddleton Argyll 275 B8
Caddonfoot Borders 261 C10
Caddonlee Borders 261 B10
Cadeby Leics 135 C8
S Yorks 198 G4
Cadeleigh Devon 26 F6
Cademuir Borders 260 B6
Cader Denb 165 C8
Cade Street E Sus 37 C10
Cadger Path Angus 287 B8
Cad Green Som 28 D4
Cadgwith Corn 2 G6
Cadham Fife 286 G6
Cadishead Gtr Man 184 C2
Cadle Swansea 56 B6
Cadley Lancs 202 G6
Wilts 47 C8
Wilts 63 F8
Cadmore End Bucks 84 G3
Cadnam Hants 32 E3
Cadney N Lincs 200 G4
Cadney Bank Wrex 149 C9
Cadole Flint 166 C2
Cadoxton V Glam 58 F6
Cadoxton-Juxta-Neath Neath 57 B9
Cadshaw Blkburn 195 D8
Cadwell Herts 104 E3
Cadzow S Lnrk 268 E4
Caeathro Gwyn 163 C7
Cae Clyd Gwyn 164 G2
Cae-gors Carms 75 E9
Caehopkin Powys 76 C4
Caemorgan Ceredig 92 B3
Caenby Lincs 189 D8
Caenby Corner Lincs 189 D7
Caerau Bridgend 57 C11
Cardiff 58 D6
Caerau Park Newport 59 B9
Cae'r-bont Powys 76 C4
Cae'r-bryn Carms 75 C9
Caerdeon Gwyn 146 F2
Caer-Estyn Wrex 166 D4
Caerfarchell Pembs 90 F5
Caer-Farchell Pembs 90 F5
Caerffili / Caerphilly Caerph 59 B7
Caerfyrddin / Carmarthen Carms 93 G8
Caergeiliog Anglesey 178 F4
Caergwrle Flint 166 D4
Caergybi / Holyhead Anglesey 178 E2
Caerhendy Neath 57 C9
Caerhun Gwyn 163 B9
Cae'r-Lan Powys 76 C4
Caerleon Newport 78 G4
Caer Llan Mon 79 D7
Caermead V Glam 58 F3
Caermeini Pembs 92 E2
Caernarfon Gwyn 163 C7
Caerphilly / Caerffili Caerph 59 B7
Caersws Powys 129 E10
Caerwedros Ceredig 111 F7
Caerwent Mon 79 G7
Caerwent Brook Mon 60 B3
Caerwych Gwyn 146 B2
Caerwys Flint 181 G10
Caethle Gwyn 128 D2
Cage Green Kent 52 D5
Caggan Highld 291 B10
Caggle Street Mon 78 B5
Cailness Stirl 285 G7
Caim Anglesey 179 E10
Cainscross Glos 80 D4
Caio Carms 94 D3
Cairinis W Isles 296 E4
Cairisiadar W Isles 304 E2
Cairminis W Isles 296 C6
Cairnbaan Argyll 275 D9
Cairnbanno Ho Aberds 303 E8
Cairnborrow Aberds 302 E4
Cairnbrogie Aberds 303 G8
Cairnbulg Castle Aberds 303 C10
Cairncross Angus 292 F6
Borders 273 C7
Cairnderry Dumfries 236 B5
Cairndow Argyll 284 F5
Cairness Aberds 303 C10
Cairneyhill Fife 279 D10
Cairnfield Ho Moray 302 C4
Cairngaan Dumfries 236 F3
Cairngarroch Dumfries 236 E2
Cairnhill Aberds 302 F6
Aberds 303 D7
N Lnrk 268 C5
Cairnie Aberds 293 C10
Aberds 302 E4
Cairnlea S Ayrs 244 G6
Cairnleith Crofts Aberds 303 F9
Cairnmuir Aberds 303 C9
Cairnorrie Aberds 303 E8
Cairnpark Aberds 293 B10
Dumfries 247 D9
Cairnryan Dumfries 236 C2
Cairnton Orkney 314 F3
Cairston Orkney 314 E2
Caister-on-Sea Norf 161 G10
Caistor Lincs 200 G6
Caistor St Edmund Norf 142 C4
Caistron Northumb 251 C11
Caitha Bowland Borders 271 G9
Cakebole Worcs 117 C7
Calais Street Suff 107 D9
Calanais W Isles 304 E4
Calbost W Isles 305 G6
Calbourne IoW 20 D4
Calceby Lincs 190 F5
Calcoed Flint 181 G11
Calcot Glos 81 C9
W Berks 65 E7
Calcot Row W Berks 65 E7
Calcott Kent 71 G7
Shrops 149 G8
Calcott's Green Glos 80 B3
Calcutt N Yorks 206 B2
Wilts 81 G10
Caldback Shetland 312 C8
Caldbeck Cumb 230 D2
Caldbergh N Yorks 213 B11
Caldecote Cambs 122 F6
Cambs 138 F2
Herts 104 D4
Northants 120 G3
Warks 135 E7
Caldecote Hill Herts 85 G11
Caldecott Northants 121 D9
Oxon 83 F7
Rutland 137 E7
Caldecotte M Keynes 103 D7
Calder Cumb 219 E10
Calderbank N Lnrk 268 C5
Calder Bridge Cumb 219 D10
Calderbrook Gtr Man 196 D2
Caldercruix N Lnrk 268 B6
Calder Grove W Yorks 197 D10
Calder Hall Cumb 219 E10
Calder Mains Highld 310 D4
Caldermill S Lnrk 268 G3
Caldermoor Gtr Man 196 D2
Calderstones Mers 182 D6
Calder Vale Lancs 202 D6
Calderwood S Lnrk 268 D2
Caldhame Angus 287 C8
Caldicot / Cil-y-coed Mon 60 B3
Caldmore W Mid 133 D10
Caldwell Derbys 152 F5
N Yorks 224 C3
Caldy Mers 182 D2
Caledrhydiau Ceredig 111 G9
Cale Green Gtr Man 184 D5
Calenick Corn 4 G6
Caleys Fields Worcs 100 C4
Calf Heath Staffs 133 B8
Calford Green Suff 106 B3
Calfsound Orkney 314 C5
Calgary Argyll 288 D5
Caliach Argyll 288 D5
Califer Moray 301 D10
California Cambs 139 G10
Falk 279 F8
Norf 161 G10
Suff 108 C3
W Mid 133 G10
Calke Derbys 153 E7
Callakille Highld 298 D6
Callaly Northumb 252 B3
Callander Stirl 285 G10
Callandrode Stirl 285 G10
Callands Warr 183 C9
Callaughton Shrops 132 D2
Callendar Park Falk 279 F7
Callert Ho Highld 290 G2
Callerton T&W 242 D5
Callerton Lane End T&W 242 D5
Callestick Corn 4 E5
Calligarry Highld 295 E8
Callington Corn 7 B7
Callingwood Staffs 152 E3
Calloose Corn 2 B3
Callop Highld 289 B11
Callow Derbys 170 E3
Hereford 97 E9
Callow End Worcs 98 B6
Callow Hill Mon 79 B8
Som 44 E4
Wilts 62 C4
Worcs 116 C4
Callow Marsh Hereford 98 B3
Callows Grave Worcs 115 D11
Calmore Hants 32 E4
Calmsden Glos 81 D8
Calne Wilts 62 E4
Calne Marsh Wilts 62 E4
Calow Derbys 186 G6
Calow Green Derbys 170 B6
Calrofold Ches E 184 G6
Calshot Hants 33 G7
Calstock Corn 7 B8
Calstone Wellington Wilts 62 F4
Calthorpe Norf 160 C3
Oxon 101 D9
Calthwaite Cumb 230 C5
Calton Glasgow 268 C2
N Yorks 204 B4
Staffs 169 E10
Calton Lees Derbys 170 B3
Calvadnack Corn 2 B5
Calveley Ches E 167 D9
Calver Derbys 186 G2
Calverhall Shrops 150 B2
Calver Hill Hereford 97 B7
Calverleigh Devon 26 E6
Calverley W Yorks 205 F10
Calver Sough Derbys 186 F2
Calvert Bucks 102 G3
Calverton M Keynes 102 D5
Notts 171 F10
Calvine Perth 291 G10
Calvo Cumb 238 G4
Cam Glos 80 F3
Camaghael Highld 290 F3
Camas an Staca Argyll 274 G5
Camas-luinie Highld 295 C11
Camasnacroise Highld 289 D10
Camas Salach Highld 289 C8
Camastianavaig Highld 295 B7
Camasunary Highld 295 D7
Camault Muir Highld 300 E5
Camb Shetland 312 D7
Camber E Sus 39 D7
Camberley Sur 65 G11
Camberwell London 67 D10
Camblesforth N Yorks 199 B7
Cambo Northumb 252 F2
Cambois Northumb 253 G8
Camborne Corn 4 G3
Cambourne Cambs 122 F6
Cambridge Borders 271 F11
Cambs 123 F9
Glos 80 E3
W Yorks 205 D10
Cambridge Batch N Som 60 F4
Cambridge Town Sthend 70 C2
Cambrose Corn 4 F3
Cambus Clack 279 C7
Cambusavie Farm Highld 309 K7
Cambusbarron Stirl 278 C5
Cambusdrenny Stirl 278 C5
Cambuskenneth Stirl 278 C6
Cambuslang S Lnrk 268 D2
Cambusmore Lodge Highld 309 K7
Cambusnethan N Lnrk 268 D6
Camden London 67 C9
Camden Hill Kent 53 F9
Camden Park Kent 52 F5
Cameley Bath 44 B6
Camelford Corn 11 E8
Camel Green Dorset 31 E10
Camelon Falk 279 E7
Camelsdale Sur 49 G11
Camer Kent 69 F7
Cameron Fife 280 B6
Cameron Bridge Fife 280 B6
Camerory Highld 301 F10
Camer's Green Worcs 98 D5
Camerton Bath 45 B7
Cumb 228 E6
E Yorks 201 B8
Camghouran Perth 285 B9
Cammachmore Aberds 293 D11
Cammeringham Lincs 188 E6
Camnant Powys 113 F11
Camoquhill Stirl 277 D10
Camore Highld 309 K7
Camp Lincs 172 E5
Campbeltown Argyll 255 E8
Camp Corner Oxon 83 E10
Camperdown T&W 243 C7
Camphill Derbys 185 F11
Camp Hill N Yorks 214 C6
Pembs 73 C10
Warks 134 E6
W Yorks 196 D5
Campion Hills Warks 118 D6
Campions Essex 87 C7
Cample Dumfries 247 E9
Campmuir Perth 286 D6
Campsall S Yorks 198 E4
Campsea Ashe Suff 126 F6
Camps End Cambs 106 C2
Campsey Ash Suff 126 F6
Campsfield Oxon 83 B7
Camps Heath Suff 143 E10
Campton C Beds 104 D2
Camptoun E Loth 281 F10
Camptown Borders 262 G5
Camp Town W Yorks 206 F2
Camquhart Argyll 275 E10
Camrose Pembs 91 G8
Camserney Perth 286 C2
Camster Highld 310 E6
Camuschoirk Highld 289 C9
Camuscross Highld 295 D8
Camusnagaul Highld 290 F2
Highld 307 L5
Camusrory Highld 295 F10
Camusteel Highld 299 E7
Camusterrach Highld 299 E7
Camusvrachan Perth 285 C10
Canada Hants 32 D3
Lincs 200 G6
Canadia E Sus 38 D2
Canal Foot Cumb 210 D6
Canal Side S Yorks 199 E7
Canbus Clack 279 C7
Candacraig Ho Aberds 292 B5
Candlesby Lincs 175 B7
Candle Street Suff 125 C10
Candy Mill S Lnrk 269 G11
Cane End Oxon 65 D7
Caneheath E Sus 23 D9
Canewdon Essex 88 G5
Canford Bottom Dorset 31 G8
Canford Cliffs Poole 19 D7
Canford Heath Poole 18 C6
Canford Magna Poole 18 B6
Cangate Norf 160 F6
Canham's Green Suff 125 D11
Canholes Derbys 185 G8
Canisbay Highld 310 B7
Canklow S Yorks 186 C6
Canley W Mid 118 B6
Cann Dorset 30 C5
Cannalidgey Corn 5 B8
Cannard's Grave Som 44 E6
Cann Common Dorset 30 C5
Cannich Highld 300 F3
Cannington Som 43 F9
Canning Town London 68 C2
Cannock Staffs 133 B9
Cannock Wood Staffs 151 G10
Cannon's Green Essex 87 D9
Cannop Glos 79 C10
Canonbie Dumfries 239 B9
Canon Bridge Hereford 97 C8
Canonbury London 67 C10
Canon Frome Hereford 98 C3
Canon Pyon Hereford 97 B9
Canons Ashby Northants 119 G11
Canonsgrove Som 28 C2
Canons Park London 85 G11
Canon's Town Corn 2 B2
Canterbury Kent 54 B6
Cantley Norf 143 C7
S Yorks 198 G6
Cantlop Shrops 131 B10
Canton Cardiff 59 D7
Cantraybruich Highld 301 E7
Cantraydoune Highld 301 E7
Cantraywood Highld 301 E7
Cantsfield Lancs 212 E2
Canvey Island Essex 69 C9
Canwick Lincs 173 B7
Canworthy Water Corn 11 C10
Caol Highld 290 F3
Caolas Argyll 288 E2
W Isles 297 M2
Caolas Fhlodaigh W Isles 296 F4
Caolas Liubharsaigh W Isles 297 G4
Caolas Scalpaigh W Isles 305 J4
Caolas Stocinis W Isles 305 J3
Caol Ila Argyll 274 F5
Caoslasnacon Highld 290 G3
Capel Carms 75 E8
Kent 52 E6
Sur 51 E7
Capel Bangor Ceredig 128 G3
Capel Betws Lleucu Ceredig 112 F2
Capel Carmel Gwyn 144 D3
Capel Coch Anglesey 179 E7
Capel Cross Kent 53 E8
Capel Curig Conwy 164 D2
Capel Cynon Ceredig 93 B7
Capel Dewi Carms 93 G9
Ceredig 93 C9
Ceredig 128 G2
Capel Garmon Conwy 164 D4
Capel Green Suff 109 B7
Capel-gwyn Anglesey 178 F4
Capel Gwyn Carms 93 G9
Capel Gwynfe Carms 94 G4
Capel Hendre Carms 75 C9
Capel Hermon Gwyn 146 D4
Capel Isaac Carms 93 F11
Capel Iwan Carms 92 D5
Capel-le-Ferne Kent 55 F8
Capel Llanilltern Cardiff 58 C5
Capel Mawr Anglesey 178 G6
Capel Newydd / Newchapel Pembs 92 D4
Capel Parc Anglesey 178 D6
Capel St Andrew Suff 109 B7
Capel St Mary Suff 107 D11
Capel Seion Carms 75 C8
Ceredig 112 B2
Capel Siloam Conwy 164 E4
Capel Tygwydd Ceredig 92 C5
Capel Uchaf Gwyn 162 F6
Capelulo Conwy 180 F2
Capel-y-ffin Powys 96 E5
Capel-y-graig Gwyn 163 B8
Capenhurst Ches W 182 G5
Capernwray Lancs 211 E10
Capheaton Northumb 252 G2
Capland Som 28 D4
Cappercleuch Borders 260 E6
Capplegill Dumfries 248 B4
Capstone Medway 69 F9
Captain Fold Gtr Man 195 E11
Capton Devon 8 E6
Som 42 F5
Caputh Perth 286 D4
Caradon Town Corn 11 G11
Carbis Corn 5 D10
Carbis Bay Corn 2 B2
Carbost Highld 294 B5
Highld 298 E4
Carbrain N Lnrk 278 G5
Carbrook S Yorks 186 D5
Carbrooke Norf 141 C9
Carburton Notts 187 G10
Carcant Borders 271 E7
Carcary Angus 287 B10
Carclaze Corn 5 E10
Carclew Corn 3 B7
Car Colston Notts 172 G2
Carcroft S Yorks 198 E4
Cardenden Fife 280 C4
Cardeston Shrops 149 G7
Cardew Cumb 230 B2
Cardewlees Cumb 239 G8
Cardiff Cardiff 59 D7
Cardigan / Aberteifi Ceredig 92 B3
Cardinal's Green Cambs 106 B2
Cardington Beds 103 B11
Shrops 131 D10
Cardinham Corn 6 B2
Cardonald Glasgow 267 C10
Cardow Moray 301 E11
Cardrona Borders 261 B8
Cardross Argyll 276 F6
Cardurnock Cumb 238 F5
Careby Lincs 155 F10
Careston Angus 293 G7
Careston Castle Angus 287 B9
Care Village Leics 136 D4
Carew Pembs 73 E8
Carew Cheriton Pembs 73 E8
Carew Newton Pembs 73 E8
Carey Hereford 97 E11
Carey Park Corn 6 E4
Carfin N Lnrk 268 D5
Carfrae E Loth 271 B11
Carfury Corn 1 C4
Cargate Common Norf 142 E2
Cargenbridge Dumfries 237 B11
Cargill Perth 286 D5
Cargo Cumb 239 F9
Cargo Fleet Mbro 234 G6
Cargreen Corn 7 C8
Carham Northumb 263 B8
Carhampton Som 42 E4
Carharrack Corn 4 G4
Carie Perth 285 B10
Perth 285 D10
Carines Corn 4 D5
Carisbrooke IoW 20 D5
Cark Cumb 211 D7
Carkeel Corn 7 C8
Carlabhagh W Isles 304 D4
Carland Cross Corn 5 E7
Carlbury N Yorks 224 B4
Carlby Lincs 155 G11
Carlecotes S Yorks 197 G7
Carleen Corn 2 C4
Carlenrig Borders 249 C9
Carlesmoor N Yorks 214 E3
Carleton Cumb 219 D10
Cumb 230 F6
Cumb 239 G10
Lancs 202 F2
N Yorks 204 D5
W Yorks 198 C3
Carleton Forehoe Norf 141 B11
Carleton Hall Cumb 219 F11
Carleton-in-Craven N Yorks 204 D5
Carleton Rode Norf 142 E2
Carleton St Peter Norf 142 C6
Carley Hill T&W 243 F9
Carlidnack Corn 3 D7
Carlincraig Aberds 302 E6
Carlingcott Bath 45 B7
Carlinghow W Yorks 197 C8
Carlingwark Devon 27 E11
Carlin How Redcar 226 B4
Carlisle Cumb 239 F10
Carloggas Corn 5 B7
Corn 5 E9
Carloonan Argyll 284 F4
Carlops Borders 270 D3
Carlton Beds 121 F9
Cambs 124 G2
Leics 135 C7
Notts 171 G10
N Yorks 198 C6
N Yorks 213 C11
N Yorks 216 B2
N Yorks 224 C3
Stockton 234 G3
Suff 127 E7
S Yorks 197 E11
W Yorks 197 B10
Carlton Colville Suff 143 F10
Carlton Curlieu Leics 136 D3
Carlton Green Cambs 124 G2
Carlton Husthwaite N Yorks 215 D9
Carlton in Cleveland N Yorks 225 E10
Carlton in Lindrick Notts 187 E9
Carlton le Moorland Lincs 172 D6
Carlton Miniott N Yorks 215 C7
Carlton on Trent Notts 172 C3
Carlton Purlieus Northants 136 F6
Carlton Scroop Lincs 172 G6
Carluddon Corn 5 D10
Carluke S Lnrk 268 E6
Carlyon Bay Corn 5 E11
Carmarthen / Caerfyrddin Carms 93 G8
Carmel Anglesey 178 E5
Carms 75 B9
Flint 181 F11
Gwyn 163 E7
Powys 113 D11
Carmichael S Lnrk 259 B10
Carminow Cross Corn 5 B11
Carmont Aberds 293 E10
Carmunnock Glasgow 268 D2
Carmyle Glasgow 268 C2
Carmyllie Angus 287 C9
Carnaby E Yorks 218 F2
Carnach Highld 299 G10
Highld 307 K5
W Isles 305 J4
Carnachy Highld 308 D7
Càrnais W Isles 304 E2
Càrnan W Isles 297 G3
Carn Arthen Corn 2 B5
Carnbahn Perth 285 C10
Carnbee Fife 287 G9
Carnbo Perth 286 G4
Carn Brea Corn 4 G3
Carn Brea Village Corn 4 G3
Carnbroe N Lnrk 268 C4
Carndu Highld 295 C10
Carnduff S Lnrk 268 F3
Carnduncan Argyll 274 G3
Carne Corn 3 B10
Corn 3 E7
Corn 5 D9
Carnebone Corn 2 C6
Carnedd Powys 129 E10
Carnetown Rhondda 77 G9
Carnforth Lancs 211 E9
Lancs 211 E10
Carnglas Swansea 56 C6
Carnhedryn Pembs 90 F6
Carnhedryn Uchaf Pembs 90 F5
Carnhell Green Corn 2 B4
Carnhot Corn 4 F4
Carnkie Corn 2 B5
Corn 2 C6
Carnkief Corn 4 E5
Carno Powys 129 D9
Carnoch Highld 300 D2
Highld 300 F3
Carnock Fife 279 D10
Carnon Downs Corn 4 G5
Carnousie Aberds 302 D6
Carnoustie Angus 287 D9
Carnsmerry Corn 5 D10
Carn Towan Corn 1 D3
Carntyne Glasgow 268 B2
Carnwadric E Renf 267 D10
Carnwath S Lnrk 269 F9
Carnyorth Corn 1 C3
Caroe Corn 11 C9
Carol Green W Mid 118 B5
Carpalla Corn 5 E9
Carpenders Park Herts 85 G10
Carpenter's Hill Worcs 117 C11
Carperby N Yorks 213 B10
Carpley Green N Yorks 213 B8
Carr Gtr Man 195 D9
S Yorks 187 C8
Carradale Argyll 255 D9
Carragraich W Isles 305 J3
Carr Bank Cumb 211 D9
Carrbridge Highld 301 G9
Carrbrook Gtr Man 196 G3
Carr Cross Lancs 193 E11
Carreglefn Anglesey 178 D5
Carreg-wen Pembs 92 C4
Carreg y Garth Gwyn 163 B9
Carr Gate W Yorks 197 C10
Carr Green Gtr Man 184 D2
Carr Hill T&W 243 E7
Carrhouse Devon 26 F3
Carr Houses Mers 193 G10
Carrick Argyll 275 E10
Dumfries 237 D7
Fife 287 E8
Carrick Castle Argyll 276 C3
Carrick Ho Orkney 314 C5
Carriden Falk 279 E10
Carrington Gtr Man 184 C2
Lincs 174 E4
Midloth 270 C6
Nottingham 171 G9
Carroch Dumfries 246 E5
Carrog Conwy 164 F3
Denb 165 G10
Carroglen Perth 285 E11
Carrol Highld 311 J2
Carron Falk 279 E7
Moray 302 E2
Carronbridge Dumfries 247 D9
Carron Bridge Stirl 278 E4
Carronshore Falk 279 E7
Carrot Angus 287 C8
Carroway Head Staffs 134 D3
Carrow Hill Mon 78 G6
Carrshield Northumb 232 B2
Carrutherstown Dumfries 238 C4
Carr Vale Derbys 171 B7
Carrville Durham 234 C2
Carry Argyll 275 G10
Carsaig Argyll 275 E8
Argyll 289 G7
Carscreugh Dumfries 236 D4
Carsegowan Dumfries 236 D6
Carse Gray Angus 287 B8
Carse Ho Argyll 275 G8
Carseriggan Dumfries 236 C5
Carsethorn Dumfries 237 D11
Carshalton London 67 G9
Carshalton Beeches London 67 G9
Carshalton on the Hill London 67 G9
Carsington Derbys 170 E3
Carskiey Argyll 255 G7
Carsluith Dumfries 236 D6
Carsphairn Dumfries 246 E3
Carstairs S Lnrk 269 F8
Carstairs Junction S Lnrk 269 F9
Carswell Marsh Oxon 82 F4
Cartbridge Sur 50 B4
Carterhaugh Borders 261 D10
Carter Knowle S Yorks 186 E4
Carter's Clay Hants 32 C4
Carter's Green Essex 87 C8
Carter's Hill Wokingham 65 F9
Carterspiece Glos 79 C9
Carterton Oxon 82 D3
Carterway Heads Northumb 242 G2
Carthamartha Corn 12 F3
Carthew Corn 2 B5
Corn 5 D10
Carthorpe N Yorks 214 C6
Cartington Northumb 252 C2
Cartland S Lnrk 269 F7
Cartledge Derbys 186 F4
Cartmel Cumb 211 D7
Cartmel Fell Cumb 211 B8
Cartsdyke Invclyd 276 F5
Cartworth W Yorks 196 F6
Carty Port Dumfries 236 C6
Carway Carms 75 D7
Carwinley Cumb 239 C10
Carwynnen Corn 2 B5
Cary Fitzpaine Som 29 B9
Carzantic Corn 12 E3
Carzield Dumfries 247 G11
Carzise Corn 2 C3
Cascob Powys 114 D4
Cashes Green Glos 80 D4
Cashlie Perth 285 C8
Cashmoor Dorset 31 E7
Cas Mael / Puncheston Pembs 91 F10
Cassey Compton Glos 81 C9
Cassington Oxon 83 C7
Cassop Durham 234 D2
Castallack Corn 1 D5
Castell Conwy 164 B3
Denb 165 B10
Castellau Rhondda 58 B5
Castell-Howell Ceredig 93 B8
Castell nedd / Neath Neath 57 B8
Castell Newydd Emlyn / Newcastle Emlyn Carms 92 C6
Castell-y-bwch Torf 78 G3
Castell-y-rhingyll Carms 75 C9
Casterton Cumb 212 D2
Castle Devon 28 G4
Som 27 B9
Castle Acre Norf 158 F6
Castle Ashby Northants 121 F7
Castle Bolton N Yorks 223 G10
Castle Bromwich W Mid 134 F2
Castle Bytham Lincs 155 F9
Castlebythe Pembs 91 F10
Castle Caereinion Powys 130 B3
Castle Camps Cambs 106 C2
Castle Carlton Lincs 190 E5
Castle Carrock Cumb 240 F2
Castlecary N Lnrk 278 F5
Castle Cary Som 44 G6
Castle Combe Wilts 61 D10
Castlecraig Highld 301 C8
Castle Craig Borders 270 G2
Castlecroft Staffs 133 D7
Castle Donington Leics 153 D8
Castle Douglas Dumfries 237 C9
Castle Eaton Swindon 81 F10
Castle Eden Durham 234 D4
Castle End Pboro 138 B2
Castlefairn Dumfries 246 F6
Castlefields Halton 183 E8
Castle Fields Shrops 149 G10
Castle Forbes Aberds 293 B8
Castleford W Yorks 198 B2
Castle Frome Hereford 98 B3
Castle Gate Corn 1 C5
Castlegreen Shrops 130 F6
Castle Green London 68 C3
Sur 66 G3
S Yorks 197 G9
Castle Gresley Derbys 152 F5
Castlehead Renfs 267 C9
Castle Heaton Northumb 273 G8
Castle Hedingham Essex 106 E5
Castlehill Argyll 254 B4
Borders 260 B6
Highld 310 C5
S Ayrs 257 E9
W Dunb 277 F7
Castle Hill E Sus 37 B9
Gtr Man 184 C6
Kent 53 E7
Suff 108 B3
Worcs 116 F5
Castle Huntly Perth 287 E7
Castle Kennedy Dumfries 236 D3
Castlemaddy Dumfries 246 F3
Castlemartin Pembs 72 F6
Castlemilk Dumfries 238 B5
Glasgow 268 D2
Castlemorris Pembs 91 E8
Castlemorton Worcs 98 D5
Castle O'er Dumfries 248 E6
Castlerigg Cumb 229 G11
Castle Rising Norf 158 E3
Castleside Durham 233 B7
Castle Street W Yorks 196 C3
Castle Stuart Highld 301 E7
Castlethorpe M Keynes 102 C6
N Lincs 200 F3
Castleton Angus 287 C7
Argyll 275 E9
Derbys 185 E11
Gtr Man 195 E11
Moray 301 G11
Newport 59 C9
N Yorks 226 D3
Castleton Village Highld 300 E6
Castle Toward Argyll 266 B2
Castletown Ches W 166 E6
Cumb 230 E6
Dorset 17 G9
Highld 301 E7
Highld 310 C5
IoM 192 F3
Staffs 151 E8
T&W 243 F9
Castle Town W Sus 36 E2
Castletump Glos 98 F4
Castle-upon-Alun V Glam 58 E2
Castle Vale W Mid 134 E2
Castleweary Borders 249 C10
Castlewigg Dumfries 236 E6
Castley N Yorks 205 D11
Castling's Heath Suff 107 C9
Caston Norf 141 D9
Castor Pboro 138 D2
Caswell Swansea 56 D5
Catacol N Ayrs 255 C10
Cat Bank Cumb 220 F6
Catbrain S Glos 60 C5
Catbrook Mon 79 E8
Catch Flint 182 G2
Catchall Corn 1 D4
Catchems Corner W Mid 118 B4
Catchems End Worcs 116 B5
Catchgate Durham 242 G5
Catchory Highld 310 D6
Catcleugh Northumb 250 C6
Catcliffe S Yorks 186 D6
Catcomb Wilts 62 D4
Catcott Som 43 F11
Caterham Sur 51 B10
Catfield Norf 161 E7
Catfirth Shetland 313 H6
Catford London 67 E11
Catforth Lancs 202 F5
Cathays Cardiff 59 D7
Cathays Park Cardiff 59 D7
Cathcart Glasgow 267 C11
Cathedine Powys 96 F2
Catherine-de-Barnes W Mid 134 G3
Catherine Slack W Yorks 196 B5
Catherington Hants 33 E11
Catherton Shrops 116 B3
Cat Hill S Yorks 197 F8
Cathiron Warks 119 B9
Catholes Cumb 222 G3
Cathpair Borders 271 F9
Catisfield Hants 33 F8
Catley Lane Head Gtr Man 195 D11
Catley Southfield Hereford 98 C3
Catlodge Highld 291 D8
Catlowdy Cumb 239 B11
Catmere End Essex 105 D9
Catmore W Berks 64 C3
Caton Devon 13 G11
Lancs 211 G10
Caton Green Lancs 211 F10
Catrine E Ayrs 258 D2
Cat's Ash Newport 78 G5
Cat's Common Norf 160 E6
Cats Edge Staffs 169 E7
Catsfield E Sus 38 E2
Catsfield Stream E Sus 38 E2
Catsgore Som 29 B8
Catsham Som 44 G5
Catshaw S Yorks 197 G8
Catshill W Mid 133 B11
Worcs 117 C9
Cat's Hill Cross Staffs 150 C6
Catslackburn Borders 261 D8
Catslip Oxon 65 B8
Catstree Shrops 132 D4
Cattadale Argyll 274 G4
Cattal N Yorks 206 C4
Cattawade Suff 108 E2
Cattedown Plym 7 E9
Catterall Lancs 202 E5
Catterick N Yorks 224 F4
Catterick Bridge N Yorks 224 F4
Catterick Garrison N Yorks 224 F3
Catterlen Cumb 230 E5
Catterline Aberds 293 F10
Catterton N Yorks 206 D6
Catteshall Sur 50 E3
Catthorpe Leics 119 B11
Cattistock Dorset 17 B7
Cattle End Northants 102 C3
Catton Northumb 241 F8
N Yorks 215 D7
Catwick E Yorks 209 D8
Catworth Cambs 121 C11
Caudle Green Glos 80 C6
Caudlesprings Norf 141 C8
Caulcott C Beds 103 C9
Oxon 101 G10
Cauld Borders 261 G11

Warks 134 E4
Warks 134 E5
Wilts 62 D4
W Mid 119 B7
Worcs 98 C6
Church Enstone
Oxon 101 G7
Churches Green
E Sus 23 B10
Church Fenton
N Yorks 206 F6
Churchfield Hereford 98 B4
W Mid 133 E10
Churchfields Wilts 31 B10
Churchgate Herts 86 E4
Churchgate Street
Essex 87 C7
Church Green Devon 15 B9
Norf 141 E11
Church Gresley
Derbys 152 F5
Church Hanborough
Oxon 82 C6
Church Hill
Ches W 167 C10
Pembs 73 C7
Staffs 151 G10
W Mid 133 D9
Worcs 117 D11
Church Hougham
Kent 55 E9
Church Houses
N Yorks 226 F3
Churchill Devon 28 G4
Devon 40 E5
N Som 44 B2
Oxon 100 G5
Worcs 117 B7
Worcs 117 G8
Churchill Green
N Som 60 G2
Churchinford Som 28 E2
Church Knowle
Dorset 18 E4
Church Laneham
Notts 188 F4
Church Langton
Leics 136 E4
Church Lawford
Warks 119 B8
Church Lawton
Ches E 168 D4
Church Leigh
Staffs 151 B10
Church Lench
Worcs 117 G10
Church Mayfield
Staffs 169 G11
Church Minshull
Ches E 167 C11
Churchmoor Rough
Shrops 131 F8
Church Norton
W Sus 22 D5
Church Oakley Hants 48 C5
Churchover Warks 135 G10
Church Preen
Shrops 131 D10
Church Pulverbatch
Shrops 131 C8
Churchstanton Som 27 E11
Churchstoke Powys 130 E5
Churchstow Devon 8 F4
Church Stowe
Northants 120 F2
Church Street
Essex 106 C5
Kent 69 E8
Church Stretton
Shrops 131 E9
Churchton Pembs 73 D10
Churchtown Corn 11 F7
Cumb 230 C3
Derbys 170 C3
Devon 24 G3
Devon 41 E7
IoM 192 C5
Lancs 202 E5
Mers 193 D11
Shrops 130 F5
Som 42 F3
Church Town Corn 4 G3
Leics 153 F7
N Lincs 199 F9
Sur 51 C11
Church Village
Rhondda 58 B5
Church Warsop
Notts 171 B9
Church Westcote
Glos 100 G4
Church Whitfield
Kent 55 D10
Church Wilne
Derbys 153 C8
Churchwood W Sus 35 D8
Churnet Grange
Staffs 169 E7
Churnsike Lodge
Northumb 240 B5
Churscombe Torbay 9 C7
Churston Ferrers
Torbay 9 D8
Churt Sur 49 F11
Churton Ches W 166 D6
Churwell W Yorks 197 B9
Chute Cadley Wilts 47 C10
Chute Standen
Wilts 47 C10
Chweffordd Conwy 180 G4
Chwilog Gwyn 145 B8
Chwitffordd / Whitford
Flint 181 F10
Chyandour Corn 1 C5
Chyanvounder Corn 2 E5
Chycoose Corn 3 B8
Chynhale Corn 2 C4
Chynoweth Corn 2 C2
Chyvarloe Corn 2 E5
Cicelyford Mon 79 E8
Cilan Uchaf Gwyn 144 E5
Cilau Pembs 91 D8
Cilcain Flint 165 B11
Cilcennin Ceredig 111 E10
Cilcewydd Powys 130 C4
Cilfor Gwyn 146 B2
Cilfrew Neath 76 E3
Cilfynydd Rhondda 77 G9
Cilgerran Pembs 92 C3
Cilgwyn Carms 94 F4
Ceredig 92 C6
Gwyn 163 E7
Pembs 91 D11
Ciliau Aeron Ceredig 111 F9
Cill Amhlaidh
W Isles 297 G3
Cill Donnain
W Isles 297 J3
Cille Bhrighde
W Isles 297 K3
Cill Eireabhagh
W Isles 297 G4
Cille Pheadair
W Isles 297 K3
Cilmaengwyn Neath 76 D2
Cilmery Powys 113 G10
Cilsan Carms 93 G11
Ciltalgarth Gwyn 164 G5
Ciltwrch Powys 96 C3
Cilybebyll Neath 76 E2
Cil y coed / Caldicot
Mon 60 B3
Cilycwm Carms 94 D5
Cimla Neath 57 B9
Cinderford Glos 79 C11
Cinderhill Derbys 170 F5
Nottingham 171 G8
Cinder Hill Gtr Man 195 F9
Kent 52 D4
W Mid 133 E8
W Sus 36 B5
Cinnamon Brow
Warr 183 C10
Cippenham Slough 66 C2
Cippyn Pembs 92 B2
Circebost W Isles 304 E3
Cirencester Glos 81 E8
Ciribhig W Isles 304 D3
City London 67 C10
Powys 130 F4
V Glam 58 D3
City Dulas Anglesey 179 D7
Clabhach Argyll 288 D3
Clachaig Argyll 276 E2
Highld 292 B2
N Ayrs 255 E10
Clachan Argyll 255 B8
Argyll 275 B8
Argyll 284 F5
Argyll 289 E10
Highld 295 B7
Highld 298 C4
Highld 307 L6
W Isles 297 G3
Clachaneasy
Dumfries 236 B5
Clachanmore
Dumfries 236 E2
Clachan na Luib
W Isles 296 E4
Clachan of Campsie
E Dunb 278 F2
Clachan of Glendaruel
Argyll 275 E10
Clachan-Seil Argyll 275 B8
Clachan Strachur
Argyll 284 G4
Clachbreck Argyll 275 F8
Clachnabrain Angus 292 G5
Clachtoll Highld 307 G5
Clackmannan Clack 279 C8
Clackmarras Moray 302 D2
Clacton-on-Sea
Essex 89 B11
Cladach N Ayrs 256 B2
Cladach Chairinis
W Isles 296 F4
Cladach Chireboist
W Isles 296 E3
Claddach Argyll 254 B2
Claddach-knockline
W Isles 296 E3
Cladich Argyll 284 E4
Cladich Steading
Argyll 284 E4
Cladswell Worcs 117 F10
Claggan Highld 289 E8
Highld 290 F3
Perth 285 D11
Claigan Highld 298 D2
Claines Worcs 117 F7
Clandown Bath 45 B7
Clanfield Hants 33 D11
Oxon 82 E3
Clanking Bucks 84 D4
Clanville Hants 47 D10
Som 44 G6
Wilts 62 D2
Claonaig Argyll 255 B9
Claonel Highld 309 J5
Clapgate Dorset 31 G8
Herts 105 G8
Clapham Beds 121 G10
Devon 14 D3
London 67 D9
N Yorks 212 F4
W Sus 35 F9
Clapham Green
Beds 121 G10
N Yorks 205 B10
Clapham Hill Kent 70 G6
Clapham Park London 67 E9
Clap Hill Kent 54 F5
Clapper Corn 10 G6
Clapper Hill Kent 53 F10
Clappers Borders 273 D8
Clappersgate Cumb 221 E7
Clapphoull Shetland 313 L6
Clapton Som 28 F6
Som 44 C6
W Berks 63 E11
Clapton in Gordano
N Som 60 E3
Clapton-on-the-Hill
Glos 81 B11
Clapton Park
London 67 B11
Clapworthy Devon 25 C11
Clarach Ceredig 128 G2
Clarack Aberds 292 D6
Clara Vale T&W 242 E4
Clarbeston Pembs 91 G10
Clarbeston Road
Pembs 91 G10
Clarborough Notts 188 E2
Clardon Highld 310 C5
Clare Oxon 83 F11
Suff 106 B5
Clarebrand
Dumfries 237 C9
Claregate W Mid 133 C7
Claremont Park Sur 66 G6
Claremount
W Yorks 196 B5
Clarencefield
Dumfries 238 D3
Clarence Park
N Som 59 G10
Clarendon Park
Leicester 135 C11
Clareston Pembs 73 C7
Clarilaw Borders 262 D3
Borders 262 F2
Clarken Green Hants 48 C5
Clark Green Ches E 184 F6
Clarksfield Gtr Man 196 G2
Clark's Green Sur 51 F7
Clark's Hill Lincs 157 E7
Clarkston E Renf 267 D11
N Lnrk 268 B5
Clase Swansea 57 B7
Clashandorran
Highld 300 E5
Clashcoig Highld 309 K6
Clasheddy Highld 308 C6
Clashgour Argyll 284 C6
Clashindarroch
Aberds 302 F4
Clashmore Highld 306 F5
Highld 309 L7
Clashnessie Highld 306 F5
Clashnoir Moray 302 G2
Clate Shetland 313 G7
Clatford Wilts 63 F7
Clatford Oakcuts
Hants 47 F10
Clathy Perth 286 F3
Clatt Aberds 302 G5
Clatter Powys 129 E9
Clatterford IoW 20 D5
Clatterford End
Essex 87 C10
Essex 87 D9
Essex 87 E8
Clatterin Bridge
Aberds 293 F8
Clatto Fife 287 F8
Clatworthy Som 42 G5
Clauchlands N Ayrs 256 C2
Claughton Lancs 202 E6
Lancs 211 F11
Mers 182 D4
Clavelshay Som 43 G9
Claverdon Warks 118 E3
Claverham N Som 60 F2
Claverhambury Essex 86 E6
Clavering Essex 105 E9
Claverley Shrops 132 E5
Claverton Bath 61 G9
Claverton Down Bath 61 G9
Clawdd-côch
V Glam 58 D5
Clawdd-newydd
Denb 165 E9
Clawdd Poncen
Denb 165 G9
Clawthorpe Cumb 211 D10
Clawton Devon 12 B3
Claxby Lincs 189 C10
Lincs 191 G7
Claxby St Andrew
Lincs 191 G7
Claxton Norf 142 C6
N Yorks 216 G3
Claybokie Aberds 292 D2
Claybrooke Magna
Leics 135 F9
Claybrooke Parva
Leics 135 F9
Clay Common Suff 143 G9
Clay Coton
Northants 119 B11
Clay Cross Derbys 170 C5
Claydon Glos 99 E8
Oxon 119 G9
Suff 126 G2
Clay End Herts 104 F6
Claygate Dumfries 239 B9
Kent 52 C6
Kent 53 E8
Sur 67 G7
Claygate Cross Kent 52 B6
Clayhall Hants 21 B8
London 86 G6
Clayhanger Devon 27 C8
Som 28 E4
W Mid 133 C10
Clayhidon Devon 27 D11
Clayhill E Sus 38 C4
Hants 32 F4
Clay Hill Bristol 60 E6
London 86 F4
W Berks 64 E5
Clayhithe Cambs 123 E10
Clayholes Angus 287 D9
Clay Lake Lincs 156 E5
Clayland Stirl 277 D11
Clay Mills Derbys 152 D5
Clayock Highld 310 D5
Claypit Hill Cambs 123 G7
Claypits Devon 27 B7
Glos 80 D3
Kent 55 B9
Suff 140 G4
Claypole Lincs 172 F5
Clays End Bath 61 G8
Claythorpe Lincs 190 F6
Clayton Gtr Man 184 B5
Staffs 168 G5
S Yorks 198 F3
W Sus 36 E3
W Yorks 205 G8
Clayton Brook
Lancs 194 C5
Clayton Green
Lancs 194 C5
Clayton Heights
W Yorks 205 G8
Clayton-le-Dale
Lancs 203 G9
Clayton-le-Moors
Lancs 203 G10
Clayton-le-Woods
Lancs 194 C5
Clayton West
W Yorks 197 E9
Clayworth Notts 188 D2
Cleadale Highld 294 G6
Cleadon T&W 243 E9
Cleadon Park T&W 243 E9
Clearbrook Devon 7 B10
Clearwell Glos 79 D9
Newport 59 B9
Clearwood Wilts 45 D10
Cleasby N Yorks 224 C5
Cleat Orkney 314 B4
Orkney 314 H4
Cleatlam Durham 224 B2
Cleator Cumb 219 C10
Cleator Moor
Cumb 219 B10
Cleave Devon 28 G2
Clebrig Highld 308 F5
Cleckheaton
W Yorks 197 B7
Cleddon Mon 79 E8
Cleedownton
Shrops 131 G11
Cleehill Shrops 115 B11
Cleekhimin N Lnrk 268 D5
Cleemarsh Shrops 131 G11
Clee St Margaret
Shrops 131 G11
Cleestanton
Shrops 115 B11
Cleethorpes
NE Lincs 201 F10
Cleeton St Mary
Shrops 116 B2
Cleeve Glos 80 C2
N Som 60 F3
Oxon 64 C6
Cleeve Hill Glos 99 F9
Cleeve Prior Worcs 99 B11
Cleghorn S Lnrk 269 F8
Clegyrnant Powys 129 B8
Clehonger Hereford 97 D9
Cleirwy / Clyro
Powys 96 C4
Cleish Perth 279 B11
Cleland N Lnrk 268 D5
Clements End Glos 79 D9
Clement's End
C Beds 85 B8
Clement Street Kent 68 E4
Clench Wilts 63 G7
Clench Common
Wilts 63 F7
Clencher's Mill
Hereford 98 D4
Clenchwarton Norf 157 E11
Clennell Northumb 251 B10
Clent Worcs 117 B8
Cleobury Mortimer
Shrops 116 B3
Cleobury North
Shrops 132 F2
Cleongart Argyll 255 D7
Clephanton Highld 301 D8
Clerkenwater Corn 5 B11
Clerkenwell London 67 C10
Clerk Green
W Yorks 197 C8
Clerklands Borders 262 E2
Clermiston Edin 280 G3
Clestrain Orkney 314 F3
Cleuch Head
Borders 262 G3
Cleughbrae
Dumfries 238 C3
Clevancy Wilts 62 D5
Clevans Renfs 267 B7
Clevedon N Som 60 E2
Cleveley Oxon 101 G7
Cleveleys Lancs 202 E2
Cleverton Wilts 62 B3
Clevis Bridgend 57 F10
Clewer Som 44 C2
Clewer Green
Windsor 66 D2
Clewer New Town
Windsor 66 D3
Clewer Village
Windsor 66 D3
Cley next the Sea
Norf 177 E8
Cliaid W Isles 297 L2
Cliasmol W Isles 305 H2
Cliburn Cumb 231 G7
Click Mill Orkney 314 D3
Cliddesden Hants 48 D6
Cliff Derbys 185 D8
Warks 134 D4
Cliffburn Angus 287 C10
Cliffe Lancs 203 G10
Medway 69 D8
N Yorks 207 G9
N Yorks 224 B4
Cliff End E Sus 38 E5
W Yorks 196 D6
Cliffe Woods Medway 69 E8
Clifford Devon 24 C4
Hereford 96 B4
W Yorks 206 E4
Clifford Chambers
Warks 118 G3
Clifford's Mesne
Glos 98 G4
Cliffs End Kent 71 G10
Clifftown Sthend 69 B11
Clifton Bristol 60 E5
C Beds 104 D3
Ches W 183 F8
Cumb 230 F6
Derbys 169 G11
Devon 40 E5
Gtr Man 195 G9
Lancs 202 G5
Northumb 252 G6
Nottingham 153 C11
N Yorks 205 D9
Oxon 101 E9
Stirl 285 D7
S Yorks 186 C6
S Yorks 187 B8
Worcs 98 B6
W Yorks 197 C7
York 207 C7
Clifton Campville
Staffs 152 G5
Cliftoncote Borders 263 E8
Clifton Green
Gtr Man 195 G9
Clifton Hampden
Oxon 83 F8
Clifton Junction
Gtr Man 195 G9
Clifton Manor
C Beds 104 D3
Clifton Maybank
Dorset 29 E9
Clifton Moor York 207 B7
Clifton Reynes
M Keynes 121 G8
Clifton upon Dunsmore
Warks 119 B10
Clifton upon Teme
Worcs 116 E4
Cliftonville Kent 71 E11
N Lnrk 268 B4
Norf 160 B6
Climping W Sus 35 G8
Climpy S Lnrk 269 D8
Clink Som 45 D9
Clinkham Wood
Mers 183 B8
Clint N Yorks 205 B11
Clint Green Norf 159 G10
Clintmains Borders 262 C4
Clints N Yorks 224 E2
Cliobh W Isles 304 E2
Clipiau Gwyn 146 G6
Clippesby Norf 161 G8
Clippings Green
Norf 159 G10
Clipsham Rutland 155 F9
Clipston Northants 136 G4
Notts 154 C2
Clipstone C Beds 103 F8
Clitheroe Lancs 203 E10
Cliuthar W Isles 305 J3
Clive Ches W 167 B11
Shrops 149 E10
Clive Green
Ches W 167 C11
Clive Vale E Sus 38 E4
Clivocast Shetland 312 C8
Clixby Lincs 200 G6
Cloatley Wilts 81 G7
Cloatley End Wilts 81 G7
Clocaenog Denb 165 E9
Clochan Aberds 303 E9
Moray 302 C4
Clock Face Mers 183 C8
Clock House London 67 G9
Clockmill Borders 272 E5
Clock Mills Hereford 96 B5
Cloddiau Powys 130 B4
Cloddymoss Moray 301 D9
Clodock Hereford 96 F6
Cloford Som 45 E8
Cloford Common
Som 45 E8
Cloigyn Carms 74 C6
Clola Aberds 303 E10
Clophill C Beds 103 D11
Clopton Northants 137 G11
Suff 126 G4
Clopton Corner
Suff 126 G4
Clopton Green Suff 124 G5
Suff 125 E9
Closeburn Dumfries 247 E9
Close Clark IoM 192 E3
Close House
Durham 233 F10
Closworth Som 29 E9
Clothall Herts 104 E5
Clothall Common
Herts 104 E5
Clotton Ches W 167 C8
Clotton Common
Ches W 167 C8
Cloudesley Bush
Warks 135 F9
Clouds Hereford 97 D11
Cloud Side Staffs 168 C6
Clough Gtr Man 196 D2
Gtr Man 196 F2
W Yorks 196 E5
Clough Dene
Durham 242 F5
Cloughfold Lancs 195 C10
Clough Foot
W Yorks 196 C2
Clough Hall Staffs 168 E4
Clough Head
W Yorks 196 C5
Cloughton
N Yorks 227 G10
Cloughton Newlands
N Yorks 227 F10
Clounlaid Highld 289 D9
Clousta Shetland 313 H5
Clouston Orkney 314 E2
Clova Aberds 302 G4
Angus 292 F5
Clovelly Devon 24 C4
Clove Lodge
Durham 223 B8
Clovenfords
Borders 261 B10
Clovenstone Aberds 293 B9
Cloves Moray 301 C11
Clovullin Highld 290 G2
Clowance Wood Corn 2 C4
Clow Bridge Lancs 195 B10
Clowne Derbys 187 F7
Clows Top Worcs 116 C4
Cloy Wrex 166 G5
Cluanie Inn Highld 290 B2
Cluanie Lodge
Highld 290 B2
Clubmoor Mers 182 C5
Clubworthy Corn 11 C11
Cluddley Telford 150 G2
Clun Shrops 130 G6
Clunbury Shrops 131 G7
Clunderwen Carms 73 B10
Clune Highld 301 D9
Highld 301 G7
Clunes Highld 290 E4
Clungunford Shrops 115 B7
Clunie Aberds 302 D6
Perth 286 C5
Clunton Shrops 130 G6
Cluny Fife 280 B4
Cluny Castle Aberds 293 B8
Highld 291 D8
Clutton Bath 44 B6
Ches W 167 E7
Clutton Hill Bath 44 B6
Clwt-grugoer
Conwy 165 C7
Clwt-y-bont Gwyn 163 C9
Clwydyfagwyr
M Tydf 77 D8
Clydach Mon 78 C2
Swansea 75 E11
Clydach Terrace
Powys 77 C11
Clydach Vale
Rhondda 77 G7
Clydebank W Dunb 277 G9
Clyffe Pypard Wilts 62 D5
Clynder Argyll 276 E4
Clyne Neath 76 E4
Clynelish Highld 311 J2
Clynnog-fawr Gwyn 162 F6
Clyro / Cleirwy
Powys 96 C4
Clyst Honiton Devon 14 C5
Clyst Hydon Devon 27 G8
Clyst St George
Devon 14 D5
Clyst St Lawrence
Devon 27 G8
Clyst St Mary Devon 14 C5
Cnip W Isles 304 E2
Cnoc Amhlaigh
W Isles 304 E7
Cnoc an t-Solais
W Isles 304 D6
Cnocbreac Argyll 274 F5
Cnoc Fhionn
Highld 295 D10
Cnoc Màiri W Isles 304 E6
Cnoc Rolum
W Isles 296 F3
Cnwch-coch
Ceredig 112 B3
Coachford Aberds 302 E4
Coad's Green Corn 11 F11
Coal Aston Derbys 186 F5
Coal Bank Darl 234 G3
Coalbrookdale
Telford 132 C3
Coalbrookvale
Bl Gwent 77 D11
Coalburn S Lnrk 259 C8
Coalburns T&W 242 E4
Coalcleugh
Northumb 232 B2
Coaley Glos 80 E3
Coaley Peak Glos 80 E3
Coalford Aberds 293 D10
Coalhall E Ayrs 257 F10
Coalhill Essex 88 F3
Coalmoor Telford 132 B3
Coalpit Field Warks 135 F7
Coalpit Heath S Glos 61 C7
Coalpit Hill Staffs 168 E4
Coal Pool W Mid 133 C10
Coalport Telford 132 C3
Coalsnaughton
Clack 279 B8
Coaltown of Balgonie
Fife 280 B5
Coaltown of Wemyss
Fife 280 B6
Coalville Leics 153 G8
Coalway Glos 79 C9
Coanwood Northumb 240 F5
Coarsewell Devon 8 E4
Coat Som 29 C7
Coatbridge N Lnrk 268 C4
Coatdyke N Lnrk 268 C5
Coate Swindon 63 C7
Wilts 62 G4
Coates Cambs 138 D6
Glos 81 E7
Lancs 204 D3
Lincs 188 E6
Midloth 270 C4
Notts 188 E4
W Sus 35 D7
Coatham Redcar 235 F7
Coatham Mundeville
Darl 233 G11
Coatsgate Dumfries 248 B3
Cobairdy Aberds 302 E5
Cobbaton Devon 25 B10
Cobbler's Corner
Worcs 116 F5
Cobbler's Green
Norf 142 E5
Cobbler's Plain Mon 79 E7
Cobbs Warr 183 D10
Cobb's Cross Glos 98 E5
Cobbs Fenn Essex 106 E5
Cobby Syke N Yorks 205 B9
Coberley Glos 81 B7
Cobhall Common
Hereford 97 D9
Cobham Kent 69 F7
Sur 66 G6
Cobleland Stirl 277 B10
Cobler's Green
Essex 87 B11
Cobley Dorset 31 C8
Cobley Hill Worcs 117 C10
Cobnash Hereford 115 E9
Cobridge Stoke 168 F5
Cobscot Shrops 150 B3
Coburty Aberds 303 C9
Cockadilly Glos 80 E4
Cock Alley Derbys 186 G6
Cock and End Suff 124 G4
Cockayne N Yorks 226 F2
Cock Bank Wrex 166 F5
Cock Bevington
Warks 117 G11
Cock Bridge Aberds 292 C4
Cockburnspath
Borders 282 G5
Cock Clarks Essex 88 E4
Cockden Lancs 204 G3
Cockenzie and Port
Seton E Loth 281 F8
Cocker Bar Lancs 194 C4
Cockerham Lancs 202 C5
Cockermouth Cumb 229 E8
Cockernhoe Herts 104 G2
Cockernhoe Green
Herts 104 G2
Cockersdale
W Yorks 197 B8
Cockerton Darl 224 B5
Cockett Swansea 56 C6
Cocketty Aberds 293 F9
Cockfield Durham 233 G8
Suff 125 G8
Cockfosters London 86 F3
Cock Gate Hereford 115 D9
Cock Green Essex 87 B11
Cockhill Som 44 G6
Cock Hill N Yorks 206 B6
Cocking W Sus 34 D5
Cocking Causeway
W Sus 34 D5
Cockington Torbay 9 C7
Cocklake Som 44 D2
Cocklaw Northumb 241 C10
Cockleford Glos 81 C7
Cockley Beck Cumb 220 E4
Cockley Cley Norf 140 C5
Cockley Hill
W Yorks 197 D7
Cock Marling E Sus 38 D5
Cocknowle Dorset 18 E4
Cockpole Green
Wokingham 65 C9
Cocks Corn 4 E5
Cocks Green Suff 125 F7
Cockshead Ceredig 112 F2
Cockshoot Hereford 97 D11
Cockshutford
Shrops 131 F11
Cockshutt Shrops 132 G4
Shrops 149 D8
Cock Street Kent 53 C9
Suff 107 D9
Cockthorpe Norf 177 E7
Cockwells Corn 2 C2
Cockwood Devon 14 E5
Som 43 E8
Cockyard Derbys 185 F8
Hereford 97 E8
Codda Corn 11 F9
Coddenham Suff 126 G2
Coddenham Green
Suff 126 F2
Coddington
Ches W 167 D7
Hereford 98 C4
Notts 172 E4
Codford St Mary
Wilts 46 F3
Codford St Peter
Wilts 46 F3
Codicote Herts 86 B2
Codicote Bottom
Herts 85 B2
Codmore Bucks 85 E7
Codmore Hill W Sus 35 C9
Codnor Derbys 170 F6
Codnor Breach
Derbys 170 F6
Codnor Gate Derbys 170 E6
Codnor Park Derbys 170 E6
Codrington S Glos 61 D8
Codsall Staffs 133 C7
Codsall Wood Staffs 132 B6
Codsend Som 41 F11
Coedcae Bl Gwent 77 D11
Torf 78 D3
Coed Cwnwr Mon 78 F6
Coedely Rhondda 58 B4
Coed Eva Torf 78 G3
Coedkernew Newport 59 C9
Coed Llai / Leeswood
Flint 166 D3
Coed Mawr Gwyn 179 G9
Coed Morgan Mon 78 C5
Coedpoeth Wrex 166 E3
Coed-Talon Flint 166 D3
Coedway Powys 148 G6
Coed-y-bryn Ceredig 93 C7
Coed-y-caerau
Newport 78 G5
Coed-y-fedw Mon 78 D6
Coed y Garth
Ceredig 128 E3
Coed y go Shrops 148 D5
Coed-y-paen Mon 78 F4
Coed-y-parc Gwyn 163 B10
Coed-yr-ynys Powys 96 G3
Coed Ystumgwern
Gwyn 145 E11
Coed-y-wlad Powys 130 B4
Coelbren Powys 76 C4
Coffee Hall
M Keynes 103 D7
Coffinswell Devon 9 B7
Cofton Devon 14 E5
Cofton Common
W Mid 117 B10
Cofton Hackett
Worcs 117 B10
Cog V Glam 59 F7
Cogan V Glam 59 E7
Cogenhoe Northants 120 E6
Cogges Oxon 82 D5
Coggeshall Essex 106 G6
Coggeshall Hamlet
Essex 107 G7
Coggins Mill E Sus 37 B9
Coignafearn Lodge
Highld 291 B8
Coignascallan
Highld 291 B9
Coig Peighinnean
W Isles 304 B7
Coig Peighinnean
Bhuirgh W Isles 304 C6
Coilacriech Aberds 292 D5
Coilantogle Stirl 285 G9
Coilessan Argyll 284 G6
Coilleag W Isles 297 K3
Coillemore Highld 300 B6
Coillore Highld 294 B5
Coirea-chrombe
Stirl 285 G9
Coisley Hill S Yorks 186 E6
Coity Bridgend 58 C2
Cokenach Herts 105 D7
Cokhay Green
Derbys 152 D5
Col W Isles 304 D6
Colaboll Highld 309 H5
Colan Corn 5 C7
Colaton Raleigh
Devon 15 D7
Colbost Highld 298 E2
Colburn N Yorks 224 F3
Colby Cumb 231 G9
IoM 192 E3
Norf 160 C4
Colchester Essex 107 F10
Colchester Green
Suff 125 F8
Colcot V Glam 58 F6
Cold Ash W Berks 64 F4
Cold Ashby
Northants 120 B3
Cold Ash Hill Hants 49 G10
Cold Ashton S Glos 61 E9
Cold Aston Glos 81 B10
Coldbackie Highld 308 D6
Coldbeck Cumb 222 E4
Coldblow London 68 E4
Cold Blow Pembs 73 C10
Cold Brayfield
M Keynes 121 G8
Coldbrook Powys 96 D3
Cold Christmas Herts 86 B5
Cold Cotes N Yorks 212 E4
Coldean Brighton 36 F4
Coldeast Devon 14 G2
Coldeaton Derbys 169 D10
Cold Elm Glos 98 E6
Colden W Yorks 196 B3
Colden Common
Hants 33 C7
Coldfair Green Suff 127 E8
Coldham Cambs 139 C8
Staffs 133 B7
Coldham's Common
Cambs 123 F9
Cold Hanworth
Lincs 189 E8
Coldharbour Corn 4 F5
Devon 27 E9
Dorset 17 E9
Glos 79 E9
Kent 52 C5
London 68 D4
Sur 50 E6
Cold Harbour Dorset 18 D4
Herts 85 B10
Kent 69 G11
Lincs 155 C9
Oxon 64 D6
Wilts 45 B11
Wilts 45 D11
Windsor 65 D10
Cold Hatton Telford 150 E2
Cold Hatton Heath
Telford 150 E2
Cold Hesledon
Durham 234 B4
Cold Hiendley
W Yorks 197 E11
Cold Higham
Northants 120 G3
Coldingham Borders 273 B8
Cold Inn Pembs 73 D10
Cold Kirby N Yorks 215 C10
Coldmeece Staffs 151 C7
Cold Moss Heath
Ches E 168 C3
Cold Newton Leics 136 B4
Cold Northcott
Corn 11 D10
Cold Norton Essex 88 E4
Coldoch Stirl 278 B3
Cold Overton Leics 154 G6
Coldra Newport 59 B11
Coldrain Perth 286 G4
Coldred Kent 55 D9
Coldridge Devon 25 F11
Cold Row Lancs 202 E3
Coldstream Angus 287 D7
Borders 263 B8
Coldvreath Corn 5 D9
Coldwaltham W Sus 35 D8
Cold Well Staffs 151 G11
Coldwells Aberds 303 E11
Coldwells Croft
Aberds 302 G5
Cole Som 45 G7
Colebatch Shrops 130 F6
Colebrook Devon 27 F8
Colebrooke Devon 13 B11
Coleburn Moray 302 D2
Coleby Lincs 173 C7
N Lincs 199 D11
Cole End Essex 105 D11
Warks 134 F3
Coleford Devon 26 G3
Glos 79 C9
Som 45 D7
Coleford Water Som 42 G6
Colegate End Norf 142 F3
Cole Green Herts 86 C3
Herts 105 E8
Colehall W Mid 134 F2
Cole Henley Hants 48 C3
Colehill Dorset 31 G8
Coleman Green
Herts 85 C11
Coleman's Hatch
E Sus 52 G3
Colemere Shrops 149 C8
Colemore Hants 49 G8
Colemore Green
Shrops 132 D4
Coleorton Leics 153 F8
Coleorton Moor
Leics 153 F8
Cole Park London 67 E7
Colerne Wilts 61 E10
Colesbourne Glos 81 C7
Colesbrook Dorset 30 B4
Cole's Cross Dorset 28 G5
Colesden Beds 122 F2
Coles Green Suff 107 C11
Worcs 116 G5
Cole's Green Suff 126 E5
Coleshill Bucks 85 F7
Oxon 82 G2
Warks 134 F4

Craigmalloch E Ayrs 245 E11
Craigmaud Aberds 303 D8
Craigmill Stirl 278 B6
Craigmillar Edin 280 G5
Craigmore Argyll 266 B2
Craig-moston Aberds 293 F8
Craignant Shrops 148 B5
Craignell Dumfries 237 B7
Craigneuk N Lnrk 268 C5
N Lnrk 268 D5
Craignish Castle Argyll 275 C8
Craignure Argyll 289 F9
Craigo Angus 293 G8
Craigow Perth 286 G4
Craig Penllyn V Glam 58 D3
Craigrory Highld 300 E6
Craigrothie Fife 287 F7
Craigroy Moray 301 D11
Craigruie Stirl 285 E8
Craig's End Essex 106 D4
Craigsford Mains Borders 262 B3
Craigshall Dumfries 237 D10
Craigshill W Loth 269 B11
Craigside Durham 233 D8
Craigston Castle Aberds 303 D7
Craigton Aberdeen 293 C10
Angus 287 B7
Angus 287 D9
Glasgow 267 C10
Highld 300 E6
Highld 309 H6
Highld 309 K6
Craigtown Highld 310 D2
Craig-y-don Conwy 180 E3
Craig-y-Duke Swansea 76 E2
Craig-y-nos Powys 76 B4
Craig-y-penrhyn Ceredig 128 E3
Craig-y-Rhacca Caerph 59 B7
Craik Borders 249 B8
Crail Fife 287 G10
Crailing Borders 262 E5
Crailinghall Borders 262 E5
Crakaig Highld 311 H3
Crakehill N Yorks 215 E8
Crakemarsh Staffs 151 B11
Crambe N Yorks 216 G4
Crambeck N Yorks 216 F4
Cramhurst Sur 50 E2
Cramlington Northumb 243 B7
Cramond Edin 280 F3
Cramond Bridge Edin 280 F3
Crampmoor Hants 32 C5
Cranage Ches E 168 B3
Cranberry Staffs 150 B6
Cranborne Dorset 31 E9
Cranbourne Brack 66 E2
Hants 48 C6
Cranbrook Devon 14 B6
Kent 53 F9
London 68 B2
Cranbrook Common Kent 53 F9
Crane Moor S Yorks 197 G10
Crane's Corner Norf 159 G8
Cranfield C Beds 103 C9
Cranford Devon 24 C4
London 66 D6
Cranford St Andrew Northants 121 B8
Cranford St John Northants 121 B8
Cranham Glos 80 C5
London 68 B5
Cranhill Glasgow 268 B2
Warks 118 G2
Crank Mers 183 B8
Crankwood Gtr Man 194 G6
Crank Wood Gtr Man 194 G6
Cranleigh Sur 50 F5
Cranley Suff 126 C3
Cranley Gardens London 67 B9
Cranmer Green Suff 125 C10
Cranmore IoW 20 D3
Som 45 E7
Cranna Aberds 302 D6
Crannich Argyll 289 E7
Crannoch Moray 302 D4
Cranoe Leics 136 D5
Cransford Suff 126 E6
Cranshaws Borders 272 C3
Cranstal IoM 192 B5
Cranswick E Yorks 208 C6
Crantock Corn 4 C5
Cranwell Lincs 173 F8
Cranwich Norf 140 E5
Cranworth Norf 141 C9
Craobh Haven Argyll 275 C8
Crapstone Devon 7 B10
Crarae Argyll 275 D10
Crask Highld 308 C7
Crask Inn Highld 309 G5
Craskins Aberds 293 C7
Crask of Aigas Highld 300 E4
Craster Northumb 265 F7
Craswall Hereford 96 D5
Crateford Shrops 132 F4
Staffs 133 B8
Cratfield Suff 126 B6
Crathes Aberds 293 D9
Crathie Aberds 292 D4
Highld 291 D7
Crathorne N Yorks 225 D8
Craven Arms Shrops 131 G8
Crawcrook T&W 242 E4
Crawford Lancs 194 G3
S Lnrk 259 E11
Crawforddyke S Lnrk 269 F7
Crawfordjohn S Lnrk 259 E9
Crawick Dumfries 259 G7
Crawley Devon 28 F3
Hants 48 G2
Oxon 82 C4
W Sus 51 F9
Crawley Down W Sus 51 F10
Crawley End Essex 105 C8
Crawley Hill Sur 65 G11
Crawleyside Durham 232 C5
Crawshaw W Yorks 197 E8
Crawshawbooth Lancs 195 B10
Crawton Aberds 293 F10
Cray N Yorks 213 D8
Perth 292 G3
Crayford London 68 E4
Crayke N Yorks 215 E11
Craymere Beck Norf 159 C11
Crays Hill Essex 88 G2
Cray's Pond Oxon 64 C6
Crazies Hill Wokingham 65 C9
Creacombe Devon 26 D4
Creagan Argyll 289 E11
Creagan Sithe Argyll 284 G6
Creag Aoil Highld 290 F3
Creagastrom W Isles 297 G4
Creag Ghoraidh W Isles 297 G3
Creaguaineach Lodge Highld 290 G5
Creaksea Essex 88 F6
Creamore Bank Shrops 149 C10
Crean Corn 1 E3
Creaton Northants 120 C4
Creca Dumfries 238 C6
Credenhill Hereford 97 C9
Crediton Devon 26 G4
Creebridge Dumfries 236 C6
Creech Dorset 18 E4
Creech Bottom Dorset 18 E4
Creech Heathfield Som 28 B3
Creech St Michael Som 28 B3
Creed Corn 5 F8
Creediknowe Shetland 312 G7
Creegbrawse Corn 4 G4
Creekmoor Poole 18 C6
Creekmouth London 68 C3
Creeksea Essex 88 F6
Creeting Bottoms Suff 126 F2
Creeting St Mary Suff 125 F11
Creeton Lincs 155 E10
Creetown Dumfries 236 D6
Creggans Argyll 284 G4
Cregneash IoM 192 F2
Creg-ny-Baa IoM 192 D4
Cregrina Powys 114 G2
Creich Fife 287 E7
Creigau Mon 79 F7
Creighton Staffs 151 B11
Creigiau Cardiff 58 C5
Crelly Corn 2 C5
Cremyll Corn 7 E9
Crendell Dorset 31 E9
Crepkill Highld 298 E4
Creslow Bucks 102 G6
Cressage Shrops 131 C11
Cressbrook Derbys 185 G11
Cresselly Pembs 73 D9
Cressex Bucks 84 G4
Cress Green Glos 80 E3
Cressing Essex 106 G5
Cresswell Northumb 253 E7
Staffs 151 B9
Cresswell Quay Pembs 73 D9
Creswell Derbys 187 G8
Staffs 151 D7
Staffs 151 D8
Creswell Green Staffs 151 G11
Cretingham Suff 126 E4
Cretshengan Argyll 275 G8
Creunant/Crynant Neath 76 E3
Crewe Ches E 168 D2
Ches W 166 E6
Crewe-by-Farndon Ches W 166 E6
Crewgarth Cumb 231 E8
Crewgreen Powys 148 F6
Crewkerne Som 28 F6
Crews Hill London 86 F4
Crew's Hole Bristol 60 E6
Crewton Derby 153 C7
Crianlarich Stirl 285 E7
Cribbs Causeway S Glos 60 C5
Cribden Side Lancs 195 C9
Cribyn Ceredig 111 G10
Criccieth Gwyn 145 B9
Crich Derbys 170 E5
Crich Carr Derbys 170 E4
Crichie Aberds 303 E9
Crichton Midloth 271 C7
Crick Mon 79 G7
Northants 119 C11
Crickadarn Powys 95 C11
Cricket Hill Hants 65 G10
Cricket Malherbie Som 28 E5
Cricket St Thomas Som 28 F5
Crickham Som 44 D2
Crickheath Shrops 148 E5
Crickheath Wharf Shrops 148 E5
Crickhowell Powys 78 B2
Cricklade Wilts 81 G10
Cricklewood London 67 B8
Crickmery Shrops 150 D3
Crick's Green Hereford 116 G2
Criddlestyle Hants 31 E11
Cridling Stubbs N Yorks 198 C4
Cridmore IoW 20 E5
Crieff Perth 286 E2
Criggan Corn 5 C10
Criggion Powys 148 F5
Crigglestone W Yorks 197 D10
Crimble Gtr Man 195 E11
Crimchard Som 28 F4
Crimdon Park Durham 234 D5
Crimond Aberds 303 D10
Crimonmogate Aberds 303 D10
Crimp Corn 24 D3
Crimplesham Norf 140 C3
Crimscote Warks 100 B4
Crinan Argyll 275 D8
Crinan Ferry Argyll 275 D8
Crindau Newport 59 B10
Crindledyke N Lnrk 268 D6
Cringleford Norf 142 B3
Cringles W Yorks 204 D6
Cringletie Borders 270 G4
Crinow Pembs 73 C10
Cripple Corner Essex 107 E7
Cripplesease Corn 2 B2
Cripplestyle Dorset 31 E9
Cripp's Corner E Sus 38 C3
Crispie Argyll 275 F10
Crist Derbys 185 E8
Critchell's Green Hants 32 B3
Critchill Som 45 D9
Critchmere Sur 49 G11
Crit Hall Kent 53 G9
Crizeley Hereford 97 E8
Croanford Corn 10 G6
Croasdale Cumb 219 B11
Crobeag W Isles 304 F5
Crockenhill Kent 68 F4
Crocker End Oxon 65 B8
Crockerhill Hants 33 F9
W Sus 22 B6
Crockernwell Devon 13 C11
Crockers Devon 40 F5
Crocker's Ash Hereford 79 B8
Crockerton Wilts 45 E11
Crockerton Green Wilts 45 E11
Crocketford or Ninemile Bar Dumfries 237 B10
Crockey Hill York 207 D8
Crockham Heath W Berks 64 G2
Crockham Hill Kent 52 C2
Crockhurst Street Kent 52 E6
Crockleford Heath Essex 107 F10
Crockleford Hill Essex 107 F10
Crockness Orkney 314 G3
Crock Street Som 28 E4
Croesau Bach Shrops 148 D4
Croeserw Neath 57 B11
Croes-goch Pembs 87 E11
Croes-Hywel Mon 78 C4
Croes-lan Ceredig 93 C7
Croes Llanfair Mon 78 D4
Croesor Gwyn 163 G10
Croespenmaen Caerph 77 F11
Croes-wian Flint 181 G10
Croesyceiliog Carms 74 B6
Torf 78 F4
Croes-y-mwyalch Torf 78 G4
Croes y pant Mon 78 E4
Croesywaun Gwyn 163 D8
Croft Hereford 115 D9
Leics 135 D10
Lincs 175 C8
Pembs 92 C3
Warr 183 C10
Croftamie Stirl 277 D9
Croftfoot S Lnrk 268 C2
Crofthandy Corn 4 G4
Croftlands Cumb 210 D5
Croftmalloch W Loth 269 C8
Croft Mitchell Corn 2 B5
Croftmoraig Perth 285 C11
Croft of Tillymaud Aberds 303 F11
Crofton Cumb 239 G8
London 68 F2
Wilts 63 G9
W Yorks 197 D11
Croft-on-Tees N Yorks 224 D5
Crofts Dumfries 237 B9
Crofts Bank Gtr Man 184 B3
Crofts of Benachielt Highld 310 F5
Crofts of Haddo Aberds 303 F8
Crofts of Inverthernie Aberds 303 E7
Crofts of Meikle Ardo Aberds 303 E8
Crofty Swansea 56 B4
Croggan Argyll 289 G9
Croglin Cumb 231 B7
Croich Highld 309 K4
Croick Highld 310 D2
Croig Argyll 288 D5
Crois Dughaill W Isles 297 J3
Cromarty Highld 301 C7
Cromasaig Highld 299 C10
Crombie Fife 279 D10
Crombie Castle Aberds 302 D5
Cromblet Aberds 303 F7
Cromdale Highld 301 G10
Cromer Herts 104 F5
Norf 160 A4
Cromer-Hyde Herts 86 C2
Cromford Derbys 170 D3
Cromhall S Glos 79 G11
Cromhall Common S Glos 61 B7
Cromor W Isles 304 F6
Crompton Fold Gtr Man 196 F2
Cromra Highld 291 D7
Cromwell Notts 172 C3
Cromwell Bottom W Yorks 196 C6
Cronberry E Ayrs 258 E4
Crondall Hants 49 D9
Cronk-y-Voddy IoM 192 D4
Cronton Mers 183 D7
Crook Cumb 221 G9
Devon 27 G11
Durham 233 D9
Crookdake Cumb 229 C9
Crooke Gtr Man 194 F5
Crooked Billet London 67 E8
Crookedholm E Ayrs 257 B11
Crooked Soley Wilts 63 E10
Crooked Withies Dorset 31 F9
Crookes S Yorks 186 D4
Crookesmoor S Yorks 186 D4
Crookfur E Renf 267 D10
Crookgate Bank Durham 242 F5
Crookhall Durham 242 G4
Crookham Northumb 263 B10
W Berks 64 G4
Crookham Village Hants 49 C9
Crookhaugh Borders 260 D4
Crookhill T&W 242 E5
Crookhouse Borders 263 D7
Crooklands Cumb 211 C10
Crook of Devon Perth 286 G4
Crookston Glasgow 267 C10
Cropredy Oxon 101 B9
Cropston Leics 153 G11
Cropthorne Worcs 99 C9
Cropton N Yorks 216 B5
Cropwell Bishop Notts 154 B3
Cropwell Butler Notts 154 B3
Cros W Isles 304 B7
Crosben Highld 289 D9
Crosbost W Isles 304 F5
Crosby Cumb 229 D7
IoM 192 E4
Mers 182 B4
N Lincs 199 E11
Crosby Court N Yorks 225 G7
Crosby Garrett Cumb 222 D4
Crosby-on-Eden Cumb 239 F11
Crosby Ravensworth Cumb 222 C2
Crosby Villa Cumb 229 D7
Croscombe Som 44 E5
Crosemere Shrops 149 D8
Crosland Edge W Yorks 196 E6
Crosland Hill W Yorks 196 E6
Crosland Moor W Yorks 196 D6
Croslands Park Cumb 210 E4
Cross Devon 40 F3
Devon 40 G6
Shrops 149 B7
Som 44 C2
Crossaig Argyll 255 B9
Crossal Highld 294 B6
Crossapol Argyll 288 E1
Cross Ash Mon 78 B6
Cross-at-Hand Kent 53 D9
Cross Bank Worcs 116 C4
Crossbrae Aberds 302 D6
Crossburn Falk 279 G7
Crossbush W Sus 35 F8
Crosscanonby Cumb 229 D7
Cross Coombe Corn 4 E4
Crosscrake Cumb 211 B10
Crossdale Street Norf 160 B4
Cross End Beds 121 F11
Essex 107 E7
M Keynes 103 D8
Crossens Mers 193 D11
Crossflatts W Yorks 205 E8
Crossford Fife 279 D11
S Lnrk 268 F6
Crossgate Lincs 156 D4
Orkney 314 E4
Staffs 151 B8
Cross Gate W Sus 35 E8
Crossgatehall E Loth 271 B7
Crossgates Cumb 229 G7
Fife 280 D2
N Yorks 217 C10
Powys 113 E11
Cross Gates W Yorks 205 F7
W Yorks 206 G3
Crossgill Cumb 231 C10
Lancs 211 G11
Crossgreen Shrops 149 F9
Cross Green Devon 12 D3
Staffs 133 B8
Suff 124 G6
Suff 125 F7
Suff 125 G9
Telford 150 G2
Warks 119 F7
W Yorks 206 G2
Crosshands Carms 92 G3
Cross Hands Carms 75 C9
Cross-hands Carms 92 G3
Cross Hands Pembs 73 C9
Cross Heath Staffs 168 F4
Crosshill E Ayrs 257 E11
Fife 280 B3
S Ayrs 245 B8
Cross Hill Corn 10 G6
Derbys 170 F6
Glos 79 F9
Cross Hills N Yorks 204 E6
Cross Holme N Yorks 225 F11
Crosshouse E Ayrs 257 B9
Cross Houses Shrops 131 B10
Shrops 132 E3
Crossings Cumb 240 B2
Cross in Hand E Sus 37 C9
Leics 135 G10
Cross Inn Carms 74 C3
Ceredig 111 E10
Ceredig 111 F7
Rhondda 58 C5
Crosskeys Caerph 78 G2
Cross Keys Kent 52 C4
Wilts 61 E11
Crosskirk Highld 310 B4
Crosslands Cumb 210 B6
Cross Lane Ches E 167 C11
Cross Lane Head Shrops 132 D4
Crosslanes Shrops 148 F6
Cross Lanes Corn 2 E5
Dorset 30 G3
N Yorks 215 F10
Oxon 65 D7
Wrex 166 F5
Crosslee Borders 261 F8
Renfs 267 B8
Crossley Hall W Yorks 205 G8
Cross Llyde Hereford 97 F8
Crossmichael Dumfries 237 C9
Crossmill E Renf 267 D10
Crossmoor Lancs 202 F4
Crossmount Perth 285 B11
Cross Oak Powys 96 G2
Cross of Jackston Aberds 303 F7
Cross o' th' hands Derbys 170 F3
Cross o' th' Hill Ches W 167 F7
Crosspost W Sus 36 C3
Crossroads Aberds 293 D9
E Ayrs 257 C11
Fife 281 B7
Cross Roads Devon 12 D5
W Yorks 204 F6
Cross Stone Aberds 303 G9
Cross Street Suff 126 B3
Crosston Angus 287 B9
Crosstown Corn 24 D2
V Glam 58 F4
Cross Town Ches E 184 F3
Crosswater Sur 49 F11
Crossway Hereford 98 E2
Mon 78 B6
Powys 113 F11
Crossway Green Mon 79 G8
Worcs 116 D6
Crossways Dorset 17 D11
Kent 68 D5
Mon 96 G6
S Glos 79 G11
Sur 49 F11
Crosswell/Ffynnongroes Pembs 92 D2
Crosswood Ceredig 112 C3
Crosthwaite Cumb 221 G8
Croston Lancs 194 D3
Crostwick Norf 160 F5
Crostwight Norf 160 D6
Crothair W Isles 304 E3
Crouch Kent 52 B6
Kent 54 B5
Crouch End London 67 B9
Crouchers W Sus 22 C4
Croucheston Wilts 31 B9
Crouch Hill Dorset 30 E2
Crouch House Green Kent 52 D2
Croughly Moray 301 G11
Croughton Northants 101 E10
Crovie Aberds 303 C8
Crow Hants 31 G11
Crowan Corn 2 C4
Crowborough E Sus 52 G4
Staffs 168 D6
Crowborough Warren E Sus 52 G4
Crowcombe Som 42 F6
Crowcroft Worcs 116 G5
Crowden Derbys 185 B9
Devon 12 B5
Crowder Park Devon 8 D4
Crowdhill Hants 33 C7
Crowdicote Derbys 169 B10
Crowdleham Kent 52 B5
Crowdon N Yorks 227 F9
Crow Edge S Yorks 197 G7
Crowell Oxon 84 F2
Crowell Hill Oxon 84 F3
Crowfield Northants 102 C2
Suff 126 F2
Crowgate Street Norf 160 E6
Crowgreaves Shrops 132 D4
Crow Green Essex 87 F9
Crowhill Gtr Man 184 B6
M Keynes 102 D6
Crow Hill Hereford 98 F2
Crowhole Derbys 186 F4
Crowhurst E Sus 38 E3
Sur 51 D11
Crowhurst Lane End Sur 51 D11
Crowland Lincs 156 G4
Crowlas Corn 2 C2
Crowle N Lincs 199 E9
Worcs 117 F8
Crowle Green Worcs 117 F8
Crowle Hill N Lincs 199 E9
Crowle Park N Lincs 199 E9
Crowmarsh Gifford Oxon 64 B6
Crown Corner Suff 126 C5
Crown East Worcs 116 G6
Crow Nest W Yorks 205 F8
Crownfield Bucks 84 F4
Crownhill Plym 7 D9
Crown Hills Leicester 136 C2
Crownland Suff 125 D10
Crownpits Sur 50 E3
Crownthorpe Norf 141 C11
Crowntown Corn 2 C4
Crown Wood Brack 65 F11
Crows-an-wra Corn 1 D3
Crow's Green Essex 106 F3
Crowshill Norf 141 B8
Crowsley Oxon 65 D8
Crowsnest Shrops 131 C7
Crow's Nest Corn 6 B5
Crowther's Pool Powys 96 B4
Crowthorne Brack 65 G10
Crowton Ches W 183 G9
Crow Wood Halton 183 D8
Croxall Staffs 152 G3
Croxby Lincs 189 B11
Croxby Top Lincs 189 B11
Croxdale Durham 233 D11
Croxden Staffs 151 B11
Croxley Green Herts 85 F9
Croxteth Mers 182 B6
Croxton Cambs 122 E4
N Lincs 200 E5
Norf 141 F7
Norf 159 C9
Staffs 150 C5
Croxtonbank Staffs 150 C5
Croxton Green Ches E 167 E8
Croxton Kerrial Leics 154 D6
Croy Highld 301 E7
N Lnrk 278 F4
Croyde Devon 40 F2
Croyde Bay Devon 40 F2
Croydon Cambs 104 B6
London 67 F10
Crozen Hereford 97 B11
Crubenbeg Highld 291 D8
Crubenmore Lodge Highld 291 D8
Cruckmeole Shrops 131 B8
Cruckton Shrops 149 G8
Cruden Bay Aberds 303 F10
Crudgington Telford 150 F2
Crudie Aberds 303 D7
Crudwell Wilts 81 G7
Crug Powys 114 C3
Crugmeer Corn 10 F4
Crugybar Carms 94 D3
Cruise Hill Worcs 117 E10
Crulabhig W Isles 304 E3
Crumlin Caerph 78 F2
Crumplehorn Corn 6 E4
Crumpsall Gtr Man 195 G10
Crumpsbrook Shrops 116 B2
Crumpton Hill Worcs 98 B5
Crundale Kent 54 D5
Pembs 73 B7
Cruwys Morchard Devon 26 E5
Crux Easton Hants 48 B2
Cruxton Dorset 17 B8
Crwbin Carms 75 C7
Crya Orkney 314 F3
Cryers Hill Bucks 84 F5
Crymlyn Gwyn 179 G10
Crymych Pembs 92 E3
Crynant/Creunant Neath 76 E3
Crynfryn Ceredig 111 E11
Cuaich Highld 291 E8
Cuaig Highld 299 D7
Cuan Argyll 275 B8
Cubbington Warks 118 D6
Cubeck N Yorks 213 B9
Cubert Corn 4 D5
Cubitt Town London 67 D11
Cubley S Yorks 197 G8
Cubley Common Derbys 152 B3
Cublington Bucks 102 G6
Hereford 97 D8
Cuckfield W Sus 36 B4
Cucklington Som 30 B3
Cuckney Notts 187 G9
Cuckold's Green Suff 143 G9
Wilts 46 B3
Cuckoo Green Suff 143 D10
Cuckoo Hill Notts 188 C2
Cuckoo's Corner Hants 49 E8
Wilts 46 B4
Cuckoo's Knob Wilts 63 G7
Cuckoo Tye Suff 107 C7
Cuckron Shetland 313 H6
Cucumber Corner Norf 143 B7
Cuddesdon Oxon 83 E10
Cuddington Bucks 84 C2
Ches W 183 G10
Cuddington Heath Ches W 167 F7
Cuddy Hill Lancs 202 F5
Cudham London 52 B2
Cudlipptown Devon 12 F6
Cudliptown Devon 12 F6
Cudworth Som 28 E5
Sur 51 E8
S Yorks 197 F11
Cudworth Common S Yorks 197 F11
Cuerden Green Lancs 194 C5
Cuerdley Cross Warr 183 D8
Cufaude Hants 48 B6
Cuffern Pembs 91 G7
Cuffley Herts 86 E4
Cuiashader W Isles 304 C7
Cuidhir W Isles 297 L2
Cuidhtinis W Isles 296 C6
Cuiken Midloth 270 C4
Cuilcheanna Ho Highld 290 G2
Cuin Argyll 288 D6
Culbo Highld 300 C6
Culbokie Highld 300 D6
Culburnie Highld 300 E4
Culcabock Highld 300 E6
Culcairn Highld 300 C6
Culcharry Highld 301 D8
Culcheth Warr 183 B11
Culcronchie Dumfries 237 C7
Cùl Doirlinn Highld 289 B8
Culdrain Aberds 302 F5
Culduie Highld 299 E7
Culeave Highld 309 K5
Culford Suff 124 D6
Culfordheath Suff 125 C7
Culfosie Aberds 293 C9
Culgaith Cumb 231 F8
Culham Oxon 83 F8
Culkein Highld 306 F5
Culkein Drumbeg Highld 306 F6
Culkerton Glos 80 F6
Cullachie Highld 301 G9
Cullen Moray 302 C5
Cullercoats T&W 243 C9
Cullicudden Highld 300 C6
Cullingworth W Yorks 205 F7
Cullipool Argyll 275 B8
Cullivoe Shetland 312 C7
Culloch Perth 285 F11
Culloden Highld 301 E7
Cullompton Devon 27 F8
Culmaily Highld 311 K2
Culmazie Dumfries 236 D5
Culm Davy Devon 27 D10
Culmer Sur 50 F2
Culmers Kent 70 G5
Culmington Shrops 131 G9
Culmore Stirl 278 B3
Culmstock Devon 27 E10
Culnacraig Highld 307 J5
Cul na h-Aird W Isles 305 H3
Culnaightrie Dumfries 237 D9
Culnaknock Highld 298 C5
Culnaneam Highld 294 C6
Culpho Suff 108 B4
Culrain Highld 309 K5
Culra Lodge Highld 291 F7
Culross Fife 279 D9
Culroy S Ayrs 257 G8
Culscadden Dumfries 236 E6
Culsh Aberds 292 D5
Aberds 303 E8
Culshabbin Dumfries 236 D5
Culswick Shetland 313 J4
Cultercullen Aberds 303 G9
Cults Aberdeen 293 C10
Aberds 302 F5
Dumfries 236 E6
Fife 287 G7
Culverlane Devon 8 C4
Culverstone Green Kent 68 G6
Culverthorpe Lincs 173 G8
Culworth Northants 101 B10
Culzie Lodge Highld 300 B5
Cumberlow Green Herts 104 E6
Cumbernauld N Lnrk 278 G5
Cumbernauld Village N Lnrk 278 F5
Cumber's Bank Wrex 149 B8
Cumberworth Lincs 191 G8
Cumdivock Cumb 230 B2
Cumeragh Village Lancs 203 F7
Cuminestown Aberds 303 D8
Cumledge Borders 272 D5
Cumlewick Shetland 313 L6
Cumlodden Argyll 275 D11
Cumloden Dumfries 236 C6
Cummersdale Cumb 239 G9
Cummerton Aberds 303 C8
Cummertrees Dumfries 238 D4
Cummingston Moray 301 C11
Cumnock E Ayrs 258 E3
Cumnor Oxon 83 E7
Cumnor Hill Oxon 83 D7
Cumrew Cumb 240 G2
Cumwhinton Cumb 239 G10
Cumwhitton Cumb 240 G2
Cundall N Yorks 215 E8
Cundy Cross S Yorks 197 F11
Cundy Hos S Yorks 186 B4
Cunninghamhead N Ayrs 267 G7
Cunnister Shetland 312 D7
Cupar Fife 287 F7
Cupar Muir Fife 287 F7
Cupernham Hants 32 C5
Cupid Green Herts 85 D9
Cupid's Hill Mon 97 F8
Curbar Derbys 186 G3
Curborough Staffs 152 G2
Curbridge Hants 33 E8
Oxon 82 D4
Curdridge Hants 33 E8
Curdworth Warks 134 E3
Curgurrell Corn 3 B9
Curin Highld 300 D3
Curland Som 28 D3
Curland Common Som 28 D3
Curlew Green Suff 127 D7
Curling Tye Green Essex 88 D4
Curload Som 28 B4
Currarie S Ayrs 244 E5
Currian Vale Corn 5 D9
Curridge W Berks 64 E3
Currie Edin 270 B3
Currock Cumb 239 G10
Curry Lane Corn 11 C11
Curry Mallet Som 28 C4
Curry Rivel Som 28 B5
Cursiter Orkney 314 E3
Curteis' Corner Kent 53 F11
Curtisden Green Kent 53 E8
Curtisknowle Devon 8 E4
Curtismill Green Essex 87 F8
Cury Corn 2 E5
Cusbay Orkney 314 C5
Cusgarne Corn 4 G5
Cushnie Aberds 303 C7
Cushuish Som 43 G7
Cusop Hereford 96 C4
Custards Hants 32 F3
Custom House London 68 C2
Cusveorth Coombe Corn 4 G5
Cusworth S Yorks 198 G4
Cutcloy Dumfries 236 F6
Cutcombe Som 42 F2
Cutgate Gtr Man 195 E11
Cuthill E Loth 281 G7
Cutiau Gwyn 146 F2
Cutlers Green Essex 105 E11
Cutler's Green Som 44 C5
Cutmadoc Corn 5 C11
Cutmere Corn 6 C6
Cutnall Green Worcs 117 D7
Cutsdean Glos 99 E11
Cutsyke W Yorks 198 C2
Cutteslowe Oxon 83 C8
Cutthorpe Derbys 186 G4
Cuttiford's Door Som 28 E4
Cutts Shetland 313 K6
Cuttybridge Pembs 72 B6
Cuttyhill Aberds 303 D10
Cuxham Oxon 83 F11
Cuxton Medway 69 F8
Cuxwold Lincs 201 G7
Cwm Bl Gwent 77 D11
Denb 181 F9
Neath 57 C10
Powys 129 D11
Powys 130 E5
Shrops 114 B6
Swansea 57 B7
Cwmafan Neath 57 C9
Cwmaman Rhondda 77 F8
Cwmann Carms 93 B11
Cwmavon Torf 78 D3
Cwmbach Carms 75 E7
Carms 92 F5
Powys 96 D3
Rhondda 77 E8
Cwmbâch Rhondda 77 E8
Cwmbach Llechrhyd Powys 113 G10
Cwmbelan Powys 129 G8
Cwmbran Torf 78 G3
Cwmbrwyno Ceredig 128 G4
Cwm-byr Carms 94 E2
Cwm Capel Carms 75 E7
Cwmcarn Caerph 78 G2
Cwmcarvan Mon 79 D7
Cwm-celyn Bl Gwent 78 D2
Cwm-Cewydd Gwyn 147 G7
Cwmcoednerth Ceredig 92 B6
Cwm-cou Ceredig 92 C5
Cwmcrawnon Powys 77 B10
Cwmcych Carms 92 D5
Cwmdare Rhondda 77 E7
Cwm Dows Caerph 78 F2
Cwmdu Carms 94 E2
Powys 96 G3
Swansea 56 C6
Cwmduad Carms 93 E7
Cwm-Dulais Swansea 75 E10
Cwmdwr Carms 94 E4
Cwmerfyn Ceredig 128 G3
Cwmfelin Bridgend 57 D11
M Tydf 77 E9
Cwmfelin Boeth Carms 73 B11
Cwm felin fach Caerph 77 G11
Cwmfelin Mynach Carms 92 G4
Cwmffrwd Carms 74 B6
Cwm Ffrwd-oer Torf 78 E3
Cwm-Fields Torf 78 E3
Cwm Gelli Caerph 77 F11
Cwmgiedd Powys 76 C3
Cwmgors Neath 76 C2
Cwmgwili Carms 75 C9
Cwmgwrach Neath 76 E5
Cwm Gwyn Swansea 56 C6
Cwm Head Shrops 131 F8
Cwm-hesgen Gwyn 146 D5
Cwmhiraeth Carms 92 D6
Cwm-hwnt Rhondda 76 D6
Cwmifor Carms 94 F3
Cwm Irfon Powys 95 B7
Cwmisfael Carms 75 B7
Cwm-Llinau Powys 128 B6
Cwmllynfell Neath 76 C2
Cwm-mawr Carms 75 C8
Cwm-miles Carms 92 G3
Cwm Nant-gam Bl Gwent 78 C2
Cwmnantyrodyn Caerph 77 F11
Cwmorgan Pembs 92 E5
Cwmparc Rhondda 77 F7
Cwm-parc Rhondda 77 F7
Cwmpengraig Carms 92 D6
Cwm Penmachno Conwy 164 F3
Cwmpennar Rhondda 77 E8
Cwm Plysgog Ceredig 92 C3
Cwmrhos Powys 96 G3
Cwmrhydyceirw Swansea 57 B7

Cwmsychpant
Ceredig 93 B9
Cwmsyfiog Caerph 77 E11
Cwmsymlog Ceredig 128 G4
Cwmtillery Bl Gwent 78 D2
Cwm-twrch Isaf
Powys 76 C3
Cwm-twrch Uchaf
Powys 76 C3
Cwmwdig Water
Pembs 90 E6
Cwmwysg Powys 95 F7
Cwm-y-glo Carms 75 C9
Gwyn 163 C8
Cwmynyscoy Torf 78 F3
Cwmyoy Mon 96 G5
Cwmystwyth
Ceredig 112 C5
Cwrt Gwyn 128 C3
Cwrt-newydd Ceredig 93 B9
Cwrt-y-cadno Carms 94 C3
Cwrt-y-gollen Powys 78 B2
Cydweli/
Kidwelly Carms 74 D6
Cyffordd Llandudno/
Llandudno Junction
Conwy 180 F3
Cyffylliog Denb 165 D9
Cyfronydd Powys 130 B2
Cymau Flint 166 D3
Cymdda Bridgend 58 C2
Cymer Neath 57 B11
Cymmer Rhondda 77 G8
Cyncoed Cardiff 59 C7
Cynghordy Carms 94 C6
Cynheidre Carms 75 D7
Cynonville Neath 57 B10
Cyntwell Cardiff 58 D6
Cynwyd Denb 165 G9
Cynwyl Elfed Carms 93 F7
Cywarch Gwyn 147 F7

D

Daccombe Devon 9 B8
Dacre Cumb 230 F5
N Yorks 214 G3
Dacre Banks
N Yorks 214 G3
Daddry Shield
Durham 232 D3
Dadford Bucks 102 D3
Dadlington Leics 135 D8
Dafarn Faig Gwyn 163 F7
Dafen Carms 75 E8
Daffy Green Norf 141 B9
Dagdale Staffs 151 C11
Dagenham London 68 C3
Daggons Dorset 31 E10
Daglingworth Glos 81 D7
Dagnall Bucks 85 B7
Dagtail End Worcs 117 E10
Dagworth Suff 125 E10
Dail Beag W Isles 304 D4
Dail bho Dheas
W Isles 304 B6
Dail bho Thuath
W Isles 304 B6
Daill Argyll 274 G4
Dailly S Ayrs 245 C7
Dail Mor W Isles 304 D4
Dainton Devon 9 B7
Dairsie or Osnaburgh
Fife 287 F8
Daisy Green Suff 125 D10
Suff 125 D11
Daisy Hill Gtr Man 195 G7
W Yorks 197 B9
W Yorks 205 G8
Daisy Nook
Gtr Man 196 G2
Dalabrog W Isles 297 J3
Dalavich Argyll 275 B10
Dalbeattie
Dumfries 237 C10
Dalbeg Highld 291 B8
Dalblair E Ayrs 258 F4
Dalbog Angus 293 F7
Dalbrack Stirl 285 G11
Dalbury Derbys 152 C5
Dalby IoM 192 E3
Lincs 190 G6
N Yorks 216 E2
Dalchalloch Perth 291 G9
Dalchalm Highld 311 J3
Dalchenna Argyll 284 G4
Dalchirach Moray 301 F11
Dalchonzie Perth 285 E11
Dalchork Highld 309 H5
Dalchreichart
Highld 290 B4
Dalchruin Perth 285 F11
Dalderby Lincs 174 B2
Dale Cumb 230 C6
Gtr Man 196 F3
Pembs 72 D4
Shetland 312 G6
Dale Abbey Derbys 153 B8
Dalebank Derbys 170 C5
Dale Bottom Cumb 229 G11
Dale Brow Ches E 184 F6
Dale End Derbys 170 C2
N Yorks 204 D5
Dale Head Cumb 221 B8
Dale Hill E Sus 53 G7
E Sus 53 G8
Dalelia Highld 289 C9
Dale Moor Derbys 153 B8
Dale of Walls
Shetland 313 H3
Dales Brow
Gtr Man 195 G9
Dales Green Staffs 168 D5
Dalesss Highld 301 F8
Dalestie Moray 292 B3
Dalestorth Notts 171 C8
Dalfaber Highld 291 B11
Dalfoil Stirl 277 D11
Dalganachan Highld 310 E4
Dalgarven N Ayrs 266 F5
Dalgety Bay Fife 280 E3
Dalginross Perth 285 F11
Dalguise Perth 286 C3
Dalhalvaig Highld 310 D2
Dalham Suff 124 E4
Dalhastnie Angus 293 F7
Dalhenzean Perth 292 G3
Dalinlongart Argyll 276 E2
Dalkeith Midloth 270 B6
Dallam Warr 183 C9
Dallas Moray 301 D11
Dallas Lodge
Moray 301 D11
Dallcharn Highld 308 D6
Dalleagles E Ayrs 258 G3
Dallicott Shrops 132 E5
Dallimores IoW 20 C6
Dallinghoo Suff 126 G5
Dallington E Sus 23 B11
Northants 120 E4
Dallow N Yorks 214 E3
Dalmadilly Aberds 293 B9
Dalmally Argyll 284 E5
Dalmarnock
Glasgow 268 C2
Perth 286 C3
Dalmary Stirl 277 B10
Dalmellington
E Ayrs 245 B11
Dalmeny Edin 280 F2
Dalmigavie Highld 291 B9
Dalmigavie Lodge
Highld 301 G7
Dalmilling S Ayrs 257 E9
Dalmore Highld 300 C6
Dalmuir W Dunb 277 G9
Dalnabreck Highld 289 C8
Dalnacardoch Lodge
Perth 291 F9
Dalnacroich Highld 300 D3
Dalnaglar Castle
Perth 292 G3
Dalnahaitnach
Highld 301 G8
Dalnamein Lodge
Perth 291 G9
Dalnarrow Argyll 289 F9
Dalnaspidal Lodge
Perth 291 F8
Dalnavaid Perth 292 G2
Dalnavie Highld 300 B6
Dalnaw Dumfries 236 B5
Dalnawillan Lodge
Highld 310 E4
Dalness Highld 284 B5
Dalnessie Highld 309 H6
Dalphaid Highld 309 H3
Dalqueich Perth 286 G4
Dalrannoch Argyll 289 E11
Dalreavoch Highld 309 J7
Dalriach Highld 301 F10
Dalrigh Stirl 285 E7
Dalry Edin 280 G4
N Ayrs 266 F5
Dalrymple E Ayrs 257 G9
Dalscote Northants 120 G3
Dalserf S Lnrk 268 E6
Dalshannon N Lnrk 278 G4
Dalston Cumb 239 G9
London 67 C10
Dalswinton
Dumfries 247 F10
Dalton Cumb 211 D10
Dumfries 238 C4
Lancs 194 F3
Northumb 241 F10
Northumb 242 C4
N Yorks 215 D8
N Yorks 224 D2
S Lnrk 268 D3
S Yorks 187 C7
W Yorks 197 D7
Dalton-in-Furness
Cumb 210 E4
Dalton-le-Dale
Durham 234 B4
Dalton Magna
S Yorks 187 C7
Dalton-on-Tees
N Yorks 224 D5
Dalton Parva
S Yorks 187 C7
Dalton Piercy Hrtlpl 234 E5
Dalveallan Highld 300 F6
Dalveich Stirl 285 E10
Dalvina Lo Highld 308 E6
Dalwey Telford 132 B3
Dalwhinnie Highld 291 E8
Dalwood Devon 28 G3
Dalwyne S Ayrs 245 D8
Damask Green
Herts 104 F5
Damems W Yorks 204 F6
Damerham Hants 31 D10
Damery Glos 80 G2
Damgate Norf 143 B8
Norf 161 F9
Dam Green Norf 141 F11
Damhead Moray 301 D10
Dam Head W Yorks 196 B6
Damhead Holdings
Midloth 270 B5
Dam Mill Staffs 133 C7
Damnaglaur
Dumfries 236 F3
Dam of Quoiggs
Perth 286 G2
Damside Borders 270 F3
Dam Side Lancs 202 D4
Danaway Kent 69 G11
Danbury Essex 88 E3
Danbury Common
Essex 88 E3
Danby N Yorks 226 D4
Danby Wiske
N Yorks 224 F6
Dan Caerlan Rhondda 58 C5
Dancers Hill Herts 86 F2
Dancing Green
Hereford 98 G2
Dandaleith Moray 302 E2
Danderhall Midloth 270 B6
Dandy Corner Suff 125 D11
Danebank Ches E 185 E7
Dane Bank Gtr Man 184 B6
Danebridge Ches E 169 B7
Dane End Herts 104 G6
Danegate E Sus 52 G5
Danehill E Sus 36 B6
Dane in Shaw
Ches E 168 C5
Danemoor Green
Norf 141 B11
Danesbury Herts 86 B2
Danesfield Bucks 65 C10
Danesford Shrops 132 E4
Daneshill Hants 49 C7
Danesmoor Derbys 170 C6
Danes Moss Ches E 184 G6
Dane Street Kent 54 C5
Daneway Glos 80 E6
Dangerous Corner
Gtr Man 195 G7
Lancs 194 E4
Daniel's Water Kent 54 E3
Danna na Cloiche
Argyll 275 F7
Dannonchapel Corn 10 E6
Danskine E Loth 271 B11
Danthorpe E Yorks 209 G10
Danygraig Caerph 78 G2
Danzey Green
Warks 118 D2
Dapple Heath
Staffs 151 D10
Darby End W Mid 133 F9
Darby Green Hants 65 G10
Darbys Green
Worcs 116 F4
Darby's Hill W Mid 133 F9
Darcy Lever
Gtr Man 195 F8
Dardy Powys 78 B2
Darenth Kent 68 E5
Daresbury Halton 183 E9
Daresbury Delph
Halton 183 E9
Darfield S Yorks 198 G2
Darfoulds Notts 187 F9
Dargate Kent 70 G5
Dargate Common
Kent 70 G5
Darite Corn 6 B5
Darkland Moray 302 C2
Darland Wrex 166 D5
Darlaston W Mid 133 D9
Darlaston Green
W Mid 133 D9
Darley N Yorks 205 B10
Shrops 132 D3
Darley Abbey Derby 153 B7
Darley Bridge
Derbys 170 C3
Darley Dale Derbys 170 C3
Darleyford Corn 11 G11
Darley Green Warks 118 C3
Darleyhall Herts 104 G2
Darley Head
N Yorks 205 B9
Darley Hillside
Derbys 170 C3
Darlingscott Warks 100 C4
Darlington Darl 224 C5
Darliston Shrops 149 C11
Darlton Notts 188 G3
Darmsden Suff 125 G11
Darnall S Yorks 186 D5
Darnaway Castle
Moray 301 D9
Darnford Staffs 134 B2
Darnhall Ches W 167 C10
Darnhall Mains
Borders 270 F4
Darn Hill Gtr Man 195 E10
Darnick Borders 262 C2
Darowen Powys 128 C6
Darra Aberds 303 E7
Darracott Devon 24 D2
Devon 40 F3
Darras Hall
Northumb 242 C5
Darrington W Yorks 198 D3
Darrow Green Norf 142 F5
Darsham Suff 127 D8
Darshill Som 44 E6
Dartford Kent 68 E4
Dartford Crossing
Kent 68 D5
Dartington Devon 8 C5
Dartmeet Devon 13 G9
Dartmouth Devon 9 E7
Dartmouth Park
London 67 B9
Darton S Yorks 197 F10
Darvel E Ayrs 258 B3
Darvillshill Bucks 84 F4
Darwell Hole E Sus 23 B11
Darwen Blkburn 195 C7
Dassels Herts 105 F7
Datchet Windsor 66 D3
Datchet Common
Windsor 66 D3
Datchworth Herts 86 B3
Datchworth Green
Herts 86 B3
Daubhill Gtr Man 195 F8
Daugh of Kinermony
Moray 302 E2
Dauntsey Wilts 62 C3
Dauntsey Lock Wilts 62 C3
Dava Moray 301 F10
Davenham
Ches W 183 G11
Davenport Ches E 168 B4
Gtr Man 184 D5
Davenport Green
Ches E 184 F4
Gtr Man 184 D4
Daventry Northants 119 E11
Davidson's Mains
Edin 280 F4
Davidston Highld 301 C7
Davidstow Corn 11 D9
David Street Kent 68 G6
David's Well Powys 113 B11
Davington Dumfries 248 C6
Kent 70 G4
Daviot Aberds 303 G7
Highld 301 F7
Davis's Town E Sus 23 B8
Davoch of Grange
Moray 302 D4
Davo Mains Aberds 293 F9
Davyhulme Gtr Man 184 B3
Daw Cross
N Yorks 205 C11
Dawdon Durham 234 B4
Daw End W Mid 133 C10
Dawesgreen Sur 51 D8
Dawker Hill N Yorks 207 F7
Dawley Telford 132 B3
Dawley Bank Telford 132 B3
Dawlish Devon 14 F5
Dawlish Warren
Devon 14 F5
Dawn Conwy 180 G5
Daw's Cross Essex 107 E7
Daw's Green Som 27 C11
Daws Heath Essex 69 B10
Dawshill Worcs 116 G6
Daw's House Corn 12 E2
Dawsmere Lincs 157 C8
Daybrook Notts 171 F9
Day Green Ches E 168 D3
Dayhills Staffs 151 C9
Dayhouse Bank
Worcs 117 B9
Daylesford Glos 100 F4
Daywall Shrops 148 C5
Ddol Flint 181 G10
Ddôl Cownwy
Powys 147 F10
Ddrydwy Anglesey 178 G5
Deacons Hill Herts 85 F11
Deadman's Cross
C Beds 104 C2
Deadman's Green
Staffs 151 B10
Deadwater Hants 49 F10
Northumb 250 D4
Deaf Hill Durham 234 D3
Deal Hall Essex 89 F8
Kent 55 C11
Dean Cumb 229 F7
Devon 8 C4
Devon 40 D6
Devon 40 E4
Devon 41 D8
Dorset 31 D7
Edin 280 G4
Hants 33 D9
Hants 48 G2
Lancs 195 B11
Oxon 100 G6
Som 45 E7
Dean Bank Durham 233 E11
Deanburnhaugh
Borders 261 G9
Dean Court Oxon 83 D7
Dean Cross Devon 40 E4
Deane Gtr Man 195 F7
Hants 48 C4
Deanend Dorset 31 D7
Dean Head S Yorks 197 G9
Deanich Lodge
Highld 309 L3
Deanland Dorset 31 D7
Deanlane End W Sus 34 E2
Dean Lane Head
W Yorks 205 G7
Dean Park Renfs 267 B10
Dean Prior Devon 8 C4
Dean Row Ches E 184 E5
Deans W Loth 269 B10
Deans Bottom Kent 69 G11
Deanscales Cumb 229 F7
Deansgreen
Ches E 183 D11
Dean's Green
Warks 118 D2
Deanshanger
Northants 102 D5
Deans Hill Kent 69 G11
Deanston Stirl 285 G11
Dean Street Kent 53 C8
Dearham Cumb 229 D7
Dearnley Gtr Man 196 D2
Debach Suff 126 G4
Debdale Gtr Man 184 B5
Debden Essex 86 F6
Essex 105 E11
Debden Cross
Essex 105 E11
Debden Green Essex 86 F6
Essex 105 E11
De Beauvoir Town
London 67 C10
Debenham Suff 126 E3
Deblin's Green Worcs 98 B6
Dechmont W Loth 279 G10
Deckham T&W 243 E7
Deddington Oxon 101 E9
Dedham Essex 107 E11
Dedham Heath
Essex 107 E11
Dedridge W Loth 269 B11
Dedworth Windsor 66 D2
Deebank Aberds 293 D8
Deecastle Aberds 292 D6
Deene Northants 137 E8
Deenethorpe
Northants 137 E9
Deepcar S Yorks 186 B3
Deepclough Derbys 185 B8
Deepcut Sur 50 B2
Deepdale C Beds 104 B4
Cumb 212 C4
N Yorks 213 D7
Deepdene Sur 51 D7
Deepfields W Mid 133 E8
Deeping Gate Lincs 138 B2
Deeping St James
Lincs 138 B3
Deeping St Nicholas
Lincs 156 F4
Deepthwaite Cumb 211 C10
Deepweir Mon 60 B3
Deerhill Moray 302 D4
Deerhurst Glos 99 F7
Deerhurst Walton
Glos 99 F7
Deerland Pembs 73 C7
Deerness Orkney 314 F5
Deer's Green Essex 105 E9
Deerstones N Yorks 205 C7
Deerton Street Kent 70 G3
Defford Worcs 99 C8
Defynnog Powys 95 F8
Deganwy Conwy 180 F3
Degar V Glam 58 D4
Degibna Corn 2 D5
Deighton N Yorks 225 E7
W Yorks 197 D7
York 207 E8
Deiniolen Gwyn 163 C9
Deishar Highld 291 B11
Delabole Corn 11 E7
Delamere Ches W 167 B9
Delfour Highld 291 C10
Delfrigs Aberds 303 G9
Delliefure Highld 301 F10
Dell Lodge Highld 292 B2
Dell Quay W Sus 22 C4
Delly End Oxon 82 C5
Delnabo Moray 292 B3
Delnadamph Aberds 292 C4
Delnamer Angus 292 G3
Delph Gtr Man 196 F3
Delves Durham 233 B8
Delvine Perth 286 C5
Delvin End Essex 106 D5
Dembleby Lincs 155 B10
Demelza Corn 5 C9
Denaby Main
S Yorks 187 B7
Denbeath Fife 281 B7
Denbigh Denb 165 B9
Denbury Devon 8 B6
Denby Derbys 170 F5
Denby Bottles
Derbys 170 F5
Denby Common
Derbys 170 F6
Denby Dale
W Yorks 197 F8
Denchworth Oxon 82 G5
Dendron Cumb 210 E4
Denel End C Beds 103 D10
Denend Aberds 302 F6
Dene Park Kent 52 C5
Deneside Durham 234 B4
Denford Northants 121 B9
Staffs 169 E7
Dengie Essex 89 E7
Denham Bucks 66 B4
Bucks 102 G5
Suff 124 E5
Suff 126 C3
Denham Corner
Suff 126 C3
Denham End Suff 124 E5
Denham Green Bucks 66 B4
Denham Street Suff 126 C3
Denhead Aberds 303 D9
Fife 287 F8
Denhead of Arbilot
Angus 287 C9
Denhead of Gray
Dundee 287 D7
Denholm Borders 262 F3
Denholme W Yorks 205 G7
Denholme Clough
W Yorks 205 G7
Denholme Edge
W Yorks 205 G7
Denholme Gate
W Yorks 205 G7
Denholmhill Borders 262 F3
Denio Gwyn 145 B7
Denmead Hants 33 E11
Denmore Aberdeen 293 B11
Denmoss Aberds 302 E6
Dennington Suff 126 D5
Dennington Corner
Suff 126 D5
Dennington Hall
Suff 126 D5
Denny Falk 278 E6
Denny Bottom Kent 52 F5
Denny End Cambs 123 D9
Dennyloanhead
Falk 278 E6
Denny Lodge Hants 32 F4
Dennystown
W Dunb 277 F7
Denshaw Gtr Man 196 E3
Denside Aberds 293 D10
Densole Kent 55 E8
Denston Suff 124 G5
Denstone Staffs 169 G9
Denstroude Kent 70 G6
Dent Cumb 212 B4
Dent Bank Durham 232 F4
Denton Cambs 138 F2
Darl 224 B4
E Sus 23 E7
Gtr Man 184 B6
Kent 55 D8
Kent 69 E7
Lincs 155 C7
Norf 142 F5
Northants 120 F6
N Yorks 205 D8
Oxon 83 E9
Denton Burn T&W 242 D5
Denton Holme
Cumb 239 G10
Denton's Green
Mers 183 B7
Denver Norf 140 C2
Denvilles Hants 22 B2
Denwick Northumb 264 G6
Deopham Norf 141 C11
Deopham Green
Norf 141 D10
Deopham Stalland
Norf 141 D10
Depden Suff 124 F5
Depden Green Suff 124 F5
Deppers Bridge
Warks 119 F7
Deptford London 67 D11
T&W 243 F9
Wilts 46 F4
Derby Derbys 153 B7
Devon 40 G5
Derbyhaven IoM 192 F3
Derbyshire Hill
Mers 183 C8
Dereham Norf 159 G9
Dergoals Dumfries 236 D4
Deri Caerph 77 E10
Derriford Plym 7 D9
Derril Devon 24 G4
Derringstone Kent 55 D8
Derrington Shrops 132 E2
Staffs 151 E7
Derriton Devon 24 G4
Derry Stirl 285 E10
Derrydaroch Stirl 285 E7
Derry Downs London 68 F3
Derry Fields Wilts 81 G8
Derryguaig Argyll 288 F6
Derry Hill Wilts 62 E3
Derry Lodge Aberds 292 D2
Derrythorpe
N Lincs 199 F10
Dersingham Norf 158 C3
Dertfords Wilts 45 D10
Dervaig Argyll 288 D6
Derwen Bridgend 58 C2
Denb 165 E9
Derwenlas Powys 128 D4
Desborough
Northants 136 G6
Desford Leics 135 C9
Deskryshiel Aberds 292 B6
Detchant Northumb 264 B3
Detling Kent 53 B9
Deuchar Angus 292 G6
Deuddwr Powys 148 F4
Deuxhill Shrops 132 F3
Devauden Mon 79 F7
Deveral Corn 2 B3
Devil's Bridge/
Pontarfynach
Ceredig 112 B4
Devitts Green
Warks 134 E5
Devizes Wilts 62 G4
Devol Invclyd 276 G6
Devonport Plym 7 E9
Devonside Clack 279 B8
Devon Village Clack 279 B8
Devoran Corn 3 B7
Dewar Borders 270 F6
Dewartown Midloth 271 C7
Dewes Green Essex 105 E9
Dewlands Common
Dorset 31 F9
Dewlish Dorset 17 B11
Dewsbury W Yorks 197 C8
Dewsbury Moor
W Yorks 197 C8
Dewshall Court
Hereford 97 E9
Dhoon IoM 192 D5
Dhoor IoM 192 C5
Dhowin IoM 192 B5
Dhustone Shrops 115 B11
Dial Green W Sus 34 B6
Dial Post W Sus 35 D11
Dibberford Dorset 29 G7
Dibden Hants 32 F6
Dibden Purlieu Hants 32 F6
Dickens Heath
W Mid 118 B2
Dickleburgh Norf 142 G3
Dickleburgh Moor
Norf 142 G3
Dickon Hills Lincs 174 D6
Didbrook Glos 99 E11
Didcot Oxon 64 B4
Diddington Cambs 122 D3
Diddlebury Shrops 131 F10
Diddywell Devon 25 B7
Didley Hereford 97 E9
Didling W Sus 34 D4
Didlington Norf 140 D5
Didmarton Glos 61 B10
Didsbury Gtr Man 184 C4
Didworthy Devon 8 C3
Diebidale Highld 309 L4
Digbeth W Mid 133 F11
Digby Lincs 173 E9
Digg Highld 298 C4
Diggle Gtr Man 196 F4
Diglis Worcs 116 G6
Digmoor Lancs 194 F3
Digswell Herts 86 B3
Digswell Park Herts 86 C2
Digswell Water Herts 86 C3
Dihewyd Ceredig 111 F9
Dilham Norf 160 D6
Dilhorne Staffs 169 G7
Dillarburn S Lnrk 268 G6
Dill Hall Lancs 195 B8
Dillington Cambs 122 D2
Som 28 D5
Dilston Northumb 241 E11
Dilton Marsh Wilts 45 D11
Dilwyn Hereford 115 G8
Dimlands V Glam 58 F3
Dimmer Som 44 G6
Dimple Derbys 170 C3
Gtr Man 195 D8
Dimsdale Staffs 168 F4
Dimson Corn 12 G4
Dinas Carms 92 E5
Corn 10 G4
Gwyn 144 B5
Gwyn 163 D7
Dinas Cross Pembs 91 D10
Dinas Dinlle Gwyn 162 D6
Dinas-Mawddwy
Gwyn 147 G7
Dinas Mawr Conwy 164 E4
Dinas Powys V Glam 59 E7
Dinbych y Pysgod/
Tenby Pembs 73 E10
Dinckley Lancs 203 F9
Dinder Som 44 E5
Dinedor Hereford 97 D10
Dinedor Cross
Hereford 97 D10
Dines Green Worcs 116 F6
Dingestow Mon 79 C7
Dinghurst N Som 44 B2
Dingle Mers 182 D5
Dingleden Kent 53 G10
Dingleton Borders 262 C2
Dingley Northants 136 F5
Dingwall Highld 300 D5
Dinlabyre Borders 250 E2
Dinmael Conwy 165 G8
Dinnet Aberds 292 D6
Dinnington Som 28 E6
S Yorks 187 D8
T&W 242 C6
Dinorwic Gwyn 163 C9
Dinton Bucks 84 C3
Wilts 46 G4
Dinwoodie Mains
Dumfries 248 E4
Dinworthy Devon 24 D4
Dipford Som 28 C2
Dipley Hants 49 B8
Dippenhall Sur 49 D10
Dippertown Devon 12 E4
Dippin N Ayrs 256 E2
Dipple Devon 24 D4
Moray 302 D3
S Ayrs 244 C6
Diptford Devon 8 D4
Dipton Durham 242 G5
Diptonmill
Northumb 241 E10
Dirdhu Highld 301 G10
Direcleit W Isles 305 J3
Dirleton E Loth 281 E10
Dirt Pot Northumb 232 B3
Discoed Powys 114 E5
Discove Som 45 G7
Diseworth Leics 153 E9
Dishes Orkney 314 D6
Dishforth N Yorks 215 E7
Dishley Leics 153 E10
Disley Ches E 185 E7
Diss Norf 126 B2
Disserth Powys 113 F10
Distington Cumb 228 G6
Ditchampton Wilts 46 G5
Ditcheat Som 44 F6
Ditchfield Bucks 84 G4
Ditchford Hill
Worcs 100 D4
Ditchingham Norf 142 E6
Ditchling E Sus 36 D4
Ditherington
Shrops 149 G10
Ditteridge Wilts 61 F10
Dittisham Devon 9 E7
Ditton Halton 183 D7
Kent 53 B8
Ditton Green Cambs 124 F3
Ditton Priors Shrops 132 F2
Dittons E Sus 23 E10
Divach Highld 300 G4
Divlyn Carms 94 D5
Dixton Glos 99 E9
Mon 79 C8
Dizzard Corn 11 B9
Dobcross Gtr Man 196 F3
Dobs Hill Flint 166 C4
Dobson's Bridge
Shrops 149 C9
Dobwalls Corn 6 C4
Doccombe Devon 13 D11
Dochfour Ho Highld 300 F6
Dochgarroch Highld 300 E6
Dockeney Norf 143 E7
Dockenfield Sur 49 E10
Docker Lancs 211 E11
Docking Norf 158 B5
Docklow Hereford 115 F11
Dockray Cumb 230 G3
Dockroyd W Yorks 204 F6
Doc Penfro/Pembroke
Dock Pembs 73 E7
Docton Devon 24 C2
Dodbrooke Devon 8 G4
Dodburn Borders 249 B11
Doddenham Worcs 116 F5
Doddinghurst Essex 87 F9
Doddington Cambs 139 E7
Kent 54 B2
Lincs 188 G6
Northumb 263 C11
Shrops 116 B2
Doddiscombsleigh
Devon 14 D3
Doddshill Norf 158 C3
Doddycross Corn 6 C6
Dodford Northants 120 E2
Worcs 117 C8
Dodington S Glos 61 C9
Som 43 E7
Dodleston Ches W 166 C5
Dodmarsh Hereford 97 C11
Dodscott Devon 25 D8
Dods Leigh Staffs 151 C10
Dodworth S Yorks 197 F10
Dodworth Bottom
S Yorks 197 G10
Dodworth Green
S Yorks 197 G10
Doe Bank W Mid 134 D2
Doe Green Warr 183 D9
Doehole Derbys 170 D5
Doe Lea Derbys 171 B7
Doffcocker Gtr Man 195 E7
Dogdyke Lincs 174 D2
Dog & Gun Mers 182 B5
Dog Hill Gtr Man 196 F3
Dogingtree Estate
Staffs 151 G9
Dogley Lane
W Yorks 197 E7
Dogmersfield Hants 49 C9
Dogridge Wilts 62 B5
Dogsthorpe Pboro 138 C3
Dog Village Devon 14 B5
Doirlinn Highld 289 D8
Dolanog Powys 147 G11
Dolau Powys 114 D2
Rhondda 58 C3
Dolbenmaen Gwyn 163 G8
Dole Ceredig 128 F2
Dolemeads Bath 61 G9
Doley Staffs 150 D4
Dolfach Powys 129 C8
Dol-ffanog Gwyn 146 G4
Dolfor Powys 130 F2
Dol-fôr Powys 128 B6
Dolgarrog Conwy 164 B3
Dolgellau Gwyn 146 F4
Dolgerdd Ceredig 111 G8
Dolgoch Gwyn 128 C3
Dolgran Carms 93 E8
Dolhelfa Powys 113 C8
Dolhendre Gwyn 147 C7
Doll Highld 311 J2
Dollar Clack 279 B9
Dolley Green Powys 114 D5
Dollis Hill London 67 B8
Dollwen Ceredig 128 G3
Dolphin Flint 181 G11
Dolphingstone
E Loth 281 G7
Dolphinholme
Lancs 202 C6
Dolphinston Borders 262 F5
Dolphinton S Lnrk 270 F2
Dolton Devon 25 E9
Dolwen Conwy 180 G5
Powys 129 B9
Dolwyd Conwy 180 F4
Dolwyddelan Conwy 164 E2
Dôl-y-Bont Ceredig 128 F2
Dol-y-cannau Powys 96 B3
Dolydd Gwyn 163 D7
Dolyhir Powys 114 F4
Dolymelinau
Powys 129 D11
Dolywern Wrex 148 B4
Domewood Sur 51 E10
Domgay Powys 148 F5
Dommett Som 28 E3
Doncaster S Yorks 198 G5
Doncaster Common
S Yorks 198 G6
Dones Green
Ches W 183 F10
Donhead St Andrew
Wilts 30 C6
Donhead St Mary
Wilts 30 C6
Donibristle Fife 280 D3
Doniford Som 42 E5
Donington Lincs 156 B4
Shrops 132 C6
Donington Eaudike
Lincs 156 B4
Donington le Heath
Leics 153 G8
Donington on Bain
Lincs 190 E2
Donington South Ing
Lincs 156 C4
Donisthorpe Leics 152 G6
Don Johns Essex 106 F6
Donkey Street Kent 54 G6
Donkey Town Sur 66 G2
Donna Nook Lincs 190 B6
Donnington Glos 100 F3
Hereford 98 E4
Shrops 131 B11
Telford 150 G4
W Berks 64 F3
W Sus 22 C5
Donnington Wood
Telford 150 G4
Donwell T&W 243 F7
Donyatt Som 28 E4
Doomsday Green
W Sus 35 B11
Doonfoot S Ayrs 257 F8
Dora's Green Hants 49 D10
Dorback Lodge
Highld 292 B2
Dorcan Swindon 63 C7
Dorchester Dorset 17 C9
Oxon 83 G9
Dordale Worcs 117 C8
Dordon Warks 134 C5
Dore S Yorks 186 E4
Dores Highld 300 F5
Dorking Sur 51 D7
Dorking Tye Suff 107 D8
Dorley's Corner
Suff 127 D7
Dormansland Sur 52 E2
Dormans Park Sur 51 E11
Dormanstown
Redcar 235 G7
Dormer's Wells
London 66 C6
Dormington
Hereford 97 C11
Dormston Worcs 117 F9
Dorn Glos 100 E4
Dornal S Ayrs 236 B4
Dorney Bucks 66 D2
Dorney Reach Bucks 66 D2
Dorn Hill Worcs 100 E3
Dornie Highld 295 C10
Dornoch Highld 309 L7
Dornock Dumfries 238 D6
Dorrery Highld 310 D4
Dorridge W Mid 118 B3
Dorrington Lincs 173 E9
Shrops 131 C9
Dorsington Warks 100 B2
Dorstone Hereford 96 C6
Dorton Bucks 83 C11
Dorusduain Highld 295 C11
Doseley Telford 132 B3
Dosmuckeran
Highld 300 C2
Dosthill Staffs 134 C4
Staffs 134 D4
Dothan Anglesey 178 G5
Dothill Telford 150 G2
Dottery Dorset 16 B5
Doublebois Corn 6 C3
Double Hill Bath 45 B8
Dougarie N Ayrs 255 D9
Doughton Glos 80 G5
Norf 159 D7
Douglas IoM 192 E4
S Lnrk 259 C8
Douglas & Angus
Dundee 287 D8
Douglastown Angus 287 C8
Douglas Water S
Lnrk 259 B9
Douglas West S
Lnrk 259 C8
Doulting Som 44 E6
Dounby Orkney 314 D2
Doune Highld 291 C10
Highld 309 J4
Stirl 285 G11
Doune Park Aberds 303 C7
Douneside Aberds 292 C6
Dounie Argyll 275 D8
Highld 309 K5
Highld 309 L6
Dounreay Highld 310 C3
Doura N Ayrs 266 G6
Dousland Devon 7 B10
Dovaston Shrops 149 E7
Dovecot Mers 182 C6
Dovecothall
Glasgow 267 D10
Dove Green Notts 171 E7
Dove Holes Derbys 185 F9
Dovenby Cumb 229 E7
Dovendale Lincs 190 E4
Dove Point Mers 182 C2
Dover Gtr Man 194 G6

Kent 55 E10
Dovercourt Essex 108 E5
Doverdale Worcs 117 D7
Doverhay Som 41 D11
Doveridge Derbys 152 C2
Doversgreen Sur 51 D9
Dowally Perth 286 C4
Dowanhill Glasgow 267 B11
Dowbridge Lancs 202 G4
Dowdeswell Glos 81 B7
Dowe Hill Norf 161 F10
Dowlais M Tydf 77 D10
Dowlais Top M Tydf 77 D9
Dowland Devon 25 E9
Dowles Worcs 116 B5
Dowlesgreen
Wokingham 65 F10
Dowlish Ford Som 28 E5
Dowlish Wake Som 28 E5
Downall Green
Gtr Man 194 G5
Down Ampney Glos 81 F10
Downan Moray 301 F11
S Ayrs 244 G3
Downcraig Ferry
N Ayrs 266 D3
Downderry Corn 6 E6
Downe London 68 G2
Downend Glos 80 F4
IoW 20 D6
S Glos 60 D6
W Berks 64 D3
Down End Som 43 E10
Downfield Dundee 287 D7
Down Field Cambs 124 C2
Downgate Corn 11 G11
Corn 12 G3
Down Hall Cumb 239 G7
Downham Essex 88 F2
Lancs 203 E11
London 67 E11
Northumb 263 C9
Downham Market
Norf 140 C2
Down Hatherley Glos 99 G7
Downhead Som 29 B9
Som 45 D7
Downhead Park
M Keynes 103 C7
Downhill Corn 5 B7
Perth 286 D4
T&W 243 F9
Downholland Cross
Lancs 193 F11
Downholme
N Yorks 224 F2
Downicary Devon 12 C3
Downies Aberds 293 D11
Downinney Corn 11 C10
Downley Bucks 84 G4
Down Park W Sus 51 F10
Downs V Glam 58 E6
Down St Mary Devon 26 G2
Downside C Beds 103 G10
E Sus 23 E9
N Som 60 F3
Som 44 D6
Sur 50 B6
Sur 51 B7
Down Street E Sus 36 C6
Down Thomas Devon 7 E10
Downton Hants 19 C11
Powys 114 E4
Shrops 149 G10
Wilts 31 C11
Downton on the Rock
Hereford 115 C8
Dowsby Lincs 156 D2
Dowsdale Lincs 156 G5
Dowslands Som 28 C2
Dowthwaitehead
Cumb 230 G3
Doxey Staffs 151 E8
Doxford Park T&W 243 G9
Doynton S Glos 61 E8
Drabblegate Norf 160 D4
Draethen Newport 59 B8
Draffan S Lnrk 268 F5
Dragley Beck Cumb 210 D5
Dragonby N Lincs 200 E2
Dragons Green
W Sus 35 C10
Drakehouse
S Yorks 186 E6
Drakeland Corner
Devon 7 D11
Drakelow Worcs 132 G6
Drakemyre Aberds 303 F9
N Ayrs 266 E5
Drake's Broughton
Worcs 99 B8
Drakes Cross
Worcs 117 B11
Drakestone Green
Suff 107 B9
Drakewalls Corn 12 G4
Draughton
Northants 120 B5
N Yorks 204 C6
Drawbridge Corn 6 B3
Drax N Yorks 199 B7
Draycot Oxon 83 D10
Draycot Cerne Wilts 62 D2
Draycote Warks 119 C8
Draycot Fitz Payne
Wilts 62 G6
Draycot Foliat
Swindon 63 D7
Draycott Derbys 153 C8
Glos 80 E2
Glos 100 D3
Shrops 132 E6
Som 29 C8
Som 44 C3
Worcs 99 B7
Draycott in the Clay
Staffs 152 D3
Draycott in the Moors
Staffs 169 G7
Drayford Devon 26 E3
Drayton Leics 136 E6
Lincs 156 B4
Norf 160 G3
Northants 119 E11
Oxon 83 G7
Oxon 101 C8
Ptsmth 33 F11
Som 28 C6
Som 29 D7
Warks 118 F3
Worcs 117 B8
Drayton Bassett
Staffs 134 C3
Drayton Beauchamp
Bucks 84 C6
Drayton Parslow
Bucks 102 F6
Drayton St Leonard
Oxon 83 F10
Drebley N Yorks 205 B7
Dreemskerry IoM 192 C5
Dreenhill Pembs 72 C6
Drefach Carms 75 C8
Carms 92 G5
Carms 93 D7
Dre-fach Carms 75 B11
Ceredig 93 B10
Drefelin Carms 93 D7
Dreggie Highld 301 G10
Dreghorn Edin 270 B4
N Ayrs 257 B9
Dre-gôch Denb 165 B10
Drellingore Kent 55 E8
Drem E Loth 281 F10
Dresden Stoke 168 G6
Dreumasdal
W Isles 297 H3
Drewsteignton
Devon 13 C10
Driby Lincs 190 G5
Driffield E Yorks 208 B6
Glos 81 F9
Drift Corn 1 D4
Drigg Cumb 219 F11
Drighlington
W Yorks 197 B8
Drimnin Highld 289 D7
Drimnin Ho Highld 289 D7
Drimpton Dorset 28 F6
Drimsynie Argyll 284 G5
Dringhoe E Yorks 209 C9
Dringhouses York 207 D7
Drinisiadar W Isles 305 J3
Drinkstone Suff 125 E9
Drinkstone Green
Suff 125 E9
Drishaig Argyll 284 F5
Drissaig Argyll 275 B10
Drive End Dorset 29 F9
Driver's End Herts 86 B2
Drochedlie Aberds 302 C5
Drochil Borders 270 G3
Drointon Staffs 151 D10
Droitwich Spa
Worcs 117 E7
Droman Highld 306 D6
Dromore Dumfries 237 C7
Dron Perth 286 F5
Dronfield Derbys 186 F5
Dronfield Woodhouse
Derbys 186 F4
Drongan E Ayrs 257 F10
Dronley Angus 287 D7
Droop Dorset 30 F3
Drope Cardiff 58 D6
Dropping Well
S Yorks 186 C5
Droughduil
Dumfries 236 D3
Droxford Hants 33 D10
Droylsden Gtr Man 184 B6
Drub W Yorks 197 B7
Druggers End Worcs 98 D5
Druid Denb 165 G8
Druidston Pembs 72 B5
Druim Highld 301 D9
Druimarbin Highld 290 F2
Druimavuic Argyll 284 C4
Druimdrishaig
Argyll 275 F8
Druimindarroch
Highld 295 G8
Druimkinnerras
Highld 300 F4
Druimnacroish
Argyll 288 E6
Druimsornaig Argyll 289 F9
Druimyeon More
Argyll 255 B7
Drum Argyll 275 F10
Edin 270 B6
Perth 286 G4
Drumardoch Stirl 285 F10
Drumbeg Highld 306 F6
Drumblade Aberds 302 E5
Drumblair Aberds 302 E6
Drumbuie Dumfries 246 G3
Highld 295 B9
Drumburgh Cumb 239 F7
Drumburn
Dumfries 237 C11
Drumchapel
Glasgow 277 G10
Drumchardine
Highld 300 E5
Drumchork Highld 307 L3
Drumclog S Lnrk 258 B4
Drumdelgie Aberds 302 E4
Drumderfit Highld 300 D6
Drumdollo Aberds 302 F6
Drumeldrie Fife 287 G8
Drumelzier Borders 260 C4
Drumfearn Highld 295 D8
Drumgask Highld 291 D8
Drumgelloch N Lnrk 268 B5
Drumgley Angus 287 B8
Drumgreen Angus 292 F6
Drumguish Highld 291 D9
Drumhead Aberds 293 B11
Drumin Moray 301 F11
Drumindorsair
Highld 300 E4
Drumlasie Aberds 293 C8
Drumlean Stirl 285 G8
Drumlemble Argyll 255 F7
Drumliah Highld 309 K6
Drumligair Aberds 293 B11
Drumlithie Aberds 293 E9
Drumloist Stirl 285 G10
Drummersdale
Lancs 193 E11
Drummick Perth 286 E3
Drummoddie
Dumfries 236 E5
Drummond Highld 300 C6
Drummore Dumfries 236 F3
Drummuir Moray 302 E3
Drummuir Castle
Moray 302 E3
Drumnadrochit
Highld 300 G5
Drumnagorrach
Moray 302 D5
Drumness Perth 286 F2
Drumoak Aberds 293 D9
Drumore Argyll 255 E8
Drumpark Dumfries 247 G9
Drumpellier N Lnrk 268 B4
Drumphail Dumfries 236 C4
Drumrash Dumfries 237 B8
Drumrunie Highld 307 J6
Drumry W Dunb 277 G10
Drums Aberds 303 G9
Drumsallie Highld 289 B11
Drumsmittal Highld 300 E6
Drumstinchall
Dumfries 237 D10
Drumsturdy Angus 287 D8
Drumtochty Castle
Aberds 293 F8
Drumtroddan
Dumfries 236 E5
Drumuie Highld 298 E4
Drumuillie Highld 301 G9
Drumvaich Stirl 285 G10
Drumwalt Dumfries 236 D5
Drumwhindle
Aberds 303 F9
Drunkendub Angus 287 C10
Drury Flint 166 C3
Drurylane Norf 141 C8
Drury Lane Wrex 167 G7
Drury Square Norf 159 F8
Drybeck Cumb 222 B3
Drybridge Moray 302 C4
N Ayrs 257 B9
Drybrook Glos 79 B10
Dryburgh Borders 262 C3
Dryden Borders 261 E11
Dry Doddington
Lincs 172 F4
Dry Drayton Cambs 123 E7
Dryhill Kent 52 B3
Dry Hill Hants 49 F7
Dryhope Borders 261 E7
Drylaw Edin 280 F4
Drym Corn 2 C4
Drymen Stirl 277 D9
Drymere Norf 140 B5
Drymuir Aberds 303 E9
Drynachan Lodge
Highld 301 F8
Drynain Argyll 276 D3
Drynham Wilts 45 B11
Drynie Park Highld 300 D5
Drynoch Highld 294 B6
Dry Sandford Oxon 83 E7
Dryslwyn Carms 93 G11
Dry Street Essex 69 B7
Dryton Shrops 131 B11
Drywells Aberds 302 D6
Duag Bridge Highld 309 K3
Duartbeg Highld 306 F6
Duartmore Bridge
Highld 306 F6
Dubbs Cross Devon 12 C3
Dubford Aberds 303 C8
Dubhchladach
Argyll 275 G9
Dublin Suff 126 D3
Dubton Angus 287 B9
Dubwath Cumb 229 E9
Duchally Highld 309 H3
Duchlage Argyll 276 D6
Duchrae Dumfries 246 G5
Duck Corner Suff 109 C7
Duck End Beds 103 C11
Beds 121 G9
Bucks 102 F5
Cambs 122 E4
Essex 105 G10
Essex 106 E3
Essex 106 F3
Duckend Green
Essex 106 G4
Duckhole S Glos 79 G10
Duckington Ches W 167 E7
Ducklington Oxon 82 D5
Duckmanton Derbys 186 G6
Duck's Cross Beds 122 F2
Ducks Island London 86 F2
Duckswich Worcs 98 D6
Dudbridge Glos 80 E4
Dudden Hill London 67 B8
Duddenhoe End
Essex 105 D9
Duddingston Edin 280 G5
Duddington
Northants 137 C9
Duddlestone Som 28 C2
Duddleswell E Sus 37 B7
Duddlewick Shrops 132 G3
Duddo Northumb 273 G8
Duddon Ches W 167 C8
Duddon Bridge
Cumb 210 B3
Duddon Common
Ches W 167 B8
Dudleston Shrops 148 B6
Dudleston Grove
Shrops 149 B7
Dudleston Heath
(Criftins) Shrops 149 B7
Dudley T&W 243 C7
W Mid 133 E8
Dudley Hill W Yorks 205 G9
Dudley Port W Mid 133 E9
Dudley's Fields
W Mid 133 C9
Dudley Wood
W Mid 133 F8
Dudlows Green
Warr 183 E10
Dudsbury Dorset 19 B7
Dudswell Herts 85 D7
Dudwells Pembs 91 G8
Duerdon Devon 24 D4
Duffield Derbys 170 G4
Duffieldbank
Derbys 170 G5
Duffryn Neath 57 B10
Newport 59 B9
Shrops 130 G4
Dufftown Moray 302 F3
Duffus Moray 301 C11
Dufton Cumb 231 F9
Duggleby N Yorks 217 F9
Duich Argyll 254 B4
Duiletter Argyll 284 D5
Duinish Perth 291 G8
Duirinish Highld 295 B9
Duisdalebeg Highld 295 D8
Duisdalemore
Highld 295 D9
Duisky Highld 290 F2
Duke End Warks 134 F4
Dukesfield
Northumb 241 F10
Dukestown
Bl Gwent 77 C10
Dukinfield Gtr Man 184 B6
Dulas Anglesey 179 D7
Dulcote Som 44 E5
Dulford Devon 27 F9
Dull Perth 286 C2
Dullatur N Lnrk 278 F4
Dullingham Cambs 124 F2
Dullingham Ley
Cambs 124 F2
Dulnain Bridge
Highld 301 G9
Duloch Fife 280 D2
Duloe Beds 122 E3
Corn 6 D4
Dulsie Highld 301 E9
Dulverton Som 26 B6
Dulwich London 67 E10
Dulwich Village
London 67 E10
Dumbarton W Dunb 277 F7
Dumbleton Glos 99 D10
Dumcrieff Dumfries 248 C4
Dumfries Dumfries 237 B11
Dumgoyne Stirl 277 E10
Dummer Hants 48 D5
Dumpford W Sus 34 C4
Dumpinghill Devon 24 F6
Dumpling Green
Norf 159 G10
Dumplington
Gtr Man 184 B3
Dumpton Kent 71 F11
Dun Angus 287 B10
Dunach Argyll 289 G10
Dunadd Argyll 275 D9
Dunain Ho Highld 300 E6
Dunalastair Perth 285 B11
Dunan Highld 295 C7
Dunans Argyll 275 D9
Argyll 275 D11
Dunball Som 43 E10
Dunbar E Loth 282 F3
Dunbeath Highld 311 G5
Dunbeg Argyll 289 F10
Dunblane Stirl 285 G11
Dunbog Fife 286 F6
Dunbridge Hants 32 B4
Duncanscleft
Shetland 313 K5
Duncanston Highld 300 D5
Duncanstone
Aberds 302 G5
Dun Charlabhaigh
W Isles 304 D3
Dunchideock Devon 14 D3
Dunchurch Warks 119 C9
Duncombe Lancs 202 F6
Duncote Northants 120 G3
Duncow Dumfries 247 G11
Duncraggan Stirl 285 G9
Duncrievie Perth 286 G5
Duncroisk Stirl 285 D9
Duncton W Sus 35 D7
Dundas Ho Orkney 314 H4
Dundee Dundee 287 D8
Dundeugh Dumfries 246 F3
Dundon Som 44 G3
Dundonald Fife 280 C4
S Ayrs 257 C9
Dundon Hayes Som 44 G3
Dundonnell Highld 307 L5
Dundonnell Hotel
Highld 307 L5
Dundonnell House
Highld 307 L6
Dundraw Cumb 229 B10
Dundreggan Highld 290 B5
Dundreggan Lodge
Highld 290 B5
Dundrennan
Dumfries 237 E9
Dundridge Hants 33 D9
Dundry N Som 60 F5
Dundurn Perth 285 E11
Dundyvan N Lnrk 268 C4
Dunecht Aberds 293 C9
Dunfermline Fife 279 D11
Dunfield Glos 81 F10
Dunford Bridge
S Yorks 197 G7
Dungate Kent 54 B2
Dunge Wilts 45 C11
Dungeness Kent 39 D9
Dungworth S Yorks 186 D3
Dunham Notts 188 G4
Dunham-on-the-Hill
Ches W 183 G7
Dunham on Trent
Notts 188 G4
Dunhampstead
Worcs 117 E8
Dunhampton Worcs 116 D6
Dunham Town
Gtr Man 184 D2
Dunham Woodhouses
Gtr Man 184 D2
Dunholme Lincs 189 F8
Dunino Fife 287 F9
Dunipace Falk 278 E6
Dunira Perth 285 E11
Dunkeld Perth 286 C4
Dunkerton Bath 45 B8
Dunkeswell Devon 27 F10
Dunkeswick
N Yorks 206 D2
Dunkirk Cambs 139 F10
Ches W 182 G5
Kent 54 B5
Norf 160 D4
Nottingham 153 B11
S Glos 61 B9
Staffs 168 E4
Wilts 62 G3
Dunk's Green Kent 52 C6
Dunlappie Angus 293 G7
Dunley Hants 48 C3
Worcs 116 D5
Dunlichity Lodge
Highld 300 F6
Dunlop E Ayrs 267 F8
Dunmaglass Lodge
Highld 300 G5
Dunmere Corn 5 B10
Dunmore Argyll 275 G8
Falk 279 D7
Highld 300 E5
Dunnerholme Cumb 210 D4
Dunnet Highld 310 B6
Dunnichen Angus 287 C9
Dunnikier Fife 280 C5
Dunninald Angus 287 B11
Dunning Perth 286 F4
Dunnington
E Yorks 209 C9
Warks 117 G11
York 207 C9
Dunningwell Cumb 210 C3
Dunnockshaw
Lancs 195 B10
Dunnose IoW 21 F7
Dunnsheath Shrops 149 F9
Dunn Street Kent 54 D3
Kent 69 G9
Dunollie Argyll 289 F10
Dunoon Argyll 276 F3
Dunragit Dumfries 236 D3
Dunrobin Mains
Highld 311 J2
Dunrostan Argyll 275 E8
Duns Borders 272 E5
Dunsa Derbys 186 G2
Dunsby Lincs 156 D2
Dunscar Gtr Man 195 E8
Dunscore Dumfries 247 G9
Dunscroft S Yorks 199 F7
Dunsdale Redcar 226 B2
Dunsden Green Oxon 65 D8
Dunsfold Sur 50 F4
Dunsfold Common
Sur 50 F4
Dunsfold Green Sur 50 F4
Dunsford Devon 14 D2
Sur 50 F4
Dunshalt Fife 286 F6
Dunshillock Aberds 303 E9
Dunsill Notts 171 C7
Dunsinnan Perth 286 D5
Dunskey Ho
Dumfries 236 D2
Dunslea Corn 11 G11
Dunsley N Yorks 227 C7
Staffs 133 G7
Dunsmore Bucks 84 D5
Warks 119 B10
Dunsop Bridge
Lancs 203 C9
Dunstable C Beds 103 G10
Dunstal Staffs 151 D11
Dunstall Staffs 152 E3
Dunstall Common
Worcs 99 C7
Dunstall Green Suff 124 E4
Dunstall Hill W Mid 133 C8
Dunstan Northumb 265 F7
Dunstan Steads
Northumb 264 E6
Dunster Som 42 E3
Duns Tew Oxon 101 F9
Dunston Derbys 186 G5
Lincs 173 C9
Norf 142 C4
Staffs 151 F8
T&W 242 E6
Dunstone Devon 7 E11
Devon 8 G5
Dunston Heath
Staffs 151 F8
Dunston Hill T&W 242 E6
Dunsville S Yorks 198 F6
Dunswell E Yorks 209 F7
Dunsyre S Lnrk 269 F11
Dunterton Devon 12 F3
Dunthrop Oxon 101 F7
Duntisbourne Abbots
Glos 81 D7
Duntisbourne Leer
Glos 81 D7
Duntisbourne Rouse
Glos 81 D7
Duntish Dorset 29 F11
Duntocher W Dunb 277 G9
Dunton Bucks 102 G6
C Beds 104 C4
Norf 159 C7
Dunton Bassett
Leics 135 E10
Dunton Green Kent 52 B4
Dunton Patch Norf 159 C7
Dunton Wayletts
Essex 87 G11
Duntrune Castle
Argyll 275 D8
Duntulm Highld 298 B4
Dunure S Ayrs 257 F7
Dunvant/Dynfant
Swansea 56 C5
Dunvegan Highld 298 E2
Dunveth Corn 10 G5
Dunwear Som 43 F10
Dunwich Suff 127 C9
Dunwood Staffs 168 D6
Dupplin Castle
Perth 286 F4
Durdar Cumb 239 G10
Durgan Corn 3 D7
Durgates E Sus 52 G6
Durham Durham 233 C11
Durisdeer Dumfries 247 C9
Durisdeermill
Dumfries 247 C9
Durkar W Yorks 197 D10
Durleigh Som 43 F9
Durleighmarsh
W Sus 34 C3
Durley Hants 33 D8
Wilts 63 G8
Durley Street Hants 33 D8
Durlock Kent 55 B9
Durlow Common
Hereford 98 D2
Durn Gtr Man 196 D2
Durnamuck Highld 307 K5
Durness Highld 308 C4
Durnfield Som 29 C7
Durno Aberds 303 G7
Durns Town Hants 19 B11
Duror Highld 289 D11
Durran Argyll 275 C10
Highld 310 C5
Durrant Green Kent 53 F11
Durrants Hants 22 B2
Durrington Wilts 47 E7
W Sus 35 F10
Durrisdale Orkney 314 D3
Dursley Glos 80 F3
Wilts 45 C11
Dursley Cross Glos 98 G3
Durston Som 28 B3
Durweston Dorset 30 F5
Dury Shetland 313 G6
Duryard Devon 14 C4
Duston Northants 120 E4
Dutch Village Essex 69 C9
Duthil Highld 301 G9
Dutlas Powys 114 B4
Duton Hill Essex 106 F2
Dutson Corn 12 D2
Dutton Ches W 183 F9
Duxford Cambs 105 B9
Oxon 82 F5
Duxmoor Shrops 115 B8
Dwygyfylchi Conwy 180 F2
Dwyran Anglesey 162 B6
Dwyrhiw Powys 129 C11
Dyce Aberdeen 293 B10
Dyche Som 43 E7
Dye House
Northumb 241 F10
Dyer's Common
S Glos 60 C5
Dyer's Green Cambs 105 B7
Dyffryn Bridgend 57 C11
Carms 92 G6
Ceredig 110 G5
Pembs 91 D8
Dyffryn Ardudwy
Gwyn 145 E11
Dyffryn-bern
Ceredig 110 G5
Dyffryn Castell
Ceredig 128 G5
Dyffryn Ceidrych
Carms 94 F4
Dyffryn Cellwen
Neath 76 D5
Dyke Lincs 156 E2
Moray 301 D9
Dykehead Angus 292 G5
N Lnrk 269 D7
Stirl 277 B11
Dykelands Aberds 293 G9
Dykends Angus 286 B6
Dykeside Aberds 303 E7
Dykesmains N Ayrs 266 G5
Dylife Powys 129 E7
Dymchurch Kent 39 B9
Dymock Glos 98 E4
Dynfant/Dunvant
Swansea 56 C5
Dyrham S Glos 61 D8
Dysart Fife 280 C6
Dyserth Denb 181 F9

E

Eabost Highld 294 B5
Eabost West Highld 298 E3
Each End Kent 55 B10
Eachway Worcs 117 B9
Eachwick Northumb 242 C4
Eadar Dha Fhadhail
W Isles 304 E2
Eagland Hill Lancs 202 D4
Eagle Lincs 172 B5
Eagle Barnsdale
Lincs 172 B5
Eagle Moor Lincs 172 B5
Eaglesfield Cumb 229 F7
Dumfries 238 C6
Eaglesham E Renf 267 E11
Eaglestone
M Keynes 103 D7
Eaglethorpe
Northants 137 E11
Eagle Tor Derbys 170 C2
Eagley Gtr Man 195 E8
Eairy IoM 192 E3
Eakley Lanes
M Keynes 120 G6
Eakring Notts 171 C11
Ealand N Lincs 199 E9
Ealing London 67 C7
Eals Northumb 240 F5
Eamont Bridge
Cumb 230 F6
Earby Lancs 204 D3
Earcroft Blkburn 195 C7
Eardington Shrops 132 E4
Eardisland Hereford 115 F8
Eardisley Hereford 96 B6
Eardiston Shrops 149 D7
Worcs 116 D3
Earith Cambs 123 C7
Earle Northumb 263 D11
Earlestown Mers 183 B9
Earley Wokingham 65 E9
Earlham Norf 142 B4
Earlish Highld 298 C3
Earls Barton
Northants 121 E7
Earls Colne Essex 107 F7
Earl's Common
Worcs 117 F9
Earl's Court London 67 D9
Earl's Croome Worcs 99 C7
Earlsdon W Mid 118 B6
Earl's Down E Sus 23 B10
Earlsferry Fife 281 B9
Earlsfield Lincs 155 B8
London 67 E9
Earlsford Aberds 303 F8
Earl's Green Suff 125 D10
Earlsheaton
W Yorks 197 C9
Earl Shilton Leics 135 D9
Earlsmill Moray 301 D9
Earl Soham Suff 126 E4
Earl Sterndale
Derbys 169 B9
Earlston Borders 262 B3
E Ayrs 257 B10
Earlstone Common
Hants 64 G3
Earl Stoneham Suff 126 F2
Earl Stonham Suff 126 F2
Earlstoun Dumfries 246 G4
Earlswood Mon 79 F7
Sur 51 D9
Warks 118 C2
Earnley W Sus 22 D4
Earnock S Lnrk 268 E3
Earnshaw Bridge
Lancs 194 C4
Earsairidh W Isles 297 M3
Earsdon T&W 243 C8
Earsham Norf 142 F6
Earsham Street Suff 126 B4
Earswick York 207 B8
Eartham W Sus 22 B6
Earthcott Green
S Glos 61 B7
Easby N Yorks 224 E3
N Yorks 225 D11
Easdale Argyll 275 B8
Easebourne W Sus 34 C5
Easenhall Warks 119 B9
Eashing Sur 50 E2
Easington Bucks 83 C11
Durham 234 C4
E Yorks 201 D11
Lancs 203 C10
Northumb 264 C4
Oxon 83 F11
Oxon 101 D9
Redcar 226 B4
Easington Colliery
Durham 234 C4
Easington Lane
T&W 234 B3
Easingwold
N Yorks 215 F10
Easole Street Kent 55 C9
Eason's Green E Sus 23 B8
Eassie Angus 287 C7
East Aberthaw
V Glam 58 F4
Eastacombe Devon 25 B8
Devon 25 C9
Eastacott Devon 25 C10
East Acton London 67 C8
East Adderbury
Oxon 101 D9
East Allington Devon 8 F5
East Amat Highld 309 K4
East Anstey Devon 26 B5
East Anton Hants 47 D11
East Appleton
N Yorks 224 F4
East Ardsley
W Yorks 197 B10
East Ashling W Sus 22 B4
East Aston Hants 48 D2
East Auchronie
Aberds 293 C10
East Ayton N Yorks 217 B9
East Bank Bl Gwent 78 D2
East Barkwith
Lincs 189 E11
East Barming Kent 53 C8
East Barnby
N Yorks 226 C6
East Barnet London 86 F3
East Barns E Loth 282 F4
East Barsham Norf 159 C8
East Barton Suff 125 D8
East Beach W Sus 22 E5
East Beckham
Norf 177 E11
East Bedfont London 66 E5
East Bergholt Suff 107 D11
East Bierley
W Yorks 197 B7
East Bilney Norf 159 F9
East Blackdene
Durham 232 D3
East Blatchington
E Sus 23 E7
East Bloxworth
Dorset 18 C3
East Boldon T&W 243 E9
East Boldre Hants 32 G5
East Bonhard Perth 286 E5
Eastbourne Darl 224 C6
E Sus 23 F10
East Bower Som 43 F10
East Brent Som 43 C11
Eastbridge Suff 127 D9
East Bridgford
Notts 171 G11
East Briscoe
Durham 223 B9
Eastbrook Som 28 C2
V Glam 59 E7
East Buckland Devon 41 G7
East Budleigh Devon 15 E7
Eastburn E Yorks 208 B5
W Yorks 204 E6
Eastburn Br
W Yorks 204 E6
East Burnham Bucks 66 C3
East Burrafirth
Shetland 313 H5
East Burton Dorset 18 D2
Eastbury London 85 G9
W Berks 63 D10
East Butsfield
Durham 233 B8
East Butterleigh
Devon 27 F7
East Butterwick
N Lincs 199 F10
Eastby N Yorks 204 C6
East Cairnbeg
Aberds 293 F9
East Calder
W Loth 269 B11
East Carleton Norf 142 C3
East Carlton
Northants 136 F6
W Yorks 205 E10
East Chaldon or Chaldon
Herring Dorset 17 E11
East Challow Oxon 63 B11
East Charleton Devon 8 G5
East Chelborough
Dorset 29 F9
East Chiltington
E Sus 36 D5
East Chinnock Som 29 E7
East Chisenbury
Wilts 46 C6
East Cholderton
Hants 47 D9
Eastchurch Kent 70 E3
East Clandon Sur 50 C5
East Claydon Bucks 102 F4
East Clevedon
N Som 60 E2
East Clyne Highld 311 J3
East Clyth Highld 310 F7
East Coker Som 29 E8
Eastcombe Glos 80 E5
East Combe Som 43 G7
East Common
N Yorks 207 G8
East Compton Dorset 30 D5
Som 44 E6
East Cornworthy
Devon 8 D6
Eastcote London 66 B6
Northants 120 G3
W Mid 118 B3
Eastcote Village
London 66 B6
Eastcott Corn 24 D3
Wilts 46 B4
East Cottingwith
E Yorks 207 E10
Eastcotts Beds 103 B11
Eastcourt Wilts 63 G8
Wilts 81 G7
East Cowes IoW 20 B6
East Cowick
E Yorks 199 C7
East Cowton
N Yorks 224 E6
East Cramlington
Northumb 243 B7
East Cranmore Som 45 E7
East Creech Dorset 18 E4
East Croachy Highld 300 G6
East Croftmore
Highld 291 B11
East Curthwaite
Cumb 230 B2
East Dean E Sus 23 F9
Glos 98 G3
Hants 32 B3
W Sus 34 E6
East Dene S Yorks 186 C6
East Denton T&W 242 D6
East Didsbury
Gtr Man 184 C5
Eastdon Devon 14 F5
Eastdown Devon 8 F6
East Down Devon 40 E6
East Drayton Notts 188 F3
East Dulwich
London 67 E10
East Dundry N Som 60 F5
East Ella Hull 200 B5
Eastend Essex 86 C6
Oxon 100 G6
East End Beds 122 F2
Bucks 84 B4
C Beds 103 C9
Dorset 18 B5
Essex 89 D8
E Yorks 201 B9
E Yorks 209 B9
E Yorks 209 G9
Glos 81 E11
Hants 20 B3
Hants 33 C11
Hants 64 G2
Herts 105 F9
Kent 53 E11
Kent 53 F10
Kent 70 E3
M Keynes 103 C8
N Som 60 E3
Oxon 82 C5
Oxon 101 D9
Oxon 101 E7
S Glos 61 E9
Som 29 B10
Som 44 C5
Som 45 D7
Suff 108 E2
Suff 126 F3
East End Green Herts 86 C3
Easter Aberchalder
Highld 291 B7
Easter Ardross
Highld 300 B6
Easter Balgedie
Perth 286 G5
Easter Balmoral
Aberds 292 D4
Easter Boleskine
Highld 300 G5
Easter Brackland
Stirl 285 G10
Easter Brae Highld 300 C6
Easter Cardno
Aberds 303 C9
Easter Compton
S Glos 60 C5
Easter Cringate
Stirl 278 D4
Easter Culfosie
Aberds 293 C9
Easter Davoch
Aberds 292 C6
Easter Earshaig
Dumfries 248 C2
Easter Ellister Argyll 254 B3
Easter Fearn Highld 309 L6
Easter Galcantray
Highld 301 E8
Eastergate W Sus 22 B6

Easterhouse Glasgow 268 B3
Easter Housebyres Borders 262 B2
Easter Howgate Midloth 270 C4
Easter Howlaws Borders 272 G4
Easter Kinkell Highld 300 D5
Easter Knox Angus 287 D9
Easter Langlee Borders 262 B2
Easter Lednathie Angus 292 G5
Easter Milton Highld 301 D9
Easter Moniack Highld 300 E5
Eastern Green W Mid 134 G5
Easter Ord Aberdeen 293 C10
Easter Quarff Shetland 313 K6
Easter Rhynd Perth 286 F5
Easter Row Stirl 278 B5
Easterside Mbro 225 B10
Easter Silverford Aberds 303 C7
Easter Skeld Shetland 313 J5
Easter Softlaw Borders 263 C7
Easterton Wilts 46 C4
Easterton of Lenabo Aberds 303 E10
Easterton Sands Wilts 46 B4
Eastertown Som 43 C10
Eastertown of Auchleuchries Aberds 303 F10
Easter Tulloch Highld 291 B11
Easter Whyntie Aberds 302 C6
East Everleigh Wilts 47 C8
East Ewell Sur 67 G8
East Farleigh Kent 53 C8
East Farndon Northants 136 F4
East Fen Common Cambs 124 C2
East Ferry Lincs 188 B4
Eastfield Borders 262 D2
Bristol 60 D5
N Lnrk 269 C7
N Lnrk 278 G4
Northumb 243 B7
N Yorks 217 C10
Pboro 138 D4
S Lnrk 268 C2
S Yorks 197 G9
Eastfield Hall Northumb 252 B6
East Fields W Berks 64 F3
East Finchley London 67 B9
East Finglassie Fife 280 B5
East Firsby Lincs 189 D8
East Fleet Dorset 17 E8
East Fortune E Loth 281 F10
East Garforth W Yorks 206 G4
East Garston W Berks 63 D11
Eastgate Durham 232 D5
Norf 160 E2
Pboro 138 D4
East Gateshead T&W 243 E7
East Ginge Oxon 64 B2
East Gores Essex 107 G7
East Goscote Leics 154 G2
East Grafton Wilts 63 G9
East Grange Moray 301 C10
East Green Hants 49 E9
Suff 124 G3
Suff 127 D8
East Grimstead Wilts 32 B2
East Grinstead W Sus 51 F11
East Guldeford E Sus 38 C6
East Haddon Northants 120 D3
East Hagbourne Oxon 64 B4
Easthall Herts 104 G3
East Halton N Lincs 200 D6
Eastham Mers 182 E5
Worcs 116 D3
East Ham London 68 C2
Eastham Ferry Mers 182 E5
East Hampnett W Sus 22 B6
Easthampstead Brack 65 F11
Easthampton Hereford 115 E8
East Hanney Oxon 82 G6
East Hanningfield Essex 88 E3
East Hardwick W Yorks 198 D3
East Harling Norf 141 F9
East Harlsey N Yorks 225 F8
East Harnham Wilts 31 B10
East Harptree Bath 44 B5
East Hartford Northumb 243 B7
East Harting W Sus 34 D3
East Hatch Wilts 30 B6
East Hatley Cambs 122 G5
Easthaugh Norf 159 F11
East Hauxwell N Yorks 224 G3
East Haven Angus 287 D9
Eastheath Wokingham 65 F10
East Heckington Lincs 173 G11
East Hedleyhope Durham 233 C9
East Helmsdale Highld 311 H4
East Hendred Oxon 64 B3
East Herringthorpe S Yorks 187 C7
East Herrington T&W 243 G9
East Heslerton N Yorks 217 D8
East Hewish N Som 59 G11
East Hill Kent 68 G5
East Hoathly E Sus 23 B8
East Hogaland Shetland 313 K5
East Holme Dorset 18 D3
East Holton Dorset 18 C5
East Holywell Northumb 243 C8
Easthope Shrops 131 D11
Easthopewood Shrops 131 D11
East Horndon Essex 68 B6
Easthorpe Essex 107 G8
Leics 154 B6
Notts 172 E2
East Horrington Som 44 D5
East Horsley Sur 50 C5
East Horton Northumb 264 C2
Easthouse Shetland 313 J5
Easthouses Midloth 270 B6
East Howdon T&W 243 D8
East Howe Bmouth 19 B7
East Huntspill Som 43 E10
East Hyde C Beds 85 B10
East Ilkerton Devon 41 D8
East Ilsley W Berks 64 C3
Easting Orkney 314 A7
Eastington Devon 26 F2
Glos 80 D3
Glos 81 C10
East Keal Lincs 174 C5
East Kennett Wilts 62 F6
East Keswick W Yorks 206 E3
East Kilbride S Lnrk 268 E2
East Kimber Devon 12 B5
East Kingston W Sus 35 G9
East Kirkby Lincs 174 C4
East Knapton N Yorks 217 D7
East Knighton Dorset 18 D2
East Knowstone Devon 26 C4
East Knoyle Wilts 45 G11
East Kyloe Northumb 264 B3
East Kyo Durham 242 G5
East Lambrook Som 28 D6
East Lamington Highld 301 B7
Eastland Gate Hants 33 E11
East Langdon Kent 55 D10
East Langton Leics 136 E4
East Langwell Highld 309 J7
East Lavant W Sus 22 B5
East Lavington W Sus 34 D6
East Law Northumb 242 G3
East Layton N Yorks 224 D3
Eastleach Martin Glos 82 D2
Eastleach Turville Glos 81 D11
East Leake Notts 153 D11
East Learmouth Northumb 263 B9
Eastleigh Devon 25 B7
Hants 32 D6
East Leigh Devon 8 E3
Devon 25 F11
East Lexham Norf 159 F7
East Lilburn Northumb 264 E2
Eastling Kent 54 B3
East Linton E Loth 281 F11
East Liss Hants 34 B3
East Lockinge Oxon 64 B2
East Loftus Redcar 226 B4
East Looe Corn 6 E5
East Lound N Lincs 188 B3
East Lulworth Dorset 18 E3
East Lutton N Yorks 217 F8
East Lydeard Som 27 B11
East Lydford Som 44 G5
East Lyng Som 28 B4
East Mains Aberds 293 D8
Borders 271 F11
S Lnrk 268 E2
East Malling Kent 53 B8
East Malling Heath Kent 53 B7
East March Angus 287 D8
East Marden W Sus 34 E4
East Markham Notts 188 G2
East Marsh NE Lincs 201 E9
East Martin Hants 31 D9
East Marton N Yorks 204 C4
East Melbury Dorset 30 C5
East Meon Hants 33 C11
East Mere Devon 27 D7
East Mersea Essex 89 C9
East Mey Highld 310 B7
East Molesey Sur 67 F7
Eastmoor Derbys 186 G4
Norf 140 C4
East Moor W Yorks 197 C10
East Moors Cardiff 59 D8
East Morden Dorset 18 B4
East Morton W Yorks 205 E7
East Moulsecoomb Brighton 36 F4
East Ness N Yorks 216 D3
East Newton E Yorks 209 F11
N Yorks 216 D2
Eastney Ptsmth 21 B9
Eastnor Hereford 98 D4
East Norton Leics 136 C5
East Nynehead Som 27 C11
East Oakley Hants 48 C5
Eastoft N Lincs 199 D10
East Ogwell Devon 14 G2
Eastoke Hants 21 B10
Easton Bristol 60 E6
Cambs 122 C2
Cumb 239 C10
Cumb 239 F7
Devon 8 F3
Devon 13 D10
Dorset 17 G9
Hants 48 G4
IoW 20 D2
Lincs 155 D8
Norf 160 G2
Som 44 D4
Suff 126 F5
W Berks 64 E2
Wilts 61 E11
Easton Grey Wilts 61 B11
Easton in Gordano N Som 60 D4
Easton Maudit Northants 121 F7
Easton on the Hill Northants 137 C10
Easton Royal Wilts 63 G8
Easton Town Som 44 G5
Wilts 61 B11
East Orchard Dorset 30 D4
East Ord Northumb 273 E9
Eastover Som 43 F10
East Panson Devon 12 C3
Eastpark Dumfries 238 D2
East Parley Dorset 19 B8
East Peckham Kent 53 D7
East Pennard Som 44 F5
East Perry Cambs 122 D3
East Portholland Corn 5 G9
East Portlemouth Devon 9 G9
East Prawle Devon 9 G10
East Preston W Sus 35 G9
East Pulham Dorset 30 F2
East Putford Devon 24 D5
East Quantoxhead Som 42 E6
East Rainton T&W 234 B2
East Ravendale NE Lincs 190 B2
East Raynham Norf 159 D7
Eastrea Cambs 138 D5
East Rhidorroch Lodge Highld 307 K7
Eastriggs Dumfries 238 D6
East Rigton W Yorks 206 E3
Eastrington E Yorks 199 B9
Eastrip Wilts 61 E10
East Rolstone N Som 59 G11
Eastrop Hants 48 C6
East Rounton N Yorks 225 E8
East Row N Yorks 227 C7
East Rudham Norf 158 D6
East Runton Norf 177 E11
East Ruston Norf 160 D6
Eastry Kent 55 C10
East Saltoun E Loth 271 B9
East Sheen London 67 D8
East Skelston Dumfries 247 F8
East Sleekburn Northumb 253 G7
East Somerton Norf 161 F9
East Stanley Durham 242 G6
East Stockwith Lincs 188 C3
East Stoke Dorset 18 D3
Notts 172 F3
Som 29 D7
East Stour Dorset 30 C4
East Stour Common Dorset 30 C4
East Stourmouth Kent 71 G9
East Stowford Devon 25 B10
East Stratton Hants 48 F4
East Street Kent 55 B10
Som 44 F4
East Studdal Kent 55 D10
East Suisnish Highld 295 B7
East Taphouse Corn 6 C3
East-the-Water Devon 25 B7
East Third Borders 262 B4
East Thirston Northumb 252 D5
East Tilbury Thurrock 69 D7
East Tisted Hants 49 G8
East Torrington Lincs 189 E10
East Town Som 42 G6
Som 44 E6
Wilts 45 B11
East Trewent Pembs 73 F8
East Tuddenham Norf 159 G11
East Tuelmenna Corn 6 B4
East Tytherley Hants 32 B3
East Tytherton Wilts 62 E3
East Village Devon 26 F4
V Glam 58 E3
Eastville Bristol 60 E6
Lincs 174 D6
East Wall Shrops 131 E10
East Walton Norf 158 F4
East Water Som 44 C4
East Week Devon 13 C9
Eastwell Leics 154 D5
East Wellow Hants 32 C4
Eastwell Park Kent 54 D4
East Wemyss Fife 280 B6
East Whitburn W Loth 269 B9
Eastwick Herts 86 C6
Shetland 312 F5
East Wickham London 68 D3
East Williamston Pembs 73 E9
East Winch Norf 158 F3
East Winterslow Wilts 47 G8
East Wittering W Sus 21 B11
East Witton N Yorks 214 B2
Eastwood Hereford 98 C2
Notts 171 F7
Sthend 69 B10
S Yorks 186 C6
W Yorks 196 B3
East Woodburn Northumb 251 F10
Eastwood End Cambs 139 E8
Eastwood Hall Notts 171 F7
East Woodhay Hants 64 G2
East Woodlands Som 45 E9
East Worldham Hants 49 F8
East Worlington Devon 26 E3
East Worthing W Sus 35 G11
East Wretham Norf 141 E8
East Youlstone Devon 24 D3
Eathorpe Warks 119 D7
Eaton Ches E 168 B5
Ches W 167 C9
Hereford 115 F10
Leics 154 D5
Norf 142 B4
Notts 188 F2
Oxon 82 E6
Shrops 131 F7
Shrops 131 F10
Eaton Bishop Hereford 97 D8
Eaton Bray C Beds 103 G9
Eaton Constantine Shrops 131 B11
Eaton Ford Cambs 122 E3
Eaton Green C Beds 103 G9
Eaton Hastings Oxon 82 F3
Eaton Mascott Shrops 131 B10
Eaton on Tern Shrops 150 E3
Eaton Socon Cambs 122 F3
Eaton upon Tern Shrops 150 E3
Eau Brink Norf 157 F11
Eau Withington Hereford 97 C10
Eaves Green W Mid 134 G5
Eavestone N Yorks 214 F4
Ebberly Hill Devon 25 D9
Ebberston N Yorks 217 C7
Ebbesbourne Wake Wilts 31 C7
Ebblake Hants 31 F10
Ebbw Vale Bl Gwent 77 D11
Ebchester Durham 242 F4
Ebdon N Som 59 G11
Ebernoe W Sus 35 B7
Ebford Devon 14 D5
Ebley Glos 80 D4
Ebnal Ches W 167 F7
Ebnall Hereford 115 F9
Ebreywood Shrops 149 F10
Ebrington Glos 100 C3
Ecchinswell Hants 48 B4
Ecclaw Borders 272 B5
Ecclefechan Dumfries 238 C5
Eccle Riggs Cumb 210 B4
Eccles Borders 272 G5
Gtr Man 184 B3
Kent 69 G8
Ecclesall S Yorks 186 E4
Ecclesfield S Yorks 186 C5
Ecclesgreig Aberds 293 G9
Eccleshall Staffs 150 D6
Eccleshill W Yorks 205 F9
Ecclesmachan W Loth 279 G11
Eccles on Sea Norf 161 D8
Eccles Road Norf 141 E10
Eccleston Ches W 166 C6
Lancs 194 D4
Mers 183 B7
Eccleston Park Mers 183 C7
Eccliffe Dorset 30 B3
Eccup W Yorks 205 E11
Echt Aberds 293 C9
Eckford Borders 262 D6
Eckfordmoss Borders 262 D6
Eckington Derbys 186 F6
Worcs 99 C8
Eckington Corner E Sus 23 D8
Ecklands S Yorks 197 G8
Eckworthy Devon 24 D6
Ecton Northants 120 E6
Staffs 169 D9
Ecton Brook Northants 120 E6
Edale Derbys 185 D10
Edale End Derbys 185 D11
Edbrook Som 43 E8
Edburton W Sus 36 E2
Edderside Cumb 229 B7
Edderton Highld 309 L7
Eddington Kent 71 F7
W Berks 63 F10
Eddistone Devon 24 C3
Eddleston Borders 270 F4
Eddlewood S Lnrk 268 E4
Edenbridge Kent 52 D2
Edenfield Lancs 195 D9
Edenhall Cumb 231 E7
Edenham Lincs 155 E11
Eden Mount Cumb 211 D8
Eden Park London 67 F11
Edensor Derbys 170 B2
Edentaggart Argyll 276 C6
Edenthorpe S Yorks 198 F6
Edentown Cumb 239 F9
Eden Vale Durham 234 D4
Wilts 45 C11
Ederline Argyll 275 C9
Edern Gwyn 144 B5
Edford Som 45 D7
Edgarley Som 44 F4
Edgbaston W Mid 133 G11
Edgcote Northants 101 B10
Edgcott Bucks 102 G3
Som 41 F10
Edgcumbe Corn 2 C6
Edge Glos 80 D4
Shrops 131 B7
Edgebolton Shrops 149 E11
Edge End Glos 79 C9
Lancs 203 G10
Edgefield Norf 159 C11
Edgefield Street Norf 159 C11
Edge Fold Blkburn 195 D8
Gtr Man 195 F8
Edge Green Ches W 167 E7
Gtr Man 183 B9
Norf 141 F10
Edgehill Warks 101 B7
Edge Hill Mers 182 C5
Warks 134 D4
Edgeley Gtr Man 184 D5
Edge Mount S Yorks 186 C3
Edgerley Shrops 148 F6
Edgerston Borders 262 G5
Edgerton W Yorks 196 D6
Edgeside Lancs 195 C10
Edgeworth Glos 80 D6
Edginswell Devon 9 B7
Edgiock Worcs 117 E10
Edgmond Telford 150 F4
Edgmond Marsh Telford 150 E4
Edgton Shrops 131 F7
Edgware London 85 G11
Edgwick W Mid 134 G6
Edgworth Blkburn 195 D8
Edham Borders 262 B6
Edial Staffs 133 B11
Edinample Stirl 285 E9
Edinbane Highld 298 D3
Edinburgh Edin 280 G5
Edinchip Stirl 285 E9
Edingale Staffs 152 G4
Edingight Ho Moray 302 D5
Edinglassie Ho Aberds 292 B5
Edingley Notts 171 D11
Edingthorpe Norf 160 C6
Edingthorpe Green Norf 160 C6
Edington Som 43 E11
Wilts 46 C2
Edingworth Som 43 C11
Edintore Moray 302 E4
Edistone Devon 24 C2
Edithmead Som 43 D10
Edith Weston Rutland 137 B8
Edlaston Derbys 169 G11
Edlesborough Bucks 85 B7
Edlingham Northumb 252 B4
Edlington Lincs 190 G2
Edmondsham Dorset 31 E9
Edmondsley Durham 233 B10
Edmondstown Rhondda 77 G8
Edmondthorpe Leics 155 F7
Edmonston S Lnrk 269 G11
Edmonstone Orkney 314 D5
Edmonton Corn 10 G5
London 86 G4
Edmundbyers Durham 242 G2
Ednam Borders 262 B6
Ednaston Derbys 170 G2
Edney Common Essex 87 E11
Edradynate Perth 286 B2
Edrom Borders 272 D6
Edstaston Shrops 149 C10
Edstone Warks 118 E3
Edvin Loach Hereford 116 F3
Edwalton Notts 153 B11
Edwardstone Suff 107 C8
Edwardsville M Tydf 77 F9
Edwinsford Carms 94 E2
Edwinstowe Notts 171 B10
Edworth C Beds 104 C4
Edwyn Ralph Hereford 116 F2
Edzell Angus 293 G7
Efail-fôch Neath 57 B9
Efail Isaf Rhondda 58 C5
Efailnewydd Gwyn 145 B7
Efailwen Carms 92 F2
Efenechtyd Denb 165 D10
Effingham Sur 50 C6
Effirth Shetland 313 H5
Effledge Borders 262 F3
Efflinch Staffs 152 F3
Efford Devon 26 G5
Plym 7 D10
Egbury Hants 48 C2
Egdon Worcs 117 G8
Egerton Gtr Man 195 E8
Kent 54 D2
Egerton Forstal Kent 53 D11
Egerton Green Ches E 167 E8
Egford Som 45 D9
Eggbeare Corn 12 D2
Eggborough N Yorks 198 C5
Eggbuckland Plym 7 D10
Eggesford Station Devon 25 E11
Eggington C Beds 103 F9
Egginton Derbys 152 D5
Egginton Common Derbys 152 D5
Egglesburn Durham 232 G5
Egglescliffe Stockton 225 C8
Eggleston Durham 232 G5
Egham Sur 66 E4
Egham Hythe Sur 66 E4
Egham Wick Sur 66 E3
Egleton Rutland 137 B7
Eglingham Northumb 264 F4
Egloshayle Corn 10 G5
Egloskerry Corn 11 D11
Eglwysbach Conwy 180 G4
Eglwys-Brewis V Glam 58 F4
Eglwys Cross Wrex 167 G7
Eglwys Fach Ceredig 128 D3
Eglwyswen Pembs 92 D3
Eglwyswrw Pembs 92 D2
Egmanton Notts 172 B2
Egmere Norf 159 B8
Egremont Cumb 219 C10
Mers 182 C4
Egton N Yorks 226 D6
Egton Bridge N Yorks 226 D6
Egypt Bucks 66 B3
Hants 48 E3
W Berks 64 D2
W Yorks 205 G7
Eiden Highld 309 J7
Eight Ash Green Essex 107 F8
Eighton Banks T&W 243 F7
Eignaig Highld 289 E9
Eign Hill Hereford 97 D10
Eil Highld 291 B10
Eilanreach Highld 295 D10
Eildon Borders 262 C3
Eileanach Lodge Highld 300 C5
Eilean Anabaich W Isles 305 H4
Eilean Darach Highld 307 L6
Eilean Shona Ho Highld 289 B8
Einacleite W Isles 304 F3
Einsiob / Evenjobb Powys 114 E5
Eisgean W Isles 305 G5
Eisingrug Gwyn 146 C2
Eland Green Northumb 242 C5
Elan Village Powys 113 D8
Elberton S Glos 60 B6
Elborough N Som 43 B11
Elbridge Shrops 149 E7
W Sus 22 C6
Elburton Plym 7 E10
Elcho Perth 286 E5
Elcock's Brook Worcs 117 E10
Elcombe Glos 80 F3
Swindon 62 C6
Elcot W Berks 63 F11
Eldene Swindon 63 C7
Eldernell Cambs 138 D6
Eldersfield Worcs 98 E6
Elderslie Renfs 267 C8
Elder Street Essex 105 E11
Eldon Durham 233 F10
Eldon Lane Durham 233 F10
Eldrick S Ayrs 245 G7
Eldroth N Yorks 212 F5
Eldwick W Yorks 205 E8
Elemore Vale T&W 234 B3
Elerch / Bont-goch Ceredig 128 F3
Elfhowe Cumb 221 F9
Elford Northumb 264 C5
Staffs 152 G3
Elford Closes Cambs 123 C10
Elgin Moray 302 C2
Elgol Highld 295 D7
Elham Kent 55 E7
Eliburn W Loth 269 B10
Elie Fife 287 G8
Elim Anglesey 178 D5
Eling Hants 32 E5
W Berks 64 D4
Elishader Highld 298 C5
Elishaw Northumb 251 D9
Elizafield Dumfries 238 C2
Elkesley Notts 187 F11
Elkington Northants 120 B2
Elkins Green Essex 87 E10
Elkstone Glos 81 C7
Ellacombe Torbay 9 C8
Ellan Highld 301 G8
Elland W Yorks 196 C6
Elland Lower Edge W Yorks 196 C6
Elland Upper Edge W Yorks 196 C6
Ellary Argyll 275 F8
Ellastone Staffs 169 G10
Ellel Lancs 202 B5
Ellemford Borders 272 C4
Ellenborough Cumb 228 D6
Ellenbrook Herts 86 D2
IoM 192 E4
Ellenglaze Corn 4 D5
Ellenhall Staffs 150 D6
Ellen's Green Sur 50 F5
Ellerbeck N Yorks 225 F8
Ellerburn N Yorks 216 C6
Ellerby N Yorks 226 C5
Ellerdine Telford 150 E2
Ellerdine Heath Telford 150 E2
Ellerhayes Devon 27 G7
Elleric Argyll 284 C4
Ellerker E Yorks 200 B2
Ellerton E Yorks 207 F10
N Yorks 224 F5
Shrops 150 D4
Ellesborough Bucks 84 D4
Ellesmere Shrops 149 C8
Ellesmere Park Gtr Man 184 B3
Ellesmere Port Ches W 182 F6
Ellicombe Som 42 E3
Ellingham Hants 31 F10
Norf 143 E7
Northumb 264 D5
Ellingstring N Yorks 214 C3
Ellington Cambs 122 C3
Northumb 253 E7
Ellington Thorpe Cambs 122 C3
Elliot Angus 287 D10
Elliots Green Som 45 D9
Elliot's Town Caerph 77 E10
Ellisfield Hants 48 D6
Elliston Borders 262 D3
Ellistown Leics 153 G8
Ellon Aberds 303 F9
Ellonby Cumb 230 D4
Ellough Suff 143 F8
Elloughton E Yorks 200 B2
Ellwood Glos 79 D9
Elm Cambs 139 B9
Elmbridge Glos 80 B5
Worcs 117 D8
Elm Corner Sur 50 B5
Elm Cross Wilts 62 D6
Elmdon Essex 105 D9
W Mid 134 G3
Elmdon Heath W Mid 134 G3
Elmer W Sus 35 G7
Elmers End London 67 F11
Elmers Green Lancs 194 F3
Elmers Marsh W Sus 34 B5
Elmesthorpe Leics 135 D9
Elmfield IoW 21 C8
Elm Hill Dorset 30 B4
Elmhurst Bucks 84 B4
Staffs 152 G2
Elmley Castle Worcs 99 C9
Elmley Lovett Worcs 117 D7
Elmore Glos 80 B3
Elmore Back Glos 80 B3
Elm Park London 68 B4
Elmscott Devon 24 C2
Elmsett Suff 107 B11
Elms Green Hereford 115 F10
Worcs 116 D4
Elmslack Lancs 211 D9
Elmstead Essex 107 F11
London 68 E2
Elmstead Heath Essex 107 G11
Elmstead Market Essex 107 G11
Elmsted Kent 54 E6
Elmsthorpe Leics 135 D9
Elmstone Kent 71 G9
Elmstone Hardwicke Glos 99 F8
Elmswell E Yorks 208 B5
Suff 125 E9
Elmton Derbys 187 G8
Elness Orkney 314 C6
Elphin Highld 307 H7
Elphinstone E Loth 281 G7
Elrick Aberds 293 C10
Elrig Dumfries 236 E5
Elrigbeag Argyll 284 F5
Elrington Northumb 241 E9
Elscar S Yorks 197 G11
Elsdon Hereford 114 G6
Northumb 251 E10
Elsecar S Yorks 186 B5
S Yorks 197 G11
Elsenham Essex 105 F10
Elsenham Sta Essex 105 F10
Elsfield Oxon 83 C8
Elsham N Lincs 200 E4
Elsing Norf 159 F11
Elslack N Yorks 204 D4
Elson Hants 33 G10
Shrops 149 B7
Elsrickle S Lnrk 269 G11
Elstead Sur 50 E2
Elsted W Sus 34 D4
Elsthorpe Lincs 155 E11
Elstob Durham 234 G2
Elston Devon 26 G3
Notts 172 F3
Wilts 46 E5
Elstone Devon 25 D11
Elstow Beds 103 B11
Elstree Herts 85 F11
Elstronwick E Yorks 209 G10
Elswick Lancs 202 F4
T&W 242 E6
Elswick Leys Lancs 202 F4
Elsworth Cambs 122 E6
Elterwater Cumb 220 E6
Eltham London 68 E2
Eltisley Cambs 122 F5
Elton Cambs 137 E11
Ches W 183 F7
Derbys 170 C2
Glos 80 C2
Gtr Man 195 E9
Hereford 115 C9
Notts 154 B5
Stockton 225 B8
Elton Green Ches W 183 G7
Elton's Marsh Hereford 97 C9
Eltringham Northumb 242 E3
Elvanfoot S Lnrk 259 F11
Elvaston Derbys 153 C8
Elveden Suff 124 B6
Elvet Hill Durham 233 C11
Elvingston E Loth 281 G9
Elvington Kent 55 C9
York 207 D9
Elwell Devon 41 G7
Dorset 17 E9
Elwick Hrtlpl 234 E5
Northumb 264 B4
Elworth Ches E 168 C2
Elworthy Som 42 G5
Ely Cambs 139 G10
Cardiff 58 D6
Emberton M Keynes 103 B7
Embleton Cumb 229 E9
Durham 234 F4
Northumb 264 E6
Embo Highld 311 K2
Emborough Som 44 C6
Embo Street Highld 311 K2
Embsay N Yorks 204 C6
Emerson Park London 68 B4
Emerson's Green S Glos 61 D7
Emerson Valley M Keynes 102 E6
Emery Down Hants 32 F3
Emley W Yorks 197 E8
Emmbrook Wokingham 65 F9
Emmer Green Reading 65 D8
Emmett Carr Derbys 187 F7
Emmington Oxon 84 E2
Emneth Norf 139 B9
Emneth Hungate Norf 139 B10
Emorsgate Norf 157 E10
Empingham Rutland 137 B8
Empshott Hants 49 G9
Empshott Green Hants 49 G8
Emscote Warks 118 D5
Emstrey Shrops 149 G10
Emsworth Hants 22 B2
Enborne W Berks 64 F2
Enborne Row W Berks 64 G2
Enchmarsh Shrops 131 D10
Enderby Leics 135 D10
Endmoor Cumb 211 C10
Endon Staffs 168 E6
Endon Bank Staffs 168 E6
Energlyn Caerph 58 B6
Enfield London 86 F4
Worcs 117 D10
Enfield Highway London 86 F5
Enfield Lock London 86 F5
Enfield Town London 86 F4
Enfield Wash London 86 F5
Enford Wilts 46 C6
Engamoor Shetland 313 H4
Engedi Anglesey 178 F5
Engine Common S Glos 61 C7
Englefield W Berks 64 E6
Englefield Green Sur 66 E3
Englesea-brook Ches E 168 E3
English Bicknor Glos 79 B9
Englishcombe Bath 61 G8
English Frankton Shrops 149 D9
Engollan Corn 10 G3
Enham Alamein Hants 47 D11
Enis Devon 25 B9
Enisfirth Shetland 312 F5
Enmore Som 43 G8
Enmore Field Hereford 115 E9
Enmore Green Dorset 30 C5
Ennerdale Bridge Cumb 219 B11
Enniscaven Corn 5 D9
Enoch Dumfries 247 C9
Enochdhu Perth 292 G2
Ensay Argyll 288 E5
Ensbury Bmouth 19 B7
Ensbury Park Bmouth 19 C7
Ensdon Shrops 149 F8
Ensis Devon 25 B9
Enslow Oxon 83 B7
Enstone Oxon 101 G7
Enterkinfoot Dumfries 247 C9
Enterpen N Yorks 225 D9
Enton Green Sur 50 E3
Enville Staffs 132 F6
Eolaigearraidh W Isles 297 L3
Eorabus Argyll 288 G5
Eòropaidh W Isles 304 B7
Epney Glos 80 C3
Epperstone Notts 171 F11
Epping Essex 87 E7
Epping Green Essex 86 D6
Herts 86 D3
Epping Upland Essex 86 E6
Eppleby N Yorks 224 C3
Eppleworth E Yorks 208 G6
Epsom Sur 67 G8
Epwell Oxon 101 C7
Epworth N Lincs 199 G9
Epworth Turbary N Lincs 199 G9
Erbistock Wrex 166 G5
Erbusaig Highld 295 C9
Erchless Castle Highld 300 E4
Erdington W Mid 134 E2
Eredine Argyll 275 C10
Eriboll Highld 308 D4
Ericstane Dumfries 260 G3
Eridge Green E Sus 52 F5
Erines Argyll 275 F9
Eriswell Suff 124 B4
Erith London 68 D4
Erlestoke Wilts 46 C3
Ermine Lincs 189 G7
Ermington Devon 8 E2
Ernesettle Plym 7 D8
Erpingham Norf 160 C3
Erriottwood Kent 54 B2
Errogie Highld 300 G5
Errol Perth 286 E6
Errol Station Perth 286 E6
Erskine Renfs 277 G9
Erskine Bridge Renfs 277 G9
Ervie Dumfries 236 C2
Erwarton Suff 108 E4
Erwood Powys 95 C11
Eryholme N Yorks 224 D6
Eryrys Denb 166 D2
Escomb Durham 233 E9
Escott Som 42 F5
Escrick N Yorks 207 E8
Esgairdawe Carms 94 C2
Esgairgeiliog Powys 128 B5
Esgyryn Conwy 180 F4
Esh Durham 233 C9
Esher Sur 66 G6
Eshiels Borders 261 B7
Esholt W Yorks 205 E9
Eshott Northumb 252 D6
Eshton N Yorks 204 B4
Esh Winning Durham 233 C9
Eskadale Highld 300 F4
Eskbank Midloth 270 B6
Eskdale Green Cumb 220 E2
Eskdalemuir Dumfries 249 D7

Eske E Yorks 209 E7
Eskham Lincs 190 B5
Eskholme S Yorks 198 D6
Esknish Argyll 274 G4
Esk Valley N Yorks 226 E6
Eslington Park
Northumb 264 G2
Esperley Lane Ends
Durham 233 G8
Esprick Lancs 202 F4
Essendine Rutland 155 G10
Essendon Herts 86 D3
Essich Highld 300 F6
Essington Staffs 133 C9
Esslemont Aberds 303 G9
Eston Redcar 225 B11
Estover Plym 7 D10
Eswick Shetland 313 H6
Etal Northumb 263 B10
Etchilhampton Wilts 62 G4
Etchingham E Sus 38 B2
Etchinghill Kent 55 F7
Staffs 151 F10
Etchingwood E Sus 37 C8
Etherley Dene
Durham 233 F9
Ethie Castle Angus 287 C10
Ethie Mains Angus 287 C10
Etling Green Norf 159 G10
Etloe Glos 79 D11
Eton Windsor 66 D3
Eton Wick Windsor 66 D2
Etruria Stoke 168 F5
Etsell Shrops 131 C7
Etterby Cumb 239 F9
Etteridge Highld 291 D8
Ettersgill Durham 232 F3
Ettiley Heath
Ches E 168 C2
Ettingshall W Mid 133 D8
Ettingshall Park
W Mid 133 D8
Ettington Warks 100 B5
Etton E Yorks 208 E5
Pboro 138 B2
Ettrick Borders 261 G7
Ettrickbridge
Borders 261 E9
Ettrickdale Argyll 275 G11
Ettrickhill Borders 261 G7
Etwall Derbys 152 C5
Etwall Common
Derbys 152 C5
Eudon Burnell
Shrops 132 F3
Eudon George
Shrops 132 F3
Euston Suff 125 B7
Euximoor Drove
Cambs 139 D9
Euxton Lancs 194 D5
Evanstown Bridgend 58 B3
Evanton Highld 300 C6
Evedon Lincs 173 F9
Eve Hill W Mid 133 E8
Evelix Highld 309 K7
Evendine Hereford 98 C5
Evenjobb / Einsiob
Powys 114 E5
Evenley Northants 101 E11
Evenlode Glos 100 F4
Even Pits Hereford 97 D11
Even Swindon
Swindon 62 B6
Evenwood Durham 233 G9
Evenwood Gate
Durham 233 G9
Everbay Orkney 314 D6
Evercreech Som 44 F6
Everdon Northants 119 F11
Everingham E Yorks 208 E2
Everland Shetland 312 D8
Everleigh Wilts 47 C8
Everley N Yorks 217 B9
Eversholt C Beds 103 E9
Evershot Dorset 29 G9
Eversley Essex 69 B8
Hants 65 G9
Eversley Centre
Hants 65 G9
Eversley Cross Hants 65 G9
Everthorpe E Yorks 208 G4
Everton C Beds 122 G4
Hants 19 C11
Mers 182 C5
Notts 187 C11
Evertown Dumfries 239 B9
Evesbatch Hereford 98 B3
Evesham Worcs 99 C10
Evington Kent 54 D6
Leicester 136 C2
Ewanrigg Cumb 228 D6
Ewden Village
S Yorks 186 B3
Ewell Sur 67 G8
Ewell Minnis Kent 55 E9
Ewelme Oxon 83 G10
Ewen Glos 81 F8
Ewenny V Glam 58 D2
Ewerby Lincs 173 F10
Ewerby Thorpe
Lincs 173 F10
Ewes Dumfries 249 E9
Ewesley Northumb 252 E3
Ewhurst Sur 50 E5
Ewhurst Green
E Sus 38 C3
Sur 50 F5
Ewloe Flint 166 B4
Ewloe Green Flint 166 B3
Ewood Blkburn 195 B7
Ewood Bridge
Lancs 195 C9
Eworthy Devon 12 C5
Ewshot Hants 49 D10
Ewyas Harold
Hereford 97 F7
Exbourne Devon 25 G10
Exbury Hants 20 B4
Exceat E Sus 23 F8
Exebridge Devon 26 C6
Exelby N Yorks 214 B5
Exeter Devon 14 C4
Exford Som 41 F11
Exfords Green
Shrops 131 B9
Exhall Warks 118 F2
Warks 135 F7
Exlade Street Oxon 65 C7
Exley W Yorks 196 C5
Exley Head W Yorks 204 F6
Exminster Devon 14 D4
Exmouth Devon 14 E6
Exnaboe Shetland 313 M5
Exning Suff 124 D2
Exted Kent 55 E7
Exton Devon 14 D5
Hants 33 C10
Rutland 155 G8
Som 42 G2
Exwick Devon 14 C4
Eyam Derbys 186 F2
Eydon Northants 119 G10
Eye Hereford 115 E9
Pboro 138 C4
Suff 126 C2
Eye Green Pboro 138 C4
Eyemouth Borders 273 C8
Eyeworth C Beds 104 B4
Eyhorne Street Kent 53 C10
Eyke Suff 126 G6
Eynesbury Cambs 122 F3
Eynort Highld 294 C5
Eynsford Kent 68 F4
Eynsham Oxon 82 D6
Eype Dorset 16 C5
Eyre Highld 295 B7
Highld 298 D4
Eyres Monsell
Leicester 135 D11
Eythorne Kent 55 D9
Eyton Hereford 115 E9
Shrops 131 F7
Shrops 149 G7
Wrex 166 G4
Eyton on Severn
Shrops 131 B11
Eyton upon the Weald
Moors Telford 150 G3

F

Faberstown Wilts 47 C9
Faccombe Hants 47 B11
Faceby N Yorks 225 E9
Fachell Gwyn 163 B8
Fachwen Gwyn 163 C9
Facit Lancs 195 D11
Fackley Notts 171 C7
Faddiley Ches E 167 E9
Faddonch Highld 295 C11
Fadmoor N Yorks 216 B3
Faerdre Swansea 75 E11
Fagley W Yorks 205 G9
Fagwyr Swansea 75 E11
Faichem Highld 290 C4
Faifley W Dunb 277 G10
Failand N Som 60 E4
Failford S Ayrs 257 D11
Failsworth
Gtr Man 195 G11
Fain Highld 299 B11
Faindouran Lodge
Moray 292 C2
Fairbourne Gwyn 146 G2
Fairbourne Heath
Kent 53 C11
Fairburn N Yorks 198 B3
Fairburn House
Highld 300 D4
Fair Cross London 68 B3
Fairfield Clack 279 C7
Derbys 185 G9
Gtr Man 184 B6
Gtr Man 195 E10
Kent 39 B7
Mers 182 C5
Stockton 225 B8
Worcs 99 C10
Worcs 117 B8
Fairfield Park Bath 61 F9
Fairfields Glos 98 E4
Fairford Glos 81 E11
Fair Green Norf 158 F3
Fairhaven Lancs 193 B10
N Ayrs 255 C10
Fairhill S Lnrk 268 E4
Fair Hill Cumb 230 E6
Fairlands Sur 50 C3
Fairlee IoW 20 C6
Fairlie N Ayrs 266 D4
Fairlight E Sus 38 E5
Fairlight Cove E Sus 38 E5
Fairlop London 87 G7
Fairmile Devon 15 B7
Dorset 19 C9
Sur 66 G6
Fairmilehead Edin 270 B4
Fair Moor Northumb 252 F5
Fairoak Caerph 77 F11
Staffs 150 C5
Fair Oak Hants 33 D7
Hants 64 G5
Lancs 203 D8
Fair Oak Green
Hants 65 G7
Fairseat Kent 68 G6
Fairstead Essex 88 B3
Norf 158 F2
Fairview Glos 99 G9
Fairwarp E Sus 37 B7
Fairwater Cardiff 58 D6
Torf 78 G3
Fairwood Wilts 45 C10
Fairy Cottage IoM 192 D5
Fairy Cross Devon 24 C6
Fakenham Norf 159 D8
Fakenham Magna
Suff 125 B8
Fala Midloth 271 C8
Fala Dam Midloth 271 C8
Falahill Borders 271 D7
Falcon Hereford 98 E2
Falcon Lodge
W Mid 134 D2
Falconwood London 68 D3
Falcutt Northants 101 C11
Faldingworth Lincs 189 E9
Faldonside Borders 262 C2
Falfield Fife 287 G8
S Glos 79 G11
Falkenham Suff 108 D5
Falkenham Sink
Suff 108 D5
Falkirk Falk 279 F7
Falkland Fife 286 G6
Falla Borders 262 G6
Fallgate Derbys 170 C5
Fallin Stirl 278 C6
Fallinge Derbys 170 B3
Fallings Heath
W Mid 133 D9
Fallowfield Gtr Man 184 C5
Fallside N Lnrk 268 C4
Falmer E Sus 36 F5
Falmouth Corn 3 C8
Falnash Borders 249 B9
Falsgrave N Yorks 217 B10
Falside W Loth 269 B9
Falsidehill Borders 272 G3
Falstone Northumb 250 F6
Fanagmore Highld 306 E6
Fancott C Beds 103 F10
Fangdale Beck
N Yorks 225 G11
Fangfoss E Yorks 207 C11
Fanich Highld 311 J2
Fankerton Falk 278 E5
Fanmore Argyll 288 E6
Fanner's Green
Essex 87 C11
Fannich Lodge
Highld 300 C2
Fans Borders 272 G2
Fanshowe Ches E 184 G5
Fant Kent 53 B8
Faoilean Highld 295 C7
Far Arnside Cumb 211 D8
Far Bank S Yorks 198 E6
Far Banks Lancs 194 C2
Far Bletchley
M Keynes 103 E7
Farcet Cambs 138 E4
Far Coton Leics 135 C7
Far Cotton
Northants 120 F4
Farden Shrops 115 B11
Fareham Hants 33 F9
Far End Cumb 220 F6
Farewell Staffs 151 G11
Far Forest Worcs 116 C4
Farforth Lincs 190 F4
Far Green Glos 80 E3
Farhill Derbys 170 C5
Far Hoarcross
Staffs 152 E2
Faringdon Oxon 82 F3
Farington Lancs 194 B4
Farington Moss
Lancs 194 C4
Farlam Cumb 240 F3
Farlands Booth
Derbys 185 D9
Farlary Highld 309 J7
Far Laund Derbys 170 F5
Farleigh N Som 60 F3
Sur 67 G11
Farleigh Court Sur 67 G11
Farleigh Green Kent 53 C8
Farleigh Hungerford
Som 45 B10
Farleigh Wallop
Hants 48 D6
Farleigh Wick Wilts 61 G10
Farlesthorpe Lincs 191 G7
Farleton Cumb 211 C10
Lancs 211 F11
Farley Bristol 60 E2
Derbys 170 C3
Shrops 131 B7
Shrops 132 C2
Staffs 169 G9
Wilts 32 B2
Far Ley Staffs 132 D5
Farley Green Suff 124 G4
Sur 50 D5
Farley Hill Luton 103 G11
Wokingham 65 G8
Farleys End Glos 80 B3
Farlington N Yorks 216 F2
Ptsmth 33 F11
Farlow Shrops 132 G2
Farmborough Bath 61 G7
Farmbridge End
Essex 87 C10
Farmcote Glos 99 F11
Shrops 132 E5
Farmington Glos 81 B10
Farmoor Oxon 82 D6
Far Moor Gtr Man 194 G4
Farms Common Corn 2 C5
Farmtown Moray 302 D5
Farm Town Leics 153 F7
Farnah Green
Derbys 170 F4
Farnborough Hants 49 C11
London 68 G2
Warks 101 B8
W Berks 64 C2
Farnborough Green
Hants 49 B11
Farnborough Park
Hants 49 B11
Farnborough Street
Hants 49 B11
Farncombe Sur 50 E3
Farndish Beds 121 E8
Farndon Ches W 166 E6
Notts 172 E3
Farnell Angus 287 B10
Farnham Dorset 31 D7
Essex 105 G9
N Yorks 215 G7
Suff 127 E7
Sur 49 D10
Farnham Common
Bucks 66 C3
Farnham Green
Essex 105 F9
Farnham Park Bucks 66 C3
Farnham Royal Bucks 66 C3
Farnhill N Yorks 204 D6
Farningham Kent 68 F4
Farnley N Yorks 205 D10
W Yorks 205 G11
Farnley Bank
W Yorks 197 E7
Farnley Tyas
W Yorks 197 E7
Farnsfield Notts 171 D10
Farnworth Gtr Man 195 F8
Halton 183 D8
Far Oakridge Glos 80 E6
Farr Highld 291 C10
Highld 300 F6
Highld 308 C7
Farraline Highld 300 G5
Farr House Highld 300 F6
Farringdon Devon 14 C6
T&W 243 G9
Farrington Dorset 30 D4
Farrington Gurney
Bath 44 B6
Far Royds
W Yorks 205 G11
Far Sawrey Cumb 221 F7
Farsley W Yorks 205 F10
Farsley Beck Bottom
W Yorks 205 F10
Farther Howegreen
Essex 88 E4
Farthing Corner
Medway 69 G10
Farthing Green
Kent 53 D10
Farthinghoe
Northants 101 D10
Farthingloe Kent 55 E9
Farthingstone
Northants 120 F2
Far Thrupp Glos 80 E5
Fartown W Yorks 196 D6
Farway Devon 15 B9
Farway Marsh Devon 28 G4
Fasach Highld 297 G7
Fasag Highld 299 D8
Fascadale Highld 289 B7
Faslane Port Argyll 276 D4
Fasnacloich Argyll 284 C4
Fasnakyle Ho
Highld 300 G3
Fassfern Highld 290 F2
Fatfield T&W 243 G8
Fattahead Aberds 302 D6
Faucheldean
W Loth 279 G11
Faugh Cumb 240 G2
Faughill Borders 262 C2
Fauld Staffs 152 D3
Fauldhouse W Loth 269 C8
Fauldiehill Angus 287 D9
Fauldshope
Borders 261 D10
Faulkbourne Essex 88 B3
Faulkland Som 45 C8
Fauls Shrops 149 C11
Faverdale Darl 224 B5
Faversham Kent 70 G4
Favillar Moray 302 F2
Fawdington
N Yorks 215 E8
Fawdon Northumb 264 F2
T&W 242 D6
Fawfieldhead Staffs 169 C9
Fawkham Green Kent 68 F5
Fawler Oxon 63 B10
Oxon 82 B5
Fawley Bucks 65 B9
Hants 33 G7
W Berks 63 C11
Fawley Bottom Bucks 65 B8
Fawley Chapel
Hereford 97 F11
Faxfleet E Yorks 199 C11
Faygate W Sus 51 G8
Fazakerley Mers 182 B5
Fazeley Staffs 134 C4
Feagour Highld 291 D7
Fearby N Yorks 214 C3
Fearn Highld 301 B8
Fearnan Perth 285 C11
Fearnbeg Highld 299 D7
Fearnhead Warr 183 C10
Fearn Lodge Highld 309 L6
Fearnmore Highld 299 C7
Fearn Station
Highld 301 B8
Fearnville W Yorks 206 F2
Featherstone Staffs 133 B8
W Yorks 198 C2
Featherwood
Northumb 251 C8
Feckenham Worcs 117 E10
Fedw Fawr
Anglesey 179 E10
Feering Essex 107 G7
Feetham N Yorks 223 F9
Fegg Hayes Stoke 168 E5
Fèith Mhor Highld 301 G8
Feizor N Yorks 212 F5
Felbridge Sur 51 F11
Felbrigg Norf 160 B4
Felcourt Sur 51 E11
Felden Herts 85 E8
Felderland Kent 55 B10
Feldy Ches E 183 F11
Felhampton Shrops 131 F8
Felin-Crai Powys 95 G7
Felindre Carms 75 C7
Carms 93 D7
Carms 93 G11
Carms 94 E3
Carms 94 F4
Ceredig 111 F10
Powys 96 D3
Powys 96 G3
Powys 130 C3
Powys 130 G3
Rhondda 58 C3
Swansea 75 E10
Felindre Farchog
Pembs 92 D2
Felinfach Ceredig 111 F10
Powys 95 E11
Felinfoel Carms 75 E8
Felingwmisaf
Carms 93 G10
Felingwmuchaf
Carms 93 G10
Felin Newydd Carms 94 D3
Felin-newydd Powys 96 D2
Felin Newydd /
New Mills Powys 129 C11
Felin Puleston Wrex 166 F4
Felin-Wnda Ceredig 92 B6
Felinwynt Ceredig 110 G4
Felixkirk N Yorks 215 C9
Felixstowe Suff 108 E5
Felixstowe Ferry
Suff 108 D6
Felkington
Northumb 273 G8
Felkirk W Yorks 197 E11
Felldyke Cumb 219 B11
Fell End Cumb 222 F4
Fellgate T&W 243 E8
Felling T&W 243 E7
Felling Shore T&W 243 E7
Fell Lane W Yorks 204 E6
Fellside T&W 242 E5
Fell Side Cumb 230 D2
Felmersham Beds 121 F9
Felmingham Norf 160 D5
Felmore Essex 69 B8
Felpham W Sus 35 H7
Felsham Suff 125 F8
Felsted Essex 106 G3
Feltham London 66 E6
Som 28 D2
Felthamhill London 66 E5
Felthorpe Norf 160 F3
Felton Hereford 97 B11
Northumb 252 C5
N Som 60 F4
Felton Butler
Shrops 149 F7
Feltwell Norf 140 E4
Fenay Bridge
W Yorks 197 D7
Fence Lancs 204 F2
Fence Houses T&W 243 G8
Fencott Oxon 83 B9
Fen Ditton Cambs 123 E9
Fen Drayton Cambs 122 D6
Fen End Lincs 156 E4
W Mid 118 B4
Fengate Norf 160 E3
Pboro 138 D4
Fenham Northumb 273 G11
T&W 242 D6
Fenhouses Lincs 174 G3
Feniscliffe Blkburn 195 B7
Feniscowles Blkburn 194 B6
Feniton Devon 15 B8
Fenlake Beds 103 B11
Fenn Green Shrops 132 G5
Fennington Som 27 B11
Fenn's Bank Wrex 149 B10
Fenn Street Medway 69 D9
Fenny Bentley
Derbys 169 E11
Fenny Bridges Devon 15 B8
Fenny Castle Som 44 E4
Fenny Compton
Warks 119 G8
Fenny Drayton
Leics 134 D6
Fenny Stratford
M Keynes 103 E7
Fenrother Northumb 252 E5
Fen Side Lincs 174 D4
Fenstanton Cambs 122 D6
Fenstead End Suff 124 G6
Fen Street Norf 141 G11
Suff 125 B9
Suff 125 B11
Fenton Cambs 122 B6
Cumb 240 F2
Lincs 172 E5
Lincs 188 F4
Northumb 263 C11
Stoke 168 G5
Fentonadle Corn 11 F7
Fenton Barns
E Loth 281 E10
Fenton Low Stoke 168 F5
Fenton Pits Corn 5 C11
Fenton Town
Northumb 263 C11
Fenwick E Ayrs 267 G9
Northumb 242 C3
Northumb 273 G11
S Yorks 198 D5
Feochaig Argyll 255 F8
Feock Corn 3 B8
Feolin Ferry Argyll 274 G5
Ferguslie Park
Renfs 267 C9
Ferindonald Highld 295 E8
Feriniquarrie Highld 296 F7
Ferlochan Argyll 289 E11
Fern Angus 292 G6
Bucks 65 B11
Fern Bank Gtr Man 185 B7
Ferndale Kent 52 E5
Rhondda 77 F7
Ferndown Dorset 31 G9
Ferne Wilts 30 C6
Ferness Highld 301 E9
Ferney Green Cumb 221 F8
Fernham Oxon 82 G3
Fernhill Gtr Man 195 E10
Rhondda 77 F8
W Sus 51 E10
Fern Hill Suff 106 B6
Fernhill Gate
Gtr Man 195 F7
Fernhill Heath
Worcs 117 F7
Fernhurst W Sus 34 B5
Fernie Fife 287 F7
Ferniebrae Aberds 303 D9
Ferniegair S Lnrk 268 E4
Ferniehirst Borders 271 G8
Fernilea Highld 294 B5
Fernilee Derbys 185 F8
Fernsplatt Corn 4 G5
Ferrensby N Yorks 215 G7
Ferring W Sus 35 G9
Ferrybridge
W Yorks 198 C3
Ferryden Angus 287 B11
Ferryhill Aberdeen 293 C11
Durham 233 E11
Ferry Hill Cambs 139 G7
Ferryhill Station
Durham 234 E2
Ferry Point Highld 309 L7
Ferryside / Glan-y-Fferi
Carms 74 C5
Ferryton Highld 300 C6
Fersfield Norf 141 G11
Fersit Highld 290 F5
Feshiebridge
Highld 291 C10
Fetcham Sur 50 B6
Fetterangus Aberds 303 D9
Fettercairn Aberds 293 F8
Fetterdale Fife 287 E8
Fettes Highld 300 D5
Fewcott Oxon 101 F10
Fewston N Yorks 205 C9
Fewston Bents
N Yorks 205 C9
Ffairfach Carms 94 G2
Ffair-Rhos Ceredig 112 D4
Ffaldybrenin Carms 94 C2
Ffarmers Carms 94 C3
Ffawyddog Powys 78 B2
Ffodun / Forden
Powys 130 C4
Ffont y gari /
Font y gary V Glam 58 F5
Fforddlas Powys 96 D4
Ffordd-las Denb 165 C10
Ffordd-y-Gyfraith
Bridgend 57 E11
Fforest Carms 75 E9
Fforest-fach Swansea 56 B6
Fforest Gôch Neath 76 E2
Ffostrasol Ceredig 93 B7
Ffos-y-ffin Ceredig 111 E8
Ffos-y-go Wrex 166 E4
Ffridd Powys 130 D3
Ffrith Wrex 166 D3
Ffrwd Gwyn 163 D7
Ffrwd y mwn / Fonmon
V Glam 58 F4
Ffynnon Carms 74 B5
Ffynnon ddrain
Carms 93 G8
Ffynnongroes /
Crosswell Pembs 92 D2
Ffynnon Gron Pembs 91 F8
Ffynnongroyw
Flint 181 E10
Ffynnon Gynydd
Powys 96 C3
Ffynnon-oer
Ceredig 111 G10
Fickleshole Sur 67 G11
Fidden Argyll 288 G5
Fiddes Aberds 293 E10
Fiddington Glos 99 E8
Som 43 E8
Fiddington Sands
Wilts 46 C4
Fiddleford Dorset 30 E4
Fiddlers' Green
Norf 141 D10
Fiddler's Ferry
Mers 193 C11
Warr 183 D9
Fiddler's Green Glos 99 G8
Hereford 97 D11
Fiddlers Hamlet
Essex 87 E7
Field Hereford 114 G6
Som 44 E6
Staffs 151 C10
Field Assarts Oxon 82 C4
Field Broughton
Cumb 211 C7
Field Common Sur 66 F6
Field Dalling Norf 159 B10
Field Green Kent 38 B3
Field Head Leics 135 B9
Fields End Herts 85 D8
Field's Place
Hereford 115 G8
Fifehead Magdalen
Dorset 30 C3
Fifehead Neville
Dorset 30 E3
Fifehead St Quintin
Dorset 30 E3
Fife Keith Moray 302 D4
Fifield Oxon 82 B2
Wilts 46 C6
Windsor 66 D2
Fifield Bavant Wilts 31 B8
Figheldean Wilts 47 D7
Filands Wilts 62 B2
Filby Norf 161 G9
Filby Heath Norf 161 G9
Filchampstead Oxon 83 D7
Filey N Yorks 218 C2
Filgrave M Keynes 103 B7
Filham Devon 8 D2
Filkins Oxon 82 E2
Filleigh Devon 25 B11
Devon 26 E2
Fillingham Lincs 188 D6
Fillongley Warks 134 F5
Filmore Hill Hants 33 B11
Filton S Glos 60 D6
Filwood Park Bristol 60 F5
Fimber E Yorks 217 G7
Finavon Angus 287 B8
Fincastle Ho Perth 291 G10
Finchairn Argyll 275 C10
Fincham Mers 182 C6
Norf 140 B3
Finchampstead
Wokingham 65 G9
Finchdean Hants 34 E2
Finchingfield Essex 106 E3
Finchley London 86 G3
Findern Derbys 152 C6
Findhorn Moray 301 C10
Findhorn Bridge
Highld 301 G8
Findochty Moray 302 C4
Findo Gask Perth 286 E4
Findon Aberds 293 D11
W Sus 35 F10
Findon Mains
Highld 300 C6
Findon Valley
W Sus 35 F10
Findrack Ho Aberds 293 C8
Finedon Northants 121 C8
Fineglen Argyll 275 B10
Fine Street Hereford 96 D6
Fingal Street Suff 126 D4
Fingask Aberds 303 G7
Fingerpost Worcs 116 C4
Fingest Bucks 84 G3
Finghall N Yorks 214 B3
Fingland Cumb 239 F7
Dumfries 259 F7
Finglesham Kent 55 C10
Fingringhoe Essex 107 G10
Finham W Mid 118 B6
Finkle Street
S Yorks 186 B4
Finlarig Stirl 285 D9
Finmere Oxon 102 E2
Finnart Perth 285 B9
Finney Green
Ches E 184 E5
Staffs 168 F3
Finningham Suff 125 D11
Finningley S Yorks 187 B11
Finnygaud Aberds 302 D5
Finsbury London 67 C10
Finsbury Park
London 67 B10
Finstall Worcs 117 D9
Finsthwaite Cumb 211 B7
Finstock Oxon 82 B5
Finstown Orkney 314 E3
Fintry Aberds 303 D7
Dundee 287 D8
Stirl 278 D2
Finwood Warks 118 D3
Finzean Aberds 293 D8
Finzean Ho Aberds 293 D7
Fionnphort Argyll 288 G5
Fionnsbhagh
W Isles 296 C6
Firbank Cumb 222 G2
Firbeck S Yorks 187 D9
Firby N Yorks 214 B5
N Yorks 216 F4
Firemore Highld 307 L3
Firgrove Gtr Man 196 E2
Firkin Argyll 285 G7
Firle E Sus 23 D7
Firsby Lincs 175 C7
Firsdown Wilts 47 G8
Firs Lane Gtr Man 194 G6
First Coast Highld 307 K4
Firswood Gtr Man 184 B4
Firth Borders 262 E2
Firth Moor Darl 224 C6
Firth Park S Yorks 186 C5
Fir Toll Kent 54 E2
Fir Tree Durham 233 E8
Fir Vale S Yorks 186 C5
Firwood Fold
Gtr Man 195 E8
Fishbourne IoW 21 C7
W Sus 22 C4
Fishburn Durham 234 E3
Fishcross Clack 279 B7
Fisherford Aberds 302 F6
Fishermead
M Keynes 103 D7
Fisher Place Cumb 220 B6
Fisherrow E Loth 280 G6
Fishersgate Brighton 36 F3
Fishers Green Herts 104 F4
Fisher's Pond Hants 33 C7
Fisherstreet W Sus 50 G3
Fisherton Highld 301 D7
S Ayrs 257 F7
Fisherton de la Mere
Wilts 46 F4
Fisherwick Staffs 134 B3
Fishery Windsor 65 C11
Fishguard / Abergwaun
Pembs 91 D9
Fishlake S Yorks 199 E7
Fishleigh Devon 25 F8
Fishleigh Barton
Devon 25 C9
Fishleigh Castle
Devon 25 F8
Fishley Norf 161 G8
W Mid 133 C10
Fishmere End Lincs 156 B5
Fishponds Bristol 60 D6
Fishpool Glos 98 F3
Gtr Man 195 F10
N Yorks 205 D10
Fishpools Powys 114 D3
Fishtoft Lincs 174 G5
Fishtoft Drove Lincs 174 F4
Fishtown of Usan
Angus 287 B11
Fishwick Borders 273 E8
Lancs 194 B5
Fiskavaig Highld 294 B5
Fiskerton Lincs 189 G8
Notts 172 E2
Fitling E Yorks 209 G11
Fittleton Wilts 46 D6
Fittleworth W Sus 35 D8
Fitton End Cambs 157 G8
Fitton Hill Gtr Man 196 G2
Fitz Shrops 149 F8
Fitzhead Som 27 B10
Fitzwilliam W Yorks 198 D2
Fiunary Highld 289 E8
Five Acres Glos 79 C9
Five Ash Down E Sus 37 C7
Five Ashes E Sus 37 C9
Five Bells Som 42 E5
Five Bridges Hereford 98 B3
Fivecrosses Ches W 183 F8
Fivehead Som 28 C5
Five Houses IoW 20 D4
Five Lane Ends
Lancs 202 C6
Fivelanes Corn 11 E10
Five Lanes Mon 78 G6
Five Oak Green Kent 52 D6
Five Oaks W Sus 35 B9
Five Roads Carms 75 D7
Five Ways Warks 118 D4
Five Wents Kent 53 C10
Fixby W Yorks 196 C6
Flackley Ash E Sus 38 C5
Flack's Green Essex 88 B3
Flackwell Heath
Bucks 65 B11
Fladbury Worcs 99 B9
Fladbury Cross
Worcs 99 B9
Fladda Shetland 312 E5
Fladdabister
Shetland 313 K6
Flagg Derbys 169 B10
Flaggoners Green
Hereford 116 G2
Flamborough
E Yorks 218 E4
Flamstead Herts 85 C9
Flamstead End Herts 86 E4
Flansham W Sus 35 G7
Flanshaw W Yorks 197 C10
Flappit Spring
W Yorks 205 F7
Flasby N Yorks 204 B4
Flash Staffs 169 B8
Flashader Highld 298 D3
Flask Inn N Yorks 227 E8
Flathurst W Sus 35 C7
Flaunden Herts 85 E8
Flawborough Notts 172 G3
Flawith N Yorks 215 F9
Flax Bourton N Som 60 F4
Flaxby N Yorks 206 B3
Flaxholme Derbys 170 G4
Flaxlands Norf 142 E2
Flaxley Glos 79 B11
Flax Moss Lancs 195 C9
Flaxpool Som 42 F6
Flaxton N Yorks 216 G3
Fleckney Leics 136 E2
Flecknoe Warks 119 E10
Fledborough Notts 188 G4
Fleet Dorset 17 E8
Hants 22 C2
Hants 49 C10
Lincs 157 E7
Fleet Downs Kent 68 E5
Fleetend Hants 33 F8
Fleet Hargate Lincs 157 E7
Fleetlands Hants 33 G9
Fleets N Yorks 213 G9
Fleetville Herts 85 D11
Fleetwood Lancs 202 D2
Fleggburgh / Burgh St
Margaret Norf 161 G8
Fleming Field
Durham 234 C3
Flemings Kent 55 B9
Flemingston V Glam 58 E4
Flemington S Lnrk 268 D3
S Lnrk 268 G4
Flempton Suff 124 D6
Fleoideabhagh
W Isles 296 C6
Fletchersbridge Corn 6 B2
Fletcher's Green
Kent 52 C4
Fletchertown
Cumb 229 C10
Fletching E Sus 36 C6
Fletching Common
E Sus 36 C6
Fleuchary Highld 309 K7
Fleuchlang
Dumfries 237 D8
Fleur-de-lis Caerph 77 F11
Flexbury Corn 24 F2
Flexford Hants 32 C6
Sur 50 D2
Flimby Cumb 228 E6
Flimwell E Sus 53 G8
Flint Flint 182 G2
Flint Cross Cambs 105 C8
Flintham Notts 172 F2
Flint Hill Durham 242 G5
Flint Mountain /
Mynydd Fflint
Flint 182 G2
Flinton E Yorks 209 F10
Flint's Green W Mid 134 G5
Flintsham Hereford 114 F6
Flishinghurst Kent 53 F9
Flitcham Norf 158 D4
Flitholme Cumb 222 B5
Flitton C Beds 103 D11
Flitwick C Beds 103 D10
Flixborough
N Lincs 199 D11
Flixborough Stather
N Lincs 199 E11
Flixton Gtr Man 184 C2
N Yorks 217 D10
Suff 142 F6
Flockton W Yorks 197 E8
Flockton Green
W Yorks 197 D8
Flockton Moor
W Yorks 197 E8
Flodaigh W Isles 296 F4
Flodden Northumb 263 B10
Flodigarry Highld 298 B4
Floodgates Hereford 114 F5
Flood's Ferry Cambs 139 E7
Flood Street Hants 31 D10
Flookburgh Cumb 211 D7
Flordon Norf 142 D3
Flore Northants 120 E2
Florence Stoke 168 G6
Flotterton
Northumb 251 C11
Flowers Bottom
Bucks 84 F4
Flowers Green
E Sus 23 C10
Flowery Field
Gtr Man 184 B6
Flowton Suff 107 B11
Fluchter E Dunb 277 G11
Flugarth Shetland 313 G6
Flushdyke W Yorks 197 C9
Flush House
W Yorks 196 F6
Flushing Aberds 303 E10
Corn 3 C8
Corn 3 D7
Flyford Flavell
Worcs 117 G9
Foals Green Suff 126 C5
Fobbing Thurrock 69 C8
Fochabers Moray 302 D3
Fochriw Caerph 77 D10
Fockerby N Lincs 199 D10
Fodderletter
Moray 301 G11
Fodderstone Gap
Norf 140 B3
Fodderty Highld 300 D5
Foddington Som 29 B9
Foel Powys 147 G9

Foel-gastell Carms 75 C8
Foffarty Angus 287 C8
Foggathorpe
E Yorks 207 F11
Foggbrook Gtr Man 184 D6
Fogo Borders 272 F5
Fogorig Borders 272 F5
Fogrigarth Shetland 313 H4
Fogwatt Moray 302 D2
Foindle Highld 306 E6
Folda Angus 292 G3
Fold Head Lancs 195 D11
Fold Hill Lincs 175 E7
Foldrings S Yorks 186 C3
Fole Staffs 151 B10
Foleshill W Mid 135 G7
Foley Park Worcs 116 B6
Folke Dorset 29 E11
Folkestone Kent 55 F8
Folkingham Lincs 155 C11
Folkington E Sus 23 E9
Folksworth Cambs 138 F2
Folkton N Yorks 217 D11
Folla Rule Aberds 303 F7
Folley Shrops 132 D5
Follifoot N Yorks 206 C2
Follingsby T&W 243 E8
Folly Dorset 30 G2
Pembs 91 G8
Folly Cross Devon 25 F7
Folly Gate Devon 13 B7
Folly Green Essex 106 F6
Fonmon/Ffwl-y-mwn
V Glam 58 F4
Fonston Corn 11 C10
Fonthill Bishop Wilts 46 G2
Fonthill Gifford Wilts 46 G2
Fontmell Magna
Dorset 30 D5
Fontmell Parva
Dorset 30 E4
Fontwell W Sus 35 F7
Font-y-gary/
Ffont-y-gari V Glam 58 F5
Foodieash Fife 287 F7
Foolow Derbys 185 F11
Footbridge Glos 99 F10
Footherley Staffs 134 C2
Footrid Worcs 116 C3
Foots Cray London 68 E3
Forbestown Aberds 292 B5
Force Forge Cumb 220 G6
Force Green Kent 52 B2
Force Mills Cumb 220 G6
Forcett N Yorks 224 C3
Ford Argyll 275 C9
Bucks 84 D3
Derbys 186 E6
Devon 8 E2
Devon 8 G5
Devon 24 C6
Devon 28 G2
Glos 99 F11
Hereford 115 F10
Kent 71 F8
Mers 182 B4
Northumb 263 B10
Pembs 91 F9
Plym 7 D9
Shrops 149 G8
Som 27 B9
Som 44 C5
Staffs 169 E9
Wilts 47 G7
Wilts 61 E10
W Sus 35 G7
Forda Devon 12 C6
Devon 40 F3
Fordbridge W Mid 134 F3
Fordcombe Kent 52 E4
Fordell Fife 280 D3
Ford End Essex 87 B11
Essex 105 E9
Forden/Ffodun
Powys 130 C4
Forder Corn 7 D8
Forder Green Devon 8 B5
Ford Forge
Northumb 263 B10
Fordgate Som 43 G10
Ford Green Lancs 202 D5
Stoke 168 E5
Fordham Cambs 124 C2
Essex 107 F8
Norf 140 D2
Fordham Heath
Essex 107 F8
Ford Heath Shrops 149 G8
Ford Hill Northumb 263 B11
Fordhouses W Mid 133 C8
Fordingbridge
Hants 31 E10
Fordington Lincs 190 G6
Fordley T&W 243 C7
Fordon E Yorks 217 D10
Fordoun Aberds 293 F9
Ford's Green E Sus 36 B6
Suff 125 D11
Fordstreet Essex 107 F8
Ford Street Som 27 D11
Fordton Devon 14 B2
Fordwater Devon 28 G4
Fordwells Oxon 82 C4
Fordwich Kent 55 B7
Fordyce Aberds 302 C5
Forebridge Staffs 151 E8
Foredale N Yorks 212 F6
Forehill S Ayrs 257 E8
Foreland Fields IoW 21 D9
Foreland Ho Argyll 274 G3
Foremark Derbys 152 D6
Forest Becks
Lancs 203 C11
Forestburn Gate
Northumb 252 D3
Forest Coal Pit Mon 96 G5
Forestdale London 67 G11
Foresterseat
Moray 301 D11
Forest Gate Hants 33 E10
London 68 C2
Forest Green Glos 80 E4
Sur 50 E6
Forest Hall Cumb 221 E10
T&W 243 D7
Forest Head Cumb 240 F3
Forest Hill London 67 E11
Oxon 83 D9
Wilts 63 F8
Forest Holme
Lancs 195 B10
Forest-in-Teesdale
Durham 232 F3
Forest Lane Head
N Yorks 206 B2
Forest Lodge Argyll 284 C6
Highld 292 B2
Perth 291 F11
Forest Mill Clack 279 C9
Forest Moor
N Yorks 206 B2
Forestreet Devon 24 E5
Forest Row E Sus 52 G2
Forestside W Sus 34 E3
Forest Side IoW 20 D5
Forest Town Notts 171 C9
Forewoods Common
Wilts 61 G10
Forfar Angus 287 B8
Forgandenny Perth 286 F4
Forge Corn 4 F3
Powys 128 D5
Forge Hammer Torf 78 F3
Forge Side Torf 78 D2
Forgewood N Lnrk 268 D4
Forgie Moray 302 D3
Forglen Ho Aberds 302 D6
Forgue Aberds 302 E6
Forhill Worcs 117 B11
Formby Mers 193 F10
Forncett End Norf 142 E2
Forncett St Mary
Norf 142 E3
Forncett St Peter
Norf 142 E3
Forneth Perth 286 C4
Fornham All Saints
Suff 124 D6
Fornham St Genevieve
Suff 124 D6
Fornham St Martin
Suff 125 D7
Fornighty Highld 301 D9
Forrabury Corn 11 C7
Forres Moray 301 D10
Forrestfield N Lnrk 269 B7
Forrest Lodge
Dumfries 246 F3
Forry's Green Essex 106 E5
Forsbrook Staffs 169 G7
Forse Highld 310 F6
Forse Ho Highld 310 F6
Forshaw Heath
Warks 117 C11
Forsinain Highld 310 E3
Forsinard Highld 310 E2
Forsinard Station
Highld 310 E2
Forstal Kent 53 B8
Forston Dorset 17 B9
Fort Augustus
Highld 290 C5
Forteviot Perth 286 F4
Fort George Highld 301 D7
Forth S Lnrk 269 E8
Forthampton Glos 99 E7
Forthay Glos 80 F2
Forth Road Bridge
Edin 280 F2
Fortingall Perth 285 C11
Fortis Green London 67 B9
Fort Matilda Invclyd 276 F5
Forton Hants 33 G10
Hants 48 E2
Lancs 202 C5
Shrops 149 F8
Som 28 F4
Staffs 150 E5
Forton Heath
Shrops 149 F8
Fortrie Aberds 302 E6
Aberds 303 D7
Fortrose Highld 301 D7
Fortuneswell Dorset 17 G9
Fort William Highld 290 F3
Forty Green Bucks 84 E3
Bucks 84 G6
Forty Hill London 86 F4
Forward Green
Suff 125 F11
Forwood Glos 80 E5
Fosbury Wilts 47 B10
Foscot Oxon 100 G4
Foscote Bucks 102 D4
Northants 102 B3
Wilts 61 D11
Fosdyke Lincs 156 C6
Fosdyke Bridge
Lincs 156 C6
Foss Perth 285 B11
Foss Cross Glos 81 D9
Fossebridge Glos 81 C9
Fostall Kent 70 G5
Fosten Green Kent 53 F10
Fosterhouses
S Yorks 199 E7
Foster's Booth
Northants 120 G3
Foster's Green
Worcs 117 D9
Foster Street Essex 87 D7
Foston Derbys 152 C3
Leics 136 D2
Lincs 172 G5
N Yorks 216 F3
Foston on the Wolds
E Yorks 209 B8
Fotherby Lincs 190 C4
Fothergill Cumb 228 E6
Fotheringhay
Northants 137 E11
Foubister Orkney 314 F5
Foul Anchor Cambs 157 F9
Foulbridge Cumb 230 B4
Foulby W Yorks 197 D11
Foulden Borders 273 D8
Norf 140 D5
Foul End Warks 134 E4
Foulford Hants 31 F11
Foulis Castle Highld 300 C5
Foul Mile E Sus 23 B10
Foulride Green
E Sus 23 E9
Foulridge Lancs 204 E3
Foulsham Norf 159 E10
Foundry Corn 2 B3
Foundry Hill Norf 159 D11
Fountain Bridgend 57 E11
Fountainhall
Borders 271 F8
Four Ashes Bucks 84 F5
Staffs 132 F6
Staffs 133 B8
Suff 125 C10
W Mid 118 B3
Four Crosses
Powys 129 B11
Powys 148 F5
Staffs 133 B9
Wrex 166 E3
Four Elms Devon 28 F3
Kent 52 D3
Four Foot Som 44 G5
Four Forks Som 43 F8
Four Gates Gtr Man 194 F6
Four Gotes Cambs 157 F9
Four Houses Corner
W Berks 64 F6
Four Lane End
S Yorks 197 G9
Fourlane Ends
Derbys 170 D5
Four Lane Ends
Blkburn 195 B7
Ches W 167 C9
Gtr Man 195 E9
W Yorks 205 G8
Four Lanes Corn 2 B5
Fourlanes End
Ches E 168 D4
Four Marks Hants 49 G7
Four Mile Bridge
Anglesey 178 F3
Four Mile Elm Glos 80 C4
Four Oaks E Sus 38 C5
Glos 98 F3
Kent 70 G3
W Mid 134 D2
W Mid 134 G4
Four Oaks Park
W Mid 134 D2
Fourpenny Highld 311 K2
Four Points W Berks 64 D5
Four Pools Worcs 99 C10
Four Roads Carms 74 D6
IoM 192 F3
Fourstones
Northumb 241 D9
Four Throws Kent 38 B3
Four Wantz Essex 87 C10
Four Wents Kent 53 F9
Fovant Wilts 31 B8
Foveran Aberds 303 G9
Fowey Corn 6 E2
Fowler's Plot Som 43 F10
Fowley Common
Warr 183 B11
Fowlis Angus 287 D7
Fowlis Wester Perth 286 E3
Fowlmere Cambs 105 B8
Fownhope Hereford 97 E11
Foxash Estate
Essex 107 E11
Foxbar Renfs 267 C9
Foxbury London 68 E2
Foxcombe Hill Oxon 83 E7
Fox Corner C Beds 103 F8
Sur 50 C3
Foxcote Glos 81 B8
Som 45 B8
Foxcotte Hants 47 D10
Foxdale IoM 192 E3
Foxdown Hants 48 C4
Foxearth Essex 106 C6
Foxendown Kent 69 F7
Foxfield Cumb 210 B4
Foxford W Mid 135 G7
Foxham Wilts 62 D3
Fox Hatch Essex 87 F9
Fox Hill Bath 61 G9
Hereford 98 B3
Foxhills Hants 32 E4
Foxhole Corn 5 E9
Norf 142 D4
Swansea 57 C7
Fox Hole Swansea 56 D5
Foxholes N Yorks 217 E10
Fox Holes Wilts 45 E11
Foxhunt Green E Sus 23 B8
Fox Lane Hants 49 B11
Foxley Hereford 97 B8
Norf 159 E10
Staffs 168 E3
Wilts 61 B11
Foxlydiate Worcs 117 D10
Fox Royd W Yorks 197 D8
Fox Street Essex 107 F10
Foxt Staffs 169 F8
Foxton Cambs 105 B8
Durham 234 F3
Leics 136 E4
N Yorks 225 F8
Foxup N Yorks 213 D7
Foxwist Green
Ches W 167 B10
Foxwood Shrops 116 B2
Foy Hereford 97 F11
Foyers Highld 300 G4
Foynesfield Highld 301 D8
Fraddam Corn 2 C3
Fraddon Corn 5 D8
Fradley Staffs 152 G3
Fradley Junction
Staffs 152 G2
Fradswell Staffs 151 C9
Fraisthorpe E Yorks 218 G3
Framfield E Sus 37 C7
Framingham Earl
Norf 142 C5
Framingham Pigot
Norf 142 C5
Framlingham Suff 126 E5
Frampton Dorset 17 B8
Lincs 156 B6
Frampton Cotterell
S Glos 61 C7
Frampton Court
Glos 99 E10
Frampton End
S Glos 61 C7
Frampton Mansell
Glos 80 E6
Frampton on Severn
Glos 80 D2
Frampton West End
Lincs 174 G3
Framsden Suff 126 F3
Framwellgate Moor
Durham 233 C11
France Lynch Glos 80 E6
Franche Worcs 116 B6
Frandley Ches W 183 F10
Frankby Mers 182 D2
Frankfort Norf 160 E6
Franklands Gate
Hereford 97 B10
Frankley Worcs 133 G9
Frankley Green
Worcs 133 G9
Frankley Hill Worcs 117 B9
Frank's Bridge
Powys 114 F2
Frankton Warks 119 C8
Frankwell Shrops 149 G9
Frans Green Norf 160 G2
Frant E Sus 52 F5
Fraserburgh Aberds 303 C9
Frating Essex 107 G11
Frating Green
Essex 107 G11
Fratton Ptsmth 21 B9
Freasley Warks 134 D4
Freathy Corn 7 E8
Frecheville S Yorks 186 E5
Freckenham Suff 124 C3
Freckleton Lancs 194 B2
Fredley Sur 51 C7
Freebirch Derbys 186 G4
Freeby Leics 154 E6
Freefolk Hants 48 D3
Freehay Staffs 169 G8
Freeland Oxon 82 C6
Renfs 267 B9
Freeland Corner
Norf 160 F3
Freemantle Soton 32 E6
Freester Shetland 313 H6
Freethorpe Norf 143 B8
Free Town
Gtr Man 195 E10
Freezy Water London 86 F5
Freiston Lincs 174 G5
Freiston Shore
Lincs 174 G5
Fremington Devon 40 G4
N Yorks 223 F10
Frenchay S Glos 60 D6
Frenchbeer Devon 13 D9
Frenches Green
Essex 106 G4
Frenchmoor Hants 32 B3
French Street Kent 52 C3
Frenchwood Lancs 194 B4
Frenich Stirl 285 G8
Frensham Sur 49 E10
Frenze Norf 142 G2
Fresgoe Highld 310 C3
Freshbrook Swindon 62 C6
Freshfield Mers 193 F9
Freshford Bath 61 G9
Freshwater IoW 20 D2
Freshwater Bay IoW 20 D2
Freshwater East
Pembs 73 F8
Fressingfield Suff 126 B5
Freston Suff 108 D3
Freswick Highld 310 C7
Fretherne Glos 80 D2
Frettenham Norf 160 F4
Freuchie Fife 286 G6
Freuchies Angus 292 G4
Freystrop Pembs 73 C7
Friarn Som 43 F7
Friar Park W Mid 133 E10
Friars Cliff Dorset 19 C9
Friar's Gate E Sus 52 G3
Friar's Hill E Sus 38 E5
Friarton Perth 286 E5
Friday Bridge
Cambs 139 C9
Friday Hill London 86 G5
Friday Street E Sus 23 E10
Suff 126 G6
Suff 127 E7
Sur 50 D6
Fridaythorpe
E Yorks 208 B3
Friendly W Yorks 196 C5
Friern Barnet London 86 G3
Friesland Argyll 288 D3
Friesthorpe Lincs 189 E9
Frieston Lincs 172 F6
Frieth Bucks 84 G3
Frieze Hill Som 28 B2
Friezeland Notts 171 E7
Frilford Oxon 82 F6
Frilford Heath Oxon 82 F6
Frilsham W Berks 64 E4
Frimley Sur 49 B11
Frimley Green Sur 49 B11
Frimley Ridge Sur 49 B11
Frindsbury Medway 69 E8
Fring Norf 158 C4
Fringford Oxon 102 F2
Friningham Kent 53 B10
Frinkle Green Essex 106 C4
Frinsted Kent 53 B11
Frinton-on-Sea
Essex 108 G4
Friockheim Angus 287 C9
Friog Gwyn 146 G2
Frisby Leics 136 C4
Frisby on the Wreake
Leics 154 F3
Friskney Lincs 175 D7
Friskney Eaudyke
Lincs 175 D7
Friskney Tofts Lincs 175 E7
Friston E Sus 23 F8
Suff 127 E8
Fritchley Derbys 170 E5
Frith Kent 54 B2
Fritham Hants 32 E2
Frith Bank Lincs 174 F4
Frith Common
Worcs 116 D3
Frithelstock Devon 25 D7
Frithelstock Stone
Devon 25 D7
Frithend Hants 49 F10
Frith-hill Bucks 84 E6
Frith Hill Sur 50 E3
Frithsden Herts 85 D8
Frithville Lincs 174 E4
Frittenden Kent 53 E10
Frittiscombe Devon 8 G6
Fritton Norf 142 E4
Norf 143 C9
Norf 161 F8
Fritwell Oxon 101 F10
Frizinghall W Yorks 205 F8
Frizington Cumb 219 B10
Frizzeler's Green
Suff 124 E5
Frobost W Isles 297 J3
Frocester Glos 80 E3
Frochas Powys 148 G5
Frodesley Shrops 131 C10
Frodingham
N Lincs 199 E11
Frodsham Ches W 183 F8
Frogden Borders 263 D7
Frog End Cambs 123 F10
Cambs 123 G8
Froggatt Derbys 186 F2
Froghall Staffs 169 F8
Frogham Hants 31 E11
Kent 55 C9
Froghole Kent 52 C2
Frogholt Kent 55 F7
Frogland Cross
S Glos 60 C6
Frog Moor Swansea 56 C3
Frogmore Devon 8 G5
Hants 33 C11
Hants 49 B10
Herts 85 E11
Frognal S Ayrs 257 D8
Frognall Lincs 156 G3
Frogpool Corn 4 G5
Frog Pool Worcs 116 D5
Frogs' Green
Essex 105 D11
Frogshail Norf 160 B5
Frogwell Corn 6 B6
Frolesworth Leics 135 E10
Frome Som 45 D9
Fromebridge Glos 80 D3
Fromefield Som 45 D9
Frome St Quintin
Dorset 29 G9
Fromes Hill Hereford 98 B3
Fromington
Hereford 97 B10
Fron Denb 165 B9
Gwyn 145 B7
Gwyn 163 D8
Powys 113 D11
Powys 129 C8
Powys 130 C4
Powys 130 D3
Shrops 148 B5
Fron-Bache Denb 166 G2
Froncysyllte Wrex 166 G3
Fron-dêg Wrex 166 F3
Frongoch Gwyn 147 B8
Fron Isaf Wrex 166 G3
Frost Devon 26 F3
Frostenden Suff 143 G9
Frostenden Corner
Suff 143 G9
Frosterley Durham 232 D6
Frost Hill N Som 60 G2
Frostlane Hants 32 F6
Frost Row Norf 141 C10
Frotoft Orkney 314 D4
Froxfield C Beds 103 E9
Wilts 63 F9
Froxfield Green
Hants 34 B2
Froyle Hants 49 E9
Fryern Hill Hants 32 C6
Fryerning Essex 87 E10
Fryerns Essex 69 B8
Fryton N Yorks 216 E3
Fugglestone St Peter
Wilts 46 G6
Fulbeck Lincs 172 E6
Northumb 252 F5
Fulbourn Cambs 123 F10
Fulbrook Oxon 82 C3
Fulflood Hants 33 B7
Fulford Som 28 B2
Staffs 151 B9
York 207 D8
Fulham London 67 D8
Fulking W Sus 36 E2
Fullabrook Devon 40 E4
Fullarton Glasgow 268 C2
N Ayrs 257 B8
Fuller's End Essex 105 F10
Fuller's Moor
Ches W 167 E7
Fuller Street Essex 88 B2
Fullerton Hants 47 F11
Fulletby Lincs 190 G3
Fullshaw S Yorks 197 G8
Full Sutton
E Yorks 207 B10
Fullwell Cross
London 86 G6
Fullwood E Ayrs 267 E8
Gtr Man 196 F2
Fulmer Bucks 66 B3
Fulmodestone Norf 159 C9
Fulneck W Yorks 205 G10
Fulnetby Lincs 189 F9
Fulney Lincs 156 E5
Fulready Warks 100 B5
Fulshaw Park
Ches E 184 E4
Fulstone W Yorks 197 F7
Fulstow Lincs 190 B4
Fulthorpe Stockton 234 G4
Fulwell Oxon 101 G7
T&W 243 F9
Fulwood Lancs 202 G6
Som 28 C2
S Yorks 186 D4
Fundenhall Norf 142 D3
Fundenhall Street
Norf 142 D2
Funtington W Sus 22 B3
Funtley Hants 33 F9
Funtullich Perth 285 E11
Funzie Shetland 312 D8
Furley Devon 28 G3
Furnace Argyll 284 G4
Carms 74 E6
Carms 75 E8
Ceredig 128 D3
Highld 299 B9
Furnace End Warks 134 E4
Furnace Green
W Sus 51 F9
Furnace Wood
W Sus 51 F11
Furneaux Pelham
Herts 105 F8
Furner's Green E Sus 36 B6
Furness Vale Derbys 185 E8
Furneux Pelham
Herts 105 F8
Furnham Som 28 F4
Further Ford End
Essex 105 E9
Further Quarter
Kent 53 F11
Furtho Northants 102 C5
Furze Devon 25 B10
Furzebrook Dorset 18 E4
Furzedown Hants 32 B5
London 67 E9
Furzehill Devon 41 D8
Dorset 31 G8
Furze Hill Hants 31 E11
Furzeley Corner
Hants 33 E11
Furze Platt Windsor 65 C11
Furzey Lodge Hants 32 G5
Furzley Hants 32 D3
Furzton M Keynes 102 D6
Fyfett Som 28 E2
Fyfield Essex 87 D9
Glos 82 E2
Hants 47 D9
Oxon 82 F6
Wilts 63 F7
Wilts 63 G7
Fylingthorpe
N Yorks 227 D8
Fyning W Sus 34 C4
Fyvie Aberds 303 F7

G

Gabalfa Cardiff 59 D7
Gabhsann bho Dheas
W Isles 304 C6
Gabhsann bho Thuath
W Isles 304 C6
Gable Head Hants 21 B10
Gablon Highld 309 K7
Gabroc Hill E Ayrs 267 E9
Gadbrook Sur 51 D8
Gaddesby Leics 154 G3
Gadebridge Herts 85 D8
Gadfa Anglesey 179 D7
Gadfield Elm Worcs 98 E5
Gadlas Shrops 149 B7
Gadlys Rhondda 77 E7
Gadshill Kent 69 E8
Gaer Newport 59 B9
Powys 96 G3
Gaer-fawr Mon 78 F6
Gaerllwyd Mon 78 F6
Gaerwen Anglesey 179 G7
Gagingwell Oxon 101 F8
Gaick Lodge Highld 291 E9
Gailey Staffs 151 G8
Gailey Wharf Staffs 151 G8
Gainfield Oxon 82 F4
Gainford Durham 224 B3
Gain Hill Kent 53 D8
Gainsborough Lincs 188 C4
Suff 108 C3
Gainsford End
Essex 106 D4
Gairletter Argyll 276 E3
Gairloch Highld 299 B8
Gairlochy Highld 290 E3
Gairney Bank Perth 280 B2
Gairnshiel Lodge
Aberds 292 C4
Gaisgill Cumb 222 D2
Gaitsgill Cumb 230 B3
Galadean Borders 271 G11
Galashiels Borders 261 B11
Galdlys Flint 182 G2
Gale Gtr Man 196 D2
Galgate Lancs 202 B5
Galhampton Som 29 B10
Gallaberry
Dumfries 247 G11
Gallachoille Argyll 275 E8
Gallanach Argyll 288 C4
Argyll 289 G10
Highld 294 G6
Gallantry Bank
Ches E 167 E8
Gallatown Fife 280 C5
Galley Common
Warks 134 E6
Galleyend Essex 88 E2
Galley Hill Cambs 122 D6
Lincs 190 F6
Galleywood Essex 88 E2
Galligill Cumb 231 B11
Gallin Perth 285 C9
Gallovie Highld 291 E7
Gallowfauld Angus 287 C8
Gallowhill Glasgow 267 D11
Renfs 267 B9
Gallowhills Aberds 303 D10
Gallows Corner
London 87 G8
Gallowsgreen Torf 78 D3
Gallows Green
Essex 106 F2
Essex 107 F8
Staffs 169 G9
Worcs 117 E8
Gallows Inn Derbys 171 G7
Gallowstree Common
Oxon 65 C7
Galltair Highld 295 C10
Galltegfa Denb 165 D10
Gallt Melyd/Meliden
Denb 181 E9
Gallt-y-foel Gwyn 163 C9
Gallypot Street
E Sus 52 F3
Galmington Som 28 C2
Galmisdale Highld 294 G6
Galmpton Devon 8 G3
Torbay 9 D7
Galon Uchaf M Tydf 77 D9
Galphay N Yorks 214 E5
Galston E Ayrs 258 B2
Galtrigill Highld 296 F7
Gam Corn 11 F7
Gamble Hill
W Yorks 205 G11
Gamblesby Cumb 231 D8
Gamble's Green
Essex 88 C3
Gamelsby Cumb 239 G7
Gamesley Derbys 185 C8
Gamlingay Cambs 122 G4
Gamlingay Cinques
Cambs 122 G4
Gamlingay Great Heath
Cambs 122 G4
Gammaton Devon 25 B7
Gammaton Moor
Devon 25 C7
Gammersgill
N Yorks 213 C11
Gamston Notts 154 B2
Notts 188 F2
Ganarew Hereford 79 B8
Ganavan Argyll 289 F10
Ganders Green Glos 98 G4
Gang Corn 6 B6
Ganllwyd Gwyn 146 E4
Gannetts Dorset 30 D3
Gannochy Angus 293 F7
Perth 286 E5
Gansclet Highld 310 E7
Ganstead E Yorks 209 G9
Ganthorpe N Yorks 216 E3
Ganton N Yorks 217 D9
Gants Hill London 68 B2
Ganwick Corner
Herts 86 F3
Gaodhail Argyll 289 F8
Gappah Devon 14 F3
Garafad Highld 298 C4
Garamor Highld 295 F8
Garbat Highld 300 C4
Garbhallt Argyll 275 D11
Garboldisham
Norf 141 G10
Garbole Highld 301 G7
Garden City
Bl Gwent 77 D11
Flint 166 B4
Gardeners Green
Wokingham 65 F10
Gardenstown
Aberds 303 C7
Garden Village
Swansea 56 B5
S Yorks 186 B3
Wrex 166 E4
W Yorks 206 G4
Garderhouse
Shetland 313 J5
Gardham E Yorks 208 E5
Gardie Shetland 312 D7
Gardin Shetland 312 G6
Gare Hill Som 45 E9
Garelochhead
Argyll 276 C4
Garford Oxon 82 F6
Garforth W Yorks 206 G4
Gargrave N Yorks 204 C4
Gargunnock Stirl 278 C4
Garizim Conwy 179 F11
Garker Corn 5 E10
Garlandhayes
Devon 27 D11
Garlands Cumb 239 G10
Garleffin S Ayrs 244 G3
Garlic Street Norf 142 G4
Garlieston Dumfries 236 E6
Garliford Devon 26 B3
Garlinge Kent 71 F10
Garlinge Green Kent 54 C6
Garlogie Aberds 293 C9
Garmelow Staffs 150 D5
Garmond Aberds 303 D8
Garmondsway
Durham 234 E2
Garmony Argyll 289 E8
Garmouth Moray 302 C3
Garmston Shrops 132 B2
Garn Powys 130 G2
Garnant Carms 75 C11
Garndiffaith Torf 78 E3
Garndolbenmaen
Gwyn 163 G7
Garnedd Conwy 164 E2
Garnett Bridge
Cumb 221 F10
Garnetts Essex 87 B10
Garnfadryn Gwyn 144 C5
Garnkirk N Lnrk 268 B3
Garnlydan Bl Gwent 77 C11
Garnsgate Lincs 157 E8
Garnswllt Swansea 75 D10
Garn-swllt Swansea 75 D10
Garn-yr-erw Torf 78 C2
Garrabost W Isles 304 E7
Garrachra Argyll 275 E11
Garra Eallabus
Argyll 274 F3
Garralburn Moray 302 D4
Garraron Argyll 275 C9
Garras Corn 2 E6
Garreg Flint 181 F10
Gwyn 163 G10
Garrets Green
W Mid 134 F2
Garrick Perth 286 F2
Garrigill Cumb 231 C10
Garrison Stirl 285 G7
Garriston N Yorks 224 G3
Garroch Dumfries 246 G3
Garrogie Lodge
Highld 291 B7
Garros Highld 298 C4
Garrow Perth 286 C2
Garrowhill Glasgow 268 C3
Garrygualach Highld 290 C3
Garryhorn Dumfries 246 E2
Garsdale Cumb 212 B4
Garsdale Head
Cumb 222 G5
Garsdon Wilts 62 B3
Garshall Green
Staffs 151 C9
Garsington Oxon 83 E9
Garstang Lancs 202 D5
Garston Herts 85 F10
Mers 182 E6
Garswood Mers 183 B9
Gartachoil Stirl 277 C10
Gartbreck Argyll 254 B3
Gartcosh N Lnrk 268 B3
Garth Bridgend 57 C11
Ceredig 128 G2
Flint 181 E10
Gwyn 179 G9
Newport 59 B9
Newport 78 G4
Perth 285 B11
Powys 95 B9
Powys 114 C5
Shetland 313 H4
Shetland 313 H6
Wrex 166 G3
Garthamlock
Glasgow 268 B3
Garthbeg Highld 291 B7
Garthbrengy Powys 95 E10
Garthdee Aberdeen 293 C11
Gartheli Ceredig 111 F11
Garthmyl Powys 130 D3
Garthorpe Leics 154 E6
N Lincs 199 D11
Garth Owen Powys 130 E2
Garth Row Cumb 221 F10
Garth Trevor Wrex 166 G3
Gartlea N Lnrk 268 C5
Gartloch Glasgow 268 B3
Gartly Aberds 302 F5
Gartmore Stirl 277 B10
Gartmore Ho Stirl 277 B10
Gartnagrenach
Argyll 255 B8
Gartness N Lnrk 268 C5
Stirl 277 D10
Gartocharn W Dunb 277 D8
Garton E Yorks 209 F11
Garton-on-the-Wolds
E Yorks 208 B5
Gartsherrie N Lnrk 268 B4
Gartur Stirl 277 B11
Gartymore Highld 311 H4
Garvald E Loth 281 G11
Garvamore Highld 291 D7
Garvard Argyll 274 D4
Garvault Hotel
Highld 308 F7
Garve Highld 300 C3
Garvestone Norf 141 B10
Garvock Aberds 293 F9
Invclyd 276 G5
Garvock Hill Fife 280 D2
Garway Hereford 97 G9
Garway Hill Hereford 97 F8
Gaskan Highld 289 B9
Gasper Wilts 45 G9
Gastard Wilts 61 F11
Gasthorpe Norf 141 G9
Gaston Green Essex 87 B7
Gatacre Park Shrops 132 F5
Gatcombe IoW 20 D5
Gateacre Mers 182 D6
Gatebeck Cumb 211 B10
Gate Burton Lincs 188 E4
Gateford Notts 187 E9
Gateford Common
Notts 187 E9
Gateforth N Yorks 198 B5
Gatehead E Ayrs 257 B9
Gate Helmsley
N Yorks 207 B9
Gatehouse Northumb 251 F7
Gatehouse of Fleet
Dumfries 237 D8
Gatelawbridge
Dumfries 247 D10
Gateley Norf 159 E9
Gatenby N Yorks 214 B6
Gatesgarth Cumb 220 B3
Gateshead T&W 243 E7
Gatesheath Ches W 167 C7
Gateside Aberds 293 B8
Angus 287 C8
Dumfries 248 E4
E Renf 267 D9
Fife 286 G5
N Ayrs 267 E7
Shetland 312 F4
Gatewen Wrex 166 E4
Gatherley Devon 12 E3
Gathurst Gtr Man 194 F4
Gatlas Newport 78 G4
Gatley End Cambs 104 C5
Gtr Man 184 D4
Gatton Sur 51 C9
Gattonside Borders 262 B2
Gatwick Glos 80 C2
Gatwick Airport
W Sus 51 E9
Gaufron Powys 113 D9
Gaulby Leics 136 C3
Gauldry Fife 287 E7
Gauntons Bank
Ches E 167 F9
Gaunt's Common
Dorset 31 F8
Gaunt's Earthcott
S Glos 60 C6
Gaunt's End Essex 105 F10
Gautby Lincs 189 G11
Gavinton Borders 272 E5
Gawber S Yorks 197 F10
Gawcott Bucks 102 E3
Gawsworth Ches E 168 B5
Gawthorpe W Yorks 197 C9
W Yorks 197 D7
Gawthrop Cumb 212 B3
Gawthwaite Cumb 210 C5
Gay Bowers Essex 88 E3
Gaydon Warks 119 G7
Gayfield Orkney 314 A4
Gayhurst M Keynes 103 B7

Gayle N Yorks 213 B7
Gayles N Yorks 224 D2
Gay Street W Sus 35 C9
Gayton Mers 182 E3
Norf 158 F4
Northants 120 G4
Staffs 151 D9
Gayton Engine
Lincs 191 D7
Gayton le Marsh
Lincs 190 E6
Gayton le Wold
Lincs 190 D2
Gayton Thorpe Norf 158 F4
Gaywood Norf 158 E2
Gaza Shetland 312 F5
Gazeley Suff 124 E4
Geanies House
Highld 301 B8
Gearraidh Bhailteas
W Isles 297 J3
Gearraidh Bhaird
W Isles 304 F5
Gearraidh Dubh
W Isles 296 F4
Gearraidh na h-Aibhne
W Isles 304 E4
Gearraidh na Monadh
W Isles 297 K3
Geàrraidh Sheilidh
W Isles 297 J3
Geary Highld 298 C2
Geat Wolford Warks 100 E4
Geddes House
Highld 301 D8
Gedding Suff 125 F9
Geddington
Northants 137 G7
Gedgrave Hall Suff 109 B8
Gedintailor Highld 295 B7
Gedling Notts 171 G10
Gedney Lincs 157 E8
Gedney Broadgate
Lincs 157 E8
Gedney Drove End
Lincs 157 D9
Gedney Dyke Lincs 157 D8
Gedney Hill Lincs 156 G6
Gee Cross Gtr Man 185 C7
Geeston Rutland 137 C9
Gegin Wrex 166 E3
Geilston Argyll 276 F6
Geinas Denb 165 B9
Geirinis W Isles 297 G3
Geise Highld 310 C5
Geisiadar W Isles 304 E3
Geldeston Norf 143 E7
Gell Conwy 164 B5
Gelli Pembs 73 B9
Rhondda 77 G7
Gellideg M Tydf 77 D8
Gellifor Denb 165 C10
Gelligaer Caerph 77 F10
Gelli-gaer Neath 57 C9
Gelligroes Caerph 77 G11
Gelli-hôf Caerph 77 F11
Gellilydan Gwyn 146 B3
Gellinud Neath 76 E2
Gellinudd Neath 76 E2
Gellyburn Perth 286 D4
Gellygron Neath 76 E2
Gellywen Carms 92 G5
Gelsmoor Leics 153 F8
Gelston Dumfries 237 D9
Lincs 172 G6
Gembling E Yorks 209 B8
Gemini Warr 183 C9
Gendros Swansea 56 B6
Genesis Green Suff 124 F4
Gentleshaw Staffs 151 G11
Geocrab W Isles 305 J3
Georgefield
Dumfries 249 E7
George Green Bucks 66 C4
Georgeham Devon 40 F3
George Nympton
Devon 26 C2
Georgetown
Bl Gwent 77 D10
Georgia Corn 1 B5
Gergask Highld 291 D8
Gerlan Gwyn 163 B10
Germansweek Devon 12 C4
Germiston Glasgow 268 B2
Germoe Corn 2 D3
Gernon Bushes Essex 87 E7
Gerrans Corn 3 B9
Gerrard's Bromley
Staffs 150 C5
Gerrards Cross Bucks 66 B4
Gerrick Redcar 226 C4
Geseilfa Powys 129 E8
Gestingthorpe
Essex 106 D6
Gesto Ho Highld 294 B5
Geuffordd Powys 148 G4
Geufron Denb 166 G2
Gibbet Hill Warks 135 G10
W Mid 118 C6
Gibb Hill Ches W 183 F10
Gibbshill Dumfries 237 B9
Gib Heath W Mid 133 F11
Gibraltar Beds 103 B10
Bucks 84 C3
Kent 55 F8
Gibralter Oxon 83 B7
Gibshill Invclyd 276 G6
Gibsmere Notts 172 F2
Giddeahall Wilts 61 E11
Giddy Green Dorset 18 D2
Gidea Park London 68 B4
Gidleigh Devon 13 D9
Giffard Park
M Keynes 103 C7
Giffnock E Renf 267 D11
Gifford E Loth 271 B10
Giffordland N Ayrs 266 F5
Giffordtown Fife 286 F6
Gigg Gtr Man 195 F10
Giggetty Staffs 133 E7
Giggleswick
N Yorks 212 G6
Giggshill Sur 67 F7
Gignog Pembs 91 G7
Gilberdyke E Yorks 199 B10
Gilbert's Coombe Corn 4 G3
Gilbert's End Worcs 98 C6
Gilbert's Green
Warks 118 C2
Gilbertstone W Mid 134 G2
Gilbert Street Hants 49 G7
Gilchriston E Loth 271 B9
Gilcrux Cumb 229 D8
Gildersome
W Yorks 197 B8
Gildersome Street
W Yorks 197 B8
Gildingwells
S Yorks 187 D9
Gilesgate Durham 233 C11
Gilesgate Moor
Durham 233 C11
Gileston V Glam 58 F4
Gilfach Caerph 77 F11
Hereford 96 E6
Gilfach Goch
Rhondda 58 B3
Gilfachrheda
Ceredig 111 F8
Gilgarran Cumb 228 G6
Gill N Yorks 204 E5
Gillamoor N Yorks 216 B3
Gillan Corn 3 E7
Gillar's Green Mers 183 B7
Gillbank Cumb 221 F7
Gillbent Gtr Man 184 E5
Gillen Highld 298 D2
Gillesbie Dumfries 248 E5
Gilling East N Yorks 216 D2
Gillingham Dorset 30 B4
Medway 69 F9
Norf 143 E8
Gilling West
N Yorks 224 D3
Gillmoss Mers 182 B6
Gillock Highld 310 D6
Gillow Heath Staffs 168 D5
Gills Highld 310 B7
Gill's Green Kent 53 G9
Gillway Staffs 134 C4
Gilmanscleuch
Borders 261 E8
Gilmerton Edin 270 B5
Perth 286 E2
Gilmonby Durham 223 C9
Gilmorton Leics 135 F11
Gilmourton S Lnrk 268 G3
Gilnow Gtr Man 195 F8
Gilroyd S Yorks 197 G10
Gilsland Northumb 240 D4
Gilsland Spa Cumb 240 D4
Gilson Warks 134 E3
Gilstead W Yorks 205 F8
Gilston Borders 271 D8
Herts 86 C6
Gilston Park Herts 86 C6
Giltbrook Notts 171 F7
Gilver's Lane Worcs 98 C6
Gilwell Park Essex 86 F5
Gilwern Mon 78 C2
Gimingham Norf 160 B5
Ginclough Ches E 185 F7
Ginger's Green
E Sus 23 C10
Giosla W Isles 304 F3
Gipping Suff 125 E11
Gipsey Bridge Lincs 174 F3
Gipsy Row Suff 107 D11
Gipsyville Hull 200 B5
Gipton W Yorks 206 F2
Gipton Wood
W Yorks 206 F2
Girdle Toll N Ayrs 266 G6
Girlington W Yorks 205 G8
Girlsta Shetland 313 H6
Girsby Lincs 190 D2
N Yorks 225 D7
Girt Som 29 C10
Girtford C Beds 104 B3
C Beds 122 G3
Girthon Dumfries 237 D8
Girton Cambs 123 E8
Notts 172 B4
Girvan S Ayrs 244 D5
Gisburn Lancs 204 D2
Gisleham Suff 143 F10
Gislingham Suff 125 C11
Gissing Norf 142 F2
Gittisham Devon 15 B8
Givons Grove Sur 51 C7
Glachavoil Argyll 275 F11
Glackmore Highld 300 D6
Glack of Midthird
Moray 302 E3
Gladestry Powys 114 F4
Gladsmuir E Loth 281 G9
Glaichbea Highld 300 F5
Glais Swansea 76 E2
Glaisdale N Yorks 226 D5
Glame Highld 298 E5
Glamis Angus 287 C7
Glan Adda Gwyn 179 G9
Glanafon Pembs 73 B7
Glanaman Carms 75 C11
Glan-Conwy Conwy 164 E4
Glandford Norf 177 E8
Glan-Duar Carms 93 C10
Glandwr Caerph 78 E2
Pembs 92 F3
Glan-Dwyfach
Gwyn 163 G7
Glandy Cross Carms 92 F2
Glandyfi Ceredig 128 D3
Glan Gors Anglesey 179 F7
Glangrwyney Powys 78 B2
Glanhanog Powys 129 D8
Glanmule Powys 130 E3
Glanrafon Ceredig 128 G2
Glanrhyd Gwyn 144 B5
Pembs 92 C2
Glan-rhyd Gwyn 163 D7
Powys 76 D3
Glantlees Northumb 252 B4
Glanton Northumb 264 G3
Glanton Pike
Northumb 264 G3
Glan-traeth
Anglesey 178 F3
Glantwymyn/Cemmaes
Road Powys 128 C6
Glanvilles Wootton
Dorset 29 F11
Glanwern Ceredig 128 F2
Glanwydden Conwy 180 E4
Glan-y-don Flint 181 F11
Glan y Ffer/Ferryside
Carms 74 C5
Glan-y-llyn Rhondda 58 C6
Glan-y-môr Carms 74 C4
Glan-y-nant Caerph 77 F10
Powys 129 G8
Glan-yr-afon
Anglesey 179 E10
Flint 181 E10
Gwyn 164 G6
Gwyn 165 G8
Shrops 148 E4
Glan-y-wern Gwyn 146 C2
Glapthorn
Northants 137 E10
Glapwell Derbys 171 B7
Glas-allt Shiel
Aberds 292 E4
Glasbury Powys 96 D3
Glaschoil Highld 301 F10
Glascoed Denb 181 G7
Mon 78 E4
Powys 129 F11
Powys 148 G2
Wrex 166 E3
Glascorrie Aberds 292 D5
Perth 286 E2
Glascote Staffs 134 C4
Glascwm Powys 114 G3
Glasdir Flint 181 E10
Glasdrum Argyll 284 C4
Glasfryn Conwy 164 E6
Glasgoed Ceredig 92 B6
Glasgoforest
Aberds 293 B10
Glasgow Glasgow 267 B11
Glashvin Highld 298 C4
Glasinfryn Gwyn 163 B9
Glasllwch Newport 59 B9
Glasnacardoch
Highld 295 F8
Glasnakille Highld 295 D7
Glasphein Highld 297 G7
Glaspwll Powys 128 D4
Glassburn Highld 300 F3
Glassenbury Kent 53 F8
Glasserton Dumfries 236 F6
Glassford S Lnrk 268 F4
Glassgreen Moray 302 C2
Glass Houghton
W Yorks 198 C2
Glasshouse Glos 98 G4
Glasshouse Hill Glos 98 G4
Glasshouses
N Yorks 214 G3
Glasslie Fife 286 G6
Glasson Cumb 228 D6
Cumb 239 E7
Lancs 202 B4
Glassonby Cumb 231 D7
Glasterlaw Angus 287 B9
Glaston Rutland 137 C7
Glastonbury Som 44 F4
Glatton Cambs 138 F3
Glazebrook Warr 183 C11
Glazebury Warr 183 B11
Glazeley Shrops 132 F4
Gleadless S Yorks 186 E5
Gleadless Valley
S Yorks 186 E5
Gleadmoss Ches E 168 B4
Gleadsmoss Ches E 168 B4
Gleanhead
Dumfries 245 G10
Gleann Tholàstaidh
W Isles 304 D7
Gleaston Cumb 210 E5
Glebe Hants 33 D9
Shetland 313 J6
T&W 243 F8
Glecknabae Argyll 275 G11
Gledhow W Yorks 206 F2
Gledrid Shrops 148 B5
Gleiniant Powys 129 E9
Glemsford Suff 106 B6
Glen Dumfries 237 B10
Dumfries 237 D7
Glenallachie Moray 302 E2
Glenalmond College
Perth 286 E3
Glenalmond Ho
Perth 286 E3
Glenamachrie
Argyll 289 G11
Glenample Stirl 285 E9
Glenancross Highld 295 F8
Glenapp Castle
S Ayrs 244 G3
Glenaros Ho Argyll 289 E7
Glen Auldyn IoM 192 C5
Glenbarr Argyll 255 D7
Glenbeg Highld 289 C7
Highld 301 G10
Glen Bernisdale
Highld 298 E4
Glenbervie Aberds 293 E9
Glenboig N Lnrk 268 B4
Glenborrodale
Highld 289 C8
Glenbranter Argyll 276 B2
Glenbreck Borders 260 E3
Glenbrein Lodge
Highld 290 B6
Glenbrittle House
Highld 294 C6
Glenbrook Edin 270 B2
Glenbuchat Castle
Aberds 292 B5
Glenbuchat Lodge
Aberds 292 B5
Glenbuck E Ayrs 259 D7
Glenburn Renfs 267 C9
Glenbyre Argyll 289 G7
Glencalvie Lodge
Highld 309 L4
Glencanisp Lodge
Highld 307 G6
Glencaple
Dumfries 237 C11
Glencarron Lodge
Highld 299 D10
Glencarse Perth 286 E5
Glencassley Castle
Highld 309 J4
Glencat Aberds 293 D7
Glenceitlein Highld 284 C5
Glencoe Highld 284 B4
Glencraig Fife 280 B3
Glencripesdale
Highld 289 D8
Glencrosh Dumfries 247 F7
Glendavan Ho
Aberds 292 C6
Glendearg Borders 262 B2
Glendevon Perth 286 G3
Glendoebeg Highld 290 C6
Glendoe Lodge
Highld 290 C6
Glendoick Perth 286 E6
Glendoll Lodge
Angus 292 F4
Glendoune S Ayrs 244 D5
Glenduckie Fife 286 F6
Glendye Lodge
Aberds 293 E8
Gleneagles Hotel
Perth 286 F3
Gleneagles House
Perth 286 G3
Glenearn Perth 286 F5
Glenegedale Argyll 254 B4
Glenelg Highld 295 D10
Glenernie Moray 301 E10
Glenfarg Perth 286 F5
Glenfarquhar Lodge
Aberds 293 E9
Glenferness House
Highld 301 E9
Glenfeshie Lodge
Highld 291 D10
Glenfiddich Lodge
Moray 302 F3
Glenfield Leics 135 B10
Glenfinnan Highld 295 G10
Glenfinnan Lodge
Highld 295 G11
Glenfintaig Ho
Highld 290 E4
Glenfoot Perth 286 F5
Glenfyne Lodge
Argyll 284 F6
Glengap Dumfries 237 D8
Glengarnock
N Ayrs 266 E6
Glengolly Highld 310 C5
Glengorm Castle
Argyll 288 D6
Glengoulandie
Perth 285 B11
Glengrasco Highld 298 E4
Glenhead Farm
Angus 292 G4
Glen Ho Borders 261 C7
Glenholt Plym 7 C10
Glenhoul Dumfries 246 F4
Glenhurich Highld 289 C10
Glenkerry Borders 261 G7
Glenkiln Dumfries 237 B10
Glenkindie Aberds 292 B6
Glenlair Dumfries 237 B9
Glenlatterach
Moray 301 D11
Glenlee Dumfries 246 G4
Glenleigh Park E Sus 38 F2
Glenleraig Highld 306 F6
Glenlichorn Perth 285 F11
Glenlicht Ho Highld 290 B2
Glenlivet Moray 301 G11
Glenlochar Dumfries 237 C9
Glenlochsie Perth 292 F2
Glenlocksie Lodge
Perth 292 F2
Glenloig N Ayrs 255 D10
Glenlomond Perth 286 G5
Glenluce Dumfries 236 D4
Glenlussa Ho Argyll 255 E8
Glenmallan Argyll 276 B5
Glenmark Angus 292 E6
Glenmarkie Lodge
Angus 292 G4
Glenmarksie Highld 300 D3
Glenmavis N Lnrk 268 B4
W Loth 269 B9
Glenmaye IoM 192 E3
Glenmayne
Borders 261 C11
Glenmeanie Highld 300 D2
Glenmidge Dumfries 247 F9
Glenmoidart Ho
Highld 289 B9
Glen Mona IoM 192 D5
Glen Mor Highld 295 B10
Glenmore Argyll 275 B9
Argyll 275 G11
Highld 298 E4
Glenmore Lodge
Highld 291 C11
Glenmoy Angus 292 G6
Glen Nevis House
Highld 290 F3
Glennoe Argyll 284 D4
Glen of Newmill
Moray 302 D4
Glenogil Angus 292 G6
Glenowen Pembs 73 D7
Glen Parva Leics 135 D11
Glenprosen Lodge
Angus 292 G4
Glenprosen Village
Angus 292 G5
Glenquaich Lodge
Perth 286 D2
Glenquiech Angus 292 G6
Glenquithlie Aberds 303 C8
Glenrath Borders 260 C6
Glenrazie Dumfries 236 C5
Glenreasdell Mains
Argyll 255 B9
Glenree N Ayrs 255 E10
Glenridding Cumb 221 B7
Glenrosa N Ayrs 256 B2
Glenrossal Highld 309 J4
Glenrothes Fife 286 G6
Glensanda Highld 289 E10
Glensaugh Aberds 293 F8
Glensburgh Falk 279 E8
Glenshero Lodge
Highld 291 D7
Glenshoe Lodge
Perth 292 G3
Glen Sluain Argyll 275 D11
Glenstockadale
Dumfries 236 C2
Glenstriven Argyll 275 F11
Glentaggart S Lnrk 259 D8
Glen Tanar House
Aberds 292 D6
Glentarkie Perth 286 F5
Glenternie Borders 260 B6
Glentham Lincs 189 C8
Glentirranmuir Stirl 278 C3
Glenton Aberds 302 G6
Glentress Borders 261 B7
Glentromie Lodge
Highld 291 D9
Glen Trool Lodge
Dumfries 245 G10
Glentrool Village
Dumfries 236 B5
Glentruan IoM 192 B5
Glentruim House
Highld 291 D8
Glentworth Lincs 188 D6
Glenuaig Lodge
Highld 299 E11
Glenuig Highld 289 B8
Glenure Argyll 284 C4
Glenurquhart Highld 301 C7
Glen Vic Askil
Highld 298 E3
Glenview Argyll 284 E5
Glen Village Falk 279 F7
Glen Vine IoM 192 E4
Glespin S Lnrk 259 D8
Gletness Shetland 313 H6
Glewstone Hereford 97 G11
Glinton Pboro 138 B3
Globe Town London 67 C11
Glodwick Gtr Man 196 G2
Glogue Pembs 92 E4
Glooston Leics 136 D4
Glororum Northumb 264 C5
Glossop Derbys 185 C8
Gloster Hill
Northumb 253 C7
Gloucester Glos 80 B4
Gloup Shetland 312 C7
Gloweth Corn 4 G5
Glusburn N Yorks 204 E6
Glutt Lodge Highld 310 F3
Glutton Bridge
Staffs 169 B9
Gluvian Corn 5 C8
Glympton Oxon 101 G8
Glyn Mon 79 F7
Powys 129 F8
Glynarthen Ceredig 92 B6
Glynbrochan Powys 129 G8
Glyn Castle Neath 76 E4
Glyn-Ceiriog Wrex 148 B4
Glyncoch Rhondda 77 G9
Glyncoed Bl Gwent 77 C11
Glyncorrwg Neath 57 B11
Glyn-cywarch Gwyn 146 C2
Glynde E Sus 23 D7
Glyndebourne E Sus 23 C7
Glyndyfrdwy Denb 165 G10
Glynedd/Glyn neath
Neath 76 D5
Glyne Gap E Sus 38 F3
Glyn Etwy Bl Gwent 77 D11
Glynhafren Powys 129 G7
Glynllan Bridgend 58 B2
Glynmorlas Shrops 148 B6
Glyn-neath/Glynedd
Neath 76 D5
Glynogwr Bridgend 58 B3
Glyntaff Rhondda 58 B5
Glyntawe Powys 76 B4
Gnosall Staffs 150 E6
Gnosall Heath
Staffs 150 E6
Goadby Leics 136 D4
Goadby Marwood
Leics 154 D5
Goatacre Wilts 62 D4
Goatham Green
E Sus 38 C4
Goathill Dorset 29 D11
Goathland N Yorks 226 E6
Goathurst Som 43 G9
Goathurst Common
Kent 52 C3
Goat Lees Kent 54 D4
Gobernuisgach Lodge
Highld 308 E4
Gobernuisgeach
Highld 310 F3
Gobhaig W Isles 305 H2
Gobley Hole Hants 48 D6
Gobowen Shrops 148 C6
Godalming Sur 50 E3
Goddards Bucks 84 G3
Goddard's Corner
Suff 126 D5
Goddard's Green
Kent 53 G10
W Berks 65 F7
Goddards' Green
W Sus 36 C3
Godden Green Kent 52 B5
Goddington London 68 F3
Godley Gtr Man 185 B7
Godleybrook Staffs 169 G7
Godley Hill Gtr Man 185 C7
Godleys Green E Sus 36 D5
Godmanchester
Cambs 122 C4
Godmanstone Dorset 17 B9
Godmersham Kent 54 C5
Godney Som 44 E3
Godolphin Cross Corn 2 C4
Godre'r-graig Neath 76 D3
God's Blessing Green
Dorset 31 G8
Godshill Hants 31 E11
IoW 20 E6
Godstone Sur 51 C10
Godswinscroft Hants 19 B9
Godwell Devon 8 D2
Godwick Norf 159 E8
Godwinscroft Hants 19 B9
Goetre Mon 78 D4
Goferydd Anglesey 178 E2
Goff's Oak Herts 86 E4
Gogar Edin 280 G3
Goginan Ceredig 128 G3
Goirtean a'Chladaich
Highld 290 F2
Golan Gwyn 163 G8
Golant Corn 6 E2
Golberdon Corn 12 G2
Golborne Gtr Man 183 B10
Golcar W Yorks 196 D6
Golch Flint 181 F11
Goldcliff Newport 59 C11
Golden Balls Oxon 83 F9
Golden Cross E Sus 23 C8
E Sus 23 C10
Golden Green Kent 52 D6
Golden Grove Carms 75 B9
Goldenhill Stoke 168 E5
Golden Hill Bristol 60 D5
Hants 19 B11
Pembs 73 E7
Pembs 91 G9
Golden Park Devon 24 C2
Golden Pot Hants 49 E8
Golden Valley
Derbys 170 E6
Glos 99 G8
Hereford 98 B3
Golder Field
Hereford 115 E11
Golders Green
London 67 B9
Goldfinch Bottom
W Berks 64 G4
Goldhanger Essex 88 D6
Gold Hill Dorset 30 E4
Norf 139 E10
Golding Shrops 131 C10
Goldington Beds 121 G11
Goldsborough
N Yorks 206 B3
N Yorks 226 C6
Gold's Cross Bath 60 G5
Golds Green W Mid 133 E9
Goldsithney Corn 2 C2
Goldstone Shrops 150 D4
Goldthorn Park
W Mid 133 D8
Goldthorpe S Yorks 198 G3
Goldworthy Devon 24 C5
Golford Kent 53 F9
Golftyn Flint 182 G3
Golgotha Kent 55 D9
Gollanfield Highld 301 D8
Gollawater Corn 4 E5
Gollinglith Foot
N Yorks 214 C3
Golly Wrex 166 D4
Golsoncott Som 42 F4
Golspie Highld 311 J2
Golval Highld 310 C2
Golynos Torf 78 E3
Gomeldon Wilts 47 F7
Gomersal W Yorks 197 B8
Gometra Ho Argyll 288 E5
Gomshall Sur 50 D5
Gonalston Notts 171 F11
Gonamena Corn 11 G11
Gonerby Hill Foot
Lincs 155 B8
Gonfirth Shetland 313 G5
Good Easter Essex 87 C10
Gooderstone Norf 140 C5
Goodleigh Devon 40 G6
Goodley Stock Kent 52 C2
Goodmanham
E Yorks 208 E3
Goodmayes London 68 B3
Goodnestone Kent 55 C9
Kent 70 G4
Goodrich Hereford 79 B9
Goodrington Torbay 9 D7
Good's Green
Worcs 132 G5
Goodshaw Lancs 195 B10
Goodshaw Chapel
Lancs 195 B10
Goodshaw Fold
Lancs 195 B10
Goodstone Devon 13 G11
Goodwick/Wdig
Pembs 91 D8
Goodworth Clatford
Hants 47 E11
Goodyers End
Warks 134 F6
Goodyhills Cumb 229 B8
Goole E Yorks 199 C8
Goom's Hill Worcs 117 G10
Goonabarn Corn 5 E9
Goonbell Corn 4 F4
Goon Gumpas Corn 4 G4
Goonhavern Corn 4 E5
Goonhusband Corn 2 D5
Goonlaze Corn 2 B6
Goonown Corn 4 E4
Goonpiper Corn 3 B8
Goonvrea Corn 4 F4
Gooseberry Green
Essex 87 F11
Goose Eye W Yorks 204 E6
Gooseford Devon 13 C9
Goose Green
Cumb 211 C10
Essex 108 F2
Gtr Man 194 G5
Hants 32 F4
Herts 86 D5
Kent 52 C6
Kent 53 F10
Lancs 194 C3
Norf 142 F2
S Glos 61 C8
W Sus 34 C3
W Sus 35 D10
Gooseham Mill
Devon 24 D2
Goosehill W Yorks 197 C11
Goose Hill Hants 64 G4
Goosehill Green
Worcs 117 E8
Goosemoor Staffs 150 F6
Goosemoor Green
Staffs 151 G11
Goosenford Som 28 B2
Goose Pool Hereford 97 D9
Goosewell Devon 40 D5
Goosey Oxon 82 G5
Goosnargh Lancs 203 F7
Goostrey Ches E 184 G3
Gorbals Glasgow 267 C11
Gorcott Hill Warks 117 D11
Gord Shetland 313 L6
Gorddinog Conwy 179 G11
Gordon Borders 272 G2
Gordonbush Highld 311 J2
Gordonsburgh
Moray 302 C4
Gordonstoun
Moray 301 C11
Gordonstown
Aberds 302 D5
Aberds 303 F7
Gore Dorset 29 D9
Kent 55 B10
Gorebridge Midloth 270 C6
Gore Cross Wilts 46 C4
Gore End Hants 64 G2
Gorefield Cambs 157 G8
Gorehill W Sus 35 C7
Gore Pit Essex 88 B5
Gore Street Kent 71 F9
Gorgie Edin 280 G4
Gorhambury Herts 85 D10
Goring Oxon 64 C6
Goring-by-Sea
W Sus 35 G10
Goring Heath Oxon 65 D7
Gorleston-on-Sea
Norf 143 C10
Gornalwood W Mid 133 E8
Gorrachie Aberds 303 D7
Gorran Churchtown
Corn 5 G9
Gorran Haven Corn 5 G10
Gorran High Lanes
Corn 5 G9
Gorrenberry
Borders 249 D11
Gorrig Ceredig 93 C8
Gorse Covert Warr 183 C11
Gorsedd Flint 181 F11
Gorse Hill Gtr Man 184 B4
Swindon 63 B7
Gorseinon Swansea 56 B5
Gorseness Orkney 314 E4
Gorsethorpe Notts 171 B9
Gorseybank Derbys 170 E3
Gorsgoch Ceredig 111 G9
Gorslas Carms 75 C9
Gorsley Glos 98 F3
Gorsley Common
Hereford 98 F3
Gorsley Ley Staffs 133 B11
Gorstage Ches W 183 G10
Gorstan Highld 300 C3
Gorstanvorran
Highld 289 B10
Gorstella Ches W 166 C5
Gorsteyhill Ches E 168 E2
Gorst Hill Worcs 116 C4
Gorstyhill Staffs 168 E2
Gorsty Hill Staffs 151 D11
Gortan Argyll 274 G3
Gortantaoid Argyll 274 F4
Gortenacullish
Highld 295 G8
Gorteneorn Highld 289 C8
Gortenfern Highld 289 C8
Gortinanane Argyll 255 C8
Gorton Gtr Man 184 B5
Gortonallister
N Ayrs 256 D2
Gosbeck Suff 126 F3
Gosberton Lincs 156 C4
Gosberton Cheal
Lincs 156 D4
Gosberton Clough
Lincs 156 D3
Goscote W Mid 133 C10
Goseley Dale
Derbys 152 E6
Gosfield Essex 106 F5
Gosford Hereford 115 D10
Oxon 83 C7
Gosford Green
W Mid 118 B6
Gosforth Cumb 219 E11
T&W 242 D6
Gosforth Valley
Derbys 186 F4
Gosland Green Suff 124 G5
Gosling Green Suff 107 C9
Gosmere Kent 54 B4
Gosmore Herts 104 F3
Gospel Ash Staffs 132 E6
Gospel End Village
Staffs 133 E7
Gospel Green W Sus 50 G2
Gospel Oak London 67 B9
Gosport Hants 21 B8
Hants 32 C5
Gossabrough
Shetland 312 E7
Gossard's Green
C Beds 103 C9
Gossington Glos 80 E2
Gossops Green
W Sus 51 F9
Goswick Northumb 273 F11
Gotham Dorset 31 E9
E Sus 38 F2
Notts 153 C10
Gothelney Green
Som 43 F9
Gotherington Glos 99 F9
Gothers Corn 5 D9
Gott Argyll 288 E2
Shetland 313 J6
Gotton Som 28 B2
Goudhurst Kent 53 F8
Goukstone Moray 302 D4
Goulceby Lincs 190 F3
Goulton N Yorks 225 E9
Gourdas Aberds 303 E7
Gourdon Aberds 293 F10
Gourock Invclyd 276 F4
Govan Glasgow 267 B11
Govanhill Glasgow 267 C11
Gover Hill Kent 52 C6
Goverton Notts 172 E2
Goveton Devon 8 F5
Govilon Mon 78 C3
Gowanhill Aberds 303 C10
Gowanwell Aberds 303 E8
Gowdall E Yorks 198 C6
Gowerton/Tre-Gwyr
Swansea 56 B5
Gowhole Derbys 185 E8
Gowkhall Fife 279 D11
Gowkthrapple N
Lnrk 268 E5
Gowthorpe
E Yorks 207 C11
Goxhill E Yorks 209 E9
N Lincs 200 C6
Goxhill Haven
N Lincs 200 B6
Goybre Neath 57 D9
Goytre Neath 57 D9
Gozzard's Ford Oxon 83 F7
Grabhair W Isles 305 G5
Graby Lincs 155 D11
Gracca Corn 5 D10
Gracemount Edin 270 B5
Grade Corn 2 G6
Graffham W Sus 34 D6
Grafham Cambs 122 D3
Sur 50 E4
Grafton Hereford 97 D9
N Yorks 215 G8
Oxon 82 E3
Shrops 149 F8
Worcs 99 D9
Worcs 115 E11
Grafton Flyford
Worcs 117 F9
Grafton Regis
Northants 102 B5
Grafton Underwood
Northants 137 G8
Grafty Green Kent 53 D11
Grahamston Falk 279 E7
Graianrhyd Denb 166 D2
Graig Carms 74 E6
Conwy 180 G4
Denb 181 G9
Rhondda 58 B5
Wrex 148 B4
Graig-Fawr
Swansea 75 E10
Graig-fechan
Denb 165 E10
Graig Felen
Swansea 75 E11
Graig Penllyn
V Glam 58 D3
Graig Trewyddfa
Swansea 57 B7
Grain Medway 69 D11
Grains Bar Gtr Man 196 F3
Grainsby Lincs 190 B3
Grainthorpe Lincs 190 B5
Grainthorpe Fen
Lincs 190 B5
Graiselound N Lincs 188 B3
Grampound Corn 5 F8
Grampound Road
Corn 5 E8
Gramsdal W Isles 296 F4
Granborough Bucks 102 F5
Granby Notts 154 B5
Grandborough
Warks 119 D9
Grandpont Oxon 83 D8
Grandtully Perth 286 B3
Grange Cumb 220 B5
Dorset 31 G8
E Ayrs 257 B10
Fife 287 G8
Halton 183 E8
Lancs 203 G7
Medway 69 F9
Mers 182 D2
NE Lincs 201 F9
N Yorks 223 G8
Perth 286 E6
Warr 183 C10
Grange Crossroads
Moray 302 D4
Grange Estate
Dorset 31 G10
Grangehall Moray 301 C10
Grange Hill
Durham 233 F10
Essex 86 G6
Grangemill Derbys 170 D2
Grange Moor
W Yorks 197 D8
Grangemouth Falk 279 E8
Grangemuir Fife 287 G9
Grange of Cree
Dumfries 236 D6
Grange of Lindores
Fife 286 F6
Grange-over-Sands
Cumb 211 D8
Grangepans Falk 279 E10
Grange Park London 86 F4
Mers 183 C7
Northants 120 F5
Swindon 62 C6
Grangetown Cardiff 59 E7
Redcar 235 G7
T&W 243 G10
Grange Villa
Durham 242 G6
Grange Village Glos 79 C11
Granish Highld 291 B11
Gransmoor E Yorks 209 B8
Gransmore Green
Essex 106 G3
Granston/Treopert
Pembs 91 E7
Grantchester Cambs 123 F8
Grantham Lincs 155 B8
Grantley N Yorks 214 F4
Grantley Hall
N Yorks 214 F4
Grantlodge Aberds 293 B9
Granton Dumfries 248 B3
Edin 280 F4
Grantown Aberds 302 D6
Grantown-on-Spey
Highld 301 G10
Grantsfield
Hereford 115 E10
Grantshouse
Borders 272 B6
Grant Thorold
NE Lincs 201 F9
Graplin Dumfries 237 E8
Grappenhall Warr 183 D10
Grasby Lincs 200 G5

Gtr Man 196 E2
Lincs 190 F6
Haugham Lincs 190 E4
Haugh-head
Borders 261 B8
Haugh Head
Northumb 264 D2
Haughland Orkney 314 E5
Haughley Suff 125 E10
Haughley Green
Suff 125 E10
Haughley New Street
Suff 125 E10
Haugh of Glass
Moray 302 F4
Haugh of Kilnmaichlie
Moray 301 F11
Haugh of Urr
Dumfries 237 C10
Haughs of Clinterty
Aberdeen 293 B10
Haughton Ches E 167 D9
Notts 187 G11
Powys 148 F6
Shrops 132 B4
Shrops 132 D3
Shrops 149 D7
Shrops 149 F11
Staffs 151 E7
Haughton Castle
Northumb 241 C10
Haughton Green
Gtr Man 184 C6
Haughton Le Skerne
Darl 224 B6
Haughurst Hill
W Berks 64 G5
Haulkerton Aberds 293 F9
Haultwick Herts 104 G6
Haunn Argyll 288 E5
W Isles 297 K3
Haunton Staffs 152 G4
Hauxton Cambs 123 G8
Havannah Ches E 168 C5
Havant Hants 22 B2
Haven Hereford 97 B11
Hereford 115 G8
Haven Bank Lincs 174 E2
Haven Side E Yorks 201 B7
Havenstreet IoW 21 C7
Havercroft
W Yorks 197 E11
Haverfordwest/
Hwlffordd Pembs 73 B7
Haverhill Suff 106 B3
Haverigg Cumb 210 D3
Havering-atte-Bower
London 87 G8
Haveringland Norf 160 E3
Haversham
M Keynes 102 C6
Haverthwaite Cumb 210 C6
Haverton Hill
Stockton 234 G5
Haviker Street Kent 53 D8
Havyatt Som 44 F4
Havyatt Green
N Som 60 G3
Hawarden/Penarlâg
Flint 166 B4
Hawbridge Worcs 99 B8
Hawbush Green
Essex 106 G5
Hawcoat Cumb 210 E4
Hawcross Glos 98 E5
Hawddamor Gwyn 146 F3
Hawen Ceredig 92 B6
Hawes N Yorks 213 B7
Hawes' Green Norf 142 D4
Hawes Side Blkpool 202 G2
Hawford Worcs 116 E6
Hawgreen Shrops 150 D2
Hawick Borders 262 F2
Hawkchurch Devon 28 G4
Hawkcombe Som 41 D11
Hawkedon Suff 124 G5
Hawkenbury Kent 52 F5
Kent 53 E10
Hawkeridge Wilts 45 C11
Hawkerland Devon 15 D7
Hawkersland Cross
Hereford 97 B10
Hawkesbury S Glos 61 B9
Warks 135 G7
Hawkesbury Upton
S Glos 61 B9
Hawkes End W Mid 134 G6
Hawkesley W Mid 117 B10
Hawk Green
Gtr Man 185 D7
Hawkhill Northumb 264 G6
Hawk Hill Cumb 228 F6
Hawkhope Northumb 250 F6
Hawkhurst Kent 53 G9
Hawkhurst Common
E Sus 23 B8
Hawkinge Kent 55 F8
Hawkin's Hill Essex 106 E3
Hawkley Gtr Man 194 G5
Hants 34 B2
Hawkridge Som 41 G11
Hawksdale Cumb 230 B3
Hawks Green Staffs 151 G9
Hawkshaw Blkburn 195 D9
Hawkshead Cumb 221 F7
Hawkshead Hill
Cumb 220 F6
Hawks Hill Bucks 66 B2
Hawk's Hill Sur 51 B7
Hawksland S Lnrk 259 B8
Hawkspur Green
Essex 106 E3
Hawks Stones
W Yorks 196 B2
Hawkswick N Yorks 213 E9
Hawksworth Notts 172 G3
W Yorks 205 E9
W Yorks 205 F11
Hawkwell Essex 88 G4
Hawley Hants 49 B11
Kent 68 E4
Hawley Bottom
Devon 28 G2
Hawley Lane Hants 49 B11
Hawling Glos 99 G11
Hawn Orkney 314 D4
Hawnby N Yorks 215 B10
Hawne W Mid 133 G9
Haworth W Yorks 204 F6
Haws Bank Cumb 220 F6
Hawstead Suff 125 F7
Hawstead Green
Suff 125 F7
Hawthorn Durham 234 B4
Hants 49 G7
Rhondda 58 B6
Wilts 61 F11
Hawthorn Corner
Kent 71 F8
Hawthorn Hill Brack 65 E11
Lincs 174 D2
Hawthorns Staffs 168 F4
Hawthorpe Lincs 155 D10
Hawton Notts 172 E3
Haxby York 207 B8
Haxey N Lincs 188 B3
N Lincs 199 G9
Haxey Carr N Lincs 199 G9
Haxted Sur 52 D2
Haxton Wilts 46 D6
Hay Corn 10 G5
Haybridge Shrops 116 C2
Som 44 D4
Telford 150 G3
Hayden Glos 99 G8
Haydock Mers 183 B9
Haydon Bath 45 C7
Dorset 29 D11
Som 28 C3
Som 44 D5
Swindon 62 B6
Haydon Bridge
Northumb 241 E8
Haydon Wick
Swindon 62 B6
Haye Corn 7 B7
Haye Fm Corn 6 B6
Hayes Bromley 68 F2
Hillingdon 66 C6
Staffs 169 C9
Hayes End London 66 C5
Hayes Knoll Wilts 81 G10
Hayes Town London 66 C6
Hayfield Derbys 185 D8
Fife 280 C5
Hay Field S Yorks 187 B10
Hayfield Green
S Yorks 187 B11
Haygate Telford 150 G2
Haygrass Som 28 C2
Hay Green Essex 87 E10
Herts 104 D6
Norf 157 F10
Hayhill E Ayrs 257 F11
Hayhillock Angus 287 C9
Haylands IoW 21 C7
Hayle Corn 2 B3
Hayley Green
W Mid 133 G8
Hay Mills W Mid 134 G2
Haymoor End Som 28 B4
Haymoor Green
Ches E 167 E11
Hayne Devon 26 F5
Haynes C Beds 103 C11
Haynes Church End
C Beds 103 C11
Haynes West End
C Beds 103 C11
Hay-on-Wye Powys 96 C4
Hayscastle Pembs 91 F7
Hayscastle Cross
Pembs 91 G8
Haysford Pembs 91 G8
Hayshead Angus 287 C10
Hayston E Dunb 278 G2
Haystoun Borders 261 B7
Hay Street Herts 105 F7
Haythorne Dorset 31 F8
Hayton Aberdeen 293 C11
Cumb 229 C8
Cumb 240 F2
E Yorks 208 D2
Notts 188 E2
Hayton's Bent
Shrops 131 G10
Haytor Vale Devon 13 F11
Haytown Devon 24 E5
Haywards Heath
W Sus 36 C4
Haywood S Lnrk 269 E9
S Yorks 198 E5
Haywood Oaks
Notts 171 D10
Hazard's Green
E Sus 23 C11
Hazelbank S Lnrk 268 F6
Hazelbeach Pembs 72 E6
Hazelbury Bryan
Dorset 30 F2
Hazeleigh Essex 88 E4
Hazel End Essex 105 G9
Hazeley Hants 49 B8
Hazeley Bottom
Hants 49 B9
Hazeley Heath Hants 49 B9
Hazeley Lea Hants 49 B8
Hazelgrove Notts 171 F8
Hazel Grove
Gtr Man 184 D6
Hazelhurst Gtr Man 195 D9
Gtr Man 195 G9
Gtr Man 196 G3
Hazelslack Cumb 211 D9
Hazelslade Staffs 151 G10
Hazel Street Kent 53 B11
Kent 53 F7
Hazel Stub Suff 106 C3
Hazelton Glos 81 B9
Hazelton Walls Fife 287 E7
Hazelwood Derbys 170 F4
Devon 8 E4
London 68 G2
Hazlehead S Yorks 197 G7
Hazlemere Bucks 84 F5
Hazler Shrops 131 E9
Hazlerigg T&W 242 C6
Hazles Staffs 169 F8
Hazlescross Staffs 169 F8
Hazleton Glos 81 B9
Hazlewood N Yorks 205 C7
Hazon Northumb 252 C5
Heacham Norf 158 B3
Headbourne Worthy
Hants 48 G3
Headbrook Hereford 114 F6
Headcorn Kent 53 E10
Headingley
W Yorks 205 F11
Headington Oxon 83 D8
Headington Hill
Oxon 83 D8
Headlam Durham 224 B3
Headless Cross
Cumb 211 D7
Worcs 117 D10
Headley Hants 49 F10
Hants 64 G4
Sur 51 C8
Headley Down
Hants 49 F10
Headley Heath
Worcs 117 B11
Headley Park Bristol 60 F5
Head of Muir Falk 278 E6
Headon Devon 24 G5
Notts 188 F2
Heads S Lnrk 268 F4
Headshaw Borders 261 E11
Heads Nook Cumb 239 F11
Headstone London 66 B6
Headwell Fife 279 D11
Heady Hill Gtr Man 195 E10
Heage Derbys 170 E5
Healaugh N Yorks 206 D5
N Yorks 223 F10
Heald Green
Gtr Man 184 D4
Healds Green
Gtr Man 195 F11
Heale Devon 40 D6
Som 28 B5
Som 28 D2
Som 45 E7
Healey Gtr Man 195 D11
Northumb 242 F2
N Yorks 214 C3
W Yorks 197 C8
W Yorks 197 D9
Healey Cote
Northumb 252 C4
Healeyfield Durham 233 B7
Healey Hall
Northumb 242 F2
Healing NE Lincs 201 E8
Heamoor Corn 1 C5
Heaning Cumb 221 F8
Heanish Argyll 288 E2
Heanor Derbys 170 F6
Heanor Gate Derbys 170 F6
Heanton Punchardon
Devon 40 F4
Heap Bridge
Gtr Man 195 E10
Heapham Lincs 188 D5
Hearn Hants 49 F10
Hearnden Green
Kent 53 D10
Hearthstane
Borders 260 D4
Hearthstone Derbys 170 D4
Hearts Delight Kent 69 G11
Heasley Mill Devon 41 G8
Heast Highld 295 D8
Heath Cardiff 59 D7
Derbys 170 B6
Halton 183 E8
Heath and Reach
C Beds 103 F8
Heath Charnock
Lancs 194 E5
Heath Common
W Sus 35 E10
W Yorks 197 D11
Heathcot Aberds 293 C10
Heathcote Derbys 169 C10
Shrops 150 D3
Warks 118 E6
Heath Cross Devon 13 B10
Devon 14 C2
Heath End Bucks 84 F5
Bucks 85 D7
Derbys 153 E7
Hants 64 G2
Hants 64 G5
S Glos 61 B7
Sur 49 D10
Warks 118 E4
W Mid 133 C10
W Sus 35 D7
Heather Leics 153 G7
Heathercombe
Devon 13 E10
Heatherfield Highld 298 E4
Heather Row Hants 49 C8
Heatherside Sur 50 B2
Heatherwood Park
Highld 311 K2
Heatherybanks
Aberds 303 E7
Heathfield Cambs 105 B9
Devon 14 F2
E Sus 37 C9
Glos 80 F2
Hants 33 F9
Lincs 189 C10
N Yorks 214 F2
S Ayrs 257 E9
Som 27 B11
Som 43 G7
Heathfield Village
Oxon 83 B8
Heath Green Hants 48 F6
Worcs 117 C11
Heathhall Dumfries 237 B11
Heath Hayes Staffs 151 G10
Heath Hill Shrops 150 G5
Heath House Som 44 D2
Heathlands
Wokingham 65 F10
Heath Lanes Telford 150 E2
Heath Park London 68 B4
Heathrow Airport
London 66 D5
Heath Side Kent 68 E4
Heathstock Devon 28 G2
Heathton Shrops 132 E6
Heathtop Derbys 152 C4
Heath Town W Mid 133 D8
Heathwaite Cumb 221 F8
N Yorks 225 E9
Heatley Staffs 151 D11
Warr 184 D2
Heaton Gtr Man 195 F7
Lancs 211 G8
Staffs 169 C7
T&W 243 D7
W Yorks 205 G8
Heaton Chapel
Gtr Man 184 C5
Heaton Mersey
Gtr Man 184 C5
Heaton Moor
Gtr Man 184 C5
Heaton Norris
Gtr Man 184 C5
Heaton Royds
W Yorks 205 F8
Heaton's Bridge
Lancs 194 E2
Heaton Shay
W Yorks 205 F8
Heaven's Door Som 29 C10
Heaverham Kent 52 B5
Heaviley Gtr Man 184 D6
Heavitree Devon 14 C4
Hebburn T&W 243 E8
Hebburn Colliery
T&W 243 D8
Hebburn New Town
T&W 243 E8
Hebden N Yorks 213 G10
Hebden Bridge
W Yorks 196 B3
Hebden Green
Ches W 167 B10
Hebing End Herts 104 G6
Hebron Anglesey 179 E7
Carms 92 F3
Northumb 252 F5
Heck Dumfries 248 G3
Heckdyke N Lincs 188 B3
Heckfield Hants 65 G8
Heckfield Green
Suff 126 B3
Heckfordbridge
Essex 107 G8
Heckingham Norf 143 D7
Heckington Lincs 173 G10
Heckmondwike
W Yorks 197 C8
Heddington Wilts 62 F3
Heddington Wick
Wilts 62 F3
Heddle Orkney 314 E3
Heddon Devon 25 B11
Heddon-on-the-Wall
Northumb 242 D4
Hedenham Norf 142 E6
Hedge End Dorset 30 F4
Hants 33 E7
Hedgehog Bridge
Lincs 174 F3
Hedgerley Bucks 66 B3
Hedgerley Green
Bucks 66 B3
Hedgerley Hill Bucks 66 B3
Hedging Som 28 B4
Hedley Hill Durham 233 C9
Hedley on the Hill
Northumb 242 F3
Hednesford Staffs 151 G9
Hedon E Yorks 201 B7
Hedsor Bucks 66 B2
Hedworth T&W 243 E8
Heelands M Keynes 102 D6
Heeley S Yorks 186 E5
Hegdon Hill
Hereford 115 G11
Heggerscales Cumb 222 C6
Heggle Lane Cumb 230 D3
Heglibister Shetland 313 H5
Heighington Darl 233 G11
Lincs 173 B8
Heighley Staffs 168 F3
Height End Lancs 195 C9
Heightington Worcs 116 C5
Heights Gtr Man 196 F3
Heights of Brae
Highld 300 C5
Heights of Kinlochewe
Highld 299 C10
Heilam Highld 308 C4
Heiton Borders 262 C6
Helbeck Cumb 222 B5
Hele Devon 12 C2
Devon 13 G10
Devon 27 G7
Devon 40 D4
Som 27 C11
Torbay 9 B8
Helebridge Corn 24 G2
Helensburgh Argyll 276 E5
Helford Corn 3 D7
Helford Passage Corn 3 D7
Helham Green Herts 86 B5
Helhoughton Norf 159 D7
Helions Bumpstead
Essex 106 C3
Hellaby S Yorks 187 C8
Helland Corn 11 G7
Som 28 C4
Hellandbridge Corn 11 G7
Hell Corner
W Berks 63 G11
Hellesdon Norf 160 G4
Hellesveor Corn 2 A2
Hellidon Northants 119 F10
Hellifield N Yorks 204 B3
Hellifield Green
N Yorks 204 B3
Hellingly E Sus 23 C9
Hellington Norf 142 C6
Hellister Shetland 313 J5
Hellman's Cross
Essex 87 B9
Helm Northumb 252 D5
N Yorks 223 G8
Helmburn Borders 261 E9
Helmdon Northants 101 C11
Helme W Yorks 196 E5
Helmingham Suff 126 F3
Helmington Row
Durham 233 D9
Helmsdale Highld 311 H4
Helmshore Lancs 195 C9
Helmside Cumb 212 B3
Helmsley N Yorks 216 C2
Helperby N Yorks 215 F8
Helperthorpe
N Yorks 217 E9
Helpringham Lincs 173 G10
Helpston Pboro 138 B2
Helsby Ches W 183 F7
Helscott Corn 24 G2
Helsey Lincs 191 G8
Helston Corn 2 D5
Helstone Corn 11 E7
Helston Water Corn 4 G5
Helton Cumb 230 G6
Helwith Bridge
N Yorks 212 F6
Helygain/Halkyn
Flint 182 G2
Hemblington Norf 160 G6
Hemblington Corner
Norf 160 G6
Hembridge Som 44 F5
Hemel Hempstead
Herts 85 D9
Hemerdon Devon 7 D11
Hemford Shrops 130 C6
Hem Heath Stoke 168 G5
Hemingbrough
N Yorks 207 G9
Hemingby Lincs 190 G2
Hemingfield
S Yorks 197 G11
Hemingford Abbots
Cambs 122 C5
Hemingford Grey
Cambs 122 C5
Hemingstone Suff 126 G3
Hemington Leics 153 D9
Northants 137 F11
Som 45 C8
Hemley Suff 108 C5
Hemlington Mbro 225 C10
Hemp Green Suff 127 D7
Hempholme
E Yorks 209 C7
Hempnall Norf 142 E4
Hempnall Green
Norf 142 E4
Hempriggs House
Highld 310 E7
Hemp's Green Essex 107 F8
Hempshill Vale
Notts 171 G8
Hempstead Essex 106 D2
Medway 69 G9
Norf 160 B2
Norf 161 D8
Hempsted Glos 80 B4
Hempton Norf 159 D8
Oxon 101 E8
Hempton Wainhill
Oxon 84 E3
Hemsby Norf 161 F9
Hemsted Kent 54 E6
Hemswell Lincs 188 C6
Hemswell Cliff
Lincs 188 D6
Hemsworth Dorset 31 F7
S Yorks 186 E5
W Yorks 198 E2
Hemyock Devon 27 E10
Henaford Devon 24 D2
Hen Bentref Llandegfan
Anglesey 179 G9
Henbrook Worcs 117 D8
Henbury Bristol 60 D5
Ches E 184 G5
Dorset 18 B5
Hendomen Powys 130 D4
Hendon London 67 B8
T&W 243 F10
Hendra Corn 2 B6
Corn 2 C5
Corn 2 D3
Corn 2 F6
Corn 5 C9
Corn 5 D9
Corn 11 E7
Hendrabridge Corn 6 B5
Hendraburnick Corn 11 D8
Hendra Croft Corn 4 D5
Hendre Flint 165 B11
Gwyn 110 B2
Powys 129 D9
Hendre-ddu Conwy 164 B5
Hendredenny Park
Caerph 58 B6
Hendreforgan
Rhondda 58 B3
Hendrerwydd
Denb 165 C10
Hendrewen
Swansea 75 D10
Hendy Carms 75 E9
Hendy-Gwyn Carms 74 B2
Hendy Gwyn/Whitland
Carms 73 B11
Hên-efail Denb 165 C9
Heneglwys Anglesey 178 F6
Hen-feddau fawr
Pembs 92 E4
Henfield S Glos 61 D7
W Sus 36 D2
Henford Devon 12 C3
Henfords Marsh
Wilts 45 E11
Henghurst Kent 54 F3
Hengoed Caerph 77 F10
Denb 165 D9
Powys 114 G4
Shrops 148 C5
Hengrave Norf 160 F2
Suff 124 D6
Hengrove Bristol 60 F6
Hengrove Park
Bristol 60 F5
Henham Essex 105 F10
Heniarth Powys 130 B2
Henlade Som 28 C3
Henleaze Bristol 60 D5
Henley Dorset 29 G11
Glos 80 B6
Shrops 115 B10
Shrops 131 F9
Som 44 G2
Suff 126 G3
Wilts 47 B10
Wilts 61 F10
W Sus 34 B5
Henley Common
W Sus 34 B5
Henley Green
W Mid 135 G7
Henley-in-Arden
Warks 118 D3
Henley-on-Thames
Oxon 65 C9
Henley's Down E Sus 38 E2
Henley Street Kent 69 F7
Henllan Ceredig 93 C7
Denb 165 B8
Henllan Amgoed
Carms 92 G3
Henlle Shrops 148 C6
Henllys Torf 78 G3
Henllys Vale Torf 78 G3
Henlow C Beds 104 D3
Hennock Devon 14 E2
Henny Street Essex 107 D7
Henryd Conwy 180 G3
Henry's Moat Pembs 91 F10
Hensall N Yorks 198 C5
Henshaw Northumb 241 E7
W Yorks 205 E10
Hensingham Cumb 219 B9
Hensington Oxon 83 B7
Henstead Suff 143 F9
Hensting Hants 33 C7
Henstridge Devon 40 E5
Som 30 D2
Henstridge Ash Som 30 C2
Henstridge Bowden
Som 29 C11
Henstridge Marsh
Som 30 C2
Henton Oxon 84 E3
Som 44 D3
Henwood Corn 11 G11
Oxon 83 E7
Henwood Green Kent 52 E6
Heogan Shetland 313 J6
Heol-ddu Carms 75 E7
Swansea 56 B6
Heolgerrig M Tydf 77 D8
Heol-laethog
Bridgend 58 C2
Heol-las Bridgend 58 C2
Swansea 57 B7
Heol Senni Powys 95 G8
Heol-y-gaer Powys 96 D3
Heol-y-mynydd
V Glam 57 G11
Hepburn Northumb 264 E3
Hepple Northumb 251 C11
Hepscott Northumb 252 G6
Hepthorne Lane
Derbys 170 C6
Heptonstall
W Yorks 196 B3
Hepworth Suff 125 C9
W Yorks 197 F7
Herbrandston Pembs 72 D5
Hereford Hereford 97 C10
Heribusta Highld 298 B4
Heriot Borders 271 E7
Hermiston Edin 280 G3
Hermitage Borders 250 D2
Dorset 29 F10
W Berks 64 E4
W Sus 22 B3
Hermitage Green
Mers 183 C10
Hermit Hill
S Yorks 197 G10
Hermit Hole
W Yorks 205 F7
Hermon Anglesey 162 B5
Carms 93 E7
Carms 94 F3
Pembs 92 E4
Herne Kent 71 F7
Herne Bay Kent 71 F7
Herne Common Kent 71 F7
Herne Hill London 67 E10
Herne Pound Kent 53 C7
Herner Devon 25 B9
Hernhill Kent 70 G5
Herniss Corn 2 C6
Herodsfoot Corn 6 C4
Heron Cross Stoke 168 G5
Heronden Kent 55 C9
Herongate Essex 87 G10
Heronsford S Ayrs 244 G4
Heronsgate Herts 85 G8
Heron's Ghyll E Sus 37 B7
Herons Green Bath 44 B5
Heronston Bridgend 58 D2
Herra Shetland 312 D8
Herriard Hants 49 D7
Herringfleet Suff 143 D9
Herring's Green
Beds 103 C11
Herringswell Suff 124 C4
Herringthorpe
S Yorks 186 C6
Hersden Kent 71 G8
Hersham Corn 24 F3
Sur 66 G6
Herstmonceux
E Sus 23 C10
Herston Dorset 18 F6
Orkney 314 G4
Hertford Herts 86 C4
Hertford Heath Herts 86 C4
Hertingfordbury
Herts 86 C4
Hesketh Bank Lancs 194 C2
Hesketh Lane Lancs 203 E8
Hesketh Moss
Lancs 194 C2
Hesket Newmarket
Cumb 230 D2
Heskin Green Lancs 194 D4
Hesleden Durham 234 D4
Hesleyside
Northumb 251 G8
Heslington York 207 C8
Hessay York 206 C6
Hessenford Corn 6 D6
Hessett Suff 125 E8
Hessle E Yorks 200 B4
W Yorks 198 D2
Hest Bank Lancs 211 F9
Hester's Way Glos 99 G8
Hestinsetter
Shetland 313 J4
Heston London 66 D6
Hestwall Orkney 314 E2
Heswall Mers 182 E3
Hethe Oxon 101 F11
Hethel Norf 142 C3
Hethelpit Cross Glos 98 F5
Hethersett Norf 142 C3
Hethersgill Cumb 239 D11
Hetherside Cumb 239 D10
Hetherson Green
Ches W 167 F8
Hethpool Northumb 263 D9
Hett Durham 233 D11
Hetton N Yorks 204 B5
Hetton Downs T&W 234 B3
Hetton-le-Hill T&W 234 B3
Hetton-le-Hole
T&W 234 B3
Hetton Steads
Northumb 264 B2
Heugh Northumb 242 C3
Heugh-head Aberds 292 B5
Heveningham Suff 126 C6
Hever Kent 52 E3
Heversham Cumb 211 C9
Hevingham Norf 160 E3
Hewas Water Corn 5 F9
Hewelsfield Glos 79 E9
Hewelsfield Common
Glos 79 E8
Hewer Hill Cumb 230 D3
Hew Green
N Yorks 205 B10
Hewish N Som 60 G2
Som 28 F6
Hewood Dorset 28 G5
Heworth T&W 243 E7
York 207 C8
Hexham Northumb 241 E10
Hextable Kent 68 E4
Hexthorpe S Yorks 198 G5
Hexton Herts 104 E2
Hexworthy Devon 13 G9
Hey Lancs 204 E3
Heybridge Essex 87 F10
Essex 88 D5
Heybridge Basin
Essex 88 D5
Heybrook Bay Devon 7 F10
Heydon Cambs 105 C8
Norf 160 D2
Heydour Lincs 155 B10
Hey Green W Yorks 196 E4
Heyheads Gtr Man 196 G3
Hey Houses Lancs 193 B10
Heylipol Argyll 288 E1
Heylor Shetland 312 E4
Heyope Powys 114 C4
Heyrod Gtr Man 185 B7
Heysham Lancs 211 G8
Heyshaw N Yorks 214 G3
Heyshott W Sus 34 D5
Heyshott Green
W Sus 34 D5
Heyside Gtr Man 196 F2
Heytesbury Wilts 46 E2
Heythrop Oxon 101 F7
Heywood Gtr Man 195 E11
Wilts 45 C11
Hibaldstow N Lincs 200 G3
Hibb's Green Suff 125 G7
Hickford Hill Essex 106 C5
Hickleton S Yorks 198 F3
Hickling Norf 161 E8
Notts 154 D3
Hickling Green Norf 161 E8
Hickling Heath Norf 161 E8
Hickling Pastures
Notts 154 D3
Hickmans Green
Kent 54 B5
Hicks Forstal Kent 71 G7
Hicks Gate Bath 60 F6
Hick's Mill Corn 4 G5
Hickstead W Sus 36 C3
Hidcote Bartrim
Glos 100 C3
Hidcote Boyce Glos 100 C3
Hifnal Shrops 132 D4
Higginshaw
Gtr Man 196 F2
High Ackworth
W Yorks 198 D2
Higham Derbys 170 D5
Fife 286 F6
Kent 69 E8
Lancs 204 F2
Suff 107 D10
Suff 124 E4
S Yorks 197 F10
Higham Common
S Yorks 197 F10
Higham Dykes
Northumb 242 B4
Higham Ferrers
Northants 121 D9
Higham Gobion
C Beds 104 E2
Higham Hill London 86 G5
Higham on the Hill
Leics 135 D7
Highampton Devon 25 G7
Highams Park
London 86 G5
Higham Wood Kent 52 D5
High Angerton
Northumb 252 F3
High Bankhill Cumb 231 C7
High Banton N Lnrk 278 E4
High Barn Lincs 174 C5
High Barnes T&W 243 F9
High Barnet London 86 F2
High Beach Essex 86 F6
High Bentham
N Yorks 212 F3
High Bickington
Devon 25 C10
High Biggins Cumb 212 D2
High Birkwith
N Yorks 212 D5
High Birstwith
N Yorks 205 B10
High Blantyre S
Lnrk 268 D3
High Bonnybridge
Falk 278 F6
High Bradfield
S Yorks 186 C3
High Bradley
N Yorks 204 D6
High Bray Devon 41 G7
Highbridge Cumb 230 C3
Hants 33 C7
Highld 290 E3
Som 43 D10
W Mid 133 C10
Highbrook W Sus 51 G11
High Brooms Kent 52 E5
High Brotheridge
Glos 80 C5
High Bullen Devon 25 C8
Highburton
W Yorks 197 E7
Highbury London 67 B10
Ptsmth 33 G11
Som 45 D7
Highbury Vale
Nottingham 171 G8
High Buston
Northumb 252 B6
High Callerton
Northumb 242 C5
High Cark Cumb 211 C7
High Casterton
Cumb 212 D2
High Catton
E Yorks 207 C10
High Church
Northumb 252 F5
Highclere Hants 64 G2
Highcliffe Derbys 186 F2
Dorset 19 C10
High Cogges Oxon 82 D5
High Common Norf 141 B9
High Coniscliffe
Darl 224 B4
High Crompton
Gtr Man 196 F2
High Cross Cambs 123 F8
Corn 2 D6
E Sus 37 B9
Hants 34 B2
Herts 85 F10
Herts 86 B5
Newport 59 B9
Warks 118 D3
W Sus 36 D2
High Crosshill S
Lnrk 268 C2
High Cunsey Cumb 221 G7
High Dubmire T&W 234 B2
High Dyke Durham 232 F5
High Easter Essex 87 C10
High Eggborough
N Yorks 198 C5
High Eldrig
Dumfries 236 C4
High Ellington
N Yorks 214 C3
Higher Alham Som 45 E7
Higher Ansty Dorset 30 G3
Higher Ashton Devon 14 E3
Higher Audley
Blkburn 195 B7
Higher Bal Corn 4 E4
Higher Ballam
Lancs 202 G3
Higher Bartle Lancs 202 G6
Higher Bebington
Mers 182 D4
Higher Berry End
C Beds 103 E9
Higher Blackley
Gtr Man 195 G10
Higher Boarshaw
Gtr Man 195 F11
Higher Bockhampton
Dorset 17 C10
Higher Bojewyan Corn 1 C3
Higher Boscaswell
Corn 1 C3
Higher Brixham
Torbay 9 D8
Higher Broughton
Gtr Man 195 G10
Higher Burrow Som 28 C6
Higher Burwardsley
Ches W 167 D8
High Ercall Telford 149 F11
Higher Chalmington
Dorset 29 G9
Higher Cheriton
Devon 27 G10
Higher Chillington
Som 28 E5
Higher Chisworth
Derbys 185 C7
Highercliff Corn 6 D4
Higher Clovelly
Devon 24 C4
Higher Condurrow
Corn 2 B5
Higher Crackington
Corn 11 B9
Higher Cransworth
Corn 5 B9
Higher Croft
Blkburn 195 B7
Higher Denham
Bucks 66 B4
Higher Dinting
Derbys 185 C8
Higher Disley
Ches E 185 E7
Higher Downs Corn 2 C3
Higher Durston Som 28 B3
Higher End Gtr Man 194 G4
Higher Folds
Gtr Man 195 G7
Higherford Lancs 204 E3
Higher Gabwell Torbay 9 B8
Higher Green
Gtr Man 195 G8
Higher Halstock Leigh
Dorset 29 F8
Higher Heysham
Lancs 211 G8
Higher Hogshead
Lancs 195 C11
Higher Holton Som 29 B11

Hig–Hoo 389

Higher Hurdsfield Ches E 184 G6
Higher Kingcombe Dorset 16 B6
Higher Kinnerton Flint 166 C4
Higher Land Corn 12 G3
Higher Marsh Som 30 C2
Higher Melcombe Dorset 30 G2
Higher Menadew Corn 5 D10
Higher Molland Devon 41 G8
Higher Muddiford Devon 40 F5
Higher Nyland Dorset 30 C2
Higher Penwortham Lancs 194 B4
Higher Pertwood Wilts 45 F11
Higher Porthpean Corn 5 E10
Higher Poynton Ches E 184 E6
Higher Prestacott Devon 12 B3
Higher Rads End C Beds 103 E9
Higher Ridge Shrops 149 C7
Higher Rocombe Barton Devon 9 B8
Higher Row Dorset 31 G8
Higher Runcorn Halton 183 E8
Higher Sandford Dorset 29 C10
Higher Shotton Flint 166 B4
Higher Shurlach Ches W 183 G11
Higher Slade Devon 40 D4
Higher Street Som 42 E6
Higher Tale Devon 27 G9
Higher Tolcarne Corn 5 B7
Higher Totnell Dorset 29 F10
Highertown Corn 4 G6
Corn 11 E8
Higher Town Corn 5 C10
Scilly 1 F4
Som 42 D3
Higher Tremarcoombe Corn 6 B5
Higher Vexford Som 42 F6
Higher Walreddon Devon 12 G5
Higher Walton Lancs 194 B5
Warr 183 D9
Higher Wambrook Som 28 F3
Higher Warcombe Devon 40 D3
Higher Weaver Devon 27 G9
Higher Whatcombe Dorset 30 G4
Higher Wheelton Lancs 194 C6
Higher Whitley Ches W 183 E10
Higher Wincham Ches W 183 F11
Higher Woodsford Dorset 17 D11
Higher Wraxall Dorset 29 G9
Higher Wych Ches W 167 G7
High Etherley Durham 233 F9
High Ferry Lincs 174 F5
Highfield E Yorks 207 F10
Glos 79 E10
Gtr Man 194 G5
Gtr Man 195 F8
Herts 85 D9
N Ayrs 266 E6
Oxon 101 G11
Soton 32 E6
S Yorks 186 D5
T&W 242 F4
High Field Lancs 203 C10
Highfields Cambs 123 F7
Derbys 170 B6
Essex 88 B5
Glos 80 F3
Leicester 136 C2
Northumb 273 E9
Staffs 151 E8
S Yorks 198 F4
High Flatts W Yorks 197 F8
High Forge Durham 242 G6
High Friarside Durham 242 F5
High Gallowhill E Dunb 278 G2
High Garrett Essex 106 F5
Highgate E Sus 52 G2
Kent 53 G9
London 67 B9
Powys 130 D2
S Yorks 198 G3
W Mid 133 F11
High Grange Durham 233 E9
High Grantley N Yorks 214 F4
High Green Cumb 221 E8
Norf 141 B8
Norf 142 B2
Norf 159 G8
Shrops 132 G4
Suff 125 E7
S Yorks 186 B4
Worcs 99 B7
W Yorks 197 E7
High Halden Kent 53 F11
High Halstow Medway 69 D9
High Ham Som 44 G2
High Handenhold Durham 242 G6
High Harrington Cumb 228 F6
High Harrogate N Yorks 206 B2
High Haswell Durham 234 C3
High Hatton Shrops 150 E2
High Hauxley Northumb 253 C7
High Hawsker N Yorks 227 D8
High Heath Shrops 150 D3
W Mid 133 C10
High Hesket Cumb 230 C5
High Hesleden Durham 234 D5
High Hill Cumb 229 G11
High Houses Essex 87 C11
High Hoyland S Yorks 197 E9
High Hunsley E Yorks 208 F4
High Hurstwood E Sus 37 B7
High Hutton N Yorks 216 F5
High Ireby Cumb 229 D10
High Kelling Norf 177 E10
High Kilburn N Yorks 215 D10
High Lands Durham 233 F8
Highlane Ches E 168 B5
Derbys 186 E6
High Lane Gtr Man 185 D7
Worcs 116 E3
Highlanes Corn 10 G4
Staffs 150 C5
High Lanes Corn 2 B3
High Laver Essex 87 D8
Highlaws Cumb 229 B8
Highleadon Glos 98 G5
High Legh Ches E 184 E2
Highleigh W Sus 22 D4
High Leven Stockton 225 C8
Highley Shrops 132 G4
High Littleton Bath 44 B6
High Longthwaite Cumb 229 B11
High Lorton Cumb 229 F9
High Marishes N Yorks 216 D6
High Marnham Notts 188 G4
High Melton S Yorks 198 G4
High Mickley Northumb 242 E3
High Mindork Dumfries 236 D5
Highmoor Cumb 229 B11
Oxon 65 B8
High Moor Derbys 187 E7
Lancs 194 E4
Highmoor Cross Oxon 65 C8
Highmoor Hill Mon 60 B3
High Moorsley T&W 234 B2
Highnam Glos 80 B3
Highnam Green Glos 98 G5
High Nash Glos 79 C9
High Newton Cumb 211 C8
High Newton-by-the-Sea Northumb 264 D6
High Nibthwaite Cumb 210 B5
Highoak Norf 141 C11
High Oaks Cumb 222 G2
High Offley Staffs 150 D5
High Ongar Essex 87 E9
High Onn Staffs 150 F6
High Onn Wharf Staffs 150 F6
High Park Cumb 221 G10
Mers 193 D11
Highridge Bristol 60 F5
High Risby N Lincs 200 E2
Highroad Well Moor W Yorks 196 B5
High Roding Essex 87 B10
High Rougham Suff 125 E8
High Row Cumb 230 D3
Cumb 230 G3
High Salvington W Sus 35 F10
High Scales Cumb 229 B9
High Sellafield Cumb 219 E10
High Shaw N Yorks 223 G7
High Shields T&W 243 D9
High Shincliffe Durham 233 C11
High Side Cumb 229 E10
High Southwick T&W 243 F9
High Spen T&W 242 F4
High Stakesby N Yorks 227 C7
Highstead Kent 71 F8
Highsted Kent 70 G2
High Stoop Durham 233 C8
Highstreet Kent 70 G5
High Street Corn 5 E9
Kent 53 G8
Pembs 73 B11
Suff 107 B7
Suff 127 C8
Suff 127 F8
Suff 143 G7
Highstreet Green Essex 106 E5
Sur 50 F3
High Street Green Suff 125 F10
High Sunderland Borders 261 C11
Hightae Dumfries 238 B3
Highter's Heath W Mid 117 B11
High Throston Hrtlpl 234 E5
High Tirfergus Argyll 255 F7
Hightown Ches E 168 C5
Hants 31 G11
Mers 193 G10
Soton 33 E7
Wrex 166 F4
W Yorks 197 C7
High Town Luton 103 G11
Shrops 132 E4
Staffs 151 G9
Hightown Green Suff 125 F9
Hightown Heights W Yorks 197 C7
High Toynton Lincs 174 B3
High Trewhitt Northumb 252 B2
High Urpeth Durham 242 G6
High Valleyfield Fife 279 D10
High Walton Cumb 219 C9
High Warden Northumb 241 D10
High Water Head Cumb 220 F6
Highway Corn 4 G4
Hereford 97 B9
Som 29 C7
Wilts 62 E4
Windsor 65 C11
Highweek Devon 14 G2
High Westwood Durham 242 F4
High Whinnow Cumb 239 G8
Highwood Devon 27 F10
Dorset 18 D3
Essex 87 E10
Hants 31 F11
Worcs 116 D3
Highwood Hill London 86 G2
High Woolaston Glos 79 F9
High Worsall N Yorks 225 D7
Highworth Swindon 82 G2
Highworthy Devon 24 F6
High Wray Cumb 221 F7
High Wych Herts 87 C7
High Wycombe Bucks 84 G5
Hilborough Norf 140 C6
Hilborough Ho Norf 140 C6
Hilcot Glos 81 B7
Hilcote Derbys 171 D7
Hilcot End Glos 81 E9
Hilcott Wilts 46 B6
Hildenborough Kent 52 D5
Hilden Park Kent 52 D5
Hildersham Cambs 105 B10
Hildersley Hereford 98 G2
Hilderstone Staffs 151 C8
Hilderthorpe E Yorks 218 F3
Hilfield Dorset 29 F10
Hilgay Norf 140 D2
Hill S Glos 79 G10
Warks 119 D9
W Mid 134 D2
Hillam N Yorks 198 B4
Hillbeck Cumb 222 B5
Hillblock Pembs 73 B8
Hillborough Kent 71 F8
Hill Bottom Oxon 64 D6
Hillbourne Poole 18 C6
Hillbrae Aberds 302 E6
Aberds 303 G7
Hill Brow W Sus 34 B3
Hillbutts Dorset 31 G7
Hill Chorlton Staffs 150 B5
Hillcliffe Warr 183 D10
Hillclifflane Derbys 170 F3
Hillcommon Som 27 B11
Hill Common Norf 161 E8
Hill Corner Som 45 D10
Hill Croome Worcs 99 C7
Hillcross Derbys 152 C6
Hill Dale Lancs 194 E3
Hill Deverill Wilts 45 E11
Hilldyke Lincs 174 F4
Hill Dyke Lincs 174 F4
Hillend Fife 280 E2
N Lnrk 268 B6
N Som 43 B11
Shrops 132 E6
Swansea 56 C2
Hill End Durham 232 D6
Fife 279 B10
Glos 99 D8
London 85 G8
N Yorks 205 C7
Som 29 E8
Worcs 117 E8
Hillend Green Glos 98 F4
Hillersland Glos 79 C9
Hillerton Devon 13 B10
Hillesden Bucks 102 F3
Hillesden Hamlet Bucks 102 E3
Hillesley Glos 61 B9
Hillfarance Som 27 C11
Hillfarrance Som 27 C11
Hillfield Devon 8 E6
W Mid 118 B2
Hillfields S Glos 60 D6
W Mid 118 B6
Hillfoot Aberds 303 D9
W Yorks 205 G10
Hillfoot End C Beds 104 E2
Hill Furze Worcs 99 B9
Hill Gate Hereford 97 F9
Hillgreen W Berks 64 D3
Hill Green Essex 105 E9
Kent 69 G10
Hillgrove W Sus 34 B6
Hillhampton Hereford 97 B11
Hillhead Aberds 302 F5
Aberds 303 G8
Corn 5 C11
Devon 9 E8
E Ayrs 257 B10
S Ayrs 257 F10
Hill Head Hants 33 G8
Northumb 241 D10
Hillhead of Auchentumb Aberds 303 D9
Hillhead of Blairy Aberds 302 D6
Hillhead of Cocklaw Aberds 303 E10
Hill Hoath Kent 52 E3
Hill Hook W Mid 134 C2
Hillhouse Borders 271 D10
Hill Houses Shrops 116 B2
Hilliard's Cross Staffs 152 G3
Hilliclay Highld 310 C5
Hillingdon London 66 C5
Hillingdon Heath London 66 C5
Hillington Glasgow 267 C10
Norf 158 D4
Hillis Corner IoW 20 C5
Hillmoor Devon 27 E10
Hillmorton Warks 119 C10
Hill Mountain Pembs 73 D7
Hillockhead Aberds 292 B6
Aberds 292 C5
Hillock Vale Lancs 195 B9
Hill of Beath Fife 280 C3
Hill of Drip Stirl 278 B5
Hill of Fearn Highld 301 B8
Hill of Keillor Angus 286 C6
Hill of Mountblairy Aberds 302 D6
Hill of Overbrae Aberds 303 C8
Hill Park Hants 33 F9
Kent 52 B2
Hillpool Worcs 117 B7
Hillpound Hants 33 D9
Hill Ridware Staffs 151 F11
Hillsborough S Yorks 186 C4
Hillside Aberds 293 D11
Angus 293 G9
Devon 8 C4
Devon 27 F11
Hants 49 C9
Mers 193 E10
Orkney 314 D3
Orkney 314 G4
Shetland 313 G6
Shrops 131 F11
Wilts 81 G9
Hill Side Hants 34 B3
S Yorks 197 G8
Worcs 116 E5
W Yorks 197 D7
Hill Somersal Derbys 152 C2
Hills Town Derbys 171 B7
Hillstreet Hants 32 D4
Hill Street Kent 54 D6
Hillswick Shetland 312 F4
Hilltop Bl Gwent 77 D11
Bucks 85 E7
Derbys 170 C4
Hill Top Derbys 186 F5
Durham 232 G5
Durham 233 C10
Durham 242 G5
Gtr Man 195 G8
Hants 32 G6
Notts 171 F7
N Yorks 214 G3
N Yorks 214 G5
Staffs 133 B7
S Yorks 186 C5
S Yorks 186 D3
S Yorks 187 B7
S Yorks 197 F9
Warks 134 E5
Warks 135 E7
W Mid 133 E9
W Sus 34 C5
W Yorks 196 E5
W Yorks 197 D10
W Yorks 205 G7
W Yorks 205 G11
Hillview T&W 243 G9
Hill View Dorset 18 B5
Hillway IoW 21 D8
Hillwell Shetland 313 M5
Hill Wood W Mid 134 C2
Hill Wootton Warks 118 D6
Hillyfields Hants 32 D5
Hilmarton Wilts 62 D4
Hilperton Wilts 45 B11
Hilperton Marsh Wilts 45 B11
Hilsea Ptsmth 33 G11
Hilston E Yorks 209 G11
Hiltingbury Hants 32 C6
Hilton Aberds 303 F9
Borders 273 E7
Cambs 122 D5
Cumb 231 G10
Derbys 152 C4
Dorset 30 G3
Durham 233 G9
Highld 309 L7
Highld 311 L3
Shrops 132 D5
Staffs 133 B11
Stockton 225 C9
Hilton House Gtr Man 194 F6
Hilton Lodge Highld 300 G2
Hilton of Cadboll Highld 301 B8
Hilton Park Gtr Man 195 G10
Himbleton Worcs 117 F8
Himley Staffs 133 E7
Hincaster Cumb 211 C10
Hinchley Wood Sur 67 F7
Hinchliffe Mill W Yorks 196 F6
Hinchwick Glos 100 E2
Hinckley Leics 135 E8
Hinderclay Suff 125 B10
Hinderton Ches W 182 F4
Hinderwell N Yorks 226 B5
Hindford Shrops 148 C6
Hindhead Sur 49 F11
Hindle Fold Lancs 203 G10
Hindley Gtr Man 194 G6
Northumb 242 F2
Hindley Green Gtr Man 194 G6
Hindlip Worcs 117 F7
Hindolveston Norf 159 D10
Hindon Wilts 46 G2
Hindpool Cumb 210 F3
Hindringham Norf 159 B9
Hindsford Gtr Man 195 G7
Hingham Norf 141 C10
Hinstock Shrops 150 D3
Hintlesham Suff 107 C11
Hinton Glos 79 E11
Hants 19 B10
Hereford 96 D6
Northants 119 G10
S Glos 61 D8
Shrops 131 B8
Som 29 C9
Hinton Ampner Hants 33 B9
Hinton Blewett Bath 44 B5
Hinton Charterhouse Bath 45 B9
Hinton Cross Worcs 99 C10
Hinton-in-the-Hedges Northants 101 D11
Hinton Martell Dorset 31 F8
Hinton on the Green Worcs 99 C10
Hinton Parva Dorset 31 G7
Swindon 63 C8
Hinton St George Som 28 E6
Hinton St Mary Dorset 30 D3
Hinton Waldrist Oxon 82 F5
Hints Shrops 116 C2
Staffs 134 C3
Hinwick Beds 121 E8
Hinwood Shrops 131 B7
Hinxhill Kent 54 E5
Hinxton Cambs 105 B9
Hinxworth Herts 104 C4
Hipperholme W Yorks 196 B6
Hipplecote Worcs 116 F4
Hipsburn Northumb 264 G6
Hipswell N Yorks 224 F3
Hirael Gwyn 179 G9
Hiraeth Carms 92 G3
Hirn Aberds 293 C9
Hirnant Powys 147 E11
Hirst N Lnrk 269 C7
Northumb 253 F7
Hirst Courtney N Yorks 198 C6
Hirwaen Denb 165 C10
Hirwaun Rhondda 77 D7
Hirwaun Common Bridgend 58 C2
Hiscott Devon 25 B8
Hislop Borders 249 C9
Hisomley Wilts 45 D11
Histon Cambs 123 E8
Hitcham Suff 125 G9
Hitchill Dumfries 238 D4
Hitchin Herts 104 F3
Hitchin Hill Herts 104 F3
Hitcombe Bottom Wilts 45 E10
Hither Green London 67 E11
Hittisleigh Devon 13 C10
Hittisleigh Barton Devon 13 B10
Hive E Yorks 208 G2
Hixon Staffs 151 D10
Hoaden Kent 55 B9
Hoar Cross Staffs 152 E2
Hoarwithy Hereford 97 F10
Hoath Kent 71 G8
Hoath Corner Kent 52 E3
Hobarris Shrops 114 B6
Hobbister Orkney 314 F3
Hobble End Staffs 133 B10
Hobbles Green Suff 124 G4
Hobbs Cross Essex 87 C7
Essex 87 F7
Hobbs Wall Bath 61 G7
Hob Hill Ches W 167 E7
Hobkirk Borders 262 G3
Hobroyd Derbys 185 C8
Hobson Durham 242 F5
Hoby Leics 154 F3
Hoccombe Som 27 B10
Hockenden London 68 F3
Hockerill Herts 105 G9
Hockering Norf 159 G11
Hockering Heath Norf 159 G11
Hockerton Notts 172 D2
Hockholler Som 27 C11
Hockholler Green Som 27 C11
Hockley Ches E 184 E6
Essex 88 G4
Kent 54 B3
Staffs 134 C4
W Mid 118 B5
Hockley Heath W Mid 118 C3
Hockliffe C Beds 103 F9
Hockwold cum Wilton Norf 140 F4
Hockworthy Devon 27 D8
Hocombe Hants 32 C6
Hoddesdon Herts 86 D5
Hoddlesden Blkburn 195 C8
Hoddomcross Dumfries 238 C5
Hoddom Mains Dumfries 238 C5
Hoden Worcs 99 B11
Hodgefield Staffs 168 E6
Hodgehill Ches E 168 B4
W Mid 134 F2
Hodgeston Pembs 73 F8
Hodley Powys 130 E3
Hodnet Shrops 150 D2
Hodnetheath Shrops 150 D2
Hodsock Notts 187 D10
Hodsoll Street Kent 68 G6
Hodson Swindon 63 C7
Hodthorpe Derbys 187 F8
Hoe Hants 33 D9
Norf 159 F9
Sur 50 D5
Hoe Benham W Berks 64 F2
Hoe Gate Hants 33 E10
Hoff Cumb 222 B3
Hoffleet Stow Lincs 156 B4
Hogaland Shetland 312 F5
Hogben's Hill Kent 54 B4
Hogganfield Glasgow 268 B2
Hoggard's Green Suff 125 F7
Hoggeston Bucks 102 G6
Hoggington Wilts 45 B10
Hoggrill's End Warks 134 E4
Hogha Gearraidh W Isles 296 D3
Hog Hatch Sur 49 D10
Hoghton Lancs 194 B6
Hoghton Bottoms Lancs 194 B6
Hogley Green W Yorks 196 F6
Hognaston Derbys 170 E2
Hogpits Bottom Herts 85 E8
Hogsthorpe Lincs 191 G8
Hogstock Dorset 31 F7
Holbeach Lincs 157 E7
Holbeach Bank Lincs 157 D7
Holbeach Clough Lincs 156 D6
Holbeach Drove Lincs 156 G6
Holbeache Worcs 116 B5
Holbeach Hurn Lincs 157 D7
Holbeach St Johns Lincs 156 F6
Holbeach St Marks Lincs 157 C7
Holbeach St Matthew Lincs 157 C8
Holbeck Notts 187 G8
W Yorks 205 G11
Holbeck Woodhouse Notts 187 G8
Holberrow Green Worcs 117 F10
Holbeton Devon 8 E2
Holborn London 67 C10
Holborough Kent 69 G8
Holbrook Derbys 170 G5
Suff 108 D3
S Yorks 186 E6
Holbrook Common S Glos 61 E7
Holbrook Moor Derbys 170 F5
Holbrooks W Mid 134 G6
Holburn Northumb 264 B2
Holbury Hants 32 G6
Holcombe Devon 14 G5
Gtr Man 195 D9
Som 45 D7
Holcombe Brook Gtr Man 195 E9
Holcombe Rogus Devon 27 D9
Holcot Northants 120 D5
Holdbrook London 86 F5
Holden Lancs 203 D11
Holdenby Northants 120 D3
Holden Fold Gtr Man 196 F2
Holdenhurst Bmouth 19 B8
Holder's Green Essex 106 F2
Holders Hill London 86 G2
Holdfast Worcs 99 D7
Holdgate Shrops 131 F11
Holdingham Lincs 173 F9
Holditch Dorset 28 G4
Holdsworth W Yorks 196 B5
Holdworth S Yorks 186 C3
Hole Devon 24 D4
W Yorks 204 F6
Hole Bottom W Yorks 196 C2
Holefield Borders 263 C8
Holehills N Lnrk 268 B5
Holehouse Derbys 185 C8
Holehouses Ches E 184 F2
Hole-in-the-Wall Hereford 98 F2
Holemill Aberdeen 293 C10
Holemoor Devon 24 F6
Hole's Hole Devon 7 B8
Holestane Dumfries 247 D9
Holestone Derbys 170 C4
Hole Street W Sus 35 E10
Holewater Devon 41 F8
Holford Som 43 E7
Holgate York 207 C7
Holker Cumb 211 D7
Holkham Norf 176 E5
Hollacombe Devon 24 G5
Devon 26 G4
Hollacombe Hill Devon 7 E10
Holland Orkney 314 A4
Orkney 314 D6
Sur 52 C2
Holland Fen Lincs 174 F2
Holland Lees Lancs 194 F4
Holland-on-Sea Essex 89 B12
Hollands Som 29 D9
Hollandstoun Orkney 314 A7
Hollee Dumfries 239 D7
Hollesley Suff 109 C7
Hollicombe Torbay 9 C7
Hollies Common Staffs 150 E6
Hollinfare Warr 183 C11
Hollingbourne Kent 53 B10
Hollingbury Brighton 36 F4
Hollingdean Brighton 36 F4
Hollingdon Bucks 103 F7
Hollingrove E Sus 37 C11
Hollingthorpe W Yorks 197 D10
Hollington Derbys 152 B4
E Sus 38 E3
Hants 48 B2
Staffs 151 B11
Hollington Cross Hants 48 B2
Hollington Grove Derbys 152 B4
Hollingwood Derbys 186 G6
Hollingworth Gtr Man 185 B8
Hollin Hall Lancs 204 F4
Hollin Park W Yorks 206 F2
Hollins Cumb 222 G3
Derbys 186 G4
Gtr Man 195 F8
Gtr Man 195 F10
Gtr Man 195 F11
Staffs 168 D6
Staffs 168 E4
Staffs 169 F7
Hollinsclough Staffs 169 B9
Hollins End S Yorks 186 E5
Hollinsgreen Ches E 168 C2
Hollins Green Warr 183 C11
Hollins Lane Lancs 202 C5
Shrops 149 B10
Hollinswood Telford 132 B4
Hollinthorpe W Yorks 206 G3
Hollinwood Gtr Man 196 G2
Shrops 149 B10
Hollis Green Devon 27 F9
Hollis Head Devon 27 G7
Hollocombe Devon 25 E10
Hollocombe Town Devon 25 E10
Holloway Derbys 170 D4
Wilts 45 G11
Windsor 65 C10
Holloway Hill Sur 50 E3
Hollow Brook Bath 60 G5
Hollowell Northants 120 C3
Hollow Meadows S Yorks 186 D2
Hollowmoor Heath Ches W 167 B7
Hollow Oak Dorset 18 C2
Hollows Dumfries 239 B9
Hollow Street Kent 71 G8
Holly Bank W Mid 133 C11
Hollyberry End W Mid 134 G5
Holly Brook Som 44 D4
Hollybush Caerph 77 E11
E Ayrs 257 G9
Stoke 168 G5
Torf 78 G3
Worcs 98 D5
Holly Bush Wrex 166 G6
Hollybush Corner Bucks 66 B3
Suff 125 F8
Hollybushes Kent 54 B2
Hollybush Hill Bucks 66 C3
Essex 89 B10
Hollycroft Leics 135 E8
Holly Cross Windsor 65 C10
Holly End Norf 139 B9
Holly Green Bucks 84 E3
Worcs 99 C7
Holly Hill N Yorks 224 E3
Hollyhurst Shrops 131 D9
Warks 135 F7
Hollym E Yorks 201 B10
Hollywaste Shrops 116 B2
Hollywater Hants 49 G10
Hollywood Worcs 117 B11
Holmacott Devon 25 B8
Holman Clavel Som 28 D2
Holmbridge W Yorks 196 F6
Holmbury St Mary Sur 50 E6
Holmbush Corn 5 E10
Dorset 28 G5
Holmcroft Staffs 151 D8
Holme Cambs 138 F3
C Beds 104 C3
Cumb 211 D10
N Lincs 200 F2
Notts 172 D4
N Yorks 215 C7
W Yorks 196 F6
W Yorks 205 G9
Holmebridge Dorset 18 D3
Holme Chapel Lancs 195 B11
Holme Green C Beds 104 C3
N Yorks 207 E7
Wokingham 65 F10
Holme Hale Norf 141 B7
Holme Hill NE Lincs 201 F9
Holme Lacy Hereford 97 D11
Holme Lane Notts 154 B2
Holme Marsh Hereford 114 G6
Holme Mills Cumb 211 D10
Holme next the Sea Norf 176 E2
Holme-on-Spalding-Moor E Yorks 208 F2
Holme on the Wolds E Yorks 208 D5
Holme Pierrepont Notts 154 B2
Holmer Hereford 97 C10
Holmer Green Bucks 84 F6
Holmes Lancs 194 D2
Holme St Cuthbert Cumb 229 B8
Holmes Chapel Ches E 168 B3
Holmesdale Derbys 186 F5
Holmesfield Derbys 186 F4
Holme Slack Lancs 203 G7
Holme's Hill E Sus 23 C8
Holmeswood Lancs 194 D2
Holmethorpe Sur 51 C9
Holmewood Derbys 170 B6
Holme Wood W Yorks 205 G9
Holmfield W Yorks 196 B5
Holmfirth W Yorks 196 F6
Holmhead Angus 293 F7
Dumfries 246 F6
E Ayrs 258 E3
Holmhill Dumfries 247 D9
Holmisdale Highld 297 G7
Holmley Common Derbys 186 F5
Holmpton E Yorks 201 C11
Holmrook Cumb 219 F11
Holmsgarth Shetland 313 J6
Holmside Durham 233 B10
Holmsleigh Green Devon 28 G2
Holmston S Ayrs 257 E9
Holmwood Corner Sur 51 E7
Holmwrangle Cumb 230 B6
Holne Devon 8 B4
Holnest Dorset 29 E11
Holnicote Som 42 D2
Holsworthy Devon 24 G4
Holsworthy Beacon Devon 24 F5
Holt Dorset 31 G8
Hants 49 C8
Mers 183 C7
Norf 159 B11
Wilts 61 G11
Worcs 116 E6
Wrex 166 E6
Holtby York 207 C9
Holt End Hants 49 F7
Worcs 117 D11
Holt Fleet Worcs 116 E6
Holt Green Lancs 193 G11
Holt Head W Yorks 196 E5
Holt Heath Dorset 31 G9
Worcs 116 E6
Holt Hill Kent 53 B8
Staffs 152 D2
Holton Oxon 83 D10
Som 29 B11
Suff 127 B7
Holton cum Beckering Lincs 189 E10
Holton Heath Dorset 18 C4
Holton le Clay Lincs 201 G9
Holton le Moor Lincs 189 B9
Holton St Mary Suff 107 D11
Holt Park W Yorks 205 E11
Holt Pound Hants 49 E10
Holts Gtr Man 196 G3
Holtspur Bucks 84 G6
Holt Wood Dorset 31 F8
Holtye E Sus 52 F3
Holway Dorset 28 G5
Dorset 29 C10
Flint 181 F11
Som 28 C2
Holwell Dorset 30 E2
Herts 104 E3
Leics 154 E4
Oxon 82 D2
Som 45 D8
Holwellbury C Beds 104 E3
Holwick Durham 232 F4
Holworth Dorset 17 E11
Holybourne Hants 49 E8
Holy City Devon 28 G3
Holy Cross T&W 243 D8
Worcs 117 B8
Holyfield Essex 86 E5
Holyhead / Caergybi Anglesey 178 E2
Holy Island Northumb 273 B11
Holylee Borders 261 B9
Holymoorside Derbys 170 B4
Holyport Windsor 65 D11
Holystone Northumb 251 C11
Holytown N Lnrk 268 C5
Holy Vale Scilly 1 G4
Holywell Cambs 122 C6
C Beds 85 B8
Corn 4 D5
Dorset 29 G9
E Sus 23 F9
Glos 80 G3
Hereford 97 C7
Herts 85 F9
Northumb 243 C8
Som 29 E8
Warks 118 D3
Holywell Green W Yorks 196 D5
Holywell Lake Som 27 C10
Holywell Row Suff 124 B4
Holywell / Treffynnon Flint 181 F11
Holywood Dumfries 247 G10
Homedowns Glos 99 E8
Homer Shrops 132 C2
Homer Green Mers 193 G10
Homersfield Suff 142 F5
Homerton London 67 B11
Hom Green Hereford 97 G11
Homington Wilts 31 B10
Honeybourne Worcs 100 C2
Honeychurch Devon 25 G10
Honeydon Beds 122 F2
Honey Hall N Som 60 G2
Honeyhill Wokingham 65 F10
Honey Hill Kent 70 G6
Honeystreet Wilts 62 G6
Honey Street Wilts 62 G6
Honey Tye Suff 107 D9
Honeywick C Beds 103 G9
Honicknowle Plym 7 D9
Honiley Warks 118 C4
Honing Norf 160 D6
Honingham Norf 160 G2
Honington Lincs 172 G6
Suff 125 C8
Warks 100 C5
Honiton Devon 27 G11
Honkley Wrex 166 D4
Honley W Yorks 196 E6
Honley Moor W Yorks 196 E6
Honnington Telford 150 F4
Honor Oak London 67 E11
Honor Oak Park London 67 E11
Honresfeld Gtr Man 196 D2
Hoo Kent 71 G9

Lan–Lit 393

Som 28 B2
Langford Budville
Som 27 C10
Langford Green
Devon 27 G8
N Som 44 B3
Langham Dorset 30 B3
Essex 107 E10
Norf 177 E8
Rutland 154 G6
Som 28 E4
Suff 125 C9
Langhaugh Borders 260 C6
Langho Lancs 203 G10
Langholm Dumfries 249 G9
Langholme N Lincs 188 B3
Langhope Borders 261 E10
Langland Swansea 56 D6
Langlee Borders 262 B2
Langleeford
Northumb 263 E10
Langlee Mains
Borders 262 B2
Langlees Falk 279 E7
Langley Ches E 184 G6
Derbys 170 F6
Essex 105 D8
Glos 99 F10
Gtr Man 195 F11
Hants 32 G6
Herts 104 G4
Kent 53 C10
Northumb 241 E8
Oxon 82 B4
Slough 66 D4
Som 27 B9
Warks 118 E3
W Mid 133 F9
W Sus 34 B4
Langley Burrell Wilts 62 D2
Langleybury Herts 85 E9
Langley Common
Derbys 152 B5
Wokingham 65 F9
Langley Corner
Bucks 66 C4
Langley Green
Derbys 152 B5
Essex 107 G7
Warks 118 E3
W Mid 133 F9
W Sus 51 F9
Langley Heath Kent 53 C10
Langley Marsh Som 27 B9
Langley Mill Derbys 170 F6
Langley Moor
Durham 233 C11
Langley Park
Durham 233 C10
Langley Street Norf 143 C7
Langley Vale Sur 51 B8
Langloan N Lnrk 268 C4
Langney E Sus 23 E10
Langold Notts 187 D9
Langore Corn 12 D2
Langport Som 28 B6
Langrick Lincs 174 F3
Langrick Bridge
Lincs 174 F3
Langridge Bath 61 F8
Langridge Ford
Devon 25 C9
Langrigg Cumb 222 C5
Cumb 229 B9
Langrish Hants 34 C2
Langsett S Yorks 197 G8
Langshaw Borders 262 B2
Langside Glasgow 267 C11
Perth 285 F11
Langskaill Orkney 314 B4
Langstone Devon 13 E10
Hants 22 C2
Newport 78 G5
Langthorne N Yorks 224 G5
Langthorpe N Yorks 215 F7
Langthwaite
N Yorks 223 E10
Langtoft E Yorks 217 F10
Lincs 156 G2
Langton Durham 224 B3
Lincs 174 B2
Lincs 190 G5
N Yorks 216 F5
Langton by Wragby
Lincs 189 F11
Langton Green Kent 52 F4
Suff 126 C2
Langton Herring
Dorset 17 E8
Langton Long Blandford
Dorset 30 F5
Langton Matravers
Dorset 18 F6
Langtree Devon 25 D7
Langtree Week
Devon 25 D7
Langwathby Cumb 231 E7
Langwell Ho Highld 311 G5
Langwell Lodge
Highld 307 J6
Langwith Derbys 171 B8
Langwith Junction
Derbys 171 B8
Langworth Lincs 189 F9
Lanham Green
Essex 106 G5
Lanivet Corn 5 C10
Lanjeth Corn 5 E9
Lanjew Corn 5 C9
Lank Corn 11 F7
Lanlivery Corn 5 D11
Lanner Corn 2 B6
Lanreath Corn 6 D3
Lanrick Stirl 285 G10
Lansallos Corn 6 E3
Lansbury Park
Caerph 59 B7
Lansdown Bath 61 F8
Glos 99 G8
Lanstephan Corn 12 D2
Lanteglos Corn 11 E7
Lanteglos Highway
Corn 6 E3
Lanton Borders 262 E4
Northumb 263 C10
Lantuel Corn 5 B9
Lantyan Corn 6 D2
Lapal W Mid 133 G9
Lapford Devon 26 F2
Lapford Cross Devon 26 F2
Laphroaig Argyll 254 C4
Lapley Staffs 151 G7
Lapworth Warks 118 C3
Larachbeg Highld 289 E8
Larbert Falk 279 E7
Larbreck Lancs 202 E4
Larches Lancs 202 G6
Larden Green
Ches E 167 E9
Larg Highld 292 B2
Largie Aberds 302 F6
Largiebaan Argyll 255 F7
Largiemore Argyll 275 E10
Largoward Fife 287 G8
Largs N Ayrs 266 D4
Largue Aberds 302 E6
Largybeg N Ayrs 256 E3
Largymeanoch
N Ayrs 256 E2
Largymore N Ayrs 256 E2
Larkfield Invclyd 276 F4
Kent 53 B8
W Yorks 205 F10
Larkhall Bath 61 F9
S Lnrk 268 E5
Larkhill Wilts 46 E6
Lark Hill Gtr Man 195 G7
Larklands Derbys 171 G7
Larks' Hill Suff 108 B3
Larling Norf 141 F9
Larport Hereford 97 D11
Larrick Corn 12 F2
Larriston Borders 250 E2
Lartington Durham 223 B10
Lary Aberds 292 C5
Lasborough Glos 80 G4
Lasham Hants 49 E7
Lashenden Kent 53 E10
Lask Edge Staffs 168 D6
Lassington Glos 98 G5
Lassodie Fife 280 C2
Lastingham
N Yorks 226 G4
Latcham Som 44 D2
Latchbrook Corn 7 D8
Latchford Herts 105 G7
Oxon 83 E11
Warr 183 D10
Latchingdon Essex 88 E5
Latchley Corn 12 G4
Latchmere Green
Hants 64 G6
Latchmore Bank
Essex 87 B7
Lately Common
Warr 183 B11
Lathallan Mill Fife 287 G8
Lathbury M Keynes 103 B7
Latheron Highld 310 F5
Latheronwheel
Highld 310 F5
Latheronwheel Ho
Highld 310 F5
Lathom Lancs 194 E3
Lathones Fife 287 G8
Latimer Bucks 85 F8
Latteridge S Glos 61 C7
Lattiford Som 29 B11
Lattinford Hill Suff 107 D11
Latton Wilts 81 F9
Latton Bush Essex 87 D7
Lauchintilly Aberds 293 B9
Laudale Ho Highld 289 D9
Lauder Borders 271 F10
Lauder Barns
Borders 271 F10
Laugharne/Talacharn
Carms 74 C4
Laughern Hill Worcs 116 F5
Laughterton Lincs 188 F4
Laughton E Sus 23 C8
Leics 136 F3
Lincs 155 C11
Lincs 188 B4
Laughton Common
E Sus 23 C7
S Yorks 187 D8
Laughton en le Morthen
S Yorks 187 D8
Launcells Corn 24 F2
Launcells Cross Corn 24 F3
Launceston Corn 12 D2
Launcherley Som 44 E4
Laund Lancs 195 C10
Launton Oxon 102 G2
Laurencekirk
Aberds 293 F9
Laurieston Dumfries 237 C8
Falk 279 F8
Lavendon M Keynes 121 G8
Lavenham Suff 107 B8
Laverackloch
Moray 301 C11
Laverhay Dumfries 248 D4
Laverlaw Borders 261 B7
Laverley Som 44 F5
Lavernock V Glam 59 F7
Laversdale Cumb 239 E11
Laverstock Wilts 47 G7
Laverstoke Hants 48 D3
Laverton Glos 99 D11
N Yorks 214 E4
Som 45 C9
Lavington Sands
Wilts 46 B4
Lavister Wrex 166 D5
Lavrean Corn 5 D10
Lawers Perth 285 D10
Perth 285 E11
Lawford Essex 107 E11
Som 42 F6
Lawford Heath
Warks 119 C9
Lawhill Perth 286 F3
Law Hill S Lnrk 268 E6
Lawhitton Corn 12 E3
Lawkland N Yorks 212 F5
Lawkland Green
N Yorks 212 F5
Lawley Telford 132 B3
Lawn Swindon 63 C7
Lawnhead Staffs 150 E6
Lawns W Yorks 197 C10
Lawnswood
W Yorks 205 F11
Lawnt Denb 165 B8
Lawrence Hill
Newport 59 B10
Lawrence Weston
Bristol 60 D4
Lawrenny Pembs 73 D8
Lawrenny Quay
Pembs 73 D8
Lawshall Suff 125 G7
Lawshall Green
Suff 125 G7
Lawton Hereford 115 F8
Shrops 131 G10
Lawton-gate
Ches E 168 D4
Lawton Heath End
Ches E 168 D3
Laxey IoM 192 D5
Laxfield Suff 126 C5
Laxfirth Shetland 313 H6
Shetland 313 J6
Laxford Bridge
Highld 306 E7
Laxo Shetland 313 G6
Laxobigging
Shetland 312 F6
Laxton E Yorks 199 B9
Northants 137 D8
Notts 172 B2
Laycock W Yorks 204 E6
Layer Breton Essex 88 B6
Layer de la Haye
Essex 89 B7
Layer Marney Essex 88 B6
Layerthorpe York 207 C8
Layham Suff 107 C10
Laymore Dorset 28 G5
Layters Green Bucks 85 G7
Laytham E Yorks 207 F10
Layton Blkpool 202 F2
Lazenby Redcar 225 B11
Lazonby Cumb 230 D6
Lea Derbys 170 D4
Hereford 98 G3
Lancs 202 G5
Lincs 188 D4
Shrops 131 B8
Shrops 131 F7
Wilts 62 B3
Lea Bridge London 67 B11
Leabrooks Derbys 170 E6
Lea by Backford
Ches W 182 G5
Leacainn W Isles 305 H3
Leac a Li W Isles 305 J3
Leachkin Highld 300 E6
Leacnasaide Highld 299 B7
Leadburn Midloth 270 D4
Leadendale Staffs 151 B8
Leadenham Lincs 173 E7
Leaden Roding Essex 87 C9
Leadgate Cumb 231 C10
Durham 242 G4
T&W 242 F4
Leadhills S Lnrk 259 G9
Leadingcross Green
Kent 53 C11
Leadmill Derbys 186 E2
Flint 166 C2
Lea End Worcs 117 B10
Leafield Oxon 82 B4
Wilts 61 F11
Lea Forge Ches E 168 F2
Leagrave Luton 103 G10
Leagreen Hants 19 C11
Lea Green Mers 183 C8
Lea Hall W Mid 134 F2
Lea Heath Staffs 151 D10
Leake Lincs 174 F6
N Yorks 225 G8
Leake Commonside
Lincs 174 E5
Leake Fold Hill
Lincs 174 E6
Lealholm N Yorks 226 D5
Lealholm Side
N Yorks 226 D5
Lea Line Hereford 98 G3
Lealt Argyll 275 D7
Highld 298 C5
Leam Derbys 186 F2
Lea Marston Warks 134 E4
Leamington Hastings
Warks 119 D8
Leamoor Common
Shrops 131 F8
Leamore W Mid 133 C9
Leamside Durham 234 B2
Leanach Argyll 275 D11
Leanachan Highld 290 F4
Leanaig Highld 300 D5
Leapgate Worcs 116 C6
Leargybreck Argyll 274 F6
Lease Rigg N Yorks 226 E6
Leasey Bridge Herts 85 C11
Leasgill Cumb 211 C9
Leasingham Lincs 173 F9
Leasingthorne
Durham 233 F11
Leason Swansea 56 C3
Leasowe Mers 182 C3
Leatherhead Sur 51 B7
Leatherhead Common
Sur 51 B7
Leathern Bottle Glos 80 E2
Leathley N Yorks 205 D10
Leaths Dumfries 237 C9
Leaton Shrops 149 F9
Telford 150 G2
Leaton Heath
Shrops 149 F9
Lea Town Lancs 202 G5
Lea Valley Herts 85 B11
Leaveland Kent 54 C4
Leavenheath Suff 107 D9
Leavening N Yorks 216 G5
Leavesden Green
Herts 85 E9
Leaves Green London 68 G2
Lea Yeat Cumb 212 B5
Leazes Durham 242 F5
Lebberston
N Yorks 217 C11
Leburnick Corn 12 E3
Lechlade-on-Thames
Glos 82 F2
Leck Lancs 212 D2
Leckford Hants 47 F11
Leckfurin Highld 308 D7
Leckgruinart Argyll 274 G3
Leckhampstead
Bucks 102 D4
W Berks 64 D2
Leckhampstead Thicket
W Berks 64 D2
Leckhampton Glos 80 B6
Leckie Highld 299 C10
Leckmelm Highld 307 K6
Leckuary Argyll 275 D9
Leckwith V Glam 59 E7
Leconfield E Yorks 208 E6
Ledaig Argyll 289 F11
Ledburn Bucks 103 G8
Ledbury Hereford 98 D4
Ledcharrie Stirl 285 E9
Leddington Glos 98 E3
Ledgemoor
Hereford 115 G8
Ledgowan Highld 299 D11
Ledicot Hereford 115 E8
Ledmore Angus 293 G7
Highld 307 H7
Lednagullin Highld 308 C7
Ledsham Ches W 182 G5
W Yorks 198 B3
Ledston W Yorks 198 B2
Ledstone Devon 8 F4
Ledston Luck
W Yorks 206 G4
Ledwell Oxon 101 F8
Lee Argyll 288 G6
Devon 40 D3
Devon 40 D5
Hants 32 D5
Lancs 203 B7
London 67 E11
Northumb 241 F10
Shrops 149 C8
Leeans Shetland 313 J5
Lee Bank W Mid 133 F11
Leebotten Shetland 313 L6
Leebotwood Shrops 131 D9
Lee Brockhurst
Shrops 149 D10
Leece Cumb 210 F4
Lee Chapel Essex 69 B7
Leechpool Mon 60 B4
Lee Clump Bucks 84 E6
Lee Common Bucks 84 E6
Leeds Kent 53 C10
W Yorks 205 G11
Leedstown Corn 2 C4
Leeford Devon 41 D9
Lee Gate Bucks 84 D5
Leegomery Telford 150 G3
Lee Ground Hants 33 F8
Lee Head Derbys 185 C8
Leeholme Durham 233 E10
Leek Staffs 169 D7
Leekbrook Staffs 169 E7
Leek Wootton
Warks 118 D5
Lee Mill Devon 8 D2
Leeming N Yorks 214 B5
W Yorks 204 G6
Leeming Bar
N Yorks 224 G5
Leemings Lancs 203 D10
Lee Moor Devon 7 C11
W Yorks 197 B10
Lee-on-the-Solent
Hants 33 G9
Lee-over-Sands
Essex 89 C10
Lees Derbys 152 B5
Gtr Man 196 G3
W Yorks 204 F6
Leesthorpe Leics 154 G5
Leeswood/Coed-Llai
Flint 166 D3
Leetown Perth 286 E6
Leftwich Ches W 183 G11
Legar Powys 78 B2
Legbourne Lincs 190 E5
Legburthwaite
Cumb 220 B6
Legerwood
Borders 271 G11
Leggatt Hill W Sus 34 C6
Legsby Lincs 189 D10
Leicester Leicester 135 C11
Leicester Forest East
Leics 135 C10
Leicester Grange
Warks 135 E8
Leigh Devon 26 E2
Dorset 18 B6
Dorset 29 F10
Dorset 30 F3
Glos 99 F7
Gtr Man 195 G7
Kent 52 D4
Shrops 130 C6
Sur 51 D8
Wilts 81 G9
Worcs 116 G5
Leigham Plym 7 D10
Leigh Beck Essex 69 C10
Leigh Common Som 30 B2
Leigh Delamere
Wilts 61 D11
Leigh Green Kent 54 G2
Leighland Chapel
Som 42 F4
Leigh-on-Sea
Shend 69 B10
Leigh Park Hants 22 B2
Leigh Sinton Worcs 116 G5
Leighswood
W Mid 133 C11
Leighterton Glos 80 G4
Leighton N Yorks 214 D3
Shrops 132 B2
Som 45 E8
Leighton Bromswold
Cambs 122 B2
Leighton Buzzard
C Beds 103 F8
Leighton/Tre'r llai
Powys 130 B4
Leigh upon Mendip
Som 45 D7
Leigh Woods N Som 60 E5
Leinthall Earls
Hereford 115 D8
Leinthall Starkes
Hereford 115 D8
Leintwardine
Hereford 115 C8
Leire Leics 135 E10
Leirinmore Highld 308 C4
Leiston Suff 127 E8
Leitfie Perth 286 C6
Leith Edin 280 F5
Leithenhall
Dumfries 248 D4
Leitholm Borders 272 G5
Lelant Corn 2 B2
Lelant Downs Corn 2 B2
Lelley E Yorks 209 G10
Lem Hill Worcs 116 C4
Lemington T&W 242 E5
Lemmington Hall
Northumb 264 G4
Lempitlaw Borders 263 C7
Lemsford Herts 86 C2
Lenacre Cumb 212 B3
Lenborough Bucks 102 E3
Lenchwick Worcs 99 B10
Lendalfoot S Ayrs 244 F4
Lendrick Lodge
Stirl 285 G9
Lenham Kent 53 C11
Lenham Forstal Kent 54 C2
Lenham Heath Kent 54 D2
Lennel Borders 273 G7
Lennoxtown E Dunb 278 F2
Lent Bucks 66 C2
Lenten Pool Denb 165 B8
Lenton Lincs 155 C10
Nottingham 153 B11
Lenton Abbey
Nottingham 153 B10
Lentran Highld 300 E5
Lent Rise Bucks 66 C2
Lenwade Norf 159 F11
Leny Ho Stirl 285 G10
Lenzie E Dunb 278 G3
Lenziemill N Lnrk 278 G5
Leoch Angus 287 D7
Leochel-Cushnie
Aberds 293 B7
Leominster Hereford 115 F9
Leomonsley Staffs 134 B2
Leonard Stanley Glos 80 E4
Leonardston Pembs 72 D6
Leorin Argyll 254 C4
Lepe Hants 20 B5
Lephin Highld 297 G7
Lephinchapel
Argyll 275 D10
Lephinmore Argyll 275 D10
Leppington N Yorks 216 G5
Lepton W Yorks 197 D8
Lepton Edge
W Yorks 197 D8
Lerigoligan Argyll 275 C9
Lerrocks Stirl 285 G11
Lerryn Corn 6 D2
Lerwick Shetland 313 J6
Lesbury Northumb 264 G6
Leschangie Aberds 293 B9
Le Skerne Haughton
Darl 224 B6
Leslie Aberds 302 G5
Fife 286 G6
Lesmahagow S Lnrk 259 B8
Lesnewth Corn 11 C8
Lessendrum Aberds 302 E5
Lessingham Norf 161 D7
Lessness Heath
London 68 D3
Lessonhall Cumb 238 G6
Leswalt Dumfries 236 C2
Letchmore Heath
Herts 85 F11
Letchworth Herts 104 E4
Letcombe Bassett
Oxon 63 B11
Letcombe Regis
Oxon 63 B11
Letham Angus 287 C9
Falk 279 D7
Fife 287 F7
Perth 286 E4
Letham Grange
Angus 287 C10
Lethem Borders 250 B5
Lethen Ho Highld 301 D9
Lethenty Aberds 303 E8
Aberds 303 G7
Letheringham Suff 126 F5
Letheringsett Norf 159 B11
Lettaford Devon 13 E10
Lettan Orkney 314 B7
Letter Aberds 293 B9
Letterewe Highld 299 B9
Letterfearn Highld 295 C10
Letterfinlay Highld 290 D4
Lettermay Argyll 284 G5
Lettermorar Highld 295 G9
Lettermore Argyll 288 E6
Letters Highld 307 L6
Letterston/Treletert
Pembs 91 F8
Lettoch Highld 292 B2
Highld 301 F10
Moray 302 F3
Perth 291 G11
Letton Hereford 96 B6
Hereford 115 C7
Letton Green Norf 141 B9
Lett's Green Kent 52 B3
Letty Brongu
Bridgend 57 D11
Letty Green Herts 86 C3
Letwell S Yorks 187 D9
Leuchars Fife 287 E8
Leuchars Ho Moray 302 C2
Leumrabhagh
W Isles 305 G5
Levalsa Meor Corn 5 F10
Levan Invclyd 276 F4
Levaneap Shetland 313 G6
Levedale Staffs 151 F7
Level of Mendalgief
Newport 59 B10
Level's Green Essex 105 G9
Leven E Yorks 209 D8
Fife 287 G7
Levencorroch
N Ayrs 256 E2
Levenhall E Loth 281 G7
Levens Cumb 211 B9
Leven Seat W Loth 269 D8
Levens Green Herts 105 G7
Levenshulme
Gtr Man 184 C5
Leventhorpe
W Yorks 205 G8
Levenwick Shetland 313 L6
Lever-Edge
Gtr Man 195 F8
Leverington Cambs 157 G8
Leverington Common
Cambs 157 G8
Leverstock Green
Herts 85 D9
Leverton Lincs 174 F6
W Berks 63 E10
Leverton Highgate
Lincs 174 F6
Leverton Lucasgate
Lincs 174 F6
Leverton Outgate
Lincs 174 F6
Levington Suff 108 D4
Levisham N Yorks 226 G6
Levishie Highld 290 B6
Lew Oxon 82 D4
Lewannick Corn 11 E11
Lewcombe Dorset 29 F9
Lewdown Devon 12 D4
Lewes E Sus 36 E6
Leweston Pembs 91 G8
Lewisham London 67 D11
Lewiston Highld 300 G5
Lewistown Bridgend 58 B2
Lewknor Oxon 84 F2
Leworthy Devon 24 G4
Devon 41 F7
Lewson Street Kent 70 G3
Lewth Lancs 202 F5
Lewthorn Cross
Devon 13 F11
Lewtrenchard Devon 12 D5
Lexden Essex 107 G9
Ley Aberds 293 B7
Corn 6 B3
Som 41 F10
Leybourne Kent 53 B7
Leyburn N Yorks 224 G2
Leycett Staffs 168 F3
Leyfields Staffs 134 B4
Ley Green Herts 104 G3
Ley Hey Park
Gtr Man 185 D7
Leyhill Bucks 85 E7
S Glos 79 G11
Ley Hill W Mid 134 D2
Leyland Lancs 194 C4
Leylodge Aberds 293 B9
Leymoor W Yorks 196 D6
Leys Aberds 292 C6
Aberds 303 D10
Cumb 219 B11
Perth 286 D6
Staffs 169 F8
Leys Castle Highld 300 E6
Leysdown-on-Sea
Kent 70 E4
Leys Hill Hereford 79 B9
Leysmill Angus 287 C10
Leys of Cossans
Angus 287 C7
Leysters Hereford 115 E11
Leysters Pole
Hereford 115 E11
Leyton London 67 B11
Leytonstone London 67 B11
Lezant Corn 12 F2
Lezerea Corn 2 C5
Leziate Norf 158 F3
Lhanbryde Moray 302 C2
Liatrie Highld 300 F2
Libanus Powys 95 F9
Libberton S Lnrk 269 G9
Libbery Worcs 117 F9
Liberton Edin 270 B5
Liceasto W Isles 305 J3
Lichfield Staffs 134 B2
Lick Perth 286 B2
Lickey Worcs 117 B9
Lickey End Worcs 117 C9
Lickfold W Sus 34 B6
Lickhill Worcs 116 C6
Lickleyhead Castle
Aberds 302 G6
Liddaton Devon 12 E5
Liddel Orkney 314 H4
Liddesdale Highld 289 D9
Liddeston Pembs 72 D5
Liddington Swindon 63 C8
Liden Swindon 63 C7
Lidgate Suff 124 F4
Lidget S Yorks 199 G7
Lidget Green
W Yorks 205 G8
Lidgett Notts 171 B10
Lidgett Park
W Yorks 206 F2
Lidham Hill E Sus 38 D4
Lidlington C Beds 103 D9
Lidsey W Sus 22 C6
Lidsing Kent 69 G9
Lidstone Oxon 101 G7
Lieurary Highld 310 C4
Liff Angus 287 D7
Lifford W Mid 117 B11
Lifton Devon 12 D3
Liftondown Devon 12 D3
Lightcliffe W Yorks 196 B6
Lighteach Shrops 149 C10
Lightfoot Green
Lancs 202 G6
Lighthorne Warks 118 F6
Lighthorne Heath
Warks 119 F7
Lighthorne Rough
Warks 118 F6
Lightmoor Telford 132 B3
Light Oaks Staffs 168 E6
Lightpill Glos 80 E4
Lightwater Sur 66 G2
Lightwood Shrops 132 E2
Shrops 150 D3
Staffs 169 G8
Stoke 168 G6
S Yorks 186 E5
Lightwood Green
Ches E 167 G10
Wrex 166 G5
Liglartrie S Ayrs 244 F6
Lilbourne
Northants 119 B11
Lilburn Tower
Northumb 264 E2
Lilford Gtr Man 195 G7
Lillesdon Som 28 C4
Lilleshall Telford 150 F4
Lilley Herts 104 F2
W Berks 64 D2
Lilliesleaf Borders 262 E2
Lillingstone Dayrell
Bucks 102 D4
Lillingstone Lovell
Bucks 102 C4
Lillington Dorset 29 E10
Warks 118 D6
Lilliput Poole 18 C6
Lilstock Som 43 E7
Lilybank Invclyd 276 G6
Lilyhurst Shrops 150 G4
Lilyvale Kent 54 F5
Limbrick Lancs 194 D6
Limbury Luton 103 G11
Limebrook Hereford 115 D7
Limefield Gtr Man 195 E10
Limehouse London 67 C11
Limehurst Gtr Man 196 G2
Limekilnburn S Lnrk 268 E4
Limekiln Field
Derbys 187 G7
Limekilns Fife 279 E11
Limerigg Falk 279 G7
Limerstone IoW 20 E4
Lime Side Gtr Man 196 G2
Limestone Brae
Northumb 231 B11
Lime Street Worcs 98 E6
Lime Tree Park
W Mid 118 B5
Limington Som 29 C8
Limpenhoe Norf 143 C7
Limpenhoe Hill
Norf 143 C8
Limpers Hill Wilts 45 G10
Limpley Stoke Wilts 61 G9
Limpsfield Sur 52 C2
Limpsfield Chart Sur 52 C2
Limpsfield Common
Sur 52 C2
Linbriggs Northumb 251 B9
Linburn W Loth 270 B2
Linby Notts 171 E8
Linchmere W Sus 49 G11
Lincluden Dumfries 237 B11
Lincoln Lincs 189 G7
Lincomb Worcs 116 D6
Lincombe Devon 8 D4
Devon 40 D3
Lindale Cumb 211 C8
Lindal in Furness
Cumb 210 D5
Lindean Borders 261 C11
Linden Glos 80 B4
Lindfield W Sus 36 B4
Lindford Hants 49 F10
Lindifferon Fife 287 F7
Lindley N Yorks 205 D10
W Yorks 196 D6
Lindley Green
N Yorks 205 D10
Lindores Fife 286 F6
Lindow End Ches E 184 F4
Lindrick Dale
S Yorks 187 E8
Lindridge Worcs 116 D3
Lindsell Essex 106 F2
Lindsey Suff 107 C9
Lindsey Tye Suff 107 B9
Lindwell W Yorks 196 C5
Lineholt Worcs 116 D6
Lineholt Common
Worcs 116 D6
Liney Som 43 F11
Linfitts Gtr Man 196 F3
Linford Hants 31 F11
Thurrock 69 D7
Lingague IoM 192 E3
Lingards Wood
W Yorks 196 E5
Lingbob W Yorks 205 F7
Lingdale Redcar 226 B3
Lingen Hereford 115 D7
Lingfield Darl 224 C6
Sur 51 E11
Lingfield Common
Sur 51 E11
Lingley Green Warr 183 D9
Lingley Mere Warr 183 D10
Lingreabhagh
W Isles 296 C6
Lingwood Norf 143 B7
Linhope Borders 249 C10
Northumb 263 F11
Linicro Highld 298 C3
Link N Som 44 B3
Linkend Worcs 98 E6
Linkenholt Hants 47 B11
Linkhill Kent 38 B4
Linkinhorne Corn 12 G2
Linklater Orkney 314 H4
Linklet Orkney 314 A7
Linksness Orkney 314 E5
Orkney 314 F2
Linktown Fife 280 C5
Linley Shrops 131 E7
Shrops 132 D3
Linley Brook Shrops 132 D3
Linleygreen Shrops 132 D3
Linley Green
Hereford 116 G3
Linlithgow W Loth 279 F10
Linlithgow Bridge
W Loth 279 F9
Linndhu Ho Argyll 289 D7
Linneraineach
Highld 307 J6
Linns Angus 292 F3
Linnyshaw Gtr Man 195 G8
Linshiels Northumb 251 B9
Linsiadar W Isles 304 E4
Linsidemore Highld 309 K5
Linslade C Beds 103 F8
Linstead Parva Suff 126 B6
Linstock Cumb 239 F10
Linthorpe Mbro 225 B9
Linthurst Worcs 117 C9
Linthwaite W Yorks 196 E6
Lintlaw Borders 272 D6
Lintmill Moray 302 C5
Linton Borders 263 D7
Cambs 105 B11
Derbys 152 F5
Hereford 98 F3
Kent 53 D9
Northumb 253 E7
N Yorks 213 G9
W Yorks 206 D3
Linton Heath Derbys 152 F5
Linton Hill Hereford 98 G3
Linton-on-Ouse
N Yorks 215 G9
Lintridge Glos 98 E4
Lintz Durham 242 F5
Lintzford T&W 242 F4
Lintzgarth Durham 232 C4
Linwood Hants 31 F11
Lincs 189 D10
Renfs 267 C8
Lionacleit W Isles 297 G3
Lional W Isles 304 B7
Lions Green E Sus 23 B9
Liphook Hants 49 G10
Lipley Shrops 150 C4
Lippitts Hill Essex 86 F5
Liquo or Bowhousebog N
Lnrk 269 D7
Liscard Mers 182 C4
Liscombe Som 41 G11
Liskeard Corn 6 C5
Liss Hants 34 B3
Lissett E Yorks 209 B8
Liss Forest Hants 34 B3
Lissington Lincs 189 E10
Lisson Grove London 67 C9
Listerdale S Yorks 187 C7
Listock Som 28 C4
Listoft Lincs 191 G8
Liston Essex 107 C7
Liston Garden Essex 106 B6
Lisvane Cardiff 59 C7
Liswerry Newport 59 B10
Litcham Norf 159 F7
Litchard Bridgend 58 C2
Litchborough
Northants 120 G2
Litchfield Hants 48 C3
Litchurch Derbys 153 B7
Litherland Mers 182 B4
Litlington Cambs 104 C6
E Sus 23 E8
Litmarsh Hereford 97 B10
Little Abington
Cambs 105 B10
Little Addington
Northants 121 C9
Little Airmyn
E Yorks 199 B8
Little Almshoe
Herts 104 F3
Little Alne Warks 118 E2
Little Altcar Mers 193 F10
Little Ann Hants 47 E10
Little Arowry Wrex 167 G7
Little Asby Cumb 222 D3
Little Ashley Wilts 61 G10
Little Assynt Highld 307 G6
Little Aston Staffs 133 C11
Little Atherfield IoW 20 E5
Little Ayre Orkney 314 G3
Little-ayre Shetland 313 G5
Little Ayton
N Yorks 225 C11
Little Baddow Essex 88 D3
Little Badminton
S Glos 61 C10
Little Ballinluig
Perth 286 B3
Little Bampton
Cumb 239 F7
Little Bardfield
Essex 106 E3
Little Barford Beds 122 F3
Little Barningham
Norf 160 C2
Little Barrington
Glos 82 C2
Little Barrow
Ches W 183 G7
Little Barugh
N Yorks 216 D5
Little Bavington
Northumb 241 B11
Little Bayham E Sus 52 F6
Little Bealings Suff 108 B4
Littlebeck N Yorks 227 D7
Little Beckford Glos 99 E9
Little Bedwyn Wilts 63 F9
Little Bentley Essex 108 F2
Little Berkhamsted
Herts 86 D3
Little Billing
Northants 120 E6
Little Billington
C Beds 103 G8
Little Birch Hereford 97 E10
Little Bispham
Blkpool 202 E2
Little Blakenham
Suff 108 B2
Little Blencow
Cumb 230 E5
Little Bloxwich
W Mid 133 C10
Little Bognor W Sus 35 C8
Little Bolehill
Derbys 170 E3
Little Bollington
Ches E 184 D2
Little Bolton
Gtr Man 184 B3
Little Bookham Sur 50 C6
Littleborough Devon 26 E4

Gtr Man 196 D2
Notts 188 E4
Little Bosullow Corn 1 C4
Littlebourne Kent 55 B8
Little Bourton Oxon 101 C9
Little Bowden Leics 136 F4
Little Boys Heath Bucks 84 F6
Little Bradley Suff 124 G3
Little Braithwaite Cumb 229 G10
Little Brampton Shrops 131 G7
Little Braxted Essex 88 C4
Little Bray Devon 41 F7
Little Brechin Angus 293 G7
Littlebredy Dorset 17 D7
Little Brickhill M Keynes 103 E8
Little Bridgeford Staffs 151 D7
Little Brington Northants 120 E3
Little Bristol S Glos 80 G2
Little Britain Warks 118 G2
Little Bromley Essex 107 F11
Little Bromwich W Mid 134 F2
Little Broughton Cumb 229 E7
Little Budworth Ches W 167 B9
Little Burstead Essex 87 G11
Littlebury Essex 105 D10
Littlebury Green Essex 105 D9
Little Bytham Lincs 155 F10
Little Cambridge Essex 106 F2
Little Canfield Essex 105 G11
Little Canford Poole 18 B6
Little Carleton Lancs 202 F2
Little Carlton Lincs 190 D5
Notts 172 D3
Little Casterton Rutland 137 B10
Little Catwick E Yorks 209 E8
Little Catworth Cambs 122 C2
Little Cawthorpe Lincs 190 E5
Little Chalfield Wilts 61 G11
Little Chalfont Bucks 85 F7
Little Chart Kent 54 D2
Little Chart Forstal Kent 54 D3
Little Chell Stoke 168 E5
Little Chester Derby 153 B7
Little Chesterford Essex 105 C10
Little Chesterton Oxon 101 G11
Little Cheverell Wilts 46 C3
Little Chishill Cambs 105 D8
Little Clacton Essex 89 B11
Little Clanfield Oxon 82 E3
Little Clegg Gtr Man 196 E2
Little Clifton Cumb 229 F7
Little Coates NE Lincs 201 F8
Little Colp Aberds 303 E7
Little Comberton Worcs 99 C9
Little Comfort Corn 12 E2
Little Common E Sus 38 F2
Lincs 156 D6
Shrops 115 B7
W Sus 34 C6
Little Compton Warks 100 E5
Little Corby Cumb 239 F11
Little Cornard Suff 107 D7
Littlecote Bucks 102 G6
Littlecott Wilts 46 C6
Little Cowarne Hereford 116 G2
Little Coxwell Oxon 82 G3
Little Crakehall N Yorks 224 G4
Little Cransley Northants 120 B6
Little Crawley M Keynes 103 B8
Little Creaton Northants 120 C4
Little Creich Highld 309 L6
Little Cressingham Norf 141 D7
Little Crosby Mers 193 G10
Little Cubley Derbys 152 B3
Little Dalby Leics 154 G5
Little Dawley Telford 132 B3
Littledean Glos 79 C11
Littledean Hill Glos 79 C11
Little Dens Aberds 303 E10
Little Dewchurch Hereford 97 E10
Little Ditton Cambs 124 F3
Little Doward Hereford 79 B8
Littledown Bmouth 19 C8
Hants 47 B10
Little Downham Cambs 139 G10
Little Drayton Shrops 150 C3
Little Driffield E Yorks 208 B6
Little Drybrook Glos 79 D9
Little Dunham Norf 159 G7
Little Dunkeld Perth 286 C4
Little Dunmow Essex 106 G3
Little Durnford Wilts 46 G6
Little Eastbury Worcs 116 F6
Little Easton Essex 106 G2
Little Eaton Derbys 170 G5
Little Eccleston Lancs 202 E4
Little Ellingham Norf 141 D10
Little End Cambs 122 F3
Essex 87 E8
E Yorks 208 F2
Little Everdon Northants 119 F11
Little Eversden Cambs 123 G7
Little Faringdon Oxon 82 E2
Little Fencote N Yorks 224 G5
Little Fenton N Yorks 206 F6
Littleferry Highld 311 K2
Littlefield NE Lincs 201 F9
Littlefield Common Sur 50 C3
Littlefield Green Windsor 65 D11
Little Finborough Suff 125 G10
Little Fransham Norf 159 G8
Little Frith Kent 54 B2
Little Gaddesden Herts 85 C7
Littlegain Shrops 132 D5
Little Gidding Cambs 138 G2
Little Gight Aberds 303 F8
Little Glemham Suff 126 F6
Little Glenshee Perth 286 D3
Little Gorsley Glos 98 F3
Little Gransden Cambs 122 F5
Little Green Cambs 104 B5
Notts 172 G2
Som 45 D8
Suff 125 C11
Wrex 167 G7
Little Grimsby Lincs 190 C4
Little Gringley Notts 188 E2
Little Gruinard Highld 307 L4
Little Habton N Yorks 216 D4
Little Hadham Herts 105 G8
Little Hale Lincs 173 G10
Norf 141 B8
Little Hallam Derbys 171 G7
Little Hallingbury Essex 87 B7
Littleham Devon 14 E6
Devon 24 C6
Little Hampden Bucks 84 E5
Littlehampton W Sus 35 G8
Little Haresfield Glos 80 D4
Little Harrowden Northants 121 C7
Little Harwood Blkburn 195 B7
Little Haseley Oxon 83 E10
Little Hatfield E Yorks 209 E9
Little Hautbois Norf 160 E5
Little Haven Pembs 72 C5
W Sus 51 G7
Little Hay Staffs 134 C2
Little Hayfield Derbys 185 D8
Little Haywood Staffs 151 E10
Little Heath Ches E 167 G11
Ches W 166 B6
Herts 85 D8
Herts 86 E3
London 68 B3
Staffs 151 F8
Sur 66 G6
W Berks 65 E7
W Mid 134 G6
Little Heck N Yorks 198 C5
Littlehempston Devon 8 C6
Little Henham Essex 105 E10
Little Henny Essex 107 D7
Little Herbert's Glos 81 B7
Little Hereford Hereford 115 D11
Little Hill Hereford 97 F9
Som 28 E3
Little Holbury Hants 32 G6
Little Honeyborough Pembs 73 D7
Little Hoole Moss Houses Lancs 194 C3
Little Horkesley Essex 107 E9
Little Hormead Herts 105 F8
Little Horsted E Sus 23 B7
Little Horton Wilts 62 G4
W Yorks 205 G9
Little Horwood Bucks 102 E5
Littlehoughton Northumb 264 F6
Little Houghton Northants 120 F6
S Yorks 198 G2
Little Hucklow Derbys 185 F11
Little Hulton Gtr Man 195 G8
Little Humber E Yorks 201 C8
Little Hungerford W Berks 64 E4
Little Ilford London 68 B2
Little Ingestre Staffs 151 E9
Little Inkberrow Worcs 117 F10
Little Irchester Northants 121 D8
Little Keyford Som 45 D9
Little Kimble Bucks 84 D4
Little Kineton Warks 118 G6
Little Kingshill Bucks 84 F5
Little Knowles Green Suff 124 F5
Little Langdale Cumb 220 E6
Little Langford Wilts 46 F4
Little Laver Essex 87 D8
Little Lawford Warks 119 B9
Little Layton Blkpool 202 F2
Little Leigh Ches W 183 F10
Little Leighs Essex 88 B2
Little Lepton W Yorks 197 E8
Little Leven E Yorks 209 D8
Little Lever Gtr Man 195 F9
Little Limber Lincs 200 E6
Little Linford M Keynes 102 C6
Little Load Som 29 C7
Little London Bucks 83 C10
Bucks 84 D5
Cambs 139 D8
Essex 105 F9
Essex 106 D3
E Sus 23 B9
Glos 80 B2
Hants 47 D11
Hants 48 B6
Lincs 156 E4
Lincs 157 E8
Lincs 189 D10
Lincs 190 F4
Norf 140 D5
Norf 160 C2
Norf 160 C5
Norf 160 E3
Oxon 83 E8
Powys 129 F10
Shrops 131 F10
Som 44 D6
Suff 125 F10
Worcs 116 C2
W Yorks 205 F10
Little Longstone Derbys 185 G11
Little Lynturk Aberds 293 B7
Little Lyth Shrops 131 B9
Little Madeley Staffs 168 F3
Little Malvern Worcs 98 C5
Little Mancot Flint 166 B4
Little Maplestead Essex 106 E6
Little Marcle Hereford 98 D3
Little Marlow Bucks 65 B11
Little Marsden Lancs 204 F3
Little Marsh Bucks 102 G3
Norf 159 B10
Wilts 45 B11
Little Marton Blkpool 202 G2
Little Mascalls Essex 88 E2
Little Massingham Norf 158 E5
Little Melton Norf 142 B3
Little Merthyr Hereford 96 B5
Little Milford Pembs 73 C7
Littlemill Aberds 292 D5
E Ayrs 257 F11
Highld 301 D9
Northumb 264 F6
Little Mill Kent 53 D7
Mon 78 E4
Little Milton Newport 59 B11
Oxon 83 E10
Little Minster Oxon 82 C4
Little Missenden Bucks 84 F6
Little Mongeham Kent 55 C10
Littlemoor Derbys 170 C5
Dorset 17 E9
Little Moor Gtr Man 184 D6
Lancs 203 E10
Little Moor End Lancs 195 B8
Littlemore Oxon 83 E8
Little Morrell Warks 118 F6
Littlemoss Gtr Man 184 B6
Little Mountain Flint 166 C3
Little Musgrave Cumb 222 C5
Little Ness Shrops 149 F8
Little Neston Ches W 182 F3
Little Newcastle Pembs 91 F9
Little Newsham Durham 224 B2
Little Norlington E Sus 23 C7
Little Norton Som 29 D7
Little Oakley Essex 108 F4
Northants 137 F7
Little Odell Beds 121 F9
Little Offley Herts 104 F2
Little Onn Staffs 150 F6
Little Ormside Cumb 222 B4
Little Orton Cumb 239 F9
Leics 134 B6
Little Ouse Norf 140 F2
Little Ouseburn N Yorks 215 G8
Littleover Derby 152 C6
Little Overton Wrex 166 G5
Little Oxney Green Essex 87 D11
Little Packington Warks 134 G4
Little Parndon Essex 86 C6
Little Paxton Cambs 122 E3
Little Petherick Corn 10 G4
Little Pitlurg Moray 302 E4
Little Plumpton Lancs 202 G3
Little Plumstead Norf 160 G6
Little Ponton Lincs 155 C8
Littleport Cambs 139 F11
Little Posbrook Hants 33 G8
Little Poulton Lancs 202 F3
Little Preston Kent 53 B8
W Yorks 206 G3
Littler Ches W 167 B10
Little Raveley Cambs 122 B5
Little Reedness E Yorks 199 C10
Little Reynoldston Swansea 56 D3
Little Ribston N Yorks 206 C3
Little Rissington Glos 81 B11
Little Rogart Highld 309 J7
Little Rollright Oxon 100 E5
Little Ryburgh Norf 159 D9
Little Ryle Northumb 264 G2
Little Ryton Shrops 131 C9
Little Salisbury Wilts 63 G7
Little Salkeld Cumb 231 D7
Little Sampford Essex 106 E3
Little Sandhurst Brack 65 G10
Little Saredon Staffs 133 B8
Little Saxham Suff 124 E5
Little Scatwell Highld 300 D3
Little Scotland Gtr Man 194 E6
Little Sessay N Yorks 215 E9
Little Shelford Cambs 123 G9
Little Shoddesden Hants 47 D9
Little Shrewley Warks 118 D4
Little Shurdington Glos 80 B6
Little Silver Devon 26 F6
Devon 40 E4
Little Singleton Lancs 202 F3
Little Skillymarno Aberds 303 D9
Little Skipwith N Yorks 207 F9
Little Smeaton N Yorks 198 D4
N Yorks 224 E6
Little Snoring Norf 159 C9
Little Sodbury S Glos 61 C9
Little Sodbury End S Glos 61 C8
Little Somborne Hants 47 G11
Little Somerford Wilts 62 C3
Little Soudley Shrops 150 D4
Little Stainforth N Yorks 212 F6
Little Stainton Darl 234 G2
Little Stanmore London 85 G11
Little Stanney Ches W 182 G6
Little Staughton Beds 122 E2
Littlestead Green Oxon 65 D8
Little Steeping Lincs 174 C6
Little Stoke S Glos 60 C6
Staffs 151 C8
Littlestone-on-Sea Kent 39 C9
Little Stonham Suff 126 E2
Little Stretton Leics 136 C3
Shrops 131 E8
Little Strickland Cumb 221 B11
Little Studley N Yorks 214 E6
Little Stukeley Cambs 122 B4
Little Sugnall Staffs 150 C6
Little Sutton Ches W 182 F5
Lincs 157 E9
Shrops 131 G10
Little Swinburne Northumb 241 B10
Little Tarrington Hereford 98 C2
Little Tew Oxon 101 F7
Little Tey Essex 107 G7
Little Thetford Cambs 123 B10
Little Thirkleby N Yorks 215 D9
Little Thornage Norf 159 B11
Little Thornton Lancs 202 E3
Littlethorpe Leics 135 D10
N Yorks 214 F6
Little Thorpe Durham 234 C4
W Yorks 197 C7
Little Thurlow Suff 124 G3
Little Thurlow Green Suff 124 G3
Little Thurrock Thurrock 68 D6
Littleton Bath 60 G5
Ches W 166 B6
Dorset 30 G5
Guildford, Sur 50 D3
Hants 48 G3
Perth 286 D6
Som 44 G3
Wilts 62 G2
Littleton Common Sur 66 E5
Littleton Drew Wilts 61 C10
Littleton-on-Severn S Glos 60 B5
Littleton Panell Wilts 46 C4
Littleton Spelthorne, Sur 66 F5
Littleton-upon-Severn S Glos 79 G9
Little Torboll Highld 309 K7
Little Torrington Devon 25 D7
Little Totham Essex 88 C5
Little Toux Aberds 302 D5
Littletown Durham 234 C2
IoW 20 C6
W Yorks 197 C8
Little Town Cumb 220 B4
Lancs 203 F9
Warr 183 C10
Little Tring Herts 84 C6
Little Twycross Leics 134 B6
Little Urswick Cumb 210 E5
Little Vantage W Loth 270 C2
Little Wakering Essex 70 B2
Little Walden Essex 105 C10
Little Waldingfield Suff 107 B8
Little Walsingham Norf 159 B8
Little Waltham Essex 88 C2
Little Walton Warks 135 G9
Little Warley Essex 87 G10
Little Warton Warks 134 C5
Little Washbourne Glos 99 E9
Little Weighton E Yorks 208 G5
Little Weldon Northants 137 F8
Little Welland Worcs 98 D6
Little Welnetham Suff 125 E7
Little Welton Lincs 190 D4
Little Wenham Suff 107 D11
Little Wenlock Telford 132 B2
Little Weston Som 29 B10
Little Whitehouse IoW 20 C5
Little Whittingham Green Suff 126 B5
Littlewick Green Windsor 65 D10
Little Wigborough Essex 89 B7
Little Wilbraham Cambs 123 F10
Littlewindsor Dorset 28 G6
Little Wisbeach Lincs 156 C2
Little Wishford Wilts 46 F5
Little Witcombe Glos 80 B6
Little Witley Worcs 116 E5
Little Wittenham Oxon 83 G9
Little Wolford Warks 100 D5
Littlewood Staffs 133 B9
Little Wood Corner Bucks 84 E6
Little Woodcote London 67 G9
Littlewood Green Warks 117 E11
Little Woolgarston Dorset 18 E5
Littleworth Beds 103 C11
Glos 80 E4
Glos 100 D2
Oxon 82 F4
Oxon 83 D9
Oxon 83 G10
Staffs 151 E8
Staffs 151 G10
S Yorks 187 B10
Warks 118 E4
Wilts 63 G7
Worcs 117 G9
Worcs 117 G7
W Sus 35 C11
Littleworth Common Bucks 66 B2
Little Worthen Shrops 130 B6
Littleworth End Warks 134 D3
Little Wratting Suff 106 B3
Little Wymington Beds 121 D9
Little Wymondley Herts 104 F4
Little Wyrley Staffs 133 B10
Little Wytheford Shrops 149 F11
Little Yeldham Essex 106 D5
Littley Green Essex 87 B11
Litton Derbys 185 F11
N Yorks 213 E8
Som 44 C5
Litton Cheney Dorset 17 C7
Litton Mill Derbys 185 G11
Liurbost W Isles 304 F5
Livermead Torbay 9 C8
Liverpool Mers 182 C4
Liverpool Airport Mers 182 E6
Liversedge W Yorks 197 C8
Liverton Devon 14 F2
Redcar 226 B4
Liverton Mines Redcar 226 B4
Liverton Street Kent 53 C11
Livesey Street Kent 53 C8
Livingshayes Devon 27 G7
Livingston W Loth 269 B11
Livingston Village W Loth 269 B10
Lix Toll Stirl 285 D9
Lixwm Flint 181 G11
Lizard Corn 2 G6
Llaingoch Anglesey 178 E2
Llaithddu Powys 129 G11
Llampha V Glam 58 D2
Llan Powys 129 C7
Llanaber Gwyn 146 F2
Llanaelhaearn Gwyn 162 G5
Llanafan Ceredig 112 C3
Llanafan-fawr Powys 113 F9
Llanallgo Anglesey 179 D7
Llananno Powys 113 C11
Llanarmon Gwyn 145 B8
Llanarmon Dyffryn Ceiriog Wrex 148 C3
Llanarmon Mynydd-mawr Powys 148 D2
Llanarmon-yn-Ial Denb 165 D11
Llanarth Ceredig 111 F8
Mon 78 C5
Llanarthne Carms 93 G10
Llanasa Flint 181 E10
Llanbabo Anglesey 178 D5
Llanbad Rhondda 58 C3
Llanbadarn Fawr Ceredig 128 G2
Llanbadarn Fynydd Powys 114 B2
Llanbadarn-y-Garreg Powys 96 B2
Llanbadoc Mon 78 E5
Llanbadrig Anglesey 178 C5
Llanbeder Newport 78 G5
Llanbedr Gwyn 145 D11
Powys 96 B2
Powys 96 G4
Llanbedr-Dyffryn-Clwyd Denb 165 D10
Llanbedrgoch Anglesey 179 E8
Llanbedrog Gwyn 144 C6
Llanbedr Pont Steffan / Lampeter Ceredig 93 B11
Llanbedr-y-cennin Conwy 164 B3
Llanberis Gwyn 163 C9
Llanbethery V Glam 58 F4
Llanbister Powys 114 C2
Llanblethian / Llanfleiddan V Glam 58 E3
Llanboidy Carms 92 G4
Llanbradach Caerph 77 G10
Llanbrynmair Powys 129 C7
Llancadle / Llancatal V Glam 58 F4
Llancaiach Caerph 77 F10
Llancarfan V Glam 58 E5
Llancatal / Llancadle V Glam 58 F4
Llancayo Mon 78 E5
Llancloudy Hereford 97 G9
Llancowrid Powys 130 E3
Llancynfelyn Ceredig 128 E2
Llan-dafal Bl Gwent 77 E11
Llandaff Cardiff 59 D7
Llandaff North Cardiff 59 D7
Llandanwg Gwyn 145 D11
Llandarcy Neath 57 B8
Llandawke Carms 74 C3
Llanddaniel Fab Anglesey 179 G7
Llanddarog Carms 75 B8
Llanddeiniol Ceredig 111 C11
Llanddeiniolen Gwyn 163 B8
Llandderfel Gwyn 147 B9
Llanddeusant Anglesey 178 D4
Carms 94 G5
Llanddew Powys 95 E11
Llanddewi Swansea 56 D3
Llanddewi-Brefi Ceredig 112 F3
Llanddewi Fach Mon 78 F4
Llanddewi'r Cwm Powys 95 B10
Llanddewi Rhydderch Mon 78 C5
Llanddewi Skirrid Mon 78 B4
Llanddewi Velfrey Pembs 73 B10
Llanddewi Ystradenni Powys 114 D2
Llanddoged Conwy 164 C4
Llanddona Anglesey 179 F9
Llanddowror Carms 74 C3
Llanddulas Conwy 180 F6
Llanddwywe Gwyn 145 E11
Llanddyfnan Anglesey 179 F8
Llandecwyn Gwyn 146 B2
Llandefaelog Powys 95 E10
Llandefaelog Fach Powys 95 E10
Llandefaelog-tre'r-graig Powys 96 F2
Llandefalle Powys 96 D2
Llandegai Gwyn 179 G9
Llandegfan Anglesey 179 G9
Llandegla Denb 165 E11
Llandegley Powys 114 E2
Llandegveth Mon 78 F4
Llandegwning Gwyn 144 C5
Llandeilo Carms 94 G2
Llandeilo Graban Powys 95 C11
Llandeilo'r Fan Powys 95 E7
Llandeloy Pembs 91 F7
Llandenny Mon 78 E6
Llandenny Walks Mon 78 E5
Llandevaud Newport 78 G6
Llandevenny Mon 60 B2
Llandewi Ystradenny Powys 114 D2
Llandilo Pembs 92 F2
Llandilo-yr-ynys Carms 93 G9
Llandinabo Hereford 97 F10
Llandinam Powys 129 F10
Llandissilio Pembs 92 G2
Llandogo Mon 79 E8
Llandough V Glam 58 E3
V Glam 59 E7
Llandovery / Llanymddyfri Carms 94 E5
Llandow / Llandw V Glam 58 E2
Llandre Carms 94 C3
Ceredig 128 F2
Llandrillo Denb 147 B10
Llandrillo-yn-Rhôs Conwy 180 E4
Llandrindod Wells Powys 113 E11
Llandrinio Powys 148 F5
Llandruidion Pembs 90 G5
Llandudno Conwy 180 E3
Llandudno Junction / Cyffordd Llandudno Conwy 180 F3
Llandudoch / St Dogmaels Pembs 92 B3
Llandw / Llandow V Glam 58 E2
Llandwrog Gwyn 163 D7
Llandybie Carms 75 B10
Llandyfaelog Carms 74 C6
Llandyfan Carms 75 B10
Llandyfriog Ceredig 92 C6
Llandyfrydog Anglesey 178 D6
Llandygwydd Ceredig 92 C4
Llandynan Denb 165 F11
Llandyrnog Denb 165 B10
Llandysilio Powys 148 F5
Llandyssil Powys 130 D3
Llandysul Ceredig 93 C8
Llanedeyrn Cardiff 59 C8
Llanedi Carms 75 D9
Llanedwen Anglesey 163 B8
Llaneglwys Powys 95 D11
Llanegryn Gwyn 110 B2
Llanegwad Carms 93 G10
Llaneilian Anglesey 179 C7
Llanelian yn-Rhôs Conwy 180 F5
Llanelidan Denb 165 E10
Llanelieu Powys 96 E3
Llanellen Mon 78 C4
Llanelli Carms 56 B4
Llanelltyd Gwyn 146 F4
Llanelly Mon 78 C2
Llanelly Hill Mon 78 C2
Llanelwedd Powys 113 G10
Llanelwy / St Asaph Denb 181 G8
Llanenddwyn Gwyn 145 E11
Llanengan Gwyn 144 D5
Llanerch Powys 130 E6
Llanerch Emrys Powys 148 E4
Llanerchymedd Anglesey 178 E6
Llanerfyl Powys 129 B10
Llaneuddog Anglesey 179 D7
Llan eurgain / Northop Flint 166 B2
Llanfabon Caerph 77 G10
Llanfachraeth Anglesey 178 E4
Llanfachreth Gwyn 146 E5
Llanfaelog Anglesey 178 G4
Llanfaelrhys Gwyn 144 D4
Llanfaenor Mon 78 B6
Llanfaes Anglesey 179 F10
Powys 95 F10
Llanfaethlu Anglesey 178 D4
Llanfaglan Gwyn 163 C7
Llanfair Gwyn 145 D11
Llanfair Caereinion Powys 130 B2
Llanfair Clydogau Ceredig 112 G2
Llanfair-Dyffryn-Clwyd Denb 165 D10
Llanfairfechan Conwy 179 F11
Llanfair Kilgeddin Mon 78 D4
Llanfair Kilgheddin Mon 78 D4
Llanfair-Nant-Gwyn Pembs 92 D3
Llanfairpwll-gwyngyll Anglesey 179 G8
Llanfair Talhaiarn Conwy 180 G6
Llanfair Waterdine Shrops 114 B4
Llanfairyneubwll Anglesey 178 F4
Llanfairynghornwy Anglesey 178 C4
Llanfallteg Carms 73 B11
Llanfallteg West Carms 73 B10
Llanfaredd Powys 113 G11
Llanfarian Ceredig 111 B11
Llanfechain Powys 148 E3
Llanfechan Powys 113 G9
Llanfechell Anglesey 178 C5
Llanferres Denb 165 C11
Llan Ffestiniog Gwyn 164 G2
Llanfflewyn Anglesey 178 D5
Llanfigael Anglesey 178 E4
Llanfihangel-ar-arth Carms 93 D9
Llanfihangel-Crucorney Mon 96 G6
Llanfihangel Glyn Myfyr Conwy 165 F7
Llanfihangel-helygen Powys 113 E10
Llanfihangel Nant Bran Powys 95 E8
Llanfihangel-nant-Melan Powys 114 F3
Llanfihangel Rhydithon Powys 114 D3
Llanfihangel Rogiet Mon 60 B2
Llanfihangel Tal-y-llyn Powys 96 F2
Llanfihangel Tor y Mynydd Mon 79 E7
Llanfihangel-uwch-Gwili Carms 93 G9
Llanfihangel-y-Creuddyn Ceredig 112 B3
Llanfihangel-yng-Ngwynfa Powys 147 F11
Llanfihangel yn Nhowyn Anglesey 178 F4
Llanfihangel-y-pennant Gwyn 128 B3
Gwyn 163 F8
Llanfilo Powys 96 E2
Llanfleiddan / Llanblethian V Glam 58 E3
Llanfoist Mon 78 C3
Llanfor Gwyn 147 B8
Llanfrechfa Torf 78 G4
Llanfrothen Gwyn 163 G10
Llanfrynach Powys 95 F11
Llanfwrog Anglesey 178 E4
Denb 165 D10
Llanfyllin Powys 148 F2
Llanfynydd Carms 93 F11
Flint 166 D3
Llanfyrnach Pembs 92 E4
Llangadfan Powys 147 G10
Llangadog Carms 74 D6
Carms 94 F4
Llangadwaladr Anglesey 162 B5
Powys 148 C3
Llangaffo Anglesey 162 B6
Llangain Carms 74 B5
Llangammarch Wells Powys 95 B8
Llangan V Glam 58 D3
Llangarron Hereford 97 G10
Llangasty Talyllyn Powys 96 F2
Llangathen Carms 93 G11
Llangattock Powys 78 B2
Llangattock Lingoed Mon 97 G7
Llangattock nigh Usk Mon 78 D4
Llangattock-Vibon-Avel Mon 79 B7
Llangedwyn Powys 148 E3
Llangefni Anglesey 179 F7
Llangeinor Bridgend 58 B2
Llangeitho Ceredig 112 F2
Llangeler Carms 93 D7
Llangendeirne Carms 75 C7
Llangennech Carms 75 E9
Llangennith Swansea 56 C2
Llangenny Powys 78 B2
Llangernyw Conwy 164 B5
Llangeview Mon 78 E5
Llangewydd Court Bridgend 57 E11
Llangian Gwyn 144 D5
Llangloffan Pembs 91 E8
Llanglydwen Carms 92 F3
Llangoed Anglesey 179 F10
Llangoedmor Ceredig 92 B3
Llangollen Denb 166 G2
Llangolman Pembs 92 F2
Llangors Powys 96 F2
Llangorwen Ceredig 128 G2
Llangovan Mon 79 D7
Llangower Gwyn 147 C8
Llangrannog Ceredig 110 G6
Llangristiolus Anglesey 178 G6
Llangrove Hereford 79 B8
Llangua Mon 97 F7
Llangunllo Powys 114 C4
Llangunnor Carms 74 B6
Llangurig Powys 113 B8
Llangwm Conwy 165 G7
Mon 78 E6
Pembs 73 D7
Llangwnnadl Gwyn 144 C4
Llangwyfan Denb 165 B10
Llangwyfan-isaf Anglesey 162 B4
Llangwyllog Anglesey 178 F6
Llangwyryfon Ceredig 111 C11
Llangybi Ceredig 112 G2
Gwyn 162 G6
Mon 78 F5
Llangyfelach Swansea 56 B6
Llangyndeyrn Carms 75 C7
Llangynhafal Denb 165 C10
Llangynidr Powys 77 B11
Llangyniew Powys 130 B2
Llangynin Carms 74 B2
Llangynog Carms 74 B4
Powys 147 D11
Llangynwyd Bridgend 57 D11
Llanhamlach Powys 95 F11
Llanharan Rhondda 58 C4
Llanharry Rhondda 58 C4
Llanhennock Mon 78 G5
Llanhilleth Bl Gwent 78 E2
Llanhowel Pembs 90 F6
Llanidloes Powys 129 G9
Llaniestyn Gwyn 144 C5
Llanifyny Powys 129 G7
Llanigon Powys 96 D4
Llanilar Ceredig 112 C2
Llanilid Rhondda 58 C3
Llanilltud Fawr / Llantwit Major V Glam 58 F3
Llanio Ceredig 112 F2
Llanion Pembs 73 E7
Llanishen Cardiff 59 C7
Mon 79 E7
Llanllawddog Carms 93 F9
Llanllechid Gwyn 163 B10
Llanllowell Mon 78 F5
Llanllugan Powys 129 C11
Llanllwch Carms 74 B5
Llanllwchaiarn Powys 130 E2

396 Low–Man

Lower Horncroft W Sus 35 D8
Lower Horsebridge E Sus 23 C9
Lowerhouse Ches E 184 F6
Lancs 204 G2
Lower House Halton 183 D8
Lower Houses W Yorks 197 D7
Lower Howsell Worcs 98 B5
Lower Illey Worcs 133 G9
Lower Island Kent 70 F6
Lower Kersal Gtr Man 195 G10
Lower Kilburn Derbys 170 F5
Lower Kilcott Glos 61 B9
Lower Killeyan Argyll 254 C3
Lower Kingcombe Dorset 17 B7
Lower Kingswood Sur 51 C8
Lower Kinnerton Ches W 166 C4
Lower Kinsham Hereford 115 E7
Lower Knapp Som 28 B4
Lower Knightley Staffs 150 E6
Lower Knowle Bristol 60 E5
Lower Langford N Som 60 G3
Lower Largo Fife 287 G8
Lower Layham Suff 107 C10
Lower Ledwyche Shrops 115 C10
Lower Leigh Staffs 151 B10
Lower Lemington Glos 100 E4
Lower Lenie Highld 300 G5
Lower Lode Glos 99 E7
Lower Lovacott Devon 25 B8
Lower Loxhore Devon 40 F6
Lower Lydbrook Glos 79 B9
Lower Lye Hereford 115 D8
Lower Machen Newport 59 B8
Lower Maes-coed Hereford 96 E6
Lower Mains Clack 279 B9
Lower Mannington Dorset 31 F9
Lower Marsh Som 30 C2
Lower Marston Som 45 E9
Lower Meend Glos 79 E9
Lower Menadue Corn 5 D10
Lower Merridge Som 43 G8
Lower Mickletown W Yorks 198 B2
Lower Middleton Cheney Northants 101 C10
Lower Midway Derbys 152 E6
Lower Mill Corn 3 B10
Lower Milovaig Highld 296 F7
Lower Milton Som 44 D4
Lower Moor Wilts 81 G8
Worcs 99 B9
Lower Morton S Glos 79 G10
Lower Mountain Flint 166 D4
Lower Nazeing Essex 86 D5
Lower Netchwood Shrops 132 E2
Lower Netherton Devon 14 G3
Lower New Inn Torf 78 F4
Lower Ninnes Corn 1 C5
Lower Nobut Staffs 151 C10
Lower North Dean Bucks 84 F5
Lower Norton Warks 118 E4
Lower Nyland Dorset 30 C2
Lower Ochrwyth Caerph 59 B8
Lower Odcombe Som 29 D8
Lower Oddington Glos 100 F4
Lower Ollach Highld 295 B7
Lower Padworth W Berks 64 F6
Lower Penarth V Glam 59 F7
Lower Penn Staffs 133 D7
Lower Pennington Hants 20 C2
Lower Penwortham Lancs 194 B4
Lower Peover Ches W 184 G2
Lower Pexhill Ches E 184 G5
Lower Pilsley Derbys 170 C6
Lower Pitkerrie Highld 311 L2
Lower Place Gtr Man 196 E2
London 67 C8
Lower Pollicot Bucks 84 C2
Lower Porthkerry V Glam 58 F5
Lower Porthpean Corn 5 E10
Lower Quinton Warks 100 B3
Lower Rabber Hereford 114 G5
Lower Race Torf 78 E3
Lower Radley Oxon 83 F8
Lower Rainham Medway 69 F10
Lower Ratley Hants 32 C4
Lower Raydon Suff 107 D10
Lower Rea Glos 80 B4
Lower Ridge Devon 28 G2
Shrops 148 C6
Lower Roadwater Som 42 F4
Lower Rochford Worcs 116 D2
Lower Rose Corn 4 E5
Lower Row Dorset 31 G8
Lower Sapey Worcs 116 E3
Lower Seagry Wilts 62 C3
Lower Sheering Essex 87 C7
Lower Shelton C Beds 103 C9
Lower Shiplake Oxon 65 D9
Lower Shuckburgh Warks 119 E9
Lower Sketty Swansea 56 C6
Lower Slackstead Hants 32 B5
Lower Slade Devon 40 D4
Lower Slaughter Glos 100 G3
Lower Solva Pembs 87 G11
Lower Soothill W Yorks 197 C9
Lower Soudley Glos 79 D11
Lower Southfield Hereford 98 C3
Lower Stanton St Quintin Wilts 62 C2
Lower Stoke Medway 69 D10
W Mid 119 B7
Lower Stondon C Beds 104 D3
Lower Stone Glos 79 G11
Lower Stonnall Staffs 133 C11
Lower Stow Bedon Norf 141 E9
Lower Stratton Som 28 D6
Swindon 63 B7
Lower Street E Sus 38 E2
Norf 160 B5
Norf 160 C3
Norf 160 F6
Suff 108 E3
Suff 124 G5
Lower Strensham Worcs 99 C8
Lower Stretton Warr 183 E10
Lower Studley Wilts 45 B11
Lower Sundon C Beds 103 F10
Lower Swainswick Bath 61 F9
Lower Swanwick Hants 33 F7
Lower Swell Glos 100 F3
Lower Sydenham London 67 E11
Lower Tadmarton Oxon 101 D8
Lower Tale Devon 27 G9
Lower Tasburgh Norf 142 D3
Lower Tean Staffs 151 B10
Lower Thorpe Northants 101 B10
Lower Threapwood Wrex 166 G6
Lower Thurlton Norf 143 D8
Lower Thurnham Lancs 202 C5
Lower Thurvaston Derbys 152 B4
Lower Todding Hereford 115 B8
Lower Tote Highld 298 C5
Lowertown Corn 2 D5
Corn 5 C11
Devon 12 E5
Lower Town Devon 27 E8
Hereford 98 C2
Pembs 91 D9
Worcs 117 F7
W Yorks 204 G6
Lower Trebullett Corn 12 F2
Lower Tregunnon Corn 11 E10
Lower Treworrick Corn 6 B4
Lower Tuffley Glos 80 C4
Lower Turmer Hants 31 F10
Lower Twitchen Devon 24 D5
Lower Twydall Medway 69 F10
Lower Tysoe Warks 100 B6
Lower Upham Hants 33 D8
Lower Upnor Medway 69 E9
Lower Vexford Som 42 F6
Lower Wainhill Oxon 84 E3
Lower Walton Warr 183 D10
Lower Wanborough Swindon 63 C8
Lower Weacombe Som 42 E6
Lower Weald M Keynes 102 D5
Lower Wear Devon 14 D4
Lower Weare Som 44 C2
Lower Weedon Northants 120 F2
Lower Welson Hereford 114 G5
Lower Westholme Som 44 E5
Lower Westhouse N Yorks 212 E3
Lower Westmancote Worcs 99 D8
Lower Weston Bath 61 F8
Lower Whatcombe Dorset 30 G4
Lower Whatley Som 45 D8
Lower Whitley Ches W 183 F10
Lower Wick Glos 80 F2
Worcs 116 G6
Lower Wield Hants 48 E6
Lower Willingdon E Sus 23 E9
Lower Winchendon or Nether Winchendon Bucks 84 C2
Lower Withington Ches E 168 B4
Lower Wolverton Worcs 117 G8
Lower Woodend Aberds 293 B8
Bucks 65 B10
Lower Woodford Wilts 46 G6
Lower Woodley Corn 5 B10
Lower Woodside Herts 86 D2
Lower Woolston Som 29 B11
Lower Woon Corn 5 C10
Lower Wraxall Dorset 29 G9
Som 44 F6
Wilts 61 G10
Lower Wych Ches W 167 G7
Lower Wyche Worcs 98 C5
Lower Wyke W Yorks 197 B7
Lower Yelland Devon 40 G3
Lower Zeals Wilts 45 G9
Lowes Barn Durham 233 C11
Lowesby Leics 136 B4
Lowestoft Suff 143 E10
Loweswater Cumb 229 G8
Low Etherley Durham 233 F9
Low Fell T&W 243 F7
Lowfield S Yorks 186 D5
Lowfield Heath W Sus 51 E9
Low Fold W Yorks 205 F10
Lowford Hants 33 E7
Low Fulney Lincs 156 E5
Low Garth N Yorks 226 D4
Low Gate Northumb 241 E10
N Yorks 214 F5
Low Geltbridge Cumb 240 F2
Lowgill Cumb 222 F2
Lancs 212 G3
Low Grantley N Yorks 214 E4
Low Green N Yorks 205 B10
Suff 125 E7
W Yorks 205 F10
Low Greenside T&W 242 E4
Low Habberley Worcs 116 B6
Low Ham Som 28 B6
Low Hauxley Northumb 253 C7
Low Hawsker N Yorks 227 D8
Low Hesket Cumb 230 B5
Low Hesleyhurst Northumb 252 D3
Low Hill W Mid 133 C8
Low Hutton N Yorks 216 F5
Lowick Cumb 210 B5
Northants 137 G9
Northumb 264 B2
Lowick Bridge Cumb 210 B5
Lowick Green Cumb 210 B5
Low Knipe Cumb 230 G6
Low Laithe N Yorks 214 G3
Low Laithes S Yorks 197 G11
Lowlands Torf 78 F3
Low Leighton Derbys 185 D8
Low Lorton Cumb 229 F9
Low Marishes N Yorks 216 D6
Low Marnham Notts 172 B4
Low Mill N Yorks 226 F3
Low Moor Lancs 203 E10
W Yorks 197 B7
Lowmoor Row Cumb 231 F8
Low Moorsley T&W 234 B2
Low Moresby Cumb 228 G5
Lowna N Yorks 226 G3
Low Newton Cumb 211 C8
Low Newton-by-the-Sea Northumb 264 E6
Lownie Moor Angus 287 C8
Lowood Borders 262 B2
Low Prudhoe Northumb 242 E4
Low Risby N Lincs 200 E2
Low Row Cumb 229 C9
Cumb 240 E3
N Yorks 223 F9
Low Salchrie Dumfries 236 C2
Low Smerby Argyll 255 E8
Low Snaygill N Yorks 204 D5
Lowsonford Warks 118 D3
Low Street Norf 141 B10
Thurrock 69 D7
Low Tharston Norf 142 D3
Lowther Cumb 230 G6
Lowthertown Dumfries 238 D6
Lowtherville IoW 21 F7
Low Thornley T&W 242 E5
Lowthorpe E Yorks 217 G11
Lowton Gtr Man 183 B10
Som 27 D11
Lowton Common Gtr Man 183 B10
Lowton Heath Gtr Man 183 B10
Lowton St Mary's Gtr Man 183 B10
Low Torry Fife 279 D10
Low Town Shrops 132 E4
Low Toynton Lincs 190 G3
Low Valley S Yorks 198 G2
Low Valleyfield Fife 279 D10
Low Walton Cumb 219 C9
Low Waters S Lnrk 268 E4
Low Westwood Durham 242 F4
Low Whinnow Cumb 239 G8
Low Whita N Yorks 223 F10
Low Wood Cumb 210 C6
Low Worsall N Yorks 225 C7
Low Wray Cumb 221 E7
Loxbeare Devon 26 D6
Loxford London 68 B2
Loxhill Sur 50 F4
Loxhore Devon 40 F6
Loxhore Cott Devon 40 F6
Loxley S Yorks 186 D4
Warks 118 G5
Loxley Green Staffs 151 C11
Loxter Hereford 98 C4
Loxton N Som 43 B11
Loxwood W Sus 50 G4
Loyter's Green Essex 87 C8
Loyterton Kent 70 G3
Lozells W Mid 133 F11
Lubachlaggan Highld 300 B3
Lubachoinnich Highld 309 K4
Lubberland Shrops 116 B2
Lubcroy Highld 309 J3
Lubenham Leics 136 F4
Lubinvullin Highld 308 C5
Lucas End Herts 86 E4
Lucas Green Lancs 194 C5
Sur 50 B2
Luccombe Som 42 E2
Luccombe Village IoW 21 F7
Lucker Northumb 264 C5
Luckett Corn 12 G3
Lucking Street Essex 106 E6
Luckington Wilts 61 C10
Lucklawhill Fife 287 E8
Luckwell Bridge Som 42 F2
Lucton Hereford 115 E8
Ludag W Isles 297 K3
Ludborough Lincs 190 B3
Ludbrook Devon 8 E3
Ludchurch Pembs 73 C10
Luddenden W Yorks 196 B4
Luddenden Foot W Yorks 196 C4
Ludderburn Cumb 221 G8
Luddesdown Kent 69 F7
Luddington N Lincs 199 D10
Warks 118 G3
Luddington in the Brook Northants 138 G2
Lude House Perth 291 G10
Ludford Lincs 190 D2
Shrops 115 C10
Ludgershall Bucks 83 B11
Wilts 47 C9
Ludgvan Corn 2 C2
Ludham Norf 161 F7
Ludlow Shrops 115 C10
Ludney Lincs 190 B5
Som 28 E5
Ludstock Hereford 98 D3
Ludstone Shrops 132 E6
Ludwell Wilts 30 C6
Ludworth Durham 234 C3
Luffenhall Herts 104 F5
Luffincott Devon 12 C2
Lufton Som 29 D8
Lugar E Ayrs 258 E3
Lugate Borders 271 G8
Luggate Burn E Loth 282 G2
Lugg Green Hereford 115 E9
Luggiebank N Lnrk 278 G5
Lugsdale Halton 183 D8
Lugton E Ayrs 267 E8
Lugwardine Hereford 97 C11
Luib Highld 295 C7
Luibeilt Highld 290 G4
Lulham Hereford 97 C8
Lullenden Sur 52 E2
Lullington Derbys 152 G5
Som 45 C9
Lulsgate Bottom N Som 60 F4
Lulsley Worcs 116 F4
Lulworth Camp Dorset 18 E2
Lumb Lancs 195 C10
Lancs 195 D9
W Yorks 196 C4
W Yorks 197 E7
Lumb Foot W Yorks 204 F6
Lumburn Devon 12 G5
Lumbutts W Yorks 196 C3
Lumby N Yorks 206 G5
Lumley W Sus 22 B3
Lumley Thicks Durham 243 G8
Lumloch E Dunb 268 B2
Lumphanan Aberds 293 C7
Lumphinnans Fife 280 C3
Lumsdaine Borders 273 B7
Lumsden Aberds 302 G4
Lunan Angus 287 B10
Lunanhead Angus 287 B8
Luncarty Perth 286 E4
Lund E Yorks 208 D5
N Yorks 207 G9
Shetland 312 C7
Lundal W Isles 304 E3
Lundavra Highld 290 G2
Lunderton Aberds 303 E11
Lundie Angus 286 D6
Highld 290 B3
Lundin Links Fife 287 G8
Lundwood S Yorks 197 F11
Lundy Green Norf 142 E4
Lunga Argyll 275 C8
Lunna Shetland 312 G6
Lunning Shetland 312 G7
Lunnister Shetland 312 F5
Lunnon Swansea 56 D4
Lunsford Kent 53 B7
Lunsford's Cross E Sus 38 E2
Lunt Mers 193 G10
Luntley Hereford 115 F7
Lunts Heath Halton 183 D8
Lupin Staffs 152 F2
Luppitt Devon 27 F11
Lupridge Devon 8 E4
Lupset W Yorks 197 D10
Lupton Cumb 211 C11
Lurg Aberds 293 C8
Lurgashall W Sus 34 B6
Lurignich Argyll 289 D11
Lurley Devon 26 E6
Lusby Lincs 174 B4
Lushcott Shrops 131 D11
Luson Devon 8 F2
Luss Argyll 277 C7
Lussagiven Argyll 275 E7
Lusta Highld 298 D2
Lustleigh Devon 13 E11
Lustleigh Cleave Devon 13 E11
Luston Hereford 115 E9
Lusty Som 45 G7
Luthermuir Aberds 293 G8
Luthrie Fife 287 F7
Lutley W Mid 133 G8
Luton Devon 14 F4
Devon 27 G9
Luton 103 G11
Medway 69 F9
Lutsford Devon 24 D3
Lutterworth Leics 135 G10
Lutton Devon 7 D11
Devon 8 C3
Lincs 157 D8
Northants 138 F2
Lutton Gowts Lincs 157 E8
Lutworthy Devon 26 D3
Luxborough Som 42 F3
Luxley Glos 98 G3
Luxted London 68 G2
Luxton Devon 28 E2
Luxulyan Corn 5 D11
Luzley Gtr Man 196 G3
Luzley Brook Gtr Man 196 F2
Lyatts Som 29 E8
Lybster Highld 310 F6
Lydbury North Shrops 131 F7
Lydcott Devon 41 F7
Lydd Kent 39 C8
Lydden Kent 55 D9
Kent 71 F11
Lyddington Rutland 137 D7
Lydd on Sea Kent 39 C9
Lyde Orkney 314 E3
Shrops 130 C6
Lydeard St Lawrence Som 42 G6
Lyde Cross Hereford 97 C10
Lyde Green Hants 49 B8
S Glos 61 D7
Lydford Devon 12 E6
Lydford Fair Place Som 44 G5
Lydford-on-Fosse Som 44 G5
Lydgate Derbys 186 F4
Gtr Man 196 G3
W Yorks 196 B2
Lydham Shrops 130 E6
Lydiard Green Wilts 62 B5
Lydiard Millicent Wilts 62 B5
Lydiard Plain Wilts 62 B5
Lydiard Tregoze Swindon 62 C6
Lydiate Mers 193 G11
Lydiate Ash Worcs 117 B9
Lydlinch Dorset 30 E2
Lydmarsh Som 28 F5
Lydney Glos 79 E10
Lydstep Pembs 73 F9
Lye W Mid 133 G8
Lye Cross N Som 60 G3
Lye Green Bucks 85 E7
E Sus 52 G4
Warks 118 D3
Wilts 45 B10
Lye Head Worcs 116 C5
Lye Hole N Som 60 G4
Lyewood Common E Sus 52 F4
Lyford Oxon 82 G5
Lymbridge Green Kent 54 E6
Lyme Green Ches E 184 G6
Lyme Regis Dorset 16 C2
Lymiecleuch Borders 249 C9
Lyminge Kent 55 E7
Lymington Hants 20 B2
Lyminster W Sus 35 G8
Lymm Warr 183 D11
Lymore Hants 19 C11
Lympne Kent 54 F6
Lympsham Som 43 C10
Lympstone Devon 14 E5
Lynbridge Devon 41 D8
Lynch Hants 48 D4
Som 42 D2
Lynchat Highld 291 C9
Lynchgate Shrops 131 F7
Lynch Hill Hants 48 D3
Slough 66 C2
Lyndale Ho Highld 298 D3
Lyndhurst Hants 32 F4
Lyndon Rutland 137 C8
Lyndon Green W Mid 134 F2
Lyne Borders 270 G4
Sur 66 F4
Lyneal Shrops 149 C8
Lyneal Mill Shrops 149 C9
Lyneal Wood Shrops 149 C9
Lyne Down Hereford 98 E2
Lyneham Oxon 100 G5
Wilts 62 D4
Lynemore Highld 301 G10
Lynemouth Northumb 253 E7
Lyne of Gorthleck Highld 300 G5
Lyne of Skene Aberds 293 B9
Lyness Orkney 314 G3
Lyne Station Borders 260 B6
Lynford Norf 140 E6
Lyng Norf 159 F11
Som 28 B4
Lyngate Norf 160 C5
Lyngford Som 28 B2
Lynmore Highld 301 F10
Lynmouth Devon 41 D8
Lynn Staffs 133 C11
Telford 150 F5
Lynnwood Borders 261 G11
Lynsore Bottom Kent 55 D7
Lynsted Kent 70 G2
Lynstone Corn 24 F2
Lynton Devon 41 D8
Lynwilg Highld 291 B10
Lynworth Glos 99 G9
Lyons T&W 234 B3
Lyon's Gate Dorset 29 F11
Lyon's Green Norf 159 G8
Lyonshall Hereford 114 F6
Lyons Hall Essex 88 B2
Lypiatt Glos 80 D6
Lyrabus Argyll 274 G3
Lytchett Matravers Dorset 18 B4
Lytchett Minster Dorset 18 C5
Lyth Highld 310 C6
Lytham Lancs 193 B11
Lytham St Anne's Lancs 193 B10
Lythbank Shrops 131 B9
Lythe N Yorks 226 C6
Lythes Orkney 314 H4
Lythmore Highld 310 C4

M

Maam Argyll 284 F5
Mabe Burnthouse Corn 3 C7
Mabie Dumfries 237 B11
Mableden Kent 52 E5
Mablethorpe Lincs 191 D8
Macclesfield Ches E 184 G6
Macclesfield Forest Ches E 185 G7
Macduff Aberds 303 C7
Mace Green Suff 108 C2
Machan S Lnrk 268 E5
Macharioch Argyll 255 G8
Machen Caerph 59 B8
Machrie N Ayrs 255 D9
Machrie Hotel Argyll 254 C4
Machrihanish Argyll 255 E7
Machroes Gwyn 144 D6
Machynlleth Powys 128 C4
Machynys Carms 56 B4
Mackerel's Common W Sus 35 B8
Mackerye End Herts 85 B11
Mackham Devon 27 F11
Mackney Oxon 64 B5
Mackside Borders 262 G4
Mackworth Derbys 152 B6
Macmerry E Loth 281 G8
Madderty Perth 286 E3
Maddington Wilts 46 E5
Maddiston Falk 279 F8
Maddox Moor Pembs 73 C7
Madehurst W Sus 35 E7
Madeley Staffs 168 G3
Telford 132 C3
Madeley Heath Staffs 168 F3
Worcs 117 B9
Madeley Park Staffs 168 G3
Madeleywood Telford 132 C3
Maders Corn 12 G2
Madford Devon 27 E10
Madingley Cambs 123 E7
Madjeston Dorset 30 B4
Madley Hereford 97 D8
Madresfield Worcs 98 B6
Madron Corn 1 C5
Maenaddwyn Anglesey 179 E7
Maenclochog Pembs 91 F11
Maendy V Glam 58 D4
Maenporth Corn 3 D7
Maentwrog Gwyn 163 G11
Maen-y-groes Ceredig 111 F7
Maer Corn 24 F2
Staffs 150 B5
Maerdy Carms 94 G2
Conwy 165 G8
Rhondda 77 F7
Maes-bangor Ceredig 128 G3
Maesbrook Shrops 148 E5
Maesbury Shrops 148 D6
Maesbury Marsh Shrops 148 D6
Maesgeirchen Gwyn 179 G9
Maes-glas Newport 59 B9
Maes Glas / Greenfield Flint 181 F11
Maesgwyn-Isaf Powys 148 G3
Maeshafn Denb 166 C2
Maesllyn Ceredig 93 C7
Maes Llyn Ceredig 93 C7
Maesmynis Powys 95 B10
Maes Pennant Flint 181 F11
Maesteg Bridgend 57 C10
Maes-Treylow Powys 114 D5
Maesybont Carms 75 B9
Maesycoed Rhondda 58 B5
Maesycrugiau Carms 93 C9
Maesycwmmer Caerph 77 G11
Maes-y-dre Flint 166 C2
Maesygwartha Mon 78 C2
Maesymeillion Ceredig 93 B8
Maesypandy Powys 129 D9
Maesyrhandir Powys 129 E11
Magdalen Laver Essex 87 D8
Maggieknockater Moray 302 E3
Maggots End Essex 105 F9
Magham Down E Sus 23 C10
Maghull Mers 193 G11
Magor Mon 60 B2
Magpie Green Suff 125 B11
Mahaar Dumfries 236 B2
Maida Vale London 67 C9
Maidenbower W Sus 51 F9
Maiden Bradley Wilts 45 F10
Maidencombe Torbay 9 B8
Maidenhall Suff 108 C3
Maidenhead Windsor 65 C11
Maiden Head N Som 60 F5
Maidenhead Court Windsor 66 C2
Maiden Law Durham 233 B9
Maiden Newton Dorset 17 B7
Maidenpark Falk 279 E9
Maidens S Ayrs 244 B6
Maidensgrave Suff 108 B5
Maiden's Green Brack 65 E11
Maidensgrove Oxon 65 B8
Maiden's Hall Northumb 252 D6
Maidenwell Corn 11 G8
Lincs 190 F4
Maiden Wells Pembs 73 F7
Maidford Northants 120 G2
Maids Moreton Bucks 102 D4
Maidstone Kent 53 B9
Maidwell Northants 120 B4
Mail Shetland 313 L6
Mailand Shetland 312 C8
Mailingsland Borders 270 G4
Main Powys 148 F3
Maindee Newport 59 B10
Maindy Cardiff 59 D7
Mainholm S Ayrs 257 E9
Mains Cumb 229 G7
Mainsforth Durham 234 E2
Mains of Airies Dumfries 236 C1
Mains of Allardice Aberds 293 F10
Mains of Annochie Aberds 303 E9
Mains of Ardestie Angus 287 D9
Mains of Arnage Aberds 303 F9
Mains of Auchoynanie Moray 302 E4
Mains of Baldoon Dumfries 236 D6
Mains of Balhall Angus 293 G7
Mains of Ballindarg Angus 287 B8
Mains of Balnakettle Aberds 293 F8
Mains of Birness Aberds 303 F9
Mains of Blackhall Aberds 303 G7
Mains of Burgie Moray 301 D10
Mains of Cairnbrogie Aberds 303 G8
Mains of Cairnty Moray 302 D3
Mains of Clunas Highld 301 E8
Mains of Crichie Aberds 303 E9
Mains of Daltulich Highld 301 E7
Mains of Dalvey Highld 301 F11
Mains of Dellavaird Aberds 293 E9
Mains of Drum Aberds 293 D10
Mains of Edingight Moray 302 D5
Mains of Fedderate Aberds 303 E8
Mains of Flichity Highld 300 G6
Mains of Hatton Aberds 303 D9
Aberds 303 E7
Mains of Inkhorn Aberds 303 F9
Mains of Innerpeffray Perth 286 F3
Mains of Kirktonhill Aberds 293 G8
Mains of Laithers Aberds 302 E6
Mains of Mayen Moray 302 E5
Mains of Melgund Angus 287 B9
Mains of Taymouth Perth 285 C11
Mains of Thornton Aberds 293 F8
Mains of Towie Aberds 303 E7
Mains of Ulbster Highld 310 E7
Mains of Watten Highld 310 D6
Mainsriddle Dumfries 237 D11
Mainstone Shrops 130 F5
Maisemore Glos 98 G6
Maitland Park London 67 C9
Major's Green W Mid 118 B2
Makeney Derbys 170 G5
Malacleit W Isles 296 D3
Malborough Devon 9 G9
Malcoff Derbys 185 E9
Malden Rushett London 67 G7
Maldon Essex 88 D4
Malehurst Shrops 131 B7
Malham N Yorks 213 G8
Maligar Highld 298 C4
Malinbridge S Yorks 186 D4
Malinslee Telford 132 B3
Malkin's Bank Ches E 168 D3
Mallaig Highld 295 F8
Mallaig Bheag Highld 295 F8
Malleny Mills Edin 270 B3
Malling Stirl 285 G9
Mallows Green Essex 105 F9
Malltraeth Anglesey 162 B6
Mallwyd Gwyn 147 G7
Malmesbury Wilts 62 B2
Malmsmead Devon 41 D9
Malpas Ches W 167 F7
Corn 4 G6
Newport 78 G4
W Berks 64 E6
Malswick Glos 98 F4
Maltby Lincs 190 E4
Stockton 225 C9
S Yorks 187 C8
Maltby le Marsh Lincs 191 E7
Malting End Suff 124 G4
Malting Green Essex 107 G9
Maltings Angus 293 G9
Maltman's Hill Kent 54 E2
Malton N Yorks 216 E5
Malvern Common Worcs 98 C5
Malvern Link Worcs 98 B5
Malvern Wells Worcs 98 C5
Mambeg Argyll 276 D4
Mamble Worcs 116 C3
Mamhilad Mon 78 E4
Manaccan Corn 3 E7
Manadon Plym 7 D9
Manafon Powys 130 C2
Manais W Isles 296 C7
Manar Ho Aberds 303 G7
Manaton Devon 13 E11
Manby Lincs 190 D5
Mancetter Warks 134 D6
Manchester Gtr Man 184 B4
Manchester Airport Gtr Man 184 D4
Mancot Flint 166 B4
Mancot Royal Flint 166 B4
Mandally Highld 290 C4
Manea Cambs 139 F9
Maney W Mid 134 D2
Manfield N Yorks 224 C4
Mangaster Shetland 312 F5
Mangotsfield S Glos 61 D7
Mangrove Green Herts 104 G2
Mangurstadh W Isles 304 E2
Manhay Corn 2 C5
Manian-fawr Pembs 92 B3
Mankinholes W Yorks 196 C3
Manley Ches W 183 G8
Devon 27 E7
Manley Common Ches W 183 G8
Manmoel Caerph 77 E11
Man-moel Caerph 77 E11
Mannal Argyll 288 E1
Mannamead Plym 7 D9
Mannerston W Loth 279 F10
Manningford Abbots Wilts 46 B6
Manningford Bohune Wilts 46 B6
Manningford Bruce Wilts 46 B6
Manningham W Yorks 205 G9
Mannings Heath W Sus 36 B2
Mannington Dorset 31 F9
Manningtree Essex 107 E11
Mannofield Aberdeen 293 C11
Manor London 68 B2
Manorbier Pembs 73 F9
Manorbier Newton Pembs 73 F8
Manor Bourne Devon 7 F9
Manordeilo Carms 94 F3
Manor Estate S Yorks 186 D5
Manorhill Borders 262 C5
Manor Hill Corner Lincs 157 F8
Manor House W Mid 135 G7
Manorowen Pembs 91 D8
Manor Park Bucks 84 C4
Ches W 167 B11
E Sus 37 C7
London 68 B2
Notts 153 C11
Slough 66 C3
S Yorks 186 D5
W Yorks 205 D9
Manor Parsley Corn 4 F4
Manor Royal W Sus 51 F9
Man's Cross Essex 106 D5
Mansegate Dumfries 247 G9
Manselfield Swansea 56 D5
Mansel Lacy Hereford 97 B8
Mansell Gamage Hereford 97 C7
Manselton Swansea 57 B7
Mansergh Cumb 212 C2

Mansewood
Glasgow 267 C11
Mansfield E Ayrs 258 G4
Notts 171 C8
Mansfield Woodhouse
Notts 171 C8
Manson Green
Norf 141 C10
Mansriggs Cumb 210 C5
Manston Dorset 30 D4
Kent 71 F10
W Yorks 206 F3
Manswood Dorset 31 F7
Manthorpe Lincs 155 B8
Lincs 155 F11
Mantles Green Bucks 85 F7
Manton N Lincs 200 G2
Notts 187 F9
Rutland 137 C7
Wilts 63 F7
Manton Warren
N Lincs 200 F2
Manuden Essex 105 F9
Manwood Green
Essex 87 C8
Manywells Height
W Yorks 205 F7
Maperton Som 29 B11
Maplebeck Notts 172 C2
Maple Cross Herts 85 G8
Mapledurham Oxon 65 D7
Mapledurwell Hants 49 C7
Maple End Essex 105 D11
Maplehurst W Sus 35 C11
Maplescombe Kent 68 G5
Mapleton Derbys 169 F11
Mapperley Derbys 170 G6
Nottingham 171 G9
Mapperley Park
Nottingham 171 G9
Mapperton Dorset 16 B6
Dorset 18 B4
Mappleborough Green
Warks 117 D11
Mappleton E Yorks 209 E10
Mapplewell
S Yorks 197 F10
Mappowder Dorset 30 F2
Maraig W Isles 305 H3
Marazanvose Corn 4 E6
Marazion Corn 2 C2
Marbhig W Isles 305 G6
Marbrack Dumfries 246 E3
Marbury Ches E 167 F9
March Cambs 139 D8
S Lnrk 259 G11
Marcham Oxon 83 F7
Marchamley
Shrops 149 D11
Marchamley Wood
Shrops 149 C11
Marchington Staffs 152 C2
Marchington Woodlands
Staffs 152 D2
Marchroes Gwyn 144 D6
Marchwiel Wrex 166 F5
Marchwood Hants 32 E5
Marcross V Glam 58 F2
Marden Hereford 97 B10
Kent 53 E8
T&W 243 C9
Wilts 46 B5
Marden Ash Essex 87 E9
Marden Beech Kent 53 E8
Marden's Hill E Sus 52 G3
Marden Thorn Kent 53 E9
Mardleybury Herts 86 B3
Mardu Shrops 130 G5
Mardy Mon 78 B4
Shrops 148 C5
Marefield Leics 136 B4
Mareham le Fen
Lincs 174 C3
Mareham on the Hill
Lincs 174 B3
Marehay Derbys 170 F5
Marehill W Sus 35 D9
Maresfield E Sus 37 C7
Maresfield Park
E Sus 37 C7
Marfleet Hull 200 B6
Marford Wrex 166 D5
Margam Neath 57 D9
Margaret Marsh
Dorset 30 D4
Margaret Roding
Essex 87 C9
Margaretting Essex 87 E11
Margaretting Tye
Essex 87 E11
Margate Kent 71 E11
Margery Sur 51 C9
Margnaheglish
N Ayrs 256 C2
Margreig Dumfries 237 B10
Margrove Park
Redcar 226 B3
Marham Norf 158 G4
Marhamchurch Corn 24 G2
Marholm Pboro 138 C2
Marian Flint 181 F9
Marian Cwm Denb 181 F9
Mariandyrys
Anglesey 179 E10
Marianglas Anglesey 179 E8
Marian-glas
Anglesey 179 E8
Mariansleigh Devon 26 C2
Marian y de/
South Beach Gwyn 145 C7
Marian y mor/West
End Gwyn 145 C7
Marine Town Kent 70 E2
Marionburgh
Aberds 293 C9
Marishader Highld 298 C4
Marjoriebanks
Dumfries 248 G3
Mark Dumfries 236 D3
Dumfries 237 C7
S Ayrs 236 B2
Som 43 D11
Markbeech Kent 52 E3
Markby Lincs 191 F7
Mark Causeway
Som 43 D11
Mark Cross E Sus 23 C7
E Sus 52 G5
Markeaton Derbys 152 B6
Market Bosworth
Leics 135 C8
Market Deeping
Lincs 138 B2
Market Drayton
Shrops 150 C3
Market Harborough
Leics 136 F4
Markethill Perth 286 D6
Market Lavington
Wilts 46 C4
Market Overton
Rutland 155 F7
Market Rasen
Lincs 189 D10
Market Stainton
Lincs 190 F2
Market Warsop
Notts 171 B9
Market Weighton
E Yorks 208 E3
Market Weston Suff 125 B9
Markfield Leics 153 G9
Mark Hall North
Essex 87 C7
Mark Hall South
Essex 87 C7
Markham Caerph 77 E11
Markham Moor
Notts 188 G2
Markinch Fife 286 G6
Markington N Yorks 214 F5
Markland Hill
Gtr Man 195 F7
Markle E Loth 281 F11
Marksbury Bath 61 G7
Mark's Corner IoW 20 C5
Marks Gate London 87 G7
Marks Tey Essex 107 G8
Markyate Herts 85 B9
Marland Gtr Man 195 E11
Marlas Hereford 97 F8
Marl Bank Worcs 98 C5
Marlborough Wilts 63 F7
Marlbrook
Hereford 115 G10
Worcs 117 C9
Marlcliff Warks 117 G11
Marldon Devon 9 C7
Marle Green E Sus 23 B9
Marle Hill Glos 99 G9
Marlesford Suff 126 F6
Marley Kent 55 C7
Kent 55 C10
Marley Green
Ches E 167 F9
Marley Heights
W Sus 49 G11
Marley Hill T&W 242 F6
Marley Pots T&W 243 F9
Marlingford Norf 142 B2
Mar Lodge Aberds 292 D2
Marloes Pembs 72 D3
Marlow Bucks 65 B10
Hereford 115 B8
Marlow Bottom
Bucks 65 B11
Marlow Common
Bucks 65 B10
Marlpit Hill Kent 52 D2
Marlpits E Sus 38 E2
Marlpool Derbys 170 F6
Marnhull Dorset 30 D3
Marnoch Aberds 302 D5
Marnock N Lnrk 268 B4
Marple Gtr Man 185 D7
Marple Bridge
Gtr Man 185 D7
Marpleridge
Gtr Man 185 D7
Marr S Yorks 198 F4
Marrel Highld 311 H4
Marr Green Wilts 63 G8
Marrick N Yorks 223 F11
Marrister Shetland 313 G7
Marros Carms 74 D2
Marsden T&W 243 E9
W Yorks 196 E4
Marsden Height
Lancs 204 F3
Marsett N Yorks 213 B8
Marsh Bucks 84 D4
Devon 28 E3
W Yorks 196 D6
W Yorks 204 F6
Marshall Meadows
Northumb 273 D9
Marshall's Cross
Mers 183 C8
Marshall's Elm Som 44 G3
Marshall's Heath
Herts 85 B11
Marshalsea Dorset 28 G5
Marshalswick Herts 85 D11
Marsham Norf 160 E3
Marshaw Lancs 203 C7
Marsh Baldon Oxon 83 F9
Marsh Benham
W Berks 64 F2
Marshborough Kent 55 B10
Marshbrook Shrops 131 F8
Marshchapel Lincs 190 B5
Marsh Common
S Glos 60 C5
Marsh End Worcs 98 D6
Marshfield Newport 59 C9
S Glos 61 E9
Marshfield Bank
Ches E 167 D11
Marshgate Corn 11 C9
Marsh Gate
W Berks 63 F10
Marsh Gibbon
Bucks 102 G2
Marsh Green
Ches W 183 F8
Devon 14 C6
Gtr Man 194 F5
Kent 52 E2
Staffs 168 D5
Telford 150 G2
Marsh Houses
Lancs 202 C5
Marshland St James
Norf 139 B10
Marsh Lane Derbys 186 F6
Glos 79 D9
Marsh Mills Som 43 F7
Marshmoor Herts 86 D2
Marshside Kent 71 F8
Mers 193 D11
Marsh Side Norf 176 E3
Marsh Street Som 42 E3
Marshwood Dorset 16 B3
Marske N Yorks 224 E2
Marske-by-the-Sea
Redcar 235 G8
Marston Ches W 183 F11
Hereford 115 F7
Lincs 172 G5
Oxon 83 D8
Staffs 150 G6
Staffs 151 D8
Warks 119 B8
Warks 134 E4
Wilts 46 B3
Marston Bigot Som 45 E9
Marston Doles
Warks 119 F9
Marston Gate Som 45 D9
Marston Green
W Mid 134 F3
Marston Hill Glos 81 F10
Marston Jabbett
Warks 135 F7
Marston Magna Som 29 C9
Marston Meysey
Wilts 81 F10
Marston Montgomery
Derbys 152 B2
Marston Moretaine
C Beds 103 C9
Marston on Dove
Derbys 152 D4
Marston St Lawrence
Northants 101 C10
Marston Stannett
Hereford 115 F11
Marston Trussell
Northants 136 F3
Marstow Hereford 79 B9
Marsworth Bucks 84 C6
Marten Wilts 47 B9
Marthall Ches E 184 F4
Martham Norf 161 F9
Marthwaite Cumb 222 G2
Martin Hants 31 D9
Kent 55 D10
Lincs 173 D10
Lincs 174 B2
Martindale Cumb 221 B8
Martin Dales Lincs 173 C11
Martin Drove End
Hants 31 C9
Martinhoe Devon 41 D7
Martinhoe Cross
Devon 41 D7
Martin Hussingtree
Worcs 117 E7
Martin Mill Kent 55 D10
Martin Moor Lincs 174 C2
Martinscroft Warr 183 D11
Martin's Moss
Ches E 168 C4
Martinstown Dorset 17 D8
Martinstown or
Winterbourne St
Martin Dorset 17 D8
Martlesham Suff 108 B4
Martlesham Heath
Suff 108 B4
Martletwy Pembs 73 C8
Martley Worcs 116 E5
Martock Som 29 D7
Marton Ches E 168 B5
Ches W 167 B10
Cumb 210 D4
E Yorks 209 F9
Lincs 188 E4
Mbro 225 B10
N Yorks 215 G8
N Yorks 216 C4
Shrops 130 C5
Shrops 149 E8
Warks 119 D8
Marton Green
Ches W 167 B10
Marton Grove Mbro 225 B9
Marton-in-the-Forest
N Yorks 215 F11
Marton-le-Moor
N Yorks 215 E7
Marton Moor Warks 119 D8
Marton Moss Side
Blkpool 202 G2
Martyr's Green Sur 50 B5
Martyr Worthy Hants 48 G4
Marwick Orkney 314 D2
Marwood Devon 40 F4
Marybank Highld 300 D4
Highld 301 B7
Maryburgh Highld 300 D5
Maryfield Aberds 293 D7
Corn 7 D8
Maryhill Glasgow 267 B11
Marykirk Aberds 293 G8
Maryland Mon 79 D8
Marylebone
Gtr Man 194 F5
Marypark Moray 301 F11
Maryport Cumb 228 D6
Dumfries 236 F3
Mary Tavy Devon 12 F6
Maryton Angus 287 B7
Angus 287 B10
Marywell Aberds 293 D7
Aberds 293 D11
Angus 287 C10
Masbrough S Yorks 186 C6
Mascle Bridge
Pembs 73 D7
Masham N Yorks 214 C4
Mashbury Essex 87 C11
Masongill N Yorks 212 D3
Masonhill S Ayrs 257 E9
Mastin Moor Derbys 187 F7
Mastrick Aberdeen 293 C10
Matchborough
Worcs 117 D11
Matching Essex 87 C8
Matching Green
Essex 87 C8
Matching Tye Essex 87 C8
Matfen Northumb 242 C2
Matfield Kent 53 E7
Mathern Mon 79 G8
Mathon Hereford 98 B4
Mathry Pembs 91 E7
Matlaske Norf 160 C3
Matley Gtr Man 185 B7
Matlock Derbys 170 C3
Matlock Bank
Derbys 170 C3
Matlock Bath
Derbys 170 D3
Matlock Bridge
Derbys 170 D3
Matlock Cliff
Derbys 170 D4
Matlock Dale
Derbys 170 D3
Matshead Lancs 202 E6
Matson Glos 80 B4
Matterdale End
Cumb 230 G3
Mattersey Notts 187 D11
Mattersey Thorpe
Notts 187 D11
Matthewsgreen
Wokingham 65 F10
Mattingley Hants 49 B8
Mattishall Norf 159 G11
Mattishall Burgh
Norf 159 G11
Mauchline E Ayrs 257 D11
Maud Aberds 303 E9
Maudlin Corn 5 C11
Dorset 28 F5
W Sus 22 B5
Maudlin Cross Dorset 28 F5
Maugersbury Glos 100 F4
Maughold IoM 192 C5
Mauld Highld 300 F4
Maulden C Beds 103 D11
Maulds Meaburn
Cumb 222 B2
Maunby N Yorks 215 B7
Maund Bryan
Hereford 115 G11
Maundown Som 27 B9
Mauricewood
Midloth 270 C4
Mautby Norf 161 G9
Mavesyn Ridware
Staffs 151 F11
Mavis Enderby Lincs 174 B5
Maviston Highld 301 D9
Mawbray Cumb 229 B7
Mawdesley Lancs 194 E3
Mawdlam Bridgend 57 E10
Mawgan Corn 2 D6
Mawgan Porth Corn 5 B7
Maw Green Ches E 168 D2
Mawla Corn 4 F4
Mawnan Corn 3 D7
Mawnan Smith Corn 3 D7
Mawsley Northants 120 B6
Mawson Green
S Yorks 198 D6
Mawthorpe Lincs 191 G7
Maxey Pboro 138 B2
Maxstoke Warks 134 F4
Maxted Street Kent 54 E6
Maxton Borders 262 C4
Kent 55 E10
Maxwellheugh
Borders 262 C6
Maxwelltown
Dumfries 237 B11
Maxworthy Corn 11 C11
Mayals Swansea 56 C6
May Bank Staffs 168 F5
Maybole S Ayrs 257 G8
Maybury Sur 50 B4
Maybush Soton 32 E5
Mayer's Green
W Mid 133 E10
Mayes Green Sur 50 F6
Mayeston Pembs 73 E8
Mayfair London 67 C9
Mayfield E Sus 37 B9
Midloth 271 C7
Northumb 243 B7
Staffs 169 F11
W Loth 269 B8
Mayford Sur 50 B3
Mayhill Swansea 56 C6
May Hill Mon 79 C8
May Hill Village Glos 98 G4
Mayland Essex 88 E6
Maylandsea Essex 88 E6
Maynard's Green
E Sus 23 B9
Mayne Ho Moray 302 C2
Mayon Corn 1 D3
Maypole Bromley 68 G3
Dartford 68 E4
Kent 71 G7
Mon 79 B7
Scilly 1 G4
Maypole Green
Essex 107 G9
Norf 143 D8
Suff 125 F8
Suff 126 D5
Mays Green Oxon 65 C8
May's Green N Som 59 G11
Sur 50 B5
Mayshill S Glos 61 C7
Maythorn S Yorks 197 F7
Maythorne Notts 171 D11
Maywick Shetland 313 L5
Mead Devon 13 G11
Devon 24 D2
Mead End Hants 19 B11
Hants 33 E11
Wilts 31 C8
Meadgate Bath 45 B7
Meadle Bucks 84 D4
Meadowbank
Ches W 167 B11
Edin 280 G5
Meadowend Essex 106 C4
Meadowfield
Durham 233 D10
Meadowfoot N Ayrs 266 F4
Meadow Green
Hereford 116 F4
Meadow Hall
S Yorks 186 C5
Meadow Head
S Yorks 186 E4
Meadowley Shrops 132 E3
Meadowmill E Loth 281 G8
Meadows
Nottingham 153 B11
Meadowtown
Shrops 130 C6
Meads E Sus 23 F10
Meadside Oxon 83 G9
Mead Vale Sur 51 D9
Meadwell Devon 12 E4
Meaford Staffs 151 B7
Meagill N Yorks 205 B9
Mealabost W Isles 304 E6
Mealabost Bhuirgh
W Isles 304 C6
Mealasta W Isles 304 F1
Meal Bank Cumb 221 F10
Meal Hill W Yorks 197 F7
Mealrigg Cumb 229 B8
Mealsgate Cumb 229 C10
Meanwood
W Yorks 205 F11
Mearbeck N Yorks 212 G6
Meare Som 44 E3
Meare Green Som 28 B4
Som 28 C3
Mearns Bath 45 B7
E Renf 267 D10
Mears Ashby
Northants 120 D6
Measborough Dike
S Yorks 197 F11
Measham Leics 152 G6
Meath Green Sur 51 E9
Meathop Cumb 211 C8
Meaux E Yorks 209 F7
Meaver Corn 2 F5
Meavy Devon 7 B10
Medbourne Leics 136 E5
M Keynes 102 D6
Medburn Northumb 242 C4
Meddon Devon 24 D3
Meden Vale Notts 171 B9
Medhurst Row Kent 52 D3
Medlam Lincs 174 D4
Medlar Lancs 202 F4
Medlicott Shrops 131 E8
Medlyn Corn 2 C6
Medmenham Bucks 65 C10
Medomsley Durham 242 G4
Medstead Hants 49 F7
Meerbrook Staffs 169 C7
Meer Common
Hereford 115 G7
Meer End W Mid 118 C4
Meerhay Dorset 29 G7
Meers Bridge Lincs 191 D7
Meersbrook
S Yorks 186 E5
Meesden Herts 105 E8
Meeson Telford 150 E3
Meeson Heath
Telford 150 E3
Meeth Devon 25 F8
Meethe Devon 25 C11
Meeting Green Suff 124 F4
Meeting House Hill
Norf 160 D6
Meggernie Castle
Perth 285 C9
Meggethead
Borders 260 E5
Meidrim Carms 92 G5
Meifod Denb 165 D8
Powys 148 G3
Meigle N Ayrs 266 B3
Perth 286 C6
Meikle Earnock S
Lnrk 268 E4
Meikle Ferry Highld 309 L7
Meikle Forter
Angus 292 G3
Meikle Gluich
Highld 309 L6
Meikle Obney Perth 286 D4
Meikleour Perth 286 D5
Meikle Pinkerton
E Loth 282 F4
Meikle Strath
Aberds 293 F8
Meikle Tarty Aberds 303 G9
Meikle Wartle
Aberds 303 F7
Meinciau Carms 75 C7
Meir Stoke 168 G6
Meir Heath Staffs 168 G6
Melbourn Cambs 105 C7
Melbourne Derbys 153 D7
E Yorks 207 E11
S Lnrk 269 G11
Melbury Abbas
Dorset 30 D5
Melbury Bubb Dorset 29 F9
Melbury Osmond
Dorset 29 F9
Melbury Sampford
Dorset 29 F9
Melby Shetland 313 H3
Melchbourne Beds 121 D10
Melcombe Som 43 G9
Melcombe Bingham
Dorset 30 G3
Melcombe Regis
Dorset 17 E9
Meldon Devon 13 C7
Northumb 252 G4
Meldreth Cambs 105 B7
Meldrum Ho Aberds 303 G8
Melfort Argyll 275 B9
Melgarve Highld 290 D6
Meliden/Gallt Melyd
Denb 181 E9
Melinbyrhedyn
Powys 128 D6
Melin Caiach Caerph 77 F10
Melincourt Neath 76 E4
Melincryddan Neath 57 B8
Melinsey Corn 3 B10
Melin-y-coed
Conwy 164 C4
Melin-y-ddôl
Powys 129 B11
Melin-y-grug
Powys 129 B11
Melin-y-Wig Denb 165 F8
Melkington
Northumb 273 G7
Melkinthorpe Cumb 231 F7
Melkridge Northumb 240 E6
Melksham Wilts 62 G2
Melksham Forest
Wilts 62 G2
Mellangaun Highld 307 L3
Mellangoose Corn 2 D5
Melldalloch Argyll 275 F10
Mell Green W Berks 64 D3
Mellguards Cumb 230 B4
Melling Lancs 211 E11
Mers 193 G11
Mellingey Corn 10 G4
Melling Mount
Mers 194 G2
Mellis Suff 126 C2
Mellis Green Suff 125 C11
Mellon Charles
Highld 307 K3
Mellon Udrigle
Highld 307 K3
Mellor Gtr Man 185 D7
Lancs 203 G9
Mellor Brook Lancs 203 G8
Mells Som 45 D8
Suff 127 B8
Mells Green Som 45 D8
Melmerby Cumb 231 D8
N Yorks 213 B11
N Yorks 214 D6
Melon Green Suff 124 F6
Melplash Dorset 16 B5
Melrose Borders 262 C2
Melsetter Orkney 314 H2
Melsonby N Yorks 224 D3
Meltham W Yorks 196 E6
Meltham Mills
W Yorks 196 E6
Melton E Yorks 200 B3
Suff 126 G5
Meltonby E Yorks 207 C11
Melton Constable
Norf 159 C10
Melton Mowbray
Leics 154 F5
Melton Ross
N Lincs 200 E5
Melvaig Highld 307 L2
Melverley Shrops 148 F6
Melverley Green
Shrops 148 F6
Melvich Highld 310 C2
Membland Devon 7 F11
Membury Devon 28 G3
Memsie Aberds 303 C9
Memus Angus 287 B8
Mena Corn 5 C10
Menabilly Corn 5 E11
Menadarva Corn 4 G2
Menagissey Corn 4 F4
Menai Bridge/
Porthaethwy
Anglesey 179 G9
Mendham Suff 142 G5
Mendlesham Suff 126 D2
Mendlesham Green
Suff 125 E11
Menethorpe
N Yorks 216 F5
Mengham Hants 21 B10
Menheniot Corn 6 C5
Menherion Corn 2 B6
Menithwood Worcs 116 D4
Menna Corn 5 E8
Mennock Dumfries 247 B8
Menston W Yorks 205 E9
Menstrie Clack 278 B6
Mentmore Bucks 84 B6
Menzion Borders 260 E3
Meoble Highld 295 G9
Meole Brace Shrops 149 G9
Meols Mers 182 C2
Meon Hants 33 G8
Meonstoke Hants 33 D10
Meopham Kent 68 F6
Meopham Green
Kent 68 F6
Meopham Station
Kent 68 F6
Mepal Cambs 139 G8
Meppershall
C Beds 104 D2
Merbach Hereford 96 B6
Mercaton Derbys 170 G3
Merchant Fields
W Yorks 197 B7
Merchiston Edin 280 G4
Mere Ches E 184 E2
Wilts 45 G10
Mere Brow Lancs 194 D2
Mereclough Lancs 204 G3
Mere Green W Mid 134 D2
Worcs 117 E9
Merehead Wrex 149 B9
Mere Heath
Ches W 183 G11
Meresborough
Medway 69 G10
Mereside Blkpool 202 G2
Meretown Staffs 150 E5
Mereworth Kent 53 C7
Mergie Aberds 293 E9
Meriden Herts 85 F10
W Mid 134 G4
Merkadale Highld 294 B5
Merkland Dumfries 237 B9
N Ayrs 256 B2
S Ayrs 244 E6
Merkland Lodge
Highld 309 G4
Merle Common Sur 52 D2
Merley Poole 18 B6
Merlin's Bridge
Pembs 72 C6
Merlin's Cross Pembs 73 E7
Merridale W Mid 133 D7
Merridge Som 43 G8
Merrie Gardens IoW 21 E7
Merrifield Devon 8 F6
Devon 24 G3
Merrington Shrops 149 E9
Merrion Pembs 72 F6
Merriott Dorset 16 B6
Som 28 E6
Merriottsford Som 28 E6
Merritown Dorset 19 B8
Merrivale Devon 12 F6
Hereford 98 G2
Merrow Sur 50 C4
Merrybent Darl 224 C4
Merry Field Hill
Dorset 31 G8
Merry Hill Herts 85 G10
W Mid 133 D7
Merryhill Green
Wokingham 65 E9
Merrylee E Renf 267 D11
Merry Lees Leics 135 B9
Merrymeet Corn 6 B5
Merry Meeting Corn 11 G7
Merry Oak Soton 32 E6
Mersham Kent 54 F5
Merstham Sur 51 C9
Merston W Sus 22 C5
Merstone IoW 20 E6
Merther Corn 5 G7
Merther Lane Corn 5 G7
Merthyr Carms 93 G7
Merthyr Cynog
Powys 95 D9
Merthyr-Dyfan
V Glam 58 F6
Merthyr Mawr
Bridgend 57 F11
Merthyr Tydfil
M Tydf 77 D8
Merthyr Vale M Tydf 77 F9
Merton Devon 25 E8
London 67 E9
Norf 141 D8
Oxon 83 B9
Merton Park London 67 F9
Mervinslaw Borders 262 G5
Meshaw Devon 26 D3
Messing Essex 88 B5
Messingham
N Lincs 199 G11
Mesty Croft W Mid 133 E9
Mesur-y-dorth
Pembs 87 E11
Metal Bridge
Durham 233 E11
Metfield Suff 142 G5
Metherell Corn 7 B8
Metheringham
Lincs 173 C9
Methersgate Suff 108 B5
Methil Fife 281 B7
Methilhill Fife 281 B7
Methlem Gwyn 144 C3
Methley W Yorks 197 B11
Methley Junction
W Yorks 197 B11
Methley Lanes
W Yorks 197 B11
Methlick Aberds 303 F8
Methven Perth 286 E4
Methwold Norf 140 E4
Methwold Hythe
Norf 140 E4
Mettingham Suff 143 F7
Metton Norf 160 B3
Mevagissey Corn 5 G10
Mewith Head
N Yorks 212 F4
Mexborough
S Yorks 187 B7
Mey Highld 310 B6
Meyrick Park Bmouth 19 C7
Meysey Hampton
Glos 81 F10
Miabhag W Isles 305 H2
W Isles 305 J3
Miabhig W Isles 304 E2
Mial Highld 299 B7
Michaelchurch
Hereford 97 F10
Michaelchurch Escley
Hereford 96 E6
Michaelchurch on Arrow
Powys 114 G4
Michaelston-le-Pit
V Glam 59 E7
Michaelston-y-Fedw
Newport 59 C8
Michaelstow Corn 11 F7
Michealston-super-Ely
Cardiff 58 D6
Michelcombe Devon 8 B3
Micheldever Hants 48 F4
Michelmersh Hants 32 B4
Mickfield Suff 126 E2
Micklebring
S Yorks 187 C8
Mickleby N Yorks 226 C6
Micklefield Bucks 84 G5
W Yorks 206 G4
Micklefield Green
Herts 85 F8
Mickleham Sur 51 C7
Micklehurst
Gtr Man 196 G3
Mickleover Derby 152 C6
Micklethwaite
Cumb 239 G7
W Yorks 205 E8
Mickleton Durham 232 G5
Glos 100 C3
Mickletown
W Yorks 197 B11
Mickle Trafford
Ches W 166 B6
Mickley Derbys 186 F4
N Yorks 214 D5
Shrops 150 C2
Mickley Green Suff 124 F6
Mickley Square
Northumb 242 E3
Midanbury Hants 33 E7
Mid Ardlaw Aberds 303 C9
Mid Auchinleck
Invclyd 276 G6
Midbea Orkney 314 B4
Mid Beltie Aberds 293 C8
Mid Calder W Loth 269 B11
Mid Cloch Forbie
Aberds 303 D7
Mid Clyth Highld 310 F6
Middle Assendon
Oxon 65 B8
Middle Aston Oxon 101 F9
Middle Balnald
Perth 286 B4
Middle Barton Oxon 101 F8
Middle Bickenhill
W Mid 134 G4
Middlebie Dumfries 238 B6
Middle Bockhampton
Dorset 19 B9
Middle Bourne Sur 49 E10
Middle Bridge
N Som 60 D3
Middle Burnham
Som 43 D10
Middle Cairncake
Aberds 303 E8
Middlecave N Yorks 216 E5
Middle Chinnock
Som 29 E7
Middle Claydon
Bucks 102 F4
Middle Cliff Staffs 169 E8
Middlecliffe
S Yorks 198 F2
Middlecott Devon 13 D10
Devon 24 F6
Devon 26 F3
Middle Crackington
Corn 11 B9
Middlecroft Derbys 186 G6
Middle Drums
Angus 287 B9
Middle Duntisbourne
Glos 81 D7
Middlefield Falk 279 E7
Middleforth Green
Lancs 194 B4
Middle Green Bucks 66 C4
Som 27 D10
Suff 124 D4
Middleham N Yorks 214 B2
Middle Handley
Derbys 186 F6
Middle Harling Norf 141 F9
Middle Herrington
T&W 243 G9
Middlehill Corn 6 B5
Wilts 61 F10
Middle Hill Pembs 73 C7
Staffs 133 B9
Middlehope Shrops 131 F9
Middle Kames
Argyll 275 E10
Middle Littleton
Worcs 99 B11
Middle Luxton Devon 28 E2
Middle Madeley
Staffs 168 F3
Middle Maes-coed
Hereford 96 E6
Middlemarsh Dorset 29 F11
Middle Marwood
Devon 40 F4
Middle Mayfield
Staffs 169 G10
Middle Mill Pembs 87 F11
Middlemoor Devon 12 G5
Middlemuir Aberds 303 D9
Aberds 303 E8
Aberds 303 G9
Middleport Stoke 168 F5
Middle Quarter Kent 53 F11
Middle Rainton
T&W 234 B2
Middle Rasen Lincs 189 D9
Middlerig Falk 279 F8
Middle Rigg Perth 286 G4
Middle Rocombe
Devon 9 B8
Middlesbrough
Mbro 234 G5
Middlesceugh
Cumb 230 C4
Middleshaw Cumb 211 B11
Middle Side Durham 232 F4
Middlesmoor
N Yorks 213 E11
Middle Stoford Som 27 C11
Middle Stoke Devon 13 G9
Medway 69 D10
W Mid 119 B7
Middlestone
Durham 233 E11
Middlestone Moor
Durham 233 E10
Middle Stoughton
Som 44 D2
Middlestown
W Yorks 197 D9
Middle Strath
W Loth 279 G8
Middle Street Glos 80 E3
Middle Taphouse Corn 6 C3
Middlethird Borders 272 G3
Middlethorpe York 207 D7
Middleton Aberds 293 B10
Argyll 288 E1
Cumb 212 B2
Derbys 169 C11
Derbys 170 D3
Essex 107 D7
Gtr Man 195 F11
Hants 48 E2
Hereford 115 D10
Hrtlpl 234 E6
IoW 20 D2
Lancs 202 B4
Midloth 271 D7
Norf 158 F3
Northants 136 F6
Northumb 252 F3
Northumb 264 B4
N Yorks 204 E5
N Yorks 205 D8
N Yorks 216 B5
Perth 286 C5
Perth 286 F2
Perth 286 G5
Shrops 115 B10
Shrops 130 D5
Shrops 148 D6
Suff 127 D8

New Cheltenham
S Glos 61 E7
New Cheriton Hants 33 B9
Newchurch
Bl Gwent 77 C11
Carms 93 G7
Hereford 115 G7
IoW 21 D7
Kent 54 G5
Lancs 195 C10
Mon 79 F7
Powys 114 G4
Staffs 152 E2
Newchurch in Pendle
Lancs 204 F2
New Clipstone
Notts 171 C9
New Costessey
Norf 160 G3
Newcott Devon 28 F2
New Coundon
Durham 233 E10
New Cowper Cumb 229 B8
Newcraighall Edin 280 G6
New Crofton
W Yorks 197 D11
New Cross Ceredig 112 B2
London 67 D11
Oxon 65 D9
Som 28 D6
New Cross Gate
London 67 D11
New Cumnock
E Ayrs 258 G4
New Deer Aberds 303 E8
New Delaval
Northumb 243 B7
New Delph Gtr Man 196 F3
New Denham Bucks 66 C4
Newdigate Sur 51 E7
New Downs Corn 1 C3
Corn 4 E4
New Duston
Northants 120 E4
New Earswick York 207 B8
New Eastwood
Notts 171 F7
New Edlington
S Yorks 187 B8
New Elgin Moray 302 C2
New Ellerby E Yorks 209 F9
Newell Green Brack 65 E11
New Eltham London 68 E2
New End Lincs 190 G2
Warks 118 E2
Worcs 117 F11
Newenden Kent 38 B4
New England Essex 106 C4
Lincs 175 D8
Pboro 138 C3
Som 28 E4
Newent Glos 98 F4
Newerne Glos 79 E10
New Farnley
W Yorks 205 G10
New Ferry Mers 182 D4
Newfield Durham 233 E10
Durham 242 G6
Highld 301 B7
Stoke 168 E6
New Fletton Pboro 138 D3
Newford Scilly 1 G4
Newfound Hants 48 C5
New Fryston
W Yorks 198 B3
Newgale Pembs 90 G6
New Galloway
Dumfries 237 B8
Newgarth Orkney 314 E2
Newgate Lancs 194 F4
Norf 177 E9
Newgate Corner
Norf 161 G8
Newgate Street
Herts 86 D4
New Gilston Fife 287 G8
New Greens Herts 85 D10
New Grimsby Scilly 1 F3
New Ground Herts 85 C7
Newgrounds Hants 31 E11
Newhailes Edin 280 G6
New Hainford Norf 160 F4
Newhall Ches E 167 F10
Derbys 152 E5
Newhall Green
Warks 134 F5
New Hall Hey
Lancs 195 C10
Newhall House
Highld 300 C6
Newhall Point
Highld 301 C7
Newham Lincs 174 E3
Northumb 264 D5
New Hartley
Northumb 243 B8
Newhaven Derbys 169 C11
Devon 24 C5
Edin 280 F5
E Sus 36 G6
New Haw Sur 66 G5
Newhay N Yorks 207 G9
New Headington
Oxon 83 D9
New Heaton
Northumb 273 G7
New Hedges Pembs 73 E10
New Herrington
T&W 243 G8
Newhey Gtr Man 196 E2
Newhill Fife 286 F6
Perth 286 G5
S Yorks 186 B6
Newhills Aberdeen 293 C10
New Hinksey Oxon 83 E8
New Ho Durham 232 D3
New Holkham Norf 159 B7
New Holland
N Lincs 200 C5
W Yorks 205 F7
Newholm N Yorks 227 C7
New Horwich
Derbys 185 E8
New Houghton
Derbys 171 B7
Norf 158 D5
Newhouse Borders 262 E2
N Lnrk 268 C5
Shetland 313 G6
New House Kent 68 E6
Newhouses
Borders 271 G10
New Houses
Gtr Man 194 G5
N Yorks 212 E6
New Humberstone
Leicester 136 B2
New Hunwick
Durham 233 E9
New Hutton Cumb 221 G11
New Hythe Kent 53 B8
Newick E Sus 36 C6
Newingreen Kent 54 F6
Newington Edin 280 G5
Kent 55 F7
Kent 69 G11
Kent 71 F11
London 67 D10
Notts 187 C11
Oxon 83 F10
Shrops 131 G8
Newington Bagpath
Glos 80 G4
New Inn Carms 93 D9
Devon 24 F6
Mon 79 E7
Pembs 91 E11
Torf 78 F4
New Invention
Shrops 114 B5
W Mid 133 C9
New Kelso Highld 299 E9
New Kingston
Notts 153 D10
New Kyo Durham 242 G5
New Ladykirk
Borders 273 F7
New Lanark S Lnrk 269 G7
Newland Cumb 210 D6
E Yorks 199 B10
Glos 79 D9
Hull 209 G7
N Yorks 199 C7
Oxon 82 C5
Worcs 98 B5
Newland Bottom
Cumb 210 C5
Newland Common
Worcs 117 E8
Newland Green Kent 54 D2
Newlandrig Midloth 271 C7
Newlands Borders 250 E2
Borders 262 E2
Cumb 229 G10
Cumb 230 D2
Derbys 170 F6
Dumfries 247 F11
Glasgow 267 C11
Highld 301 E7
Moray 302 D3
Northumb 242 F3
Notts 171 C9
Staffs 151 E11
Newlands Corner
Sur 50 D4
Newlandsmuir S
Lnrk 268 E2
Newlands of Geise
Highld 310 C4
Newlands of Tynet
Moray 302 C3
Newlands Park
Anglesey 178 E3
New Lane Lancs 194 E2
New Lane End
Warr 183 B10
New Langholm
Dumfries 249 G9
New Leake Lincs 174 D6
New Leeds Aberds 303 D9
Newliston Edin 280 G2
Fife 280 C5
New Lodge
S Yorks 197 F10
New Longton Lancs 194 B4
Newlot Orkney 314 E5
New Luce Dumfries 236 C3
Newlyn Corn 1 D5
Newmachar
Aberds 293 B10
Newmains N Lnrk 268 D6
New Malden London 67 F8
Newman's End Essex 87 C8
Newman's Green
Suff 107 C7
Newman's Place
Hereford 96 B5
Newmarket Glos 80 F4
Suff 124 E2
W Isles 304 E6
New Marske Redcar 235 G8
New Marston Oxon 83 D8
New Marton Shrops 148 C6
New Micklefield
W Yorks 206 G4
Newmill Borders 261 G11
Corn 1 C5
Moray 302 D4
New Mill Aberds 293 E9
Borders 262 G2
Corn 1 C5
Corn 4 F6
Cumb 219 E11
Herts 84 C6
Wilts 63 G7
W Yorks 197 F7
Newmillerdam
W Yorks 197 D10
Newmill of Inshewan
Angus 292 G6
Newmills Corn 11 D11
Fife 279 D10
Highld 300 C6
New Mills Borders 271 F10
Ches E 184 E3
Corn 5 E7
Derbys 185 D7
Glos 79 E10
Hereford 98 D4
New Mills / Felin
Newydd Powys 129 C11
Newmills of Boyne
Aberds 302 D5
Newmiln Perth 286 D5
Newmilns E Ayrs 258 B2
New Milton Hants 19 B10
New Mistley Essex 108 E2
New Moat Pembs 91 F11
Newmore Highld 300 D5
Highld 300 E5
New Moston
Gtr Man 195 G11
Newnes Shrops 149 C7
Newney Green
Essex 87 D11
Newnham Cambs 123 F8
Glos 79 C11
Hants 49 C8
Herts 104 D4
Kent 54 B3
Northants 119 F11
Warks 118 E3
Newnham Bridge
Worcs 116 D2
New Ollerton
Notts 171 B11
New Oscott W Mid 133 E11
New Pale Ches W 183 G8
Newpark Fife 287 F8
New Park N Yorks 205 B11
New Parks
Leicester 135 B11
New Passage S Glos 60 B4
New Pitsligo Aberds 303 D8
New Polzeath Corn 10 F4
Newpool Staffs 168 D5
Newport Corn 12 D2
Devon 40 G5
Dorset 18 C3
Essex 105 E10
E Yorks 208 G3
Glos 79 F11
Highld 311 G5
IoW 20 D6
Newport 59 B10
Norf 161 F10
Som 28 C4
Telford 150 F4
Newport-on-Tay
Fife 287 E8
Newport Pagnell
M Keynes 103 C7
Newport / Trefdraeth
Pembs 91 D11
Newpound Common
W Sus 35 B9
Newquay Corn 4 C6
New Quay / Ceinewydd
Ceredig 111 F7
New Rackheath
Norf 160 G5
New Radnor Powys 114 E4
New Rent Cumb 230 D5
New Ridley
Northumb 242 F3
New Road Side
N Yorks 204 E5
W Yorks 197 B7
New Romney Kent 39 C9
New Rossington
S Yorks 187 B10
New Row Ceredig 112 C4
Lancs 203 F8
N Yorks 226 C2
Newsam Green
W Yorks 206 G3
New Sarum Wilts 46 G6
New Sawley Derbys 153 C9
Newsbank Ches E 168 B4
New Scarbro
W Yorks 205 G10
Newseat Aberds 303 E10
Aberds 303 F7
Newsells Herts 105 D7
Newsham Lancs 202 F6
Northumb 243 B8
N Yorks 215 C7
N Yorks 224 C2
New Sharlston
W Yorks 197 C11
Newsholme E Yorks 199 B8
Lancs 204 C2
W Yorks 204 F6
New Silksworth
T&W 243 G9
New Skelton Redcar 226 B3
New Smithy Derbys 185 E9
Newsome W Yorks 196 E6
New Southgate
London 86 G3
New Springs
Gtr Man 194 F6
New Sprowston
Norf 160 G4
New Stanton Derbys 153 B9
Newstead Borders 262 C3
Northumb 264 D5
Notts 171 E8
Staffs 168 G5
W Yorks 197 E11
New Stevenston N
Lnrk 268 D5
New Street Kent 68 G6
Staffs 169 E9
Newstreet Lane
Shrops 150 B2
New Swanage Dorset 18 E6
New Swannington
Leics 153 F8
Newtake Devon 14 G3
New Thirsk N Yorks 215 C8
Newthorpe Notts 171 F7
N Yorks 206 G5
Newthorpe Common
Notts 171 F7
New Thundersley
Essex 69 B9
Newtoft Lincs 189 D8
Newton Argyll 275 D11
Borders 262 E3
Borders 262 F2
Bridgend 57 F10
Cambs 105 B8
Cambs 157 G8
Cardiff 59 D8
C Beds 104 C4
Ches W 166 B6
Ches W 167 D8
Ches W 183 F8
Corn 5 C11
Cumb 210 E4
Derbys 170 D6
Dorset 30 E3
Dumfries 239 C7
Dumfries 248 E4
Gtr Man 185 B7
Hereford 96 C5
Hereford 96 E6
Hereford 115 D7
Hereford 115 G10
Highld 301 C7
Highld 301 E7
Highld 306 F7
Highld 310 E7
Lancs 202 F2
Lancs 202 G4
Lancs 203 C9
Lancs 211 E11
Lincs 155 B10
Mers 182 D2
Moray 301 C11
Norf 158 F6
Northants 137 G7
Northumb 242 E2
Notts 171 G11
Perth 286 D2
S Glos 79 G10
Shetland 312 E5
Shetland 313 K5
Shrops 132 D4
Shrops 149 C8
S Lnrk 259 C10
S Lnrk 268 C3
Som 42 F6
Staffs 151 D10
Suff 107 C8
Swansea 56 D6
S Yorks 198 G5
Warks 119 B10
Wilts 32 C2
W Loth 279 F11
W Mid 133 E10
Newton Abbot Devon 14 G3
Newtonairds
Dumfries 247 G9
Newton Arlosh
Cumb 238 F5
Newton Aycliffe
Durham 233 G11
Newton Bewley
Hrtlpl 234 F5
Newton Blossomville
M Keynes 121 G8
Newton Bromswold
Northants 121 D9
Newton Burgoland
Leics 135 B7
Newton by Toft
Lincs 189 D9
Newton Cross Pembs 91 F7
Newton Ferrers
Devon 7 F10
Newton Flotman
Norf 142 D4
Newtongrange
Midloth 270 C6
Newton Green Mon 79 G8
Newton Hall
Durham 233 B11
Northumb 242 D2
Newton Harcourt
Leics 136 D2
Newton Heath
Gtr Man 195 G11
Newtonhill Aberds 293 D11
Highld 300 E5
Newton Hill
W Yorks 197 C10
Newton Ho Aberds 302 G6
Newton Hurst
Staffs 151 D11
Newtonia Ches E 167 B11
Newton Ketton Darl 234 G2
Newton Kyme
N Yorks 206 E5
Newton-le-Willows
Mers 183 B9
N Yorks 214 B4
Newton Longville
Bucks 102 E6
Newton Mearns
E Renf 267 D10
Newtonmill Angus 293 G8
Newtonmore Highld 291 D9
Newton Morrell
N Yorks 224 D4
Oxon 102 F2
Newton Mulgrave
N Yorks 226 B5
Newton of Ardtoe
Highld 289 B8
Newton of Balcanquhal
Perth 286 F5
Newton of Balcormo
Fife 287 G9
Newton of Falkland
Fife 286 G6
Newton of Mountblairy
Aberds 302 D6
Newton of Pitcairns
Perth 286 F4
Newton on Ayr
S Ayrs 257 E8
Newton on Ouse
N Yorks 206 B6
Newton-on-Rawcliffe
N Yorks 226 G6
Newton on the Hill
Shrops 149 E9
Newton on the Moor
Northumb 252 B5
Newton on Trent
Lincs 188 G4
Newton Park Argyll 266 B2
Mers 183 C9
Newton Peveril
Dorset 18 B4
Newton Poppleford
Devon 15 D7
Newton Purcell
Oxon 102 E2
Newton Regis
Warks 134 B5
Newton Reigny
Cumb 230 E5
Newton Rigg Cumb 230 E5
Newton St Boswells
Borders 262 C3
Newton St Cyres
Devon 14 B3
Newton St Faith
Norf 160 F4
Newton St Loe Bath 61 G8
Newton St Petrock
Devon 24 E6
Newton Solney
Derbys 152 D5
Newton Stacey Hants 48 E2
Newton Stewart
Dumfries 236 C6
Newton Tony Wilts 47 E8
Newton Tracey
Devon 25 B8
Newton under
Roseberry
Redcar 225 C11
Newton Underwood
Northumb 252 F4
Newton upon Derwent
E Yorks 207 D10
Newton Valence
Hants 49 G8
Newton with Scales
Lancs 202 G4
Newton Wood
Gtr Man 184 B6
New Totley S Yorks 186 F4
Newtown Argyll 284 G4
Bl Gwent 77 C11
Bucks 85 E7
Caerph 78 G2
Cambs 121 D11
Ches E 184 E6
Ches W 183 F8
Corn 2 D3
Corn 11 F11
Cumb 229 B7
Cumb 239 F9
Cumb 240 E2
Derbys 185 E7
Devon 26 B3
Dorset 29 G7
Falk 279 E9
Glos 79 E11
Glos 80 D3
Glos 99 E8
Gtr Man 194 F5
Gtr Man 195 G9
Hants 21 B8
Hants 32 C4
Hants 32 E3
Hants 33 D8
Hants 33 E10
Hants 33 F7
Hants 49 F8
Hants 49 G10
Hants 64 G3
Hereford 97 E10
Hereford 98 C2
Highld 290 C5
IoM 192 E4
IoW 20 C4
Mers 183 B7
Norf 143 B10
Northumb 252 C2
Northumb 263 C11
Northumb 264 D2
Oxon 65 C9
Poole 18 C6
Powys 130 E2
Rhondda 77 F9
Shrops 132 C2
Shrops 149 C9
Shrops 149 E8
Som 28 E3
Som 43 F9
Staffs 133 C9
Staffs 168 C6
Staffs 169 C9
Wilts 30 B6
Wilts 63 G10
W Mid 133 F11
Worcs 116 F5
Worcs 117 E7
New Town Bath 45 B9
Bath 60 G5
Dartford 68 E4
Dorset 30 C3
Dorset 30 D6
Dorset 31 D7
Dorset 31 F7
Edin 280 G4
Edin 280 G5
E Loth 281 G8
E Sus 37 C7
Glos 99 E10
Lancs 203 F8
Luton 103 G11
Maidstone 53 B7
Medway 69 G8
Oxon 100 F5
Reading 65 E8
Shetland 312 E6
Som 29 D9
Som 29 D11
Som 44 D3
Soton 33 E7
Swindon 63 C7
T&W 234 B2
T&W 243 E8
W Berks 64 D6
Wilts 46 C6
Wilts 63 E9
W Mid 133 B11
W Mid 133 E9
W Sus 35 B11
W Yorks 198 C3
Newtown-in-St Martin
Corn 2 E6
Newtown Linford
Leics 135 B10
Newtown St Boswells
Borders 262 C3
Newtown Unthank
Leics 135 C9
New Tredegar
Caerph 77 E10
New Trows S Lnrk 259 B8
Newtyle Angus 286 C6
New Ulva Argyll 275 E8
New Village
E Yorks 209 G7
S Yorks 198 F5
New Walsoken
Cambs 139 B9
New Waltham
NE Lincs 201 G9
New Well Powys 113 B11
New Wells Powys 130 D3
New Whittington
Derbys 186 F5
New Wimpole
Cambs 104 B6
New Winton E Loth 281 G8
New Woodhouses
Shrops 167 G9
New Works Telford 132 B3
New Wortley
W Yorks 205 G11
New Yatt Oxon 82 C5
Newyears Green
London 66 B5
New York Lincs 174 D2
N Yorks 214 G3
T&W 243 C8
New Zealand Wilts 62 D4
Nextend Hereford 114 F6
Neyland Pembs 73 D7
Niarbyl IoM 192 E3
Nib Heath Shrops 149 F8
Nibley Glos 79 D11
S Glos 61 C7
Nibley Green Glos 80 F2
Nibon Shetland 312 F5
Nicholashayne
Devon 27 D10
Nicholaston Swansea 56 D4
Nidd N Yorks 214 G6
Niddrie Edin 280 G5
Nigg Aberdeen 293 C11
Highld 301 B8
Nigg Ferry Highld 301 C7
Nightcott Som 26 B5
Nilig Denb 165 D8
Nimble Nook
Gtr Man 196 G2
Nimlet S Glos 61 E8
Nimmer Som 28 E4
Nine Ashes Essex 87 E9
Ninebanks
Northumb 241 G7
Nine Elms London 67 D9
Swindon 62 B6
Nine Maidens Downs
Corn 2 B5
Nine Mile Burn
Midloth 270 D3
Nineveh Worcs 116 C3
Worcs 116 E2
Ninewells Glos 79 C9
Nine Wells Pembs 90 G5
Ninfield E Sus 38 E2
Ningwood IoW 20 D3
Ningwood Common
IoW 20 D3
Ninnes Bridge Corn 2 B2
Nisbet Borders 262 D5
Nisthouse Orkney 314 E3
Shetland 313 G7
Nithbank Dumfries 247 D9
Niton IoW 20 F6
Nitshill Glasgow 267 C10
Noah's Arks Kent 52 B5
Noah's Green
Worcs 117 E10
Noak Bridge Essex 87 G11
Noak Hill Essex 87 G11
London 87 G8
Nob End Gtr Man 195 F9
Nobland Green Herts 86 B5
Noblethorpe
S Yorks 197 F9
Nobold Shrops 149 G9
Nobottle Northants 120 E3
Nob's Crook Hants 33 C7
Nocton Lincs 173 C9
Noctorum Mers 182 D3
Nodmore W Berks 64 D2
Noel Park London 86 G4
Nogdam End Norf 143 C7
Nog Tow Lancs 202 G6
Noke Oxon 83 C8
Noke Street Medway 69 E8
Nolton Pembs 72 B5
Nolton Haven Pembs 72 B5
No Man's Heath
Ches W 167 F8
Warks 134 B5
Nomansland Devon 26 E4
Herts 85 C11
Wilts 32 D3
No Man's Land Corn 6 D5
Hants 33 B8
Noneley Shrops 149 D9
Noness Shetland 313 L6
Nonikiln Highld 300 B6
Nonington Kent 55 C9
Nook Cumb 211 C10
Noon Nick W Yorks 205 F8
Noonsbrough
Shetland 313 H4
Noonsun Ches E 184 F4
Noonvares Corn 2 C3
Noranside Angus 292 G6
Norbiton London 67 F7
Norbreck Blkpool 202 E2
Norbridge Hereford 98 C4
Norbury Ches E 167 F9
Derbys 169 G10
London 67 F10
Shrops 131 E7
Staffs 150 E5
Norbury Common
Ches E 167 F9
Norbury Junction
Staffs 150 E5
Norbury Moor
Gtr Man 184 D6
Norby N Yorks 215 C8
Shetland 313 H3
Norchard Worcs 116 D6
Norcote Glos 81 E8
Norcott Brook
Ches W 183 E10
Norcross Blkpool 202 E2
Nordelph Norf 139 C11
Nordelph Corner
Norf 141 C10
Norden Dorset 18 E4
Gtr Man 195 E11
Norden Heath Dorset 18 E4
Nordley Shrops 132 D3
Norham Northumb 273 F8
Norham West Mains
Northumb 273 F8
Nork Sur 51 B8
Norland Town
W Yorks 196 C5
Norleaze Wilts 45 C11
Norley Ches W 183 G9
Devon 25 G8
Norley Common Sur 50 E4
Norleywood Hants 20 B3
Norlington E Sus 36 E6
Normacot Stoke 168 G6
Normanby N Lincs 199 D11
N Yorks 216 C4
Redcar 225 B10
Normanby-by-Spital
Lincs 189 D7
Normanby by Stow
Lincs 188 E5
Normanby le Wold
Lincs 189 B10
Norman Cross
Cambs 138 E3
Normandy Sur 50 C2
Norman Hill Glos 80 F3
Norman's Bay
E Sus 23 D11
Norman's Green
Devon 27 G9
Normanston Suff 143 E10
Normanton Derby 152 C6
Leics 172 G4
Lincs 172 F6
Notts 172 E2
Rutland 137 B8
Wilts 46 E6
W Yorks 197 C11
Normanton le Heath
Leics 153 G7
Normanton on Soar
Notts 153 E10
Normanton-on-the-
Wolds Notts 154 C2
Normanton on Trent
Notts 172 B3
Normanton Spring
S Yorks 186 E6
Normanton Turville
Leics 135 D9
Normoss Lancs 202 F2
Norney Sur 50 E2
Norr W Yorks 205 F7
Norrington Common
Wilts 61 G11
Norris Green Corn 7 B8
Mers 182 C5
Norris Hill Leics 152 F6
Norristhorpe
W Yorks 197 C8
Norseman Orkney 314 E3
Northacre Norf 141 D9
North Acton London 67 C8
Northall Bucks 103 G9
Northallerton
N Yorks 225 G7
Northall Green Norf 159 G9
Northam Devon 24 B6
Soton 32 E6
Northampton
Northants 120 E5
North Anston
S Yorks 187 E8
North Ascot Brack 66 F2
North Aston Oxon 101 F9
Northaw Herts 86 E3
Northay Devon 28 G5
Som 28 E3
North Ayre Shetland 312 F6
North Baddesley
Hants 32 D5
North Ballachulish
Highld 290 G2
North Barrow Som 29 B10
North Barsham
Norf 159 C8
North Batsom Som 41 G10
Northbeck Lincs 173 G9
North Beer Corn 12 C2
North Benfleet Essex 69 B9
North Bersted
W Sus 22 C6
North Berwick
E Loth 281 D11
North Bitchburn
Durham 233 E9
North Blyth
Northumb 253 G8
North Boarhunt
Hants 33 E10
North Bockhampton
Dorset 19 B9
Northborough
Pboro 138 B3
Northbourne Bmouth 19 B7
Kent 55 C10
North Bovey Devon 13 E10
North Bradley Wilts 45 C11
North Brentor Devon 12 E5
North Brewham Som 45 F8
Northbridge Street
E Sus 38 C2
Northbrook Dorset 17 C10
Hants 33 D9
Hants 48 F4
Oxon 101 G9
Wilts 46 C4
North Brook End
Cambs 104 C5
North Broomage
Falk 279 E7
North Buckland
Devon 40 E3
North Burlingham
Norf 161 G7
North Cadbury Som 29 B10
North Cairn
Dumfries 236 B1
North Camp Hants 49 C11
North Carlton Lincs 188 F6
Notts 187 E9
North Carrine Argyll 255 G7
North Cave E Yorks 208 G3
North Cerney Glos 81 D8
North Chailey E Sus 36 C5
Northchapel W Sus 35 B7
North Charford
Wilts 31 D11
North Charlton
Northumb 264 E5
North Cheam London 67 F8
North Cheriton Som 29 B11
Northchurch Herts 85 D7
North Cliff E Yorks 209 D10
North Cliffe E Yorks 208 F3
North Clifton Notts 188 G4
North Close
Durham 233 E11
North Cockerington
Lincs 190 C5
North Coker Som 29 E8
North Collafirth
Shetland 312 E5
North Common
S Glos 61 E7
Suff 125 B9
North Connel
Argyll 289 F11
North Cornelly
Bridgend 57 E10
North Corner Corn 3 F7
S Glos 61 C7
North Corriegills
N Ayrs 256 C2
North Corry Highld 289 D10
Northcote Devon 27 G11
North Cotes Lincs 201 G11
Northcott Corn 24 F2
Devon 12 C2
Devon 27 E9
Devon 27 F10
North Country Corn 4 G3
Northcourt Oxon 83 F8
North Court Som 41 F11
North Cove Suff 143 F9
North Cowton
N Yorks 224 E5
North Craigo Angus 293 G8
North Crawley
M Keynes 103 C8
North Cray London 68 E3
North Creake Norf 159 B7
North Curry Som 28 B4
North Dalton
E Yorks 208 C4
North Darley Corn 11 G11
North Dawn Orkney 314 F4
North Deighton
N Yorks 206 C3
North Denes Norf 161 G10
Northdown Kent 71 E11
North Dronley
Angus 287 D7
North Drumachter
Lodge Highld 291 F8
North Duffield
N Yorks 207 F9
Northdyke Orkney 314 D2
North Dykes Cumb 230 D6
North Eastling Kent 54 B3
Northedge Derbys 170 B5
North Elham Kent 55 E7
North Elkington
Lincs 190 C3
North Elmham Norf 159 E9
North Elmsall
W Yorks 198 E3
North Elmshall
W Yorks 198 E3
North Elphinestone
E Loth 281 G7
Northend Bath 61 F9
Bucks 84 G2
Essex 89 E7
Essex 105 D10
Warks 119 G7
North End Bath 60 G6
Beds 103 B9
Beds 121 F10
Bexley 68 D4
Bucks 102 F4
Bucks 102 F6
Camden 67 B9
Cumb 239 F8
Devon 27 D10
Dorset 30 B4
Durham 233 C11
Essex 87 B11
Essex 106 D5
E Yorks 209 C9
E Yorks 209 E9
E Yorks 209 G11
Hants 31 D10
Hants 33 B9
Hants 64 G2
Leics 153 F11
Lincs 174 G2
Lincs 189 B8
Lincs 190 C5
Lincs 190 D6
Lincs 191 D7
Lincs 201 G10
N Lincs 200 C6
Norf 141 E10
Northumb 252 C4
N Som 60 F2
Ptsmth 33 G11
Som 28 B3
Wilts 81 G8
W Sus 35 F10
W Sus 35 G7
W Sus 51 F11
Northenden
Gtr Man 184 C4
Northern Moor
Gtr Man 184 C4
North Erradale
Highld 307 L2
North Evington
Leicester 136 C2
North Ewster
N Lincs 199 G10
North Fambridge
Essex 88 F5
North Fearns Highld 295 B7
North Featherstone
W Yorks 198 C2

North Feltham London 66 E6
North Feorline N Ayrs 255 E10
North Ferriby E Yorks 200 B3
Northfield
Aberdeen 293 C11
Borders 262 D3
Borders 273 B8
Edin 280 G5
E Yorks 200 B4
Highld 301 B7
M Keynes 103 C7
Northants 137 E7
Som 43 F9
W Mid 117 B10
Northfields Hants 33 B7
Lincs 137 B10
North Finchley London 86 G3
Northfleet Kent 68 E6
Northfleet Green Kent 68 E6
North Flobbets Aberds 303 F7
North Frodingham E Yorks 209 C8
Northgate Lincs 156 D3
Som 27 B9
W Sus 51 F9
North Gluss Shetland 312 F5
North Gorley Hants 31 E11
North Green Norf 141 B10
Norf 142 F4
Suff 126 B6
Suff 126 E6
Suff 127 D7
North Greetwell Lincs 189 G8
North Grimston N Yorks 216 F6
North Halley Orkney 314 F5
North Halling Medway 69 F8
North Harrow London 66 B6
North Hayling Hants 22 C2
North Hazelrigg Northumb 264 C3
North Heasley Devon 41 G8
North Heath W Berks 64 E3
W Sus 35 C9
North Hill Corn 11 F11
North Hillingdon London 66 C5
North Hinksey Oxon 83 D7
North Hinksey Village Oxon 83 D7
North Ho Shetland 313 J5
North Holmwood Sur 51 D7
North Houghton Hants 47 G10
Northhouse Borders 249 B10
North Howden E Yorks 207 G11
North Huish Devon 8 D4
North Hyde London 66 D6
North Hykeham Lincs 172 B6
North Hylton T&W 243 F8
Northiam E Sus 38 B4
Northill C Beds 104 B2
Northington Glos 80 D2
Hants 48 F5
North Kelsey Lincs 200 G4
North Kelsey Moor Lincs 200 G5
North Kensington London 67 C8
North Kessock Highld 300 E6
North Killingholme N Lincs 200 D6
North Kilvington N Yorks 215 B8
North Kilworth Leics 136 G2
North Kingston Hants 31 G11
North Kirkton Aberds 303 D11
North Kiscadale N Ayrs 256 D2
North Kyme Lincs 173 E11
North Laggan Highld 290 D4
North Lancing W Sus 35 F11
North Landing E Yorks 218 E4
Northlands Lincs 174 E4
Northlea Durham 243 G10
Northleach Glos 81 C10
North Lee Bucks 84 D4
North Lees N Yorks 214 E6
Northleigh Devon 15 B9
Devon 40 G6
North Leigh Kent 54 D6
Oxon 82 C5
North Leverton with Habblesthorpe Notts 188 E3
Northlew Devon 12 B6
North Littleton Worcs 99 B11
North Looe Sur 67 G8
North Lopham Norf 141 G10
North Luffenham Rutland 137 C8
North Marden W Sus 34 D4
North Marston Bucks 102 G5
North Middleton Midloth 271 D7
Northumb 264 E2
North Millbrex Aberds 303 E8
North Molton Devon 26 B2
Northmoor Devon 24 D4
Oxon 82 E6
Northmoor Corner Som 43 G10
Northmoor Green or Moorland Som 43 G10
North Moreton Oxon 64 B5
North Mosstown Aberds 303 D10
North Motherwell N Lnrk 268 D4
North Moulsecoomb Brighton 36 F4
Northmuir Angus 287 B7
North Mundham W Sus 22 C5
North Muskham Notts 172 D3
North Newbald E Yorks 208 F4
North Newington Oxon 101 D8
North Newnton Wilts 46 B6
North Newton Som 43 G9
Northney Hants 22 C2
North Nibley Glos 80 F2
North Oakley Hants 48 C4
North Ockendon London 68 C5
Northolt London 66 C6
Northop Hall Flint 166 B3
Northop/Llan-eurgain Flint 166 B2
North Ormesby Mbro 234 G6
North Ormsby Lincs 190 C3
Northorpe Lincs 155 F11
Lincs 156 B4
Lincs 188 B5
W Yorks 197 C8
North Otterington N Yorks 215 B7
Northover Som 29 C8
Som 44 F3
North Owersby Lincs 189 C9
Northowram W Yorks 196 B6
Northpark Argyll 275 G11
North Perrott Som 29 F7
North Petherton Som 43 G9
North Petherwin Corn 11 D11
North Pickenham Norf 141 B7
North Piddle Worcs 117 G9
North Poorton Dorset 16 B6
Northport Dorset 18 D4
North Port Argyll 284 E4
North Poulner Hants 31 F11
Northpunds Shetland 313 L6
North Queensferry Fife 280 E2
North Radworthy Devon 41 G9
North Rauceby Lincs 173 F8
North Reddish Gtr Man 184 C5
Northrepps Norf 160 B4
North Reston Lincs 190 E5
North Rigton N Yorks 205 D11
North Ripley Hants 19 B9
North Rode Ches E 168 B5
North Roe Shetland 312 E5
North Row Cumb 229 E10
North Runcton Norf 158 F2
North Sandwick Shetland 312 D7
North Scale Cumb 210 F3
North Scarle Lincs 172 B5
North Seaton Northumb 253 F7
North Seaton Colliery Northumb 253 F7
North Sheen London 67 D7
North Shian Argyll 289 E11
North Shields T&W 243 D9
North Shoebury Sthend 70 B2
North Shore Blkpool 202 F2
Northside Aberds 303 D8
Orkney 314 D2
North Side Cumb 228 F6
Pboro 138 D5
North Skelmanae Aberds 303 D9
North Skelton Redcar 226 B3
North Somercotes Lincs 190 B6
North Stainley N Yorks 214 D5
North Stainmore Cumb 222 B6
North Stifford Thurrock 68 C6
North Stoke Bath 61 F8
Oxon 64 B6
W Sus 35 E8
North Stoneham Hants 32 D6
North Street Hants 31 D11
Hants 48 G6
Kent 54 B4
Medway 69 E10
W Berks 64 E6
North Sunderland Northumb 264 C6
North Synton Borders 261 E11
North Tamerton Corn 12 B2
North Tawton Devon 25 G11
North Thoresby Lincs 190 B3
North Tidworth Wilts 47 D8
North Togston Northumb 252 C6
Northton Aberds 293 C9
Northtown Orkney 314 G4
Shetland 313 M5
North Town Devon 25 F8
Hants 49 C11
Som 29 B10
Som 44 E5
Windsor 65 C11
North Tuddenham Norf 159 G10
Northumberland Heath London 68 D4
Northville Torf 78 F3
North Walbottle T&W 242 D5
North Walney Cumb 210 F3
North Walsham Norf 160 C5
North Waltham Hants 48 D5
North Warnborough Hants 49 C8
North Water Bridge Angus 293 G8
North Waterhayne Devon 28 F3
North Watford Herts 85 F10
North Watten Highld 310 D6
Northway Devon 24 C5
Glos 99 E8
Som 27 B10
Swansea 56 D5
North Weald Bassett Essex 87 E7
North Weirs Hants 32 G3
North Wembley London 67 B7
North Weston N Som 60 D3
Oxon 83 D11
North Wheatley Notts 188 D3
North Whilborough Devon 9 B7
North Whiteley Moray 302 E4
Northwich Ches W 183 G11
Northwick S Glos 60 B5
Som 43 D11
Worcs 116 F6
North Wick Bath 60 F5
North Widcombe Bath 44 B5
North Willingham Lincs 189 D11
North Wingfield Derbys 170 B6
North Witham Lincs 155 E8
Northwold Norf 140 D5
Northwood Derbys 170 C3
IoW 20 C5
Kent 71 F11
London 85 G9
Mers 182 B6
Shrops 149 C9
Staffs 168 G5
Stoke 168 F5
Northwood Green Glos 80 B2
Northwood Hills London 85 G9
North Woolwich London 68 D2
North Wootton Dorset 29 E11
Norf 158 E2
Som 44 E5
North Wraxall Wilts 61 D10
North Wroughton Swindon 63 C7
Norton Devon 9 E7
Devon 24 B3
E Sus 23 E7
Glos 99 G7
Halton 183 E9
Herts 104 E4
IoW 20 D2
Mon 78 B6
Northants 120 E2
Notts 187 G9
N Som 59 G10
Powys 114 D6
Shrops 131 B11
Shrops 131 G9
Shrops 132 C4
Stockton 234 G4
Suff 125 D9
Swansea 56 D3
Swansea 56 D6
S Yorks 186 E5
S Yorks 198 D4
Wilts 61 C11
W Mid 133 G7
Worcs 99 B10
Worcs 117 G7
W Sus 22 B6
W Sus 22 D5
Norton Ash Kent 70 G3
Norton Bavant Wilts 46 E2
Norton Bridge Staffs 151 C7
Norton Canes Staffs 133 B10
Norton Canon Hereford 97 B7
Norton Corner Norf 159 D11
Norton Disney Lincs 172 D5
Norton East Staffs 133 B10
Norton Ferris Wilts 45 F9
Norton Fitzwarren Som 27 B11
Norton Green Herts 104 G4
IoW 20 D2
Staffs 168 E6
W Mid 118 C3
Norton Hawkfield Bath 60 G5
Norton Heath Essex 87 E10
Norton in Hales Shrops 150 B4
Norton-in-the-Moors Stoke 168 E5
Norton-Juxta-Twycross Leics 134 B6
Norton-le-Clay N Yorks 215 E8
Norton Lindsey Warks 118 E4
Norton Little Green Suff 125 D9
Norton Malreward Bath 60 F6
Norton Mandeville Essex 87 E9
Norton-on-Derwent N Yorks 216 E5
Norton St Philip Som 45 B9
Norton Subcourse Norf 143 D8
Norton sub Hamdon Som 29 D7
Norton's Wood N Som 60 E2
Norton Woodseats S Yorks 186 E5
Norwell Notts 172 C3
Norwell Woodhouse Notts 172 C2
Norwich Norf 142 B4
Norwick Shetland 312 B8
Norwood Derbys 187 E7
Dorset 29 F8
Norwood End Essex 87 D9
Norwood Green London 66 D6
W Yorks 196 B6
Norwood Hill Sur 51 E8
Norwood New Town London 67 E10
Norwoodside Cambs 139 D8
Noseley Leics 136 D4
Noss Highld 310 D7
Shetland 313 M5
Noss Mayo Devon 7 F11
Nosterfield N Yorks 214 C5
Nosterfield End Cambs 106 C2
Nostie Highld 295 C10
Notgrove Glos 100 G2
Nottage Bridgend 57 F10
Notter Corn 7 C7
Nottingham Nottingham 153 B11
Notting Hill London 67 C8
Nottington Dorset 17 E9
Notton Wilts 62 F2
W Yorks 197 E10
Nounsley Essex 88 C3
Noutard's Green Worcs 116 D5
Novar House Highld 300 C6
Nova Scotia Ches W 167 B10
Novers Park Bristol 60 F5
Noverton Glos 99 G9
Nowton Suff 125 E7
Nox Shrops 149 G8
Noyadd Trefawr Ceredig 92 B5
Noyadd Wilym Ceredig 92 C4
Nuffield Oxon 65 B7
Nun Appleton N Yorks 207 F7
Nunburnholme E Yorks 208 D2
Nuncargate Notts 171 E8
Nunclose Cumb 230 B5
Nuneaton Warks 135 E7
Nuneham Courtenay Oxon 83 F9
Nuney Green Oxon 65 D7
Nunhead London 67 D10
Nun Hills Lancs 195 C11
Nun Monkton N Yorks 206 B6
Nunney Som 45 D8
Nunney Catch Som 45 E8
Nunnington N Yorks 216 D3
Nunnykirk Northumb 252 E3
Nunsthorpe NE Lincs 201 F9
Nunthorpe Mbro 225 C10
York 207 C8
Nunton Wilts 31 B11
Nunwick N Yorks 214 E6
Nupdown S Glos 79 F10
Nupend Glos 80 D3
Glos 80 F4
Nup End Bucks 84 B5
Herts 86 B2
Nuper's Hatch Essex 87 G8
Nuppend Glos 79 E10
Nuptown Brack 65 E11
Nursling Hants 32 D5
Nursted Hants 34 C3
Nursteed Wilts 62 G4
Nurston V Glam 58 F5
Nurton Staffs 132 D6
Nurton Hill Staffs 132 D6
Nutbourne W Sus 22 B3
W Sus 35 D9
Nutbourne Common W Sus 35 D9
Nutburn Hants 32 C5
Nutcombe Sur 49 G11
Nutfield Sur 51 C10
Nut Grove Mers 183 C7
Nuthall Notts 171 G8
Nuthampstead Herts 105 E8
Nuthurst Warks 118 C3
W Sus 35 B11
Nutley E Sus 36 B6
Hants 48 E6
Nuttall Gtr Man 195 D9
Nutwell S Yorks 198 G6
Nybster Highld 310 C7
Nye N Som 60 G2
Nyetimber W Sus 22 D5
Nyewood W Sus 34 C4
Nyland Som 44 C3
Nymet Rowland Devon 26 F2
Nymet Tracey Devon 26 G2
Nympsfield Glos 80 E4
Nynehead Som 27 C10
Nythe Som 44 G2
Swindon 63 B7
Nyton W Sus 22 B6

O

Oadby Leics 136 C2
Oad Street Kent 69 G11
Oakall Green Worcs 116 E6
Oakamoor Staffs 169 G9
Oakbank W Loth 269 B11
Oak Bank Gtr Man 195 F10
Oak Cross Devon 12 B6
Oakdale Caerph 77 F11
N Yorks 205 B11
Poole 18 C6
Oake Som 27 B11
Oake Green Som 27 B11
Oaken Staffs 133 C7
Oakenclough Lancs 202 D6
Oakengates Telford 150 G4
Oakenholt Flint 182 G3
Oakenshaw Durham 233 D10
Lancs 203 G10
W Yorks 197 B7
Oakerthorpe Derbys 170 E5
Oakes W Yorks 196 D6
Oakfield Herts 104 F3
IoW 21 C7
Torf 78 G4
Oakford Ceredig 111 F9
Devon 26 C6
Oakfordbridge Devon 26 C6
Oakgrove Ches E 168 B6
M Keynes 103 D7
Oakham Rutland 137 B7
W Mid 133 F9
Oakhanger Ches E 168 E3
Hants 49 F9
Oakhill Som 44 D6
W Sus 51 G7
Oak Hill Stoke 168 G5
Suff 109 B7
Oakhurst Kent 52 C4
Oakington Cambs 123 E8
Oaklands Carms 74 B6
Herts 86 B2
Powys 113 G10
Oakleigh Park London 86 G3
Oakle Street Glos 80 B3
Oakley Beds 121 G10
Bucks 83 C10
Fife 279 D10
Glos 99 G9
Hants 48 C5
Oxon 84 E3
Poole 18 B6
Staffs 150 B4
Suff 126 B3
Oakley Court Oxon 64 B6
Oakley Green Windsor 66 D2
Oakley Park Powys 129 F9
Suff 126 B3
Oakley Wood Oxon 64 B6
Oakmere Ches W 167 B9
Oakridge Glos 80 E6
Hants 48 C6
Oakridge Lynch Glos 80 E6
Oaks Shrops 131 C8
Oaksey Wilts 81 G7
Oaks Green Derbys 152 C3
Oakshaw Ford Cumb 240 B2
Oakshott Hants 34 B2
Oaks in Charnwood Leics 153 F9
Oakthorpe Leics 152 G6
Oak Tree Darl 225 C7
Oakwell W Yorks 197 B8
Oakwood Derby 153 B7
London 86 F3
Northumb 241 D10
Warr 183 C11
W Yorks 206 F2
Oakwoodhill Sur 50 F6
Oakworth W Yorks 204 F6
Oape Highld 309 J4
Oare Kent 70 G4
Som 41 D10
W Berks 64 E4
Wilts 63 G7
Oareford Som 41 D10
Oasby Lincs 155 B10
Oath Som 28 B5
Oathill Dorset 28 F6
Oathlaw Angus 287 B8
Oatlands Glasgow 267 C11
N Yorks 205 C11
Oatlands Park Sur 66 G5
Oban Argyll 289 G10
Highld 295 G10
W Isles 305 H3
Obley Shrops 114 B6
Oborne Dorset 29 D11
Obthorpe Lincs 155 F11
Obthorpe Lodge Lincs 156 F2
Occlestone Green Ches W 167 C11
Occold Suff 126 C3
Ocean Village Soton 32 E6
Ochiltree E Ayrs 258 E2
Ochr-y-foel Denb 181 F9
Ochtermuthill Perth 286 F2
Ochtertyre Perth 286 E2
Ochtow Highld 309 J4
Ockbrook Derbys 153 B8
Ocker Hill W Mid 133 E9
Ockeridge Worcs 116 E5
Ockford Ridge Sur 50 E3
Ockham Sur 50 B5
Ockle Highld 289 B7
Ockley Sur 50 F6
Ocle Pychard Hereford 97 B11
Octon E Yorks 217 F10
Octon Cross Roads E Yorks 217 F10
Odam Barton Devon 26 D2
Odcombe Som 29 D8
Odd Down Bath 61 G8
Oddendale Cumb 221 C11
Odder Lincs 188 G6
Oddingley Worcs 117 F8
Oddington Glos 100 F4
Oxon 83 C9
Odell Beds 121 F9
Odham Devon 25 G7
Odie Orkney 314 D6
Odiham Hants 49 C8
Odsal W Yorks 197 B7
Odsey Cambs 104 D5
Odstock Wilts 31 B10
Odstone Leics 135 B7
Offchurch Warks 119 D7
Offenham Worcs 99 B11
Offenham Cross Worcs 99 B11
Offerton Gtr Man 184 D6
T&W 243 F8
Offerton Green Gtr Man 184 D6
Offham E Sus 36 E5
Kent 53 B7
W Sus 35 F8
Offleyhay Staffs 150 D5
Offleymarsh Staffs 150 D5
Offleyrock Staffs 150 D5
Offord Cluny Cambs 122 D4
Offord D'Arcy Cambs 122 D4
Offton Suff 107 B11
Offwell Devon 15 B9
Ogbourne Maizey Wilts 63 E7
Ogbourne St Andrew Wilts 63 E7
Ogbourne St George Wilts 63 E8
Ogden W Yorks 205 G7
Ogdens Hants 31 E11
Ogil Angus 292 G6
Ogle Northumb 242 B4
Ogmore V Glam 57 F11
Ogmore-by-Sea/Aberogwr V Glam 57 F11
Ogmore Vale Bridgend 76 G6
Okeford Fitzpaine Dorset 30 E4
Okehampton Devon 13 B7
Okehampton Camp Devon 13 C7
Oker Derbys 170 C3
Okewood Hill Sur 50 F6
Okle Green Glos 98 F5
Okraquoy Shetland 313 K6
Okus Swindon 62 C6
Olchard Devon 14 F3
Old Northants 120 C5
Old Aberdeen Aberdeen 293 C11
Old Alresford Hants 48 G5
Oldany Highld 306 F6
Old Arley Warks 134 E5
Old Balornock Glasgow 268 B2
Old Basford Nottingham 171 G8
Old Basing Hants 49 C7
Old Belses Borders 262 E3
Oldberrow Warks 118 D2
Old Bewick Northumb 264 E3
Old Bexley London 68 E3
Old Blair Perth 291 G10
Old Bolingbroke Lincs 174 B4
Oldborough Devon 26 F3
Old Boston Mers 183 B9
Old Bramhope W Yorks 205 E10
Old Brampton Derbys 186 G4
Old Bridge of Tilt Perth 291 G10
Old Bridge of Urr Dumfries 237 C9
Oldbrook M Keynes 103 D7
Old Buckenham Norf 141 E11
Old Burdon T&W 243 G9
Old Burghclere Hants 48 B3
Oldbury Kent 52 B5
Shrops 132 E4
Warks 134 E6
W Mid 133 F9
Oldbury Naite S Glos 79 G10
Oldbury-on-Severn S Glos 79 G10
Oldbury on the Hill Glos 61 B10
Old Byland N Yorks 215 B11
Old Cambus Borders 272 B6
Old Cardinham Castle Corn 6 B2
Old Carlisle Cumb 229 B11
Old Cassop Durham 234 D2
Oldcastle Mon 96 G6
Oldcastle Heath Ches W 167 F7
Old Castleton Borders 250 E2
Old Catton Norf 160 G4
Old Chalford Oxon 100 F6
Old Church Stoke Powys 130 E5
Old Clee NE Lincs 201 F9
Old Cleeve Som 42 E4
Old Colwyn Conwy 180 F5
Old Coppice Shrops 131 B9
Old Corry Highld 295 C8
Oldcotes Notts 187 D9
Old Coulsdon London 51 B10
Old Country Hereford 98 C4
Old Craig Aberds 303 G9
Angus 292 G4
Oldcroft Glos 79 D10
Old Crombie Aberds 302 D5
Old Cryals Kent 53 E7
Old Cullen Moray 302 C5
Old Dailly S Ayrs 244 D6
Old Dalby Leics 154 E3
Old Dam Derbys 185 F10
Old Deer Aberds 303 E9
Old Denaby S Yorks 187 B7
Old Ditch Som 44 D4
Old Dolphin W Yorks 205 G8
Old Down S Glos 60 B6
Old Duffus Moray 301 C11
Old Edlington S Yorks 187 B8
Old Eldon Durham 233 F10
Old Ellerby E Yorks 209 F9
Oldend Glos 80 D3
Old Fallings W Mid 133 C8
Oldfallow Staffs 151 G9
Old Farm Park M Keynes 103 D8
Old Felixstowe Suff 108 D6
Oldfield Cumb 229 F7
Shrops 132 F3
Worcs 116 E6
W Yorks 196 E6
W Yorks 204 F6
Old Field Shrops 115 B9
Oldfield Brow Gtr Man 184 D3
Oldfield Park Bath 61 G8
Old Fletton Pboro 138 D3
Old Fold T&W 243 E7
Oldford Som 45 C9
Old Ford London 67 C11
Old Forge Hereford 79 B9
Oldfurnace Staffs 169 G8
Old Furnace Torf 78 E3
Old Gate Lincs 157 E8
Old Glossop Derbys 185 C8
Old Goginan Ceredig 128 G3
Old Goole E Yorks 199 C8
Old Gore Hereford 98 F2
Old Graitney Dumfries 239 D8
Old Grimsby Scilly 1 F3
Oldhall Renfs 267 C10
Old Hall Powys 129 G8
Oldhall Green Suff 125 F7
Old Hall Green Herts 105 G7
Oldhall Ho Highld 310 D6
Old Hall Street Norf 160 C6
Oldham Gtr Man 196 F2
Oldham Edge Gtr Man 196 F2
Oldhamstocks E Loth 282 G4
Old Harlow Essex 87 C7
Old Hatfield Herts 86 D2
Old Heath Essex 107 G10
Old Heathfield E Sus 37 C9
Old Hill W Mid 133 F9
Old Hills Worcs 98 B6
Old Hunstanton Norf 175 G11
Oldhurst Cambs 122 B6
Old Hurst Cambs 122 B5
Old Hutton Cumb 211 B11
Oldington Shrops 132 D4
Old Johnstone Dumfries 248 D6
Old Kea Corn 4 G6
Old Kilpatrick W Dunb 277 G9
Old Kinnernie Aberds 293 C9
Old Knebworth Herts 104 G4
Oldland S Glos 61 E7
Oldland Common S Glos 61 E7
Old Langho Lancs 203 F10
Old Laxey IoM 192 D5
Old Leake Lincs 174 E6
Old Leckie Stirl 278 C3
Old Lindley W Yorks 196 D5
Old Linslade C Beds 103 F8
Old Llanberis/Nant Peris Gwyn 163 D10
Old Malden London 67 F8
Old Malton N Yorks 216 E5
Old Marston Shrops 148 C6
Old Mead Essex 105 F10
Oldmeldrum Aberds 303 G8
Old Micklefield W Yorks 206 G4
Old Mill Corn 12 G3
Old Milton Hants 19 C10
Old Milverton Warks 118 D5
Oldmixon N Som 43 B10
Old Monkland N Lnrk 268 C4
Old Nenthorn Borders 262 B5
Old Netley Hants 33 F7
Old Neuadd Powys 129 F11
Old Newton Suff 125 E11
Old Oak Common London 67 C8
Old Park Corn 6 B4
Telford 132 B3
Old Passage S Glos 60 B5
Old Perton Staffs 133 D7
Old Philpstoun W Loth 279 F11
Old Polmont Falk 279 F8
Old Portsmouth Ptsmth 21 B8
Old Quarrington Durham 234 D2
Old Radnor Powys 114 F5
Old Rattray Aberds 303 D10
Old Rayne Aberds 302 G6
Old Romney Kent 39 B8
Old Shirley Soton 32 E5
Oldshore Beg Highld 306 D6
Old Shoreham W Sus 36 F2
Oldshoremore Highld 306 D7
Old Snydale W Yorks 198 C2
Old Sodbury S Glos 61 C9
Old Somerby Lincs 155 C9
Oldstead N Yorks 215 C10
Old Stillington Stockton 234 G3
Old Storridge Common Worcs 116 G4
Old Stratford Northants 102 C5
Old Struan Perth 291 G10
Old Swan Mers 182 C5
Old Swarland Northumb 252 C5
Old Swinford W Mid 133 G8
Old Tame Gtr Man 196 F3
Old Tebay Cumb 222 D2
Old Thirsk N Yorks 215 C8
Old Tinnis Borders 261 D9
Old Toll S Ayrs 257 E9
Oldtown Aberds 293 C7
Aberds 302 G5
Highld 309 L5
Old Town Cumb 211 C11
Cumb 230 C5
Edin 280 G5
E Sus 23 F9
E Sus 38 F2
E Sus 38 F4
E Yorks 218 F3
Herts 104 F4
Scilly 1 G4
Swindon 63 C7
W Yorks 196 B3
Oldtown of Ord Aberds 302 D6
Old Trafford Gtr Man 184 B4
Old Tree Kent 71 G8
Old Tupton Derbys 170 B5
Oldwalls Swansea 56 C3
Old Warden C Beds 104 C2
Old Warren Flint 166 C4
Oldway Swansea 56 D5
Torbay 9 C7
Old Way Som 28 D5
Oldways End Devon 26 B5
Old Weston Cambs 121 B11
Old Wharf Hereford 98 D4
Oldwhat Aberds 303 D8
Old Whittington Derbys 186 G5
Oldwich Lane W Mid 118 C4
Old Wick Highld 310 D7
Old Wimpole Cambs 122 G6
Old Windsor Windsor 66 E3
Old Wingate Durham 234 D3
Old Wives Lees Kent 54 C5
Old Woking Sur 50 B4
Old Wolverton M Keynes 102 C6
Oldwood Worcs 115 D11
Old Woodhall Lincs 174 B2
Old Woodhouses Shrops 167 G9
Old Woodstock Oxon 82 B6
Olgrinmore Highld 310 D4
Olive Green Staffs 152 F2
Oliver's Battery Hants 33 B7
Ollaberry Shetland 312 E5
Ollag W Isles 297 G3
Ollerbrook Booth Derbys 185 D10
Ollerton Ches E 184 F3
Notts 171 B11
Shrops 150 D2
Ollerton Fold Lancs 194 C6
Ollerton Lane Shrops 150 D3
Olmarch Ceredig 112 F2
Olmstead Green Essex 106 C2
Olney M Keynes 121 G7
Olrig Ho Highld 310 C5
Olton W Mid 134 G2
Olveston S Glos 60 B6
Olwen Ceredig 93 B11
Ombersley Worcs 116 E6
Ompton Notts 171 B11
Omunsgarth Shetland 313 J5
Onchan IoM 192 E4
Onecote Staffs 169 D9
Onehouse Suff 125 F10
Onen Mon 78 C6
Onesacre S Yorks 186 C3
Ongar Hill Norf 157 E11
Ongar Street Hereford 115 D7
Onibury Shrops 115 B9
Onich Highld 290 G2
Onllwyn Neath 76 C4
Onneley Staffs 168 G3
Onslow Village Sur 50 D3
Onthank E Ayrs 267 G8
Onziebust Orkney 314 D4
Openshaw Gtr Man 184 B5
Openwoodgate Derbys 170 F5
Opinan Highld 299 B7
Highld 307 K3
Orange Lane Borders 272 G5
Orange Row Norf 157 E10
Orasaigh W Isles 305 G5
Orbiston N Lnrk 268 D4
Orbliston Moray 302 D3
Orbost Highld 298 E2
Orby Lincs 175 B7
Orchard Hill Devon 24 B6
Orchard Leigh Bucks 85 E7
Orchard Portman Som 28 C2
Orcheston Wilts 46 D5
Orcop Hereford 97 F9
Orcop Hill Hereford 97 F9
Ord Highld 295 D8
Ordale Shetland 312 C8
Ordhead Aberds 293 B8
Ordie Aberds 292 C6
Ordiequish Moray 302 D3
Ordighill Aberds 302 D5
Ordley Northumb 241 F10
Ordsall Gtr Man 184 B4
Notts 187 E11
Ore E Sus 38 E4
Oreston Plym 7 E10
Oreton Shrops 132 G3
Orford Suff 109 B8
Warr 183 C10
Organford Dorset 18 C4
Orgreave Staffs 152 F3
S Yorks 186 D6

Oridge Street Glos 98 F5
Orlandon Pembs 72 D4
Orlestone Kent 54 G3
Orleton Hereford 115 D9
Worcs 116 D3
Orleton Common
Hereford 115 D9
Orlingbury
Northants 121 C7
Ormacleit W Isles 297 H3
Ormathwaite Cumb 229 F11
Ormesby Redcar 225 B10
Ormesby St Margaret
Norf 161 G9
Ormesby St Michael
Norf 161 G9
Ormiclate Castle
W Isles 297 H3
Ormidale Lodge
Argyll 275 F11
Ormiscaig Highld 307 K3
Ormiston Borders 262 G2
E Loth 271 B8
Ormsaigbeg Highld 288 C6
Ormsaigmore
Highld 288 C6
Ormsary Argyll 275 F8
Ormsgill Cumb 210 E3
Ormskirk Lancs 194 F2
Ornsby Hill Durham 233 B9
Orpington London 68 F3
Orrell Gtr Man 194 F4
Mers 182 B4
Orrell Post Gtr Man 194 G4
Orrisdale IoM 192 C4
Orrock Fife 280 D4
Orroland Dumfries 237 E9
Orsett Thurrock 68 C6
Orsett Heath
Thurrock 68 D6
Orslow Staffs 150 F6
Orston Notts 172 G3
Orthwaite Cumb 229 E11
Ortner Lancs 202 C6
Orton Cumb 222 D2
Northants 120 B6
Staffs 133 D7
Orton Brimbles
Pboro 138 D3
Orton Goldhay
Pboro 138 D3
Orton Longueville
Pboro 138 D3
Orton Malborne
Pboro 138 D3
Orton-on-the-Hill
Leics 134 C6
Orton Rigg Cumb 239 G8
Orton Southgate
Pboro 138 E2
Orton Waterville
Pboro 138 D3
Orton Wistow
Pboro 138 D2
Orwell Cambs 123 G7
Osbaldeston Lancs 203 G8
Osbaldeston Green
Lancs 203 G8
Osbaldwick York 207 C8
Osbaston Leics 135 C8
Shrops 148 E6
Telford 149 F11
Osbaston Hollow
Leics 135 B8
Osbournby Lincs 155 B11
Oscroft Ches W 167 B8
Ose Highld 298 E3
Osea Island Essex 88 D6
Osehill Green
Dorset 29 F11
Osgathorpe Leics 153 F8
Osgodby Lincs 189 C9
N Yorks 207 G8
N Yorks 217 C11
Osgodby Common
N Yorks 207 F8
Osidge London 86 G3
Oskaig Highld 295 B7
Oskamull Argyll 288 E6
Osleston Derbys 152 B4
Osmaston Derby 153 C7
Derbys 170 G2
Osmington Dorset 17 E10
Osmington Mills
Dorset 17 E10
Osmondthorpe
W Yorks 206 G2
Osmotherley
N Yorks 225 F9
Osney Oxon 83 D8
Ospisdale Highld 309 L7
Ospringe Kent 70 G4
Ossaborough Devon 40 E3
Ossemsley Hants 19 B10
Osset Spa W Yorks 197 D9
Ossett W Yorks 197 C9
Ossett Street Side
W Yorks 197 C9
Ossington Notts 172 C3
Ostend Essex 88 F6
Norf 161 C7
Osterley London 66 D6
Oswaldkirk N Yorks 216 D2
Oswaldtwistle Lancs 195 B8
Oswestry Shrops 148 D5
Otby Lincs 189 C10
Oteley Shrops 149 C8
Otford Kent 52 B4
Otham Kent 53 C9
Otham Hole Kent 53 C10
Otherton Staffs 151 G8
Othery Som 43 G11
Otley Suff 126 F4
W Yorks 205 D10
Otterbourne Hants 33 C7
Otterburn Northumb 251 E9
N Yorks 204 B3
Otterburn Camp
Northumb 251 D9
Otterden Place Kent 54 C2
Otter Ferry Argyll 275 E10
Otterford Som 28 E2
Otterham Corn 11 C9
Otterhampton Som 43 E8
Otterham Quay Kent 69 F10
Otterham Station
Corn 11 D9
Otter Ho Argyll 275 F10
Ottershaw Sur 66 G4
Otterspool Mers 182 D5
Otterswick Shetland 312 E7
Otterton Devon 15 D7
Otterwood Hants 32 G6
Ottery St Mary Devon 15 B8
Ottinge Kent 55 E7
Ottringham E Yorks 201 C9
Oughterby Cumb 239 F7
Oughtershaw
N Yorks 213 C7
Oughterside Cumb 229 C8
Oughtibridge
S Yorks 186 C4
Oughtrington
Warr 183 D11
Oulston N Yorks 215 E10
Oulton Cumb 238 G6
Norf 160 D2
Staffs 150 E5
Staffs 151 B8
Suff 143 D10
W Yorks 197 B11
Oulton Broad Suff 143 E10
Oultoncross Staffs 151 C8
Oulton Grange
Staffs 151 B8
Oulton Heath Staffs 151 B8
Oulton Street Norf 160 D3
Oundle Northants 137 F10
Ounsdale Staffs 133 E7
Ousby Cumb 231 E8
Ousdale Highld 311 G4
Ousden Suff 124 F4
Ousefleet E Yorks 199 C10
Ousel Hole W Yorks 205 E8
Ouston Durham 243 G7
Northumb 241 G7
Northumb 242 C3
Outcast Cumb 210 D6
Out Elmstead Kent 55 C8
Outer Hope Devon 8 G3
Outertown Orkney 314 E2
Outgate Cumb 221 F7
Outhgill Cumb 222 E5
Outhill Warks 118 D2
Outhills Aberds 303 D10
Outlands Staffs 150 C5
Outlane W Yorks 196 D5
Outlane Moor
W Yorks 196 D5
Outlet Village
Ches W 182 G6
Outmarsh Wilts 61 G11
Out Newton
E Yorks 201 C11
Out Rawcliffe Lancs 202 E4
Outwell Norf 139 C10
Outwick Hants 31 D10
Outwood Gtr Man 195 F9
Som 28 B4
Sur 51 D10
W Yorks 197 C10
Outwoods Leics 153 F8
Staffs 150 F5
Staffs 152 E4
Warks 134 G4
Ouzlewell Green
W Yorks 197 B10
Ovenden W Yorks 196 B5
Ovenscloss
Borders 261 C11
Over Cambs 123 C7
Ches W 167 B10
Glos 80 B4
S Glos 60 C5
Overa Farm Stud
Norf 141 F9
Overbister Orkney 314 B6
Over Burrow Lancs 212 D2
Over Burrows
Derbys 152 B5
Overbury Worcs 99 D9
Overcombe Dorset 17 E9
Over Compton
Dorset 29 D9
Overend W Mid 133 G9
Over End Cambs 137 E11
Derbys 186 G3
Overgreen Derbys 186 G4
Over Green W Mid 134 E3
Over Haddon
Derbys 170 B2
Over Hulton
Gtr Man 195 F7
Over Kellet Lancs 211 E10
Over Kiddington
Oxon 101 G8
Over Knutsford
Ches E 184 F3
Over Langshaw
Borders 271 G10
Overleigh Som 44 F3
Overley Staffs 152 F3
Overley Green
Warks 117 F11
Over Monnow Mon 79 C8
Overmoor Staffs 169 F7
Over Norton Oxon 100 F6
Over Peover Ches E 184 G3
Overpool Ches W 182 F5
Overs Shrops 131 D7
Overscaig Hotel
Highld 309 G4
Overseal Derbys 152 F5
Over Silton N Yorks 225 G9
Overslade Warks 119 C9
Oversland Kent 54 B5
Oversley Green
Warks 117 F11
Overstone Northants 120 D6
Over Stowey Som 43 F7
Overstrand Norf 160 A4
Over Stratton Som 28 D6
Over Tabley Ches E 184 E2
Overthorpe
Northants 101 C9
W Yorks 197 D8
Overton Aberdeen 293 B10
Aberds 293 B9
Ches W 183 F8
Dumfries 237 C11
Glos 80 C2
Hants 48 D4
Invclyd 276 G5
Lancs 202 B4
N Yorks 207 B7
Shrops 115 C10
Staffs 151 B10
Swansea 56 D3
W Yorks 197 D9
Overton Bridge
Wrex 166 G5
Overton/Owrtyn
Wrex 166 G5
Overtown Lancs 212 D2
N Lnrk 268 E6
Swindon 63 D7
W Yorks 197 D11
Over Town Lancs 195 B11
Over Wallop Hants 47 F9
Over Whitacre
Warks 134 E5
Over Worton Oxon 101 F8
Oving Bucks 102 G5
W Sus 22 C6
Ovingdean Brighton 36 G5
Ovingham Northumb 242 E3
Ovington Durham 224 C2
Essex 106 C5
Hants 48 G5
Norf 141 C8
Northumb 242 E3
Owen's Bank Staffs 152 D4
Ower Hants 32 D4
Owermoigne Dorset 17 D11
Owlbury Shrops 130 E6
Owlcotes Derbys 170 B6
Owl End Cambs 122 B4
Owler Bar Derbys 186 F3
Owlerton S Yorks 186 D4
Owlet W Yorks 205 F9
Owlpen Glos 80 F4
Owl's Green Suff 126 D5
Owlsmoor Brack 65 G11
Owlswick Bucks 84 D3
Owlthorpe S Yorks 186 E6
Owmby Lincs 200 G5
Owmby-by-Spital
Lincs 189 D8
Ownham W Berks 64 E2
Owrtyn/Overton
Wrex 166 G5
Owslebury Hants 33 C8
Owston Leics 136 B5
S Yorks 198 E5
Owston Ferry
N Lincs 199 G10
Owstwick E Yorks 209 G11
Owthorne E Yorks 201 B10
Owthorpe Notts 154 C3
Owton Manor Hrtlpl 234 F5
Oxborough Norf 140 C4
Oxclose S Yorks 186 E6
T&W 243 F7
Oxcombe Lincs 190 F4
Oxcroft Derbys 187 G7
Oxcroft Estate
Derbys 187 G7
Oxen End Essex 106 F3
Oxenhall Glos 98 F4
Oxenholme Cumb 211 B10
Oxenhope W Yorks 204 F6
Oxen Park Cumb 210 B6
Oxenpill Som 44 E2
Oxenton Glos 99 E9
Oxenwood Wilts 47 B10
Oxford Oxon 83 D8
Stoke 168 E5
Oxgang E Dunb 278 G3
Oxgangs Edin 270 B4
Oxhey Herts 85 F10
Oxhill Durham 242 G5
Warks 100 B6
Oxlease Herts 86 D2
Oxley W Mid 133 C8
Oxley Green Essex 88 C6
Oxley's Green E Sus 37 C11
Oxlode Cambs 139 F9
Oxnam Borders 262 F5
Oxnead Norf 160 E4
Oxshott Sur 66 G6
Oxspring S Yorks 197 G9
Oxted Sur 51 C11
Oxton Borders 271 E9
Mers 182 D3
Notts 171 E10
N Yorks 206 E6
Oxton Rakes Derbys 186 G4
Oxwich Swansea 56 D3
Oxwich Green
Swansea 56 D3
Oxwick Norf 159 D8
Oykel Bridge Highld 309 J3
Oyne Aberds 302 G6
Oystermouth
Swansea 56 D6
Ozleworth Glos 80 G3

P

Pabail Iarach
W Isles 304 E7
Pabail Uarach
W Isles 304 E7
Pabo Conwy 180 F4
Pace Gate N Yorks 205 C8
Pachesham Park Sur 51 B7
Packers Hill Dorset 30 E2
Packington Leics 153 G7
Packmoor Staffs 168 E5
Packmores Warks 118 D5
Packwood W Mid 118 C3
Packwood Gullet
W Mid 118 C3
Padanaram Angus 287 B8
Padbury Bucks 102 E4
Paddington London 67 C9
Warr 183 D10
Paddlesworth Kent 55 F7
Kent 69 G7
Paddock Kent 54 C3
W Yorks 196 D6
Paddockhaugh
Moray 302 D2
Paddockhill Ches E 184 F4
Paddockhole
Dumfries 248 G6
Paddock Wood Kent 53 E7
Paddolgreen
Shrops 149 C10
Padfield Derbys 185 B8
Padgate Warr 183 D10
Padham's Green
Essex 87 F10
Padiham Lancs 203 G11
Padney Cambs 123 C10
Padog Conwy 164 E4
Padside N Yorks 205 B9
Padside Green
N Yorks 205 B9
Padson Devon 13 B7
Padstow Corn 10 F4
Padworth W Berks 64 F6
Padworth Common
Hants 64 G6
Paganhill Glos 80 D4
Page Bank Durham 233 D10
Page Moss Mers 182 C6
Page's Green Suff 126 D2
Pagham W Sus 22 D5
Paglesham Churchend
Essex 88 G6
Paglesham Eastend
Essex 88 G6
Paibeil W Isles 296 E3
Paible W Isles 305 J2
Paignton Torbay 9 C7
Pailton Warks 135 G9
Painleyhill Staffs 151 C10
Painscastle Powys 96 B3
Painshawfield
Northumb 242 E3
Pains Hill Sur 52 C2
Painsthorpe
E Yorks 208 B2
Painswick Glos 80 D5
Painter's Forstal
Kent 54 B3
Painters Green
Wrex 167 G8
Painter's Green Herts 86 B3
Painthorpe
W Yorks 197 D10
Paintmoor Som 28 F4
Pairc Shiaboist
W Isles 304 D4
Paisley Renfs 267 C9
Pakefield Suff 143 E10
Pakenham Suff 125 D8
Pale Gwyn 147 B9
Pale Green Essex 106 C3
Palehouse Common
E Sus 23 B7
Palestine Hants 47 E9
Paley Street
Windsor 65 D11
Palfrey W Mid 133 D10
Palgowan Dumfries 245 G9
Palgrave Suff 126 B2
Pallaflat Cumb 219 C9
Pallington Dorset 17 C11
Pallion T&W 243 F9
Pallister Mbro 225 B10
Palmarsh Kent 54 G6
Palmer Moor
Derbys 152 C2
Palmersbridge Corn 11 F9
Palmers Cross
Staffs 133 C7
Sur 50 E4
Palmer's Flat Glos 79 D9
Palmers Green
London 86 G4
Palmer's Green Kent 53 E7
Palmerstown V Glam 58 F6
Palmersville T&W 243 C7
Palmstead Kent 55 D7
Palnackie Dumfries 237 D10
Palnure Dumfries 236 C6
Palterton Derbys 171 B7
Pamber End Hants 48 B6
Pamber Green Hants 48 B6
Pamber Heath Hants 64 G6
Pamington Glos 99 E8
Pamphill Dorset 31 G7
Pampisford Cambs 105 B9
Pan IoW 20 D6
Orkney 314 G3
Panborough Som 44 D3
Panbride Angus 287 D9
Pancakehill Glos 81 C9
Pancrasweek Devon 24 F3
Pancross V Glam 58 F4
Pandy Gwyn 128 C2
Gwyn 146 F4
Gwyn 147 D7
Mon 96 G6
Powys 129 C8
Wrex 148 B3
Wrex 166 G6
Pandy'r Capel Denb 165 E9
Pandy Tudur Conwy 164 C5
Panfield Essex 106 F4
Pangbourne
W Berks 64 D6
Panhall Fife 280 C6
Panks Bridge
Hereford 98 B2
Pannal N Yorks 206 C2
Pannal Ash
N Yorks 205 C11
Pannel's Ash Essex 106 C5
Panpunton Powys 114 C5
Panshanger Herts 86 C3
Pant Denb 166 E2
Flint 181 G10
Gwyn 144 C4
M Tydf 77 D9
Powys 129 C11
Shrops 148 E5
Wrex 166 D5
Wrex 166 F3
Pantasaph Flint 181 F11
Pantdu Neath 57 C9
Panteg Ceredig 111 E9
Torf 78 F4
Pantersbridge Corn 6 B3
Pant-glas Gwyn 163 F7
Pant-glâs Powys 128 D5
Pant-glas Shrops 148 C5
Pantgwyn Carms 93 F11
Ceredig 92 B4
Pant-lasau Swansea 57 B7
Pantmawr Cardiff 58 C6
Pant Mawr Powys 129 G7
Panton Lincs 189 F11
Pant-pastynog
Denb 165 C8
Pantperthog Gwyn 128 C4
Pantside Caerph 78 F2
Pant-teg Carms 93 F9
Pant-y-Caws Carms 92 F3
Pant-y-crûg
Ceredig 112 B3
Pant-y-dwr Powys 113 B9
Powys 113 C9
Pant-y-ffridd
Powys 130 C3
Pantyffynnon Carms 75 C10
Pantygasseg Torf 78 F3
Pantymwyn Flint 165 C11
Pant-y-pyllau
Bridgend 58 C2
Pant-yr-awel
Bridgend 58 B2
Pant-y-Wacco
Flint 181 F10
Panxworth Norf 161 G7
Papcastle Cumb 229 E8
Papermill Bank
Shrops 149 D11
Papigoe Highld 310 D7
Papil Shetland 313 K5
Papley Northants 138 F2
Orkney 314 G4
Papple E Loth 281 G11
Papplewick Notts 171 E8
Papworth Everard
Cambs 122 E5
Papworth St Agnes
Cambs 122 E5
Papworth Village
Settlement Cambs 122 E5
Par Corn 5 E11
Paradise Glos 80 C5
Paradise Green
Hereford 97 B10
Paramoor Corn 5 F9
Paramour Street
Kent 71 G9
Parbold Lancs 194 E3
Parbrook Som 44 F5
W Sus 35 B9
Parc Gwyn 147 C7
Parc Erissey Corn 4 G3
Parc-hendy Swansea 56 B4
Parchey Som 43 F10
Parciau Anglesey 179 E7
Parcllyn Ceredig 110 G4
Parc Mawr Caerph 77 G10
Parc-Seymour
Newport 78 G6
Parc-y-rhôs Carms 93 B11
Pardown Hants 48 D5
Pardshaw Cumb 229 G7
Pardshaw Hall
Cumb 229 F8
Parham Suff 126 E6
Park Corn 10 G6
Devon 14 B2
Dumfries 247 E10
Som 44 G3
Swindon 63 C7
Park Barn Sur 50 C3
Park Bottom Corn 4 G3
Park Bridge
Gtr Man 196 G2
Park Broom Cumb 239 F10
Park Close Lancs 204 E3
Park Corner Bath 45 B9
E Sus 23 C8
E Sus 52 F4
Oxon 65 B7
Windsor 65 C11
Parkend Glos 79 D10
Glos 80 C3
Park End Beds 121 G9
Cambs 123 E11
Mbro 225 B10
Northumb 241 B9
Som 43 G7
Staffs 168 E3
Worcs 116 C5
Parkengear Corn 5 F8
Parker's Corner
W Berks 64 E6
Parker's Green
Herts 104 F6
Kent 52 D6
Parkeston Essex 108 E4
Parkfield Corn 6 B6
S Glos 61 D7
W Mid 133 D8
Parkfoot Falk 278 F6
Parkgate Ches E 184 G3
Ches W 182 F3
Cumb 229 B10
Dumfries 248 F2
Essex 87 B11
Kent 53 G11
Sur 51 E8
S Yorks 186 B6
Park Gate Dorset 30 F2
Hants 33 F8
Kent 55 D7
Suff 124 F4
Worcs 117 C8
W Yorks 197 E8
Park Green Essex 105 F9
Park Hall Shrops 148 C6
Parkham Devon 24 C5
Parkham Ash Devon 24 C5
Parkhead Cumb 230 C2
Glasgow 268 C2
S Yorks 186 E4
Park Head Cumb 231 C7
Derbys 170 E5
W Yorks 197 F7
Parkhill Aberds 303 E10
Invclyd 277 G7
Park Hill Glos 79 F9
Kent 54 G3
Mers 194 G3
Notts 171 E11
N Yorks 214 F6
S Yorks 186 D5
Parkhill Ho Aberds 293 B10
Parkhouse Mon 79 E7
Parkhouse Green
Derbys 170 C6
Parkhurst IoW 20 C5
Parklands W Yorks 206 F3
Park Lane Staffs 133 B7
Wrex 149 B8
Park Langley London 67 F11
Park Mains Renfs 277 G9
Parkmill Swansea 56 D4
Park Mill W Yorks 197 E9
Parkneuk Aberds 293 F9
Fife 279 D11
Park Royal London 67 C7
Parkside C Beds 103 G10
Cumb 219 B10
Durham 234 B4
N Lnrk 268 D6
Staffs 151 D8
Wrex 166 D5
Parkstone Poole 18 C6
Park Street Herts 85 E10
W Sus 50 G6
Park Town Luton 103 G11
Oxon 83 D8
Park Village
Northumb 240 E5
W Mid 133 C8
Park Villas W Yorks 206 F2
Parkway Hereford 98 D4
Som 29 C9
Park Wood Kent 53 C9
Medway 69 G10
Parkwood Springs
S Yorks 186 D4
Parley Cross Dorset 19 B7
Parley Green Dorset 19 B7
Parliament Heath
Suff 107 C9
Parlington W Yorks 206 F4
Parmoor Bucks 65 B9
Parnacott Devon 24 F4
Parney Heath
Essex 107 E10
Parr Mers 183 C8
Parracombe Devon 41 E7
Parr Brow Gtr Man 195 G8
Parrog Pembs 91 D10
Parsley Hay
Derbys 169 C10
Parslow's Hillock
Bucks 84 E4
Parsonage Green
Essex 88 D2
Parsonby Cumb 229 D8
Parson Cross
S Yorks 186 C5
Parson Drove
Cambs 139 B7
Parsons Green
London 67 D9
Parson's Heath
Essex 107 F10
Partick Glasgow 267 B11
Partington Gtr Man 184 C2
Partney Lincs 174 B6
Parton Cumb 228 G5
Cumb 239 G7
Dumfries 237 B8
Glos 99 G7
Hereford 96 B6
Partridge Green
W Sus 35 D11
Partrishow Powys 96 G5
Parwich Derbys 169 E11
Pasford Staffs 132 D6
Passenham
Northants 102 D5
Passfield Hants 49 G10
Passingford Bridge
Essex 87 F8
Passmores Essex 86 D6
Paston Norf 160 C6
Pboro 138 C3
Paston Green Norf 160 C6
Pasturefields Staffs 151 D9
Patchacott Devon 12 B5
Patcham Brighton 36 F4
Patchetts Green
Herts 85 F10
Patching W Sus 35 F9
Patchole Devon 40 E6
Patchway S Glos 60 C6
Pategill Cumb 230 F6
Pateley Bridge
N Yorks 214 F3
Paternoster Heath
Essex 88 C6
Pathe Som 43 G11
Pather N Lnrk 268 E5
Pathfinder Village
Devon 14 C2
Pathhead Aberds 293 G9
E Ayrs 258 G4
Fife 280 C5
Midloth 271 C7
Path Head T&W 242 E5
Pathlow Warks 118 F3
Path of Condie
Perth 286 F4
Pathstruie Perth 286 F4
Patient End Herts 105 F8
Patmore Heath
Herts 105 F8
Patna E Ayrs 257 G10
Patney Wilts 46 B5
Patrick IoM 192 D3
Patrick Brompton
N Yorks 224 G4
Patricroft Gtr Man 184 B3
Patrington E Yorks 201 C10
Patrington Haven
E Yorks 201 C10
Patrixbourne Kent 55 B7
Patsford Devon 40 F4
Patterdale Cumb 221 B7
Pattiesmuir Fife 279 E11
Pattingham Staffs 132 D6
Pattishall Northants 120 G3
Pattiswick Essex 106 G6
Patton Shrops 131 E11
Patton Bridge
Cumb 221 F11
Paul Corn 1 D5
Paulerspury
Northants 102 B4
Paull E Yorks 201 B7
Paul's Green Corn 2 C4
Paulsgrove Ptsmth 33 F10
Paulton Bath 45 B7
Paulville W Loth 269 B9
Pave Lane Telford 150 F5
Pavenham Beds 121 F9
Pawlett Som 43 E10
Pawlett Hill Som 43 E9
Pawston Northumb 263 C9
Paxford Glos 100 D3
Paxton Borders 273 D9
Payden Street Kent 54 C2
Payhembury Devon 27 G9
Paynes Green Sur 50 F6
Paynter's Cross Corn 7 C7
Paynter's Lane End
Corn 4 G3
Paythorne Lancs 204 C2
Payton Som 27 C10
Peacehaven E Sus 36 G6
Peacehaven Heights
E Sus 36 G6
Peacemarsh Dorset 30 B4
Peak Dale Derbys 185 F9
Peak Forest
Derbys 185 F10
Peak Hill Lincs 156 F5
Peakirk Pboro 138 B3
Pean Hill Kent 70 G6
Pear Ash Som 45 G9
Pearsie Angus 287 B7
Pearson's Green Kent 53 E7
Peartree Herts 86 C2
Pear Tree Derby 153 C7
Peartree Green
Essex 87 F9
Hereford 97 E11
Soton 32 E6
Sur 50 F3
Peas Acre W Yorks 205 E8
Peasedown St John
Bath 45 B8
Peasehill Derbys 170 F6
Peaseland Green
Norf 159 F11
Peasemore W Berks 64 D3
Peasenhall Suff 127 D7
Pease Pottage
W Sus 51 G9
Peas Hill Cambs 139 D8
Peaslake Sur 50 E5
Peasley Cross Mers 183 C8
Peasmarsh E Sus 38 C5
Som 28 E4
Sur 50 D3
Peaston E Loth 271 B8
Peastonbank E Loth 271 B8
Peathill Aberds 303 C9
Peat Inn Fife 287 G8
Peatling Magna
Leics 135 E11
Peatling Parva
Leics 135 F11
Peaton Shrops 131 G10
Peatonstrand
Shrops 131 G10
Peats Corner Suff 126 E3
Pebmarsh Essex 107 E7
Pebsham E Sus 38 F3
Pebworth Worcs 100 B2
Pecket Well
W Yorks 196 B3
Peckforton Ches E 167 D8
Peckham London 67 D10
Peckham Bush Kent 53 D7
Peckingell Wilts 62 E2
Pecking Mill Som 44 F6
Peckleton Leics 135 C9
Pedair-ffordd
Powys 148 E2
Pedham Norf 160 G6
Pedlars End Essex 87 D8
Pedlar's Rest
Shrops 131 G9
Pedlinge Kent 54 F6
Pedmore W Mid 133 G8
Pednor Bottom
Bucks 84 E6
Pednormead End
Bucks 85 E7
Pedwell Som 44 F2
Peebles Borders 270 G5
Peel Borders 261 B10
IoM 192 D3
Lancs 202 G3
Peel Common Hants 33 G9
Peel Green Gtr Man 184 B2
Peel Hall Gtr Man 184 D4
Peel Hill Lancs 202 G3
Peel Park S Lnrk 268 E2
Peene Kent 55 F7
Peening Quarter
Kent 38 B5
Peggs Green Leics 153 F8
Pegsdon C Beds 104 E2
Pegswood Northumb 252 F6
Pegwell Kent 71 G11
Peinaha Highld 298 D4
Peinchorran Highld 295 B7
Peingown Highld 298 B4
Peinlich Highld 298 D4
Peinmore Highld 298 E4
Pelaw T&W 243 E7
Pelcomb Pembs 72 B6
Pelcomb Bridge
Pembs 72 B6
Pelcomb Cross
Pembs 72 B6
Peldon Essex 89 B7
Pelhamfield IoW 21 C7
Pell Green E Sus 52 G6
Pellon W Yorks 196 B5
Pelsall W Mid 133 C10
Pelsall Wood
W Mid 133 C10
Pelton Durham 243 G7
Pelton Fell Durham 243 G7
Pelutho Cumb 229 B8
Pelynt Corn 6 D4
Pemberton Carms 75 E8
Gtr Man 194 G5
Pembles Cross Kent 53 D11
Pembre/Pembrey
Carms 74 E6
Pembrey/Pembre
Carms 74 E6
Pembridge Hereford 115 F7
Pembroke Pembs 73 E7
Pembroke Dock/Doc
Penfro Pembs 73 E7
Pembroke Ferry
Pembs 73 E7
Pembury Kent 52 E6
Pempwell Corn 12 F3
Penallt Mon 79 C8
Pen-allt Hereford 97 F11
Penally/Penalun
Pembs 73 F10
Penalt Hereford 97 F11
Penalun/Penally
Pembs 73 F10
Penare Corn 5 G9
Penarlâg/Hawarden
Flint 166 B4
Penarron Powys 130 F2
Penarth V Glam 59 E7
Penarth Moors
Cardiff 59 E7
Penbeagle Corn 2 B2
Penbedw Flint 165 B11
Pen-bedw Pembs 92 D4
Penberth Corn 1 E4
Penbidwal Mon 96 G6
Penbodlas Gwyn 144 C5
Pen-bont Rhydybeddau
Ceredig 128 G3
Penboyr Carms 93 D7
Penbryn Ceredig 110 G5
Pencader Carms 93 D8
Pencaenewydd
Gwyn 162 G6
Pencaerau Neath 57 B8
Pen-caer-fenny
Swansea 56 B4
Pencaitland E Loth 271 B8
Pencarnisiog
Anglesey 178 G5
Pencarreg Carms 93 B10
Pencarrow Corn 11 E8
Penceiliogi Carms 75 E8
Pencelli Powys 95 F11
Pen-clawdd Swansea 56 B4
Pencoed Bridgend 58 C3
Pencombe
Hereford 115 G11
Pen-common Powys 76 D6
Pencoyd Hereford 97 F10
Pencoys Corn 2 B5
Pencraig Anglesey 179 F7
Hereford 97 G11
Powys 147 D10
Pencroesoped Mon 78 D4
Pencuke Corn 11 C9
Pendas Fields
W Yorks 206 F3
Pendeen Corn 1 C3
Pendeford W Mid 133 C7
Penderyn Rhondda 77 D7
Pendine/Pentywyn
Carms 74 D2
Pendlebury
Gtr Man 195 G9
Pendleton Gtr Man 184 B4
Lancs 203 F11
Pendock Worcs 98 E5
Pendoggett Corn 10 F6
Pendomer Som 29 E8
Pendoylan V Glam 58 D5
Pendre Bridgend 58 C2
Gwyn 110 C2
Powys 95 F10
Pendrift Corn 11 G8
Penegoes Powys 128 C5
Penelewey Corn 4 G6
Penenden Heath
Kent 53 B9
Penffordd Pembs 91 G11
Penffordd Lâs/
Staylittle Powys 129 E7
Pengam Caerph 77 F11
Penge London 67 E11
Pengegon Corn 2 B5
Pengelly Corn 11 E7
Pengenffordd Powys 96 E3
Pengersick Corn 2 D3
Pen-gilfach Gwyn 163 C9
Pengold Corn 11 C8
Pengorffwysfa
Anglesey 179 C7
Pengover Green Corn 6 B5
Pen-groes-oped
Mon 78 D4
Penguithal Hereford 97 G10
Pengwern Denb 181 F8
Penhale Corn 2 F5
Corn 5 D8
Penhale Jakes Corn 2 D4
Penhallick Corn 3 F7
Corn 4 G3
Penhallow Corn 4 E5
Penhalurick Corn 2 B6
Penhalvean Corn 2 B6
Penhelig Gwyn 128 D2
Penhill Devon 40 G4
Swindon 63 B7
Penhow Newport 78 G6
Penhurst E Sus 23 B11
Peniarth Gwyn 128 B2
Penicuik Midloth 270 C4
Peniel Carms 93 G8
Denb 165 C8
Penifiler Highld 298 E4
Peninver Argyll 255 E8
Penisa'r Waun
Gwyn 163 C9
Penistone S Yorks 197 G8
Penjerrick Corn 3 C7
Penketh Warr 183 D9
Penkhull Stoke 168 G5
Penkill S Ayrs 244 D6
Penknap Wilts 45 D11
Penkridge Staffs 151 G8
Pen-lan Swansea 56 B6
Pen-Lan-mabws
Pembs 91 F7
Penleigh Wilts 45 C11
Penley Wrex 149 B8
Penllech Gwyn 144 C4
Penllergaer Swansea 56 B6
Penllwyn Caerph 77 F11
Ceredig 128 G3
Penllyn V Glam 58 D3
Pen-llyn Anglesey 178 E4
Pen-lon Anglesey 162 B6
Penmachno Conwy 164 E3
Penmaen Caerph 77 F11
Swansea 56 D4

Ramsey Cambs 138 F5
Essex 108 E4
IoM 192 C5
Ramseycleuch
Borders 261 G7
Ramsey Forty Foot
Cambs 138 F6
Ramsey Heights
Cambs 138 F5
Ramsey Island Essex 89 D7
Ramsey Mereside
Cambs 138 F5
Ramsey St Mary's
Cambs 138 F5
Ramsgate Kent 71 G11
Ramsgill N Yorks 214 E2
Ramshaw Durham 232 B5
Durham 233 F8
Ramsholt Suff 108 C6
Ramshorn Staffs 169 F9
Ramsley Devon 13 C8
Ramslye Kent 52 F5
Ramsnest Common
Sur 50 G2
Ranais W Isles 304 F6
Ranby Lincs 190 F2
Notts 187 E11
Rand Lincs 189 F10
Randwick Glos 80 D4
Ranfurly Renfs 267 C7
Rangag Highld 310 E5
Rangemore Staffs 152 E3
Rangeworthy S Glos 61 B7
Rankinston E Ayrs 257 G11
Rank's Green Essex 88 B3
Ranmoor S Yorks 186 D4
Ranmore Common
Sur 50 C6
Rannerdale Cumb 220 B3
Rannoch Lodge
Perth 285 B9
Rannoch Station
Perth 285 B8
Ranochan Highld 295 G10
Ranskill Notts 187 D11
Ranton Staffs 151 E7
Ranton Green Staffs 150 E6
Ranworth Norf 161 G7
Rapkyns W Sus 50 G6
Raploch Stirl 278 C5
Rapness Orkney 314 B5
Rapps Som 28 D4
Rascal Moor
E Yorks 208 F2
Rascarrel Dumfries 237 E9
Rashielee Renfs 277 G9
Rashiereive Aberds 303 G9
Rashwood Worcs 117 D8
Raskelf N Yorks 215 E9
Rassal Highld 299 E8
Rassau Bl Gwent 77 C11
Rastrick W Yorks 196 C6
Ratagan Highld 295 D11
Ratby Leics 135 B10
Ratcliff London 67 C11
Ratcliffe Culey
Leics 134 D6
Ratcliffe on Soar
Leics 153 D9
Ratcliffe on the Wreake
Leics 154 G2
Ratford Wilts 62 E3
Ratfyn Wilts 47 E7
Rathen Aberds 303 C10
Rathillet Fife 287 E7
Rathmell N Yorks 204 B2
Ratho Edin 280 G2
Ratho Station Edin 280 G2
Rathven Moray 302 C4
Ratlake Hants 32 C6
Ratley Warks 101 B7
Ratling Kent 55 C8
Ratlinghope Shrops 131 D8
Ratsloe Devon 14 B5
Rattar Highld 310 B6
Ratten Row Cumb 230 B3
Cumb 230 C2
Lancs 202 E4
Norf 157 G10
Rattery Devon 8 C4
Rattlesden Suff 125 F9
Rattray Perth 286 C5
Raughton Cumb 230 B3
Raughton Head
Cumb 230 B3
Raunds Northants 121 C9
Ravelston Edin 280 G4
Ravenfield S Yorks 187 B7
Ravenglass Cumb 219 F11
Ravenhead Mers 183 C8
Ravenhills Green
Worcs 116 G4
Raveningham Norf 143 D7
Ravenscar N Yorks 227 E9
Ravenscliffe Stoke 168 E4
W Yorks 205 F9
Ravenscraig Invclyd 276 F5
Ravensdale IoM 192 C4
Ravensden Beds 121 G11
Ravenseat N Yorks 223 E7
Raven's Green
Essex 108 G2
Ravenshall Staffs 168 F3
Ravenshead Notts 171 E9
Ravensmoor
Ches E 167 E10
Ravensthorpe
Northants 120 C3
Pboro 138 C3
W Yorks 197 C8
Ravenstone Leics 153 G8
M Keynes 120 G6
Ravenstonedale
Cumb 222 E4
Ravenstown Cumb 211 D7
Ravenstruther S
Lnrk 269 F8
Ravenswood Village
Settlement
Wokingham 65 G10
Ravensworth
N Yorks 224 D2
Raw N Yorks 227 D8
Rawcliffe E Yorks 199 C7
York 207 C7
Rawcliffe Bridge
E Yorks 199 C7
Rawdon W Yorks 205 F10
Rawdon Carrs
W Yorks 205 F10
Rawfolds W Yorks 197 C7
Rawgreen
Northumb 241 F10
Raw Green S Yorks 197 F9
Rawmarsh S Yorks 186 B6
Rawnsley Staffs 151 G10
Rawreth Essex 88 G3
Rawreth Shot Essex 88 G3
Rawridge Devon 28 F2
Rawson Green
Derbys 170 F5
Rawtenstall Lancs 195 C10
Rawthorpe W Yorks 197 D7
Rawyards N Lnrk 268 B5
Raxton Aberds 303 F8
Raydon Suff 107 D11
Raygill N Yorks 204 D4
Raylees Northumb 251 E10
Rayleigh Essex 88 G4
Rayne Essex 106 G4
Rayners Lane London 66 B6
Raynes Park London 67 F8
Reabrook Shrops 131 C7
Reach Cambs 123 D11
Read Lancs 203 G11
Reader's Corner
Essex 88 E2
Reading Reading 65 E8
Readings Glos 79 B10
Reading Street Kent 54 G2
Kent 71 F11
Readymoney Corn 6 E2
Ready Token Glos 81 E10
Reagill Cumb 222 B2
Rearquhar Highld 309 K7
Rearsby Leics 154 G3
Reasby Lincs 189 F9
Rease Heath
Ches E 167 E10
Reaster Highld 310 C6
Reaulay Highld 299 D7
Reawick Shetland 313 J5
Reawla Corn 2 B4
Reay Highld 310 C3
Rechullin Highld 299 D8
Reculver Kent 71 F8
Red Ball Devon 27 D9
Redberth Pembs 73 E9
Redbourn Herts 85 C10
Redbournbury
Herts 85 C10
Redbourne N Lincs 189 B7
N Lincs 200 G3
Redbridge Dorset 17 D11
London 68 B2
Soton 32 E5
Red Bridge Lancs 211 D9
Redbrook Mon 79 C8
Wrex 167 G8
Red Bull Ches E 168 D4
Staffs 150 B4
Redburn Highld 300 C5
Highld 301 E9
Northumb 241 E7
Redcar Redcar 235 G8
Redcastle Angus 287 B10
Highld 300 E5
Redcliff Bay N Som 60 D2
Redcroft Dumfries 237 B9
Redcross Worcs 117 C7
Red Dial Cumb 229 B11
Reddicap Heath
W Mid 134 D2
Redding Falk 279 F8
Reddingmuirhead
Falk 279 F8
Reddish Gtr Man 184 C5
Warr 183 D11
Redditch Worcs 117 D10
Rede Suff 124 F6
Redenhall Norf 142 G5
Redenham Hants 47 D10
Redesdale Camp
Northumb 251 D8
Redesmouth
Northumb 251 G9
Redford Aberds 293 F9
Angus 287 C9
Dorset 29 F10
Durham 233 E7
W Sus 34 B5
Redfordgreen
Borders 261 F9
Redgorton Perth 286 E4
Redgrave Suff 125 B10
Redheugh Angus 292 G6
Redhill Aberds 293 C9
Aberds 302 F6
Herts 104 E6
Notts 171 F9
N Som 60 G4
Shrops 131 B9
Shrops 150 G4
Staffs 150 D6
Sur 51 C9
Telford 150 G4
Red Hill Bmouth 19 B7
Hants 34 E2
Hereford 97 D10
Kent 53 C7
Leics 135 D10
Pembs 72 B6
Warks 118 F2
Worcs 117 G7
W Yorks 198 B2
Redhills Cumb 230 F6
Devon 14 C4
Redhouse Argyll 275 G9
Red House Common
E Sus 36 C5
Redhouses Argyll 274 G4
Redisham Suff 143 G8
Red Lake Telford 150 G3
Redland Bristol 60 D5
Orkney 314 D3
Redland End Bucks 84 E4
Redlands Dorset 17 E9
Som 44 G3
Swindon 81 G11
Redlane Som 28 E2
Redlingfield Suff 126 C3
Red Lodge Suff 124 C3
Red Lumb Gtr Man 195 D10
Redlynch Som 45 G8
Wilts 32 C2
Redmain Cumb 229 E8
Redmarley D'Abitot
Glos 98 E5
Redmarshall
Stockton 234 G3
Redmile Leics 154 B5
Redmire N Yorks 223 G10
Redmonsford Devon 24 D4
Redmoor Corn 5 C11
Redmoss Aberds 303 F8
Rednal Shrops 149 D7
W Mid 117 B10
Redpath Borders 262 B3
Red Pits Norf 159 D11
Redpoint Highld 299 C7
Red Post Corn 24 F3
Red Rail Hereford 97 F10
Red Rice Hants 47 E10
Red Rock Gtr Man 194 F5
Red Roses Carms 74 C2
Red Row Northumb 253 D7
Redruth Corn 4 G3
Red Scar Lancs 203 G7
Redscarhead
Borders 270 G4
Redstocks Wilts 62 G2
Red Street Staffs 168 E4
Redtye Corn 5 C10
Redvales Gtr Man 195 F10
Red Wharf Bay
Anglesey 179 E8
Redwick Newport 60 C2
S Glos 60 B4
Redwith Shrops 148 E6
Redworth Darl 233 G10
Reed Herts 105 D7
Reed End Herts 104 D6
Reedham Lincs 174 D2
Norf 143 C8
Reedley Lancs 204 F2
Reedness E Yorks 199 C9
Reed Point Lincs 174 E2
Reeds Beck Lincs 174 B2
Reedsford Northumb 263 C9
Reeds Holme
Lancs 195 C10
Reedy Devon 14 D2
Reen Manor Corn 4 E5
Reepham Lincs 189 G8
Norf 159 E11
Reeth N Yorks 223 F10
Reeves Green
W Mid 118 B5
Refail Powys 130 C3
Regaby IoM 192 C5
Regil Bath 60 G4
Regoul Highld 301 D8
Reiff Highld 307 H4
Reigate Sur 51 C9
Reigate Heath Sur 51 C8
Reighton N Yorks 218 D2
Reighton Gap
N Yorks 218 D2
Reinigeadal
W Isles 305 H4
Reisque Aberds 293 B10
Reiss Highld 310 D7
Rejerrah Corn 4 D5
Releath Corn 2 C5
Relubbus Corn 2 C3
Relugas Moray 301 E9
Remenham
Wokingham 65 C9
Remenham Hill
Wokingham 65 C9
Remony Perth 285 C11
Rempstone Notts 153 E11
Remusaig Highld 309 J7
Rendcomb Glos 81 D8
Rendham Suff 126 E6
Rendlesham Suff 126 G6
Renfrew Renfs 267 B10
Renhold Beds 121 G11
Renishaw Derbys 186 F6
Renmure Angus 287 B10
Rennington
Northumb 264 F6
Renshaw Wood
Shrops 132 B6
Renton W Dunb 277 F7
Renwick Cumb 231 C7
Repps Norf 161 F8
Repton Derbys 152 D6
Reraig Highld 295 C10
Reraig Cot Highld 295 B10
Rerwick Shetland 313 M5
Rescassa Corn 5 G9
Rescobie Angus 287 B9
Rescorla Corn 5 D10
Resipole Highld 289 C9
Reskadinnick Corn 4 G2
Resolfen / Resolven
Neath 76 E4
Resolis Highld 300 C6
Resolven / Resolfen
Neath 76 E4
Restalrig Edin 280 G5
Reston Borders 273 C7
Cumb 221 F9
Restronguet Passage
Corn 3 B8
Restrop Wilts 62 B5
Resugga Green Corn 5 D10
Reswallie Angus 287 B9
Retallack Corn 5 B8
Retew Corn 5 D8
Retford Notts 188 E2
Retire Corn 5 C10
Rettendon Essex 88 F3
Rettendon Place
Essex 88 F3
Revesby Lincs 174 C3
Revesby Bridge
Lincs 174 C4
Revidge Blkburn 195 B7
Rew Devon 9 G9
Devon 13 G11
Dorset 29 F11
Rewe Devon 14 B4
Rew Street IoW 20 C5
Rexon Devon 12 D4
Rexon Cross Devon 12 D4
Reybridge Wilts 62 F2
Reydon Suff 127 B9
Reydon Smear Suff 127 B9
Reymerston Norf 141 B10
Reynalton Pembs 73 D9
Reynoldston Swansea 56 C3
Rezare Corn 12 F3
Rhadyr Mon 78 E5
Rhaeadr Gwy /
Rhayader Powys 113 D9
Rhandir Conwy 180 G4
Rhandirmwyn Carms 94 C5
Rhayader / Rhaeadr
Gwy Powys 113 D9
Rhedyn Gwyn 144 C5
Rhegreanoch
Highld 307 H5
Rhemore Highld 289 D7
Rhencullen IoM 192 C4
Rhenetra Highld 298 D4
Rhes-y-cae Flint 181 G11
Rhewl Denb 165 C10
Denb 165 F11
Shrops 148 C6
Wrex 149 B7
Rhewl-fawr Flint 181 E10
Rhewl-Mostyn
Flint 181 E11
Rhian Highld 309 H5
Rhicarn Highld 307 G5
Rhiconich Highld 306 D7
Rhicullen Highld 300 B6
Rhidorroch Ho
Highld 307 K6
Rhiews Shrops 150 B2
Rhifail Highld 308 E7
Rhigolter Highld 308 D3
Rhigos Rhondda 76 D6
Rhilochan Highld 309 J7
Rhippinllwyd Ceredig 92 C5
Ceredig 110 G6
Rhiroy Highld 307 L6
Rhitongue Highld 308 D6
Rhivichie Highld 306 D7
Rhiw Gwyn 144 D4
Rhiwabon / Ruabon
Wrex 166 G4
Rhiwbebyll Denb 165 B10
Rhiwbina Cardiff 59 C7
Rhiwbryfdir Gwyn 163 F11
Rhiwceiliog Bridgend 58 C3
Rhiwderin Newport 59 B9
Rhiwen Gwyn 163 C9
Rhiwfawr Neath 76 C2
Rhiwinder Rhondda 58 B4
Rhiwlas Gwyn 147 B8
Gwyn 163 B9
Powys 148 C3
Rhode Som 43 G9
Rhode Common Kent 54 B5
Rhodes Gtr Man 195 F11
Rhodesia Notts 187 F9
Rhodes Minnis Kent 55 E7
Rhodiad Pembs 90 F5
Rhonadale Argyll 255 D8
Rhondda Rhondda 77 F7
Rhonehouse or Kelton
Hill Dumfries 237 D9
Rhoose V Glam 58 F5
Rhos Carms 93 D7
Rhôs Denb 165 C10
Neath 76 E2
Rhos Powys 148 F5
Rhosaman Carms 76 C2
Rhosbeirio Anglesey 178 C5
Rhoscefnhir
Anglesey 179 F8
Rhoscolyn Anglesey 178 F3
Rhôs Common
Powys 148 F5
Rhoscrowther Pembs 72 E6
Rhosddu Wrex 166 E4
Rhos-ddû Gwyn 144 B5
Rhosdylluan Gwyn 147 D7
Rhosesmor Flint 166 B2
Rhosfach Pembs 92 F2
Rhos-fawr Gwyn 145 B7
Rhosgadfan Gwyn 163 D8
Rhosgoch Anglesey 178 D6
Powys 96 B3
Rhos-goch Powys 96 B3
Rhosgyll Gwyn 163 G7
Rhos Haminiog
Ceredig 111 E10
Rhos-hill Pembs 92 C3
Rhoshirwaun Gwyn 144 D3
Rhos Isaf Gwyn 163 D7
Rhoslan Gwyn 163 G7
Rhoslefain Gwyn 110 B2
Rhosllanerchrugog
Wrex 166 F3
Rhôs Lligwy
Anglesey 179 D7
Rhosmaen Carms 94 G2
Rhosmeirch
Anglesey 179 F7
Rhosneigr Anglesey 178 G4
Rhosnesni Wrex 166 E5
Rhôs-on-Sea
Conwy 180 E4
Rhosrobin Wrex 166 E4
Rhossili Swansea 56 D2
Rhosson Pembs 90 F4
Rhostrehwfa
Anglesey 178 G6
Rhostryfan Gwyn 163 D7
Rhostyllen Wrex 166 F4
Rhoswiel Shrops 148 B5
Rhosybol Anglesey 178 D6
Rhos-y-brithdir
Powys 148 E2
Rhosycaerau Pembs 91 D8
Rhosygadair Newydd
Ceredig 92 B4
Rhosygadfa Shrops 148 C6
Rhos-y-garth
Ceredig 112 C2
Rhosygilwen Pembs 92 C4
Rhos-y-gwaliau
Gwyn 147 C8
Rhos-y-llan Gwyn 144 B4
Rhos-y-Madoc
Wrex 166 G4
Rhosymedre Wrex 166 G3
Rhos-y-meirch
Powys 114 D5
Rhosyn-coch Carms 92 G5
Rhu Argyll 275 G9
Argyll 276 E5
Rhuallt Denb 181 F9
Rhubodach Argyll 275 F11
Rhuddall Heath
Ches W 167 C9
Rhuddlan Ceredig 93 C9
Denb 181 F8
Rhue Highld 307 K5
Rhulen Powys 96 B2
Rhunahaorine
Argyll 255 C8
Rhyd Ceredig 92 C5
Gwyn 163 G10
Powys 129 C9
Rhydaman / Ammanford
Carms 75 C10
Rhydargaeau Carms 93 F8
Rhydcymerau
Carms 93 D11
Rhydd Worcs 98 B6
Rhyd-Ddu Gwyn 163 E9
Rhydd Green Worcs 98 B6
Rhydding Neath 57 B8
Rhydfudr Ceredig 111 D11
Rhydgaled Conwy 165 C7
Rhydgaled / Chancery
Ceredig 111 B11
Rhydlewis Ceredig 92 B6
Rhydlios Gwyn 144 C3
Rhydlydan Conwy 164 E5
Powys 129 E11
Rhydmoelddu
Powys 113 B11
Rhydness Powys 96 C2
Rhydowen Carms 92 F3
Ceredig 93 B8
Rhyd-Rosser
Ceredig 111 D11
Rhydspence Hereford 96 B4
Rhydtalog Flint 166 D2
Rhyd-uchaf Gwyn 147 B8
Rhydwen Gwyn 146 F4
Rhydwyn Anglesey 178 D4
Rhyd-y-Brown
Pembs 91 G11
Rhyd-y-clafdy
Gwyn 144 B6
Rhydycroesau
Powys 148 C4
Rhyd-y-cwm
Shrops 130 G3
Rhydyfelin Carms 92 D5
Ceredig 111 B11
Powys 129 E11
Rhondda 58 B5
Rhyd-y-foel Conwy 180 F6
Rhyd-y-fro Neath 76 D2
Rhydygele Pembs 91 G7
Rhyd-y-gwin
Swansea 75 E11
Rhyd-y-gwystl
Gwyn 145 B8
Rhydymain Gwyn 146 E6
Rhyd-y-meirch Mon 78 D4
Rhyd-y-meudwy
Denb 165 E10
Rhydymwyn Flint 166 B2
Rhyd-y-pandy
Swansea 75 E11
Rhyd-yr-onen
Gwyn 128 C2
Rhyd-y-sarn Gwyn 163 G11
Rhydywrach Carms 73 B11
Rhyl Denb 181 E8
Rhymney Caerph 77 D10
Rhyn Wrex 148 B6
Rhynd Fife 287 E8
Perth 286 E5
Rhynie Aberds 302 G4
Highld 301 B8
Ribbesford Worcs 116 C5
Ribblehead N Yorks 212 D5
Ribble Head
N Yorks 212 D5
Ribbleton Lancs 203 G7
Ribby Lancs 202 G4
Ribchester Lancs 203 F8
Riber Derbys 170 D4
Ribigill Highld 308 D5
Riby Lincs 201 F7
Riby Cross Roads
Lincs 201 F7
Riccall N Yorks 207 F8
Riccarton E Ayrs 257 B10
Richards Castle
Hereford 115 D9
Richborough Port
Kent 71 G10
Richings Park Bucks 66 D4
Richmond London 67 E7
N Yorks 224 E3
S Yorks 186 D6
Richmond Hill
W Yorks 206 G2
Richmond's Green
Essex 106 F2
Rich's Holford Som 42 G6
Rickard's Down
Devon 24 B6
Rickarton Aberds 293 E10
Rickerby Cumb 239 F10
Rickerscote Staffs 151 E8
Rickford N Som 44 B3
Rickinghall Suff 125 B10
Rickleton T&W 243 G7
Rickling Essex 105 E9
Rickling Green
Essex 105 F10
Rickmansworth
Herts 85 G9
Rickney E Sus 23 D10
Riddell Borders 262 E2
Riddings Derbys 170 E6
Riddlecombe Devon 25 E10
Riddlesden W Yorks 205 E7
Riddrie Glasgow 268 B2
Ridgacre W Mid 133 G10
Ridge Bath 44 B5
Dorset 18 D4
Hants 32 D4
Herts 86 E2
Lancs 211 G9
Som 28 F3
Wilts 46 G3
Ridgebourne
Powys 113 E11
Ridge Common
Hants 34 C2
Ridge Green Sur 51 D10
Ridgehill N Som 60 G4
Ridge Hill Gtr Man 185 B7
Ridge Lane Warks 134 E5
Ridgemarsh Herts 85 G8
Ridge Row Kent 55 E8
Ridgeway Bristol 60 D6
Derbys 170 E5
Derbys 186 E6
Kent 54 E5
Newport 59 B9
Pembs 73 D10
Som 45 D8
Staffs 168 E5
Ridgeway Cross
Hereford 98 B4
Ridgeway Moor
Derbys 186 E6
Ridgewell Essex 106 C4
Ridgewood E Sus 23 B7
Ridgmont C Beds 103 D9
Ridgway Shrops 131 F7
Sur 50 B4
Riding Gate Som 30 B2
Riding Mill
Northumb 242 E2
Ridley Kent 68 G6
Northumb 241 E7
Ridley Stokoe
Northumb 250 F6
Ridleywood Wrex 166 E6
Ridlington Norf 160 C6
Rutland 136 C6
Ridlington Street
Norf 160 C6
Ridsdale Northumb 251 G10
Riechip Perth 286 C4
Riemore Perth 286 C4
Rienachait Highld 306 F5
Rievaulx N Yorks 215 B11
Riff Orkney 314 E4
Riffin Aberds 303 E7
Rifle Green Torf 78 D3
Rift House Hrtlpl 234 E5
Rigg Dumfries 239 D7
Riggend N Lnrk 278 G5
Rigsby Lincs 190 F6
Rigside S Lnrk 259 B9
Riley Green Lancs 194 B6
Rileyhill Staffs 152 F2
Rilla Mill Corn 11 G11
Rillaton Corn 11 G11
Rillington N Yorks 217 E7
Rimac Lincs 191 C7
Rimington Lancs 204 D2
Rimpton Som 29 C10
Rimswell E Yorks 201 B10
Rimswell Valley
E Yorks 201 B10
Rinaston Pembs 91 F9
Rindleford Shrops 132 D4
Ringasta Shetland 313 M5
Ringford Dumfries 237 D8
Ringing Hill Leics 153 F9
Ringinglow S Yorks 186 E3
Ringland Newport 59 B11
Norf 160 G2
Ringles Cross E Sus 37 C7
Ringlestone Kent 53 B9
Kent 53 B11
Ringley Gtr Man 195 F9
Ringmer E Sus 36 E6
Ringmore Devon 8 F3
Ring o' Bells Lancs 194 E3
Ringorm Moray 302 E2
Ring's End Cambs 139 C7
Ringsfield Suff 143 F8
Ringsfield Corner
Suff 143 F8
Ringshall Herts 85 C7
Suff 125 G10
Ringshall Stocks
Suff 125 G10
Ringstead Norf 176 E2
Northants 121 B9
Ringtail Green
Essex 87 B11
Ringwood Hants 31 F11
Ringwould Kent 55 D11
Rinmore Aberds 292 B6
Rinnigill Orkney 314 G3
Rinsey Corn 2 D3
Rinsey Croft Corn 2 D4
Riof W Isles 304 E3
Ripe E Sus 23 C8
Ripley Derbys 170 E5
Hants 19 B9
N Yorks 214 G5
Sur 50 B5
Riplingham E Yorks 208 G5
Ripon N Yorks 214 E6
Ripper's Cross Kent 54 E3
Rippingale Lincs 155 D11
Ripple Kent 55 D10
Worcs 99 D7
Ripponden W Yorks 196 D4
Rireavach Highld 307 K5
Risabus Argyll 254 C4
Risbury Hereford 115 G10
Risby E Yorks 208 G6
Lincs 189 C10
Suff 124 D5
Risca Caerph 78 G2
Rise E Yorks 209 E9
Rise Carr Darl 224 B5
Riseden E Sus 52 G6
Kent 53 F8
Rise End Derbys 170 D3
Risegate Lincs 156 D4
Riseholme Lincs 189 F7
Risehow Cumb 228 E6
Riseley Beds 121 E10
Wokingham 65 G8
Rise Park London 87 G8
Nottingham 171 F9
Rishangles Suff 126 D3
Rishton Lancs 203 G10
Rishworth W Yorks 196 D4
Rising Bridge Lancs 195 B9
Risingbrook Staffs 151 E8
Risinghurst Oxon 83 D9
Rising Sun Corn 12 G3
Risley Derbys 153 B9
Warr 183 C10
Risplith N Yorks 214 F4
Rispond Highld 308 C4
Rivar Wilts 63 G10
Rivenhall Essex 88 B4
Rivenhall End Essex 88 B4
River Kent 55 E9
W Sus 34 C6
River Bank Cambs 123 D10
Riverhead Kent 52 B4
Rivers' Corner Dorset 30 E3
Riverside Cardiff 59 D7
Plym 7 D8
Stirl 278 C6
Worcs 117 D10
Riverside Docklands
Lancs 194 B4
Riverton Devon 40 G6
Riverview Park Kent 69 E7
Rivington Lancs 194 E6
Rixon Dorset 30 E3
Rixton Warr 183 C11
Roach Bridge Lancs 194 B5
Roaches Gtr Man 196 G3
Roachill Devon 26 C4
Roade Northants 120 G5
Road Green Norf 142 E5
Roadhead Cumb 240 C2
Roadmeetings S
Lnrk 269 F7
Roadside Highld 310 C5
Roadside of Catterline
Aberds 293 F10
Roadside of Kinneff
Aberds 293 F10
Roadwater Som 42 F4
Road Weedon
Northants 120 F2
Roag Highld 298 E2
Roa Island Cumb 210 G4
Roast Green Essex 105 E9
Roath Cardiff 59 D7
Roath Park Cardiff 59 D7
Roberton Borders 261 G10
S Lnrk 259 D10
Robertsbridge E Sus 38 C2
Robertstown Moray 302 E2
Rhondda 77 E8
Roberttown
W Yorks 197 C7
Robeston Back
Pembs 73 B9
Robeston Cross
Pembs 72 D5
Robeston Wathen
Pembs 73 B9
Robeston West
Pembs 72 D5
Robhurst Kent 54 G2
Robin Hill Staffs 168 D6
Robin Hood Derbys 186 G3
Lancs 194 E4
W Yorks 197 B10
Robinhood End
Essex 106 D4
Robin Hood's Bay
N Yorks 227 D9
Robins W Sus 34 B4
Robinson's End
Warks 134 E6
Roborough Devon 7 C10
Devon 25 D9
Rob Roy's House
Argyll 284 F5
Robroyston Glasgow 268 B2
Roby Mers 182 C6
Roby Mill Lancs 194 F4
Rocester Staffs 152 B2
Roch Pembs 91 G7
Rochdale Gtr Man 195 E11
Roche Corn 5 C9
Roche Grange
Staffs 169 C7
Rochester Medway 69 F8
Northumb 251 D8
Rochford Essex 88 G5
Worcs 116 D2
Roch Gate Pembs 91 G7
Rock Caerph 77 F11
Corn 10 F4
Devon 28 G3
Neath 57 C9
Northumb 264 E6
Som 28 C4
Worcs 116 C4
W Sus 35 E10
Rockbeare Devon 14 C6
Rockbourne Hants 31 D10
Rockcliffe Cumb 239 E9
Dumfries 237 D10
Flint 182 G3
Lancs 195 C11
Rockcliffe Cross
Cumb 239 E8
Rock End Staffs 168 D5
Rock Ferry Mers 182 D4
Rockfield Highld 311 L3
Mon 79 C7
Rockford Devon 41 D9
Hants 31 F11
Rockgreen Shrops 115 B10
Rockhampton
S Glos 79 G11
Rockhead Corn 11 E7
Rockhill Shrops 114 B5
Rockingham
Northants 137 E7
Rockland All Saints
Norf 141 D9
Rockland St Mary
Norf 142 C6
Rockland St Peter
Norf 141 D9
Rockley Notts 188 G2
Wilts 63 E7
Rockley Ford Som 45 C8
Rockness Glos 80 F4
Rockrobin E Sus 52 G6
Rocksavage Halton 183 E8
Rocks Park E Sus 37 C7
Rockstowes Glos 80 F3
Rockville Argyll 276 C4
Rockwell End Bucks 65 B9
Rockwell Green
Som 27 C10
Rocky Hill Scilly 1 G4
Rodbaston Staffs 151 G8
Rodborough Glos 80 E4
Rodbourne Swindon 62 C6
Wilts 62 C2
Rodbourne Bottom
Wilts 62 C2
Rodbourne Cheney
Swindon 62 B6
Rodbridge Corner
Essex 107 C7
Rodd Hereford 114 E6
Roddam Northumb 264 E2
Rodden Dorset 17 E8
Rodd Hurst Hereford 114 E6
Roddymoor Durham 233 D9
Rode Som 45 C10
Rodeheath Ches E 168 B5
Rode Heath Ches E 168 D3
Rode Hill Som 45 C10
Roden Telford 149 F11
Rodford S Glos 61 C7
Rodgrove Som 30 C2
Rodhuish Som 42 F4
Rodington Telford 149 G11
Rodington Heath
Telford 149 G11
Rodley Glos 80 C2
W Yorks 205 F10
Rodmarton Glos 80 F6
Rodmell E Sus 36 F6
Rodmer Clough
W Yorks 196 B3
Rodmersham Kent 70 G2
Rodmersham Green
Kent 70 G2
Rodney Stoke Som 44 C3
Rodsley Derbys 170 G2
Rodway Som 43 F9
Telford 150 F3
Rodwell Dorset 17 F9
Roebuck Low
Gtr Man 196 F3
Roecliffe N Yorks 215 F7
Roe Cross Gtr Man 185 B7
Roedean Brighton 36 G4
Roe End Herts 85 B8
Roe Green Gtr Man 195 G9
Herts 86 D2
Herts 104 E6
Roehampton London 67 E8
Roe Lee Blkburn 203 G9
Roesound Shetland 312 G5
Roestock Herts 86 D2
Roffey W Sus 51 G7
Rogart Highld 309 J7
Rogart Station
Highld 309 J7
Rogate W Sus 34 C4
Roger Ground Cumb 221 F7
Rogerstone Newport 59 B9
Rogerton S Lnrk 268 D2
Roghadal W Isles 296 C6
Rogiet Mon 60 B3
Rogue's Alley
Cambs 139 B7
Roke Oxon 83 G10
Rokemarsh Oxon 83 G10
Roker T&W 243 F10
Rollesby Norf 161 F8
Rolleston Leics 136 C4
Notts 172 E2
Rollestone S Yorks 186 E5
Wilts 46 E5
Rollestone Camp
Wilts 46 E5
Rolleston-on-Dove
Staffs 152 D4
Rolls Mill Dorset 30 E3
Rolston E Yorks 209 D10
Rolstone N Som 59 G11
Rolvenden Kent 53 G10
Rolvenden Layne
Kent 53 G11
Romaldkirk Durham 232 G5
Romanby N Yorks 225 G7
Roman Hill Suff 143 E10
Romannobridge
Borders 270 F3
Romansleigh Devon 26 C2
Rome Angus 293 G7
Romesdal Highld 298 D4
Romford Dorset 31 F9
Kent 52 E6
London 68 B4
Romiley Gtr Man 184 C6
Romney Street Kent 68 G4
Rompa Shetland 313 L6
Romsey Hants 32 C5
Romsey Town
Cambs 123 F9
Romsley Shrops 132 G5
Worcs 117 B9
Romsley Hill Worcs 117 B9
Ronachan Ho Argyll 255 B8
Ronague IoM 192 E3
Rondlay Telford 132 B4
Ronkswood Worcs 117 G7
Rood End W Mid 133 F10
Rookby Cumb 222 C6
Rook End Essex 105 E11
Rookhope Durham 232 C4
Rooking Cumb 221 B8
Rookley IoW 20 E6
Rookley Green IoW 20 E6
Rooks Bridge Som 43 C11
Rooksey Green Suff 125 G8
Rooks Hill Kent 52 C5
Rooksmoor Glos 80 E4
Rook's Nest Som 42 G5
Rook Street Wilts 45 G10
Rookwith N Yorks 214 B4
Rookwood W Sus 21 B11
Roos E Yorks 209 G11
Roose Cumb 210 F4
Roosebeck Cumb 210 F5
Roosecote Cumb 210 F4
Roost End Essex 106 C4
Rootham's Green
Beds 122 F2
Rooting Street Kent 54 D3
Rootpark S Lnrk 269 E9
Ropley Hants 48 G6
Ropley Dean Hants 48 G6
Ropley Soke Hants 49 G7
Ropsley Lincs 155 C9
Rora Aberds 303 D10
Rorandle Aberds 293 B8
Rorrington Shrops 130 C5
Rosarie Moray 302 E3
Roscroggan Corn 4 G3

N Som 44 B2
Shrops 148 E6
Shrops 149 C11
S Lnrk 268 G4
Worcs 99 B7
W Yorks 205 F11
Sandford Batch
N Som 44 B2
Sandfordhill
Aberds 303 E11
Sandford Hill Stoke 168 G6
Sandford on Thames
Oxon 83 E8
Sandford Orcas
Dorset 29 C10
Sandford St Martin
Oxon 101 F8
Sandgate Kent 55 G7
Sand Gate Cumb 211 D7
Sandgreen Dumfries 237 D7
Sandhaven Aberds 303 C9
Argyll 276 E3
Sandhead Dumfries 236 E2
Sandhill Bucks 102 F4
Cambs 139 F11
S Yorks 198 F2
Sandhills Dorset 29 E11
Dorset 29 G9
Mers 182 C4
Oxon 83 D9
Sur 50 F2
W Yorks 206 F3
Sandhoe Northumb 241 D11
Sandhole Argyll 275 D11
Sand Hole E Yorks 208 F2
Sandholme E Yorks 208 G2
Lincs 156 B6
Sandhurst Brack 65 G10
Glos 98 G6
Kent 38 B3
Sandhurst Cross
Kent 38 B3
Sandhutton N Yorks 215 C7
Sand Hutton
N Yorks 207 B9
Sandiacre Derbys 153 B9
Sandilands Lincs 191 E8
S Lnrk 259 B9
Sandiway Ches W 183 G10
Sandleheath Hants 31 E10
Sandling Kent 53 B9
Sandlow Green
Ches E 168 B3
Sandness Shetland 313 H3
Sandon Essex 88 E2
Herts 104 E6
Staffs 151 C8
Sandonbank Staffs 151 D8
Sandown IoW 21 E7
Sandown Park Kent 52 E6
Sandpit Dorset 28 G6
Sandpits Glos 98 F6
Sandplace Corn 6 D5
Sandridge Herts 85 C11
Wilts 62 F2
Sandringham Norf 158 D3
Sands Bucks 84 G4
Sandsend N Yorks 227 C7
Sands End London 67 D9
Sandside Cumb 210 D6
Cumb 211 C9
Orkney 314 F2
Sand Side Cumb 210 C4
Lancs 202 C4
Sandside Ho Highld 310 C3
Sandsound Shetland 313 J5
Sandtoft N Lincs 199 F8
Sandvoe Shetland 312 D5
Sandway Kent 53 C11
Sandwell W Mid 133 F10
Sandwich Kent 55 B10
Sandwich Bay Estate
Kent 55 B11
Sandwick Cumb 221 B8
Orkney 314 H4
Shetland 313 L6
Sandwith Cumb 219 C9
Sandwith Newtown
Cumb 219 C9
Sandy Carms 75 E7
C Beds 104 B3
Sandybank Orkney 314 C5
Sandy Bank Lincs 174 E3
Sandy Carrs Durham 234 C3
Sandycroft Flint 166 B4
Sandy Cross E Sus 37 C9
Sur 49 D11
Sandy Down Hants 20 B2
Sandyford Dumfries 248 E6
Stoke 168 E5
Sandygate Devon 14 G3
IoM 192 C4
S Yorks 186 D4
Sandy Gate Devon 14 C5
Sandy Haven Pembs 72 D5
Sandyhills
Dumfries 237 D10
Sandylake Corn 6 C2
Sandylands Lancs 211 G8
Som 27 C10
Sandylane Swansea 56 D5
Sandy Lane Wilts 62 F3
Wrex 166 G5
W Yorks 205 F8
Sandypark Devon 13 D10
Sandysike Cumb 239 D9
Sandy Way IoW 20 E5
Sangobeg Highld 308 C4
Sangomore Highld 308 C4
Sanham Green
W Berks 63 F10
Sankey Bridges
Warr 183 D9
Sankyns Green
Worcs 116 E5
Sanna Highld 288 C6
Sanndabhaig
W Isles 297 G4
W Isles 304 E6
Sannox N Ayrs 255 C11
Sanquhar Dumfries 247 B7
Sansaw Heath
Shrops 149 E10
Santon Cumb 220 E2
N Lincs 200 E2
Santon Bridge
Cumb 220 E2
Santon Downham
Suff 140 F6
Sapcote Leics 135 E9
Sapey Bridge Worcs 116 F4
Sapey Common
Hereford 116 E4
Sapiston Suff 125 B8
Sapley Cambs 122 C4
Sapperton Derbys 152 C3
Glos 80 E6
Lincs 155 C10
Saracen's Head
Lincs 156 D6
Sarclet Highld 310 E7
Sardis Carms 75 D9
Pembs 73 D10
Sarisbury Hants 33 F8
Sarn Bridgend 58 C2
Flint 181 F10
Powys 130 E4
Sarnau Carms 74 B4
Ceredig 110 G6
Gwyn 147 B9
Powys 95 E10
Powys 148 F4
Sarn Bach Gwyn 144 D6
Sarnesfield
Hereford 115 G7
Sarn Meyllteyrn
Gwyn 144 C4
Saron Carms 75 C10
Carms 93 D7
Denb 165 C8
Gwyn 163 B8
Gwyn 163 D7
Sarratt Herts 85 F8
Sarratt Bottom Herts 85 F8
Sarre Kent 71 G9
Sarsden Oxon 100 G5
Sarsden Halt Oxon 100 G5
Sarsgrum Highld 308 C3
Sasaig Highld 295 E8
Sascott Shrops 149 G8
Satley Durham 233 C8
Satmar Kent 55 F9
Satran Highld 294 B6
Satron N Yorks 223 F8
Satterleigh Devon 25 C11
Satterthwaite Cumb 220 G6
Satwell Oxon 65 C8
Sauchen Aberds 293 B8
Saucher Perth 286 D5
Sauchie Clack 279 C7
Sauchieburn Aberds 293 G8
Saughall Ches W 182 G5
Saughall Massie
Mers 182 D3
Saughton Edin 280 G4
Saughtree Borders 250 D3
Saul Glos 80 D2
Saundby Notts 188 D3
Saundersfoot
Pembs 73 E10
Saunderton Bucks 84 E3
Saunderton Lee
Bucks 84 F4
Saunton Devon 40 F3
Sausthorpe Lincs 174 B5
Saval Highld 309 J5
Savary Highld 289 E8
Saveock Corn 4 F5
Saverley Green
Staffs 151 B9
Savile Park
W Yorks 196 C5
Savile Town
W Yorks 197 C8
Sawbridge Warks 119 D10
Sawbridgeworth
Herts 87 B7
Sawdon N Yorks 217 B8
Sawley Derbys 153 C9
Lancs 203 D11
N Yorks 214 F4
Sawood W Yorks 204 G6
Sawston Cambs 105 B9
Sawtry Cambs 138 G3
Sawyers Hill Wilts 81 G8
Sawyer's Hill Som 27 C11
Saxby Leics 154 F6
Lincs 189 D8
W Sus 35 G7
Saxby All Saints
N Lincs 200 D3
Saxelbye Leics 154 E4
Saxham Street
Suff 125 E11
Saxilby Lincs 188 F5
Saxlingham Norf 159 B10
Saxlingham Green
Norf 142 D4
Saxlingham Nethergate
Norf 142 D4
Saxlingham Thorpe
Norf 142 D4
Saxmundham Suff 127 E7
Saxondale Notts 154 B3
Saxon Street Cambs 124 F3
Saxtead Suff 126 E5
Saxtead Green Suff 126 E5
Saxtead Little Green
Suff 126 D5
Saxthorpe Norf 160 C2
Saxton N Yorks 206 F5
Sayers Common
W Sus 36 D3
Scackleton N Yorks 216 E2
Scadabhagh
W Isles 305 J3
Scaftworth Notts 187 C11
Scagglethorpe
N Yorks 216 E6
Scaitcliffe Lancs 195 B9
Scaladal W Isles 305 G3
Scalan Moray 292 B4
Scalasaig Argyll 274 D4
Scalby E Yorks 199 B10
N Yorks 227 G10
Scald End Beds 121 F10
Scaldwell Northants 120 C5
Scaleby Cumb 239 E11
Scalebyhill Cumb 239 E10
Scale Hall Lancs 211 G9
Scale Houses Cumb 231 B7
Scales Cumb 210 E5
Cumb 230 F2
Cumb 231 C7
Lancs 202 G5
Scalford Leics 154 E5
Scaling Redcar 226 C4
Scaliscro W Isles 304 F3
Scallasaig Highld 295 D10
Scallastle Argyll 289 F8
Scalloway Shetland 313 K6
Scalpay W Isles 305 J4
Scalpay Ho Highld 295 C8
Scalpsie Argyll 255 B11
Scamadale Highld 295 F9
Scamblesby Lincs 190 F3
Scamland E Yorks 207 E11
Scammadale
Argyll 289 G10
Scamodale Highld 289 B10
Scampston N Yorks 217 D7
Scampton Lincs 189 F7
Scaniport Highld 300 F6
Scapa Orkney 314 F4
Scapegoat Hill
W Yorks 196 D5
Scar Orkney 314 B6
Scarborough
N Yorks 217 B10
Scarcewater Corn 5 E8
Scarcliffe Derbys 171 B7
Scarcroft W Yorks 206 E3
Scarcroft Hill
W Yorks 206 E3
Scardroy Highld 300 D2
Scarff Shetland 312 E4
Scarfskerry Highld 310 B6
Scargill Durham 223 C11
Scar Head Cumb 220 G5
Scarinish Argyll 288 E2
Scarisbrick Lancs 193 E11
Scarness Cumb 229 E10
Scarning Norf 159 G9
Scarrington Notts 172 G2
Scarth Hill Lancs 194 F2
Scarthingwell
N Yorks 206 F5
Scartho NE Lincs 201 F9
Scarvister Shetland 313 J5
Scarwell Orkney 314 D2
Scatness Shetland 313 M5
Scatraig Highld 301 F7
Scatwell Ho Highld 300 D3
Scawby N Lincs 200 F3
Scawsby S Yorks 198 G5
Scawthorpe S Yorks 198 F5
Scawton N Yorks 215 C10
Scayne's Hill W Sus 36 C5
Scethrog Powys 96 F2
Scholar Green
Ches E 168 D4
Scholemoor
W Yorks 205 G8
Scholes Gtr Man 194 F5
S Yorks 186 B5
W Yorks 197 B7
W Yorks 197 F7
W Yorks 204 F6
W Yorks 206 F3
Scholey Hill
W Yorks 197 B11
School Aycliffe
Durham 233 G11
Schoolgreen
Wokingham 65 F8
School Green
Ches W 167 C10
Essex 106 E4
IoW 20 D2
W Yorks 205 G8
Schoolhill Aberds 293 D11
School House Dorset 28 G5
Sciberscross Highld 309 H7
Scilly Bank Cumb 219 B9
Scissett W Yorks 197 E8
Scleddau Pembs 91 E8
Scofton Notts 187 E10
Scole Norf 126 B2
Scole Common
Norf 142 G2
Scolpaig W Isles 296 D3
Scone Perth 286 E5
Sconser Highld 295 B7
Scoonie Fife 287 G7
Scoor Argyll 274 B5
Scopwick Lincs 173 D9
Scoraig Highld 307 K5
Scorborough
E Yorks 208 D6
Scorrier Corn 4 G4
Scorriton Devon 8 B4
Scorton Lancs 202 D6
N Yorks 224 E5
Sco Ruston Norf 160 E5
Scotbheinn W Isles 296 F4
Scotby Cumb 239 G10
Scotch Corner
N Yorks 224 E4
Scotches Derbys 170 F4
Scotforth Lancs 202 B5
Scotgate W Yorks 196 E6
Scot Hay Staffs 168 F4
Scothern Lincs 189 F8
Scotland Leics 136 D3
Leics 153 E7
Lincs 155 C10
W Berks 64 F5
Scotland End Oxon 100 E6
Scotland Gate
Northumb 253 G7
Scotlands W Mid 133 C8
Scotland Street
Suff 107 D9
Scot Lane End
Gtr Man 194 F6
Scotsburn Highld 301 B7
Scotscalder Station
Highld 310 D4
Scotscraig Fife 287 E8
Scots' Gap Northumb 252 F2
Scotston Aberds 293 F9
Perth 286 C3
Scotstoun Glasgow 267 B10
Scotstown Highld 289 C10
Scotswood T&W 242 E5
Windsor 66 F2
Scottas Highld 295 E9
Scotter Lincs 199 G11
Scotterthorpe
Lincs 199 G11
Scottlethorpe
Lincs 155 E11
Scotton Lincs 188 B5
N Yorks 206 B2
N Yorks 224 F3
Scottow Norf 160 E5
Scott Willoughby
Lincs 155 B11
Scoughall E Loth 282 E2
Scoulag Argyll 266 D2
Scoulton Norf 141 C9
Scounslow Green
Staffs 151 D11
Scourie Highld 306 E6
Scourie More
Highld 306 E6
Scousburgh
Shetland 313 M5
Scout Dike S Yorks 197 G8
Scout Green Cumb 221 D11
Scouthead Gtr Man 196 F3
Scowles Glos 79 C9
Scrabster Highld 310 B4
Scraesburgh
Borders 262 F5
Scrafield Lincs 174 B4
Scragged Oak Kent 69 G10
Scrainwood
Northumb 251 B11
Scrane End Lincs 174 G5
Scrapsgate Kent 70 E2
Scraptoft Leics 136 B2
Scrapton Som 28 E3
Scratby Norf 161 F10
Scrayingham
N Yorks 216 G4
Scredda Corn 5 E10
Scredington Lincs 173 G9
Screedy Som 27 B9
Scremby Lincs 174 B6
Scremerston
Northumb 273 F10
Screveton Notts 172 G2
Scrivelsby Lincs 174 B3
Scriven N Yorks 206 B2
Scronkey Lancs 202 D4
Scrooby Notts 187 C11
Scropton Derbys 152 C3
Scrub Hill Lincs 174 D2
Scruton N Yorks 224 G5
Scrwgan Powys 148 E3
Scuddaborg Highld 298 C3
Scuggate Cumb 239 C10
Sculcoates Hull 209 G7
Sculthorpe Norf 159 C7
Scunthorpe
N Lincs 199 E11
Scurlage Swansea 56 D3
Sea Som 28 E4
Seaborough Dorset 28 F6
Seabridge Staffs 168 G4
Seabrook Kent 55 G7
Seaburn T&W 243 F10
Seacombe Mers 182 C4
Seacox Heath Kent 53 G8
Seacroft Lincs 175 C9
W Yorks 206 F3
Seadyke Lincs 156 B6
Seafar N Lnrk 278 G5
Seafield Highld 311 L3
Midloth 270 C5
S Ayrs 257 E8
W Loth 269 B10
Seaford E Sus 23 F7
Seaforth Mers 182 B4
Seagrave Leics 154 F2
Seagry Heath Wilts 62 C3
Seaham Durham 234 B4
Seahouses
Northumb 264 C6
Seal Kent 52 B4
Sealand Flint 166 B5
Seale Sur 49 D11
Seamer N Yorks 217 C10
N Yorks 225 C9
Seamill N Ayrs 266 F4
Sea Mill Cumb 210 F5
Sea Mills Bristol 60 D5
Corn 10 G4
Sea Palling Norf 161 D8
Searby Lincs 200 F5
Seasalter Kent 70 F5
Seascale Cumb 219 E10
Seathorne Lincs 175 B9
Seathwaite Cumb 220 C4
Cumb 220 F4
Seatle Cumb 211 C7
Seatoller Cumb 220 C4
Seaton Corn 6 E6
Cumb 228 E6
Devon 15 C10
Durham 243 G9
E Yorks 209 D9
Kent 55 B8
Northumb 243 B8
Rutland 137 D8
Seaton Burn T&W 242 C6
Seaton Carew Hrtlpl 234 F6
Seaton Delaval
Northumb 243 B8
Seaton Ross
E Yorks 207 E11
Seaton Sluice
Northumb 243 B8
Seatown Aberds 302 C5
Aberds 303 D11
Dorset 16 C4
Seaureaugh Moor
Corn 2 B6
Seave Green
N Yorks 225 E11
Seaview IoW 21 C8
Seaville Cumb 238 G5
Seavington St Mary
Som 28 E6
Seavington St Michael
Som 28 D6
Seawick Essex 89 C10
Sebastopol Torf 78 F3
Sebay Orkney 314 F5
Sebergham Cumb 230 C3
Sebiston Velzian
Orkney 314 D2
Seckington Warks 134 B5
Second Coast
Highld 307 K4
Second Drove
Cambs 139 F10
Sedbergh Cumb 222 G3
Sedbury Glos 79 G8
Sedbusk N Yorks 223 G7
Seddington C Beds 104 B3
Sedgeberrow
Worcs 99 D10
Sedgebrook Lincs 155 B7
Sedgefield Durham 234 F3
Sedgeford Norf 158 B4
Sedgehill Wilts 30 B5
Sedgemere W Mid 118 B4
Sedgley W Mid 133 E8
Sedgley Park
Gtr Man 195 G10
Sedgwick Cumb 211 B10
Sedlescombe E Sus 38 D3
Sedlescombe Street
E Sus 38 D3
Sedrup Bucks 84 C3
Seed Kent 54 B2
Seed Lee Lancs 194 C5
Seedley Gtr Man 184 B4
Seend Wilts 62 G2
Seend Cleeve Wilts 62 G2
Seend Head Wilts 62 G2
Seer Green Bucks 85 G7
Seething Norf 142 D6
Seething Wells
London 67 F7
Sefton Mers 193 G11
Segensworth Hants 33 F8
Seggat Aberds 303 E7
Seghill Northumb 243 C7
Seifton Shrops 131 G9
Seighford Staffs 151 D7
Seilebost W Isles 305 J2
Seion Gwyn 163 B8
Seisdon Staffs 132 E6
Seisiadar W Isles 304 E7
Selattyn Shrops 148 C5
Selborne Hants 49 G8
Selby N Yorks 207 G8
Selgrove Kent 54 B4
Selham W Sus 34 C6
Selhurst London 67 F10
Selkirk Borders 261 D11
Sellack Hereford 97 F11
Sellack Boat
Hereford 97 F11
Sellafirth Shetland 312 D7
Sellan Corn 1 C4
Sellibister Orkney 314 B7
Sellick's Green Som 28 D2
Sellindge Kent 54 F6
Selling Kent 54 B4
Sells Green Wilts 62 G3
Selly Hill N Yorks 227 D7
Selly Oak W Mid 133 G10
Selly Park W Mid 133 G11
Selmeston E Sus 23 D8
Selsdon London 67 G10
Selsey W Sus 22 E5
Selsfield Common
W Sus 51 G10
Selside Cumb 221 F10
N Yorks 212 D5
Selsley Glos 80 E4
Selsmore Hants 21 B10
Selson Kent 55 B10
Selsted Kent 55 E8
Selston Notts 171 E7
Selston Common
Notts 171 E7
Selston Green Notts 171 E7
Selwick Orkney 314 F2
Selworthy Som 42 D2
Semblister Shetland 313 H5
Semer Suff 107 B9
Sem Hill Wilts 30 B5
Semington Wilts 61 G11
Semley Wilts 30 B5
Sempringham Lincs 156 C2
Send Sur 50 B4
Send Grove Sur 50 C4
Send Marsh Sur 50 B4
Senghenydd Caerph 77 G10
Sennen Corn 1 D3
Sennen Cove Corn 1 D3
Sennybridge / Pont
Senni Powys 95 F8
Serlby Notts 187 D10
Serrington Wilts 46 F5
Sessay N Yorks 215 D9
Setchey Norf 158 G2
Setley Hants 32 G4
Seton E Loth 281 G8
Seton Mains E Loth 281 F8
Setter Shetland 312 E6
Shetland 313 H5
Shetland 313 J7
Shetland 313 L6
Settiscarth Orkney 314 E3
Settle N Yorks 212 G6
Settrington N Yorks 216 E6
Seven Ash Som 43 G7
Sevenhampton Glos 99 G10
Swindon 82 G2
Seven Kings London 68 B3
Sevenoaks Kent 52 C4
Sevenoaks Common
Kent 52 C4
Sevenoaks Weald
Kent 52 C4
Seven Sisters /
Blaendulais Neath 76 D4
Seven Springs Glos 81 B7
Seven Star Green
Essex 107 F8
Severn Beach S Glos 60 B4
Severnhampton
Swindon 82 G2
Severn Stoke Worcs 99 C7
Sevick End Beds 121 G11
Sevington Kent 54 E4
Sewards End
Essex 105 D11
Sewardstone Essex 86 F5
Sewardstonebury
Essex 86 F5
Sewell C Beds 103 G9
Sewerby E Yorks 218 F3
Seworgan Corn 2 C6
Sewstern Leics 155 E7
Sexhow N Yorks 225 D9
Sezincote Glos 100 E3
Sgarasta Mhor
W Isles 305 J2
Sgiogarstaigh
W Isles 304 B7
Sgiwen / Skewen
Neath 57 B8
Shabbington Bucks 83 D11
Shab Hill Glos 80 B6
Shackerley Shrops 132 B6
Shackerstone Leics 135 B7
Shacklecross
Derbys 153 C8
Shackleford Sur 50 D2
Shackleton W Yorks 196 B3
Shacklewell London 67 B10
Shacklford Sur 50 D2
Shade W Yorks 196 C2
Shadforth Durham 234 C2
Shadingfield Suff 143 G8
Shadoxhurst Kent 54 F3
Shadsworth Blkburn 195 B8
Shadwell Glos 80 F3
London 67 C11
Norf 141 G8
W Yorks 206 F2
Shaffalong Staffs 169 E7
Shaftenhoe End
Herts 105 D8
Shaftesbury Dorset 30 C5
Shafton S Yorks 197 E11
Shafton Two Gates
S Yorks 197 E11
Shaggs Dorset 18 E3
Shakeford Shrops 150 D3
Shakerley Gtr Man 195 G7
Shakesfield Glos 98 E3
Shalbourne Wilts 63 G10
Shalcombe IoW 20 D3
Shalden Hants 49 E7
Shalden Green Hants 49 E8
Shaldon Devon 14 G4
Shalfleet IoW 20 D4
Shalford Essex 106 F4
Som 45 G8
Sur 50 D4
Shalford Green
Essex 106 F4
Shalloch Moray 302 D3
Shallowford Devon 25 B11
Devon 41 E8
Staffs 151 D7
Shalmsford Street
Kent 54 C5
Shalstone Bucks 102 D2
Shamley Green Sur 50 E4
Shandon Argyll 276 D5
Shandwick Highld 301 B8
Shangton Leics 136 D4
Shankhouse
Northumb 243 B7
Shanklin IoW 21 E7
Shannochie
N Ayrs 255 E10
Shannochill Stirl 277 B10
Shanquhar Aberds 302 F5
Shanwell Fife 287 E8
Shanzie Perth 286 B6
Shap Cumb 221 B11
Shapridge Glos 79 B11
Shapwick Dorset 30 G6
Som 44 F2
Sharcott Wilts 46 B6
Shard End W Mid 134 F3
Shardlow Derbys 153 C8
Shareshill Staffs 133 B8
Sharlston W Yorks 197 D11
Sharlston Common
W Yorks 197 D11
Sharmans Cross
W Mid 118 B2
Sharnal Street
Medway 69 E9
Sharnbrook Beds 121 F9
Sharneyford Lancs 195 C11
Sharnford Leics 135 E9
Sharnhill Green
Dorset 30 F2
Sharoe Green Lancs 202 G6
Sharow N Yorks 214 E6
Sharpenhoe
C Beds 103 E11
Sharperton
Northumb 251 C11
Sharples Gtr Man 195 E8
Sharpley Heath
Staffs 151 B9
Sharpness Glos 79 E11
Sharpsbridge E Sus 36 C6
Sharp's Corner E Sus 23 B9
Sharpstone Bath 45 B9
Sharp Street Norf 161 E7
Sharpthorne W Sus 51 G11
Sharptor Corn 11 G11
Sharpway Gate
Worcs 117 D9
Sharrington Norf 159 B10
Sharrow S Yorks 186 D4
Sharston Gtr Man 184 D4
Shatterford Worcs 132 G5
Shatterling Kent 55 B9
Shatton Derbys 185 E11
Shaugh Prior Devon 7 C10
Shavington Ches E 168 E2
Shaw Gtr Man 196 F2
Swindon 62 B6
W Berks 64 F3
Wilts 61 F11
W Yorks 204 F6
Shawbank Shrops 131 G9
Shawbirch Telford 150 G2
Shawbury Shrops 149 E11
Shawclough
Gtr Man 195 E11
Shaw Common Glos 98 F3
Shawdon Hall
Northumb 264 G3
Shawell Leics 135 G10
Shawfield Gtr Man 195 E11
Staffs 169 C9
Shawfield Head
N Yorks 205 C11
Shawford Hants 33 C7
Som 45 C9
Shawforth Lancs 195 C11
Shaw Green Herts 104 E5
Lancs 194 D4
N Yorks 205 C11
Shawhead
Dumfries 237 B10
N Lnrk 268 C4
Shaw Heath Ches E 184 F3
Gtr Man 184 D5
Shawhill Dumfries 238 D6
Shawlands
Glasgow 267 C11
Shaw Lands
S Yorks 197 F10
Shaw Mills N Yorks 214 G5
Shawsburn S Lnrk 268 E5
Shaw Side Gtr Man 196 F2
Shawton S Lnrk 268 F3
Shawtonhill S Lnrk 268 F3
Shay Gate W Yorks 205 F8
Sheandow Moray 302 F2
Shear Cross Wilts 45 E11
Shearington
Dumfries 238 D2
Shearsby Leics 136 E2
Shearston Som 43 G9
Shebbear Devon 24 F6
Shebdon Staffs 150 D5
Shebster Highld 310 C4
Sheddens E Renf 267 D11
Shedfield Hants 33 E9
Sheen Staffs 169 C10
Sheepbridge
Derbys 186 G5
Sheepdrove
W Berks 63 D10
Sheep Hill Durham 242 F5
Sheeplane C Beds 103 E8
Sheepridge Bucks 65 B11
W Yorks 197 D7
Sheepscar W Yorks 206 G2
Sheepscombe Glos 80 C5
Sheepstor Devon 7 B11
Sheepwash Devon 25 F7
Northumb 253 F7
Sheepway N Som 60 D3
Sheepy Magna
Leics 134 C6
Sheepy Parva Leics 134 C6
Sheering Essex 87 C8
Sheerness Kent 70 E2
Sheerwater Sur 66 G4
Sheet Hants 34 C3
Shrops 115 C10
Sheets Heath Sur 50 B2
Sheffield Corn 1 D5
S Yorks 186 D5
Sheffield Bottom
W Berks 65 F7
Sheffield Green
E Sus 36 C6
Sheffield Park
S Yorks 186 D5
Shefford C Beds 104 D2
Shefford Woodlands
W Berks 63 E11
Sheigra Highld 306 C6
Sheildmuir N Lnrk 268 D5
Sheinton Shrops 132 C2
Shelderton Shrops 115 B8
Sheldon Derbys 169 B11
Devon 27 F10
W Mid 134 G3
Sheldwich Kent 54 B4
Sheldwich Lees Kent 54 B4
Shelf Bridgend 58 C2
W Yorks 196 B6
Shelfanger Norf 142 G2
Shelfield Warks 118 E2
W Mid 133 C10
Shelfield Green
Warks 118 E2
Shelfleys Northants 120 F4
Shelford Notts 171 G11
Warks 135 F8
Shell Worcs 117 F9
Shelland Suff 125 E10
Shellbrook Leics 152 F6
Shelley Essex 87 E9
Suff 107 D10
W Yorks 197 E8
Shelley Woodhouse
W Yorks 197 E8
Shell Green Halton 183 D8
Shellingford Oxon 82 G4
Shellow Bowells
Essex 87 D10
Shellwood Cross Sur 51 D8
Shelsley Beauchamp
Worcs 116 E4
Shelsley Walsh
Worcs 116 E4
Shelthorpe Leics 153 F10
Shelton Beds 121 D10
Norf 142 E4
Notts 172 G3
Shrops 149 G9
Stoke 168 F5
Shelton Green Norf 142 E4
Shelton Lock Derby 153 C7
Shelton under Harley
Staffs 150 B6
Shelve Shrops 130 D6
Shelvin Devon 27 G11
Shelvingford Kent 71 F8
Shelwick Hereford 97 C10
Shelwick Green
Hereford 97 C10
Shenfield Essex 87 G10
Shenington Oxon 101 C7
Shenley Herts 85 E11
Shenley Brook End
M Keynes 102 D6
Shenleybury Herts 85 E11
Shenley Church End
M Keynes 102 D6
Shenley Fields
W Mid 133 G10
Shenley Lodge
M Keynes 102 D6
Shenley Wood
M Keynes 102 D6
Shenmore Hereford 97 D7
Shennanton
Dumfries 236 C5
Shennanton Ho
Dumfries 236 C5
Shenstone Staffs 134 C2
Worcs 117 C7
Shenstone Woodend
Staffs 134 C2
Shenton Leics 135 C7
Shenval Highld 300 G4
Moray 302 G2
Shenvault Moray 301 E10
Shepeau Stow Lincs 156 G6
Shephall Herts 104 G5
Shepherd Hill
W Yorks 197 C9
Shepherd's Bush
London 67 C8
Shepherd's Gate
Norf 157 F11
Shepherd's Green
Oxon 65 C8
Shepherd's Hill Sur 50 G2
Shepherd's Patch
Glos 80 E2
Shepherd's Port
Norf 158 C3
Shepherdswell or
Sibertswold Kent 55 D9
Shepley W Yorks 197 F7
Shepperdine S Glos 79 F10
Shepperton Sur 66 F5
Shepperton Green
Sur 66 F5
Shepreth Cambs 105 B7
Shepshed Leics 153 F9
Shepton Beauchamp
Som 28 D6
Shepton Mallet Som 44 E6
Shepton Montague
Som 45 G7
Shepway Kent 53 C9
Sheraton Durham 234 D4
Sherberton Devon 13 G8
Sherborne Bath 44 B5
Dorset 29 D10
Glos 81 C11
Sherborne St John
Hants 48 B6
Sherbourne Warks 118 E5
Sherbourne Street
Suff 107 C9
Sherburn Durham 234 C2
N Yorks 217 D9
Sherburn Grange
Durham 234 C2
Sherburn Hill
Durham 234 C2
Sherburn in Elmet
N Yorks 206 G5
Shere Sur 50 D5
Shereford Norf 159 D7
Sherfield English
Hants 32 C3
Sherfield on Loddon
Hants 49 B7
Sherfin Lancs 195 B9
Sherford Devon 8 G5
Dorset 18 C4
Som 28 C2
Sheriffhales Shrops 150 G5
Sheriff Hill T&W 243 E7
Sheriff Hutton
N Yorks 216 F3
Sheriff's Lench
Worcs 99 B10
Sheringham Norf 177 E11
Sherington
M Keynes 103 B7
Sheringwood Norf 177 E11
Shermanbury W Sus 36 D2
Shernal Green
Worcs 117 E8
Shernborne Norf 158 C4
Sherrard's Green
Worcs 98 B5
Sherrardspark Herts 86 C2
Sherriffhales
Shrops 150 G5
Sherrington Wilts 46 F3
Sherston Wilts 61 B11
Sherwood
Nottingham 171 G9
Sherwood Green
Devon 25 C9
Sherwood Park Kent 52 E6
Shettleston Glasgow 268 C2
Shevington Gtr Man 194 F4
Shevington Moor
Gtr Man 194 E4
Shevington Vale
Gtr Man 194 F4
Sheviock Corn 7 D7
Shewalton N Ayrs 257 B8
Shibden Head
W Yorks 196 B5
Shide IoW 20 D5
Shiel Aberds 292 B4
Shiel Bridge
Highld 295 D11
Shieldaig Highld 299 B8
Highld 299 D8
Shieldhall Glasgow 267 B10
Shieldhill Dumfries 248 F2
Falk 279 F7
S Lnrk 269 G10
Shield Row Durham 242 G6
Shielfoot Highld 289 C8
Shielhill Angus 287 B8
Invclyd 276 G4
Shifford Oxon 82 E5
Shifnal Shrops 132 B4
Shilbottle Northumb 252 B5
Shilbottle Grange
Northumb 252 B6
Shildon Durham 233 F10
Shillford E Renf 267 D8
Shillingford Devon 27 C7
Oxon 83 G9
Shillingford Abbot
Devon 14 D4
Shillingford St George
Devon 14 D4
Shillingstone Dorset 30 E4
Shillington C Beds 104 E2
Shillmoor Northumb 251 B9
Shilton Oxon 82 D3
Warks 135 G8
Shilvington
Northumb 252 G5
Shimpling Norf 142 G3
Suff 125 G7

Shimpling Street Suff 125 G7
Shincliffe Durham 233 C11
Shiney Row T&W 243 G8
Shinfield Wokingham 65 F8
Shingay Cambs 104 B6
Shingham Norf 140 C5
Shingle Street Suff 109 C7
Shinner's Bridge Devon 8 C5
Shinness Highld 309 H5
Shipbourne Kent 52 C5
Shipdham Norf 141 B9
Shipdham Airfield Norf 141 B9
Shipham Som 44 B2
Shiphay Torbay 9 B7
Shiplake Oxon 65 D9
Shiplake Bottom Oxon 65 C8
Shiplake Row Oxon 65 D9
Shiplate N Som 43 B11
Shiplaw Borders 270 F4
Shipley Derbys 170 G6
Northumb 264 F4
Shrops 132 D6
W Sus 35 C10
W Yorks 205 F8
Shipley Bridge Sur 51 E10
Shipley Common Derbys 171 G7
Shipley Shiels Northumb 251 E7
Shipmeadow Suff 143 F7
Shipping Pembs 73 D10
Shippon Oxon 83 F7
Shipston-on-Stour Warks 100 C5
Shipton Bucks 102 F5
Glos 81 B8
N Yorks 207 B7
Shrops 131 E11
Shipton Bellinger Hants 47 D8
Shipton Gorge Dorset 16 C5
Shipton Green W Sus 22 C4
Shipton Lee Bucks 102 G4
Shipton Moyne Glos 61 B11
Shipton Oliffe Glos 81 B8
Shipton on Cherwell Oxon 83 B7
Shipton Solers Glos 81 B8
Shiptonthorpe E Yorks 208 E3
Shipton-under-Wychwood Oxon 82 B3
Shirburn Oxon 83 F11
Shirdley Hill Lancs 193 E11
Shirebrook Derbys 171 B8
Shirecliffe S Yorks 186 C4
Shiregreen S Yorks 186 C5
Shirehampton Bristol 60 D4
Shiremoor T&W 243 C8
Shirenewton Mon 79 G7
Shire Oak W Mid 133 C11
Shireoaks Derbys 185 E9
Notts 187 E9
Shires Mill Fife 279 D10
Shirkoak Kent 54 F2
Shirland Derbys 170 D6
Shirlett Shrops 132 D3
Shirley Derbys 170 G2
Hants 19 B9
London 67 F11
Soton 32 E6
W Mid 118 B2
Shirley Heath W Mid 118 B2
Shirley holms Hants 19 B11
Shirley Warren Soton 32 E5
Shirl Heath Hereford 115 F8
Shirrell Heath Hants 33 E9
Shirwell Devon 40 F5
Shirwell Cross Devon 40 F5
Shiskine N Ayrs 255 E10
Shitterton Dorset 18 C2
Shobdon Hereford 115 E8
Shobley Hants 31 F11
Shobnall Staffs 152 E4
Shobrooke Devon 26 G5
Shoby Leics 154 F3
Shocklach Ches W 166 F6
Shocklach Green Ches W 166 F6
Shoeburyness Sthend 70 C2
Sholden Kent 55 C11
Sholing Soton 32 E6
Sholing Common Soton 33 E7
Sholver Gtr Man 196 F3
Shootash Hants 32 C4
Shooters Hill London 68 D2
Shootersway Herts 85 D7
Shoot Hill Shrops 149 G8
Shop Corn 10 G3
Corn 24 E2
Devon 24 E5
Shop Corner Suff 108 E4
Shopford Cumb 240 C3
Shopnoller Som 43 G7
Shopp Hill W Sus 34 B6
Shopwyke W Sus 22 B5
Shore Gtr Man 196 D2
W Yorks 196 B2
Shore Bottom Devon 28 G2
Shoreditch London 67 C10
Som 28 C2
Shoregill Cumb 222 E5
Shoreham Kent 68 G4
Shoreham Beach W Sus 36 G2
Shoreham-by-Sea W Sus 36 F2
Shore Mill Highld 301 C7
Shoresdean Northumb 273 F9
Shores Green Oxon 82 D5
Shoreside Shetland 313 J4
Shoreswood Northumb 273 F8
Shoreton Highld 300 C6
Shorley Hants 33 B9
Shorncliffe Camp Kent 55 F7
Shorncote Glos 81 F8
Shorne Kent 69 E7
Shorne Ridgeway Kent 69 E7
Shorne West Kent 69 E7
Shortacombe Devon 12 D6
Shortacross Corn 6 D5
Shortbridge E Sus 37 C7
Short Cross W Mid 133 G9
Shortfield Common Sur 49 E10
Shortgate E Sus 23 B7
Short Green Norf 141 F11
Shorthampton Oxon 100 G6
Shortheath Hants 49 F9
Sur 49 E10
Short Heath Derbys 152 G6
W Mid 133 C9
W Mid 133 E11
Shorthill Shrops 131 B8
Shortlands London 67 F11
Shortlanesend Corn 4 F6
Shortlees E Ayrs 257 B10
Shortmoor Devon 28 G2
Dorset 29 G7
Shorton Torbay 9 C7
Shortroods Renfs 267 B9
Shortstanding Glos 79 C9
Shortstown Beds 103 B11
Short Street Wilts 45 D10
Shortwood Glos 80 F4
S Glos 61 D7
Shorwell IoW 20 E5
Shoscombe Bath 45 B8
Shoscombe Vale Bath 45 B8
Shotatton Shrops 149 E7
Shotesham Norf 142 D5
Shotgate Essex 88 G3
Shotley Northants 137 D8
Suff 108 D4
Shotley Bridge Durham 242 G3
Shotleyfield Northumb 242 G3
Shotley Gate Suff 108 E4
Shottenden Kent 54 C4
Shottermill Sur 49 G11
Shottery Warks 118 G3
Shotteswell Warks 101 B8
Shottisham Suff 108 C6
Shottle Derbys 170 F4
Shottlegate Derbys 170 F4
Shotton Durham 234 D4
Durham 234 F3
Flint 166 B4
Northumb 242 B6
Northumb 263 C8
Shotton Colliery Durham 234 C3
Shotts N Lnrk 269 C7
Shotwick Ches W 182 G4
Shouldham Norf 140 B3
Shouldham Thorpe Norf 140 B3
Shoulton Worcs 116 F6
Shover's Green E Sus 53 G7
Shraleybrook Staffs 168 F3
Shrawardine Shrops 149 F8
Shrawley Worcs 116 E6
Shreding Green Bucks 66 C4
Shrewley Warks 118 D4
Shrewley Common Warks 118 D4
Shrewsbury Shrops 149 G9
Shrewton Wilts 46 E5
Shripney W Sus 22 C6
Shrivenham Oxon 63 B8
Shropham Norf 141 E9
Shroton or Iwerne Courtney Dorset 30 E5
Shrub End Essex 107 G9
Shrubs Hill Sur 66 F3
Shrutherhill S Lnrk 268 F5
Shucknall Hereford 97 C11
Shudy Camps Cambs 106 C2
Shulishadermor Highld 298 E4
Shulista Highld 298 B4
Shuna Ho Argyll 275 C8
Shurdington Glos 80 B6
Shurlock Row Windsor 65 E10
Shurnock Worcs 117 E10
Shurrery Highld 310 D4
Shurrery Lodge Highld 310 D4
Shurton Som 43 E8
Shustoke Warks 134 E4
Shute Devon 15 B11
Devon 26 G5
Shute End Wilts 31 B11
Shutford Oxon 101 C7
Shut Heath Staffs 151 E7
Shuthonger Glos 99 D7
Shutlanger Northants 120 G4
Shutta Corn 6 E5
Shutt Green Staffs 133 B7
Shuttington Warks 134 B5
Shuttlesfield Kent 55 E7
Shuttlewood Derbys 187 G7
Shuttleworth Gtr Man 195 D10
Shutton Hereford 98 F3
Shwt Bridgend 57 D11
Siabost bho Dheas W Isles 304 D4
Siabost bho Thuath W Isles 304 D4
Siadar W Isles 304 C5
Siadar Iarach W Isles 304 C5
Siadar Uarach W Isles 304 C5
Sibbaldbie Dumfries 248 F4
Sibbertoft Northants 136 G3
Sibdon Carwood Shrops 131 G8
Sibford Ferris Oxon 101 D7
Sibford Gower Oxon 101 D7
Sible Hedingham Essex 106 E5
Sibley's Green Essex 106 F2
Sibsey Lincs 174 E5
Sibsey Fen Side Lincs 174 E4
Sibson Cambs 137 D11
Leics 135 C7
Sibster Highld 310 D7
Sibthorpe Notts 172 F3
Notts 188 G2
Sibton Suff 127 D7
Sibton Green Suff 127 C7
Sicklesmere Suff 125 E7
Sicklinghall N Yorks 206 D3
Sid Devon 15 D8
Sidbrook Som 28 B3
Sidbury Devon 15 C8
Shrops 132 F3
Sidcot N Som 44 B2
Sidcup London 68 E3
Siddal W Yorks 196 C6
Siddick Cumb 228 E6
Siddington Ches E 184 G4
Glos 81 F8
Siddington Heath Ches E 184 G4
Sidemoor Worcs 117 C9
Side of the Moor Gtr Man 195 E8
Sidestrand Norf 160 B5
Sideway Stoke 168 G5
Sidford Devon 15 C8
Sidlesham W Sus 22 D5
Sidlesham Common W Sus 22 C5
Sidley E Sus 38 F2
Sidlow Sur 51 D9
Sidmouth Devon 15 D8
Sidway Staffs 150 B5
Sigford Devon 13 G11
Sigglesthorne E Yorks 209 D9
Sighthill Edin 280 G3
Glasgow 268 B2
Sigingstone / Tresigin V Glam 58 E3
Signet Oxon 82 C2
Sigwells Som 29 C10
Silchester Hants 64 G6
Sildinis W Isles 305 G4
Sileby Leics 153 F11
Silecroft Cumb 210 C2
Silfield Norf 142 D2
Silford Devon 24 B6
Silian Ceredig 111 G11
Silkstead Hants 32 C6
Silkstone S Yorks 197 F9
Silkstone Common S Yorks 197 G9
Silk Willoughby Lincs 173 G9
Silloth Cumb 238 G4
Sills Northumb 251 C8
Sillyearn Moray 302 D5
Siloh Carms 94 D4
Silpho N Yorks 227 G9
Silsden W Yorks 204 D6
Silsoe C Beds 103 D11
Silton Dorset 30 B3
Silverburn Midloth 270 C4
Silverdale Lancs 211 E9
Staffs 168 F4
Silverdale Green Lancs 211 E9
Silver End Essex 88 B4
W Mid 133 F8
Silvergate Norf 160 D3
Silver Green Norf 142 E5
Silverhill E Sus 38 E3
Silver Hill E Sus 38 B2
Silverhill Park E Sus 38 E4
Silver Knap Som 29 C11
Silverknowes Edin 280 F4
Silverley's Green Suff 126 B5
Silvermuir S Lnrk 269 F8
Silverstone Northants 102 C3
Silver Street Glos 80 E3
Kent 69 G11
Som 27 C11
Som 44 G4
Worcs 117 B11
Silverton Devon 27 G7
W Dunb 277 F8
Silvertonhill S Lnrk 268 E4
Silvertown London 68 D2
Silverwell Corn 4 F4
Silvington Shrops 116 B2
Silwick Shetland 313 J4
Sim Hill S Yorks 197 G9
Simister Gtr Man 195 F10
Simmondley Derbys 185 C8
Simm's Cross Halton 183 D8
Simm's Lane End Mers 194 G4
Simonburn Northumb 241 C9
Simonsbath Som 41 F9
Simonsburrow Devon 27 D10
Simonside T&W 243 E8
Simonstone Lancs 203 G11
N Yorks 223 G7
Simprim Borders 272 F6
Simpson M Keynes 103 D7
Pembs 72 B5
Simpson Cross Pembs 72 B5
Simpson Green W Yorks 205 F9
Sinclair's Hill Borders 272 E6
Sinclairston E Ayrs 257 F11
Sinclairtown Fife 280 C5
Sinderby N Yorks 214 C6
Sinderhope Northumb 241 G8
Sinderland Green Gtr Man 184 C2
Sindlesham Wokingham 65 F9
Sinfin Derby 152 C6
Sinfin Moor Derby 153 C7
Singdean Borders 250 C3
Singleborough Bucks 102 E5
Single Hill Bath 45 B8
Singleton Lancs 202 F3
W Sus 34 E5
Singlewell Kent 69 E7
Singret Wrex 166 D4
Sinkhurst Green Kent 53 E10
Sinnahard Aberds 292 B6
Sinnington N Yorks 216 B4
Sinton Worcs 116 E6
Sinton Green Worcs 116 E6
Sion Hill Bath 61 F8
Sipson London 66 D5
Sirhowy Bl Gwent 77 C11
Sisland Norf 142 D6
Sissinghurst Kent 53 F9
Sisterpath Borders 272 F5
Siston S Glos 61 D7
Sithney Corn 2 D4
Sithney Common Corn 2 D4
Sithney Green Corn 2 D4
Sittingbourne Kent 70 G2
Six Ashes Staffs 132 F5
Six Bells Bl Gwent 78 E2
Sixhills Lincs 189 D11
Six Hills Leics 154 E2
Sixmile Kent 54 E6
Six Mile Bottom Cambs 123 F11
Sixpenny Handley Dorset 31 D7
Sizewell Suff 127 E9
Skaigh Devon 13 C8
Skail Highld 308 E7
Skaill Orkney 314 C4
Orkney 314 E2
Orkney 314 F5
Skares E Ayrs 258 F2
Skateraw E Loth 282 F4
Skaw Shetland 312 B8
Shetland 312 G7
Skeabost Highld 298 E4
Skeabrae Orkney 314 D2
Skeeby N Yorks 224 E4
Skeete Kent 54 E6
Skeffington Leics 136 C4
Skeffling E Yorks 201 D11
Skegby Notts 171 C7
Notts 188 G3
Skegness Lincs 175 C9
Skelberry Shetland 313 G6
Shetland 313 M5
Skelbo Highld 309 K7
Skelbo Street Highld 309 K7
Skelbrooke S Yorks 198 E4
Skeldyke Lincs 156 B6
Skelfhill Borders 249 C11
Skellingthorpe Lincs 188 G6
Skellister Shetland 313 H6
Skellorn Green Ches E 184 E6
Skellow S Yorks 198 E4
Skelmanthorpe W Yorks 197 E8
Skelmersdale Lancs 194 F3
Skelmonae Aberds 303 F8
Skelmorlie N Ayrs 266 B3
Skelmuir Aberds 303 E9
Skelpick Highld 308 D7
Skelton Cumb 230 D4
E Yorks 199 B9
N Yorks 223 E11
Redcar 226 B3
York 207 B7
Skelton-on-Ure N Yorks 215 F7
Skelwick Orkney 314 B4
Skelwith Bridge Cumb 220 E6
Skendleby Lincs 174 B6
Skendleby Psalter Lincs 190 G6
Skene Ho Aberds 293 C9
Skenfrith Mon 97 G9
Skerne E Yorks 208 B6
Skerne Park Darl 224 C5
Skeroblingarry Argyll 255 E8
Skerray Highld 308 C6
Skerricha Highld 306 D7
Skerryford Pembs 72 C6
Skerton Lancs 211 G9
Sketchley Leics 135 E8
Sketty Swansea 56 C6
Skewen / Sgiwen Neath 57 B8
Skewes Corn 5 B9
Skewsby N Yorks 216 E2
Skeyton Norf 160 D4
Skeyton Corner Norf 160 D5
Skiag Bridge Highld 307 G7
Skibo Castle Highld 309 L7
Skidbrooke Lincs 190 C6
Skidbrooke North End Lincs 190 B6
Skidby E Yorks 208 G6
Skilgate Som 27 B7
Skillington Lincs 155 D7
Skinburness Cumb 238 F4
Skinflats Falk 279 E8
Skinidin Highld 298 E2
Skinner's Bottom Corn 4 F4
Skinners Green W Berks 64 F2
Skinnet Highld 308 C5
Skinningrove Redcar 226 B4
Skipness Argyll 255 B9
Skippool Lancs 202 E3
Skiprigg Cumb 230 B3
Skipsea E Yorks 209 B9
Skipsea Brough E Yorks 209 C9
Skipton N Yorks 204 C5
Skipton-on-Swale N Yorks 215 D7
Skipwith N Yorks 207 F9
Skirbeck Lincs 174 G4
Skirbeck Quarter Lincs 174 G4
Skirethorns N Yorks 213 G9
Skirlaugh E Yorks 209 F8
Skirling Borders 260 B3
Skirmett Bucks 65 B9
Skirpenbeck E Yorks 207 B10
Skirwith Cumb 231 E8
Skirza Highld 310 C7
Skitby Cumb 239 D10
Skitham Lancs 202 E4
Skittle Green Bucks 84 E3
Skulamus Highld 295 C8
Skullomie Highld 308 C6
Skyborry Green Shrops 114 C5
Skye Green Essex 107 G7
Skye of Curr Highld 301 G9
Skyfog Pembs 90 F6
Skyreholme N Yorks 213 G11
Slack Derbys 170 C4
W Yorks 196 B3
W Yorks 196 D5
Slackcote Gtr Man 196 F3
Slackhall Derbys 185 E9
Slackhead Moray 302 C4
Slack Head Cumb 211 D9
Slackholme End Lincs 191 G8
Slacks of Cairnbanno Aberds 303 E8
Slad Glos 80 D5
Sladbrook Glos 98 F5
Slade Devon 27 F10
Devon 40 D4
Kent 54 C2
Pembs 72 B6
Slade End Oxon 83 G9
Slade Green London 68 D4
Slade Heath Staffs 133 B8
Slade Hooton S Yorks 187 D8
Sladen Green Hants 48 C2
Sladesbridge Corn 10 G6
Slades Green Worcs 99 E7
Slaggyford Northumb 240 G5
Slaidburn Lancs 203 C10
Slaithwaite W Yorks 196 E5
Slaley Derbys 170 D3
Northumb 241 F11
Slamannan Falk 279 G7
Slape Cross Som 43 F10
Slapewath Redcar 226 B2
Slapton Bucks 103 G8
Devon 8 G6
Northants 102 B2
Slateford Edin 280 G4
Slate Haugh Moray 302 C4
Slatepit Dale Derbys 170 B4
Slattocks Gtr Man 195 F11
Slaugham W Sus 36 B3
Slaughterbridge Corn 11 D8
Slaughterford Wilts 61 E10
Slaughter Hill Ches E 168 D2
Slawston Leics 136 E5
Slay Pits S Yorks 199 F7
Sleaford Hants 49 F10
Lincs 173 F9
Sleagill Cumb 221 B11
Sleap Shrops 149 D9
Sleapford Telford 150 F2
Sleapshyde Herts 86 D2
Sleastary Highld 309 K6
Slebech Pembs 73 B8
Sledge Green Worcs 98 E6
Sledmere E Yorks 217 G8
Sleeches Cross E Sus 52 G5
Sleepers Hill Hants 33 B7
Sleetbeck Cumb 240 B2
Sleet Moor Derbys 170 E6
Sleight Dorset 18 B5
Sleights N Yorks 227 D7
Slepe Dorset 18 C4
Sliabhna h-Airde W Isles 296 F3
Slickly Highld 310 C6
Sliddery N Ayrs 255 E10
Slideslow Worcs 117 C9
Sligachan Hotel Highld 294 C6
Sligneach Argyll 288 G4
Sligrachan Argyll 276 C3
Slimbridge Glos 80 E2
Slindon Staffs 150 C6
W Sus 35 F7
Slinfold W Sus 50 G6
Sling Glos 79 D9
Gwyn 163 B10
Slingsby N Yorks 216 E3
Slioch Aberds 302 F5
Slip End C Beds 85 B9
Herts 104 D5
Slippery Ford W Yorks 204 E6
Slipton Northants 121 B9
Slitting Mill Staffs 151 F10
Slochd Highld 301 G8
Slockavullin Argyll 275 D9
Slogan Moray 302 E3
Sloley Norf 160 E5
Sloncombe Devon 13 D10
Sloothby Lincs 191 G7
Slough Slough 66 D3
Slough Green Som 28 C3
W Sus 36 B3
Slough Hill Suff 125 G7
Sluggan Highld 301 G8
Sluggans Highld 298 E4
Slumbay Highld 295 B10
Sly Corner Kent 54 G3
Slyfield Sur 50 C3
Slyne Lancs 211 F9
Smailholm Borders 262 B4
Smallbridge Gtr Man 196 D2
Smallbrook Devon 14 B3
Glos 79 E9
Smallburgh Norf 160 E6
Smallburn Aberds 303 E10
E Ayrs 258 D5
Smalldale Derbys 185 E11
Derbys 185 F9
Small Dole W Sus 36 E2
Small End Lincs 174 D6
Smalley Derbys 170 G6
Smalley Common Derbys 170 G6
Smalley Green Derbys 170 G6
Smallfield Sur 51 E10
Smallford Herts 85 D11
Small Heath W Mid 134 F2
Smallholm Dumfries 238 B4
Small Hythe Kent 53 G11
Smallmarsh Devon 25 C10
Smallrice Staffs 151 C9
Smallridge Devon 28 G4
Smallshaw Gtr Man 196 G2
Smallthorne Stoke 168 E5
Small Way Som 44 G6
Smallwood Ches E 168 C4
Worcs 117 D10
Smallwood Green Suff 125 F8
Smallwood Hey Lancs 202 D3
Smallworth Norf 141 G10
Smannell Hants 47 D11
Smardale Cumb 222 D4
Smarden Kent 53 E11
Smarden Bell Kent 53 E11
Smart's Hill Kent 52 E4
Smaull Argyll 274 G3
Smeatharpe Devon 27 E11
Smeaton Fife 280 C5
Smeeth Kent 54 F5
Smeeton Westerby Leics 136 E3
Smelthouses N Yorks 214 G3
Smercleit W Isles 297 K3
Smerral Highld 310 F5
Smestow Staffs 133 E7
Smethcott Shrops 131 D9
Smethwick W Mid 133 F10
Smethwick Green Ches E 168 C4
Smirisary Highld 289 B8
Smisby Derbys 152 F6
Smite Hill Worcs 117 F7
Smithaleigh Devon 7 D11
Smithbrook W Sus 34 C6
Smith End Green Worcs 116 G5
Smithfield Cumb 239 D10
Smith Green Lancs 202 C5
Smithies S Yorks 197 F11
Smithincott Devon 27 E9
Smithley S Yorks 197 G11
Smith's End Herts 105 D8
Smiths Green Ches E 184 G4
Smith's Green Ches E 168 E3
Essex 105 G11
Essex 106 C3
Smithston Aberds 302 G5
Smithstown Highld 299 B7
Smithton Highld 301 E7
Smithwood Green Suff 125 G8
Smithy Bridge Gtr Man 196 D2
Smithy Gate Flint 181 F11
Smithy Green Ches E 184 G2
Gtr Man 184 D5
Smithy Houses Derbys 170 F5
Smithy Lane Ends Lancs 194 E2
Smock Alley W Sus 35 D9
Smockington Leics 135 F9
Smoky Row Bucks 84 D4
Smoogro Orkney 314 F3
Smug Oak Herts 85 E10
Smyrton S Ayrs 244 G4
Smythe's Green Essex 88 B6
Snagshall E Sus 38 C3
Snaigow House Perth 286 C4
Snailbeach Shrops 131 C7
Snails Hill Som 29 E7
Snailswell Herts 104 E3
Snailwell Cambs 124 D2
Snainton N Yorks 217 C8
Snaisgill Durham 232 F5
Snaith E Yorks 198 C6
Snape N Yorks 214 C5
Suff 127 F7
Snape Green Lancs 193 E11
Snape Hill Derbys 186 F5
S Yorks 198 G2
Snapper Devon 40 G5
Snaresbrook London 67 B11
Snarestone Leics 134 B6
Snarford Lincs 189 E9
Snargate Kent 39 B7
Snarraness Shetland 313 H4
Snatchwood Torf 78 E3
Snave Kent 39 B8
Sneachill Worcs 117 G8
Snead Powys 130 E6
Snead Common Worcs 116 D4
Sneads Green Worcs 117 D7
Sneath Common Norf 142 F3
Sneaton N Yorks 227 D7
Sneatonthorpe N Yorks 227 D8
Snedshill Telford 132 B4
Sneinton Nottingham 153 B11
Snelland Lincs 189 E9
Snelston Derbys 169 G11
Snetterton Norf 141 E9
Snettisham Norf 158 C3
Sneyd Green Stoke 168 F5
Sneyd Park Bristol 60 D5
Snibston Leics 153 G8
Snig's End Glos 98 F5
Snipeshill Kent 70 G2
Sniseabhal W Isles 297 H3
Snitter Northumb 252 C2
Snitterby Lincs 189 C7
Snitterfield Warks 118 F4
Snitterton Derbys 170 C3
Snitton Shrops 115 B11
Snittongate Shrops 115 B11
Snodhill Hereford 96 C6
Snodland Kent 69 G7
Snods Edge Northumb 242 G3
Snowden Hill S Yorks 197 G9
Snowdown Kent 55 C8
Snow End Herts 105 E8
Snow Hill Ches E 167 E10
W Yorks 197 C10
Snow Lea W Yorks 196 D5
Snowshill Glos 99 E11
Snow Street Norf 141 G11
Snydale W Yorks 198 D2
Soake Hants 33 E11
Soar Anglesey 178 G5
Carms 94 F2
Devon 9 G9
Gwyn 146 B2
Powys 95 E9
Soar-y-Mynydd Ceredig 112 G5
Soberton Hants 33 D10
Soberton Heath Hants 33 E10
Sockbridge Cumb 230 F6
Sockburn Darl 224 D6
Sockety Dorset 29 F7
Sodom Denb 181 G9
Shetland 313 G7
Wilts 62 C4
Sodylt Bank Shrops 148 B6
Soham Cambs 123 C11
Soham Cotes Cambs 123 B11
Soho London 67 C9
Som 45 D7
W Mid 133 F10
Solas W Isles 296 D4
Soldon Cross Devon 24 E4
Soldridge Hants 49 G7
Sole Street Kent 54 D5
Kent 69 F7
Solfach / Solva Pembs 90 G5
Solihull W Mid 118 B2
Solihull Lodge W Mid 117 B11
Sollers Dilwyn Hereford 115 F8
Sollers Hope Hereford 98 E2
Sollom Lancs 194 D3
Solva / Solfach Pembs 90 G5
Somerby Leics 154 G5
Lincs 200 F5
Somercotes Derbys 170 E6
Somerdale Bath 61 F7
Somerford Ches E 168 B4
Dorset 19 C9
Staffs 133 B7
Somerford Keynes Glos 81 G8
Somerley W Sus 22 D4
Somerleyton Suff 143 D9
Somersal Herbert Derbys 152 B2
Somersby Lincs 190 G4
Somersham Cambs 123 B7
Suff 107 B11
Somers Town London 67 C9
Ptsmth 21 B8
Somerton Newport 59 B10
Oxon 101 F9
Som 29 B7
Suff 124 G6
Somerton Hill Som 29 B7
Somerwood Shrops 149 G11
Sompting W Sus 35 G11
Sompting Abbotts W Sus 35 F11
Sonning Wokingham 65 D9
Sonning Common Oxon 65 C8
Sonning Eye Oxon 65 D9
Sontley Wrex 166 F4
Sookholme Notts 171 B8
Sopley Hants 19 B9
Sopwell Herts 85 D11
Sopworth Wilts 61 B10
Sorbie Dumfries 236 E6
Sordale Highld 310 C5
Sorisdale Argyll 288 C4
Sorley Devon 8 F4
Sorn E Ayrs 258 D3
Sornhill E Ayrs 258 C2
Sortat Highld 310 C6
Sotby Lincs 190 F2
Sothall S Yorks 186 E6
Sots Hole Lincs 173 C10
Sotterley Suff 143 G9
Soudley Shrops 131 E9
Shrops 150 D4
Soughley S Yorks 197 G7
Soughton / Sychdyn Flint 166 B2
Soulbury Bucks 103 F7
Soulby Cumb 222 C4
Cumb 230 F5
Souldern Oxon 101 E10
Souldrop Beds 121 E9
Sound Ches E 167 F10
Shetland 313 H5
Shetland 313 J6
Sound Heath Ches E 167 F10
Soundwell S Glos 60 D6
Sourhope Borders 263 E8
Sourin Orkney 314 C4
Sourlie N Ayrs 266 G6
Sour Nook Cumb 230 C3
Sourton Devon 12 C6
Soutergate Cumb 210 C4
South Acre Norf 158 G6
South Acton London 67 D7
South Alkham Kent 55 E8
Southall London 66 C6
South Allington Devon 9 G10
South Alloa Falk 279 C7
Southam Cumb 219 C9
Glos 99 F9
Warks 119 E8
South Ambersham W Sus 34 C6
Southampton Soton 32 E6
South Anston S Yorks 187 E8
South Ascot Windsor 66 F2
South Ashford Kent 54 E4
South Auchmachar Aberds 303 E9
Southay Som 28 D6
South Baddesley Hants 20 B3
South Ballachulish Highld 284 B4
South Balloch S Ayrs 245 D8
South Bank Redcar 234 G6
York 207 C7
South Barrow Som 29 B10
South Beach Northumb 243 B8
South Beach / Marian-y-de Gwyn 145 C7
South Beddington London 67 G9
South Benfleet Essex 69 B9
South Bents T&W 243 E10
South Bersted W Sus 22 C6
South Blainslie Borders 271 G10
South Bockhampton Dorset 19 B9
Southborough Bromley 68 F2
Kent 52 E5
Kingston-upon-Thames 67 F7
Southbourne Bmouth 19 C8
W Sus 22 B3
South Bramwith S Yorks 198 E6
South Brent Devon 8 D3
South Brewham Som 45 F8
South Bromley London 67 C11
Southbrook Wilts 45 G10
South Broomage Falk 279 E7
South Broomhill Northumb 252 D6
Southburgh Norf 141 C9
South Burlingham Norf 143 B7
Southburn E Yorks 208 C5
South Cadbury Som 29 B10
South Cairn Dumfries 236 C1
South Carlton Lincs 189 F7
Notts 187 E9
South Carne Corn 11 E10
South Cave E Yorks 208 G4
South Cerney Glos 81 F8
South Chailey E Sus 36 D5
South Chard Som 28 F4
South Charlton Northumb 264 E5
South Cheriton Som 29 C11
Southchurch Sthend 70 B2
South Church Durham 233 F10
South Cliffe E Yorks 208 F3
South Clifton Notts 188 G4
South Clunes Highld 300 E5
South Cockerington Lincs 190 D5
South Common Devon 28 G4
Southcoombe Oxon 100 F6
South Cornelly Bridgend 57 E10
South Corriegills N Ayrs 256 C2
South Corrielaw Dumfries 248 G5
Southcote Reading 65 E7
Southcott Corn 11 B9
Devon 24 D6
Wilts 47 B7
Southcourt Bucks 84 C4
South Cove Suff 143 G9
South Creagan Argyll 289 E11
South Creake Norf 159 B7
Southcrest Worcs 117 D10
South Crosland W Yorks 196 E6
South Croxton Leics 154 G3
South Croydon London 67 G10
South Cuil Highld 298 C3
South Dalton E Yorks 208 D5
South Darenth Kent 68 F5
Southdean Borders 250 B4
Southdene Mers 182 B6
South Denes Norf 143 C10
Southdown Bath 61 G8
Corn 7 E8
South Down Hants 33 C7
Som 28 E2
South Duffield N Yorks 207 G9
South Dunn Highld 310 D5
South Earlswood Sur 51 D9
Southease E Sus 36 F6
South Elkington Lincs 190 D3
South Elmsall W Yorks 198 E3
South Elphinstone E Loth 281 G7
Southend Argyll 255 G7
Bucks 65 B9
Glos 80 F2
London 67 E11
Oxon 83 E9
W Berks 64 D2
W Berks 64 E5
Wilts 63 E7
South End Beds 103 B10
Bucks 103 F7
Cumb 210 G4
E Yorks 209 E9
Hants 31 D10

South-end Herts 86 B6
South End N Lincs 200 C6
Norf 141 E9
Southend-on-Sea
Sthend 69 B11
Southerhouse
Shetland 313 K5
Southerly Devon 12 D6
Southernby Cumb 230 D3
Southern Cross
Brighton 36 F3
Southernden Kent 53 D11
Southerndown
V Glam 57 G11
Southerness
Dumfries 237 D11
Southern Green
Herts 104 E6
South Erradale
Highld 299 B7
Southery Norf 140 E2
Southey Green
Essex 106 E5
South Fambridge
Essex 88 F5
South Farnborough
Hants 49 C11
South Fawley
W Berks 63 C11
South Ferriby
N Lincs 200 C3
Southfield Northumb 243 B7
South Field E Yorks 200 B4
Windsor 66 D3
Southfields London 67 E9
Thurrock 69 C7
Southfleet Kent 68 E6
South Flobbets
Aberds 303 F7
Southford IoW 20 F6
South Garth
Shetland 312 D7
South Garvan
Highld 289 B11
Southgate Ceredig 111 A11
London 86 G3
Norf 159 C7
Norf 160 E2
Swansea 56 D5
W Sus 51 F9
South Glendale
W Isles 297 K3
South Gluss
Shetland 312 F5
South Godstone
Sur 51 D11
South Gorley Hants 31 E11
South Gosforth
T&W 242 D6
South Green Essex 87 G11
Essex 89 B8
Kent 69 G11
Norf 157 F10
Norf 159 G11
Suff 126 B3
South Gyle Edin 280 G3
South-haa Shetland 312 E5
South Hackney
London 67 C11
South Ham Hants 48 C6
South Hampstead
London 67 C9
South Hanningfield
Essex 88 F2
South Harefield
London 66 B5
South Harrow London 66 B6
South Harting
W Sus 34 D3
South Hatfield Herts 86 D2
South Hayling Hants 21 B10
South Hazelrigg
Northumb 264 C3
South Heath Bucks 84 E6
Essex 89 B10
South Heighton
E Sus 23 E7
South-heog
Shetland 312 E5
South Hetton
Durham 234 B3
South Hiendley
W Yorks 197 E11
South Hill Corn 12 G2
N Som 43 B10
Pembs 72 C4
South Hinksey Oxon 83 E8
South Hole Devon 24 C2
South Holme
N Yorks 216 D3
South Holmwood
Sur 51 D7
South Hornchurch
London 68 C4
South Huish Devon 8 G3
South Hykeham
Lincs 172 C6
South Hylton T&W 243 F9
Southill C Beds 104 C3
Dorset 17 E9
Southington Hants 48 D4
South Kelsey Lincs 189 B8
South Kensington
London 67 D9
South Kessock
Highld 300 E6
South Killingholme
N Lincs 201 D7
South Kilvington
N Yorks 215 C8
South Kilworth
Leics 136 G2
South Kirkby
W Yorks 198 E2
South Kirkton
Aberds 293 C9
South Kiscadale
N Ayrs 256 D2
South Knighton
Devon 14 G2
Leicester 136 C2
South Kyme Lincs 173 F11
South Lambeth
London 67 D10
South Lancing
W Sus 35 G11
Southlands Dorset 17 F9
South Lane S Yorks 197 F9
Southleigh Devon 15 C10
South Leigh Oxon 82 D5
South Leverton
Notts 188 E3
South Littleton
Worcs 99 B11
South Lopham
Norf 141 G10
South Luffenham
Rutland 137 C8
South Malling E Sus 36 E6
Southmarsh Som 45 G8
South Marston
Swindon 63 B7
Southmead Bristol 60 D5
South Merstham Sur 51 C9
South Middleton
Northumb 263 E11
South Milford
N Yorks 206 G5
South Millbrex
Aberds 303 E8
South Milton Devon 8 G4
South Mimms Herts 86 E2
Southminster Essex 89 F7
South Molton Devon 26 B2
Southmoor Oxon 82 F5
South Moor Durham 242 G5
South Moreton Oxon 64 B5
South Mundham
W Sus 22 C5
South Muskham
Notts 172 D3
South Newbald
E Yorks 208 F4
South Newbarns
Cumb 210 F4
South Newington
Oxon 101 E8
South Newsham
Northumb 243 B8
South Newton Wilts 46 G5
South Normanton
Derbys 170 D6
South Norwood
London 67 F10
South Nutfield Sur 51 D10
South Ockendon
Thurrock 68 C5
Southoe Cambs 122 E3
Southolt Suff 126 D3
South Ormsby Lincs 190 F5
Southorpe Pboro 137 C11
South Ossett
W Yorks 197 D9
South Otterington
N Yorks 215 B7
Southover Dorset 17 C8
E Sus 36 F6
E Sus 37 B11
South Owersby
Lincs 189 C9
Southowram
W Yorks 196 C6
South Oxhey Herts 85 G10
South Park Sur 51 D8
South Pelaw
Durham 243 G7
South Perrott Dorset 29 F7
South Petherton
Som 28 D6
South Petherwin
Corn 12 E2
South Pickenham
Norf 141 C7
South Pill Corn 7 D8
South Pool Devon 8 G5
South Poorton
Dorset 16 B6
Southport Mers 193 D10
South Port Argyll 284 E4
Southpunds
Shetland 313 L6
South Quilquox
Aberds 303 F8
South Radworthy
Devon 41 G9
South Rauceby
Lincs 173 F8
South Raynham
Norf 159 E7
South Reddish
Gtr Man 184 C5
Southrepps Norf 160 B5
South Reston Lincs 190 E6
Southrey Lincs 173 B10
Southrop Glos 81 E11
Oxon 101 E7
Southrope Hants 49 E7
South Ruislip London 66 B6
South Runcton Norf 140 B2
South Scarle Notts 172 C4
Southsea Ptsmth 21 B8
Wrex 166 E4
South Shian Argyll 289 E11
South Shields T&W 243 D9
South Shore Blkpool 202 G2
South Side Durham 233 F8
Orkney 314 D5
South Somercotes
Lincs 190 C6
South Stainley
N Yorks 214 G6
South Stainmore
Cumb 222 C6
South Stanley
Durham 242 G5
South Stifford
Thurrock 68 D6
Southstoke Bath 61 G8
South Stoke Oxon 64 C6
W Sus 35 F8
South Stour Kent 54 F4
South Street E Sus 36 D5
Kent 54 B5
Kent 68 G6
Kent 69 G10
Kent 70 F6
London 52 B2
South Tawton Devon 13 C9
South Tehidy Corn 4 G3
South Thoresby
Lincs 190 F6
South Tidworth Wilts 47 D8
South Tottenham
London 67 B10
Southtown Norf 143 B10
Orkney 314 G4
Som 28 D4
Som 44 F5
South Town Devon 14 E5
Hants 49 F7
South Twerton Bath 61 G8
South Ulverston
Cumb 210 D6
South View Hants 48 C6
Southville Devon 8 G4
Torf 78 F3
South Voxter
Shetland 313 G5
Southwaite Cumb 230 C4
South Walsham
Norf 161 G7
Southwark London 67 D10
South Warnborough
Hants 49 D8
Southwater W Sus 35 B11
Southwater Street
W Sus 35 B11
Southway Plym 7 C9
Som 44 E4
South Weald Essex 87 G9
South Weirs Hants 32 G3
Southwell Dorset 17 G9
Notts 172 E2
South Weston Oxon 84 F2
South Wheatley
Corn 11 C10
Notts 188 D3
South Whiteness
Shetland 313 J5
Southwick Hants 33 F10
Northants 137 E10
Som 43 D11
T&W 243 F9
Wilts 45 B10
W Sus 36 F2
South Widcombe
Bath 44 B5
South Wigston
Leics 135 D11
South Willesborough
Kent 54 E4
South Willingham
Lincs 189 E11
South Wimbledon
London 67 E9
South Wingate
Durham 234 E4
South Wingfield
Derbys 170 D5
South Witham Lincs 155 F8
Southwold Suff 127 B10
South Wonford
Devon 24 F5
South Wonston
Hants 48 F3
Southwood Derbys 153 E7
Hants 49 B10
Norf 143 B7
Som 44 G5
Worcs 116 E4
South Woodford
London 86 G6
South Woodham Ferrers
Essex 88 F4
South Wootton Norf 158 E2
South Wraxall Wilts 61 G10
South Yardley
W Mid 134 G2
South Yarrows
Highld 310 E7
South Yeo Devon 25 G8
South Zeal Devon 13 C9
Soval Lodge
W Isles 304 F5
Sowber Gate
N Yorks 215 B7
Sowerby N Yorks 215 C8
W Yorks 196 C4
Sowerby Bridge
W Yorks 196 C5
Sowerby Row Cumb 230 D3
Sower Carr Lancs 202 E3
Sowley Green Suff 124 G4
Sowood W Yorks 196 D5
Sowood Green
W Yorks 196 D5
Sowton Devon 14 C5
Sowton Barton
Devon 14 D2
Soyal Highld 309 K5
Soyland Town
W Yorks 196 C4
Spacey Houses
N Yorks 206 C2
Spa Common Norf 160 C5
Spalding Lincs 156 E4
Spaldington
E Yorks 207 G11
Spaldwick Cambs 122 C2
Spalford Notts 172 B4
Spanby Lincs 155 B11
Spango Invclyd 276 G4
Spanish Green Hants 49 B7
Sparham Norf 159 F11
Sparhamhill Norf 159 F11
Spark Bridge Cumb 210 C6
Sparkbrook
W Mid 133 G11
Sparkford Som 29 B10
Sparkhill W Mid 133 G11
Sparkwell Devon 7 D11
Sparl Shetland 312 G5
Sparnon Corn 1 E3
Sparnon Gate Corn 4 G3
Sparrow Green
Norf 159 G9
Sparrow Hill Som 44 C2
Sparrowpit Derbys 185 E9
Sparrow's Green
E Sus 52 G6
Sparsholt Hants 48 G2
Oxon 63 B10
Spartylea Northumb 232 B3
Spath Staffs 151 B11
Spaunton N Yorks 226 G4
Spaxton Som 43 F8
Spean Bridge Highld 290 E4
Spear Hill W Sus 35 D10
Spearywell Hants 32 B4
Speckington Som 29 C9
Speed Gate Kent 68 F5
Speedwell Bristol 60 E6
Speen Bucks 84 F4
W Berks 64 F3
Speeton N Yorks 218 E2
Speke Mers 182 E6
Speldhurst Kent 52 E5
Spellbrook Herts 87 B7
Spelsbury Oxon 101 G7
Spelter Bridgend 57 C11
Spen W Yorks 197 B7
Spencers Wood
Wokingham 65 F8
Spen Green Ches E 168 C4
Spennells Worcs 116 C6
Spennithorne
N Yorks 214 B2
Spennymoor
Durham 233 E11
Spernall Warks 117 E11
Spetchley Worcs 117 G7
Spetisbury Dorset 30 G6
Spexhall Suff 143 G7
Speybank Highld 291 C10
Spey Bay Moray 302 C3
Speybridge Highld 301 G10
Speyview Moray 302 E2
Spillardsford
Aberds 303 D10
Spilsby Lincs 174 B6
Spindlestone
Northumb 264 C5
Spinkhill Derbys 187 F7
Spinney Hill
Northants 120 E5
Spinney Hills
Leicester 136 C2
Spinningdale Highld 309 L6
Spion Kop Notts 171 B9
Spirthill Wilts 62 D3
Spital Mers 182 E4
Windsor 66 D3
Spitalbrook Herts 86 D5
Spitalfields London 67 C10
Spitalhill Derbys 169 F11
Spital Hill S Yorks 187 C10
Spital in the Street
Lincs 189 D7
Spital Tongues
T&W 242 D6
Spithurst E Sus 36 D6
Spittal Dumfries 236 D5
E Loth 281 F9
E Yorks 207 C11
Highld 310 D5
Northumb 273 E10
Pembs 91 G9
Stirl 277 D10
Spittalfield Perth 286 C5
Spittal Houses
S Yorks 186 B5
Spittal of Glenmuick
Aberds 292 E5
Spittal of Glenshee
Perth 292 F3
Spittlegate Lincs 155 C8
Spixworth Norf 160 F4
Splatt Corn 10 F4
Corn 11 D10
Devon 25 F10
Som 43 F8
Splayne's Green
E Sus 36 C6
Splott Cardiff 59 D7
Spofforth N Yorks 206 C3
Spondon Derby 153 B8
Spon End W Mid 118 B6
Spon Green Flint 166 C3
Spooner Row Norf 141 D11
Spoonleygate
Shrops 132 D6
Sporle Norf 158 G6
Spotland Bridge
Gtr Man 195 E11
Spott E Loth 282 F3
Spratton Northants 120 C4
Spreakley Sur 49 E10
Spreyton Devon 13 B9
Spriddlestone Devon 7 E10
Spridlington Lincs 189 E8
Sprig's Alley Oxon 84 F3
Springbank Glos 99 G8
Spring Bank Cumb 229 G10
Springboig Glasgow 268 C3
Springbourne
Bmouth 19 C8
Springburn Glasgow 268 B2
Spring Cottage
Leics 152 F6
Spring End N Yorks 223 F9
Springfield Argyll 275 F11
Caerph 77 F11
Dumfries 239 D8
Essex 88 D2
Fife 287 F7
Gtr Man 194 F5
Highld 300 C6
M Keynes 103 D7
Moray 301 D10
W Mid 133 D8
W Mid 133 F9
W Mid 133 G11
Springfields Stoke 168 G5
Spring Gardens Som 45 D9
Spring Green Lancs 204 E4
Spring Grove London 67 D7
Springhead
Gtr Man 196 G3
Springhill E Renf 267 D10
IoW 20 B6
N Lnrk 269 D7
Staffs 133 B11
Staffs 133 C9
Spring Hill Gtr Man 196 F2
Lancs 195 B8
W Mid 133 D7
Springholm
Dumfries 237 C10
Springkell Dumfries 239 B7
Spring Park London 67 F11
Springside N Ayrs 257 B9
Springthorpe Lincs 188 D5
Spring Vale S Yorks 197 G9
Spring Valley IoM 192 E4
Springwell Essex 105 C10
T&W 243 F7
T&W 243 F9
Springwells
Dumfries 248 E3
Sproatley E Yorks 209 G9
Sproston Green
Ches W 168 B2
Sprotbrough
S Yorks 198 G4
Sproughton Suff 108 C2
Sprouston Borders 263 B7
Sprowston Norf 160 G4
Sproxton Leics 155 E7
N Yorks 216 C2
Sprunston Cumb 230 B3
Spunhill Shrops 149 C8
Spurlands End Bucks 84 F5
Spurstow Ches E 167 D9
Spurtree Shrops 116 D2
Spynie Moray 302 C2
Spyway Dorset 16 C6
Square and Compass
Pembs 91 E7
Squires Gate
Blkpool 202 G2
Sraid Ruadh Argyll 288 E1
Srannda W Isles 296 C6
Sronphadruig Lodge
Perth 291 F9
Stableford Shrops 132 D5
Staffs 150 B6
Stacey Bank
S Yorks 186 C3
Stackhouse N Yorks 212 F6
Stackpole Pembs 73 F7
Stackpole Quay
Pembs 73 F7
Stacksford Norf 141 E11
Stacksteads Lancs 195 C10
Stackyard Green
Suff 107 B9
Staddiscombe Plym 7 E10
Staddlethorpe
E Yorks 199 B10
Staddon Devon 24 C3
Devon 24 G5
Staden Derbys 185 G9
Stadhampton Oxon 83 F10
Stadhlaigearraidh
W Isles 297 H3
Stadmorslow Staffs 168 D5
Staffield Cumb 230 C6
Staffin Highld 298 C4
Stafford Staffs 151 E8
Stafford Park
Telford 132 B4
Stafford's Corner
Essex 89 B7
Stafford's Green
Dorset 29 C10
Stagbatch Hereford 115 F9
Stagden Cross
Essex 87 C10
Stagehall Borders 271 G9
Stagsden Beds 103 B9
Stagsden West End
Beds 103 B9
Stag's Head Devon 25 B11
Stain Highld 310 C7
Stainburn Cumb 228 F6
N Yorks 205 D10
Stainby Lincs 155 E8
Staincliffe W Yorks 197 C8
Staincross S Yorks 197 E10
Staindrop Durham 233 G8
Staines Green Herts 86 C3
Staines-upon-Thames
Sur 66 E4
Stainfield Lincs 155 D11
Lincs 189 G10
Stainforth N Yorks 212 F6
S Yorks 198 E6
Staining Lancs 202 F3
Stainland W Yorks 196 D5
Stainsacre N Yorks 227 D8
Stainsby Derbys 170 B6
Lincs 190 G4
Stainton Cumb 211 B10
Cumb 230 F5
Cumb 239 F9
Durham 223 B11
Mbro 225 C9
N Yorks 224 F2
S Yorks 187 C9
Stainton by Langworth
Lincs 189 F9
Staintondale
N Yorks 227 F9
Stainton le Vale
Lincs 189 C11
Stainton with Adgarley
Cumb 210 E5
Stair Cumb 229 G10
E Ayrs 257 E10
Stairfoot S Yorks 197 F11
Stairhaven Dumfries 236 D4
Staithes N Yorks 226 B5
Stakeford Northumb 253 F7
Stake Hill Gtr Man 195 F11
Stakenbridge Worcs 117 B7
Stake Pool Lancs 202 D4
Stalbridge Dorset 30 D2
Stalbridge Weston
Dorset 30 D2
Stalham Norf 161 D7
Stalham Green Norf 161 E7
Stalisfield Green
Kent 54 C3
Stallen Dorset 29 D10
Stallingborough
NE Lincs 201 E7
Stalling Busk
N Yorks 213 B8
Stallington Staffs 151 B8
Stalmine Lancs 202 D3
Stalmine Moss Side
Lancs 202 D3
Stalybridge Gtr Man 185 B7
Stambermill W Mid 133 G8
Stamborough Som 42 F4
Stambourne Essex 106 D4
Stambourne Green
Essex 106 D4
Stamford Lincs 137 B10
Stamford Bridge
Ches W 167 B7
E Yorks 207 B10
Stamfordham
Northumb 242 C3
Stamford Hill
London 67 B10
Stamperland
E Renf 267 D11
Stamshaw Ptsmth 33 G10
Stanah Cumb 220 B6
Lancs 202 E3
Stanborough Herts 86 C2
Stanbridge C Beds 103 G9
Dorset 31 G8
Stanbridgeford
C Beds 103 G9
Stanbrook Essex 106 F2
Worcs 98 B6
Stanbury W Yorks 204 F6
Stand Gtr Man 195 F9
N Lnrk 268 B5
Standburn Falk 279 G8
Standeford Staffs 133 B8
Standen Kent 53 E11
Standen Hall Lancs 203 E10
Standen Street
Kent 53 G10
Standerwick Som 45 C10
Standford Hants 49 G10
Standford Bridge
Telford 150 E4
Standingstone
Cumb 229 B11
Cumb 229 E7
Standish Glos 80 D4
Gtr Man 194 E5
Standish Lower Ground
Gtr Man 194 F5
Standlake Oxon 82 E5
Standon Hants 32 B6
Herts 105 G7
Staffs 150 B6
Standon Green End
Herts 86 B5
Stane N Lnrk 269 D7
Stanecastle N Ayrs 257 B8
Stanfield Norf 159 E8
Stoke 168 E5
Stanford C Beds 104 C3
Kent 54 F6
Norf 141 E7
Shrops 148 G6
Stanford Bishop
Hereford 116 G3
Stanford Bridge
Worcs 116 D4
Stanford Dingley
W Berks 64 E5
Stanford End
Wokingham 65 G8
Stanford Hills
Notts 153 E10
Stanford in the Vale
Oxon 82 G4
Stanford-le-Hope
Thurrock 69 C7
Stanford on Avon
Northants 119 B11
Stanford on Soar
Notts 153 E10
Stanford on Teme
Worcs 116 D4
Stanford Rivers
Essex 87 E8
Stanfree Derbys 187 G7
Stanground Pboro 138 D4
Stanhill Lancs 195 B8
Stanhoe Norf 158 B6
Stanhope Borders 260 D4
Durham 232 D5
Kent 54 E3
Stanion Northants 137 F8
Stank Cumb 210 E4
Stanklyn Worcs 117 C7
Stanks W Yorks 206 F3
Stanley Derbys 170 G6
Durham 242 G5
Lancs 194 F3
Notts 171 C7
Perth 286 D5
Shrops 132 G3
Shrops 132 G5
Staffs 168 E6
Wilts 62 E3
W Yorks 197 C10
Stanley Common
Derbys 170 G6
Stanley Crook
Durham 233 D9
Stanley Downton
Glos 80 E4
Stanley Ferry
W Yorks 197 C11
Stanley Gate Lancs 194 G2
Stanley Green
Ches E 184 E5
Poole 18 C6
Shrops 149 B10
Stanley Hill Hereford 98 C3
Stanley Moor Staffs 168 E6
Stanley Pontlarge
Glos 99 E9
Stanleytown Rhondda 77 G8
Stanlow Ches W 182 F6
Staffs 132 D5
Stanmer Brighton 36 F4
Stanmore Hants 33 B7
London 85 G11
Shrops 132 E4
W Berks 64 D3
Stanner Powys 114 F5
Stannergate Dundee 287 D8
Stannersburn
Northumb 250 F6
Stanners Hill Sur 66 G3
Stanningfield Suff 125 F7
Stanningley
W Yorks 205 G10
Stannington
Northumb 242 B6
S Yorks 186 D4
Stanpit Dorset 19 C9
Stansbatch Hereford 114 E6
Stansfield Suff 124 G5
Stanshope Staffs 169 E10
Stanstead Suff 106 B6
Stanstead Abbotts
Herts 86 C5
Stansted Kent 68 G6
Stansted Airport
Essex 105 G11
Stansted Mountfitchet
Essex 105 G10
Stanthorne
Ches W 167 B11
Stanton Glos 99 E11
Mon 96 G6
Northumb 252 F4
Staffs 169 F10
Suff 125 C9
Stantonbury
M Keynes 102 C6
Stanton by Bridge
Derbys 153 D7
Stanton-by-Dale
Derbys 153 B9
Stanton Chare Suff 125 C9
Stanton Drew Bath 60 G5
Stanton Fitzwarren
Swindon 81 G11
Stanton Gate Notts 153 B9
Stanton Harcourt
Oxon 82 D6
Stanton Hill Notts 171 C7
Stanton in Peak
Derbys 170 C2
Stanton Lacy Shrops 115 B9
Stanton Lees
Derbys 170 C3
Stanton Long
Shrops 131 E11
Stanton-on-the-Wolds
Notts 154 C2
Stanton Prior Bath 61 G7
Stanton St Bernard
Wilts 62 G5
Stanton St John
Oxon 83 D9
Stanton St Quintin
Wilts 62 D2
Stanton Street Suff 125 D9
Stanton under Bardon
Leics 153 G9
Stanton upon Hine
Heath Shrops 149 E11
Stanton Wick Bath 60 G6
Stantway Glos 80 C2
Stanwardine in the
Fields Shrops 149 E8
Stanwardine in the
Wood Shrops 149 D8
Stanway Essex 107 G8
Glos 99 E11
Stanway Green
Essex 107 G9
Suff 126 C4
Stanwell Sur 66 E5
Stanwell Moor Sur 66 E4
Stanwick Northants 121 C9
Stanwick-St-John
N Yorks 224 C3
Stanwix Cumb 239 F10
Stanycliffe
Gtr Man 195 F11
Stanydale Shetland 313 H4
Staoinebrig
W Isles 297 H3
Stape N Yorks 226 G5
Stapehill Dorset 31 G9
Stapeley Ches E 167 F11
Stapenhill Staffs 152 E5
Staple Kent 55 B9
Som 42 E6
Staplecross E Sus 38 C3
Staple Cross Devon 27 C8
Staplefield W Sus 36 B3
Staple Fitzpaine Som 28 D3
Stapleford Cambs 123 G9
Herts 86 B4
Leics 154 F6
Lincs 172 D5
Notts 153 B9
Wilts 46 F5
Stapleford Abbotts
Essex 87 G8
Stapleford Tawney
Essex 87 F8
Staplegrove Som 28 B2
Staplehay Som 28 C2
Staple Hill S Glos 61 D7
Worcs 117 C9
Staplehurst Kent 53 E9
Staple Lawns Som 28 D3
Staplers IoW 20 D6
Staples Hill W Sus 35 B8
Staplestreet Kent 70 G5
Stapleton Bristol 60 D6
Cumb 240 C2
Hereford 114 D6
Leics 135 D8
N Yorks 198 D4
N Yorks 224 C5
Shrops 131 C9
Som 29 C7
Stapley Som 27 E11
Staploe Beds 122 E2
Staplow Hereford 98 C3
Stapness Shetland 313 J4
Star Fife 287 G7
Pembs 92 E4
Som 44 B2
Stara Orkney 314 D2
Starbeck N Yorks 206 B2
Starbotton N Yorks 213 E9
Starcross Devon 14 E5
Stareton Warks 118 C6
Stargate T&W 242 E5
Star Hill Mon 79 E7
Starkholmes Derbys 170 D4
Starling Gtr Man 195 E9
Starlings Green
Essex 105 E9
Starr's Green E Sus 38 D3
Starston Norf 142 G4
Start Devon 8 G6
Startforth Durham 223 B10
Start Hill Essex 105 G10
Startley Wilts 62 C2
Startop's End Bucks 84 C6
Starveall S Glos 61 B9
Starvecrow Kent 52 D5
Statenborough Kent 55 B10
Statford St Andrew
Suff 127 E7
Statham Warr 183 D11
Stathe Som 28 B5
Stathern Leics 154 C5
Station Hill Cumb 229 B11
Station Town
Durham 234 D4
Statland Common
Norf 141 D10
Staughton Green
Cambs 122 D2
Staughton Highway
Cambs 122 E2
Staughton Moor
Beds 122 E2
Staunton Glos 79 C8
Glos 98 F5
Staunton in the Vale
Notts 172 G4
Staunton on Arrow
Hereford 115 E7
Staunton on Wye
Hereford 97 B7
Staupes N Yorks 205 B10
Staveley Cumb 211 B7
Cumb 221 F9
Derbys 186 G6
N Yorks 215 G7
Staveley-in-Cartmel
Cumb 211 B7
Staverton Devon 8 C5
Glos 99 G7
Northants 119 E10
Wilts 61 G11
Staverton Bridge
Glos 99 G7
Stawell Som 43 F11
Stawley Som 27 C9
Staxigoe Highld 310 D7
Staxton N Yorks 217 D10
Staylittle Ceredig 128 F2
Staylittle / Penffordd-
Lâs Powys 129 E7
Staynall Lancs 202 E3
Staythorpe Notts 172 E3
Stead W Yorks 205 D8
Steam Mills Glos 79 B10
Stean N Yorks 213 E11
Steanbow Som 44 F5
Stearsby N Yorks 216 E2
Steart Som 29 B9
Som 43 D9
Stebbing Essex 106 G3
Stebbing Green
Essex 106 G3
Stechford W Mid 134 F2
Stede Quarter Kent 53 F11
Stedham W Sus 34 C5
Steel Northumb 241 F10
Northumb 251 G9
Steel Bank S Yorks 186 D4
Steel Cross E Sus 52 G4
Steelend Fife 279 C10
Steele Road Borders 250 E2
Steeleroad-end
Borders 250 E2
Steel Green Cumb 210 D3
Steel Heath Shrops 149 B10
Steen's Bridge
Hereford 115 F10
Steep Hants 34 B2
Steephill IoW 21 F7
Steep Lane
W Yorks 196 C4
Steeple Dorset 18 E4
Essex 88 E6
Steeple Ashton Wilts 46 B2
Steeple Aston Oxon 101 F9
Steeple Barton
Oxon 101 G8
Steeple Bumpstead
Essex 106 C3
Steeple Claydon
Bucks 102 F3
Steeple Gidding
Cambs 138 G2
Steeple Langford
Wilts 46 F4
Steeple Morden
Cambs 104 C5
Steep Marsh Hants 34 B3
Steeraway Telford 132 B3
Steeton W Yorks 204 E6
Stein Highld 298 D2
Steinmanhill Aberds 303 E7
Stella T&W 242 E5
Stelling Minnis Kent 54 D6
Stelvio Newport 59 B9
Stembridge Som 28 C6
Swansea 56 C3
Stemster Highld 310 C5
Stemster Ho Highld 310 C5
Stenalees Corn 5 D10
Stenaquoy Orkney 314 C5
Stencoose Corn 4 F4
Stenhill Devon 27 E9
Stenhouse Dumfries 247 E8
Edin 280 G4
Stenhousemuir Falk 279 E7
Stenigot Lincs 190 E3
Stennack Corn 2 B5
Stenness Shetland 312 F4
Stenscholl Highld 298 C4
Stenso Orkney 314 D3
Stenson Derbys 152 D6
Stenton E Loth 282 G2
Fife 280 B5
Stentwood Devon 27 F10
Stenwith Lincs 154 B6
Stepaside Corn 5 F9
Pembs 73 D10
Powys 129 F11
Stepping Hill
Gtr Man 184 D6
Steppingley
C Beds 103 D10
Stepps N Lnrk 268 B3
Sterndale Moor
Derbys 169 B10
Sternfield Suff 127 E7
Sterridge Devon 40 D5
Stert Wilts 46 B4
Stetchworth Cambs 124 F2
Stevenage Herts 104 G4
Steven's Crouch
E Sus 38 D2
Stevenston N Ayrs 266 G5
Stevenstone Devon 25 D8

Sutton Scarsdale
Derbys ... 170 B6
Sutton Scotney Hants ... 48 F3
Sutton Street Suff ... 108 C6
Sutton under Brailes
Warks ... 100 D6
Sutton-under-Whitestonecliffe
N Yorks ... 215 C9
Sutton upon Derwent
E Yorks ... 207 D10
Sutton Valence
Kent ... 53 D10
Sutton Veny Wilts ... 45 E11
Sutton Waldron
Dorset ... 30 D5
Sutton Weaver
Ches W ... 183 F8
Sutton Wick Bath ... 44 B5
Oxon ... 83 G7
Swaby Lincs ... 190 F5
Swadlincote Derbys ... 152 F6
Swaffham Norf ... 140 B6
Swaffham Bulbeck
Cambs ... 123 E11
Swaffham Prior
Cambs ... 123 E11
Swafield Norf ... 160 C5
Swaile's Green E Sus ... 38 C3
Swainby N Yorks ... 225 E9
Swain House
W Yorks ... 205 F9
Swainshill Hereford ... 97 C9
Swainsthorpe Norf ... 142 C4
Swainswick Bath ... 61 F9
Swaithe S Yorks ... 197 G11
Swalcliffe Oxon ... 101 D7
Swalecliffe Kent ... 70 F6
Swallow Lincs ... 201 G7
Swallow Beck Lincs ... 173 B7
Swallowcliffe Wilts ... 31 B7
Swallowfield
Wokingham ... 65 G8
Swallowfields Devon ... 8 C5
Swallowhurst Cumb ... 220 G2
Swallownest
S Yorks ... 187 E7
Swallows Cross
Essex ... 87 F10
Swalwell T&W ... 242 E6
Swampton Hants ... 48 C2
Swanage Dorset ... 18 F6
Swanbach Ches E ... 167 G11
Swanbister Orkney ... 314 F3
Swanborough
Swindon ... 81 G11
Swan Bottom Bucks ... 84 D6
Swanbourne Bucks ... 102 F6
Swanbridge V Glam ... 59 F7
Swan Green
Ches W ... 184 G2
Suff ... 126 C5
Swanland E Yorks ... 200 B3
Swanley Glos ... 80 F2
Kent ... 68 F4
Swanley Bar Herts ... 86 E3
Swanley Village Kent ... 68 F4
Swanmore Hants ... 33 D9
IoW ... 21 C7
Swannay Orkney ... 314 D2
Swannington Leics ... 153 F8
Norf ... 160 F2
Swanpool Lincs ... 189 G7
Swanscombe Kent ... 68 E6
Swansea / Abertawe
Swansea ... 56 C6
Swanside Mers ... 182 C6
Swanston Edin ... 270 B4
Swan Street Essex ... 107 F7
Swanton Abbott
Norf ... 160 D5
Swanton Hill Norf ... 160 D5
Swanton Morley
Norf ... 159 F10
Swanton Novers
Norf ... 159 C10
Swanton Street
Kent ... 53 B11
Swan Village
W Mid ... 133 E9
Swanwick Derbys ... 170 E6
Hants ... 33 F8
Swanwick Green
Ches E ... 167 F9
Swarby Lincs ... 173 G8
Swarcliffe W Yorks ... 206 F3
Swardeston Norf ... 142 C4
Swarister Shetland ... 312 E7
Swarkestone
Derbys ... 153 D7
Swarland Northumb ... 252 C5
Swarraton Hants ... 48 F5
Swartha W Yorks ... 205 D7
Swarthmoor Cumb ... 210 D5
Swartland Orkney ... 314 D2
Swathwick Derbys ... 170 B5
Swaton Lincs ... 156 B2
Swavesey Cambs ... 123 D7
Sway Hants ... 19 B11
Swayfield Lincs ... 155 E9
Swaythling Soton ... 32 D6
Sweet Green Worcs ... 116 E2
Sweetham Devon ... 14 B3
Sweethaws E Sus ... 37 B8
Sweethay Som ... 28 C2
Sweetholme Cumb ... 221 B11
Sweethouse Corn ... 5 C11
Sweets Corn ... 11 B9
Sweetshouse Corn ... 5 C11
Swefling Suff ... 126 E6
Swell Som ... 28 C5
Swelling Hill Hants ... 49 G7
Swepstone Leics ... 153 G7
Swerford Oxon ... 101 E7
Swettenham Ches E ... 168 B4
Swetton N Yorks ... 214 E3
Swffryd Caerph ... 78 F2
Swiftsden E Sus ... 38 B2
Swift's Green Kent ... 53 E11
Swilland Suff ... 126 G3
Swillbrook Lancs ... 202 G5
Swillington
W Yorks ... 206 G3
Swillington Common
W Yorks ... 206 G3
Swimbridge Devon ... 25 B10
Swimbridge Newland
Devon ... 40 G6
Swinbrook Oxon ... 82 C3
Swincliffe N Yorks ... 205 B10
W Yorks ... 197 B8
Swincombe Devon ... 41 E7
Swinden N Yorks ... 204 C3
Swinderby Lincs ... 172 C5
Swindon Glos ... 99 G8
Staffs ... 133 E7
Swindon ... 63 C7
Swine E Yorks ... 209 F8
Swinefleet E Yorks ... 199 C9
Swineford S Glos ... 61 F7
Swineshead Beds ... 121 D11
Lincs ... 174 G2
Swineshead Bridge
Lincs ... 174 G2
Swinethorpe Lincs ... 172 B5
Swiney Highld ... 310 F6
Swinford Leics ... 119 B11
Oxon ... 82 D6
Swingate Notts ... 171 G8
Swingbrow Cambs ... 139 F7
Swingfield Minnis
Kent ... 55 E8
Swingfield Street
Kent ... 55 E8
Swingleton Green
Suff ... 107 B9
Swinhoe Northumb ... 264 D6
Swinhope Lincs ... 190 B2
Swining Shetland ... 312 G6
Swinister Shetland ... 312 E5
Shetland ... 313 L6
Swinithwaite
N Yorks ... 213 B10
Swinmore Common
Hereford ... 98 C3
Swinnie Borders ... 262 F4
Swinnow Moor
W Yorks ... 205 G10
Swinscoe Staffs ... 169 F10
Swinside Cumb ... 229 G10
Swinside Townfoot
Borders ... 262 F6
Swinstead Lincs ... 155 E10
Swinton Borders ... 272 F6
Glasgow ... 268 C3
Gtr Man ... 195 G9
N Yorks ... 214 D4
N Yorks ... 216 E5
S Yorks ... 186 B6
Swinton Bridge
S Yorks ... 187 B7
Swinton Hill Borders ... 272 F6
Swintonmill Borders ... 272 F6
Swinton Park
Gtr Man ... 195 G9
Swiss Valley Carms ... 75 E8
Swithland Leics ... 153 G10
Swordale Highld ... 300 C5
Highld ... 309 K6
Swordland Highld ... 295 F9
Swordly Highld ... 308 C7
Sworton Heath
Ches E ... 183 E11
Swyddffynnon
Ceredig ... 112 D3
Swynnerton Staffs ... 151 B7
Swyre Dorset ... 16 D6
Sycamore Devon ... 28 F3
Sychdyn / Soughton
Flint ... 166 B2
Sychtyn Powys ... 129 B9
Sydallt Wrex ... 166 D4
Syde Glos ... 81 C7
Sydenham London ... 67 E11
Oxon ... 84 E2
Som ... 43 F10
Sydenham Damerel
Devon ... 12 F4
Syderstone Norf ... 158 C6
Sydling St Nicholas
Dorset ... 17 B8
Sydmonton Hants ... 48 B3
Sydney Ches E ... 168 D2
Syerston Notts ... 172 F2
Syke Gtr Man ... 195 D11
Sykehouse S Yorks ... 198 D6
Sykes Lancs ... 203 C8
Syleham Suff ... 126 B4
Sylen Carms ... 75 D8
Symbister Shetland ... 313 G7
Symington Borders ... 271 F8
S Ayrs ... 257 C9
S Lnrk ... 259 B11
Symondsbury Dorset ... 16 C4
Symonds Green
Herts ... 104 F4
Symonds Yat
Hereford ... 79 B9
Synderford Dorset ... 28 G5
Synod Inn / Post Mawr
Ceredig ... 111 G8
Synton Borders ... 261 E11
Synton Mains
Borders ... 261 E11
Synwell Glos ... 80 G3
Syre Highld ... 308 E6
Syreford Glos ... 99 G10
Syresham Northants ... 102 C2
Syster Highld ... 310 C6
Syston Leics ... 154 G2
Lincs ... 172 G6
Sytchampton Worcs ... 116 D6
Sytch Ho Green
Shrops ... 132 E5
Sytch Lane Telford ... 150 E2
Sywell Northants ... 120 D6

T

Taagan Highld ... 299 C10
Tabley Hill Ches E ... 184 F2
Tabor Gwyn ... 146 F5
Tàbost W Isles ... 304 B7
Tabost W Isles ... 305 G5
Tachbrook Mallory
Warks ... 118 E6
Tacker Street Som ... 42 F4
Tackley Oxon ... 101 G9
Tacleit W Isles ... 304 E3
Tacolneston Norf ... 142 D2
Tadcaster N Yorks ... 206 E5
Tadden Dorset ... 31 G7
Taddington Derbys ... 185 G10
Glos ... 99 E11
Taddiport Devon ... 25 D7
Tadhill Som ... 45 D7
Tadley Hants ... 64 G6
Oxon ... 64 B4
Tadlow Beds ... 104 B5
C Beds ... 104 B5
Tadmarton Oxon ... 101 D7
Tadnoll Dorset ... 17 D11
Tadwick Bath ... 61 E8
Tadworth Sur ... 51 B8
Tafarnau-bach
Bl Gwent ... 77 C10
Tafarn-y-bwlch
Pembs ... 91 E11
Tafarn-y-gelyn
Denb ... 165 C11
Taff Merthyr Garden
Village M Tydf ... 77 F10
Taff's Well Rhondda ... 58 C6
Tafolwern Powys ... 129 C7
Tai Conwy ... 164 C3
Taibach Neath ... 57 D9
Tai-bach Powys ... 148 D3
Taigh a Ghearraidh
W Isles ... 296 D3
Taigh Bhalaigh
W Isles ... 296 D3
Tai-mawr Conwy ... 165 G7
Tai-morfa Gwyn ... 144 D5
Tain Highld ... 309 L7
Highld ... 310 C6
Tai-nant Wrex ... 166 F3
Tainlon Gwyn ... 162 E6
Tairbeart W Isles ... 305 H3
Tai'r-Bull Powys ... 95 F9
Tairgwaith Neath ... 76 C2
Tai'r-heol Caerph ... 77 G10
Tai'r-ysgol Swansea ... 57 B7
Tai-Ucha Denb ... 165 D8
Takeley Essex ... 105 G11
Takeley Street
Essex ... 105 G10
Talacharn / Laugharne
Carms ... 74 C4
Talachddu Powys ... 95 E11
Talacre Flint ... 181 E10
Talardd Gwyn ... 147 D7
Talaton Devon ... 15 B7
Talbenny Pembs ... 72 C4
Talbot Green
Rhondda ... 58 C4
Talbot Heath Poole ... 19 C7
Talbot's End S Glos ... 80 G2
Talbot Village Poole ... 19 C7
Talbot Woods
Bmouth ... 19 C7
Tale Devon ... 27 G9
Talerddig Powys ... 129 C8
Talgarreg Ceredig ... 111 G8
Talgarth Powys ... 96 E3
Talgarth's Well
Swansea ... 56 D2
Talisker Highld ... 294 B5
Talke Staffs ... 168 E4
Talke Pits Staffs ... 168 E4
Talkin Cumb ... 240 F3
Talladale Highld ... 299 B9
Talla Linnfoots
Borders ... 260 E4
Tallaminnoch
S Ayrs ... 245 D10
Talland Corn ... 6 E4
Tallarn Green Wrex ... 166 G6
Tallentire Cumb ... 229 D8
Talley Carms ... 94 E2
Tallington Lincs ... 137 B11
Talmine Highld ... 308 C5
Talog Carms ... 92 F6
Talsarn Carms ... 94 F5
Tal-sarn Ceredig ... 111 F10
Talsarnau Gwyn ... 146 B2
Talskiddy Corn ... 5 B8
Talwrn Anglesey ... 179 F7
Wrex ... 166 F3
Tal-y-bont Ceredig ... 128 F3
Conwy ... 164 B3
Gwyn ... 145 E11
Gwyn ... 179 G10
Talybont-on-Usk
Powys ... 96 G2
Tal-y-cafn Conwy ... 180 G3
Tal-y-coed Mon ... 78 B6
Talygarn Rhondda ... 58 C4
Talyllyn Powys ... 96 F2
Tal-y-llyn Gwyn ... 128 B4
Talysarn Gwyn ... 163 E7
Tal-y-waenydd
Gwyn ... 163 F11
Talywain Torf ... 78 E3
Tal-y-wern Powys ... 128 C6
Tamanabhagh
W Isles ... 304 F2
Tame Bridge
N Yorks ... 225 D10
Tamer Lane End
Gtr Man ... 194 G6
Tamerton Foliot Plym ... 7 C9
Tame Water
Gtr Man ... 196 F3
Tamfourhill Falk ... 279 E7
Tamworth Staffs ... 134 C4
Tamworth Green
Lincs ... 174 G5
Tancred N Yorks ... 206 B5
Tandem W Yorks ... 197 D7
Tanden Kent ... 54 F2
Tandlehill Renfs ... 267 C8
Tandridge Sur ... 51 C11
Tanerdy Carms ... 93 G8
Tanfield Durham ... 242 F5
Tanfield Lea
Durham ... 242 G5
Tang N Yorks ... 205 B10
Tangasdal W Isles ... 297 M2
Tang Hall York ... 207 C8
Tangiers Pembs ... 73 B7
Tangley Hants ... 47 C10
Tanglwst Carms ... 92 E6
Tangmere W Sus ... 22 B6
Tangwick Shetland ... 312 F4
Tangy Argyll ... 255 E7
Tan Hills Durham ... 233 B11
Tan Hinon Powys ... 129 F7
Tanhouse Lancs ... 194 F3
Tanis Wilts ... 62 G3
Tankersley
S Yorks ... 197 G10
Tankerton Kent ... 70 F6
Tanlan Flint ... 181 E10
Tan-lan Conwy ... 164 C3
Gwyn ... 163 G10
Tanlan Banks Flint ... 181 E10
Tannach Highld ... 310 E7
Tannachie Aberds ... 293 E9
Tannadice Angus ... 287 B8
Tanner's Green
Worcs ... 117 C11
Tannington Suff ... 126 D4
Tannington Place
Suff ... 126 D4
Tannochside N Lnrk ... 268 C4
Tan Office Suff ... 126 E2
Tan Office Green
Suff ... 124 F5
Tansley Derbys ... 170 D4
Tansley Hill W Mid ... 133 F9
Tansley Knoll
Derbys ... 170 C4
Tansor Northants ... 137 E11
Tanterton Lancs ... 202 G6
Tantobie Durham ... 242 G5
Tanton N Yorks ... 225 C10
Tanwood Worcs ... 117 C8
Tanworth-in-Arden
Warks ... 118 C2
Tan-y-bwlch
Gwyn ... 163 G11
Tanyfron Wrex ... 166 E3
Tan-y-fron Conwy ... 165 C7
Tan-y-graig
Anglesey ... 179 F8
Gwyn ... 144 B6
Tanygrisiau Gwyn ... 163 F11
Tan-y-groes Ceredig ... 92 B5
Tan-y-mynydd
Gwyn ... 144 C6
Tan-y-pistyll
Powys ... 147 D11
Tan-yr-allt Denb ... 181 E9
Gwyn ... 163 E7
Tanyrhydiau
Ceredig ... 112 D4
Tanysgafell Gwyn ... 163 B10
Taobh a Chaolais
W Isles ... 297 K3
Taobh a' Ghlinne
W Isles ... 305 G5
Taobh a Thuath Loch
Aineort W Isles ... 297 J3
Taobh a Tuath Loch
Baghasdail
W Isles ... 297 J3
Taobh Siar W Isles ... 305 H3
Taobh Tuath
W Isles ... 296 C5
Taplow Bucks ... 66 C2
Tapnage Hants ... 33 E9
Tapton Derbys ... 186 G5
Tapton Hill S Yorks ... 186 D4
Tarbat Ho Highld ... 301 B7
Tarbert Argyll ... 255 B7
Argyll ... 275 E7
Argyll ... 275 G9
Tarbet Argyll ... 285 G7
Highld ... 295 F9
Highld ... 306 E6
Tarbock Green
Mers ... 183 D7
Tarbolton S Ayrs ... 257 D10
Tarbrax S Lnrk ... 269 D10
Tardebigge Worcs ... 117 D10
Tardy Gate Lancs ... 194 B4
Tarfside Angus ... 292 F6
Tarland Aberds ... 292 C6
Tarleton Lancs ... 194 C3
Tarleton Moss
Lancs ... 194 C2
Tarlogie Highld ... 309 L7
Tarlscough Lancs ... 194 E2
Tarlton Glos ... 81 F7
Tarn W Yorks ... 205 F9
Tarnbrook Lancs ... 203 B7
Tarnock Som ... 43 C11
Tarns Cumb ... 229 B8
Tarnside Cumb ... 221 G8
Tarporley Ches W ... 167 C9
Tarpots Essex ... 69 B9
Tarr Som ... 42 G6
Tarraby Cumb ... 239 F10
Tarrant Crawford
Dorset ... 30 G6
Tarrant Gunville
Dorset ... 30 E6
Tarrant Hinton
Dorset ... 30 E6
Tarrant Keyneston
Dorset ... 30 G6
Tarrant Launceston
Dorset ... 30 F6
Tarrant Monkton
Dorset ... 30 F6
Tarrant Rawston
Dorset ... 30 F6
Tarrant Rushton
Dorset ... 30 F6
Tarrel Highld ... 311 L2
Tarring Neville
E Sus ... 36 G6
Tarrington Hereford ... 98 C2
Tarrington Common
Hereford ... 98 D2
Tarryblake Ho
Moray ... 302 E5
Tarsappie Perth ... 286 E5
Tarskavaig Highld ... 295 E7
Tarts Hill Shrops ... 149 B8
Tarves Aberds ... 303 F8
Tarvie Highld ... 300 D4
Perth ... 292 G2
Tarvin Ches W ... 167 B7
Tarvin Sands
Ches W ... 167 B7
Tasburgh Norf ... 142 D4
Tasley Shrops ... 132 E3
Taston Oxon ... 101 G7
Tat Bank W Mid ... 133 F9
Tatenhill Staffs ... 152 E4
Tatenhill Common
Staffs ... 152 E3
Tathall End
M Keynes ... 102 B6
Tatham Lancs ... 212 F2
Tathwell Lincs ... 190 E4
Tatling End Bucks ... 66 B4
Tatsfield Sur ... 52 B2
Tattenhall Ches W ... 167 D7
Tattenhoe
M Keynes ... 102 E6
Tatterford Norf ... 159 D7
Tattersett Norf ... 158 C6
Tattershall Lincs ... 174 D2
Tattershall Bridge
Lincs ... 173 D11
Tattershall Thorpe
Lincs ... 174 D2
Tattingstone Suff ... 108 D2
Tattingstone White
Horse Suff ... 108 D2
Tattle Bank Warks ... 118 E3
Tatton Dale Ches E ... 184 E2
Tatworth Som ... 28 F4
Taunton Gtr Man ... 196 G2
Som ... 28 C2
Taverham Norf ... 160 G3
Taverners Green
Essex ... 87 B9
Tavernspite Pembs ... 73 C11
Tavistock Devon ... 12 G5
Taw Green Devon ... 13 B9
Tawstock Devon ... 25 B9
Taxal Derbys ... 185 F8
Tay Bridge Dundee ... 287 E8
Tayinloan Argyll ... 255 C7
Taymouth Castle
Perth ... 285 C11
Taynish Argyll ... 275 E8
Taynton Glos ... 98 G4
Oxon ... 82 C2
Taynuilt Argyll ... 284 D4
Tayport Fife ... 287 E8
Tayvallich Argyll ... 275 E8
Tea Green Herts ... 104 G2
Tealby Lincs ... 189 C11
Tealing Angus ... 287 D8
Teams T&W ... 242 E6
Team Valley T&W ... 242 E6
Teanford Staffs ... 169 G8
Teangue Highld ... 295 E8
Teanna Mhachair
W Isles ... 296 E3
Teasley Mead E Sus ... 52 F4
Tebay Cumb ... 222 E2
Tebworth C Beds ... 103 F9
Tedburn St Mary
Devon ... 14 C2
Teddington Glos ... 99 E9
London ... 67 E7
Teddington Hands
Worcs ... 99 E9
Tedsmore Shrops ... 149 D7
Tedstone Delamere
Hereford ... 116 F3
Tedstone Wafer
Hereford ... 116 F3
Teesville Redcar ... 225 B10
Teeton Northants ... 120 C3
Teffont Evias Wilts ... 46 G3
Teffont Magna Wilts ... 46 G3
Tegryn Pembs ... 92 E4
Teigh Rutland ... 155 F7
Teigncombe Devon ... 13 D9
Teigngrace Devon ... 14 G2
Teignmouth Devon ... 14 G4
Teign Village Devon ... 14 E2
Telford Telford ... 132 B3
Telham E Sus ... 38 E3
Tellisford Som ... 45 B10
Telscombe E Sus ... 36 G6
Telscombe Cliffs
E Sus ... 36 G5
Templand Dumfries ... 248 F3
Temple Corn ... 11 G8
Glasgow ... 267 B10
Midloth ... 270 D6
Wilts ... 45 E10
Windsor ... 65 C10
Temple Balsall
W Mid ... 118 B4
Temple Bar Carms ... 75 B9
Ceredig ... 111 G10
W Sus ... 22 B5
Templeborough
S Yorks ... 186 C6
Temple Cloud Bath ... 44 B6
Templecombe Som ... 30 C2
Temple Cowley Oxon ... 83 E8
Temple End Essex ... 106 C6
Suff ... 124 G3
Temple Ewell Kent ... 55 E9
Temple Fields Essex ... 87 C7
Temple Grafton
Warks ... 118 G2
Temple Guiting
Glos ... 99 F11
Templehall Fife ... 280 C5
Temple Herdewyke
Warks ... 119 G7
Temple Hill Kent ... 68 D5
Temple Hirst
N Yorks ... 198 C6
Templeman's Ash
Dorset ... 28 G6
Temple Normanton
Derbys ... 170 B6
Temple Sowerby
Cumb ... 231 F8
Templeton Devon ... 26 E5
Pembs ... 73 C10
W Berks ... 63 F11
Templeton Bridge
Devon ... 26 E5
Templetown
Durham ... 242 G4
Tempsford C Beds ... 122 G3
Ten Acres W Mid ... 133 G11
Tenandry Perth ... 291 G11
Tenbury Wells
Worcs ... 115 D11
Tenby / Dinbych-y-Pysgod Pembs ... 73 E10
Tencreek Corn ... 6 E4
Tendring Essex ... 108 G2
Tendring Green
Essex ... 108 F2
Tendring Heath
Essex ... 108 F2
Ten Mile Bank Norf ... 140 D2
Tenston Orkney ... 314 E2
Tenterden Kent ... 53 G11
Terfyn Conwy ... 180 F6
Gwyn ... 163 C9
Terhill Som ... 43 G7
Terling Essex ... 88 B3
Ternhill Shrops ... 150 C2
Terpersie Castle
Aberds ... 302 G5
Terras Corn ... 5 E8
Terregles Banks
Dumfries ... 237 B11
Terrible Down E Sus ... 23 B7
Terrick Bucks ... 84 D4
Terriers Bucks ... 84 G5
Terrington N Yorks ... 216 E3
Terrington St Clement
Norf ... 157 E10
Terrington St John
Norf ... 157 G10
Terryhorn Aberds ... 302 F4
Terry's Green
Warks ... 118 C2
Terwick Common
W Sus ... 34 C4
Teston Kent ... 53 C8
Testwood Hants ... 32 E5
Tetbury Glos ... 80 G5
Tetbury Upton Glos ... 80 F5
Tetchill Shrops ... 149 C7
Tetchwick Bucks ... 83 B11
Tetcott Devon ... 12 B2
Tetford Lincs ... 190 G4
Tetley N Lincs ... 199 E9
Tetney Lincs ... 201 G10
Tetney Lock Lincs ... 201 G10
Tetsworth Oxon ... 83 E11
Tettenhall W Mid ... 133 D7
Tettenhall Wood
W Mid ... 133 D7
Tetworth Cambs ... 122 G4
Teuchan Aberds ... 303 F10
Teversal Notts ... 171 C7
Teversham Cambs ... 123 F9
Teviothead
Borders ... 249 B10
Tewel Aberds ... 293 E10
Tewin Herts ... 86 C3
Tewin Wood Herts ... 86 B3
Tewitfield Lancs ... 211 E10
Tewkesbury Glos ... 99 E7
Teynham Kent ... 70 G3
Teynham Street Kent ... 70 G3
Thackley W Yorks ... 205 F9
Thackley End
W Yorks ... 205 F9
Thackthwaite Cumb ... 229 G8
Thainston Aberds ... 293 F8
Thakeham W Sus ... 35 D10
Thame Oxon ... 84 D2
Thames Ditton Sur ... 67 F7
Thames Haven
Thurrock ... 69 C8
Thames Head Glos ... 81 F7
Thamesmead London ... 68 C3
Thanington Kent ... 54 B6
Thankerton S Lnrk ... 259 B11
Tharston Norf ... 142 E3
Thatcham W Berks ... 64 F4
Thatto Heath Mers ... 183 C8
Thaxted Essex ... 106 E2
The Aird Highld ... 298 D4
Theakston N Yorks ... 214 B6
Thealby N Lincs ... 199 D11
The Alders Staffs ... 134 C3
Theale Som ... 44 D3
W Berks ... 64 E6
The Arms Norf ... 141 D7
Thearne E Yorks ... 209 F7
The Bage Hereford ... 96 C5
The Balloch Perth ... 286 F2
The Bank Ches E ... 168 D4
The Banks Gtr Man ... 185 D7
Wilts ... 62 D4
The Barony
Ches E ... 167 E11
Orkney ... 314 D2
The Barton Wilts ... 62 D5
The Batch S Glos ... 61 E7
The Beeches Glos ... 81 E8
The Bell Gtr Man ... 194 F4
The Bents Staffs ... 151 C10
Theberton Suff ... 127 D8
The Blythe Staffs ... 151 D10
The Bog Shrops ... 131 D7
The Borough Dorset ... 30 E2
London ... 67 D10
The Bourne Sur ... 49 E10
Worcs ... 117 F9
The Bows Stirl ... 285 G11
The Braes Highld ... 295 B7
The Brampton
Staffs ... 168 F4
The Brand Leics ... 153 G10
The Bratch Staffs ... 133 E7
The Breck Orkney ... 314 F3
The Brents Kent ... 70 G4
The Bridge Dorset ... 30 E3
The Broad Hereford ... 115 E9
The Brook Suff ... 125 B11
The Brushes Derbys ... 186 F5
The Bryn Mon ... 78 D4
The Burf Worcs ... 116 D6
The Butts Hants ... 49 F8
Som ... 45 D9
The Camp Glos ... 80 D6
Herts ... 85 D11
The Cape Warks ... 118 D5
The Chart Kent ... 52 C3
The Chequer Wrex ... 167 G7
The Chuckery
W Mid ... 133 D10
The City Bucks ... 84 F3
The Cleaver
Hereford ... 97 F10
The Close W Sus ... 22 C5
The Colony Oxon ... 100 D6
The Common Bath ... 60 G6
Bucks ... 102 E5
Dorset ... 30 E3
Shrops ... 150 D3
Suff ... 108 B2
Swansea ... 56 C4
Wilts ... 47 G8
Wilts ... 61 G11
Wilts ... 62 C4
W Sus ... 51 G7
The Corner Kent ... 53 E8
Shrops ... 131 F8
The Cot Mon ... 79 F8
The Craigs Highld ... 309 K4
The Crofts E Yorks ... 218 E4
The Cronk IoM ... 192 C4
The Cross Hands
Leics ... 134 C6
The Cwm Mon ... 79 G7
Theddingworth
Leics ... 136 F3
Theddlethorpe All Saints
Lincs ... 191 D7
Theddlethorpe St Helen
Lincs ... 191 D7
The Dell Suff ... 143 D9
The Delves W Mid ... 133 D10
The Den N Ayrs ... 266 E6
The Dene Durham ... 242 G4
Hants ... 47 C11
The Down Kent ... 53 F7
Shrops ... 132 E3
The Downs Sur ... 50 F3
The Dunks Wrex ... 166 E4
The Eals Northumb ... 251 F7
The Eaves Glos ... 79 D10
The Fall W Yorks ... 197 B10
The Fence Glos ... 79 D8
The Flat Glos ... 80 B3
The Flatt Cumb ... 240 B3
The Flourish Derbys ... 153 B8
The Folly Herts ... 85 C11
S Glos ... 61 E8
The Fording Hereford ... 98 F3
The Forge Hereford ... 114 F6
The Forstal Kent ... 54 F4
The Forties Derbys ... 152 F6
The Four Alls
Shrops ... 150 C3
The Fox Wilts ... 62 B6
The Foxholes
Shrops ... 132 G2
The Frenches Hants ... 32 C4
The Frythe Herts ... 86 C2
The Garths Shetland ... 312 B8
The Gibb Wilts ... 61 D10
The Glack Borders ... 260 B6
The Gore Shrops ... 131 G11
The Grange Norf ... 160 E2
N Yorks ... 225 F11
The Green Cambs ... 122 D5
C Beds ... 85 B8
Cumb ... 210 C3
Cumb ... 211 D7
Essex ... 88 B3
Hants ... 32 B3
M Keynes ... 103 C7
Norf ... 141 C11
Norf ... 159 B11
Northants ... 102 C5
Oxon ... 101 F9
Shrops ... 130 G6
S Yorks ... 197 G8
Warks ... 118 F4
Wilts ... 45 G11
The Grove
Dumfries ... 237 B11
Durham ... 242 G3
Herts ... 85 F9
Shrops ... 131 B7
Shrops ... 131 G8
Worcs ... 99 C7
The Gutter Derbys ... 170 F5
Worcs ... 117 B9
The Hacket S Glos ... 61 B7
The Hague Derbys ... 185 C8
The Hall Shetland ... 312 D8
The Hallands
N Lincs ... 200 C5
The Ham Wilts ... 45 C11
The Handfords
Staffs ... 151 E7
The Harbour Kent ... 53 D10
The Haven W Sus ... 50 G5
The Headland Hrtlpl ... 234 E6
The Heath Norf ... 159 D8
Norf ... 160 E3
Norf ... 160 E4
Staffs ... 151 C11
Suff ... 108 D2
The Hem Shrops ... 132 B4
The Hendre Mon ... 79 C7
The Herberts V Glam ... 58 E3
The Hermitage
Cambs ... 123 C7
The High Essex ... 86 C6
The Highlands E Sus ... 38 F2
The Hill Cumb ... 210 C3
The Hobbins Shrops ... 132 E4
The Hollands Staffs ... 168 D6
The Hollies Notts ... 172 E4
The Holmes Derbys ... 153 B7
The Holt Wokingham ... 65 D10
The Hook Worcs ... 98 C6
The Hope Shrops ... 115 B10
The Howe Cumb ... 211 B9
IoM ... 192 F2
The Humbers
Telford ... 150 G3
The Hundred
Hereford ... 115 E10
The Hyde London ... 67 B8
Worcs ... 98 C6
The Hythe Essex ... 107 G10
The Inch Edin ... 280 G5
The Knab Swansea ... 56 D6
The Knap V Glam ... 58 F5
The Knapp Hereford ... 116 G3
S Glos ... 79 G11
The Knowle W Mid ... 133 F9
The Laches Staffs ... 133 B8
The Lake Dumfries ... 237 E8
The Lakes Worcs ... 116 B5
The Lawe T&W ... 243 D9
The Lawns E Yorks ... 208 G6
Thelbridge Barton
Devon ... 26 E3
The Leacon Kent ... 54 G3
The Leath Shrops ... 131 F11
The Lee Bucks ... 84 E6
The Lees Kent ... 54 C4
The Leigh Glos ... 99 F7
The Leys Staffs ... 134 C4
The Lhen IoM ... 192 B4
The Ling Norf ... 142 D6
The Lings Norf ... 141 B10
S Yorks ... 199 F7
The Linleys Wilts ... 61 F11
Thelnetham Suff ... 125 B10
The Lunt W Mid ... 133 D9
Thelveton Norf ... 142 G3
Thelwall Warr ... 183 D10
The Manor W Sus ... 22 C4
The Marsh Ches E ... 168 C4
Hereford ... 115 F9
Powys ... 130 D6
Shrops ... 150 D3
Staffs ... 150 D6
Suff ... 125 B11
Suff ... 126 B2
Wilts ... 62 C5
Themelthorpe
Norf ... 159 E11
The Middles
Durham ... 242 G6
The Mint Hants ... 34 B3
The Moor Flint ... 166 B4
Kent ... 38 B3
The Moors Hereford ... 97 E10
The Mount Hants ... 64 G2
Reading ... 65 E8
The Mumbles /
Y Mwmbwls Swansea ... 56 D6
The Murray S Lnrk ... 268 E2
The Mythe Glos ... 99 E7
The Nant Wrex ... 166 E3
The Narth Mon ... 79 D8
The Neuk Aberds ... 293 D9
Thenford Northants ... 101 C10
The Node Herts ... 104 G4
The Nook Shrops ... 149 C11
Shrops ... 150 E3
The North Mon ... 79 D8
Theobald's Green
Wilts ... 62 F4
The Oval Bath ... 61 G8
The Park Glos ... 99 G8
The Parks S Yorks ... 198 F6
The Pitts Wilts ... 31 B9
The Platt Oxon ... 83 E9
The Pludds Glos ... 79 B10
The Point Devon ... 14 E5
The Pole of Itlaw
Aberds ... 302 D6
The Port of Felixstowe
Suff ... 108 E5
The Potteries Stoke ... 168 F5
The Pound Glos ... 98 E4
The Quarry Glos ... 80 F2
Shrops ... 149 G9
The Quarter Kent ... 53 E11
Kent ... 53 G11
The Rampings Worcs ... 99 E7
The Rectory Lincs ... 156 G2
The Reddings Glos ... 99 G8
Therfield Herts ... 104 D6
The Rhos Pembs ... 73 C8
The Rhydd Hereford ... 97 E9
The Riddle Hereford ... 115 E9
The Ridge Wilts ... 61 F11
The Ridges
Wokingham ... 65 G10
The Ridgeway Herts ... 86 E3
The Riding
Northumb ... 241 D10
The Riggs Borders ... 261 C8
The Rink Borders ... 261 C11
The Rise Windsor ... 66 F2
The Rock Telford ... 132 B3
The Rocks Kent ... 53 B8
S Glos ... 61 C8
The Roe Denb ... 181 G8
The Rookery Herts ... 85 G10
Staffs ... 168 D5
The Row Lancs ... 211 D9
The Rowe Staffs ... 150 B6
The Ryde Herts ... 86 D2
The Sands Sur ... 49 D11
The Scarr Glos ... 98 F4
The Shoe Wilts ... 61 E10
The Shruggs Staffs ... 151 C8
The Slack Durham ... 233 F8
The Slade W Berks ... 64 F4
The Smeeth Norf ... 157 G10
The Smithies
Shrops ... 132 D3
The Spa Wilts ... 62 G2
The Spring Warks ... 118 C5
The Square Torf ... 78 F3
The Stocks Kent ... 38 B6
Wilts ... 62 G2
The Straits Hants ... 49 F9
W Mid ... 133 E8
The Strand Wilts ... 46 B2
The Swillett Herts ... 85 F8
The Sydnall Shrops ... 150 C3
Thetford Lincs ... 156 F2
Norf ... 141 G7
The Thrift Cambs ... 104 D6
The Throat
Wokingham ... 65 F10
The Toft Staffs ... 151 F8
The Towans Corn ... 2 B3
The Town Scilly ... 1 F3
The Twittocks Glos ... 99 D7
The Tynings Glos ... 80 B6
The Vale W Mid ... 133 G11
The Valley Ches E ... 167 D11
Kent ... 54 C3
Leics ... 154 F4
Pembs ... 73 D10
The Vauld Hereford ... 97 B10
The Village Newport ... 78 G4
Windsor ... 66 E3
W Mid ... 133 F7
The Walshes Worcs ... 116 C6
The Warren Kent ... 54 E3
Wilts ... 63 F8
The Waterwheel
Shrops ... 131 C7
The Weaven
Hereford ... 97 E10
The Wells Sur ... 67 G7
The Wern Wrex ... 166 E3
The Willows
NE Lincs ... 201 F8
The Wood Shrops ... 148 E6
Shrops ... 149 D9
The Woodlands
Leics ... 136 D3
Suff ... 107 C11
Suff ... 108 D3
The Woods W Mid ... 133 D10

Derbys 185 F11
E Yorks 207 C10
Mers 183 D7
W Yorks 196 D5
Townfield Durham 232 B5
Town Fields
Ches W 167 B10
Towngate Cumb 230 B6
Lincs 156 G2
Town Green
Gtr Man 183 B9
Lancs 194 F2
Norf 161 G7
Townhead Argyll 275 G11
Cumb 229 D7
Cumb 230 D6
Cumb 231 E8
Dumfries 237 E8
N Lnrk 268 B4
Northumb 251 E9
S Ayrs 244 C6
S Yorks 186 E4
S Yorks 197 G7
Town Head Cumb 220 D6
Cumb 221 E8
Cumb 222 C2
Cumb 222 C3
Cumb 231 F7
Cumb 231 F8
Cumb 231 G8
Cumb 231 G9
Derbys 185 F11
N Yorks 204 B2
N Yorks 212 F5
Staffs 169 F8
W Yorks 204 D6
Townhead of Greenlaw
Dumfries 237 C9
Townhill Fife 280 D2
Swansea 56 C6
Townhill Park Hants 33 E7
Town Kelloe
Durham 234 D3
Townlake Devon 12 G4
Townland Green
Kent 54 G2
Town Lane
Gtr Man 183 B11
Town Littleworth
E Sus 36 D6
Town of Lowton
Mers 183 B10
Town Park Telford 132 B3
Town Row E Sus 52 G5
Townsend Bath 44 B5
Bucks 84 D2
Devon 25 B10
Herts 85 D10
Oxon 63 B11
Pembs 72 D4
Som 44 C4
Stoke 168 F6
Wilts 46 B3
Wilts 46 B4
Towns End Hants 48 B5
Som 30 D2
Town's End Bucks 102 G2
Dorset 18 B3
Dorset 18 E5
Dorset 29 F9
Som 45 D7
Townsend Fold
Lancs 195 C10
Townshend Corn 2 C3
Town Street Glos 98 F6
Townwell S Glos 79 G11
Town Yetholm
Borders 263 D8
Towthorpe E Yorks 217 G8
York 207 B8
Towton N Yorks 206 F5
Towyn Conwy 181 F7
Toxteth Mers 182 D5
Toynton All Saints
Lincs 174 C5
Toynton Fen Side
Lincs 174 C5
Toynton St Peter
Lincs 174 C6
Toy's Hill Kent 52 C3
Trabboch E Ayrs 257 E10
Traboe Corn 2 E6
Trabrown Borders 271 F10
Tracebridge Som 27 C9
Tradespark Highld 301 D8
Orkney 314 F4
Trafford Park
Gtr Man 184 B3
Traigh Ho Highld 295 F8
Trallong Powys 95 F9
Trallwn Rhondda 77 G9
Swansea 57 B7
Tramagenna Corn 11 E7
Tram Inn Hereford 97 E9
Tranch Torf 78 E3
Tranent E Loth 281 G8
Tranmere Mers 182 D4
Trantlebeg Highld 310 D2
Trantlemore Highld 310 D2
Tranwell Northumb 252 G5
Trapp Carms 75 B11
Traprain E Loth 281 F11
Trap's Green Warks 118 D2
Trapshill W Berks 63 G11
Traquair Borders 261 C8
Trash Green W Berks 65 F7
Travellers' Rest
Carms 74 B5
Trawden Lancs 204 F4
Trawscoed Powys 95 E11
Trawsfynydd Gwyn 146 B4
Trawsnant Ceredig 111 D11
Treadam Mon 78 B5
Treaddow Hereford 97 G10
Treal Corn 2 F6
Trealaw Rhondda 77 G8
Treales Lancs 202 G4
Trearddur Anglesey 178 F3
Treaslane Highld 298 D3
Treath Corn 3 D7
Treator Corn 10 F4
Tre-Aubrey V Glam 58 E4
Trebanog Rhondda 77 G8
Trebanos Neath 76 E2
Trebarber Corn 5 C7
Trebartha Corn 11 F11
Trebarwith Corn 11 D7
Trebarwith Strand
Corn 10 D6
Trebeath Corn 11 D11
Tre-Beferad V Glam 58 F3
Trebell Green Corn 5 C11
Treberfydd Powys 96 F2
Trebetherick Corn 10 F4
Trebilcock Corn 5 C9
Treble's Holford Som 43 G7
Tre-boeth Swansea 57 B7
Treborough Som 42 F4
Trebudannon Corn 5 C7
Trebullett Corn 12 F2
Treburgett Corn 11 F7
Treburgie Corn 6 C4
Treburley Corn 12 F3
Treburrick Corn 10 G3
Trebyan Corn 5 C11
Trecastle Powys 95 F7
Trecenydd Caerph 58 B6
Trecott Devon 25 G10
Trecwn Pembs 91 E9
Trecynon Rhondda 77 E7
Tredannick Corn 10 G6
Tredaule Corn 11 E10
Tredavoe Corn 1 D5
Treddiog Pembs 91 F7
Tredegar Bl Gwent 77 D10
Trederwen Powys 148 F5
Tre-derwen Powys 148 F4
Tredethy Corn 11 G7
Tredington Glos 99 F8
Warks 100 C5
Tredinnick Corn 1 C4
Corn 5 D10
Corn 6 B3
Corn 6 D4
Corn 10 G4
Tredogan V Glam 58 F5
Tredomen Caerph 77 G10
Powys 96 E2
Tredown Devon 24 D2
Tredrizzick Corn 10 F5
Tredunnock Mon 78 G5
Tredustan Powys 96 E2
Tredworth Glos 80 B4
Treen Corn 1 B4
Corn 1 E3
Treesmill Corn 5 D11
Treeton S Yorks 186 D6
Trefaes Gwyn 144 C5
Trefanny Hill Corn 6 D4
Trefasser Pembs 91 D7
Trefdraeth Anglesey 178 G6
Trefdraeth/Newport
Pembs 91 D11
Trefecca Powys 96 E2
Trefechan Ceredig 111 A11
M Tydf 77 D8
Wrex 166 F3
Trefeglwys Powys 129 E9
Trefeitha Powys 96 E2
Trefenter Ceredig 112 D2
Treffgarne Pembs 91 G9
Treffynnon Pembs 90 F6
Treffynnon/Holywell
Flint 181 F11
Trefgarn Owen
Pembs 91 F7
Trefil Bl Gwent 77 C10
Trefilan Ceredig 111 F11
Trefin/Trevine
Pembs 90 E6
Treflach Shrops 148 D5
Trefnanney Powys 148 F4
Trefnant Denb 181 G9
Trefonen Shrops 148 D5
Trefor Anglesey 178 E5
Gwyn 162 F5
Treforda Corn 11 E7
Treforest Rhondda 58 B5
Treforgan Ceredig 92 B4
Tre-Forgan Neath 76 D3
Treforys/Morriston
Swansea 57 B7
Trefriw Conwy 164 C3
Trefrize Corn 12 F2
Tref y Clawdd/
Knighton Powys 114 C5
Trefynwy/Monmouth
Mon 79 C8
Tregada Corn 12 E2
Tregadgwith Corn 1 D4
Tregadillett Corn 12 E2
Tre-gagle Mon 79 D8
Tregaian Anglesey 178 F6
Tregajorran Corn 4 G3
Tregamere Corn 5 C8
Tregardock Corn 10 E6
Tregare Mon 78 C6
Tregarland Corn 6 D5
Tregarlandbridge
Corn 6 D4
Tregarne Corn 3 E7
Tregaron Ceredig 112 F3
Tregarrick Mill Corn 6 D4
Tregarth Gwyn 163 B10
Tregath Gwyn 163 B10
Tregatillian Corn 5 C8
Tregatta Corn 11 D7
Tregavarah Corn 1 D4
Tregear Corn 2 E5
Tregeare Corn 11 D10
Tregeiriog Wrex 148 C3
Tregele Anglesey 178 C5
Tregellist Corn 10 F6
Tregeseal Corn 1 C3
Tregew Corn 3 C8
Tre-Gibbon Rhondda 77 E7
Tregidden Corn 3 E7
Treginnis Pembs 90 G4
Treglemais Pembs 90 F6
Tregole Corn 11 B9
Tregolls Corn 2 B6
Tregolwyn/Colwinston
V Glam 58 D2
Tregona Corn 5 B7
Tregonce Corn 10 G4
Tregonetha Corn 5 C9
Tregonna Corn 10 G4
Tregonning Corn 5 D7
Tregony Corn 5 G8
Tregoodwell Corn 11 E8
Tregorden Corn 10 G6
Tregorrick Corn 5 E10
Tregoss Corn 5 C9
Tregoyd Powys 96 D4
Tregoyd Mill Powys 96 D3
Tregreenwell Corn 11 E7
Tregrehan Mills Corn 5 E10
Tregroes Ceredig 93 C8
Tregullon Corn 5 C11
Tregunna Corn 10 G5
Tregurrian Corn 5 B7
Tregurtha Downs
Corn 2 C2
Tre Gwyr/Gowerton
Swansea 56 B5
Tregyddulan Pembs 91 D7
Tregynon Powys 129 D11
Tre-gynwr Carms 74 B6
Trehafod Rhondda 77 G8
Trehafren Powys 129 E11
Trehan Corn 7 D8
Treharris M Tydf 77 F9
Trehemborne Corn 10 G3
Treherbert Rhondda 76 F6
Tre-hill V Glam 58 E5
Trehunist Corn 6 C6
Tre-Ifor Rhondda 77 D7
Trekeivesteps Corn 11 G10
Trekenner Corn 12 F2
Trekenning Corn 5 C8
Treknow Corn 11 D7
Trelales/Laleston
Bridgend 57 F11
Trelan Corn 2 F6
Tre-lan Flint 165 B11
Trelash Corn 11 C9
Trelassick Corn 5 E7
Trelawnyd Flint 181 F9
Trelech Carms 92 E5
Treleddyd-fawr
Pembs 90 F5
Treleigh Corn 4 G4
Treletert/Letterston
Pembs 91 F8
Trelew Corn 3 B8
Trelewis M Tydf 77 F10
Treligga Corn 11 E7
Trelights Corn 10 F5
Trelill Corn 10 F6
Trelion Corn 5 E8
Treliske Corn 4 F6
Trelissick Corn 3 B8
Treliver Corn 5 B9
Trellech Mon 79 D8
Trelleck Grange Mon 79 E7
Trelogan Flint 181 E10
Treloquithack Corn 2 D5
Trelowia Corn 6 D5
Trelowth Corn 5 E9
Trelystan Powys 130 C5
Tremadog Gwyn 163 G9
Tremail Corn 11 D9
Tremain Ceredig 92 B4
Tremaine Corn 11 D10
Tremains Bridgend 58 D2
Tremar Corn 6 B5
Trematon Corn 7 D7
Trematon Castle Corn 7 D8
Tremayne Corn 2 B4
Trembraze Corn 6 B5
Tremedda Corn 1 B5
Tremeirchion Denb 181 G9
Tremethick Cross
Corn 1 C4
Tremore Corn 5 C10
Tremorebridge Corn 5 C10
Tremorfa Cardiff 59 D8
Tre-Mostyn Flint 181 F10
Trenance Corn 4 C6
Corn 5 B7
Corn 5 C9
Corn 10 G4
Trenant Corn 6 B4
Corn 10 G5
Trenarren Corn 5 F10
Trenay Corn 6 B3
Trench Telford 150 G3
Trench Green Oxon 65 D7
Trench Wood Kent 52 D5
Trencreek Corn 4 C6
Trencrom Corn 2 B2
Trendeal Corn 5 E7
Trenear Corn 2 C5
Treneglos Corn 11 D10
Trenerth Corn 2 B4
Trenewan Corn 6 E3
Trengune Corn 11 C9
Trenhorne Corn 11 F11
Treninnick Corn 4 C6
Trenoon Corn 2 F6
Trenoweth Corn 3 C7
Trent Dorset 29 D9
Trentham Stoke 168 G5
Trentishoe Devon 40 D6
Trentlock Derbys 153 C9
Trent Vale Stoke 168 G5
Trenwheal Corn 2 C4
Treoes V Glam 58 D2
Treopert/Granston
Pembs 91 E7
Treorchy/Treorci
Rhondda 77 F7
Treorci/Treorchy
Rhondda 77 F7
Treowen Caerph 78 F2
Powys 130 E2
Tre-pit V Glam 58 E2
Trequite Corn 10 F6
Tre'r-ddôl Ceredig 128 E3
Trerhyngyll V Glam 58 D4
Trerise Corn 2 F6
Trer Ilai/Leighton
Powys 130 B4
Trerose Corn 3 D7
Trerulefoot Corn 6 D6
Tresaith Ceredig 110 G5
Tresamble Corn 3 B7
Tresarrett Corn 11 G7
Tresavean Corn 2 B6
Tresawle Corn 5 F7
Tresawsen Corn 4 F5
Trescoll Corn 5 C10
Trescott Staffs 132 D6
Trescowe Corn 2 C3
Tresean Corn 4 D5
Tresevern Croft Corn 2 B6
Tresham Glos 80 G3
Tresigin/Sigingstone
V Glam 58 E3
Tresillian Corn 5 F7
Tresimwn/Bonvilston
V Glam 58 E5
Tresinney Corn 11 E8
Tresinwen Pembs 91 C7
Treskerby Corn 4 G4
Treskillard Corn 2 B5
Treskilling Corn 5 D10
Treskinnick Cross
Corn 11 B10
Treslothan Corn 2 B5
Tresmeer Corn 11 D10
Tresowes Green Corn 2 D3
Tresoweshill Corn 2 D4
Tresparrett Corn 11 C8
Tresparrett Posts
Corn 11 C8
Tressady Highld 309 J7
Tressait Perth 291 G10
Tresta Shetland 312 D8
Shetland 313 H5
Treswell Notts 188 F3
Treswithian Corn 4 G2
Treswithian Downs
Corn 4 G2
Tre-Taliesin Ceredig 128 E3
Trethellan Water Corn 2 B6
Trethevy Corn 11 D7
Trethewell Corn 3 B9
Trethewey Corn 1 E3
Trethillick Corn 10 F4
Trethomas Caerph 59 B7
Trethosa Corn 5 E8
Trethowel Corn 5 E10
Trethurgy Corn 5 D10
Tretio Pembs 90 F5
Tretire Hereford 97 G10
Tretower Powys 96 G3
Treuddyn Flint 166 D3
Trevadlock Corn 11 F11
Trevail Corn 4 D5
Trevalga Corn 11 D7
Trevalgan Corn 1 A5
Trevalyn Wrex 166 D5
Trevance Corn 10 G4
Trevanger Corn 10 F5
Trevanson Corn 10 G5
Trevarrack Corn 1 C5
Trevarren Corn 5 C8
Trevarrian Corn 4 B6
Trevarrick Corn 5 G9
Trevarth Corn 4 G4
Trevaughan Carms 73 B11
Carms 93 G7
Tre-vaughan Carms 93 G8
Treveal Corn 1 A5
Trevegean Corn 1 D3
Treveighan Corn 11 F7
Trevellas Corn 4 E4
Trevelmond Corn 6 C4
Trevelver Corn 10 G5
Trevemper Corn 4 D6
Treven Corn 11 D7
Trevena Corn 2 D4
Trevenen Corn 2 D5
Trevenen Bal Corn 2 D5
Trevenning Corn 11 F7
Treveor Corn 5 G9
Treverbyn Corn 5 D10
Corn 6 B4
Treverva Corn 3 C7
Trevescan Corn 1 E3
Trevethin Torf 78 E3
Trevia Corn 11 E7
Trevigro Corn 6 B6
Trevilder Corn 10 G6
Trevilla Corn 3 B8
Trevilson Corn 4 D6
Trevine Corn 10 F5
Trevine/Trefin
Pembs 90 E6
Treviscoe Corn 5 D8
Treviskey Corn 2 B6
Trevithal Corn 1 D5
Trevoll Corn 4 D6
Trevone Corn 10 F3
Trevor Wrex 166 G3
Trevorrick Corn 10 G4
Trevor Uchaf Denb 166 G2
Trevowah Corn 4 D5
Trevowhan Corn 1 B4
Trew Corn 2 D4
Trewalder Corn 11 E7
Trewarmett Corn 11 D7
Trewartha Corn 2 B2
Corn 3 B10
Trewassa Corn 11 D8
Treween Corn 11 E10
Trewellard Corn 1 C3
Trewen Corn 2 C5
Corn 11 E11
Mon 79 G7
Trewennack Corn 2 D5
Trewennan Corn 11 E7
Trewern Powys 148 G5
Trewetha Corn 10 E6
Trewethen Corn 10 F6
Trewethern Corn 10 F6
Trewey Corn 1 B5
Trewidland Corn 6 D5
Trewindle Corn 6 C2
Trewint Corn 6 C5
Corn 11 B9
Corn 11 E10
Trewithian Corn 3 B9
Trewithick Corn 11 D11
Trewollock Corn 5 G10
Trewoodloe Corn 12 G2
Trewoofe Corn 1 D4
Trewoon Corn 2 F5
Corn 5 E9
Treworga Corn 5 G7
Treworgan Common
Mon 78 D6
Treworlas Corn 3 B9
Treworld Corn 11 C8
Trewornan Corn 10 G5
Treworrick Corn 6 B4
Treworthal Corn 3 B9
Trewyddel/Moylgrove
Pembs 92 C2
Trewyn Devon 24 G4
Tre-wyn Mon 96 G6
Treyarnon Corn 10 G3
Treyford W Sus 34 D4
Trezaise Corn 5 D9
Trezelah Corn 1 C5
Triangle Glos 79 E8
Staffs 133 B11
W Yorks 196 C4
Trickett's Cross
Dorset 31 G9
Triffleton Pembs 91 G9
Trillacott Corn 11 D11
Trimdon Durham 234 E3
Trimdon Colliery
Durham 234 D3
Trimdon Grange
Durham 234 D3
Trimingham Norf 160 B5
Trimley Lower Street
Suff 108 D5
Trimley St Martin
Suff 108 D5
Trimley St Mary
Suff 108 D5
Trimpley Worcs 116 B5
Trimsaran Carms 75 E7
Trims Green Herts 87 B7
Trimstone Devon 40 E3
Trinafour Perth 291 G9
Trinant Caerph 78 E2
Tring Herts 84 C6
Tringford Herts 84 C6
Tring Wharf Herts 84 C6
Trinity Angus 293 G8
Devon 27 F7
Edin 280 F4
Trinity Fields Staffs 151 D8
Trisant Ceredig 112 B4
Triscombe Som 43 F7
Trislaig Highld 290 F2
Trispen Corn 4 E6
Tritlington
Northumb 252 E6
Troan Corn 5 D7
Trochry Perth 286 C3
Trodigal Argyll 255 E7
Troearhiwgwair
Bl Gwent 77 D11
Troedrhiwdalar
Powys 113 G9
Troedrhiwffenyd
Ceredig 93 C8
Troedrhiwfuwch
Caerph 77 E10
Troedyraur Ceredig 92 B6
Troedyrhiw M Tydf 77 E9
Trofarth Conwy 180 G5
Trolliloes E Sus 23 C10
Tromode IoM 192 E4
Trondavoe Shetland 312 F5
Troon Corn 2 B5
S Ayrs 257 C8
Trooper's Inn Pembs 73 C7
Trosaraidh W Isles 297 K3
Trossachs Hotel
Stirl 285 G9
Troston Suff 125 C7
Trostre Carms 56 B4
Trostrey Common
Mon 78 E5
Troswell Corn 11 C11
Trotshill Worcs 117 F7
Trotten Marsh
W Sus 34 B4
Trottiscliffe Kent 68 G6
Trotton W Sus 34 C4
Trough Gate Lancs 195 C11
Troutbeck Cumb 221 E8
Cumb 230 F3
Troutbeck Bridge
Cumb 221 F8
Troway Derbys 186 F5
Trowbridge Cardiff 59 C8
Wilts 45 B11
Trowell Notts 153 B9
Trow Green Glos 79 D9
Trowle Common
Wilts 45 B10
Trowley Bottom
Herts 85 C9
Trows Borders 262 C5
Trowse Newton
Norf 142 B4
Troydale W Yorks 205 G10
Troy Town Kent 52 D2
Kent 54 E5
Medway 69 F8
Truas Corn 11 D7
Trub Gtr Man 195 F11
Trudoxhill Som 45 E8
Trueman's Heath
Worcs 117 B11
True Street Devon 8 C6
Trull Som 28 C2
Trumaisgearraidh
W Isles 296 D4
Trumfleet S Yorks 198 E6
Trumpan Highld 298 C2
Trumpet Hereford 98 D3
Trumpington Cambs 123 F8
Trumpsgreen Sur 66 F3
Trunch Norf 160 C5
Trunnah Lancs 202 E2
Truro Corn 4 G6
Truscott Corn 12 D2
Trusham Devon 14 E3
Trusley Derbys 152 B5
Trussall Corn 2 D5
Trussell Corn 11 D10
Trusthorpe Lincs 191 E8
Truthan Corn 4 E6
Truthwall Corn 2 C2
Trwstllewelyn
Powys 130 D3
Tryfil Anglesey 178 E6
Trysull Staffs 133 E7
Trythogga Corn 1 C5
Tubbs Mill Corn 5 G9
Tubney Oxon 82 F6
Tubslake Kent 53 G9
Tuckenhay Devon 8 D6
Tuckermarsh Devon 7 B8
Tuckerton Som 28 B3
Tuckhill Shrops 132 F5
Tuckingmill Corn 4 G3
Corn 11 E7
Wilts 30 B6
Tucking Mill Bath 61 G9
Tuckton Bmouth 19 C8
Tuddenham Suff 108 B3
Suff 124 C4
Tuddenham St Martin
Suff 108 B3
Tudeley Kent 52 D6
Tudeley Hale Kent 52 D6
Tudhay Devon 28 G4
Tudhoe Durham 233 D11
Tudhoe Grange
Durham 233 E11
Tudor Hill W Mid 134 D2
Tudorville Hereford 97 G11
Tudweiliog Gwyn 144 B4
Tuebrook Mers 182 C5
Tuesley Sur 50 E3
Tuesnoad Kent 54 E2
Tuffley Glos 80 C4
Tufnell Park London 67 B9
Tufton Hants 48 D3
Pembs 91 F10
Tugby Leics 136 C5
Tugford Shrops 131 F11
Tughall Northumb 264 D6
Tulchan Lodge
Angus 292 F3
Tullecombe W Sus 34 B4
Tullibardine Perth 286 F3
Tullibody Clack 279 B7
Tullich Argyll 284 F4
Highld 299 E9
Highld 300 G6
Tullich Muir Highld 301 B7
Tulliemet Perth 286 B3
Tulloch Aberds 293 F9
Aberds 303 F8
Highld 290 E5
Perth 286 E4
Tulloch Castle
Highld 300 C5
Tullochgorm
Argyll 275 D10
Tulloch-gribban
Highld 301 G9
Tullochroisk Perth 285 B11
Tullochvenus
Aberds 293 C7
Tulloes Angus 287 C9
Tullybannocher
Perth 285 E11
Tullybelton Perth 286 D4
Tullycross Stirl 277 D9
Tullyfergus Perth 286 C6
Tullymurdoch Perth 286 B5
Tullynessle Aberds 293 B7
Tulse Hill London 67 E10
Tumbler's Green
Essex 106 F6
Tumble/Y Tymbl
Carms 75 C8
Tumby Lincs 174 D2
Tumby Woodside
Lincs 174 D3
Tummel Bridge
Perth 285 B11
Tumpy Green Glos 80 E2
Tumpy Lakes
Hereford 97 B10
Tunbridge Hill
Medway 69 E10
Tunbridge Wells/Royal
Tunbridge Wells
Kent 52 F5
Tunga W Isles 304 E6
Tungate Norf 160 D5
Tunley Bath 45 B7
Glos 80 E6
Tunnel Hill Worcs 98 C6
Tunnel Pits N Lincs 199 G8
Tunshill Gtr Man 196 E2
Tunstall E Yorks 209 G12
Kent 69 G11
Lancs 212 E2
Norf 143 B8
N Yorks 224 F4
Staffs 150 D5
Stoke 168 E5
Suff 127 G7
T&W 243 G9
Tunstead Derbys 185 G10
Gtr Man 196 G4
Norf 160 E5
Tunworth Hants 49 D7
Tupsley Hereford 97 C10
Tupton Derbys 170 B5
Turbary Common
Poole 19 C7
Turfdown Corn 5 B11
Turf Hill Gtr Man 196 E2
Turfholm S Lnrk 259 B8
Turfmoor Devon 28 G3
Shrops 149 F7
Turgis Green Hants 49 B7
Turin Angus 287 B9
Turkdean Glos 81 B10
Turkey Island Hants 33 E9
W Sus 34 D3
Turkey Tump
Hereford 97 F10
Tur Langton Leics 136 E4
Turleigh Wilts 61 G10
Turleygreen Shrops 132 F5
Turlin Moor Poole 18 C5
Turmer Hants 31 F10
Turn Lancs 195 D10
Turnalt Argyll 275 C9
Turnastone Hereford 97 D7
Turnberry S Ayrs 244 B6
Turnchapel Plym 7 E9
Turnditch Derbys 170 F3
Turner Green Lancs 203 G8
Turner's Green
E Sus 23 B10
E Sus 52 G6
Warks 118 D3
W Berks 64 F4
Turners Hill W Sus 51 F10
Turners Puddle
Dorset 18 C2
Turnerwood
S Yorks 187 E8
Turnford Herts 86 E5
Turnhouse Edin 280 G3
Turnhurst Stoke 168 E5
Turnstead Milton
Derbys 185 E8
Turnworth Dorset 30 F4
Turrerich Perth 286 D2
Turriff Aberds 303 D7
Tursdale Durham 234 D2
Turton Bottoms
Blkburn 195 D8
Turves Cambs 138 D6
Turves Green
W Mid 117 B10
Turvey Beds 121 G8
Turville Bucks 84 G3
Turville Heath Bucks 84 G2
Turweston Bucks 102 D2
Tushielaw Borders 261 F8
Tutbury Staffs 152 D4
Tutnall Worcs 117 C9
Tutnalls Glos 79 E10
Tutshill Glos 79 G8
Tutt Hill Kent 54 D3
Tuttington Norf 160 D4
Tutts Clump W Berks 64 E5
Tutwell Corn 12 F3
Tuxford Notts 188 G2
Twatt Orkney 314 D2
Shetland 313 H5
Twechar E Dunb 278 F4
Tweedale Telford 132 C4
Tweeddaleburn
Borders 270 E5
Tweedmouth
Northumb 273 E9
Tweedsmuir
Borders 260 E3
Twelve Heads Corn 4 G5
Twelve Oaks E Sus 37 C11
Twelvewoods Corn 6 B4
Twemlow Green
Ches E 168 B3
Twenties Kent 71 F10
Twenty Lincs 156 E3
Twerton Bath 61 G8
Twickenham London 67 E7
Twigworth Glos 98 G6
Twineham W Sus 36 D3
Twineham Green
W Sus 36 C3
Twinhoe Bath 45 B8
Twinstead Essex 107 D7
Twinstead Green
Essex 106 D6
Twiss Green Warr 183 B11
Twist Devon 28 G3
Twiston Lancs 204 E2
Twitchen Devon 41 G9
Shrops 115 B7
Twitchen Mill Devon 41 G9
Twitham Kent 55 B9
Twitton Kent 52 B4
Two Bridges Devon 13 G8
Glos 79 D11
Two Burrows Corn 4 F4
Two Dales Derbys 170 C3
Two Gates Staffs 134 C4
Two Mile Ash
M Keynes 102 D6
W Sus 35 B10
Two Mile Hill Bristol 60 E6
Two Mile Oak Cross
Devon 8 B6
Two Mills Ches W 182 G5
Two Pots Devon 40 E4
Two Waters Herts 85 D9
Twr Anglesey 178 E2
Twycross Leics 134 C6
Twydall Medway 69 F9
Twyford Bucks 102 F3
Derbys 152 D6
Dorset 30 D5
Hants 33 C7
Leics 154 G4
Lincs 155 E8
Norf 159 E10
Oxon 101 D9
Shrops 148 D6
Wokingham 65 D9
Worcs 99 B10
Twyford Common
Hereford 97 D10
Twyn-Allws Mon 78 C3
Twynholm Dumfries 237 D8
Twyning Glos 99 D7
Twyning Green Glos 99 D8
Twynllanan Carms 94 G5
Twynmynydd Carms 75 C11
Twyn Shôn-Ifan
Caerph 77 G11
Twynyrodyn M Tydf 77 D9
Twyn-yr-odyn
V Glam 58 E6
Twyn-y-Sheriff Mon 78 D6
Twywell Northants 121 B9
Tyberton Hereford 97 D7
Tyburn W Mid 134 E2
Tyby Norf 159 D11
Ty-coch Swansea 56 C6
Tycroes Carms 75 C10
Tycrwyn Powys 148 F2
Tyddewi/St Davids
Pembs 90 F5
Tydd Gote Lincs 157 F9
Tydd St Giles Cambs 157 F8
Tydd St Mary Lincs 157 F8
Tyddyn Powys 129 F9
Tyddyn Angharad
Denb 165 F9
Tyddyn Dai Anglesey 178 C6
Tyddyn-mawr Gwyn 163 G9
Ty-draw Conwy 164 D5
Swansea 57 C7
Tye Hants 22 C2
Tye Common Essex 87 G11
Tyegate Green Norf 161 G7
Tye Green Essex 87 C10
Essex 87 D7
Essex 87 F11
Essex 105 D11
Essex 105 G10
Essex 106 G5
Tyersal W Yorks 205 G9
Ty-fry Mon 78 F6
Tyganol V Glam 58 E4
Ty-hen Carms 92 G6
Gwyn 144 C3
Ty-isaf Carms 56 B4
Tyla Mon 78 C2
Tylagwyn Bridgend 58 B2
Tyldesley Gtr Man 195 G7
Tyle Carms 94 F3
Tyle-garw Rhondda 58 C4
Tyler Hill Kent 70 G6
Tylers Causeway
Herts 86 D3
Tylers Green Bucks 84 G6
Tyler's Green Essex 87 D8
Sur 51 C11
Tyler's Hill Bucks 85 E7
Ty Llwyn Bl Gwent 77 D11
Tylorstown Rhondda 77 F8
Tylwch Powys 129 G9
Ty-mawr Anglesey 179 D7
Ty Mawr Carms 93 C10
Ty-mawr Conwy 181 F7
Ty Mawr Cwm
Conwy 164 F6
Tynant Rhondda 58 B5
Ty-nant Conwy 165 G7
Gwyn 147 D8
Tyncelyn Ceredig 112 E2
Tyndrum Stirl 285 D7
Tyne Dock T&W 243 D9
Tyneham Dorset 18 E3
Tynehead Midloth 271 D7
Tynemouth T&W 243 D9
Tyne Tunnel T&W 243 D8
Tynewydd Ceredig 92 B4
Neath 76 D4
Rhondda 76 F6
Ty-Newydd
Ceredig 111 D10
Tyning Bath 45 B7
Tyninghame E Loth 282 F2
Tyn-lon Gwyn 163 D7
Tynron Dumfries 247 E8
Tyntesfield N Som 60 E4
Tyntetown Rhondda 77 F9
Ty'n-y-bryn Rhondda 58 B4
Tyn-y-celyn Wrex 148 B3
Tyn-y-coed Shrops 148 D4
Ty'n-y-coedcae
Caerph 59 B7
Tyn-y-cwm
Swansea 75 E10
Tynyfedw Conwy 165 B7
Tyn-y-fedwen
Powys 148 C2
Ty'n-y-ffordd Denb 181 G8
Tyn-y-ffridd Powys 148 C2
Ty'n-y-garn
Bridgend 57 E11
Tynygongl Anglesey 179 E8
Tynygraig Ceredig 112 D3
Tyn-y-graig
Powys 113 G10
Ty'n-y-groes Conwy 180 G3
Ty'n-y-maes Gwyn 163 C10
Tyn-y-pwll
Anglesey 178 D6
Ty'n-yr-eithin
Ceredig 112 E3
Tynyrwtra Powys 129 F7
Tyrells End C Beds 103 E9
Tyrell's Wood Sur 51 B7
Ty'r-felin-isaf
Conwy 164 C5
Ty Rhiw Rhondda 58 C6
Tyrie Aberds 303 C9
Tyringham
M Keynes 103 B7
Tyseley W Mid 134 G2
Ty-Sign Caerph 78 G2
Tythecott Devon 24 D6
Tythegston Bridgend 57 F11
Tytherington
Ches E 184 F6
S Glos 61 B7
Som 45 D9
Wilts 46 E2
Tytherleigh Devon 28 G4
Tytherton Lucas
Wilts 62 E2
Tyttenhanger Herts 85 D11
Ty-uchaf Powys 147 E10
Tywardreath Corn 5 E11
Tywardreath Highway
Corn 5 D11
Tywyn Conwy 180 F3
Gwyn 110 C2

U

Uachdar W Isles 296 F3
Uags Highld 295 B9
Ubberley Stoke 168 F6
Ubbeston Green
Suff 126 C6
Ubley Bath 44 B4
Uckerby N Yorks 224 E4
Uckfield E Sus 37 C7
Uckinghall Worcs 99 D7
Uckington Glos 99 G8
Shrops 131 B11
Uddingston S Lnrk 268 C3
Uddington S Lnrk 259 C9
Udimore E Sus 38 D5
Udley N Som 60 G3
Udny Green Aberds 303 G8
Udny Station
Aberds 303 G9
Udston S Lnrk 268 D3
Udstonhead S Lnrk 268 F4
Uffcott Wilts 62 D6
Uffculme Devon 27 E9
Uffington Lincs 137 B11
Oxon 63 B10
Shrops 149 G10
Ufford Pboro 137 C11
Suff 126 G5
Ufton Warks 119 E7
Ufton Green W Berks 64 F6
Ufton Nervet
W Berks 64 F6
Ugadale Argyll 255 E8
Ugborough Devon 8 D3
Ugford Wilts 46 G5
Uggeshall Suff 143 G8
Ugglebarnby
N Yorks 227 D7
Ughill S Yorks 186 C3
Ugley Essex 105 F10
Ugley Green Essex 105 F10
Ugthorpe N Yorks 226 C5
Uidh W Isles 297 M2
Uig Argyll 276 E2
Argyll 288 D3
Highld 296 F7
Highld 298 C3